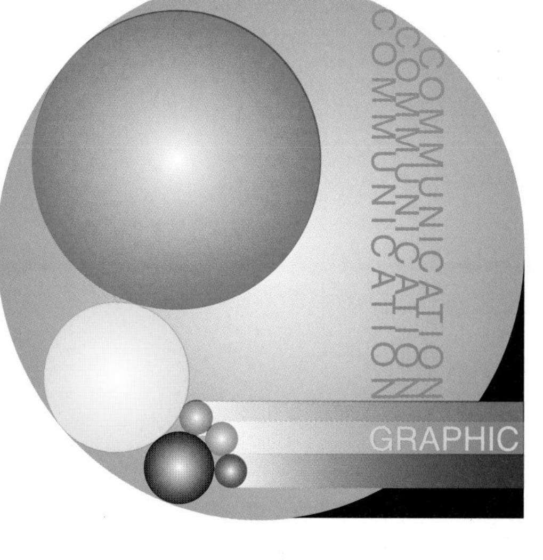

Graphic Communications

The Printed Image

Z.A. "Zeke" Prust

Publisher
The Goodheart-Willcox Company, Inc
Tinley Park, Illinois

Library of Congress Card Catalog Number 2002072710

ISBN-13: 978-1-56637-984-7
ISBN-10: 1-56637-984-9

6 7 8 9 0—03—07

Library of Congress Cataloging in Publication Data

Prust, Z.A.

Graphic communications: the printed image / by Z.A. "Zeke" Prust

p. cm.

Includes index.

ISBN 1-56637-984-9

1. Printing, Practical — United States. I. Title.

Z244.P958 2003

686.2 '0973—dc21 2002072710

CIP

Introduction

The graphic communications field (sometimes called graphic arts or simply, *printing*) has undergone sweeping changes in recent years with the introduction of computers and digital technology in virtually every aspect of the industry. Digital image capture and manipulation, electronic prepress operations, computer-based systems for managing most aspects of a business, computer-to-plate technology, electronic control systems on presses and bindery equipment, and many other advances have changed the fundamental ways that most printing and related operations are performed. It is probably safe to say that the industry has seen more extensive changes in the 15 years than have taken place in the five centuries since Johannes Gutenberg began printing from movable type in the mid-1400s.

Graphic Communications reflects these changes in the industry, with chapters devoted to in-depth coverage of color science, electronic prepress and digital printing, digital image capture, color management, and flexography. Other chapters provide important information on design and layout, text composition, page composition, stripping and imposition, contacting, the business aspects of printing, and careers in graphic communications have been extensively revised. Strong emphasis has been placed on safety and workplace health matters and on environmental considerations.

Information on new methods and equipment has been incorporated throughout the book, while information on processes that have become obsolete has been condensed and treated in a historical context. An extensive *Glossary of Technical Terms* defines and illustrates the many new words than have become part of the vocabulary of graphic communications workers in recent years. The aim is to better prepare today's graphic communication student for a career in this rapidly evolving field.

The text is divided into 28 chapters. Each chapter begins with a set of *Learning Objectives* and a list of ten *Important Terms*. Those terms, and many others, are highlighted in boldface italic type as they occur. In addition to being explained in the chapter, the terms are also defined in the *Glossary*. At the end of each chapter, *Review Questions* are presented to help assess comprehension of the material presented.

Since "a picture is worth a thousand words," **Graphic Communications** is highly illustrated. To clarify the complex processes of the industry, literally hundreds of full-color illustrations are used. Color is also used to enhance the educational value of many of the line art illustrations and to stress safety rules given throughout the text.

Graphic Communications is a valuable source of information for anyone entering any area of the printing industry today. This text will help you become well-versed in most aspects of printing technology.

Z. A. Prust, Ed.D.

Acknowledgments

A special thanks is extended to the many students, colleagues, and industry personnel who have given assistance, in some way, during the completion and revision of this text. Some of the individuals are: John Adler, Alfred (Bud) R. Anderson, Bob Baranowsky, Pat Beausoleil, Dick Benjamin, Bruce Binder, C. Ray Bradley, Blair Brouhle, Pam Carritt, Wesley Carter, Robert D. Cavin, Scott Cazel, Larry Charles, Mike Chiricuzio, Joleen Crimmins, Warren Daum, Andy Delph, Thomas Detrie, Bryce W. Drenhan, Bill Dunn, John Earle, Jon Engfer, Don Epley, Cheryl Ferrin, Michael Friel, Jim Gale, Karen Gallik, Chris Gannon, Don Gasser, D. W. Gillmore, Joseph J. Goclowski, Mark Goddard, Lynn Glasenap, Willis Hawrylkiw, Joe Hayes, R. Cameron Hitchcock, Don Hoffman, Ed Holmberg, Robert Hughes, John Jacobs, George Jenson, Nicole H. Johnson, William Kaverman, Edward Kelly, Julian (Red) Koren, Larry Kroll, William Lamparter, John Latsko, Kathryn Lauerman, Jessica Lipe, Peter Lovegrove, Tony Mancuso, Donald Marsden, William F. Martin, James McClintick, John Morton, Laura Nelson, Karen O'Brien, Stephanie Palmer, Kim Pardini, Hans Peetz-Larsen, C. Phillips, J. J. Plank, John Pollicino, Ken Robbins, Frank Roys, Pat Shudak, Jack Simich, Tony Simuel, Brent Smith, Terry Stengel, Brian P. Stephens, Kent Stumpe, John Sweeney, Daryl VanderHaar, Paul Volpe, John Walker, Robert Walker, Paul Wasserman, Art Webb, Gordon Woodard, Frank Woods, Tim Young, and Richard Zazueta.

Appreciation is extended to Sue Fogler for typing the original manuscript, to Martha Beakley Heier and Sergio Capon for artwork. Appreciation is also extended to Dr. Walter C. Brown, retired Professor, College of Technology and Applied Sciences, Arizona State University, and Professor Scott Williams, College of Science and Technology, Georgia Southern University, for their assistance. Thanks to Dr. Thomas Schildgren, College of Technology and Applied Sciences, Arizona State University, for writing the chapters relating to color theory and reproduction and gravure printing and to Dr. Ron Dahl, IKON Color Group, and Professor Thomas Detrie, College of Architecture and Environmental Design, Arizona State University, for writing the chapters relating to color science, vision and space, electronic production, and digital documents and digital printing. Thanks is also extended to Dr. Richard F. Hannemann, Professor, University of California, Chico, for writing the screen process chapter, to David L. Milburn, for writing the digital photography chapter and to Charles Weigand, retired Professor, Rochester Institute of Technology, for writing the flexography chapter. Thanks is extended to Dr. Thomas E. Gray, Retired Professor, Murray State University, Murray, Kentucky, for revising the Gravure Printing Chapter.

To my wife, Mary Ann, a sincere thanks for her patience and encouragement. Thanks to our sons, Donald L. Prust, printer, and Randall S. Prust, M.D.

The following companies have assisted greatly by providing information and pictorial material used in the textbook:

A. B. Dick Company; Adobe Acrobat; Accurate Steel Rule Die Mfg., Inc.; ACTI Products, Inc.; Advance Graphics Equipment; Advance Process Supply; Agfa; American Color Corp; American Roller Company; American Screen Printing Equipment Co.; American Wholesale Thermographers; Apple Computer, Inc.; Arizona Printing Equipment Co., Inc.; ATF; Autotype U.S.A.; AZTECH Reproductions, Inc.; Baker Perkins Limited; Baumfolder Corp.; BEI Sportswear, Inc.; Bobst Group, Inc.; Bowling Green State University, Visual Communication Technology Program; Brookfield Engineering Laboratories, Inc.; Brown Camera Co.; ByChrome Co.; Cameron-Somerset Technologies; Camex, Inc.; Caprock Development Inc.; Carpenter-Offutt Paper Co.; Central Bindery; Center for Metric Education, Western Michigan University; Center for Vocational Education, Columbus, Ohio; Central Missouri State University; Consolidated Papers, Inc.; Courier Graphics Corp.; Challenge Machinery Co.; Color Masters, Inc.; Compugraphic; Compuscan Inc.; Comsource Public Relations; Cordata; Covalent Systems; Max Daetwyler Corporation: Diagraph; Davidson International; Didde Web Press Corporation; Dienes; DK&A, Inc.; Doboy Packaging Machinery; Domino Amjet, Inc.; Donihe Graphics Co.; DuPont; Earmark, Inc.; Eastman Kodak Company; Edwards Brothers; Essex Products Group; Flexographic Technical Association, Inc.; Formatt Graphic Products, Inc.; Foster Manufacturing Company; Fuji Graphic Systems; Fuji Hunt Photographic Chemicals, Inc.; Fuji Photo Film U.S.A., Inc.; Gans Ink and Supply Co.; General Binding Corp.; Gerber Systems Corporation; Graphic Arts Technical Foundation; Gravure Association of America; GretagMacbeth; Greystone Peripherals, Inc.; GSMA; Hagen Systems, Inc.; Hantscho; Heidelberg Harris; Heidelberg Pacific, Inc.; Heidelberg West; Heidelbeg USA; Heritage Graphics; High Technology Solutions; High Water Designs Limited; Hunterlab; ICG North America; Ilford; Illinois Environmental Protection Agency, Office of Pollution Prevention; Imacon; Imation; Information International Inc.; Inter-City Paper Co.; Interlake Packaging Corp.; International Paper Co.; Interthor, Inc.; Iris Graphics, Inc.; Ironwood Lithographers, Inc.; Justrite Manufacturing Company; Kenro; Kimberly-Clark Paper Co.; King Press Corporation; Koh-I-Noor Rapidograph, Inc.; Krause; KURTA; Lab Safety Supply, Inc.; Lehigh Press; Linotype-Hell; MAN Roland; Mark Andy, Inc.; Matthias Bauerle GmbH; McCain Manufacturing Corp.; Mead Publishing Papers Division; Mee Industries, Inc.; MegaVision; Miller; Minolta Corporation; Mix & Match Corp.; Muller-Martini Corp.; Multigraphics; Murray Printing Co.; NAPL; National Association of Printing Ink Manufacturers; NAQP; National Soy Ink Information Center; Nekoosa Papers, Inc.; Nelson/Keystone; nuArc Company, Inc.; Orbotech, Inc.; Oliver; Pantone, Inc.; Paper Converting Machine Company; The Peerless Group of Graphic Services; J. J. Plank Corp.; Polychrome Corporation; Printing Industries of America, Inc.; Printing Industries Association, Inc. of Arizona; Ponte Engraving Co.; Prisma Graphics; Quantel; RAID, Inc.; Rapiline; Rob Macintosh Communications, Inc.; Rollem; Ronar; RPS; Salco, Inc.; S. D. Warren Co.; Scitex America Corp.; Screaming Color-Chapter One; Screen Printing Association International; Screen-USA; Sequel; Shanebrook Graphics; Software Publishing Corp.; Sonoco Products Co.; Southern Forest Products Assn.; Strachan Henshaw Machinery, Inc.; Supratech Systems, Inc.; Synergo; SWOP, Inc.; Teaneck Graphics; TEC Systems; Tekra; Tensor Group, Inc.; Tetko, Inc.; 3M Company; Tobias Associates, Inc.; Typography Unlimited; Ulano; Unisource Corporation; U.S. Bureau of Engraving and Printing; USA Today; Van Son Holland Ink Corporation; Variquick; Visual Graphics Corporation; Western Gear Corp.; Western Lithographic; Westvaco Corporation; Woods Lithographics; Xerox; Xitron; X-Rite, Inc.; Xyneticx-Clectroglas; Xyvision, Inc.

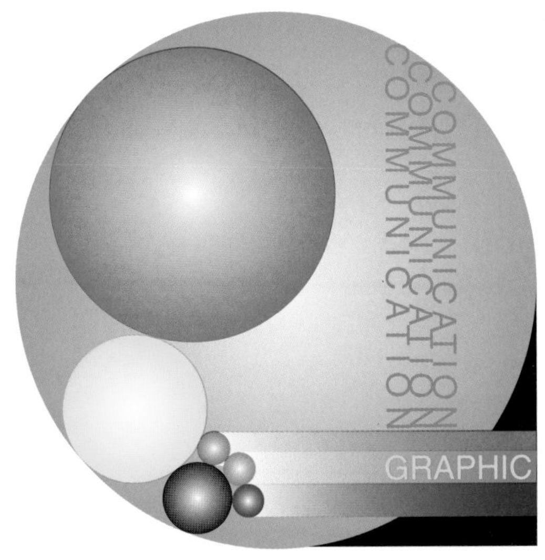

Table of Contents

Chapter 5 Design and Layout 83

Chapter 6 Text Composition 107

Chapter 7 Page Composition 131

Chapter 8 Color Science, Vision, and Space 151

Chapter 9 Electronic Prepress and Digital Printing 173

Chapter 10 Digital Image Capture 203

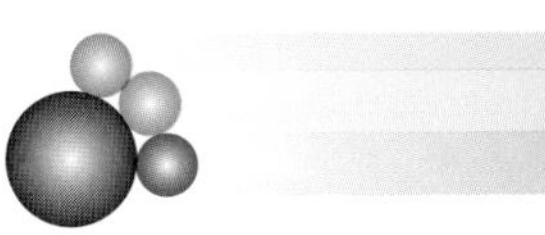

Chapter 11 Color Management 227

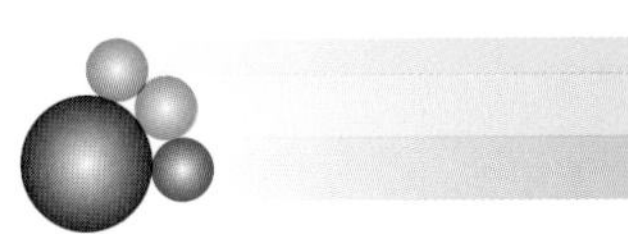

Chapter 12 Line Photography, Process Cameras 255

Chapter 13 Halftone and Special Effects Processes 277

Chapter 14 Processing Photographic Material 309

Chapter 15 Stripping and Imposition 321

Chapter 16 Contact Printing 341

Chapter 17 Lithographic Platemaking 351

Chapter 18 Lithographic Press Systems 365

Chapter 19 Lithographic Press Operation and Troubleshooting 383

Chapter 20 Relief Printing 405

Chapter 21 Flexographic Printing 415

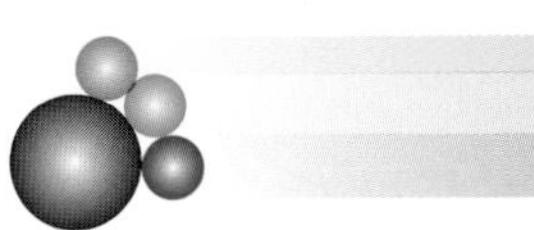

Chapter 22 Gravure Printing 429

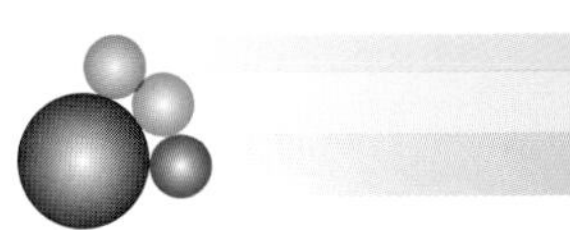

Chapter 23 Screen Printing 441

Chapter 24 Substrates 459

Chapter 25 Ink 477

Chapter 26 Finishing and Binding 493

Chapter 27 The Business of Printing 513

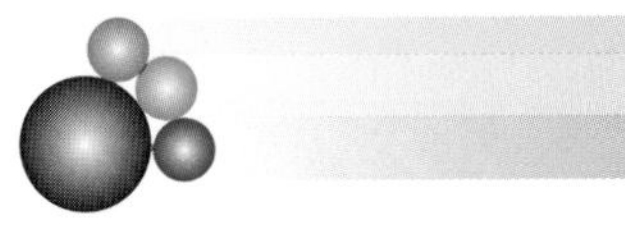

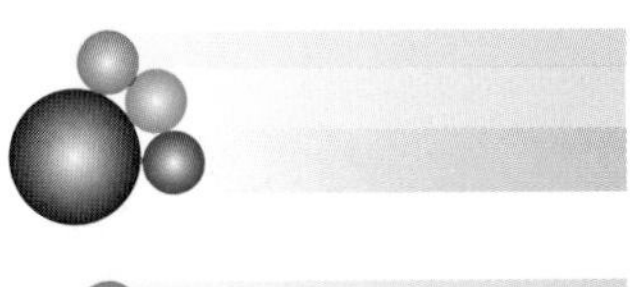

Important Safety Notice

The theory, procedures, and safety rules given in this book are typical of the industry. However, they are general and do not apply to all situations. For this reason, it is very important that you refer to the manufacturer's instructions when using any product or machine. These factory directions will give the details needed to work safely while producing quality printed products.

Graphic communications, in a relatively short period, has undergone a digital revolution. The computer and specialized software have become central to virtually every stage of the creative and production processes, from copy and image creation through prepress and press operations to bindery and finishing. (Heidelberg Prepress)

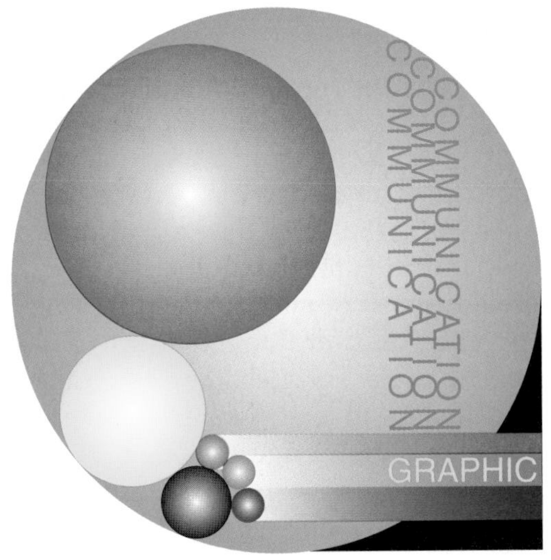

Overview of Graphic Communications 1

Learning Objectives

After studying this chapter, you will be able to:

- Explain the important role of graphic communications in our technological society.
- Identify the major processes commonly associated with the graphic communications industry.
- Summarize the four printing classifications.
- Describe the impact the computer has made and will continue to make on the graphic communications industry.

Important Terms

binding
camera-ready copy
computer-to-plate
editing
electronic page composition
image assembly
image carrier
photoconversion
photocomposing
printing

The term *"graphic"* relates to the visual, or things we can see. The term *"communication"* refers to the exchange of information in any form. Therefore, *graphic communication* means the exchange of information in a visual form, such as words, drawings, photographs, or a combination of these.

This is an extremely challenging time for anyone involved in graphic communications. Advances in electronics and the application of these advances to graphic communications processes have made it vital to keep up-to-date with changes in equipment capabilities and operating procedures. Open any graphics-related magazine and you will see advertisements for more advanced equipment. This is true in all areas of graphic communications.

"Graphic arts" used to be the common name for the study of the processes used in the printing industry. ***Graphic communications*** is now a more accurate term, because of the many methods of transferring and processing the images before printing them on a substrate. The term "graphic science" might also be used, since so many of the sciences—mechanics, physics, electronics, chemistry—are involved in various aspects of graphic communications.

One fact is crystal clear—if you fail to keep up with new technology, you could fall behind and not be aware of more efficient types of equipment and processes. This could cause your company to lose any competitive edge. The result could be antiquated techniques and inferior products or higher costs. Either could cause you to lose customers and profits.

The purpose of this chapter is to briefly explain the role of graphic communications in a technological society and identify the basic processes in this fast-changing industry. It will help prepare you to more fully comprehend the many aspects of graphic communications that are presented in detail in later chapters.

Why Is Communication Important?

People are constantly communicating. We take part in the communication process when we talk, send a letter, watch television, phone someone, read a book or newspaper, or obey a "One-way Street" sign. The ability to exchange complex data sets humans apart from other living organisms. Without the ability to communicate, the human race would live in a far different world.

The method or *medium* of communication used will vary based on the specific needs of the individuals involved. For example, speech (verbal expression) is satisfactory in certain situations, but has its limitations. With verbal communication, there is no record of the exchange of ideas or thoughts. People can misunderstand, or even totally forget the message. This is one of many reasons why *graphic images* (visual images) are and continue to be extremely important, **Figure 1-1**.

Graphic communications is the lifeblood of our technological society, influencing the population of the world wherever and whenever a product is printed. It affects education to a very high degree—how individuals think, see things, and draw conclusions, result to a great extent from what they have read and seen. Knowledge can become obsolete, but scholars often refer to the past to derive conclusions and direction for the future.

Figure 1-1. Graphic communications involves the exchange of messages in a visual form. A visual message, such as this protest sign, is less likely to be misunderstood or overlooked than a verbal message.

People often have an immediate need for practical knowledge, such as directions on how to build a shed or repair a bicycle. For such knowledge, they often turn to manuals and textbooks. Textbooks are a form of organized knowledge that can be consulted for immediate use or stored for future reference. Without books and other printed materials, people seeking knowledge would be greatly deprived. Much of our heritage and knowledge would be lost.

Textbooks, magazines, and journals all advance the information needs of our society. Advertising is another form of information. The printed advertisement, whether in a local newspaper or a national magazine, is a widely used means of conveying selling messages to potential buyers. The variety of printed products seems to be endless: books, newspapers, greeting cards, packages, stamps, fabrics, labels, order forms, advertisements, manuals, and maps are only a few examples.

Producing Visual Images

In the past, the term *"printing"* was used to cover all facets of the graphic communications industry. However, with present technology, *printing* is too limited a term to include the advanced technology found in a typical facility. Many allied systems, mostly electronic, have been added to the production of graphic images. Today, traditional printing is just one part or aspect of the rapidly growing *graphic communications* industry.

Printing is now understood to imply using ink to place an image on a *substrate* (paper, plastic, etc.). The many operations necessary to reach that point, as well as the steps completed to prepare a printed product for final use, are detailed in this book. See **Figure 1-2.**

Before any job can be printed, the product must be thought out from beginning to end. It must be properly designed. Specifications or measurements for all variables must be given, and an estimate (quote) of costs must be calculated.

Design assures that the printed image conveys the intended message. The graphic designer takes

Figure 1-2. This web of printed images is leaving the press to start the binding process. This machine folds, perforates, and chops web sheet into signatures. (Hantscho)

Figure 1-3. The quote is given to the customer after evaluation of the cost of materials, size of run, color use, etc. (Screaming Color-Chapter One)

an idea and puts it in an appropriate visual presentation. The selection of the type style and pictorial material, which includes art forms and photographs, can make the final product either acceptable or unacceptable.

Specifications are guidelines used to determine the format and cost of the final product. The development of specifications varies considerably from one facility to another, but typically includes such items as *paper weight* (thickness), color use, type of binding, and finishing methods.

A *quote* or *quotation* lists the prices and quantities for production of printed goods and services. The cost estimate is based on the job specifications and represents the final cost to manufacture the printed product. If there is agreement between two parties (the quote is accepted), work can begin. See **Figure 1-3**.

Copy and art preparation

Most printed products have a combination of written material, called ***copy*** (words), and pictures, called ***artwork*** (line art and photographs). Although one or the other may be more important in some situations, they usually are equally important in communicating information, **Figure 1-4**.

The amount of copy, also termed the *manuscript* or *text*, will vary with each type of job. For instance, a magazine article and an advertisement will differ significantly in length, style, content, and purpose.

Most writers today use a computer and word processing software to develop their manuscript.

Figure 1-4. A printed product usually includes both copy and artwork. In this example, text, photographs, and line art work together to make effective printed materials.

The use of the computer has become almost universal because it allows easy modification of copy and correction of spelling, sentence structure, and punctuation errors. The completed text can be output to a printer to provide a paper copy, and saved to a disk for use in succeeding steps of the production process. See **Figure 1-5**.

Figure 1-5. The computer has become an important part of every phase of graphic communications. Writers and editors commonly use a computer or word processor because it allows for easy revision and formatting of text.

Line art, also called line copy, is an image consisting of solid lines on a white or contrasting background. Traditionally, line art was produced manually, using technical ink pens to draw solid black lines on a white background. Most line art today is produced using special computer software (*draw* and *paint* programs). High quality line art is also available in the form of electronic "clip art." See **Figure 1-6**.

Another form of artwork is the photograph, or *continuous tone copy*. Unlike line copy, which has only solid black and white tones, continuous tone copy has gradations of tones or shades from light to dark. Continuous tone copy must be converted to a *halftone* image for printing. A computer program or a process camera may be used for the screening process, which breaks up the continuous tone image into tiny dots. The press plate or image carrier needs distinct solid and nonsolid areas (provided by the dots and surrounding spaces) to place inked images on the substrate. **Figure 1-7** shows a greatly magnified view of the dots in a halftone.

Figure 1-6. Electronic clip art is a readily available source of illustrations for printed materials. With suitable software, clip art images can be combined or altered to meet specific situations.

Editing

Editing is the final preparation of the author's or writer's manuscript for publication. It involves checking the text, line art, and photographs. There are two classifications of editing: content editing and copy editing.

In *content editing*, an editor checks the material to make sure it is up-to-date, technically accurate, organized in a logical sequence, and covers all important ideas.

Copy editing is usually done after content editing. Copy editing is done to correct spelling and punctuation, to mark for style, and to assure proper grammar. Consistency within the designated format or style is critical during copy editing.

As with writing, editing is usually done today on a computer. The writer's manuscript will typically be submitted in electronic form, either on disk or sent as digital data from computer to computer via telephone line. The edited electronic file, in effect, becomes the typeset text. In many operations, it will be imported to a page composition program and combined with graphic elements to create a finished page or other product (such as a brochure or multipage catalog). For operations still working with phototypesetting equipment and manual paste-up, the electronic text file becomes the input for the phototypesetter.

Figure 1-7. An original photo is a continuous tone that has different shades or gradations of color or light and darkness. A halftone, or screened photo, is made up of tiny dots that look like a continuous tone when printed. The screen can be seen easily in the enlarged section at right.

Text composition

As noted in the preceding paragraph, ***text composition*** today is generally done on a computer and the file imported into a page composition program. In the past, however, text composition was done using a number of other methods. The earliest method of creating text for a printed product was *hot composition,* in which molten metal was cast into individual letters or entire lines. The metal type was assembled into page forms for printing.

Within the past 50 years, *cold composition* became the dominant method of generating text. The term *"cold composition"* was derived as the opposite of hot composition, since molten metal was no longer used. Cold composition is a broad term that includes manual methods, such as freehand lettering or writing, transfer letters, and lettering devices or guides, as well as composing or image generation machines.

One of the older systems of cold composition is *photocomposing,* which uses a phototypesetting machine, **Figure 1-8**. These machines make it possible to create various size images (letters, numbers, etc.) that are very sharp and accurately positioned. Text is input manually, using a keyboard, or from a disk. The phototypesetter's circuitry deposits the image on light-sensitive paper with a laser (concentrated light beam) or CRT (cathode ray tube or electron beam). This produces a latent image on the material, which is developed in a special processor.

The copy output from the phototypesetter is in sheets called *galleys* that can be pasted up with other page elements and used as ***camera-ready copy*** (images that are good enough to be used in a printed product).

Page composition

It is essential that printed material be attractive in design, hold attention, and transmit the desired message to the reader. To make this possible, words (text) and visual images (photographs and line art) must be arranged on a page or pages. The process begins with design, progresses to layout, and finally is completed as *page composition.*

Figure 1-8. Use of phototypesetting equipment like the machine shown here has declined greatly since computers became the primary tool for text preparation and page composition.

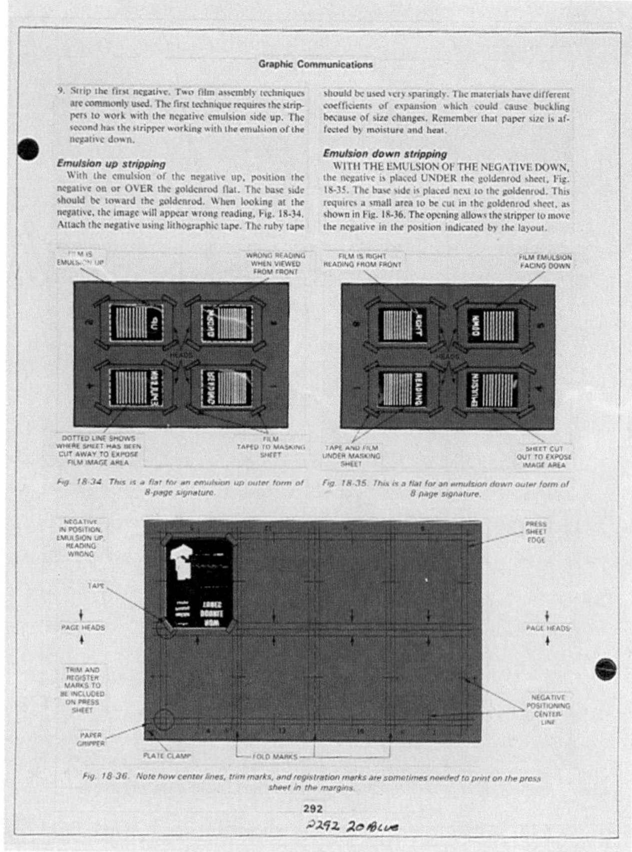

Graphic Communications

9. Strip the first negative. Two film assembly techniques are commonly used. The first technique requires the strippers to work with the negative emulsion side up. The second has the stripper working with the emulsion of the negative down.

Emulsion up stripping

With the emulsion of the negative up, position the negative on or OVER the goldenrod flat. The base side should be toward the goldenrod. When looking at the negative, the image will appear wrong reading, Fig. 18-34. Attach the negative using lithographic tape. The ruby tape should be used very sparingly. The materials have different coefficients of expansion which could cause buckling because of size changes. Remember that paper size is affected by moisture and heat.

Emulsion down stripping

WITH THE EMULSION OF THE NEGATIVE DOWN, the negative is placed UNDER the goldenrod sheet, Fig. 18-35. The base side is placed next to the goldenrod. This requires a small area to be cut in the goldenrod sheet, as shown in Fig. 18-36. The opening allows the stripper to move the negative in the position indicated by the layout.

Fig. 18-34. This is a flat for an emulsion up outer form of 8-page signature.

Fig. 18-35. This is a flat for an emulsion down outer form of 8 page signature.

Fig. 18-36. Note how center lines, trim marks, and registration marks are sometimes needed to print on the press sheet in the margins.

292

Figure 1-9. A completed mechanical consists of text and graphic elements adhered in the desired locations on a base sheet to form a page. This mechanical is ready for photoconversion.

The initial *design*, or idea in basic form, is worked out by making a series of quickly executed thumbnail sketches. Next, a rough layout is prepared. This is an actual size visual of the page that accurately shows the space for type and position of different illustrations. Finally, a comprehensive layout is done. This detailed sketch clearly shows style, size, and format to be used in the final printed piece.

The assembly of all the necessary components or elements on the page (matching the layout) can be done manually or electronically. The manual method, usually referred to as paste-up, involves arranging and adhering copy and artwork to a base sheet. The completed page, known as a *mechanical*, is photographed to create a negative for preparation of a printing plate. See **Figure 1-9.**

Electronic page composition has replaced mechanical paste-up in many printing operations. The text, line art, and photographs (all in digital form) can be arranged and manipulated on the computer monitor to assemble the final page (or multiple pages of a book, for example). See **Figure 1-10.** The completed pages are then output to an

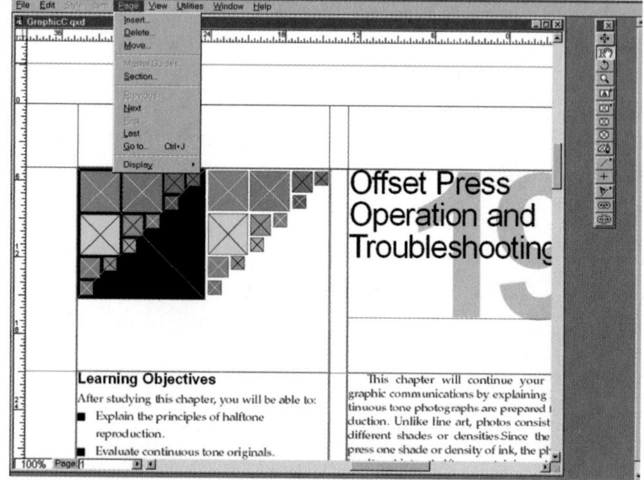

Figure 1-10. Electronic page composition has replaced manual paste-up in most operations. Page composition software allows the operator to position elements on the page and make all needed alterations.

imagesetter to produce camera-ready copy, actual negatives, or even the printing plates themselves.

Photoconversion

Photoconversion is a general term for processes that use light to place the original image onto a light-sensitive material. This broad category includes the use of process cameras to make negatives and screened (halftone) images, digital cameras and scanners used for image capture, and exposure units for platemaking. This area of the printing plant is being eliminated in many facilities that no longer use negatives or positives.

Traditionally, a ***process camera*** has been used to make enlargements, reductions, and same-size reproductions of originals for use in page composition or stripping work. Depending upon the purpose for which the reproduction is needed, the camera may be used to produce a *film negative* (opposite original), a *film positive* (film like original), or a *print* (photo like original). It is sometimes used to make a screened photo or *halftone* from a continuous-tone original.

The process camera has either horizontal or vertical facing lens, **Figure 1-11**. Some must be used in a darkroom (area that can be made devoid of light for working with photographic material). Others are *daylight* cameras and can be used in normal room light.

As is the case in most graphics communication areas, the computer has greatly changed the process of photoconversion. Scanned images are combined with text and electronically generated line art, using page composition software. The resulting electronic file of the page or pages is sent to an *imagesetter* that outputs the final film with all elements in place.

A widely used device today for many image-capture tasks is the electronic *scanner.* Both drum-type and flatbed scanners are used extensively in graphic communications work. They convert the light and dark (or color) values of the original to digital form, allowing the image to be stored as an electronic file. The image can then be altered or enhanced in a number of ways by using a computer equipped with image modification software. The image can be enlarged or reduced, color-corrected or modified, combined with other images, or processed in many other ways. Use of a scanner and computer is the most common method today for making color separations for printing.

Figure 1-11. This is a vertical process camera. This type camera is commonly used to make photostats, enlarge or reduce copies, screen halftones, and make film positives or negatives. (nuArc Company, Inc.)

Separations

When color photographs must be reproduced in a printed piece, *separations* are needed. Each separation is a halftone positive or negative representing one of the ***process colors*** used for printing: cyan (blue), magenta (red), yellow, and black. Each separation is used to make the image carrier (plate) for that color. When run on the press, each color is printed in *register* (alignment) with the others to produce a full-color illustration. See **Figure 1-12**.

Figure 1-12. To print a full-color image, color separations have to be made of a full-color photo. Each separation represents one of the three primary colors (cyan, magenta, and yellow). A fourth separation is made for black. Then, four colors of ink can be deposited in register or on top of each other on the paper when running through press. (Westvaco Corporation)

Figure 1-13. Negatives are stripped onto a masking sheet to create a flat that will be used to expose the printing plate. This stripper is checking negatives with a magnifying glass.

Image assembly

The process of assembling line and halftone negatives or positives into pages has traditionally been called stripping. Today, the process of putting together pages is more often electronic, and is referred to as ***image assembly***.

In the stripping process, pieces of negative or positive film are physically taped in place on a carrier sheet or base. The film pieces, when assembled, make up a single page or several pages, called a flat. See **Figure 1-13**. A number of pages may be assembled as a unit called a form. Location of the pages on the form is in a particular order, or *imposition*, so that the pages will be in proper order when printed and folded.

Image assembly is done electronically, with all the page elements in the proper size and place. Electronic stripping and imposition software has allowed the computer to take over these tasks as well, **Figure 1-14.** The output of the imagesetter, when used with such software, is large sheets of film with multiple pages properly imposed for making the printing plate or plates.

Platemaking

The process of placing an image on an ***image carrier*** or *press plate* is called *platemaking*. The plates are the means by which many copies can be made as duplicates of the original through the printing process. All image carriers must have the ability to transfer identical images onto a substrate.

The method used to make a plate varies with each printing process. Carriers can be produced mechanically, electronically, or photographically. The most commonly prepared type of plate is used for offset lithography, the most widely used of the printing processes. Lithographic plates have a light-sensitive coating, and are prepared by being placed in contact with a negative or positive and exposed

Figure 1-14. This is an automatic or computerized stripping system. The mouse can be moved around to outline or denote images for sizing, masking, etc. It saves time and is more accurate than manual stripping. (Screaming Color-Chapter One)

to light. See **Figure 1-15.** An alternative method of preparing printing plates does not use a negative. Called the ***computer-to-plate (CTP)*** or *direct-to-plate* system, this method uses an imagesetter to prepare the plate. The plate is prepared directly from the electronic file, without any negatives involved.

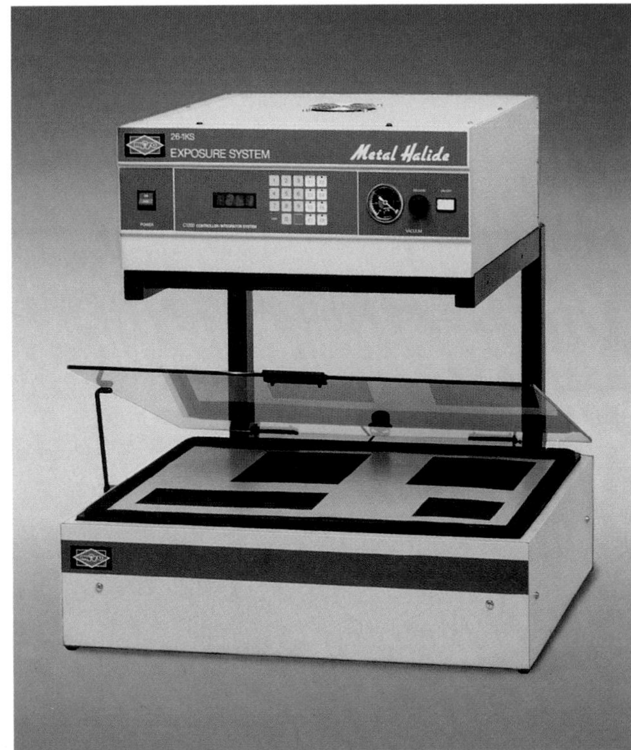

Figure 1-15. Printing plates for offset lithography are made by the contact platemaking process. A flat like the one shown here is placed on top of the plate (which has a light-sensitive coating) and a bright light is used to "burn" (expose) the images onto the plate. The plate must be developed before printing.

Printing Processes

Printing can be considered as a process involving the use of a specialized machine (a *printing press*) to transfer an image from an image carrier to a substrate, usually paper. Most often, printing involves making duplicates (the printed product) in large quantities.

Presses are of two basic types: sheet-fed and roll-fed. The *sheet-fed press* prints on single or individual sheets of paper. A *roll-fed* or *web-fed* press uses a long, single sheet or ribbon of paper. Web presses are used for longer "runs" (press operation for complete job) than sheet-fed presses. See **Figure 1-16.**

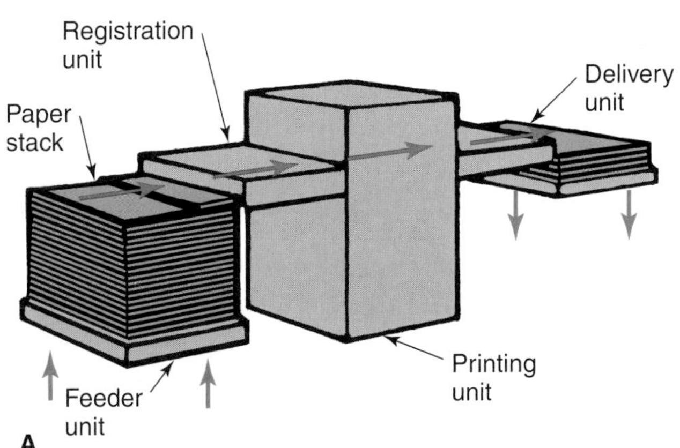

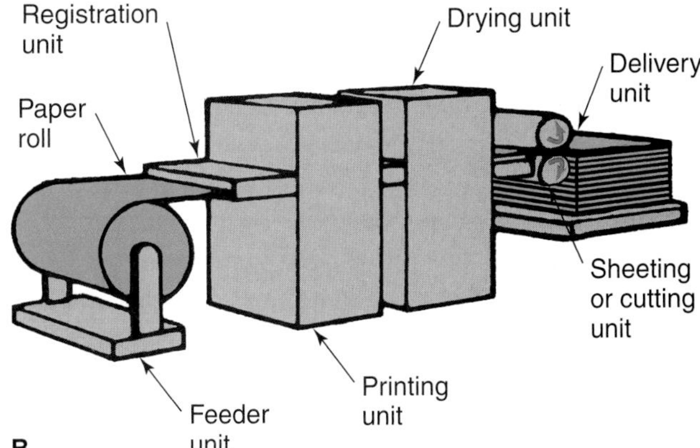

Figure 1-16. The two basic types of printing presses. A—The sheet-fed press moves single sheets of paper through impression system. B—The web-fed press prints on a long ribbon of paper. It is used for longer press runs.

The graphic communications industry generally recognizes four major printing processes: relief (letterpress and flexography), planography (lithography), intaglio (gravure), and porous printing (screen process). A fifth category, impactless printing, has come into general use in recent years.

Relief printing

The relief process is the oldest method of printing, and requires a raised image. Ink is spread upon the raised image areas, and transferred to paper by direct pressure. See **Figure 1-17**. Letterpress, the process of printing from metal plates, is seldom used today. Until recent years, however, it was the most widely used printing process. Examples of products once printed by letterpress are business cards, stationery, labels, business forms, tickets, cartons, magazines, reports, wrappings, newspapers, and books.

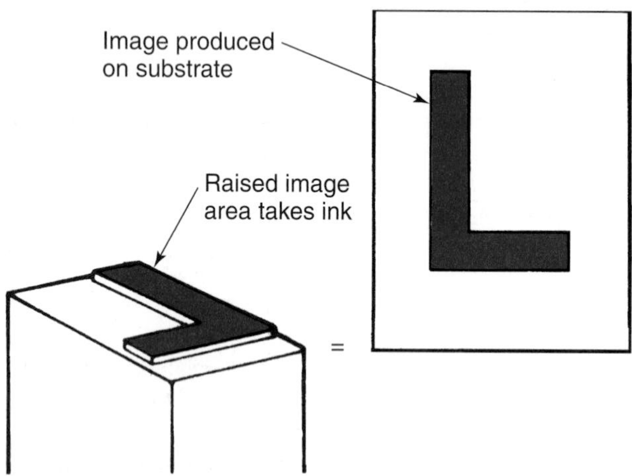

Figure 1-17. Letterpress printing transfers ink from a raised image area to a substrate.

Although letterpress has declined, another relief printing process has been growing in popularity. The process of ***flexography*** uses a flexible plastic or synthetic plate with a relief or raised image to print on a substrate. Plastic bags, labels, and other packaging materials are commonly printed by this process. Some of today's newspapers and books are printed by flexography, using large *belt presses*. See **Figure 1-18.**

Figure 1-18. A belt press used in flexographic printing has individual page plates bonded onto the belt with special adhesive. Belt presses are gaining increasing use in book and newspaper printing.
(Cameron-Somerset Technologies)

Planography

Planography is the process of printing from a flat (nonraised) surface, and is based on the concept that water and oil do not readily mix. In this process, the image areas of the printing plate accept ink and repel water; nonimage areas accept water, which keeps ink from sticking. See **Figure 1-19.**

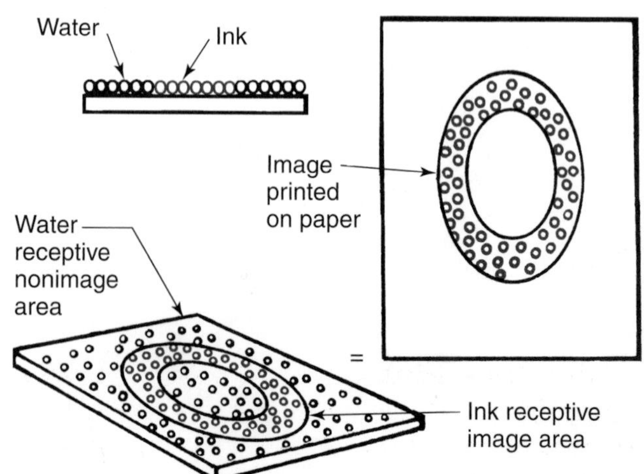

Figure 1-19. Offset lithography has the image area and nonimage areas on same plane. Image area is receptive to ink. Nonimage area is only receptive to water.

The most widely used form of planography is the printing process called *offset lithography*. In this form of printing, the inked image is first transferred (*offset*) from the printing plate to a rubber cylinder or roller, then from the roller to a substrate. Both sheet-fed, and web-fed presses are used in offset lithography. Lithography is widely used for all forms of commercial printing and publishing.

A form of offset lithography that is rapidly growing in popularity is *waterless printing*. It uses ink viscosity, rather than a dampening solution, to keep image and nonimage areas separate, and is increasingly used for both quality and environmental reasons.

Intaglio process

Gravure printing is a method most commonly known in the graphic communications industry as the *intaglio process*. The image area is sunken into the image carrier, as shown in **Figure 1-20**.

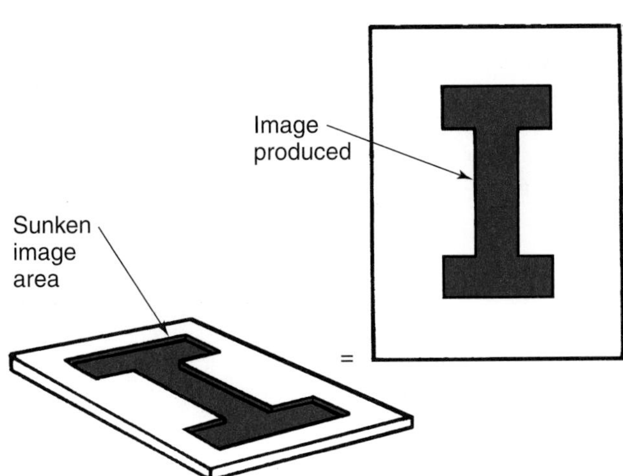

Figure 1-20. Gravure or intaglio printing has an image area that is sunken below the plate surface to hold ink.

Two characteristics are common to the gravure process. First, both line work and photographs are screened. In effect, the total cylinder or gravure plate is a halftone. Once the images are etched in the plate, it is very difficult to alter them. Second, the image and nonimage areas of the carrier surface are inked and the ink must be scraped off the carrier surface by a doctor blade. This leaves ink only in the sunken image area.

When preparing the line art, it must be remembered that the lines will be screened. The edges will appear irregular if they are very fine. Type styles with thin lines and serifs should be used with caution. Reverse type should be chosen carefully so that the letters do not fill in.

The gravure process is considered to be an excellent, high-speed, long run means of producing a superior product. Some of the typical materials printed by this method are: magazines, catalogs, newspaper supplements, package printing, metal surfaces, and vinyl surfaces.

Porous printing

Porous printing is basically a stencil process, in which an image carrier is attached to a screen and ink is forced through the open mesh areas. The *screen printing process* is the most used of the porous printing methods. See **Figure 1-21**.

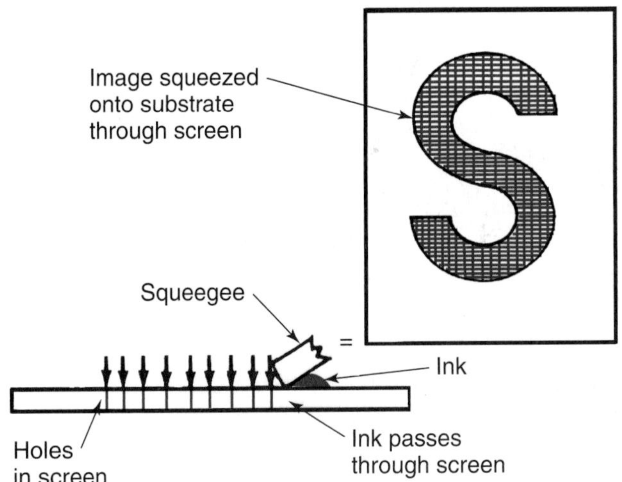

Figure 1-21. Screen printing is a form of porous printing. Small holes in the image permit ink to pass through and deposit on substrate.

Screen process is a versatile method of printing on many types of surfaces. It is capable of doing line and halftone work. Some of the screen process work in the electronic field is very precise and the equipment highly sophisticated. Special inks are required for screen printing.

The artwork is assembled much like that for lithographic work. Laying out to size, with all of the elements in position, will generally be acceptable. Overlays are necessary for additional color work. The techniques vary slightly when using photographic or hand-cut stencils. The presses for the screen process can be manual or highly automated.

A wide variety of applications exists, including packaging, clothing and other fabric items, and printing on nonabsorbent surfaces such as glass. Many tiny electronic circuits are produced with a type of screen process. Another unusual application is printing the conductive materials on automobile rear windows for defrosting circuits.

Impactless (pressureless) printing

Impactless printing does not require direct contact between an image carrier and the substrate. Impactless printing, unlike the previously discussed processes, does not require that ink be pressed against a substrate.

Ink jet printing is one of the examples of the impactless process. Ink droplets are formed and forced through very small nozzles onto the substrate. Most of the units use a computer to control the image generation. The computer controls where, and how much, ink is forced onto the substrate. See **Figure 1-22.**

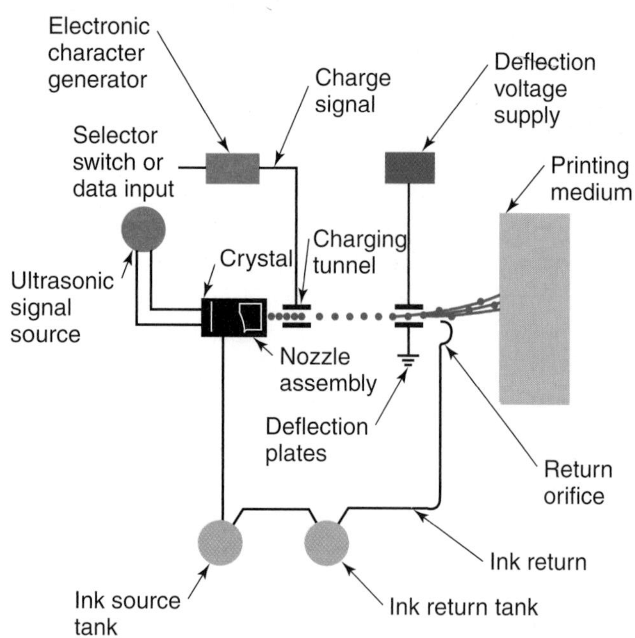

Figure 1-22. This diagram illustrates the basic principle of ink jet printing. (A.B. Dick Co.)

Electrostatic printing systems and *laser printers* are also being used to produce images which are of high quality. The electrostatic method uses the forces of electric current and static electricity. It is commonly found in office copying machines. Machines capable of producing copies in multiple colors have become common in recent years, **Figure 1-23.**

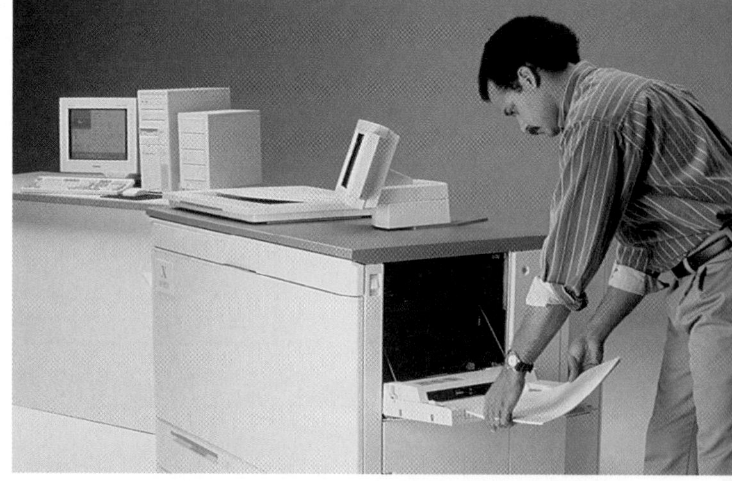

Figure 1-23. This color digital production system enables customers to send electronic files directly to the digital full-color copier/printer. It provides an affordable way to produce short-run full-color prints of documents such as proposals, menus, reports, presentations, sales flyers, brochures and other materials that are currently printed in black-and-white because of quality, turnaround and cost considerations. (Xerox)

Binding and Finishing

Once an image has been printed on a substrate, some form of binding and/or finishing is usually required. These are the final steps to completing the printing job.

Binding

Binding is the process of joining together multiple pages of a printed product by various means including sewing, stapling, spiral wire, and adhesives. Binding requires complex equipment, as shown in **Figure 1-24.**

Most printed products require one or more of the following steps that are considered part of the binding process: folding, scoring, gathering, collating, stitching, and trimming.

Figure 1-24. A bindery uses various methods to hold multiple sheets together to form one product; such as a book.

Scoring is the creasing of a heavier sheet of paper or paperboard to assist in the folding of the material.

Folding is required when a large sheet contains two or more pages of a product. Sheets containing 8, 16, or 32 pages are common in production of books and periodicals. The folded groups of pages are called *signatures*. If a product consists of several signatures, the signatures must be brought together in the proper order. This process is known as *gathering*.

Collating is the process of placing pages (usually single sheets) in the right sequence. *Stitching* is a stapling process by which pages of a signature are held together.

Trimming is the cutting of material after printing to produce even edges. **Figure 1-25** shows an example of a semiautomatic operation for cutting stock.

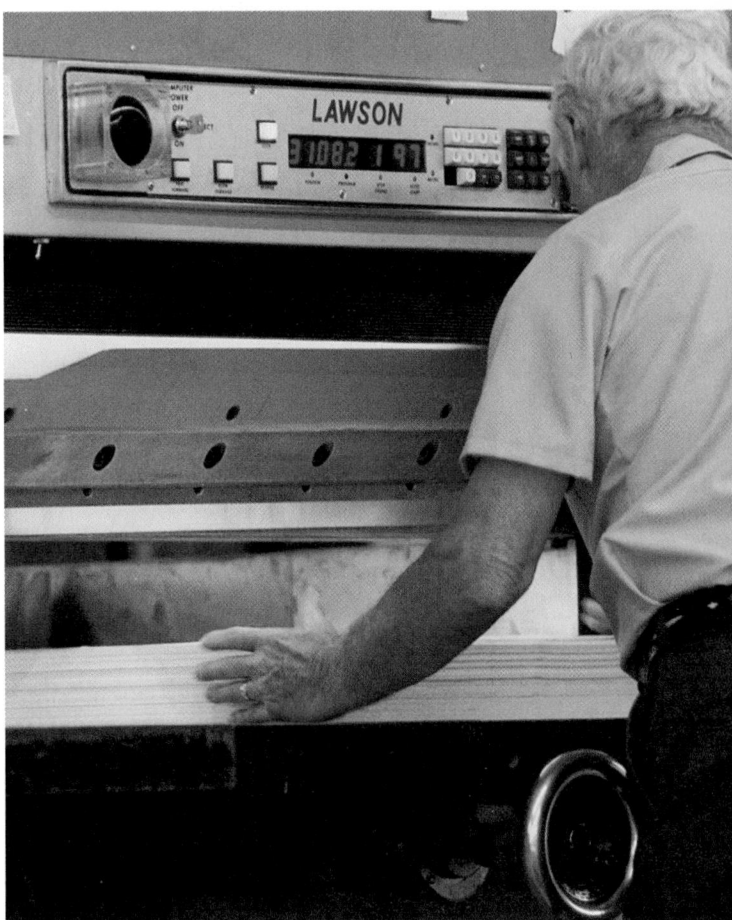

Figure 1-25. Trimming is done to make all sheets even on edges. This is a large computer-controlled cutter that automatically trims stock to size.

Finishing

Various processes that enhance the final printed product are considered ***finishing*** operations. Some of the more common finishing operations include embossing, die-cutting, stamping, punching, drilling, round cornering, and padding. Laminating and coating are also considered finishing processes.

Embossing produces a raised design on paper or other material. This process uses pressure and heat to mold the paper fibers.

Die-cutting uses rules or blades to cut paper or other sheet materials into irregular designs. *Perforating* is a similar operation that cuts a series of holes or slits in the stock to allow part of it to be torn off easily. It is used extensively for tickets and coupons, often in conjunction with the finishing operation known as *numbering* (printing numbers in sequence on each piece).

Stamping refers to the application of a metal foil to almost any type of material, such as leather, paper, or cloth. A combination of embossing and foil stamping can also be done in one operation.

Lamination is the process of bonding plastic film, by heat and pressure, to a sheet of paper to protect its surface and improve appearance. See **Figure 1-26.** *Coating* is done for the same purpose, and may be done as a finishing operation, or as part of the printing process, depending upon the application. For example, a spot coating of gloss or dull varnish to part of a page is often applied during printing. The varnish is a design element to draw attention to the area of the page where it is applied.

Figure 1-26. Laminating is just one finishing operation that puts protective coating over the image.

Segments of the Industry

The graphic communications industry can be divided into segments or classifications. A few of the major segments are described briefly in the following paragraphs.

Commercial printing

The ***commercial printing*** segment of the industry encompasses all sizes and types of printing operations. These range from small local shops with one or two employees to large companies with several plant locations and hundreds or thousands of employees. Products produced in the commercial printing segment are as varied as the company sizes, from simple one-color envelopes and letterheads to full-color product brochures and sales displays to complex and sophisticated annual reports for giant corporations. This segment of the graphic communications industry is dominated by one printing process, offset lithography. See **Figure 1-27**.

Quick printing

This is a subdivision of the commercial printing segment, consisting of shops specializing in rapidly completing short-run printing and photocopying work. ***Quick printing*** operations (both independently owned and franchised) are designed to serve the needs of business customers. Equipment in such shops may include both small offset duplicators and photocopiers with varying capabilities, including color.

Periodical printing

The ***periodical printing*** segment of the industry consists of plants that are designed primarily to print magazines. Web-fed offset lithography is used extensively, but a shift to gravure appears to be taking place in periodical publication.

Newspaper printing

Although ***newspaper printing*** was done for many years on web-fed presses using the letterpress (raised type) process, most operations have switched to offset lithography. The widespread use of computer technology and satellite transmission has made possible the publishing of national newspapers through a network of regional printing sites. This greatly simplifies distribution of the product. See **Figure 1-28**.

Book publishing and printing

Book publishing and printing includes the production of *trade books* (general interest nonfiction and fiction) sold in bookstores and other retail locations, and *textbooks* providing instruction on a great variety of subjects. At one time, many book publishers operated their own printing facilities. Today, however, most contract with large specialized printing operations. Web-fed offset lithography is the process usually used in book production.

In-plant printing

The ***in-plant printing*** segment of the industry covers printing facilities operated by companies

Figure 1-27. This is a large sheet-fed offset-litho press, one of the types widely used in commercial printing. Paper sheets are picked up on right. They are then pulled to left for printing.

Figure 1-28. These folded and gathered newspapers coming off a large web offset press are being printed at a regional site for a national publication. Electronics technology has made possible printing of the same newspaper at multiple sites for easier distribution. (USA Today)

whose business is *not* the production of printed materials. A typical use of in-plant printing is the production of owner's manuals, repair manuals, and parts lists for such products as power tools, material-handling equipment, or vehicles of various types.

Forms printing

Forms printers design and print special paper forms used in many businesses. The types of forms vary from simple sales receipts or message pads to multipart carbonless order forms to continuous perforated forms for use in special impact printers. *Label printing* is also done by some forms printers, as well as by companies specializing in labels. Most label printing is done on papers with a pressure-sensitive adhesive backing, using specially designed small web offset presses.

Review Questions

Please do not write in this text. Write your answers on a separate sheet of paper.

1. A material (such as paper) on which printing is done is called a (n) _____.
2. A quote lists the _____ and _____ for production of printed goods and services.
3. This is the most common way of generating copy for printing.
   a. Computer.
   b. Hot type.
   c. Scanning.
   d. Photocomposing.
4. *True or False?* Line art is a type of drawing consisting of continuous tones.
5. Explain the term "halftone."
6. What is a mechanical?
7. What process has replaced manual paste-up in many printing operations today?
8. Which of the following is *not* a process color used in printing a full-color photograph?
   a. Magenta.
   b. Yellow.
   c. Green.
   d. Cyan.
9. In your own words, describe the following types of printing: Flexography, Gravure, Screen printing, Impactless printing.
10. _____ is the printing process used most extensively in the commercial printing segment of the graphic communications industry.

Safety and Health 2

Learning Objectives

After studying this chapter, you will be able to:

- State the purpose of a plant safety and health program.
- Describe the importance of machine guards and personal protection.
- Demonstrate safe handling of materials, tools, and equipment, as well as proper techniques for lifting.
- Identify the correct handling, storage, and disposal of chemicals and other materials.
- Explain plans for fire prevention within a plant.
- Describe proper noise control in a plant.
- Describe an ergonomically correct computer workstation.
- Explain ways to reduce and eliminate waste for environmental compliance.

Important Terms

barrier guards
ergonomics
lockout devices
machine guards
Material Safety Data Sheet (MSDS)
nip points
personal protective devices
tagout device
volatile organic compounds (VOCs)
waste stream

Personnel in the graphic communications industry may be confronted with many hazards in the course of performing their duties. These include hazards of a mechanical, chemical, flammable, or electrical nature. While the industry has many safety and health problems common to other fields, this chapter will emphasize the recognition and control of those areas with the greatest potential for injury, illness, or environmental contamination. Later chapters will describe safety rules for specific processes performed in a graphic communications facility. Other sources of health and safety information available to you on the job are equipment instructions, manuals, and machine labels.

It is vital for workers in a graphic communications plant to know basic safety practices. Because of the wide variety of processes performed, the potential for injury, illness, or death always exists. It is up to you to keep the work environment safe and healthy for your coworkers and for yourself.

Safety and Health Program

A safety and health program is an effective means of providing a safe working environment. The purpose of such a program is to recognize, evaluate, and control potential hazards in the workplace. See **Figure 2-1.**

Unguarded machinery, improper lifting methods, chemical contaminants, flammable and combustible materials, ungrounded wires, noise, and even poorly designed computer workstations are all potential health hazards.

An effective safety program begins with informed employees. The Federal Occupational Safety and Health Administration (OSHA) has

Figure 2-1. A graphic communications facility can be a safe and enjoyable place to work. However, if safety rules are not followed, it can be very dangerous. (Variquick)

issued a Hazard Communication Standard known as the "Worker's Right to Know Law." It requires the employer to communicate information to workers about chemical hazards in the workplace. It generally requires that employees be afforded a safe and healthful work environment, be advised and trained concerning any hazardous materials to which they are routinely exposed, have access to information about chemicals used, and be advised of their rights and obligations under the act.

To ensure the success and progress of the plant safety program, management leadership is essential. The person assigned responsibility for the safety and health of the plant must have the authority to carry out the program. Everyone in the establishment must be aware of the plan. A safe operation largely depends upon all plant personnel being properly informed of potential hazards. The checklist at the end of this chapter will be helpful in performing a safety inspection of a graphic communications facility.

Mechanical Hazards

Many on-the-job physical injuries are the result of mechanical hazards that can be controlled if:

- Machines are properly guarded.
- Energy isolating devices are locked out and tagged out during maintenance.
- Workers properly use personal protective equipment.
- Workers are trained to handle materials, tools, and equipment safely.

Machine guarding

Hazards are posed by the reciprocating, rotating, pinch-pointing, and shearing actions of various types of machinery in the industry. See **Figure 2-2.** Therefore, properly placed guards on mechanical equipment are very important for the operator's protection.

Reciprocating and rotating motions create hazards in two areas — at the point of operation (where work is being done) and at the points where power or motion is being transmitted from one part to another. Any rotating part is dangerous. Contact with loose clothing, hair, and even skin can cause severe injury.

Typical rotating mechanisms are spindles, flywheels, horizontal or vertical shafts, cams, and

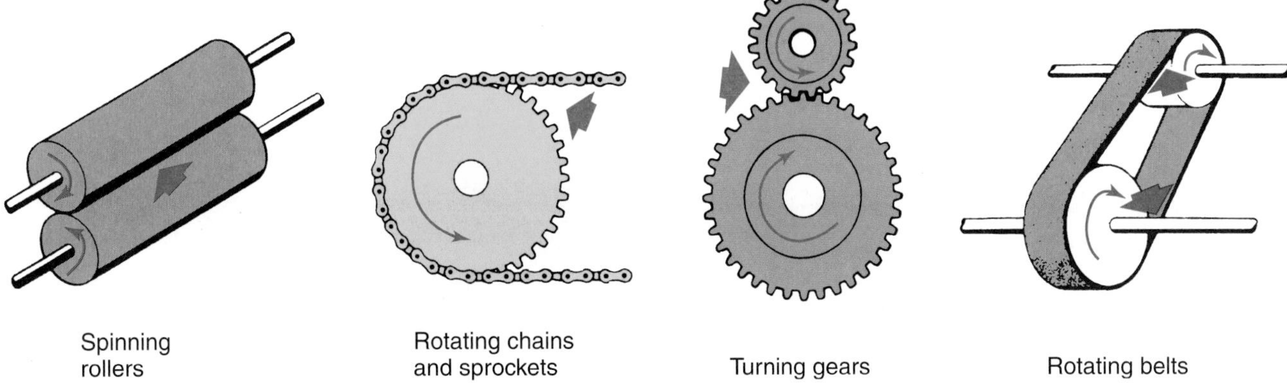

Figure 2-2. These mechanisms found in a graphic communications facility can cause serious injury.

collars, **Figure 2-3.** Whenever something projects from the rotating unit, the machine becomes even more dangerous. Extreme care must be taken when working in an area with rotating units, even though they are properly guarded.

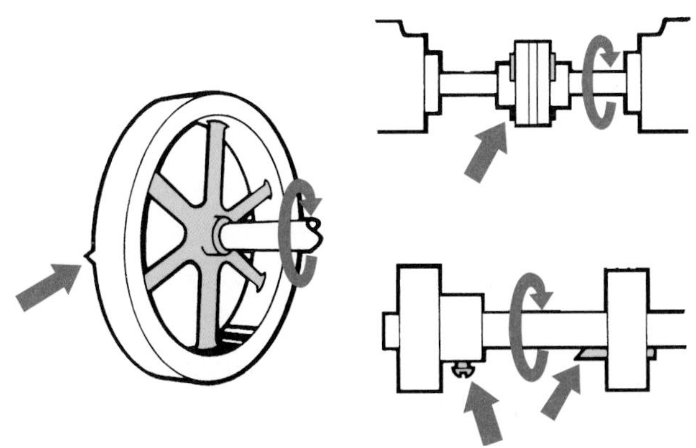

Figure 2-3 Rotating objects, especially those with projecting parts, pose a constant danger on presses and other equipment. They can cause serious cuts, wrap clothing around shafts, and pull the operator into the equipment.

Figure 2-4. Always keep guards and covers in position when operating a press or other type of equipment. Guards primarily protect people from injury, but they also keep objects from entering and damaging the press. Covers perform the same general function. (Heidelberg Harris)

Machine guards protect parts of the human body from being cut, squashed, or hit by flying fragments. Guards also protect the equipment from foreign objects. Metal and plastic are two materials commonly used as guards. Most machines in the graphic communications industry require some type of guarding. See **Figure 2-4.** If a guard is in place, do not remove it to perform an operation. Likewise, do not use equipment when guards are missing, broken, or out of adjustment. The risk of severe injury to yourself or to others is too great.

Machine guarding is necessary wherever hazardous machine parts are within reach of the operator. Make sure guards are in place over belts, chains, flywheels, cutters, pulleys, shafting, fasteners, punches, drills, clamps, gears, rollers, cylinders, shears, and all other points of operation.

Nip points exist where two cylinders meet or come close to one another. Gears and rollers also have nip points. Many guards are pressure-sensitive and automatically stop the movement of the machine when an object becomes wedged between the guard and the cylinder. See **Figure 2-5.**

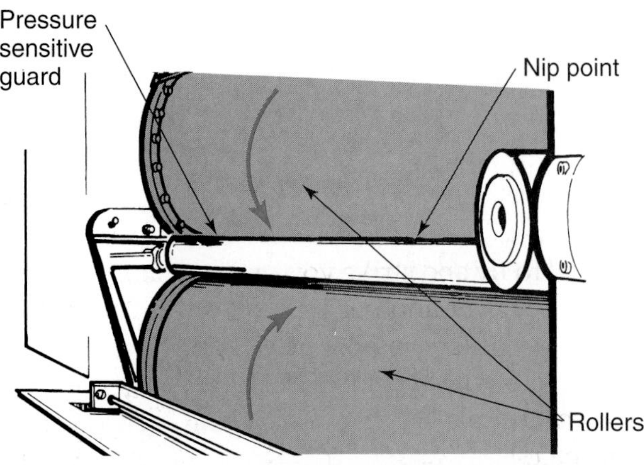

Figure 2-5. A nip point occurs where two rollers come together. Rollers produce tremendous pulling and crushing force that can severely injure a person, sometimes causing permanent disability. This press has a pressure sensitive guard that shuts it off if anything is pulled into the nip point.

Figure 2-6. Always dress properly for work. The press operator is not wearing jewelry or a watch and is wearing an apron to keep clothing out of the press.

Barrier guards keep a person out of the operation area but can be hinged or moved. When the guard is moved out of position, power is cut off, and the machine will not run.

Just because a machine or press looks small does not mean it is incapable of causing serious injury. Without a guard, the operator's clothing can easily be caught and pulled into the nip point. Long hair can also get drawn into nip points. Always wear a cap or head band and tie back long hair when operating machinery. Do not wear jewelry of any kind, not even a watch, when operating equipment, **Figure 2-6.**

Some machines required specialized types of guarding. For instance, a typical safety device on a guillotine paper cutter prevents cutting until the pressure clamp is in position. A similar safety feature is one that will not permit operation if a light beam is blocked by some object, such as a hand. A common control device on the paper cutter requires that both hands of the operator be on the operating controls, **Figure 2-7.**

Figure 2-7. Note the two control buttons on this cutter. Both red buttons must be pressed simultaneously to operate the blade. The dual mechanism ensures that hands are out of the way when cutting.

A paper cutter blade is very sharp; all precautions should be taken to avoid injury when cutting stock or handling the blade. When operating a cutter, make it a habit to never reach for a jammed piece of paper. Follow safety procedures indicated on the machine labels or operation manual.

Cleaning and maintaining equipment should be done when the machine is *not* in motion. Do not rely on a safety interlock when working on a piece of equipment. Make sure the power is *off* at the main switch!

Lockout devices

When someone is working on a piece of equipment, the electrical power supply must be cut off. "Locking out" equipment is the only sure way to prevent serious or fatal injuries that could result from unexpected energizing or startup of the machine. ***Lockout devices*** utilize either a key or combination-type lock to hold an energy isolating device (such as a manually operated electrical circuit breaker) in the safe position to prevent the machine from energizing.

A ***tagout device*** is a prominent warning, such as a tag securely fastened to an energy isolating device. When you find a tagged power box, make no attempt to restore the power until repairs are made and the tag is removed by the person who placed it. See **Figure 2-8.**

Figure 2-8. Lockout devices and tags are used to prevent accidental operation of machinery.

Many pieces of equipment have flip covers to prevent run/reverse or inch buttons from accidentally being pressed. The cover on the run/reverse button must be flipped shut during plate gumming, blanket work, or any other operation that requires a press to be inched.

Personal protection

Besides making sure that machines are properly guarded and locked out, you can take additional steps to protect yourself and others from injury.

As cautioned earlier, never wear watches, rings, ties, medallions, bracelets, scarves, or loose clothing while working with machinery. Remember that loose long hair is a hazard, as is a rag partially tucked in a pocket and hanging out.

Wear appropriate safety equipment, **Figure 2-9.** Eye protection should be worn when you are operating a saw, grinder, or any machine that can cause material to fly and strike you or other shop workers. Use earplugs or another type of hearing protection in noisy areas. Disposable plastic gloves will protect your hands when handling inks, oils, solvents, and other chemicals. Wear an apron to keep clothing from being pulled into machinery. A dust mask is suitable for some airborne particles, but an approved respirator must be worn when operations produce inks mists. Certain operations, such as press, bindery, and storage, typically require foot protection.

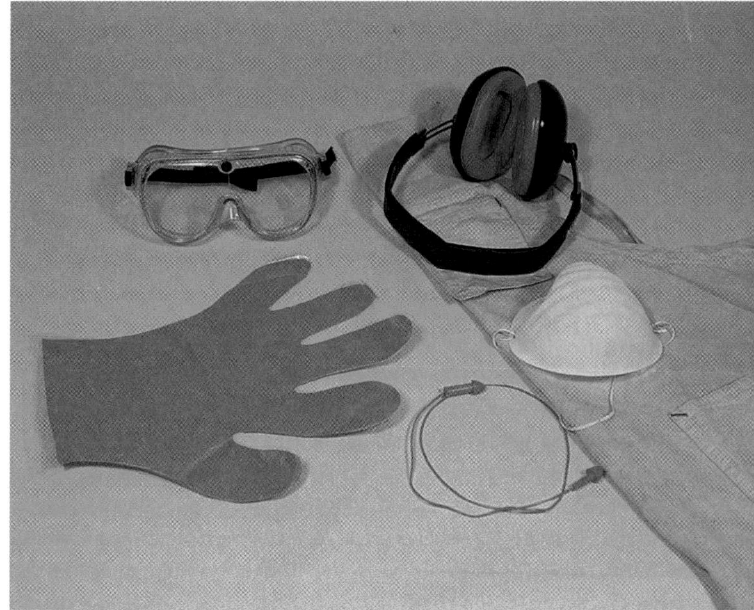

Figure 2-9. Wear personal protective equipment. Shown are approved eye protection, an apron to protect clothing, plastic gloves for handling oils and solvents, earplugs, and a dust mask. For some situations, a respirator must be worn, since it provides much greater protection than a dust mask.

Materials handling

Too often, a person lifts a heavy load without seeking assistance from another person or from a mechanical device. See **Figure 2-10.** When lifting an object, keep your knees bent and your back straight. Leaning over while lifting is poor practice, **Figure 2-11.** Follow the *Tips for Safe Lifting* on the facing page.

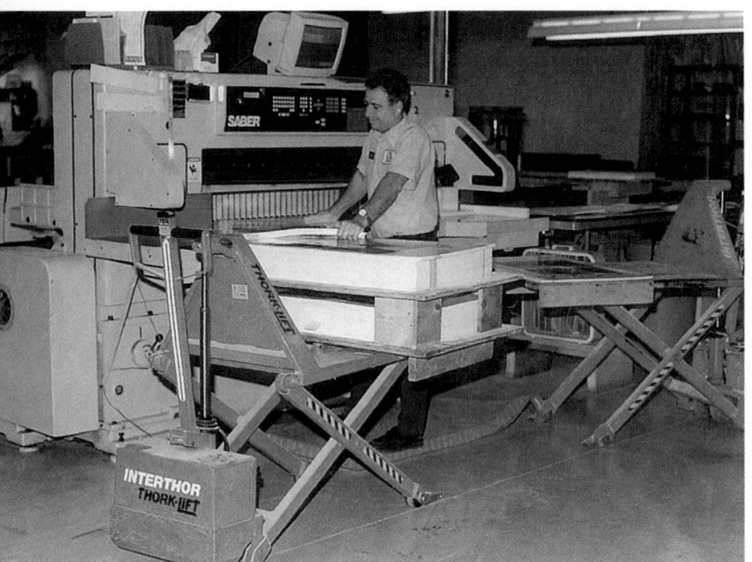

Figure 2-10. A combination lift table and pallet truck eliminates bending and lifting. (Interthor, Inc.)

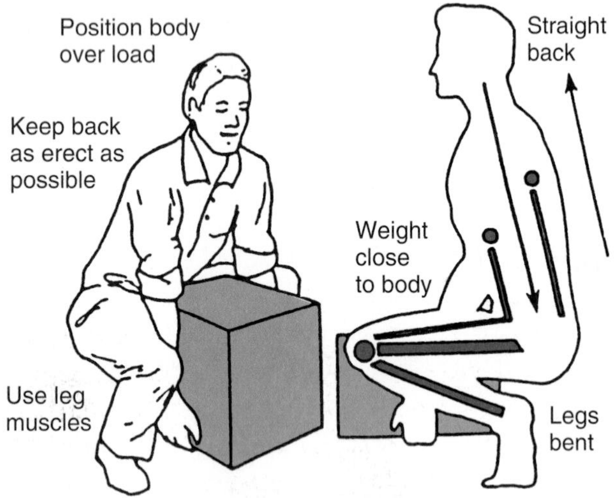

Figure 2-11. Prevent painful back injuries by using the correct lifting technique. To help maintain a straight back, keep your head up and look straight ahead.

Do not stand skid pads or pallets on edge. They are heavy enough to cause serious foot or leg injuries if they fall on someone.

Cuts from sharp materials are common injuries. Wear gloves to protect your hands when necessary. Choose gloves that suit the job while giving you the best possible protection and freedom of movement.

Some materials are banded with metal strapping. When cut, the strapping can spring and cause severe lacerations. Use extreme care if you must cut strapping, and wear proper protective equipment.

Tools and equipment handling

Keep the graphic communications facility organized. Return all tools, equipment, and supplies to their proper storage areas after use.

To prevent falls, keep floors dry and clear of tools and supplies. Clean up liquid spills immediately. Nonskid mats, adhesive strips, or coating materials may be applied to the floor around work areas, **Figure 2-12.**

Figure 2-12. Nonskid mats help prevent slipping. (Courtesy of Lab Safety Supply, Inc., Janesville, WI)

Protect your body from injury by tools or equipment. Never carry sharp objects in your pockets. They can easily puncture the skin.

As described earlier, keep all guards, shields, and covers in place. They perform the important function of keeping your hands and other body parts out of the equipment.

Tips for Safe Lifting

Routine on-the-job lifting and materials handling can lead to injury. These safety instructions will lessen the risk of serious injury to the worker who is using his or her body to lift or move materials:

- *Clear a pathway.* Before you move things from one place to another, be sure you have a clear pathway.
- *Check weight.* Check the object's weight to see if you will need help lifting it.
- *Request help.* Ask for help from another person if you need it, or use mechanical lifting equipment.
- *Keep your back straight.* Your back should be straight and vertical to the ground. Keeping your head up and looking straight ahead will help maintain this position.
- *Lift with your knees.* If you can, bend your knees when lifting; don't stoop over the object.
- *Keep objects close to your body.* Always bring the object as close to your body as possible.
- *Tighten your stomach.* Tighten your stomach muscles. This helps your back stay in balance.
- *Deliver carefully.* Use care when you put the object down. Follow the same guidelines as you would for lifting.

Never use or adjust any equipment unless you have been properly trained to do so. Make sure you have seen a demonstration or have supervision before using any equipment. Only properly certified drivers should operate a forklift. Riders are never permitted on forklifts.

Always work and act like a professional when in a graphic communications facility. Horseplay endangers the safety of individuals. A "joker" is an accident waiting to happen. If you are not sure about a safety rule or procedure, ask your supervisor.

When *operating a press,* keep these factors in mind:

- Never turn on a press unless you are sure all tools have been removed from it and all mechanisms have been set correctly.
- Make sure no one is near the press before starting the equipment.
- Check to make sure all press guards are in place.
- Keep your hands clear of the press when it is running.
- Do not try to grab paper, lubricate parts, or do anything that places your hands near the rollers and nip points while the press is running.
- Have an assistant present whenever you are cleaning or running a press. If you were to get caught in the machinery, the assistant could turn off the press.

Compressed air

Compressed air should *never* be used to clean off clothes or do general cleanup work. An air nozzle can force air through the skin and into the bloodstream, a condition that can cause death. Compressed air can also stir up paper dust, making breathing difficult and causing eye irritation.

When compressed air is used for an acceptable purpose, nozzle pressure should not exceed 30 psi (pounds per square inch) or 207 kPa (kilopascals). Always wear safety glasses when using an air nozzle.

Chemical Hazards

Chemical handling and disposal

Depending upon their chemical structure, certain substances are more harmful than others. A poisonous substance is termed a ***toxin.*** The amount of exposure to a toxic substance and the duration of exposure affect the degree of harm the substance can cause. For example, oxygen is part of the air we breathe, and in normal amounts, it keeps us alive. However, a very high concentration of oxygen can be toxic (harmful to human health).

The first line of defense against toxic materials is to know the types of chemicals you are using and the hazards involved. Chemicals should be handled with extreme care. Read the labels on chemical containers to learn specific handling procedures and potential health hazards. See **Figure 2-13.**

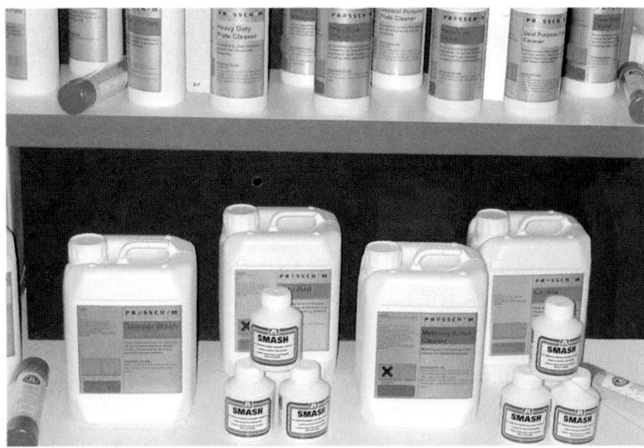

Figure 2-13. All chemical containers should be labeled. Read labels carefully before using chemicals, and note safety warnings and actions to take in an emergency.

Figure 2-14. A typical hazard identification chart with icons identifying personal protection required for various hazard categories.

Be aware of the health risks posed by hazardous materials in a graphic communications facility, and take measures to avoid harm. Chemicals can enter the body through the skin, by inhalation, or by ingestion. Wear ***personal protective devices*** appropriate to the level of hazard. Protective devices for working with chemicals include safety glasses, face shields, plastic or rubber gloves, respirators, boots, and full safety suits. See **Figure 2-14.** While exposure to some chemicals may have short-term effects, exposure to others may cause long-term health problems, even cancer.

When disposing of chemicals, do not pour them down a drain or sewer. They must be discarded in an environmentally safe manner. Some chemicals, such as photographic fixer, can be recycled to recover the silver that was dissolved from the film emulsion. Check the manufacturer's recommendations, as well as state and local environmental protection requirements, for proper disposal. Stiff fines are imposed for improper disposal of hazardous waste.

Types of chemicals and agents

The chemicals and chemical agents that pose hazards to workers in the graphic communications industry are commonly classified in four categories:

- Organic solvents.
- Platemaking chemicals.
- Ink mists.
- Gases, fumes, and dust.

Organic solvents

Some of the most common organic solvents found in the industry are blanket and roller washes, fountain solutions, plate cleaners, glaze removers, degreasers, and film cleaners. Many blanket washes used to clean the press blankets contain ***volatile organic compounds (VOCs),*** toxic substances which help the washes work well and evaporate quickly. However, the VOCs pass into the air in the pressroom, the workers' lungs, and the outside air.

Some solvents are more harmful than others, but the following ones should *not* be used: benzene, carbon tetrachloride, gasoline, chloroform, and carbon disulfide.

Breathing solvent vapors can be very harmful. Do not rely on your nose to warn you of vapors.

Specialists need to be employed to measure airborne solvents and determine safe levels.

Vapors should be exhausted away from the operator and the area kept well ventilated. Some vapors may require the operator wear a respirator. The proper respirator for each situation must be selected by an expert, **Figure 2-15.**

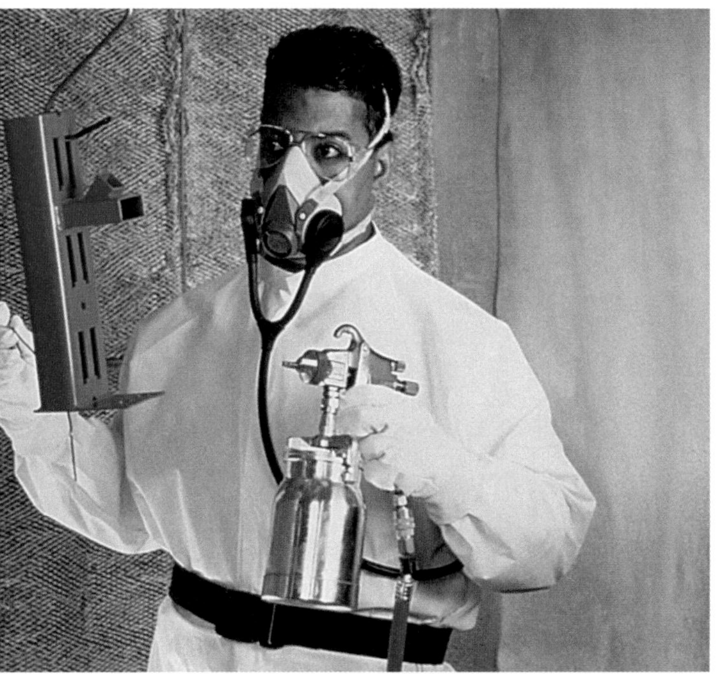

Figure 2-15. In many industrial occupations, an approved respirator is required whenever fine airborne mists of chemicals, inks, dust, paint, or other contaminants are present. (3M Company)

Solvents can also be harmful to skin or eyes. Read the container label *before* using a chemical to determine what to do in case of contact. Typically, it is recommended that the affected area be flushed with water for at least 15 minutes and then treated by a doctor. Personal protective devices such as goggles, face shields, gloves, and aprons must be worn when handling chemical solvents.

Whenever you are working with chemicals, take these general precautions against harmful solvent vapors:

- Do not attempt to identify a solvent by sniffing it.
- Keep lids and covers on cans and drums.
- Do not use large quantities of solvents in one area.
- Clean up spills immediately.
- Know the proper handling, cleanup, and disposal procedures for the chemical you are using.
- Place soiled rags in an approved safety can.
- Ventilate the press area where needed.
- Ventilate the platemaking area.
- Wash your hands before eating.

Platemaking chemicals

The chemicals used to prepare image carriers can irritate the skin and cause burns. Always wear rubber or plastic gloves or apply barrier creams when working with plate-making chemicals. Inspect gloves for pin holes before working. Never touch your face or eyes with gloves that have been in contact with a chemical.

Contact lenses should *not* be worn when working with chemicals. If splashed in the eyes, the chemicals can seep under the lenses and cause severe burning. Face shields and splash goggles are the best form of eye and face protection.

Wearing an appropriate apron will keep chemicals from reaching clothing and soaking through to the skin. Food and beverages should never be allowed to come into contact with chemicals. Chemicals that are corrosive, flammable, or poisonous should be properly labeled and stored in a safety cabinet, **Figure 2-16.**

Figure 2-16. Chemicals, safety cans, and flammable containers should be stored in an approved safety cabinet. (Justrite Manufacturing Company)

Many platemaking chemicals are concentrated. When diluting an acid, *always pour the acid into the water*. The opposite method would produce a dangerous splattering of the acid. *Never add water to concentrated acid.*

Ink mists

Rapidly rotating press rollers throw tiny droplets of ink into the air, creating an ***ink mist.*** These droplets are tiny enough to be inhaled. Ink mists often contain pigments, polymers, plasticizers, resins, and solvents that can prove harmful. Face shields and respirators should be worn for protection. Controls are necessary where a relatively large amount of ink mist is produced, such as at newspaper facilities.

Gases, fumes, and dust

Gases, fumes, and dust are chemical agents commonly found in graphic communications facilities. Proper ventilation is imperative in areas where vapors and particulate matter (dust particles) are generated.

Of much concern is ozone gas. Ozone (O_3) in the upper atmosphere, where it occurs naturally in what is known as the ozone layer, shields the earth from the sun's dangerous ultraviolet rays. However, at ground-level, it is a pollutant with highly toxic effects. Ozone damages human health, the environment, crops, and a wide range of natural and artificial materials. One source of ground-level ozone is the breakdown (oxidation) of VOCs found in solvents. Ozone gas is also created by carbon arcs, some antistatic devices, and ultraviolet ink-curing units used in printing plants.

Another hazard is carbon monoxide (CO), an odorless and colorless gas. CO is produced by the incomplete combustion of carbon-based fuels and natural and synthetic products. After being inhaled, CO molecules enter the bloodstream, where they inhibit the delivery of oxygen throughout the body. Low concentrations can cause dizziness, headaches, and fatigue; high concentrations can be fatal.

Fumes can be produced by molten materials. Acids (corrosives) also give off fumes. Rubber or plastic gloves and aprons and eye protection must be worn when handling corrosives. Many fume-producing materials are very toxic and should be considered extremely hazardous. The work area must be well-ventilated and well-lit.

Dust might be created by antisetoff powders. Another common cause of dust in graphic communication facilities is paper. Microscopic particles of dust can be inhaled and lodge in lung tissue, causing respiratory disease and lung damage. Respirators with dust filters should be worn. Systems for controlling dust and scrubbing the air are available for use in large industrial settings, **Figure 2-17.**

Figure 2-17. Tiny fog droplets sprayed by an overhead humidification system scrub dust and chemicals from the air in this graphic communications facility. (Mee Industries Inc.)

Material Safety Data Sheets

The Occupational Safety and Health Act (OSHA) requires employers to keep a list of all hazardous chemicals used on their premises, maintain a file of ***Material Safety Data Sheets (MSDS)*** on the chemicals, and train their employees to use the chemicals and respond properly should an accident occur. An MSDS gives the chemical name (common, synonyms, and formula); and the name, address, and/or telephone number of the manufacturer. See **Figure 2-18.**

The MSDS provides such information as:

- Flammability and reactivity data (vapor pressure and flash point information).
- Medical/health hazards.
- Overexposure limits/effects.
- Spill procedures.
- Personal protection information.

Material Safety Data Sheet

Preparation/Revision Date: 3/25/96

ACME Chemical Company

24 hour Emergency Phone: Chemtrec: 1-800-424-9300
Outside United States: 1-202-483-7616

Trade Name/Syn: **DICHLOROMETHANE * METHYLENE DICHLORIDE**
Chem Name/Syn: **METHYLENE CHLORIDE**
CAS Number: **75-09-2**
Formula: **Ch_2Cl_2**

NFPA Rating:
Health 4
Flammability 1
Reactivity 1

Statement of Hazard:
Possible cancer hazard. May cause cancer based on animal data. Harmful if swallowed or inhaled. Vapor irritating. May cause eye injury and/or skin irritation. May cause damage to liver, kidneys, blood, and central nervous system.

Effects of Overexposure-Toxicity-Route of Entry:
Toxic by ingestion and inhalation. Irritating on contact with skin, eyes, or mucous membranes. May cause eye injury. Inhalation of high vapor concentrations causes dizziness, nausea, headache, narcosis, irregular heartbeats, coma, and death. If vomiting occurs, methylene chloride can be aspirated into the lungs, which can cause chemical pneumonia and systemic effects. Medical conditions aggravated by exposure: heart, kidney, and liver conditions. Routes of entry: inhalation, ingestion.

Hazardous Decomposition Products:
HCL, phosgene, chlorine

Will Hazardous Polymerization Occur?
Will not occur under normal conditions.

Is the Product Stable?
Product is normally stable.

Conditions to Avoid:
Contact with open flame, welding arcs, and hot surfaces.

Spill Procedures, Disposal Requirements/Methods:
Evacuate the area of all unnecessary personnel. Wear suitable protective equipment. Eliminate any ignition sources until the area is determined to be free from explosion or fire hazard. Contain the release with a suitable absorbent. Place in a suitable container for disposal. Dispose of in accordance with all applicable federal, state, and local regulations.

Ventilation:
Local exhaust: Recommended
Mechanical (Gen): Recommended
Special: NA
Other: None

Respiratory Protection:
NIOSH/MSHA air supplied respirator.

Protective Gloves:
Viton, PVA, or equivalent to prevent skin contact.

Other Protective Equipment:
Safety glasses with side shields must be worn at all times; eyewash; fume hood.

Figure 2-18. Part of a Material Safety Data Sheet for a hazardous solvent, providing information on ventilation and personal protective equipment. Always check the MSDS before working with any chemical.

Sometimes you may need additional information about a chemical. The manufacturer or supplier should be able to supply specific information.

Fire Prevention

Most graphic communications facilities use flammable and combustible materials. Therefore, fire prevention is a crucial part of a plant safety program.

Paper dust or antisetoff powders may explode if concentrated where a spark could ignite the mixture. Solvent vapors are another source of explosion danger. Avoid spillage. When pouring solvent, make sure the area is properly vented and no ignition source is present.

Ink and solvent-soaked rags must be placed in an approved metal waste can, **Figure 2-19.** The volatile vapors are then trapped inside the container. The contents of the waste can must be disposed of daily to minimize the possibility of ***spontaneous combustion*** (ignition by rapid oxidation without an external heat source). Do not store oily or ink-soaked towels in a container that does not meet safety regulations.

Fire prevention should be a priority on the shop floor. Practice these safety precautions to reduce the risk of fire:

- Pick up dust using a vacuum cleaner; do *not* blow dust with an air hose.
- Report leaking solvent containers.
- Wipe up solvent and oil spills.
- Always use a safety can when transferring small amounts of solvent, **Figure 2-20.** Make sure flame arrestors in safety cans are intact.

Figure 2-19. An approved waste can should be used to disposed of flammable rags or towels. Empty the can regularly. (Justrite Manufacturing Company)

Figure 2-20. Flame arrestors are an important feature of safety cans. Heat is dissipated and absorbed as it passes through the arrestor. (Justrite Manufacturing Company)

- In solvent-transfer operations, properly ground and bond equipment to prevent sparking, **Figure 2-21.**
- Properly label solvents and other flammable materials.
- Do not dump solvents into drains; store and dispose of them in compliance with state and local environmental protection standards.

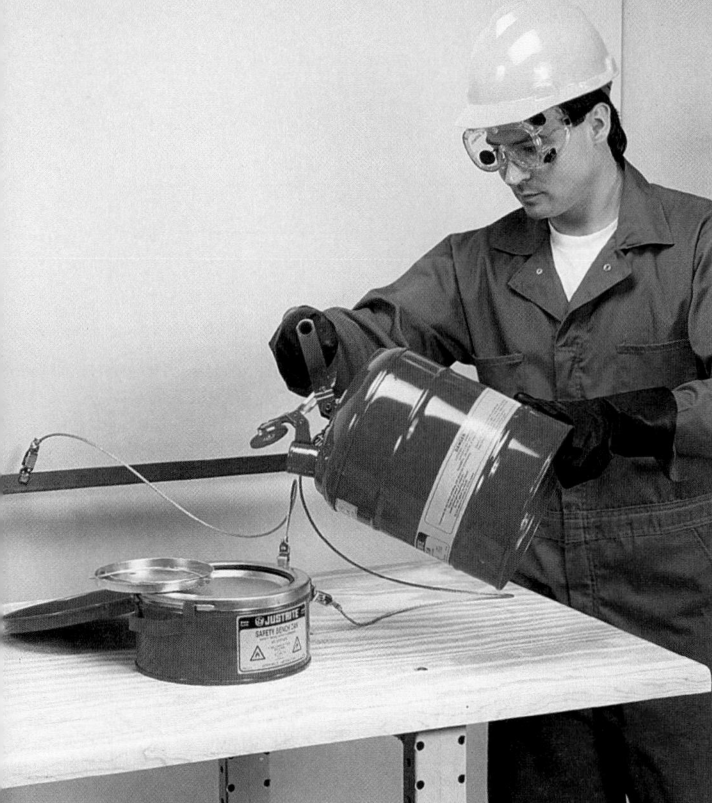

Figure 2-21. Flowing liquids can charge cans with static electricity. Static buildup can cause fires and explosions. Bonding and grounding wires prevent sparks from jumping by allowing the electric charge to balance safely. (Justrite Manufacturing Company)

- Watch for potential sources of fire, such as an overflowing safety container, dust buildup on equipment, and open chemical containers.
- No smoking! Inks, solutions, chemicals, paper, paper dust, and other substances all pose a serious fire hazard.

In case of fire, know where fire extinguishers are located and how to use them. See **Figure 2-22.** Also know the fire evacuations route. For higher visibility, many facilities outline aisles and walkways with yellow paint. Keep walkways, stairways, and exits totally free of obstruction. Being able to respond quickly and efficiently in a fire can mean the difference between a simple incident and a disaster.

Noise

Unwanted and excessively loud sound is found in many industrial facilities. Excessive noise can lead to permanent hearing loss. The best way to protect against ear damage is to control the sound. When those controls do not reduce the noise to an acceptable level, ear protection must be worn.

Sound levels are measured in units called ***decibels (dBA).*** **Figure 2-23** illustrates allowable exposure time to various decibels. A reading of 90 dBA is the maximum allowable limit for an eight -hour day. If the amount is greater than 90 dBA, a specific time limit is established.

If noise exceeds permissible levels, unwanted sound must be engineered out of the operation, or personal hearing protection devices must be provided and worn. Hearing protection devices include ear muffs, ear plugs, moldable inserts, and headsets (if they are noise-reducing), **Figure 2-24.**

Light Hazards

Light sources common to graphic communications facilities can be hazardous. Ultraviolet (UV) light, for example, can damage unprotected skin and eyes. Potentially harmful sources of light include pulsed xenon and mercury vapor lamps, UV-ink curing units, and the ozone lights used on antisetoff devices. True UV rays cannot be seen but *are* harmful; avoid contact with them. See **Figure 2-25.**

Infrared (IR) light and laser beams are also potentially harmful. When working in areas where they are in use, take special precautions to protect your eyes.

Ergonomic Hazards

A mismatch between the physical requirements of the job and the physical capacity of the worker can cause painful conditions. ***Ergonomics*** is the science of fitting the job to the worker.

In recent years, the body of knowledge about ergonomics has expanded along with the use of computers in the workplace. In graphic communications, a task such as page layout and design, formerly performed by manually cutting and pasting text and images to boards, is now done electronically utilizing desktop publishing software. Therefore, consideration must be given to the effects of computer use on human health, **Figure 2-26.**

J. J. Keller and Associates, Inc., of Neenah, Wisconsin, prepared this checklist as an evaluation tool to determine if computer workstations are appropriate for the worker.

- When seated, the operator should maintain proper posture. Are thighs horizontal?

Fire Extinguishers and Fire Classifications

Fires
Class A Fires Ordinary Combustibles (Materials such as wood, paper, textiles.) *Requires... cooling-quenching* A
Class B Fires Flammable Liquids (Liquids such as grease, gasoline, oils, and paints.) *Requires...blanketing or smothering.* B
Class C Fires Electrical Equipment (Motors, switches, and so forth.) *Requires... a nonconducting agent.* C
Class D Fires Combustible Metals (Flammable metals such as magnesium and lithium.) *Requires...blanketing or smothering.* D

Type	Use	Operation
Soda-acid Bicarbonate of soda solution and sulfuric acid 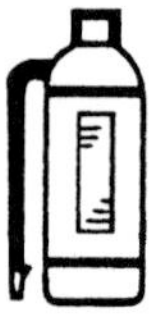	Okay for use on A Not for use on B C D	Direct stream at base of flame.
Pressurized Water Water under pressure 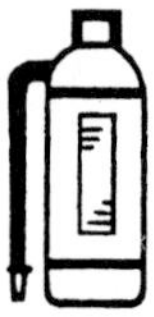	Okay for use on A Not for use on B C D	Direct stream at base of flame.
Carbon Dioxide (CO_2) Carbon dioxide (CO_2) gas under pressure 	Okay for use on B C Not for use on A D	Direct discharge as close to fire as possible, first at edge of flames and gradually forward and upward.
Foam Solution of aluminum sulfate and bicarbonate of soda 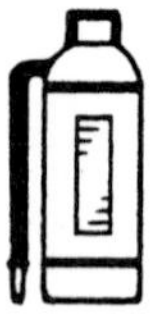	Okay for use on A B Not for use on C D	Direct stream into the burning material or liquid. Allow foam to fall lightly on fire.
Dry Chemical 	Multi-purpose type: Okay for A B C; Not okay for D Ordinary BC type: Okay for B C; Not okay for A D	Direct stream at base of flames. Use rapid left-to-right motion toward flames.
Dry Chemical Granular type material	Okay for use on D Not for use on A B C	Smother flames by scooping granular material from bucket onto burning metal.

Figure 2-22. Not every fire extinguisher will put out every kind of fire. Check the label on the extinguisher. Using the wrong extinguisher may electrocute you or produce toxic fumes.

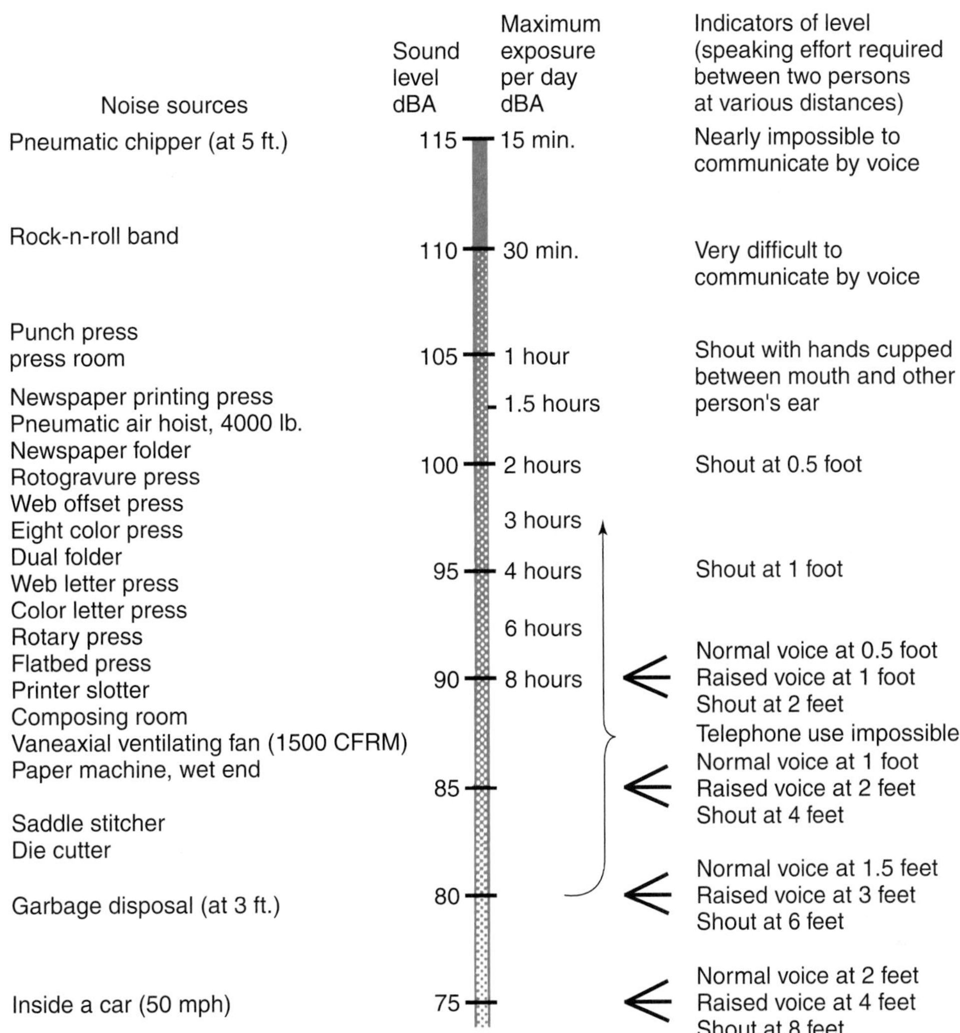

Figure 2-23. Some permissible noise exposures established by the Occupational Safety and Health Act (OSHA). When employees are subjected to sound exceeding the levels prescribed, administrative or engineering controls must be made. If such controls fail to reduce sound levels within the permissible levels, personal protective equipment must be provided.

- Are the lower legs vertical?
- Are the feet flat on the floor or on a footrest?
- Are the wrists flat?
- Is the chair easy to adjust?
- Does the chair have a padded seat with a rounded front?
- Does the chair have an adjustable backrest?
- Does the chair provide lumbar support?
- Does the chair have casters?
- Is the keyboard detachable?
- Are the height and tilt of the work surface on which the keyboard is located adjustable?
- Do keying actions require minimal force?
- Is there an adjustable document holder?
- Are the document holder and the screen the same distance from the eyes?
- Are the document holder and the screen close together to avoid excessive head movement?
- Are arm rests provided where needed?

Figure 2-24. Ear protection is often needed in the pressroom or the bindery where equipment noise is loud enough to damage your hearing. This radio headset reduces noise by 23 dBA while allowing for team communication. (Earmark, Inc.)

- Are glare and reflections avoided?
- Does the monitor have brightness and contrast controls?
- Does the operator judge the distance between eyes and work to be satisfactory for viewing?
- Is the topmost line of display no higher than the operator's eyes?
- Is there sufficient space for knees and feet?
- Are adequate rest breaks provided for task demands?
- Have employees had training for posture at the workstation?
- Have employees been trained in proper work methods?

Figure 2-25. Wear approved eye protection if you are near harmful sources of light that produce ultraviolet or infrared rays. Do not look directly at bright light when working with platemakers or cameras. (NuArc)

Figure 2-26. Workstations that are designed for health and comfort are important when you spend hours working at a computer.

Ergonomic issues are presently not regulated by the Occupational Safety and Health Act, but the "general duty" clause has been used to cite ergonomic hazards.

Environmental Compliance

Most of the safety and health guidelines discussed in this chapter are mandated by the Occupational Safety and Health Act (OSHA) for the protection of the individual worker. Another federal initiative, the Clean Air Act Amendments of 1990 (CAAA), requires the Environmental Protection Agency (EPA) to periodically review and revise national air quality standards to ensure they fully protect human health.

The CAAA continue to significantly impact lithographic printers. A 1997 EPA standard changed the National Ambient Air Quality Standards for ozone and particulate matter from 0.12 parts per million (ppm) to 0.08 ppm measured over an eight-hour period. Printers will have to fully comply with the new emission standard by 2007, or sooner if the implementation schedule is revised before then.

CAAA background

The Clean Air Act Amendments are divided into eleven titles. Not all of the titles directly affect the printing industry, however.

Title I is concerned with reducing the use of VOCs, which significantly contribute to photochemical reactions in the atmosphere. VOCs are the prime ingredient in forming ground-level ozone (smog). For example, the cleaning solvents (press washes) used in the printing industry emit VOCs and are, therefore, subject to government regulation. Plants face stiff fines for not following VOC emission regulations.

The Air Toxins Provisions of Title III has significantly affected the printing industry, as well. The Title lists 189 regulated toxic air pollutants, many found in graphic communications plants. On July 16, 1992, the EPA published a list of industry groups (known as "source categories") targeted for regulation, including major sources in the printing and publishing industry. Sources were required to install the best available air pollution control devices or Maximum Achievable Control Technology (MACT) within three years; new facilities were required to comply upon startup.

The MACT standard set emission levels for printing operations considered major sources of hazardous air pollutants, such as toluene, xylene, methanol, and hexane. Under the standard, facilities may use pollution prevention methods, which allow printers to eliminate the use of toxic chemicals or substitute non-toxic chemicals for toxic ones; traditional emissions capture and control equipment; or a combination of the two compliance options. For example, the use of substitute inks, coatings, and other materials that contain low quantities of hazardous air pollutants would preclude the need to install additional control equipment.

Most hazardous air pollutants used by printers are also VOCs. To date, the use of materials that contain low amounts of VOCs has provided a popular, alternative method for printers to meet state and federal VOC emission requirements without the costs of additional control equipment.

Under Title V, each state is required to establish rules for issuing permits for all major sources of VOCs and air toxins. The title requires facilities to obtain air permits if their emissions exceed certain limits, based on where they operate.

The Federal Clean Water Act (CWA) of 1977 governs water pollution control, regulating discharges of pollutants to U.S. waters. The commercial printing industry produces a number of pollutants potentially regulated by the CWA. Provisions and permit regulations are broad and administered by the United States EPA. Laundry effluent guidelines will most affect printers who send their shop rags to laundries. Hazardous oil spill regulations may apply to a printing facility if it works with oil and is located near a municipal storm sewer that discharges to or near a body of water.

Further information on these acts and amendments is available from the United States EPA or the appropriate state agency for environmental protection.

Reducing and eliminating waste

Typical wastes of the commercial printing industry include paper, photochemical solutions and films, inks and ink-contaminated solvents, equipment cleaning wastes (solvents, dirty rags, filters, and absorbents), and lubricating fluids from machinery.

Lithographic, gravure, flexographic, letterpress, and screen printing operations share four primary steps:

- Image (prepress) processing.
- Production of the image carrier.
- Printing.
- Finishing.

Each step generates waste and contributes to the *waste stream.* See **Figure 2-27.** However, many opportunities exist for reducing or eliminating these wastes. Described below are the wastes generated by each step in the printing operation and some pollution prevention practices that can be employed.

Image (prepress) processing

Wastes from this step include used film and wastewater containing photographic chemicals and silver.

Sending used or spoiled film and paper to silver reclaimers is currently practiced by much of the printing industry. Systems are also available for on-site reclamation; the silver is then collected by a refiner for reuse, **Figure 2-28.** Silverless films and films that use carbon black as a silver substitute are also available. Both types of silverless films are processed in a weak alkaline solution that is neutralized prior to disposal, resulting in nonhazardous wastes. Substituting silverless films eliminates the need for sending waste film to a metal reclaimer. Electrostatic films are also used frequently.

New technologies, such as computer-to-plate technology, have eliminated some of the film chemistry and the waste streams associated with films. A rapidly expanding segment of the commercial printing market is digital printing,

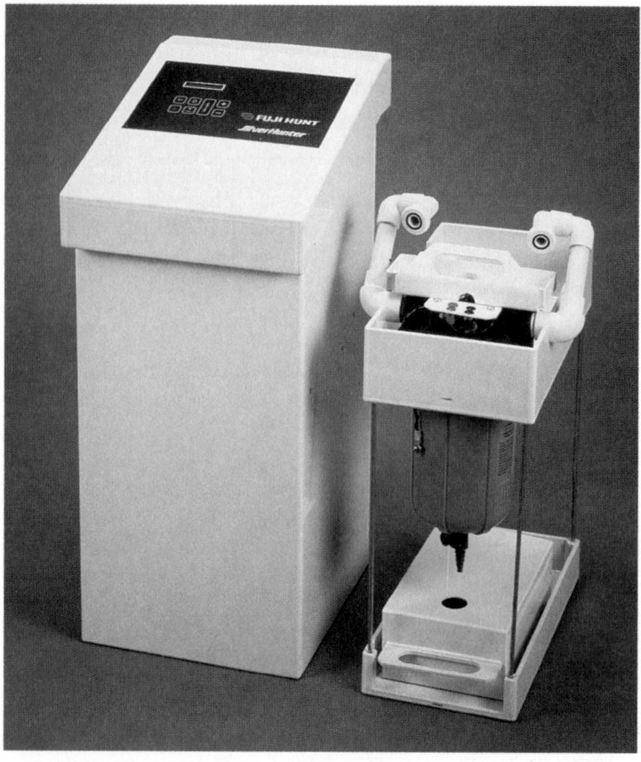

Figure 2-28. An electrolytic, recirculating silver recovery unit. The unit maintains low silver levels in the fixer tank, minimizing the amount of silver carried over into the wash tank. The complete system, including secondary metal ion exchange columns, will recover 99% or more of the available silver, meeting hazardous discharge requirements of 5.0 ppm or less. (Fuji Hunt Photographic Chemicals, Inc.)

Wastes Generated by Printing Operations

Waste Stream	Process	Composition
Solid waste	Image processing	Empty containers, used film packages, outdated material
	Platemaking	Damaged plates, developed film, dated materials
	Printing	Test production, bad printings, empty ink containers
	Finishing	Damaged products, scrap
Wastewater	Image processing	Photographic chemicals, silver
	Platemaking	Acids, alkali, solvents, plate coatings (may contain dyes, photopolymers, binders, resins, pigment, organic acids), developers (may contain isopropanol, gum arabic, lacquers, caustics), and rinse water
	Printing	Spent fountain solutions (may contain chromium)
Cleanup solvents and waste ink	Printing	Lubricating oils, waste ink, cleanup solvent (halogenated and nonhalogenated), rags
Air emissions	Makeready, printing	Solvent from heat-set inks, isopropyl alcohol fountain solution, and cleaning solvents

Illinois Environmental Protection Agency Office of Pollution Prevention

Figure 2-27. Wastes generated by printing processes.

suitable for short- to medium-run color jobs such as brochures, catalogs, direct mail pieces, fliers, and newsletters. See **Figure 2-29.**

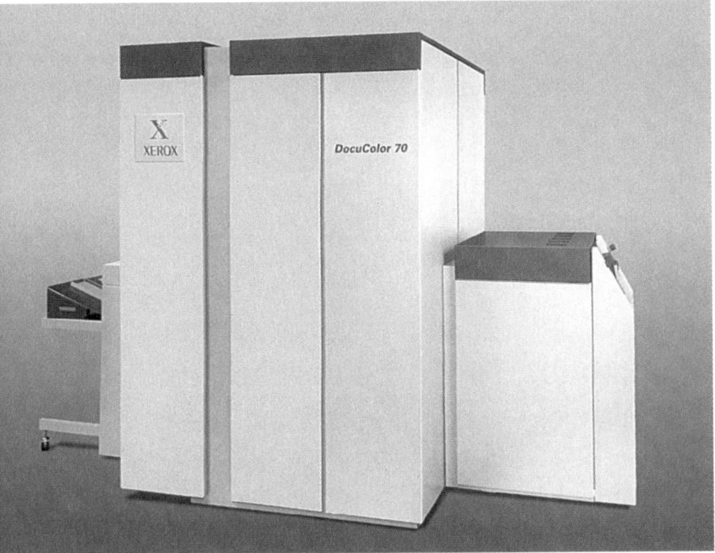

Figure 2-29. Digital color press. Digital printing is an increasingly popular alternative to offset printing for short- to medium-run length jobs. One of its benefits is minimizing impact on the environment by eliminating prepress steps requiring chemicals. (Xerox)

Production of the image carrier

Lithographic platemaking generates wastewater that may contain acids, alkalis, solvents, plate coatings, and developers. Wastewater from letterpress and flexographic plates may contain high concentrations of heavy metals. Switching from chemical processing to water processing of lithographic plates and film may eliminate development wastewaters that currently require pretreatment before discharge.

Printing

Cleaning solvents and waste ink are the primary wastes associated with the printing process. Air emissions containing VOCs from solvent-based inks and cleaning solvents are also part of the waste stream.

Typically, printers manually clean the printing equipment with a rag wetted with an organic solvent. These solvents normally contain alcohol and have low flash points (usually less than 140°F or 60°C). The rag often drips excess solvent onto the floor during cleaning. Furthermore, the solvent quickly evaporates, generating VOC emissions. Dirty rags containing solvents, waste ink, oil, dirt, and other contaminants often are sent to commercial laundries. Ink and "spent" solvents in the towels cause two major concerns for laundries and local sanitary sewer systems handling the laundry's effluent: volatility and flammability.

Several manufacturers have developed low VOC solvents with high flash points and low toxicity. Blanket washes made from vegetable oils and their fatty acid esters, terpenes (found in essential oils and plant resins), less volatile petroleum components, or a mixture have proven suitable substitutes. Compared to standard solvent-based washes that can contain up to 100% VOCs, the VOC content of vegetable ester washes is typically 12% to 30%. Vegetable and water mixtures drop to as low as 2%.

Some viable pollution prevention measures include using a less volatile solvent, applying solvents conservatively using squeeze bottles or plunger cans, or "wringing out" excess solvent from rags using a centrifuge (and reusing the recovered solvent).

Ink recovery machines make on-site reclaiming an option. Solvent recycling companies can also perform the task for printing operations that generate small quantities of ink and solvent wastes.

Substitute inks, such as UV-cured inks and water- or vegetable-based inks are suitable for some printing applications. UV-cured inks contain no solvent and dry by exposure to ultraviolet light. They are nearly 100% solids and have a VOC content of 1% or less. UV printed papers can be repulped and recycled as an added environmental benefit. Vegetable oils use less fountain additives than do mineral oils and accordingly reduce chemical use, **Figure 2-30.**

Finishing

Most of the waste from finishing operations is scrap paper. Scrap or waste paper from printing operations can be recycled into new paper. The market for recycled paper is good, shaped by depleted landfill space, tightening access to forest resources, changes in consumer awareness and preferences, and government restrictions. Technological improvements in recycled paper, such as stronger fiber and improved pulp, will continue to provide incentives for printers to send waste paper to commercial paper recyclers and to buy recycled paper for printing.

Figure 2-30. Vegetable oils in inks are a sustainable resource and free of VOCs. While soybeans are the primary oil source for these inks, oils from linseed, rapeseed, and sunflower seed are also used. (National Soy Ink Information Center)

Buying recycled paper is just the beginning. States are increasingly adopting totally chlorine-free paper purchasing policies. Chlorine, a chemical compound used to bleach paper products, has been linked with ozone depletion. Legislation for state purchase of chlorine-free paper is being modeled after laws mandating state purchase of recycled products.

Process evaluation

An excellent way to uncover new methods for reducing and eliminating waste is to evaluate the steps in the printing process. The review can be incorporated into the plant's overall safety and health program. Follow these directions for conducting a review:

- Record each step in your printing process, from purchasing raw materials to shipping the finished product.
- Diagram the process, noting every point where materials are used and wastes are created. (Include steps that are indirectly part of the process such as waste disposal and electricity use.)
- Where wastes are generated, estimate the cost of lost raw material, and costs resulting from collecting, tracking, and disposing of the wastes.
- Examine the diagram to pinpoint where the wastes are produced, and determine a plan for waste reduction. For example, you may be able to consolidate chemicals, replacing infrequently used ones with multiple-use chemicals.

Safety Audit

Safe conditions depend on a constant vigilance for possible hazards. That is why periodic inspections are one of the most important aspects of a successful safety and health program. **Figure 2-31** provides a safety checklist for identifying problems in a graphic communications facility so that corrective action can be taken.

Maintaining Tools, Equipment, and Machines

To operate safely and efficiently, the tools, equipment, and machines used in communication graphics must be regularly maintained according to the manufacturer's requirements and recommended procedures. Failing to perform required maintenance, or not following recommended procedures, can cause injury to workers, or damage to equipment and machines. It can also void the manufacturer's warranty and require costly repairs or replacement.

For many tools, equipment, and machines, maintenance procedures and requirements can be found in the owner's manual. More complex machines, such as printing presses, usually will have a separate maintenance manual.

Maintenance activities typically include:

- Cleaning, adjustment, and lubrication of specific areas or assemblies.
- Measuring to find whether tolerances are correct and making necessary adjustments to bring them "into spec."
- Checking alignment of parts and tightness of fasteners.
- Measuring wear on moving parts and adjusting or replacing parts as needed.
- Testing and calibrating electronic equipment (such as monitors) to provide correct output.

To be sure maintenance is done at the recommended intervals, many companies keep a maintenance log. It lists the procedures to be done and the time when they should be performed. As each maintenance task is completed, the worker responsible signs and dates the log.

Safety Inspection Checklist

	Satisfactory	Unsatisfactory	Not Applicable	Dangerous	Remarks
I. Housekeeping					
A. Clean and orderly work area					
B. Proper materials available for housekeeping					
C. Floor holes (drains) covered					
D. Materials available for cleaning					
E. Maintenance schedule used					
F. Properly marked aisles					
G. Proper storage facilities					
H. Proper disposal systems					
I. Warnings and cautions posted					
J. Containers labeled					
K. Open aisles and fire lanes					
L. Proper handling devices					
M. Vacuuming used where possible					
II. Personal Protective Equipment					
A. Eye protection					
B. Foot protection					
C. Head protection					
D. Protective clothing					
E. Ear protection					
F. Respiratory equipment					
III. Administration					
A. Safety program					
1. Education-safety personnel					
2. Incentives					
B. Procedures					
1. Recordkeeping					
2. Accident and injury handling					
3. Emergency evacuation plan					
4. Posting					
C. Job hazard analysis					
IV. Equipment/Machinery					
A. Fixed guarding					
B. Movable guarding					
C. Equipment placement					
D. Maintenance					
E. Mechanical controls					
F. Proper enclosure					
V. Electrical					
A. Grounding					
B. Wiring					
C. Circuits identified					
D. Switch location					
E. Extension cords					
F. Portable electrical equipment					

Figure 2-31. A safety inspection checklist that can be used for evaluating workplace safety conditions.

Figure 2-31 continued.

VI. Chemicals	Satisfactory	Unsatisfactory	Not Applicable	Dangerous	Remarks
A. Storage					
B. Ventilation					
C. Proper identification					
D. Handing devices					
E. Clean up methods					
F. Disposal					
VII. Fire Protection					
A. Flammable materials					
1. Safe storage (cabinet)					
2. Proper labeling					
3. Proper containers					
4. Disposal of rags					
B. Fire equipment					
1. Fire extinguishers					
a. Right type for location					
b. Clearly visible					
2. Automatic sprinkler					
3. Blankets (same as fire extinguishers)					
4. Smoke detectors					
5. Flame and fume arrestors					
6. Proper waste disposal					
C. Fire drills					
1. Proper exits signs					
2. Availability of exits					
3. Dissemination of exit information					
4. Education of employees					
D. Periodic checking					
VIII. First Aid					
A. First aid facility provided					
B. Qualified first aid personnel					
1. Nurse provided					
2. First aid training available					

Review Questions

Please do not write in this text. Write your answers on a separate sheet of paper.

1. What is the purpose of a workplace safety and health program?
2. Machine guarding protects the operator from hazards posed by what four types of machine action?
3. This dangerous condition exists where two cylinders meet or come close to one another.
   a. Shear point.
   b. Rip point.
   c Nip point.
   d. Cut point.
4. What is the purpose of a lockout device?
5. How should you dress when operating machinery in a graphic communications facility?
6. How can you help maintain a straight back when lifting a heavy object?
7. Inks, blanket wash, fountain solutions, and plate cleaners are examples of:
   a. inorganic solutions.
   b. organic solvents.
   c. tetrachlorides.
   d. Benzenes.
8. How should you dispose of ink and solvent-soaked rags?
9. A dBA reading of _____ is the maximum allowable limit for an eight-hour day without ear protection.
10. Standard solvent-based washes can contain up to 100% VOCs, while vegetable ester washes contain _____% VOCs.

3 Measurement

Learning Objectives

After studying this chapter, you will be able to:

- Differentiate between the US Conventional and SI Metric systems of measurement, and make conversions from one system to the other.
- Describe the point system of type measurement.
- Use a line gauge and E gauge to measure point sizes of type.
- Identify standard grades of paper and basic paper sizes.
- Measure grades of paper by basis weight, thickness, and brightness.
- Explain how visual images are produced and measured in a desktop publishing system.
- Understand the use of proportional scales, screens, and tint measurements in the reproduction of images.

Important Terms

densitometer
E gauge
ISO series
line gauge
pica
point
proportional scale
resolution
screen angles
screen tint

Measurement is used in almost every aspect of graphic reproduction. This chapter covers different systems and methods of measurement and demonstrates how vital they are to the graphic communications industry. The chapter begins with a discussion of the two most widely used systems of measurement, US Conventional and SI Metric. The point system of measurement, used throughout applications in graphics and design, is also discussed. The different standards used to measure paper sizes and weights are then covered. The chapter concludes with a discussion on developing technology in the production of images and the use of common measuring devices in the graphic communications industry. A thorough understanding of this chapter will prepare you for later chapters that apply different uses of measurement.

Measurement Principles

Throughout history, systems of measurement have been necessary in all parts of society. Different forms of measure have not only served as a means to describe quantities or values, but also provided the basic functions required for communication. Some of the first measuring terms ever used referred to parts of the human body. For instance, the distance spanned by four fingers was known as four *digits,* while the hand was also a common measuring unit, representing about 4″. The length of a forearm was once called a *cubit* or six *palms,* and the length of a person's foot represented the distance of 1′.

More sophisticated measuring systems evolved as the growth of industry and trade created the need for standardization. Common agreement on units of measure developed as more accurate and consistent methods of measurement came into use.

The two most commonly used systems of measurement today are the ***US Conventional system*** and the ***SI Metric system.*** The US Conventional system was derived from the English system of weights and measures, which evolved from traditional standards and was established in many parts of the world by the 19th century. The metric system, by contrast, was designed specifically as a standard measuring system in response to the need for standardization. It originated in France in 1790 and became recognized as a worldwide coordinated system.

The U.S. Constitution, ratified in 1788, empowered Congress to establish uniform standards for weights and measures. Today, the National Bureau of Standards assures uniformity. The most common conventional and metric measurements are listed in **Figure 3-1**.

In 1866, the United States legalized the metric system as a standard for weights and measures. But the system has remained largely unused in U.S. industry despite the Metric Conversion Act (signed in 1975), which established a national policy to coordinate conversion to metric standards.

Metric System

The metric system is the most commonly used system of weights and measures in the world. While the system is not fully understood or used in the United States, it is recognized as the international standard.

The metric system is a *decimal system* based on values of 10. The system was originally developed with the ***meter*** as the standard unit of length, the ***gram*** as the standard unit of mass, and the ***liter*** as the standard unit of capacity. The SI Metric system (the *Systeme International d'Unites,* or International

Approximate Equivalents			
Unit	**US Conventional**	**SI Metric**	**Use**
Length	inch (in) feet (ft) yard (yd) mile (mi)	millimeter (mm) meter (m) meter (m) kilometer (km)	Paper, wrapping material, plates, wire rolls, scales, press calibration Covers, tapes, binders
Pressure	pounds per square inch (psi)	kilopascal (kPa)	Web press ink pressure, air pressure, vacuum
Power	horsepower (hp)	kilowatt (kw)	Electric motor rating
Torque	pound-feet (lb-ft)	newton-meter (N•m)	Bolt tightening
Volume or Capacity	fluid ounces (oz) quart (qt) cubic inch (in^3)	milliliters (ml) liter (L) cubic centimeter (cc)	Ink, oil Plate chemicals Storage, shipping
Mass or weight	ounce (oz) pound (lb)	gram (g) kilograms (kg)	Postage, padding cement, chemicals, shipping, supplies
Speed	feet per second miles per hour (mph) revolutions per minute (rpm)	meters per second kilometers per hour (km/h) revolutions per minute (rpm)	Web press speed
Application rates	fluid ounce per square foot (fl-oz/ft^2) ounces per square feet (oz/ft^2)	milliliters per square meter (ml/m^2) grams per square meter (g/m^2)	Applying materials, ink coverage, estimating

Figure 3-1. Customary units of measure and metric equivalents. Common uses for each measurement are listed at right.

System of Units) is a modernized version of the metric system established by international agreement. The SI Metric system is built upon a foundation of seven base units of measure, as listed below:

- **Length** = *meter (m)*
- **Mass** = *kilogram (kg)*
- **Time** = *second (s)*
- **Electric current** = *ampere (A)*
- **Temperature** = *Kelvin (K)* or degree *Celsius (°C)*
- **Amount of substance** = *mole (mol)*
- **Luminous intensity** = *candela (cd)*

Metric prefixes

The process of making different computations involving measure is simpler when using the metric system, because metric units are structured in multiples of 10. ***Metric prefixes*** indicate multiples or divisions of these units. See **Figure 3-2**.

Common Metric Prefixes				
mega (M)	=	1 000 000	or	10^6
kilo (k)	=	1000	or	10^3
hecto (h)	=	100	or	10^2
centi (c)	=	0.01	or	10^{-2}
milli (m)	=	0.001	or	10^{-3}
micro (μ)	=	0.000 001	or	10^{-6}

Examples			
kilogram	=	1000	grams
milligram	=	0.001	gram
dekometer	=	10	meters
centimeter	=	0.01	meter
hectoliter	=	100	liters
decimeter	=	0.1	meter

Figure 3-2. Prefixes are used to identify units in the metric system.

Rules of metric notation

Several rules are observed when expressing figures in metric notation. The following are standards used when abbreviating metric quantities:

- Unit symbols are not capitalized unless the unit is a proper name (mm)
- Unit symbols are not followed by periods (mm)
- Unit symbols are not pluralized in an abbreviation (10 g)
- A space separates the numeral from the unit symbols (2 mm)
- Spaces, not commas, are used to separate large numbers into groups of three digits (21 210 km)
- A zero precedes the decimal point if the numeral is less than one (0.11 g)

Metric conversion

Since there is still widespread use of US Conventional measures in the graphic communications industry, it is sometimes necessary to convert to or from metric values. For instance, if a chemical quantity is given in liters and the equipment uses mixture ratios in quarts, one of the values has to be converted to the other system.

A ***metric conversion chart*** can be used to change a metric value to a conventional value or a conventional value to a metric value. See **Figure 3-3**. Values are converted from one system to another by multiplying known quantities by a given number.

Type Measurement

Type sizes are used to distinguish different measures of printed type. The units of measure most commonly used for sizes of type in English-speaking countries are the point and pica, known as the ***point system.*** Type sizes are measured in points, while line lengths are given in picas and points.

The ***point*** measures approximately 1/72 of an inch. It is also commonly expressed as 0.0138″. The ***pica*** measures approximately 1/6 of an inch. Twelve points equal a pica, and six picas equal approximately one inch (0.996″).

A ***line gauge*** is an instrument used to measure type sizes and line lengths in picas or inches. See **Figure 3-4.** Line gauges typically measure up to 72 picas (approximately 12″). One side of the gauge is marked in inches, and the other side is marked in picas and ***nonpareils*** (units equal to one-half pica).

Didot point system

The American point system was adopted for use in the United States in 1886. It was based on the Fournier point system developed in 1737 by Pierre Simon Fournier, a French typographer. The

CONVENTIONAL/METRIC CONVERSION CHART

UNIT EQUIVALENTS

Multiply:	by:	to get:	by:	to get:
ACCELERATION				
feet/sec^2	x 0.3048	= meters/sec^2 (m/s^2)	x 3.281	= feet/sec^2
inches/sec^2	x 0.0254	= meters/sec^2 (m/s^2)	x 39.37	= inches/sec^2
ENERGY OR WORK (watt–second = joule = newton–meter)				
foot–pounds	x 1.3558	= joules (J)	x 0.7376	= foot–pounds
calories	x 4.187	= joules (J)	x 0.2388	= calories
Btu	x 1055	= joules (J)	x 0.000948	= Btu
watt–hours	x 3600	= joules (J)	x 0.0002778	= watt–hours
kilowatt–hrs.	x 3.600	= megajoules (MJ)	x 0.2778	= kilowatt-hrs
FUEL ECONOMY AND FUEL CONSUMPTION				
miles/gal	x 0.42514	= kilometers/liter (km/L)	x 2.3522	= miles/gal
Note: 235.2/(mi/gal) = liters/100km; 235.2/(liters/100 km) = mi/gal				
LIGHT				
footcandles	x 10.76	= lumens/meter^2 (lm/m^2)	x 0.0929	= footcandles
PRESSURE OR STRESS (newton/sq meter = pascal)				
inches Hg(60 F)	x 3.377	= kilopascals (kPa)	x 0.2961	= inches Hg
pounds/sq in	x 6.895	= kilopascals (kPa)	x 0.145	= pounds/sq in
inches H_2O(60 F)	x 0.2488	= kilopascals (kPa)	x 4.0193	= inches H_2O
bars	x 100	= kilopascals (kPa)	x 0.01	= bars
pounds/sq ft	x 47.88	= pascals (Pa)	x 0.02088	= pounds/sq ft
POWER				
horsepower	x 0.746	= kilowatts (kW)	x 1.34	= horsepower
ft–lbf/min	x 0.0226	= watts (W)	x 44.25	= ft–lbf/min
TORQUE				
pounds–inches	x 0.11298	= newton–meters (N-m)	x 8.851	= pound–inches
pound–feet	x 1.3558	= newton–meters (N-m)	x 0.7376	= pound–feet
VELOCITY				
miles/hour	x 1.6093	= kilometers/hour (km/h)	x 0.6214	= miles/hour
feet/sec	x 0.3048	= meters/sec (m/s)	x 3.281	= feet/sec
kilometers/hr	x 0.27778	= meters/sec (m/s)	x 3.600	= kilometers/hr
miles/hour	x 0.4470	= meters/sec (m/s)	x 2.237	= miles/hour

COMMON METRIC PREFIXES

mega	(M)	= 1 000 000	or 10^6	centi	(c)	= 0.01	or 10^{-2}
kilo	(k)	= 1 000	or 10^3	milli	(m)	= 0.001	or 10^{-3}
hecto	(h)	= 100	or 10^2	micro	(μ)	= 0.000 001	or 10^{-6}

UNIT EQUIVALENTS

Multiply:	by:	to get:	by:	to get:
LINEAR				
inches	x 25.4	= millimeters (mm)	x 0.03937	= inches
feet	x 0.3048	= meters (m)	x 3.281	= feet
yards	x 0.9144	= meters (m)	x 1.0936	= yards
miles	x 1.6093	= kilometers (km)	x 0.6214	= miles
inches	x 2.54	= centimeters (cm)	x 0.3937	= inches
microinches	x 0.0254	= micrometers (μm)	x 39.37	= microinches
AREA				
inches^2	x 645.16	= millimeters^2(mm^2)	x 0.00155	= inches^2
inches^2	x 6.452	= centimeters^2(cm^2)	x 0.155	= inches^2
feet^2	x 0.0929	= meters^2(m^2)	x 10.764	= feet^2
yards^2	x 0.8361	= meters^2(m^2)	x 1.196	= yards^2
acres^2	x 0.4047	= hectares (10^{4}m^2) (ha)	x 2.471	= acres
miles^2	x 2.590	= kilometers^2 (km^2)	x 0.3861	= miles^2
VOLUME				
inches^3	x 16387	= millimeters^3 (mm^3)	x 0.000061	= inches^3
inches^3	x 16.387	= centimeters^3 (cm^3)	x 0.06102	= inches^3
inches^3	x 0.01639	= liters (L)	x 61.024	= inches^3
quarts	x 0.94635	= liters (L)	x 1.0567	= quarts
gallons	x 3.7854	= liters (L)	x 0.2642	= gallons
feet^3	x 28.317	= liters (L)	x 0.03531	= feet^3
feet^3	x 0.02832	= meters^3 (m^3)	x 35.315	= feet^3
fluid oz	x 29.57	= milliliters (mL)	x 0.03381	= fluid oz
yards^3	x 0.7646	= meters^3 (m^3)	x 1.3080	= yards^3
teaspoons	x 4.929	= milliliters (mL)	x 0.2029	= teaspoons
cups	x 0.2366	= liters (L)	x 4.227	= cups
MASS				
ounces (av)	x 28.35	= grams (g)	x 0.03527	= ounces (av)
pounds (av)	x 0.4536	= kilograms (kg)	x 2.2046	= pounds (av)
tons (2000 lb)	x 907.18	= kilograms (kg)	x 0.001102	= tons (2000 lb)
tons (2000 lb)	x 0.90718	= metric tons (t)	x 1.1023	= tons (2000 lb)
FORCE				
ounces—f (av)	x 0.278	= newtons (N)	x 3.597	= ounces—f (av)
pounds—f (av)	x 4.448	= newtons (N)	x 0.2248	= pounds—f (av)
kilograms—f	x 9.807	= newtons (N)	x 0.10197	= kilograms—f

TEMPERATURE

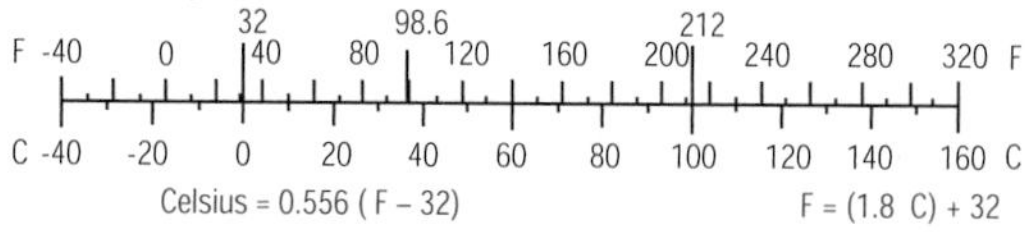

F -40 0 32 40 80 98.6 120 160 200 212 240 280 320 F

C -40 -20 0 20 40 60 80 100 120 140 160 C

Celsius = 0.556 (F – 32) F = (1.8 C) + 32

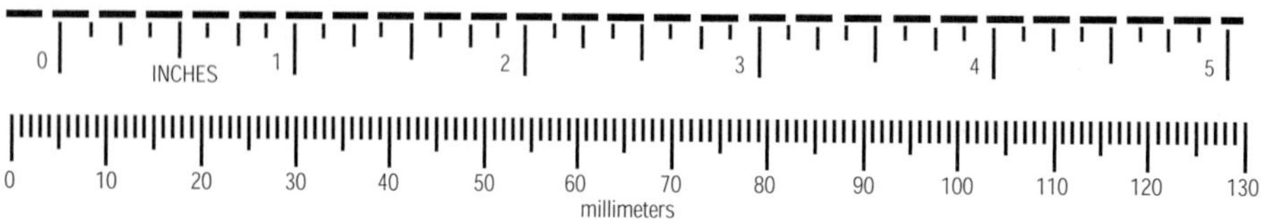

INCHES 0 1 2 3 4 5

0 10 20 30 40 50 60 70 80 90 100 110 120 130 millimeters

Figure 3-3. A metric conversion chart can be used to change values from one measuring system to another.

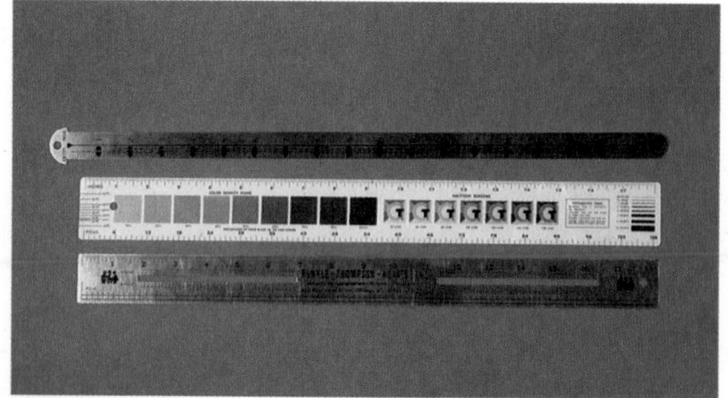

Figure 3-4. A set of line gauges with scales in both picas and inches, used to measure type sizes and line lengths.

Fournier point was later modified by a French printing family known as the Didots. The ***didot point system,*** based on the French inch, became the conventional printer's measure used in Europe and remains the standard today. The didot point is equal to 0.0148 . Twelve didot points equal the didot pica, called the ***cicero.*** A cicero is equal to 0.1776".

Metric type sizes

Metric units are also used to measure sizes of type. For example, millimeters can be used to give the equivalent sizes for either *pica point* (American point system) or *didot point* (European point system) sizes. One pica point equals 0.351 mm. One didot point equals 0.376 mm. Equivalent measures for the metric, pica, and didot point systems are shown in **Figure 3-5.**

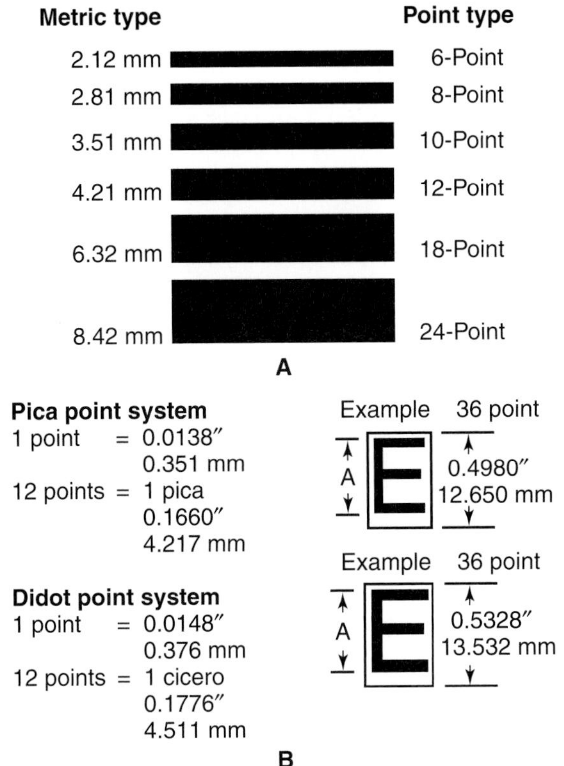

Figure 3-5. Standard point and metric sizes of type. A—Metric type is measured in millimeters, while type in the point system is measured in points. B—Different equivalents for type sizes in point, metric, and didot units.

Measuring point size

The point size or metric size of a letter is not a measurement from the top to the bottom of the letter itself. The point size also includes a small amount of white space above and below the letter for line spacing. Since different styles of type have different amounts of white space above and below the letter shape, it is difficult to measure the actual point size. Some typographers can identify a point size on sight. Others use an *E gauge* or similar measuring device, **Figure 3-6.**

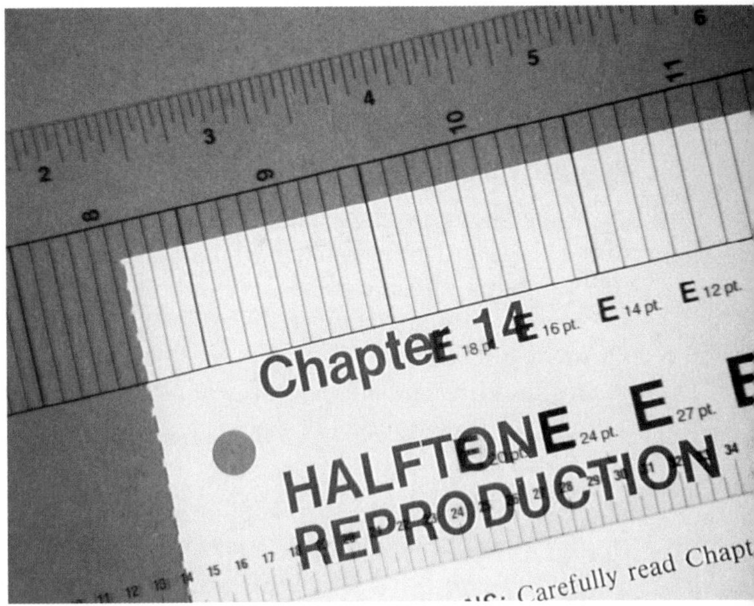

Figure 3-6. An E gauge is a measuring device for different point sizes of type and leading. The uppercase "E" in the chapter title is set in 24-point type.

The E gauge has a series of capital "E" letters with point sizes indicated for each letter. The correct point size can be determined by placing the gauge flat over a line of type and matching the letter "E" closest in size to the letters in the line.

A comparison of two different typefaces having the same point size but different letter heights is shown in **Figure 3-7.** The typefaces are both printed

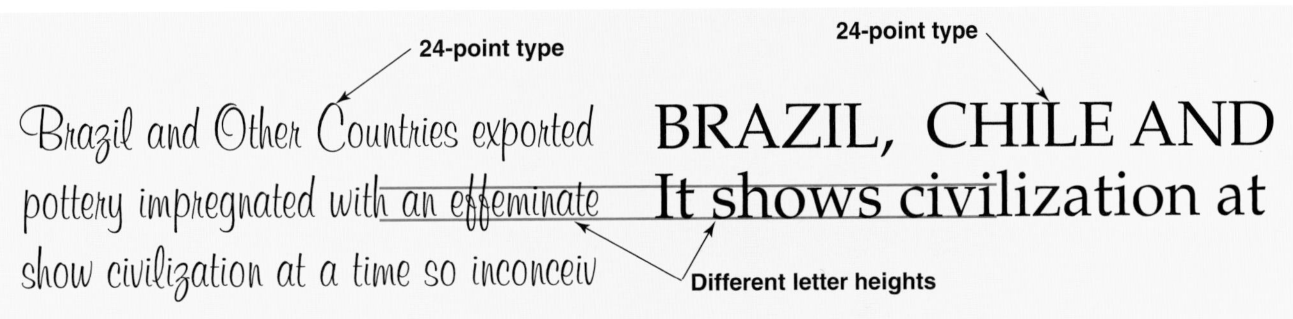

Figure 3-7. Two typefaces with the same point size but different letter heights. The point size of a letter includes the measurement of white space above and below the letter.

in 24-point type. However, the actual size of the letters is different. Identifying the correct point size is difficult without having typographical experience or using an E gauge.

The amount of vertical space between lines of type is also measured in points and is called *leading*. An E gauge has a series of line spacing grids marked with point sizes that can be used to approximate leading. When the gauge is placed over several lines of type, the grid that most closely matches the spacing between the lines indicates the leading point size.

Measuring Paper Sizes

Paper sizes are designated in length and width dimensions and are given in both inches and metric units. Paper for business use is commonly packaged in *reams,* which consist of 500 sheets. See **Figure 3-8**. Different types of paper are known as *grades* and are classified with a *basic size.* Some commonly used grades of paper, and their basic sizes, are listed below:

- **Bond,** 17″ × 22″
- **Book,** 25″ × 38″
- **Offset,** 25″ × 38″
- **Cover,** 20″ × 26″
- **Text,** 25″ × 38″

Envelopes

Envelopes are classified by size and distinguished by styles that serve a special use. Business envelope sizes are usually designated by number. The most commonly used size is a Number 10, which measures 4 1/8″ × 9 1/2″. Window envelopes are available in the same size and are generally used for invoices or statements.

Envelopes used for wedding announcements and invitations or other formal occasions commonly measure 5″ × 6″. Open-end envelopes are larger types used for mailing reports, pamphlets, magazines, and other materials. Common sizes are 9″ × 12″ and 8 3/4″ × 11 1/4″.

Postal regulations should be reviewed in order to meet current mailing standards. Envelope sizes must comply with regulations so that additional charges are not assessed for mail deliveries. See **Figure 3-9**.

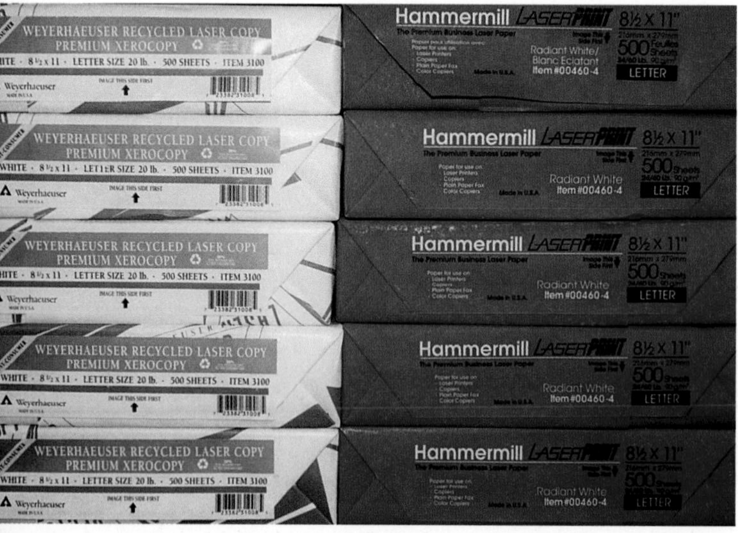

Figure 3-8. Paper packaged in reams of 500 sheets. Labels identify the paper size.

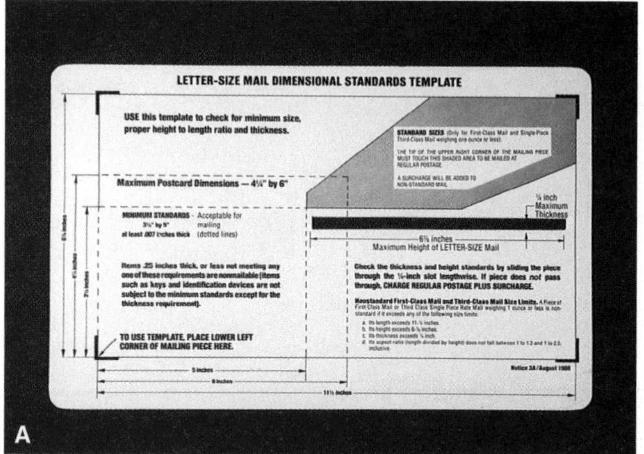

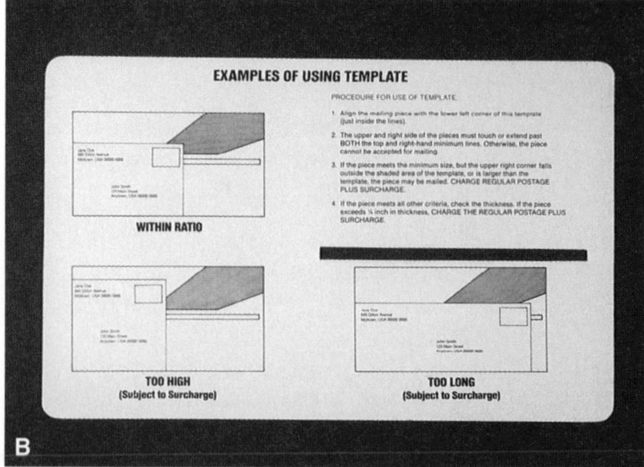

Figure 3-9. A dimensional standards template used to determine if letter size is acceptable for normal handling in mail delivery. A—Horizontal and vertical lines indicate minimum requirements for length and height. B—The upper right corner of the letter must fall within the shaded area of the template to meet standards.

ISO sizes

Standard sizes for paper and envelopes have been established by the International Organization for Standardization (ISO). The sizes, known as the ***ISO series,*** are given in both SI Metric units (millimeters) and US Conventional units (inches). ISO sizes are commonly grouped into three series. *A-series sizes* are used for general printing requirements. *B-series sizes* are used for posters. *C-series sizes* are used for postcards, folders, and envelopes.

The A-series and B-series metric paper sizes are rectangular. Their sizes are based on the ratio of the two sides having the proportion of one to the square root of two (1:1.416).

The ISO-A size of paper is based on the area of one square meter, as shown in **Figure 3-10**. Each cut reduces the size of the sheet by 50% of the previous size; for example, the size of A2 is double that of A3. Each ISO-A measurement is listed in **Figure 3-11**.

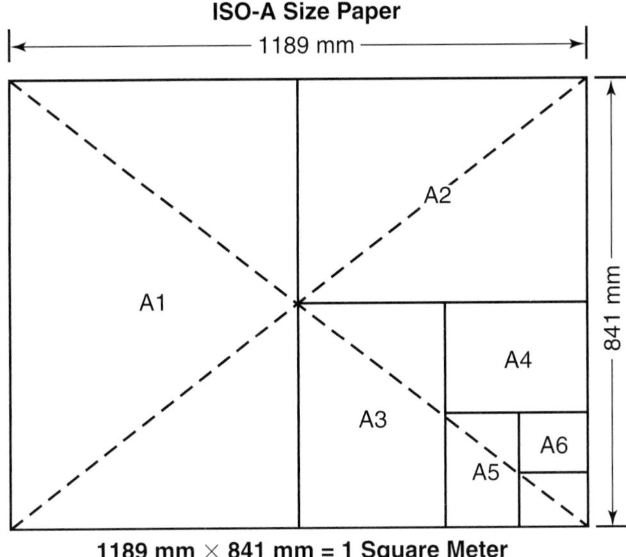

Figure 3-10. ISO-A metric size paper. The dimensions are based on the area of one square meter.

ISO-A and ISO-B metric paper sizes are considered to be trimmed sizes. However, there are other series used to classify sizes for normal trims, bleed work, and extra trims. See **Figure 3-12**.

ISO-B paper sizes are listed in **Figure 3-13**. The different sizes are based on the same ratio used in measuring ISO-A sizes (1:1.416). A comparison of ISO-A, ISO-B, and ISO-C paper sizes is shown in **Figure 3-14**.

ISO Sizes	Metric (mm)	Conventional (″)
A0	841 × 1189	33.11 × 46.81
A1	594 × 841	23.39 × 33.11
A2	420 × 594	16.54 × 23.39
A3	297 × 420	11.69 × 16.54
A4	210 × 297	8.27 × 11.69
A5	148 × 210	5.83 × 8.27
A6	105 × 148	4.13 × 5.83
A7	74 × 105	2.91 × 4.13
A8	52 × 74	2.05 × 2.91
A9	37 × 52	1.46 × 2.05
A10	26 × 37	1.02 × 1.46

Figure 3-11. ISO-A metric and conventional paper sizes.

ISO Sizes for Normal Trims		
ISO Size	Metric (mm)	Conventional (″)
RA0	860 × 1220	33.66 × 48.03
RA1	610 × 860	24.02 × 33.86
RA2	430 × 610	16.93 × 24.02
ISO Sizes for Bleed Work or Extra Trims		
ISO Size	Metric (mm)	Conventional (″)
SRA0	900 × 1280	35.43 × 50.39
SRA1	640 × 900	25.20 × 35.43
SRA2	450 × 640	17.72 × 25.20

Figure 3-12. ISO trimmed paper sizes for normal trims, bleed work, and extra trims. (Center for Metric Education, Western Michigan University)

ISO Sizes	Metric (mm)	Conventional (″)
B0	1000 × 1414	39.37 × 55.67
B1	707 × 1000	27.83 × 39.37
B2	500 × 707	19.68 × 27.83
B3	353 × 500	13.90 × 19.68
B4	250 × 353	9.84 × 13.90
B5	176 × 250	6.93 × 9.84
B6	125 × 176	4.92 × 6.93
B7	88 × 125	3.46 × 4.92
B8	62 × 88	2.44 × 3.46
B9	44 × 62	1.73 × 2.44
B10	31 × 44	1.22 × 1.73

Figure 3-13. ISO-B metric and conventional paper sizes. (Center for Metric Education, Western Michigan University)

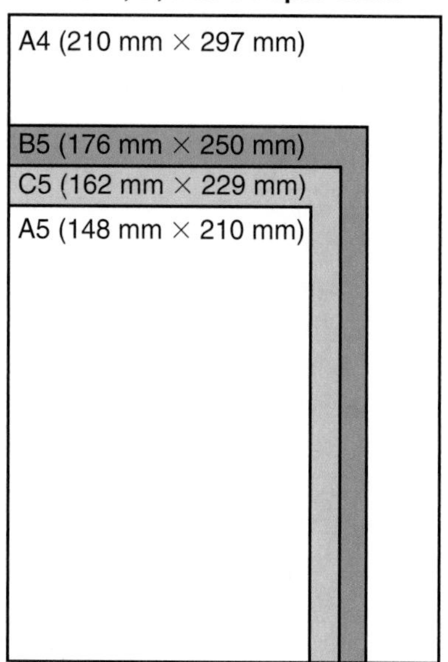

Figure 3-14. Common ISO-A, B, and C paper sizes.

The sizes for ISO-A sheets are compatible with the sizes for ISO-C envelopes. See **Figure 3-15**. One envelope size, designated DL, is not derived from ISO-A, B, or C sizes.

Paper Weight

Most grades of paper are known by their ***basis weight***, which is a measure of the number of pounds in a ream of paper cut to its basic size. Each grade of paper is available in many different weights. See **Figure 3-16**.

Usually, a quantity of paper is identified by its basis weight, such as *20-pound bond* or *70-pound book*. A package of 20-pound bond consists of 500 sheets of 17″ × 22″ writing paper and weighs 20 lbs. If an M appears after the weight, it means that the weight refers to a quantity of 1000 sheets (rather than 500). For example, 25″ × 38″—140M describes a quantity of 1000 sheets of 25″ × 38″ book paper weighing 140 lbs.

Common Paper Weights (1000 sheets)		
Grade	Size (″)	Weight (pounds)
Bond	17 × 22	26, 32, 40, 48, 56
Book	25 × 38	60, 70, 80, 90, 100
Offset	25 × 38	50, 60, 70, 80, 100
Cover	20 × 26	100, 120, 130, 160, 180

Figure 3-16. Common grades of paper are available in a number of weights.

The Technical Association of the Pulp and Paper Industry uses metric units to measure the weight of paper. The weight is expressed in grams per square meter (g/m^2). Factors for converting conventional weights of paper to metric units are listed in **Figure 3-17.** The conversion factors for changing from conventional weights of 500 sheets to grams per square meter are listed in column A. The conversion factors for changing weights from grams per square meter to conventional weights are listed in column B.

Conversion Factors for Ream Weights			
Grade of Paper	Conventional Size (″)	A Metric to Conventional	B Conventional to Metric
Writing	12 × 22	0.266	3.760
Cover	20 × 26	0.370	2.704
Cardboard	22 × 28	0.438	2.282
News	24 × 36	0.614	1.627
Book	25 × 38	0.675	1.480

Figure 3-17. Multiplying factors for converting paper weights from metric or conventional units.

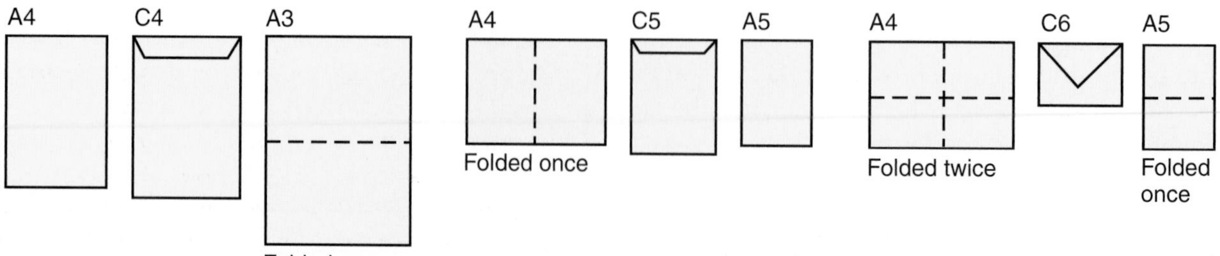

Figure 3-15. ISO-A sheets of paper and ISO-C envelopes have compatible sizes.

Using the conversion factors shown, a ream of coated book stock would be expressed as 100 g/m^2, or 67.5 lbs. (100 × 0.675). A ream of good writing paper would be listed as 85 g/m^2, or 22.61 lbs. (85 × 0.266).

Paper thickness

Several types of caliper devices are available for measuring paper thickness. The ***paper caliper*** or *micrometer* is an accurate device used to measure the thickness of paper. It can also be used to determine the thickness of a printing plate. See **Figure 3-18**.

Figure 3-18. A paper caliper or micrometer is used to measure paper thickness.

Paper brightness

Paper is classified by its brightness, according to the American Forest and Paper Association (AFPA). Number 1 quality is the brightest, reflecting 85% to 87.9% of blue light; number 5 quality is classified as having the least brightness, as shown in **Figure 3-19.** Within each grade, papers are offered as virgin or recycled stock.

Quality	Brightness
Number 1	85.0 to 87.9
Number 2	83.0 to 84.9
Number 3	79.0 to 82.9
Number 4	73.0 to 78.9
Number 5	72.9 and below

Figure 3-19. AFPA standard grade classifications for all finishes of paper. Brightness is measured by the percentage of blue light reflected from the paper's surface. (The S. D. Warren Company)

Image Measurement

The rise of desktop publishing in the graphic communications industry over the past 10 years has revolutionized the approach to the production of visual images. The use of computers has replaced many of the methods previously used in the design of printed materials. A ***desktop publishing system,*** consisting of a computer, printer, scanner, and publishing software, has taken the place of traditional methods used in operations such as typesetting and color separation. Most of the printed images found in publications and other media are now produced electronically. Equipment commonly used in desktop publishing is shown in **Figure 3-20.**

Figure 3-20. The components of a desktop publishing system include a computer, scanner, and publishing software. Output is typically to a laser printer.

The growth of digital technology has led to improvements in image quality and higher levels of productivity. As technology continues to expand, desktop publishing will play an even greater role in graphic communications.

Resolution

Resolution describes the visual quality of an image and is a measure of elements that define the image. The resolution of a printed image is measured in ***dots per inch (dpi)*** or ***pixels*** (picture elements). The image resolution of a printer or scanner is a measurement of the number of dots or pixels the unit can generate in one inch. A *pixel* is a tiny rectangle that is only visible as a dot on a computer screen. The screen display of a computer monitor is measured in horizontal rows and vertical columns of pixels. A high-resolution computer monitor rated at 1600 × 1200 pixels is able to display a resolution of 1600 pixels horizontally and 1200 pixels vertically.

Laser printers and electronic scanners used in desktop publishing are identified by a measure of dpi for image resolution. A laser printer rated at 600 dpi can produce a resolution of 600 dots for each horizontal or vertical inch. A scanner that scans images at 1200 dpi can produce a file with an image resolution of 1200 dots per inch.

Scanning and file sizes

The Warren Standard indicates that there is a simple way to govern how images should be scanned. Doubling the line screen at which the image will be printed provides the number of dots per inch at which the image should be scanned. Scanning at different resolutions will change the file size (and the amount of storage space needed); so will the type of file. A bitmap file contains the smallest amount of color information, while a CMYK color file contains the largest amount. See **Figure 3-21.**

Photoconversion Measurement

Images are generally enlarged or reduced by certain percentages for use in photographic reproduction. Traditional methods used in halftone photography relied on measuring scales, screen tints, and process cameras. While desktop publishing has introduced new methods in the printing process, traditional procedures of producing images and other forms of measurement are still used in the graphic communications industry.

Proportional scale

When images are to be enlarged or reduced, the correct percentage for reproduction can be determined by using a ***proportional scale.*** See **Figure 3-22.** The inside of the scale contains a rotating wheel that compares the size of the original to the reproduction size. The numbers along the inner scale represent the size of the original, and the numbers along the outer scale represent the size for reproduction. When the two sizes are aligned, the percentage for enlargement or reduction is indicated by an arrow pointing to a windowed scale inside the wheel.

File Sizes at Various Resolutions					
		Bitmap	Grayscale	RGB	CMYK
35mm	120 dpi	3 kb	19 kb	57 kb	76 kb
	170 dpi	6 kb	38 kb	114 kb	152 kb
	220 dpi	9 kb	64 kb	191 kb	254 kb
	300 dpi	15 kb	118 kb	353 kb	470 kb
	400 dpi	27 kb	210 kb	628 kb	838 kb
	600 dpi	60 kb	471 kb	1.38 Mb	1.84 Mb
4″ × 5″	120 dpi	36 kb	282 kb	844 kb	1.10 Mb
	170 dpi	72 kb	565 kb	1.65 Mb	2.21 Mb
	220 dpi	119 kb	946 kb	2.77 Mb	3.69 Mb
	300 dpi	220 kb	1.72 Mb	5.15 Mb	6.87 Mb
	400 dpi	391 kb	3.05 Mb	9.16 Mb	12.2 Mb
	600 dpi	879 kb	6.87 Mb	20.6 Mb	27.5 Mb
8″ × 10″	120 dpi	141 kb	1.10 Mb	3.30 Mb	4.39 Mb
	170 dpi	283 kb	2.21 Mb	6.62 Mb	8.82 Mb
	220 dpi	473 kb	3.69 Mb	11.1 Mb	14.8 Mb
	300 dpi	879 kb	6.87 Mb	20.6 Mb	27.5 Mb
	400 dpi	1.53 Mb	12.2 Mb	36.6 Mb	48.8 Mb
	600 dpi	3.43 Mb	27.5 Mb	82.4 Mb	109.9 Mb

Figure 3-21. File sizes that will result from scanning images of different sizes at various resolutions in the common formats: bitmap, grayscale, RGB color, and CMYK color. (The S. D. Warren Company)

Figure 3-22. A proportional scale is used to size images for enlargement or reduction.

A proportional scale can be used to determine percentages for both the length and width of an image in either conventional or metric units. A shooting percentage of 100% indicates that the image will be reproduced at the same size, while a shooting percentage of 50% indicates that the image will be reduced by half its original size.

Screens

Halftone photography ***screens*** are used to change continuous tone photographs into dotted halftones for printing. Screens are measured in lines per inch in conventional units and lines per centimeter in metric units. In conventional units, screen sizes below 75 lines are considered to be *coarse,* while sizes above 133 lines are considered *fine*. The larger the number of lines, the finer the screen. See **Figure 3-23.**

Screen sizes can be converted to metric units by dividing the number of lines per inch by 2.54. To convert metric screen sizes to lines per inch, multiply the number of lines per centimeter by 2.54. A comparison of conventional and metric screen sizes is shown in **Figure 3-24**.

Screen angle measurement

Different ***screen angles*** are used when making color separations for each primary color for four-color printing. Screen angles are measured in degrees. A scale giving the screen angles for each color is shown in **Figure 3-25.**

To print properly, each separation must have the correct screen angle: a 45° screen angle is normally used for black, a 75° angle for magenta, a 90° angle for yellow, and a 105° angle for cyan. The line

Figure 3-23. Screens used to make dotted halftones. The larger the screen number, the finer the screen.

Screen Rulings per Inch	Screen Rulings per Centimeter
50	20
65	26
75	30
100	40
120	48
133	54
150	60
175	70
200	80

Figure 3-24. Screen sizes compared in conventional and metric units.

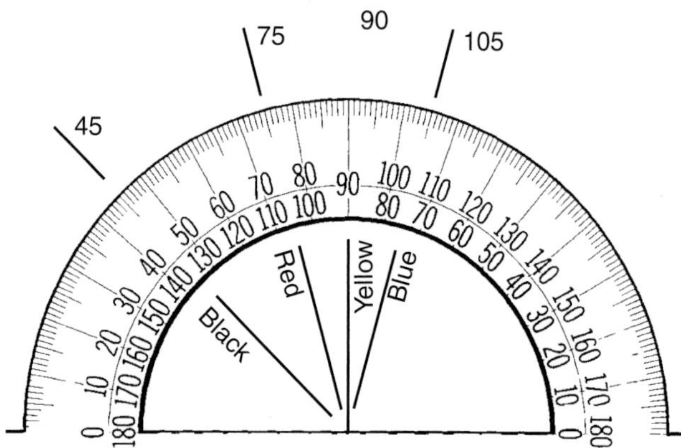

Figure 3-25. Standard screen angles used in making color separations.

patterns on each screen have a specific angular relationship to prevent a *moire pattern* (unwanted dot pattern).

Tint percentages

A ***screen tint*** is a reproduction screen that is measured as a percentage. A tint provides a hard dot screen that will produce evenly spaced dots that represent a tone percentage of a solid color. See **Figure 3-26.**

A 10% tint, for example, would result in 90% less ink deposited than an image printed without a screen tint. The resulting image would be very light. A 90% tint would print with 10% less ink and would produce a dark image.

Gray scale

A ***gray scale*** is a continuous tone strip with different shades of gray ranging from light to dark. It is used for visually gauging film exposure and development during chemical processing. Numerical values along the scale indicate the tone or *density* of an image. See **Figure 3-27.**

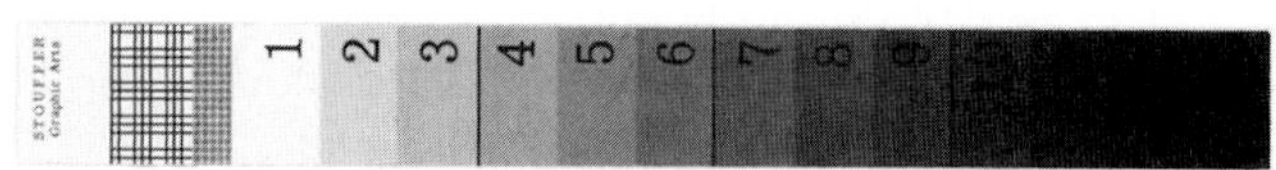

Figure 3-27. A gray scale uses a series of tones to measure image density.

Densitometer

A ***densitometer*** is a device used to measure the density or darkness of an image. See **Figure 3-28.** There are two types of densitometers commonly

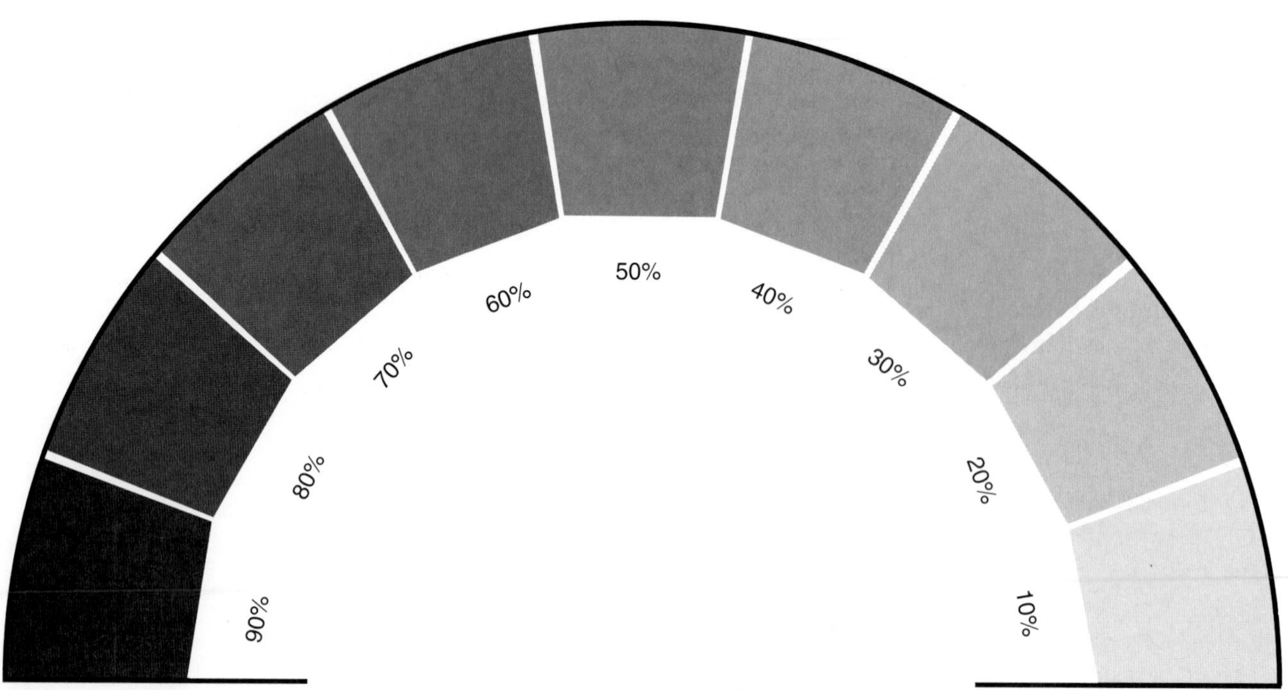

Figure 3-26. Common screen tint percentages. Larger percentages produce a darker screen, while smaller percentages result in a lighter screen.

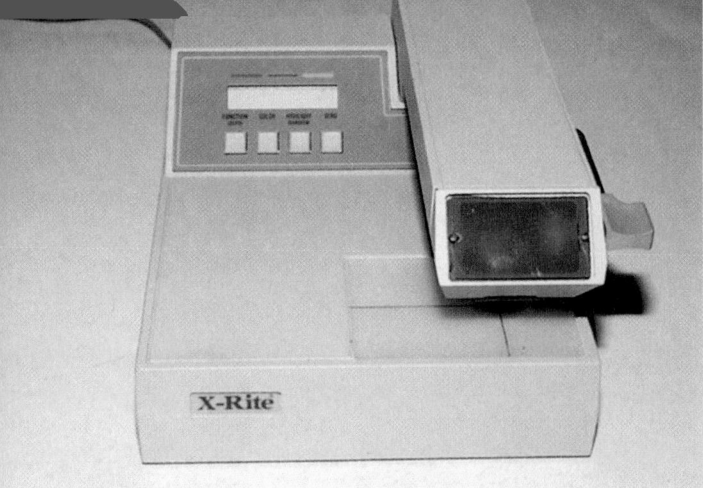

Figure 3-28. A densitometer measures reflected or transmitted light to read the density of an image.

used in graphic reproduction. One measures the reflection of light, while the other measures the transmission of light.

A ***reflection densitometer*** is used to give a reflected light measurement that indicates the tone values of printed materials or photographic prints. A ***transmission densitometer*** is used to measure light passing through a material. Both devices measure the tone range or contrast of an image.

A densitometer can be used to determine the correct exposure for making a halftone screen from a photographic print. Measurements are taken to identify the lightest and darkest areas of the print or any other areas needed to calculate exposures.

Review Questions

Please do not write in this text. Write your answers on a separate sheet of paper.

1. Name the two most commonly used systems of measurement.
2. What are the standard units for length and mass in the SI Metric system?
3. List five common metric prefixes.
4. Which of the following is an incorrect metric notation?
   a. 33 mm
   b. 0.39 km
   c. 34,000 km
   d. 42 kPa
5. Convert the following values:
   a. One inch = _____ millimeters
   b. 12 meters = _____ yards
   c. 10 quarts = _____ liters
   d. 12 milliliters = _____ fluid oz
   e. 400 pounds = _____ kilograms
   f. 25 meters/second = _____ feet/second
   g. 68°F = _____ °C
6. A point measures approximately _____ of an inch.
7. The pica is approximately _____ of an inch.
8. What are two devices commonly used to measure the point size of type?
9. The amount of vertical space between lines of type is called _____ .
10. A ream of paper consists of _____ sheets.
11. Name four common grades of paper.
12. List the three ISO series for paper and envelopes and the uses for each series.
13. What is the basis weight of paper?
14. List four components of a typical desktop publishing system.
15. Image resolution is measured in ______ or ______ .
16. Screen sizes below 75 lines are considered ______, while sizes above 133 lines are considered _____.
17. A screen angle of _____ degrees is normally used for the color black when making color separations.
18. Why must each color separation screen angle be set differently?
19. A 10% screen tint would result in _____ ink deposited than a 20% tint.
20. A _____ is used to measure the density or darkness of an image.

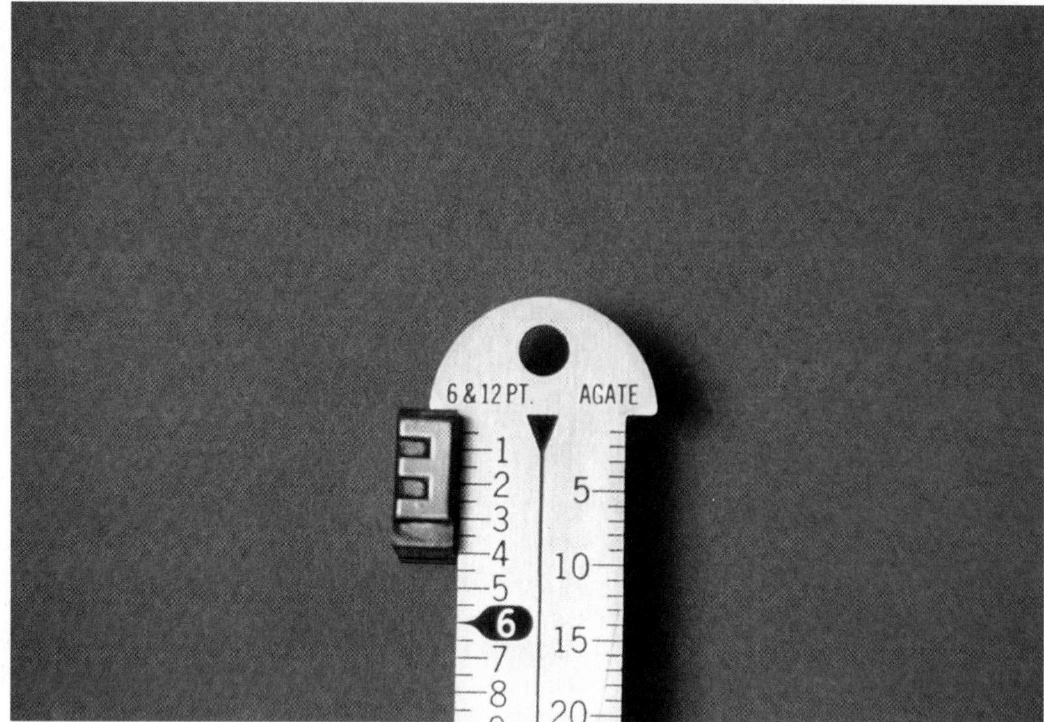

The point size of cast metal (foundry) type is measured from the top to the bottom of the metal type block—note the nonprinting space above and below the letter "E." Because the amount of white space varies from one typeface to another, the height of the actual printed letters may be considerably different, even though both typefaces are the same point size. The practice of including white space above and below the letter when determining point size has been maintained even for type that is produced by a phototypesetter or a computer. The type being measured in this photo is 48 point; the measuring device (called a "type gauge" or "pica pole") has a scale divided into increments of six and twelve points. The "4" on the scale indicates that the type is four 12-point units (or 48 points) in height.

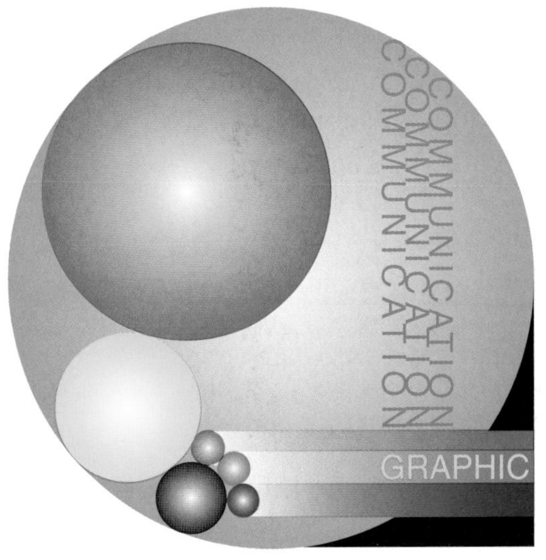

Typography 4

Learning Objectives

After studying this chapter, you will be able to:

- Describe the development of type styles.
- Identify the basic terms used to describe type.
- List seven typeface classifications.
- Explain the difference between a family, a series, and a font of type.
- Identify the common type sizes and units used in typography.
- List and explain the factors that contribute to the legibility of type.
- Summarize how the computer has increased the capabilities of typography.

Important Terms

ascender
descender
font
justify
leading
legibility
point size
Roman
sans serif
x-height

This chapter introduces the role that typefaces play in producing printed images. Typefaces are important, not only to the communication of thoughts, but to the overall appearance or aesthetic characteristics of the printed image. Careful study of this chapter will help you understand the information presented in later chapters.

Typefaces

Typefaces are distinctive designs of visual symbols (images) that are used to compose a printed page on paper or another substrate (printing surface). ***Characters*** are the individual visual symbols in a particular typeface. An assortment of characters — letters, numerals, punctuation marks, and special symbols (such as the ampersand) — is necessary to put words into print.

Just as every person has a name, every typeface has a name. It would be very difficult to identify specific typefaces without names, just as it would be difficult to identify individual human beings if there were no names. There are literally thousands of typefaces available to the producer of printed products. With the introduction of computerized typesetting, the number of new typefaces has increased dramatically and continues to grow steadily.

Typography

Typography is the art of expressing ideas in printed form through the selection of appropriate typefaces. The ***typographer*** (print designer) must determine how the manuscript should be expressed in type as well as other details of reproduction and physical format.

For example, if the typographer is selecting a typeface to use in an advertisement for a new electronic device, he or she would *not* select an old-fashioned-appearing type style with ornate, curly letters. A modern, clean-looking type would be more appropriate and representative.

Typeface terminology

The alphabet used for English and most European languages consists of only 26 letters. However, since there are thousands of typefaces, the letters of that alphabet are represented in many different ways. To be able to differentiate among the various typefaces, you must understand the basic terms relating to type and know how they affect the printed image.

The fundamental terms relating to a typeface are shown in **Figure 4-1**. They include:

- ***Uppercase***. The capital letters, usually abbreviated "caps."
- ***Lowercase***. The body letters, abbreviated "lc."
- ***Body height***. The distance from top to bottom of the lowercase letters, not including the ascenders and descenders. Also called *x-height*.
- ***Ascender***. The part of a letter that extends above the body height.
- ***Descender***. The part of a letter that extends below the body height.
- ***Base line***. An imaginary line drawn along bottom of body height letters. Descenders go below it.
- ***Waist line***. An imaginary line drawn along top of body height letters.
- ***Counter***. The nonprinting area surrounding a letter or inside the loop of a letter, such as d or p.
- ***Point size***. A vertical measurement used to identify or specify the size of a typeface. Measurement is approximately from the top of the ascender space to the bottom of the descender space.

Basic terms relating to specific characters, as shown in **Figure 4-2**, are:

- ***Hairline***. A thin line or element of the character.
- ***Stem***. The vertical part of the character.
- ***Stroke***. The thickness of a line forming a character element.
- ***Stress***. The slant or tilt of a character.
- ***Serif***. The thickened tips or short finishing-off strokes at the top and bottom of character.
- ***Set width***. The distance across a character from side to side.

Later sections of this chapter, and other chapters, will discuss these terms in greater detail. You will learn how these typeface components and characteristics can be used to alter the form and function of words, sentences, and the general "look" of the printed image.

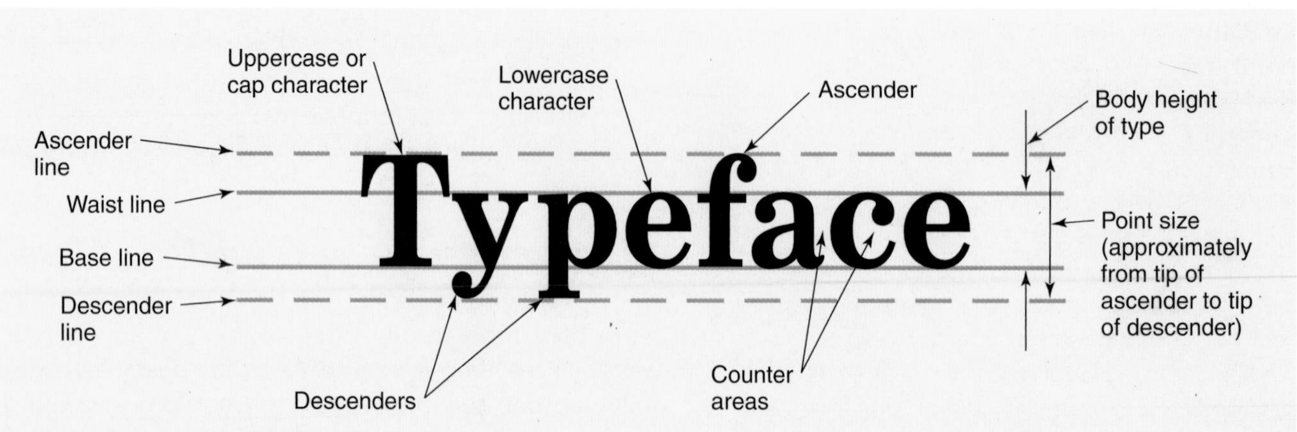

Figure 4-1. Basic terms relating to a typeface.

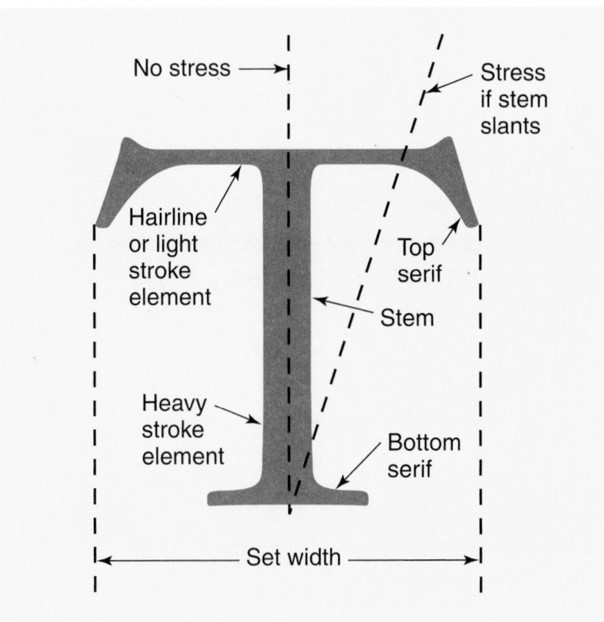

Figure 4-2. The parts of a character.

Type Style Development

Throughout history, humans have striven to perfect the art of making written or printed images. The scribes of medieval Europe produced hundreds of beautiful and masterful letter forms as they hand-lettered book pages. The scribes developed very beautiful lettering, making each character into an "art form." Across Europe, the style of the letters varied from country to country, or sometimes even from region to region within a country.

When the process of mechanical printing from individual pieces of type was introduced in Europe in the 15th Century, typographers modeled their letters upon those drawn by scribes. Each letter was cut by hand from hard metal to form a punch, which then was driven into softer metal to make a mold. The mold, in turn, was used to produce many copies of the letter. Molten ***type metal*** (an alloy of lead, tin, and antimony) was poured into the mold to form an individual piece of type that could be aligned with type containing other letters to form words and sentences. **Figure 4-3** shows a piece of ***foundry type*** produced by the modern version of this method. Although it is used only in a few specialized applications today, "hot metal" type (another term for foundry type) was the major form of type for used for printing from the 1400s through the mid-1900s.

Figure 4-3. Foundry type, cast in metal, was the major form of type used by printers for more than 500 years. Ink was applied to the raised surface of the letter and transferred to paper to form an image.

New printing methods introduced in the past 50 years have given rise to photographic and electronic (computer-based) methods of typesetting. These methods, which will be described later, also made it easier to design and produce new typefaces. Many of these new faces are radically different from those that have been widely used for many years.

Black letter

The ***manuscript*** (literally "hand written") style of lettering used by the scribes of Germany, France, Holland, and other countries was similar to the type style known today as *black letter*, *text*, or ***Old English***, **Figure 4-4**. This letter style was the basis for development of the earliest metal type, since the typographer or printer typically imitated the manuscript style common to a locality or geographic area.

Graphic Arts Display of Fine Printing Reveals
Skillful Arrangement of Type

Figure 4-4. Black letter is a style of type based on hand-lettering done by scribes in European countries. (ATF)

Development of the Roman type style

As the art of printing developed, changes in type styles also increased. This was especially true in Italy, where many of the German printers had migrated. The German black letter type styles gradually were replaced by a more delicate and lighter type style that became known the *Roman*. Several books were printed in an early version of the Roman face, known as the ***Subiaco face*** (named for the town where the printing was done).

A major figure in the development of the Roman type style was Nicolas Jenson. He was a master engraver for the French government who learned the new craft of printing in Mainz, Germany, and later moved to Italy.

Jenson is credited with designing and cutting the Roman letter forms that first appeared in printed pieces in 1469 and 1470. His designs, **Figure 4-5,** were based on the letters cut into stone monuments by the ancient Romans. Since the letters on the monuments were all capitals, Jenson developed Roman lowercase letters that would merge readily into word forms. This was significant, since we recognize words by their shape. The Jenson designs were the models used by type designers for hundreds of years. Nicolas Jenson is credited with printing about 150 books during his ten years in Italy.

ABCDEFGHIJKLMNOPQR
STUVWXYZ
abcdefghijklmnopqrstuvwxyz

Figure 4-5. Nicolas Jenson modified Roman letters and developed a lowercase alphabet so that it would more readily form words. This is a modern version of his typeface.

Jenson followed the traditions of the manuscript scribe in his lowercase letters. When enlarged, these letters revealed the feeling of the pen-drawn letter on a parchment surface. Each letter could be considered independently, yet they merged into the identity of the word.

Many other designers produced type styles in Italy during the same period. The slanted ***italic type***, modeled on a form of handwriting, was developed and first used by Aldus Manutius, a printer in Venice.

The black letter, Roman, and Italic type styles were used universally in Europe for two centuries. For a time, black letter was dominant in Germany and the Roman face was used primarily in Italy. Eventually however, Roman became the principal letter style used in all countries except Germany.

Modern typefaces

As noted, the early type styles were adapted from hand-drawn or stone-carved letters. By the 1700s, however, the emphasis changed to producing typefaces by copying from those styles that already existed, rather than working from original sources. Aesthetics were no longer an important design factor. Types became thinner and lines became much sharper.

The decline in the quality of type design throughout Europe and England continued through much of the 1800s. The decline was reflected in the poorly printed books of the era.

In 1890, William Morris, an English architect, artist, and poet, set out to demonstrate that books could again be beautiful. His interest brought about the revival of many early typefaces, such as Jenson, Garamond, Janson, and Caslon. These faces are the basis for many of the typefaces used today in book publication. See **Figure 4-6.**

BRAZIL, CHILE AND OTHER
A It shows civilization at the time so

AT BRAZIL AND OTHER
It shows civilization at a time so
B remote that it is doubtful whether

CHESS-KNIGHT
C After an apprentice

SOME KNIGHTS OF
D After an apprentice as

Figure 4-6. Roman typefaces revived for modern use are the basis of many faces employed today. A—Today's Garamond type is faithful to the original style. (ATF) B—The Caslon face is considered a classic. (ATF) C—Baskerville developed a type with letter forms designed specifically for printing. D—The extreme contrast of elements in Bodoni identifies it as a modern Roman typeface. (ATF)

Claude Garamond, a French printer, was influenced by Nicholas Jenson's Roman typeface, but designed a more elegant and refined face that was typically French. Garamond's 1540 design was redesigned in 1919 in the United States. The redesign resulted in a light-lined, more open design that would print more clearly.

The Janson typeface of today is a recutting of the face issued in about the year 1675 by Anton Janson. Janson (not to be confused with Nicholas Jenson) modified the manuscript letter by lightening the lines for better printing on a rough-surfaced stock.

Also designed for printing on rough stock was the typeface issued by William Caslon in England in about the year 1722. Caslon's typeface was an immediate success. The design by Caslon continued the trend toward lighter lines and more open design for better printing.

The English printer John Baskerville developed a typeface that is considered the beginning of the transition from letters based on manuscript to letters designed solely for printing. This type style was suitable for printing on smooth paper. Baskerville established a paper mill, type foundry, and printing office in Birmingham, England, and conducted extensive experiments with type and paper from 1750 to 1758. Baskerville's principle of considering type, paper, ink, and presswork together was the basis of today's planning of a printed job.

Another widely used type style was designed by Giambattista Bodoni, an Italian printer active in the late 1700s and early 1800s. Bodoni's typeface had greater differences between the light and heavy elements than any other face at that time, and is considered to be a modern Roman typeface. Bodoni typefaces used today show extreme difference between light and heavy elements. The typeface known as *Bodoni Book* has less pronounced contrast between elements, and closer to Bodoni's earlier designs.

Contemporary typefaces

Contemporary typefaces are primarily the contributions of the 20th century, and can be divided into three groups. First, there are the modern versions of the basic book faces of the early printers, as described in the preceding section. Second, there are the modifications of the basic book faces made for newspapers. Third, there are the many new display faces. The substantial increase in the number of typefaces paralleled the rapid growth of advertising and commercial printing during the first half of this century.

Today, thousands of faces are in existence. While this number seems large, think of the carpenter or auto technician who keeps a large chest of tools so the right one will be available when needed. In the same way, a typographer needs many "tools" so he or she can choose the correct typeface for a specific job. For use in computerized typesetting, numerous typefaces are available on CD-ROM. Printed samples of the faces available on the disk allow the designer to easily select a specific font. See **Figure 4-7.**

Figure 4-7. Literally thousands of fonts are available on disk for computer-based typesetting. This is a typical disk containing just typefaces. Most page layout and drawing programs also include sizable typeface libraries.

Sometimes, typefaces will look very much alike, yet have different names. Since typefaces cannot be copyrighted, it is possible for a designer to change a typeface slightly and gave the style a new name.

Roman typeface elements

Three elements contribute to the appearance of a character in a Roman typeface and help to differentiate between faces. They are the heavy elements, light elements, and serifs.

The ***heavy elements*** of the type character give identity, while the ***light elements*** tie the heavy elements together. The contrast between heavy and light elements help give a typeface its distinctive character. See **Figure 4-8**.

The curves of the characters should vary to emphasize difference or unlikeness of the letters and to neutralize the vertical thrusts of the letters.

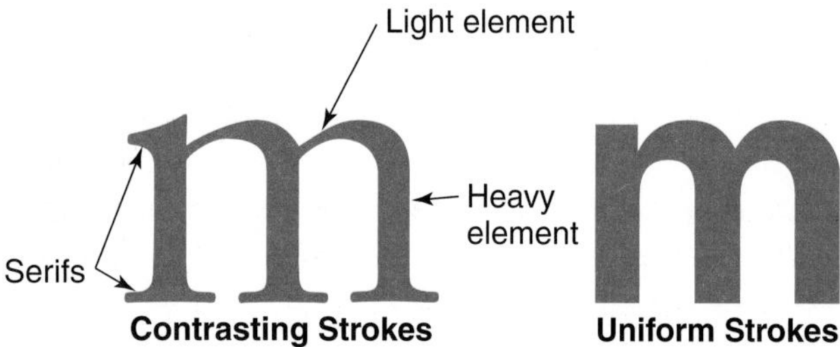

Figure 4-8. The contrast between heavy and light strokes makes differences in letter shape more pronounced. Serifs are finishing strokes at the tips of letters. Uniform strokes have the same thickness, so there is no contrast.

The *serifs* found on the *bottom* of letters imply the horizontal base line, helping tie the letters together to form words. The *top* serifs contribute to the unique appearance of the letter and help readability. The *ascenders* and *descenders* are also useful as identifiers and assist in the recognition of a word, **Figure 4-9**.

Typeface Classifications

The number of typeface classifications is not totally agreed upon, since some experts will list more classifications than others. For purposes of this book, seven classifications will be identified:

- Roman (also called serif)
- Sans serif
- Square serif (also called slab serif)
- Black letter or Text
- Script or Cursive.
- Novelty or Decorative.
- Italic (a variation of other classifications).

Roman

The ***Roman typefaces*** are numerous in number and are the most widely used. The characteristics commonly associated with Roman types are the contrast between the heavy and light elements, and the use of the finishing off lines or serifs.

Roman typefaces are further classified into three groups: Oldstyle faces, Transitional faces, and Modern faces. These are shown in **Figure 4-10**.

Oldstyle faces

The ***Oldstyle Roman*** typefaces have a rugged appearance, with relatively little contrast between heavy and light elements. The fillets of the serifs are curved. Oldstyle letters look better as words; thus, faces such as Caslon and Garamond were typically used for book text matter.

Readability

Figure 4-9. Top serifs and ascenders are critical to readability. Cover the top half of word and try to read it. Then, cover the bottom half and read. Note how ascenders help you identify the word.

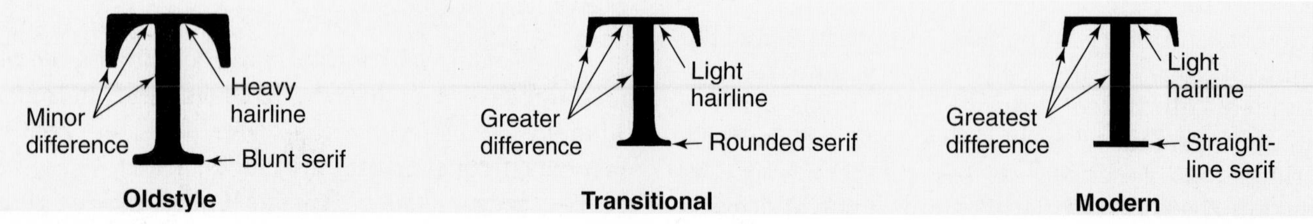

Figure 4-10. Roman typefaces are classified into three groups: Oldstyle, Transitional, and Modern. The differences in stroke weights and serifs are shown.

Transitional faces

Transitional Roman faces are a remodeling of Oldstyle typefaces. Greater contrast is evident between the heavy and light elements. The characters were also wider than the equivalent Oldstyle characters. John Baskerville improved on the Caslon typeface and produced Baskerville, the first typeface used to print on smooth paper. The Oldstyle characters were designed to print *into* thick, rough paper, rather than on the surface of thinner and smoother stock.

Modern faces

The most distinguishing feature of ***Modern Roman*** typefaces, first designed by Bodoni in 1789, is the increased contrast between the very thin, light elements and heavy elements. The Bodoni typeface has long ascenders and descenders and the serifs are straight lines without fillets.

Sans serif

"Sans" in French means "without." Thus, the classification ***sans serif*** is used for typefaces *without serifs.* See **Figure 4-11.** This typeface classification is second only to Roman in popularity today. Sans serif typefaces usually have a *monotone* appearance, meaning that the heavy and light elements are approximately the same thickness. While most are formed with strokes of uniform weight, a few sans serif faces have heavy and light elements.

Figure 4-11. A sans serif typeface is normally formed with strokes of uniform thickness, and has no finishing strokes (serifs).

Square serif

Square serif typefaces are usually formed with strokes of equal weight, like sans serif types, but have finishing-off strokes added. The shape of the serif is square or block-like and the serif has the same weight as the main portion of the letter face, **Figure 4-12**.

THE EARLY PRINTER
They instructed some of

Figure 4-12. On a square serif typeface, the serif strokes are often the same weight as the rest of the letter strokes. This sample is set in the typeface named Stymie.

Very seldom is a square serif typeface used for straight matter composition or text of a page, because it is not as easy to read as type with thinner serifs. These contemporary typefaces are most often used as display or headline types.

Black letter or text

The ***black letter*** or ***text face*** resembles the ***calligraphy*** (hand-drawn lettering) of German monks of the 1400s. Black letter is most often used for printed materials relating to special occasions. Typical examples are: certificates, wedding and graduation announcements, religious materials, diplomas, and official documents.

A text face set in all caps is very difficult to read, **Figure 4-13.** For this reason, the use of both capital and lowercase letters is recommended when setting copy.

UNIVERSITY

Figure 4-13. Black letter typefaces are very difficult to read when set in all capital letters.

Script or cursive

Both script and cursive typefaces are designed to simulate handwriting. The distinction between them is whether the individual letters in a word are joined or not. The letters in a ***script*** typeface are joined; letters in a ***cursive*** face are not. See **Figure 4-14**. The contrast of characters varies with the typeface design. Like text face types, script and cursive typefaces are used primarily for special effects. These include headlines, announcements, invitations, and letterheads. Since they are hard to read when copy length is more than a sentence or two, script and cursive types are seldom used for setting a full printed page or a large block of body copy.

Where to look for your rain-beau

for the one man in ten who

Orders regularly entered, verbal

A

Good neighbors to the North of us

Limited Time Only

Remember the sounds of San Francisco

B

Figure 4-14. Script typefaces have joined letters; cursive letters are separate. A—Examples of script typefaces. B—Examples of cursive styles.

NOVELTY

NOVELTY

NOVELTY

Novelty

Figure 4-15. Decorative typefaces are intended to draw your attention. They are normally used for headlines in advertisements and similar applications.

Novelty or Decorative

This typeface classification is used for a wide variety of types whose primary intent is to command special attention, **Figure 4-15.** A *Novelty* (sometimes called an "Occasional" or "Decorative") face must be carefully chosen to express a mood or provide a specific appearance for a theme or an occasion. Each style has individuality and is suited for a special situation. These faces are *not* intended to be used as body copy.

Italic

Italic is a slanted version of the upright letter, and is often treated as a separate classification. Most Roman faces have a companion italic of related design, **Figure 4-16.** In electronic composition, the term ***oblique*** is sometimes used to describe a simulated italic character produced by electronically slanting an upright Roman character. Italic type is often used to indicate emphasis in body copy. It is also used for titles, for foreign words, for terms being defined, and for quotations. Poetry is often typeset in an italic face.

Caslon Oldstyle Italic No. 471
Characters in complete font
A B C D E F G H I J K L M N
O P Q R S T U V W Z Y Z &
$ 1 2 3 4 5 6 7 8 9 0
a b c d e f g h i j k l m n o p q
r s t u v w x y z . , - ' : ; ! ?)
fi ff fl ffi ffl ct
Qu QU

Caslon Oldstyle Italic No. 471
Characters in complete font
A B C D E F G H I J K L M N
O P Q R S T U V W Z Y Z &
$ 1 2 3 4 5 6 7 8 9 0
a b c d e f g h i j k l m n o p q
r s t u v w x y z . , - : ; ! ? ')]
fi ff fl ffi ffl ct
Qu QU

Figure 4-16. An italic is a slanted companion version of a Roman typeface.

Reverse type

Reverse type usually consists of white characters on a solid black or color background. This is done occasionally and can be done to stress the importance of the message or information in the copy. For example, a small newspaper advertisement might be reversed to make it stand out on the page and be noticed. Care must be used in choosing a typeface and type size for reversing. Many types are difficult to read when reversed, especially in small point sizes. See **Figure 4-17.**

Typeface Families, Series, and Fonts

In addition to the classifications discussed so far, typefaces can be grouped by specific name or style of type. The term associated with a given style is called *family.*

Typeface family

A ***typeface family*** consists of the variations of one style of type, **Figure 4-18**. The design elements of the characters sets one family apart from another. Even though some typefaces are very similar in appearance, this does not make them part of the same family. As an example, Garamond is one family, and Caslon is another, even though their design is very similar. Refer to Figure 4-6.

Every variation of the designated typeface style becomes a part of that family. Knowledge of the variations in character widths and weights within a family are important to working effectively with type.

English Times Medium
English Times *Medium Italic*
English Times **Bold**
English Times ***Bold Italic***

Figure 4-18. A type family is made up of all the variations within one style of type, such as different weights or stresses.

Width variations

Some typefaces are designed to include width variations. These include the normal width types, as well as types with condensed, extra condensed, and expanded widths. Examples of such variations are found in **Figure 4-19**.

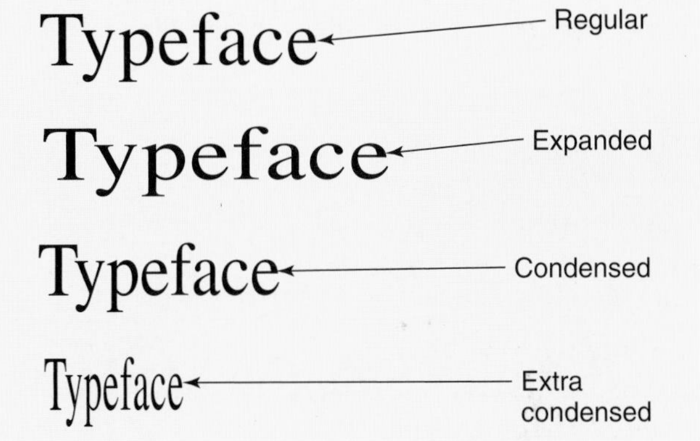

Figure 4-19. Width variations in a given typeface might include regular, expanded, condensed, and extra condensed type.

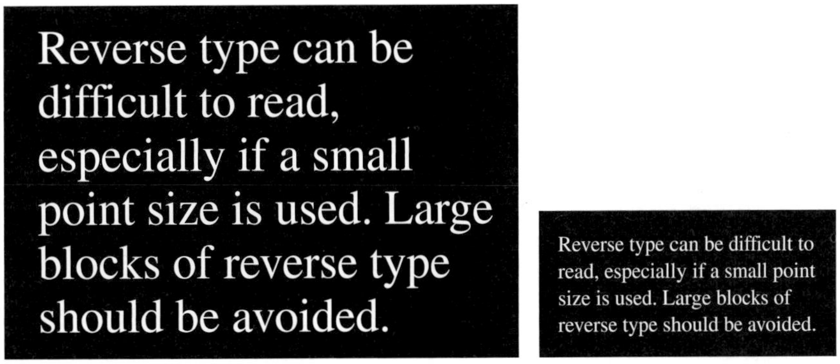

Reverse type can be difficult to read, especially if a small point size is used. Large blocks of reverse type should be avoided.

Reverse type can be difficult to read, especially if a small point size is used. Large blocks of reverse type should be avoided.

Figure 4-17. While reverse type can be effective as an attention-getting device, legibility suffers when the type is too small. Compare these examples on 18- point and 8-point type.

The *condensed typefaces* are intended to get more words in less space. They are used rather than going to a smaller typeface. *Expanded faces,* also called *extended faces,* fill more space without going to a larger point size.

Weight variations

The *weight* of a letter refers to the image area. The readable image might have a light, medium, bold, or extra-bold printing surface. Refer to Figure 4-18. With this range of weights, it is possible to vary the contrast for words or lines of type without changing the point size.

Typeface series

A *typeface series* is the range of sizes of each typeface in a family, **Figure 4-20**. The common type sizes used in printing are 6, 8, 10, 12, 14, 18, 24, 36, 48, 60, and 72 point. In traditional *relief* (raised letter) printing, type in sizes 96 points and larger was made from wood, rather than metal, **Figure 4-21**.

Figure 4-21. Type over 96 points used for letterpress printing was traditionally made from wood.

The introduction of phototypesetters allowed the use of sizes, such as 7, 9, and 11 point, that were not common to the relief process. More recently, electronic (computer-based) composition has made it possible to generate typefaces in virtually any size needed, even in hundredths of a point increments. This can be a major advantage in design and copyfitting.

8 Point Spartan Medium

10 Point Spartan Medium

12 Point Spartan Medium

18 Point Spartan Medium

24 Point Spartan Medium

36 Point Spartan Medium

48 Point Spartan Med

72 Point Spart

Figure 4-20. A typeface series is a full range of sizes of one typeface.

Type font

In computer-based or phototypesetting composition methods, a *font* consists of all the characters (letters, numerals, punctuation marks, and symbols) that make up a specific typeface, such as 9-point Bodoni or 12-point Helvetica Bold.

When applied to foundry type, where each character is on a separate piece of metal, "font" has a somewhat different meaning. As shown in **Figure 4-22**, a foundry type font consists of different quantities of each character in one size and style of type. This is necessary because the individual characters are physically assembled into words, **Figure 4-23**. Enough copies of each character must be available to make up a number of words.

The kinds and total number of characters differ from font to font. While most will include a full set of cap and lowercase letters, the numerals 0 to 9, and the usual punctuation marks, they often will differ in the symbols and special characters they include. For example, some fonts include *ligatures,* which are joined letter combinations such

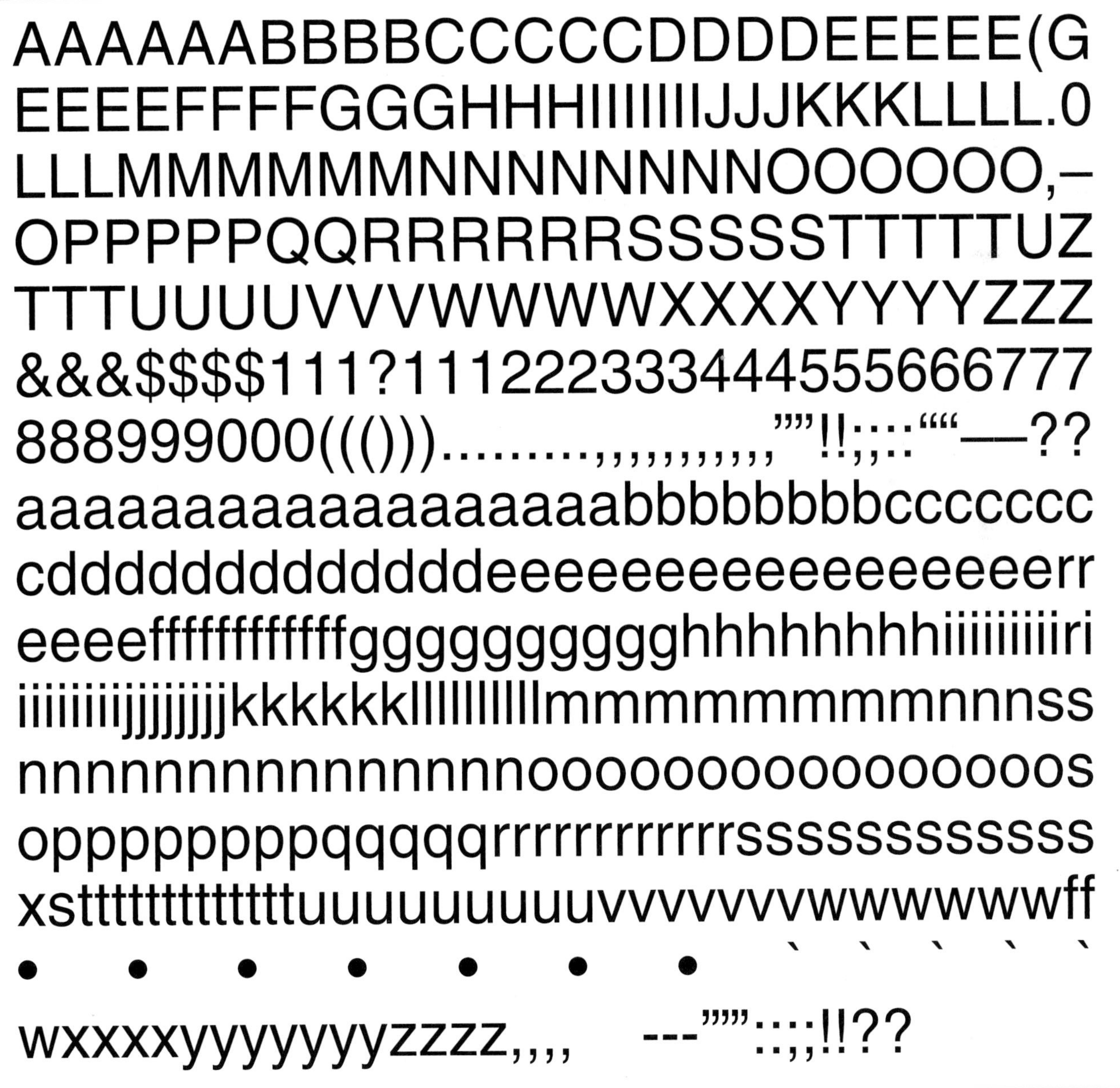

Figure 4-22. A foundry type font consists of a full assortment of characters for one size typeface. The varying number of characters is based on frequency of use: more e characters are needed than x or z characters.

Figure 4-23. Setting copy in foundry type involves selecting individual pieces of type and assembling the letters in a holder called a "stick." This method was used by printers for hundreds of years.

as **fi, ff, fl, ffi,** and **ffl.** Other fonts might include ***small caps,*** which are capital letters smaller than the normal caps of the font.

In fonts for computer or phototypesetting, such symbols as stars, asterisks, arrows, percent signs, or checkmarks are known as ***pi characters,*** **Figure 4-24.** In foundry type, such special characters are called ***sorts,*** or "dingbats."

Figure 4-24. Symbols such as these are known as pi characters, sorts, or dingbats. They add to the interest of printed materials.

Type and Typesetting Measurements

While people in most occupations measure in units of inches, fractions of inches, centimeters, or millimeters, people working in graphic communications use special measuring units with names like *points* and *picas.*

Points and picas

The two principal units of measure used in the graphic communications industry are the point and the pica. A ***point*** is equal to 0.0138″. A ***pica*** is equal to 0.166″. *Twelve points* equals one pica and *six picas* almost equals one inch (0.996″).

Points are used to measure the vertical height of a line of type, while picas are used to measure ***line lengths*** and *composition depth.* The ***point size*** of type is based on distance from the top of the ascenders to the bottom of the descenders, as shown in **Figure 4-25.** The point size of type should not be confused with the ***x-height,*** which is the height of the lowercase "x."

Figure 4-25. The point size of type is measured from the top of the ascenders to the bottom of the descenders.

The size of type is difficult to distinguish when in print, because two typefaces of the same point size may have x-heights that are quite different. The letters of one typeface may appear to be larger or smaller than the letters of the other, but lines set in the two faces would require the same amount of vertical space. See **Figure 4-26.**

Mm Mm Mm Mm

Figure 4-26. Typefaces of the same point size may vary greatly in body height (x-height), as shown by the lowercase letters here. These typefaces are all set in 36-point.

Type sizes that range from 4-point through 12-point are usually referred to as ***text*** or ***body type.*** Sizes above 12-point are referred to as ***display type.***

Ems and ens

The ***em*** is a unit of printer's measure equal to the height and width of the capital M in the given size of type. For example, in 12-point type, an em would measure 12 points wide and 12 points high; in 18-point type, an em would be 18 points wide and 18 points high. In foundry type, an ***em quad*** (nonprinting type block that was a square of the type size) was used to indent the beginning of a paragraph. Sentences set in foundry type were separated by spaces that were half an em quad in width. That spacing element was called an ***en quad.*** See **Figure 4-27**.

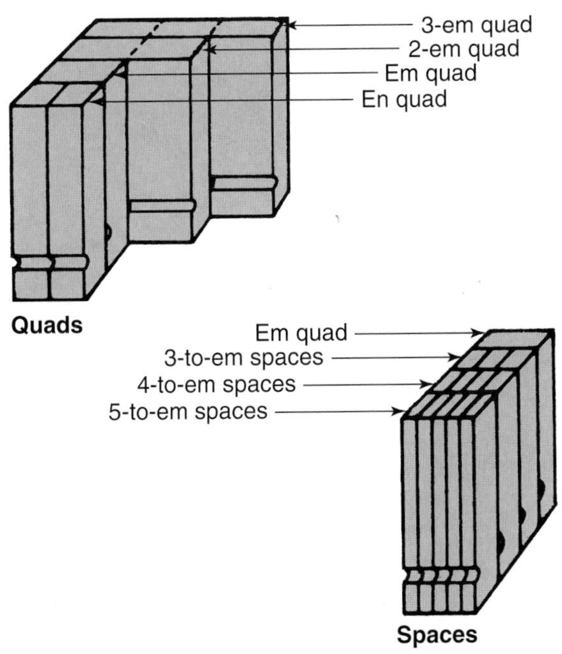

Figure 4-27. Foundry type used blocks called quads for spacing. Blocks narrower than the en quad were referred to as spaces.

Units

The ***unit*** is a measure that results from splitting the em into uniform narrow widths. The number of units per em will vary with the composing method. The most common are the 18-unit count and 54-unit count, **Figure 4-28**. Typefaces used in phototypesetting are given assigned unit widths, but a very small amount of space is allowed on each side. When the characters are composed, they will not touch.

Set size

As you learned, *point size* refers to the *height* of the type. ***Set size***, or *set width*, refers to the *width* of a character. Electronic composition has made it possible to change the set width of characters, and the words they make up.

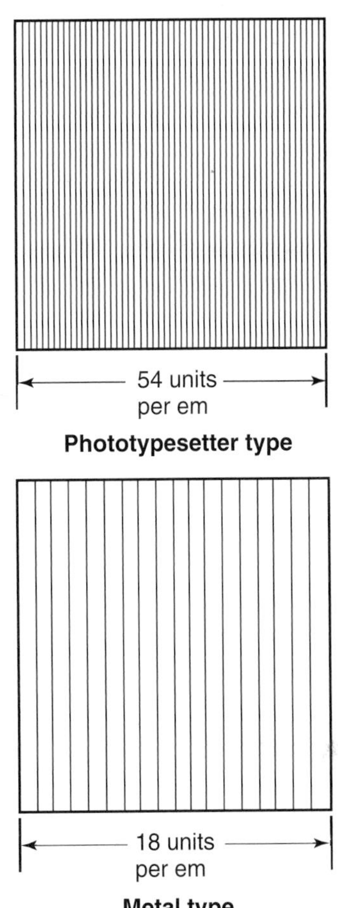

Figure 4-28. The em is typically divided into 54 units in phototypesetting. Eighteen units to the em was usual with metal type.

When the character is electronically expanded or condensed, the height is not changed, **Figure 4-29**. For example, 12-point type with a 12-set would be normal. If 12-point is programmed as "8-set," the type would be condensed. If 12-point is programmed for a "14-set," the type would be expanded. Although width of the character is changed, spacing between characters remains the same.

THIS IS 12 POINT WITH 8 SET.

THIS IS 12 POINT WITH 12 SET.

THIS IS 12 POINT WITH 14 SET.

Figure 4-29. Set size is modern term that refers to width of characters. Computerized typesetting allows letters to be condensed or expanded easily.

Letterspacing and wordspacing

Letterspacing refers to a change of spacing between letters, while ***wordspacing*** involves varying the spacing between words, **Figure 4-30**. When carefully done, increasing or decreasing the space between letters and words can improve the legibility of type. It is also possible to increase or decrease the amount of copy to fit an allocated space by altering the letterspacing or the wordspacing.

	Tight:	Letterspace changes distance between characters.
	Normal:	Letterspace changes distance between characters.
A	**Loose:**	Letterspace changes distance between characters.
	Tight:	Wordspace changes distance or space between words.
	Normal:	Wordspace changes distance or space between words.
B	**Loose:**	Wordspace changes distance or space between words.

Figure 4-30. Letterspacing compared to wordspacing. A—Letterspacing alters amount of space between each character or letter. B— Wordspacing changes space between complete words.

If letterspacing other than normal is used, it is expressed as ***loose-set*** (large spacing) or ***tight set*** (small spacing). Spacing is expressed in units, with different composing systems varying in capability. Full units and half units are common. *Plus units* (loose set) and *minus units* (tight set) give the designer freedom to change the spacing to best fit the desired style or available space.

Character compensation is a method of tight-setting copy by electronically reducing very slightly the width of each character and space. This results in a reduction of white space between characters, allowing the copy to "shrink" and fit a smaller space.

Tracking

Tracking is a feature of computer typesetting programs that allows you to control the letter and word spacing together. The common choices for tracking are very tight, tight, normal, loose, and very loose. See **Figure 4-31**.

Horizontal *scaling* of letters is often an option, as well. This is not a form of letter spacing, since the actual widths of the characters are changed, but the proportion of character to space is not.

Letter Tracking Very Tight
Letter Tracking Tight
Letter Tracking Normal
Letter Tracking Loose
Letter Tracking Very Loose

Figure 4-31. Letter tracking allows letter spacing and word spacing to be varied simultaneously.

Justifying type

Letter-spacing and word-spacing are used to ***justify*** lines of type so that the lines are all equal in length. This results in blocks of copy with even left and right margins (like the paragraph you are reading right now). Justification can be done automatically with modern typesetting equipment.

Widow

A ***widow*** is a very short word, or part of a word, forming the final line of a paragraph. The rest of the line is empty. To avoid this undesirable amount of white space, the line will usually be lengthened or the previous line will be shortened, usually by adding or deleting words.

Kerning

Kerning is a typesetting technique that that involves closing up space between certain characters in the alphabet to improve the appearance and readability of the word. Kerning is normally done for letters that are top- or bottom-heavy.

For example, as shown in **Figure 4-32,** the capital letter "T" is top-heavy and the space

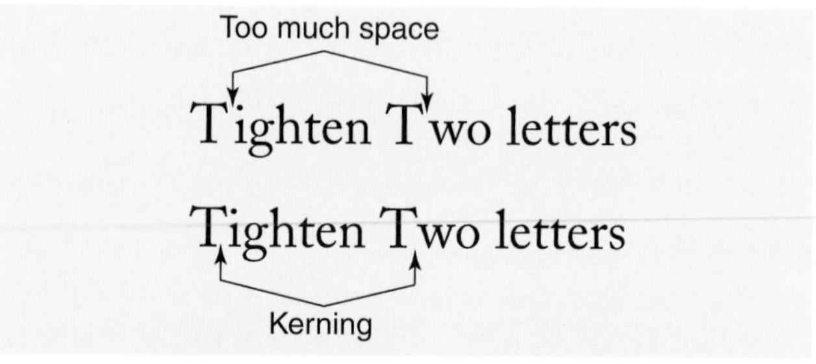

Figure 4-32. Kerning is similar to letterspacing, but changes only spaces between specific letters to improve appearance and readability.

between it and the next letter would appear to be too wide. Kerning moves the adjoining letter closer to the "T" for better appearance. **Figure 4-33** illustrates a number of letter combinations that can be improved in readability by using kerning.

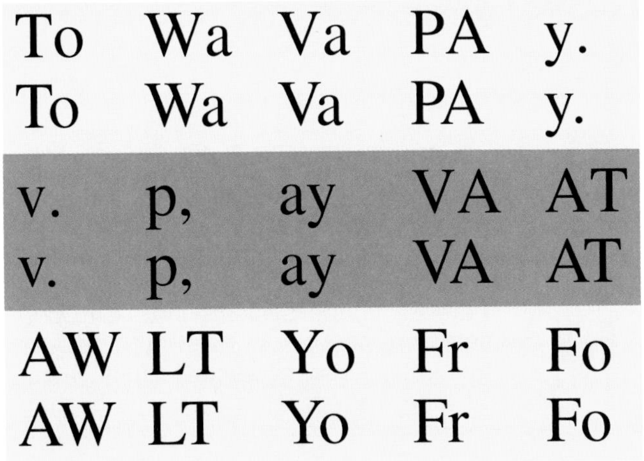

To Wa Va PA y.
To Wa Va PA y.
v. p, ay VA AT
v. p, ay VA AT
AW LT Yo Fr Fo
AW LT Yo Fr Fo

Figure 4-33. Examples of letter combinations before and after kerning. (Compugraphic)

Legibility Factors

Legibility, sometimes termed ***readability***, is a measure of how difficult or easy it is to read printed matter. When selecting a typeface, legibility can be a very critical factor.

The major consideration when selecting a typeface is *purpose*. If the content of the copy is the main purpose (for example, in a textbook), legibility of the printed page should be the aim in selecting a typeface. When appearance is of major importance, (as in designing an advertisement), then the aesthetic characteristics of the type must be given more attention.

The type you are now reading is what a printer calls ***straight matter***. Examples of products in which straight matter is used extensively are books, newspapers, magazines, and pamphlets.

Good legibility of the straight matter is the result of a proper combination of *type*, *paper*, and *ink*. It can make reading printed material less tiring to the eyes. Many printed pieces will have thousands of readers of varying ages and physical conditions. This makes good legibility a high priority.

Physical factors that contribute to legibility in the printed pages are: visibility, letter forms, definition, type size, line length, and leading.

Visibility

Visibility results from the contrast of the dark typeface against the light reflected by the paper. This is due to the paper's *brightness*, *smoothness*, and *opacity*,

The term whiteness is *not* used because ***brightness*** is a property of both white and colored papers. The brightness of paper varies greatly. The smoother the paper, the more light it reflects, therefore, paper ***smoothness*** also affects visibility of the images. A paper with high ***opacity*** does not allow print from the opposite side to show through.

The contrast of the printed material is affected by ***ink darkness.*** That term is used, rather than *ink color*, because both black and colored inks have degrees of darkness. Darkness depends on the ink's covering power — complete coverage hides the surface of the paper.

The type style is also a factor: the thicker the elements of the letter, the more ink will be deposited on the paper for contrast. As type size decreases, this factor gains in importance.

Letter forms

Readers are accustomed to the basic letter forms. The Roman letter form is the "tried and true" classification, but the sans serif classification has also become a familiar form. Straight matter is made up almost entirely of lowercase letters. Capital (uppercase) letters are used sparingly, because they do not form distinctive word shapes.

Letter forms that merge readily into words and phrases contribute to legibility. This means that the letter elements must relate to each other. The thick elements of a Roman letter give identity while the thin elements tie them together. The more unlike or dissimilar the letters, the more certain their identity. For example, **c**, **e**, and **o** should be as different as possible.

The distribution of white space within and between letters should be uniform to help shape the letters into words. Whenever letters have serifs, the intent is to aid the eye to mark the terminals or finishing marks of the letter elements. Serifs also make the letters more distinctive for easy reading.

Definition

Definition refers to the sharpness or distinction of the printed image. Sharply defined letter forms are essential for easier reading. The relationship between the typeface and paper is very important. A small type size requires a smoother paper for good definition. Top-quality pressmanship contributes to sharp images on the page.

Special consideration must be given when placing type over a screened background, because poor definition may result. See **Figure 4-34**. The same principle applies when the background for type is a halftone image, such as a photo of clouds or foliage.

Figure 4-34. Selecting the proper typeface for placement on a screen pattern is very important to legibility.

Type size

The legibility of copy, as it relates to type size, increases dramatically up to 10-point type. This increase flattens out with larger type sizes. Straight matter set in 10-point type is considered a norm for comfortable reading by young and middle-aged adults. **Figure 4-35** compares blocks of copy set in three different point sizes.

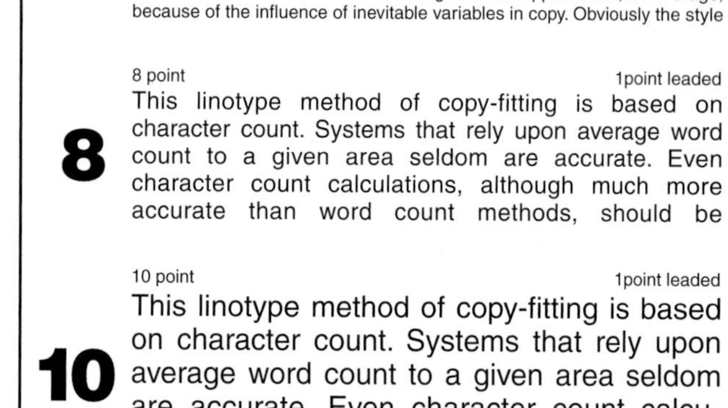

Figure 4-35. Smaller type sizes (those below 10-point) are difficult to read for the average person. The same copy is shown here in 6-point, 8-point, and 10-point type.

The x-height of the font also contributes to legibility. A large x-height would increase the size of the letters, and decrease the length of ascenders and descenders.

Line length

Line length, also called ***line width,*** is the distance from the left to right sides of a line or body of copy. It is usually measured in picas.

Eye span is the width people can see with one fixation (sweep or adjustment) of the eye muscles. With body copy, the normal eye span is about one and one-half alphabets (about 40 characters). This width will vary with typeface classification and size, however.

When the width of the line corresponds to the eye span of the reader, the physical task of reading is made easier. Longer lengths require extra physical effort when reading (the more eye fixations per line, the more effort required). Horizontal travel of the eye is considered more tiring than moving vertically from one line to the next.

Line spacing

Line spacing determines the distance separating each line of copy. It is measured in points from one line to the next. This spacing is also called ***leading*** (pronounced *"ledding"*), since lines of hand-set foundry type were separated by strips of lead-based type metal. See **Figure 4-36.**

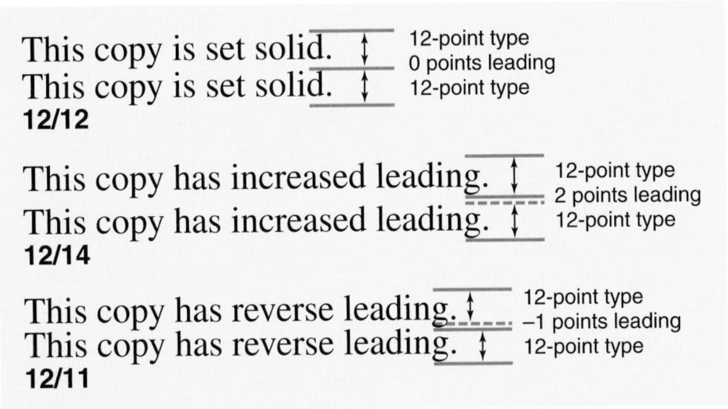

This copy is set solid. 12-point type
0 points leading
This copy is set solid. 12-point type
12/12

This copy has increased leading. 12-point type
2 points leading
This copy has increased leading. 12-point type
12/14

This copy has reverse leading. 12-point type
–1 points leading
This copy has reverse leading. 12-point type
12/11

Figure 4-36. Linespacing, usually called leading, is the amount of vertical space separating one line of type from the next.

When line spacing is equal to the size of the type, the type is said to be ***set solid***. For example, if the typeface is 12-point and there is no extra line spacing, it would be set solid. On a specification, the size would be written 12/12 (in spoken form, "twelve on twelve").

When a customer or designer wants more space between lines of type, one or more points of leading would be added. For example, 10-point type might be used with 2 points of leading. The specifications would be written as 10/12 ("ten on twelve"). The typeface point size is normally written before the line spacing.

Many of today's typesetting systems have the capability of reducing spacing below the type size. This interline spacing, is called ***negative leading*** or ***minus leading***. The specifications might be written as 10/9. This means the space between lines is to be reduced by one point ("ten on nine").

Proper leading helps the reader's eye to readily separate one line from another. The white space gives the eye better access to the top portions of the lowercase letters. As stated earlier, the tops of letters are the more unlike portions, and contribute most to word identity.

Leading also unites a line horizontally. Close word spacing will help to achieve unity in the line. Visibility is increased when extra leading is used on paper with low brightness. The extra leading lightens the tone of the page, and tends to make the type seem larger.

It is also possible to fit copy into a designated area by changing leading. By increasing leading, the copy will take up more space or area. Decreasing leading does just the opposite.

Typefaces for Display

Display type is intended to draw attention to a message. To emphasize the importance of the message and capture the reader's attention, display lines are larger in size. Generally, the smallest typeface size used in display is 14 point.

The position of the display line also gives it prominence. The words of that line supply the language and theme of the printed page or a block of copy. For this reason, it may be necessary to keep a complete thought in one line. This is shown in **Figure 4-37**.

Different weights of type can be used for emphasis by contrast. Different sizes show the relationship between principal and subordinate thoughts. Selection becomes very important to make sure that the typeface fits the intended use.

Towns getting together to fight against sprawl

By Marles Humphrey
Special to the Tribune

Residents of Crystal Lake and Lakewood long have been aware that urban sprawl threatens to blur the boundaries that preserve the two towns' distinctive characters.

Until recently, however, the two communites failed to engage in any cooperative efforts to address the issue.

That might change following a recent meeting between representatives of Crystal Lake and

Figure 4-37. Newspaper headlines are an example of display type in use. Note that the major thought, "Towns getting together," is on the first line. The subordinate or secondary thought is on the second line. This is commonly done in newspapers.

Review Questions

Please do not write in this text. Write your answers on a separate sheet of paper.

1. The art of expressing ideas through the selection of appropriate typefaces is called _____.
2. Define the term "body height."
3. An ascender extends _____ and a descender _____ the x-height letters.
4. What is the base line?
5. The finishing-off stroke at the top or bottom of a character is called a _____.
6. The _____ _____ type style is based on the hand-written lettering of German scribes
7. Who is credited with designing and cutting the first Roman typefaces?
8. Which designer first developed a typeface with letters designed solely for printing?
9. Other than the use of serifs, what is the major difference between Roman and sans serif typefaces?
10. List and describe the seven basic typeface classifications.
11. A typeface _____ consists of the variation of one style of type.
12. A type _____ consists of the letters, figures, and punctuation marks that are of one size and style.
13. On a type specification, what does "10/12" mean?
14. Changing the distance between words in a line of copy is called _____.
    a. letter spacing.
    b. leading
    c. kerning.
    d. word spacing.
15. _____ refers to changing the distance between some letters of a word to improve appearance of the type.
16. Name and describe at least three physical factors that affect legibility
17. *True or False?* The point size of a typeface is the same as its x-height.
18. When the line spacing dimension is equal to the size of the typeface, the type is said to be _____.
    a. reverse leaded.
    b. letter spaced.
    c. set solid.
    d. tight set.
19. Which is the larger unit of measure, the em or the en?
20. Briefly discuss some of the advantages the computer has brought to typography and typesetting.

Design and Layout

5

Learning Objectives

After studying this chapter, you will be able to:

- Summarize the role of the graphic designer.
- List and explain the elements of design.
- Utilize the principles of design.
- Identify the elements that make up a layout.
- Explain the factors that determine how a layout design is developed.
- Differentiate between the design methods used in layout.
- Demonstrate how copyfitting is used to estimate layout space.
- Describe the methods used in preparing illustrations for layout.
- List the layout materials needed to produce a mechanical.

Important Terms

comprehensive layout
copyfitting
elements of design
elements of layout
layout base sheet
photo cropping
principles of design
rough layout
specifications
thumbnail sketches

In graphic communications, ***design*** refers to the application of proper methods to produce a product that is both artistic and functional. A successful design requires the skillful use of design elements and principles.

This chapter will cover the primary elements and principles of design and layout. Knowledge of common design techniques is critical in producing a layout and evaluating the visual quality of a product.

The Graphic Designer

The role of the graphic designer varies greatly within the graphic communications industry. This is because of the overlapping duties that are performed throughout the process of design and layout. In some companies, the same artist who is responsible for producing artwork may also be required to perform certain layout tasks. See **Figure 5-1**. It is very important for the design person to work closely with the printer, since the planned design could cause problems when it arrives to be printed. Limitations relating to folding, press size, and paper capabilities could be potential problem areas.

Today's graphic designer might be an artist who prepares the artwork necessary for a portion of a product. Artwork could include freehand sketches, technical art, lettering, and calligraphy. In many cases, the graphic designer has little knowledge of the processes used in graphic reproduction. But the designer may also be responsible for pasting up camera-ready copy or producing a finished product with page layout software. This illustrates that the specific duties performed by design and layout personnel are very difficult to clearly define.

Figure 5-1. A graphic artist is commonly involved in several stages of production, from designing visual materials to performing layout tasks. (Screaming Color-Chapter One)

In the simplest of situations, a *design artist* would create the art images needed by the *layout artist.* Many companies, however, do not have the luxury of hiring people who only have specific design or layout skills. The design artist, in many companies, translates ideas into art and is also involved in layout and production in various stages.

Once the layout design is approved by a client or outside source, the elements are usually gathered and assembled by the same person who created the design. The design artist must initially express a visual idea. The idea becomes the foundation of the layout and is then developed into the final product.

Planning and organizing the design process is essential to having an efficient operation. A small printing facility, from a financial standpoint, often cannot afford to employ one person to perform design tasks. Therefore, designing may be left to the plant personnel, who may have very little design knowledge but are required to devise and complete layouts for production.

A knowledge of the fundamentals of design is required for both the design artist and the layout artist. The elements and principles of design are an accumulation of many factors that help solve the problem of producing an image that is both attractive and practical.

Elements of Design

Design involves the selection and arrangement of visual images to make a pleasing presentation. The text and illustrations used in a design will have a tremendous impact upon the viewer; therefore, it is essential to develop a strong layout of visual materials.

A successful graphic designer must apply the fundamental principles of design. The basic ***elements of design*** are *lines, shapes, mass, texture,* and *color.*

Lines

Lines are design elements that form the shapes of an image. Lines can be used to give the printed image a "personality." Lines can be loose and free or they can be straight and sharp. See **Figure 5-2**. The repetition of lines creates patterns and adds emotional impact to the visual image.

Figure 5-2. Lines can be used to denote a specific meaning. Curved, loose lines imply a free spirit. Lines drawn straight imply a more straightforward or disciplined theme.

Lines can also be used as a form of "universal language" in communication. In other words, lines can be designed to create a message. Arrows and other symbols are examples of lines used as a visual form. See **Figure 5-3**.

Lines are often used to enhance or change the visual quality of styles of type. They can appear very harsh or very delicate. Lines play a highly important role in designing a layout that communicates effectively.

Figure 5-3. Lines can deliver a visual message when they are drawn as arrows or other symbols.

Shapes

Shapes are elementary forms that define specific areas of space. In many cases, a shape is defined by a line. The three basic shapes are the square, circle, and triangle. See **Figure 5-4**.

Figure 5-4. The three basic design shapes are the square, circle, and triangle.

Each of the three basic shapes is associated with a psychological meaning, as shown in **Figure 5-5.** The visual attitude portrayed by the *triangle* is one of conflict or action. The *square* projects an attitude of honesty or equality, while the *circle* conveys a feeling of protection or infinity.

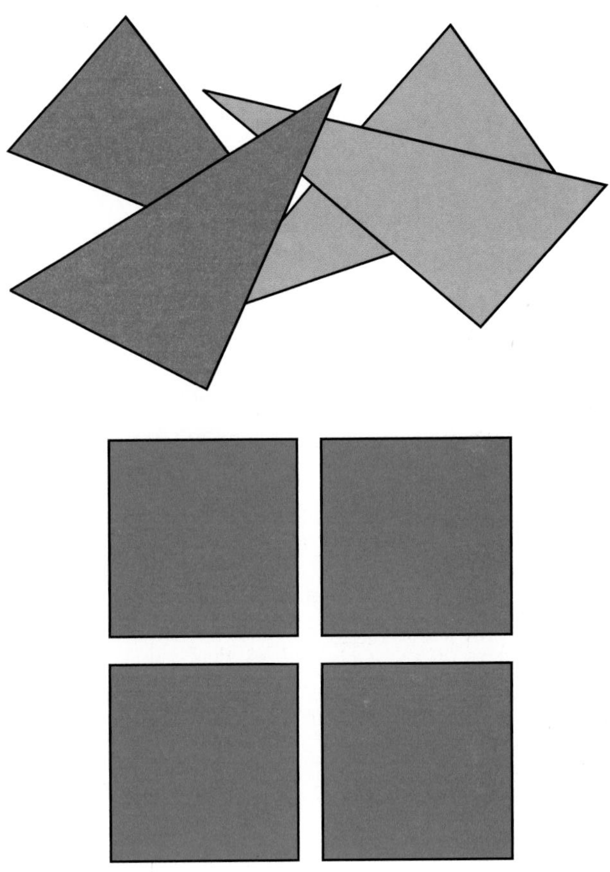

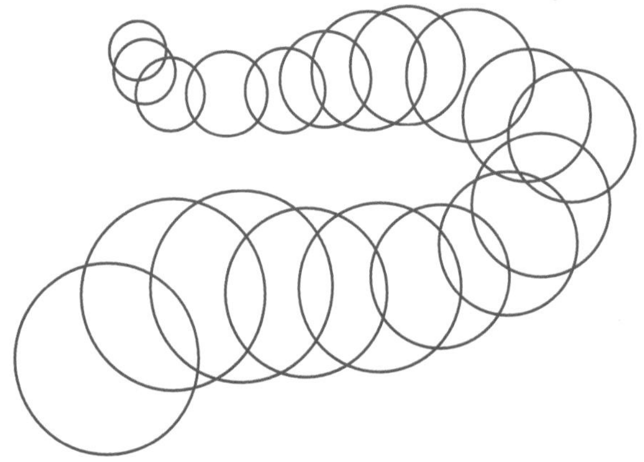

Figure 5-5. Different shapes are associated with psychological meanings. Squares show organization, while triangles display aggression and circles indicate motion.

Mass

Mass is a measure of volume that adds definition to shapes in a visual presentation. The mass or solid portion of the shape provides a visual relationship with the other elements. See **Figure 5-6**.

Figure 5-6. Mass adds volume or weight to a shape by emphasizing part of an image.

Different shapes of varying intensities, known as *weights*, can be used to emphasize or de-emphasize styles of type. See **Figure 5-7**. Physical forms are made by combining the three basic shapes. See **Figure 5-8**.

Figure 5-7. Visual emphasis can be achieved by varying the weights or sizes of type or other images.

Figure 5-8. A combination of shapes creates the physical form of an image.

Texture

The *texture* of a visual image is a projection of emphasized structure or weight. When measuring the texture of an object, the first inclination is to touch the surface. In graphic communications, texture is usually visual; there is no feeling gained through the sense of touch. See **Figure 5-9**.

Figure 5-9. Lines can provide surface variation to give texture to an image.

Texture appears as a design element when the visual images reflect the meaning of lines, as shown in **Figure 5-10**, or when mass forms images that reflect a special technique. See **Figure 5-11**.

Texture varies and depends on the structure and weight of the individual letters, the amount of space between lines, and the amount of mass in a certain space. Actual texture for a printed image can be produced by embossing, which presses a shape or irregular surface into the substrate.

Color

Color is an important element to be considered when planning or designing a printed product.

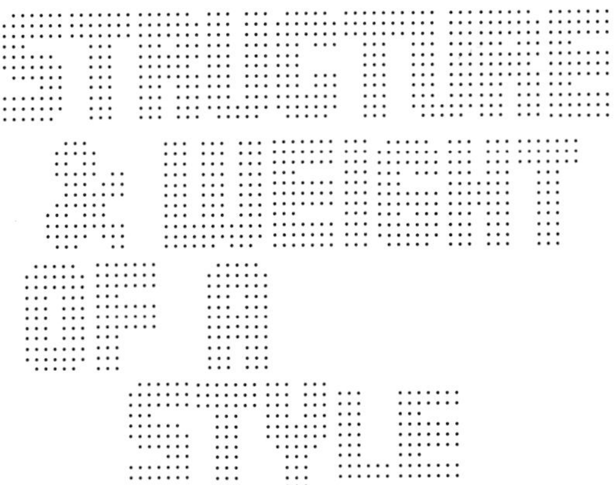

Figure 5-10. Texture of type can be a design element.

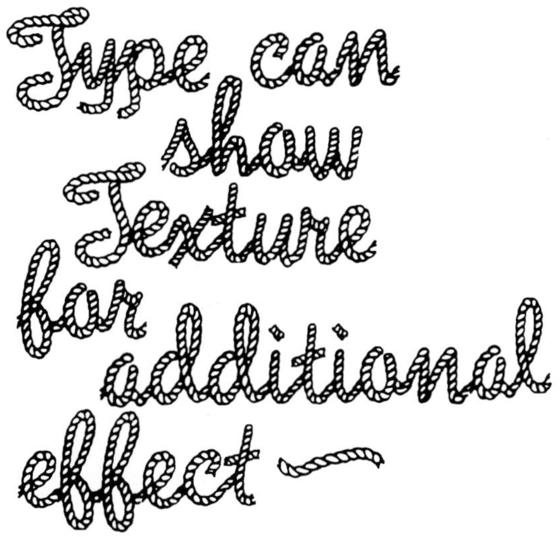

Figure 5-11. Lines added to type can provide texture. Here, they create a unique visual effect resembling rope.

Color can draw attention and produce a strong emotional and psychological impact. Different colors have traditional and symbolic meanings. A basic understanding of color is essential to creating a good design.

Color should be used to add interest and variety to a design. A small amount of color can heighten the visual quality of a page.

Color moods

Different colors project different moods. Yellow, orange, and red are considered to be *warm* colors and often denote aggression, excitement, and danger. Red is considered the most active of these three. Blue, green, and violet are considered to be *cool* colors and are associated with nature and passiveness.

Color wheel

A ***color wheel*** is a visual tool that illustrates the basics of color. It is an arrangement of colors that provides a means of identifying colors in a consistent manner. See **Figure 5-12**.

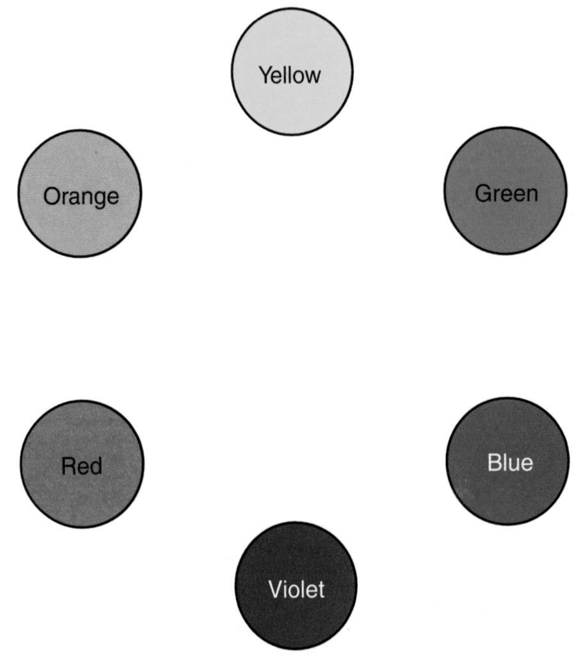

Figure 5-12. A color wheel is an arrangement of colors based on three primary colors, red, yellow, and blue.

The wheel is based on three ***primary colors***, from which all other colors can be made. The primary colors are red, yellow, and blue. Mixing any two will produce a secondary color. The secondary colors are green, orange, and violet.

Two systems of color formation, additive and subtractive, use different primary colors. The *additive* primaries are red, green, and blue. The *subtractive* primaries are cyan, magenta, and yellow. Color formation is covered in detail in Chapter 8.

The colors that are positioned across from each other on the color wheel are known as *complementary colors*. Red and green, orange and blue, and yellow and violet are complementary colors. See **Figure 5-13**.

Different shades and tints of a color, known as *values*, may be obtained by adding white or black to a color. A color can also take on a different intensity when it is mixed with its complement. For example, when green is mixed with red, it will probably produce a *brown*. Striking color effects may be

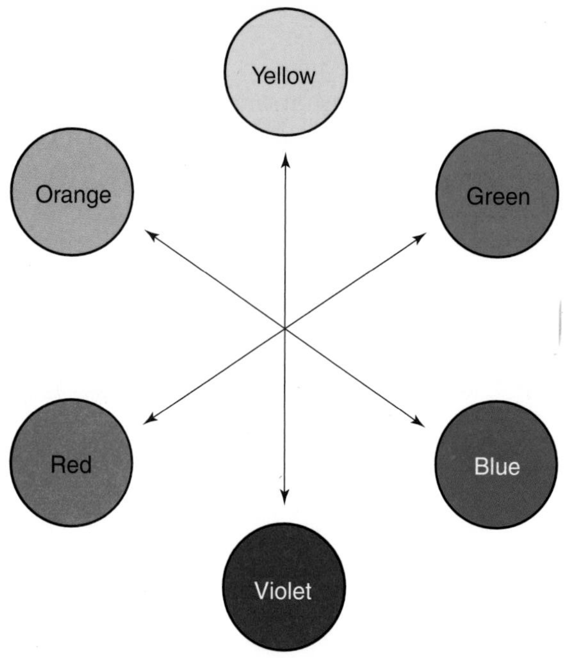

Figure 5-13. Complementary colors are the colors that are positioned across from each other on a color wheel.

produced not only by mixing colors, but also by arranging colors in a layout so they have a direct effect on each other. Chapter 8 includes a detailed description of color theory and how it relates to graphic communication.

Principles of Design

In the process of designing a printed product, many different ideas are generated through the use of design elements. To ensure the images have a pleasing relationship, design principles must be applied to sort out or select the right ideas.

The basic ***principles of design*** are *balance, contrast, unity, rhythm,* and *proportion*. These principles are used by the design artist to create an image that is both visually pleasing and functional.

Balance

Balance describes the even distribution of images to create a pleasing visual effect. Balance has one of the most important psychological influences on human perception. Consciously and unconsciously, people have a basic need for balance.

This principle can be illustrated by the placement of letters on a scale, as shown in **Figure 5-14**.

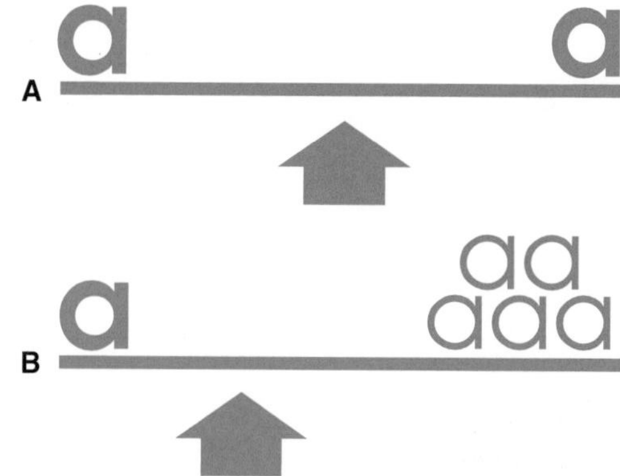

Figure 5-14. Balance in an image is produced through an equal positioning of elements. A—Letters placed symmetrically to achieve formal balance. B—Letters placed in uneven quantities to represent informal balance.

Visually, a judgment can be made by the value of each image. The type of balance in Figure 5-14A is symmetrical and is called formal. The type of balance in Figure 5-14B is asymmetrical and is called informal.

Formal balance is achieved when all of the elements on a page are of equal weight and are positioned symmetrically. ***Informal balance*** may be achieved by changing the value, size, or location of elements on a page. The use of various colors and color intensities can also create informal balance. For example, two squares of equal size but different color values (such as pink and dark red) will appear to be *unequal* in size when placed side by side.

Balance is a guiding principle of design. The layout should be considered as a whole when positioning the elements. See **Figure 5-15**.

Figure 5-15. Balance in a design can vary depending on the desired visual effect. An unbalanced layout can be used to attract attention or imply leisure.

Contrast

Contrast is the variation of elements in a printed product. When used, contrast gives meaning to a design. Lines drawn thick might have little meaning by themselves. Adding thin lines, however, can enhance the design and eliminate monotony. See **Figure 5-16**.

Figure 5-16. A variation of mass or other elements adds contrast and attracts attention to an area of an image.

Styles of type can be contrasted to produce greater legibility and design variation. Some useful contrasts are round and straight, ornate and plain, and broad and narrow. An example of contrast is shown in **Figure 5-17**. A tall tree looks much taller if it is standing on a flat plane.

Figure 5-17. Using contrast emphasizes one element in relation to another. A tree appears taller when it is placed on a flat plane.

The relationship between an unprinted area and a printed area of an image can also be enhanced through the use of contrast. White space, when used effectively, creates contrast in an image. See **Figure 5-18**.

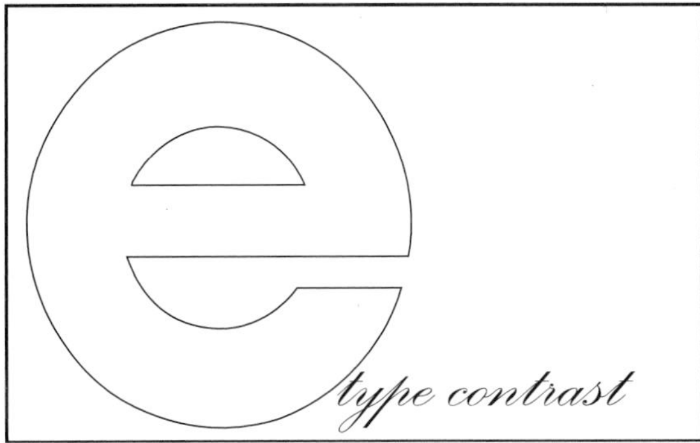

Figure 5-18. The use of white space creates contrast between the printed and unprinted areas of an image.

Care must be taken when combining contrasting elements so that the uniform effect of the total design remains unaffected. A page of many contrasting designs might create confusion. See **Figure 5-19**.

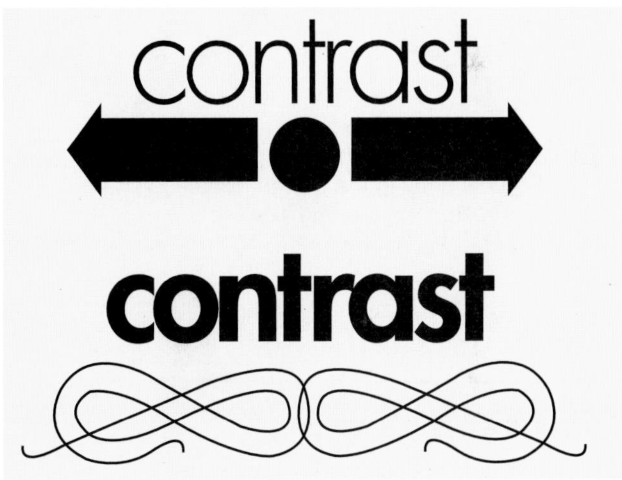

Figure 5-19. Too much contrast between elements can cause confusion.

Balance must be maintained to ensure that one primary element dominates the layout. This principle can be used to draw attention and keep the reader's attention from jumping from one element to another.

Unity

Unity is the proper balance of all elements in an image so that a pleasing whole results and the image is viewed as one piece. Every element must be in proper position to create a harmonious image. A design can be moved and manipulated to create an interesting and functional combination of elements.

Choosing type styles is also important to achieving unity. See **Figure 5-20**. A unified design is the result of viewing the layout as a whole and not as separate elements. This principle is also called *harmony*. See **Figure 5-21**.

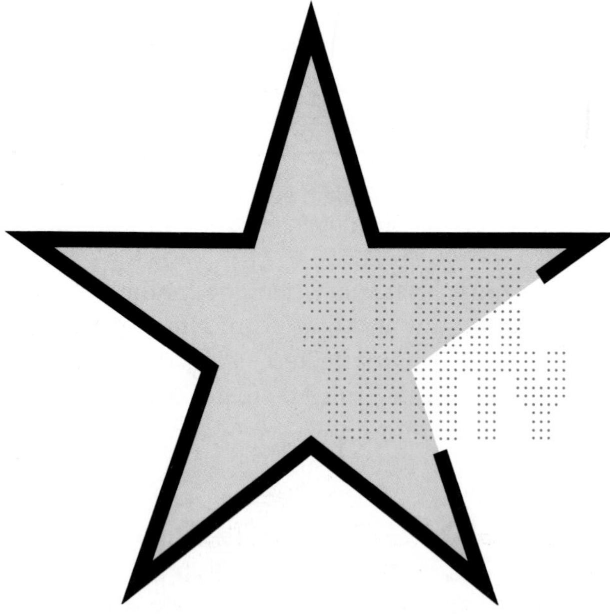

Figure 5-20. A type style that corresponds visually to the subject reflects unity in the design. Small dots forming the type represent stars in the sky.

Figure 5-21. Unity results when all of the elements in an image are arranged as a whole.

Rhythm

The movement of a reader's eye is often determined by the shapes used in the image. The square reflects horizontal and vertical movement. The triangle reflects diagonal movement, and the circle reflects a curve.

Rhythm in a design results when the elements have been properly used to create visual movement and direction. See **Figure 5-22**. Rhythm can also be achieved through the use of a pattern or repetition. Patterns can be used in contrast with an element to create an effective design. See **Figure 5-23**.

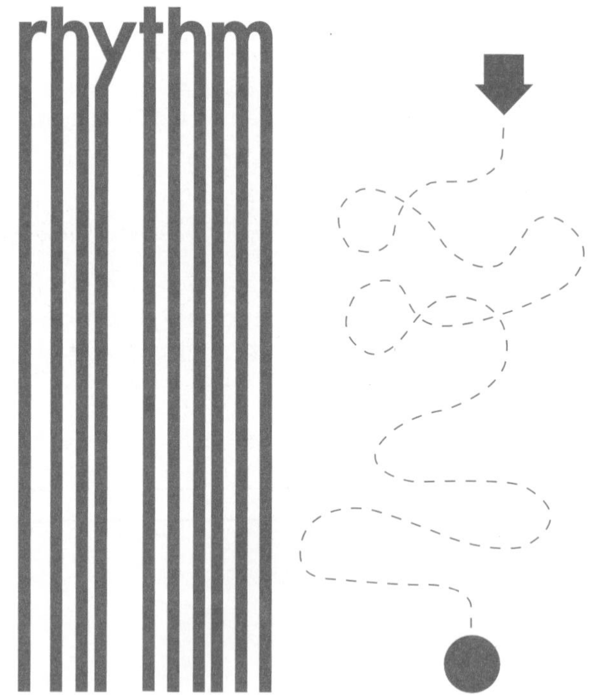

Figure 5-22. Images that imply movement or direction give rhythm to a design.

Proportion

Proportion is the relationship between elements in an image. The use of proportion helps to achieve balance and unity in a layout. All elements should be in proportion to each other. See **Figure 5-24**.

When using different type styles, it is important that they are in proportion to the other elements on the page. See **Figure 5-25**. Using proportion is a means of developing an aesthetically pleasing relationship between each of the elements in the layout.

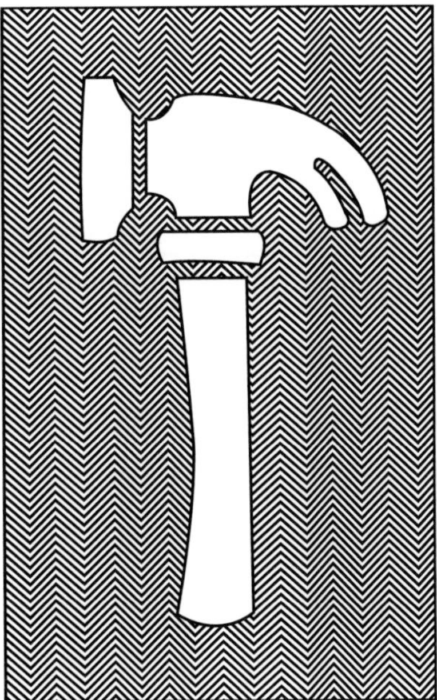

Figure 5-23. A balanced pattern of lines provides rhythm by contrasting with the rest of the image.

Figure 5-24. Elements arranged in proportion to each other produce a unified design.

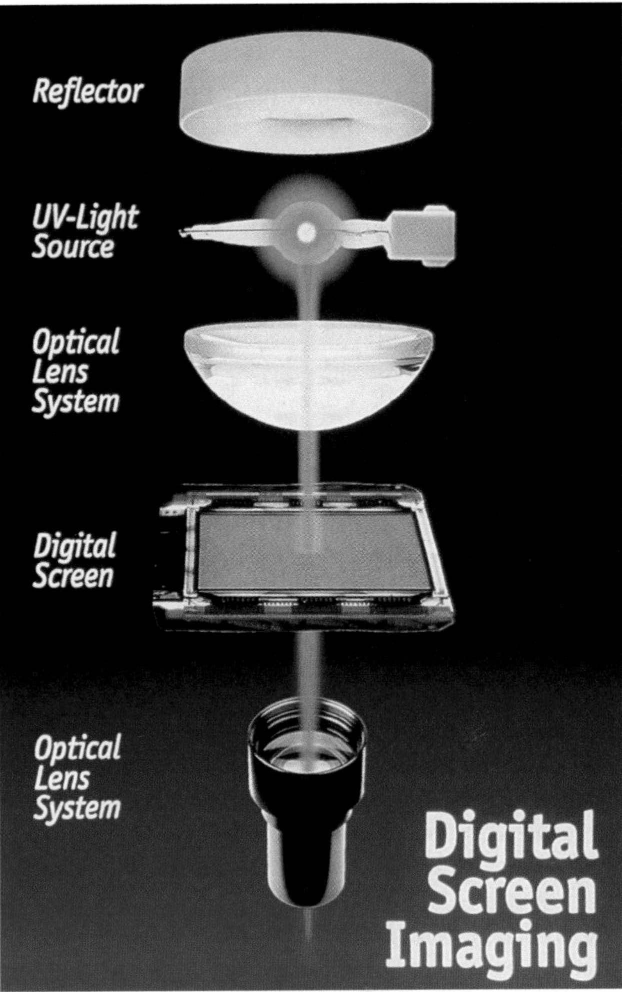

Figure 5-25. The size of type used in a design should be in proportion to the other elements.

A basic knowledge of design elements and principles is key to understanding the guidelines used in layout. The finished layout or *mechanical* must exhibit sound principles of design. The process of preparing a layout sheet is often performed by the same artist responsible for the design.

Layout Elements

Layout is the arrangement of printing elements on a layout sheet. The paste-up version of the base sheet, or mechanical, is made up of the elements ready for reproduction. Planning a layout involves choosing elements that best represent the design. The ***elements of layout*** are *body type*, *display type*, *illustrations*, and *white space*.

The arrangement of elements in a layout must be pleasing to the eye and easy to read. The layout artist or designer is responsible for assembling the elements to make a composition. The layout artist plays a very important role in planning each job.

If the same elements were given to several artists, it is very probable that different layouts would be submitted. If each layout applies valid principles of design, it might be impossible to say one is better than another. Layouts may be judged differently by different people.

The major objective of the layout is that the printed material must be clearly seen and read. The layout artist must consider each element independently and determine how each one relates to the complete product.

Body type

Body type is the printed type that makes up the text in a layout. Body type must be chosen to reflect the intent of the message. The text must be clearly legible and must relate to the topic. Typically, a topic aimed at a contemporary audience would use a modern typeface. See **Figure 5-26**. The placement of type requires proper spacing or *air*. White space can be just as important as the type itself.

Usually, the body type itself is not the focal point of the layout. The text will contain a message that expands upon the other elements. All of the elements, including type, are positioned in a logical progression of importance to meet the layout objectives. Some layout elements will be primary, while others become secondary, according to the objectives of the layout.

Figure 5-26. Selecting a proper typeface and type size for the layout is an important part of the design process.

Display type

Display type is the type that conveys the main message of the layout. It is intended to draw attention. Newspaper and magazine headlines are typical examples of display type. See **Figure 5-27**. The display line is key to the success of a message. If the display type creates interest, the reader will proceed to the body.

Figure 5-27. Headlines are a form of display type. They should draw attention and create interest in the image.

The display line in an advertisement leads the reader to other information. After reading the display material, the person must be satisfied or directed to continue reading the text.

The style of display type is very important because it must correspond to the visual message. Some type styles can be very dramatic, as illustrated in **Figure 5-28**. In such cases, the topic and type style must be compatible. Fine-line display type, for example, is usually not appropriate when used with heavy mass images.

Some type styles are directional and lead the eye of the reader. Sometimes, the layout designer organizes the display line for an ad using hand-lettered display type.

The entire layout must be looked at when choosing a display typeface. The display line must be distinctive and appropriate. To properly select a typeface, the job objective must be fully understood by the layout artist.

Figure 5-28. The style of display type used should reflect the message of the printed piece.

Figure 5-29. A meaningful illustration can be used to convey a strong message.

Illustrations

The ***illustrations*** in a layout include the ornamentation, photographs, and artwork, such as line art. Illustrations are common in most printed materials. For example, display ads typically include illustrations of the product.

The message provided by an illustration can be very revealing. See **Figure 5-29**. The old saying, "A picture is worth a thousand words," applies to many printed materials. Pictorial images are a very strong way of conveying a message. In some cases, an illustration may convey the message by itself. See **Figure 5-30**. Illustrations add another dimension to the layout; they can increase understanding of the product, as well as interest in the product.

White space

White space includes areas of the layout that are void of printed images. Filling up the entire design space will usually not produce good results. The utilization of white space or air can add to the visual quality of a layout.

The distance between elements can be very valuable when white space is used according to sound design principles. It provides a brief period for absorbing the printed matter.

If used excessively, white space can be disorienting. When ideas are too greatly separated, flow and meaning can be lost. White space is very important and must be used properly to create flow, unity, and organization for the reader.

Figure 5-30. Illustrations used in road signs can deliver a message with a minimum use of words.

Developing a Layout

There are a number of factors to consider in developing a layout. Five areas that must be addressed by the layout artist are the *objective* of the project, the *message* the product will send, the *style and format* to be used, the *layout* requirements for production, and *printing* requirements. Each factor contributes to making decisions that will influence production of the final product.

Layout objective

The layout objective is a statement that describes the intent or purpose of an identifiable end product. The objective outlines the goal of the layout artist. For example, an objective might state that the final printed piece should inform the reader, through text and illustrated material, how a piece of equipment will help in a specific production situation.

The objective describes what the information on the printed page is intended to do. Knowing the purpose helps the layout artist determine which text and illustrations will be best for the job.

Conveying a message

The message or visual effect delivered by a printed image helps determine how the layout will be planned. Identifying the audience gives direction to the layout artist. For example, one ad might be designed for young people, while another might be aimed at the elderly. The design of each ad should be unique and must reflect the intent of the printed piece.

Design of the end product also determines the tone or *mood* of the message. If a lighthearted or humorous mood is intended, a dramatic photograph might not achieve the desired effect. All of the elements should reflect the message of the end product.

Style and format

Style includes the text type, display type, and illustrations of the design. Some printed pieces will require a set style, while others do not. For instance, the style used in this textbook is quite different from the styles used in advertisements. The designer must choose the elements that will work best.

Deciding how to organize the ***format*** of the printed piece is of primary importance. Will a single sheet carry the message, or will a booklet do a better job? The format will also be determined by its intended use. For example, if the printed piece is to be posted, it should not be printed on both sides.

Layout requirements

The different methods of layout and the schedule to complete the job must be considered in planning a layout. A layout may need to be developed as a sketch, a rough, or a comprehensive. It may be necessary to perform all three.

A *sketch* is an idea in pictorial form with little detail. Sketches are often helpful because they provide a picture indicating possible placement of the elements. A *rough* is more illustrative of the final product; it provides the style of the type as well as the position of the elements. A *comprehensive* is the third and final method of layout. It is the presentation of what the finished product will indeed look like. When planning a layout, the artist should decide which methods will be necessary to reach the final product in a timely manner.

An estimate of the time it will take to complete the job is essential from a planning standpoint. Most printed pieces are produced to meet a deadline and must be delivered by a specified date. The planner must decide whether the job can be completed in the time allowed.

Printing requirements

The printing process that follows production has a strong influence on how a layout is developed. The size of the product, the quantity to be printed, paper requirements, color use, and operations following the printing must all be considered.

The finished dimension of a printed piece must be determined before beginning layout. The finished size will have a bearing on every production step. One important concern is the size of the press required to run the job. The finished size also determines the size of the paper to be used in printing.

The number of pages to be printed and the number of copies required are also factors to consider because they will help determine the printing requirements. Deciding the most economical way of printing the job is essential. The designer or editor must estimate the approximate number of pages to be printed so that final plans for printing can be made.

Printing requirements include the kind of stock or paper to be used. The necessary stock must be available at the designated time for printing. A custom stock may need to be ordered and may require additional time. Other considerations in ordering stock are the size of the order, paper weight (thickness), and opacity.

Multicolor printing is another factor to consider when planning a layout. Different jobs require different uses of color. Printing a one-color or black and white job requires different layout methods than a two-color, or four-color job. The layout artist must decide whether to use color when planning the layout.

Once the job is printed, further finishing operations might be required, such as trimming the job to the final size. Other finishing operations may include folding, scoring, creasing, varnishing, and binding. Knowing the operations that will be required after printing is important in planning the job.

Layout Methods

Choosing the right method to develop a layout can be very difficult and requires careful planning and thinking by the layout artist. The design methods used in layout are thumbnail sketches, the rough layout, and the comprehensive layout. Much of the decision depends on the factors that have already been discussed. The size of the job, the objective, and use of color are all important considerations. The layout artist must have a vision of how to arrive at the final product.

The layout can make or break the appearance of the final product. Many times, a number of layout ideas are discarded before one is chosen. Each method must be carefully analyzed to produce a strong, functional layout.

Thumbnail sketches

Thumbnail sketches are simple, rapidly drawn designs for a layout. See **Figure 5-31**. Different approaches can be taken in drawing sketches. Sketching is a means of testing the visual appeal of a printed piece.

Figure 5-31. Sketches showing the general relationship of elements provide a basis for the design.

The size of a *thumbnail* is not important. The sketch is generally smaller than the size of the printed product. The first sketch might not be the design selected, but each one will help the artist visualize the end product.

A soft pencil or felt tip pen is typically used to draw thumbnail sketches. Even though the size is not important, the general proportion is required to indicate image relationships. The purpose of the sketch is to evaluate the weight of each element. The sketch shows the basic shape and tone of the total piece.

Rough layout

A ***rough layout*** is a redrawn version of a thumbnail sketch, **Figure 5-32**. Once a specific thumbnail has been selected, refinement is necessary. The elements in a rough layout or *dummy* offer a truer visual meaning. In many cases, the dummy must be checked and approved by the designer, client, and sometimes the printer.

Figure 5-32. A rough layout is a sketched version of the final product.

Figure 5-33. A refined layout is sometimes made before doing a comprehensive layout.

The display lines and illustrations of a rough are very similar to the elements of the final product. The text material is located in a greeked (illegible) block or whatever form it will take in the finished product. The rough has a closer resemblance to the intended printed piece than the thumbnail sketches.

Sometimes, a refined layout may be made, **Figure 5-33**. Since the refined layout is closer to the final layout, it can be used as the final layout when time is a major factor. Special notations for type size, type style, or color can be made on a tissue overlay or on the layout.

Comprehensive layout

A ***comprehensive layout*** shows how the printed piece will look when finished. The layout artist is making a close version of the finished product; therefore, exact detail is essential. See **Figure 5-34**.

The body type is usually ruled in and the display type is drawn as it will appear in the finished piece. Any art sketched previously now has a photograph or accurate line art in its place. Special effects become a part of the comprehensive layout, and colors can also be added.

Instructions, specifications, and notations are not placed directly on the comprehensive. A common practice is to attach an overlay sheet with tape at the top of the base sheet. The overlay sheet is usually translucent tissue paper so that the comprehensive can be easily viewed along with any notations. The information is written on the tissue and serves as the specifications for the final preparation of art and copy.

The comprehensive should not be confused with the *mechanical*. The mechanical is pasted up and completed in the next step of production. The mechanical is the final stage of layout. It includes the body text and any other camera-ready images that are converted to film by a process camera or other means. See **Figure 5-35**.

Specifications

Specifications provide the information relating to type style, type size, line or column width, color use, page organization, and other facts pertaining to a printed product. Specifications or *specs* are the overall guidelines used in layout.

Figure 5-34. A comprehensive layout is a detailed representation of the final layout.

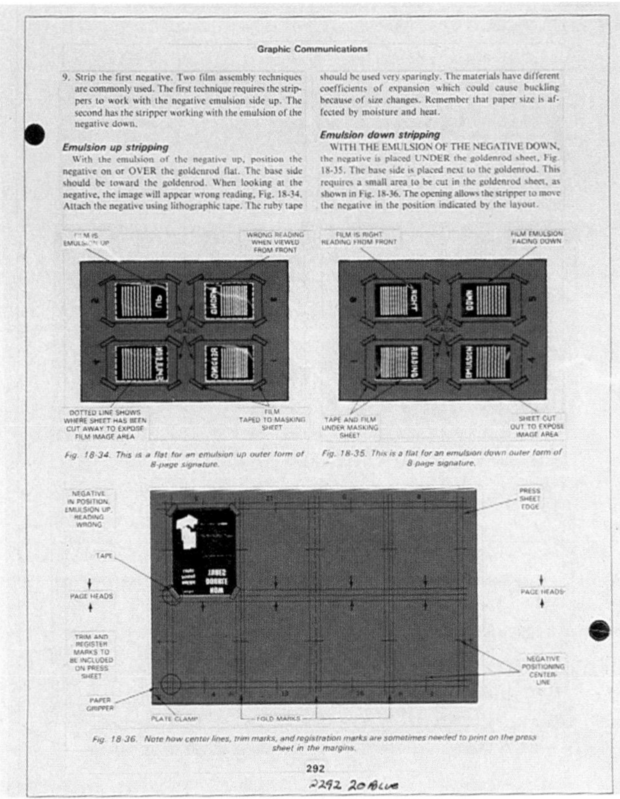

Graphic Communications

9. Strip the first negative. Two film assembly techniques are commonly used. The first technique requires the strippers to work with the negative emulsion side up. The second has the stripper working with the emulsion of the negative down.

Emulsion up stripping

With the emulsion of the negative up, position the negative on or OVER the goldenrod flat. The base side should be toward the goldenrod. When looking at the negative, the image will appear wrong reading, Fig. 18-34. Attach the negative using lithographic tape. The ruby tape should be used very sparingly. The materials have different coefficients of expansion which could cause buckling because of size changes. Remember that paper size is affected by moisture and heat.

Emulsion down stripping

WITH THE EMULSION OF THE NEGATIVE DOWN, the negative is placed UNDER the goldenrod sheet, Fig. 18-35. The base side is placed next to the goldenrod. This requires a small area to be cut in the goldenrod sheet, as shown in Fig. 18-36. The opening allows the stripper to move the negative in the position indicated by the layout.

WRONG READING WHEN VIEWED FROM FRONT

FILM IS RIGHT READING FROM FRONT

FILM EMULSION FACING DOWN

DOTTED LINE SHOWS WHERE SHEET HAS BEEN CUT AWAY TO EXPOSE FILM IMAGE AREA

FILM TAPED TO MASKING SHEET

TAPE AND FILM UNDER MASKING SHEET

SHEET CUT OUT TO EXPOSE IMAGE AREA

Fig. 18-34. This is a flat for an emulsion up outer form of 8-page signature.

Fig. 18-35. This is a flat for an emulsion down outer form of 8 page signature.

NEGATIVE IN POSITION, EMULSION UP, READING WRONG

TAPE

PAGE HEADS

TRIM AND REGISTER MARKS TO BE INCLUDED ON PRESS SHEET

PAPER GRIPPER

PLATE CLAMP

FOLD MARKS

PRESS SHEET EDGE

PAGE HEADS

NEGATIVE POSITIONING CENTER-LINE

Fig. 18-36. Note how center lines, trim marks, and registration marks are sometimes needed to print on the press sheet in the margins.

292

2292 20 Blue

Figure 5-35. A completed mechanical ready to be photographed and converted to film.

Manuscripts are commonly marked with specifications identifying the typeface and type size to be used. The specs are used to convert the original copy on the manuscript to the text in the final layout. See **Figure 5-36.**

FR Helios 11/12.3 +10.3

Our teaching staff is creative and well qualified. Our focus is geared to the family and the role of the individual. Classes are offered for every age group.

Join our staff in discovering your many talents which can help your family better understand itself. Explore careers, interests, hobbies. Exercise in our gymnasium and attend the family seminars.

Daily hours are from 9:00 to 5:00 P M. Evening sessions start at 7:00 P.M. and go until 10:00 P.M.

A

B

Figure 5-36. Specifications identify the styles and sizes of type to be used in a design. A—The manuscript is marked to indicate type specs. B—Text in the final layout is arranged according to the specs.

A *spec sheet*, sometimes called a *style sheet*, lists the specs used in production. See **Figure 5-37**. The spec sheet is created before beginning a job. It contains information on type styles and sizes, art to be used, and color usage.

Specifications for *Graphic Communications*

Trim: 8-1/2 x 10-7/8
Gutter: 5p
Bottom Margin: 5p
Thumb Margin: 4p
Top Margin: 3p to the base of the running head, 5p to the top of the first line of text
2 column format: 20p3 x 1p6 x 20p3

4-color process

Chapters are always to start a new right.

Typefaces used: Palm Springs, Helvetica (all in roman, bold, italic and/or bold italic).

Running Heads: Left hand pages, set folio flush left on left hand margin of left column. Folio sets in 10pt Helvetica Bold. On 3p indent set Book Title. Book Title sets in 10pt Helvetica. Right hand pages, set folio flush right on right hand margin of right column. Folio sets in 10pt Helvetica Bold. On 3p indent from right margin set Chapter Number and Title. Chapter number and title sets in 10pt Helvetica, flush right on indent. Allow an em space between the number and title.

Chapters: Are to start a new right. The chapter opener takes a drop folio, 10pt Helvetica Bold, prints black, flush left on the outside margin, 2p below the normal text bed.

Chapter Opening Graphic: Falls in the first column, and is made up of squares. Large black square is 10p3, and sets flush left on first column. Three large squares are each 3p, second set of squares is 1p6, and smallest set of squares is 1p3. There should be 3pt space between the various squares, follow the sample pages for general layout of graphic. The large squares should be 100% Cyan; 100% Magenta; and 100% Yellow. Secondary squares should be 100% Cyan, 100% Yellow; 100% Yellow, 50% Magenta; 50% Magenta, 50% Cyan. Tertiary squares should be 50% Yellow, 100% Cyan; 100% Yellow, 50% Cyan; 20% Magenta, 100% Yellow; 80% Magenta, 100% Yellow.

Chapter number: 190pt Arabic number, Helvetica Bold, 30% Black Screen, 2 digit numbers track -20, do not use the word chapter. Set so its top aligns with the top of nominal text bed, flush right. Underprints chapter title.

Chapter title: 30/30 Helvetica, Track -5, build down from top line, flush left, ragged right, in second column, with ascender of first line aligning with the top of the nominal text bed.

Objectives: Heading sets Helvetica Bold, 14/auto, Clc, flrr x 20p3, 6p below the bottom of the chapter graphic to the ascender of the heading. 0p3 after. Opening state-

Figure 5-37. A spec sheet lists type styles and sizes, along with information on art, the use of color, page margins, and other specific information needed to produce the printed piece.

Specifications are also used in printing, binding, and finishing. A printing spec sheet may list information on the type of paper to be used, color specifications, and other requirements. See **Figure 5-38**.

Copyfitting

Copyfitting is the process of fitting together copy and illustrations in a specific amount of space. It can be done by altering type size, leading, line

PRINTING SPECIFICATIONS

Company ______ Contact ______
Address ______
Phone ______ Fax ______
Project Title ______
Description ______

☐ Early budget ☐ Late budget ☐ Based on specs ☐ Based on art
Date ______
Date prices required ______
Release date ______
Delivery date ______

Quantities ______

☐ Overs up to ____%
☐ Unders up to ____%
☐ No overs/unders

☐ New project
☐ Exact reprint
☐ Reprint w/changes

Page count | ☐ Plus cover, no. pages ___ ☐ Self cover
Flat size | Finished size

Proofs: No:
☐ Blueline ___
☐ Colorkey ___
☐ Matchprint ___
☐ Other ___
☐ Press check

Paper

Form	# of Pages	Color	Basis Weight	Specify Cover or Book Weight	Name or Grade	Finish
Single Sheet						
Cover						
Fly						
Text 1						
Text 2						

Preparation

Electronic Prepress Output
Type of output ______
Software used and version no. ______
Fonts: ______

Disk Format ☐ Single pages ☐ Readers spreads ☐ Printers spreads

Customer Furnish
☐ Complete camera ready art
☐ Windows on art for images
☐ Flapped for colors and screens
☐ Key lined for color break
☐ Masks furnished for outlines
☐ Composite negs. in ___ pg spreads

Maps charts: No. ___ Size ___ (×3)
Line strip-ins: No. ___ Size ___ (×3)
Half-tones: No. ___ Size ___ Outline ___ (×3)
Duo-tones: No. ___ Size ___ Outline ___ (×3)
Screens: No. ___ Size ___ (×3)
Reverses: No. ___ Size ___ (×3)

Color Seps.

No.	Original size	To	Finished size	Trans.	Refl	Scan	Cam.	Outline	Crossover	Scan to file	Lo/Hi res.
No. ____	___ x ___	To	___ x ___	☐	☐	☐	☐	☐	☐	☐	☐
No. ____	___ x ___	To	___ x ___	☐	☐	☐	☐	☐	☐	☐	☐
No. ____	___ x ___	To	___ x ___	☐	☐	☐	☐	☐	☐	☐	☐
No. ____	___ x ___	To	___ x ___	☐	☐	☐	☐	☐	☐	☐	☐
No. ____	___ x ___	To	___ x ___	☐	☐	☐	☐	☐	☐	☐	☐

Press

Cover	Fly	Text 1	Text 1
out ______	Side 1 ______	Side 1 ______	Side 1 ______
in ______	Side 2 ______	Side 2 ______	Side 2 ______
% Coverage ______	% Coverage ______	% Coverage ______	% Coverage ______
Varnish ☐dry ☐wet ☐spot ☐overall	Varnish ☐dry ☐wet ☐spot ☐overall	Varnish ☐dry ☐wet ☐spot ☐overall	Varnish ☐dry ☐wet ☐spot ☐overall
Solids ☐yes ☐no	Solids ☐yes ☐no	Solids ☐yes ☐no	Solids ☐yes ☐no
Bleeds ☐yes ☐no	Bleeds ☐yes ☐no	Bleeds ☐yes ☐no	Bleeds ☐yes ☐no
Coating ☐aqueous	Coating ☐aqueous	Coating ☐aqueous	Coating ☐aqueous
Coating ☐UV ☐spot ☐overall	Coating ☐UV ☐spot ☐overall	Coating ☐UV ☐spot ☐overall	Coating ☐UV ☐spot ☐overall

Bindery

☐ Soft fold Fold to ___ x ___ No. of folds ___ ☐ Letter fold ☐ Accordion ☐ Round corner ☐ Remoistenable gum
☐ Saddle stitch ☐ Double saddle ☐ Side stitch & tape ☐ Perfect bind ☐ Case bind ☐ Spiral ☐ Wire-O ☐ GBC
☐ Perforate ______ ☐ Die Cut ______ ☐ Collate ______
☐ Drill ______ ☐ Emboss/size ______ ☐ Shrink wrap ______
☐ Score ______ ☐ Deboss/size ______ ☐ Mail ☐ Label ☐ Ink jet
☐ Glue pockets/size ______ No. ______ ☐ Foil stamp/size ______ ☐ Cust. supplies: ______
☐ Pockets no glue/size ______ No. ______ ☐ Trim only ______ x ______ ☐ Other ______

Shipping

Special packing ______
(Bulk pack in cartons unless otherwise specified.)
No. of samples required ______ Delivery date ______
F.O.B. point ______ No. of local deliveries ______

Pricing

Vendor ______ Contact ______ Phone ______
Quantity ______ Estimated price ______

Figure 5-38. A printing spec sheet provides the guidelines used in printing a finished product.

length, or letter spacing. The layout planner or artist is heavily involved in copyfitting during various stages of production. If the amount of copy is greater than the space allocated, the total design is affected.

Copyfitting also involves estimating the amount of space needed for a certain amount of text. The amount of space needed must be known by the layout artist to design a comprehensive layout.

In desktop publishing, copyfitting is commonly completed for layout on a computer screen. See **Figure 5-39**. A desktop publishing system can be used to copyfit text and illustrations, move copy, draw line art, and finalize layout.

Figure 5-39. Copyfitting for layout is commonly performed electronically using a desktop publishing system.

There are also manual counting techniques used in copyfitting. The most common method is counting the total number of characters in a body of text.

To determine the number of characters in the text, a vertical line is drawn through the printed copy at the end of the shortest line in the copy. See **Figure 5-40**. The number of characters in a single line to the left of the vertical line is then counted. Characters include all letters, spaces, and punctuation. The number of characters in one line is then multiplied by the number of full lines. If there is a partial line, the number of characters it contains is counted and added to the total from the preceding step. This total represents the number of characters to the left of the vertical line. Next, the number of characters to the right of the vertical line is counted. The total number of characters from all lines on the right side is then added to the total number of characters on the left side. As shown in Figure 5-40, the number of characters in this example is 290.

Once the number of characters in the text is determined, a type style and size is selected for the text. The line length and character size for the text, in picas, must then be determined. Typeface tables or catalogs showing different sizes of type and the number of characters per pica are commonly used. See **Figure 5-41**.

Suppose that you wish to set type in a 10-point sans serif typeface with a line width of 18 picas, and there are 310 total characters in the text. The following steps are used to determine the space required for the text:

1. Referring to Figure 5-41, find the number of characters in 10-point type that will fill one pica of space. Multiply that figure (2.9) by the line length to find the number of characters in an 18-pica line:

   $2.9 \times 18 = 52.2$ characters per line

2. Find the number of typeset lines by dividing the total number of characters in the text by the number of characters per line (rounded to the nearest whole number):

   $310 \div 52 = 5.96$ or 6 lines

3. To find the total depth of the text, multiply the point size by the number of typeset lines:

   $10 \times 6 = 60$ points

4. Convert the measure from points to picas. One pica is equal to 12 points.

   $60 \div 12 = 5$ picas

The text will measure 5 picas deep and 18 picas wide. This example was for type that is set solid. If leading is added, the amount of leading space in points must be added to the type size. If the type were set as 10 points with 2 points of leading (10/12), the calculation would be as follows:

10-point type + 2-point leading = 12 points
12 points $\times$ 6 lines = 72 points
$72 \div 12 = 6$ picas

The depth of the text, with leading added, would be 6 picas. The text would measure 6 picas deep and 18 picas wide.

Processing Illustrations

Photographs and pieces of line art used in layout are commonly edited or sized for reproduction

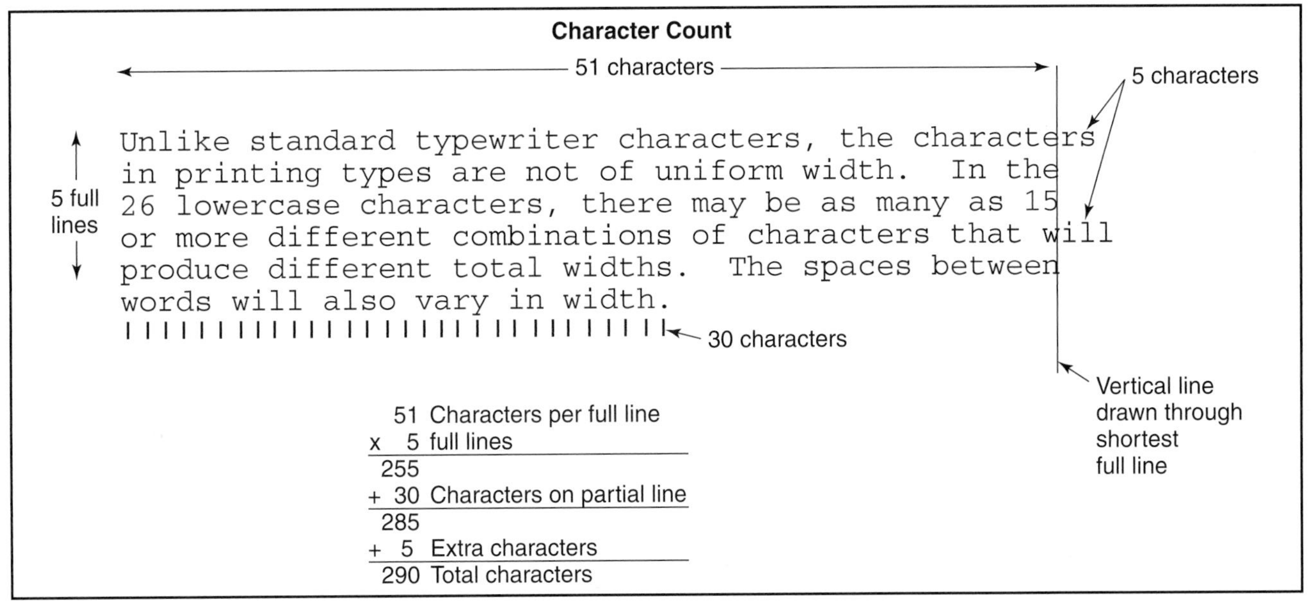

Figure 5-40. The number of characters in a block of text can be determined by drawing a vertical line through the shortest line of copy and counting characters on both sides of the line.

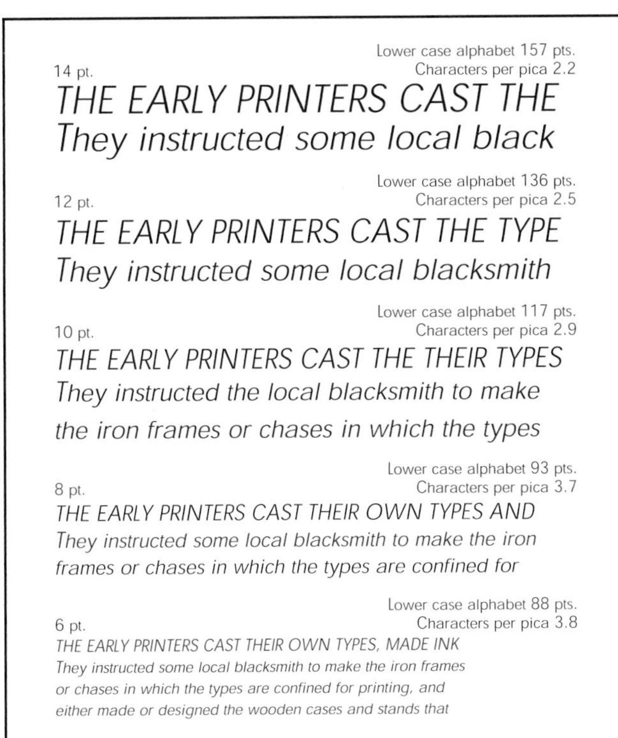

Figure 5-41. A list of typefaces showing the number of characters per pica for different type sizes. Characters per pica will differ from one typeface to another as well.

by the layout artist. The principles used in design and layout must be followed when processing illustrations. The layout artist must make sure that the illustrations are sized properly, and that they have the right contrast, unity, and proportion.

Photo cropping

The complete image of a photograph often cannot be used because some portion of the print is not needed. In many cases, the composition of the photo must be edited or cropped.

Photo cropping is a method of indicating what portion of the print is to be used or reproduced. A cropped photo separates the desired image from the unwanted areas. Crop marks border the area to be used. Marks are placed in the white margin of the print with a grease pencil or a similar marker that will not damage the photograph. See **Figure 5-42.**

Crop marks set the photograph dimensions. Two sets of marks can be used along the top and bottom of the image to establish width. Pairs of marks on each side of the image indicate depth or height. The final image will only use the portion of the photograph that lies within the crop marks.

Photo sizing

In graphic production, it is often necessary to use photographs at sizes other than the original. Many times, the photo must be enlarged or reduced by a certain percentage to fit the space. For example, if a photo measures 6″ × 6″ and the design space is only 3″ × 3″, the photo would have to be reduced to half its original size or by 50 percent. A 35 mm slide might have to be enlarged to twice its original size (200 percent) or more to provide a printed image of the required size.

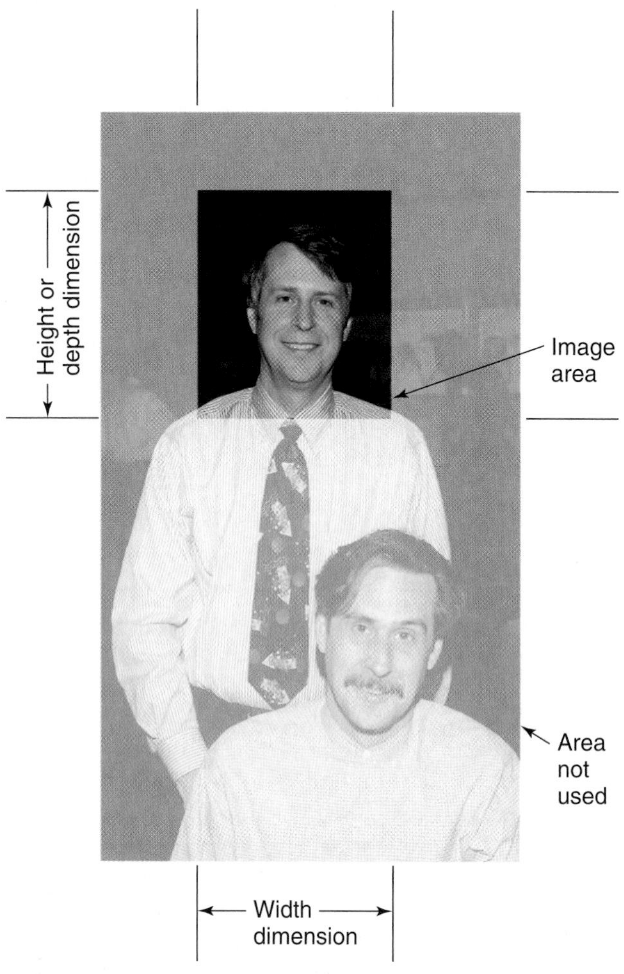

Figure 5-42. Crop marks drawn along the border of a photograph show the area of the image to be used.

A *proportional scale* or "proportion wheel" is commonly used to size illustrations for enlargement or reduction. See **Figure 5-43**. The scale can be used to determine the correct reproduction percentage by comparing the original size of the photo with the reproduction size. The numbers along the inner portion of the scale represent the original size, and the numbers along the outer portion represent the reproduction size. When the scale is rotated to match the two sizes, the resulting percentage of enlargement or reduction is indicated by an arrow pointing to a windowed scale located on the inner portion of the proportion wheel.

When sizing a photo, it is important to remember that the image will retain the same shape and proportion. For example, a rectangle will reproduce as a smaller or larger rectangle. The dimensions change, but the proportion remains the same.

Figure 5-43. A sampling of proportional scales used to determine reproduction sizes for photographs or for other illustrations.

Precise reproduction percentages and often, cropping are necessary to produce the required results and fit the design space. Sometimes, it might be necessary to use a different photograph or illustration to meet the specifications of the job.

Photo layout

Photographs are not pasted down along with the other elements on a mechanical. Usually, a space for the photo is outlined on the layout with a thin black line (called a *keyline*). A block of opaque material the exact size of the photo is sometimes used, instead of a keyline. A figure number is assigned to the space and the photo. The number indicates where to place the screened halftone of the photo when making the mechanical. See **Figure 5-44**.

Photo markup

Photo markup involves writing directions or specifications for the visual images used in layout. A marked-up photo is shown in **Figure 5-45**. Markings should be carefully placed on the border or outside the image area of photos. Crop marks should appear in the margin or in an area that will not be reproduced.

Photographs must be handled very carefully when they are used in layout. The surface of the image can scratch very easily; never write on an overlay that is placed on top of a photo. The pressure from a pen or pencil can indent the surface. Damage to a photo can leave an unwanted mark or reflection during reproduction or screening.

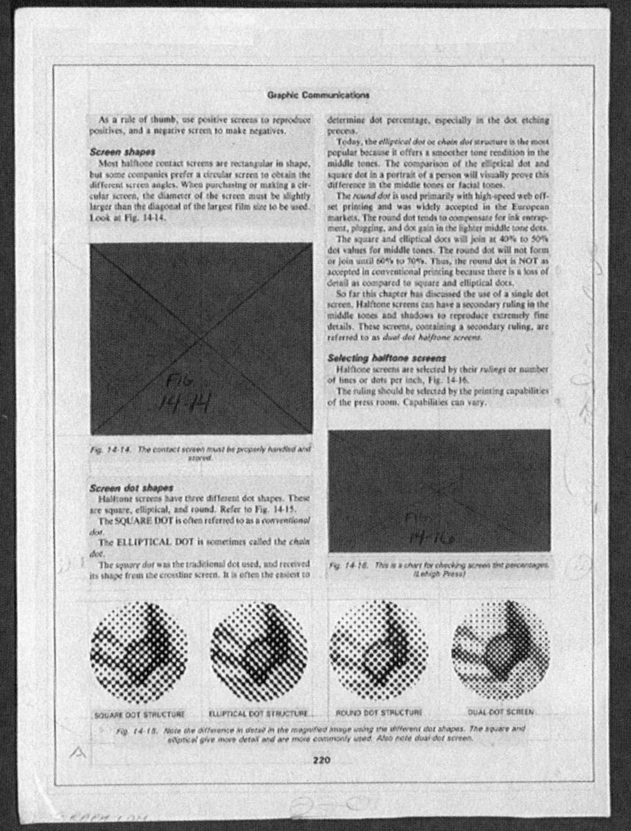

Graphic Communications

As a rule of thumb, use positive screens to reproduce positives, and a negative screen to make negatives.

Screen shapes

Most halftone contact screens are rectangular in shape, but some companies prefer a circular screen to obtain the different screen angles. When purchasing or making a circular screen, the diameter of the screen must be slightly larger than the diagonal of the largest film size to be used. Look at Fig. 14-14.

Fig 14-14

Fig. 14-14. The contact screen must be properly handled and stored.

Screen dot shapes

Halftone screens have three different dot shapes. These are square, elliptical, and round. Refer to Fig. 14-15.

The SQUARE DOT is often referred to as a *conventional dot*.

The ELLIPTICAL DOT is sometimes called the *chain dot*.

The *square dot* was the traditional dot used, and received its shape from the crossline screen. It is often the easiest to determine dot percentage, especially in the dot etching process.

Today, the *elliptical dot* or *chain dot* structure is the most popular because it offers a smoother tone rendition in the middle tones. The comparison of the elliptical dot and square dot in a portrait of a person will visually prove this difference in the middle tones or facial tones.

The *round dot* is used primarily with high-speed web offset printing and was widely accepted in the European markets. The round dot tends to compensate for ink entrapment, plugging, and dot gain in the lighter middle tone dots.

The square and elliptical dots will join at 40% to 50% dot values for middle tones. The round dot will not form or join until 60% to 70%. Thus, the round dot is NOT as accepted in conventional printing because there is a loss of detail as compared to square and elliptical dots.

So far this chapter has discussed the use of a single dot screen. Halftone screens can have a secondary ruling in the middle tones and shadows to reproduce extremely fine details. These screens, containing a secondary ruling, are referred to as *dual-dot halftone screens*.

Selecting halftone screens

Halftone screens are selected by their *rulings* or number of lines or dots per inch, Fig. 14-16.

The ruling should be selected by the printing capabilities of the press room. Capabilities can vary.

Fig 14-16

Fig. 14-16. This is a chart for checking screen tint percentages. (Lehigh Press)

SQUARE DOT STRUCTURE | ELLIPTICAL DOT STRUCTURE | ROUND DOT STRUCTURE | DUAL-DOT SCREEN

Fig. 14-15. Note the difference in detail in the magnified image using the different dot shapes. The square and elliptical give more detail and are more commonly used. Also note dual-dot screen.

220

Figure 5-44. Spaces are reserved as holes to indicate where photos are to be placed for a mechanical.

Figure 5-45. A photo marked up with crop marks indicates the size for reduction or enlargement.

Line art

Line art is artwork that is drawn by hand or electronically and is normally pasted up at the same size on a mechanical. If necessary, the original art can be enlarged or reduced. Then, the correctly sized line art can be pasted onto the mechanical. See **Figure 5-46**.

Figure 5-46. Line art is drawn to the necessary size and pasted up on the mechanical.

Sketches and drawings are marked in the same manner as photographs. They must be cropped, sized, and located. Information that is marked up on illustrations might include the job title and number, location in the printed piece, a figure number if applicable, the percentage for enlargement or reduction, the reproduction size, and the name of the layout artist.

When line art and *tone material* are used together, the tone material is placed on an overlay. For example, if the tone material is going to be used to place color in line art, it must be cut to the shape of the art and placed in register on the overlay.

Clip art

Clip art is preprinted artwork that is designed to be cut and pasted up on the mechanical. The artwork is normally cut from a sheet of clip art. See **Figure 5-47**. Today, clip art is commonly available in electronic form. It can be printed out and pasted up in the traditional manner, or added directly to an electronic page layout.

Clip art is commonly used for seasonal designs, such as Thanksgiving or Christmas newspaper ads. Pieces of clip art save the artist from having to draw Christmas trees, wreaths, turkeys, and other common images.

Clip art must have high image quality and density so that it will reproduce properly. The most common form of clip art is made up of black images on a white background. Some clip art is also available as separations for color printing. See **Figure 5-48**. Four-color clip art can be very effective if the artwork is appropriate for the layout.

Layout Materials

The two most common working surfaces used in layout and design are a ***drawing board*** and *light table*. A drawing board provides an area where the layout can be taped down for paste-up. A T-square is used to align the mechanical on the board. See **Figure 5-49**.

A light table is used in layout for the placement of translucent images, such as page negatives or color separations. Light passing through the images allows for easier alignment or registration.

Figure 5-47. Clip art. A—Preprinted clip art is available in common designs and is ready to be pasted up. B—Electronic clip art is now widely used.

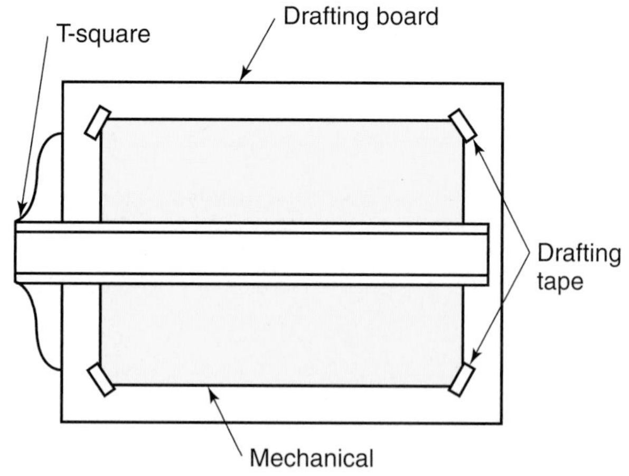

Figure 5-49. A drawing board serves as a working surface to paste up the mechanical.

Figure 5-48. Clip art used in multicolor printing. Each image is a color separation and can be used to make a plate for a primary color.

Layout base sheet

A ***layout base sheet*** is the paste-up surface or board used in layout. The elements making up the layout design are pasted up on the base sheet as it is developed into a mechanical.

Various kinds of base sheet stock are available. Base sheets must have a surface that can accept a variety of adhesives and ink drawings. Sizes typically depend on the size of the copyboard of the process camera used to photograph the finished mechanical.

Preprinted base sheets are often used to make mechanicals when the same type of job is done repeatedly. Artists using preprinted sheets do not align paste-up materials with a T-square. Preprinted base sheets have grids printed with nonreproducing blue lines that serve as a guide for image placement. The grid lines are often measured at intervals of one pica. See **Figure 5-50**.

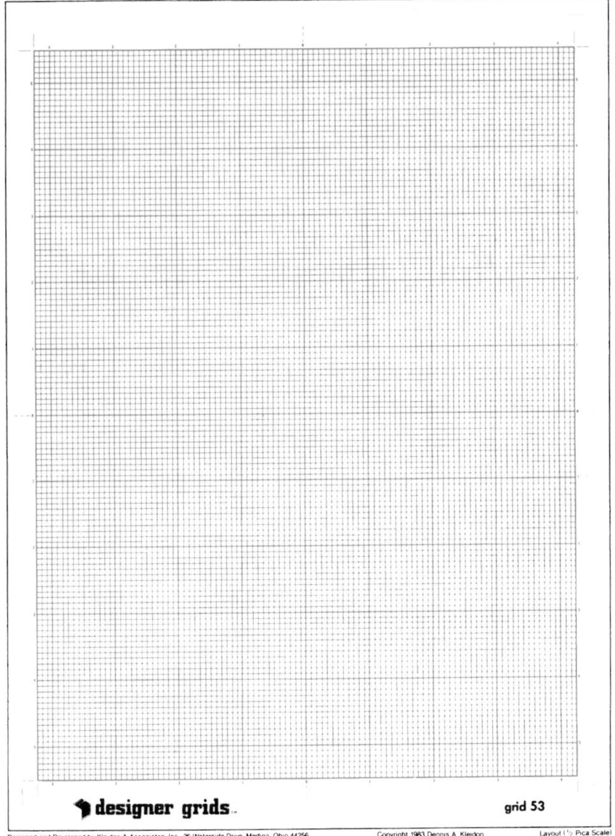

Figure 5-50. A preprinted layout base sheet often is used to make the mechanical. Grid lines serve as guides for positioning copy and art.

Thin plastic sheets are used with base sheets as *overlays* when preparing a mechanical. Overlays are usually frosted or clear plastic and are used to align images supporting color on top of the base sheet. They contain the elements that will print as color or screened color. Register marks are used to align the overlay with the mechanical. See **Figure 5-51**.

Figure 5-51. A plastic overlay sheet is used with a mechanical to align images that will print in a second color or as a percentage of black. Register marks are applied to align the parts.

Workmarks

Workmarks are lines that guide the placement of materials on a base sheet. Corner or trim marks are always placed on the sheet. Center marks are usually positioned and are essential for color work. See **Figure 5-52A**. Workmarks serve as guidelines for the paste-up artist as well as the mechanical stripper.

A nonreproducing blue pencil or pen is commonly used to draw workmarks on a layout base sheet. These lines or other marks will not appear when the page is shot.

Trim marks are usually drawn one-eighth inch in length for paste-up or to designate bleeds. Refer to **Figure 5-52B**. A ***bleed*** is an image that extends to the end of a printed sheet. A bleed image, when printed, appears outside the trim area of the sheet and is cut away when the sheet is trimmed to the final size.

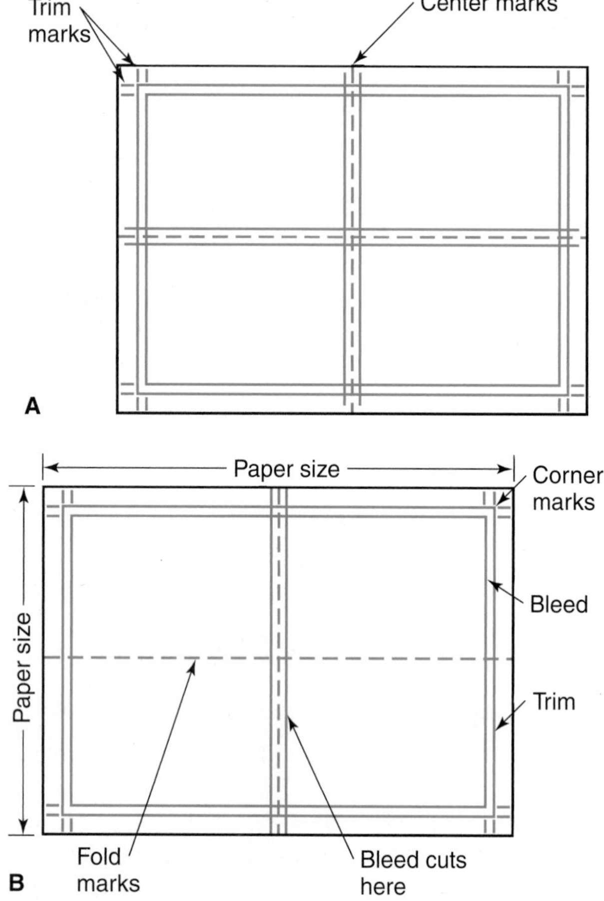

Figure 5-52. Workmarks. A—Layout sheets are commonly printed with trim and center marks to serve as guidelines when preparing the mechanical. B—Bleeds that extend to the end of a printed sheet are designated as trim margins measuring one-eighth inch.

Graphics Programs

The programs used to produce graphics electronically appear as object-oriented images or bitmapped images. Using these programs, the designer can create very complex documents. These illustration packages will be discussed in greated detail in a later chapter.

Review Questions

Please do not write in this text. Write your answers on a separate sheet of paper.

1. In graphic communications, design refers to the use of proper methods to produce a product that is both _____ and _____.
2. Explain the role of the graphic designer.
3. Which of the following is *not* an element of design?
   a. Shape.
   b. Texture.
   c. Mass.
   d. Beauty.
4. What are the three basic design shapes?
5. The _____ is a tool that illustrates the basics of color.
6. What are the three primary colors?
7. Name the five principles of design.
8. _____ is the proper balance of all elements in an image so that a pleasing whole results and the image is viewed as one piece.
9. List the four elements of layout.
10. _____ is intended to draw attention to the printed piece.
11. What are the factors to consider in developing a layout?
12. A _____ is a rapidly drawn design of a layout.
13. A _____ layout shows how the printed piece will look when finished.
14. The guidelines that list information about the type style, type size, line width, color use, and page organization of a printed product are called _____.
15. _______ is the process of fitting together copy and illustrations in a specific amount of space.
16. What is photo cropping?
17. A ____ is used to size illustrations for enlargement or reduction.
18. *True or False?* Line art is normally pasted down as the same size on the mechanical.
19. What are the two most common working surfaces used in layout and design?
20. Why is a light blue pencil or pen commonly used in paste-up?

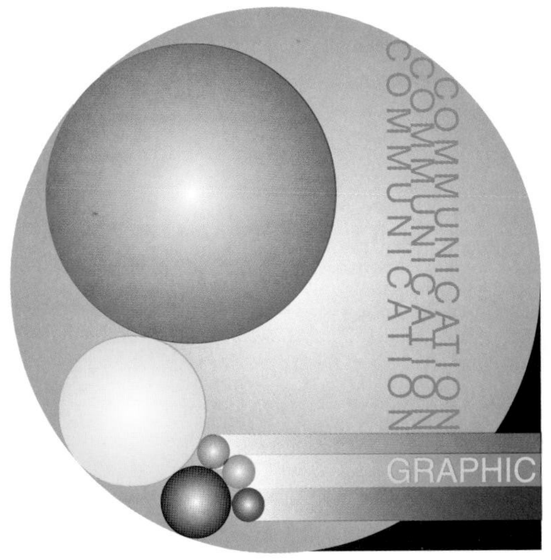

Text Composition 6

Learning Objectives

After studying this chapter, you will be able to:

- Identify the techniques and materials associated with relief type composition.
- Identify the techniques associated with "cold type" composition.
- Explain the concept of photocomposition.
- Describe the binary system as it relates to processing and storage of information by computers.
- List the various types of data storage devices and describe how they differ.
- Explain the difference between hardware and software in electronic imaging systems.
- Describe the differences between bitmapped and object-oriented images and identify the types of software used to modify them.
- Describe the duties of a proofreader.

Important Terms

bitmapped images
digital
electronic imaging system
hardware
image carrier
movable type
object-oriented images
photocomposition
relief printing
software

The term ***composition*** generally refers to the production and organization of all images to be printed. However, in graphic communications, composition can also mean setting type or words, not line art or photographs. The *typesetter* or ***compositor*** is the person who sets the type.

Composition methods have changed through history as new technology has been introduced. Hand composition of wood or metal type—physically assembling separate letters into words, sentences, paragraphs and pages—was the primary composition method from the 1400s to the early 1900s. Machine methods for rapidly assembling molds and casting an entire line of type in metal were introduced at the end of the 1800s, and were an important technology for more than a half-century. In the late 1960s, equipment permitting photographic setting of type began to appear, and remained in widespread use until the early 1990s. The role of the personal computer in composition has grown steadily since its introduction in the 1980s. Today, the computer is the primary method of composition for materials that will be presented in either printed or electronic form. This chapter will discuss each of these major composition methods.

Relief Composition

Printing from a raised surface is called ***relief printing*** or ***letterpress***. The name comes from the fact that the image area of the type (the printing surface) is *"in relief"* or raised above the nonimage area. The raised surface is covered with ink and pressed against paper or another substrate to produce an image, **Figure 6-1**.

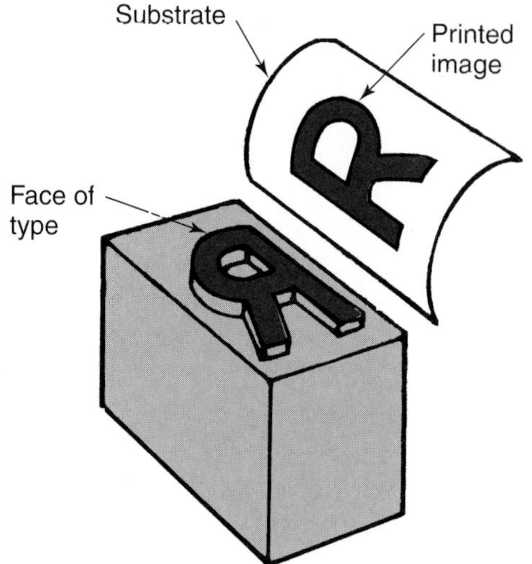

Figure 6-1. The surface of the raised image is first inked. After it is brought into contact with the substrate, an image remains on the surface of the substrate.

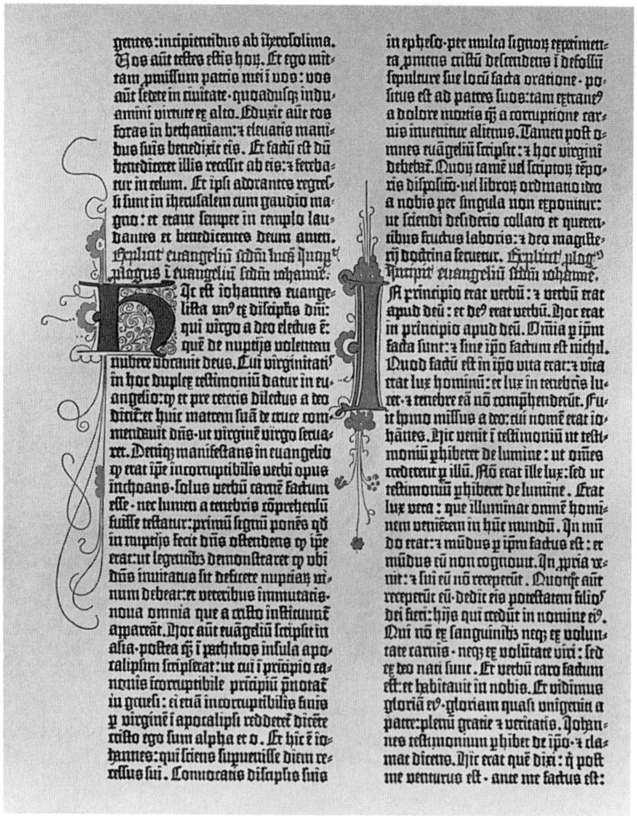

Relief or letterpress printing dates back more than ten centuries to the use of wooden relief type in China. The first relief printing was done from carved wooden blocks. This composition method was a long and tedious process, and was suitable only for pictures or a small number of words.

The modern process of printing traces its roots to the development of movable type in the mid-1400s by Johannes Gutenberg in Mainz, Germany. Gutenberg made molds that could be used to cast individual metal blocks, each holding one raised letter. The blocks could be produced in quantity and assembled into words. Since the typeset material could be taken apart and the letters reassembled into different words, the blocks were termed ***movable type***. The first books printed from movable type by Gutenberg and his associates were copies of the Christian Bible, **Figure 6-2**.

The art of printing from movable type quickly spread to other cities across Europe. Two hundred years later, in 1639, the first press in what is now the United States was established at Harvard Academy in Cambridge, Massachusetts. The first newspaper regularly published in British North America was printed in Boston by John Campbell in 1704.

Figure 6-2. Johannes Gutenberg developed movable type and used it to print books such as this Bible.

Materials used for relief type

Relief type can be made from various materials. At different times, type has been manufactured from wood, metal, rubber, or plastic. Some early printing in China was even done from plates made of ceramic materials.

- *Wood* is well suited for large-point-size characters, since it is lighter than metal. It was used in relief printing for newspaper headlines and large posters. Wood type was relatively soft and could be easily damaged. For longer wear, the face of the type was placed on the polished end grain of the wood block.
- *Metal* was widely used to produce individual pieces of foundry type by pouring molten metal into a ***matrix*** (mold) to form the characters. See **Figure 6-3**. In machine composition for relief printing, hot metal was used with a series of molds to cast a full line of type at a time. The ***type metal*** used to cast type is lead with some tin and antimony. Tin gives the type toughness and counteracts shrinkage. The antimony is added to give hardness to the type block and fluidity to the molten metal.

Figure 6-3. Individual pieces of "hot metal" foundry type were cast in molds. The type could be assembled in various combinations, sorted, and reused.

- *Rubber* can also be used to make images in relief. The most common application is the ***rubber stamp***, which can be considered a form of relief printing.
- *Plastic* is the most modern material used in relief printing. A one-piece plastic plate with a raised image surface is used to print some newspapers and other long run jobs quickly and efficiently. The printing process is termed ***flexography*** because of the flexible printing plate that is used, **Figure 6-4.**

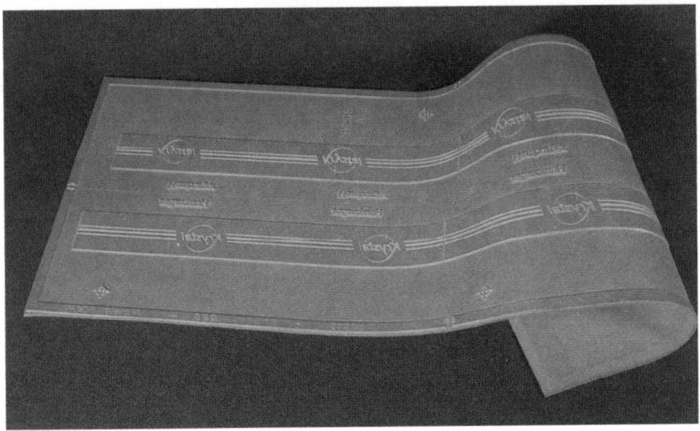

Figure 6-4. Rubber and plastic are common materials for plates used in flexography, the only raised-type printing process in commercial use today.

First- and second-generation image carriers

An ***image carrier*** is a device on a printing press that transfers an inked image to an intermediate carrier (as in lithographic or "offset" printing) or directly to a substrate such as paper. A *first-generation image carrier* is an original. Hot type that is formed by pouring molten metal into a mold would be an example of a first-generation image carrier.

A *second-generation image carrier* is a copy produced by making a mold of an original, then casting a metal plate. An example would be an advertisement consisting of type and line art, **Figure 6-5.** Such a plate might be produced for long press runs, since making many thousands of impressions can cause physical wear on the image carrier. If the second-generation plate becomes worn, the original (first-generation) image carrier can be used to make another plate for continuing the press run.

Figure 6-5. A second-generation image carrier, such as this advertisement, is produced by casting a plate from a mold of a first-generation carrier. The plate is mounted on a wood base to bring it to standard type height (0.918").

Setting metal relief type

Various methods are used to set type for the relief printing process. The oldest method of composition is hand-setting of individually cast characters known as *foundry type*. Later, machine methods were developed for linecasting of type and individual character composition.

Foundry type

A compositor who is hand-setting foundry type selects the individual letters needed from a storage drawer called a ***job case***. The case being used is positioned on top of the compositor's work station, known as a ***bank***, as shown in **Figure 6-6**.

Figure 6-6. The job case is placed on the compositor's workstation, called a bank.

Each job case holds a full font of type. A ***font*** of foundry type is the set of characters in one point size. It is made up of varying numbers of each capital and lowercase letter, numeral, punctuation mark, and special symbol.

Each character is picked from the case and placed in a ***composing stick*** held in the left hand, **Figure 6-7**. The stick has a movable knee that can be set to the determined line length. As each piece of type is positioned in the stick, the thumb is used to place pressure on the characters. This eliminates the possibility of spilling the type.

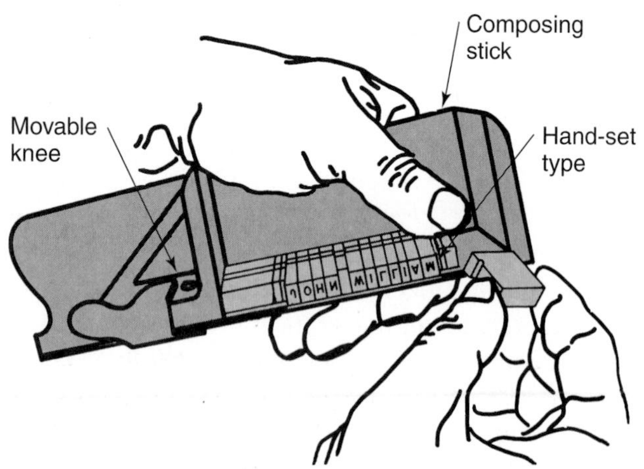

Figure 6-7. The composing stick is used to hold hand-set type. The stick is held in the left hand with the thumb holding the last character set.

Type is set from left to right. The composed type appears upside down. This reversal is necessary so that the characters read correctly when printed on paper. See **Figure 6-8.** When the stick is approximately two-thirds filled with type, the type is removed and placed in a ***galley*** (a three-sided metal tray for storing type forms), **Figure 6-9.**

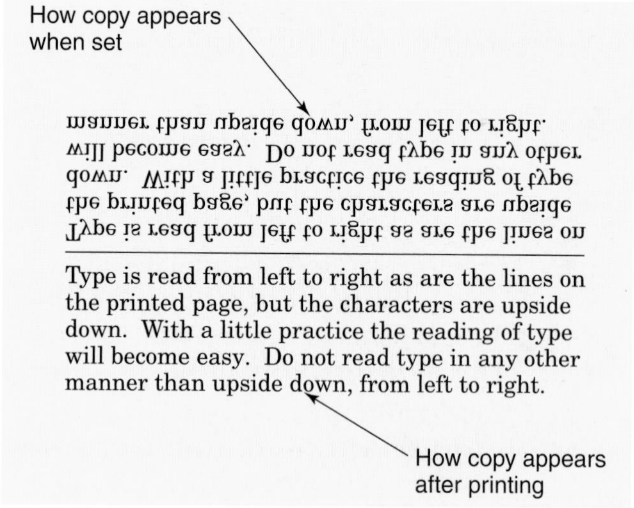

How copy appears when set

Type is read from left to right as are the lines on the printed page, but the characters are upside down. With a little practice the reading of type will become easy. Do not read type in any other manner than upside down, from left to right.

How copy appears after printing

Figure 6-8. In relief type composition, composed type is read upside down and from left to right.

Figure 6-9. A compositor sets lines of type in the stick until approximately two thirds of the stick is used. The composed type is then placed in the galley.

Additional type is set as needed and assembled in the galley. The type is then transferred to a metal frame called a ***chase***. Wood or metal spacers (*furniture*) are arranged around the block of type, as shown in **Figure 6-10**. Arrangement of the furniture properly positions the block of type (called the *form*) for printing. ***Quoins*** (expanding metal locking devices) are used to wedge the form and furniture in place in the chase. The chase supports the type when positioned in the printing press.

Figure 6-10. Type is positioned in a chase by using wood or metal furniture as spacers.

Figure 6-11. The linecasting machine made relief composition more efficient. Matrices or molds were formed into lines, cast in metal, then distributed back into the magazines for reuse.

To print properly, metal relief characters must be of uniform height, aligned, assembled in a desired length and width, and locked up in a frame (chase).

Linecasting machines

Approximately 100 years ago, hot metal typesetting machines were introduced as a faster and more efficient composing method than hand-set type. Instead of individual pieces of type, these machines produced an entire *line* of type. The lines, called ***slugs***, could be easily assembled into columns and pages for printing. Unlike the individual pieces of foundry type that had to be sorted and stored when the printing job was completed, the machine-produced slugs could simply be melted down and used to cast new lines of type.

The most common type of linecasting machine was the ***Linotype***, **Figure 6-11**. It contained hundreds of brass molds, or matrices, stored in channels inside one or more magazines. Each mold (called a matrix) had one letter or symbol cut into it.

Whenever the Linotype operator pressed a key on the keyboard, the corresponding matrix was released from the magazine and dropped down a guide to an assembly area.

Each word was assembled, letter-by-letter, with wedge-shaped ***spacebands*** between the words. Once the preset line length was reached, the line of matrices and spacebands was transferred to the casting position. Molten metal was forced into the die, creating a slug, **Figure 6-12**. The slug was automatically trimmed, forced out of the mold, and positioned in a galley.

The matrices and spacebands were then transferred to a distribution system which returned them to their proper places in the magazine, ready to be used again. The development of circulating matrices was a major breakthrough in machine metal composition allowing them to be used over and over to cast images as a single line of type.

Figure 6-12. Slugs of type contained an entire line. They were much easier to assemble into columns and pages.

Another type of linecasting machine, the ***Ludlow***, was used primarily to set larger point sizes for use as display type. Although this machine produced a cast line of type, **Figure 6-13**, it was a variation of hand-setting. The large matrices were selected and arranged in order. After the display line was cast, the matrices had to be distributed into a storage case.

Figure 6-13. This slug of line material was cast by the Ludlow machine.

A more complicated composing machine that produced individual cast letters, rather than a line of type, was called the ***Monotype***. This system was a two-part machine with a keyboard and a separate metal caster.

The operator produced a punched paper tape by pressing keys on the keyboard unit. Holes in the paper tape were codes which, when placed in the caster, produced letters in the desired order. The letters were not attached to each other.

"Cold Type" Composition

The composition methods traditionally described as "cold type" (to distinguish them from "hot metal" relief composition) range from hand and mechanical techniques, to various forms of photographic typesetting, to text generation on desktop computers. Because of the relative simplicity and low cost of computer-based text generation, the use of traditional cold type methods has declined steadily in recent years. Just as hot metal composition almost disappeared from commercial printing with widespread adoption of phototypesetting methods, the phototypesetter has almost been replaced by the computer.

Hand composition methods

Hand composition methods, using a pen, brush, template, or transfer letters, are utilized to a very limited extent today. This technique is limited to special situations, such as advertisements or posters, where special symbols or a small amount of copy in an unusual typeface might be needed.

Hand lettering

Numerous letter forms are available today, but special designs can be difficult to find. The graphic designer or artist may create specific images for specific needs by hand, using pens and brushes. Special types of lettering and drawing pens are available to produce freehand lettering. The shapes and tip sizes of the pens vary. The most common are: square, round, flat, and oval, **Figure 6-14**.

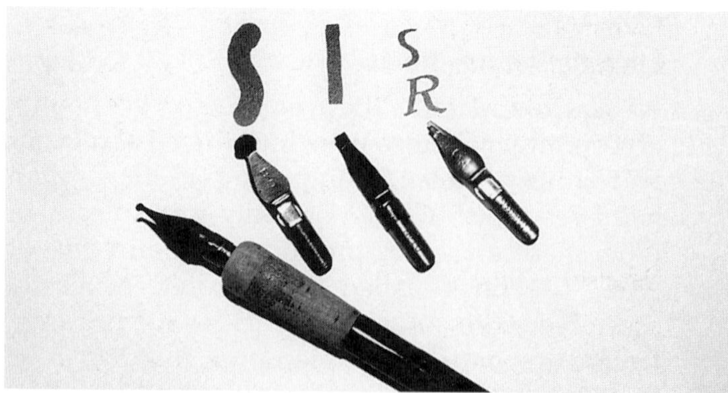

Figure 6-14. Special pens for doing hand composition have tips with varied sizes and shapes.

Hand lettering is often created oversized. This allows for reduction during the photoconversion process. Reducing the images tends to sharpen them and helps hide minor errors.

Templates

Lettering also may be done using a ***template***, which is a guide of a desired shape or letter. The template has the letter style cut into it. When the scriber (tool for following template) follows the letter or figure pattern, the attached pen will deposit ink on the sheet of paper in the matching pattern, **Figure 6-15**. Some templates are for one size and style of characters; others allow a variety of character heights and permit changing the slant of the letter or figure.

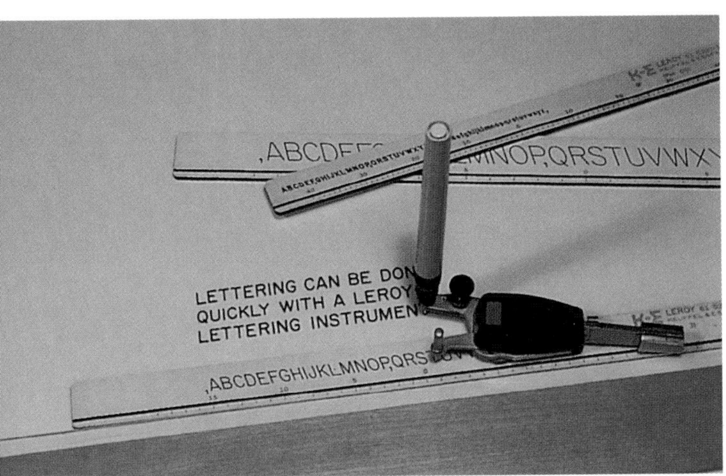

Figure 6-15. This template and scriber can be used to produce one size and style of type. A different template must be used to change size or style.

Whatever type of hand lettering device is used, the tools and work area must be kept clean to produce quality work. The paper used also contributes to the quality of the finished image. A hard, smooth surface is preferable. With such a paper surface, the line quality will be sharper.

Dry transfer type

Dry transfer sheets are an inexpensive way of producing professional, camera-ready display type. Each sheet consists of a complete alphabet of a single type style, with varying numbers of each letter. There are more of the most commonly used letters (**a, o, e**, etc.) per sheet than less-used letters (**x, y, z**, etc.). Many typestyles and sizes are available.

Each letter is placed in position and ***burnished*** (rubbed) down with a smooth wood, plastic, or metal tool, as shown in **Figure 6-16**. When properly burnished, the dry transfer image will adhere to the base sheet.

Figure 6-16. Dry transfer letters are first positioned, then, burnished to adhere the type to the base sheet. These letters are available in many styles and sizes.

Dry transfer is also used to create borders and other decorative artwork. Shading material is also available. This is a very inexpensive composition method when a limited number of camera-ready decorative images is needed.

Another form of transfer type is printed on a transparent carrier sheet with an adhesive backing. The desired letters are cut from the carrier and lifted off the base sheet. The image is then positioned very carefully and burnished down.

Strike-on composition

Before the introduction of phototypesetting systems, ***strike-on composition*** was used as a simple and rapid means of generating camera-ready text. The simplest piece of strike-on equipment was the standard typewriter. Later, special strike-on composers were introduced that could produce several different typefaces and several point sizes. They also made it possible to vary word spacing and produce justified columns (with even left and right margins).

Photocomposition

Photocomposition is the generation of type using photographic paper or film exposed to light. This system of generating text was widely used from the 1960s to the early 1990s, but is rapidly being displaced by the desktop computer. See **Figure 6-17**.

Figure 6-17. Phototypesetters like the one being used here had banks of special-function keys (keypads) to either side of the standard keyboard. One of these keypads was used for editing text, the other for file management. Computers have virtually displaced dedicated phototypesetting equipment in commercial printing applications.

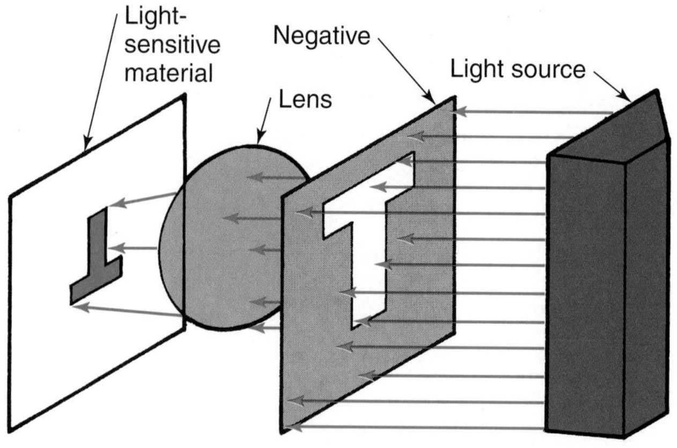

Figure 6-18. The basic principle of projection photocomposition. Light is projected through a transparent image and onto light-sensitive material.

Several methods were used to photographically compose images. Early photocomposers were of two types: one for generating large display type, the other for setting body copy or text. Both were contact-type printers, in which a negative (on a film strip or disk) was positioned over photographic paper and exposed with a bright light source. After a letter was exposed, the disk or strip was shifted to the next letter to be set. On display-type machines, this was done manually; text machines used electromechanical methods to rapidly position the images. The exposed photographic paper was developed, fixed, washed, and dried to produce camera-ready copy.

The contact method produced crisp, good-quality images, but was relatively slow. A more serious drawback was the fact that it could produce only *same-size* images — a separate film strip or disk was needed for each typeface and point size.

Projection method

The projection method used a film strip or disk, similar to the contact method. This method, however, allows enlargement or reduction of a single typeface to provide a wide range of point sizes. As shown in **Figure 6-18**, the light passes through the negative, then through a lens, and exposes an enlarged or reduced image onto the photographic paper.

Cathode ray tube method

The negative was eliminated from phototypesetting with the development of equipment based on the ***cathode ray tube*** (CRT), a large vacuum tube much like a television screen. The inside surface of the CRT is coated with a light-sensitive phosphor material that will glow when struck by a beam of electrons. Under control of a computer program, an electron beam sweeps across the screen surface from side to side and top to bottom. The beam pulses on and off to make tiny dots of phosphor (called picture elements or ***pixels***) glow in patterns corresponding to the material being typeset. See **Figure 6-19**.

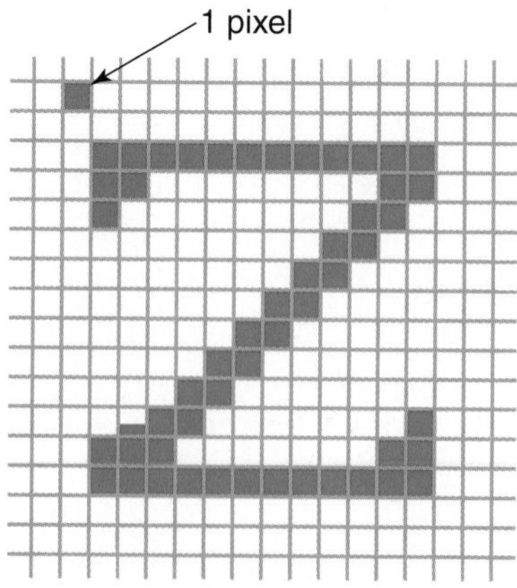

Figure 6-19. CRT and laser image generators form letter or character shapes by scanning light beam from side to side to make pixels (tiny phosphor dots) glow.

The image formed by the glowing pixels on the face of the CRT is transmitted by a system of lenses and mirrors, **Figure 6-20A**, to the photographic paper or film. The system can set large amounts of type quickly. A similar system uses a laser beam to directly "write" an image onto the photographic paper or film, **Figure 6-20B**.

Phototypesetting paper

When developed, phototypesetting paper turns black in the parts (image areas) that are exposed to light, forming a positive image. The paper containing the developed typeset image is referred to as a "galley." There are two types of photopaper: stabilization and resin-coated.

The stabilization paper has developer incorporated in its emulsion, and can be processed in rapid-access chemical systems. Resin-coated (RC) paper is more costly, but has a longer storage life than stabilization paper. It offers wide development latitude, and has a very white background and high image density. The paper has good stability and does not curl, which are plus factors when pasting up.

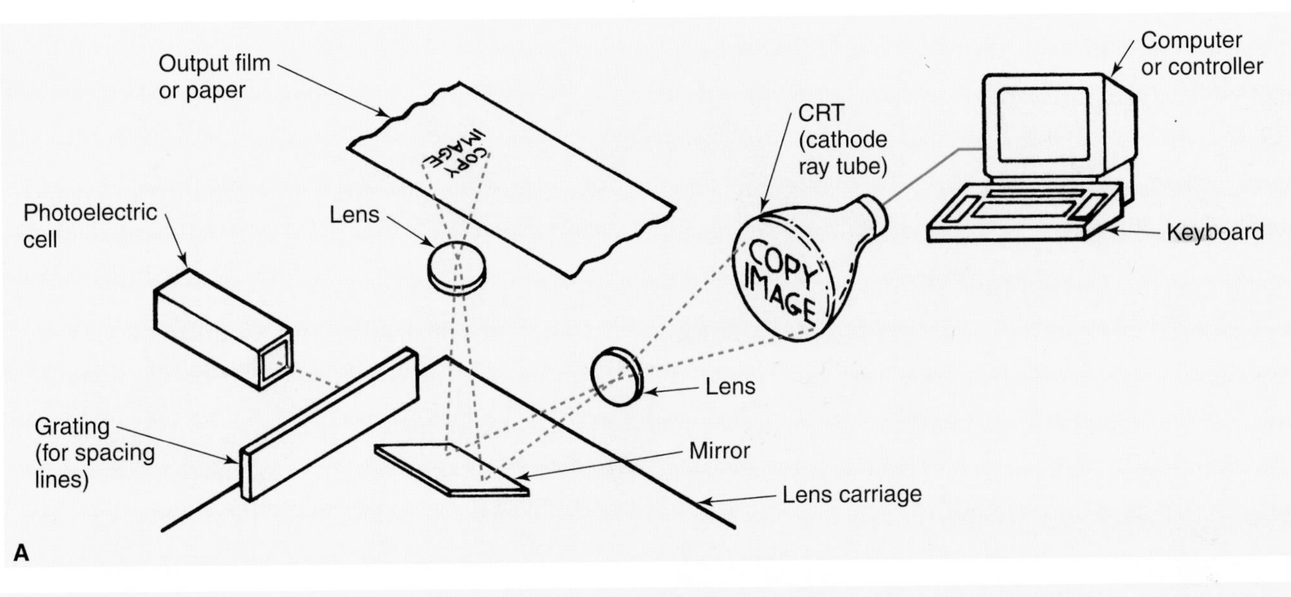

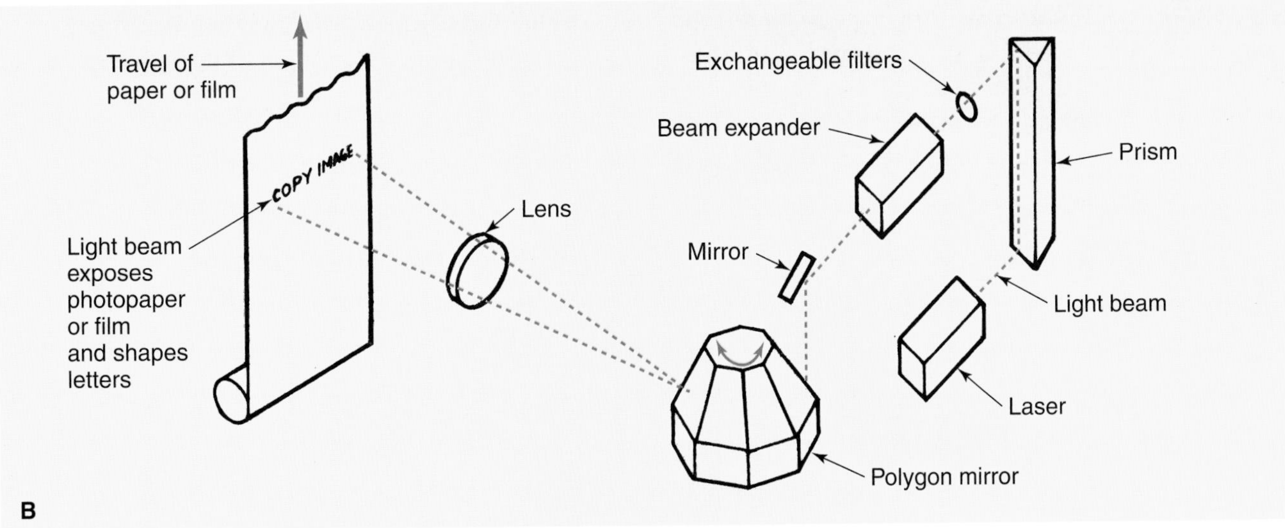

Figure 6-20. Systems used to generate type images in the latest generation of phototypesetters and imagesetters. A—The CRT system forms letter shapes on a cathode ray tube, then uses a lens and mirror system to transfer the image to the film or paper. B—A laser imagesetter directs a beam of light to shape and burn each image onto film or paper.

Processor

The ***processor*** for developing photopaper uses chemicals to make the image on the paper or film visible and permanent. The processor turns out dry galleys in a very short period of time. The chemicals that are used must be replenished at regular intervals to produce high quality images. It is also important to maintain the proper solution temperature. Processing equipment is expensive and requires proper maintenance to assure good operation and long service life. See **Figure 6-21**.

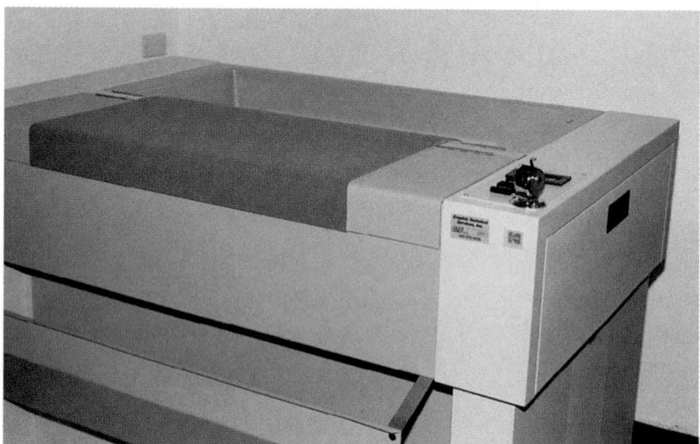

Figure 6-21. An example of a processing unit.

Figure 6-22. In recent years, the desktop computer has emerged as the most common method of composing text for printed documents. A large proportion of page layout is also done on a computer screen.

Electronic Composition

As noted at the beginning of this chapter, the desktop or personal computer has become the major tool for composition in recent years. In addition to its role in producing text, the computer has become the focal point of image handling and the assembly of text and images (artwork and photos) into page layouts. The computer (***hardware***) and the specialized graphics programs (***software***) used with it can be described as an ***electronic imaging system***. See **Figure 6-22**.

Digital basics

The computer is a device that is used to process and store information in ***digital*** form, using a ***binary*** system. This means that the computer recognizes only *two* numbers or digits: 1 and 0. Actually, rather than numbers, the computer recognizes two states: on and off (the *presence* or *absence* of an electrical charge). For convenience in notation, 1 is used to represent an "on" state and 0 represents "off."

The individual 1s and 0s are called ***bits***, or binary digits, and can be combined into groups of eight digits (a binary word, or ***byte***). Since there are 256 possible combinations of 1 and 0 in an eight-digit byte (from 11111111 to 00000000), a special code was devised to assign a specific meaning to each combination.

The American Standard Code for Information Interchange, usually referred to as ***ASCII***, provides a way to digitally store and process letters, numbers, punctuation marks, and symbols. When the letter C is pressed on a keyboard, for example, it is converted to a specific combination of 1 and 0 digits (different combinations are assigned for the cap and lowercase forms of each letter). Once it is in digital form, the information can be processed in the computer's circuits and stored as electrical or magnetic charges.

Components of computer systems

Regardless of size or complexity, a computer *system* can be thought of as having three parts or functions: input, processing, and output. See **Figure 6-23**. A simple example would be typing five words, using the computer keyboard (*input*); having the computer check the spelling and organize the words into an alphabetical list (*processing*), then sending the list to the printer to obtain a hard copy (*output*). In addition, computer systems typically have some means of storing information, either within the system or in a portable form (or both). There are a number of different methods and devices used for input, storage, and output. They are described in the following sections.

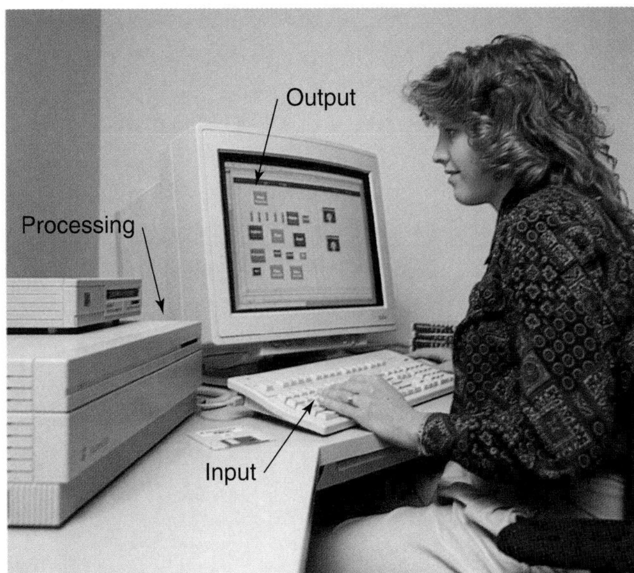

Figure 6-23. This computer system illustrates the three functions of input through the keyboard, processing through the CPU (Central Processing Unit) and output to a monitor or a printer. With the appropriate software, this workstation has the components needed to combine text and graphic images electronically for publication. (Chapter One, Screaming Color)

Input devices

There are a number of ways in which text or graphics information can be acquired by the computer system. These range from manual methods (keyboarding) to receiving electronic transmissions through a modem.

- **Keyboard.** The keyboard, similar in many respects to the one on a typewriter, is the most common way of inputting copy to a computer system. In addition to standard typing tasks, the keyboard can be used to perform special functions through dedicated keys (such as the delete and insert keys). Special *function* keys are used to carry out different tasks, depending upon the program (*software*) being used.
- **Mouse.** Many computer systems rely extensively on input from this pointing device, especially for user interfaces and graphics. A typical use for the mouse is selecting text for cutting and pasting from one document to another.
- **Digitizing tablet.** This is another form of pointing device used for input to the system. It is very useful with forms of graphics that require high precision. See **Figure 6-24**.
- **Modem.** An electronic device (technically, *modulator/demodulator*) that converts digital signals to a form that can be transmitted over telephone lines, and vice-versa. Modems allow information to be sent from one computer to another over a distance.
- **Scanner.** Four types of scanners are used today to capture images. They are: hand-held, flatbed, slide, and drum. Some types can quickly convert an entire page of type or printed material into digital form. Scanners are used extensively for graphic input (line art and photo). See **Figure 6-25.**

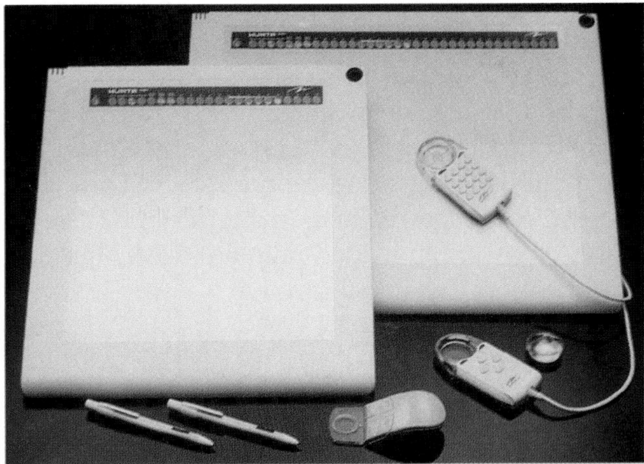

Figure 6-24. The digitizing tablet is an input device that can be used to trace a drawing and convert it to a graphic image file. The tracing work is done with a pen or a mouse-like pointing device called a puck. (KURTA)

Figure 6-25. The flatbed scanner is commonly used to convert photographs or pages of typed or printed material into digital form. Optical Character Recognition (OCR) software is used for typed or printed originals. (Heidelberg)

- **Voice recognition system.** The premise of this technology is to use voice commands to control devices (computers) and to enter text simply by speaking into a microphone. Major challenges exist. A voice recognition system is required; one of the concerns is recognizing the voices of multiple users on the same system. Consider the complication of a system's ability to distinguish homonyms — words that have different meanings but sound alike, such as "there," "their," or "they're." As the technology advances, the application will extend into common applications within the industry. Presently, voice recognition is limited to common computer commands.

Storage devices

A number of different types of devices have been developed to allow electronic files to be stored and reused. Most of these devices use disks with surfaces that contain magnetic tracks to hold the digitally encoded data (typeset or graphic material) being stored. With the exception of the hard disk drive, the storage methods make files *portable,* so that a copy can be loaded onto another computer. The major options for storage are:

- **Hard disk drive.** Although external units are available, most hard disk drives are *internal* (built into the computer unit). The hard disk drive contains one or more rigid, nonremovable aluminum disks coated with a magnetic material. When the computer is operating, the drive motor spins the disk and a read/write head (similar to a record/play head in an audio cassette recorder) moves over the disk surface, which contains densely packed magnetic tracks. The head is used to *write information to* (magnetize) portions of the tracks as they spin past the head. The head can also *read* (play back) previously stored information. The amount of information that can be stored on a hard drive has increased steadily from fewer than 10 ***megabytes*** (millions of bytes, or Mb) to capacities measured in ***gigabytes*** (billions of bytes, or Gb). Almost unlimited storage capacity is available with a configuration known as a ***RAID*** (Redundant Array of Independent Disks), which connects a number of high-capacity hard disk drives together. The "ganged" drives act like a single huge hard drive, an advantage with the extremely large files involving graphics and text. See **Figure 6-26.**
- **Floppy disk drive.** The floppy disk has long been the standard medium for storage of text files, but its limited capacity (typically 1.4 Mb) makes it unsuitable for many graphics applications. The name

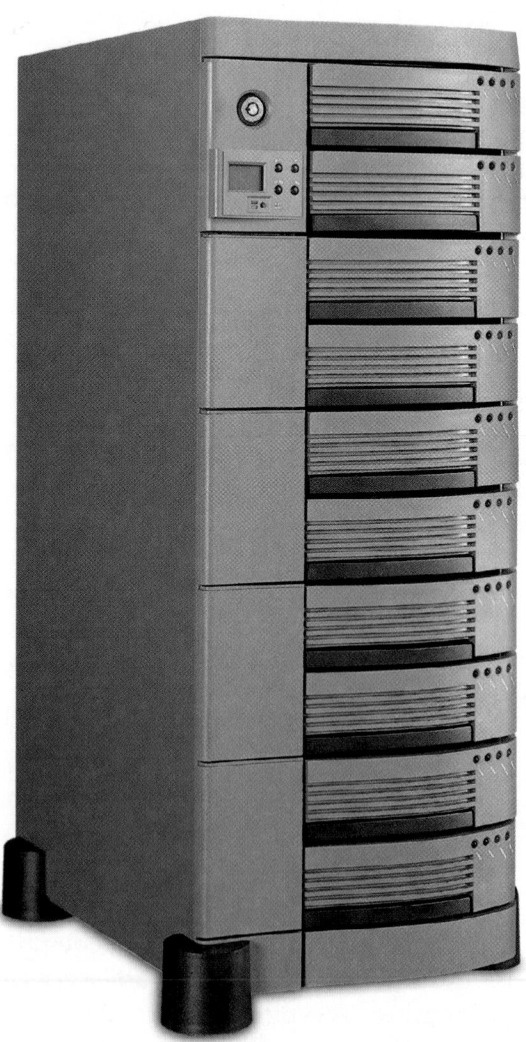

Figure 6-26. By connecting a number of high-capacity hard drives together in a RAID, an almost unlimited amount of data storage can be obtained. (The RAIDinc Z 2, courtesy of RAID, Inc.)

"floppy" comes from the earlier 8" and 5 1/4" disk sizes, which had flexible housings containing the thin plastic magnetized disk. The currently standard 3 1/2" format still uses a thin magnetized disk, but has a rigid plastic housing. The floppy disk drive functions in the same way as the hard disk drive, but the disk is removable, rather than permanent. Compared to a hard drive, the floppy has relatively slow access and data transfer speeds. Floppy disks are low in cost, take up little storage space, and allow files to be transported easily to a different computer.

- **Hard drive.** Hard drives are available as either internal or external types. Virtually all electronic imaging systems have an internal hard drive. This storage medium is also relatively inexpensive. The single most critical occurrence for a hard drive is when it becomes inoperable ("crashes"). The adage of "It isn't *if* your hard drive is going to crash, it's *when* your hard drive is going to crash" should be taken very seriously. Optimizing the drive for operational efficiency and regularly backing up the data are both considered standard operating procedures.
- **Removable cartridge devices.** These devices combine some of the advantages of the hard drive and the floppy disk—like the hard drive, they offer large capacity, while retaining the portability of the floppy. See **Figure 6-27.** Compared to a hard drive, some of these devices have rather slow access and data transfer speeds.
- **Magneto-optical (M/O) drive.** This form of removable cartridge storage is also known as "optical storage," although it is actually a magnetic medium. Like other magnetic media, it allows data to be erased and new data written to the disk. The drive incorporates two lasers, one to write the data onto a disk coated with magnetic material and the other to read the data back when the user retrieves the file. Data retrieval is quite slow although it is much faster than the process of writing the data to disk. The large capacity (up to 500 Mb) of these devices makes them an excellent choice for storing and transporting large files.

Figure 6-27. This Zip drive, with its 100 Mb removable disk, is at the low end among such storage devices, in terms of both capacity and cost. Devices with removable cartridges holding 1000 Mb or more are common in electronic imaging work. Some newer devices offer an entire high-capacity drive that is removable, rather than just a cartridge.

- **CD and DVD drives.** The compact disk (CD) drive has become a standard feature of new computers, with most drives having the capability for writing ("burning") data onto the plastic disk. Newer drives can be used to prepare disks that become "read-only" after writing (CD-R disks), or "rewritable" (CD-RW) disks that can be recorded upon many times. CDs range in capacity from 670 to more than 800 megabytes. The Digital Video Disk (DVD), although intended for the video industry, is finding its way into the graphic communications industry because of its very high storage capacity of 4.7 gigabytes.
- **Personal Digital Assistant (PDA) removable storage media.** Removable storage for these devices, based upon the sizes of the device, must remain small but have high storage capacity with fast access and retrieval speeds. Examples of PDA removable storage media are: SmartMedia

cards, CompactFlash cards, Memory Sticks, and 3″ compact disks. See **Figure 6-28.** These storage devices extend beyond the PDA market and are common in the storage of digital camera images, game machines, printers, PC cards, and audio storage devices. They range in storage sizes from 8 megabytes to 1 gigabyte and have low voltage requirements. They are small in physical size, have fast write and erase speeds, and allow for easy file management.

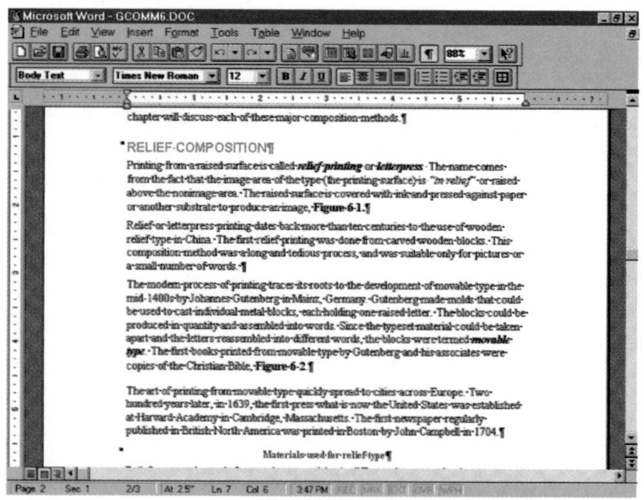

Figure 6-29. The WYSIWYG monitor display provides the user with a very close approximation of how material will appear when printed out. This screen is displaying formatted text from a word processing program. The text can later be exported to a page layout program, where its format may be altered as needed.

Output devices

As material is input by using a keyboard or other device, it is almost instantly processed by the computer and displayed on a monitor. The *monitor*, which resembles a television screen, is considered an ***output device***. Other output devices include the *modem* (used to send and receive files electronically), and two types of equipment that produce a physical output, often referred to as "hard copy." These include the dot matrix, ink jet, and laser *printers* that produce copies on paper, and the *imagesetter*, typically used to output film.

- **Monitors.** The software used for word processing and page layout on computer systems provides a *WYSIWYG* ("What You See Is What You Get") display on the monitor, **Figure 6-29**. Monitors used for page layout are large enough (17″–21″ diagonal measure) to display an entire page or even two pages.

Figure 6-28. Removable storage media for digital cameras, Personal Digital Assistants, and similar devices pack a great deal of capacity in a small space. The 3" CD will hold 156 Mb; CompactFlash cards—smaller in size than a matchbook—are available in many different capacities.

- In addition to display size, *resolution* and *dot pitch* are issues of major importance when choosing a monitor. The ***resolution*** (ability to show fine detail) of a monitor is stated in the number of pixels lined up across and down the screen. A typical high-resolution 14″ monitor would have 1280 pixels across the screen and 1024 pixels top-to-bottom, usually stated as 1280 × 1024. Monitors used in graphic communication today typically have resolutions ranging from 1024 × 768 to 1600 × 1280, or even higher. ***Dot pitch*** is a measurement of the vertical distance between rows of pixels on the monitor. The distance is stated in decimal fractions of a millimeter, with the image quality becoming crisper as the fraction becomes smaller.
- The color monitor uses the ***additive color*** theory, based upon the combination of red, green, and blue ***(RGB)*** to form white light. This creates a problem for the desktop publisher

who is trying to achieve a WYSIWYG color environment. Since colors are displayed in RGB, there is difficulty in matching the printed results of the subtractive color environment. In the ***subtractive color*** environment, inks in the colors cyan, magenta, yellow, and black (*CMYK*) are combined to produce the printed image. This means that full-color representation of images on the monitor and on the printed sheet are achieved through different principles. To overcome this problem, ***color management software (CMS)*** has been developed to provide a monitor display that is termed *WYSIWYP*, or "What You See Is What You Print."

- **Printers.** For proofing text and graphic material, a printer is typically used to make a copy on paper. Resolution of the printed image is measured in ***dots per inch*** (***dpi***), and ranges from 100 dpi or less to 1200 dpi, depending upon the type and quality of printer. In some cases, final copy or page layouts can be output by a high-resolution laser printer to attain quality sufficient for short-run reproduction by lithographic or xerographic methods. There are three basic types of printers in use today:
  - **Dot matrix.** The output quality of the dot matrix printer is the poorest of the three types of printers. Images are formed by the ends of thin wires striking an inked ribbon and transferring a dot of ink to the paper. Because of the dot structure, the images have rough edges and resolution is low (typically, 100 dots per inch or less). For these reasons, it is seldom used today, except for proofing text.
  - **Ink jet.** This type of printer forms images by using a print head that "shoots" tiny dots of ink onto the paper surface. The positioning of the dots is carefully controlled, and provides a resolution of 300 dpi or more. Ink jet printers output copy that is of much higher quality than the dot matrix printer, and are able to print images in color. They are often used for making color proofs of graphics, and page proofs to show the positioning of text and graphics, **Figure 6-30.** Printer speeds range from approximately 3 to 8 pages per minute (ppm) when printing text, but output drops dramatically when printing high-resolution color graphics.
  - **Laser.** This type of printer operates much like a photocopying machine. The copying machine uses reflected light to create an image on a drum, while the laser printer uses a laser beam to polarize an image on the drum, **Figure 6-31.** The printer has a built-in computer (called a ***print engine***) that translates the output of the computer into a bitmapped image for printing. A laser transfers the page image to a light-sensitive drum that has a positive electrical

Figure 6-30. An ink jet printer can be used to produce a high-quality proof copy of graphics or page layouts. Output is relatively slow when compared to laser printers. (Epson America, Inc.)

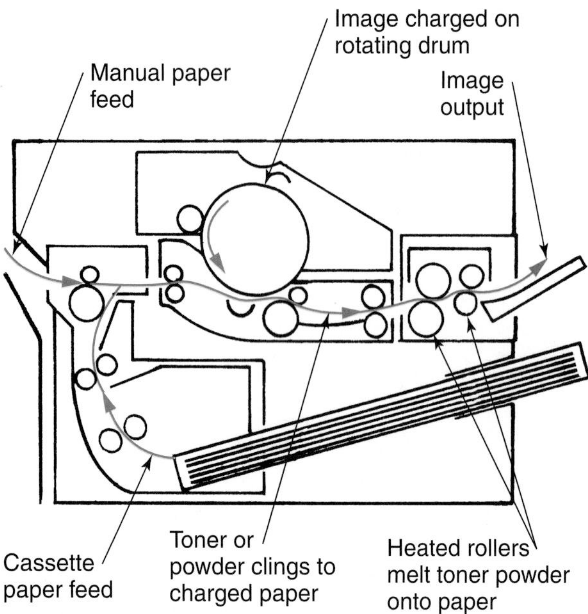

Figure 6-31. A laser printer produces an image by a scanning technique combined with electrostatic principles. Rollers feed paper through the printer at a constant speed. The paper source may be a cassette (tray) for multiple sheets, or a manual feed for single sheets.

Figure 6-32. For highest quality output on photopaper or film, an imagesetter is used. This imagesetter offers six resolution settings ranging from 1000 dpi to 3000 dpi, and can output material up to 22" (56 cm) in width. (Fuji Graphic Systems)

charge. As the laser light moves across the rotating drum, emitting the image drawn from printer memory, the polarity changes. Areas where the black part of the image would be are neutralized, leaving the surrounding area positively charged. A positively charged black powder (***toner***) is repelled by the positively charged areas and attracted to the negatively charged image dots to make up the image of the page. The paper with its toner image next passes between heated rollers that fuse (melt) the powder dots onto the paper to produce a permanent image. Laser printers have resolutions ranging from 300 dpi to 1200 dpi, depending upon the model.

- **Imagesetters.** When high-resolution images must be output for commercial printing, an *imagesetter* is used. See **Figure 6-32**. The output station consists of two parts; the raster image processor and the imagesetter. The ***Raster Image Processor (RIP)*** converts all elements of the page or image into a bitmapped image at the resolution of the selected output device. Using laser technology, the ***imagesetter*** outputs the material (text, a page of text and graphics, or a set of color separations) on the selected medium: film, resin-coated photographic paper, or printing plate material. Imagesetters provide the highest resolution output.

Platforms

The *platform* of an electronic imaging system is the computer system, or hardware, that is used to operate the software. It includes the elements necessary to create, assemble, and output type or a finished page. Although there were once many competing platforms, the major surviving ones are the Apple Macintosh, the *PC* (almost universal shorthand for the IBM personal computer and its compatible "clones"), and UNIX. There have been prototypes developed for a system (called the Common Hardware Reference Platform, or CHRP) that would allow software written for either platform to be used.

Macintosh

The *Macintosh* computer, introduced in 1984, and quickly became popular because of its ease of use and ability to generate high-quality graphic images. The Macintosh system was designed around the concept of a ***graphical user interface (GUI)***, which allowed for easy-to-understand graphic representation of computing tasks on screen. At that time, competing platforms were based on the harder-to-use method of typing commands to perform tasks. This platform was central to the development of electronic imaging, and continues to play a major role. In 1998, the iMac line was introduced. See **Figure 6-33.**

Personal computers (PCs)

The PC is the most often-used platform in business environments. In the early 1990s, the original command-based operating system for PCs was replaced by Microsoft *Windows*™, a GUI designed to give the PC the same ease of use as the Macintosh. The introduction of versatile word processing programs, sophisticated illustration and graphics software, and such powerful page composition software as QuarkXPress™, has made this platform a strong competitor to the Macintosh for electronic imaging applications. See **Figure 6-34**.

Figure 6-33. The latest version of the iMac computer features a flat screen LCD (Liquid Crystal Display) monitor instead of the bulky cathode ray tube (CRT) monitors used by most computer systems. The system requires only a small amount of desk space, since all the electronics and disk drives are contained in the dome-shaped base of the monitor. Both traditional Macintosh computers and iMac models are widely used in the graphics field. (Apple Computers, Inc.)

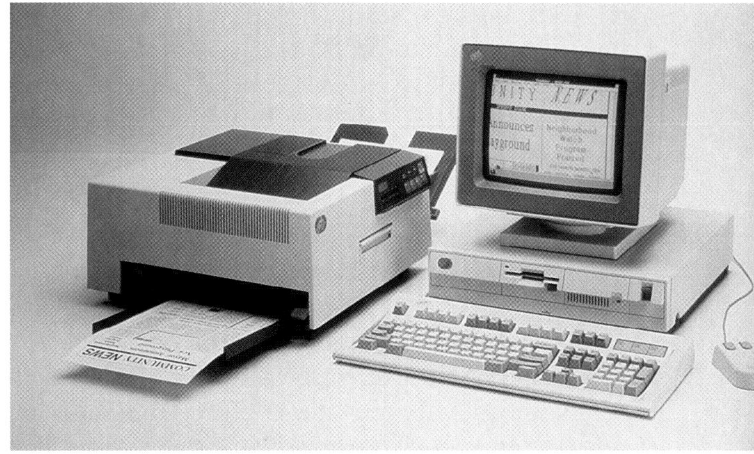

Figure 6-34. Development of the Windows GUI permitted IBM-compatible personal computers to become competitive with the Macintosh in graphic communications applications. This computer and laser printer, combined with word processing, page layout, and graphics software, form an elementary desktop publishing system.

UNIX

The computers often referred to as "UNIX boxes" use an operating system different from the Mac or PC. The Unix operating system was adapted from software that was used in large mainframe computers. UNIX systems are considered to be very reliable but they can be difficult to use because they are command driven, rather than using a graphical user interface (such as Windows or MAC OS). The easier-to-use LINUX operating system is also available for use on Mac and PC machines.

CHRP

The goal in developing the ***CHRP (Common Hardware Reference Platform)***, is *compatibility* — making it possible for users to run software written for either the Macintosh or the PC platforms. It would also make possible the connection of peripheral devices, such as printers, originally designed for either platform. Prototype CHRP systems have been introduced.

Software

Software used with electronic imaging systems is classified by its role in the ***digital prepress*** process. This process essentially consists of preparing content (text and graphics), then composing pages (design/layout), and outputting the finished file to an imagesetter, directly to a platemaker, or directly to a digital press. The classes of software used in prepress work consist of word processors, draw and paint software, graphics editors, and page composition programs.

Text preparation

Several options exist when preparing text for use in the digital prepress process. The simplest method, where small amounts of text are involved, is to enter copy directly onto the page while using page composition software. When a large amount of text is involved, however, it is better to do the composition using word processing software. It is also possible to scan text from hard copy, using an Optical Character Recognition (OCR) scanner, or to import text electronically from a disk or by use of a modem. You would then edit the text in a word processing program.

Word processing software is a highly efficient tool for creating and editing text. Originally designed for correspondence and similar tasks in the business environment, it has allowed computers to replace phototypsetters in composing text for graphic communications applications. Many word processors have the capability of providing both text and graphics formatting. However, it is generally considered better to use the word processor strictly for text entry and editing, instead of trying to create the entire publication with it. This is particularly true if the publication will require extensive text formatting and incorporation of numerous graphic elements.

Word processors typically include *proofing tools* that allow the operator to detect and correct errors in spelling, punctuation, and word division. The proofing tools go well beyond mere "spell-checking." They are usually capable of detecting such faults as incorrect, extra, or missing punctuation; incorrect hyphenation, improper abbreviation, missing or incorrect capitalization at the beginning of a sentence, or doubled words. This is a small sample of what proofing tools can do to increase typesetting efficiency.

To assist in formatting the text when it is placed in a page composition program, it is possible to incorporate special codes to identify specific attributes, such as headlines, subheads, or body text. See **Figure 6-35**. Depending upon the word processing program involved, the codes may be called styles, tags, or a similar term. When the text is imported into the page composition program, the code is recognized and assigns the specific text attributes to that copy. Such attributes may include type size, leading, alignment (centered, flush left, flush right), indents, and other considerations. This technique saves the person using the page composer many hours of work once the text has been placed in the document.

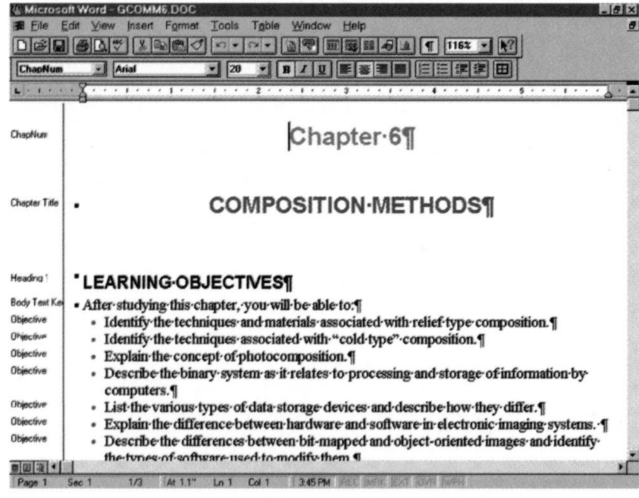

Figure 6-35. Formatting of special attributes, such as different sizes and forms of headlines or various types of lists, can be done by applying styles in a word processing program. In this screen example, the labels to the left of the vertical line are the styles associated with different text elements.

Page composition software is able to recognize the formats of the common word processing programs on the market. This allows the page composer to recognize the text files and retain much of the formatting (such as the use of boldface or italic type styles) that was applied in the word processor. The greater the compatibility of the page composer to the word processor, the less formatting needed once the text has been incorporated into the page composer.

Graphics preparation

When a designer begins using graphics in publications, he or she must be familiar with the various types of software that can be used to generate and manipulate different types of graphic images. These include draw programs, paint programs, and image editing programs (sometimes called graphics editors). In electronic imaging, graphics can be broadly divided into two groups, object-oriented images and bitmapped images.

Object-oriented images are able to be defined in terms of mathematical parameters (*Bezier curves*). A piece of line art generated by a ***draw program***, **Figure 6-36**, is an object-oriented image. The draw program also gives the designer control over shape, placement, line width, and object pattern. Because the object is defined geometrically, shapes will not break up when enlarged or reduced. An advantage of object-oriented images is that the computer can store them very efficiently.

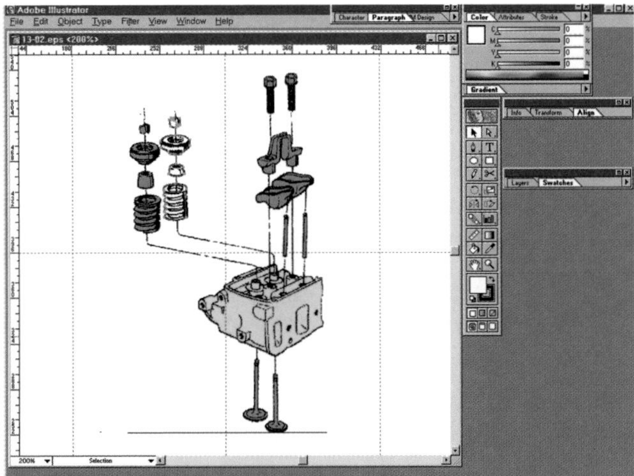

Figure 6-36. A draw program generates object-oriented images that can be easily scaled and modified. The object is defined geometrically.

Bitmapped images are graphics files that contain a map of *pixels* (tiny rectangular picture elements), each of which is assigned characteristics. See **Figure 6-37**. In a simple black and white bit map, one bit of information is assigned to each pixel: either it is "on" (black) or "off" (white). This information, in turn, determines where ink is placed on the paper when the image is printed. Graphics programs are able to also store additional information about each pixel location, providing gray scale and color data. Each of these pixels might require eight or even 32 bits of information to describe.

Artwork created by a ***paint program*** is a bitmapped image, so is a continuous tone image (photograph) that has been digitized by use of a scanner. Some graphics editing is possible with the paint program, but more extensive and precise changes should be made with an ***image editor.*** A full-featured image editor, such as Adobe Photo-

Figure 6-37. This piece of bitmapped art has been greatly enlarged to show the individual pixels.

shop™, permits manipulation of almost any aspect of the image: cropping, changing color and contrast, adding or removing visual information, even combining two or more images into a new illustration. When bitmapped images are used for reproducing photographs, they are converted to halftone dots and placed on film for printing.

Page composition

The assembly of text and graphic images into the final page is accomplished with a page composer. The most widely used page composition software packages today are PageMaker™ and QuarkXPress™. Although the specific operations of the programs are somewhat different, an experienced operator can use either of them to accomplish many of the prepress production activities on a computer monitor. These programs create a file in PostScript™ (a page description language) that is sent to an imagesetter. That device, in turn, converts the PostScript file to a bitmapped image on paper, film, or plate material.

Proofreading

A ***proof*** is any copy or art that is checked before going into print. In traditional typesetting, the proof would be a galley "pulled" (printed) from the metal type or a printout on phototypesetting paper. In today's electronic production systems, it would more commonly be a printout from a laser printer.

In traditional typesetting situations, a manuscript was edited and marked for type size and style before being sent to the compositor (typesetter). The compositor followed all editing instructions, setting the copy exactly as it was written.

After the copy was set, the ***proofreading*** process was carried out to make sure any typesetting errors were detected and marked for correction. See **Figure 6-38**. The marked proof would then be sent back to the typesetter for correction, and a corrected proof would be made and checked.

In electronic composition methods, the author and editor create the final copy, so the separate typesetting step is eliminated. This does not eliminate the need for proofreading, but changes the method and approach: the typeset copy is no longer compared to "original manuscript," since the typeset material is the manuscript. It still must be read carefully for errors and marked for correction. After corrections are made, they must be checked as well. In some operations, the checking of type corrections may be combined with proofing the laid-out pages.

Proofreading skills

The proofreader has a very important job of making sure the final product reflects quality and professionalism. In the larger publishing and printing facilities, people are hired with expertise in proofreading. In smaller facilities, a variety of people might have this responsibility. Every printer, especially in the small plant, should be able to read proofs.

The proofreader must be a meticulous person. He or she must be able to accurately check individual letters in words as well as look for combinations of letters. This person cannot scan but must study each word separately. If proofreading is done poorly, the highest quality paper, the best printing methods, excellent content, and other favorable aspects of the product will be ruined.

Proofreader's responsibilities

The typical duties of a proofreader are:

- Check the spelling of all words.
- Make sure word divisions or hyphenations are correct.
- Make sure the style (such matters as use of italic and bold type, capitalization, and similar matters) is consistent.
- Check that the size of type, line length and spacing are as specified.
- Make sure that copy has not been omitted or repeated. (In electronic composition, this could be encountered when proofing laid-out pages.)

Figure 6-38. Proofreaders must check work of the typesetter. This reader is working with an assistant, called a copyholder, to check material produced by a phototypesetting system. The reader is following the typeset copy as the copyholder works with the original manuscript.

Proofreading methods

Comparison proofing, or *one-person proofing*, is done primarily to find such major problems as copy deletion, incorrect sequence, or copy duplication It is most suitable for small jobs with little copy, since switching back and forth from proof to copy can be troublesome. Generally, the proofreader scans quickly through the proof once to check for problems. The reader then places the proof next to the manuscript and traces along the lines of the proof with a pen while reading. Placing a straightedge across the copy and moving it slowly down the page is also helpful. To be consistent, the proofreader must always compare *proof* with *copy*, not vice versa.

The ***two-person proofing system*** requires the reader to work with an assistant. This is the most common proofreading method when accuracy and speed are important. It is frequently used with larger jobs, such as a textbook.

The two people are referred to as the reader and the copyholder. The *reader* follows the camera-ready copy or a printout (or sometimes a display on the computer screen) to check closely for errors. The *copyholder* follows the original manuscript or a printout. Usually, the two take turns reading to each other. Each word must be carefully pronounced and reading must not be too fast. The reader must have time to scan the letters of each word, check punctuation, style, and other items.

A special jargon or language often develops between the reader and copyholder. For instance, some readers pronounce each capital letter as "cap" and each period as "peer" to denote the beginning and end of a sentence.

Proofreader's marks

Proofreader's marks are widely used symbols that single out and explain copy changes or errors. The symbols are used to show when something is to be taken out, added, or changed. **Figure 6-39** shows common proofreader's marks.

The most common method of noting errors in copy is to place a mark (usually the *caret*, or upside-

Mark	Punctuation
⊙	Period
^,	Comma
(:)	Colon
^;	Semicolon
’∨	Apostrophe
“∨	Open quotes
”∨	Close quotes
=/	Hyphen
1/n 1/em 2/em	Dash (show length)
( )	Parentheses
	Delete and insert
(delete mark)	Delete
(delete and close up mark)	Delete and close up
out see copy	Insert omitted matter
stet	Let it stand
	Paragraphing
¶	Paragraph
fl ¶	Flush paragraph
[1] [2]	Indent (show no. of ems)
run in	Run in
	Position
] [	Move right or left
⊓ ⊔	Raise, lower
ctr	Center
fl L fl R	Flush left, right
=	Align horizontally
‖	Align vertically
tr ∿	Transpose
tr #	Transpose space

Mark	Spacing
#	Insert space
eq #	Equalize space
⁀‿	Close up
	Style of type
wf	Wrong font
lc	Lower case
cap	Capitalize
u lc	Initial cap, then lower case
sc	Small capitals
c sc	Initial cap, then small caps
rom	Set in roman
ital	Set in italics
lf	Set in light face
bf	Set in bold face
3∨	Superior character
^3	Inferior character
	Miscellaneous
X	Broken type
(invert mark)	Invert
⊥	Push down
(sp)	Spell out
/	Shilling mark (slash)
(...)	Ellipsis
see l/o	See layout
? query	Query

Figure 6-39. This chart gives some commonly used proofreader's symbols. Although many are considered standard, there is some variation of marks from facility to facility.

down v symbol) below the error. The appropriate proofreader's mark is then placed in the margin to indicate the type of error, **Figure 6-40**. This system is an efficient means of showing the typesetter the location of the fault and the desired correction.

Proofreading marks must be written clearly and should be exaggerated so they are not overlooked. When needed, the proofreader can write special notes pertaining to the marks in the border. Sometimes an extra sheet of instructions may have to be attached to the copy or page layout.

Typesetting and checking corrections

Once the corrections are marked on the proof or layout, the typesetter must keystroke the changes following the proofreader's marks. With traditional hot metal typesetting, the correction had to be made physically in the type and a new proof made. Phototypesetting corrections were usually output as a block of copy (several lines or a paragraph) for ease of alignment with the existing galley. The corrected block of copy was either cut and taped into the galley, or adhered with wax or rubber cement on top of the paragraph containing the error. With modern computer-based typesetting, only the specific errors are corrected, and a full page of text (or the entire document) printed out for proofing.

One person can usually read and check the corrections. The corrected proofs are checked by the proofreader against the marked proof. Usually, just the changes are read and not the complete job.

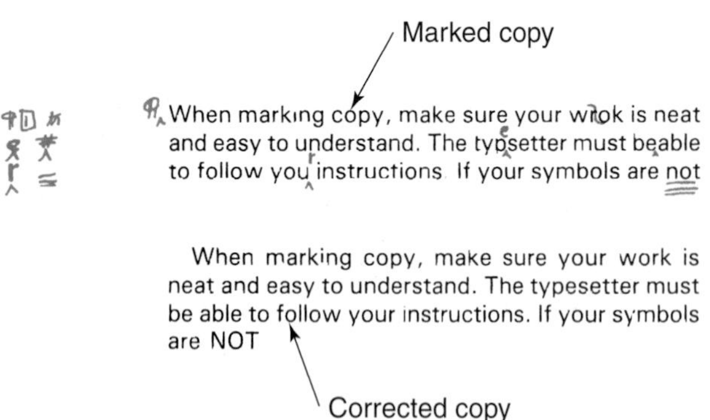

Figure 6-40. This is a sample of proofreader's marks being used to correct copy problems. Note that a caret is placed at the point of the error, and the symbol is written in the margin.

Spellchecking programs

A *spellcheck* program, also called a spellchecker or proofing program, is incorporated in major word processing software. Depending upon the operator's preference, the program will automatically check the spelling of each word as it is keystroked, or all the words in a document when typesetting is completed.

The proofing program compares words in the document with those in the program dictionary. If a word is spelled incorrectly, a suggested correction is shown on the computer screen, **Figure 6-41**. The typesetter can accept that spelling, if appropriate, or provide the proper spelling. The misspelled word will be corrected in the document. Spellcheck programs also permit unusual spellings or technical words to be added to the dictionary.

Spellcheck programs can be very helpful to production speed and quality. They can greatly reduce typos and make the correction cycle much easier for everyone involved with producing the printed piece. The proofreader must still go over the copy. However, with fewer typing errors to worry about, more effort can be given to checking style, illustration references, sequence, and other important aspects.

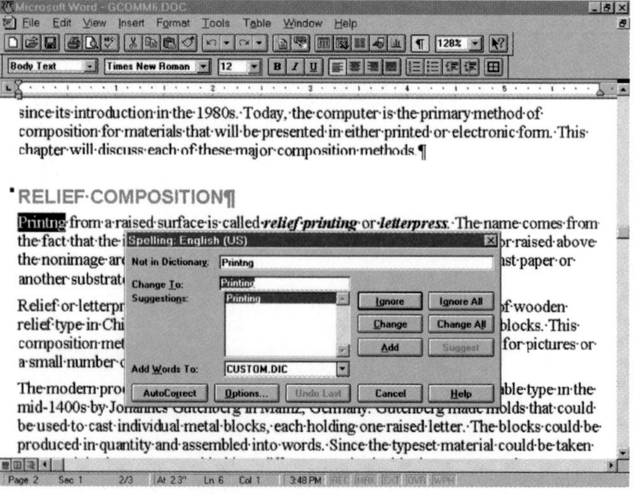

Figure 6-41. Computer programs are available to check for correct spelling. This spellchecker has highlighted the word in the text and displayed it in a window. The most likely correct spelling is shown in the "Change To" box, but one or more additional suggestions are often given.

Review Questions

Please do not write in this text. Write your answers on a separate sheet of paper.

1. Letterpress is another name used for _____ printing.
2. The person who sets type is called a _____.
3. _____ type is an assortment of individually cast, metal characters used for relief printing.
4. The _____ is the common method for storing foundry type.
5. What is furniture?
6. __________ methods involve using a pen, brush, lettering template, clip art, or transfer letters to manually generate copy.
7. ___________ is the generation of type using photographic paper or film exposed to light.
8. What was the advantage of the projection type of phototypesetter?
9. List the three basic functions of a computer system.
10. The term _____ refers to the way a computer processes and stores information as a series of 1s and 0s (or on-off states).
11. What do the letters WYSIWYG represent?
12. The colors cyan, magenta, yellow, and black are represented in the _____ color system used for printing.
13. The computer monitor is a(n) _____ device.
14. Computer equipment is referred to as _____, while programs are described as _____.
15. Which of the following images would normally be edited with the type of program called an image editor?
    A. Bitmapped artwork.
    B. Object-oriented artwork.
    C. Scanned photograph.
    D. Only A and B.
    E. Only A and C.
    F. Only B and C.
16. The process of checking typeset material for errors in spelling, hyphenation, and other areas is called _____.
17. The _____ is an upside-down v symbol used to mark the location of an error when proofreading copy.
18. *True or False?* Spellcheckers that are part of word processing programs eliminate the need for proofreading.

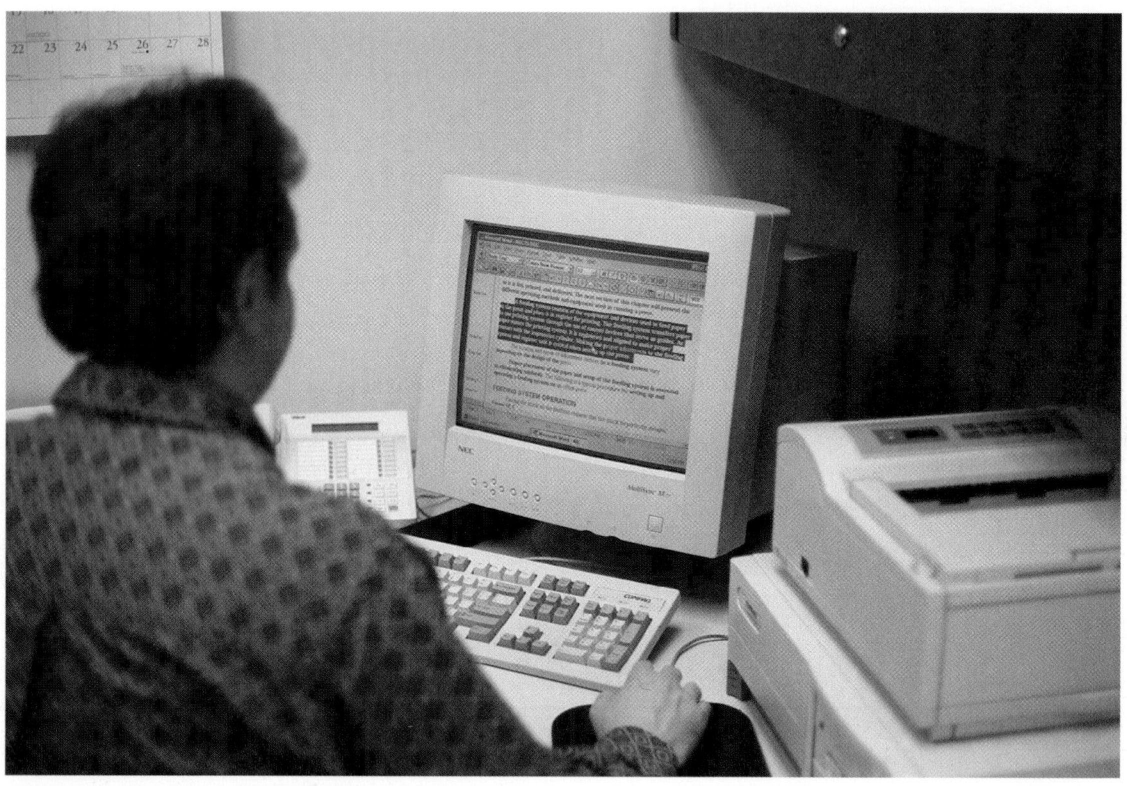

The computer has become an essential tool at almost every stage in the production of printed materials. Text creation and editing, as shown here, is typically followed by electronic page layout, in which text materials and digital images are arranged in final form. In many printing operations today, the resulting digital files are processed and eventually used to create the printing plate, or even an electrostatic image for direct digital printing.

Page Composition 7

Learning Objectives

After studying this chapter, you will be able to:

- Explain the role of the paste-up artist.
- Summarize the tools and equipment used in the paste-up process.
- Describe the paste-up steps for producing a mechanical.
- Explain the electronic page composition process used to combine text and graphic images.
- Define and correctly use the terms unique to electronic page composition.

Important Terms

camera-ready copy
dropdown menus
master page
mechanical
paste-up method
picture box
register marks
T-square
text box
workmarks

Page composition or *page layout* is the process of properly arranging the various *elements* or *components* that will make up a printed page. The components of a page typically include *text* (body type), *display type*, *illustrations* (line art and photographs), and *white space*.

The methods used to arrange elements on the page have changed dramatically during the past 50 years. From the 1400s through the first half of the 20th century, metal type was arranged into words and paragraphs, then combined with "cuts" (artwork converted into raised lines and mounted on a block of wood) to form a page. In the 1880s, the introduction of the halftone dot process made it possible to include photographs. The printing could be done directly from the page form, or from a copy made by casting type metal in a mold.

In the 1950s, the widespread adoption of phototypesetters gave rise to a paper-based method of page layout. Text and display type was produced on photographic paper that could be adhered to a base sheet, along with copies of illustrations. This process, called *paste-up*, produced a completed page referred to as a ***mechanical***. A photographic negative made from the mechanical was then used to produce a printing plate.

Today, electronic production methods have become the norm. Computers are used to generate text and display type, to create and alter line art, and to prepare photographs for printing, **Figure 7-1**. With the use of page composition software, an operator can assemble and adjust all the elements needed to produce a finished page. The page may be sent to an imagesetter for output on photographic paper, film negative, or printing plate

Figure 7-1. Computers are central to graphic communications today. They are used to generate type, to create and manipulate art, and to combine the various elements into page form.

material. Another possibility would be output directly to a digital press, without any intermediate negative or plate.

Traditional Paste-up

Although electronic page composition methods have become widely adopted in graphic communications, the traditional method of preparing a mechanical by using the ***paste-up method*** is still used to some extent. Using an approved ***layout*** (sketch or plan for the finished page), the paste-up artist assembles the needed typeset material and illustrations, then adheres them with wax or rubber cement to a base sheet. The artist may also prepare various overlays for a second-color or other special elements. See **Figure 7-2**.

Base sheet materials range from 70 lb. white offset paper to thin plastic sheets to 110 lb. index stock to illustration board. Paper is used primarily where cost is a factor, while plastic sheets provide good dimensional stability. Index stock is a good balance between cost and durability. Illustration board gives maximum durability, but is expensive. To prepare

Figure 7-2. A paste-up artist assembles all the necessary page elements and adheres them to the base sheet. Rubber cement and hot wax are the traditional materials for adhering page elements, since they allow some repositioning. For applying rules and other lines, special tapes like the one being used here are available.

the base sheet for use, the paste-up artist will usually draw various workmarks using a pencil with *light blue* lead (light blue is not picked up photographically). Typical ***workmarks*** include corner or trim marks, center marks, and fold lines, **Figure 7-3**. These marks are helpful to the paste-up artist and the stripper. Some layout sheets have location or margin lines preprinted on them. Special paste-up

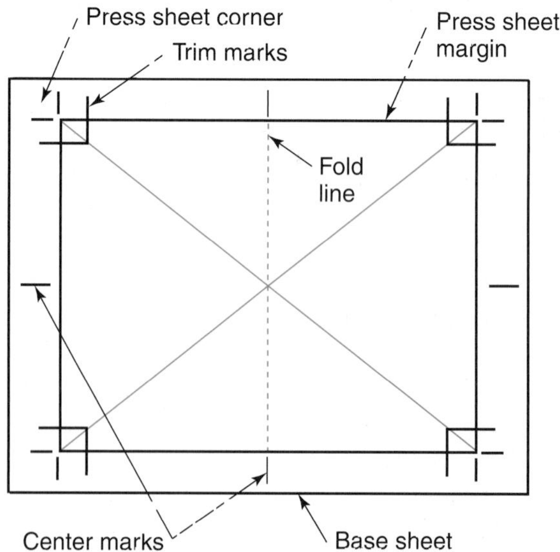

Figure 7-3. The paste-up surface, called a base sheet, will hold the type and graphic elements. It is usually made up using a T-square on a drawing board or light table. Workmarks, such as center marks, trim marks, and fold lines, are guides for the paste-up artist and printer. They must be accurate. Drafting tape is used to hold the base sheet in alignment on the board.

sheets used by newspapers and other periodicals may be preprinted with a grid of light blue lines that allows copy to be aligned without the use of a T-square.

Paste-up Tools and Equipment

A good work surface and many tools are needed for paste-up. Tools should be kept in good condition and stored where they will be convenient to the work surface. The most common paste-up tools are a T-square and triangles, scissors, art knives, rulers, tweezers, compass/dividers, tape, ink, light blue pencils, pens, brushes, burnishers, and erasers.

Working surfaces

Either a drawing board or a light table may be used as a working surface for paste-up. Wood drawing boards are most common, but various materials are used. When backlighting is needed for easier alignment or registration of two images, a light table is often used for paste-up, **Figure 7-4**. This is especially useful with paper or plastic base sheets.

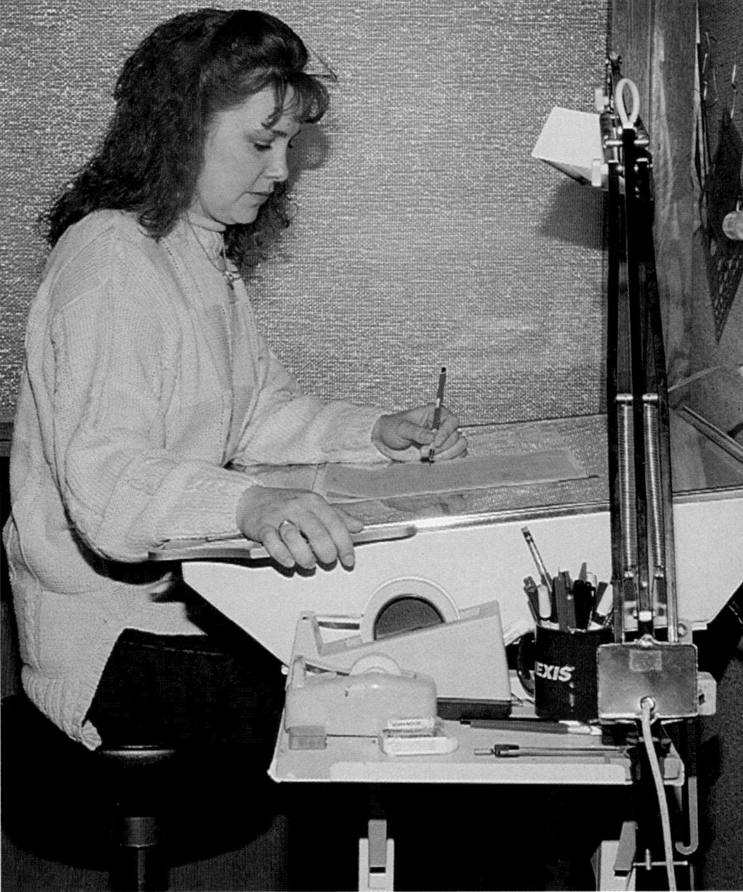

Figure 7-4. A drawing board is commonly used as a work surface for paste-up, but a light table like this one is preferable when it is necessary to see through images for alignment.

Pencils

The *pencil* is an essential tool for various layout tasks. Keeping a pencil sharp is vital for fine line accuracy. For this reason, *mechanical pencils* are often preferred over conventional wooden pencils, **Figure 7-5**. They use a small-diameter lead that can be extended out of the tip as it wears down. The lead for mechanical pencils comes in various thicknesses or diameters (0.5 mm is a popular size), and will produce consistent line weights.

When ruling with any kind of pencil, make sure the point is held against the edge of the T-square. To produce a straight uniform line, maintain the same general pencil angle as you slide the pencil along the edge.

Pencil *lead hardness* is given as a letter-number designation—7B is the softest and 9H is the hardest lead. A harder lead would be good for light lines. A softer lead would produce darker, but more easily smudged, lines. Select a lead hardness that matches the task.

As noted earlier, a *light blue pencil* is used on the base sheet for workmarks and to indicate where copy is to be placed. The lines indicate the shapes

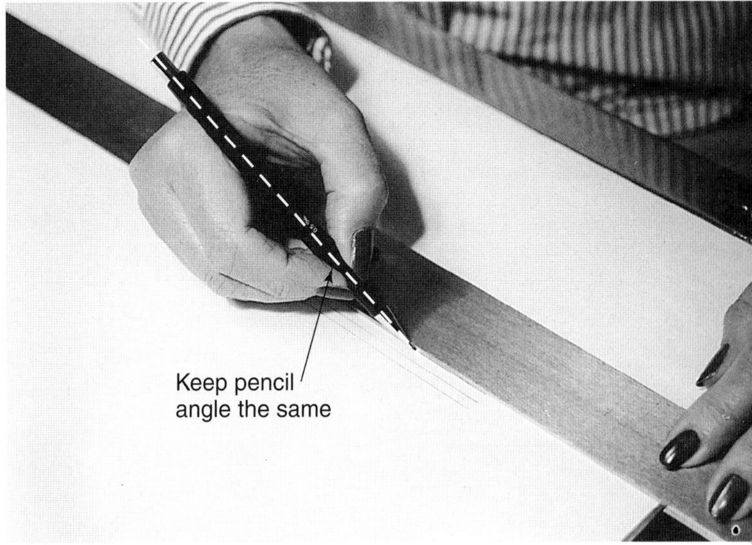

Figure 7-5. Mechanical pencils, with very small diameter lead, never need sharpening and produce consistent line weights. Hold the point at a consistent angle against the T-square for a uniform line.

and positioning of material. Instructions for sizing, tint screens, stripping, or other operations are usually written on the mechanical or on a tissue overlay in light blue pencil, as well. This type of pencil is often referred to as a *"nonrepro pencil,"* since light blue does not reproduce on litho film. This means the lines will not appear on the platemaker's negative.

Pens

There are several types of special pens that are used to produce very sharp images in ink during paste-up. All are used in the same way—held straight up and down, with even pressure applied to assure consistent density and width of lines.

The ***technical ink pen*** is most commonly used today to make camera-ready illustrations and other line work. It has a set tip or nib size that may be expressed in a number system or as a metric dimension. For example, a No. 00 is a fine tip that is 0.30 mm in diameter, while a No. 2 tip would have a 0.60 mm diameter. A color code on the pen's cap also shows pen size. **Figure 7-6** shows pen sizes and resulting line widths.

The technical ink pen screws apart and has a small reservoir for ink, **Figure 7-7**. Keep these pens clean and handle them carefully; the tip is very delicate and easily damaged. Hold the pen as straight as possible when drawing lines, because tilting the pen can upset ink flow and line weight. Allow the ink to dry before touching it; ink will smear easily when wet.

6x0	4x0	3x0	00	0	1	2	2½	3	3½	4	6	7
.13	.18	.25	.30	.35	.50	.60	.70	.80	1.00	1.20	1.40	2.00

.005 in.	.007 in.	.010 in.	.012 in.	.014 in	.020 in.	.024 in.	.028 in.	.031 in.	.039 in.	.047 in.	.055 in.	.079 in.
.13 mm	.18mm	.25mm	.30mm	.35mm	.50mm	.60 mm	.70mm	.80mm	1.00mm	1.20mm	1.40mm	2.00mm

Figure 7-6. The technical ink pen has a precisely sized tip for drawing accurate lines. Common pen sizes and actual line weights are shown on the chart.

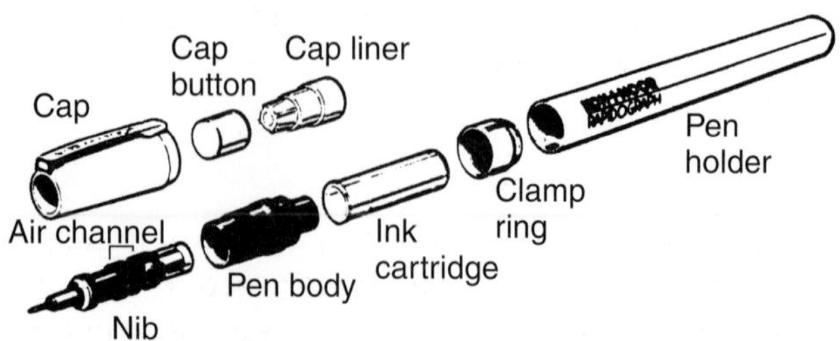

Figure 7-7. Technical pens have an ink reservoir and a point (nib). On some pens, the reservoir is actually a removable cartridge. (Koh-I-Noor Rapidograph, Inc.)

The *ruling pen* is seldom used today. It has movable *nibs* (jaws) that can be set for different line weights or widths. A ruling pen will make good straight lines, but does not draw curved lines efficiently.

Various kinds of *felt-tipped pens* have been developed specifically for making camera-ready art, but they do not produce lines as sharp-edged as those made by technical or ruling pens.

Ink

India ink is the most common type, and works very well in technical ink pens. Ink is sold in various size bottles and containers, but a small plastic bottle is often used to fill a technical pen. The bottle has a pointed outlet so the ink can be deposited in the pen's small reservoir quickly and efficiently.

Ink must be able to produce a very dense image. It should cover fully to produce a sharp black line.

Brushes

Brushes are commonly used to touch up areas of artwork. Brush size and stiffness should match the task. A wide brush can be used to fill in a large area with black ink, for example. A narrow or small brush might be used to place an opaque white paint over smeared black ink. Brushes can also be used to touch up or modify photographs. Always clean brushes thoroughly after use to extend their service life.

T-square

The ***T-square*** is commonly used to align images, as a knife guide when cutting elements, and as a support and guide for a pen or pencil when drawing straight lines. It is one of the most important pieces of equipment in layout and paste-up work. The T-square consists of a thin straightedge blade fastened to a head, **Figure 7-8**. The T-square blade should be made of thin steel and securely joined to the head. The technical fountain pen works well with such thin bladed, steel T-squares. Some blades have a beveled edge so that ink will not run under them.

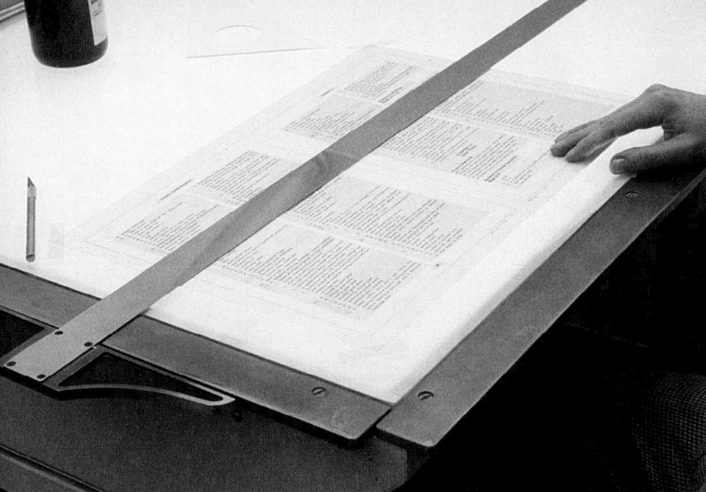

Figure 7-8. A good T-square is vital to accurate paste-up work. One with a steel blade is preferred.

Plastic T-square blades are *not* satisfactory when used as a guide for cutting. The blade of the knife can easily cut the plastic and ruin the blade.

When using the T-square, hold the head firmly against the left side of the drawing board. Always try to work near the frame end of the T-square. This will result in more accurate work. The other end of the T-square is unsupported and can flex up or down, causing images or lines to be out of alignment. It is good practice to draw lines with the upper edge of the T-square blade, **Figure 7-9**.

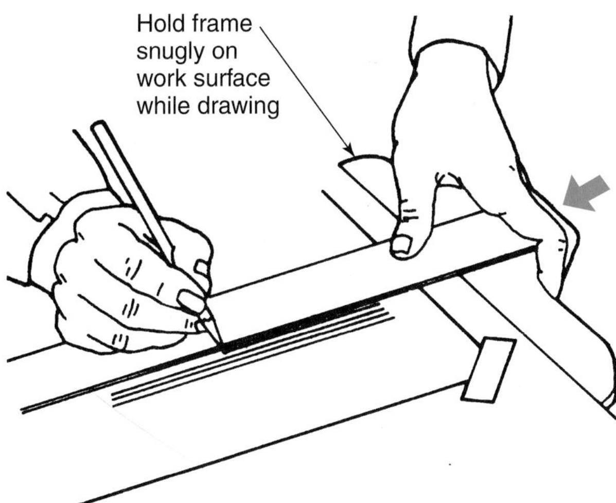

Figure 7-9. Always work near the frame end of the T-square to prevent flexing that could upset accuracy. Press the frame against the board with one hand while drawing lines with the other. Use the top edge of the T-square blade.

Triangles

The ***triangle*** is used to draw vertical and slanted lines on layouts and mechanicals. The two most common types are the 30°–60°–90° triangle and the 45° triangle. An *adjustable triangle* is available, and can be swiveled to produce any desired angle. Various triangle sizes are sold. Select a size that matches the job. The 12″ triangle is very common because it will reach all the way across an 8 1/2″ × 11″ paste-up format.

Triangles are available in metal or plastic. A clear plastic triangle is useful in paste-up work, since you can see through it when aligning elements. Plastic is acceptable for drawing but *not* for cutting.

A conventional triangle has its lower edge touching the paper, which can allow ink to flow under it and ruin the line. To prevent ink smearing, an *inking triangle* has a two-step lip that raises the edge off the paper. Some triangles make use of a tapered edge that serves the same purpose as a two-step edge.

To use a triangle, hold the T-square against the drawing board with one hand. Use the other hand to position the triangle against the T-square. This will align the triangle properly, **Figure 7-10**.

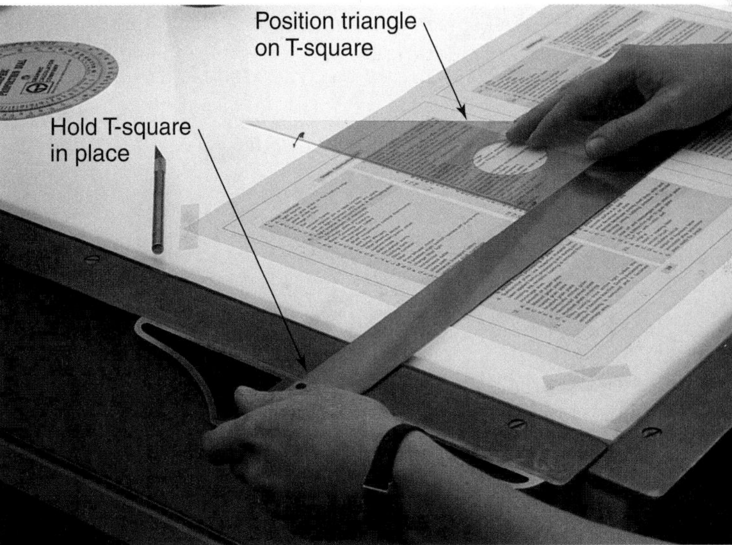

Figure 7-10. When using a triangle, hold the T-square against the drawing board and the triangle against the T-square. This will align the triangle properly.

Rulers

Rulers are used for making linear measurements during paste-up. Inch, millimeter, and pica measurements are often needed. Many sizes of rulers are available, but the 18″ length is preferred by many workers. It is long enough to handle most tasks without being cumbersome.

When measuring with a ruler, make sure you look straight down at the markings. If you sight down at an angle, an incorrect measurement can result. See **Figure 7-11**.

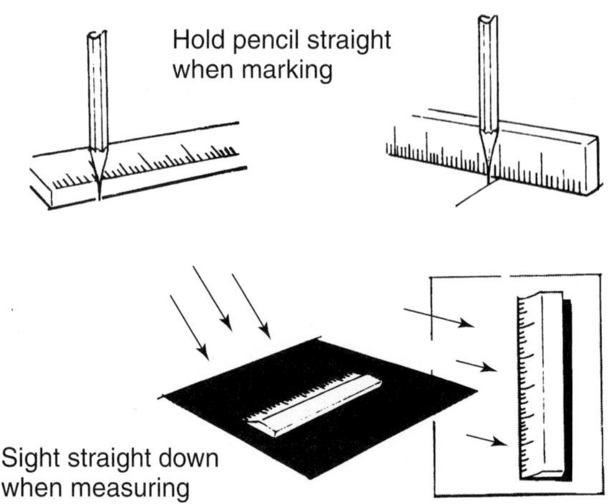

Figure 7-11. Sight down the ruler scale from directly above to get accurate measurements. If you sight down at an angle, your measurement will not be precise.

Templates

Templates can be used to draw circles, ellipses, electrical symbols, and other specialized images. They can save time and produce excellent results. See **Figure 7-12**.

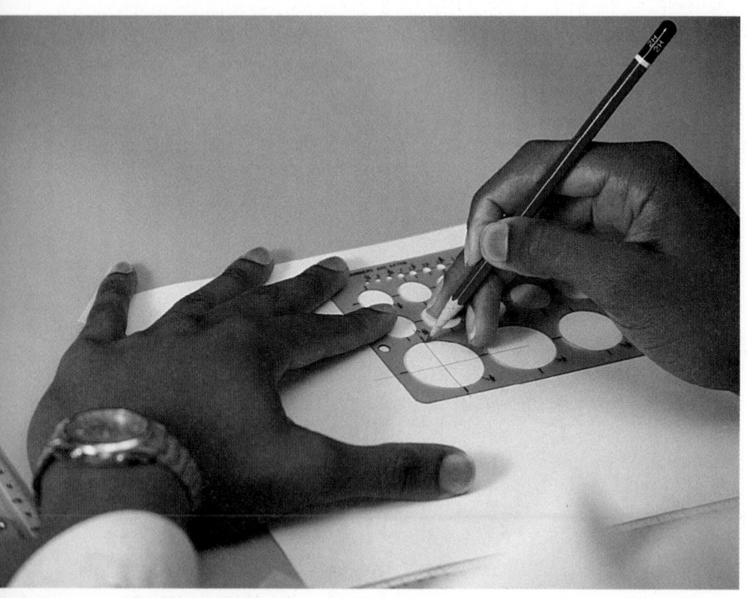

Figure 7-12. Numerous types of templates are used in layout. This is the commonly used circle template. Others are available for ellipses, electrical circuit symbols, and other special applications.

An *inking template* has small nipples or bumps on its bottom surface. This holds it off the paper surface, so that ink cannot flow under the template. When using an inking template, hold the pen straight up. Tilting the pen will produce an inaccurate shape.

Compass, dividers, tweezers

The ***compass*** is an adjustable device that can be used with a lead point or an inking point to draw circles of various sizes, **Figure 7-13**. It is also possible to use a swivel knife in a compass. The knife can be used to cut overlay film.

Dividers will measure and transfer measurements from one source to another. Dividers might be used to check the space of an area during layout.

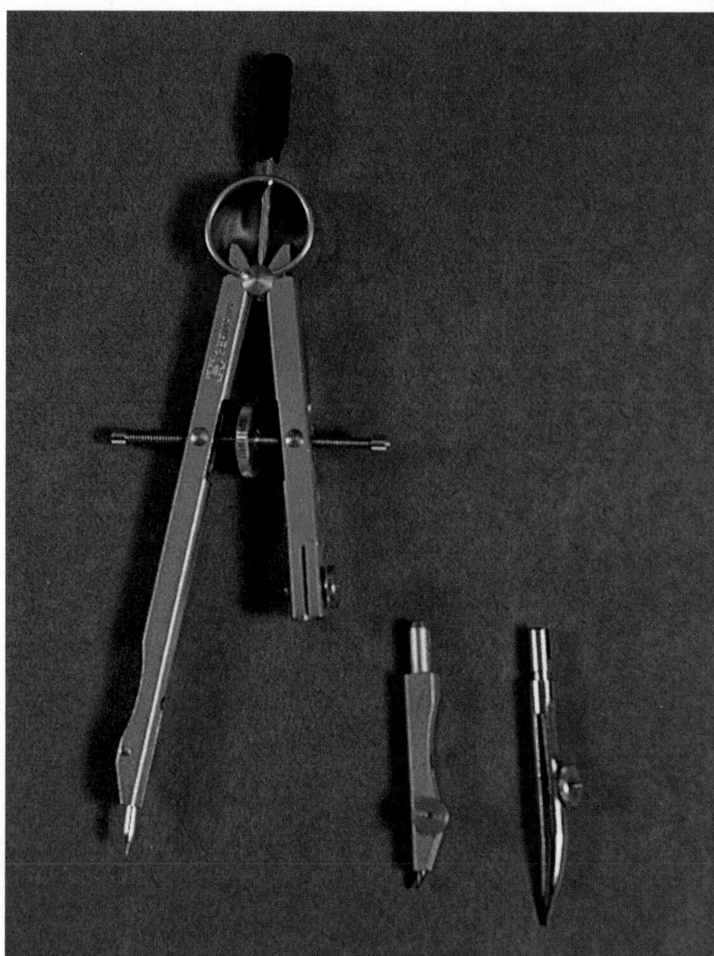

Figure 7-13. A compass will accurately draw a circle in pencil or ink. It is handy when template sizes do not match the size of circle needed.

Tweezers can be used to hold and accurately position a small piece of copy or other element during paste-up. Self-closing, pointed tweezers are recommended. Placing pressure on the tweezers opens them.

Cutting tools

The ***art knife*** is a valuable tool for making precise cuts in typeset copy and other materials, such as shading or masking films. The sharply pointed knife blade can also be used to shift or position small elements during paste-up. See **Figure 7-14**.

Figure 7-14. Art knives and razor blades can be used to make very accurate cuts. The point of an art knife is useful for shifting and accurately positioning small elements on a paste-up.

A *swivel knife* has a cutting head that rotates for cutting curved or irregular shapes. The swiveling blade will closely follow curves as you pull the knife around the shape.

Single-edge razor blades are sometimes used with a special holder. Use of the art knife is preferred, however, because it is more versatile and less dangerous to use.

Be very careful when handling art knives or razor blades. They are very sharp and can inflict deep cuts. A protective cover should be placed over the knife blade when the tool is not in use. Never place an unprotected knife in a drawer or storage tray. You could be cut when reaching in to get tools.

Scissors are used in layout to make rough cuts of materials. They will not cut as accurately as an art knife. For example, scissors might be used to cut excess white space off a galley produced by a phototypesetter.

Burnisher

The ***burnisher*** is a tool used to apply firm pressure to copy or artwork being adhered to the base sheet. See **Figure 7-15**. Proper burnishing is particularly important when using wax as the adhesive material. If material is not well-burnished, it can shift or even fall off the paste-up. In most cases, a clean sheet of paper or thin acetate sheet is placed over the copy before burnishing. The purpose of this sheet is to prevent damage to the art or copy.

Figure 7-15. Burnishing is done to make elements adhere properly to the base sheet, and is especially important when adhering waxed copy. A flat burnishing tool is being used here, but a roller-type burnisher could also be used for this task.

Two types of burnisher are commonly used: the roller type and the beveled-edge stick or rod type. The *roller* is typically made of plastic and is used to apply even pressure when adhering larger pieces of copy or art to a base sheet. The *beveled-edge* type of burnisher may have a rounded or flat shape. It can be made of plastic, wood, or metal. The flat shape is used when adhering copy or artwork, while the stick-type burnisher is most often used to apply transfer ("rub-down") lettering.

Magnifiers

Magnifiers are viewing devices for inspecting small areas on images, **Figure 7-16**. The 8× and 10× magnifiers are common. Whatever power is chosen, the figure before the "×" indicates the number of times the image is enlarged. For instance, a 10× magnifier means the image is ten times larger than the original image. The paste-up artist commonly uses a magnifier to check alignment, dot patterns, copy, and artwork.

Figure 7-16. Magnifiers are needed for close inspection of images. They are available in different powers.

Trimmers

Table-model *paper trimmers* or *paper cutters* are often used to trim off large, unwanted areas from material to be pasted up. Either blade-type or wheel-type trimmers can swiftly and accurately trim strips from galley material. Scissors are slower and less accurate. Wheel-type trimmers are used strictly for paper materials; blade-type cutters can handle heavier material, such as card stock.

Proportion scale

A *proportion scale* is a device with rotating scales used to calculate the percent of reduction or enlargement for images, **Figure 7-17**. It also permits the paste-up artist to determine the new height of an element when the width is changed, and vice versa. Use of the proportion scale was described in Chapter 3.

Paste-up Materials

All the elements to be positioned on the mechanical must be attached to the base sheet. The adhering materials most commonly used are wax, rubber cement, tape, and spray adhesives.

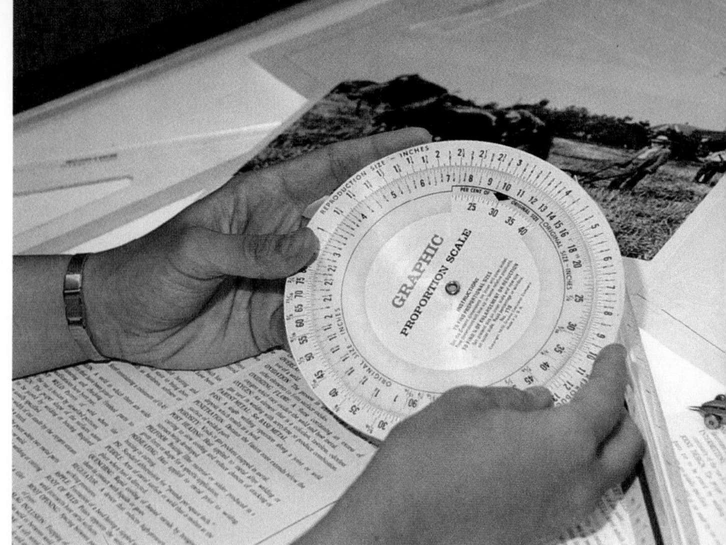

Figure 7-17. The proportion scale is commonly used to size images for paste-up.

Hot wax adhesives

Hot wax is the most common adhesive in the graphic communications industry. It provides a fast, clean, and convenient medium for adhering copy to the base sheet.

A *table top waxer,* **Figure 7-18**, is a motorized device that feeds the type and image materials through the waxing roller at a constant speed. This applies an even coating of wax to the underside of the materials. The elements will then stick to the paste-up sheet when positioned and burnished.

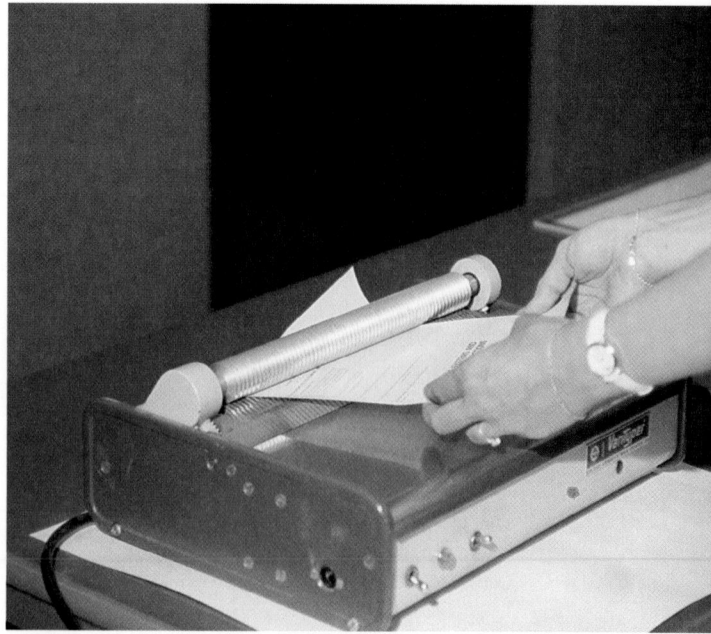

Figure 7-18. Elements to be adhered to the base sheet are fed through a waxing machine. It will deposit a thin layer of melted wax on the back of the element, which can then be easily positioned and burnished down.

Wax is an excellent paste-up adhesive because you can move elements, even after it has hardened. This is very useful when changing layout or making corrections. You can lift or pull up the images without damaging them. If necessary, heat can be applied to soften the wax and help free the copy.

Rubber cement

Rubber cement is also used as an adhesive during layout. A thin coat of the cement is placed on the underside of the copy using a brush. Since the entire surface should be coated, it is a good idea to place scrap paper under the copy, **Figure 7-19**.

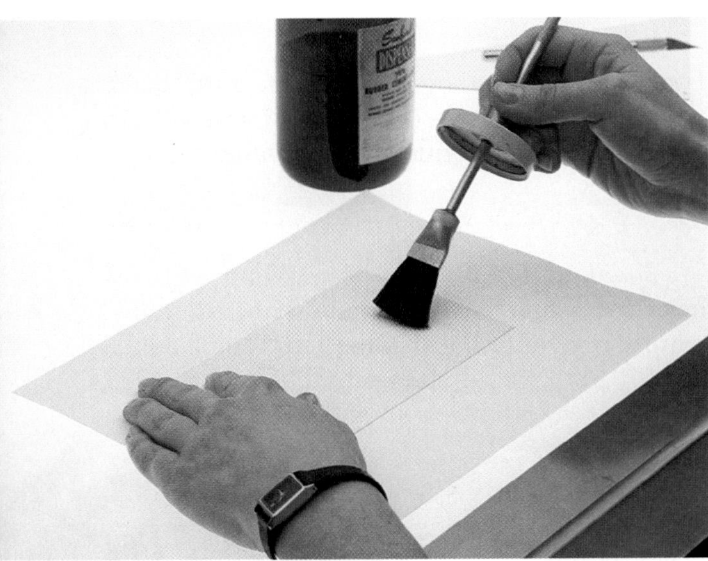

Figure 7-19. Rubber cement can be used to adhere elements, but is not as handy as wax in most instances. Place a sheet of paper under the element when coating it with rubber cement.

Rubber cement dries quite rapidly. Placement must be done immediately after coating the copy. Slight movement is initially possible. However, once the rubber cement is set, movement is very difficult without damaging the copy.

To assure greater holding power, you can coat both surfaces (base sheet and copy) with the rubber cement. Both surfaces are allowed to partially dry, then placed together. Be careful, however, since bonding is immediate and image movement for adjustment is not possible.

Rubber cement tends to be messy. It is possible to clean dried rubber cement from the sheet by rubbing or using a soft eraser. It is also possible to take old rubber cement and roll it into a ball as a means of removal. Even though the excess cement is removed, the edges of adhered elements tend to collect dirt.

Spray adhesives

Extreme care must be taken when using *spray adhesives*, since the overspray sticks to everything. Place a scrap piece of paper under the image as a precaution. Spray adhesives usually bond instantly, making adjustment almost impossible without damaging the copy. Placement must be accurate the first time.

Tape

Tape is commonly used for various tasks, such as holding the base sheet to the drawing board or light table, hinging flaps, or attaching overlays.

- ***Drafting tape*** is similar to masking tape, but its adhesive is not as sticky. It can be pulled off paper without damage. Drafting tape is commonly used for temporary holding tasks, as when holding the base sheet to the drawing board.
- *Transparent plastic tape* is also used in paste-up, but its adhesive is slightly more permanent. It is frequently used to hold overlays in place on the base sheet.
- *White paper tape* can be used in place of drafting tape in some situations. However, it is more difficult to remove and is considered more permanent.
- *Double-coated tape* has adhesive on both sides. It is sometimes used instead of an adhesive to bond elements to the base sheet. This is only done when the mechanical will not be retained or reused, however. The tape makes it very difficult to remove and reposition images without damage, especially after a period of storage.

Masking film

Masking film is a material which has two layers: a plastic base and an emulsion layer. The base layer is a thicker sheet of clear plastic. The masking film emulsion is a very thin pliable plastic sheet with either ruby or amber coloring. See **Figure 7-20**.

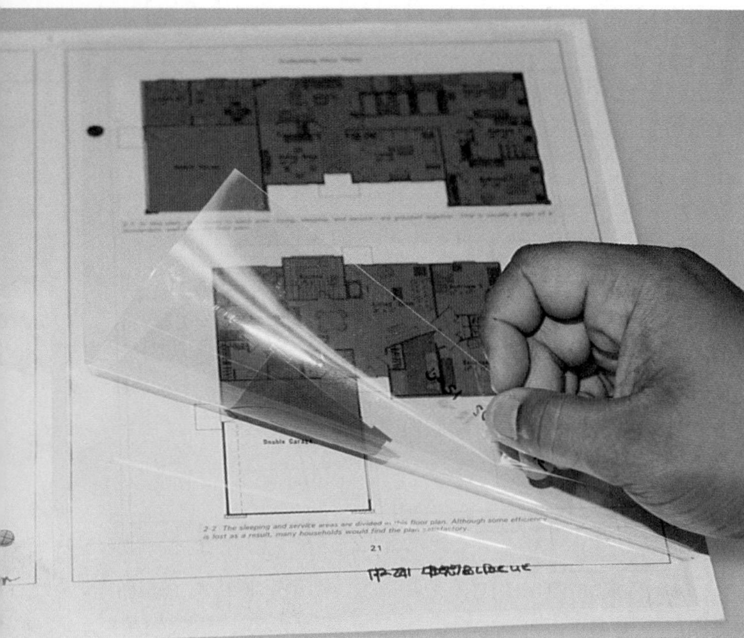

Figure 7-20. Masking film consists of a flexible sheet of clear plastic with a thin layer of ruby- or amber-colored emulsion on top. The film can be registered over an image, and unwanted areas of the thin emulsion cut and stripped away with an art knife.

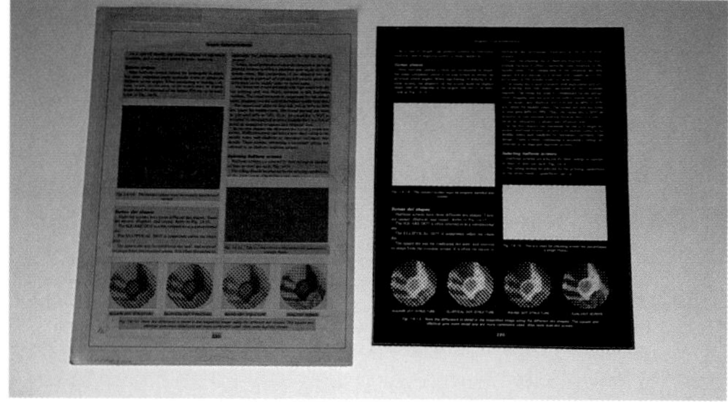

Figure 7-21. Masking film used to make a window in a negative. At left, paste-up with masking film in place. It blocks light when the film negative is exposed. At right, negative made from the paste-up, with clear area (window) where masking film was positioned.

Masking film blocks light, creating a clear area when a film negative is exposed. For this reason, it is used to make windows, solid areas, color overlays, and dropouts during paste-up. The colored layer is cut with an art knife and the unwanted material peeled off. The remaining color film is positioned on an overlay for the mechanical.

The purpose of a *window* is to make a clear area in the negative, **Figure 7-21**. Most often, the clear window will be used to position a halftone negative before exposing the printing plate. The process of converting a photograph (continuous-tone print) to a halftone negative is described in Chapter 13.

Masking film is also used whenever a *dropout* is called for. The dropped-out area might appear as a silhouette of an object, and can easily be cut on the masking film.

Overlays cut from masking film are commonly used to produce additional colors on the printed image. The material on the paste-up base sheet is printed black. The images on each of the film overlays are printed in a color, **Figure 7-22**. Registration marks are placed on the base sheet and overlay for proper alignment. Instructions for the printer are commonly printed on the overlay, as well. For example, one overlay might print in 70% magenta. Another overlay might print in 50% cyan. Still another might print as 100% yellow.

Shading film

Shading film is similar to masking film, but it has a pattern on the emulsion. A shape cut from the emulsion layer of the shading film can be adhered directly to the paste-up to print black, or placed on an overlay to produce a second color.

Border material

Border material is available in roll and sheet form. It has a pressure-sensitive back that bonds to the layout when burnished in place. It provides a quick and efficient method of placing a border around an image. Some examples are shown in **Figure 7-23**.

To use preprinted border material, draw blue layout lines showing the dimensions or location of the border. Place the border tape along the guide line. Overlap the corners of the tape, and press the border firmly in position. To make a mitered or square corner, use a sharp knife to cut each piece at a 45° angle, **Figure 7-24**. This technique works well when the borders are intricate images. Straight line borders can be cut off square.

A technical ink pen can be used to carefully draw straight line borders. Round corners on border tape also can be produced with the technical ink pen. First, use the pen to make square corners at the ends of the border tape. Then, use the same pen and a circle template to draw a circle that fits properly

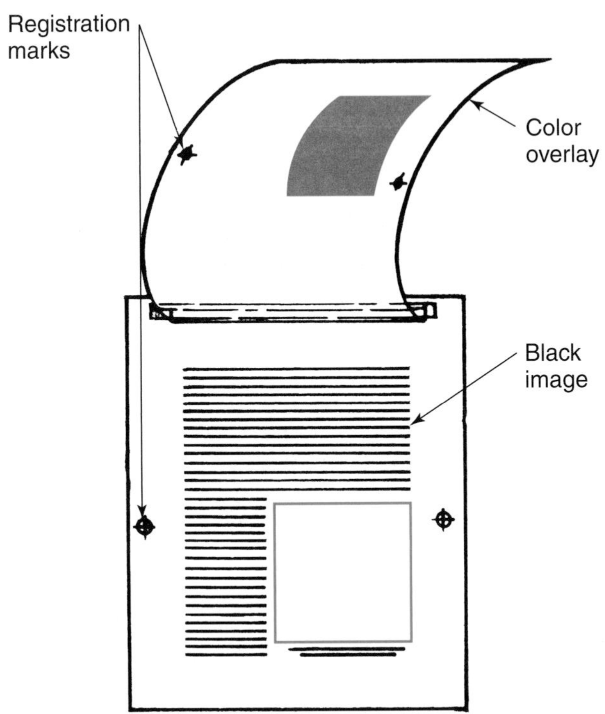

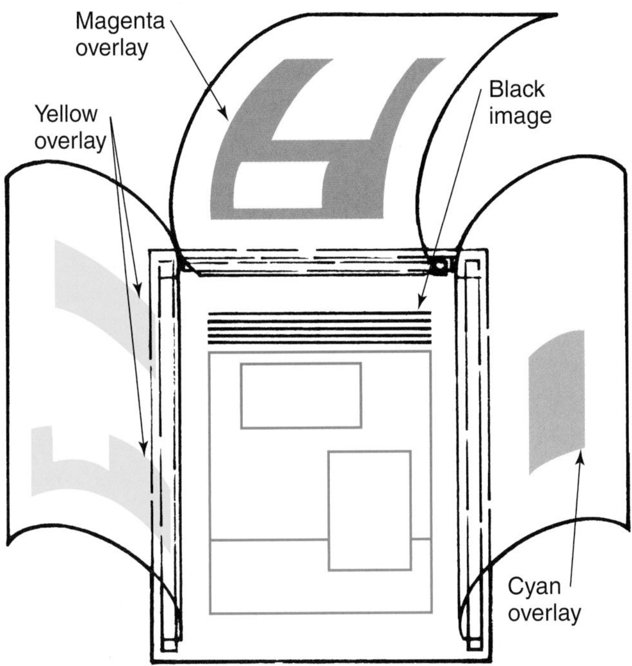

Figure 7-22. Masking film overlays are commonly used to add one or more colors to the black base image. Shown are methods of taping a single overlay and multiple overlays to the base sheet.

Figure 7-23. Some examples of preprinted border material.

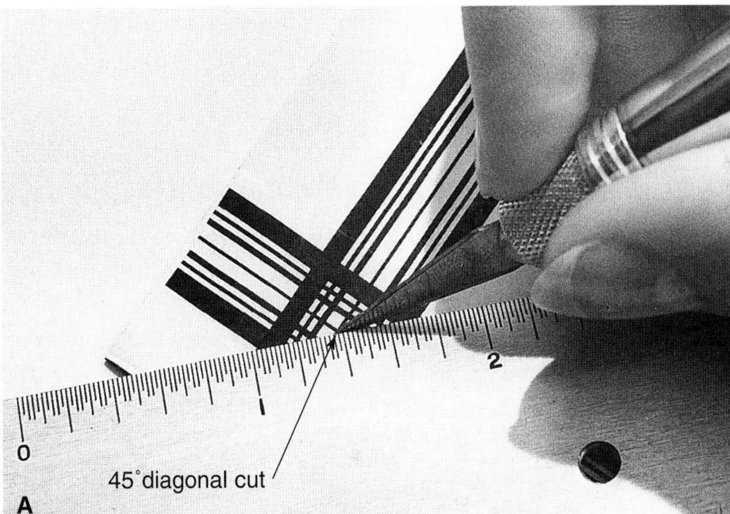

Figure 7-24. Making a mitered corner in preprinted border material. A—Overlap the border tape, then cut through the corner at a 45° angle. B—Carefully remove the overlapping pieces of tape to leave a perfect corner. (Formatt Graphic Products, Inc.)

on the corner. Use a knife to cut the inked circle into quarters. Adhere each piece of the circle over a square corner to complete the border with rounded corners. See **Figure 7-25**.

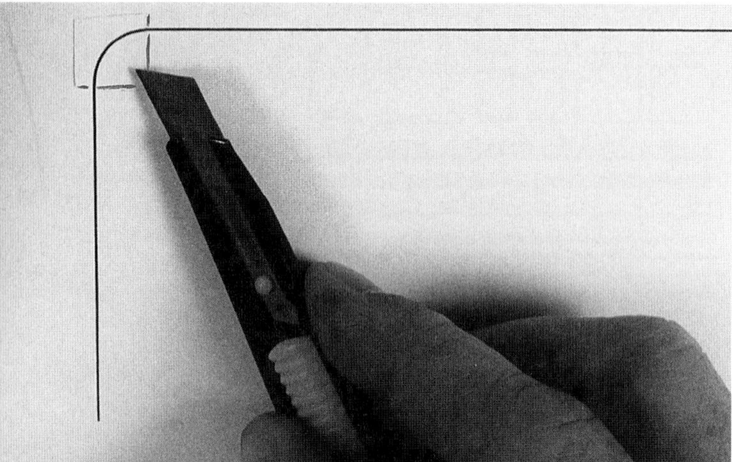

Figure 7-25. One way to draw a round-cornered border is to first draw square corners. Then, draw a complete circle sized to fit the corner. Cut the circle into four equal parts or quadrants. Then, adhere one quadrant over each corner to form the rounded corners.

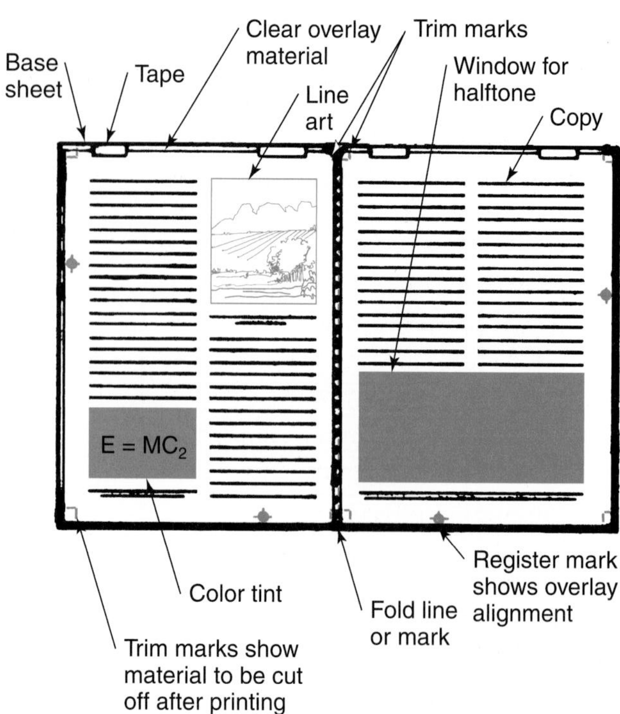

Figure 7-26. A typical mechanical has a number of elements, including various types of guides, type, illustrations, and (often) overlays of masking film used for second colors or windows to permit stripping in halftones.

Assembling the Mechanical

As discussed earlier, a *mechanical* is a pasted-up version of the final printed piece or the camera-ready copy. ***Camera-ready copy*** is material in final form, ready for the photomechanical techniques that convert it to film. The term "mechanical" comes from the word *photomechanical* (photographic and hand assembly).

A mechanical is made up of many elements, **Figure 7-26**. This would include all line work such as: illustrations, type, and any other material that has high contrast and single tonal value. If all the elements are to be printed as one color, it is often possible to have a single mechanical.

The mechanical can be prepared with all elements pasted in place or submitted as a mechanical plus separate art. The positions for the separate pieces of art are indicated on the mechanical as *strip-ins*. The correct location is on the mechanical. The stripping process is described in Chapter 15.

Preparing the base sheet

A base sheet of a size and material appropriate to the job should be selected and adhered to the work surface, such as a drawing board or light table. Usually, drafting tape is used across the corners of the base sheet to hold it firmly in place but allow removal without damaging the surface. If a T-square will be used to align elements during paste-up, it should also be used to properly align the base sheet.

Workmarks are then placed on the base sheet as guides. These marks typically include corner marks, trim marks, centerlines, fold line, and bleed marks. Some workmarks (fold lines, for example) are made with a sharp, nonreproducing blue pencil so they will not appear on the final negative. Others, such as trim marks, are drawn in black. Preprinted marks are available as rub-off or pressure-sensitive images, but many paste-up artists prefer to draw them as a fine inked line. The lines must be drawn with accuracy. These marks are photographed and printed, but are cut off during the binding-finishing process.

Collecting elements

Before paste-up, it is important to collect all the various elements. Gathering all the photos, illustrations, display lines, and body copy contributes to an efficient operation. It is a good idea to check and make sure that all the elements can be positioned according to the layout. Incorrect material must be given immediate attention.

Attaching elements

Since the mechanical becomes the original for photomechanical production, all the elements must be made ready for a single shot by the process or copy camera. When overlays are used, or where material will later be stripped in, more than one shot will be necessary. Typical steps in assembling the mechanical are as follows:

1. Before beginning work on the mechanical, make sure the layout has been approved by an authorized person.
2. Identify the required size of the mechanical and check all job specifications.
3. Lay out the job on the base sheet, using a T-square, triangle, and pencil. Measurements are critical. Make sure the base sheet is large enough to provide margins for all workmarks and instructions. Actual size is preferable.
4. All guidelines and workmarks must be carefully positioned and precisely made. Include register marks, trim marks, bleed marks, fold lines, and image lines as needed.
5. The paste-up artist is responsible for making any irregular shapes. This would also include the positioning of borders and other line materials.
6. Trim the line image materials. Repro proofs, phototypesetter copy, clip art, and other images should be trimmed to leave a margin of about 1/8″ from the image area. Scissors, paper cutter, knife, and razor blade are common tools to trim material. See **Figure 7-27.**
7. Adhere all line copy (artwork, photocomposed type, and lettering) to the base sheet in the required positions, following the layout. Elements are adhered with wax, rubber cement, or tape.
8. Attach any necessary overlays and adhere all necessary elements to them. Place register marks on the base sheet and overlay.
9. Prepare any windows necessary for material to be stripped into the page. Indicate the outline of the window with a thin black keyline, or cut masking film the exact size of the desired window area.
10. Indicate any separate art on the mechanical. Key each piece of art to the mechanical for positive identification. Use a spray fixative on artwork and other elements, where necessary, to assure that the surface will not smudge.
11. Clean excess wax or other adhering material from the mechanical. Dirty mechanical art is not acceptable.
12. If additional instructions are needed, write them on a vellum or tissue sheet hinged to the base sheet.
13. Cover the mechanical with a paper flap for protection. Kraft paper is commonly used.
14. Make sure the mechanical is properly identified with the name of the source, the job number, and other necessary information.

Figure 7-27. A scissors or other cutting tool should be used to closely trim art and other page elements before they are adhered to the base sheet.

Applying overlays

As noted earlier, an ***overlay*** often must be attached to the mechanical base sheet. The transparent or translucent overlay sheet is often the base for the second color material. Each additional color usually requires a separate overlay sheet. Overlay preparation includes drawing the guidelines necessary for the additional color and positioning all workmarks. The art or type is then placed in proper position on the overlay.

Register marks

Register marks are control devices that assure the proper positioning of overlays on the layout sheet. As an example, if one color overlay is used with a layout sheet, register marks are placed on the outside border of the layout sheet. Then, with the overlay in exact position, another set of register marks is adhered to the overlay sheet, **Figure 7-28**. The layout sheet marks and the overlay marks must be directly on top of each other or "in register." If additional overlays are used, they must also be aligned with the original set of register marks.

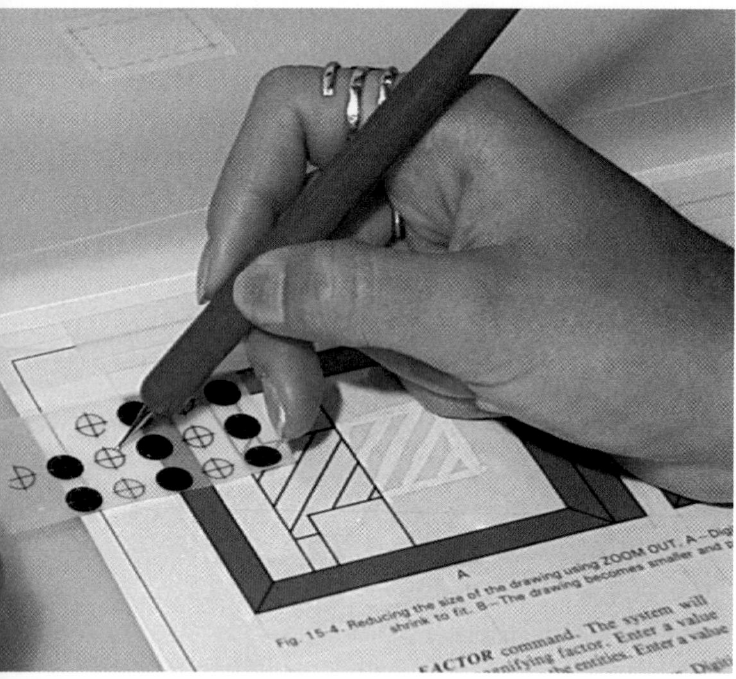

Figure 7-28. Register marks must be carefully placed on both the base sheet and overlay to help ensure that the two are properly aligned. If more than one overlay is used, each must have a set of register marks. (Jack Klasey)

The number and positioning of register marks will vary from one facility to another. You can place register marks on one side and the bottom of the page, but for best control, the marks should be placed on three sides.

Register may be loose or tight, depending upon the job requirements. ***Loose register***, also called *non-critical register*, can be used when copy does not need extremely accurate alignment. For example, this can be used when images are next to each other but are printed in different colors. One image is not placed on top of the other. ***Tight register*** (sometimes referred to as *hairline register*) refers to registration that must be very accurate. Color registration is usually critical and would require tight register.

The term ***out-of-register*** refers to images that are not properly aligned. This could be due to layout error or misalignment during printing. See **Figure 7-29**.

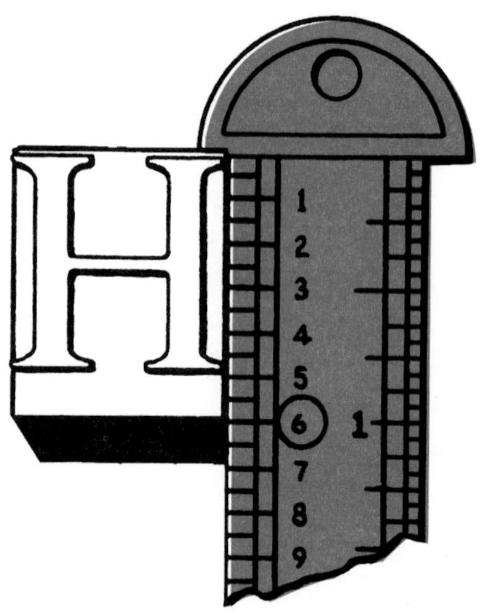

Figure 7-29. When images are not properly aligned on the printed product, they are said to be "out-of-register." The problem can result from a paste-up error, a mistake in stripping, or misalignment on the press.

Producing good quality mechanicals

Although paste-up methods can vary from one person to another, a properly prepared mechanical will present few difficulties for any of the printing processes. Keeping these factors in mind will help you produce good quality work:

- Carefully proofread all type elements. Proofreading is essential to producing a quality product.
- Size all elements properly. Accurate sizing is critical.
- Check all line elements for proper density.
- Inspect continuous tone prints to be sure they display proper tonal range.
- Correct or replace any defective elements.
- Determine if "in position" (pasted-up) or separate art is required.

- Accurately position all elements on the mechanical. Make sure that registration of overlays is precise.
- Clearly state any instructions for the job.
- Clean all artwork carefully following paste-up. Protecting the mechanical with a paper flap will help it stay clean.

Figure 7-30. A page composition program (in this case, Adobe PageMaker) is used to perform "electronic paste-up," permitting the operator to combine text and graphics into individual or multiple pages. (Apple Computer, Inc.)

Electronic Page Composition

Today, the major tool for page composition is the computer. Software specifically designed for page composition, such as QuarkXPress™ or Adobe PageMaker™, allows the operator to combine text and graphics into page formats that can be output to a laser printer, imagesetter, or even directly to a digital press. See **Figure 7-30**. Although the programs have individual differences in the way they accomplish page composition, many of the features are similar.

Screen display

The screen display produced by different page composition programs will vary in details, but also have many features in common. As shown in **Figure 7-31**, a menu bar occupies the top of the screen, while scroll bars are on the bottom and one side. The scroll bars, when used with a mouse pointer, shift the screen view up and down or left and right.

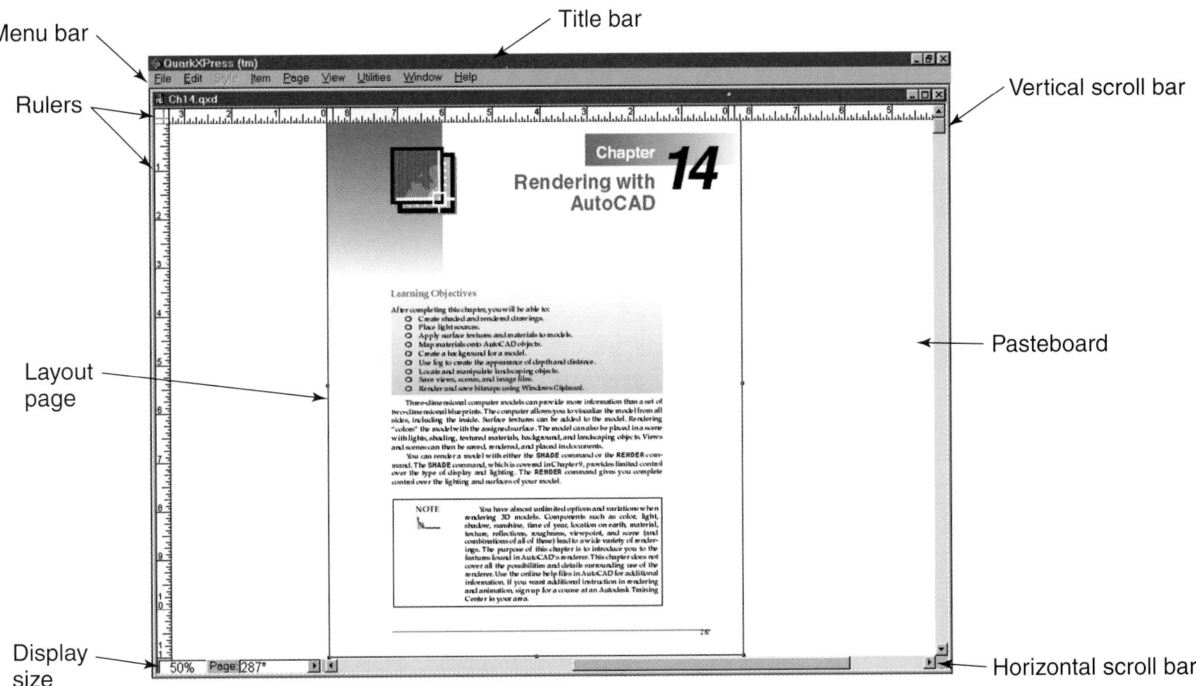

Figure 7-31. Screen layout of one popular page composition program (QuarkXPress), with menu bar along the top and scroll bars down the right side and at bottom. The Pasteboard is a work area, outside the page being composed, used for temporary storage and preliminary assembly of page elements.

Pasteboard

The major portion of the screen display includes the page or pages being laid out, and a work area usually called the ***pasteboard.*** This area of the screen is used for temporary storage of layout elements (such as a piece of art or a section of typeset material) before moving them onto the layout page. The pasteboard also can be used to try out ideas for design elements, type treatments, and other manipulations.

Page grid

The *page grid,* sometimes called a *frame* or *baseline grid,* is a nonprinting set of guidelines on each layout page. Guidelines for margins, columns, gutters and other basic page elements are included in the grid. One important function of the grid is to align type horizontally when the page is arranged in two or more columns. The page composition software allows the operator to display or hide the grid lines, depending upon preference.

Dropdown menus

Selecting one of the items on the menu bar, using a mouse or the keyboard, will cause a menu of choices to extend downward from the bar. These ***dropdown menus*** contain a number of choices that can be used to create or modify documents, **Figure 7-32.** The Page menu, for example, is used to insert, delete, or move pages within a document, as well as providing choices for quickly moving from page to page. Other menus available from the menu bar are *File, Edit, Style, Item, View, Utilities, Window,* and *Help.*

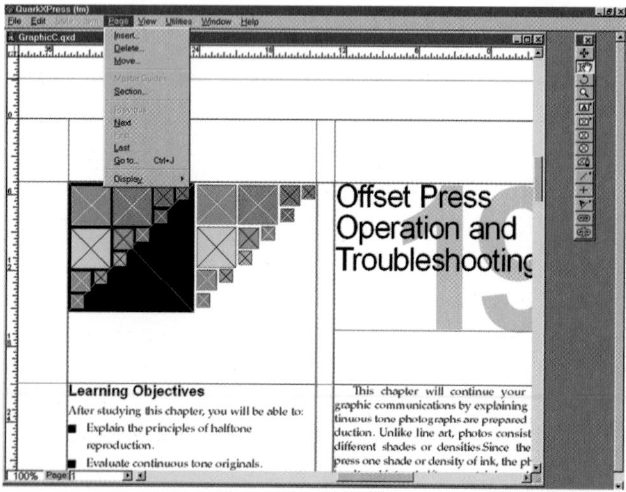

Figure 7-32. Selecting one of the items on the menu bar will open a dropdown menu with a number of choices.

Some menus are *context-sensitive.* This means the menu which appears depends on the type of material being worked on at the time the menu is selected. The *Style* menu, for example, may display a list of choices for text, for pictures, or for lines. Selecting some items on a dropdown menu will display a *submenu* that is used to make a choice. See **Figure 7-33.**

Dialog boxes

Selecting an item on a dropdown menu often will open a ***dialog box,*** which permits the operator to input information, **Figure 7-34.** This information might include specifying an action, inputting measurements, selecting colors, or applying a style. Some dialog boxes include *dropdown lists,* similar to submenus, that can be used to make a selection.

Palettes

These are a modified form of menu that can be resized and positioned on the screen to suit the operator's preferences. A ***palette*** can also be displayed or hidden. When displayed, it will always remain visible, overlaying any other images on the screen, as shown in **Figure 7-35.**

Although there are more than a half-dozen palettes available, the ***Tool palette*** is the most-often used, since it allows the operator to perform many different layout functions. The tool palette displays icons (symbols) for the different tools that can be selected. These include

- The *Item tool* is used to select a box, line, or other item on the screen so that it can be moved, resized, or reshaped.
- Although it can duplicate most of the tasks performed by the Item tool, the most important functions of the *Content tool* are importing and editing text and pictures.
- The *Rotation tool* is used to establish a point, then rotate an item (box or line) around that point.
- The view of an item displayed on the screen can be enlarged or reduced with the *Zoom tool.*

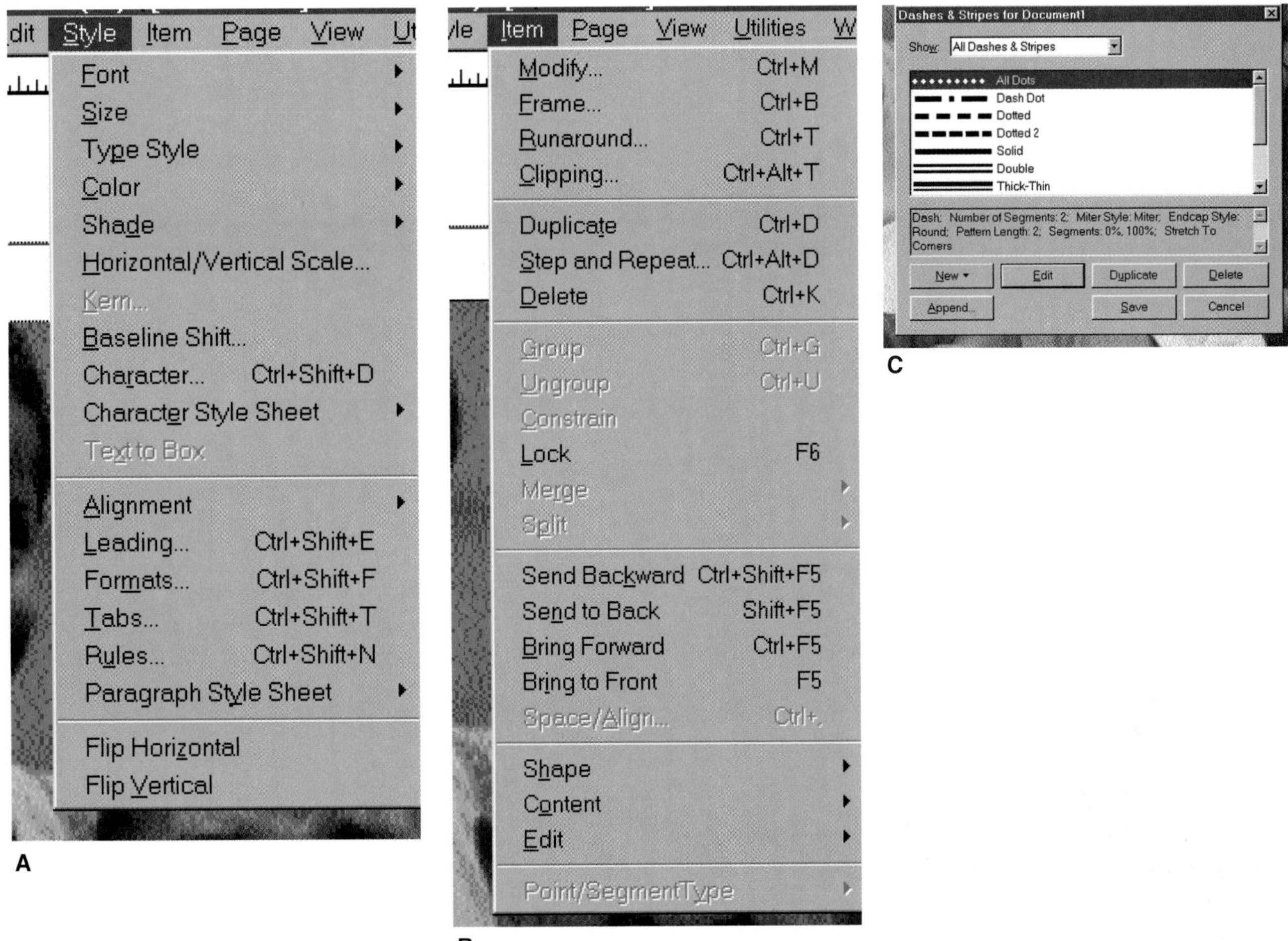

Figure 7-33. Context sensitive menus will change, depending upon the type of material being worked on. When Style is selected on the menu bar, one of these three dropdown menus will appear. A—Style text menu. B—Style picture menu. C—Style line menu.

- A text box must be created on a layout page to position text. The *Text Box tool* performs this task. A submenu that pops out to the side of the palette allows selection of different text box shapes.
- Several *Picture Box tools* (rectangular, rounded-corner, etc.) are displayed on the Tool palette. Selecting the rectangular Picture Box tool icon will open a popout menu with additional choices.
- The *Line tool* is used to draw a straight line that can be at any angle. A popout menu allows selection of tools for drawing freehand line shapes.
- To draw a line that is precisely horizontal or vertical on a page, the *Orthogonal Line tool* is used.
- The *Line-Text Path tool* allows straight lines of text to be positioned at any angle. A popout menu provides other options, such as arranging text along a freehand-drawn line.
- Text that is contained in two or more text boxes can be chained together with the *Linking tool*. This permits text to reflow freely from box to box as dimensions or type sizes are changed.
- The *Unlinking tool* disconnects text chains between boxes.

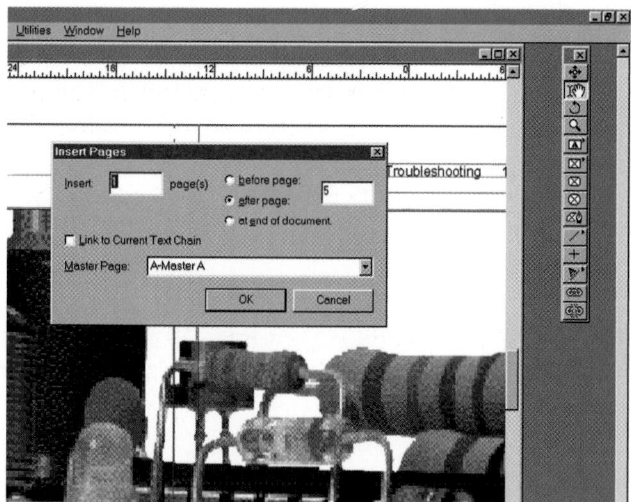

Figure 7-34. A dialog box permits the operator to input information. This dialog box appeared when the operator selected Insert from the Page menu. As shown, it allows specification of the number of pages to be inserted, and where they are to be placed. The down-pointing triangle to the right of the Master Page window indicates a drop-down list. Clicking on the triangle would reveal a list of Master Pages that have been created for this document.

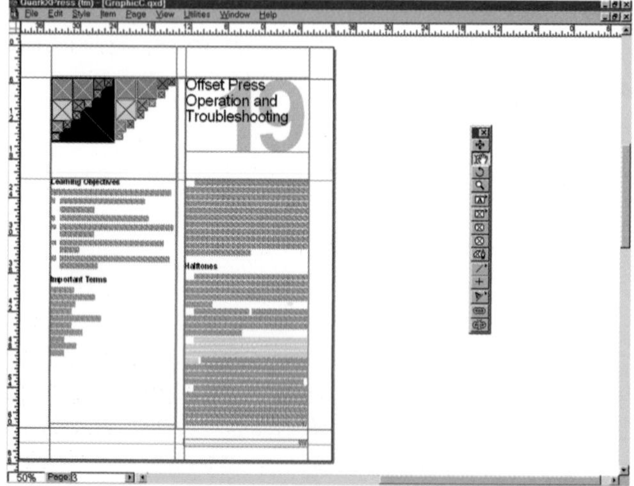

Figure 7-35. A palette is a form of list or menu that can be displayed or hidden and can be positioned at any place on the screen that the operator chooses. This is the Tool Palette, used for many layout functions.

Master pages and templates

The design of a document typically will result in certain common attributes that are repeated from page to page or section to section. Attributes such as column widths, margins, page numbers, and headers and footers, will often be repeated. It is also common to have several different page formats within a document. The page geometry, typography, and other elements in each of these page formats can be set up as a ***master page***.

A ***template*** that incorporates all the master pages and other formatting can then be created and saved. The operator can easily set up a new publication or page with similar attributes by opening the reusable template, then customizing the page formats as necessary. The main advantage of using a template is increased operator productivity and reduced time spent recreating the same page information.

Page composition

In QuarkXPress, devices called "boxes" are the basis of page composition. A box (which is a closed figure of any shape from rectangular to freeform) can be either a ***text box*** or a ***picture box***. Text can also be placed along a ***text path***, which allows for various forms of typographic manipulation. See **Figure 7-36**.

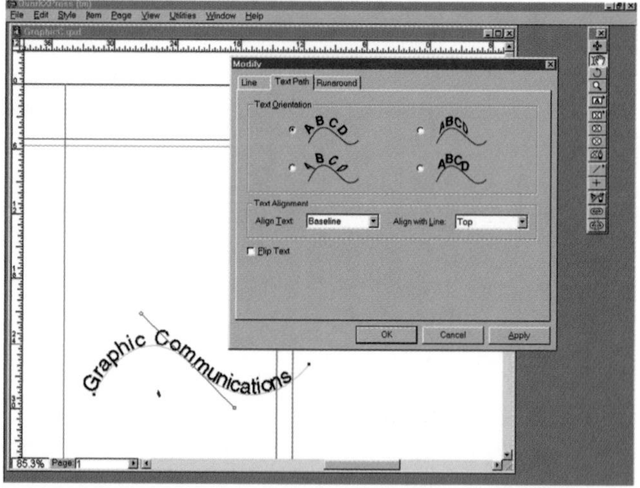

Figure 7-36. In addition to being placed in a text box, words may also be shaped along a text path, providing interesting effects.

Importing text

Although page composition programs have capabilities for the input and editing of text, documents of more than a few paragraphs in length are usually created with a word processing program. The text file is then imported into the page composition program and placed in one or more text boxes.

Formatting of the text (boldface and italics, tabs, indents, line spacing, and similar parameters) that was done in the original word processing document may be retained when the text is imported through use of a ***text filter***. Text filters are available for major word processing programs. If no filter is available or the imported material is unformatted ***ASCII*** (American Standard Code For Information Interchange) text, formatting must be done in the page composition program.

Style sheets used in page composition programs (and some word processing programs) are formatting tools that combine a number of attributes. A *paragraph style sheet* can include such information as alignment (left, right, centered), indents (paragraph, hanging, etc.), leading between lines, space before and after the paragraph, and such typeface information as font, point size, bold, or italic. Usually, different paragraph style sheets are created to format specific elements of the document: body text, major headings, subheadings, numbered lists, lists with bullets, or illustration captions.

A *character style sheet* is more specialized, and is typically applied to single letters, words, or phrases. A character style sheet might be used to set off all figure (illustration) references in the text by specifying a type font and point size different from body text, for example. A major advantage of using style sheets is the ability to accomplish changes quickly and thoroughly. For example, changing the attributes of a heading style from centered 18-point Helvetica Bold to flush left 16-point Cooper Black would take only seconds, and would switch every occurrence of that heading from one to the other.

Importing graphics

As is the case with text, *line art* is usually imported, rather than being created with the limited capabilities of the page composition program. Both bitmapped graphics created with paint programs and object-oriented graphics created with draw or illustration programs can be imported and placed in a picture box. *Photographs* are first scanned to convert them to a digital format, then imported to a picture box.

Once the graphic image is in a picture box, it can be manipulated in various ways to suit the page layout. The graphic image can be enlarged or reduced, cropped, moved around on the page, changed in color, or edited and distorted in various ways. The amount of manipulation, and its success visually, is affected by the format in which it was imported. For example, bitmap images do not enlarge very well — as they are increased in size, the tiny blocks (pixels) that make them up increase as well, giving the image a blocky, ragged-edged look. The image is said to be "pixeled." See **Figure 7-37**. Graphics file formats are covered in detail in Chapter 9.

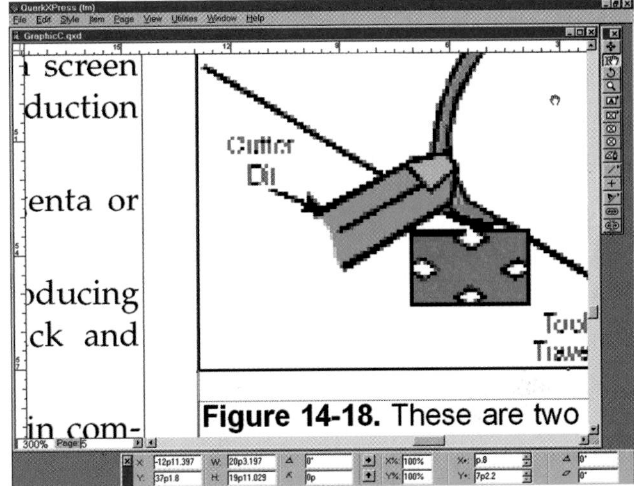

Figure 7-37. Bitmapped image cannot be enlarged by more than a small percentage, or the individual pixels will begin to become apparent. The image is said to be "pixeled," and exhibits a blocky and ragged-edged appearance.

"Drag-and-drop" manipulation

Although keyboard commands are used for many functions of the page composition program, a mouse or other pointing device is commonly employed for quickly and easily manipulating page elements. A text box or picture box, for example, can be resized by clicking the mouse pointer on a side or corner, then stretching or "dragging" it to the desired new size. See **Figure 7-38**. In the same way, a section of text can be selected, then dragged and "dropped" into a new position on the layout. Material can be dragged off the page to the pasteboard for temporary storage or manipulation, or dragged off the pasteboard and dropped into the page.

Color separations

Instead of the physical overlays used in paste-up to prepare material for color printing, page composition software produces ***separation plates*** for

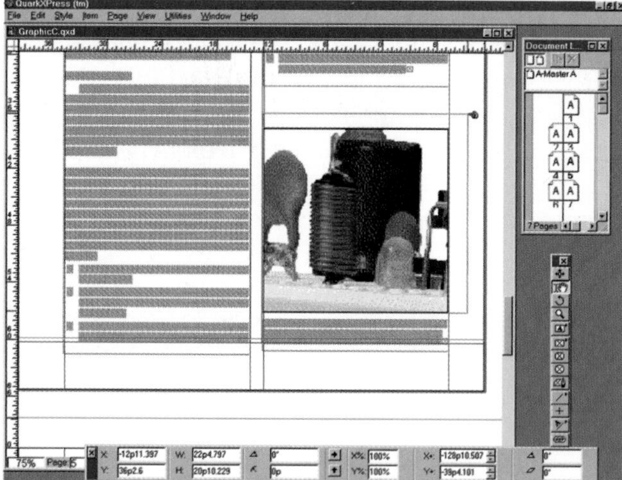

Figure 7-38. Boxes can be changed in size and shape by dragging with the mouse pointer to the desired size. With "drag-and-drop" manipulation, text or illustration elements can be selected, moved to a new location, then released.

each color on a page. For example, a page with black type and an illustration of a large red apple would be put out as two "plates." If an imagesetter was used for output, one plate would be used to create a negative or actual press plate to print the black material; the other plate would be used for the material that would print red. If the page contained a full-color photograph, *four* separation plates would be created: one each for printing with cyan, magenta, yellow, and black inks. These four "process colors" are used in combination to print all colors. Color science and its relation to printing processes is explored in detail in Chapter 8.

Review Questions

Please do not write in this text. Write your answers on a separate sheet of paper.

1. What is the difference between a layout and a mechanical?
2. Why is a light blue pencil commonly used by the paste-up artist?
3. A _____ is commonly used to rule lines and to make camera-ready illustrations in ink.
4. Explain two methods of positioning very small pieces of copy.
5. _____ is most commonly used in paste-up work to adhere elements to the base sheet.
   a. Double-sided tape
   b. Heated wax
   c. Rubber cement
   d. Spray adhesive
6. A _____ is a tool used to firmly adhere waxed copy to the base sheet.
7. _____ is commonly used to hold the paste-up base sheet on the drawing board or light table.
8. Describe two uses for masking film.
9. Why are register marks used with overlays?
10. What does the term "camera-ready copy" mean?
11. What is page composition software?
12. Which of the following is not a common feature of the computer screen display for a page composition program?
    a. Scroll bars.
    b. Pasteboard.
    c. Scanner port.
    d. Menu bar.
13. The baseline grid displayed by a page composition program includes a variety of nonprinting _____ used for aligning elements.
14. In relation to menus for a page composition program, what does the term "context sensitive" mean?
15. A program feature that allows the operator to input information (such as a measurement) is called a _____.
16. What is the function of the Zoom tool in a page composition program?
17. A reusable _____ contains all the master pages and other formatting that make up a multi-page document.
18. The QuarkXPress page composition program is based on the use of _____ boxes and _____ boxes for positioning elements on a page.
19. A _____ is used to retain the original formatting of text when it is imported from a word processing program.
20. Why do bitmapped images not enlarge well?

Color Science, Vision, and Space

8

Learning Objectives

After studying this chapter, you will be able to:

- Describe the basic principles of visible light.
- Explain how we perceive colors.
- Define color space.
- Use the color wheel to explain the relationships between primary, secondary, and tertiary colors.
- Define the HSB, HVC, CIE, and Pantone color systems.
- Describe both the additive color mixing and subtractive color mixing methods.
- Explain the basics principles of color separation.
- Describe how viewing deficiencies and external conditions affect color perception.
- Identify the various color measurement instruments.

Important Terms

electromagnetic spectrum
visible light
additive primary colors
brightness
adaptation
saturation
hue
value
chroma
primary subtractive colors

Color plays many important roles in our daily lives. Besides the aesthetic benefits to our surroundings, the use of color on any medium can greatly enhance communication. Color can be used to grab attention, set a mood, or clarify images.

Colors should maintain consistency throughout the production process. This is especially true when so many products are recognized simply by the colors on their labels or logos. To accomplish this type of consistency, everyone from the graphic designer to the press operator should have a basic understanding of color.

Color Science

Without light, there is no color. Therefore, before being able to understand color science, you must understand a few principles of light.

Principles of light

Our eyes are sensitive only to the small part of the ***electromagnetic spectrum*** known as ***visible light***. The electromagnetic spectrum consists of bands of different wavelengths ranging from radio waves to gamma rays, **Figure 8-1**. The wavelengths are usually measured in nanometers (nm). A nanometer is equal to one billionth of a meter. Another unit used to measure the wavelength of light is the Angstrom (Å). Ten angstroms are equal to 1 nm. Visible light includes wavelengths ranging from 400 nm—770 nm and contains all the colors we can see. Each wavelength is seen as a different color. Red light has the longest visible wavelength (630 nm—770 nm) and violet has the shortest (410 nm—440 nm).

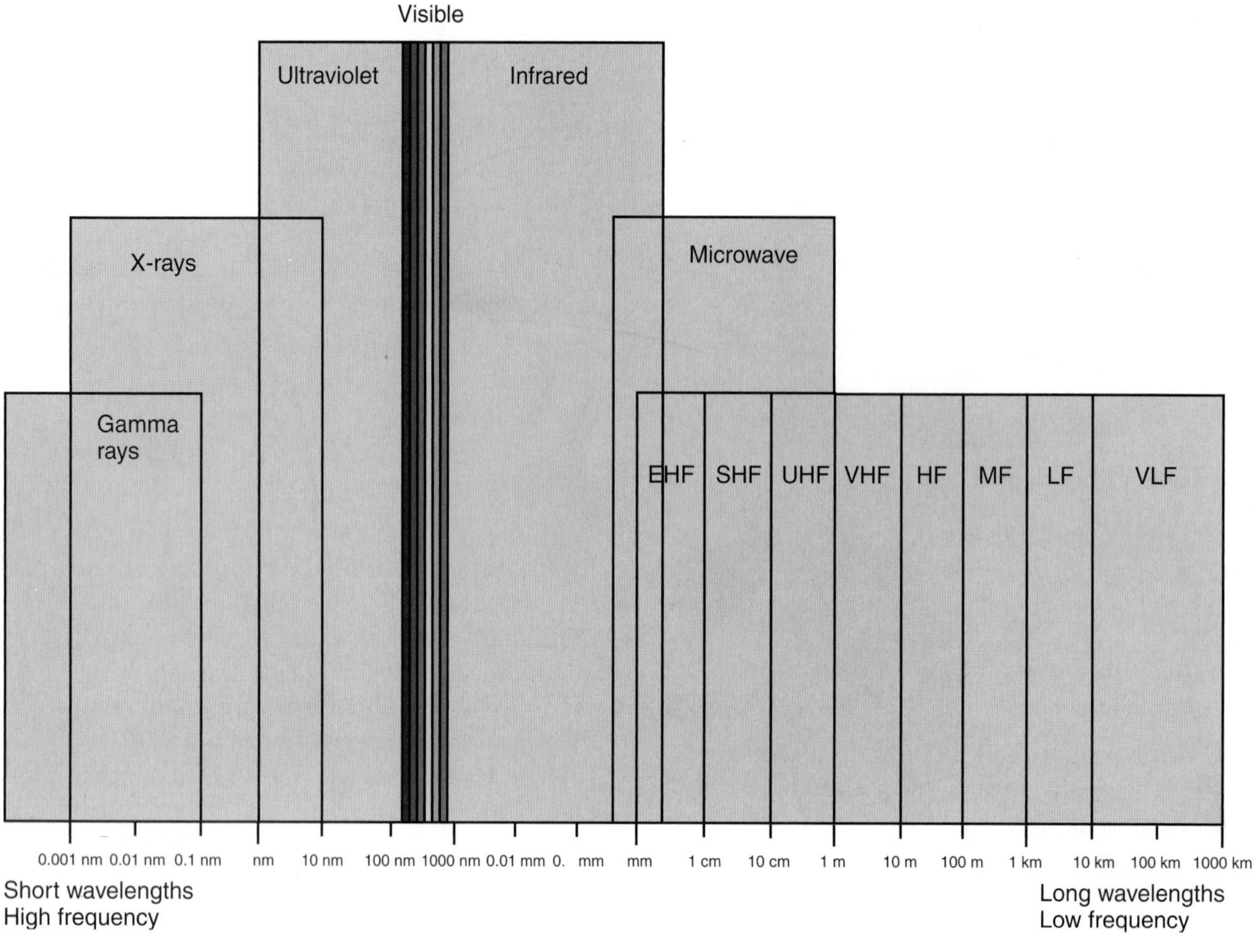

Visible

Ultraviolet

Infrared

X-rays

Microwave

Gamma rays

EHF SHF UHF VHF HF MF LF VLF

0.001 nm 0.01 nm 0.1 nm nm 10 nm 100 nm 1000 nm 0.01 mm 0. mm mm mm 1 cm 10 cm 1 m 10 m 100 m 1 km 10 km 100 km 1000 km

Short wavelengths
High frequency

Long wavelengths
Low frequency

Figure 8-1. The electromagnetic spectrum illustrated above shows how small the range of visible light actually is. Each color has its own wavelength or frequency.

Most light sources, including the sun, emit what appears to be white light, but that light is actually a combination of roughly equal parts of all the visible wavelengths. Using a prism, white light can be broken down into six major colors, **Figure 8-2**. A ***continuous spectrum*** is created when sunlight is passed through a prism. The spectrum blends smoothly from one color to the next. Many other

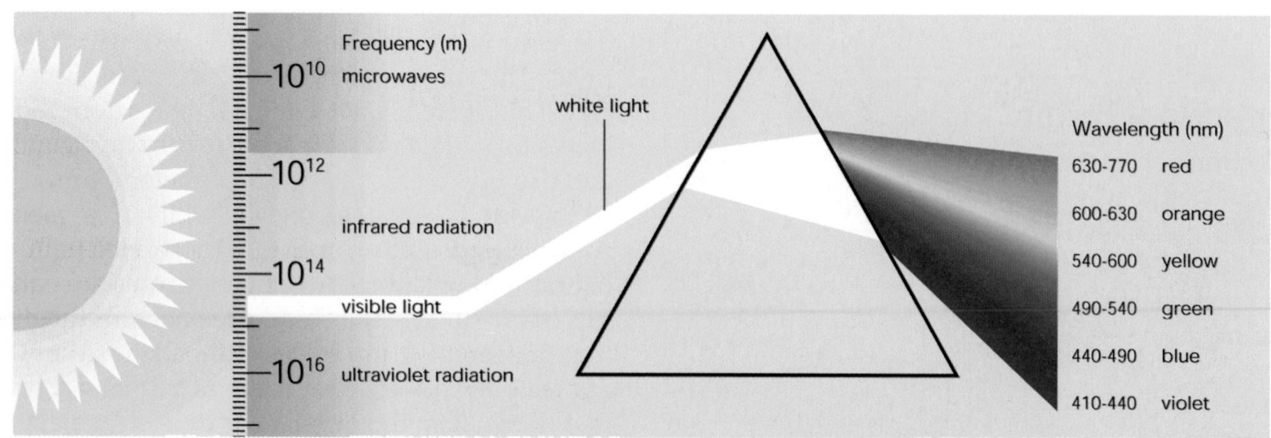

Figure 8-2. Passing light through a prism disperses the light so that our eyes can perceive individual wavelengths. The shorter waves are dispersed more than the longer waves so violet is always at the bottom and red is always at the top. (Thomas Detrie and C. Phillips)

sources of light do not produce a continuous spectrum. For example, a sodium vapor street light may produce bright yellow, blue, and a few dimmer colors, but it also has dark regions in its spectrum. This difference in light sources greatly influences individual perception of colors.

Temperature of light

The color of light is measured in Kelvin (K). In terms of ***color temperature***, the blues and violets are the warmest colors and the reds and oranges are the coolest. This range of colors can be demonstrated by heating a piece of metal called a *black body*. As the black body is heated to higher and higher temperatures, it emits a light in a range of colors. Beginning with dull red, it moves through orange, yellow, and white. If no chemical or physical change occurred, the metal would eventually emit blue light. The color of light emitted from the black body can therefore be described by its temperature. The chart in **Figure 8-3** lists the approximate color temperatures of some common light sources.

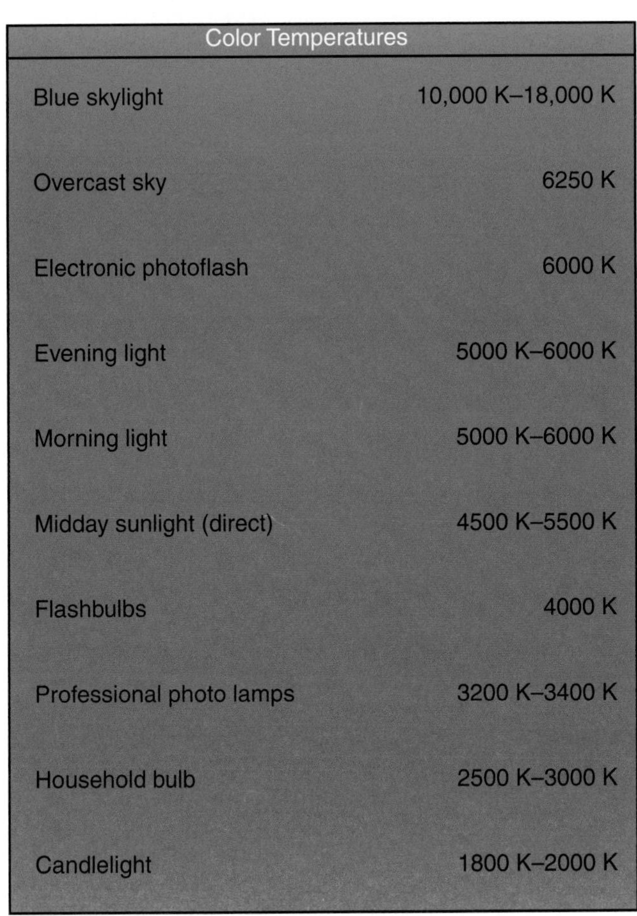

Color Temperatures	
Blue skylight	10,000 K–18,000 K
Overcast sky	6250 K
Electronic photoflash	6000 K
Evening light	5000 K–6000 K
Morning light	5000 K–6000 K
Midday sunlight (direct)	4500 K–5500 K
Flashbulbs	4000 K
Professional photo lamps	3200 K–3400 K
Household bulb	2500 K–3000 K
Candlelight	1800 K–2000 K

Figure 8-3. Approximate color temperatures of some common light sources.

Behavior of light

When light travels through a continuous medium, it travels in a straight line. However, when light reaches a surface or boundary between two types of material, such as air and water, several things can happen. Some of the light may reflect from the surface, while some may pass through it. The light that enters the second material may refract (bend). In addition, some of the light may be scattered or absorbed.

Reflection

A beam of light coming toward a surface is called the ***incident beam***. After the beam has been reflected, it is called the ***reflected beam***, **Figure 8-4**. Depending on the type of material, the reflected beam may contain a different mixture of light waves than the incident beam. If the mixture is different, the new combination of wavelengths gives the object its color. For instance, a red book exposed to white light appears red because the surface absorbs all other colors in the light. In other words, the only light waves reflected off the red cover are the wavelengths in the red portion of the spectrum.

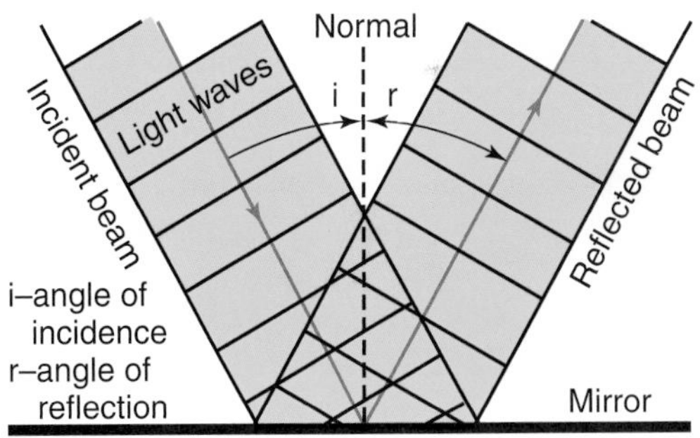

Figure 8-4. The angle that the incident beam makes with an imaginary line (*normal*) at right angles to the surface, is equal to the angle made by the reflected beam.

Refraction

When light passes through a surface at any angle except a right angle (perpendicular to the surface), the change in the light's speed alters its direction. In other words, the light refracts (bends), **Figure 8-5**. The amount of bending depends on the type of material the light wave enters. Refraction can be demonstrated by placing a pencil in a glass of water. The pencil appears to be bent at the water surface. The light from the top part of the pencil

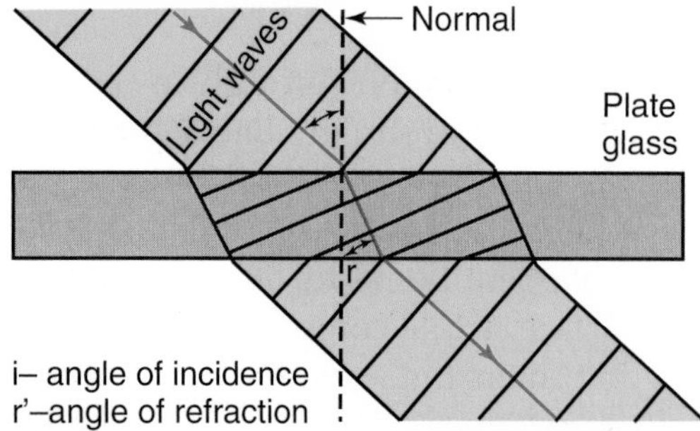

Figure 8-5. Refraction causes a beam of light to bend as it passes from one substance into another. The beam bends toward the normal (imaginary line) if it slows down when entering a substance. The angle of refraction would be less than the angle of incidence. If light travels faster in the substance, the beam bends away from the normal.

comes directly to your eyes, while the light from the bottom passes through the surface between the water and the air.

Scattering

Scattering occurs when light waves strike the molecules of another substance. The molecules cause the waves to scatter. A clear sky appears blue because air molecules scatter more of the shorter (blue) wavelengths of white sunlight than the longer wavelengths.

Interference

When two light waves cross through the same spot, they interfere with each other. The interference between light waves can occur in two ways, as ***constructive interference*** or as ***destructive interference***. If you think of light in the form of a wave with crests and troughs, constructive interference occurs when the crests of more than one light wave pass through the same point at the same time. At this point, the light is brighter than any one wave emits alone. Destructive interference occurs when the crest of one wave crosses the same point as the trough of another wave. The trough reduces the height of the crest, leaving the spot very dim or even dark.

Diffraction

As stated earlier, light waves usually travel in straight lines. However, when passing through an opening or slit, around a small object, or beyond an edge, light waves ***diffract*** (spread out) into curving waves.

The diffraction of light is useful when studying colors in a light beam. For instance, scientists are able to separate colors in the light from a star using a ***diffraction grating***. The grating uses thousands of thin slits to diffract light. Each color in the light diffracts by a slightly different amount and the spread of colors can be large enough to make each color visible. Astronomers use this information to determine the makeup of the star.

Diffraction can also be a hindrance. For example, as the magnifying power of a high-quality microscope is increased, the edges of the object being viewed begin to blur. The edges blur because the light passing over the edge on its way to the eye diffracts.

The Human Visual System

A photomechanical reaction that occurs in the eye when light stimulates retinal receptors allows us to see. These receptors supply electrical impulse patterns to the brain. The images are formed in the mind and take on meaning for the viewer, **Figure 8-6**. Exactly how the brain makes us aware of colors is still much of a mystery.

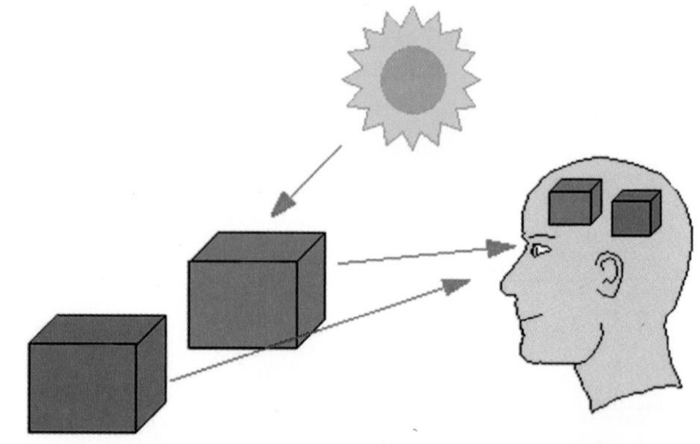

Figure 8-6. Color perception is based upon the light-sensitive receptors of the eye. After information is collected by the eye, electrical impulses are sent to the brain where the images take on meaning for the viewer.

When light reaches the eye, it is focused onto the ***retina***, a layer of light-sensitive cells at the back of the eye. This occurs mainly by refraction at the front of the ***cornea***, a transparent window at the front of the eye. A special lens behind the pupil and the eye's muscles control adjustments made for focusing. The ***iris*** controls the amount of light entering the eye by altering the size of the pupil—from 0.08″ (2 mm) in bright sunlight to 0.3″ (8 mm) at night. See **Figure 8-7**.

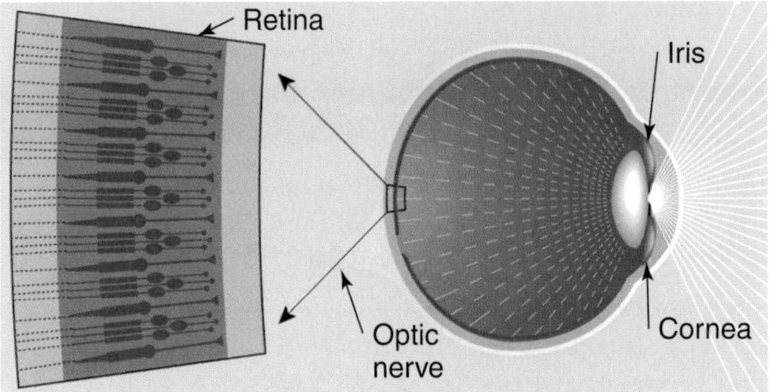

Figure 8-7. The rods and cones are located in the retina of the human eye.

Our perception of light and color is determined by the light-sensitive nerve cells of the retina known as ***rods*** and ***cones***. There are about twelve million rods and seven million cones in the human eye. The rods detect light intensity and are most sensitive to black, white, and shades of gray. Very little light is needed to stimulate the rods, so they are particularly important for night vision.

The retina has three types of cones that detect both intensity and wavelength (color). The cones contain light-sensitive chemicals called ***photopigments*** that respond to either red, green, or blue. These three colors are the ***additive primary colors*** and are usually referred to as RGB. All colors are mixtures of signals from these three types of cone receptors. In other words, colors are perceived according to which cones are stimulated by wavelengths of the light entering the eye.

This color-mixing ability allows us to perceive a multitude of colors derived from the three primaries. For example, despite yellow's pure appearance, it is not a pure color. There is no retinal receptor sensitive to the yellow frequency. The color yellow is perceived through the combined activity of the red-sensitive and green-sensitive cones.

The ***macula*** is a small hollow in the middle of the retina. The cones are concentrated in the macula and diminish in concentration toward the edges of the retina. At the center of the macula is the ***fovea***, the most sensitive part of the retina. The fovea is packed with cone cells and is the area of sharpest vision. Unlike rods, the cones need high levels of light. This is why colors often appear muted or absent at night.

Brightness and intensity

The cones and rods of the retina are extremely sensitive light detectors. Even the smallest amount of radiant energy stimulates them. It is the intensity of light entering the eye that causes the sensation of ***brightness***. Brightness is often referred to as ***lightness*** or ***luminosity***, and can be defined as a value indicating how light or dark a color is.

Bright light bleaches the color-sensitive cones of the retina. This "bleaching" stimulates the nerves. After exposure to bright light, it takes time for the photochemical activity of the eye to return to normal. A good example of this effect is when a subject is temporarily blinded by a camera flash. During the time a region of the retina is "bleached," that region is less sensitive than surrounding regions. This can cause both positive and negative ***afterimages***.

Afterimages are created by the eyes' attempt to restore equilibrium. After gazing for some time at a *green* square and then closing his or her eyes, a viewer will see a *red* square as an afterimage. If the square is red, a green square will be seen as an afterimage. This experiment may be repeated with any color and the afterimage will always be of the complementary color. **Figure 8-8** illustrates this effect. The technical name for this color-vision effect is ***successive contrast***.

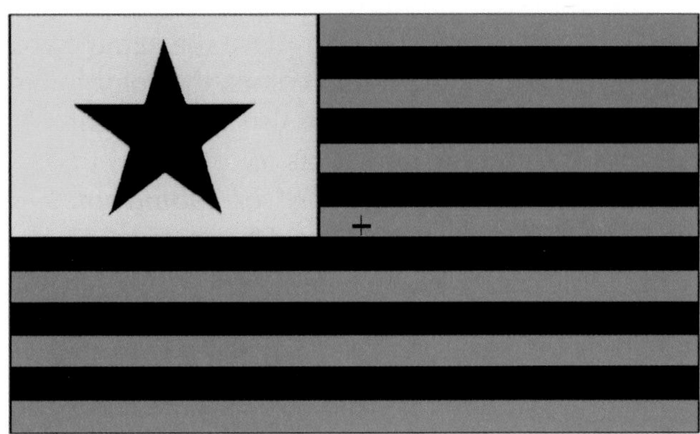

Figure 8-8. To see an afterimage, stare at the center of the flag for about 30 seconds. Then look at a white sheet of paper. You will see an image of the flag with its proper colors.

Adaptation

The adjustment your eyes make to light conditions is called ***adaptation***. If the eyes experience low light for some time, the cones and rods grow more sensitive and light appears brighter. This is ***dark adaptation***. Just as a photographer increases exposure time in a dim lighting situation, the dark adaptation of the eyes increases vision "exposure time" to raise sensitivity.

Your eyes adapt to the color of light in much the same way. This is called ***chromatic adaptation***. A good example of this effect is reading at night using a tungsten lamp that emits light with a yellow cast. The reader's eyes quickly adapt to the yellow color to the point that it is not even noticeable. If the reader steps outside and looks in the window, he or she would clearly see that the light has a yellow cast.

Adaptation makes it difficult to use your naked eye to determine such things as the amount of light needed in certain photographic situations. Adaptation is also part of the reason ***viewing booths*** are used when proofing printed materials. A viewing booth has color-balanced lighting so that anyone viewing the same printed materials will be seeing them under the same lighting conditions.

The cones and rods adapt at different rates. Cone adaptation occurs in about seven minutes, while rod adaptation continues for an hour or more. Decreased light and increased visual sensitivity will reduce the ability to make out fine detail.

Adjacency

The colors surrounding, or ***adjacent*** to, a subject affect color perception. If you place the same color against different background colors, the color looks different in each case. A color also looks brighter if the surroundings are dark. This color-vision effect is called ***chromatic induction*** or ***simultaneous contrast***.

A color will also look more ***saturated*** if surrounded by a complementary color. ***Saturation*** is the attribute of color that defines its degree of strength, or difference from white. It can also be defined as the extent to which one or two of the three RGB primaries predominates in a color. The contrast enhancement created by the surrounding color is related to the general importance of borders in perception. It is primarily the color area borders that signal the mind, **Figure 8-9**.

Figure 8-9. When a color is viewed against a light background, it appears darker. When the same color is viewed against a dark background, it appears lighter.

Color constancy

Color constancy is the tendency to perceive inaccurate nature-specific and object-specific colors as true. Some examples of these "memory" colors are eggshell white, fire engine red, and sky blue. The misperception of skin tones also falls under color constancy. For example, when viewing the printed image of a person, the skin color may appear correct due to the color maintained in the viewer's memory. Color differences become apparent when the person's actual flesh tone is compared to the printed color.

Color space

Science, as well as the graphic communications industry, requires precise color definition and classification. Words are imprecise when used to distinguish and describe color. What one person identifies as yellow-green might be described by another as light green, or "greenish." For this reason, various systems have been devised to establish universal terms for color classification.

The various color systems and color models describe colors through numerical or coordinate means. The numerical values or coordinates allow the colors to be defined within the system's parameters. These parameters define the system's ***color space***. The term *space* is used because color data occur in three dimensions. The color space defines the limits by which the color model can be used. The full range of colors that can be defined by a color model is called a color ***gamut***.

To better define color space, many of the color models are ***triaxial***. A triaxial system involves three axes (vertical, side-to-side, front-to-back). This section addresses the various color spaces in common use today.

Color organization

Color organization begins with two small groups: the pure ***chromatic colors*** or hues, and the ***achromatic colors*** (white, grays, black). All other colors exist within these two extremes.

The color wheel

Although the color wheel is not a triaxial system, it is useful for demonstrating the relationships among colors, **Figure 8-10**. A color wheel consists of a range of colors in the form of a circle. The main colors on the wheel are the primary colors: red, yellow, and blue. The ***secondary colors*** are orange, green, and violet. The other colors on the wheel—yellow-green, blue-green, blue-violet, red-violet, red-orange, and yellow-orange—are called the ***tertiary*** or ***intermediate colors***.

Note that the primary colors shown on the color wheel (red, yellow, blue) differ from the additive primary colors (red, green, blue) mentioned earlier in the discussion of human vision. The colors on the wheel are similar to those involved in the

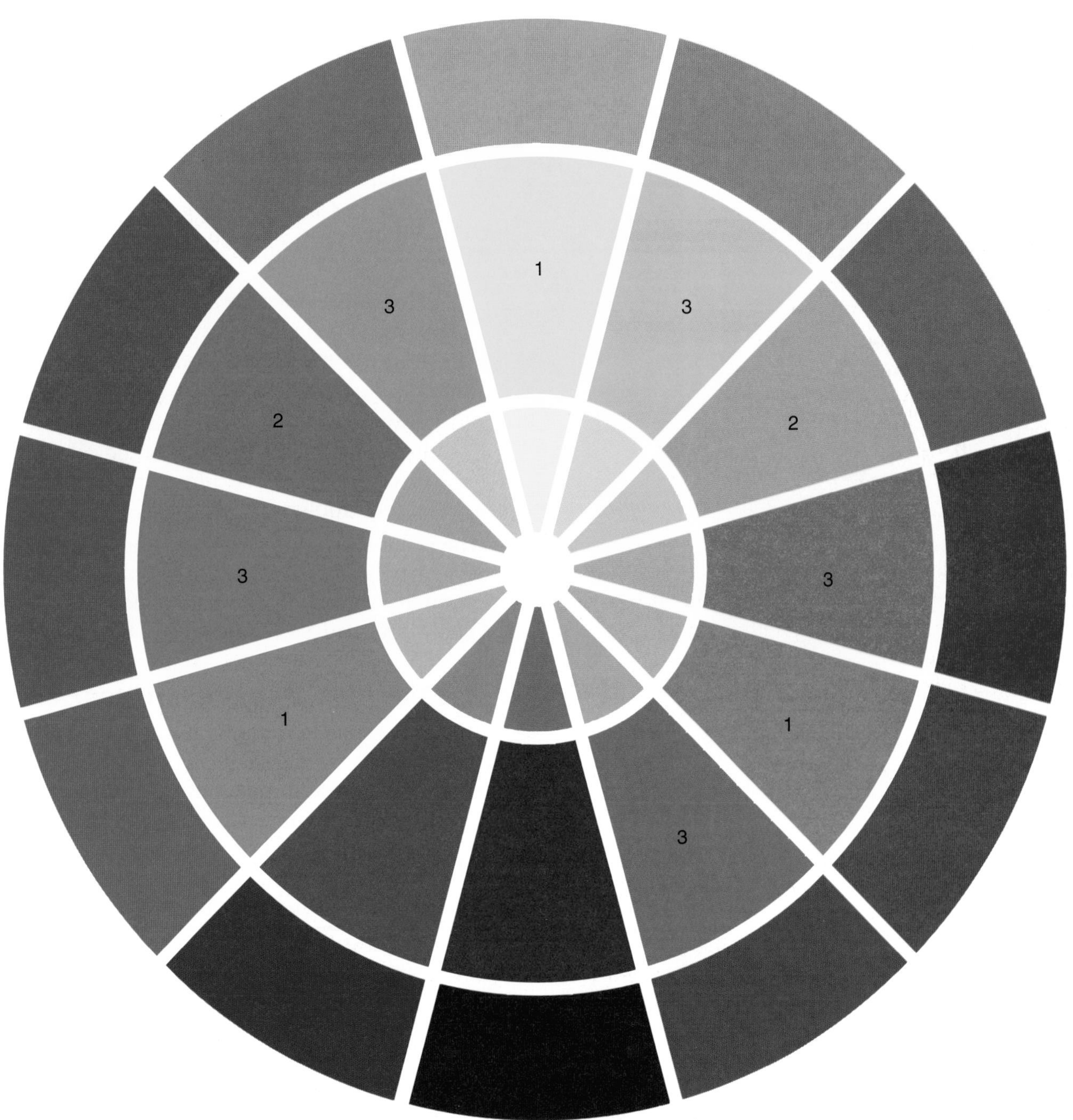

Figure 8-10. This color wheel shows the primary (1), secondary (2), and tertiary colors (3). The middle ring shows the normal values of the colors. The center ring shows the tints and the outer ring shows the shades.

subtractive method of color formation. That method deals with colors provided by pigments (in paint or printing ink, for example) that are viewed by reflected light. Additive and subtractive color formation methods are covered in greater detail later in this chapter.

The secondary colors are created by mixing equal amounts of two of the primaries. For example, orange is made by mixing yellow and red. Green is made by mixing yellow and blue. Violet is made by mixing blue and red. The secondary colors are positioned between the primaries on the color wheel.

The tertiary colors are made by mixing a primary color with a secondary color. They are named after the two colors used to make them. The primary color is always listed first. For example, yellow-orange is created by mixing the primary color yellow with the secondary color orange.

Color triads

Any three colors an equal distance apart on the color wheel compose a color triad. The colors in a triad often go well together so they are important design tools. The primary, secondary, and tertiary colors on the color wheel all form triads, **Figure 8-11**.

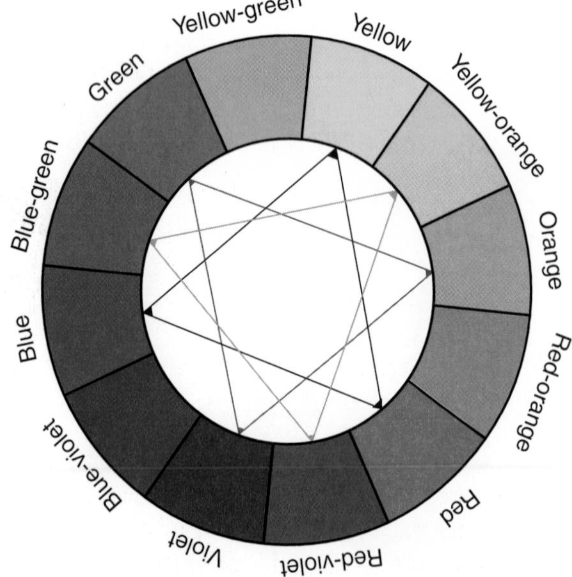

Figure 8-11. The triangles drawn in the center of the color wheel identify three different triads.

Complementary colors

Any two colors that lie directly opposite each other on the color wheel are called ***complementary colors***. Such pairs of complementary colors include red and green, orange and blue, and yellow and violet. A color may also harmonize with colors that lie on either side of its complement, such as red with blue-green or yellow-green. Such colors are called ***near-complementary*** colors or ***split complementary*** colors.

Shades, tints, and tones

Monochromatic color schemes are made up of ***shades***, ***tints***, and ***tones*** of a single color, **Figure 8-12**.

- *Shades* are created by adding black to a color. For example, if black is added to red, the color maroon is created. Maroon is a shade of red.
- *Tints* are created by adding white to a color. When white is added to red, it results in pink. Pink is a tint of red.
- The *tone* or intensity of a color may be lowered or heightened by adding some of its complement. The tone of the color red can be dulled by adding a small amount of its complement, green.

The number of pure chromatic and achromatic colors is small compared to all color possibilities. The human eye can differentiate about 300 colors and about 150 shades of gray.

Hue, saturation, and brightness (HSB)

It is impossible to describe the appearance of a color definitively. However, it is possible to describe a color's appearance in relationship to its environment. The eye differentiates colors according to the three basic criteria of every color: ***hue***, ***saturation***, and ***brightness***, or ***HSB***. Together, these three criteria define the relationship between colors in the HSB color model, **Figure 8-13**.

- ***Hue*** is the color of an object perceived by the eye, determined by the dominant light wavelengths that are reflected or transmitted.
- ***Saturation*** is the attribute of color that defines its degree of strength or difference from white. It can also be defined

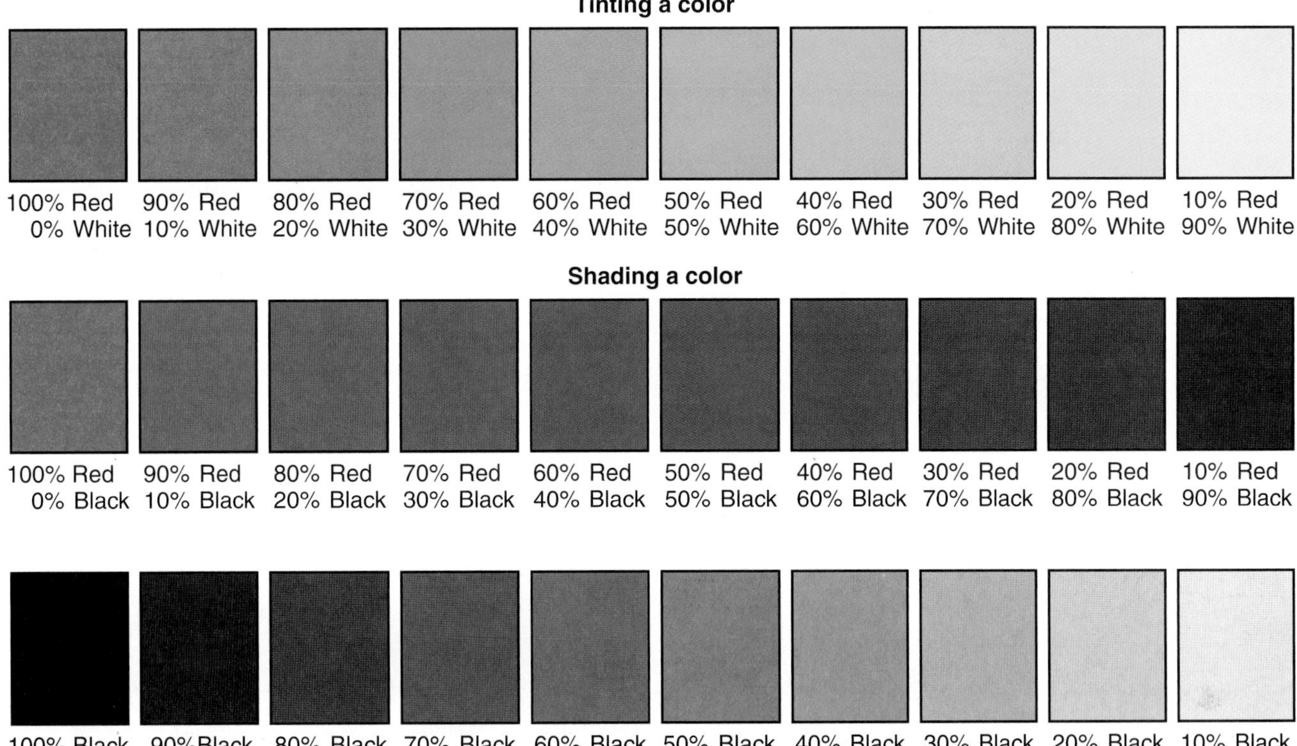

Figure 8-12. The top row shows the various tints of red that are created when different percentages of white are added. The center row illustrates the shades of red created with different percentages of black. The bottom row shows different array values (percentages of black).

as the extent to which one or two of the three RGB primaries predominates in a color.

- ***Brightness*** is often referred to as lightness or luminosity and is defined as a value indicating how light or dark a color is.

Hue, value, and chroma (HVC)

In the early 1900s, Albert H. Munsell developed a color organization and definition system based on human perception. The Munsell system identifies color's three attributes as hue, value, and ***chroma*** (HVC). In Munsell's system, chroma indicates the intensity or strength of a color and its saturation, **Figure 8-14**.

- ***Hue*** is the color name and is indicated by the letter H, followed by a fraction. The fraction's top number (numerator), represents the value. The bottom number (denominator) indicates the chroma.
- ***Value*** is the lightness or darkness of a color. It is shown on the central axis of the Munsell model as nine visible steps. The darkest value is at the bottom and the lightest value is at the top. The value of pure black is designated as 0/, pure white as 10/, and middle gray is 5/.
- ***Chroma*** is shown by the horizontal band extending outward from the value axis. The chroma value shows the amount a given hue deviates from a neutral gray of the same value. The number of chroma steps vary because hues vary in their saturation strength.

The popularity of Munsell's color system continues today because it separates the color-independent component, *brightness* (Munsell's *value*), from *hue* and *saturation* (Munsell's *chroma*). This enables two-dimensional color representation. In addition, it is perceptually uniform. Color distances on the

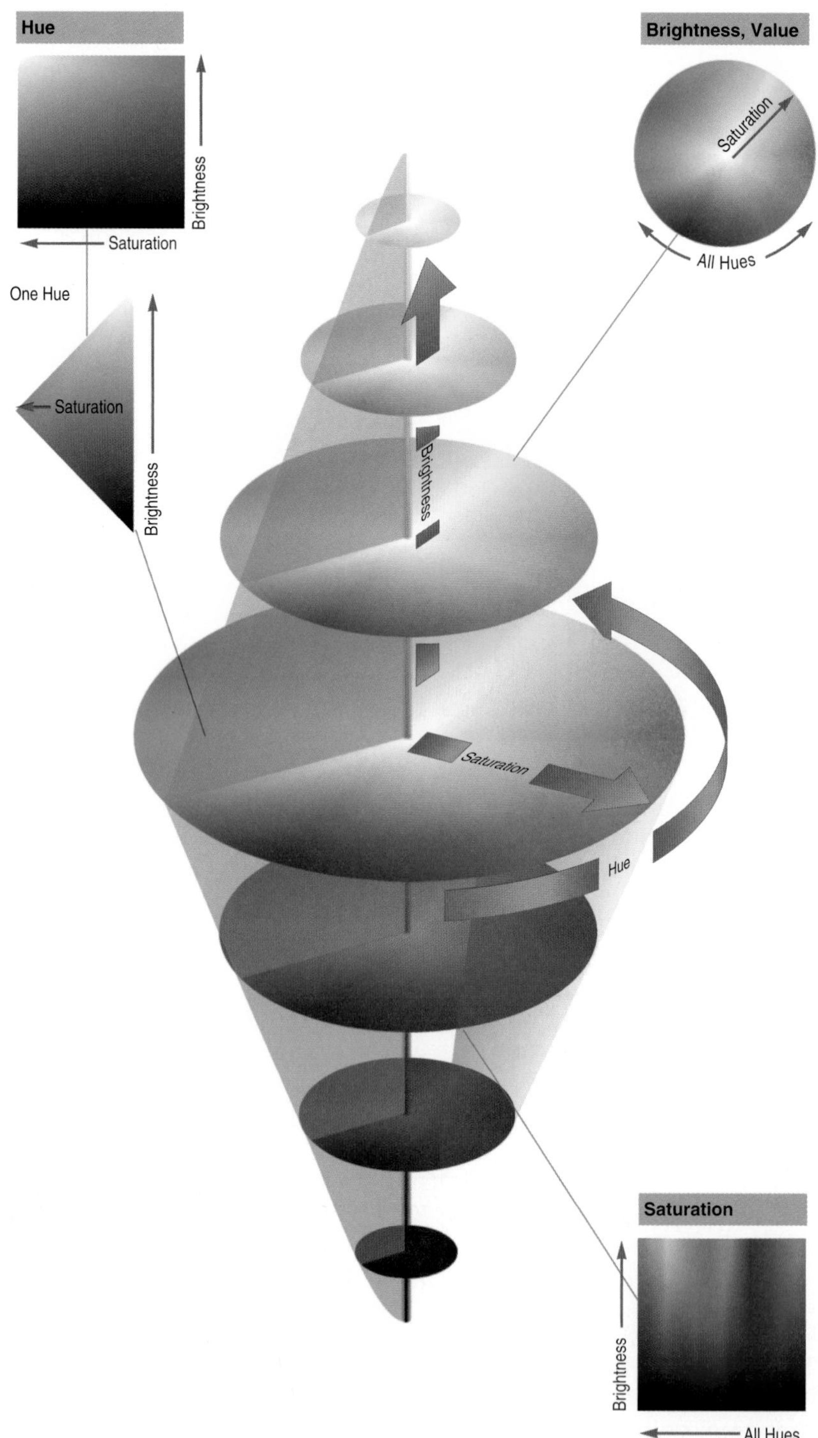

Figure 8-13. This diagram illustrates the tristimulus color space. Circular movement around each circle varies the hue. Upward movement increases brightness. Radial movement from the center of each circle increases saturation. (AGFA)

model correspond to perceived differences between the colors. Every color has a specific location with this system. ***HVC*** is often used interchangeably with ***HSL*** (hue, saturation, and lightness) and ***HSV*** (hue, saturation, and value).

The International Commission on Illumination (CIE)

To precisely match colors in the graphic communications industry, most ink and paper

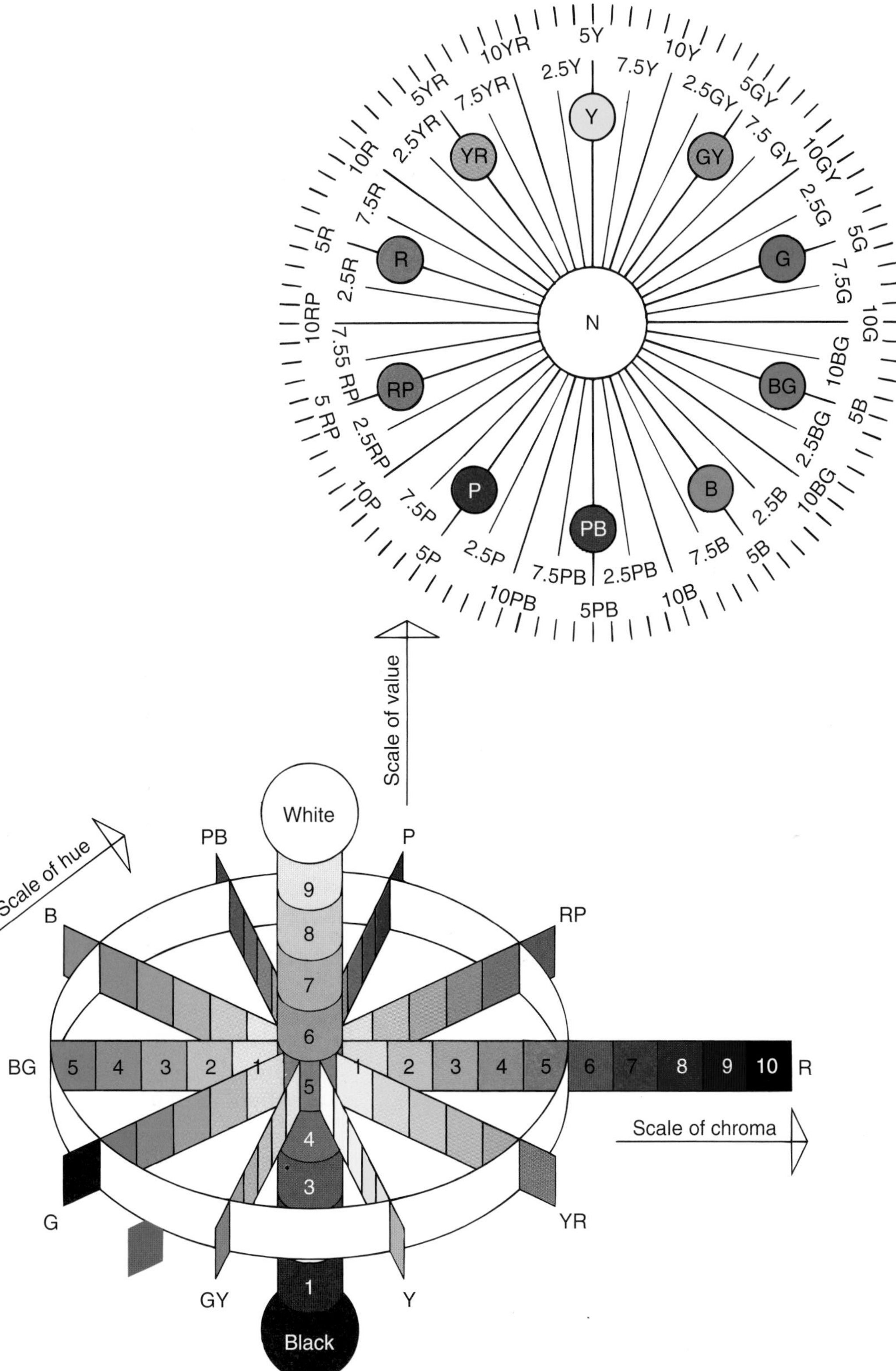

Figure 8-14. The Munsell color system (top), includes hue notations of the five principal and five intermediate hue families. Each hue family is broken down into four parts: 2.5, 5, 7.5, and 10. The outer circle markings represent the 100 hues included. The adjacent graphic (bottom) represents the relationship of hue, value, and chroma. The circular band represents the hues in their proper sequences. The center axis represents the scale of value. The bands pointing outward from the center show the steps of chroma, increasing in strength as indicated by the numbers.

manufacturers have adopted the CIE system of color specification. CIE stands for *Commission Internationale de l'Eclairage* or the International Commission on Illumination. In 1931, the CIE established a worldwide color measurement standard. The CIE system is a mathematical model of human color perception, **Figure 8-15**. Numerical values are used to quantify the responses of the average human eye to different wavelengths of light.

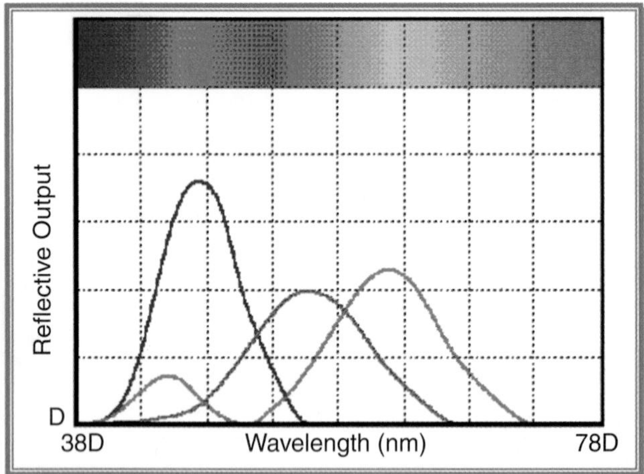

Figure 8-15. The responses of the average human eye to different lightwaves have been used to establish the CIE color standard. As illustrated above, the human eye does not perceive color as being equally spaced. Human perception of color is much greater in the center of the spectrum than on the ends.

Illuminant	Temperature
CIE source A, tungsten	2856 K
CIE source B, sunlight	4870 K
CIE source C, daylight	6770 K
CIE source D_{50}, daylight	5000K
CIE source D_{55}, daylight	5500 K
CIE source D_{65}, daylight	6500 K

Figure 8-16. The CIE Standard Illuminants (light sources). D_{65} is the most widely used to represent average daylight conditions. D_{55} and D_{50} are other commonly used daylight sources.

The CIE defined several standard light sources, **Figure 8-16**; a standard observer, and standard viewing conditions. The standard observer was chosen to have color vision representing that of the average person. Standard viewing conditions were determined using a dark background and only foveal vision. The *fovea*, as stated earlier, is the most sensitive part of the eye's retina and the area of sharpest vision. Foveal vision only covers about a 2° angle of vision so the CIE changed the angle of vision to 10° in 1964. The wider angle provides a more accurate correlation with the visual perception for larger samples.

The CIE uniform color space (CIE XYZ)

In order to determine accurate color measurements, information from three variables is required. The three variables are the light source, the color sample, and the receiver. After the information is gathered from these three variables, it is possible to determine a sample's ***tristimulus values (X, Y, Z)***. The X, Y, and Z stand for red, green, and blue (RGB) respectively. (Any color may be specified on the CIE XYZ color model by listing the amounts of the three primary colors required to match it.) Specific methods are used to manipulate the data graphically or mathematically. Modern technology allows us to quickly determine these values through the use of color measurement devices, computers, and computer software.

The **CIE XYZ** color space is the parent system for nearly all color standards. Variations such as the *CIE Yxy*, *CIELAB*, and *CIE Luminance Y* models serve different scientific and technical purposes.

The CIE chromaticity diagram

The CIE chromaticity diagram (*CIE Yxy color space*) is a two-dimensional graph of hue and chroma, **Figure 8-17A**. ***Chromaticity*** refers to a quality of color that includes hue and saturation (chroma), but not brightness (lightness).

As with Munsell's HVC color model, the CIE Yxy separates the achromatic component (Y) from the two chromatic components (xy). Two colors, the same except for luminance, would have the same chromatic definition, and therefore the same ***chromaticity coordinates***. The chromaticity coordinates are represented by the *x* and *y* values. The color's brightness (Y) is specified by a number, not a location on the graph, **Figure 8-17B**.

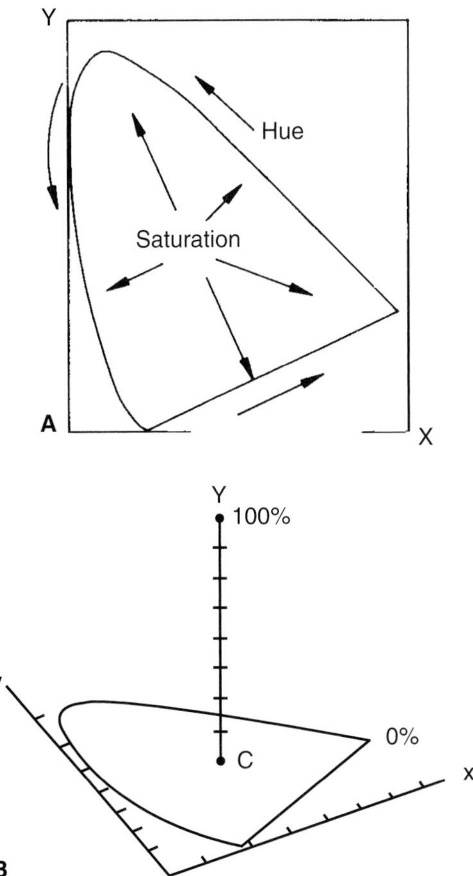

Figure 8-17. A. The CIE chromaticity diagram represents the hue and saturation of a specific color or the chromaticity coordinates of that color. **B.** The luminance value (Y) would be seen as a vertical axis rising up from the neutral position of the illuminant or light source.

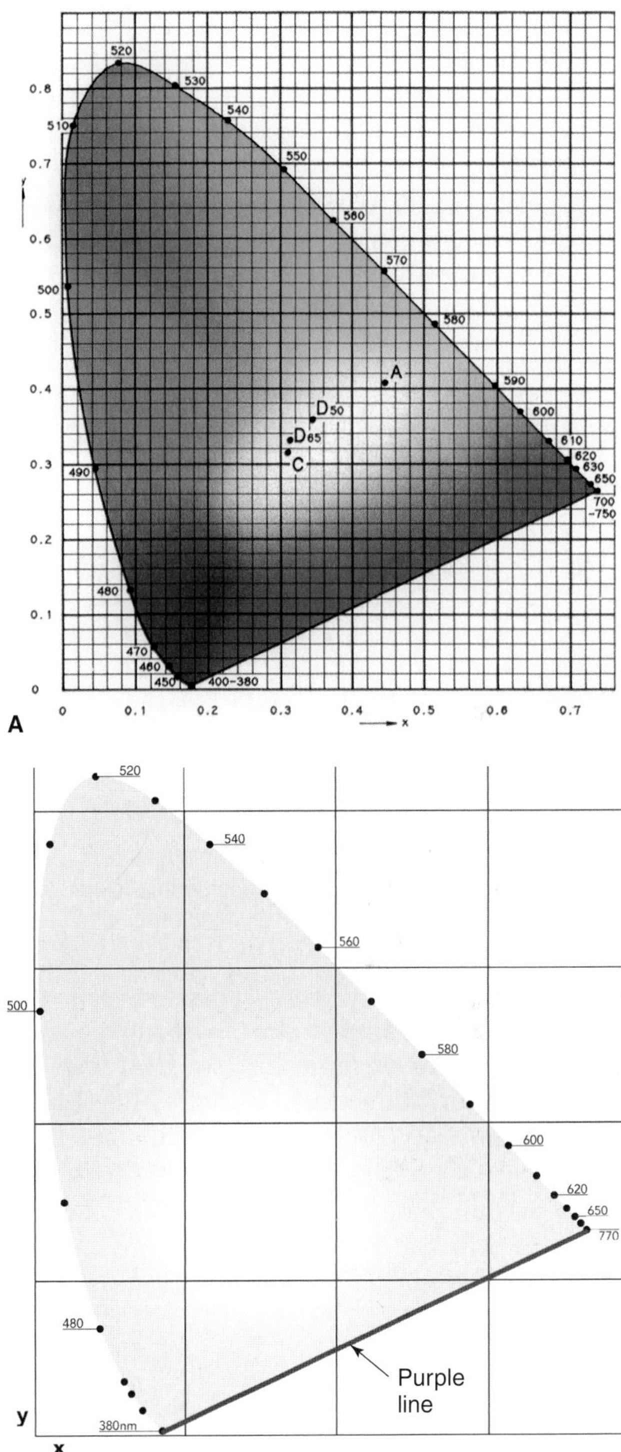

Figure 8-18. A. The CIE chromaticity chart. **B.** The bold line between 380 nm and 770 nm represents the purple line or purple boundary at the base of the spectrum locus. (Thomas Detrie)

The CIE chromaticity diagram has a horizontal x axis and a vertical y axis. When we convert and plot the chromaticity coordinates of visible light (380 nm to 770 nm), the resulting points fall on a horseshoe-shaped curve known as the ***spectrum locus***, **Figure 8-18A**. By definition, since all visible colors comprise mixtures of these wavelengths, all visible colors must occur within the boundary formed by this curve. Connecting the spectrum locus curve endpoints forms a line called the ***purple line*** or the ***purple boundary***. Colors on this line are mixtures of pure 380 nm (violet) and 770 nm (red) light, **Figure 8-18B**.

The colors plotted on the chromaticity diagram are relative to the light source used. The A, C, D_{50}, and D_{65} on Figure 8-18A represent the location of the CIE standard light sources. The CIE values of dominant wavelength, purity, and luminosity are dependent on the color temperature of the light source used in making the measurements. In the CIE system, dominant wavelength relates to hue, and purity relates to chroma or saturation.

CIELAB

In 1976, the CIE revised the standards to create a more even distribution of colors. This resulted in the creation of the CIELAB model, which is also known as the CIE L*a*b* model, **Figure 8-19**. The distances between colors correspond to perceived color differences. The CIELAB model is the current standard for measuring the color of light.

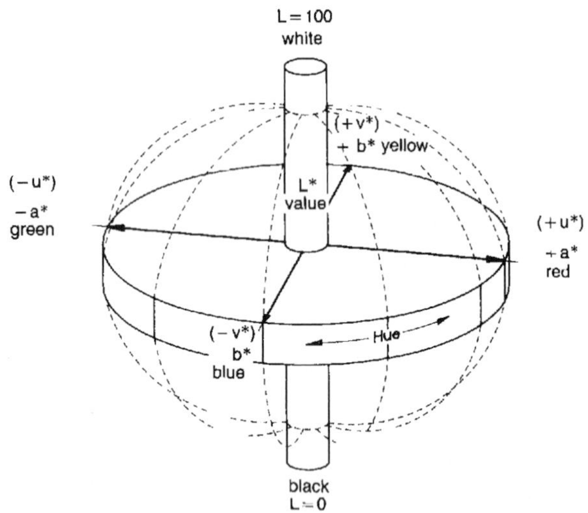

Figure 8-19. The CIELAB color space defines color based upon our visual system's perception of color.

The CIELAB color space separates color and luminance into discrete color space dimensions. These dimensions are represented by the *L*a*b**.

- The first dimension, *L**, represents lightness. All colors of the same lightness lie in a plane. Lightness varies vertically.
- The *a** indicates the red to green value. Positive a* values (+a*) appear reddish and negative a* values (–a*) appear greenish.
- The *b** represents the yellow to blue value. Positive b* values (+b*) are yellowish and negative b* values (–b*) are bluish.
- The a* and b* both represent a two-dimensional color subspace.

The human visual system is more sensitive to the *L* component, so digital systems allocate more data space to it than to the color components. This allows even more efficient coding of the color values (luminance). On the whole, the CIELAB model is very similar to Munsell's color model.

The Pantone® system

The Pantone system of color specification is the most widely used system in the graphic communications industry. Unlike the HVC or HSB color models, the Pantone system is not based on equal visual differences in color. The colors used are based on ink colors common to the printing industry.

Using manuals or swatchbooks containing representations of the Pantone colors, designers, clients, and printers can effectively communicate color selections. The manuals and swatchbooks provide color simulations, names, and mixing formulas, **Figure 8-20**. The colors are usually shown on both coated and uncoated paper.

Figure 8-20. Pantone® offers printers, designers, and color professionals a variety of materials for choosing and using the Pantone colors. The Pantone Color Formula guide is useful in specifying colors for a planned printed product and the Pantone Process Color Imaging Guide is useful in comparing electronic RGB color to printed CMYK color. (Pantone, Inc.)

Printed Color

Creating colors can be done by one of two methods: ***additive color formation*** and ***subtractive color formation***, **Figure 8-21**. Additive color

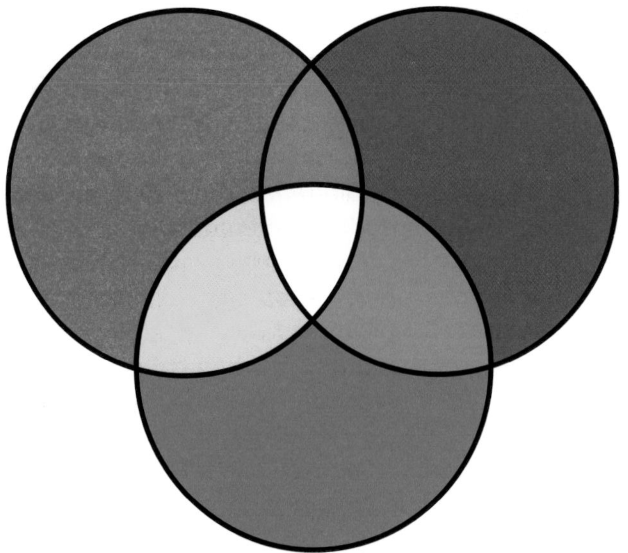

Figure 8-21. Additive color formation. The red, green, and blue additive primaries can be mixed in pairs to form magenta, yellow, and cyan. Mixing all three will result in white light.

formation is based on mixing light; subtractive color formation is based on mixing ***colorants***. Colorants are chemical substances that give color to such materials as ink, paint, crayons, and chalk. Colorants that dissolve in liquids are called dyes. Coorants that do not dissolve but spread as tiny solid particles through liquids or other substances (such as ink) are called ***pigments***.

Additive and subtractive color formation

In additive (RGB) color formation, the primary colors of light (red, green, blue) combine to form other colors. As shown in **Figure 8-22**, blue and green form cyan (a blue-green), red and blue form magenta (a blue-red), and red and green form yellow. When all three primaries combine in equal proportions, white light results. The human vision system, with its cones sensitive to red, green, and blue light, uses additive color mixing. Television sets and computer monitors create images in a full range of colors by combining dots of red, green, and blue light.

In subtractive (CMY) color formation, color is seen by reflected light. Each of the primary subtractive colors—cyan, magenta, and yellow—absorbs (subtracts) other colors from the white light and reflects only its own. As shown in **Figure 8-22**, a spot of cyan printed on a page will absorb the red wavelengths of light, and reflect back to the viewer only the blue and green wavelengths that form the color cyan. A spot of magenta will absorb green and reflect back the blue-red combination (magenta). A yellow spot will absorb blue light and reflect the red and green wavelengths that form yellow. A spot printed with black ink (or a black made by combining equal parts of cyan, magenta, and yellow) will absorb all the wavelengths. No color will be

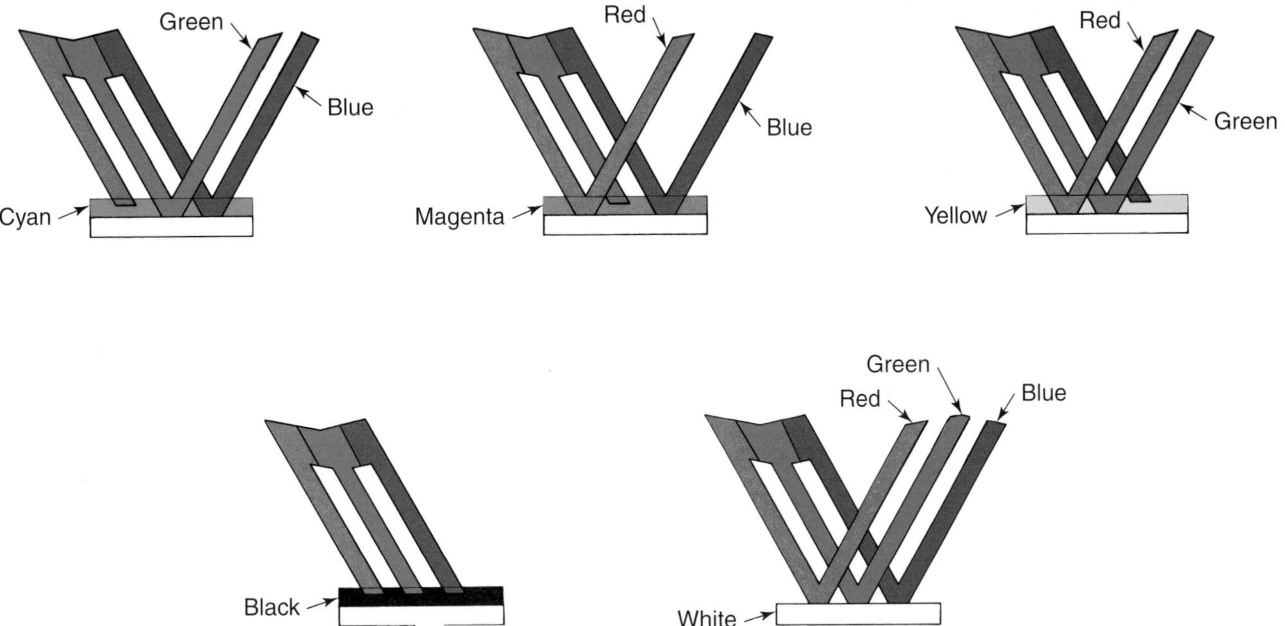

Figure 8-22. Subtractive color formation. Cyan, magenta, and yellow absorb wavelengths of some colors and reflect others back to the viewer. Black absorbs all the wavelengths, white reflects all of them.

reflected. In the same way, the white paper surface will reflect all the wavelengths, producing white light.

Colorants (such as ink pigments) of the subtractive primaries (CMY) can be mixed together in equal proportions to form the additive primaries (RGB). As shown in **Figure 8-23**, cyan and magenta colorants when mixed will absorb red and green, reflecting blue light. Magenta and yellow combined will absorb green and blue light and reflect red. Yellow and cyan together will absorb red and blue and reflect green.

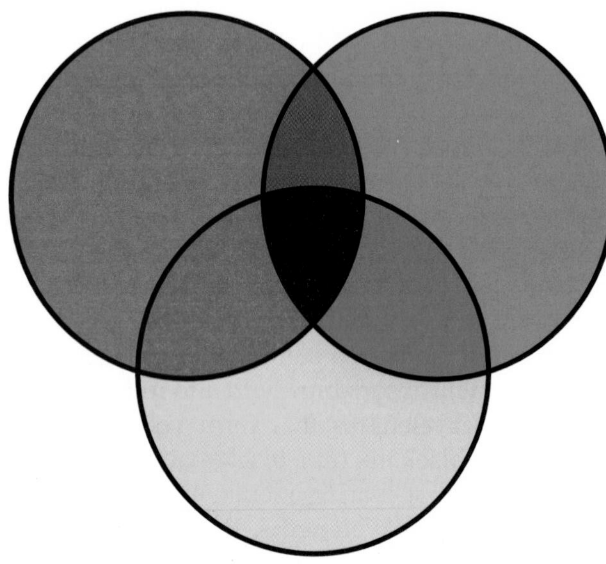

Figure 8-23. Mixing subtractive colorants. Mixing the magenta, yellow, and cyan subtractive primaries in pairs will form red, green, and blue. Mixing all three will produce black.

In ***process color printing***, where only the subtractive primary colors (plus black) are used, the same principle applies, except the colors are mixed *visually*, rather than physically. Tiny, closely spaced dots of cyan, magenta, and yellow ink, in varying combinations absorb and reflect the different wavelengths of light to produce different colors.

As noted earlier, black can be formed by mixing equal quantities of the subtractive primaries. In most process color printing, however, a black ink is actually used as the fourth printing color or "channel." In descriptions of color systems, black is designated with the letter "K." Thus, the four "process colors" are described in abbreviated form as ***CMYK***. Using black as the fourth color ensures a truer printed black and faster ink drying time. A black created from the other three colors would be muddy and require a heavier (and thus slower-drying) ink deposit on the paper. Using black ink is also more cost-effective, since it is less expensive than the color inks.

Color separation

Color separation is the process of dividing the colors of a multicolored original into the subtractive, or printing, primaries (CMY) and black (K). The CMYK color separations are made into films and used to prepare printing plates, **Figure 8-24**. The common methods of making color separations are ***direct screen photographic***, ***indirect screen photographic***, and ***electronic***. The following section briefly covers these processes.

Figure 8-24. These four-color process printers were created with computer software. When printed, the combined images will create the four-color image.

Direct screen photographic color separation uses a process camera, a contact printing frame, or an enlarger to make color separation exposures. These exposures are made through a photographic mask and halftone screen onto high-contrast film. The color-corrected halftone separation negatives are produced in one step. The direct screen process can be used to make color separations from transparent and reflective copy. Additional information on this process can be found in Chapter 13.

The ***indirect color separation method*** is a two-step process in which ***continuous tone*** separations are produced from full-color originals. Continuous tone implies there is an infinite number of tone gradations on the image. Halftone negatives or positives are then made from the continuous-tone separation. Color values are separated in the first step, and tone values are screened in the second step. The greatest advantage of the indirect method is that the negative can be retouched or enlarged. The opportunity to enlarge during the separation process allows the printer to produce large posters and display work. The indirect method can be used with transparent copy and reflective copy. Additional information on this process can be found in Chapter 13.

Electronic color separation is performed with a ***scanner.*** A scanner is an electronic device that measures color densities of an original, stores those measurements as digital information, manipulates or alters the data, and uses the manipulated data to create four film separations. With so much of the work involved in the graphic communications industry being performed electronically, electronic color separation has replaced many of the older methods.

Depending on the type of scanner, almost any type or size of original can be scanned. This includes film negatives, transparencies, photos, printed media, drawings, graphs, and text copy. Many scanners allow the operator to specify what type of color separations (RGB or CMYK) are to be made. Scanners and their operation are covered in detail in Chapter 10.

Color separation filters

The color separation process uses red, green, and blue filters to divide the original image into the CMYK process colors. Each color filter will separate the necessary colors of light to produce its complementary color or ***printer.***

To produce an image that represents each of the three subtractive primary inks (CMY), the complementary additive color filter is used, **Figure 8-25.**

The blue filter is used to produce the yellow printer. If an exposure is made with a blue filter, only the blue elements of the copy pass through and expose the film. The black, or exposed, areas of the negative represent the blue areas of the original color copy. The unexposed, or clear, areas of the negative represent the colors absorbed by the filter. When the blue-light image is printed in positive

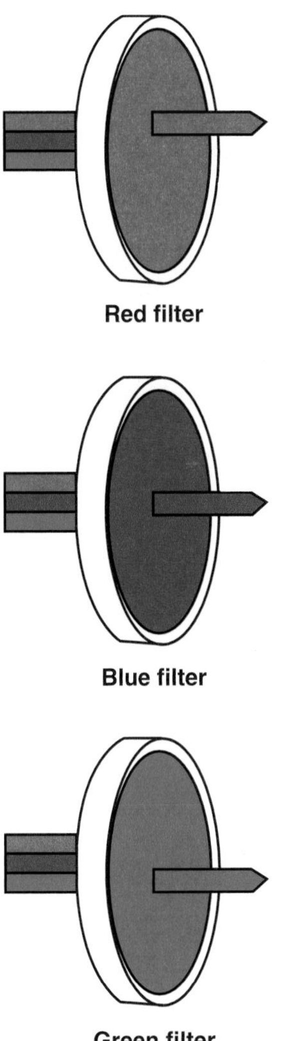

Figure 8-25. The principle of separating colors can be illustrated by looking at the results obtained from using red, green, and blue filters. The red filter transmits red and absorbs blue and green. The green filter transmits green and absorbs blue and red. The blue filter transmits blue and absorbs red and green.

form with yellow ink (a blue light absorber), only red and green lightwaves will reflect, allowing the viewer to see the color yellow.

The green filter is used to produce the magenta printer. Only the green elements of the copy will pass through the green filter and expose the film. The exposed areas of the negative will represent the green areas of the original; the unexposed areas represent the blue and red lightwaves absorbed by the filter. When the image is printed in positive form with magenta ink (a green light absorber), only the blue and red lightwaves will reflect. The viewer will see the color magenta.

Finally, the red filter is used to produce the cyan printer. The red filter allows only the red elements of the copy to pass through and expose the film. The black areas of the negative represent the red areas of the original, and the clear areas of the negative represent the green and blue colors that were absorbed by the filter. When the image is printed in positive form with cyan ink (a red light absorber), only the green and blue lightwaves will reflect, so the viewer will see the color cyan.

The black printer, often referred to as the ***skeleton*** or ***detail printer***, can also be created through the use of different filters. The black printer is created with white light. The black printer is used to extend shadow details or density ranges. Printing a black ink over the three primaries improves and enhances shadow details of the reproduction. The black printer also helps compensate for CMY register problems.

Color Viewing Variables

Although the human vision system is both highly sensitive and accurate, it is also very subjective. Visual perception varies among individuals for many reasons and can even change with varying emotional and physical states. Therefore, if color evaluation is to be both accurate and consistent, several variables must be taken into account.

Color blindness

The ability to see in color is not inherent to all animals. Although some birds, fish, reptiles, and insects have highly-developed color vision systems, it is almost certain that very few mammals below the primates possess color vision. Among humans, approximately 10% of males and about 1% of females, experience some degree of color blindness. ***Color blindness*** is the inability to tell colors apart.

A person with normal vision has cones that respond to all three of the additive primary colors. A color-blind person lacks one, two, or all three types of cones. Most color blind people have ***dichromatic vision*** and can see only yellows and blues. They confuse reds with greens, and some reds or greens with some yellows. Very few people are truly blind to all colors. Those that are, see only in shades of white, gray, and black. They are said to have ***achromatic vision***.

Vision fatigue

Random retinal impulses and involuntary rapid eye movements keep the vision system perpetually active. Both are essential to vision. Vision soon fades when an image becomes optically fixed on the retina. Part of the function of eye movement is to sweep the light pattern over the receptors to continually signal to the mind the presence of the image. However, overuse fatigues the system, and this fatigue can impair color judgment. For example, viewing a saturated color for an extended period of time will cause a second color to appear different because vision fatigue subtracts some of the first color from the image.

Aging

Even with the complete absence of light, there are random retinal impulses reaching the brain. This continuous background of random activity sets a continuous problem for the mind. The mind must "decide" whether this neural activity is "noise" or information. Internal visual noise increases with age and is partly responsible for the gradual loss of visual discrimination. Visual accuracy and adaptation also decline with aging.

Viewing conditions

Along with vision deficiencies and variation, external conditions also affect color judgment. External variables include diverse lighting types, different substrates, disparate viewing angles, unconventional illumination angles, and the size and shape of the color area, **Figure 8-26**.

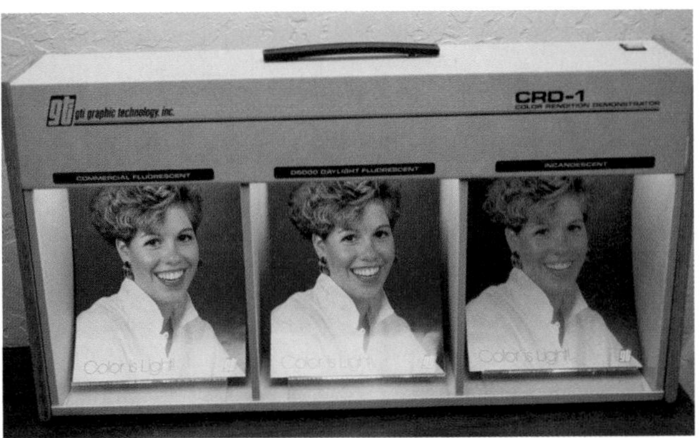

Figure 8-26. Differences in viewing conditions under 2500 K, 5000 K, and 6500 K illumination.

Because color vision requires sensory data, it is impossible to actually remember color. We can only compare color. However, accurate color comparison is almost impossible unless items are viewed under exactly the same viewing conditions. For this reason, the graphic arts industry has established an illumination standard. Viewing booths have been designed with a neutral color environment and 5000 K illumination. This light temperature appears clear and color-balanced and is ideal for making color comparisons, **Figure 8-27**.

Figure 8-27. Standardized viewing conditions are needed in order to properly evaluate color reproduction. This viewing booth emits 5000 K illumination. (Photo courtesy of GretagMacbeth, New Windsor, NY)

Color Measurement

Precise standardized measurement is also part of color evaluation. Measuring instruments vary in both design and function. Some measure density, some measure color values, and others measure lightwaves. The most common color measuring instruments are ***spectrophotometers, densitometers, colorimeters***, and ***spectrodensitometers***.

Spectrophotometers

A ***photometer*** is used to measure light intensity. The prefix *spectro* indicates that the instrument is capable of measuring light of different colors or wavelengths. When used for measurement in the graphic communications industry, a spectrophotometer converts this data to CIE color specifications. The ***spectrophotometer*** is the most accurate type of color measurement device.

The spectrophotometer's readout system either plots spectrophotometric curves or provides data from which the reader can plot the curves. ***Spectrophotometric curves*** provide a contour or envelope that describes the reflection or transmission characteristics of a sample. The sample can be the image area on printed media, a color negative, or a positive color transparency. Spectrophotometers are also used for monitor calibrations. Their use for this purpose is covered in Chapter 11, *Color Management*.

Spectrophotometric curves describe the physical characteristics of the viewing samples. They do *not* describe the colors that would be perceived by a person viewing the samples. For example, the curves for skin colors in **Figure 8-28** show that human skin has the lowest reflectance in the blue region and the highest in the red region of the spectrum. Light skin has the highest reflectance at all wavelengths, but the curve is not very smooth. The reflectance for any specific wavelength is easily obtained from the curves. In this example at 700 nm, light skin has a reflectance of 70%, dark skin 45%, and very dark skin 15%.

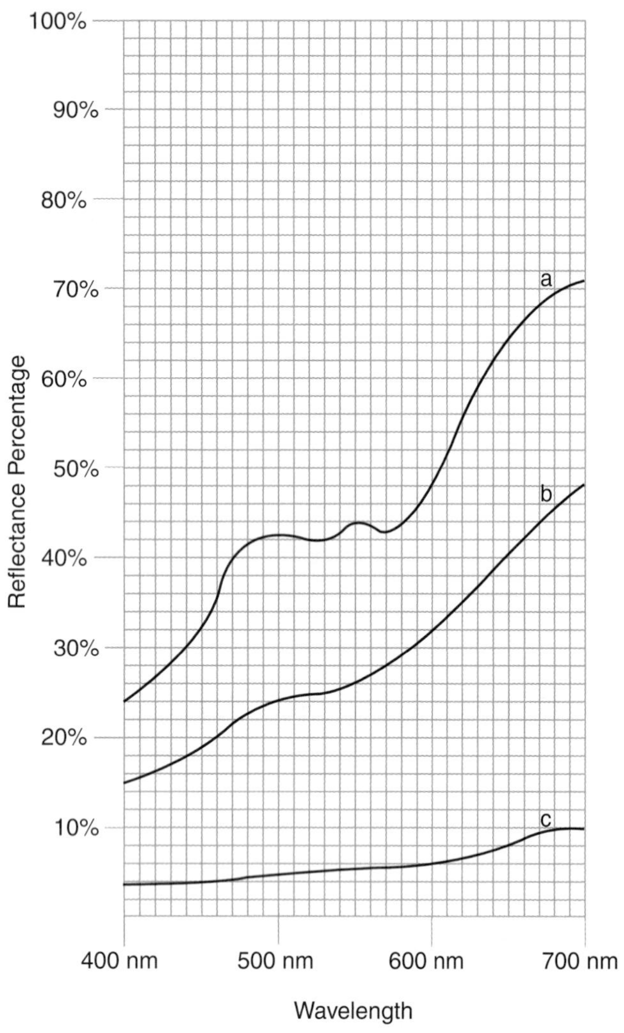

Figure 8-28. The spectrophotometric curves illustrate the reflectance of skin tones. Line *a* represents light skin, Line *b* represents dark skin, and Line *c* represents very dark skin.

Most of the spectrophotometers used in the graphic arts industry are limited to reading lightwaves in the visible spectrum. When reading lightwaves in the visible spectrum, scattering of light by the system is a great problem and the samples must be placed as close to the detector as possible, **Figure 8-29**.

Densitometers

Densitometers compute ***optical density***, the light-stopping or light absorption ability of an image or surface material. The fundamental difference between a color densitometer and a spectrophotometer is in the bandwidth of light being used. A densitometer uses red, green, and blue filters to isolate broad bands of light about 55 nm wide. A spectrophotometer uses a prism or diffraction grating to spread the light and a slit to isolate narrow bands of light between 1 nm and 10 nm. The densitometer uses numbers, not curves, to express density.

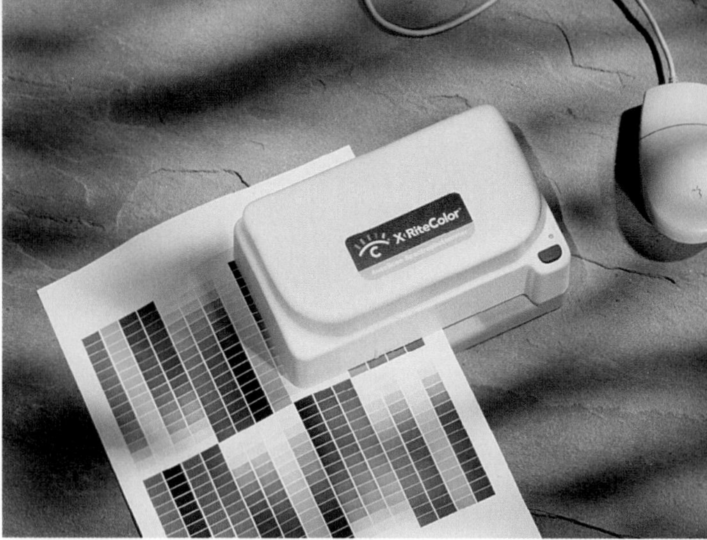

Figure 8-29. This strip-reading spectrophotometer can measure up to 800 color patches on A3 (11″ × 17″) media in eight minutes. It then sends a resulting range of detailed color measurement data, including colorimetric (CIELAB) and densitometric, as well as spectral data information, directly to computer software. (X-Rite, Incorporated)

Depending on the type being used, densitometers can be used on negative or positive transparencies, photographs, or printed images.

- ***Reflection densitometers*** measure the amount of light that bounces off a photographic print or printed sheet at a 90° angle. See **Figure 8-30.**
- ***Transmission densitometers*** measure the fraction of incident light conveyed through a negative or positive transparency without being absorbed or scattered.
- ***Combination densitometers*** measure both reflection and transmission densities.

Colorimeters

Colorimeters measure and compute XYZ color values in a way that models vision. The results are usually reported in a CIE color space. Colorimeters record all visible colors, but generally are not as precise as densitometers or spectrophotometers. Two types of colorimeters are the ***trichromatic colorimeter*** and the ***monochromatic colorimeter***.

Figure 8-30. This reflection densitometer offers all the functions needed for prepress and print production in one single unit. It is designed so the user can personalize their version with only the functions required for their specific application. It can also be configured to make direct measurements of halftone values on printing plates. (Photo courtesy of GretagMacbeth, New Windsor, NY)

The ***trichromatic colorimeter*** allows the user to match a patch of light by combination of the three primary colors. Even though this instrument relies on the perception of the eye, it is a useful device for color measurement.

The ***monochromatic colorimeter*** does not measure types of color but more specifically measures the intensity of a particular color. Unlike the trichromatic colorimeter, it does not depend on the perception of color by the eye.

Spectrodensitometers

Spectrodensitometers serve all the functions of a spectrophotometer, densitometer, and colorimeter in a single instrument, **Figure 8-31**. Besides measuring color value and optical density, many instruments can also be used to measure paper attributes and special colors.

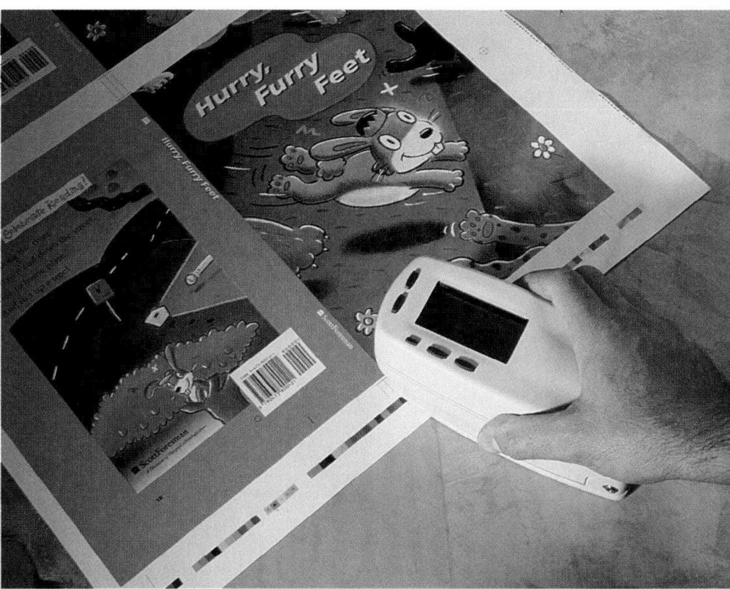

Figure 8-31. Spectrodensitometers are extremely valuable for color processing and quality control. The hand-held device illustrated above provides both CIELAB and density data. (X-Rite, Incorporated)

Review Questions

Please do not write in this book. Write your answers on a separate sheet of paper.

1. Our eyes are only sensitive to a small part of the electromagnetic spectrum. What is this range called?
2. What is the composition of white light?
3. What can happen to light when it reaches a surface or boundary between two types of material?
4. A beam of light coming toward a surface is called the _____ beam.
5. Explain the difference between the constructive interference of light and the destructive interference of light.
6. A diffraction _____ is used to separate colors in light.
7. Which part(s) of the eye determine(s) our perception of light and color?
8. What does the acronym *RGB* represent?
9. To what does the term *brightness* refer?
10. _____ is the adjustment our eyes make to light conditions.
11. What is *saturation*?
12. How is a tint produced? A shade? A tone?
13. What is a *color triad?*
14. Identify the three criteria used in the HSB color system.
15. What three color attributes are identified in Munsell's color system?
16. What are Pantone colors based on?
17. In Munsell's color system, what does the term *chroma* identify?

18. The CIE color standard uses _____ values to quantify the responses of the average human eye to different wavelengths of light.
19. What do the letters *LAB* represent in the CIELAB color model?
20. What is the additive color formation system?
21. What are the subtractive primary colors?
22. Why is black ink used as a fourth printing channel?
23. What is color separation?
24. Why is it necessary to use a viewing booth for comparing colors?
25. Name four color measurement instruments and what they measure.

Electronic Prepress and Digital Printing

9

Learning Objectives

After studying this chapter, you will be able to:

- Explain how and why text is formatted for import into a page composition program.
- Cite the differences and explain the advantages of bitmap and vector graphics.
- Define the basic functions of raster image processors and imagesetters.
- Explain the functions of page description languages.
- Explain file compression and list its applications.
- List the most commonly used file formats and their applications.
- List the types of internal and external storage devices along with their advantages and disadvantages.
- Define preflighting and explain its importance to prepress production.
- Explain the importance of font formats and font management.
- Define digital printing and list its advantages and limitations as well as the various types of technology used.

Important Terms

cross-platform
bitmap
vector graphics
raster image processor (RIP)
imagesetter
page description language (PDL)
lossy compression
lossless compression
preflighting
computer-to-plate (CTP)

Digital systems have penetrated every stage of the printing process—from the author's manuscript to platemaking and running the press. Maintaining a smooth workflow requires the consistency of digital data throughout the production process. Sustaining consistency as well as compatibility requires that everyone involved in the production process have an understanding of electronic media.

In a perfect world, every piece of electronic equipment, as well as every computer program, would be compatible. Unfortunately, this isn't the case. For this reason, many organizations such as the ***American National Standards Institute (ANSI)***, the ***International Standards Organization (ISO)***, and the ***Joint Photographic Experts Group (JPEG)*** have created standards by which electronic media and equipment must operate in order to be compatible. Due to the amount of information and the vast number of products available, this chapter covers the most general of information that applies to different platforms and software.

Computer Platforms

The ***platform*** of an electronic imaging system is the computer system, or ***hardware***, that is used to operate the ***software***. Software is the computer program, or instructions, that initiate the functions of a computer. Among these functions are word processing, page composition, and drawing creation. Computer platforms include the elements necessary to create, assemble, and output data in the form of type or finished pages, **Figure 9-1**. The major platforms are the PC (based on the IBM personal computer), the Apple Macintosh, and the UNIX system. The platform defines the

Figure 9-1. Desktop publishing allows graphic designers to create and edit both text and art. (Xyvision, Inc.)

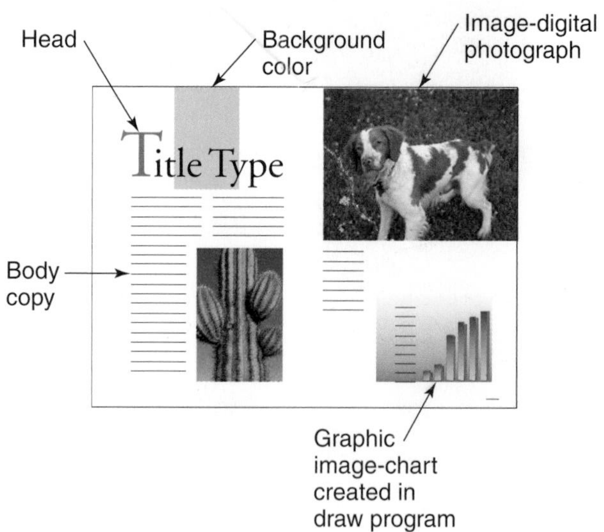

Figure 9-2. Many elements can be used in page composition including photographs, charts, background color, body copy, and specialized type styles.

standard around which a system can be developed. Once the platform has been defined, software developers can design and produce different software.

The term ***cross-platform*** refers to applications, formats, or devices that work on different platforms. For example, a cross-platform programming environment would enable a programmer to develop programs for different platforms at the same time. This is the concept behind the ***Common Hardware Reference Platform (CHRP).*** CHRP is a prototype system that allows users to run software written for either the Macintosh or PC platforms. It also makes possible the connection of peripheral devices, such as printers, originally designed for either platform.

Content Creation

In page composition, ***text*** is the body matter. The graphic images are the artwork and may consist of line drawings, photographs, charts, and graphs, **Figure 9-2**. Text files arecreated in word processing programs. Even though many word processors are capable of providing both text and graphics formatting, it is better to use the word processor strictly for text entry and editing. This is particularly true if the publication will require extensive text formatting and numerous graphic elements.

Word processing programs allow the user to assign codes and formats to text. When you format text, you assign font type, alignment, margins, line spacing, numbering, and other properties. The user identifies specific attributes, such as headlines, subheads, or body text. These formats are called styles or tags.

When the text is imported into a page composition program, the formats are recognized by name and specific attributes are assigned to that copy. The styles or attributes usually have been chosen before page composition is begun. For example, the publisher may decide that all Heading 1 styles will be blue, 14-point Helvetica bold, and all body text will be black 12-point Times New Roman.

Style names must be assigned consistently. Even though the author uses a different font size or type, if the proper style names are applied, the production department's attributes will override the author's style attributes.

Files that have been formatted with a word processor must be stored and transmitted as binary files to preserve the formatting.

Most word processing programs allow the user to save text files as ***ASCII files.*** (***ASCII*** stands for the American Standard Code for Information Interchange.) An ASCII file is a text file that contains no special formatting. Each byte in an ASCII file represents one character according to the ASCII code. The ASCII code represents English characters as numbers, with each assigned a number from zero to 127.

Although formatting is lost when a file is saved as an ASCII file, the text can still be repurposed. ***Repurposing*** is reusing content intended for one medium by reformatting it for another. Most computers use ASCII codes to represent text so it is possible to transfer data from one computer to another.

It is important to maintain your original text and image files. You should make copies and work from the copies. If data is lost or destroyed during prepress production and you need to recreate your work, or if you need to drastically resize or modify graphics, you will be able to do so.

Creating computer images

Graphic images can be created and saved in a variety of ways. Digital images can be created through ***paint programs, draw programs, digital photography,*** and ***electronic scanning,*** **Figure 9-3.** The electronic images created are saved as one of many formats. File formats of the graphics are very important because they determine how much manipulation can be done to the image and how well it will be reproduced. (Paint and draw programs are discussed in the following sections. Digital camera and electronic scanner operation are covered in detail in Chapter 10.)

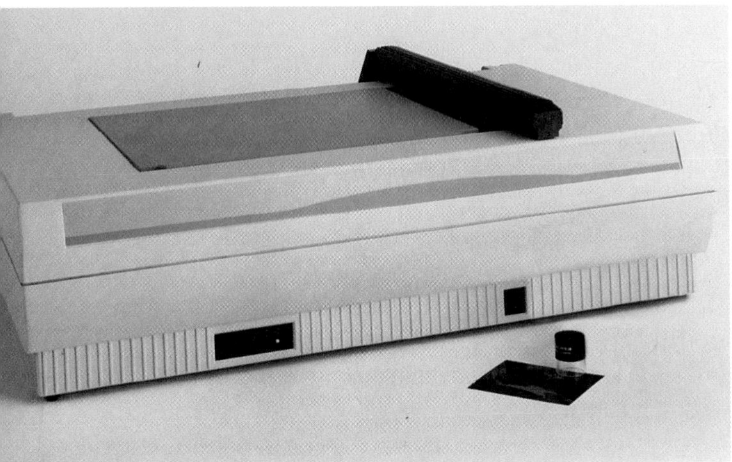

Figure 9-3. Flatbed scanners can be used to capture images from many different types of originals. Scanners vary in size, capabilities, and method of operation. (FUJI Photo Film U.S.A., Inc.)

Paint programs

Paint programs allow the user to create freehand drawings. The images are stored as ***bitmaps,*** or ***raster graphics,*** and can be edited easily. Bitmap images use a grid of small squares (pixels) to represent graphics. The bitmap image is represented as rows and columns of dots on this grid. The value of each dot is stored in one or more ***bits*** of data. Each pixel is encoded as a single binary digit. For simple black and white images, one bit is sufficient to represent each dot. However, for colors and shades of gray, each dot may require anywhere from 8 to 32 bits of information. The more bits that are used to represent a dot, the more colors and shades of gray can be represented.

When using a paint program, the user can see the rows and columns of dots that compose the image by zooming in on any given area, **Figure 9-4.** The user is able to add or delete color by filling in or "emptying" each square on the grid. In other words, when you work with bitmap images, you edit pixels rather than objects or shapes. Through these actions, the user is able to modify the image size, shape, or colors. When bitmaps are enlarged or reduced, the edges become ragged because they are composed of "squares" that do not create a smooth line. This process is referred to as ***aliasing,*** **Figure 9-5.**

Aliasing is the process by which smooth curves and other lines become jagged ***(jaggies)*** because the resolution of the graphics device or file is reduced. ***Antialiasing*** is a software technique for diminishing jaggies. Jaggies are stairstep-like lines that occur because the output device doesn't have high enough resolution to represent a smooth line.

Antialiasing reduces the prominence of jaggies by surrounding them with intermediate shades of gray or color. The gray, of course, would be for gray-scaling devices and the color for color devices. Although this reduces the jagged appearance of the lines, it also makes them fuzzier. Many programs provide an antialiasing option that is extremely useful when placing text in an image.

Another method for reducing jaggies is called ***smoothing.*** Refer to Figure 9-5. Some printers change the size and horizontal alignment of dots to make curves smoother. Other printers reduce dot size of those dots that make up a curved line.

Simple paint programs are usually included on most personal computers and are adequate for home use or simple office functions. More advanced

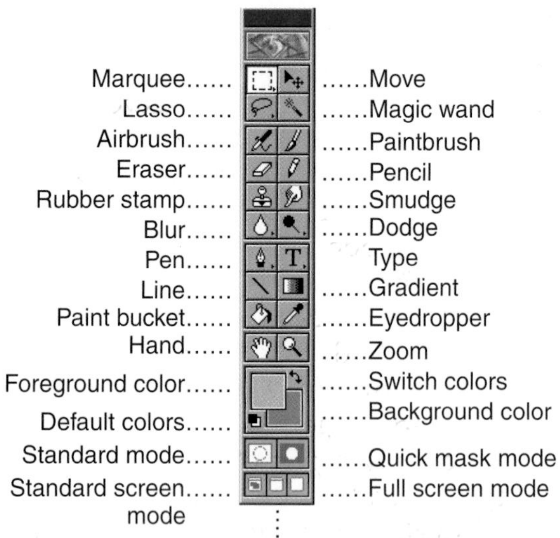

Figure 9-4. Most paint programs are limited to the basic tools indicated above.

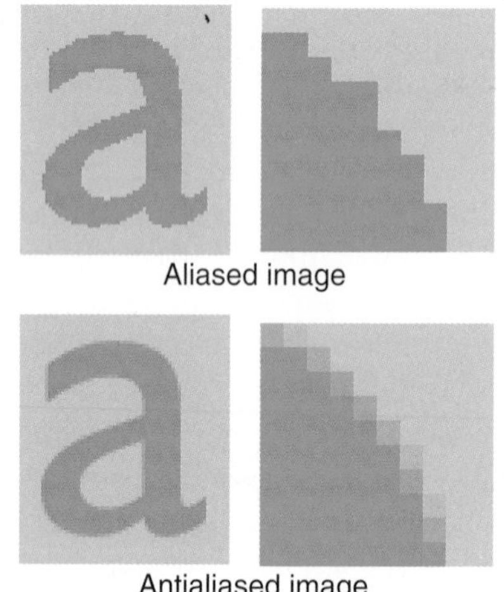

Figure 9-5. The antialiasing technique helps smooth jaggies by filling in squares along the edge with color that varies slightly from that on the image.

Figure 9-6. Digitizing tablets, paint pens, and a computer mouse can be used with most professional paint programs. (Graphic Paintbox 2 by Quantel)

paint programs are used professionally for creating print, electronic, and video images, **Figure 9-6**. Many graphic designers also use ***draw*** or ***illustration/design programs***.

Draw programs

Like paint programs, draw programs enable the user to create, store, and merge images into documents. Unlike paint programs, draw programs use ***vector graphics*** instead of raster graphics, **Figure 9-7**. In computer graphics, a ***vector*** is a line that is defined by its start and end point. With vector graphics, images are represented as mathematical formulas that define all the shapes in the image as well as their placement on a document. Vector graphics are more flexible than raster graphics because they look the same even when they are scaled to different sizes and they can be represented at any resolution. This makes them ideal for high-resolution output. Vector graphics are also referred to as ***object-oriented graphics.***

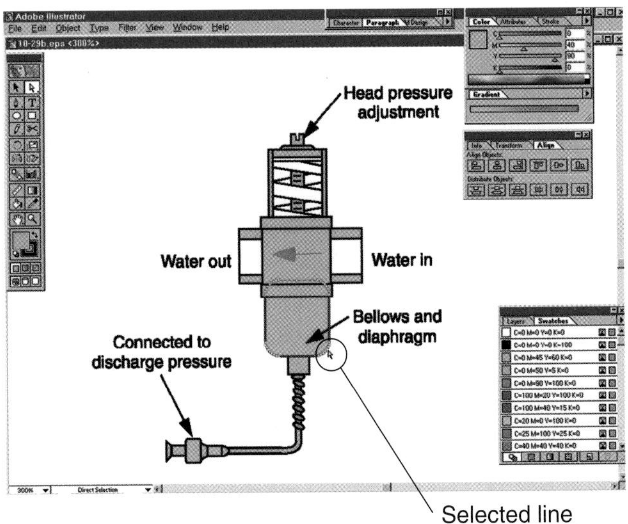

Figure 9-7. When a line is selected on a vector image, the nodes will be visible. The object selected can be modified by grabbing and dragging the line.

A ***Bezier curve*** is a vector graphic named after French mathematician Pierre Bezier. It is defined mathematically by two endpoints and two or more other points that control its shape, **Figure 9-8.** Nearly all draw programs support Bezier curves. The two endpoints of the curve are called anchor points. The other points, which define the shape of the curve, are called handles, tangent points, or nodes. Attached to each handle are two control points. By moving the handles or the control points, you can modify the shape of the curve.

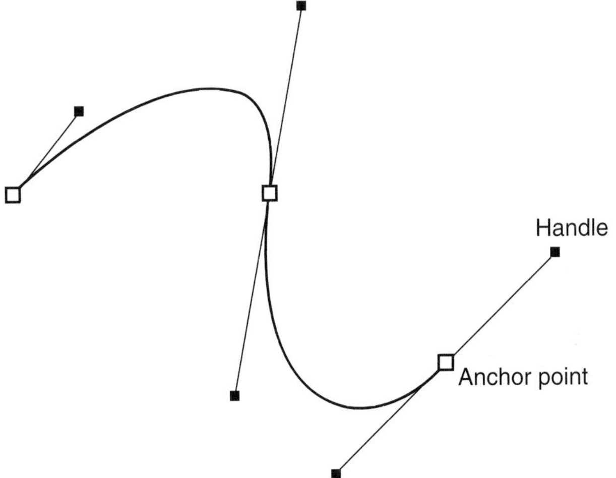

Figure 9-8. By moving the handles or the control points, you can modify the shape of a Bezier curve.

Manipulating Images

Some graphics editing is possible with paint and draw programs, but more extensive and precise changes should be made with an ***image manipulation program***, or ***image editor***. Some of the most commonly used image manipulation programs include Adobe Photoshop™, Macromedia Freehand™, CorelDRAW!™, and Adobe Illustrator™. The type of program that can be used will depend on your computer platform and the image format (vector or bitmap).

Full-featured image editors permit manipulation of almost any aspect of the image including cropping, color and contrast, adding or removing visual information, and even combining images. See **Figure 9-9**. As you gain experience with image manipulation programs, you will be able to sharpen, blur, and smudge edges; mix, choose, and apply colors; paint, draw, work with multiple layers, clone, apply filters, create gradients and textures, adjust color, and print color separations as well as composites.

Figure 9-9. When cropping an image in an imaging program such as Adobe Photoshop, you would use a marquee tool to make a selection, then trim the image.

Many programs allow the user to restrict modifications to one area of a picture or to make picture-wide changes. Additional information on creating and modifying images is included in Chapters 10 and 11.

Raster image processors (RIPs)

In electronic publishing, vector graphics information is transferred from a design workstation to a ***raster image processor (RIP)***, **Figure 9-10**. A raster image processor is a hardware-software combination that converts all elements of the vector images into a bitmapped image at the resolution of the selected output device. Most RIPs have many useful features and are able to perform multiple functions, some of which are listed below. Because each device is unique and supports different applications, the following list is not all-inclusive.

- Allows the operator to view screened files before imaging.
- Supports many font types, allowing for quick and easy downloading, proofing, and listing of fonts.
- Offers different dot shapes.
- Can drive multiple output devices simultaneously.
- Allows interpretation and output to occur simultaneously.
- Interprets color composite files directly and separates them into CMYK, RGB, and/or spot colors.
- Has high-quality screening technology that reduces or eliminates moiré patterns.

Dot-gain calibration can also be performed by many RIPs. ***Dot gain*** is the optical increase in the size of a halftone dot during prepress operations or the mechanical increase in halftone dot size that occurs as the image is transferred from plate-to-blanket-to-paper in lithography.

The RIP allows different sets of calibration tables to be selected depending on the parameters, such as screen ruling and type of printing. By controlling specific on-press calibrations, throughput and consistency can be greatly improved. Dot gain can also be adjusted by individual color channel and for numerous screen rulings and resolution combinations.

Imagesetters

The RIP interprets the page composition information for the marking engine of the ***imagesetter***, **Figure 9-11**. The imagesetter is a typesetting device used to output fully-paginated text and graphic images at a high resolution onto photographic film, paper, or plates. **Figure 9-12** compares output results from an ink-jet printer, a laser printer, and an imagesetter. Output problems are likely to occur during the transmission of files from the RIP to the imagesetter. It is usually the responsibility of the imagesetter operator to troubleshoot these

Figure 9-10. Raster image processors (RIPs) have many useful features and are able to perform multiple functions including job management and color composite file interpretation and separation. (Xitron)

Figure 9-11. With the addition of an add-on device, many imagesetters are able to create plates as well as film. (FUJI Photo Film U.S.A., Inc.)

Imagesetter

Laser printer

Ink-jet printer

Figure 9-12. Compare reproduction of the same original image by three different output devices. An imagesetter will normally produce the most accurate reproduction.

problems. However, if the files have not been properly prepared, they may need to be returned to their point of origination.

Using laser technology, the imagesetter outputs the page or color separations on the selected medium. To ensure high-quality output, especially with color separations, special attention must be given to calibration and maintenance of the imagesetter. Imagesetters are manufactured by a number of companies and they differ in speed, precision, resolution, screening technology, and media capability.

Page description languages (PDLs)

A ***page description language (PDL)*** serves as the interface between the page composition workstation and the RIP. PDLs are used in electronic publishing as a format by which all the elements to be placed on the page, their respective positions on the page, and the page's position within the larger document are identified in a manner that the output device can understand.

Several common PDLs are ***Adobe PostScript™***, ***Adobe portable document format (PDF)***, and ***Hewlett-Packard PCL (Printer Control Language)***. PDLs enable imagesetters developed by different companies to interpret electronic files from any number of personal computers and software programs. PostScript, PDF, and PCL are object-oriented, meaning that they describe a page in terms of geometrical objects such as lines, arcs, and circles.

Adobe PostScript™

The most common use of Adobe PostScript is to describe the appearance of a page to an output device. Output devices use an interpreter to interpret PostScript files. An ***interpreter*** is a computer program that resides on a controller board in the printer. The interpreter receives the PostScript page descriptions and translates them into patterns of dots for a printer or pixels for a display.

The interpreter allows PostScript files to be used on various output devices. After receiving a page description, the interpreter constructs a representation of the page to suit the output device. For example, the interpreter can determine whether the output device is a black-and-white or color printer, an RGB video monitor, or a 2000 dpi imagesetter. Once these parameters have been defined, the interpreter modifies its instructions accordingly.

Since the introduction of the original Adobe PostScript, PostScript Levels 2 and 3 have been added. These new levels integrate the original PostScript language, all previous language extensions, and new language features into the core PostScript language imaging model. The newer interpreters are not fully compatible with the original.

Portable document format (PDF)

Adobe Portable Document Format (PDF) has become the standard for electronic document distribution throughout the world. PDF is a universal file format that preserves all aspects of a native file regardless of the application or platform that uses the Adobe Acrobat™ application to create the PDF file. Anyone using the Adobe Acrobat Reader can view, navigate, and print the file exactly as the author intended. The PDF file is the leading electronic document workflow element in the paradigm *"Create, Distribute, and Print as needed."*

In the PDF workflow, the PDF file is used to create the film or plates needed by the print production facility. Within that file, all of the necessary information is contained. The fonts, graphics, images, text, and document layout are already present — no further prepress steps remain to be completed by the production department.

The Acrobat program consists of the applications ***Acrobat Distiller, Acrobat Exchange,*** and ***Acrobat Catalog,*** along with a distributable reader. See **Figure 9-13.**

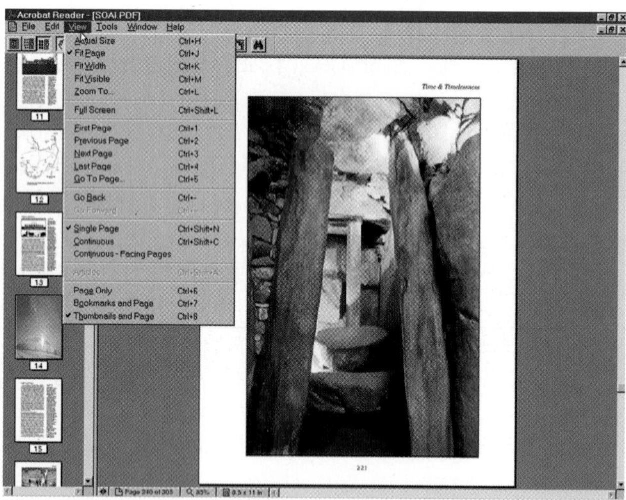

Figure 9-13. Adobe Acrobat simplifies the creation of PDF files. The Adobe Reader screen capture above illustrates a pull-down menu, thumbnails of pages in the document, and a completed page. (Adobe Acrobat)

The Acrobat Distiller is the engine that creates PDF files. Acrobat Exchange is the segment of PDF that allows minimal editing, linking, and final formatting, as well as the ability to create hypertext links to other portions of the document, to other PDF files, or to Web sites.

The Acrobat Catalog provides extensive indexing and searching capabilities. The Catalog searches through the text of PDF, indexing, referencing, and cataloging information. This application can be performed with one PDF, an entire directory, or CD full of PDF files.

The Adobe Acrobat Reader has now been extended to the hand-held Palm device (a PDA, or Personal Digital Assistant), allowing mobile professionals the flexibility to easily view PDF files. This gives the PDA user the ability to view visually rich documents that were previously accessible only on a desktop or laptop computer. Additionally, these documents can be secured, so only users with passwords can view them. This makes possible greater flexibility in viewing complex documents for "on the go" professionals, streamlining their business processes.

Unlike the complex, continuous stream of data in PostScript files, PDF files are simple, compact, object-oriented files. They process quickly and are also page-independent so single pages can be replaced or altered without reprocessing the other pages. Page independence also allows printing pages in any order from a single file. PDF files are also self-contained. This means the file has all the fonts and other resources needed to image it.

PostScript was designed with the print industry in mind. PDF, on the other hand, has been created to support CD-ROM, Internet and intranet page production, digital printing technologies, and the 100% digital workflow requirements of computer-to-plate technology. An ***intranet*** is an internal network within an organization or institution that is based on the same network protocols as the Internet. Rather than redesigning materials, companies often recycle or *repurpose* the content of their printed media. The PDF format was created with repurposing in mind.

PDF files are also much smaller than comparable PostScript files so they can be sent quickly across the Internet or a network for remote proofing or printing. To save mailing and printing costs, many government forms are available as PDF files. The files may be downloaded off the Internet or copied from compact disks.

The PDF file format allows incorporation of an ***extended job ticket.*** An extended job ticket is an electronic document that contains all of the instructions required for processing a job, **Figure 9-14.** It includes customer information, proofing directives, trapping, imposition and ripping parameters, and even finishing and shipping instructions. The job ticket specifications can be easily viewed and modified by everyone who has access to the file.

PDF is almost the ideal preflighting tool. If all the elements are not present at the time of the cre-

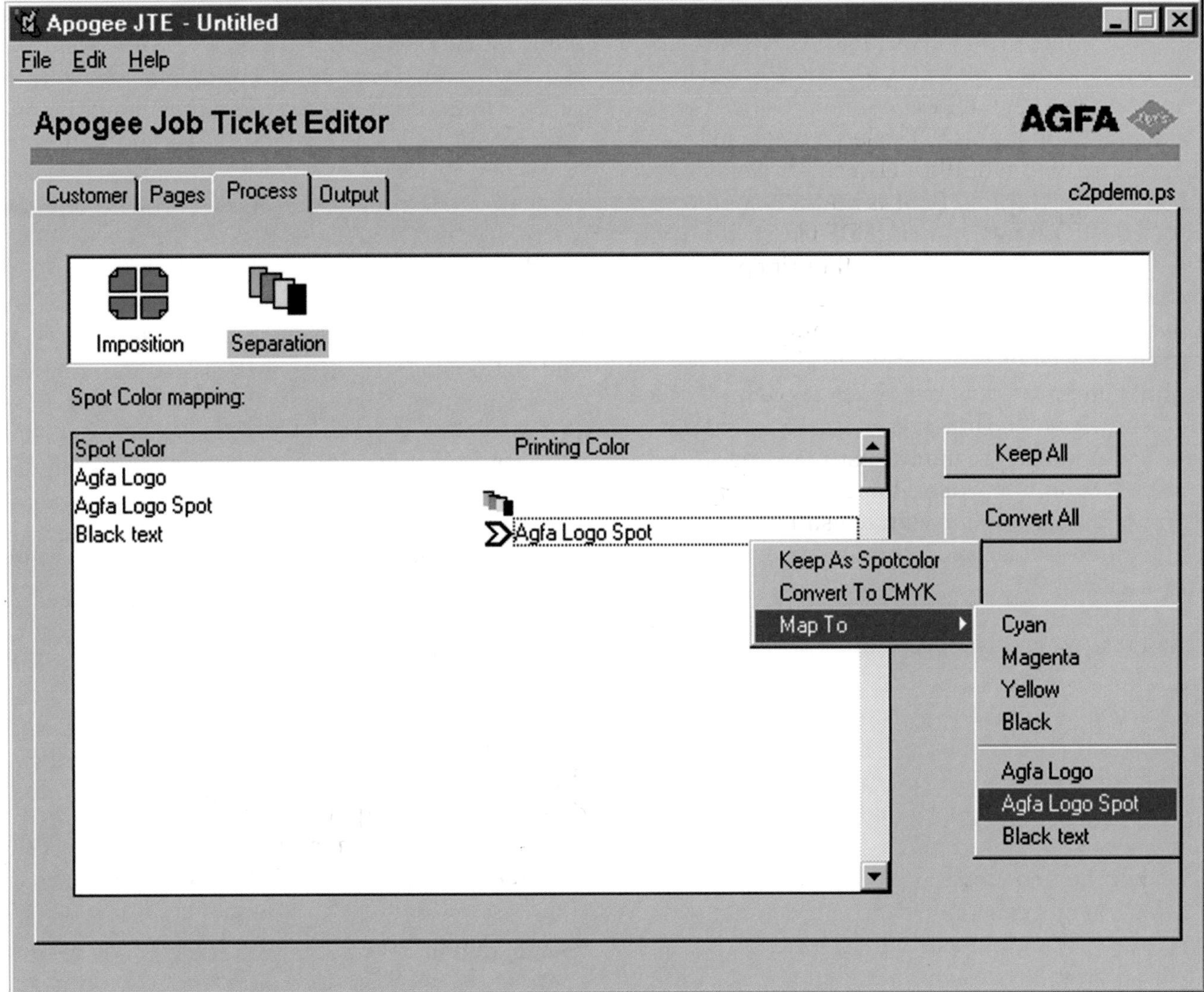

Figure 9-14. A job ticket contains several files allowing the operator access to customer information, specific page data, the type of processes involved, and the type of output. (AGFA)

ation of the file, the user is warned. Other key features and benefits of PDF are the provision of a single file for viewing, distributing, archiving, editing and printing small file sizes and the provision of built-in preview. PDF also has the ability to access many types of files including EPS, TIFF, PICT, QuarkXPress™, PageMaker™, and PostScript from applications in both Macintosh and PC platforms.

Portable document software typically will save a document bitmap, the ASCII text, and the font data. Even with compression, most PDF files are many times larger than the original file.

File compression

Before sending digital data to a service bureau or printer, most publishers will ***compress***, or reduce, the size of the files. Some programs automatically compress when the file is converted and then decompress when it is viewed. File compression requires less storage space, and enables easier data management and quicker transmission by eliminating the redundancies and other unnecessary elements from the original. Two common compression types are ***lossless compression*** and ***lossy compression***.

Lossless compression refers to data compression techniques in which no data is lost. The ***PKZIP*** compression technology is an example of lossless compression. The files are often referred to as *zip files*. Decompressing them is called unzipping. ***Decompression***, simply put, is a reversal of the compression process. Files that have been compressed with PKZIP usually end with a .ZIP extension. ZIP files that end with an .EXE extension are self-extracting files which can be unzipped simply by opening the file.

For most types of data, lossless compression techniques can reduce the space needed by about 50%. Lossless algorithms used for image compression assume that the likely value of a pixel can be inferred from the values of surrounding pixels. Because lossless compression does not discard any of the data, the decompressed image is identical to the original.

Other common lossless compression methods are the ***Huffman method, Lempel-Ziv-Welch (LZW)***, and ***run-length encoding (RLE)***. Both the Huffman and LZW methods of compression are data compression techniques in which adjacent bits are replaced with codes of varying lengths. For example, this technique would encode the fact that zero occurs 20 times, rather than using 20 zeros. This information would use 4 bytes instead of 20.

Run-length encoding (RLE) encodes digital data to reduce the amount of storage needed to hold the data without any loss of information. Each coded item consists of a data value and the number of adjacent pixels with the same data value. (In other words, strings of the same character are encoded as a single number.) This is a very efficient way of encoding large areas of flat color used in linework and text.

Lossy compression refers to data compression techniques in which some data is lost. Lossy compression technologies attempt to eliminate redundant or unnecessary information. Most video compression technologies use a lossy compression. This improves the speed of data transfer but causes a slight degradation when the image is decompressed so it can be used.

Lossless compression is preferred for images that are to be printed because each time a lossy compression is applied, more information is lost. The loss of data may not be noticeable on screen but it will be very noticeable in high-resolution printed output.

Lossy compression techniques include ***quantization, Delta Pulse Code Modification (DPCM)***, and ***JPEG***. Quantization is a filtering process that determines the amount and selection of data to eliminate so the data can be encoded with fewer bits. DPCM measures one set of bits and then measures differences from that set. The differences are then encoded into fewer bits.

The ***JPEG file format*** was created by the Joint Photographic Experts Group in collaboration with the ***International Standards Organization (ISO)*** and the ***Consultative Committee for International Telegraphy and Telephony (CCITT)***. The JPEG format was designed to establish an international data compression standard for continuous-tone digital still images. JPEG compression is an open-system, cross-platform, cross-device standard that can reduce files to about 5% of their normal size.

JPEG is based on the discrete cosine transform (DCT) algorithm. The DCT is a lossy compression algorithm that analyzes each pixel block, identifies color frequencies, and removes data redundancy. The JPEG algorithm requires the same processing amount to compress or decompress an image. JPEG compression can incorporate other algorithms, including quantization algorithms and one-dimensional modified Huffman encoding.

JPEG is a popular standard on the Internet due to extreme compression and the ability to support 24-bit color. The JPEG file format allows the user to control the compression ratio and reproduction quality at the point of compression, **Figure 9-15** The JPEG file format contains bitmap information only and supports grayscale, RGB, and CMYK color models.

A major goal of JPEG is to maintain the appearance of an image rather than the actual data that constituted the original. This works because we are visually less sensitive to high-frequency color. JPEG is a lossy compression and therefore deletes some image information, but the expanded image remains visually whole.

JPEG functions best for color and gray-scale continuous-tone images. Compressing images with high-contrast edges (line graphics or text) enough to reduce the file size significantly will adversely affect the portion containing the text. ***Selective compression*** enables users to specify different compression levels for different elements within a single image. EPS color image files embedded in a

Figure 9-15. Encoding options available when saving a file using the JPEG compression option.

digital document result in a very large file. EPS-JPEG compression creates files for incorporation into page composition software that are significantly smaller than standard EPS files. Images vary in amount of compressible data without detracting from visible quality. The user should experiment with quality settings to determine the maximum compression usable without perceptibly altering appearance. Since data is lost in each compression/decompression cycle, experienced users recommend using JPEG compression only on final images, and using it at the maximum quality setting, **Figure 9-16.**

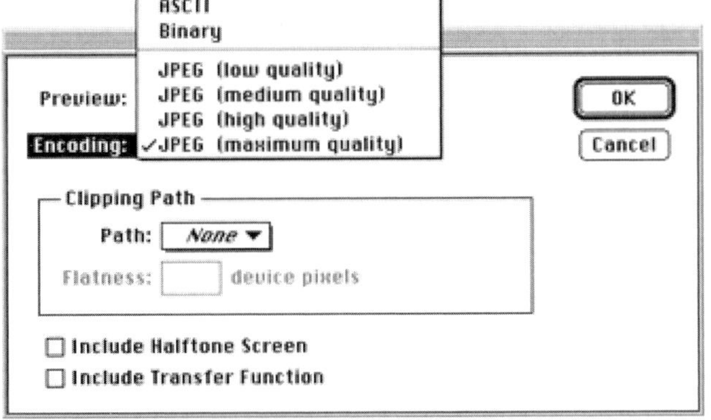

Figure 9-16. JPEG compression should be used at maximum quality to preserve the integrity of the data being compressed.

File Formats

Many different file formats exist; each type varies in the way images are saved, how they can be modified, and how well they will reproduce. File formats contain a number of important aspects, including image placement, resolution, color, and background. The following are some of the most commonly used formats.

Tagged image file format (TIFF or TIF)

The ***tagged image file format (TIFF*** or ***TIF)*** is a raster graphic file used for exchanging bitmapped images between applications. Depending on the source application, a TIFF file can allow lossless or JPEG compression. The format supports bitmap, grayscale, RGB, CMYK, and indexed color models. It also allows the inclusion of embedded paths and alpha channels. TIFF files can be exchanged among several platforms, including Mac OS, DOS, PC, and UNIX.

Tagged image file format for image technology (TIFF/IT-P1)

The ***tagged image file format for image technology (TIFF/IT-P1)*** is a device-dependent format used for describing four-color documents, including specifications for printing presses. TIFF/IT-P1 is a raster-based input format designed to be used with high-end CEPS (Color Electronic Prepress Systems). It is favored by the magazine industry for digital delivery of color advertising files. The *P1* or *"profile one"* component was added when the format was accepted by the International Standards Organization (ISO) for consideration as an international standard.

TIFF/IT-P1 is designed to reduce the need for additional time and labor created when CEP systems cannot communicate easily.

Encapsulated PostScript (EPS)

The ***Encapsulated PostScript (EPS)*** is one of the most stable of the file formats used in outputting to an imagesetter. It is less convenient than a TIFF but will usually provide more stable results when output. EPS provides a very reliable format for graphic images because it handles both vector and raster images.

The EPS format allows inclusion of low-resolution previews for screen display and nonPostScript printing. It is also possible to display just a box with the file name of an image instead of the image itself, **Figure 9-17**. The EPS format supports bitmap, grayscale, RGB, CMYK, spot color, and indexed color models.

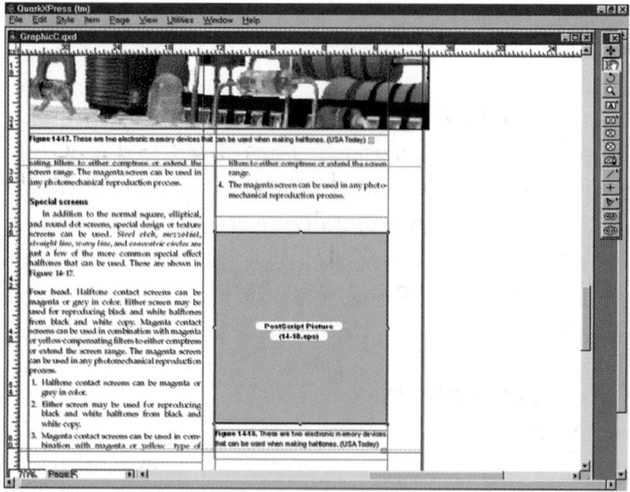

Figure 9-17. Since image files are usually very large and tend to slow a system down, the EPS file format allows the user to display just a box with the filename of an image instead of the image itself.

EPS files also allow the inclusion of ***open press interface (OPI)*** comments and the creation of embedded paths. The open press interface (OPI) file format allows the replacement of low-resolution images in files from one system with high-resolution image files on another. If saved in ASCII data format, EPS pictures can be opened and read in a text editor.

Windows Metafile (WMF) and PICT

The ***Windows Metafile (WMF)*** is the Windows 95/NT version of the ***PICT*** file format. The PICT is a Mac graphics file based on the original Mac OS QuickDraw drawing routines. Both the WMF and the PICT format can hold both bitmapped and object-oriented images. The original PICT format could only support 8 colors, but a newer version called PICT2 supports up to 256 colors.

Desktop color separations (DCS 1.0 and DCS 2.0)

The desktop color separations 2.0 (DCS 2.0) file format is an EPS graphic saved as a single file that can include up to six plates (cyan, magenta, yellow, black, and two spot colors) and a master image. The master file is used for composite printing. The DCS format supports grayscale, RGB, spot color, and CMYK color models. DCS files print faster than standard EPS files and can contain both bitmap and object-oriented information.

The desktop color separations 1.0 (DCS 1.0) creates five separate files, one for each process color (CMYK), and a data or master file. DCS 1.0 is also referred to as five-file format.

The Photo CD™

The Photo CD™ or proprietary Eastman Kodak Company format is designed for storing compressed photographic images on CD-ROM. It can only contain raster information. The format supports grayscale, RGB, and CIELAB color models. The digital images can be viewed on-screen or retrieved with the proper system.

Graphics interchange format (GIF)

The ***graphics interchange format (GIF)*** was originally designed by CompuServe to transfer graphic files between computer systems. GIF files can support only raster images, but can handle up to 256 colors, and various resolutions. GIF includes data compression, making it especially effective for scanned photos and a popular graphics format for images on the Internet.

Autotracing

Some graphics programs incorporate an ***autotracing*** feature. Autotracing is a process for converting a raster image into a vector image. Most autotracing packages read files in a variety of bitmapped formats (PCX and TIFF are the most common) and produce a file in a vector format such as an EPS. The conversion techniques used, and the accuracy of the conversion process, differ from one package to another.

File names

File naming conventions are often overlooked or even ignored. However, carefully naming your files will help keep your work organized. Whether you create a standard in-house convention or take advice from your service bureau, the format must be applied in a consistent manner.

Computer platforms and programs are subject to their own conventions. Macintosh file names should be kept under 20 characters in length, and although the latest versions of Windows allow file names to contain up to 255 characters, PC file names should be limited to less then 20 characters with a three character extension. In addition to these built-in limitations, there are several general rules you should follow.

- Only alphanumeric characters should be used. The use of symbols should be avoided.
- File names should not begin with a space.
- Each file name should be unique.
- The appropriate file extensions should be used to identify file type, such as *.TIFF*, *.EPS*, or *.FPO*.

To avoid confusion, revised files should not be submitted with the same name as the original file. However, if you are using ***automatic picture replacement (APR)*** or OPI files, it is important that you do not rename them. The name of the file serves as the link to the high-resolution image and changing the name will cause delays while the link is reestablished.

Internal and External Storage Devices

Every computer system comes with a certain amount of physical memory, usually referred to as ***main memory*** or ***RAM***. RAM is the short-term memory the computer uses to store information in process. Systems can be updated and memory capabilities can be increased to support additional programs. In addition to having a computer system that is capable of running your programs, you must have some means for storing and transmitting data. The term ***memory*** identifies data storage that comes in the form of chips, while the word ***storage*** is used for memory that exists on tapes or disks. Although compression methods can be used to reduce file size, most page composition files remain very large. Fortunately, there are many types of storage devices available that will accommodate large files. Storage devices vary in terms of size (physical and memory), access capabilities, speed, reusability, and integrity. Storage capacity is measured in kilobytes (1024 bytes), megabytes (1024 kilobytes), and gigabytes (1024 megabytes).

Disk storage

There are two basic types of disks, ***magnetic*** and ***optical***. (A disk is a round plate on which data can be encoded.) Data is encoded as microscopic magnetized needles on a disk's surface. You can record and erase data on a magnetic disk any number of times, just as you can with a cassette tape used for recording music. Magnetic disks come in a number of different forms, including ***hard*** and ***floppy***.

The ***hard disk drive***, or ***hard drive***, is a machine that reads data from and writes data to a hard disk. Hard disk drives are usually built into the computer system. The hard disk drive contains one or more permanent aluminum hard disks coated with a magnetic material, **Figure 9-18**. The aluminum disks are rotated very quickly and a read/write head moves over the disk surface, which contains densely packed magnetic tracks. The read/write head is used to write (record) or read (retrieve) information as the magnetic tracks spin past the head.

Storage capacity varies and can be increased by adding another hard drive, replacing your hard drive with a higher-capacity one, or using a new configuration known as ***RAID (redundant array of independent disks)***, **Figure 9-19**.

Figure 9-18. Storage capacity varies and can be increased by adding another hard drive or replacing your hard drive with a higher-capacity one.

Figure 9-19. RAID storage devices consist of a base unit, expansion units, and a removable cover. Most configurations are hot-swappable, allowing the removal and replacement of failed drives or power supplies without shutting down the system. (The RAIDinc Cobra LTE, courtesy of RAID, Inc.)

RAID offers almost unlimited storage capacity. The RAID configuration connects a number of high-capacity hard disk drives together to act as a single huge hard drive. In addition to increased storage capacity, RAID increases file-access speeds and data-transfer rates while providing varying degrees of data protection and failure-proofing the storage subsystem. RAID continually copies data to each of its drives so, if and when a drive crashes, it can be replaced without system downtime or loss of data.

Removable hard disk drives are often referred to as ***removable cartridge devices***. Removable hard drives are hard disks encased in a metal or plastic cartridge so you can remove them just like a floppy disk. Removable hard disk drives are very fast (often faster than fixed hard disks) and have a typical storage capacity ranging from 60 Mb to 250 Mb.

Floppy disk drives function in the same way as a hard disk drive but they use a removable disk known as a ***floppy disk.*** Floppy disk drives are relatively slow and have a limited capacity, making them unsuitable for graphics applications. Floppy disks, however, are portable, inexpensive, and fairly reliable for text files. A high-density 3 1/2″ floppy disk can hold 1.44 Mb of data. Hard disk drives are from two to 20 times faster than a floppy so it is recommended that you work from your hard drive and save to the floppy.

ZIP, JAZ, and SyQuest SparQ disks are essentially floppy disks with a vast amount of storage capacity. The disks themselves are, like a floppy disk, 3 1/2″ in size, but they are twice the thickness and can typically store more than 100 Mb of data. Some disks can hold over 1 Gb of data. Special ZIP, JAZ, and SparQ disk drives are required, **Figure 9-20**.

Figure 9-20. ZIP drives are available as external or internal units.

Unlike floppy and hard disks, which use electromagnetism to encode data, ***optical disk drives*** use a laser to read and write data. ***Optical disks*** have very large storage capacity but they are not as fast as hard disks. Five and one-quarter inch opticals may hold up to 2.3 Gb of digital information per side while 3 1/2″ opticals hold 230 Mb. The less expensive optical disk drives are read-only.

Read/write optical disk systems record data by burning microscopic pits in the surface of the disk with a laser. To read the disk, another laser beam shines on the disk and detects the pits by changes in the reflection pattern. Optical disks have a much larger data capacity than magnetic disks. Optical disks come in three forms, CD-ROM, WORM, and erasable optical.

CD-ROMs are read-only disks, **Figure 9-21**. You can read the data from a CD-ROM but you cannot

Figure 9-21. Although CD drives are included with most computer systems, external units are available.

Figure 9-22. Because of their high storage capacity, magneto-optical disks are an efficient storage medium for image files.

modify, delete, or write new data. CDs are currently the most stable storage medium and are therefore ideal for long-term storage.

WORM (write-once, read many) or ***CD-R (compact disc-recordable)*** disks can be written once and then read any number of times. However, you need a special disk drive to write data onto a WORM disk. This type of media storage is inexpensive and reliable. However, a number of disks will need to be disposed of when they are used for backup of works in progress.

Erasable optical (EO) disks can be read, written to, and erased just like magnetic disks. EO disks may be referred to as ***CD-RWs (compact disc-rewritable)***. The CD-RW disks are ideal for intermediate backup of works in progress because they can be erased about 1000 times before their recording capabilities deteriorate. Many of the CD-RW disk drives can be used to read CD-ROMs and are capable of moving two or more megabytes per second.

Magneto-optical (MO) drives combine magnetic disk technologies with CD-ROM technologies. Like magnetic disks, MO disks can be read, written to, and removed, **Figure 9-22**. However, their storage capacity can be more than 200 megabytes. In terms of data access speed, they are faster than floppies and CD-ROMs, but not as fast as hard disk drives.

Other forms of data storage

Tape drives, like tape recorders, read data from and write to a magnetic tape. Tape drives have data capacities ranging from a few hundred kilobytes to several gigabytes. Their transfer speeds also vary considerably. See **Figure 9-23**.

Figure 9-23. Tape drives are a relatively inexpensive storage medium, but because they use magnetism, they are an unstable storage medium and should only be used for temporary backup.

The main disadvantage of tape drives is that they are ***sequential-access devices***. Sequential access refers to reading or writing data records in sequence, that is, one record after the other. To read record 10, for example, you would first need to read records 1-9. This differs from random access in which you can read and write records in any order. Sequential access makes tape drives much too slow for general-purpose storage operations.

Tapes are a relatively inexpensive storage medium, but because they use magnetism, they are an unstable storage medium and should only be used for temporary backup.

Photographers using digital cameras use a removable storage device known as ***digital film*** or ***PCMCIA cards***, **Figure 9-24**. PCMCIA cards (Personal Computer Memory Card International Association), or PC cards, were originally designed for adding memory to portable computers. The PCMCIA standard has been expanded several times and the cards are now suitable for use with many types of devices, including digital cameras and scanners.

Figure 9-24. Many PCMCIA internal reader/writer units can support numerous Type I, II, or III cards simultaneously. (Greystone Peripherals Inc., CA)

Whether you are sending your files to the service bureau on disk or via a modem, you must make backup copies. When you make backup copies, you are copying your files to a second medium as a precaution in case the first medium fails or is destroyed. You should always back up your files on a regular basis.

Page Composition Programs

Page composition programs allow the user to format pages of text and graphics. Many word processing systems support their own page composition functions. However, using page composition software designed specifically for this purpose generally gives you more control over areas such as text flow, kerning, and positioning of graphics. In addition, word processing programs usually do not allow the importation of many graphic file formats, as do page composition programs.

There are many page composition programs available; if you learn with one program, you shouldn't encounter too much difficulty using another. Two popular page composition programs are PageMaker and QuarkXPress. Manuals from the specific manufacturer will provide you with detailed instructions and troubleshooting guides.

When creating image files to import into any page composition program, you must decide which format best meets your needs. If you are unfamiliar with color or unsure about your final output device, PICTs and RGB TIFFs may be a good choice. Many page composition programs provide the user with the means for converting colors in these formats. This will assure that output from your color printer will be similar to output from the imagesetter or printing press.

If you are using an illustration program to create images, you should probably use the EPS format. It is compact and will produce well-defined output. However, you must be sure the page composition program provides some means of converting colors in EPS files. If it doesn't, you might need to save different versions of the file and adjust the colors for different output devices.

If you are familiar with color and require extensive control over photographs, CMYK TIFF, DCS, and OPI may work best. You should evaluate the merits for each based on your work environment and the quality of the images you need. Software packages that create files to these specifications generally enable you to retouch and color-correct them as well as specify such printer functions as dot shape, dot gain, and screen angles.

In most page composition programs, vector graphics can be scaled in the page composition program itself. However, making drastic size reductions in a page composition program can result in distorted images. You may be better off sizing the art in the graphics software and bringing it into the page at near actual size. When you size art in a graphics program, check the resulting line widths. They should be 0.25 point or greater. Anything thinner will disappear when output on an imagesetter.

Preflighting

In addition to generating various types of proofs before sending files to the film house or printer, you should ***preflight*** your files. Preflighting is an orderly review of files to identify things that could cause problems at the output or prepress stage. To make your preflighting go smoothly, it is a good idea to discuss file format and preparation with the service bureau or printer while the project is still in the design stage. If you know their requirements ahead of time, it will save you and your company time and money.

According to the Graphic Arts Technical Foundation (GATF), some of the most common recurring problems with customer-furnished files are:

- Missing or incorrect fonts.
- Missing or incorrect trapping.
- File defined with incorrect color (RGB vs. CMYK).
- Scans supplied in wrong file format.
- Graphics not linked.
- Incorrectly defined or underdefined bleeds.
- No laser proofs supplied.
- Missing graphics.
- Resolution too high or too low in customer-supplied scans.

After the documents or pages have been created, proofed, and corrected, they are ready to send to the service bureau or printer for output. At this point, the production department can begin preflighting. Preflighting begins with the printing out of color separations and composite hard copies. The service bureau or printer can refer to these when they encounter problems with production, pagination, color, or even text flow.

Once the separations and composites are printed, all of the graphics should be linked. All page composition programs allow the user to select link or reference options as the art is imported. For example, if you are using QuarkXPress, all of the graphics in the document are linked to the Quark file unless the art was created with the drawing tools in Quark. Benefits of linking art files are numerous. Besides being easier to handle, if a graphics file corrupts, only that piece of art needs to be recreated. In contrast, if all the graphics are embedded in the document file and one piece of art is corrupted, you can lose the entire project.

When preflighting files, you should check that every graphic used in the file is on the disk or the art will print as low-resolution images or bitmapped placeholders. If the linked graphics are in a noneditable format, include the original art files in a separate directory. It is advisable to include a printed list of all files included on the disk(s) as well as how many disks are included for the project. To avoid the omission of data, you should prepare a checklist to help verify that all graphic, font, and color components are present and correct.

After the basic preflighting is complete and proofs have been output, create a letter that outlines the software and fonts that were used to create the files, trapping requirements, print specifications, and any other pertinent information, **Figure 9-25**. Preflighting also requires checking fonts and the color palette. Font formats and management are covered in the following section. For detailed information on color management, refer to Chapter 11.

The ***Scitex Graphic Arts Users Association (SGAUA)*** publishes the ***CREF II Guidelines*** to improve prepress productivity. (CREF is the acronym for Computer Ready Electronic File.) Professionals recommend consulting the CREF II Guidelines as well the service bureau before beginning any prepress work, **Figure 9-26**.

Font Formats and Management

Most applications that support text allow you to choose from a variety of fonts. The printer or film house should use the same fonts used for the original page composition, provided they can support them. The entire page composition can change if fonts are substituted. Font substitution can cause document reflow, bad word or line breaks, and loss of kerning and tracking.

File Submission Form

Book title/Part number ______
Order date ______ Blues date ______
Press date ______ Bill to P.O. number ______
Sales representative ______

CUSTOMER INFORMATION

Company name	Design house
Contact name	Design contact
Address	Address
City State Zip	City State Zip
Phone Fax	Phone Fax
Modem Baud rate	Modem Baud rate

FILE INFORMATION

Platform ❑ Macintosh ❑ IBM-PC (or compatible) ❑ UNIX (DEC) ❑ UNIX (Sun) ❑ VMS (VAX) ❑ Other ____

Operating system ❑ Macintosh version _____ ❑ MS-DOS version _____ ❑ Windows version _____

Media ❑ 3.5 inch disk ❑ 5.25 inch disk ❑ SyQuest (size___) ❑ 150 Mb DC (QIC tape) ❑ Bernoulli cartridge (size___)
❑ Zip cartridge ❑ Jaz cartridge ❑ Magneto-optical cartridge (size___) ❑ CD-ROM

Fonts ❑ Type 1 ❑ TrueType ❑ Complete font list, including manufacturer names, is attached on a separate sheet ❑ All printer and screen fonts are included on submission media

Files Files listed on other side are: ❑ Application files ❑ PostScript files
Are files compressed? ❑ No ❑ Yes (if yes, what compression software was used?_______version___)
Please complete the file list on the other side of this form.

Trapping ❑ Files do not need trapping ❑ Please trap the files for us
❑ Files need trapping, but we have taken the responsibility and done it ourselves

Proofs ❑ Single blueline ❑ Folded blueline ❑ Blackprint ❑ Matchprint ❑ Iris

Artwork ❑ Digital scanning (to be placed in file) ❑ Conventional scanning (to be stripped into film)

Pagination ❑ Total page count _________ ❑ Page map included on separate sheets

Other Special instructions attached on separate sheet

A

File Name	Application/version	Trim size	Bleed amount	No. of pages	Halftone screen	Neg. or Pos.	RREU or RRED	Color separations
Chapter 01	QuarkXPress 3.31	8.5x11	1/8in.	16	133	Neg	RRED	(C)(M)(Y)(K)/ PMS 467
								C M Y K/ PMS
								C M Y K/ PMS
								C M Y K/ PMS

B

Figure 9-25. If your service bureau does not provide a form, design a file submission form and file list similar to those illustrated above.

Documentation
____100% size laser proofs (color if possible). If not practical, mark percentage reduction of proof on all pages.
____Black & white proofs have been printed with "Print Colors as Gray" turned on.
____If the file is sent via modem, a printed proof must follow.
____Registration marks are in place.
____Proofs are properly marked identifying LIVE and FPO images, color specifications, and special instructions.
____Printed directory of contents of disk/cartridge is included.
Digital Media
____Media are clearly labeled with company name, disk number, contact, project name, and date.
____File-naming conventions have been agreed upon and followed.
____Each file has a unique and useful name.
____Revised files have a new file name.
____Disks contain copies of all layout files.
____Disks contain copies of all companion graphic files (EPS, TIFF, etc.)
____Files have been copies so that all links will be maintained when the file is opened in a new environment.
____Appropriate software programs have been used in compatible versions.
____Compression programs used match the vendor's (service bureau, printer).
Fonts
____All fonts are Type I.
____If fonts are not Type I, will service bureau be able to accommodate them?
____Do your versions match the service bureau's?
____Have you included keyboard maps for custom fonts or foreign language?
____Have you sent screen and printer fonts with the job?
Text
____Have your type styles been properly applied?
____Have reverses and outlines been properly built?
____Have you avoided the use of tiny type or graphic elements?
____Is all type aligned with tabs?
____Have you given attention to text within graphics, provided the fonts, or converted to paths or outlines?
Graphic elements
____Are borders and rules properly built?
____Hairlines are specified no less than .25 points.
____Minimal nesting of EPS graphics.
____Knowledgeable use of scaling, cropping, and rotating.
____Attention to blends: avoid shade-stepping and other processing implications.
____Imported graphics contain single subjects.
____UPC codes have been properly built.
____Resizing LIVE images has been thoughtfully implemented with careful consideration given to resolution.
____LIVE images have been provided in the proper format.
Colors
____Colors are properly defined with attention to separation on or off.
____Unused colors have been deleted.
____Trapping has been discussed and recommendations followed.
____Special colors have been properly applied.
Miscellaneous
____Document size does not exceed the limits of the imagesetter or press.
____Unwanted items have been deleted, not covered with a white box.
____Bleed and trim are properly applied.
____Image replacement considerations have been followed.
____Have you included all transparencies or reflective copy required for the job?
____Have clear instructions been written down about how to handle scans?

Figure 9-26. Create a checklist similar to the one illustrated above. Use the checklist while building your files and when preparing them to send to the service bureau.

If the production house or printer is to use your fonts, you must include them in your files. Font utility software like ***Adobe Type Manager™ (ATM), Adobe Type Reunion™, Symantec Suitcase™***, and ***FontMinder™*** can help you manage and collect your fonts.

Font utility software

Adobe Type Manager (ATM) creates bitmapped fonts in any size or style from PostScript outline fonts. This provides WYSIWYG (what-you-see-is-what-you-get) font representations on the screen (the fonts on screen will be very similar to printed fonts). ATM also converts any missing font sizes and helps improve fonts printed on nonPostScript output devices, **Figure 9-27**.

Adobe Type Reunion collects style variations in a pull-down menu. It also lists the style variations of a typeface together in a pop-up menu. Normally, the font menu displays active typefaces alphabetically by attribute, not alphabetically by name. Type Reunion unifies a type family into a list that makes true typeface selection easier.

Font utility programs enable easier font activation or deactivation. They also enable the designation of ***font sets***. Font sets provide a quick list of the fonts used in a job, **Figure 9-28**. When a supplier requests the font list for a document, that list is the same as the font set. Font sets can be created for individual jobs and activate only the set needed.

Even though the page composition program may give a list of fonts contained in a document, they may not list the fonts used in imported EPS graphics. Therefore, you must record all fonts used in supporting files because they become part of the page composition file. Fonts used within bitmapped graphics automatically convert into pixels and lose any font information so it is not necessary to record the fonts used within these files.

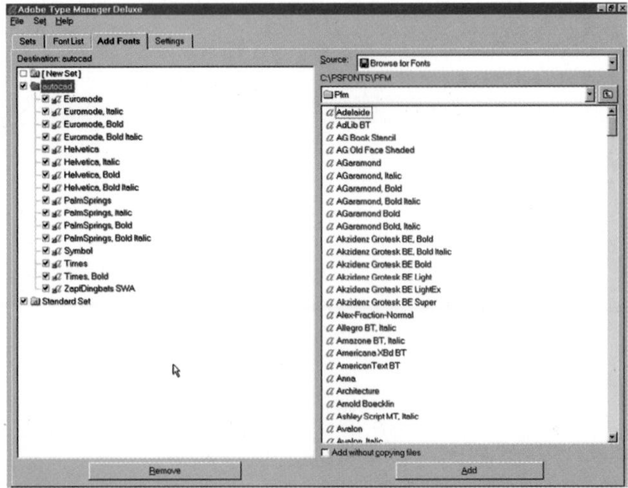

Figure 9-27. The Adobe Type Manager provides lists of all the fonts available.

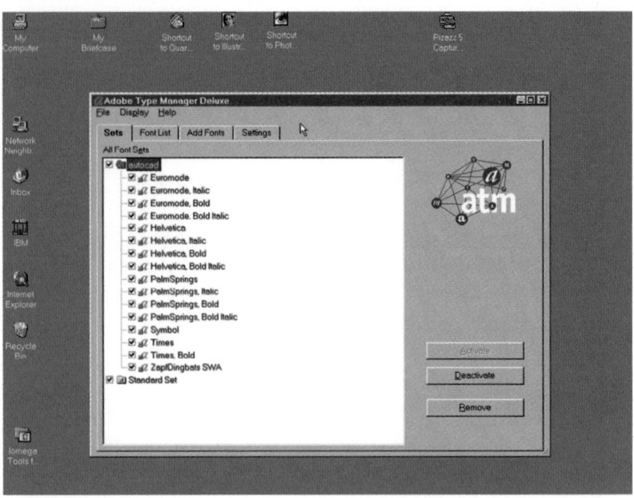

Figure 9-28. The font list above indicates all fonts used in a particular job.

Fonts represented with vector graphics are called ***scaleable fonts, outline fonts,*** or ***vector fonts***. The best-known example of a vector font system is ***PostScript***. The PostScript font characters have no specific size and are described as mathematical definitions of the outline. PostScript output devices render the characters as designated. Outline fonts require less memory than bitmapped font data because they are mathematical formulas.

As with vector images, vector fonts retain smooth contours when slanted, rotated, or scaled to any size. However, converting illustration fonts into vector graphics or object outlines can create problems for small type sizes and large text blocks. For example, outlining small type can create shapes too complex to print. Converting text to outline also makes editing more difficult since the image is now a "graphic" instead of a font.

PostScript Type 1 Fonts

PostScript Type 1 is a format for outline fonts where each character in a typeface is stored as a PostScript language program. Outline fonts have many advantages over bitmapped fonts. They take up less space in a printer's memory; they do not suffer in appearance or legibility when scaled to different sizes; they can be easily rotated, outlined, or filled with patterns; and they produce smooth curves even at large sizes when used as display fonts.

PostScript Type 1 fonts are device-independent. This allows them to be used across a broad range of output devices because any device that contains a PostScript interpreter can read them. Although resolution varies among output devices, type generated from outline fonts will be as sharp as a particular device can produce.

PostScript Type I fonts have two component files, one for screen display and one for PostScript output. These two component files are the ***PostScript printer typeface file*** and the ***suitcase file***. Together these two components make a ***type family***. Digital fonts require two files because the images on the video screen are created differently than those reproduced on film or paper. The screen font is a low-resolution pixel representation of the printer typeface. While the low-resolution image is suitable for the screen, the limited digital information of the screen font prevents high-resolution output.

The suitcase file contains a set of screen font sizes and styles. Although the size range available depends on the program, sizes usually range anywhere from 8 point to 72 point. The usual style choices are the primary font, italic, bold, and bold italic. Some font packages also include a variety of weights and widths.

The printer typefaces are the actual PostScript files. A PostScript file defines the shape of the letters through Bezier curve outlines. Every typeface requires a separate printer file. One component will not function without the other. A monitor can display screen fonts, but PostScript equipment cannot print screen fonts. PostScript devices can output printer typefaces, but a monitor cannot display printer typefaces. The two files require proper location and coupling.

TrueType fonts

TrueType font technology was developed jointly by Microsoft and Apple as a cross-platform outline font. Although TrueType support is built into all Windows and Macintosh operating systems, they do not always translate well.

TrueType fonts have no specific sizes and work by combining the screen fonts and the printer typeface into one file (instead of the separate files used in PostSript). PostScript output devices must either convert TrueType fonts or substitute a PostScript font. This complicates and slows processing and the TrueType fonts may not print well on PostScript output equipment.

If they can be imported successfully, TrueType fonts can provide many benefits in a mixed platform environment. However, most prepress suppliers use PostScript fonts (Type I fonts) as a standard, and may have only a few TrueType fonts. To maintain a smoother workflow, it would be best to avoid using both PostScript and TrueType fonts in the same document.

Multiple master fonts

Traditionally, standard type families had limited style variation. However, Adobe Systems developed ***multiple master fonts*** that allow you to create your own variations on the base design. Each multiple master font consists of the ***base font*** (the multiple master font itself) and one or more ***instances*** of the font, **Figure 9-29**. An instance is a rendition of the font that varies from other instances in one or more attributes such as weight or width.

Multiple master fonts include one or more ***design axes*** for almost unlimited variations of typeface weight and width. A design axis is a variable typeface attribute (weight, width, style, optical size). The base design determines the range of variations available.

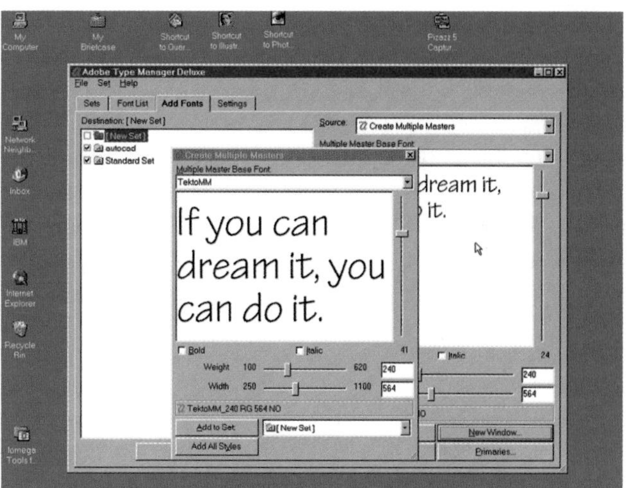

Figure 9-29. Settings for multiple master fonts can be modified within the program's type management utility.

Font organization

Along with the acquisition of fonts, it is advisable to develop an internal filing system on your hard drive. A good filing system makes it easier to collect and send the fonts associated with a document, or to reconstruct a document if problems occur. A good filing system will help prevent mistakes caused by using the wrong font, mixing font types, or mixing typeface publishers.

It is best not to store job fonts in the system folder because every font added to your system takes up Random Access Memory (RAM). Large numbers of active fonts encumber RAM, leaving less memory available for applications. Create a separate font folder inside the system font folder and file each font by its name. Use separate folders to avoid mixing fonts from different publishers. For example, you might have a font named Adobe Garamond and one named Agja Garamond, **Figure 9-30**.

Font report

Service bureaus recommend that you create a report to verify document fonts. Customers often overlook fonts used in PostScript files. Most current software can compile a document report, **Figure 9-31**. For example, QuarkXPress can create a report that indicates the fonts used and lists the EPS files. Adobe Illustrator also indicates the fonts used. Adobe PageMaker provides a font report that lists every open font on the computer and indicates the fonts used in the active file.

Font Sneak is a standalone Mac-only program that supports EPS files and reports to the user all fonts used by the document. It reports any fonts used by the document that are not currently installed and offers the user several font collection options. The options collect all document fonts for prepress output or collect fonts not currently installed for quick system installation via the System Font Folder or Symantec Suitcase.

```
ELECTRONIC OUTPUT REQUEST FOR: YOUR COMPANY NAME HERE                PAGE 2

DOCUMENT
Source Pathname:  O:\CATHY\R14A_TX\CH14\Ch14.qxd
Destination Pathname:     O:\Grph_com\quark\
Last modified: 11:03 AM; 11/18/97
Document Size: 2884K
Most recently saved version: 3.3 Windows format
Document has been saved by the following versions of QuarkXPress:
        3.31r5 Windows format
        3.32r3 Windows format
        3.31r5 Windows format
Total Pages: 60
Page Width: 8.5"
Page Height: 10.875"
Required XTensions:
        None
Active XTensions:
        Cool Blends;     CPSI Fixer;  Kern-Track XTension;    Immedia Project Menu;    JPEG
Import;     LZW Import; MS-Word Filter;    MS-Write Import;    WordPerfect Filter;  XPress Tags
Filter;  PhotoCD Import

DOCUMENT FONTS
External Name     Internal Name     Printer Font Filename
<Helvetica   Helvetica-Bold     C:\PSFONTS\PFM\HVB_____.PFM
<PalmSprings      PalmSprings-Bold   C:\PSFONTS\PFM\PALMSPRB.PFM
<PalmSprings      PalmSprings-Normal      C:\PSFONTS\PFM\PALMSPRN.PFM
<ZapfDingbats SWA      ITC-Zapf-Dingbats-SWA    C:\PSFONTS\PFM\3030X___.PFM
<Helvetica   Helvetica-BoldOblique    C:\PSFONTS\PFM\HVBO____.PFM
<Helvetica   Helvetica     C:\PSFONTS\PFM\HV______.PFM
<PalmSprings      PalmSprings-BoldItalic   C:\PSFONTS\PFM\PALMSPRT.PFM
<Symbol      Symbol        C:\PSFONTS\PFM\SY______.PFM
<PalmSprings      PalmSprings-Italic   C:\PSFONTS\PFM\PALMSPRI.PFM
<Times       Times-Roman       C:\PSFONTS\PFM\TIR_____.PFM
<Symbol      Symbol        C:\PSFONTS\PFM\SY______.PFM

PICTURE FONTS
Picture       External Name
note_c.eps    No fonts used.
r14opnr.eps   No fonts used.
00_aug.eps    No fonts used.
note_c.eps    No fonts used.
protip_c.eps  No fonts used.
protip_c.eps  No fonts used.
note_c.eps    No fonts used.
00_aug.eps    No fonts used.
protip_c.eps  No fonts used.
00_aug.eps    No fonts used.
```

Figure 9-31. The layout and design of font reports will vary from program to program and will often include additional file information.

Preflighting fonts

When preflighting files, all necessary font components should be copied to disk. By using one of the software utilities mentioned earlier, you can turn off all the fonts on your system and load the fonts directly to your printer-ready disk. A prompt will appear if any fonts are missing when you open the files. Some programs will substitute fonts or resort to the default if the fonts are missing from the file.

Problems also occur when fonts in a document have the same name as the printer's fonts but they are actually different fonts. Computer systems cannot distinguish fonts with the same name from different publishers. They are not always able to distinguish the difference or substitute one pub-

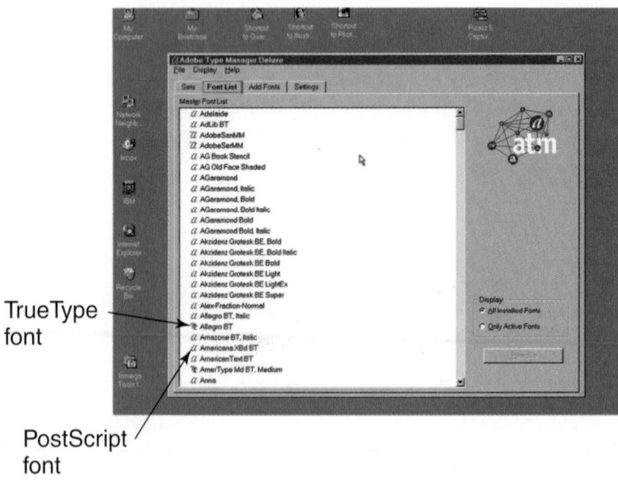

Figure 9-30. TrueType and PostScript fonts may be identified by the icons used within the type management utility.

lisher for another. Avoid mixing publishers within the same typeface family because it complicates and slows workflow.

Fonts are software and subject to strict licensing agreement. Professional practice honors font license agreements. It is the user's responsibility to maintain licensed versions of the fonts used at their location.

Turnaround Time and Proofing

The nature and complexity of a job will determine turnaround time, but in general, the workflow remains the same.

Depending on the complexity of a project and the arrangement you have with the service bureau or printer, you will review a number of proofs before the job goes to press. Proofs serve as samples for the customer and guidelines for the press operators. Proofs can be made directly from digital files, generated directly from film, or run off on a proof press. Cost variations will often determine what type of proofs you will request at different stages of prepress production. Some common proofs are ***Iris proofs, Matchprints, bluelines (diazo), Chromalin, Color Key, Dylux,*** and ***press proofs,*** **Figure 9-32**.

Iris proofs

Iris proofs are produced by an inkjet printing process that produces four-color proofs directly from the digital files. Iris proofing is often used as a contract proof, replacing the conventional Matchprint. The color simulates what you will see on press. However, there is no halftone dot, so conventional screening problems such as moiré patterns cannot be predicted. Iris proofs are initial proofs presented early in the proofing process and are very expensive.

Figure 9-32. Color proofs can be checked for dot pattern and registration with a loupe.

Matchprints

Matchprints have been used for many years and have become an industry-standard contract proof. They are produced from the actual film that will create the printing pages. This enables accurate evaluation of the film for trapping, moiré, and other conventional printing problems.

Bluelines or diazo proofs

Bluelines or diazo proofs are produced from imageset film. The process is a photographic procedure in which light-sensitive compounds are applied to paper, plastic, or metal sheets. The substrate is then exposed to intense blue and/or ultraviolet light and developed with ammonia vapors or an alkaline solution to form an image. This process produces proofs from positive film flats. The images and text on the proofs are usually blue in color.

Although bluelines are relatively inexpensive to produce, they are extremely valuable for showing the position and registration of the printed material. Bluelines can be imaged on both sides, folded, and trimmed. They are usually presented as unbound signatures that provide an accurate proof of pagination and how the finished piece will be folded, bound, and trimmed.

Bluelines are not meant to be checked for editorial corrections. Bluelines should be used only to ensure that there are no scratches, missing type or art, and that the pagination and trim are correct. Making corrections at the blueline stage is expensive and time-consuming because new film must be generated for each modified page.

Press proofs

Press proofs are generated with a ***proof press.*** A proof press is a printing machine used to produce photomechanical proofs. It has most of the elements of a true production machine but is not meant for long press runs. Press proofs may be one of the best verification proofs, but press proofing is slow and expensive.

Color proofing

The primary purpose of a ***color proofing system*** is to catch errors or mistakes prior to the press run where corrections would be expensive. Traditional methods include proofing with a set of inks on the press and using a photographic or photomechanical proofing system. Color proofs should be accurate representations of what the printed result will be. Once again, cost will often determine what types of proofs occur at specific production stages. For further discussion on color proofing, refer to Chapter 11.

Digital Printing Technology

Prior to computerization, the production of printed materials did not lend itself to complete integration. However, the application of digital technology to all aspects of the workflow has reduced the number of steps and made the process simple and more productive, **Figure 9-33**.

Digital technology is now used to create text, capture or create images, create film and printing plates, and even apply ink directly to the page. Computer applications and digital presses have made possible many printing options that were once never imaginable. Entire four-color jobs can be produced within hours, rather than days or weeks. Print runs can range from just a few to a few thousand. Materials can easily be customized to suit different target groups and individuals and documents can be transmitted electronically to multiple locations for distributed printing.

This systemization of distributed printing permits great flexibility because the physical scanner, RIP, and output devices can be spread throughout a wide area network (WAN). A print job can be spread across many printers at the same time, resulting in very high output rates for jobs that once required expensive dedicated copier/printing systems.

Digital printing can be defined as any reproduction technology that receives electronic files and uses spot (or dots) for replication. An ink, toner, ink-jet, or any other dye- or pigment-based transfer system may be used. Digital printing technologies include "computer-to-imagesetter," ***computer-to-plate (CTP)*** and ***digital-to-paper***. As discussed earlier, computer-to-imagesetter technology involves the electronic creation of materials up to the output of film by the imagesetter. Once the film is produced, conventional platemaking and printing processes are carried out.

Computer-to-plate (CTP)

Computer-to-plate (CTP) technology uses imaging systems that take fully-paginated digital materials and expose this information to plates in platesetters or imagesetters without creating film intermediates, **Figure 9-34**. CTP is also referred to as ***direct-to-plate (DTP)*** or ***digital-to-plate***. The most obvious advantage of CTP is enhanced workflow that functions as well for long-run projects as it does for short production runs.

CTP provides superior imaging as a result of the elimination of an entire generation in the prepress schedule. Problems associated with dirt, misregistration, and dot gain from film-to-plate exposure are eliminated. Halftones reproduce better, dot patterns are sharper, and there is less gain on the press. Although the elimination of films can reduce a project's cycle time, most publishers will use this "additional" time at the creative end and/or to review and revise digital proofs.

CTP applications are especially useful for projects that routinely undergo extensive revision after a publisher has forwarded files for prepress processing. This includes revisions made during the proofing process. Because changes are made to electronic files and the plates are created directly from the digital data, customers are able to make changes within hours before printing.

In CTP, plates are usually created with heat, lasers, or ultraviolet light. The method used may depend on the type of plate material. Although lasers have become one of the most commonly used methods, high-quality metal printing plates are being created with ink-jet technology. The plates are created directly from digital data by spraying fine droplets of a proprietary fluid onto aluminum. The plates do not require any processing and can be mounted directly onto a printing press, **Figure 9-35**.

Plates vary in thickness and can be made of a variety of materials including aluminum, photopolymers, and polyester resins, **Figure 9-36**. When intended for long print runs, most of the CTP plates are heat-treated to preserve quality. Plates created by CTP method can be intended for use on conventional presses or digital printers. There are still projects that will be more cost-effective when

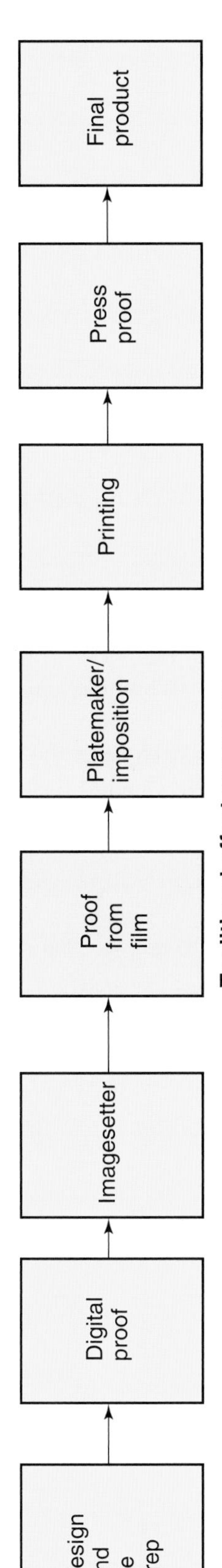

Traditional offset processes

Traditional offset printing demands plenty of time, people, materials, and steps to produce quality color output. Traditional presses are usually more economical than digital presses when printing large volumes and they also offer a greater variety of inks, paper, and other printing material. However, four-color short runs are usually cost-prohibitive.

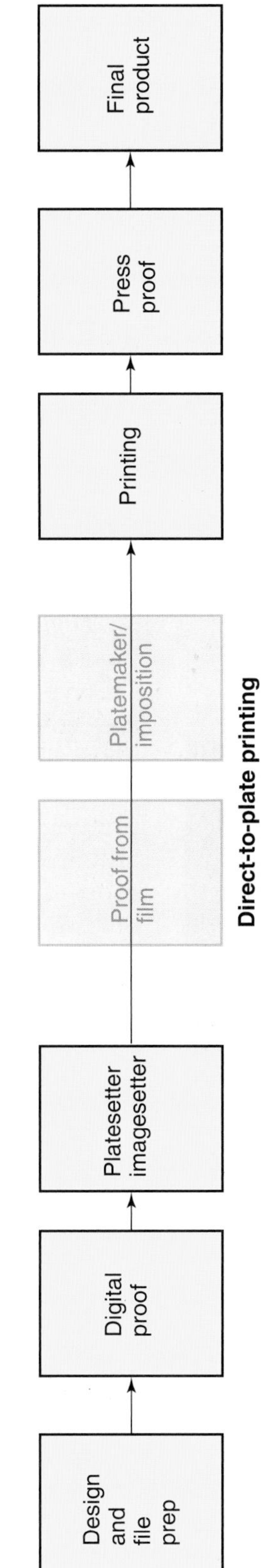

Direct-to-plate printing

Direct-to-plate technology (DTP) eliminates film production from the workflow. Instead of exposing film, fully paginated digital materials are exposed to plates in platesetters or imagesetters.

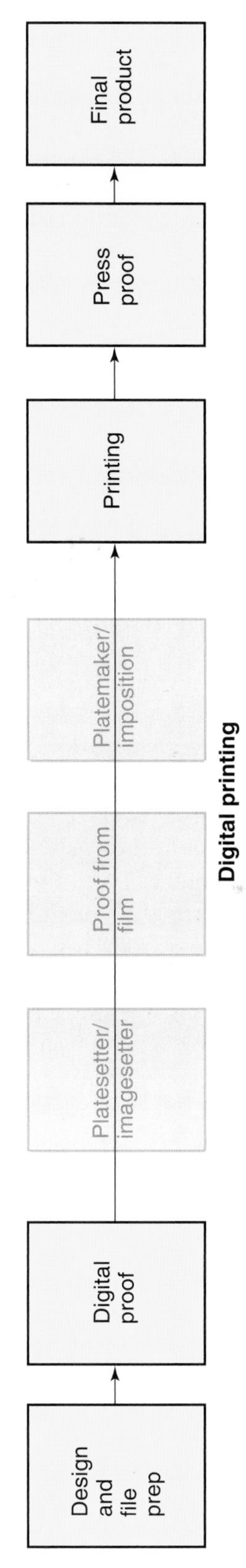

Digital printing

Digital printing eliminates film creation as well as platemaking from the workflow. It automates make-ready and provides proofs directly from the press. Plates and drums can be easily reimaged allowing the customer to make less expensive last-minute changes or to easily personalize regional publications.

Figure 9-33. Comparing traditional offset processes with digital printing technology.

Figure 9-34. This flatbed CTP system covers a wide range of printing applications including Hexachrome printing and stochastic (FM) screening. (High Water Designs Limited)

Figure 9-35. After imaging, no-process plates can be mounted directly to the printing press. (Imation)

Figure 9-36. Plates made with a high-speed polymer have medium-run-length capability. A baking process is used to extend their range to long-run capability. (FUJI Photo Film U.S.A., Inc.)

printed with traditional methods. Sometimes the costs associated with replating for straight reprints favor films over CTP. Plates made directly from stored film shorten the manufacturing cycle, saving publishers time and money.

Digital prepress proofing systems

Noncontact digital proofs are still the only method of proofing when using CTP; publishers will have to determine if they are comfortable relying on digital proofs. There are many different types of digital prepress proofing systems, with each type varying in its capabilities. The publisher's needs will determine what type of proof will be acceptable. The discussion of color proofing systems can be found in Chapter 11, *Color Management*.

Digital-to-paper

Digital-to-paper technology is the printing of images directly on the press from electronic files. This type of printing eliminates the time-consuming and costly preparation of film, plates, and inks. Though not without limitations, digital presses provide customers with options that bring professional printing closer to the desktop with quick turnaround, flexibility, and cost-effective four-color short runs. Because digital-to-paper printing does not use traditional printing processes, it is referred to as ***totally electronic printing (TEP)***.

Totally electronic printing uses a reimageable image carrier or no image carrier for the transfer of ink-jet ink or toner to paper. TEP usually uses pixels (bitmapped images) for printing.

Ink-jet printing

Ink-jet printing is a direct-to-paper technology with no intermediate image carrier. It uses digital data to control streams of very fine dye drops to produce images directly on paper. Types of ink-jet printers include ***continuous-drop, drop-on-demand,*** and ***bubblejet***. Most ink-jet printing is ***variable information printing*** of single or spot colors, such as direct mail advertising or large format posters for limited distribution, **Figure 9-37**.

Variable information printing is unique to digital printing systems because it enables quick and easy content change at varying points of a print run. Variable printing allows the production of ***customized*** and ***personalized printing*** for target marketing purposes. Customized printing means

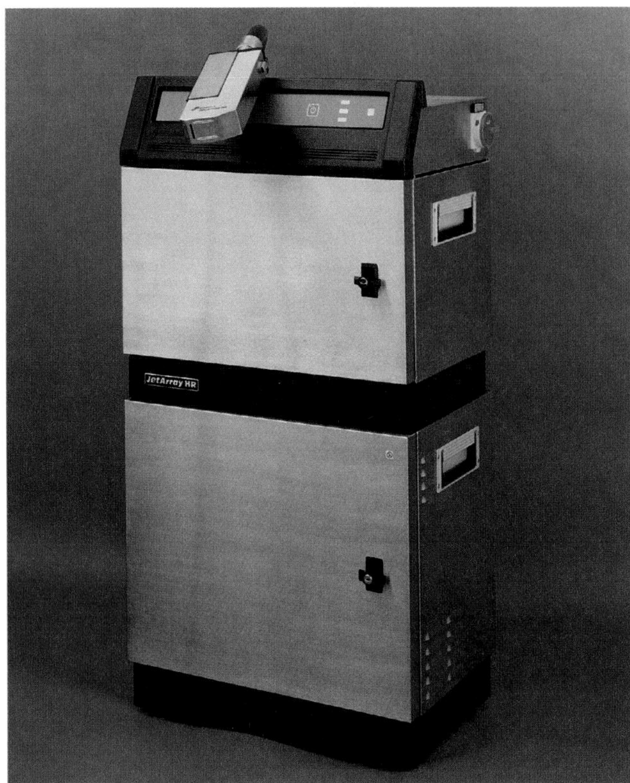

Figure 9-37. Many ink-jet printers can print high-resolution images on a variety of substrates including coated or uncoated paper stock or plastic wrapping. The ink-jet printer illustrated above can be used for printing personalized text and addresses, barcodes, and graphics. (Domino Amjet, Inc.)

that documents can be assembled that are particular to selected audiences. Personalized printing means that each unit is particular to a specific person. Variable-information products include localized editions of national magazines, catalogs, newsletters, and other publications.

These printers are classified as either desktop or large-format, based on the size of the reproduced image. Desktop printers are those that can produce images up to 13″ × 19″. Large-format printers are those that produce images, typically from paper rolls larger than 13″ in width and technically limited only by the length of the roll of substrate material (often, 150″ or more). Large-format inkjet printers, **Figure 9-38,** are used extensively within the graphic communications industry for critical proofing applications. Still larger inkjet printers, beyond the classification of "large-format," are called grand format. They are commonly used to create outdoor signage.

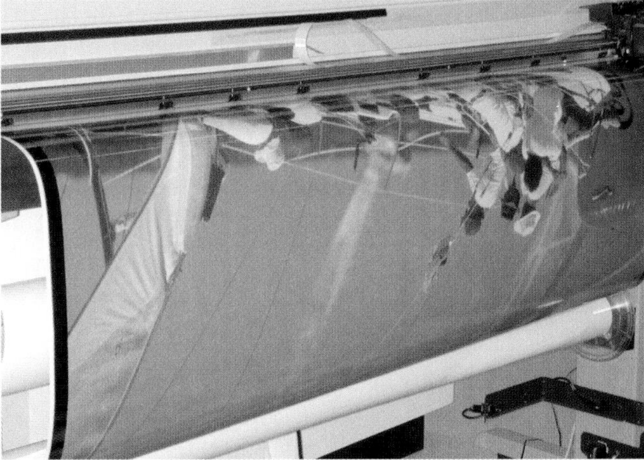

Figure 9-38. The large-format printers commonly make products that are highly pictorial, individualized, and delivered in a wide variety of sizes.

Toner-based printing

Toner-based reproduction requires a drum or belt to create the toned image and then transfer it to paper. In essence, the drum or belt is an image carrier, like any printing plate. The difference is that the printing plate content is fixed (the image does not change during reproduction). The *toner-based image carrier* must create a new image for every reproduction and is thus reimageable. Toner-based printing technologies include ***ionography, magnetography,*** and ***electrophotographic printing.***

Ionography, also known as ***ion deposition*** or ***electron charge deposition printing,*** produces images with negative charges from an electron cartridge transferred onto a heated nonconductive (dielectric) surface using magnetic toner. Ionography is used mainly for single or spot color printing because the pressure of image transfer and cold fusion toner fixing can distort the substrate. Ionography systems are used for high volume and variable information printing.

Magnetography converts an electronic image to a magnetic charge on a drum that then attracts magnetized toner. Because the toners are dark and opaque, magnetography is suited for spot color but not process color. Magnetographic systems are commonly used for variable information printing.

Electrophotographic printing systems use drums or metal plates coated with chargeable photoconductors that discharge to the nonimage areas after exposure to light. The image receives toners in the charged area, transfers to a substrate, and fuses or fixes by heat, solvent vapor, or other fixing method. Most electrophotographic systems accomodate a wide range of paper finishes, weights, and sizes. Some systems also include a scanning bed, **Figure 9-39**.

Electrophotographic printing is subject to three deficiencies:

- Charge voltage decay that affects image density and tone reproduction.
- Toner chemistry variations and expensive toner formulation.
- Environmental regulations governing some system chemistry.

Toner-based printing has become more systemized by connecting the device to a network and viewing the copier as part of a system consisting of a scanner, a RIP, and a printer. The development of color output, the changes in RIP technology, and increased processor speeds have contributed to significant improvements in the versatility of copier technology. These advances have brought about consistent, repeatable color images at speeds that challenge the output produced by small printing presses. In some instances, these copier/printing systems are being used to produce content proofing as well as final or contract proofs.

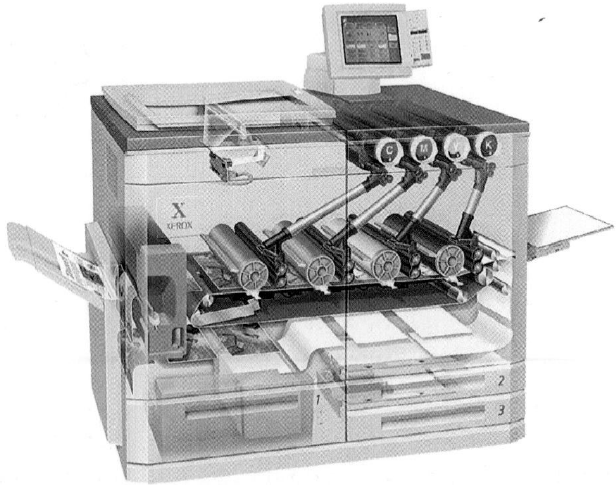

Figure 9-39. The electrophotographic printing system illustrated above includes a flatbed scanner and a pre-viewing screen. It also allows the addition of a sorter and automatic document feeder. (Xerox)

Other electronic printing technologies

Field effect imaging is high-speed, high-quality color printing composed of variable density pixels. Field effect imaging uses a write head to generate powerful electrostatic fields across a thin-film insulator surface. These fields cause the pickup of pixel-sized ink bits whose thickness is proportional to the strength of the fields. The writing surface carries these ink bits to a print surface where the complete ink amount is transferred to the print substrate.

Thermal transfer printing or ***dye sublimation printing***, uses digital data to control a thermal printhead to melt spots of dry ink on a ribbon and transfer them to a receiver. When sublimable dye replaces solid ink, the thermal head converts the dye spots to gas spots which condense on the receiver. This technique is commonly used for color proofing.

Distributed digital printing

National newspapers and magazines have been using ***distributed printing*** technology to print regional editions for quite some time. However, digital printing presses now make distributed printing possible for anyone with access to a network or modem.

With ***distributed digital printing***, electronic files can be sent anywhere and printed near to the point of distribution. For example, a brochure can be sent electronically to a service bureau near a trade show location a few days before the show. The brochure can then be printed and delivered to the convention center or hotel near the service bureau, saving time and shipping costs.

Distributed printing does have its limitations. File transfer can be slow due to inefficient telecommunication systems. As new fiber optic and ISDN lines are being established, file transfer will become more efficient. ***Color management systems*** at both ends will help make colors consistent, but it may still be necessary to send hard copies (swatches/document examples) in addition to the electronic files.

Most companies prefer to proof their own printed documents prior to a press run and most printers require final approval from the customer before a press run. Businesses using distributed printing on a regular basis may be able to provide local representatives for on-site approval; however, most jobs will require sending proofs back to the original site for review.

Printing jobs that are distributed electronically can be output on digital or conventional presses. Digital files can also be sent to remote locations to make plates.

Print services facility

The Print Services Facility (PSF) is an outgrowth of the digital print revolution. These facilities produce print jobs for clients at locations where either excess capacity exists or where conventional transportation costs would make production of the printed piece otherwise prohibitive. The transfer of large files over the Internet is a viable option. The ability to get consistent, predictable, and repeatable color has also allowed distribution of jobs across facilities that may reside in the same location or can be spread across great geographic areas. By applying ICC profiles to image color management, tools exist to interpret this information, spread the print job across digital color devices, and get consistent results. The paradigm of Create, Print, and Distribute has given way to the paradigm of Create, Distribute, and Print.

Digital printing—advantages and limitations

There are certain areas in which digital and conventional printing each have a production and economic advantage. There are also an increasing number of areas where they overlap as emerging and conventional technologies adapt to the short-run market demands.

Conventional color printing requires long runs (1000+ copies) to absorb high makeready costs. Although computer-to-plate technology has eliminated many of the time-consuming and expensive steps involved in traditional printing, digital printing has not yet surpassed the quality traditional printing provides, **Figure 9-40**.

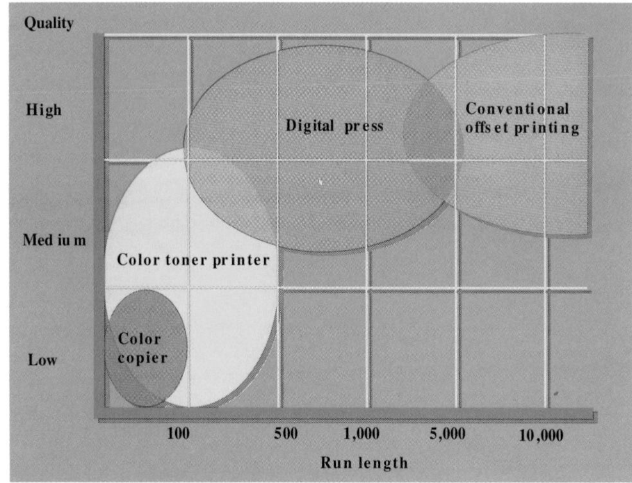

Figure 9-40. Color printing technology is available in varying levels of quality and all types of run lengths.

The term ***on-demand printing*** is often used solely to describe digital-to-paper printing. This is a misnomer because all printers print on demand. If a customer "demands" an order, the printer will print it. On-demand printing is better defined as short-run, distributed, just-in-time printing, no matter how it is produced.

Digital presses offer quick turnaround times, a great deal of flexibility, and cost-effective four-color short runs. Depending on finishing requirements, an experienced printshop using a digital press can generally turn around a document in 48 hours or less. With the proper full-color digital printers, digital printing can also provide a means to produce quick, cost-effective, high quality proofs for gravure and offset printing.

The flexibility factor of digital printing exists because plates or drums on many digital presses can be reimaged *on-the-fly*. Last-minute changes can be made while incurring little or no extra cost. Digital printing allows the customization of individual pages during print runs and the ability to transmit electronic files for printing almost anywhere in the world. Digital printing provides a cost-effective means for printing out-of-print titles and black and white short-run manuals, books, and textbooks, **Figure 9-41**.

By eliminating much of the traditional press preparation, digital presses make the overall cost of four-color short runs affordable. Short-run process color printing includes very short printing runs ranging from 1–500 copies or 501–2000 copies. The unit cost may be higher with digital printing, but the overall cost of the same short run on a traditional press would be prohibitively expensive.

Although digital printing has many advantages, it also has its limitations. Most digital presses do not yet produce the rich deep look of material printed on a seven-color traditional offset press. Document design is limited in that it should not be overly complicated or dependent on exact color matching. Digital presses are not intended as replacements for conventional printing presses.

Figure 9-41. This Docutech system is extremely efficient for printing out-of-print titles and black and white short-run manuals, books, and textbooks. (Xerox)

They are meant for the types of jobs that aren't practical or even possible on their traditional counterparts.

As the quality of digital graphic arts technology continues to improve, the advantages it promises are certain to grow. These promises include lower costs, greater flexibility, and faster production times. New technology will also require the mastery of new skills in every step of the production process.

The trend toward all-digital design, storage, production, and reproduction is very exciting. However, this trend also involves the expansion of complex input and output options that will require the use of consistent standards in the way that products are created, transmitted, and reproduced. As with all technology, you must continually update your knowledge and equipment to remain competitive.

Review Questions

Please do not write in this book. Write your answers on a separate sheet of paper.

1. What is meant by the term *cross-platform*?
2. Reusing content intended for one medium by reformatting it for another is called _____.
3. List four methods that can be used to create computer images.
4. What are two methods for diminishing jaggies that should be smooth?
5. List at least five forms of manipulation that are allowed by image editors/image manipulation programs.
6. What is a *raster image processor (RIP)*? What is its major function?
7. What is an *imagesetter*? What is its major function?
8. What purpose does a *page description language (PDL)* serve?
9. What is *portable document format (PDF)* and what are some of its main advantages?
10. What does it mean when a file format is defined as device-independent?
11. What is the main difference between *lossless* and *lossy* compression?
12. Which type of compression technique is preferred for images that are to be printed? Why?
13. Name at least four of the commonly used file formats.
14. Why is it better to use a page composition program to lay out material than a word-processing program?
15. What is *preflighting* and why is it so important in prepress production?
16. List five of the most common recurring problems with customer-furnished files.
17. What problems can occur if fonts are substituted in a final document file?
18. What are some of the ways in which prepress proofs are generated?
19. What is *CTP*?
20. What are some of the advantages of *totally electronic printing*?

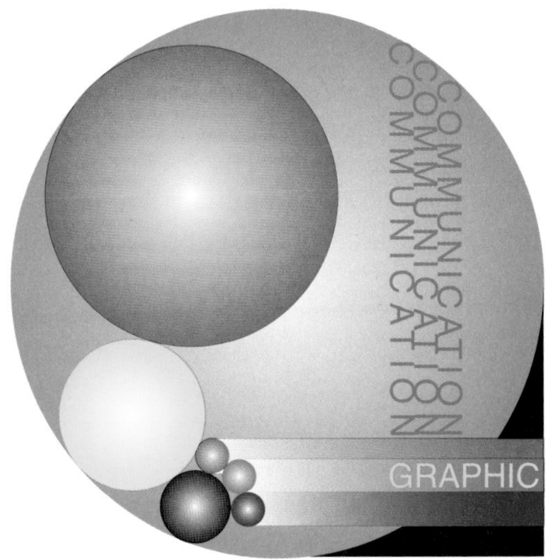

10 Digital Image Capture

Learning Objectives

After studying this chapter, you will be able to:

- Explain the difference between analog form and digital form.
- List the various types of light sensors used in imaging devices.
- Identify the array configurations of charge-coupled devices (CCDs).
- Define the different types of resolution.
- Identify what type of imaging device should be used for specific results.
- List the tools and applications available in imaging programs.
- Identify the various types of scanners.
- Describe how image capture time can limit the performance of digital imaging devices.
- Identify different types of digital cameras.
- List lighting considerations associated with the use of digital cameras.

Important Terms

analog form
digital form
bit depth
charge-coupled device (CCD)
resolution
dynamic range
interpolation
photomultiplier tube (PMT)
spatial resolution
tonal resolution

Since its introduction, digital imaging has had an increasing impact on the printing industry. Advances in computer software make it possible to quickly modify images by changing or adding colors, removing unwanted components, or even combining multiple images. When paired with a computer modem, digital imaging technology makes it possible to transmit electronic images almost instantly around the world.

Many prepress institutions still depend on scanners for film and photo reproduction. However, as digital cameras become less costly, acquire more storage capacity, and increase image quality, they will become more integrated in the printing process. Digital cameras with accurate RGB-to-CMYK conversion capabilities will allow image files to bypass scanning and color separation procedures and move directly into the production flow.

Analog and Digital Image Forms

Photos taken with a film-based camera are in ***analog form***. The principal feature of something in analog form is that it is continuous. Just as the volume control on a TV increases the sound in smooth gradations from soft to loud, the image on a film negative has smooth gradations of tone from light to dark.

In contrast, the principal feature of something in ***digital form*** is that it consists of values measured at distinct points or positions, **Figure 10-1**. When an image in analog form is converted to digital form, each of these distinct points represents the variances in brightness and color of the image. These points are recorded as pixels (picture elements). Pixels are arranged in rows and columns to form a grid. The

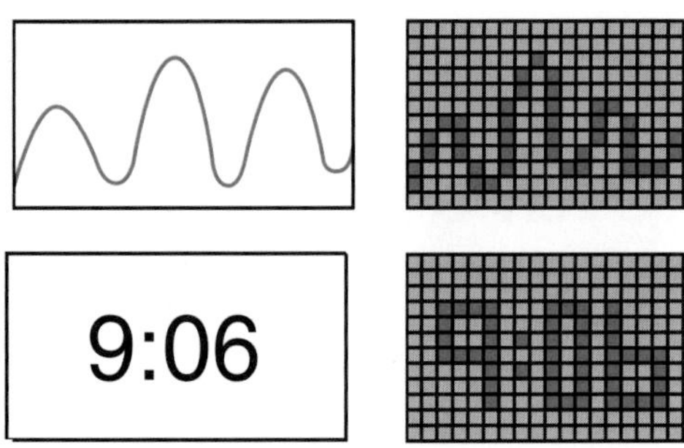

Figure 10-1. Both the line and the numbers on the left are in analog form. The images on the right are the same line and numbers in digital form.

analog image is recorded in digital form by assigning each pixel a set of numbers to designate position, brightness, and color.

The greater the number of pixels, or ***dots per inch (dpi)***, at the time an image is digitized, the greater the amount of detail or the better the resolution. The greater the number of bits used to represent each pixel, or ***bit depth***, the smoother the gradation. The greater the bit depth, the more colors or grayscales can be represented. For example, a 24-bit color scanner can represent 2^{24} (16.7 million) colors. However, a large color range is useless if the light-sensors of an imaging device are capable of detecting only a small number of distinct colors.

All digital imaging input devices function approximately in the same way—they expose the original with light and measure the amount of red, green, and blue light reflected back off or transmitted through the object. These measurements are converted into digital data, which is then recorded onto an internal or external disk. The type of light-gathering sensors the imaging device uses determines both the dpi and bit depth. Herein lies the main difference between the various types of digital cameras, camera backs, and scanners available.

CCD Array Configurations

Both flatbed scanners and digital cameras use the same type of light-gathering sensors, known as ***charge-coupled devices (CCDs)***. A CCD is a solid-state chip composed of hundreds or even thousands of separate photosensitive elements known as ***well sites*** or ***photosites***. Each of the well sites in an array has a slightly different sensitivity from every other site.

Just as the film in a conventional camera records an image when light strikes it, the CCD uses light to record an image electronically. The CCD converts light reflected from the subject matter into a series of electrical impulses, or ***analog charge***. The charge is converted from analog to digital form through an ***A/D converter***, and stored as pixels using a binary code to represent the tonal values and detail of the subject. The A/D converter creates the digital image by converting the analog charge generated by the CCD into a series of steps. This process is called *quantisizing*.

Efficient CCD design is a trade-off between ***resolution***, the sharpness and clarity of an image, and ***dynamic range***, the gradations from light to dark. As the individual well sites become smaller, the resolution of the CCD array increases. However, smaller well sites are less efficient at registering light intensity, so dynamic range suffers if they become too small. Most CCDs are designed to strike a balance between resolution and dynamic range.

CCD performance is often measured by its output resolution, which in turn is a function of the number of well sites on the CCD's surface and the shape of its pixels. CCDs using video technology have rectangular pixels, while sensors with square pixels were created specifically for use on computers.

The needs of the photographer or publisher, as well as the desired result, will determine the type of CCD array and exposure configuration that should be used. Cameras are available with a variety of CCD configurations, including single-array/single-exposure, single-array/three- or four-exposure, single-array/one-, three-, or four-exposure, and trilinear-array/single-exposure. Scanners using CCD technology always use a trilinear array. The type of CCD configuration used by a camera, camera back, or scanner determines its cost as well as the quality of the images it produces.

Because CCD sensors are inherently monochromatic, special filters are needed to separate the red, green, and blue (RGB) light reflected by an object. Designers have developed a number of ways to enable their digital imaging devices to capture color.

Single-array/single-exposure

Cameras that use a single CCD array and a single exposure rely on RGB filtration decals to gather red, green, and blue color information, **Figure 10-2**.

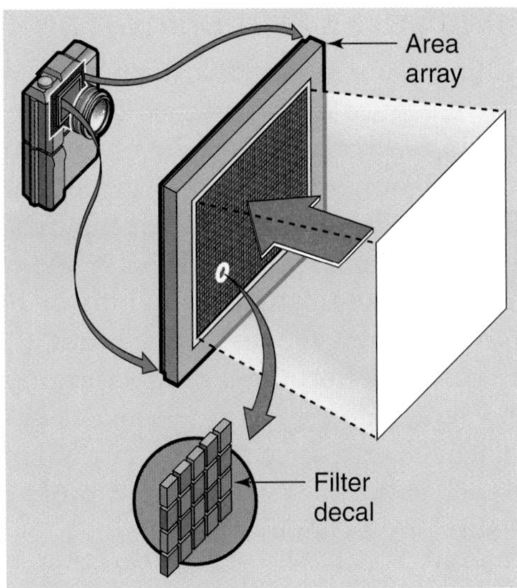

Figure 10-2. The resolution for a specific CCD corresponds to the total number of pixels and is determined by multiplying the horizontal by vertical pixel counts. This number is the resolution for a single channel and must be multiplied by three when working with RGB files. For example, a CCD with dimensions of 1000 × 1500 pixels has a resolution of 1.5 Mb per channel and an RGB resolution of 4.5 Mb.

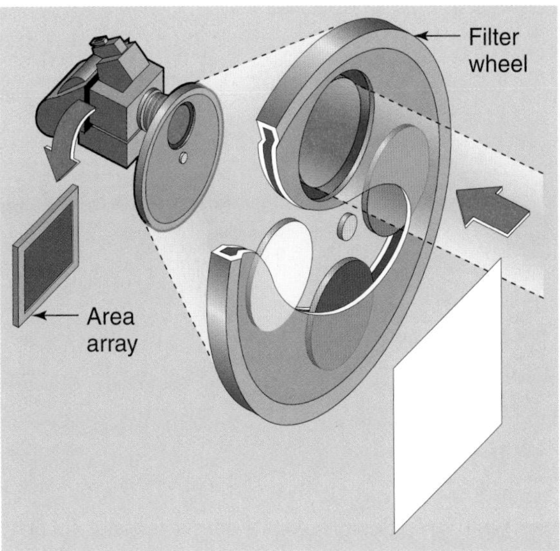

Figure 10-3. A three-exposure CCD area array captures tricolor image information through RGB filters positioned in a rotating wheel in front of the lens or the film plane.

The filter decals may be arranged in rows to create a striped array or in a discontinuous pattern to create a mosaic array. With this method, three or four CCD well sites are used to gather RGB data for a single pixel. This results in a single-channel resolution that is one-third or one-fourth what it would otherwise be. (Channels represent the color separations.) Therefore, it is necessary to compensate for these low values by *interpolating* additional RGB data from neighboring pixels.

Interpolation is a mathematical technique used to increase the apparent resolution of an image. Interpolation increases image resolution by adding data in intermediate shades of gray or color to surrounding areas. This may reduce the jagged appearance at the edges of the image, but it may also make them fuzzier. Interpolation yields higher resolution, but color purity is frequently compromised by the interpolation scheme and is often visible at high magnification.

Single-array/three- or four-exposure

Instead of filtration over the CCD well sites, this design uses three or four exposures to create pure RGB data for each pixel, **Figure 10-3**. The fourth exposure, when used, is a double pass to improve green rendition. The exposures are made through a rotating color-filter wheel positioned in front of the camera lens or CCD array. The advantage of individual exposures for RGB capture is more accurate color rendition, since no interpolation is needed. The drawback is longer overall exposure times that do not allow movement during exposure.

Single-array/one-, three-, or four-exposure

This design uses a single mosaic CCD array with one or more exposures. When RGB data is captured using three or four exposures, the CCD array is repositioned between each of the exposures, **Figure 10-4**. The CCD array changes position to align itself with the appropriately filtered light path that provides data for the respective pixels. This approach allows for pure RGB data to be gathered for each pixel without resorting to interpolation.

Digital cameras using this design often provide a single-exposure mode to stop motion and extend the camera's versatility. When operating in single-exposure mode, the mosaic CCD array gathers 25% of the total pixel resolution for the red and blue channels and 50% for the green channel. The remaining pixel resolution is interpolated to bring each channel up to 100%.

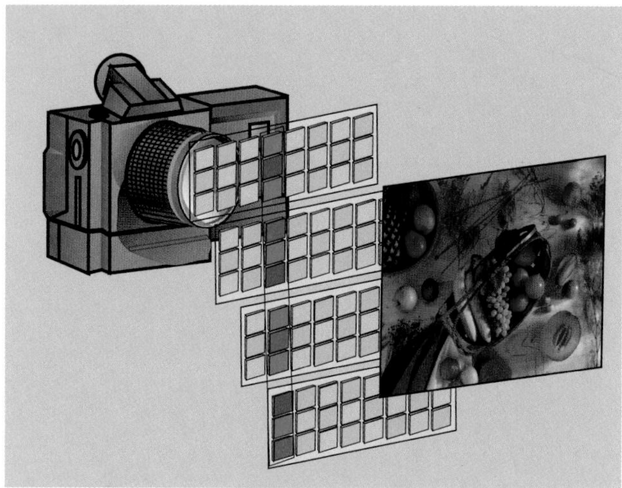

Figure 10-4. This design uses a single mosaic CCD array with one or more exposures. The CCD array is repositioned between exposures by piezoelectric motors.

Trilinear-array/single-exposure

Three CCD chips are built into a camera with this design, **Figure 10-5**. After light passes through the lens, it is split into three portions that travel to individual CCD arrays filtered to independently record red, green, and blue. The configuration achieves a noninterpolated RGB image capture without the need for multiple exposures. The disadvantage of cameras with this design is that they tend to be both bulky and costly. In order to keep the camera competitively priced, it is necessary to use CCD chips of moderate resolution.

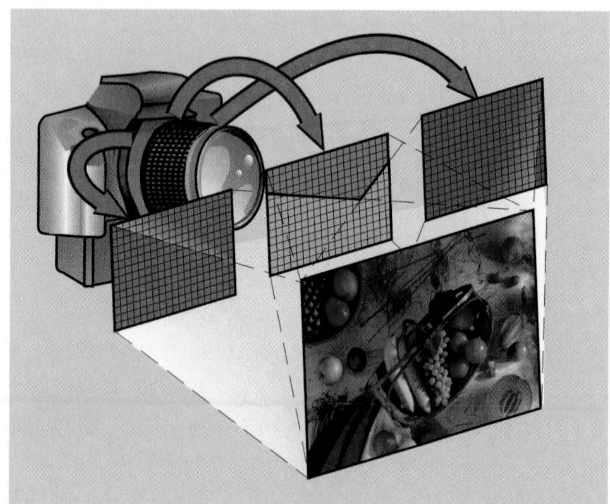

Figure 10-5. Three CCD arrays are built into a trilinear array/single-exposure camera.

Scanning backs with trilinear arrays

Scanning camera backs usually use trilinear CCD arrays, **Figure 10-6**. In place of a square or rectangular chip, a trilinear array uses three rows of CCD elements (one each for red, green, and blue) that run across the shortest side of the image capture area. When an exposure is made, the trilinear array moves slowly across the width of the film plane. As the array moves, it measures the light intensity of a predetermined number of pixel positions and writes image information as a stream of digital data. To scan at maximum resolution using this type of camera back, the image capture process may take as long as ten minutes.

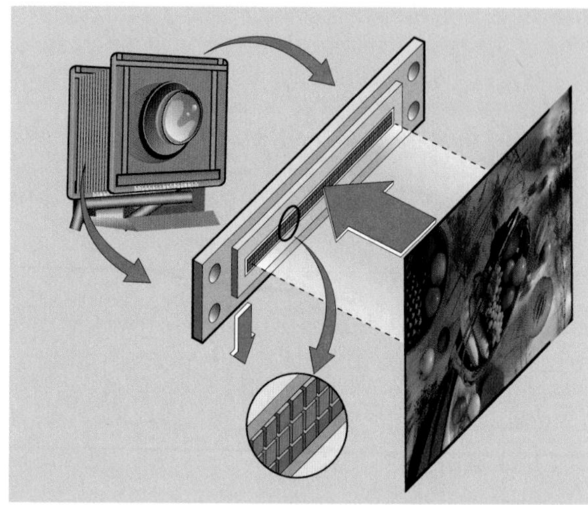

Figure 10-6. A trilinear array CCD camera back with three embedded color filters that captures RGB data in a single pass.

Scanners with linear arrays

Flatbed scanners employing CCD technology use a linear array and a single pass to capture images. Depending on the scanner design, either the bed or the array moves, **Figure 10-7**.

When the scan is performed, the array (or bed) moves slowly across the width of the ***scan area***. The scan area on a flatbed scanner is the glass bed or platen on which images are placed for scanning. As the array (or bed) moves, it measures the intensity of light as it passes through, or is reflected from, the image. The light is split into portions that travel to individual CCD arrays filtered to record, red, green, and blue independently.

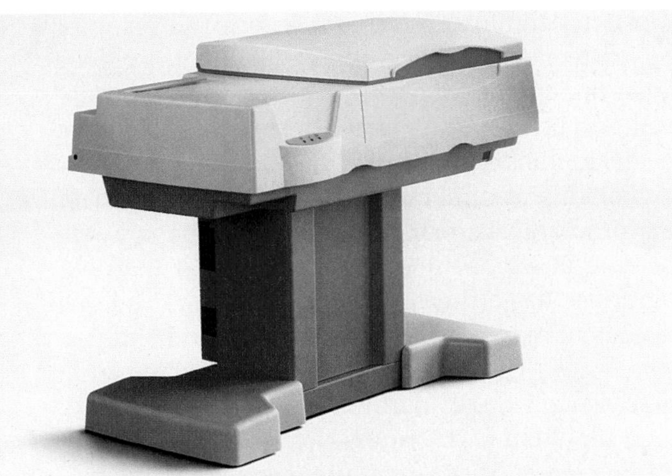

Figure 10-7. The scanning head on this multipurpose flatbed scanner can be positioned at any point beneath the platen, allowing XY scanning. (Fuji Photo Film U.S.A., Inc.)

The linear array in a scanner is arranged in a row on a single silicon chip. If the bed is stationary, the movement of the light source within the scanner, along with a mirror, directs consecutive lines of image data onto the CCD array via a second mirror and a lens unit. The full length of the image is read simultaneously as a line. Some manufacturers have eliminated the mirrors and use a more advanced optical system.

Image capture time depends on the scanner's resolution capabilities, and the type and number of images being scanned. Some flatbed scanners provide the user with a choice of resolution. Higher resolution images commonly require the interpolation of data.

CMOS APS Sensors

The ***CMOS APS (complementary metal oxide semiconductor)*** is a low-cost light sensor chip that is finding use in low-end digital cameras. An introductory point-and-shoot camera using a CMOS APS sensor can capture images at 1000 × 800 dpi. This is 2.6 times the resolution obtained by the common 640 × 480 dpi digital camera.

CMOS APS chips potentially have many advantages, including lower power consumption (up to 100 times less power than CCDs). Other advantages include the possibility of integrating analog-to-digital conversion on the CMOS processor, and even integrating signal processing, such as image compression and color encoding. As technology improves, the CMOS APS chips may replace CCDs in scanners and digital cameras.

Photomultiplier Tubes (PMTs)

Photomultiplier tubes (PMTs) are composed of highly sensitive photocells that transform variations in light into electric currents. The photocells create the input signals to the computing circuits in electronic scanners. In electronic prepress production, PMT technology is usually limited to use in drum scanners, **Figure 10-8**.

Figure 10-8. Drum scanners use photomultiplier tubes (PMTs) as a light-sensing device instead of a CCD array. (Fuji Photo Film U.S.A., Inc.)

Image File Size and Resolution

The size of a digital image file in megabytes (Mb) determines the reproduction size that can be accommodated within a specific ***screen ruling.*** The screen ruling is the number of ruled ***lines per inch (lpi)*** on a halftone screen.

To calculate file size, multiply the number of horizontal pixels by the number of vertical pixels in the CCD array. The result is the file size for a single channel or black-and-white rendition. For RGB color, multiply the file size for one channel times three. For example, if the horizontal and vertical dimensions of a CCD array are 3060 × 2036 pixels, multiply these dimensions to find the file size for a single channel. In this case, it is just over six megabytes. To get RGB color, multiply 6 Mb × 3 to get a file size of 18 Mb.

The next step in this example is to determine if there is enough pixel resolution to output a 5″ × 7″ image at a 200 lpi screen ruling. High quality reproduction requires two pixel samples for each line of resolution. Accordingly, you need a minimum image resolution of 400 dpi to use a screen ruling of 200 lpi. If you multiply the 5″ × 7″ image dimensions by 400 dpi, resolution is 2000 × 2800. The total minimum file size would be 5.6 Mb per channel. Therefore, in this example, the original file size of 6 Mb per channel is slightly more than needed to maintain the desired quality. Typically, the high-resolution image should be about twice the line screen value.

Spatial and tonal resolution

Spatial resolution refers to the capability of a digital imaging device to address data in two dimensions, horizontal and vertical. In addition to spatial resolution, digital imaging devices can also be evaluated in terms of ***tonal resolution***, **Figure 10-9**. Tonal resolution, or bit depth, is the number of bits of color or grayscale information that can be recorded per pixel. An 8-bit digital image capture device can record 256 colors or levels of gray per channel.

With digital cameras, the advantage of increased tonal resolution is that the camera has better exposure latitude. This allows the photographer to shoot in difficult lighting situations with greater confidence.

When using an 8-bit digital camera, shooting the subject at the correct exposure is critical to obtaining good highlight and shadow rendition. In many lighting situations, an 8-bit tonal scale is just long enough to provide good highlight and shadow detail—*if* the midtone is placed exactly in the correct position.

The exposure latitude is similar to what photographers experience when shooting fine grain transparency films. If it is not within 1/3 f-stop of the correct midtone position, the image will be either underexposed or overexposed. Overexposure results in the loss of highlight detail, underexposure results in the loss of shadow detail.

For digital cameras and camera backs with 12 bits or more of tonal resolution per channel, the increase in exposure latitude means that the photographer has a greater margin for error. Midtone placement may be off by as much as a full f-stop in some cases. The longer tonal range resulting from increased bit depth permits the camera to render good highlight and shadow detail, despite difficult lighting situations or exposure miscalculation.

To properly evaluate image capture files, it is necessary to open them in an image-editing software program that provides a ***histogram*** display of the pixel information, **Figure 10-10**. In graphic form, the histogram appears as a horizontal display of highlight, midtone, and shadow values corresponding to the number of pixels affected in each part of the tonal scale.

A good exposure is characterized by smooth tapering of the highlight and shadow values at opposite ends of the scale. If the display of pixel values appears cut off at either end, then highlight or shadow information has been lost due to incorrect exposure. To ensure correct highlight, midtone, and shadow detail, it is best to make a new image capture of the subject using the predetermined exposure adjustment.

Image Manipulation

Once the image has been captured electronically, editing can be done through an image manipulation program. Some of the most commonly used manipulation programs are Adobe Photoshop™, Macromedia Freehand™, CorelDRAW!™, and Adobe Illustrator™. The type of program that can be used will depend on your computer platform and the image format.

It is better to use first generation images (slides or film negative) for scanning because for every photographic generation, a little of the integrity or sharpness and tone quality of the original is lost.

With full-featured image editors, the user can manipulate any aspect of the image including cropping, color and contrast, adding or removing visual

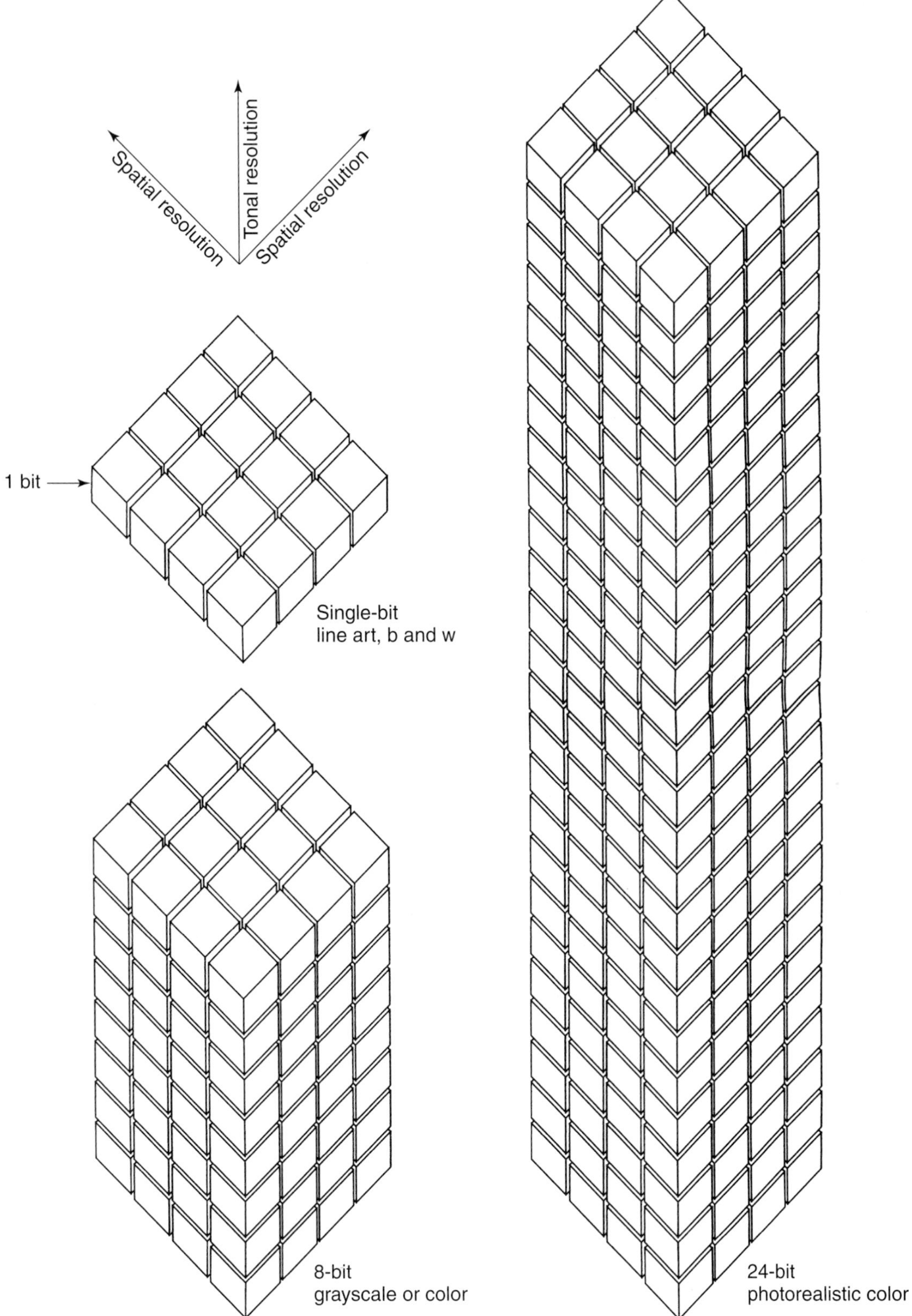

Figure 10-9. Spatial resolution refers to the capability of a digital imaging device to address data in two dimensions—horizontal and vertical.

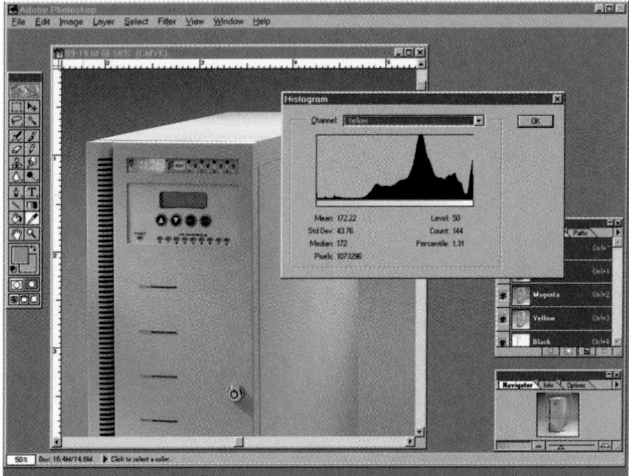

Figure 10-10. The histogram provides a picture of how the pixel values in an image are distributed.

Figure 10-11. Image manipulation can be used to improve the aesthetic quality of a photographic print. A—In the original, the woman's jacket did not line up at the neckline. B—The editor used an image manipulation program to align the top of the jacket. (The Peerless Group of Graphic Services)

information, and even combining images. The user can eliminate background clutter and erase such things as a coatrack that appears to be coming out of a subject's head. See **Figure 10-11**.

To begin working with an image, you must first open the image in the manipulation program. Once the image is onscreen, you must decide what type of changes you will be making. The programs vary so one may be better for performing certain functions than another. You should refer to the user's manual for detailed instructions.

Most image editing programs offer similar tools and applications and will allow you to select and make changes to a single area, multiple areas, or the entire image. Most programs will also allow you to work in layers, apply filters, paint, retouch, and apply masks.

Layers allow the user to create multiple levels of artwork that reside on separate overlapping layers in the same document. The layers can be thought of as resembling a stack of clear acetate sheets. Each sheet contains one or more objects. Where there are no objects, the layer is transparent and you can see through any layer to the layer below. When the image is first opened, it will usually include the RGB or CMYK channels and the user will need to create the layers, **Figure 10-12**.

By creating and working in layers, it is easier to modify objects without affecting all aspects of the artwork. You can blend between layers, create and modify layer masks, link layers, and merge layers. Separate layers take up storage space so they should be merged or flattened when you are finished working on an image.

Filters are used to apply special effects to bitmap images. Textures and patterns can be applied, **Figure 10-13**. Adobe Illustrator allows you to apply an impressionistic or mosaic effect, apply different types of lighting, or distort images, **Figure 10-14**. Applying filters to large bitmap images can be time-consuming. To save time, some filters allow you to preview the effect that they create.

Figure 10-12. The image above is displayed in the magenta channel of the CMYK color mode. The box on the right allows the user to display the image in full color or in one of the channels.

Figure 10-13. When applying filters, you can preview the effect and make a variety of adjustments to the filter including the direction of light.

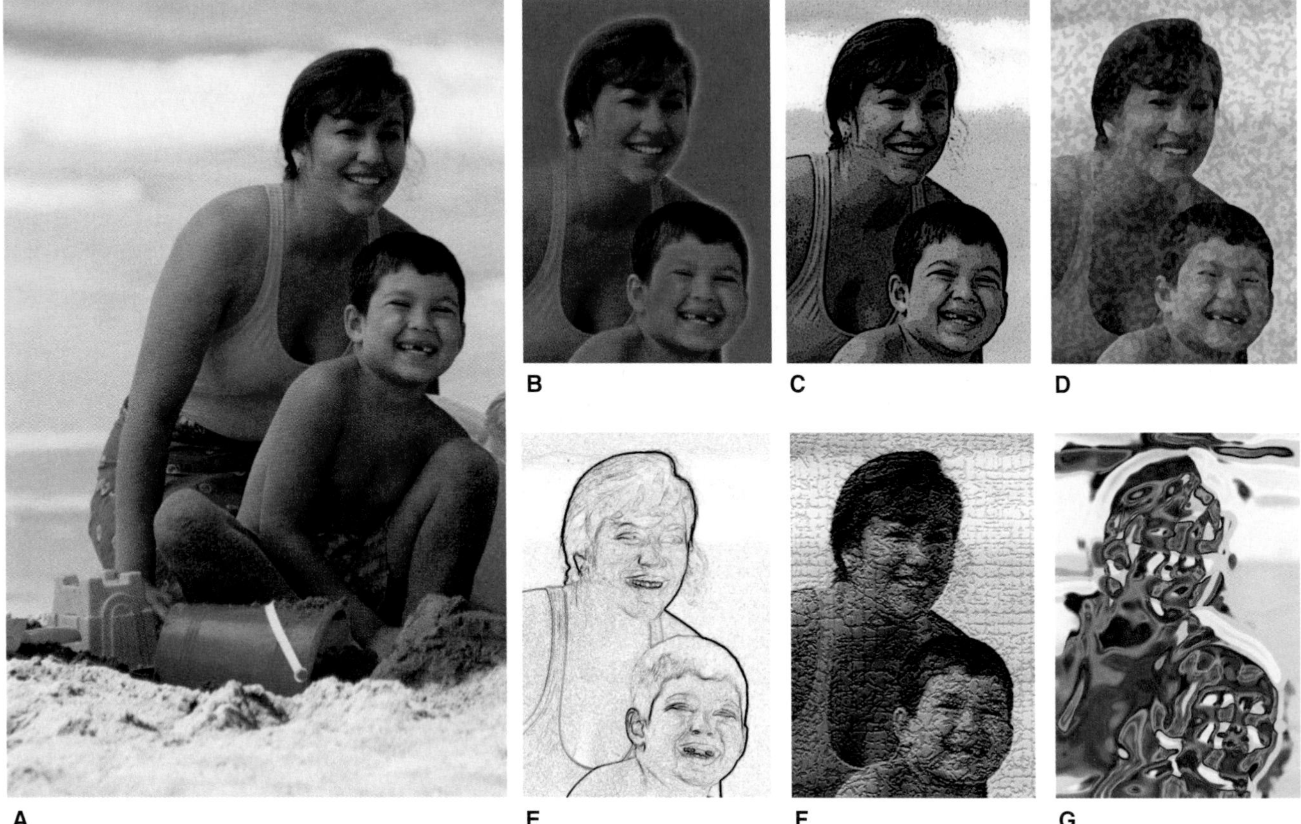

Figure 10-14. Applying filters. A—The original image. Examples B–G illustrate the application of six Adobe Illustrator filters to a cropped portion of the image. B—Diffuse glow. C—Poster edges. D—Sponge. E—Find edges. F—Craquelure. G—Chrome.

In Adobe Illustrator, the color halftone filter simulates the effect of using an enlarged halftone screen on each channel, or color separation, of the bitmap image. A channel is one of the semi-transparent overlays that compose electronic images. For example, an image in RGB color is composed of red, green, and blue channels. In CMYK color, the image is composed of the four color separations—cyan, magenta, yellow, and black. For each channel, the halftone filter divides the image into rectangles and replaces each rectangle with a circle, **Figure 10-15**.

Figure 10-15. The user must indicate a number of settings when applying a halftone filter.

The ***paint*** feature of most image manipulation programs performs the same functions as a paint or draw program. Through a number of tools, the user can create and add color to images. Various tools also allow the user to fill in and erase colors as well as assign and adjust color values and gradations.

Some programs also include tools for ***retouching*** images. These tools perform in ways similar to the methods used in darkroom photography. The user is able to *dodge* areas that are too dark and lack detail. *Burn* tools allow the user to increase "exposure" to areas that are too light. Retouching tools also include features for adjusting color, contrast, hue, and saturation.

Masks are used to isolate an area that you want to protect from change while applying color changes, filters, or other effects to the rest of the image. When you select part of an image, the area that is not selected is "masked" or protected from editing. Semitransparent masks enable the user to partially affect an area of an image. Masks can consist of a single path or a compound path, **Figure 10-16**.

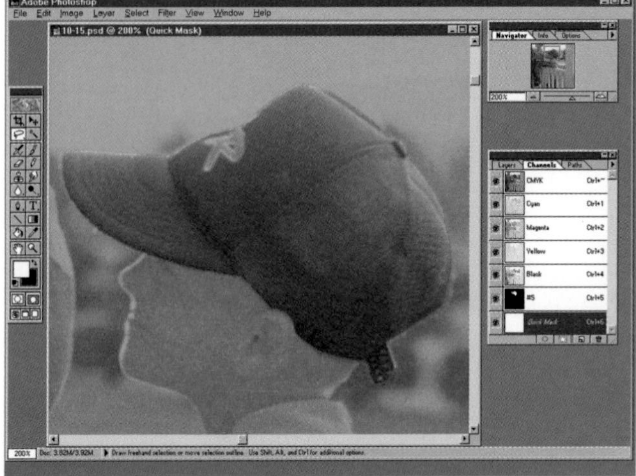

Figure 10-16. The mask applied to the baseball cap will allow the user to modify its color and pattern without affecting the rest of the image.

Image replacement

Automatic picture replacement (APR) and ***open prepress interface (OPI)*** are systems where images are scanned at high-resolution. Low-resolution FPO (for-position-only) images are then sent for placement in the layouts. When files are returned for imagesetting, the high-resolution images are automatically swapped for the low-resolution FPO files. This saves time and avoids storage problems that are created when working with large files created by high-resolution images. It also allows the prepress professional to work on color-correcting the images while they are being placed in layouts, cropped, and proofed.

APR/OPI limitations

Artwork must be properly sized and rotated before it is scanned. All art should be labeled with the percentage enlargement or reduction and the angle of rotation, **Figure 10-17**. When the low-resolution scans are returned, they should be placed in the layout at 100% size and 0° rotation. The images may be cropped and (if absolutely necessary) resized. Resizing after scanning should be kept to a minimum of ±20% to prevent loss in quality. If the image must be rotated or resized drastically, it should be rescanned.

Figure 10-17. The size and rotation (if any) of an original must be clearly marked when sent to a service bureau for scanning.

APR/OPI files should not be renamed. The file name serves as the link to the high-resolution image, and changing the name will cause delays while the link is reestablished. The FPO images should never be opened with image-editing software and resaved in a different format.

Scanners

A ***scanner*** is an electronic device that measures color densities of an original, stores those measurements as digital information, manipulates or alters the data, and uses the manipulated data to create four color separations. Scanners use either a CCD array or PMTs to capture the image as a raster or bit-mapped graphic.

A scanner's imaging quality is a function of many variables including dynamic range, resolution, quality of optics, the light source used, the number of bits per color, and aperture. Differences between these variables explain why sharpness of a 4000 dpi resolution varies from one scanner to another.

Depending on the type of scanner, almost any type or size of original can be scanned. This includes film negatives or positives (transparencies), photographic prints, printed media, drawings, graphs, and text. Text scanning requires the use of an ***OCR (optical character recognition)*** system. Scanners do not distinguish text from illustrations and represent all images as bit maps. Therefore, you cannot directly edit text that has been scanned. To edit text read by an optical scanner, you must use an OCR system to translate the image into ASCII characters.

Many scanners allow the operator to specify what type of color separations, RGB or CMYK, are to be made. There are four basic types of scanners in use: ***hand-held, drum, flatbed,*** and ***film***.

Hand-held

Hand-held scanners are small devices that you move across the paper or image by hand. Hand-held scanners are often called ***half-page scanners*** because they can only scan 2″–5″ at a time. Hand-held scanners are adequate for small pictures and photos, but they are impractical if you need to scan a large amount of text or graphics, **Figure 10-18.**

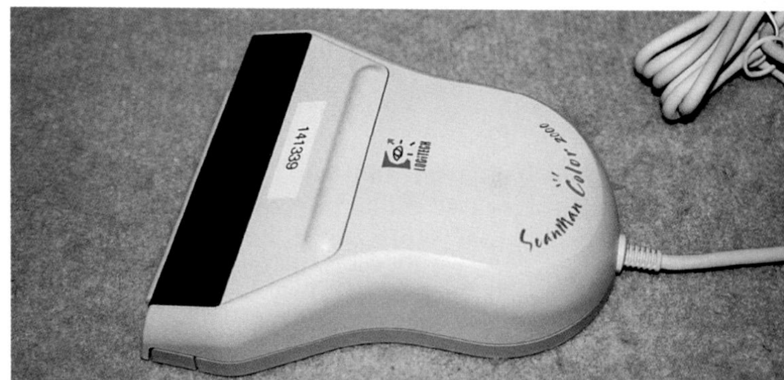

Figure 10-18. Hand-held scanners can only scan small photos or areas of text at a time.

Drum

The drum, or ***rotary***, scanner scans images mounted on a rotating drum, **Figure 10-19.** The drum spins quickly in front of a stationary reading

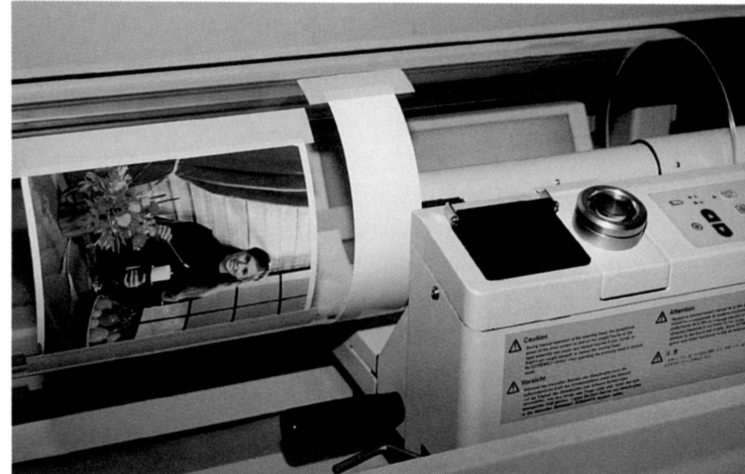

Figure 10-19. Images are mounted on a rotating drum for image capture on a drum (rotary) scanner.

head. As the drum rotates, the originals are illuminated by a halogen or pulsed xenon arc (PXA) lamp that pans slowly across the front of the drum. Light is transmitted through or reflected from the original, then passed through an aperture to the PMT light sensors where the color measurements are made.

Most drum scanners use a set of three PMTs. Each of these sensors gathers information on one of the three additive primary colors (red, green, and blue). This allows all color information to be gathered in a single pass. Less-expensive drum scanners may have only one sensor and require three passes to gather the RGB information. Drum scanners may also use a fourth PMT sensor for *unsharp masking (USM)*.

Unsharp masking (USM) is the increase of tonal contrast where light and dark tones come together at the edges of an image. USM is accomplished electronically on a color scanner by comparing readings taken through two different-size apertures and then adding the signal difference between the two readings to the signal from the larger aperture. This signal reduces density in the lighter areas of the original, and increases density in the darker areas, creating the illustration of a sharper picture.

PMTs are extremely sensitive to light, as well as to changes in light intensity measured at each pixel. PMT technology allows the scanner to "see" a wider dynamic range than scanners based on CCD arrays. The same physical limitations of CCDs also explain why image data from CCD arrays often needs to be interpolated.

PMTs can detect optical densities from 0.0 D to 4.0 D, while even the best CCD scanners can only detect optical densities up to 3.7 D, and most cannot exceed 2.8 D. (Density is represented by *D*.) In a scanner with a range of 3.0 D, the difference between the lightest and darkest detectable intensities is 1000:1. In a scanner with a range of 4.0 D, this difference is 10,000:1. This means that PMT scanners typically distinguish ten times more shades or tones for each pixel than typical CCD scanners. This is especially important in the shadow areas of an image, where PMT scanners deliver much more shadow detail than CCD scanners. It is also one reason why PMT scanners can detect more subtle differences in color.

Some drum scanners have resolution abilities that go as high 12,000 dpi or 12,000 scanning samples per inch (spi). This is enough to enlarge an image by close to 50 times. The practical limit of noninterpolated images of the high-end flatbed scanners is about 5000 dpi. Interpolation may increase the resolution to ±11,000 dpi.

The versatility of the scanner determines the kinds of jobs and volume of work that can be performed. Drum scanners can handle mixed media without any special masks, frames, or carriers. They can perform batch scans of mixed media, and permit the operator to mount artwork on removable drums while another drum is in use.

Oil mounting can also be used with drum scanners. In this process, transparent originals are coated with a small amount of oil or gel to reduce scratches and imperfections, **Figure 10-20**.

Figure 10-20. Transparencies are held in place with a flexible insert and a small amount of fluid is applied between the original and the scanner drum surface. When the scanner begins to rotate, the originals press against the interior wall of the drum, forcing the oil into a uniform layer. (ICG North America)

In general, drum scanners have a larger scanning area than flatbed units. Many offer scanning drums of 20″ × 24″ or greater. Large drum sizes allow the scanning of large originals or batch scanning of a greater number of smaller originals. One important limitation of drum scanners is that originals must be thin (1.8″ or less) and flexible enough to be wrapped around a drum.

Drum scanners are available as horizontal or vertical units, **Figure 10-21**. Vertical drum scanners take up less space; some of the drums have "pockets" to hold images in place. With some vertical scanners, the centrifugal force within the spinning drum holds images in place. The needs of the publication as well as the final output will determine what type of scanner will best suit your needs, **Figure 10-22**.

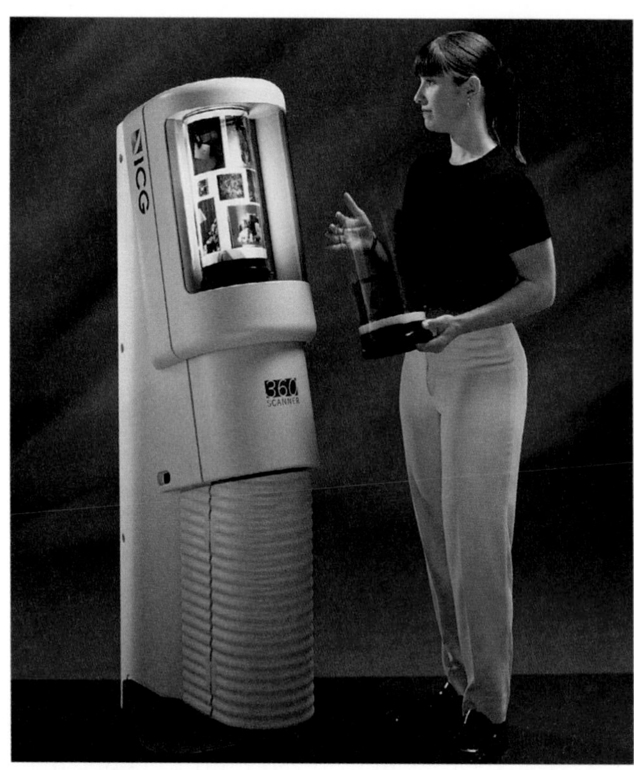

Figure 10-21. Vertical drum scanners take up less floor space. (ICG North America)

Flatbed

Flatbed scanners process images that are placed on the glass bed, or scan area, with or without some type of holder, **Figure 10-23**. Scan area varies in size from machine to machine and can be as small

Type of shop	Application	Useful features
Newspaper, weekly	Photos, color ads	Flatbed, 600 dpi 24-bit color
Newspaper, daily	Color photos and ads	Drum, 3.0+ Dmax* Batch processing
Quick printer	Line art and logos	Flatbed, 600 dpi 24-bit color
Commercial printer	133 lpi 4-color work	Drum, 3.0+ Dmax Batch processing
Commercial printer	175 lpi 4/5/6 color work	Drum, 3.8+ Dmax Batch processing
Corporate publisher	Technical manuals	Flatbed, 600 dpi 24-bit color
Corporate publisher	Marketing manuals 133 lpi 4-color work	Drum, 3.0+ Dmax, 36-bit color Batch processing
Service bureau	35 mm scans 133 lpi 4-color work	Multiformat, 2000 dpi Batch processing
Magazine publisher	FPO scans	Flatbed, 600 dpi 24-bit color

* Dmax: maximum density

Figure 10-22. This chart provides basic guidelines for determining what type of scanner would best suit your needs.

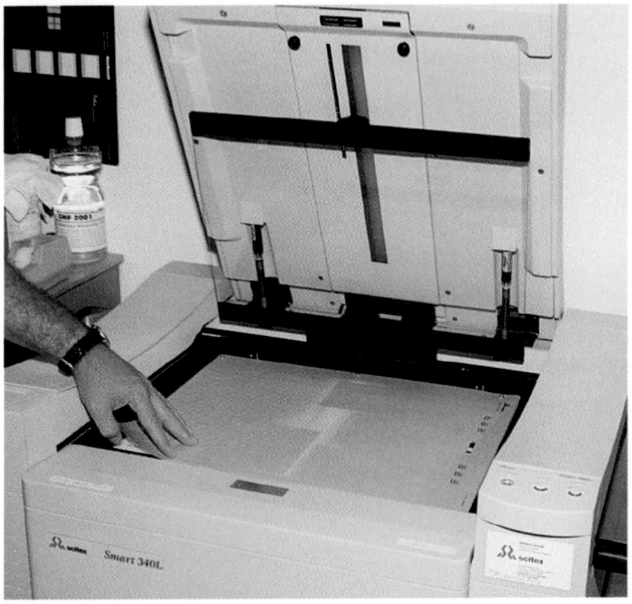

Figure 10-23. Images have been placed on the glass bed of the scanner and covered with a translucent sheet.

as 8.5″ × 11″ (216 mm × 280 mm) to larger than 13″ × 18″ (330 mm × 457 mm). Flatbed scanners are designed with either a stationary or moving bed. If the bed is stationary, the scanning head moves. If the bed moves, the scanning head is stationary, **Figure 10-24**.

Most flatbed scanners use trilinear CCD arrays and a single pass to capture images. After light passes through or is reflected from the image, it is split into three portions that travel to individual CCD arrays filtered to record red, green, and blue independently. Some flatbed scanners provide the user with a choice of resolution. The higher resolution image commonly requires the interpolation of data.

With the use of a magnetic image holder, some manufacturers have eliminated the glass between the image and the optics, **Figure 10-25**. This helps preserve sharpness, and reduces distortion and Newton's rings (although "Newton's rings" is the correct term, common usage in the graphic arts field is "Newton rings"). These rings are undesirable color patterns that result from interference between the exposure light and its reflected beam from the closely adjacent surface. They sometimes reproduce

Figure 10-24. This desktop scanner uses a stationary bed.

Figure 10-25. This scanner does not use glass between the image and the optics. Images (reflective or transparent) are mounted in a magnetic holder and placed on the light table. The original is automatically flexed into the scanner and rolled past the image sensor. (imacon)

as unwanted mottling of halftones or tint areas. Mottling is the blotchy or cloudy appearance of an image instead of a smooth, continuous tone.

As with drum scanners, the versatility of the flatbed scanner determines the kinds of jobs and volume of work that can be performed. Flatbed units can scan originals of varying thickness and many units are even able to scan three-dimensional objects. Flatbeds are also adaptable to automation features such as page feeders. Templates (holders) can be used to set up work with bar codes that specify size, location, and resolution requirements, **Figure 10-26.**

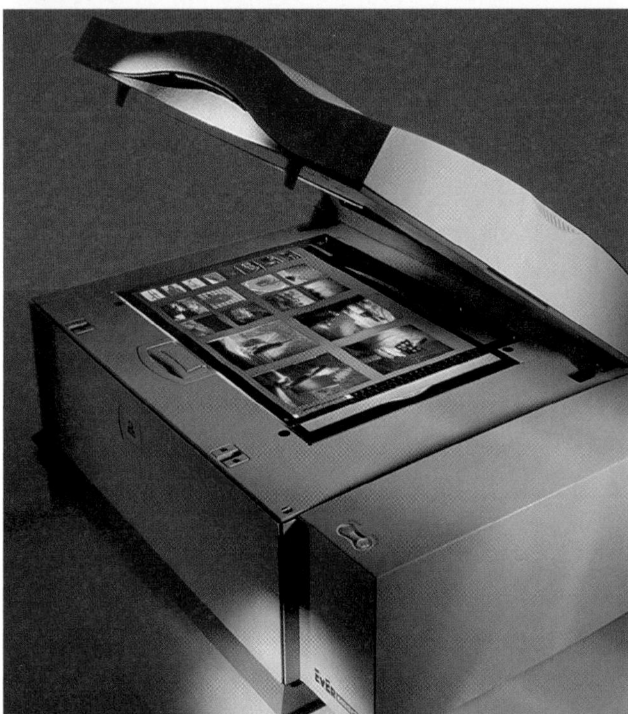

Figure 10-26. Many scanner manufacturers provide both formatted and unformatted templates or holders for use with flatbed scanners. (Scitex America Corp.)

Although flatbed scanners are versatile and lower in cost than drum scanners, they do not match the output quality of drum scanners. However, for most ink-on-paper output, it is difficult to tell the difference between comparably priced flatbed and drum scanners.

One of the most common complaints about flatbed scanners is the degradation of quality outside the 3″ area in the center of the bed called the ***sweet spot***. Conventional flatbeds do not scan at full resolution across the entire bed. Therefore, unless the original is small enough and centered directly in the sweet spot, resolution quality will decrease toward the outer edges of the image. This also makes batch scanning more difficult.

A new technology, ***XY scanning***, overcomes this problem. The XY scanning technology optimally positions its scanning head along an XY axis. The scanner head slides both horizontally and vertically beneath the bed, **Figure 10-27.** In traditional flatbed scanners, the scanning head moves in one direction only.

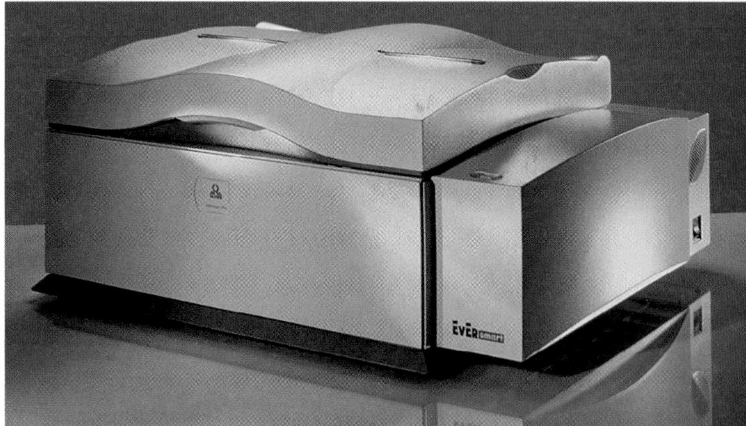

Figure 10-27. The XY technology used by flatbed scanners assures uniform sharpness and high resolution of images regardless of where they are positioned on the scanning area. (Scitex America Corp.)

This dual motion allows the capture of images with uniformly high resolution and sharpness over the entire bed surface, regardless of the original's placement. For example, an 8″ × 10″ original scanned at 300 dpi using an XY scanner may be enlarged up to 2700% for top-quality poster production. If the same job were performed on a conventional flatbed, the uneven resolution would limit enlargement to about 400%.

Film

Film scanners are specially designed CCD scanners that allow the user to capture images from various types of film. Although some scanners are designed specifically for 35 mm film or slides, many include adaptors for scanning the APS (Advanced Photo System) film format as well as slides, **Figure 10-28**. Film scanners are usually small enough to place on a desktop. As with flatbed CCD scanners, imaging speed and resolution capabilities depend on the quality of the CCDs.

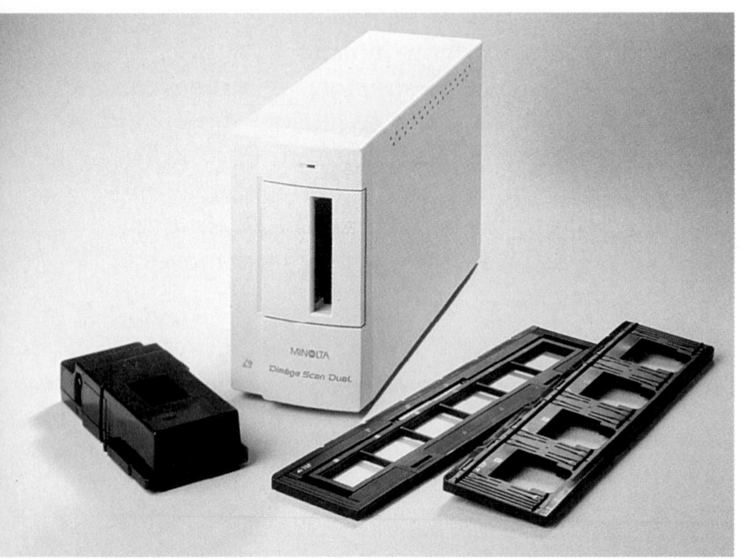

Figure 10-28. When used with an APS adapter, this film scanner is compatible with the APS film format. The frames at right are for conventional films. (Photo courtesy of Minolta Corporation)

Image capture time

Image capture time varies from scanner to scanner and may be hindered only by your system's hard drive capabilities. Many scanners provide a preview image within 8–15 seconds and can complete a high-resolution scan within 60 seconds.

A scanner can be set up to send image files directly to your hard drive or to an external storage medium. However, when working with image files, or any large file, it is recommended that you work off your hard drive. It will be faster and more stable.

Many scanners provide background processing, allowing the operator to view scans while the scanner continues working. For example, when batch-scanning 25 originals, the operator can call up the first two or three prescans as soon as they are done. The operator can begin tightening crops, specifying magnification, color-correcting, and submitting them to the scan queue. By the time all 25 prescans are completed, several high-resolution scans will have been completed.

As the scanner continues working on the high-resolution scans, the operator can begin opening and examining the first scans in an illustration program. If a high-resolution image is not acceptable, it can be disposed of, and the prescan can be recalled and sent back to the scan queue. All initial cropping, sharpening, and other parameters will still be valid and very little time is wasted.

Light sources

Most flatbed and film scanners use a fluorescent light source. Some systems may even use dual fluorescent lamps. Active cooling systems are required to keep the unit from overheating and to keep CCD sensitivity at its highest levels. Drum scanners use tungsten halogen, quartz halogen, or PXA lamps as a light source.

Digital Cameras and Camera Backs

Currently, there is no single digital camera design adaptable for shooting a broad range of subject matter. Photojournalists require easy-to-handle cameras that can freeze motion in a single exposure. Product or still-life photography requires cameras with the ability to capture fine detail and tonal nuances. The needs of the photographer, as well as the desired result, determine what digital camera or camera back design should be used.

The photographer can choose a digital camera or camera back (for attachment to a conventional camera) from an ever-increasing number of designs. Digital cameras and camera backs can be divided into three main categories: ***studio, field,*** and ***point-and-shoot.***

Studio cameras

Most of the high-end digital camera backs designed for commercial use fall into this category. These designs are most often based on trilinear scanning CCD arrays and single-array three- or four-exposure backs that make individual RGB exposures. Studio cameras are characterized by high- or ultra-high resolution and excellent noninterpolated color rendition, **Figure 10-29**.

Figure 10-29. Studio cameras are versatile and available in several sizes. (MegaVision)

When digital cameras are used in a photography studio, images can be viewed on a computer monitor to evaluate progress. The ability to refine composition and lighting by viewing progressive changes eliminates the need for film, chemical processing, and, most importantly, the one-to-two hour wait for film verification.

Low-resolution ***for-position-only (FPO)*** image files are available within minutes. FPO files can be dropped into the client's layout while work continues in the studio. The client is quickly provided with materials that allow visual assessment of the project. The client can take the FPO files, which are typically 72 dpi, and use them to complete the project's design. The final color-separated CMYK images are often ready for placement in the master document within 24 hours.

Field cameras

Field cameras are so named because of their portability. The major prerequisite is that they must be capable of stopping motion. This means the RGB data is usually gathered in a single exposure with a single CCD array. Although several manufacturers offer designs that use multiple arrays and gather pure RGB data, most field cameras use interpolation schemes to produce moderately high RGB resolution. As a result, their color fidelity is usually somewhat below that of the studio cameras.

Point-and-shoot cameras

When first introduced, most point-and-shoot cameras were highly automated. They lacked provisions for manual aperture and shutter speed adjustments and tended to be autofocus designs. Point-and-shoot cameras were characterized by low-resolution, single-exposure CCD arrays that produced RGB files well under a megabyte (Mb) in size. The popular 640 × 480 pixel array provided a working resolution of about 72 dpi. This low resolution has made these cameras well suited for capturing images intended for newsletters or on-line use.

Although the digital point-and-shoot camera does not completely rival its conventional counterpart, the constant introduction of affordable, higher-quality point-and-shoot cameras has increased their use by nonprofessionals. See **Figure 10-30**. Many lower-end cameras now offer advanced features originally found only on professional equipment. Some of these features include:

- LCD viewing screens that display a scrollable "filmstrip" of the pictures stored in the camera.
- Controls for changing resolution and quality mode. This allows the user to shoot higher resolution images in several compression modes.
- Internal storage averaging 40 to 65 images (depending on the compression mode).
- Override of the automatic functions for exposure and color balance.
- External storage using a standard 3.5" floppy or PCMCIA card.
- Powerful zoom lens as standard.
- The ability to blend several images for a panoramic effect.
- Direct attachment to a printer.

Most cameras come with photo editing software, a video output connector for viewing on a television screen, and a serial cable for downloading to a computer.

Format differences

With many digital camera backs, the CCD array is often smaller than the film format for which the

Figure 10-30. The SLR (single-lens reflex) digital camera illustrated above has a built-in flash, and allows the user to choose several automatic or manual settings. (Photo courtesy of Minolta Corporation)

camera was initially designed, **Figure 10-31**. The size difference between the CCD array and the format of the host camera creates two significant problems. The first problem is that the image seen in the viewfinder is larger than the live image area. The second is that the narrow angle of view created by the CCD array increases the lens focal length.

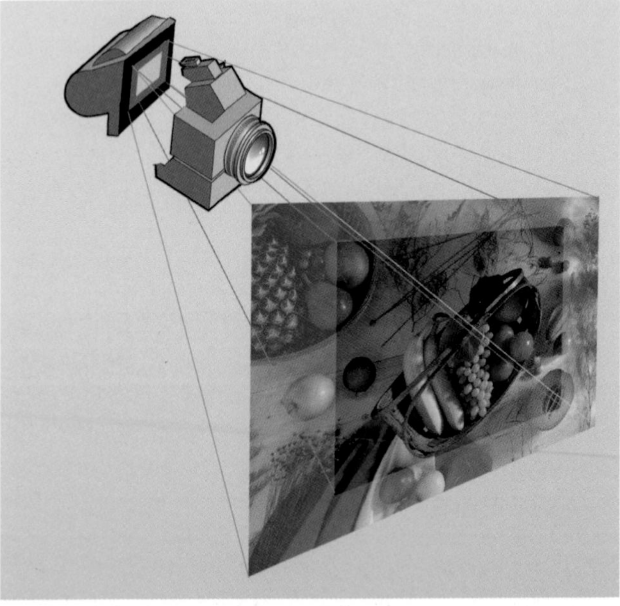

Figure 10-31. With digital camera backs, the CCD array is often smaller than the film format.

When the image seen in the viewfinder is larger than the live image area, it must be cropped to accurately display the angle of view corresponding to the CCD array. For instance, with a 35 mm film-based camera, the live image area is 24 mm × 36 mm. However, the CCD array fitted to a 35 mm camera reduces the live image area to approximately 8 mm × 12 mm. A similar size discrepancy occurs with medium-format cameras. The potential live image area of a 6 cm × 6 cm square format design is reduced to about 3 cm × 3 cm, approximately 1/4 of the original area.

With the viewing area cropped to 25% or less of its original size, arranging the compositional elements becomes increasingly difficult. This is especially true when trying to distinguish subtle tonal differences or fine detail.

The second problem caused by a difference in the CCD array and the film format of a camera concerns lens focal length. The narrow angle of view created by the live image area of the CCD array increases lens focal length 2 to 2.6 times. For example, a 50 mm normal focal length lens placed on a 35 mm camera with an 8 mm × 12 mm CCD array becomes, in effect, a 130 mm medium-length telephoto. To compensate and approximate the *normal* angle of view, a 20 mm lens is required. With medium-format cameras using a 3 cm × 3 cm CCD array, a normal focal length lens of 80 mm is transformed into a 160 mm telephoto. A 40 mm lens is needed to provide a more accurate angle of view.

Most digital camera backs introduce a different format when used in place of the host camera's native film back, **Figure 10-32**. However, manufacturers have introduced camera backs with CCD arrays that measure the same size as their film counterparts. The capability of using a camera back with a full-format CCD array offers two advantages over other hybrid designs. First, the dimensions of the image seen in the viewfinder are close to, if not identical, with those of the image captured by the CCD array. Second, there is no change in lens focal length between film and digital formats.

Image capture time

The amount of time required to write image-capture files to disk limits the performance of all digital cameras and digital camera backs. Write times tend to be longer for trilinear scanning backs, but field cameras and some point-and-shoot

Figure 10-32. This camera back is mounted on a high-quality medium-format camera. (MegaVision)

designs face a similar problem. Even though image capture by an area array requires only a fraction of a second, the size of the camera's internal ***buffer*** determines how many sequential exposures can be made before the camera must pause to write the files to an internal or external storage disk.

The buffer is a temporary storage area that enables the manipulation of data before it is transferred to internal or external storage. With a small buffer or with high-resolution files, the camera may need to pause after every exposure. More sophisticated designs may permit up to a dozen sequential exposures before a pause is required to write to disk.

With lower-resolution single-array/single-exposure cameras, the write-to-disk time often takes 1–3 seconds. Higher resolution field cameras may need as long as 12 seconds. Digital cameras that depend on a rotating filter wheel to make individual RGB exposures on a single CCD usually require 5–30 seconds to write the image-capture files to disk. Because trilinear arrays use a wide range of resolution settings, the write-to-disk time may be as short as 30 seconds or as long as 10 minutes.

When digital cameras are used to photograph active subjects, the write-to-disk time must be figured into the photographer's needs. Peak action on a football field or a desired facial expression must be anticipated so the camera is ready to shoot an exposure sequence. If the desired subject composition occurs while the camera is in pause mode and writing to disk, the photographer's only hope is to have a second camera ready to shoot.

Lighting considerations

When shooting with film-based cameras, lighting adjustments are usually made by changing the direction of light, its degree of diffusion, its color, or its intensity. The photographer can use lens filters, light deflectors, different types of lightbulbs, or different types of film to acquire the desired results. Although many of the same lighting methods are used when shooting with digital cameras, there are several special requirements.

The standard color temperature reference for digital cameras and daylight film emulsions is 5500 K, **Figure 10-33**. This reference corresponds to lighting conditions under a clear blue sky with unobstructed sunlight (roughly between 10:00 a.m. and 2:00 p.m.) These qualifications are necessary because daylight, being subject to the movement of sun, clouds, and weather fronts, is extremely variable. For instance, if the sun is obscured by clouds, color temperature will rise because the proportion of warm, direct light is decreased.

There is also great variability resulting from the geographic direction of the daylight falling on a subject being photographed. If the light is from the north sky with the sun obscured, the color temperature may rise to 10,000 K or higher resulting in very cool, bluish light. In early morning or late evening, when the sun is low on the horizon, color temperature may fall to the range of 2500 K to 3500 K.

A secondary color temperature reference is 3200 K. Before the advent of electronic flash, this was the standard for tungsten lighting used by studio photographers and cinematographers. During the last few decades, the widespread use of electronic flash has decreased the use of tungsten lighting. However, certain digital camera designs have caused a resurgence in the use of tungsten lighting.

Cameras using trilinear scanning arrays depend on constant (steady) lighting conditions because RGB exposure times often extend to between 3–10 minutes. Scanning backs record pixel information three rows at a time as they step across the image-capture plane. Slight variations in light intensity can cause banding in regions of the image that would otherwise display even tonality.

The sensitivity of scanning CCD arrays is such that normal surges in the electrical current cause fluctuations in light intensity that result in tonal irregularities in the image. To counteract these problems, several manufacturers offer flicker-free lighting solutions that smooth out current surges.

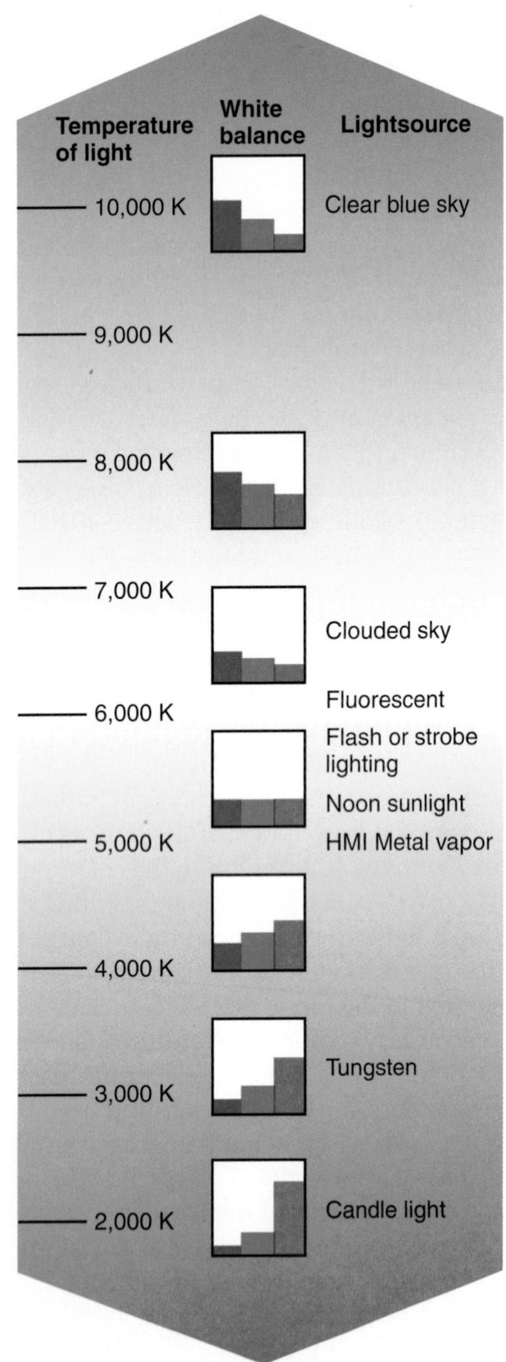

Figure 10-33. Approximate color temperatures of some common light sources. (Agfa)

HMI lighting provides another alternative to the problems presented by tungsten lighting. HMI lights are a high-intensity flicker-free source of illumination balanced for 5500 K output. The greater illumination intensity allows photographers to shoot at smaller lens apertures, producing greater depth of field. The drawback with HMI lighting is the extreme heat output relative to tungsten sources. This makes it difficult to place filters and screens in front of the lamps or to photograph perishable food items.

The most commonly used lighting for commercial studio photography is electronic flash or tungsten. Due to its variability and the additional lighting controls required to maintain consistent color temperature, actual daylight is not usually used. Aside from the ability to freeze motion, the advantage of electronic flash is its consistent color temperature. It simulates the effect of shooting under constant daylight conditions. This, in turn, lends a consistent visual appearance to ongoing photographic projects such as product catalogs.

When a digital camera uses multiple exposures to gather RGB data, it is important the color temperature be constant throughout the exposure cycle. Most manufacturers build their electronic flash equipment to deliver a color temperature of 5500 K regardless of flash duration or intensity. If the color temperature shifts during exposure, it affects the gray balance of the resulting image capture. When this occurs, it is necessary to make additional color corrections using image-editing software. For this reason, it is not practical to shoot with three- or four-exposure RGB image-capture cameras under variable daylight conditions.

Hand-held digital cameras designed for single-exposure use have much more flexibility in terms of their lighting requirements, **Figure 10-34**. Moderately expensive field cameras have built-in flash synch connections that simplify their use with a variety of electronic flash equipment. Focal plane shutters permit a range of flash-synchronized shutter speeds and make it possible to combine multiple light sources for a single exposure. Many of these cameras provide an electronic bias for often-used light sources such as electronic flash, daylight, tungsten, and fluorescent.

Less expensive point-and-shoot digital cameras include built-in electronic flash capability. This feature enables them to provide greater consistency under variable shooting conditions including daylight, tungsten, and fluorescent. Since the flash is designed to be the primary light source, off-color secondary lighting is less detrimental to good gray balance.

Figure 10-34. Besides have a built-in flash, this camera offers the photograher many options. The lens can be rotated to shoot from almost any angle, or it can be detached completely and used with a cable connection. When detached from the camera, the lens can be held above a crowd or around a corner while the user views the shot on the LCD color monitor. (Photo courtesy of Minolta Corporation)

Image File Storage and Transfer

Ongoing technological advances have made it possible to design cameras and scanners that offer increasingly high resolution capabilities. The 2000 × 2000 CCD array used in many medium- and large-format cameras produces a file size of 4 Mb per channel (12 Mb for an RGB file). For hand-held 35 mm cameras, resolutions as high as 2036 × 3060 pixels (18 Mb RGB file) are available. Ultra-high resolution CCDs with pixel dimensions of 4000 × 4000 (48 Mb), are commonly used by commercial photographers.

Internal and external storage devices

With higher resolution capabilities, image capture files have steadily grown in size. Storage devices such as magneto-optical (MO) disks (*opticals*), magnetic disks, and internal/external hard drives are used to store the larger image files. Three and one-half inch opticals may hold up to 230 Mb. Three and one-half inch magnetic disks, twice the thickness of a floppy diskette, store 100 Mb of data. These kinds of storage devices are frequently used with digital camera backs and scanners that rely on a computer workstation to store the image-capture files.

Because digital cameras are often used to capture images *on-the-fly*, they face unique transfer speed and storage requirements. For example, quick and adequate file storage is essential for digital cameras used in news gathering and sports coverage. Some field cameras include internal hard drives with storage capacities ranging from 300 Mb to 1 Gb. While it is convenient to have digital images write automatically to a disk drive, files cannot be downloaded without temporarily removing the camera from an active shooting situation. To avoid this problem, photographers can use a removable storage device known as ***"digital film"*** or ***PCMCIA cards***.

PCMCIA cards

PCMCIA cards (Personal Computer Memory Card International Association), or PC cards, were originally designed for adding memory to portable computers. The PCMCIA standard has been expanded several times and the cards are now suitable for use with many types of devices including digital cameras and scanners. In digital photography, PC cards offer the advantage of quick image downloading without tying up the host camera. A PC card is about the size of a credit card, but slightly thicker.

The PC card is inserted into a slot on the camera body in preparation for storing image files. After the card is filled to capacity, it is removed from the camera and files are downloaded with a PC card reader. Meanwhile, the photographer can insert another card into the camera and continue shooting. With this type of shoot-and-download capability, PC cards provide photographers with *ease-of-use* that is comparable to film.

There are three kinds of PC cards in use: Type I, Type II, and Type III. The three types all have the same rectangular size, but differ in thickness. Type I can be up to 3.3 mm thick. This card provides for memory enhancements and is most frequently used with proprietary digital cameras. Type II cards can be up to 5.5 mm thick and are used for modems and LAN (local area network) adaptors. Type III cards can be up to 10.5 mm thick and are used for miniature hard-disks and similar storage devices. See **Figure 10-35.**

Hybrid field cameras that couple conventional 35 mm camera bodies with digital camera backs usually use Type II and Type III cards. Some

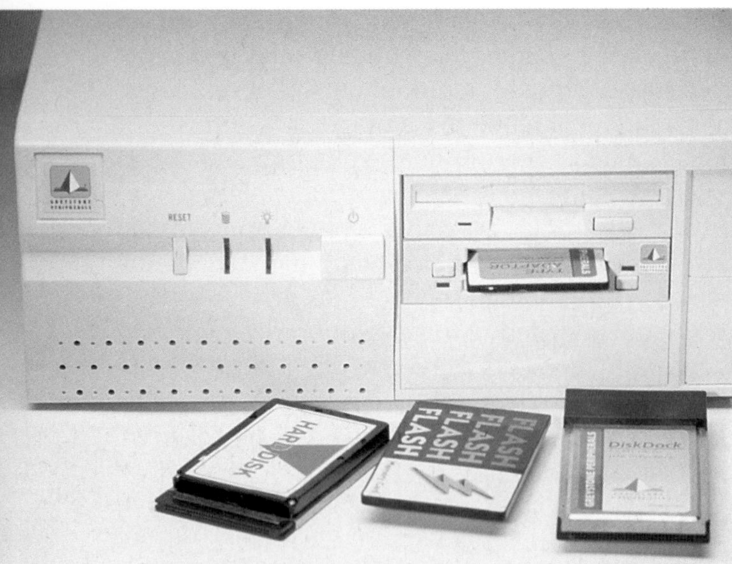

Figure 10-35. PCMCIA technology allows for easy backup and storage of data. (Greystone Peripherals, Inc.)

point-and-shoot digital cameras also make use of Type III cards. Due to size and power limitations, most cameras accept only one type of card at a time.

PC card readers or PC slots also come in three sizes. A Type I slot will accept one Type I card. A Type II slot can hold one Type II card or two Type I cards. The Type III slot can hold one Type III card or a Type I and a Type II card. Unfortunately, because of deficiencies in the original PCMCIA standard and poor implementation by card manufacturers, not all card readers can read all three types of cards, **Figure 10-36**.

Figure 10-36. PCMCIA readers can be installed on most computer systems. (Greystone Peripherals, Inc.)

Data transfer

The connecting cables used between the digital camera or scanner and the computer workstation have a significant impact on the rate of data transfer. Serial and parallel cables are used for most personal computers (PCs). All Macintosh computers use ***SCSI (small computer systems interface)*** cables. SCSI interfaces provide faster data transmission rates than standard serial and parallel ports. ANSI (American National Standards Institute) standard SCSI II cables can support rates as fast as 10 Mbps and SCSI III cables can support rates as fast as 20 Mbps.

Although SCSI is an ANSI standard, there are many variations so not all SCSI interfaces are compatible. However, SCSI devices can be attached to most PCs by installing a SCSI board in one of the expansion slots. Although most new PCs come with a built-in SCSI, the lack of a single SCSI standard means that some devices may not work with some SCSI boards.

Cable length also affects the rate of data transfer. SCSI II cables should not exceed 18′ while SCSI I cables should be 6′ or less. File transfer rate begins to lag when these specifications are exceeded.

Future Trends

Digital imaging devices have become a driving force in redefining the traditional boundaries that separate the disciplines of photography and printing. Personal computer technology and the desktop publishing revolution have transformed the prepress end of the printing industry. It is no longer commonplace to make color separation films by hand from original artwork and make localized color corrections by etching halftone dots. Today, the original artwork is likely to be a digital file produced in a paint or draw program, or captured with a scanner or digital camera.

With advances in digital imaging technology, the role of the photographer as a member of the creative team is evolving. When shooting film-based images, photographers have often been preoccupied with pushing the limits of the medium to achieve the best visual result for viewing on a light table. From the photographers' perspective, it is imperative to make maximum use of the film's tonal image range and color gamut.

Color separators long ago realized that the full tonal range of a photographic transparency could not be transferred to ink on paper. The transparency color gamut, using high-quality dye pigments, far exceeded what could be reproduced with a CMYK ink set on a lithographic press. Photographers were not necessarily concerned with these production complications until digital photography provided the ability to control how an RGB-to-CMYK conversion affects the appearance of their images.

A few years ago, the photographer's job was finished when the art director signed off on the transparency film. The transformation from film to digital image file was in the hands of the color separator. With a digital camera, the photographer is compelled to take on new responsibilities. In place of common transparent media, the end result is an RGB image-capture file.

Many photographers, seeking to gain a competitive advantage, are taking the next step and delivering print-ready CMYK files that can be dropped into a document layout. In doing so, they have assumed what was formerly the job of the color separator. Along with the new responsibility is the opportunity to have the final say in how the image-capture file will print on press.

Review Questions

Please do not write in this book. Write your answers on a separate sheet of paper.

1. The colors and lines of an image in _____ form are continuous. The colors and lines of an image in _____ form consist of values measured at distinct points.
2. CCD sensors are _____ and require special filters to separate the RGB light reflected by an object.
3. What is *interpolation*?
4. How does a single mosaic CCD array capture RGB data?
5. What is *spatial resolution*? *tonal resolution*?
6. What purpose do *layers* serve in an image manipulation program?
7. _____ are used to apply special effects to bitmap images.
8. _____ are used to isolate an area to protect it from change while applying color changes or special effects to the rest of the image.
9. When scanning text, you must use a(n) _____ system to translate the bitmapped image into ASCII characters.
10. Drum scanners use _____ for gathering color information.
    a. CMOS APS sensors
    b. PMTs
    c. CCDs
    d. All of the above.
11. What is *unsharp masking (USM)*?
12. List the three main categories of digital cameras and camera backs.
13. What are the two main problems created when there is a difference in the film format size of the original camera and the CCD array of a camera back?
14. Why do cameras using trilinear arrays require constant lighting conditions?
15. What advantage do PCMCIA cards offer photographers using digital cameras?

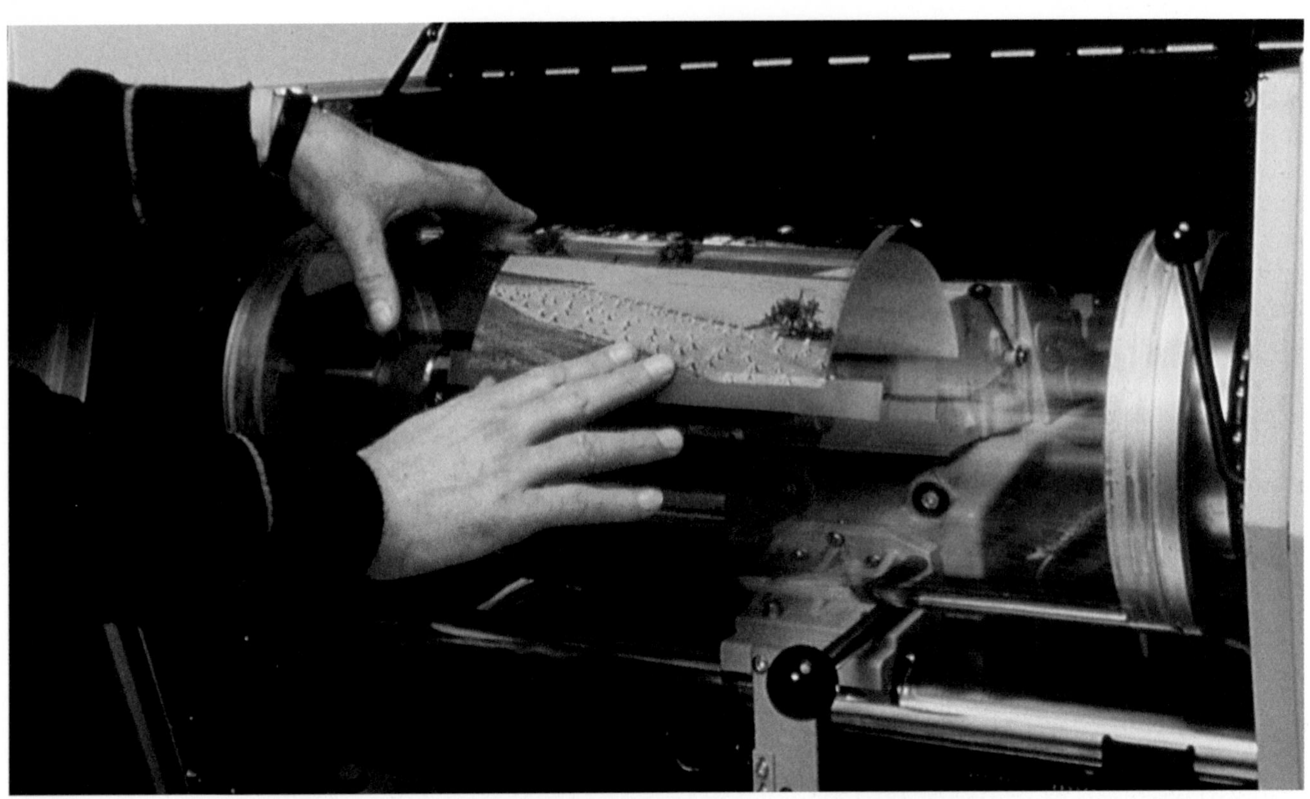

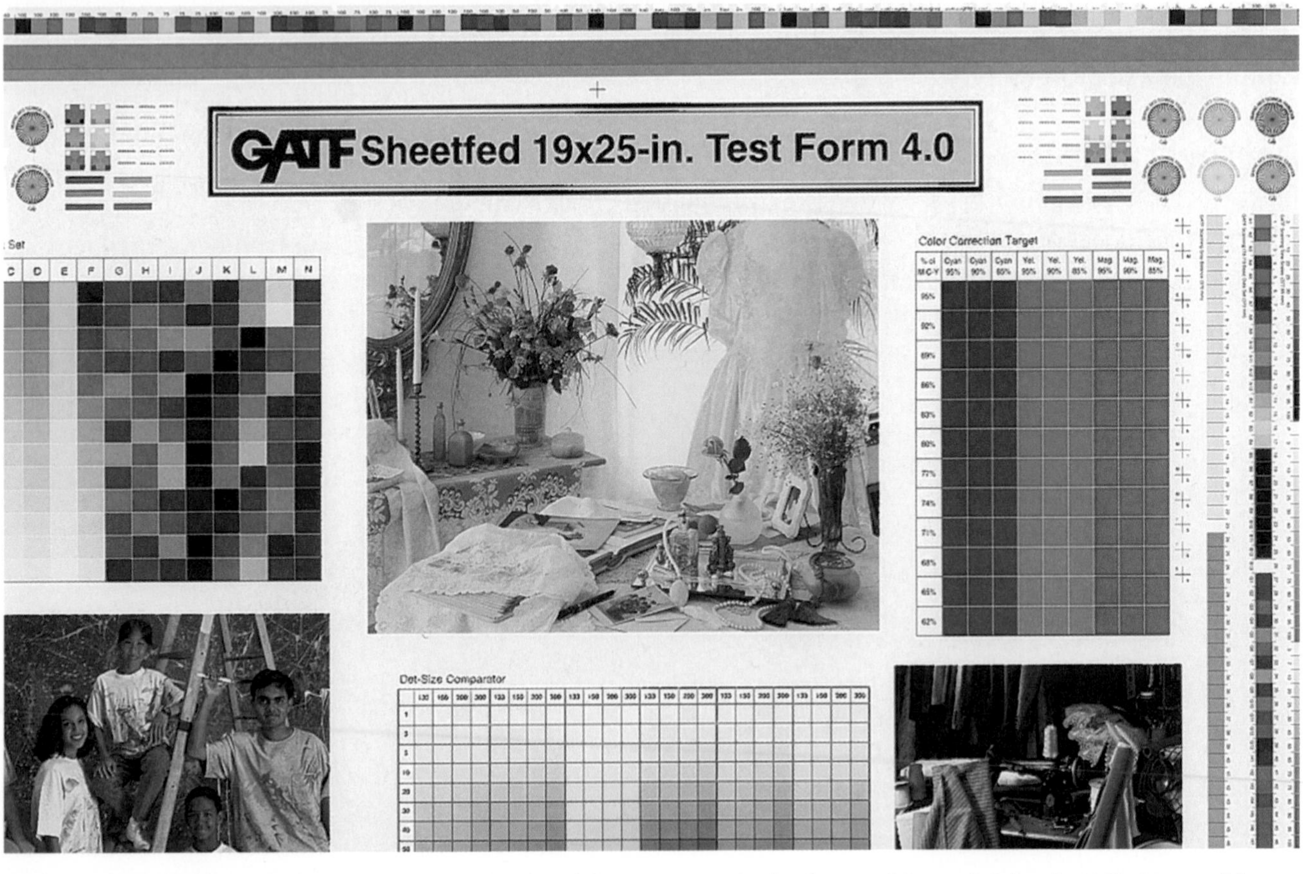

GATF Sheetfed 19x25-in. Test Form 4.0

Color Correction Target

Dot-Size Comparator

For optimum results in the final printed product, careful management of color must be maintained at all stages of the graphic communications process, from original image scanning to actual presswork. (Graphic Arts Technical Foundation)

Color Management

11

Learning Objectives

After studying this chapter, you will be able to:

- Explain the CIELAB color space.
- Define gamut reduction and explain its effect on color reproduction.
- Explain ICC color profiles.
- Describe the Pantone system of color.
- Explain how spot and process colors are defined in page composition files.
- Explain how a color management system (CMS) regulates color conversion through the workflow.
- Cite reasons why characterization and calibration are essential to accurate color reproduction.
- Describe how color monitors produce color and cite their limitations.
- List several methods used for color correction.
- Define shadow clarity and list several methods used for its improvement.
- Explain trapping and list conventional and electronic methods.
- Explain the various screening methods used in graphic arts.
- List proofing methods used in the graphic communications industry.

Important Terms

gamut reduction
ICC color profile
color management system (CMS)
calibration
undercolor removal (UCR)
gray component replacement (GCR)
undercolor addition (UCA)
trapping
stochastic screening
color control bar

Color management in graphic arts describes the systematic approach to color conversions from input to output devices. The conversions can involve output to monitors, digital color printers or presses, or to film or plate material. The primary issue is getting the color transformation correct to ensure consistent and accurate color reproduction, regardless of the number or types of devices involved.

Computer monitors, digital proofing devices, and printing presses all render color differently. Documents viewed onscreen and output to different devices will have widely varying results. With an effective color management system, images can be scanned accurately, displayed onscreen correctly, and output as close to the original colors as possible.

Standards, Regulations, and Color Models

Numerous means of regulating, testing, and reproducing color have been adopted by the graphic communications industry. Because ink and toner composition, printing presses (conventional and digital), and substrate quality also affect the accuracy of color reproduction, their design and operation are also covered under many of the same standards.

The International Commission on Illumination (CIE)

Many computer, ink, and paper manufacturers have adopted the CIE (*Commission Internationale de l'Eclairage* or the International Commission on Illumination) system of color specification. In 1976, CIE revised its 1931 color measurement standards and created the three-dimensional, device-independent *CIELAB color model,* **Figure 11-1**.

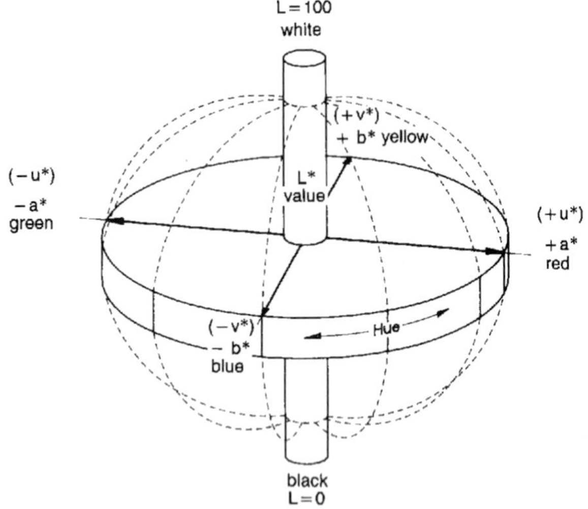

Figure 11-1. The CIE LAB color space defines color based upon our visual system's perception of color. The distances between colors in the CIELAB color space correspond to perceived color differences.

With regard to electronic devices, the CIELAB color space is usually referred to as *LAB*. The LAB color space separates color and luminance into discrete color space dimensions, or channels, that are represented by the letters *L*, *a*, and *b*. The first dimension, *L*, represents lightness. The *a* indicates the red-to-green value, and the *b* represents the yellow-to-blue value. Together, the *a* and *b* represent a two-dimensional color subspace.

The human visual system is most sensitive to the *L* component, so digital systems allocate more data space to it than to the color components. This allows even more efficient coding of the color values (luminance).

The LAB color model is an ideal color space for performing ***color correction*** (adjusting images to optimize values for highlight and shadow, neutral tones, skin tones, and sharpness). Instead of representing a color as a percentage of other colors, the LAB model puts the ***grayscale*** information in the *L* channel and uses the *a* and *b* channels for color information.

Grayscale is a means of showing the shades of gray that represent the image. When an image is converted to grayscale, all color information is discarded. The gray levels, or shades, of the converted pixels represent the luminosity of the original pixels. Because the grayscale channel is isolated in the LAB model, the user is able to apply sharpening and tonal settings without distorting the relationships of colors.

Grayscaling is the process of converting a continuous-tone image to an image in shades of gray. Continuous tone images, such as black and white photographs, use an almost unlimited number of shades of gray. Computers, however, can only represent a limited number of shades of gray (typically 16-256). Grayscaling requires large amounts of memory because each individual pixel can be a different shade of gray and is represented by 4-8 bits.

Although many image-editing programs allow the user to enhance the "crispness" of an RGB or CMYK image, halos and other distortions often occur when sharpening commands are applied. If possible, images should be captured and modified in the LAB color space and then converted to RGB or CMYK, depending on its final purpose. The LAB mode is also recommended for moving images between systems.

The color gamut of a device is usually displayed using the *CIE chromaticity diagram,* **Figure 11-2**. The CIE chromaticity diagram shows just two dimensions of the *CIE Yxy color space*—hue and chroma. (See Chapter 8 for a discussion of the Yxy color space.) The achromatic component, or color's brightness, is represented by *Y* and is specified by a number, not a location on the graph.

The degree of inability of a device to display or print color is called its ***gamut reduction***. If the color plot of a computer monitor is superimposed on the CIE chromaticity diagram, it can be seen that the monitor can display only a fraction of the visible spectrum, **Figure 11-3A**. If the plot of printable colors is superimposed on the same chart, it is clearly visible that the gamut of most printing presses is even more limited, **Figure 11-3B**.

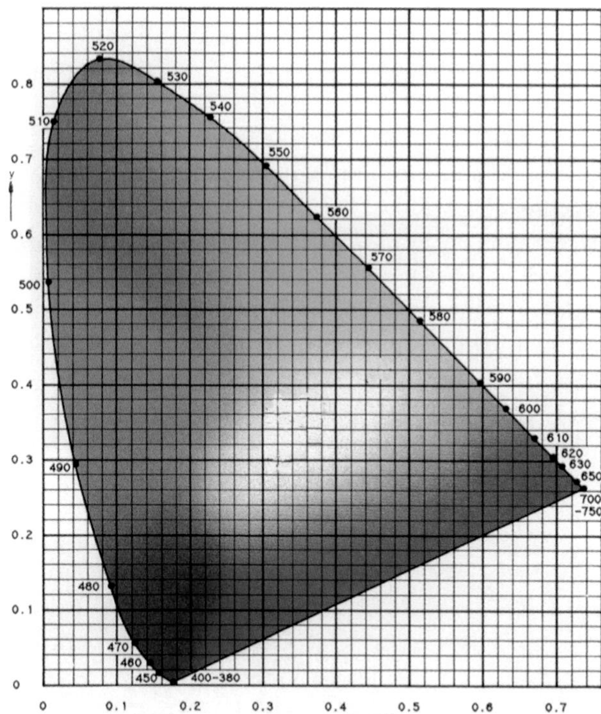

Figure 11-2. The horseshoe-shaped CIE chromaticity diagram contains the colors of the visible spectrum.

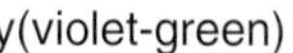

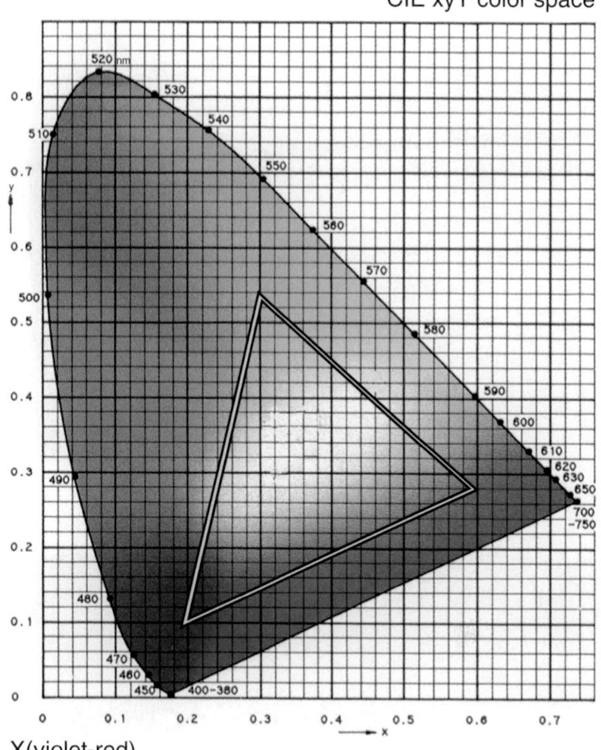

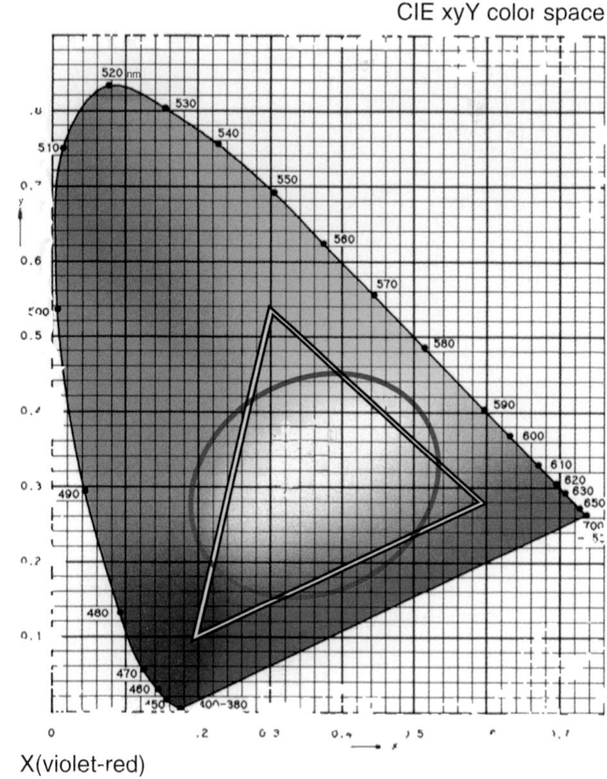

Figure 11-3. Gamut reduction. A—The triangle represents the color space of a computer monitor. B—The oval represents the CMYK space of a printer.

No matter what type of color mode is used, some quality is lost each time an image is converted. To preserve image quality, use conversions sparingly and apply them only to the final image.

The International Color Consortium (ICC)

Until 1993, the formats used to describe the color behavior of particular devices varied by manufacturer. These multiple color standards were extremely impractical, because most graphic art professionals use a combination of devices from different manufacturers.

In 1993, several leading manufacturers founded the *International Color Consortium (ICC)*. The ICC created a cross-platform standard for color management using ***ICC color profiles***. These profiles are based on the CIELAB color space and function as standards for describing color characterizations of different devices. ICC color profiles contain information on the device's color space and the compensation required to bring the device to its ideal level of performance. Most graphic arts manufacturers have developed applications that support ICC color profiles.

Once a device profile has been created, the profile is then used by a color transformation engine, or ***color management module (CMM)***. The CMM translates data from one device's color space to another.

Specifications for Web Offset Publications (SWOP)

In 1975, a review committee was formed to establish specifications to help eliminate variations in the materials being supplied to printers by prepress service bureaus. In 1976, the committee adopted its present name, *Specifications for Web Offset Publications* or *SWOP®*. Although they are not mandated as such, the SWOP specifications are accepted as industry standards, **Figure 11-4**.

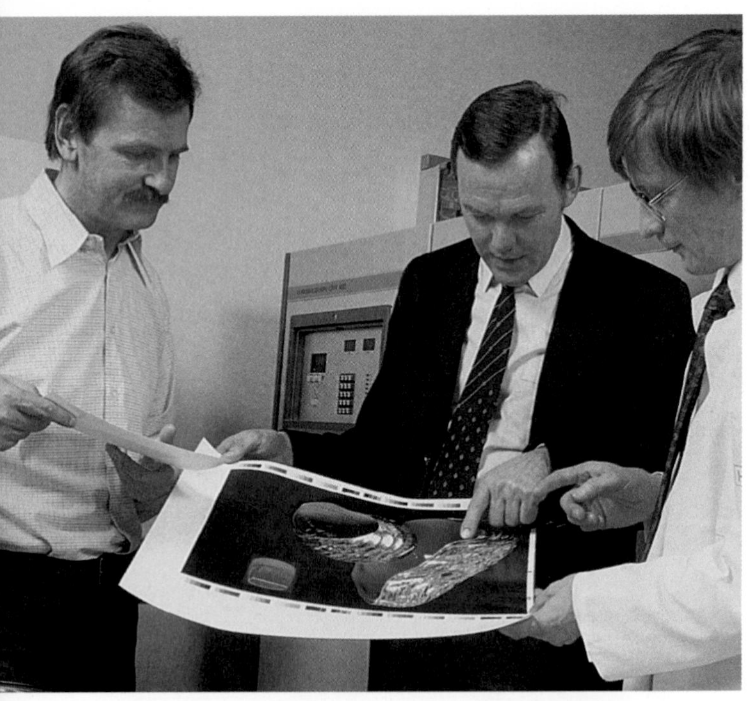

Figure 11-4. SWOP has established standards in the graphic communications industry under which professionals create, proof, and print materials.

Initially, the specifications covered only the production of film and proofs for offset printing. However, as electronic technology has become more integrated in the production process, the specifications now concentrate on the use of electronic files and their impact on publication production. Electronic files are expected to meet the same high quality standards that have been expected of the graphic arts films and proofs supplied to the printer under SWOP.

SWOP has developed its specifications in accordance with many of the graphic communications standards established by such organizations as the *American National Standards Institute (ANSI)*, the *International Organization for Standardization (ISO)*, and the *Committee for Graphic Arts Technologies Standards (CGATS)*. The SWOP specifications are presented as an appendix to this book.

Areas covered under the specifications include standard lighting for viewing proofs, electronic file formats, register marks, film requirements, ink measurement and control, and proofing (on and off press). The specifications were also adopted for gravure publications.

YCC Color Space

Kodak's YCC color space is also important to the digital workflow. Developed for the Kodak Photo CD, this color space is device-independent and is suited for data compression and decompression. YCC is a variant of the RGB color space.

Color rendition charts

Color changes with time and environmental conditions. Many professionals use color test charts to make objective measurements. Charts such as the Macbeth ColorChecker™ are commonly used by photographers but can also be useful to the graphic communications professional, **Figure 11-5**.

Figure 11-5. The ColorChecker chart has twenty-four 2″ (50 mm) square color patches that closely match real-object colors such as dark and light human skin, foliage, and blue flowers. (Photo Courtesy of GretagMacbeth, New Windsor, NY)

The ColorChecker chart is composed of twenty-four 2″ (50 mm) square color patches made of matte paint applied to a smooth paper. The patches are selected *Munsell* colors that closely match real-object colors such as dark and light human skin, foliage, and blue flowers. The additive and subtractive primary colors and a six-step neutral scale are also included.

Each patch can be identified by number; name; its CIE-Yxy chromaticity coordinates; Munsell's hue, value, and chroma; an ISCC-NBS standard name (*Inter-Society Color Council-National Bureau of Standards*); and an assigned name, **Figure 11-6.**

Subjective evaluations can be made by comparing the reproduction to the chart or by comparing the reproductions of different systems.

		CIE (1931)			Munsell Notation		ISCC/NBS Name
No.	Name	x	y	Y*	Hue	Value/Chroma	
1	Dark skin	.4002	.3504	10.05	3.05YR	3.69/3.20	Moderate brown
2	Light skin	.3773	.3446	35.82	2.2YR	6.47/4.10	Light reddish brown
3	Blue sky	.2470	.2514	19.33	4.3PB	4.95/5.55	Moderate blue
4	Foliage	.3372	.4220	13.29	6.65GY	4.19/4.15	Moderate olive green
5	Blue flower	.2651	.2400	24.27	9.65PB	5.47/6.70	Light violet
6	Bluish green	.2608	.3430	43.06	2.5BG	7/6	Light bluish green
7	Orange	.5060	.4070	30.05	5YR	6/11	Strong orange
8	Purplish blue	.2110	.1750	12.00	7.5PB	4/10.7	Strong purplish blue
9	Moderate red	.4533	.3058	19.77	2.5R	5/10	Moderate red
10	Purple	.2845	.2020	6.56	5P	3/7	Deep purple
11	Yellow green	.3800	.4887	44.29	5GY	7.08/9.1	Strong yellow green
12	Orange yellow	.4729	.4375	43.06	10YR	7/10.5	Strong orange yellow
13	Blue	.1866	.1285	6.11	7.5PB	2.90/12.75	Vivid purplish blue
14	Green	.3046	.4782	23.39	0.1G	5.38/9.65	Strong yellowish green
15	Red	.5385	.3129	12.00	5R	4/12	Strong red
16	Yellow	.4480	.4703	59.10	5Y	8/11.1	Vivid yellow
17	Magenta	.3635	.2325	19.77	2.5RP	5/12	Strong reddish purple
18	Cyan	.1958	.2519	19.77	5B	5/8	Strong greenish blue
19	White	.3101	.3163	90.01	N	9.5/	White
20	Neutral 8	.3101	.3163	59.10	N	8/	Light gray
21	Neutral 6.5	.3101	.3163	36.20	N	6.5/	Light-medium gray
22	Neutral 5	.3101	.3163	19.77	N	5/	Medium gray
23	Neutral 3.5	.3101	.3163	9.00	N	3.5	Dark gray
24	Black	.3101	.3163	3.13	N	2/	Black

Figure 11-6. This table provides the names and specification of color patches in the Macbeth ColorChecker Rendition Chart.

Comparisons should be made under the proper viewing conditions.

The Pantone System

The Pantone® System of color specification is the most widely used system in the graphic communications industry. It is a universal color language that helps to ensure color consistency throughout production. The Pantone System is based on ink colors common to the printing industry.

Designers, clients, and printers can communicate color selections using manuals or swatchbooks containing representations of the Pantone colors. The manuals and swatchbooks provide color simulations, names, and mixing formulas.

Pantone has developed software programs that allow the users of most computer systems to specify Pantone colors, **Figure 11-7**. The Pantone Matching System and the Pantone Process Color System provide color control for solid color printing and process color printing.

The designer can select from one of the 1000 Pantone colors in the solid color range when using the Pantone Color Formula Guide. With the Pantone Process Color System Guide, the user can specify any one of 3000 process tints. The colors are viewed with a fan guide displaying the colors in a spectrum, **Figure 11-8**.

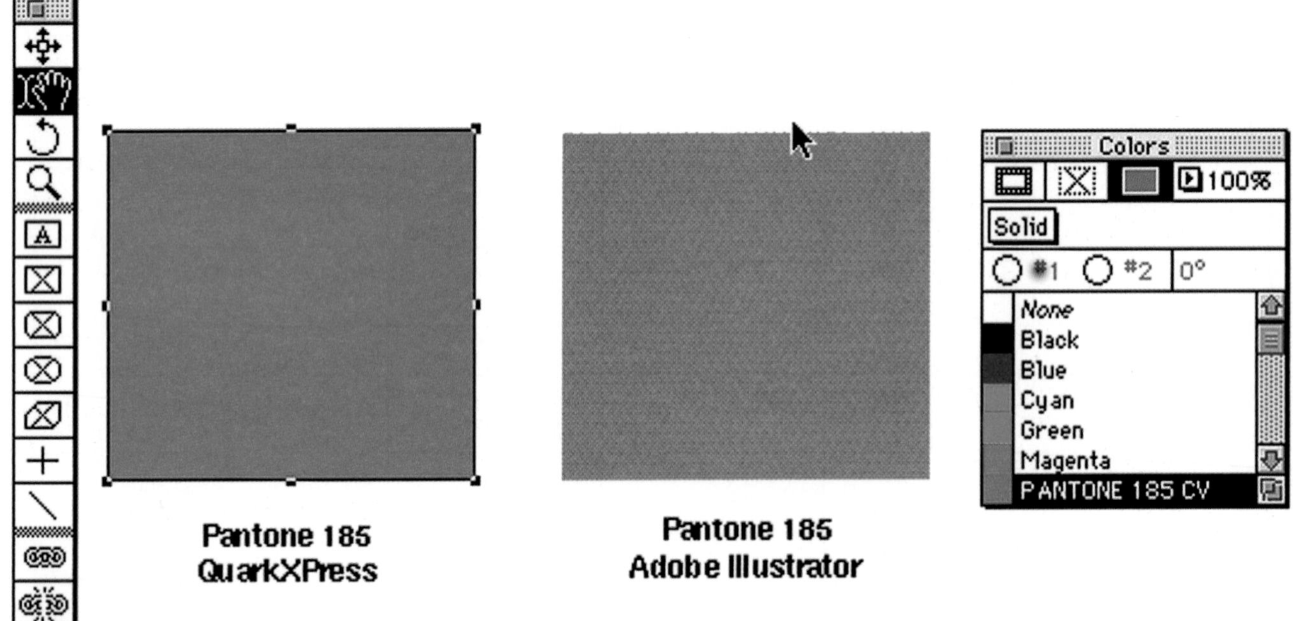

Figure 11-7. Many page composition and illustration programs allow the user to specify Pantone colors. Each program may render a color differently onscreen, as shown, even though the printed color would be as specified.

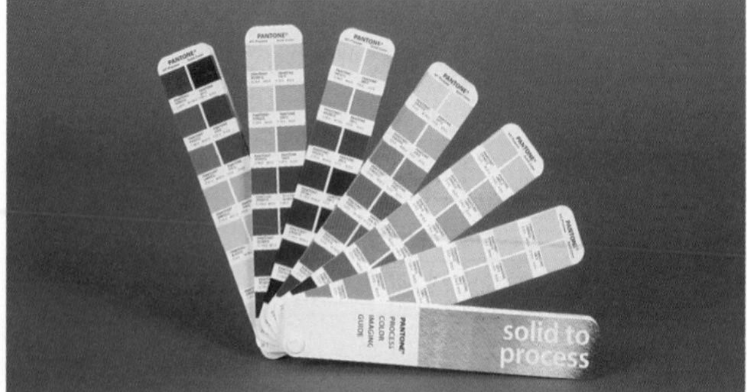

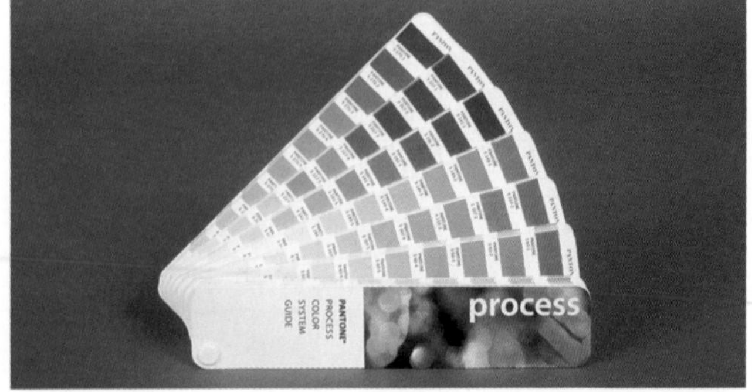

Figure 11-8. Pantone Color System. A—Pantone's Solid to Process Guide allows the user to compare Pantone Colors to their closest CMYK version. B—Pantone's Process Guide displays over 3000 CMYK color combinations. Colors are chromatically arranged and displayed with their CMYK percentages. (Pantone, Inc.)

Pantone has also developed chromaticity values for both Pantone Colors and monitor phosphors. These values allow monitors to display Pantone Colors that accurately represent the ink on paper. A color calibrator that compensates for monitor drift and phosphor decay is also available. The white balance can also be adjusted so the white screen on the monitor looks more like a press sheet illuminated in a printing plant.

Many printer manufacturers have been licensed to produce Pantone colors but results vary with the resolution of the printer as well as the purity of the cyan, magenta, and yellow inks.

Using spot and process colors

Defining spot and process colors correctly is essential for proper color separation. Most page composition programs provide editing features that allow the user to indicate the desired separation, **Figure 11-9**.

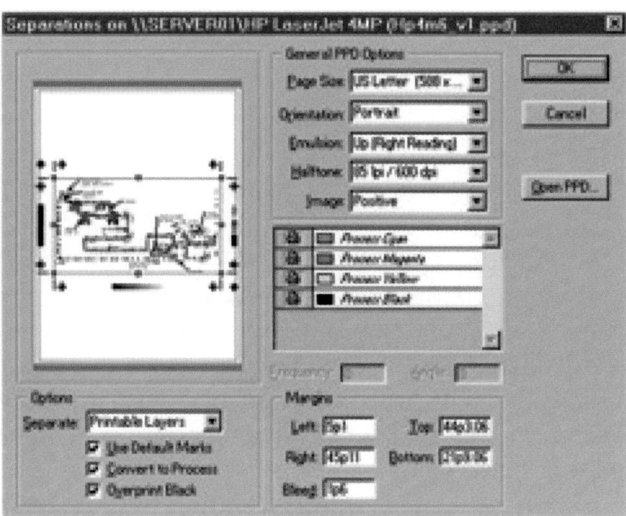

Figure 11-9. If you want a process color to separate to the proper CMYK plates, the process separation feature of the software should be turned on. When working with spot colors, you can have the color separate to its own plate by turning the separation feature off or simulate it in its corresponding 4-color equivalent by keeping it on.

If spot colors are used in imported graphic files, the same color must be defined in the page composition files. Illustration or image editing programs may name colors differently from page composition programs. Therefore, it is necessary to change the name in one file so that it matches the other exactly. If the names do not match, spot colors will separate as their CMYK equivalents. Some page composition programs automatically add the spot color to the color palette when importing graphics using that color, but do not automatically change the name.

When building process colors for output on a press, you should keep in mind that it is better to avoid too heavy an ink coverage. Maximum densities for the process colors vary for different types of presses and colors should be created with these values in mind.

Color Management Systems (CMS)

Color management for electronic imaging and reproduction involves more than the management of film color separations and ink composition. Electronic color reproduction requires a system of color management that will enable operators throughout the production process to maintain and produce accurate color reproduction.

A ***color management system (CMS)*** uses software as well as hardware to ensure that colors remain the same regardless of the device or medium used to display the colors. Color management systems can correct for color shifts on a scanner, adjust color display on a monitor, and make proofing, printing, and viewing of color more accurate.

Correlating the color-rendering capabilities of input and output devices is a difficult task because different devices use different technologies and color models to produce colors. In addition, color is highly subjective.

There is quite a variety of color management systems available; the type you use will depend on your operating system as well as your output needs. As with most computer systems, similar applications operate in a similar manner and changing from one to another is a fairly simple process. Color management can be divided into three primary steps—***characterization, calibration,*** and ***conversion.***

Characterization

Characterization describes the color limitations, or profile, of a particular device. The profile defines how the device's specific color space relates to a device-independent color space. The profile can also be used to define the ***color gamut,*** or color range, of a device.

All color management systems depend on the device profiles that store the color characteristics of the devices being used. As a means of standardization, most device profiles are described with the device-independent CIELAB color space.

Some color management systems have a generic device profile describing the manufacturer's specifications for the product. However, if the device is not performing to those specifications, the profiles will not be accurate.

Calibration

One of the most important steps when setting up a CMS is calibrating the input device(s). The calibration process allows the user to understand the small color changes to an image that a particular device introduces each time the device is used (for example, a scanner). Regular calibration is necessary to bring the device in line with its intended specifications.

The calibration of any device requires the use of a standard. The device can then be calibrated by first determining its deviation from the standard. Once the deviation has been determined, the proper correction factors can be identified and applied. In graphic communications, it is necessary to calibrate everything from the scanner through the monitor, the proofing device, and the actual press and paper on which the job will run.

Monitors

It is important to understand that the colors displayed on a computer monitor are different from those printable on a press. This is obvious when you look at the superimposed color gamut of a monitor on the CIE chromaticity diagram. Refer to Figure 11-3A. A monitor can be calibrated but it will never match the printed page perfectly because of the physics of color involved.

Color management systems can be used to ensure that your monitor provides as accurate color representation as possible. Before the CMS can begin characterization, four calibration elements must be set on the monitor to characterize it properly. These elements are the monitor's ***brightness, contrast, gamma levels,*** and ***white point***.

Brightness is the attribute of light-source colors by which emitted light is ordered continuously from light to dark in correlation with its intensity. *Contrast* is the relationship between the lightest and the darkest areas of an image. Brightness and contrast levels are set manually with the controls on your monitor, **Figure 11-10**.

Figure 11-10. The brightness and contrast controls allow manual adjustment of a computer monitor. Controls should be set at levels that correspond to the monitor's everyday working environment.

The *gamma levels* of a monitor are the degrees of contrast of the screen image. Gamma levels affect the distribution of tones between highlight and shadow areas of the original. The *white point* is the color that results when red, green, and blue channels are operating at full intensity. (In the RGB color system, a combination of equal parts of red, green, and blue light produce white light.) The white point defines the lightest area in an image. It is a movable reference point that, when changed, causes all other areas to be adjusted accordingly.

White point temperature defines the coolness (bluish) or warmness (yellowish) of video white. In some monitors, the white point will tend toward blue; in others, toward orange or another color. The white point can be set to match the light under which proofs will be viewed to help standardize color at different stages of production.

The gamma levels and white point temperature of your monitor are set within the monitor's software and are typically adjustable from the control panel within the system software, **Figure 11-11**. Both the gamma level and white point of your monitor may vary according to the computer's age and operating temperature.

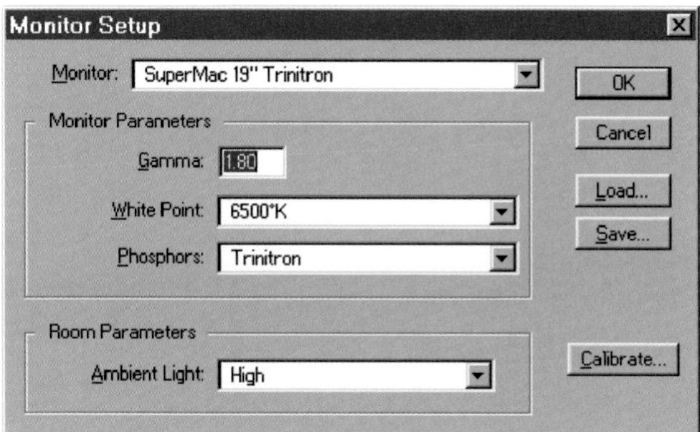

Figure 11-11. Monitor setup boxes vary between manufacturers, but most provide similar controls.

The next step involves the use of a colorimeter or spectrophotometer. When used for color measurement on a monitor, these devices use a rubber suction cup that affixes directly to the glass of the monitor, **Figure 11-12**.

Once prompted, the CMS commands the monitor to broadcast different colors on the screen. The device measures the colors emitted and sends the data back to the CMS. The CMS creates a profile of the monitor's performance by relating the color values measured to ideal colors. If the monitor tends slightly toward blue, the CMS will know that it will need to subtract that percentage of blue from every color it processes.

It is not necessary to perform a complete measurement procedure every time the white point or gamma level setting is altered. Some color management systems can automatically adapt to a new white point and gamma level.

Along with regular monitor calibration, you should eliminate light glare from windows, skylights, and overhead lighting. This can be done by constructing a glare hood for your monitor and placing egg-crate diffusers on overhead lighting.

Do not display the same pattern on your monitor for an extended time. If the same pattern is left onscreen for too long, the brightness of that area will be decreased due to the degradation of phosphors, or increased because the electrode surface will be activated more than in other areas.

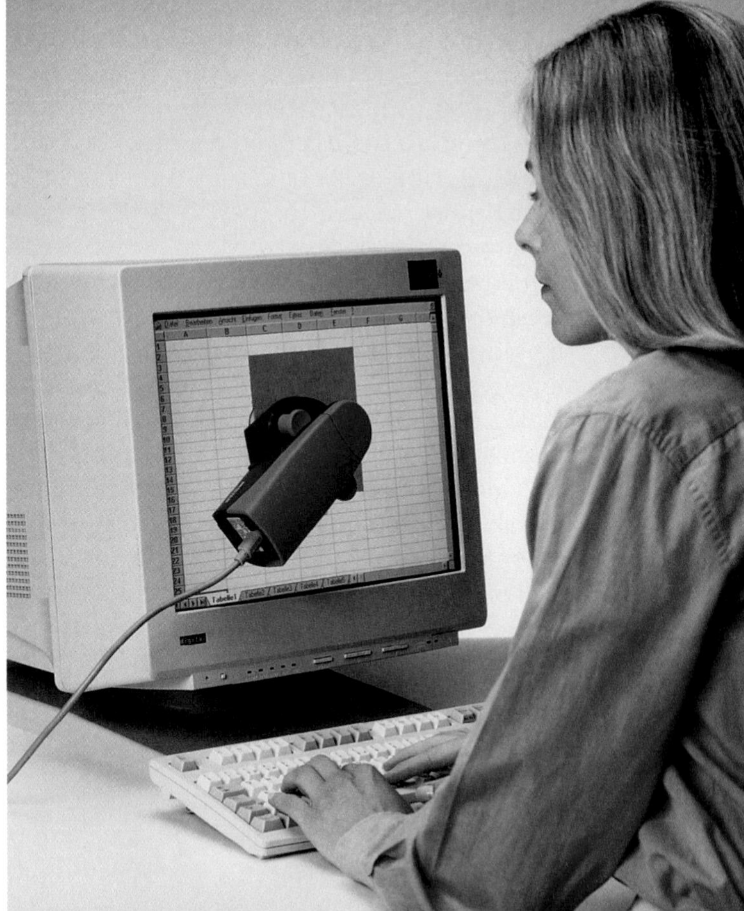

Figure 11-12. Spectrophotometers are designed for use in many areas of graphic communications. A suction cup device is used for mounting the device on a computer monitor.

Monitor limitations

It is not easy to accurately reproduce color on a computer monitor and it is practically impossible to display the exact colors of a printed image on a monitor. This problem exists because monitors and printing devices produce color through two entirely different processes. Monitors use additive color formation and printed images are formed by subtractive color formation.

In *additive color formation* (RGB), the primary colors of light (red, green, blue) combine to form other colors. Monitors produce color by exciting red, green, and blue phosphors with a sweeping beam of electrons generated from a CRT (cathode ray tube). The screen starts out as black and images are created when the electrons hitting the phosphors generate combinations of red, green and blue light. The screen becomes white when all the red, green, and blue phosphors are illuminated at the same time.

Monitors are analog devices and must translate an image's binary data before being able to display it. Computers use a ***video card*** to translate and generate the corresponding electrical voltage levels needed to produce the colors on the monitor. For a monitor to display at its optimum resolution, the video card must be able to operate at the proper level. For example, at least 4 Mb of video RAM (VRAM) is required when doing color work with a 24-bit display (16.7 million colors).

The video card uses color ***lookup tables*** and a digital-to-analog converter to coordinate the digital and analog color information. Lookup tables store the dot sizes needed to produce given colors. The type of video card used and the accuracy of the lookup tables will determine the quality of the conversion process.

In *subtractive* (CMY) *color formation*, color is seen by reflected light. Each of the subtractive primary colors—cyan, magenta, and yellow—absorbs other colors from the white light and reflects only its own. In process color printing, colors are mixed *visually*, rather than physically. Tiny, closely spaced dots of cyan, magenta, and yellow ink absorb and reflect the different wavelengths of light to produce different colors. (Refer to Chapter 8 for a review of RGB and CMY color formation.)

Monitors vary by size and resolution quality. They should be chosen based on the tasks they are to perform. The overall size of the monitor should be considered first. For example, a 15″ screen may be the most cost-effective for an RIP station, but a 17″ screen would be more suitable for a scanning station. Designers working on page composition need monitors with screens measuring at least 21″, **Figure 11-13**.

Other criteria to consider are ***dot pitch, maximum resolution,*** and ***refresh rate***. Dot pitch is the size of the pixels that make up the screen matrix (the smaller the dot, the sharper the image). Maximum resolution is the maximum number of pixels that the screen can represent in both horizontal and vertical dimensions. Higher resolution provides a clearer image and allows the user to have more windows open on the screen at the same time.

The refresh rate is the speed with which the screen is redrawn. The refresh rate controls the amount of detectable ***screen flicker*** (rapid changes in display screen light level). Screen flicker can also be affected by lighting and the persistence of the screen phosphors.

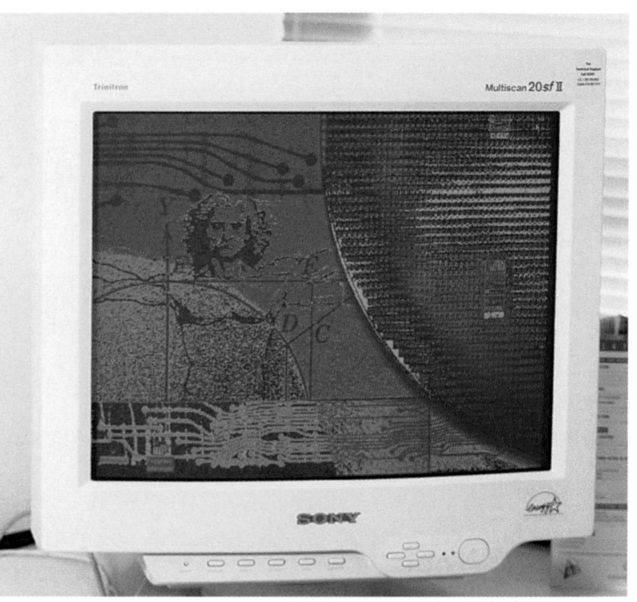

Figure 11-13. Designers working with page composition software should use as large a screen as possible. Larger screens are able to display the layout for a full two-page spread or an entire book cover image.

Scanners

Most digital imaging equipment provides a means of performing characterization and calibration. For example, to assist in determining the characterization of a scanner, manufacturers will include a ***reference image*** and a set of reference values for that image. The reference image contains well-defined color patches and will typically be the ***IT8 reflective target*** or ***pattern***, **Figure 11-14**.

IT8 reflective target

The IT8 pattern is a standard color reference tool used to calibrate input and output devices. It is also known as a *color target*. Samples from the CIELAB color space are used to create the IT8 reference charts.

Two charts currently used in the graphic communications industry are the IT8.7/1-1993 and the IT8.7/2-1993. The IT8.7/1 chart is used for scanner calibration. The chart is used to measure the values of transmissive color being read by the input device. The IT8.7/2 is also used for input scanner calibration, but it is used to measure reflective color. *Transmissive color* is light conveyed through a negative or positive transparency without being absorbed or scattered. *Reflective color* is color that is seen by reflected light.

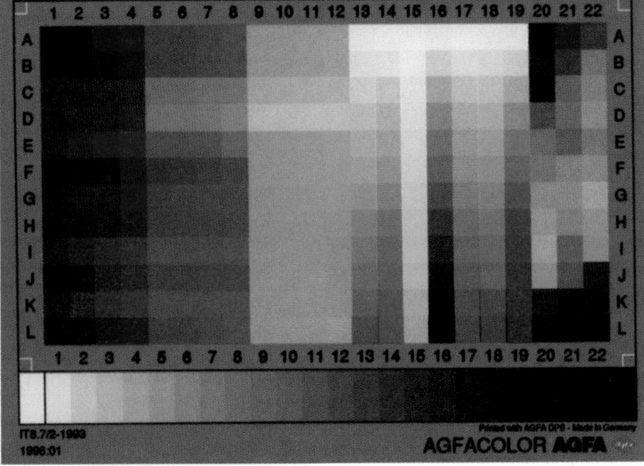

Figure 11-14. IT8 targets are available for various uses and from many different manufacturers. A—Kodak target. (Eastman Kodak Company) B—Agfa target. (Agfa)

The reference image is scanned and the measured results are related to the ideal values measured in the manufacturer's lab. The reference values are supplied to the user on disk.

An ideal scanner would allow the user to scan images directly into an independent color space such as CIELAB. However, most scanners are limited to the RGB and CMYK color spaces. All scanners start with an RGB signal and many allow conversions to CMYK as the scan is being made. If the LAB color space is not available, RGB should be used because it provides greater flexibility for the scanned image.

Some scanners convert from the RGB scan signal to CMYK *on-the-fly*, automatically creating a color-separated file from the original image. This is a less desirable approach to scanning in RGB because it makes the file device-dependent and limits the potential uses of the image. CMYK files are locked into the color gamut of the output process for which they are separated. This makes the conversion to other spaces difficult or impossible, and causes the conversion back to RGB to result in a less-than-optimum image for RGB purposes. A color management system is usually capable of making CMYK to RGB conversions, but the color quality is reduced because the original scan was made to a reduced gamut CMYK space. Therefore, scans should be saved in the original CIELAB or RGB format to preserve the maximum amount of color, and to ensure the image can be used for a number of different purposes.

Color correction and modification are easier to perform in the LAB or RGB mode than in CMYK. An RGB or LAB image file is also about 25% smaller than the same image saved in CMYK. Some imaging programs allow the user to preview an image in CMYK and still keep the file in RGB or LAB color.

Calibration schedules

Most circumstances do not warrant daily equipment calibration. However, some situations warrant device calibration on at least a monthly (if not weekly) basis. An example would be a service bureau that deals with large amounts of work. Operators can also develop a regimen for scanner characterization and calibration.

Determining a scanner's characteristics is a methodical process. Situations as well as equipment will vary, but by performing the following steps you will be able to determine the characteristics of a scanner.

- Gather an assortment of media and scan them at the scanner's default settings. Media will vary according to your scanner's capabilities, but when applicable, should include both transparent and reflective originals.
- Output the scans to your printer or imagesetter. Composite color proofs should be made from the film if you are using an imagesetter.
- Compare the color proofs to the originals under correct lighting.
- If a color measurement device is available, use it to obtain accurate readings.

Characteristics of the scanner can be identified at this point. You can determine whether the scans have a common color cast, if they are flat, or if they are all too heavy. Most scanning software provides controls in the form of highlight and shadow selection or ***tone curve adjustment*** to correct most common problems.

Tone curve adjustment involves the use of curves to make tonal adjustments. You can use curves to make precise adjustments to one area of the tonal range while maintaining the effect on other areas. For example, curves can be used to add or decrease the contrast of an image without changing the colors.

A lookup table listing the standard settings for all the scans should be created. This table should compensate for the scanner's characteristics. This lookup table will provide a good starting point for all your scans.

Save the original media, file, films, and proofs from one or two images that have been scanned with the new standard settings. The files should be output to film and a new composite color proof should be made at least once a month. The new color proof can be compared with the original to verify consistency. If the proofs are not close, you should check the output device calibration and processor status (chemical strength, temperature, speed), among other variables.

It is important to set all the controls of the scanner to neutral points before performing characterization. The neutral settings allow the user to return to the same starting point to continuously make successful scans.

Printers

Characterization and calibration of printing devices is also important to the accurate reproduction of color. The first step is to output a target file that is appropriate for the final printing process. After the target file is printed, it should be measured with a color spectrophotometer, **Figure 11-15**.

After the target is evaluated, profiling software can be used to create the printer's color profile. This profile is used by the color management system to adjust color inaccuracies in the printer as files are output.

The time needed to establish color management standards depends on the complexity of the operation. The calibration of monitors takes just a few minutes, while the calibration of scanners can require two hours. However, the procedure does not need to be repeated often because most scanners are stable performers. Printing presses and proof printers require more time because the number of color spot readings needed to build a profile is high. However, for larger operations, automated color measurement instruments are available and are capable of making hundreds of readings in just a few minutes.

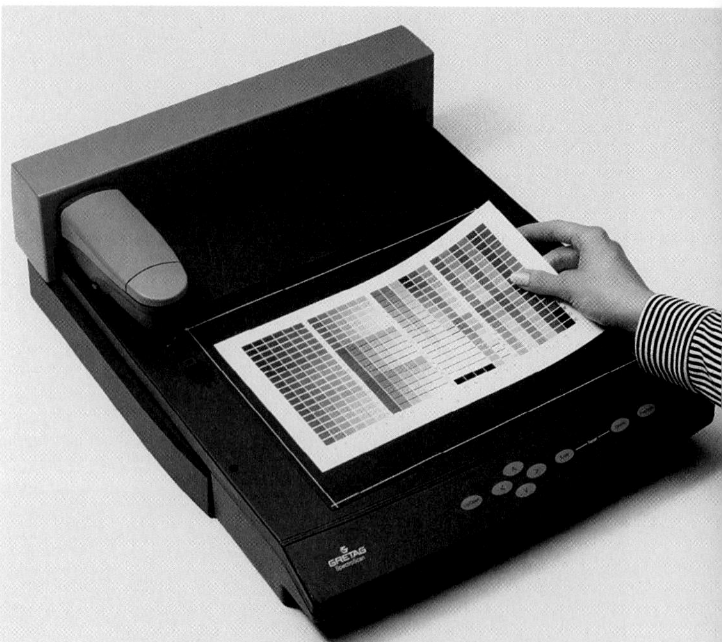

Figure 11-15. This spectrophotometer is mounted on an x/y table for automatic color measurement. (Photo courtesy of GretagMacbeth, New Windsor, NY)

Color Conversion

The conversion step performs color correction between imaging devices. Color management systems are used to compensate for and select from the possible range of colors available on each device. In most imaging programs, images can be converted to, displayed in, and edited in eight image modes. These eight modes are bitmap, duotone, indexed color, grayscale, multichannel, RGB, CMYK, and CIELAB, **Figure 11-16**.

Your system and output needs determine which image mode best suits your work. For instance, if a publication is to be printed in black and white, the grayscale mode can be used to convert color images into high-quality black-and-white images.

When converting images from one mode to another, the conversion creates a permanent change to the color values in the image. For example, the

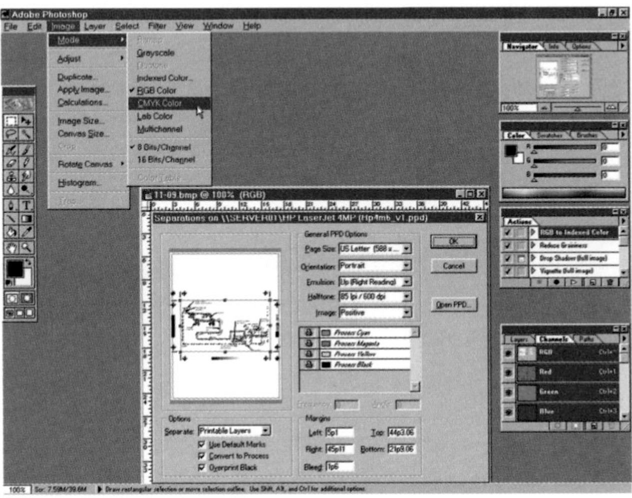

Figure 11-16. The user can easily choose image modes from a pull-down menu.

four-channel CMYK space contains far fewer colors, a narrower dynamic range, and a much smaller color gamut than the three-channel RGB space. Therefore, colors must be compressed to fit into the smaller color gamut. ***Gamut compression*** or gamut reduction is used to fit the original RGB image colors into the CMYK color gamut. Gamut compression gives the illusion that all color chroma, saturation, and value are present, but there is always a loss of color.

Each conversion changes data so you should always save a backup copy of the original file.

One of the most effective ways of performing color conversions is to begin with the CIELAB color space. Because it is device-independent, based on numerical values, and has a large color gamut, the LAB color space allows the CMS to make calculations and conversions without damaging color values.

Color Separation and Color Correction

Color separation is the process of dividing the colors of a multicolored original into the subtractive primaries cyan *(C)*, magenta *(M)*, yellow *(Y)*, and black *(K)*. The CMYK color separations can be made into films used to prepare printing plates or made directly into plates. Although there are several methods for making color separations, almost all color separation is now performed with an electronic scanner.

One of the biggest challenges in graphic communications is getting color to reproduce the way it should or even to predict what the printed colors will look like. Color correction is complex because color functions are interconnected. For example, in an RGB system (an additive or light-dependent system like a computer monitor or television set), a change in value changes chroma. For a brighter, more saturated red, the percentages of red, green, and blue must be adjusted. The percentage of red cannot simply be increased because that would increase lightness as well. To achieve a brighter red in a CMYK system, the cyan and black would need to be reduced and the yellow and magenta would need to be increased.

What used to be the job of prepress technicians is now often the responsibility of the designer. Before the advent of computers in prepress production, methods such as ***photographic masking*** and ***dot etching (dry or wet)*** were used for color correction and manipulation.

Photographic masking

Photographic masking is accomplished by creating film images from the original using filters. Photographic masks are measured by their percentage of light-stopping ability. For example, a 100% positive mask would block out all illumination when placed on a light table if it was in register and overlapping a negative image.

Dot etching

Dot etching is used for modifying isolated areas of an image, **Figure 11-17**. *Wet etching* involves the use of chemicals to erode or build up the silver deposits on the film that form the different dot sizes. *Dry etching* refers to contacting techniques used to spread or choke the dot structure.

Color correction is now performed almost exclusively in electronic format. Most color management systems provide both automatic and manual means for color correction. Imaging programs provide tools and filters for setting highlights and shadows, adjusting midtones and color balance, modifying hue and saturation values, image sharpening, and changing both brightness and contrast. Although most imaging programs allow the user to perform these types of adjustments, the need for and the amount of color correction is still best determined by the results in the pressroom.

Figure 11-17. Dot etching was performed by hand directly on film before the color correction process became almost entirely electronic.

Shadow clarity

In theory, by combining equal parts of cyan, magenta, and yellow, you can produce black. However, due to impurities present in all printing inks, a mix of these colors actually yields a muddy brown. To compensate, some cyan, magenta, and yellow is removed from areas where the three colors overlap, and black is added. Printing black ink over the three primaries improves and enhances shadow details of the reproduction.

This effect can be achieved in a number of ways, but prepress operators typically use ***undercolor removal (UCR)***, ***gray component replacement (GCR)***, and ***undercolor addition (UCA)***.

Undercolor removal (UCR)

Undercolor removal (UCR) is a process of color correction typically associated with high-speed web printing. Undercolor removal can be accomplished with an electronic scanner, an image editing program, or photographic masking techniques, **Figure 11-18**.

The shadow details of a four-color separation will typically be represented as the three process colors overprinted with black. When printing with high-speed presses, it is not desirable to overlap layers of ink that are too heavy. Drying problems as well as ink trapping problems can occur with saturated ink layers.

The theory of undercolor removal is to reduce the amount of magenta, yellow, and cyan in shadows and neutral areas of an image, and replace them with an appropriate amount of black. This is accomplished by reducing the shadow dot structure in the overlapping areas of the yellow, magenta, and cyan inks. UCR produces good shadow densities by using the black printer to its fullest capacity.

Gray component replacement (GCR)

Gray component replacement (GCR) is an electronic technique used to substitute black ink for calculated amounts of cyan, magenta, and yellow inks, **Figure 11-19**. Substitutions occur mainly in the neutral tones and in gray components of

Figure 11-18. The image on the left is a full-range color separation. The image on the right illustrates the same image with a 30% undercolor removal, providing better shadow details.

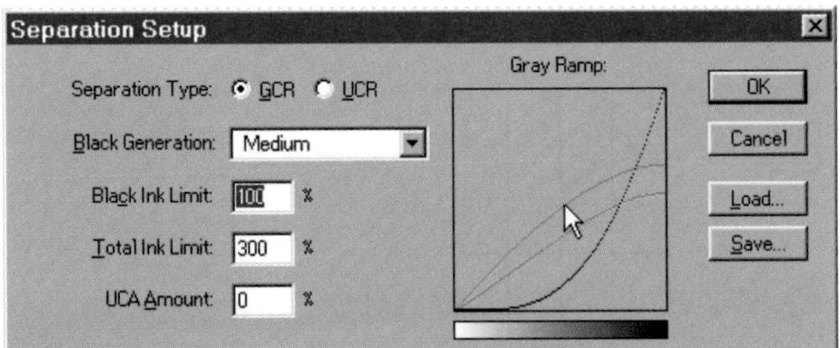

Figure 11-19. The separation setup box in most page composition programs allows the user to specify separation types and ink limits.

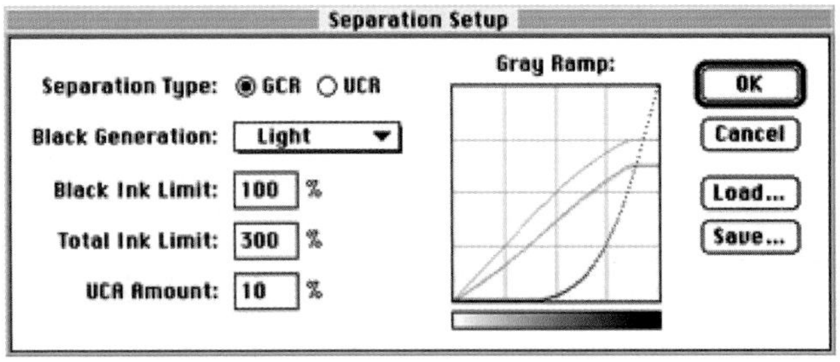

Figure 11-20. The amount of undercolor addition is set with the same control used for gray component replacement.

desaturated colors. When applying GCR, the black printer is used to replace a proportionate amount of cyan, magenta, and yellow anywhere the three colors overlap.

GCR separations tend to reproduce dark, saturated colors better than UCR operations. GCR separations also maintain better gray balance on press. Other advantages include better detail and contrast within the reproduction, reduced ink costs, reduction of ink setoff (unwanted ink transferring to adjoining sheet of paper), and reduced drying time.

Many scanner and electronic prepress equipment manufacturers have developed specific software packages for GCR. The type of separation you should use will depend on the substrate and requirements of the printer.

Undercolor addition (UCA)

Undercolor addition (UCA) is the inverse function of undercolor removal. Undercolor addition is used to add cyan, magenta, and yellow after removing some of the black in the shadow areas. Undercolor addition is applied with gray component replacement because 100% GCR does not produce a good saturated black in print.

UCA helps produce rich, dark shadows in areas that might appear flat if they are printed with only black ink. The color added to the shadow or black areas will determine the warmth or coldness of the black.

The amount of undercolor addition is set with the same control used for GCR, **Figure 11-20**. Increasing the UCA amount increases the amount of cyan, magenta, or yellow added to the shadow areas. Check with your service bureau or printer for the appropriate values.

Trapping

When colors printed from separate plates border one another, the slightest amount of misregistration can cause gaps between printed objects (graphics and type). Printers use a method called ***trapping*** to create a small area of overlap (*trap*) between colors to compensate for potential gaps. Trapping can be defined as how well one color overlaps another without leaving a white space between the two or generating a third color.

Because responsibilities for color separation have shifted from trade shops to electronic page-production artists, trapping is typically performed during electronic page and image composition, **Figure 11-21**. Trapping must be considered any time two colors meet. Methods used to set traps include ***spread, choke,*** and ***automatic***.

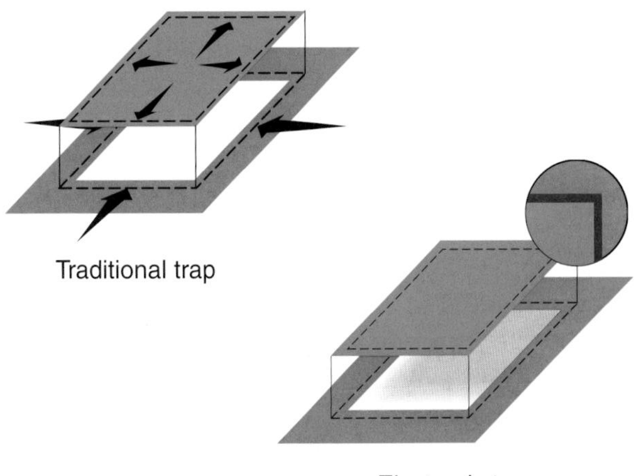

Figure 11-21. No matter which method is used, traditional or electronic, trapping still performs the same function.

A *spread trap* is created by spreading the foreground over the background color, **Figure 11-22.** Spread traps are used when a lighter object knocks out of a darker background. Illustration programs that are limited to one type of trapping usually use spread traps.

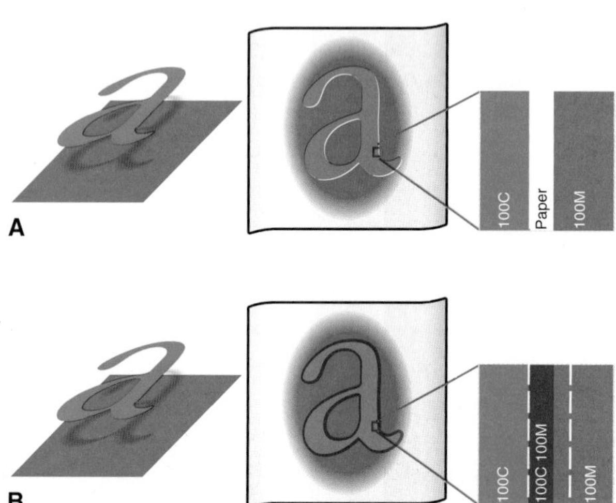

Figure 11-22. Spread trap. A—If no allowance is made for misregistration (i.e. trapping), the paper will show through as white lines around the image. B—When trapping with uncommon colors, the stroke should be the same color as the object being trapped. Half the width will fall outside the edge and blend with the other color.

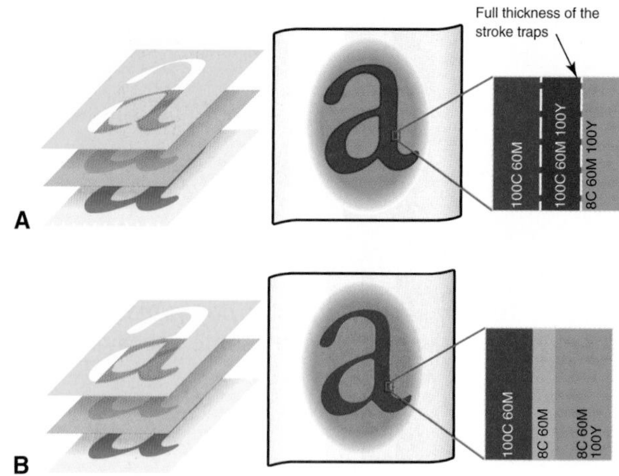

Figure 11-23. Trapping with common colors. A—Although it is not always necessary to set a trap with objects using common colors, the trap tends to blend the object colors better. B—If a trap is not used, the common color may or may not show through as a third color surrounding the object.

Chokes are performed by spreading the background under the foreground object. The object may appear to be squeezed or reduced in size. Chokes and spreads are often referred to as *fatties* and *skinnies*.

Automatic traps are set by building art with common colors. As long as a ***knockout*** (clean break between elements) is not specified, and common colors are used, the shared component compensates for the space between the objects. For example, if two overlapping objects contain cyan as part of their CMYK values, any gap between them is covered by the cyan content of the object underneath. In **Figure 11-23**, no background shows through because both the letter and the background contain the same percentage of magenta.

Some illustration programs allow the user to perform trapping automatically by applying a *trap filter.* This type of trapping is intended for simple objects where parts can be selected and trapped individually. It does not work with gradients or patterns, however. Fortunately, most illustration programs provide an alternative trapping method that allows more complex work to be performed.

It is best to scale graphics to their final size before adding a trap, otherwise the amount of trapping will increase or decrease if you scale the object. For example, if you create a graphic that has a 0.5-point trap and scale it four times its original size, the result will be a 2.0-point trap for the enlarged graphic. Trapped files should also be imported into the page composition program at actual size. If they are scaled after they are imported, the traps will also be scaled and will need to be recreated.

Trapping type

There are a variety of factors that must be considered when setting traps. They include everything from the kind of paper to pressroom conditions. These variables are extremely important when applying traps to type because spreading or choking may cause character distortion.

Applying process colors to type at small point sizes should be avoided because any amount of misregistration can make the text difficult to read. Trapping type at small point sizes can also result in hard-to-read copy. However, if it is necessary to trap type, always remember that smaller type requires a smaller trap to prevent distortion, **Figure 11-24.**

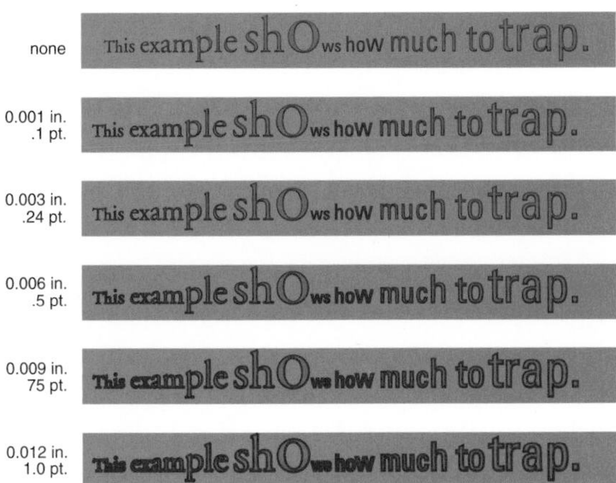

Figure 11-24. As the size of the trap is increased, the letter elements thicken and the serifs lose their delicacy.

Text can also be trapped by first converting it to outlines and then placing a copy behind the original. A trap could then be created as with any other graphic object. However, when type is converted to outlines, ***hinting*** is lost. Hinting optimizes how type prints at small point sizes on printers with a resolution of 600 dpi or lower. Text can no longer be edited when converted to outlines because it is no longer type but a graphic. You should contact your service bureau or printer for recommendations.

Special considerations

Trapping tools and capabilities vary with each illustration program, so you should refer to the user's guide for detailed instructions. However, there are several points that should be considered when creating traps—regardless of the program being used.

- In general, the lighter color is spread into the darker color. If there is no obvious lighter or darker color, then content is considered when determining the trap. For example, if text is one of the elements, it probably would not be spread over the background. However, it is okay to spread type over the background if the type is a very light color against a dark background. The dark background will hold the character shapes.
- When trapping two light-colored objects, the trap line may show through the darker of the two colors, resulting in an unsightly dark border. For example, if you trap a light blue object into a light yellow object, a bright green border is visible where the trap is created. You can specify a tint of the trapping color (in this case, yellow) to downplay the trap line. Your service bureau or printer can recommend the correct percentage of tint.
- When using an illustration program, artwork can be trapped by applying a colored ***stroke*** or outline to the elements requiring a trap. Half the width of a stroke will fall inside and half will fall outside the element it outlines. When a stroke is specified to overprint, the adjoining color will be trapped beneath the outside half. See **Figure 11-25.**

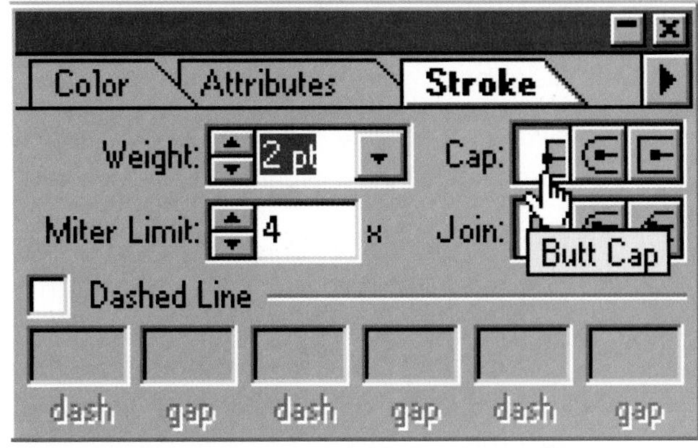

Figure 11-25. The most common method of trapping within an illustration program is to add a stroke on each element, and set the stroke to overprint. The width of the stroke should be twice the width of the desired trap.

- Color gradations are difficult to trap because the best trap would be a gradation of colors. When trapping a gradation to a solid color, a common color between the background and gradation should be selected. After a common color has been selected, a trap can be created.
- To trap lines electronically into a background of a different color, create two lines, one directly on top of the other, **Figure 11-26A**. The first line should be wide enough to create a trap.
- The need for trapping is eliminated if ***overprinting*** of colors is specified, **Figure 11-26B** and **C**.

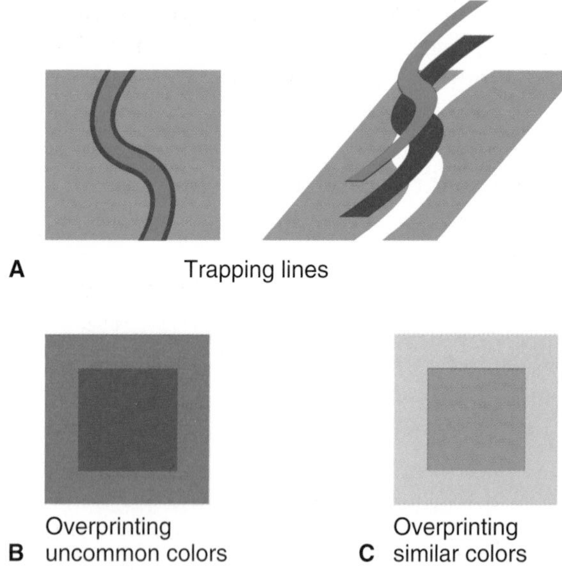

Figure 11-26. A—The trap line must be wider than the original line in order to overprint it. B—The overprinted image adds its color completely to the background. C—The background color contains 30% cyan, and the image has 8% cyan. The largest percentage of color is used for the overprint, so the overprinting area contains 30% cyan instead of 38%.

- Trapping is intended to correct misalignment of solid tints in CMYK images and should not be created for continuous-tone images. Excessive trapping may generate a keyline effect (or even crosshair lines) in C, M, and Y plates. These problems may not be visible in the composite image on screen and might show up only when output to film or plates.
- When using black to trap a black object that is a mixture of process colors, you should apply a 100% black stroke knocking out of the object to be trapped, **Figure 11-27**. This prevents misregistration from revealing the colors in the mixed black.

Figure 11-27. If 100% black is used for the stroke, none of the other process colors will show through.

- EPS art should be trapped in the image creation program, because page composition programs cannot trap EPS artwork.
- If photos are to be printed on a color background, they should always be choked by the surrounding background color.

Trapping can be an extremely complex process. Although most page composition programs can be used to set traps, they are not always sophisticated enough to handle complex situations. Besides layout considerations, factors such as the type of paper, printing process, pressroom conditions, and expected ***dot gain*** (the optical or mechanical increase in the size of a halftone dot) must be considered. In most cases, your printer will determine if any trapping is needed and will tell you what parameters or values you will need to apply.

Screening

Proper screening is vital to producing high-quality output. Before computers took over most prepress functions, screening patterns were applied with a process camera. A screening pattern is the strategic placement of dots to create the illusion of a continuous-tone image. Conventional printing uses variable-sized dots in fixed spacing to reproduce photos, **Figure 11-28**. Digital printing uses smaller, fixed-size dots to create photorealistic images.

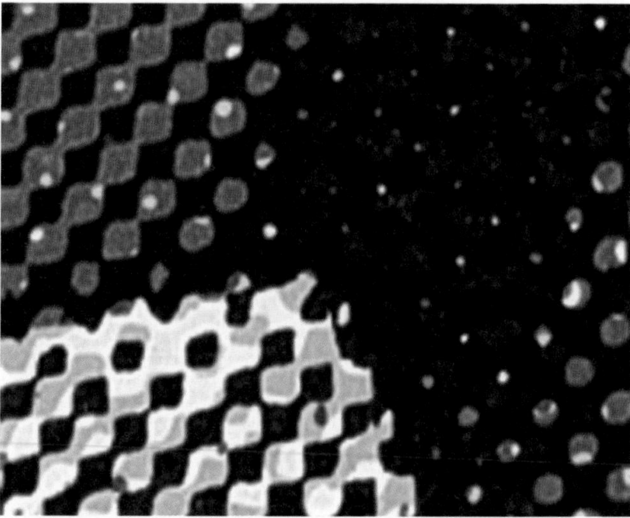

Figure 11-28. This is an enlargement of a halftone separation dot structure within a four-color reproduction.

Presently, most imaging programs, raster image processors, and imagesetters provide the user with a variety of screening options. Screening options allow the user to do such things as eliminate moiré patterns while holding rosettes across the page, and apply higher screen frequencies at lower resolutions. Features often include the ability to shift angles to accommodate gravure, screen printing and flexography, and to render dots in a variety of shapes.

Spot screening

Spot screening or ***amplitude modulation***, is a screening method in which dots are laid in a grid pattern based on the color tone. The spacing between the dot center is held constant, but the dot size (amplitude) is varied to produce different shades or tones. Because the grids for different colors are offset at angles, a distinctive rosette pattern is created in the image. Stochastic screening attempts to overcome the rosette pattern that frequently mars images created with spot screening.

Stochastic screening

Stochastic screening is a halftoning method that creates the illusion of tones by varying the number (frequency) of micro-sized dots (spots) in a small area. Unlike conventional halftoning, the spots are not positioned in a grid-like pattern. The placement of each spot is determined as a result of a complex algorithm that evaluates and distributes spots under a fixed set of parameters. In stochastic screening, the spacing of dots varies, **Figure 11-29.** Stochastic screening is also referred to as *frequency modulation (FM) dots* or *FM screening*.

Figure 11-29. Dot variation in placement and shapes is evident in this enlargement of a printed image.

Stochastic screens provide greater definition and detail in irregular shapes and expand the range of tones that can be reproduced through increased ink densities and improved color saturation. The disadvantage of stochastic screens is that tints or solid-color areas can sometimes appear grainy because the tiny dots are not really replaced in a random pattern.

To correct this problem and maintain the image's photographic attributes, most raster image processors (RIPs) provide additional screening options. Multiple screening options allow the user to select the best screening method for the type of image used. For best results, photos, line art, and vector graphics may each require different screening methods. One of the most common is *error-diffusion screening*.

Error-diffusion screening

Error-diffusion screening places dots more randomly than stochastic screening. It uses data from surrounding cells to determine dot placement. The difference between the color tone requested and that printed for a cell is fed through a filter and carried to other cells as they are processed, diffusing the error across surrounding cells. Although this reduces graininess in solid areas, it can also cause the loss of image sharpness. However, error diffusion can create smoother transitions of colors or tones for certain types of images and result in better printed output. The type of screening method used will depend on the output device and the intended use of the image.

When RIPs were first introduced, they were designed for use with 200-dpi electrostatic printers. Variations of stochastic and error-diffusion screening between different manufacturers had an obvious impact on the visual appearance of printed images. RIP software developers have since developed screening patterns to the point that it is almost impossible to detect the difference.

Screening patterns can affect file-processing speed. If one pattern adds more dots for image sharpness, then the file size will be larger and take longer to process. On the other hand, to process blends more quickly, the screening pattern on some RIPs will eliminate the top 5% and bottom 5% of the data.

Preflighting

During the design process, many colors may be defined, tested, and rejected. Rejected colors may remain in the files and should be removed from the color palette to speed printing and to ensure they are not accidentally used.

Ideally, the color palette in a page composition program would display *only* the colors used in the job. Unfortunately, this is not the case and unused colors will often be left in a layout. If an unused color is present, a warning or ***gamut alarm,*** will appear when preflighting the files and you will need to find and delete the color, **Figure 11-30**. If you cannot delete a color, it is probably an extra spot color from an imported graphic file. You will have to go back to the imaging program to delete the stray color. If stray color is not deleted, it will increase the chance that an incorrect color will be applied to the text or to a graphic.

Some composition programs include the additive primary colors red, green, and blue in the default color palette. These colors should be removed from your files because they are made of components of red, green, and blue *light*, not the CMYK colors.

Special colors, such as metallics or fluorescents, are not always available in an application's color palette. When using a special color, it should be defined as a spot color and given a unique name. You should contact your service bureau or printer for detailed instructions.

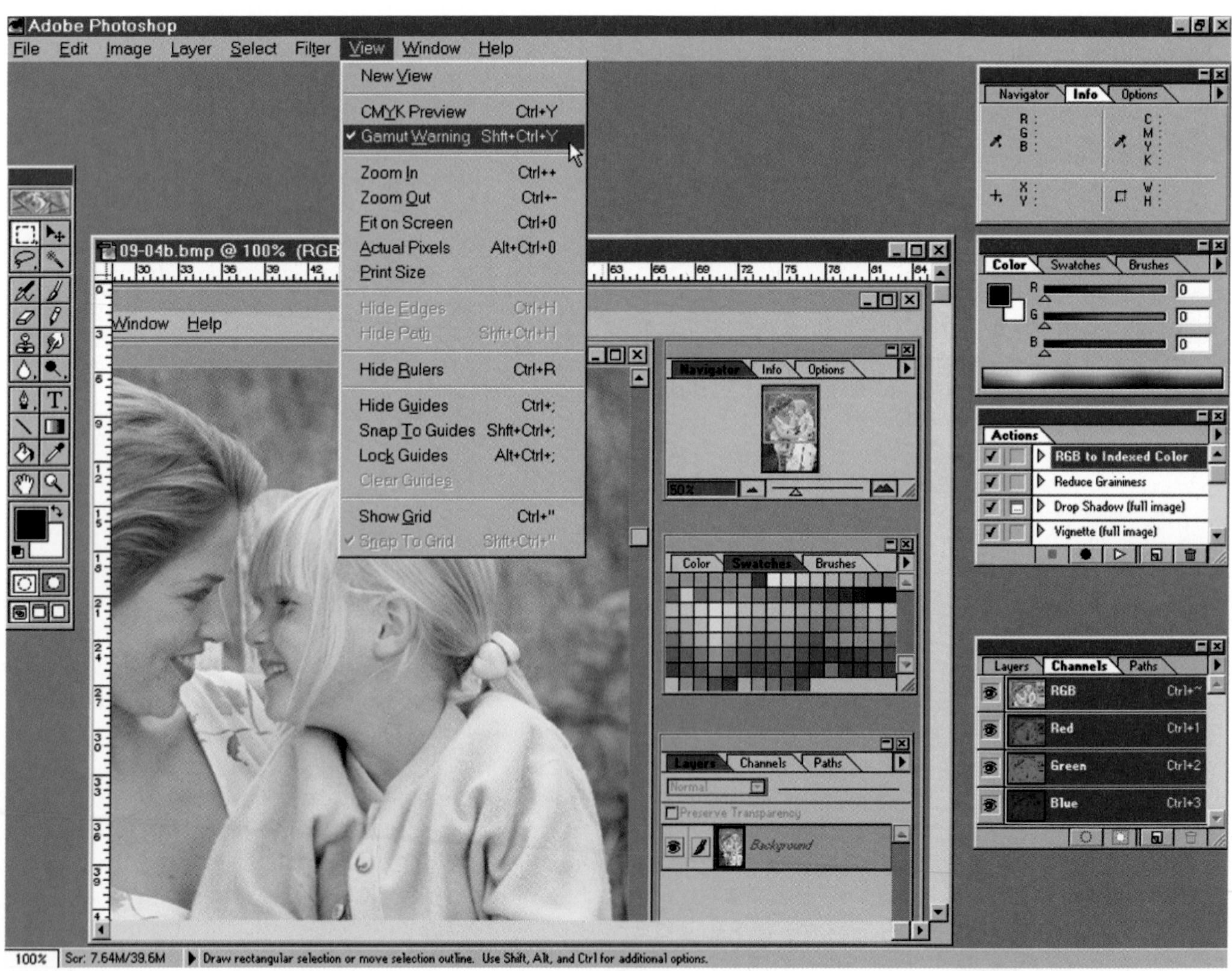

Figure 11-30. If there is an unused color present in the layout, a gamut alarm or warning will appear when preflighting files.

CREF II Guidelines

The Scitex Graphic Arts Users Association (SGAUA) publishes the CREF II Guidelines to improve prepress productivity. (CREF is the acronym for *Computer Ready Electronic File.*) Professionals recommend consulting the CREF II Guidelines and discussing file preparation with your service bureau or printer.

Proofing

Depending on the complexity of a project and the arrangement you have with the service bureau or printer, you will review a number of proofs before the job goes to press. Proofs are generated for performing corrections (text, layout, and color), and to provide a means for confirming a contract. Besides confirming that layout, fonts, and other design elements were not lost or deformed before reaching the output stage, proofs should be generated for checking color accuracy and resolution, **Figure 11-31**.

Proofs can be generated directly from film, run off on a proof press, or made directly from digital files. Cost variations will often determine what type of proofs you will request at different stages of prepress production. ***Soft proofing*** is the proofing of images onscreen.

Press proofs (those run off a press) may still be one of the best verification proofs, but the digital proof is fast becoming the standard. ***Digital proofs*** are generated by outputting files on a high-resolution, high-quality printer, **Figure 11-32**. Initially, professionals in the industry could not place much

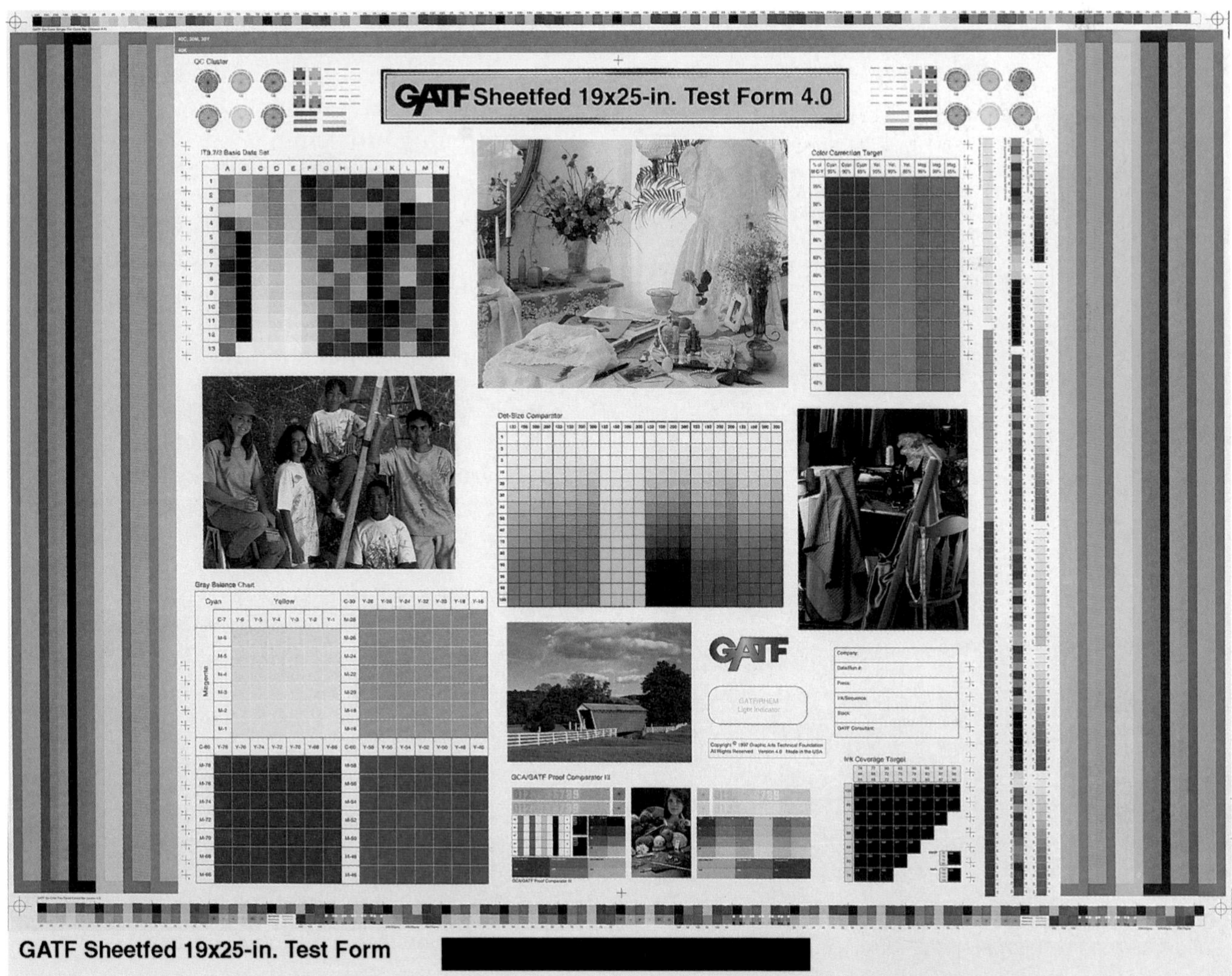

Figure 11-31. Test forms are available to check the capabilities of presses. (Graphic Arts Technical Foundation)

Figure 11-32. Digital test forms contain the same information as a conventional press form.

faith in digital proofs. However, technological advancements have allowed many types of digital output devices to meet industry color standards for prepress proofing. Because of the accuracy and cost savings, digital proofs are replacing the conventional film-generated contract proofs that have been used for decades.

Film-generated proofs

Photomechanical proofing systems are categorized into single sheet or laminate color proofing systems and overlay color proofing systems. The advantage of single sheet or laminate proofing is that the viewing light is reflected from a single surface and light refraction is limited. Film-generated proofs include Matchprints™, bluelines (diazo), Cromalin™, brownlines, and Color Key™.

- *Matchprints* are four-color proofs produced from the film that will be used to create the printed pages. They enable accurate evaluation of the film for trapping, moiré, and other conventional printing problems.
- *Bluelines* or *diazo proofs* are produced from positive imageset film. Bluelines can be imaged on both sides, folded and trimmed, and are extremely valuable for showing the position and registration of the printed material.
- *Cromalin™ proofs* are four-color proofs created from halftones using process toners and special film. Heat and pressure are used to transfer the image to the proofing substrate.
- *Brownlines* or *silverprint proofs* are created by exposing brownline paper through the negative flat on a platemaker. This method is commonly used to proof single-color flats.
- *Color Key™* proofs are transparent sheets that are imaged from film, then physically fastened together in register. Proofs can be made from process-color separations, or from mechanically-separated art to show spot color. See **Figure 11-33**.

Figure 11-33. Color Key proofing is an inexpensive means of presenting a visual likeness of the finished product. It is less widely used today than other color proofing methods.

Figure 11-34. Color proofing systems vary in size and capabilities. This system can produce proofs ranging in sizes from 11″ × 17″ to 25″ × 38″ at about one-third the cost of traditional methods. (Western Lithographic®)

Digital proofing

As more of the industry moves to a computer-to-plate workflow, digital proofing has become extremely important. For digital proofs to replace film-generated proofs, they must accurately represent all the features of the traditional proof, including color fidelity, traps and overprints, representative screening, and quality in fine line details, **Figure 11-34**.

Color management systems can be used to compensate for all factors affecting the printing process. A quality CMS will compensate for such factors as ink hues, color contamination, press gains and losses, plate gains and losses, and the paper's color and absorptivity.

Depending on the system's capabilities, digital proofs can simulate results from any type of printing press. Most dye-sublimation printers and ink-jet printers are able to simulate both process inks and spot colors. These machines produce dotless color images that closely simulate the press sheet, at a much lower cost than conventional methods.

Many digital proofing systems can also simulate dot patterns and the dot gain expected on final output. This is especially useful because most customers insist on seeing the halftone dots or screen pattern before accepting the proof as a true indication of color and quality. Many digital output devices can be connected to the same RIP that runs the imagesetter and output halftone patterns that are identical to those that will appear on the final sheet.

Some electrostatic printers and high-quality printer/copiers can also simulate the printing inks of a press. They are commonly used for proof production as well as short-run impressions of finished color printing. The same process used to calibrate printers is used for calibrating proofing devices.

Digital bluelines

Computer-to-plate workflows originally lacked a proof for checking final imposition before output to the platesetter. Several manufacturers have designed and produced two-sided signature proofs that have are referred to as *digital blueline proofs*.

The digital blueline can be defined as a two-sided digital position proof for eight-page impositions (sixteen-page signatures). These proofs are usually printed on wide format ink jet proofers, **Figure 11-35**. In some proofers, after imaging on one side of the ink jet media, the paper is flipped and repositioned. Other systems print both sides at once. Most systems allow proofs to be output in full color or in a single color to check basic layout and imposition. It is unlikely that this type of digital proof will eliminate the need for contract color digital proofs.

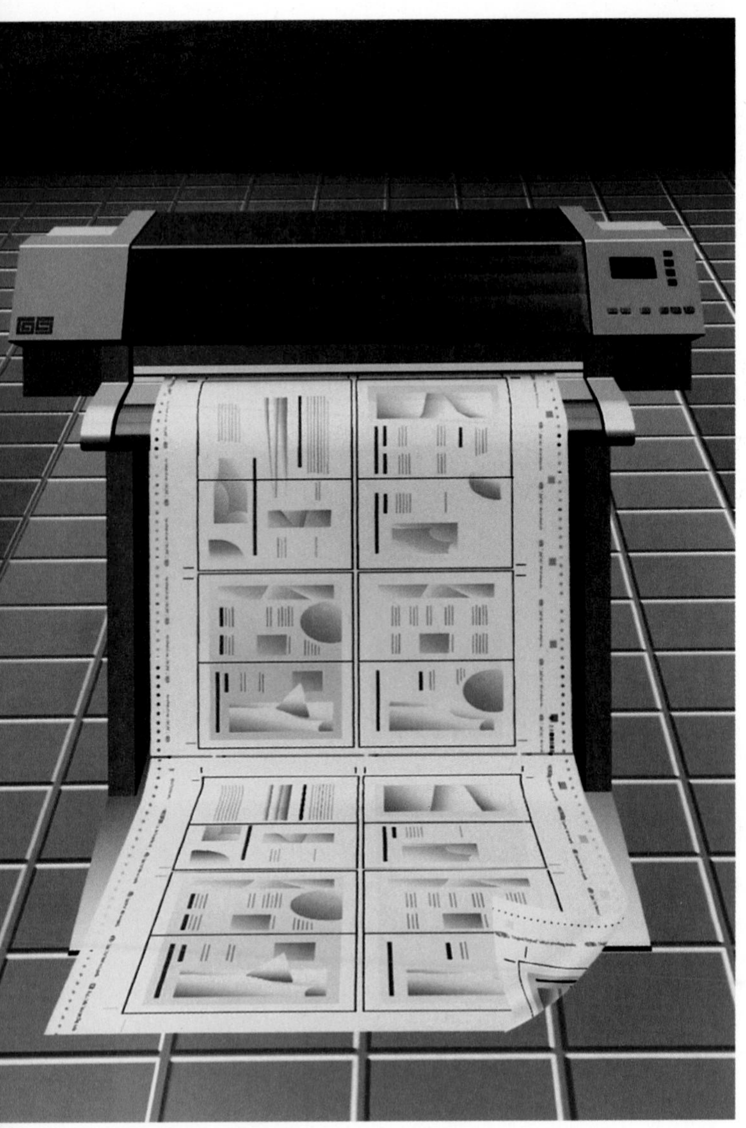

Figure 11-35. This ink jet proofing system produces two-sided digital imposition proofs. (DuPont)

Automatic proofreading systems

Automatic systems can be used for proofreading plates, film, carton stock, stuffer sheets, label stock, textbooks and a variety of other printed material. Some systems are capable of detecting details as fine as missing or partially missing periods in 3-point type, **Figure 11-36**. Sensors are mounted at various press stations to identify and warn the operator of defects such as streaking, stains, and under- or over-inking.

Figure 11-36. Automatic proofreading systems are able to complete their proofreading process in as little as three percent of the time required for traditional proofreading. (GSMA)

A database of pixels that make up the text and graphics of each sheet is generated by the system. During the inspection process, charge-coupled devices (CCDs) are used to inspect printed sheets by searching for missing or unwanted pixels. Therefore, any combination of different languages, symbols, and graphics can be accurately proofread at the same speed as simple text. The operator can call up the file of inspected images that is made during proofreading and magnify any highlighted discrepancies.

Color control bars

A ***color control bar*** is a strip of colors printed in the trim area of a press sheet. It is used to monitor printing variables such as trapping, ink density, dot gain, and print contrast. It usually consists of overprints of two- and three-color solids and tints; solid and tint blocks of cyan, magenta, yellow, and black; and additional aids such as resolution targets and dot gain scales, **Figure 11-37**. Color control bars may also be referred to as *color bars, color control strips,* or *proofing bars.*

Color control bars should be output on any type of color proof. SWOP includes a list of characteristics that should be included on a color control bar as well as its position on the proof. Color control bars created for computer-to-plate (CTP) systems may require additional features than color bars generated for film.

Calibration and characterization

Just as the calibration of scanners and monitors is vital to accurate color reproduction, proper characterization and calibration of proofing devices is vital to the production of accurate digital proofs. Before outputting a job to any type of digital output device, an output profile should be created. The output profile can be used to correct color inaccuracies in the printer, or it can be combined with a printing press profile to simulate the effect of the press on the proof printer.

The first step is to create a target file that is appropriate to the printing process. A four-color file is made for a printing press and an RGB file is made for a color film recorder that produces transparent film. The target file is printed and then measured with a color spectrophotometer.

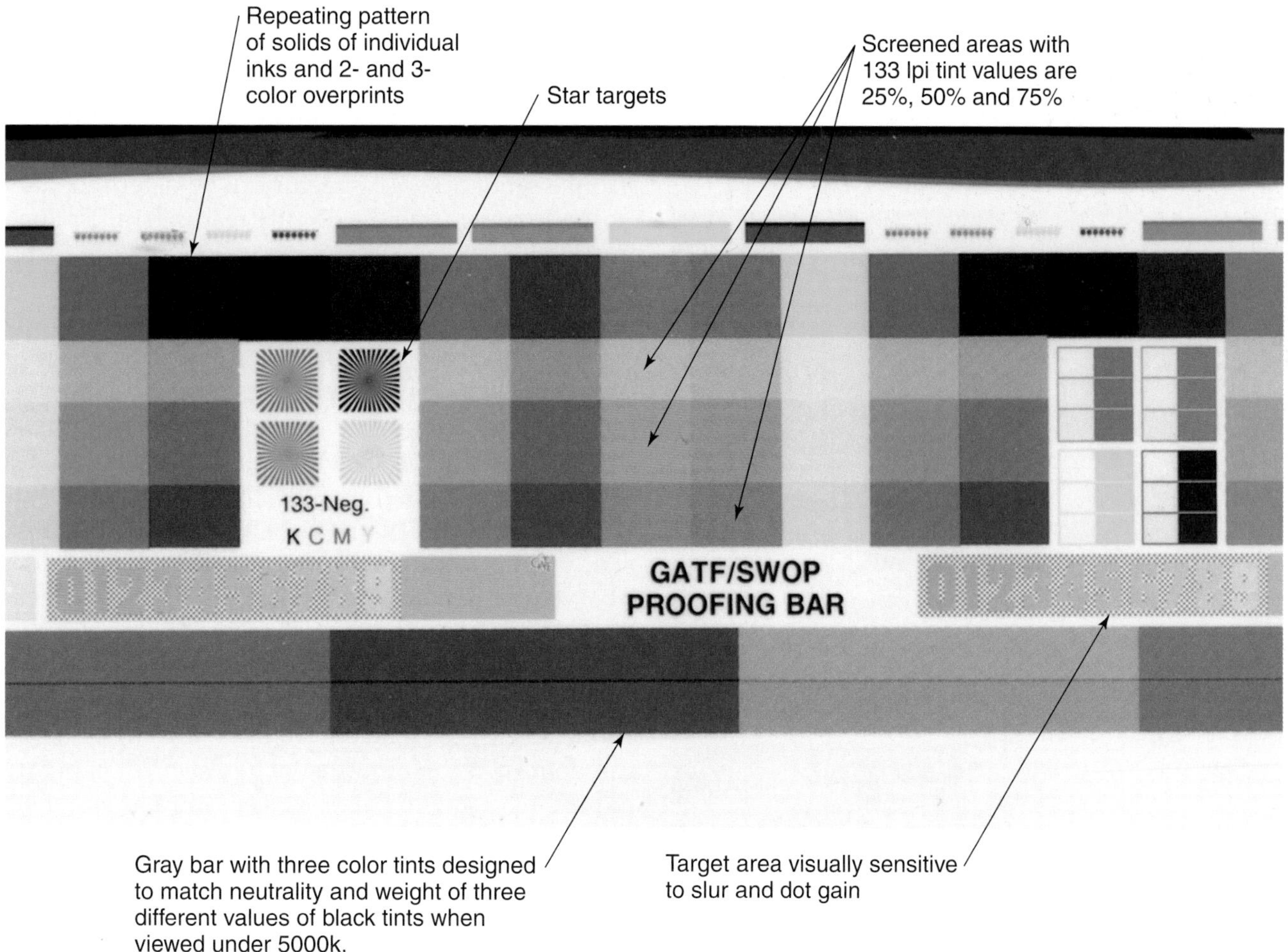

Figure 11-37. This color control bar is used to assess whether color proofs meet SWOP specifications. (Graphic Arts Technical Foundation)

After the target is printed and evaluated, the profiling software creates a profile that describes the color capabilities of the device. This profile then becomes the output profile, which adjusts the color of the file as it is output. Using this output file, the proofing system can output proofs that will accurately depict what the job will look like when printed on the printing press. This can be done before film or plates are made.

Viewing variables

As discussed in Chapter 8, there are many variables to be considered when viewing or judging color. In addition to inherent human variables (color blindness, vision fatigue, aging), viewing conditions must also be considered.

Accurate color comparison is almost impossible unless items are viewed under exactly the same viewing conditions. For this reason, the graphic arts industry has established an illumination standard. Viewing booths have been designed with a neutral color environment and 5000 K illumination, **Figure 11-38**. This light temperature is color-balanced and is ideal for making color comparisons. Viewing booths are usually available in service bureaus and printers. Unfortunately, many customers do not have standardized viewing areas and cannot view proofs under the same lighting conditions as service bureau agents and printers.

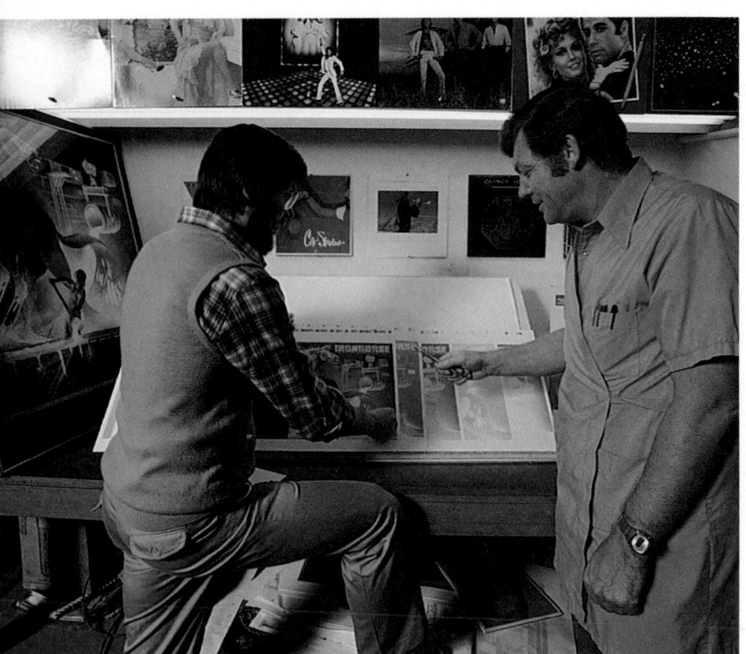

Figure 11-38. Viewing booths are used to review originals, reproductions, and color separation film.

Ink Colors

Color reproduction systems should be engineered from the *pressroom* back to the point of creation. Thus, one of the first steps in the engineering of a color reproduction system is the analysis of process inks.

Process inks differ from one ink manufacturer to another. To evaluate the set of inks used in a specific printing facility, a set of color bars is printed under normal printing conditions. Most service bureaus or printers will furnish test patterns for comparison purposes.

Ink film density is read with a reflection densitometer. The densities recorded can be used to determine the working characteristics of a set of process inks. The four factors that best describe the working characteristics or impurities of the inks are *strength, hue, grayness,* and *efficiency*.

Ink strength is important because it will identify the range and depth of colors that can be produced from a set of inks. This factor can be determined by visually comparing the density readings, and selecting the highest reading for the yellow, magenta, and cyan inks.

Ink hue error determines the percentage of the reflection of colored light from a specific color of ink. A hue or color is determined by the eye in terms of cone stimulation to colors of light. For example, the color or hue of magenta ink should absorb and prevent green light from reflecting off the paper surface, and allow all of the blue and red light to reflect. The ink impurities in the magenta ink pigmentation that distort this normal reflection ratio can be measured as a percentage of hue error.

The *grayness factor* for a set of process inks identifies the purity for the process colors. A color is considered grayed when it reflects less light of its predominant color than the white sheet of paper on which it is printed. For example, cyan should reflect 100% blue and green light, but is considered grayed in percentage because it reflects less blue than the white paper.

Ink efficiency is similar to hue error, but instead of measuring the percentage of error in the reflection of light, a positive percentage is expressed. The ability of the ink's color to filter out its complementary additive color and reflect the other two-thirds of the spectrum is the measurement of its efficiency. The higher the percentage of an ink's efficiency, the greater the gamut of possible colors, and the less color correction will be required. For additional information on inks and their formulation, see Chapter 25.

Review Questions

Please do not write in this book. Write your answers on a separate sheet of paper.

1. What is the primary purpose of color management in the graphic communications industry?
2. Why is the CIELAB color space ideal for performing color correction?
3. What is grayscaling?
4. Why shouldn't color conversions be applied more than once to an image?
5. What areas of graphic communications are covered under SWOP?
6. What are the three primary steps of color management?
7. How is a color management system used to calibrate a computer monitor?
8. The _____ is a standard color reference tool used to calibrate scanners and printers.
9. Why does scanning an image into a CMYK color space limit its potential uses?
10. _____ replaces measured amounts of magenta, yellow, and cyan in shadows and neutral areas of an image with black.
    a. GCR
    b. UCR
    c. UCA
    d. RGB
11. When must *trapping* be considered?
12. Graphics should be scaled _____ (after/before) adding a trap.
13. What is the disadvantage of the stochastic screening method?
14. What is a *digital blueline*?
15. Color control bars are used to monitor _____.
    a. dot gain
    b. print contrast
    c. trapping
    d. All of the above.

Process camera operators are skilled technicians who must be capable of working with both reflection and transmission copy originals of many sizes. This operator is adjusting the aperture scale on a large horizontal camera. (Screaming Color–Chapter One)

12 Line Photography, Process Cameras

Learning Objectives

After studying this chapter, you will be able to:

- Describe the various light sources and how to adjust them.
- Identify the major parts of a process camera.
- Explain the differences between horizontal and vertical cameras.
- Describe the structure of film.
- Identify the classifications and types of films commonly used in graphic arts photography.
- Explain the basic procedure for shooting line images.
- Describe the operation of a camera-processor.
- Explain the diffusion transfer process.
- Describe the use of silverless light-sensitive materials.

Important Terms

antihalation backing
characteristic curve
density capacity
electromagnetic spectrum
emulsion
f-stop
filter
light spectrum
overhead camera
process camera

This chapter discusses the conversion of original line art (line drawings and copy) to film negatives or positives (intermediates). See **Figure 12-1**. These high-contrast intermediates are used to produce printing plates and a final printed product. The importance of photoconversion has changed significantly over the last few years. Film negatives and positives are beginning to be used less as intermediates. Larger sizes and thicker films are being used in electronic imagesetters and scanners. Matte films have greater applications in the flexographic process. A strong desire exists to improve ecology by eliminating wet chemistry. This is a contributing factor in the development of dry processing film systems.

Figure 12-1. Line art, including text and drawings that are not continuous tone, is converted to film negatives like these to produce printing plates.
(Screaming Color–Chapter One)

Camera operators must be competent and highly skilled at producing quality negatives and positives. These operators must understand the photomechanical methods used for producing graphic arts photography. They must have the theoretical knowledge relating to physics, chemistry, and electronics, and completely comprehend the nature of light, optics, and processing. Photomechanical methods are common to relief, intaglio, planography, and screen process image carriers. Although photomechanical techniques are still used in some graphic communications facilities, many have eliminated these techniques as they move to digital applications.

Light

Line photography for graphic reproduction requires light to cause a physical change of the film, or light-sensitive material. The light source, or illumination, is an important aspect affecting the operation of a process camera. It can greatly affect the quality of the finished product. As the light strikes the original copy, some of that light is reflected into the camera lens. The lens directs the reflected light onto the film, exposing it to form a latent image. See **Figure 12-2**. A complete understanding of different light sources, how to control them, and how to rate their quality is a necessity.

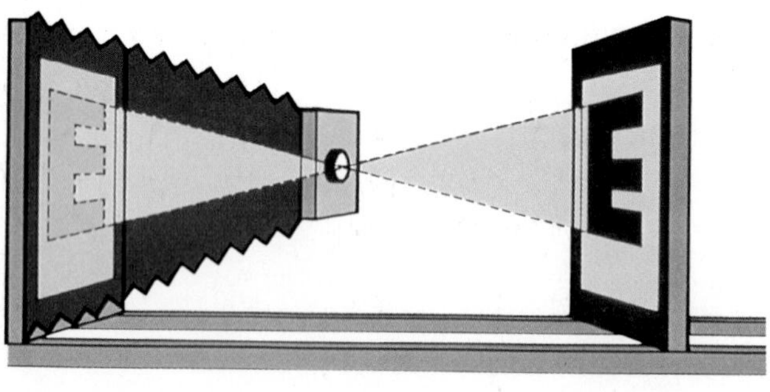

Figure 12-2. Light strikes the image and reflects into the camera lens. A lens directs the image onto light-sensitive material or film. This exposes image on film for reproduction.

Light sources

Sunlight is an excellent source of light, because it contains all colors of the light spectrum. The ***light spectrum***, or ***visible spectrum***, is the part of electromagnetic spectrum visible with the human eye. The ***electromagnetic spectrum*** is the entire range of wavelengths of electromagnetic radiation.

It is not practical to use sunlight as a light source for process camerawork. Other light sources used to expose film include tungsten-filament lights, quartz-iodine lamps, pulsed xenon lamps, mercury vapor lamps, and metal halide lamps. **Figure 12-3** compares two of these common light sources. Note how their spectral outputs differ. The intended use of the light source must be considered when selecting equipment.

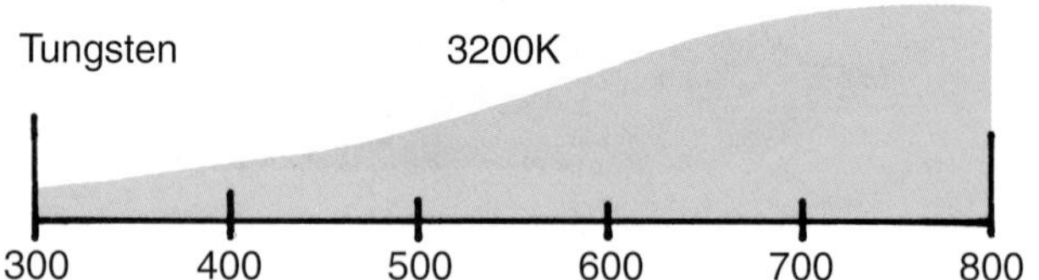

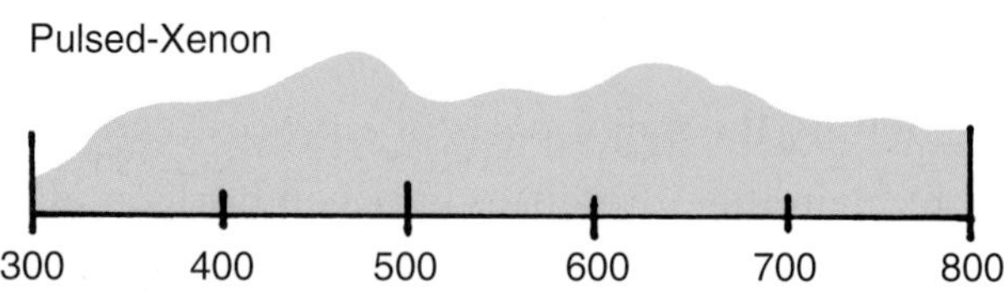

Figure 12-3. These graphs show the spectral outputs of two common light sources.

Never look directly into a light source. The rays may be harmful to your eyes. They may also damage your skin.

Pulsed xenon

Pulsed xenon lamps are the primary light source for many process cameras found in graphic communication facilities. They are an excellent light source with spectral output close to daylight. See **Figure 12-4**.

Mercury vapor

Mercury vapor lamps produce radiation by passing an electrical current through gaseous mercury. At one time, these lamps were the primary means of exposing sensitive printing plates, but this is no longer true.

These lamps are high in ultraviolet radiation and provide a good light source for platemaking. The warm-up period is eliminated. Mercury lamps are a good means of exposing materials that require long periods of light exposure. These lamps are of value to the color separation specialist.

Figure 12-4. One of the many types of exposure lights used on process cameras.

Metal halide

Metal halide lamps are mercury lamps that have metal halide additives. They are high in blue-violet radiation. They provide a good light source for platemaking and are of value to the color separation specialist. Metal halide lamps are three to four times stronger than other light sources.

Tungsten-filament

Tungsten-filament lights are incandescent lamps with a tungsten filament surrounded by gases. The filament and gases are enclosed in a glass bulb. Tungsten-filament lights are deficient in the blue and ultraviolet rays and are excessive in the red rays.

These lights are sometimes used, but they are not highly recommended. Another drawback is that some of the tungsten evaporates at high temperature and deposits on the inside of the lightbulb. The intensity of light is decreased. It is impossible to clean the inside surface of the bulb.

Quartz-iodine

Quartz-iodine lamps are incandescent lamps with a tungsten filament surrounded by iodine and inert gases. The tungsten filament, iodine, and inert gases are enclosed in a quartz bulb. The quartz bulb is smaller and can withstand higher temperatures than the glass bulb. The color temperature of this light source is greater than the tungsten-filament lights.

Cleaning the quartz-iodine bulb with a soft cloth is essential. The bulb should never be touched by your hands. This will greatly reduce the usable life of the bulb. Surface heat becomes greater in the touched area, because of oils from your skin. This can cause rapid failure of the lightbulb.

Adjusting and controlling the light source

Proper illumination is a critical consideration. The light source should be adjusted to the correct distance and angle. If adjustments are done improperly, then reflections, overexposure, underexposure, or other problems can occur. For most exposures, the typical light source angle is 45°. See **Figure 12-5.** However, you should refer to the operating manual for details of specific equipment.

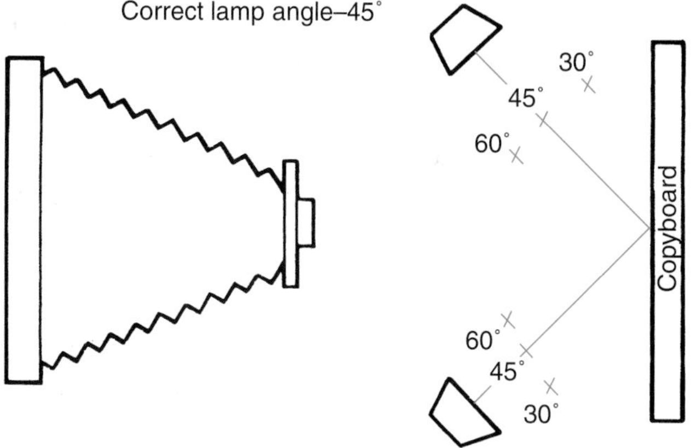

Figure 12-5. This is a typical lamp angle adjustment for most exposures. Refer to the camera operating instructions for details.

Whatever equipment is selected, the line voltage to the lights often fluctuates. Whenever the voltage changes, a different amount of light can strike the film. The final product will not be consistent when this happens. Regulators and integrators can give the necessary exposure consistency. ***Regulators*** will give constant voltage, while ***integrators*** will make sure the amount of light striking the light-sensitive surface will be the same. This topic is discussed later in the chapter.

Light spectrum

As previously mentioned, the electromagnetic spectrum is the entire range of wavelengths of electromagnetic radiation, which extends from gamma rays (very short) to radio waves (very long). All forms of electromagnetic radiation travel in waves. The type of radiation is determined by measuring wavelengths. Wavelength is the distance from the crest of one wave to the crest of the next wave. See **Figure 12-6**. Wavelengths are measured in millimicrons, also known as ***nanometers***. One nanometer (millimicron) is equal to one billionth of a meter. Another unit of measure used for measurement of wavelengths is the ***angstrom***. Ten angstoms equals one nanometer.

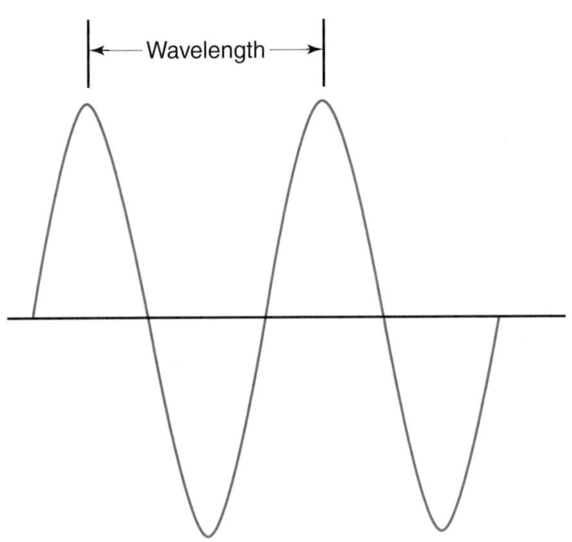

Figure 12-6. Wavelength is measured from the crest of one wave to the crest of the next.

The light spectrum is a very small part of the electromagnetic spectrum, falling between gamma rays and radio waves. The light spectrum is made up of various wavelengths. These wavelengths correspond to the different colors of the light spectrum. The approximate positioning for each color in the visible spectrum, and its relationship to the electromagnetic spectrum, is shown in **Figure 12-7**. Color is discussed in detail in Chapter 8.

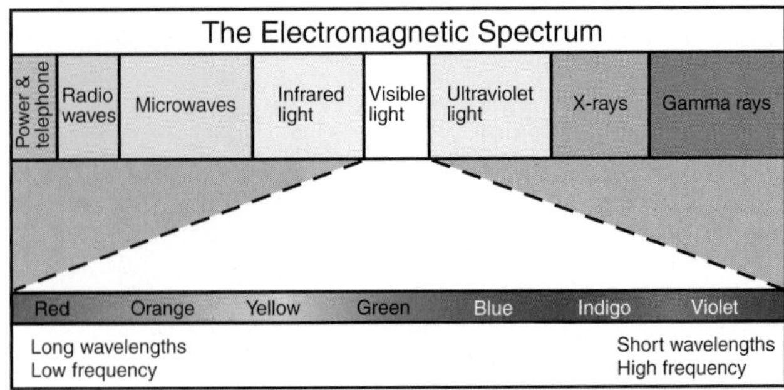

Figure 12-7. The light spectrum is made up of various wavelengths, which correspond to the different colors.

Color temperature

Color temperature is the degree to which a black body must be heated to produce a certain color radiation. It is the method of rating the quality of a light source for color reproduction. Color temperature refers to the *visual* aspect of the light and does not necessary apply to the photographic effect it will have on film. For example, mercury-vapor and metal halide light sources may have the same visual aspects, but because they have slightly different spectral emissions (wavelengths), they might produce significantly different results on film.

Color temperature is measured using the Kelvin (K) temperature scale. On the Kelvin scale, 1K is equal to 1° Celsius (°C). Absolute zero (0K) equals –273.15°C. Color temperature must be considered whenever color separations are to be prepared for full-color work. Actual sunlight is rated at 5400K, but for practical purposes *daylight* is considered 5000K. Most full-color work is viewed at 5000K. This temperature is the standard used for viewing and judging proofs and prints for consistencies.

The color temperature is a very important factor to be considered whenever viewing color work. A color viewing booth provides the correct color temperature for accurate color evaluation. See **Figure 12-8**. Remember, printed pieces will not look the same under different light sources. Viewing in room light may *not* give a true representation of color.

Graphic Arts Cameras

The ***process camera***, or ***copy camera***, is used to produce graphic images on photosensitive materials. Process cameras are designed to produce single-plane (flat) images, but some computerized cameras can also photograph three-dimensional objects.

The process camera must be capable of producing single-plane images from line work (line

Figure 12-8. A color viewing booth provides the consistent light source essential for true and dependable perception of color. (Screaming Color–Chapter One)

drawing), continuous tone work (black and white photograph), and full-color work (color photograph). This chapter deals with line work only. The other types of images are discussed in separate chapters.

Process cameras are available in a variety of styles and sizes. The two major types of process cameras are the horizontal camera and the vertical camera. See **Figure 12-9**. The principles used for both cameras are the same, but their capabilities vary. The major parts of the two types of cameras also are the same, but the orientation of the optical axis of the lens is different.

When selecting a process camera, make sure the frame is sturdy and will withstand extended use. The structural arrangement of the shutter and timer cannot be overlooked. Ease of focusing and viewing of the image must be considered, because the image must be sharp and not fuzzy. The degree of enlargement and reduction of images is also an important factor. Many cameras are capable of enlarging to 200% or reducing to 20% of the original size. Electronic (computerized) controls are used to control focusing, enlarging, reducing, illumination, and exposure. See **Figure 12-10**.

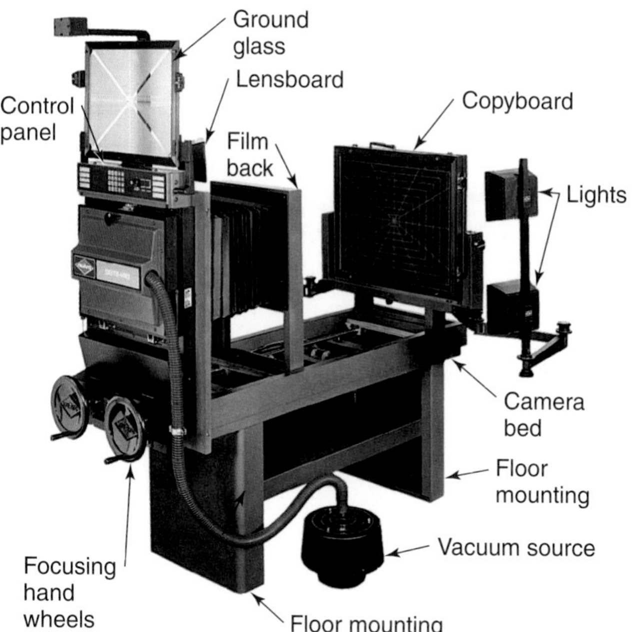

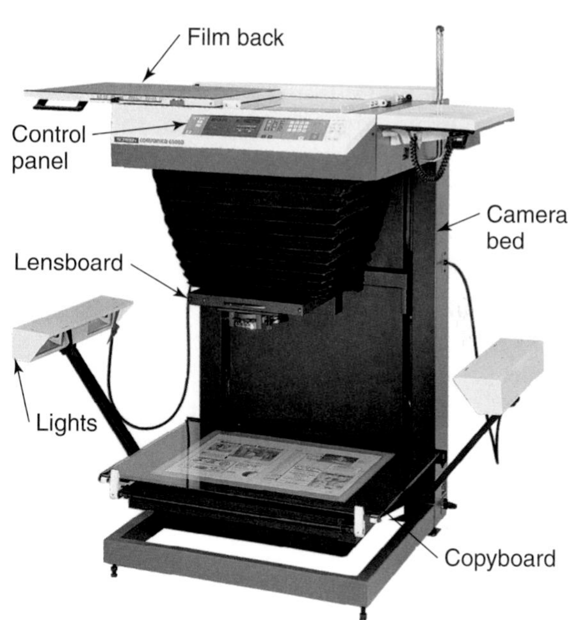

Figure 12-9. There are two types of process cameras. The major parts are the same for both. A—Horizontal camera. B—Vertical camera.

Camera parts

As previously mentioned, the major parts of the horizontal and vertical process cameras are the same. Many subparts are required and may vary from camera to camera. The major parts for both types of cameras are the camera bed, lighting system, copyboard, lensboard, film back, copyboard and lensboard controls, and ground glass.

Camera bed

The ***camera bed,*** or ***frame,*** is the main support for the other camera parts. It determines the sturdiness of the camera. A well-constructed bed is

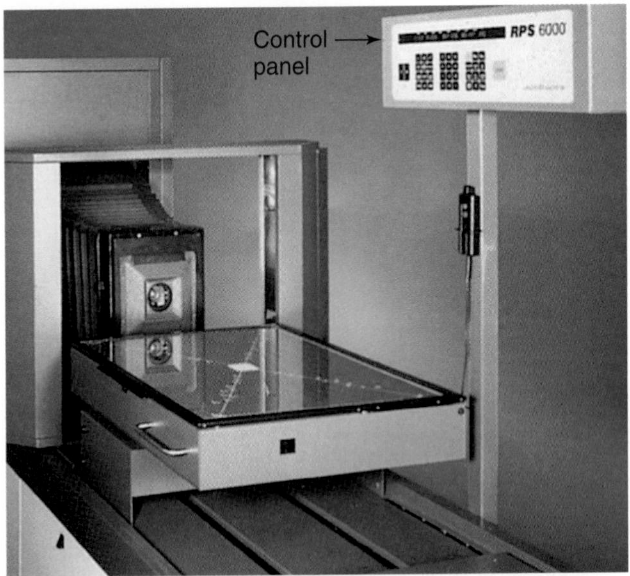

Figure 12-10. Electronic controls shown on this process camera control panel are used to adjust the focusing, enlarging, reducing, illumination, and exposure.

essential for eliminating the possibility of poor alignment. The copyboard, lensboard, and film back must be in perfect alignment to assure quality reproduction.

Lighting system

The lighting system varies from one manufacturer to another, but the manner in which lights are adjusted is of great importance. The lights must be capable of giving off even light and be sturdy enough to take the abuse of handling. They must also be designed for easy positioning and adjusting.

Copyboard

The ***copyboard*** is a glass-covered frame that holds the original image while it is being shot. The glass must be of high quality to eliminate the possibility of light distortion, which is a cause of reproduction problems. To ensure contact between the copy and the glass, the copyboard is either spring-loaded or uses a sponge material under the glass. The copy must have even contact with the glass. Some copyboards have a vacuum back that holds the copy in place.

All copyboards using glass must be handled with extreme care. If register pins are used, make sure they are of proper height. A pin that is too high or misaligned could break the copyboard glass. Handle the copyboard with care.

Lensboard

The ***lensboard*** is the support that holds the lens in alignment with the optical axis of the camera. This part must be well constructed, because it holds the very expensive lens of the camera. The lens must be held in constant alignment.

Film back

Process cameras have a hinged ***film back*** that supports the film in the ***focal plane*** (the plane on which camera images transmitted by the lens are brought to sharpest focus). See **Figure 12-11**. Some film backs have channels to hold various sizes of film, while others are perforated and use vacuum to support the film evenly over its surface.

Figure 12-11. The film back has a vacuum that holds the film in place for exposure. The film must be located properly and must be slightly larger than image area.

Copyboard and lensboard controls

Copyboard controls are used to position the copyboard in relation to other parts of the camera. ***Lensboard controls*** are for positioning the lensboard and making other adjustments to the lens. These controls are essential for same size reproduction, enlarging, or reducing. **Figure 12-12** shows how moving the copyboard and lensboard changes reproduction size. Controls may vary with make and model of camera. Always refer to operating manual for specifics about a camera.

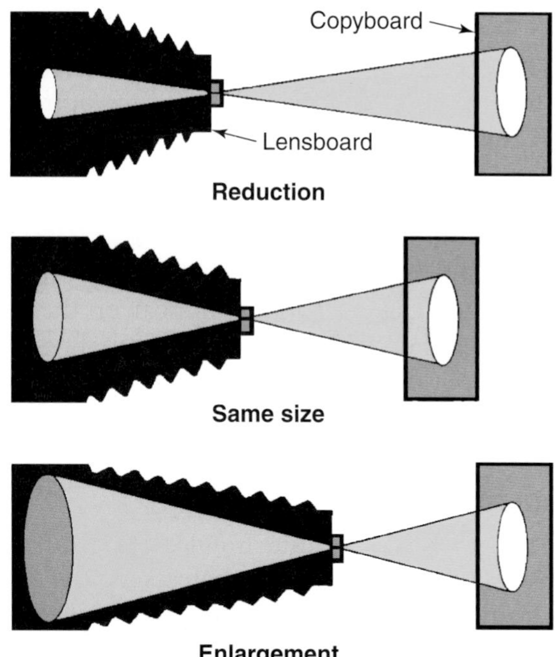

Figure 12-12. The process camera can be used to enlarge or reduce the size of the image by adjusting the lensboard and/or the copyboard. (Screaming Color–Chapter One)

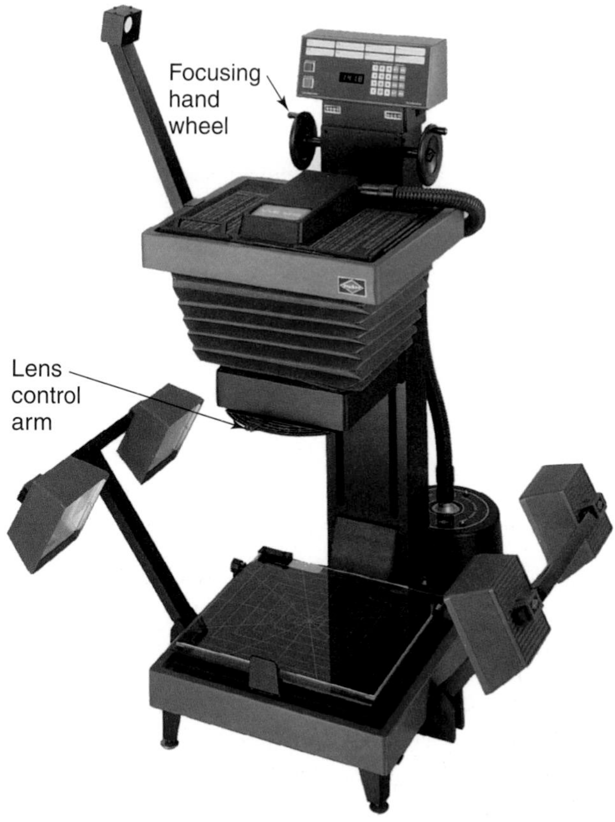

Figure 12-13. Process cameras that are not computerized have handwheels for making adjustments to the copyboard and lensboard, and an arm for making adjustments to the lens.

On most cameras, these controls are computerized and are manipulated using a control panel. Once the camera operator has the original image in place, the reproduction requirements (size and exposure) are entered using the control panel. All positioning and adjustments then are done automatically. Some cameras only have certain controls computerized and others have no computer controls. These cameras may have handwheels for making adjustments to the copyboard and lensboard, and an arm for making adjustments to the lens. See **Figure 12-13**.

Ground glass

The *ground glass* is used to check for proper focus on the original copy before exposing a latent image on film. See **Figure 12-14**. The glass has a grained, matte, or frosted surface, and is mounted onto the back of the camera with hinges or on rails. It can be swung or slid into the focal plane in place of the film.

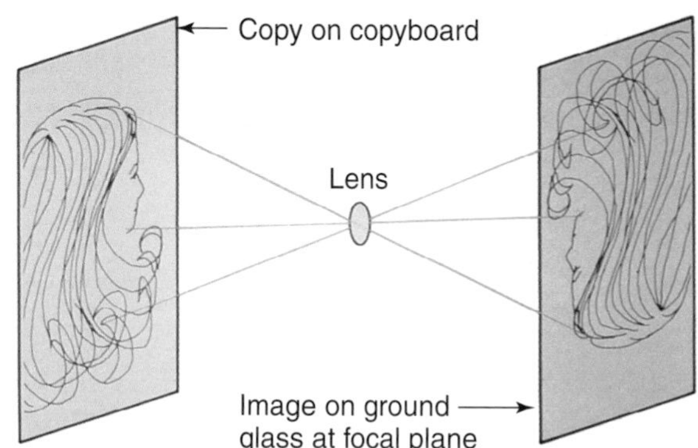

Figure 12-14. The image that will appear can be viewed on ground glass. Focus, sizing, and location of image on focal plane can be checked. (Screaming Color-Chapter One)

Vertical camera

The *vertical camera*, or *gallery camera*, has a vertical (up and down) optical axis. The copyboard and filmholder are perpendicular to the optical axis. Refer to Figure 12-9B. The vertical camera is a space-saving camera. It usually must be entirely housed in a darkroom or an adjacent light-tight room. The size of the copy and film is limited with the vertical camera, but it is still commonly found in graphic communication facilities. Even though it is space-saving, this requirement can be a drawback, because allocating space in a darkroom can pose problems. The ***daylight camera*** is a vertical camera that uses a special filmholder so it can be used outside of the darkroom.

Horizontal camera

The ***horizontal camera***, or ***darkroom camera***, has a horizontal (side-to-side) viewing plane. It is referred to as the darkroom camera, because the film is loaded in the darkroom while the rest of the camera is outside the darkroom. This allows for an efficient operation. The two variations of horizontal cameras are the floor type and the overhead type.

Floor type

The ***floor horizontal camera*** has a large bed that mounts on the floor of the facility. Refer to Figure 12-9A. The copyboard and lensboard slide on this bed.

Overhead type

The ***overhead horizontal camera*** has the camera bed and copyboard attached to the overhead framework of the camera. See **Figure 12-15**. It allows for easy access around the copyboard and lensboard, and tends to eliminate potential vibration problems.

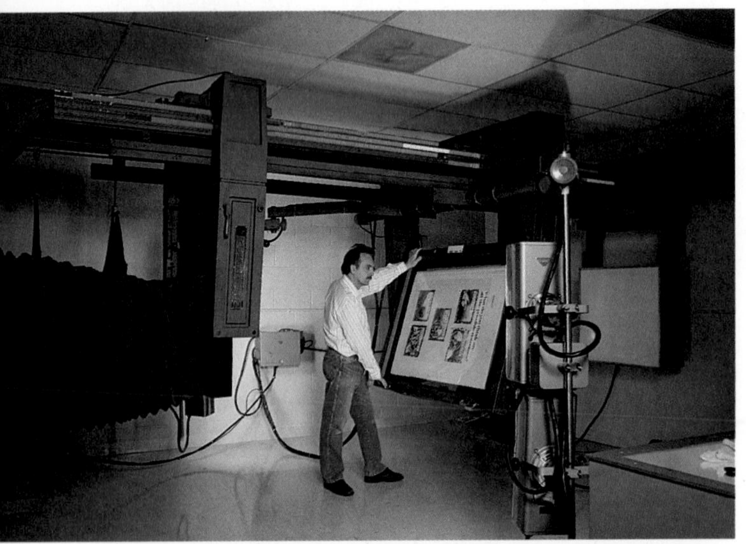

Figure 12-15. The overhead horizontal camera has the camera bed and copyboard attached to the overhead framework. It can be used for very large originals.

Film Structure

Film is a material that is chemically altered after it is exposed to light. This allows it to capture an image that can be made permanent by chemical development. It is made up of the protective overcoating, emulsion, base material, and antihalation backing. See **Figure 12-16A**.

Choosing the right film can be very difficult. New technologies continue to appear on the horizon, making the task even more difficult. Presently, an ideal replacement for film that meets all possible applications and output criteria is not available.

Protective overcoating

The emulsion is quite fragile. The ***protective overcoating*** is a material that helps keep the emulsion from being scratched and marred while film is handled.

Emulsion

The ***emulsion*** is made up of chemical compounds that form a light-sensitive coating on the base material. The emulsion is usually made up of silver halides suspended in a gelatin. Although silverless light-sensitive materials are available, the silver halides are still the most common. Silver halides are compounds of silver and chlorine, bromine, or iodine. The three compounds formed are silver chloride (AgCl), silver bromide (AgBr), and silver iodide (AgI).

The lighting used by graphic arts photography exposes the particles of silver halides in the emulsion. This produces a latent image. The parts of the emulsion that are exposed to light (the latent image) will change to black metallic silver during developing, or processing. This makes the latent image visible. See **Figure 12-16B**.

A negative and a positive are the two types of intermediates common to graphic arts photography. The negative appears opposite of the original (the dark areas of the original appear clear), while the positive appears the same as the original (dark areas of the original appear dark).

Conventional emulsions are generally thought of as being negative-forming, but it is possible to produce positives by special treatment of the film. *Image reversal* is the making of a positive from conventional emulsions. This can be done by a pretreating process from the manufacturer.

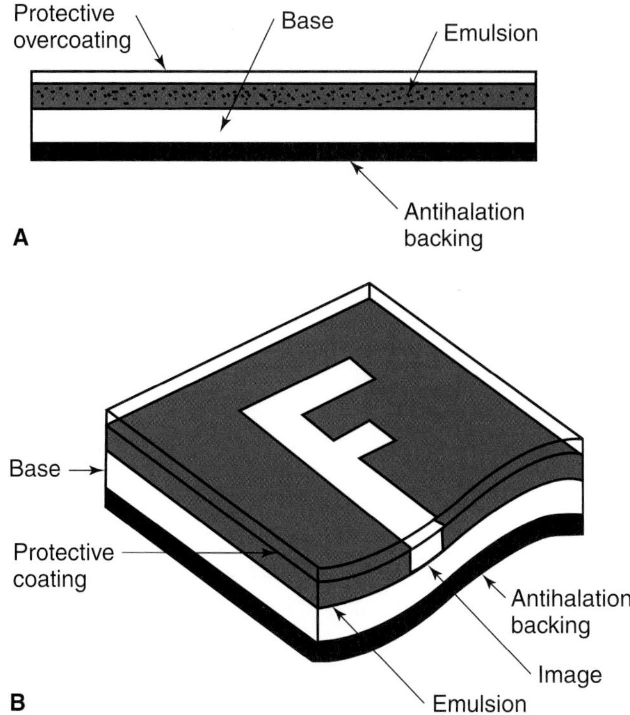

Figure 12-16. A—Film, or light-sensitive material, consists of four layers. B—When light strikes the film, it generates latent image on the film. Processing or developing will make the image visible.

Posttreatment might also produce a positive image. This means the processing steps change. Use the manufacturer's guide to produce the desired results.

Base material

The ***base material*** of a film is the support for the emulsion. The two most common base materials are made of plastic or a special grade of paper. Most of today's graphic films use a plastic (polyester) base. The ***polyester base*** is a very stable material and its size changes very little with relative humidity and temperature. This base has a long storage life; the manufacturer's special handling instructions should be followed.

Acetate base films are not as stable as the polyester-based materials. Humidity will affect the base, causing it to change size. ***Polystyrene base films*** are not affected by humidity, but temperature control is important.

Special paper photographic bases often have stability problems. They are subject to curl. The cost of this type of film is much less than the plastic-type bases.

Another base is glass. ***Glass base films*** are used for special applications, such as those that require extreme dimensional stability. Glass is a very costly type of support material for film.

Antihalation backing

The ***antihalation backing*** is a biodegradable dye coating on the back of most films. It absorbs light so light rays will not reflect back to the emulsion and produce a shadow or double image.

Film Density

The amount of darkness in the negative or positive is referred to as its *density*. ***Density*** is the light-stopping ability of a material—the ability to hold back or block light. ***Densitometry*** is the measurement of density, using an instrument called a ***densitometer***. Density values are expressed using logarithms. The density of a negative or positive is influenced by the length of exposure to a light source, the chemical composition, the developing temperature, and the amount of developing time.

Film also has a density capacity. ***Density capacity*** is the theoretical maximum density allowed by a film (emulsion). Up to a certain point of exposure, the film will continue to have greater density. Once that point has been reached, density no longer increases and the film has reached its capacity.

Measuring the effects of exposure and development is called ***sensitometry***. Generally, increased exposure increases density. Many factors affect exposure. Exposure is affected by the intensity of the light reaching the film. The intensity depends on the brightness of the camera lights, the distance the lights are located from the copy, and the direction or angle of lights. Exposure also depends on the quality of the image on the copy, the quality of the lens system, and the aperture of the lens. Changing any one of these factors will affect exposure.

Characteristic curves

The ***characteristic curve***, or ***D log E chart***, is a graphic representation of the relationship between exposure and density. It indicates how a given film reacts to light and development. On the chart, the vertical scale is typically the density (D) scale, and the horizontal scale is the logarithm (log) of exposure. See **Figure 12-17**. The examples are

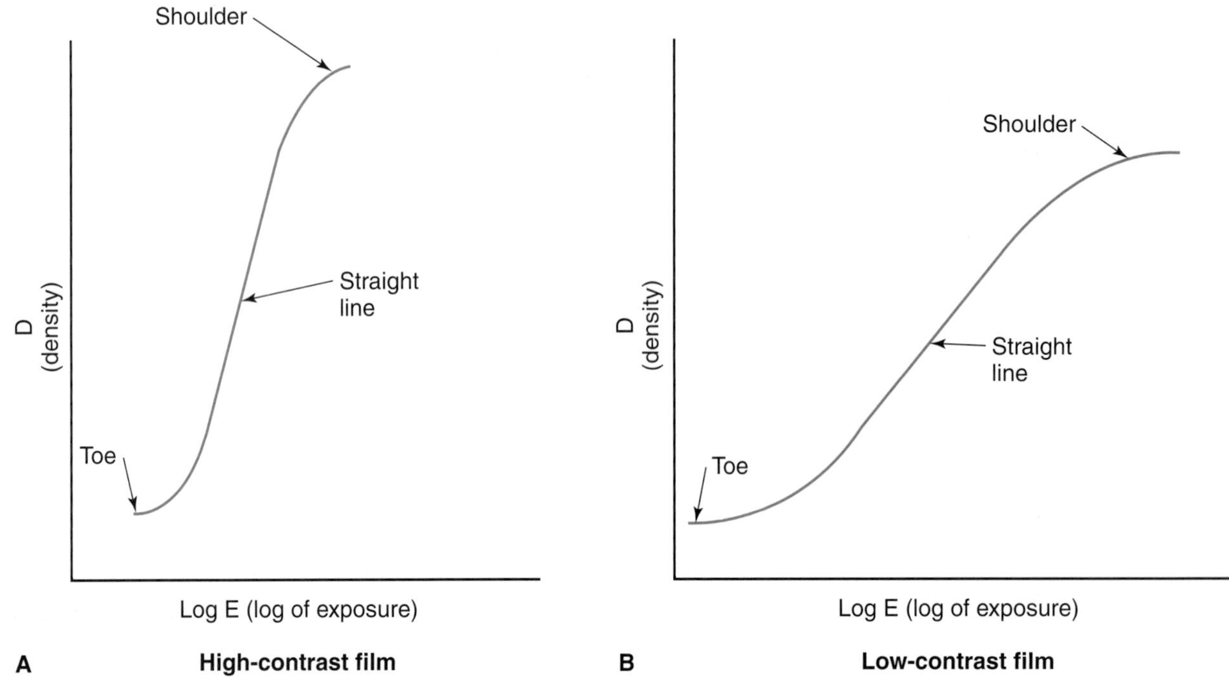

Figure 12-17. The typical characteristic curve for film has a toe, straight line, and shoulder. The characteristic curve for high-contrast film is steeper than the characteristic curve for low-contrast film.

typical of negative type films. A positive film (such as a slide film) would have the slant in the opposite direction.

The three segments of the characteristic curve are the toe, straight line, and the shoulder. The *toe* represents the initial response to exposure. The *straight line* portion represents the exposure range that identifies the density development for each exposure. The *shoulder* is that portion in which more exposure would not increase the density.

The film used for line and halftone work is considered to be high-contrast film. As shown in Figure 12-17, the characteristic curve for this film would be steeper than a low-contrast film. The slope of the curve is given as ***gamma*** (γ). Gamma is affected by development time. The longer an exposed piece of film is developed, the higher the gamma. Films do have *latitude*, which means that minor errors can take place without wasting materials. However, high-contrast films have less latitude than low-contrast films.

Color Sensitivity

Color sensitivity is a measure of how receptive a material is to the colors of light. Silver halide emulsions are normally sensitive to ultraviolet, blue-violet, and blue regions of the spectrum.

Film classifications

The three classifications of film that are common to the graphic communications industry are blue-sensitive, orthochromatic, and panchromatic. Each one is sensitive to a certain portion, or band, of the electromagnetic spectrum. See **Figure 12-18**.

Blue-sensitive film

The ***blue-sensitive films*** are highly sensitive to just the blue portion of the spectrum. Sometimes, this film is referred to as *color blind*. It is commonly used to copy black and white photographs.

Orthochromatic films

The ***orthochromatic films***, or ***ortho films***, are sensitive to a wider range of the spectrum but are not sensitive to red. Therefore, a red bulb is used as the safelight in the darkroom when handling ortho films.

The film is commonly used to photograph black and white images, but will work very satisfactorily with some filters to create color images on film. The ortho materials tend to be faster-acting than the blue-sensitive materials.

Panchromatic film

The ***panchromatic films***, or ***pan films***, have color sensitivity closest to the human eye. This film

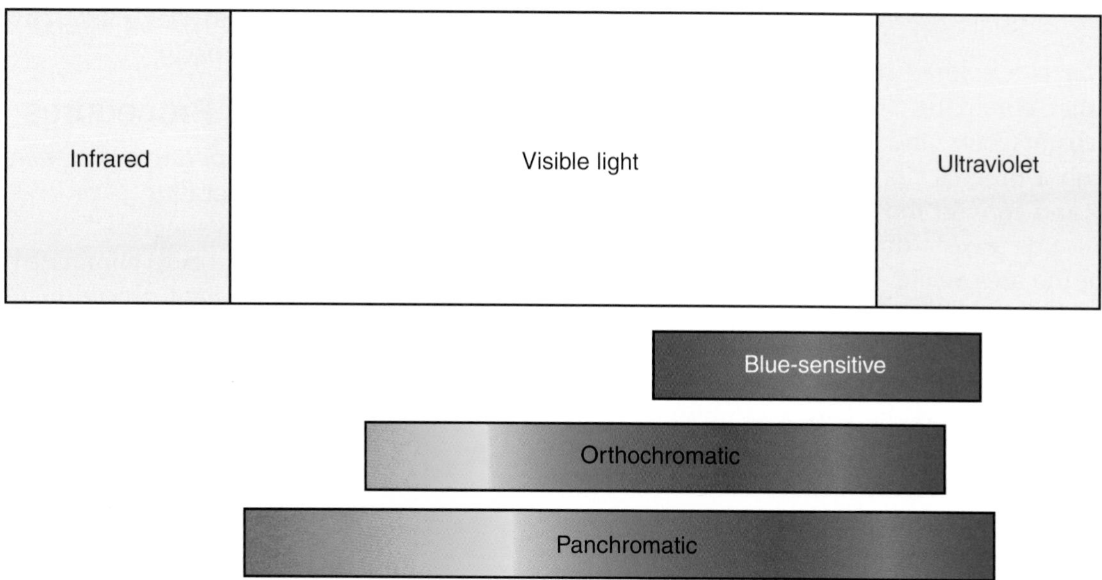

Figure 12-18. The color sensitivity for film varies. The three classifications of film are sensitive to specific bands of the electromagnetic spectrum.

will reproduce the total range of the visible spectrum. It is an ideal type of film for reproducing colored copy in monochromatic form. Pan film, however, must be handled in total darkness.

Film Types

There are a number of film types manufactured today. Each of these types has specific characteristics and uses.

Rapid access film

Rapid access film is used to make negatives with the process camera. It is also used to produce contact negatives and film positives. The film is processed in rapid access chemicals, and is a very fast way to make film intermediates.

Recording film

Recording film has been developed to be used with imagesetters and scanners. This film creates very sharp stochastic and/or halftone dots. It also creates sharp line images.

Contact film

Contact film is a blue-sensitive film used to make positives from negatives or to make negatives from film positives. This film has a great amount of latitude. Latitude means that in the processing cycle, slight variations have very little effect on the film reproduction.

Daylight film

Daylight film is used with very high-intensity light sources, because it has emulsion that is not very sensitive to light. Most of these films are intended for use in emulsion-to-emulsion contacting. A base-to-emulsion contact would create a poor quality reproduction.

Duplicating film

To make a duplicate of a negative or positive, ***duplicating film*** is used. A duplicate negative can be made from a negative or a duplicate positive from a positive.

With duplicating film, a longer exposure will create *less density*. The film has been pre-exposed to maximum density. Therefore, greater exposure causes density to decrease.

A high-intensity light source should be used when exposing regular duplicating film. A high-speed duplicating film can be exposed by using a point source light on a contacting frame. A super-speed duplicating film can also be used.

Filters

A *filter* is a colored material, usually glass or acetate, that eliminates some wavelengths of the light spectrum (color) and lets others through. It can be used on a process camera to photograph color line copy and convert the color image to black. Filters can also be used to drop out specific line colors and leave the area white. The resulting *stat* (reproduction) will be black and white only. To produce the desired results, filters must be used with recommended films.

Filters mount onto the lens assembly, so that light passes through them before striking the film. Filters also affect exposure, because they block out part of the light spectrum and less light can pass through the camera and onto the film. Adjustments must be made for more exposure when using a filter. **Figure 12-19** is a chart showing how specific filters and films can be used to *photograph as black* (hold a color as black) or to *photograph as white* (drop out color, leaving white space).

Camera Operating Procedures

For efficiency, it is imperative to understand the basic procedures for operating a process camera. Each facility might have a suggested procedure, but following a basic plan can help eliminate the possibility of mistakes. Consistent procedures lead to a more profitable operation. The following basic steps are used for operating a process camera:

1. Mounting the copy (loading the copyboard).
2. Setting the light source.
3. Making exposure adjustments.
4. Focusing.
5. Mounting the film.
6. Setting exposure time.
7. Exposing film.

To Photograph Black (to hold a color) use film and filter* suggested:			Color of Copy	To Photograph White (to drop a color) use film and filter* suggested:		
Blue-sensitive Film	Orthochromatic Film	Panchromatic Film		Blue-sensitive Film	Orthochromatic Film	Panchromatic Film
Not recommended	Orange (16) Yellow (15, 12) Green (61, 58) Yellow (9, 8)	Green (61, 58)	Magneta (process red)	No filter needed* *	Can try:* * Blue (47B) Magenta (30) Blue (47)	Red (25, 29)* * Magenta (30) Blue (47B)
No filter needed	No filter needed or Blue (47B)	Blue (47B, 47)	Red	Not recommended	Not recommended	Red (29, 25, 23A) Orange (16)
No filter needed	Blue (47B) Magenta (30) Blue (47)	Blue (47B, 47)	Orange	Not recommended	Not recommended	Orange (16) Red (29, 25, 23A)
No filter needed	Blue (47B) Magenta (30) Blue (47)	Blue (47B, 47)	Yellow	Not recommended	Orange (16) Yellow (15, 12) Green (61, 58) Yellow (9, 8)	Red (29, 25, 23A) Orange (16) Yellow (15, 12, 9, 8) Green (61, 58)
No filter needed	Blue (47B) Magenta (30) Blue (47)	Magenta (30) Red (25) Blue (47B, 47)	Green	Not recommended	Orange (16) Yellow (15, 12) Green (61, 58) Yellow (9, 8)	Green (58)
Not recommended	Not recommended	Red (25)	Cyan (process blue)	No filter needed	No filter needed	Blue (47B, 47)
Not recommended	Orange (16) Yellow (15, 12) Green (61, 58) Yellow (9, 8)	Green (58) Red (25)	Blue or Violet	No filter needed	Magenta (30) Blue (47B, 47)	Blue (47B, 47)

*Numbers are for Wratten filters. Filters are used singly. Where more than one is listed, try in order presented. Variations in color of copy may require other filters.

* * To drop magenta, use pan film and a 25 filter.

Figure 12-19. Filters can be used on a process camera to drop out color on an original or to change a color to black. This chart shows recommended filters and film. (Eastman Kodak)

Mounting the copy

The glass used in the copyboard should be perfectly clean, polished plate glass. The hinged frame allows the operator to place the original image in position before clamping it in place.

Most copyboards will accommodate various material thicknesses. Care must be taken so that a buildup of materials on a small area does not create an excessive amount of pressure. This could break the glass.

Check the copyboard glass for dirt because it could create an unwanted image on the film. Most manufacturers will recommend a good graphic arts glass cleaner that will not affect the copy.

The copy is placed on the copyboard so that it is readable on the ground glass. This means the image that appears at the top of the copyboard will appear on the bottom of the ground glass when using a horizontal camera. It is also important to position the copy in the approximate center of the copyboard. Most copyboards have a *mat* that is zoned to assist in copy placement. A minimal amount of copy handling eliminates the possibility of getting dirt on the copy surface.

Extreme care must be taken to make sure the copyboard is eased into position. If the copyboard is forced or dropped, it could shift out of alignment. Thus, all planes (copyboard and film back) would not be parallel with one another, and the reproduction would not be exact.

Setting the light source

The lamps or light sources are often a part of the copyboard housing. The lamps are positioned approximately 30° to 45° from the copy, with a slight crossing of the highest intensity portion of the lamps. There should not be a reflection back to the lens. The distance from the copyboard is around 3′ (1 m) as shown in **Figure 12-20**.

The lighting must be controlled to give even illumination. Do not touch the lamps when positioning the lamp housing. This may reduce the useful life of the lamp.

Making exposure adjustments

With a computerized camera, some or all exposure adjustments are made using a control panel. Exposure adjustments include reproduction size, diaphragm control, and length of exposure. On manual cameras, these adjustments are made by physically setting controls.

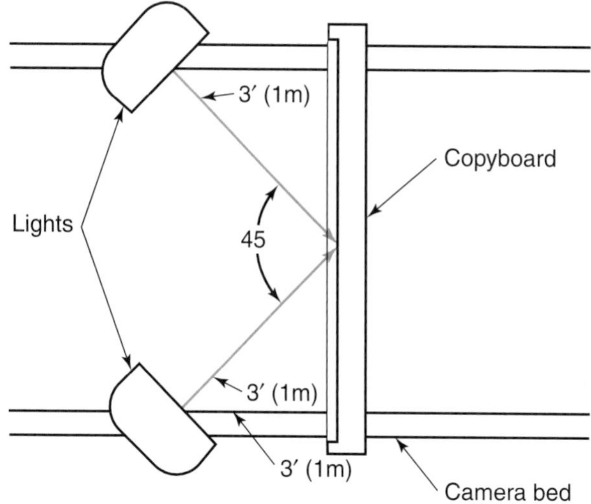

Figure 12-20. Camera lights must be adjusted properly. They should be set to the correct distance and at the correct angle.

Setting size

Not all finished negatives or positives will be shot the same size as the original copy. When the original copy is larger than the final work, the process is commonly called ***reduction***. When the images must be increased in size, it is called ***enlargement***. The process camera has capability for reducing and enlarging.

The term *scaling* is associated with enlarging or reducing copy. As explained in earlier chapters, when reducing the original size of 12′ to 6′, it would be a reduction of 50%. The negative or positive would be 50% (half) of the original size. Going from 6′ to 12′ would be a 200% enlargement, or double the original size. Percentage calculators are used to determine the reduction or enlargement.

Process cameras have various types of gauging devices to regulate the size. Many cameras have micrometer-type settings that are programmed and automatically positioned for proper focus. As previously mentioned, the operator simply enters the scaling requirements and the camera automatically makes the adjustments. Extreme exactness is possible with these cameras. The photographic lens determines the positioning of each scale for the lensboard as well as the copyboard. Scales are calibrated individually, which means they are specifically designed for each process camera.

Another common scaling method is the use of *tapes* and manual adjustment of the scaling. The tape readings appear on a calibrated scale. Often, the tapes can be regulated from the darkroom or the copyboard end of the camera. What is important to remember is that both tapes (copyboard and lensboard) must have the *same reading* to be in focus.

Some cameras have scales attached to the camera base. The indicators must line up with the scale markings. This is true of the lensboard as well as the copyboard.

Diaphragm control

The ***diaphragm*** is an adjustable opening mounted behind or between the lens elements of a camera. It is used to control the amount of light that reaches the film. The ***aperture*** is the actual opening created by the diaphragm. The fixed sizes at which the aperture can be set are called ***f-stops***.

Cameras can have computerized (automatic) or manually controlled diaphragms. On the automatic type, the operator inputs the desired aperture (f-stop). The diaphragm opening is automatically set or a suggested opening is given and adjustment is then made manually. On a manually controlled camera, an arm is used to regulate the f-stop. The arm is aligned with the desired percentage of enlargement or reduction, or the appropriate f-stop scale. See **Figure 12-21**.

f-stops

The size of the f-stop is determined by the ratio of the aperture to the focal length of the lens. The f-stops on process cameras generally range from f/8 to f/90. The smaller the f-stop number, then the larger the lens opening. The smaller the lens opening, the larger the f-stop number. See **Figure 12-22**. Typical f-stops are f/8, f/11, f/16, f/22, f/32, f/45, f/64, and f/90.

Figure 12-21. Adjusting f-stops can be done manually by aligning the arm with the desired percentage on the appropriate f-stop scale.

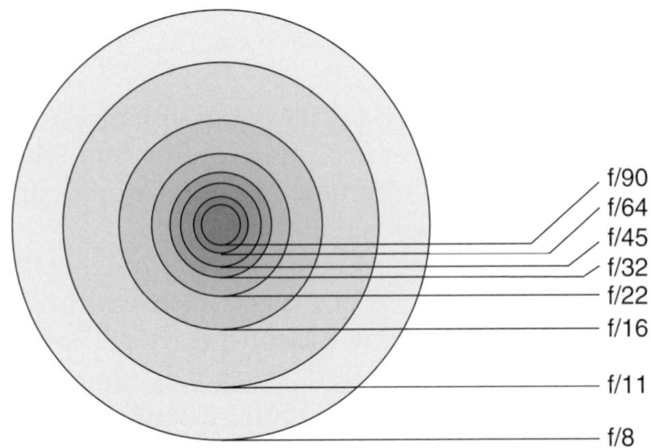

Figure 12-22. Lens opening diameters correspond with f-stop numbers. The smaller the f-stop the larger the lens opening.

As shown in **Figure 12-23**, the size of the diaphragm opening (aperture) doubles as f-stop numbers get smaller, and is cut in half as f-stop numbers become larger. For example, a setting of f/16 permits half as much light to pass as a setting of f/11, but twice as much light as a setting of f/22. If the f-stop is changed, but an **equivalent exposure** (the same amount of light reaching the film) is needed, the exposure time must be adjusted. The same "double or half" rule applies, but *in reverse*: if the original exposure was 40 seconds at f/16, the equivalent exposure would be doubled at f/22 (80 seconds), but cut in half at f/11 (20 seconds).

A process camera's best resolution is achieved with the middle f-stops. For best results, the manufacturer usually recommends the correct f-stop, typically three or four stops down from the largest opening. If f/8 is the largest opening, the sharpest images would be obtained at f/16 or f/22.

Focal length

Each lens has a focal length. The ***focal length*** is the distance from the optical center of the lens to the surface of the film (focal plane). See **Figure 12-24**. When the process camera is set at its maximum reduction, it is commonly referred to as an *infinity*

Diameter of Opening	1″	8/11″	1/2″	4/11″	1/4″
F-Stop/ Number	f/8	f/11	f/16	f/22	f/32
Exposure Time	10 sec = equivalent exposure	20 sec = equivalent exposure	40 sec = equivalent exposure	80 sec = equivalent exposure	160 sec = equivalent exposure

Figure 12-23. This chart shows f-stop numbers with the diameter of lens opening and typical amount of time needed for exposure of film. The time becomes longer as the f-stop number becomes larger (aperture becomes smaller).

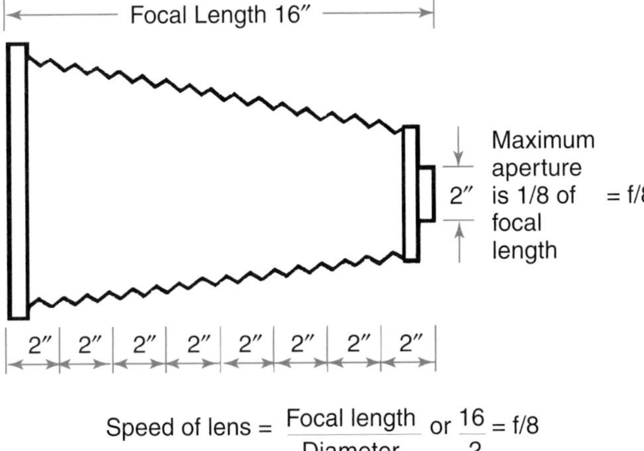

Figure 12-24. How focal length of the lens and maximum aperture are determined. (Screaming Color-Chapter One)

setting. The focal length of a *camera* is one-fourth of the distance from the copyboard to the focal plane when the camera is in focus and set for the same size (100%) reproduction. Much of the necessary information such as the diameter of the lens, f-stop, and focal length are stamped on the lens barrel.

Focusing

To be in *focus* (produce a sharp image), the copyboard and lensboard must be correctly positioned. Depending on the camera, the proper values must be entered in at the control panel, or the copyboard and lensboard must be manually adjusted so that the tapes or scales *read the same.* If the copy is to be reduced by 50%, each of the scales must read 50%. On a manually adjusted camera, the lens diaphragm must be positioned to correspond to the readings on the scales.

In order to see the image, the ground glass must be brought into position for viewing. The ground glass is in the same plane where the film will be located.

The camera master controls must be turned on. The next step is to turn on the focus switch, or exposure unit. Each camera has its own shutter design. Most have movable metal leaves that open and close automatically when the camera's focus switch is turned on.

When the focus switch has been activated, the camera lights go on and the shutter opens. The image is now visible on the ground glass. The operator often uses a magnifying glass to check the images for sharpness. See **Figure 12-25.**

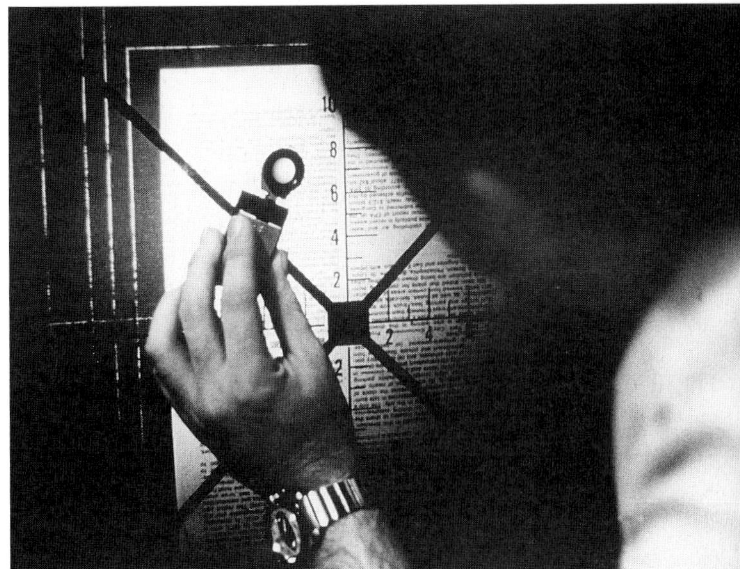

Figure 12-25. The image must be in focus and located properly. A magnifier should be used to inspect the image on the ground glass.

The image area also indicates the size of film needed for photoconversion. If the critical settings are correct, the image will be the desired size and will be in sharp focus. The focus switch must be turned off before mounting the film. Return the ground glass so that the film back is positioned and ready for use. See **Figure 12-26**.

Make sure that boxes of film are closed while checking the focus. Any film in the darkroom that is left out will be exposed and ruined.

Figure 12-26. Positioning film in the image area of film back must be done with safelights on.

Mounting the film

Positioning film on the vacuum area of the film back must be done precisely. Most camera backs have positioning indications that correspond to the copyboard markings. In most cases, the film should be centered on the back, with the emulsion side of the film toward the lens for exposure. It is imperative that the film be perfectly flat on the focal plane.

The size of the piece of film is determined by the final reproduction size. Make sure there is enough margin, so the image does not extend beyond the edge of the film.

Carefully handle the film by the edges, to avoid leaving finger marks. As previously mentioned, the emulsion of the film will scratch very easily. Make sure the film box is closed after a piece of film has been removed.

Setting exposure time

The amount of time it takes to properly expose a piece of film is determined by the speed of the film, the illumination, copyboard distance from the lens, and the distance the film is from the lens. The ratios of distance for the copyboard, film plane, and the lens has been set by the manufacturer. The illumination will vary from camera to camera. The lamp distance from the copyboard may also be set by the manufacturer or the camera may allow the operator to establish the lamp-to-copyboard distance.

Basic exposure for line copy

Each camera will have a best exposure time for reproducing the camera-ready copy. This is the ***basic main exposure***. The technique recommended by the Graphic Arts Technical Foundation to prepare settings is known as the ***step-off method***, or ***test exposure***. Using this system, the operator places an 8″ × 10″ sheet of film on the film back. All but 1″–2″ of the film is covered with a masking sheet (a material that does not allow light to pass through it). See **Figure 12-27**. If the masking sheet does not make good contact, tape down the edge.

Figure 12-27. To make a test exposure with step-off method, cover a portion of the film with a light-stopping masking sheet. Make exposure and then slide the mask approximately 1″. Repeat this procedure (a total of five times), process the film, and analyze the results.

Make the first exposure using a selected number of seconds or units. Four seconds might be an acceptable starting point. After each exposure, move the mask 1″ or the distance necessary to make at least five exposures on the one piece of film.

As you step the mask, each of the five steps will have a decreasing amount of total exposure. Using four as an increment, the first step will have 20 seconds exposure; the second, 16 seconds; the third, 12 seconds; the fourth, 8 seconds; and the last, 4 seconds.

Once all of the exposures have been made, the film must be processed according to the manufacturer's recommendations. The right exposure time should give the sharpest image with high density and no filling in of the copy. See **Figure 12-28**.

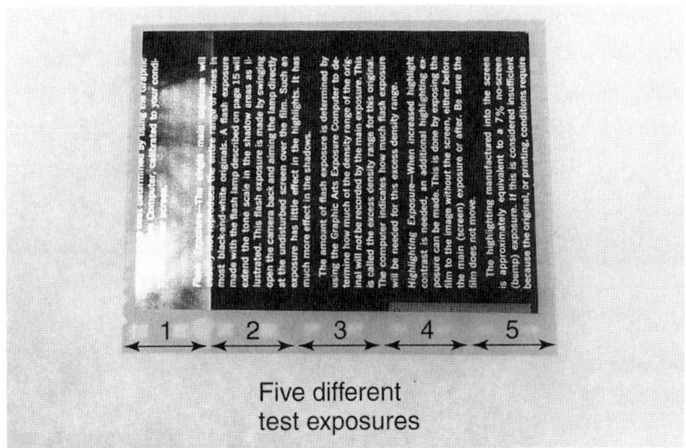

Figure 12-28. After using the step-off method, the sharpest image on the test film indicates the best exposure time. This exposure should be used to shoot the actual shot.

Exposures in memory

Some *computerized cameras* are very sophisticated and account for the exposure and density values of copy. See **Figure 12-29**. These cameras have memories that store basic exposures and conditions for a variety of exposures. An operator need only to enter the sizing information and then indicate which exposure program is desired by entering its code at the control panel. This information is used to automatically adjust the camera to exposures programmed in memory.

Light integrator

Even though the duration of exposure is set and the voltage is controlled by a regulator, the line voltage to the exposure lights can fluctuate. This means that the light intensity could vary and the exposure could be unequal even though the time is the same. This can cause exposure difficulties.

Figure 12-29. This is a modern computer-controlled horizontal camera. The control console at left is used for entering data. It can store exposure data and reproduce the same exposure upon command. It also has a photocell that serves as a light integrator to assure consistent exposures. (Screen-USA)

A ***light integrator*** regulates the intensity and the length of an exposure according to a predetermined setting. In other words, it controls the amount of light striking the film. It accounts for any change in voltage to the lights, so that the same amount of light strikes the film for a given exposure setting. See **Figure 12-30**. This device ensures a consistent amount of light striking the film, or light-sensitive surface, each time an exposure is made. An ordinary timer only allows for time, *not* for the amount of light.

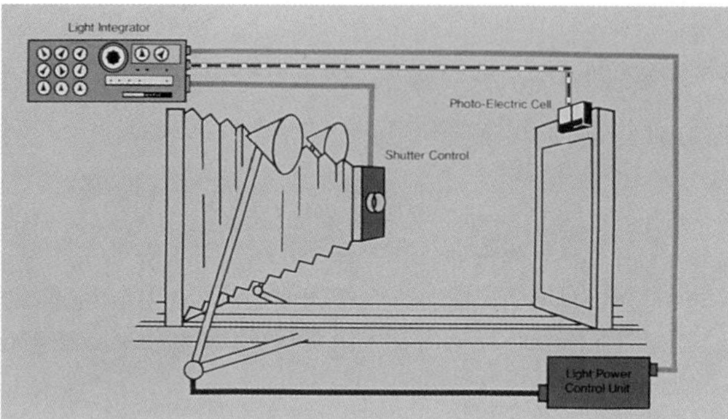

Figure 12-30. The light integrator regulates amount of light striking film. It can compensate or adjust for any variations in voltage that might upset exposure. (Screaming Color–Chapter One)

Exposing film

Once the basic main exposure has been determined for line copy, the camera-ready material is placed on the copyboard. A control device, called a ***gray scale***, or ***step table***, should be positioned next to the copy. See **Figure 12-31**. A gray scale is used to determine best exposure time, and whether an image has been underexposed or overexposed. Make sure the lamps are properly positioned. Double-check all settings.

Select the film size and place the film on the camera back, working only under red safelight conditions. The next step is to activate the timing unit to expose the film. The exposed film can then be processed. Film processing is covered in detail in Chapter 14.

Camera-Processor

A ***camera-processor*** combines a process camera and a developer into a single unit. See **Figure 12-32**. This unit is a daylight reproduction camera for line, screen, and continuous tone work. It is computer-controlled and automatically does sizing, focusing, exposure, and processing.

Most camera-processors have an on-line scanning densitometer that checks the minimum and maximum densities of the image to assure quality reproduction. The film is usually in roll form and can be fed over the camera back and then into the processor after exposure. A developed image is ejected from one end of the unit.

Figure 12-31. A gray scale is used to determine best exposure time. It also is used to determine if an image has been underexposed or overexposed.

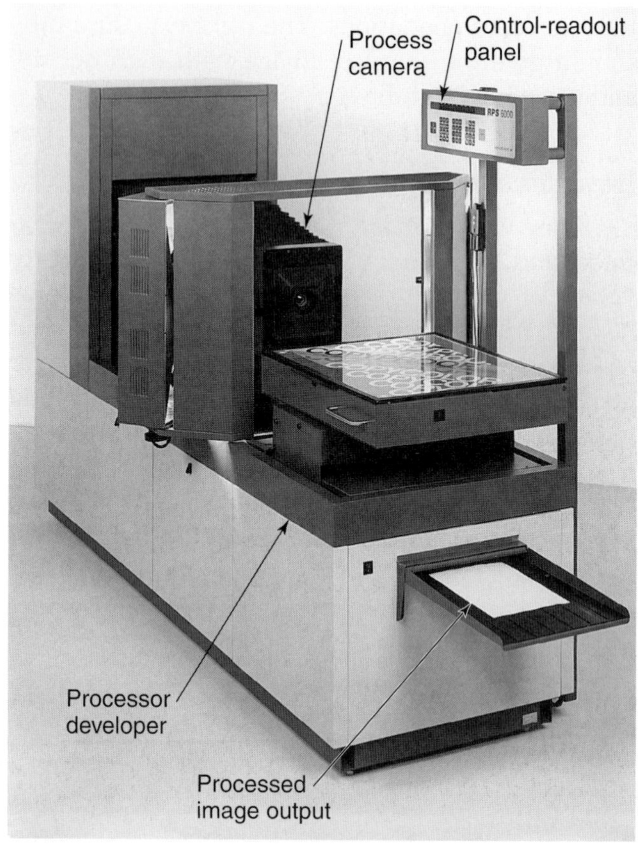

Figure 12-32. A daylight camera-processor unit consisting of a horizontal camera and a film processor. A roll of light-sensitive material is fed through the back. After exposure, it is automatically processed and cut into sheets. Sizing, focusing, exposure, and developing are all computer-controlled. (Visual Graphics Corporation)

Figure 12-33 shows the control panel for one brand of camera-processor. Control keys are provided for the lighting system, focus, processor, sizing, exposure, screen density, lens movement, copyboard movement, and other functions. Since cameras vary, always follow the operating manual for the specific make or model.

Diffusion Transfer

The *diffusion transfer process* is capable of making a line positive, screened positive, or lithographic printing plate using a process camera. This process bypasses conventional film developing, opaquing, stripping, and film contacting. With diffusion transfer, a negative sheet is exposed to the image on the process camera. The negative and a receiver sheet are fed into a diffusion transfer processor. The emulsion side of the negative must face the coated side of the receiver sheet. The negative and a receiver sheet are slightly separated as they are fed into the processor and into the processing solution. See **Figure 12-34**. Then, they are fed together through sheet rollers. The unexposed part of the emulsion transfers to the receiver sheet. This system gives good dense copy in a positive form. For most short-term uses, the negative and the receiver sheet are left in contact for approximately 30 seconds, pulled apart, and then used. See **Figure 12-35**. If the print is going to be used for an extended period of time, the receiver sheet is fed through a washing unit and drying unit. See **Figure 12-36**.

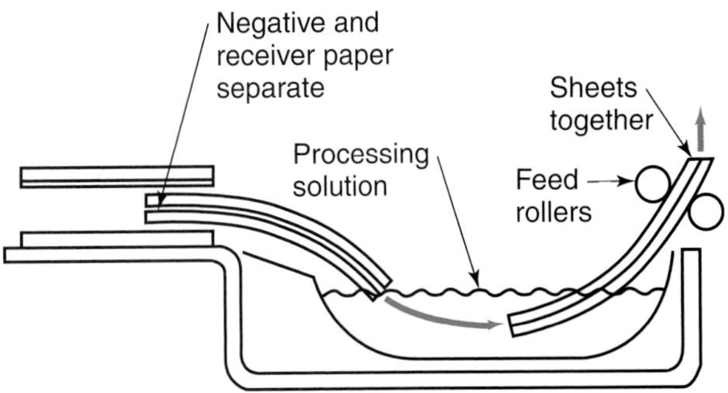

Figure 12-34. During the diffusion transfer process, the negative (image) is almost in contact with the receiver sheet as they are fed through processor. They are squeezed together by the feed rollers.

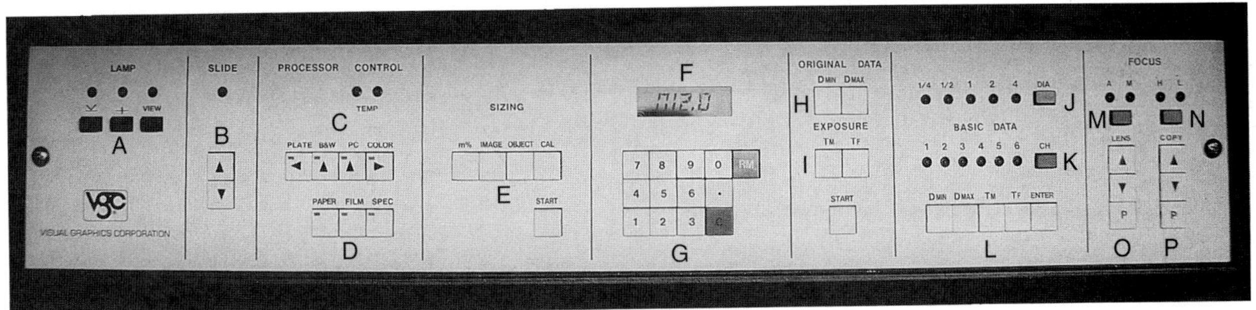

A. **Lighting system**
- reflective lighting
- transparency lighting
- operator viewing

B. **Slide enlarger focus**
- enlarge
- reduce

C. **Processor control mode**
- platemaker
- black & white
- photocomp
- color

D. **Processor speed control**
- paper
- film
- special materials

E. **Sizing control**
- manual input of % enlargement/reduction
- percentage enlargement/ reduction calculator input
- Start button

F. **4-digit LED readout**

G. **Keyboard for data input, calculation, and memory recall**

H. **Original data, halftones**
- enter minimum copy density
- enter maximum copy density

I. **Exposure time, halftones**
- to display main exposure time
- to display flash exposure time

J. **Exposure compensator**

K. **Memory selector for up to 6 channels of stored programs**

L. **Basic data entry**
- enter minimum screen density
- enter maximum screen density
- enter main exposure time
- enter flash exposure time for halftone work

M. **Automatic or manual mode for focus**

N. **Fast/slow speed for separate manual drives –lensboard or copyboard**

O. **Forward-back movement of lens**

P. **Forward-back movement of copyboard**

Figure 12-33. This electronic control panel for a camera-processor controls lighting, processing, and many other functions. (Visual Graphics Corporation)

Figure 12-35. After exposure, the two diffusion sheets are left in contact for approximately 30 seconds, then pulled apart.

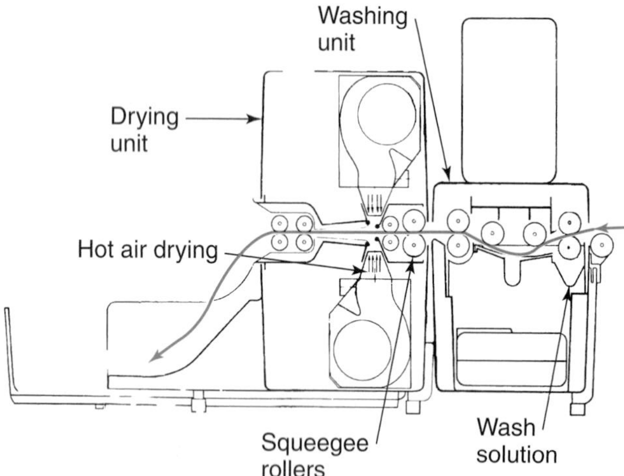

Figure 12-36. This cutaway view shows how image transfer material is fed through the washing-drying unit. Washing and drying helps keep image uniform. (Agfa-Gevaert)

The materials commonly associated with the diffusion transfer process are:

- **Negative paper.** This is a light-sensitive, camera-speed, negative material. It must be handled in red safe light.
- **Reflex paper.** This is a light-sensitive, contact-speed, negative material. It can be handled in subdued room light.
- **Receiver sheet.** This is a chemically sensitized material designed to receive the image. It is *not* light-sensitive.
- **Transparency receiver.** This is a chemically sensitized clear film made to produce a positive. It is *not* light-sensitive.
- **Offset plate.** This is a chemically sensitized metal plate made to receive the image for specific presses.
- **Activator.** This is a chemical, in liquid form, used to process the transfer material.

Exposing negative materials

To expose negative diffusion transfer materials, the following procedure is suggested:

1. Place the emulsion side of the negative material toward the lens of the camera. The emulsion side of the negative paper is black.
2. Expose the negative material. The exact exposure time must be determined by a test exposure. The same f-stop and time for ortho type film would be a satisfactory place to begin.
3. For halftones, a diffusion transfer contact screen should be used. A main white light and a yellow flash exposure are suggested. Again, tests must be made. Remember to use red safe lights.
4. To process the material, the processor must be filled to the proper level with activator liquid.
5. Place the exposed side of the diffusion transfer paper in contact with the coated side of the receiver sheet. Refer to **Figure 12-34**. The exposed material should go into the processor facing up and the receiver material goes into the processor facing down. The two sheets must travel together and be square with each other.
6. During the processing, the sheets are squeezed together after they pass through the chemicals. They exit the processor in contact. Typically, allow the two sheets to remain in contact for 30 seconds before pulling them apart.
7. A quality positive should be the result. Do not stack the prints until they are thoroughly dry.

Reflex paper

Reflex paper is a light-sensitive material that is used for making a same-size, positive proof of an original copy without the use of the camera. This material can be handled in subdued light. The emulsion side of this paper has a glossy appearance.

The original copy is placed in the vacuum printing frame face up toward the light source. See **Figure 12-37**. The reflex paper is placed over the copy with the emulsion side down. The frame is closed and the vacuum is turned on before exposing.

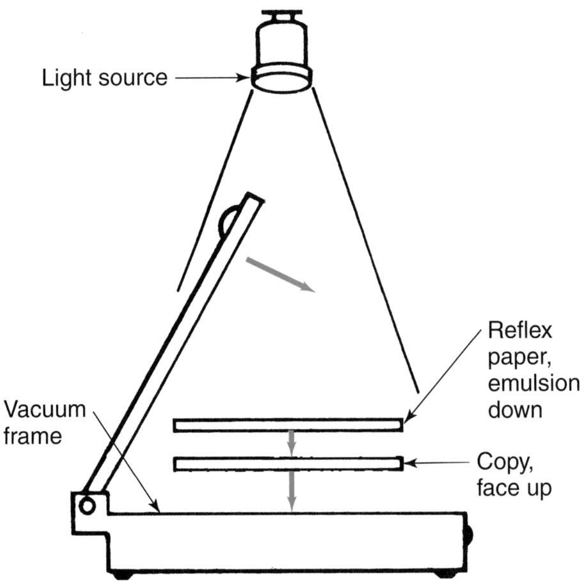

Figure 12-37. This shows the correct method of exposing reflex material.

Exposure should be with a quartz lamp at about 4′ (122 cm). Exact exposure times must be determined by a test. A typical example would be a 30-second exposure with a quartz light at 4′. The processing is the same as for the negative material.

Silverless Light-Sensitive Materials

Silverless materials have a very definite place in the industry. A wide variety of silverless materials is used for special purposes, such as proofing. Some materials require the use of heat to make film negatives. Some of the material is crystal coated and has applications ranging from photography and microfilming to lithographic platemaking. The type of development depends on the type of light-sensitive materials used. The development process can be either dry (gas) or wet (liquid).

The most used silverless process is called ***diazo***. The diazo coating, which is a diazonium salt, is exposed by ultraviolet, violet, or blue light. The image areas must absorb these light rays while the nonimage areas allow light to pass through to the diazo coating. When this type of light-sensitive material has been exposed to the copy, it must be developed. Chemical development is done with either a liquid or gas (ammonia fumes).

Review Questions

Do not write in this book. Write your answers on a separate sheet of paper.

1. *True or false?* It is not practical to use sunlight as a light source for process camera work.
2. This light source is weak in the blue and ultraviolet rays, but is excessive in the red rays.
   a. quartz-iodine lamps
   b. metal halide lamps
   c. mercury vapor lamps
   d. tungsten-filament lamps
3. The _____ is the entire range of wavelengths of electromagnetic radiation.
4. _____ is the degree to which a black body must be heated to produce a certain color radiation, and is the method of rating the quality of the light source.
5. Which of the following temperatures is closest to daylight?
   a. 5000K
   b. 4000K
   c. 6000K
   d. 3000K
6. List and explain the basic parts of a process camera.
7. *True or false?* Vertical cameras are also referred to as darkroom cameras.
8. Name the four layers of film.
9. _____ is the light-stopping ability of a negative or positive.
10. The _____ is the graphic representation of the relationship between exposure and density, and indicates how a given film will react to light and development.
11. Name the three classifications of film.

12. _____ film is used with a very high-intensity light source, because it has an emulsion that is not very sensitive to light.
13. How are filters used to copy colored line art and make it black and white? How are filters used to drop out certain colors?
14. The f-stops on a process camera range from _____ to _____; the smaller the f-stop number, the _____ the lens opening.
15. List the seven basic steps for operating a process camera.
16. How do you use the step-off method to make a test exposure?
17. What is a light integrator?
18. A(n) _____ is a control device used to determine the best exposure time and whether an image has been overexposed or underexposed.
19. A(n) _____ combines a process camera and a developer into one unit.
20. What is diffusion transfer?

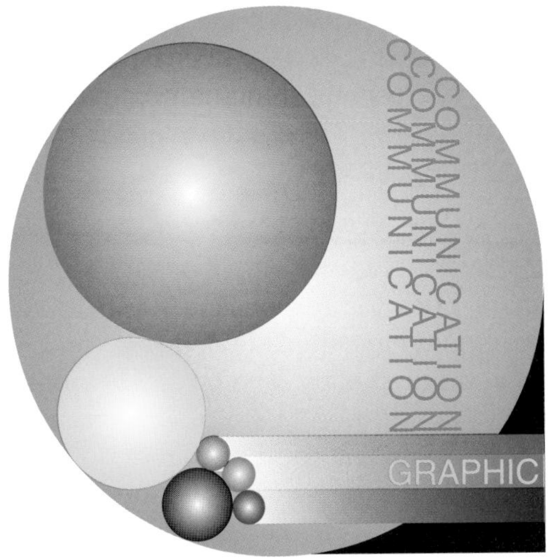

13 Halftone and Special Effects Processes

Learning Objectives

After studying this chapter, you will be able to:

- Evaluate continuous tone originals.
- Describe the role of densitometry in halftone reproduction.
- Explain the principles of halftone reproduction.
- Explain and use halftone contact screens.
- Discuss nonconventional methods to reproduce halftones.
- Describe the techniques available for producing duotones.
- Create graphic appeal by using special effects screens.
- Explain the process of producing different classifications of posterizations.
- Produce a detailed outline reproduction from a continuous tone image.

Important Terms

bump exposure
color separation
continuous tone
duotone
flash exposure
halftone
high-key
low-key
main exposure
posterization

Today, most continuous tone reproduction is done electronically using a scanner. However, this chapter will explain how continuous tone photographs are prepared photomechanically using the halftone process. The halftone process is the procedure of converting a continuous tone original into a pattern of dots.

Unlike line art, a photograph consists of many different shades or densities. Since a printing press only uses one shade or density of ink, the photo must be altered into a halftone containing a dot pattern corresponding to the many shades in the photo. Then, the printing press can deposit ink on paper so that the image will resemble a continuous tone photograph.

It is important to understand that the printing press reproduces the image on the plate with only one color and density of ink. The reproduction of high-contrast copy or line copy conforms to this limitation. If the press operator is printing from a plate that has type matter and simple line art, then the press sheet will have the same image printed in one uniform color and density of ink. See **Figure 13-1**. Halftone reproduction is the process of printing a continuous tone image, such as a photograph or painting, using the same one-color-per-plate printing process. Full-color images like **Figure 13-1A** require four plates to print the process colors of cyan, magenta, yellow, and black. Refer to the color separations section later in this chapter.

Before halftone reproduction is attempted, camera operators should have a complete grasp on the classifications of camera copy. They should also understand the principles and tools used for evaluating camera copy used for creating halftone images.

Figure 13-1. A photograph must normally be converted into a halftone before it can be reproduced on a printing press. A—Look closely to see the small dot pattern in this reproduced photo. (Jack Klasey) B—Line art does not have to be screened.

This chapter also discusses special effects such as prescreened diffusion process, stochastic screening, special effect screening, duotone process, posterization, and outlines. These effects are used to create unique printed images.

Camera Copy

The camera operator responsible for halftone reproduction should have the knowledge necessary to evaluate the original copy. The operator should understand that in addition to simple line art and continuous tone original copy, they may encounter mechanical shading (a complex form of line art) and prescreened copy (halftones). Each of these has certain characteristics and should be evaluated and handled differently.

Line art

Line art is one classification of camera copy. It was discussed in the preceding chapter. Refer to **Figure 13-1.**

Mechanical shading

Mechanical shading is considered to be a form of line art, but requires more attention because of the fine details and intricate nature of the images. Mechanical shading, like line art, will contrast the image and nonimage areas by the use of only light colors (white) and dark colors (black). Tints, textures, and some coarse or stippling airbrush techniques can also be classified as mechanical shading.

Most mechanical shading is accomplished using shading sheets. ***Shading sheets*** are materials with a visible pattern of lines or dots on an acetate base. The sheet is positioned over selected areas of the line art to prepare them for tone or tint effects.

Camera copy that consists of mechanical shading often requires the use of a halftone-sensitive film rather than the less-sensitive line film. The alignment and focus capabilities of the process camera are critical considerations. The use of a magnifying lens on the ground glass is suggested to check for accuracy. Also, it is suggested that a slight reproduction enlargement be used when possible with copy containing 133 lines or finer tint screen rulings.

Continuous tone

Continuous tone is a term used for an original that has not been screened, and has infinite tone gradations between the lightest highlights and the deepest shadows. Continuous tone can be broken down into the two subcategories of reflection and transmission copy. See **Figure 13-2**.

Figure 13-2. Continuous tone images can be reflection copy, like the photo at right, or they can be transmission copy, as in the 35mm slide or the large color transparency.

Reflection copy is an original image that is opaque (light cannot pass through it). It reflects different amounts of light from the different tone values. Examples of reflection copy include photographs, oil paintings, chalk or charcoal renderings, and water color work. See **Figure 13-3A**.

Transmission copy, or *transparent copy*, is an original that allows light to pass through the image. Examples of transparent copy include 35 mm black-and-white or color slides and larger transparencies. They will commonly require backlighting techniques on the process camera. This form of continuous tone copy will require the use of a process camera that has a semitransparent backing on the copyboard. See **Figure 13-3B**. When the copyboard lights are positioned behind the transparent copy, the amount of light transmitted through the different densities of the original will record corresponding densities on the film being exposed through the process lens.

Both reflection or transmission forms of continuous tone copy will require the use of a ***halftone grade film***. This type of film is considered to be more sensitive and dimensionally stable than *line film*. The reproduction of continuous tone copy will

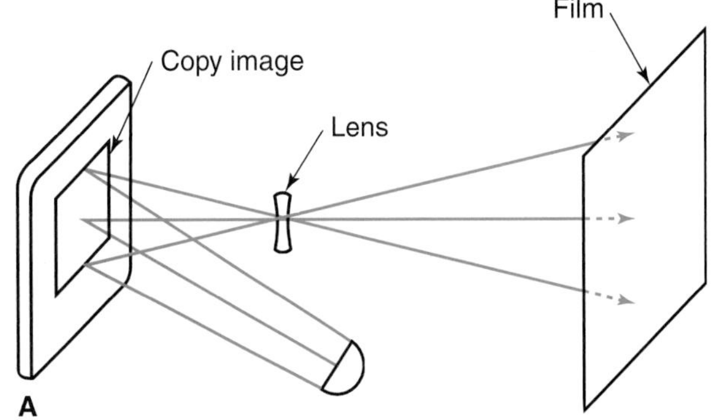

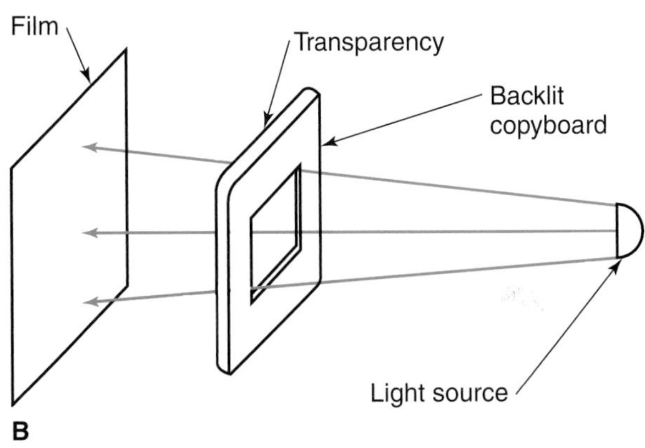

Figure 13-3. Reflection and transmission copy. A—Reflection copy is opaque and reflects light. It cannot be seen through. B—Transmission copy allows light to pass through, so it must be handled differently on the process camera.

also require the use of a halftone *contact screen* to record the dot pattern that is needed for the printing press.

With some printing processes, such as gravure, all of the images, including type and line art, are screened. Further information on gravure image generation is covered in Chapter 22 of this text.

Continuous tone copy may consist of black-and-white or color images. Your initial experiences in halftone photography should be limited to black-and-white photographs. The hues or colors in a color photograph can reproduce differently on black-and-white film. This concept is sometimes hard to understand. For example, depending on the nature of the film emulsion used (orthochromatic or panchromatic) the red lipstick on the color portrait of a woman may turn out black or gray when printed as a black-and-white halftone. It will take the practice and experience in the evaluation of color originals to make quality black-and-white halftones. Different types of filters can be used for converting a color original into black-and-white halftones.

Prescreened images

Prescreened images, or ***preprinted halftones***, are camera copy that already contain a screen or dot pattern. This category can be treated as mechanical shading or can be rescreened into halftones. Prescreened images can be made in the camera or enlarger. If shot as line work, the same considerations used for mechanical shading should be given to these presceened images.

Rescreening can be done using different techniques. Using a contact halftone screen is one method to make a rescreened halftone reproduction.

Another method is to angle the halftone screen 30° from the original screen angle to prevent a moiré pattern. A ***moiré pattern*** is a visually undesirable dot-exaggerating effect that occurs when two different screen patterns are randomly positioned or superimposed. See **Figure 13-4**.

A simpler method is to move the lensboard 2% to 4% out of focus from the desired reproduction percentage. This is done as an effort to diffuse the halftone image by a soft focus technique.

Figure 13-4. A moiré pattern will result if the screen angles are not correct.

Evaluating Continuous Tone Originals

The continuous tone original to be used as camera copy for halftone reproduction will contain a wide range of tones. These tones range from the whitest value, referred to as the ***highlight***, through gray values referred to as the ***midtones*** (middletones), to the darkest black called the ***shadow***. See **Figure 13-5**.

Density

Density is the light-stopping ability of a material—its ability to hold back or block light. Density refers to the degree of blackness and is a measurement system used in photography. For example, a high-density image would be solid or almost solid black, and a low-density image would have an absence of black (white).

Density is expressed as a numerical value. Refer to Figure 13-5. For transmitted light, 0.00 would be clear film and 3.00 would be black. For reflected light, 2.00 would be the black and 0.00 would be

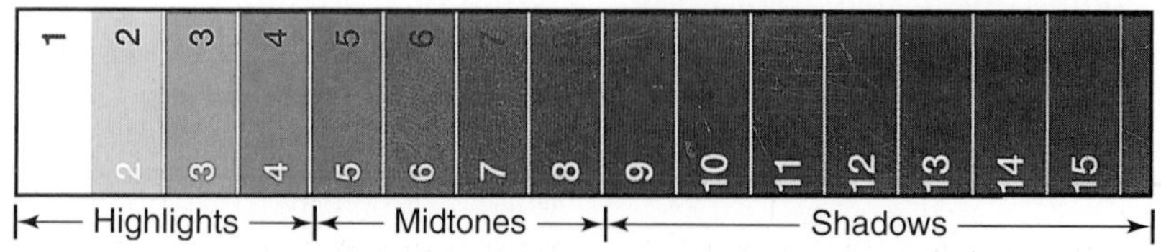

Figure 13-5. This gray scale shows the areas of highlights, midtones, and shadows. (Eastman Kodak)

white. Near the middle of these two densities would be gray with a density value around 0.30-0.60. As you can see, as the density value becomes larger, the image becomes darker and vice versa.

There are a number of methods used to measure density. Density can be measured with a reflection density guide or a reflection or transmission densitometer.

Reflection density guide

A *reflection density guide*, or *gray scale*, is used to compare a sample density to the image density. It has precalibrated density steps that are assigned a numerical value, which represent the photo-density range, or copy density range. The *photo-density range*, or *copy density range*, is the density difference between the highlight value and shadow value. See **Figure 13-6**. Using this method, you have to visually compare the example density to the image density. This method is limited to visual accuracy.

Densitometer

A *densitometer* is an electronic instrument that uses a photocell to accurately measure the amount of light reflected from or passing through different tone values. Densitometers provide an accurate way of assigning density values or determining if the values have been attained. There are several types of densitometers: those that read reflected light, those that read transmitted light, and those that read either reflection or transmission copy. The significant differences in the types of densitometers is the amount of detailed information they give and the type of materials that can be measured. See **Figure 13-7**.

High-key and low-key

Another set of terms used to evaluate continuous tone originals are high-key illustrations and low-key illustrations. A *high-key photograph* contains the most important details in the highlights, or lighter tones. A *low-key photograph* is primarily shadows, or darker tones. See **Figure 13-8**. The important details fall between the midtones and shadows.

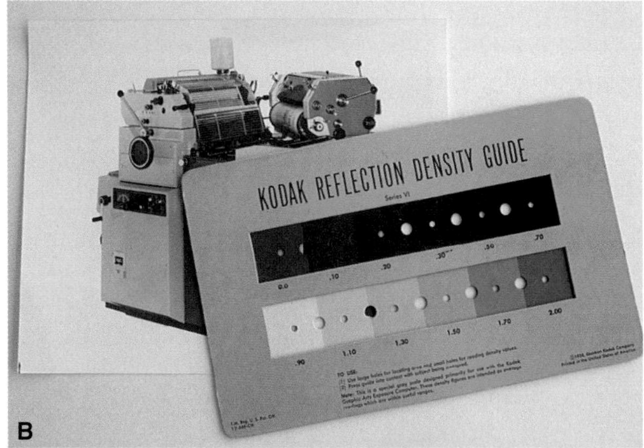

Figure 13-6. Density measurement. A—A reflection density guide can be compared to areas on image to visually assign a density value to the shade or the tone. The guide is laid directly over image and the holes are used to match up densities. B—This density guide is being used to check highlight and shadow areas on a photo.

Dot geometry

When reproducing halftones, the camera operator must pay close attention to tone reproduction or selection of dot geometry. The camera operator's ability to place the 50% midtone dot in the proper gray tone depends on their evaluation of the camera copy.

When reproducing high-key copy, the midtone dot placement should be closer to the dark tones, so the important details in the highlights are recorded. The opposite is true when reproducing low-key copy. The midtone dot placement (through selected exposures) is in close proximity to the highlights (light tones).

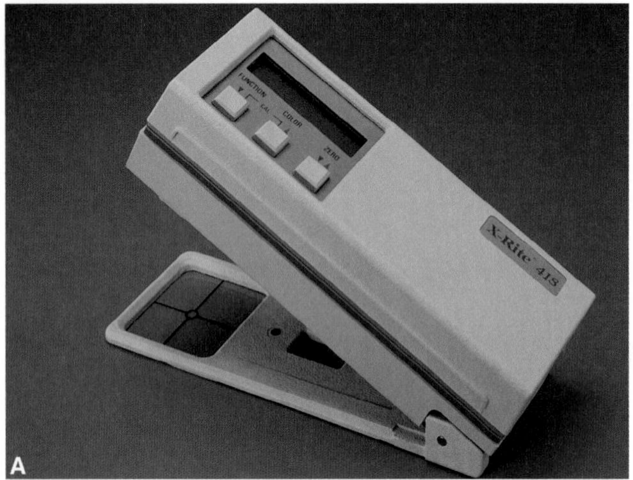

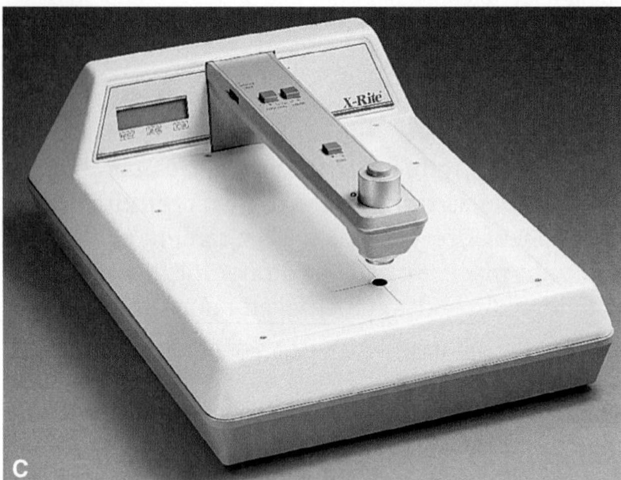

Figure 13-7. Densitometers and density identification systems. A—This is a digital color transmission/reflection densitometer. It will read the density of a photograph or the density of a negative or positive. B—This hand-held spectrodensitometer gives very specific information. C—This digital transmission densitometer is used to measure densities of negatives or positives. (X-Rite, Inc.)

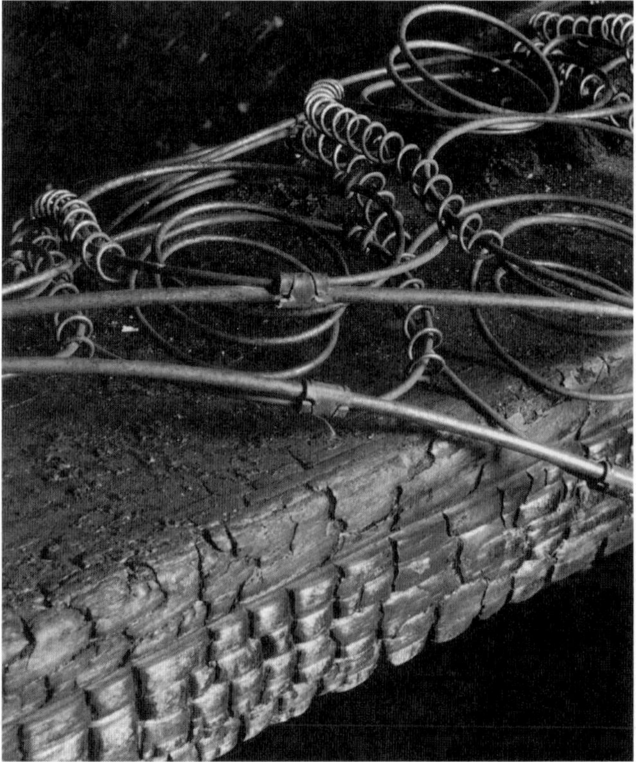

Figure 13-8. High-key and low-key photographs. A—A high-key photo will have the important image area in highlight and the less important areas in shadow. B—A low-key illustration will have the important image area more shadow than highlight.

Paper absorption

Another factor controlling tone reproduction and location is the type of paper surface used. An absorbent paper will cause the dot sizes to increase (dot gain) as the ink is absorbed into the paper and spreads.

Determining halftone exposures

To determine halftone exposures for the reproduction of a continuous tone photograph, the highlight and shadow densities will have to be measured. Whether a reflection density guide or a densitometer is used, the camera operator should read several possible highlight and shadow locations to determine the true densities of the copy.

Spectral highlights and shadows should *not* be used in determining the copy density range. *Spectral highlights* and *shadows* may be the lightest and darkest details of the original, but are considered too small in size to be used to determine tone reproduction requirements. An example of spectral highlights could be fine white pinstripes on a piece of clothing in a portrait.

Fluorescing agents

When evaluating the continuous tone original, it must be determined whether the photographic paper contains *fluorescing agents* or *optical brighteners*. It is increasingly common for a camera operator to receive a photograph for reproduction that has fluorescing agents in the paper to make the highlights more brilliant.

A black light, rich in ultraviolet light, will identify papers with fluorescing agents. Unfortunately, these agents will affect your predetermined exposures and change the desired dot sizes in the halftone. To reduce the effects of this problem, place an ultraviolet filtering agent in front of the camera lights.

Tone range limitations

When accepting original copy for halftone reproduction, the limitations of tone range should be explained. Most photographs will have a *reflection density range* of about 1.70. This is the difference between the highlight density value and the shadow density value in the photograph. Some professionally produced glossy prints can have a density range in excess of 2.00.

The client should be told that when using a coated stock and only one pass through the press, the printed press sheet has a density range capability of only about 1.60. This concern is magnified with the use of transparent originals that have a density range capability of about 3.00. The client should understand that the longer density ranges of the original will be compressed, or reduced, due to the nature of the printing process. Facsimile tone reproduction is the ultimate concern in halftone photography, but due to the total printing process limitations, some loss of detail and tonal separation will be experienced.

Densitometry

Densitometry is the science of measuring density, tone, or optical values with either reflection or transmission techniques. Density measurements provide quantitative information or specifications for halftones. A density value is a numerical value that is used universally between different departments in a printing company, as well as between different companies.

In halftone photography, the camera operator uses a ***reflection densitometer*** to accurately determine different tone values such as the highlight and shadows of a reflection original. A ***transmission densitometer*** can be used to determine the opacity or amount of light-stopping capability for different areas of an original transparency or of the processed film negative.

Using densitometers

When using either reflection or transmission densitometers, certain considerations should be observed. For black-and-white halftone applications, the densitometer should be set for a tristimulus reading. ***Tristimulus*** means that the densitometer is reading through all three color separation filters and not one specific part of the light spectrum.

Always zero and calibrate the densitometer to manufacturer's specifications before use. It is suggested that densitometers warm up before they are used. In a few cases, they are left on around the clock. Maintenance records should be kept to keep track of dates for the replacement of light sources, filters, and any other necessary components.

A block of *magnesium oxide* can be used as a white standard to internally zero a reflection densitometer. Always keep the densitometer clean. It is a precision instrument and should be treated as such.

Sensitometry

Sensitometry is the study and measurement of the sensitivity of photographic materials, in relationship to exposure and development. Before understanding the functions of the different exposures used in the production of a halftone, the nature of film emulsions should be identified. Primarily, a film emulsion is composed of microscopic silver halide crystals suspended in a layer of pure gelatin.

Emulsion sensitivity is described by a standard numerical system known as the ISO (International Standards Organization) rating. The higher the number rating assigned to a film emulsion, the faster the film will react to a light exposure. For example, ISO 200 film is half as *fast* (sensitive to light) as ISO 400 film.

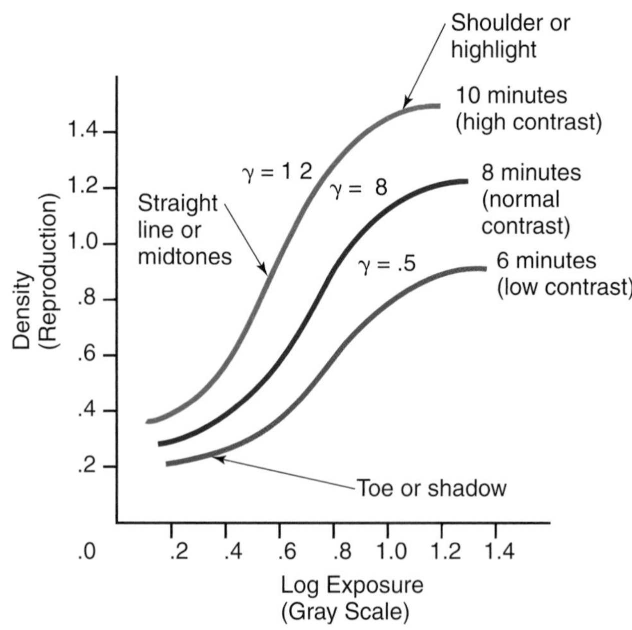

Figure 13-9. This is an example of three characteristic curves for one film emulsion. The degree of contrast, and the shape of the curve, varies with development time.

Emulsion contrast

Another characteristic of film is the emulsion contrast, or density reaction. Each film emulsion responds differently to exposure and development techniques. This response can be graphically plotted as a *characteristic curve*.

To plot a characteristic curve for a specific film emulsion, a controlled exposure is given through a transmission gray scale. This will give a uniform stepped density to the carefully processed film. The different density steps of the processed negative will be read by a transmission densitometer.

The test data is then plotted on a graph with the X-axis (horizontal) representing exposure factor, or original gray scale density. The Y-axis (vertical) represents the reproduced density. See **Figure 13-9**. The plotted density steps will form a curved shape that represents the film emulsion's contrast and sensitivity to light exposure. This curve is the ***characteristic curve***. The shape of the characteristic curve is divided into three distinct portions: the toe, the straight line portion (average gradient), and the shoulder. The *toe* of the characteristic curve is the lower part of the graph and represents the dark tones (shadow areas) of the original. The *straight line* will determine the contrast of a film by representing the midtone value of the original. The *shoulder* is the upper part of the curve and defines the light tones (highlights) of an original.

The slope of the curve is given as gamma (γ). From Figure 13-9, it can be seen that the steeper the slope of the curve, the higher the gamma. This means the film emulsion is high contrast. Basically, the same film emulsion developed longer will yield a higher contrast than will shorter development times. The ability to control the contrast by exposure and development is beneficial in the selection of different films for specific applications.

Base density fog

The action of the developer will cause a slight amount of density increase in the unexposed areas of the film. This action is referred to as ***chemical fog***, or ***developmental fog***. To measure this type of fog, develop an unexposed sheet of film. Then, take a transmission densitometer reading (value) to determine the exact amount of fog (density) added to the film base as a result of the development. This value is referred to as ***film-plus-base fog density***.

Dichroic fog is a deposit of silver particles that are suspended in the developer solution and appear to leave a purplish coating on the emulsion. This is a problem affecting the film emulsion density during processing. This is typically caused by the developer being contaminated with small amounts of fixer.

Halftone

The term *halftone* comes from an old hand-engraving process that involved breaking the image up into quarter tones, halftones, and three-quarter tones. A halftone reproduction gives the viewer an *illusion* of a continuous tone image when it is actually a tone pattern composed of dots that vary in size, but not density. See **Figure 13-10.**

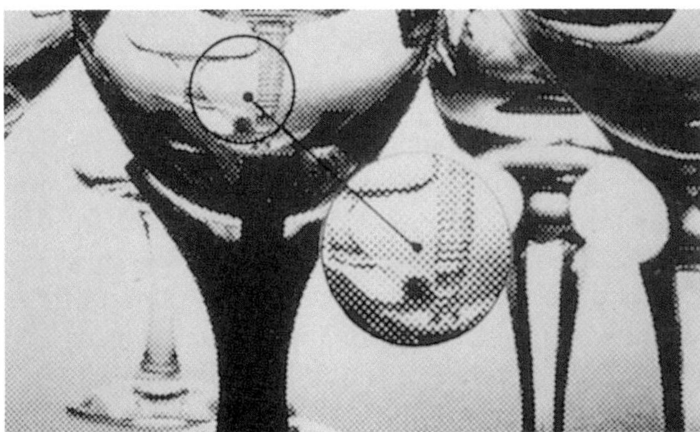

Figure 13-10. The close-up section of this halftone shows the dot structure.

As previously mentioned, continuous tone copy is composed of tones ranging from white (highlights) to black (shadows). See **Figure 13-11.** White or light colors will reflect light from the copyboard, through the lens to the film emulsion. Also, black or dark colors absorb light and reflect limited amounts of light through the lens to the film emulsion.

To record the other intermediate tone values in the continuous tone original, the camera operator needs a slightly more sensitive film. A halftone screen is also needed to record different size dots that represent *highlight values* (whites), *midtone values* (grays), and *shadow values* (blacks). See **Figure 13-12.** The screen is placed over the film, and then light from the original, continuous tone copy passes through the dot pattern before it exposes the film. The *halftone screen* records dots that vary in size according to the amount of light reflected from the original copy. This halftone light structure, when printed with a uniform density of ink on the paper, creates the illusion of many different shades or tones.

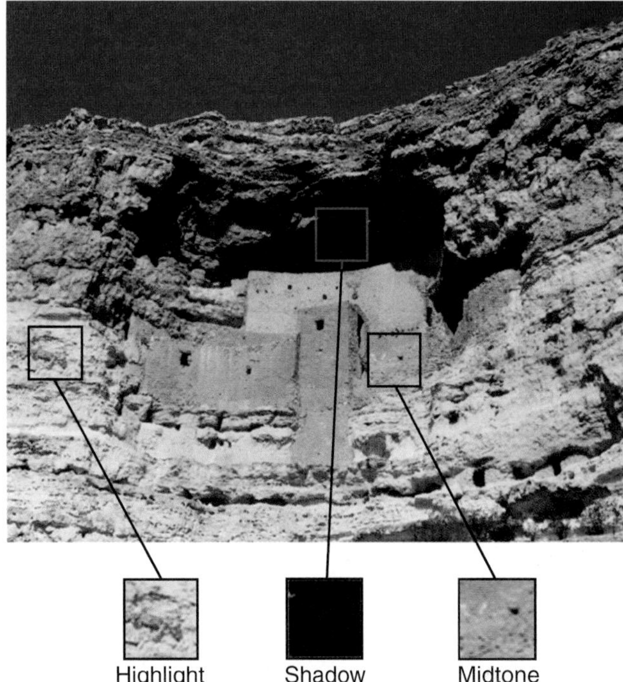

Figure 13-11. This photo consists of many shades or tones.

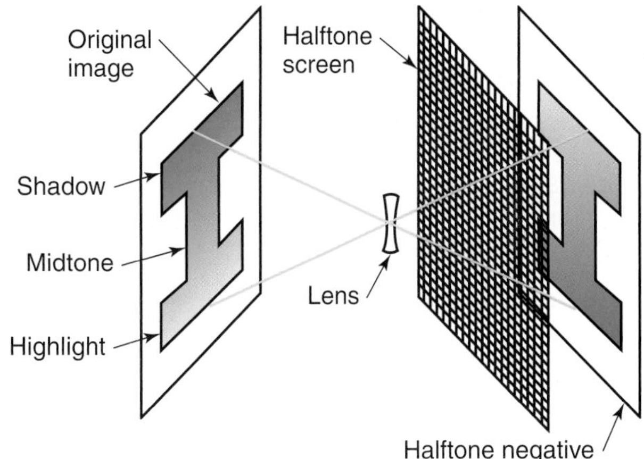

Figure 13-12. To convert a continuous tone photo into a halftone, a screen is placed over the film. Then the light from the original image must pass through the dot pattern before exposing the film. You can see that a halftone negative is the opposite image of the original.

Halftone Screen Process

The ***halftone screen process*** is the procedure of converting a continuous tone original into a pattern of dots. This conversion is made with either a halftone contact screen or crossline (glass) screen placed over the film. A fresh sheet of film is placed in the path of the imaging or main exposure.

The traditional crossline screen consisted of two pieces of ruled glass cemented together at right angles. See **Figure 13-13**. The ruled glass depressions were filled with an opaque pigment. For black-and-white work, the screen is positioned at a 45° angle, so that when the human eye focuses on the printed halftone in vertical or horizontal orientation, the rows of dots appear less obvious.

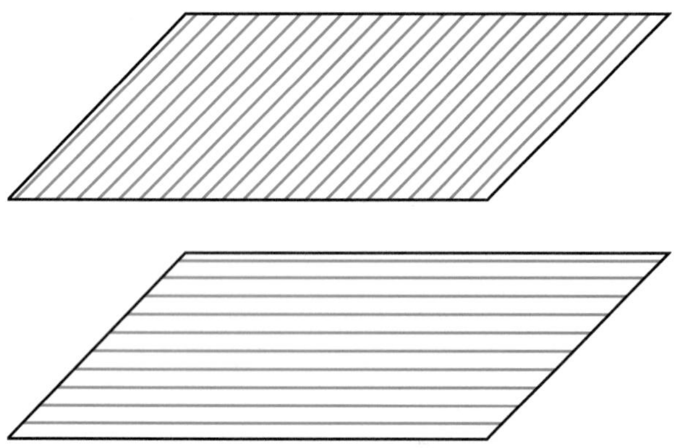

Figure 13-13. The older crossline screen used for making halftones consisted of two pieces of glass with opaque lines ruled on them.

Today, when halftones are created photomechanically they are done using the less expensive, simpler, and faster contact screen. This is the process that is covered in this chapter.

Contact screen

A ***contact screen*** is a series of uniform vignetted (soft) dots mounted on a flexible support base. Unlike the sharp ruled lines in the crossline screen, the *vignetted dot structure* in the contact screen is diffused. As a result, it appears out of focus when magnified. See **Figure 13-14**.

A halftone contact screen differs from a tint screen. A ***tint screen*** is used in the platemaking process to create the uniform tone pattern, and contains a hard dot structure that is specified by a dot percentage.

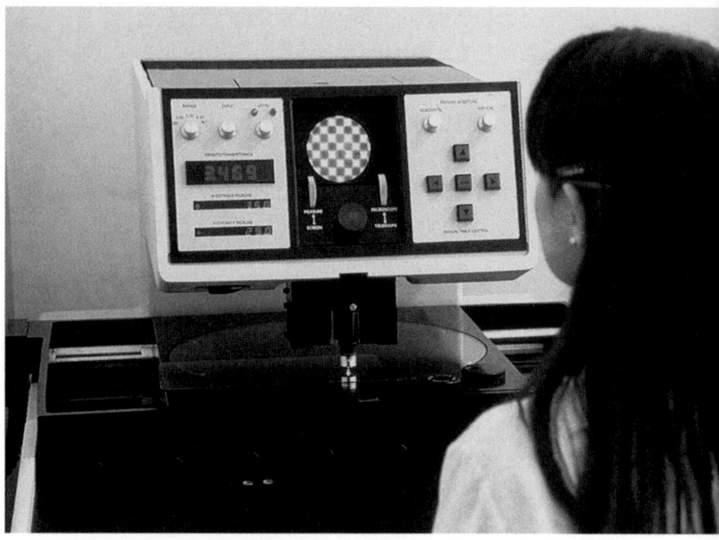

Figure 13-14. This machine is showing an enlarged area of a magenta contact screen.

The halftone contact screen is used as the name suggests—it is held in close vacuum *contact* with the film emulsion. During the camera exposure, the different amounts of light reflected from the differing tone values of the original copy will penetrate the vignetted dot structure of the contact screen. The result is a latent image recorded on the film.

Where the highlights of the original copy reflected considerable light, the dots are larger on the film. This results from the extra light passing through the fringe of the vignetted dots. Where dim light is reflected from the shadow areas of the original copy, the dot structure will be smaller. This is because the light has passed through only the transparent center of the vignetted dots.

Percent dot sizes

The ***halftone dot sizes*** are specified as percentages of ink density on a printed sheet. The highlight dots will usually be 5% to 10% in size, the midtone dots range from 30% to 70%, and the shadow dots will be around 90% to 95%. The halftone negative will represent a reversal of the original, but the dot structure is given in reference to the positive printed image. See **Figure 13-15**.

Screen color

Halftone contact screens can be magenta or gray in color. Either screen may be used for reproducing black-and-white halftones from black-and-white copy.

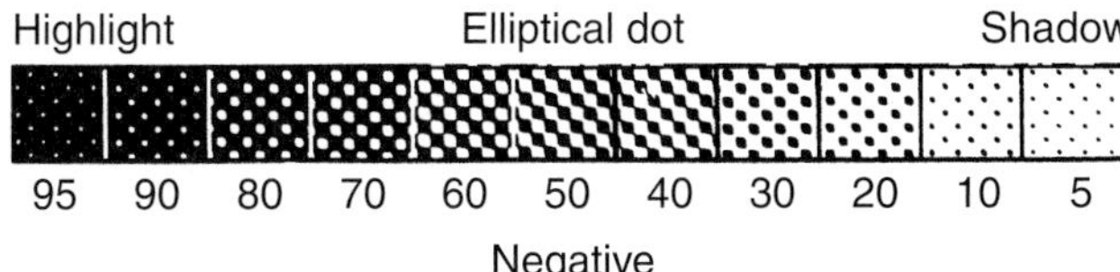

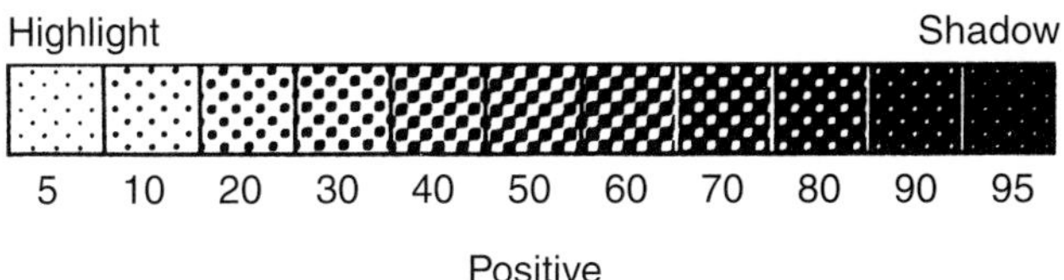

Figure 13-15. The highlight and the shadow areas of a negative or a positive are denoted by varying dot sizes. Note the inverse relationship—a shadow dot is small on the negative and large on the positive.

Magenta contact screens can be used in combination with magenta or yellow color-compensating filters to either compress or extend the screen range. The magenta screen can be used in any photomechanical reproduction process, except direct screen color separation where the magenta dye in the screen will alter the effects of the color separation filters.

Perhaps the most commonly used contact screen is the gray contact screen. This is because the silver, or gray, color is neutral. It will not alter the effects of color separation filters.

Negative and positive screens

Contact screens can be designated for negative or positive purposes. Usually, the positive screen will have a longer screen range or tone reproduction capability than the negative screen. Using different exposure techniques, it is possible to make a halftone negative with a positive screen. As a rule of thumb, use positive screens to reproduce positives, and a negative screen to make negatives.

Screen shapes

Most halftone contact screens are rectangular in shape. Some are circular in shape, making it easier to obtain different screen angles. When purchasing or making a circular screen, the diameter of the screen must be slightly larger than the diagonal of the largest film size to be used.

Screen dot shapes

Halftone screens have square, elliptical, or round dots. See **Figure 13-16**. The square dot is often referred to as a *conventional dot*. It was the traditional dot used, and received its shape from the crossline screen. It is often the easiest to determine dot percentage, especially in the dot etching process.

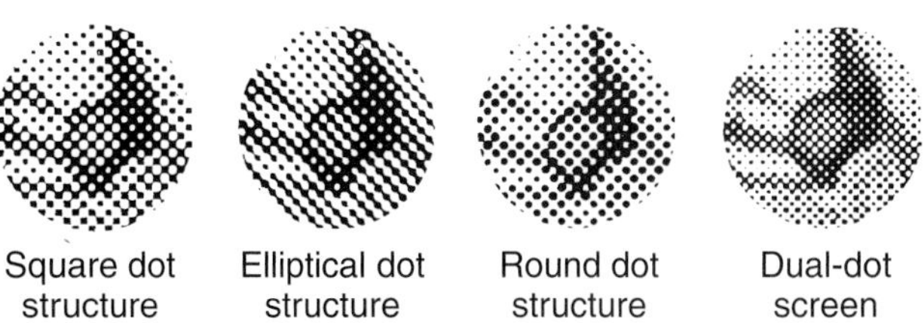

Square dot structure | Elliptical dot structure | Round dot structure | Dual-dot screen

Figure 13-16. This shows the difference in detail in the magnified image using the different dot shapes. The square and elliptical dot structures give more detail.

The elliptical dot is sometimes called the *chain dot*. It is the most popular because it offers a smoother rendition of the middle tones. A comparison of elliptical dot and square dot in a portrait of a person will visually prove this difference in the middle tones or facial tones.

The *round dot* is used primarily with high-speed web offset printing. It was widely accepted in the European markets. The round dot tends to compensate for ink entrapment, plugging, and dot gain in the lighter middle tone dots.

The square and elliptical dots will join at 40% to 50% dot values for middle tones. The round dot will not form or join until 60% to 70%. Thus, the round dot is *not* as accepted in conventional printing, because there is a loss of detail as compared to square and elliptical dots.

So far this chapter has discussed the use of a single dot screen. Halftone screens can have a secondary ruling in the middle tones and shadows to reproduce extremely fine details. The screens containing a secondary ruling are referred to as ***dual-dot halftone screens***.

Selecting halftone screens

Halftone screens are selected by their *rulings*. This means the number of lines or dots per inch. The ruling selected should be determined by the printing capabilities of the pressroom.

If the camera operator selects a 150- or 300-line screen for high-quality work and sends it to a pressroom containing small offset duplicators, the efforts will probably be wasted. The paper used for printing also should be considered in screen ruling selection. Some papers will be more absorbent and will produce dot gain.

Handling halftone screens

The life and quality of a halftone contact screen depends upon its care and handling. Be careful to treat the contact screen like a piece of film. Protect it from dirt, scratches, processing chemicals, and finger marks.

The gray contact screen is a delicate film base that has a continuous tone emulsion on one side. To wash the gray screen, use a clean tray of water at room temperature with a neutral wetting agent, dishwashing detergent, or a commercial screen cleaner. Do not rub or squeegee the screen. It is recommended that the solution drain uniformly off the screen. Most developer or fixer stains will not wash off. Magenta screens cannot be washed. The magenta dye used to make magenta screens could run or change density unevenly.

Stochastic screening

Stochastic screening is a halftone reproduction method that creates the illusion of tones by varying the number (frequency) of dots in a small area. This is different than the conventional halftone screens where spaced rows of dots of varying sizes give the illusion of various tones. Stochastic screening is done electronically, and is covered in greater detail in Chapter 11.

Halftone Exposures and Screen Ranges

All effects and results in photomechanical reproduction are directly related to the laws of physics and applied mathematics. For this reason, all exposures required in halftone reproduction are predictable and the results are explainable. The typical halftone negative will require two exposures; however, in some selective situations, three exposures are required. Each exposure serves a purpose in the successful facsimile reproduction of the original image.

Main exposure

The ***main exposure*** is the primary exposure made through a halftone screen to produce a halftone negative. Its main purpose is to reproduce the highlight, midtone, and shadow details of the original.

The main exposure of an original photograph will reproduce only the tonal range of the contact halftone screen. So, if the photo density range is equal to the density range of the screen, only a main exposure is required. Rarely will the photo range equal the screen range, thus ***supplementary exposures*** known as the *flash* or *bump exposures* will be needed after the main exposure.

Determining the main exposure

To determine the main exposure for a specific camera, halftone screen, and type of film, the camera operator will need to make a basic main exposure test. A ***main exposure test*** for a halftone requires an exposure, usually two to three times longer than used for a normal line shot of a reflection density guide or of a gray scale.

All variables affecting halftone results, such as flare, camera light positioning, f/stop selecting, and processing techniques, must be controlled and recorded. Place the film, emulsion-side up, with the halftone contact screen emulsion-side down on top of the film. After making the estimated basic main exposure, process the film in a controlled environment. Keep the temperature, time, agitation, and chemistry exhaustion under control.

Examine the dry negative on a light table with a magnifying lens to determine highlight and shadow locations. See **Figure 13-17**. If the highlight dot structure (10% dot) is located between the 0.00 step and the 0.30 step on the scale, your estimated exposure will become your basic main exposure. If the reflection density guide or gray scales are *not* precalibrated, you will have to read the steps on a reflection densitometer to accurately determine the density of tone values.

Understand that normal highlights in an original photo will fall between 0.00 and 0.30 in density. If your test exposure does not contain a 10% dot between and including the 0.00 and 0.30 step, you will have to either increase or decrease the exposure and retest.

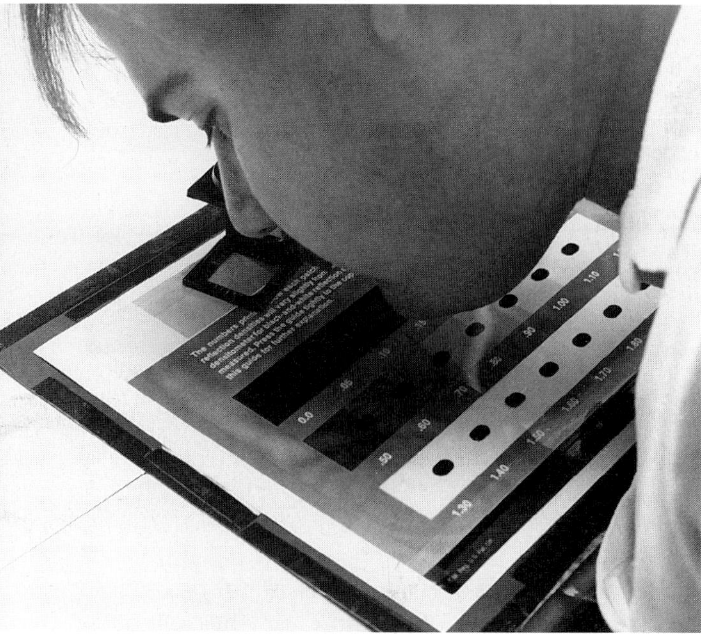

Figure 13-17. After making a test exposure, the negative should be inspected closely so that accurate camera adjustments can be made.

Finding screen range

The test used to determine the basic main exposure will also identify the effective or basic screen range. If an acceptable highlight dot placement is obtained, then identify the density step where a 90% to 95% shadow dot is located. The difference in density between the highlight and the shadow steps will numerically determine the screen range for the specific camera, film, and processing conditions.

Flash exposure

The *flash exposure* is a supplementary exposure used to strengthen the dots in the shadows of negatives, thereby lengthening the screen's tonal reproduction range. The flash exposure is a nonimaging, yellow or white light exposure made through the halftone screen and the lens. *Nonimaging* means that the exposure affects the entire emulsion surface uniformly and does *not* record the original image or copy.

The highlight areas recorded on the film by the light reflectance from the main exposure will have little or no effect from the flash exposure. However, the shadow areas of the original that have a density exceeding the screen range will appear to have either a clear or latent gray dot structure on the processed film. The flash exposure will form the shadow dot structure in halftone reproductions where the copy density range exceeds the screen range.

The flash exposure, by itself, is considered to be meaningless other than its ability to expose uniform dots through the center of the vignetted screen structure. When used in conjunction with the main exposure, the flash exposure will reinforce or add supplemental exposure to shadow dots that have not received enough main exposure to become hard dots.

Determining flash exposure

The amount of flash exposure is determined by the excess density or the difference between the screen range and the copy range. Understand that too much flash exposure will alter the tone reproduction of the highlights and midtones.

It is suggested that a flash lamp with a 7 1/2W or 15W bulb be mounted about 5′ to 6′ (1.5 m to 1.8 m) from the camera back. The filter commonly used is either a safelight filter 00, or a white light diffusion filter or sheeting.

If a magenta screen is used, the flash lamp should contain a 00 safelight filter. With a gray contact screen, either light source is appropriate.

With newer cameras, an internal flashing lamp often is housed in the bellows section. Some vertical cameras will still require a flash exposure through the lens with white paper on the copyboard. Though this is not a conventional technique for flash exposure, it will still yield the same results.

Basic flash test

To determine the basic flash exposure for a specific film, halftone screen, and camera, a step-test exposure will be needed. The basic flash exposure will be the amount of light needed to record an acceptable shadow dot (90% to 95%) on a fresh piece of film using a halftone contact screen.

For this test, position a piece of halftone-grade film on the vacuum back, emulsion side out. Cover it with the halftone contact screen emulsion-to-emulsion. Using an opaque template or shield, make a series of step exposures with the auxiliary flash lamp. It is important to keep the film plane stationary.

Process the test exposure using the time and temperature instructions furnished with the film. Using a magnification lens and a light table, inspect and select the exposure step that has the first usable 90% to 95% shadow dot. This is the basic flash exposure time. Later, this will be used in determining the halftone exposures for specific copy.

Bump exposure

Remember, the purpose of the *flash exposure* is to extend the screen range capabilities to match the photo density range. The purpose of the ***bump exposure***, or ***no-screen highlight exposure***, is to shorten the screen range to compensate for camera copy or photos with a density range *less than* the screen range. Essentially, the bump exposure is a no-screen, or line shot, of the continuous tone camera copy. This will enhance the highlight details by *reducing* the size of dots with the additional exposure.

The bump exposure is calculated as a percentage of the main exposure. It should be between 2% to 15% of the time used for the main exposure.

Often, neutral density filters are used in front of the camera lens during the bump exposure due to the extremely short exposure times. ***Neutral density filters*** reduce the amount of light passing through the camera lens without changing the rendition of the colors in the light spectrum.

When exposure times become extremely short, the accuracy of the camera timing device can present a problem.

To determine the effect of a bump exposure for a specific reproduction situation, the basic main exposure test is given with a 10% bump exposure. After processing, magnified inspection of the film negative will identify the extent of density compression. See **Figure 13-18**. Many large manufacturers provide tables to predict density changes for the difference in bump exposure percentages.

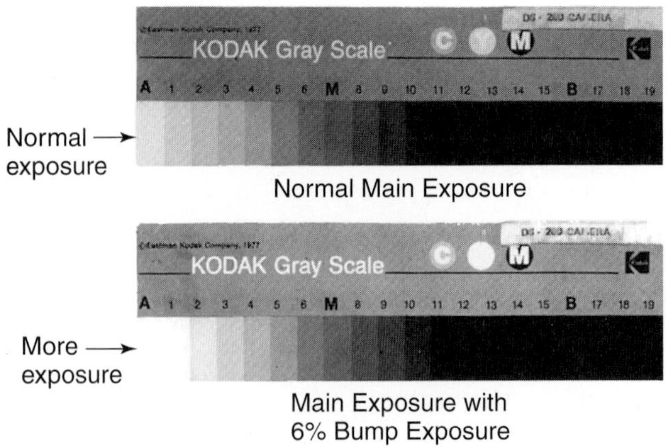

Figure 13-18. A bump exposure affects the highlight areas. When needed, it can be used to enhance the highlights of photo.

Exposure determining devices

An ***exposure determining device*** should be used to decide the different exposures required to make a good halftone from the original continuous tone copy. Most exposure determining devices are easy to use and will yield consistent and predictable results.

The three categories of exposure determining devices are the halftone exposure calculator (hand-operated dials), electronic memory devices, and data centers. Depending on the extent of camera work being completed and the sophistication of equipment in the facility, any of these systems should eliminate the guesswork involved with halftone exposures.

To gain the most benefit possible from any of the electronic memory devices or data center, all reproduction variables must be controlled. A calibrated densitometer, an automated film processor, and camera equipped with a light integrator should be used to keep all variables constant. A *light integrator* is a photocell attached to the copyboard that will control the camera timing device. If the voltage to the camera lights fluctuate, the photocell will adjust the length of the exposure to compensate and preserve accuracy. The same amount of light will thus strike the film with the same exposure setting.

Halftone exposure calculator

The ***halftone exposure calculator*** (hand-operated dial) is a device used to determine exposures for halftone production. It is the least expensive and easiest to use. These devices have been in the industry for a long time. The Kodak Q-12 Halftone Calculator not only determines halftone exposures, but can easily be used for duotones and special effects, such as posterizations. The Q-15 (shown in **Figure 13-19**) was introduced by Kodak as a more accurate device to replace the Q-12. The Q-15 compensates for reciprocity failure and other exposure factors, such as the effect of the flash exposure to the highlight dot structure.

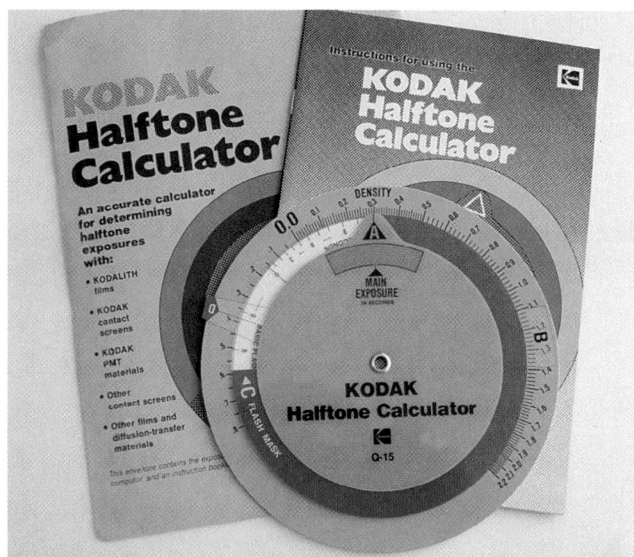

Figure 13-19. Hand-operated devices, such as this halftone calculator, provide a simple way of calculating camera settings.

When using any halftone calculator, always remember that all test data must be accurate before calibrating the device. The technique used to determine the basic main and flash exposures should be typical of production operations.

To use one of these devices, rotate the dials to program the device with basic main exposure, screen range, and basic flash exposure. After the dials have been set, the only data the camera operator must use is the original copy highlight, shadow, and photo density range. The main exposure is directly related to the highlight of the copy.

The flash exposure, if required, is relative to the photo density range in comparison to the effective screen range.

When looking at original continuous tone copy, the camera operator should be able to develop an instinct for exposure. Simply stated, a continuous tone original that has *extreme contrast* will probably require a flash exposure due to its large photo density range. The continuous tone original that is *lacking contrast* will probably require little or no flash exposure, because the screen range will be more comparable to the photo range. The continuous tone original that is *flat* (has poor contrast) will probably require a bump exposure to enhance the reproduction, or compress the screen range to match the photo range.

Electronic memory devices

The development of electronic memory devices used to determine exposure information has eliminated much of the manual calculation work. See **Figure 13-20.** After these devices are calibrated with test data, they require only the specific density information from the original. In most cases, these units will override or act as the timing device for the process camera.

Figure 13-20. This is an electronic memory device that can be used when making halftones.

Data centers

Photomechanical data centers are separate from the camera, and do a wide variety of exposure computations based on reproduction requirements. In addition, the programmable memory chips in these centers determine the placement of the midtone dot, copy sizing requirements, chemistry mixing proportions, filter selections, and a combination of other typical photomechanical functions.

The data center uses a programmable memory chip to run specific programs with a minimum of input data. Data centers do more calculations than the other devices, but will require the same test data to perform exposure calibrations.

Production of a Halftone

To produce a halftone of an original continuous tone photograph, the camera operator must first evaluate the photo density range. The highlight or whitest white of the photograph must be identified with either the use of a precalibrated reflection density guide or a reflection densitometer.

Before using the reflection densitometer, be sure to zero and calibrate it against the standard plate provided by the manufacturer. Read more than one highlight location to determine the true highlight density reading. After recording the highlight, use the same procedure to determine the shadow density reading. Do *not* read the spectral highlights and shadows of the photograph. To determine the *photodensity range,* simply subtract the highlight density value from the shadow density value. See **Figure 13-21**.

Figure 13-21. The highlight and shadow density readings are used to determine the photograph's density range.

To determine the exposure times for the halftone, select one of the exposure determining devices and follow the manufacturer's directions. To use the exposure determining devices, calibrate the exposure dials with the following test data.

- Basic main exposure.
- Basic flash exposure.
- In some cases, the main exposure with a predetermined percentage of bump exposure.

After calibration and the identification of the effective screen range, the photo density information is input. This information is used to calculate the desired exposures. Once the proper exposure is determined, mount the photo on the camera copyboard with a reflection gray scale next to it. Set the copyboard and lensboard at the predetermined reproduction percentages.

The normal f-stop for halftone work is f/16, but be sure to set the f-stop for the same setting as used in the basic main exposure test. The rest of the halftone process will be completed in the darkroom.

In the darkroom, use the ground glass to determine focus, film size, and film location. See **Figure 13-22**. Once the image is in focus, place the halftone-grade film emulsion-up on the vacuum film back. Then, place the halftone contact screen emulsion-down on top of the film. See **Figure 13-23**. Be sure to allow adequate vacuum drawdown time. A screen roller or photo chamois may be used to ensure screen drawdown is uniform.

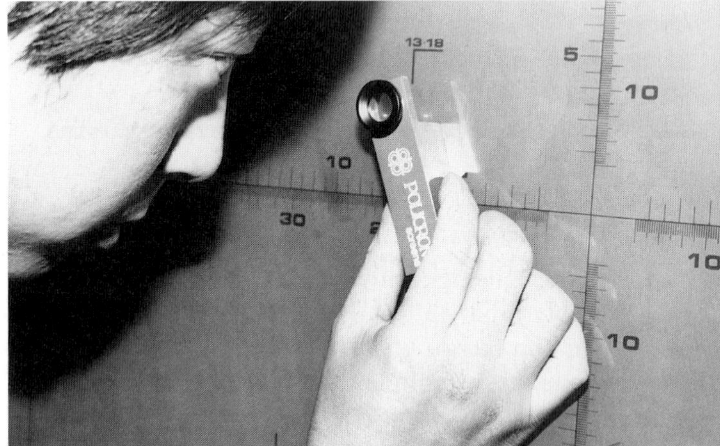

Figure 13-22. This camera operator is using a magnifier to check the focus before making an exposure.

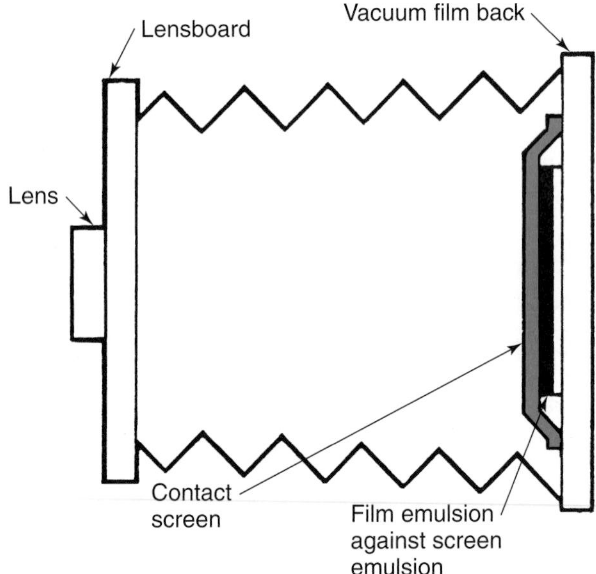

Figure 13-23. The screen is placed over the film on the film back of the process camera. This will make the light from the original pass through the screen dot structure before striking the film.

Make the required halftone exposures. The sequence of exposures should remain consistent from halftone to halftone. It makes relatively little difference as to whether the main exposure is given first or last.

To make the main exposure, simply close the film back. Adjust the camera and actuate the camera lights.

To make a flash exposure, position the focal plane perpendicular to the flash lamp. Then, expose without releasing the vacuum or halftone contact screen.

The bump exposure is made without releasing the vacuum pressure. The halftone contact screen is carefully removed and placed back into its protective folder or sleeve. After removing the screen, expose with the camera lights and lens for the predetermined percentage of the main exposure. When the exposures are complete, release the vacuum pressure.

Processing Film

Processing the halftone can be completed either in an automatic film processor or in processing trays using manual techniques. If a film processor is used, be sure to use the appropriate control strips to determine if the chemistry level is stabilized. ***Control strips*** are continuous wedges of film with graduated densities that are pre-exposed under exacting conditions, and are used to test development solution in automatic processors.

To use processing trays, the camera operator can either use a time and temperature development or development by inspection. Place the film with the latent or nonvisible image in a tray of fresh developer. If the basic test times prove consistent, processing to time and temperature is the most accurate method.

Development by inspection

As developer becomes exhausted by either film use or oxidation, ***development by inspection*** should be done. In development by inspection, the operator processing the film first looks for an acceptable highlight dot. Then they check for an acceptable shadow dot in reference to the original artwork or photograph.

Still development

One benefit of processing by the inspection method is the ability to use still development, or development without agitation. ***Still development*** requires a period of about 45 seconds where no agitation of the developing tray takes place. This stillness allows the shadow dot structure to develop faster than the highlight dot structure.

In theory, the dense or black highlight areas of the halftone negative have exhausted the developer covering that part of the emulsion, faster than the developer covering the less dense shadow areas. Without agitation, new developer cannot relocate, so highlight development stops while shadow development continues.

Stop bath

After the appropriate development occurs or the development time expires, transfer the negative to the stop bath to stabilize the film. The ***stop bath*** is an acetic acid rinse used to halt the development process. Neutralizing the effects of the alkaline developer on the negative will require approximately 15 seconds.

Fixing

The negative is next transferred to the fixer. The ***fixer*** is a solution that makes the developed image on a film permanent by dissolving or neutralizing the remaining unexposed silver particles. With fresh rapid or liquid fixer (ammonium thiosulfate), the unexposed silver removal and emulsion hardening process will require about four minutes.

Washing

After fixing, the negative is washed in running water for ten minutes. If the wash cycle does not remove the fixer from the film emulsion, it will possibly transfer to the film dryer, contaminating film placed on the dryer later.

Drying

The washed film then must be dried. Drying can be done using mechanical devices, such as drying cabinets with forced air. Drying also can be accomplished by clipping the film on a line and allowing it to drip dry.

Evaluating Halftone Negatives

Once the halftone negative has been dried, the camera operator uses a light table and a magnification device to inspect the results. Always view the negative on the *base* or *plastic side* of the film to avoid scratches. See **Figure 13-24**.

Figure 13-24. These camera operators are checking halftone images on the film after development.

Inspecting the highlight (dense) areas of the negative should reveal a 5% to 10% dot structure. Remember that the dot percentage represents ink on paper or the *positive* image. Thus, the shadow or least dense areas of the halftone *negative* should be represented by a 90% to 95% dot structure. See **Figure 13-25**. If the highlight dot structure is smaller in size than the desired 5% dot, simply *reduce* the main exposure. If the dot structure was too large a percentage, the main exposure will need to be *increased*.

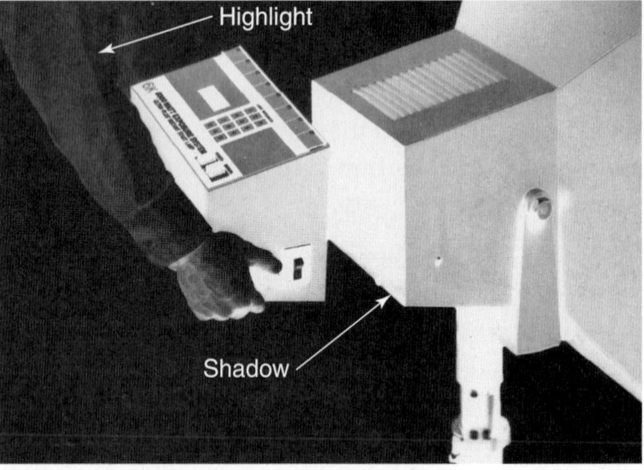

Figure 13-25. The highlight area of a halftone negative is the most dense, with the smallest dots. This area will be the lightest area of the printed piece, since the least amount of ink will be applied. The least dense (shadow) area of the halftone negative will result in the heaviest ink coverage.

The highlight dot structure of the printed halftone will look muddy or dull if the percentage is larger than the desired 10%. Remember that the main exposure will have the most influence in controlling the highlight dot structure.

Upon the evaluation of the shadow dot structure, it should be understood that the greater the flash exposure, the *larger* the shadow dot size. This means that if the dot structure in the shadows is *not* a hard dense dot or it appears latent, the flash exposure should be *increased*.

As the developer becomes exhausted or oxidized, it will tend to become high contrast in nature. This high-contrast effect will be most noticeable in the development of the shadow details or dot structure. Either still development or increased flash exposure will compensate and allow for the full 90% to 95% dot structure to develop.

Prescreened Diffusion Transfer Halftones

Another alternative method of producing halftones is the use of the *diffusion transfer process*. This process will produce a positive halftone print on photographic paper.

The advantage to this method is that the halftone illustration can be pasted-up with the line copy, and be exposed as one line shot. The diffusion transfer or *PMT* (photo-mechanical transfer) halftone should be reproduced at the desired size. This will prevent further enlargement or reduction from distorting the dot structure.

The use of a special diffusion transfer halftone contact screen will be required. Remember that diffusion transfer products react to light exposure in the direction opposite to normal film emulsions. The longer exposure of light to the diffusion transfer emulsion will result in *less* density. To determine the screen range and other basic exposure times, follow the same procedures previously mentioned. The one consideration is to use a 15% to 20% highlight dot structure and a 85% to 90% shadow dot structure. This will produce a desired *flat reproduction* (lower contrast), as it is re-exposed in the line work process. The exposure computers or calculators, described earlier, will determine individual photo requirements and times.

Halftones Using Rapid Access Process

Rapid access films are designed to have extreme latitude in the development process. For this reason, the exposure time will remain critical, but the development will be a more controlled reaction.

The rapid access process once was used for typesetting and line art only. Then, the production of a rapid access contact screen made it possible to produce a hard dot for reproduction purposes. Thus, halftone reproduction benefits from the many advantages typical to the rapid access process. Some of the advantages of using rapid access films and chemistry are as follows:

- The speed and ease in processing the films—no chemicals to mix.
- No real temperature control required for processing film in trays.
- Total repeatability and consistency in results.
- Economical in cost for most operations.

Color Separations

Color separation is the process of using red, green, and blue filters to divide the many colors of an original image into the three process colors (yellow, magenta, and cyan) and black. This process requires four halftone film negatives. Each halftone is exposed at different screen angles on pan film so that each represents a different printing ink. See **Figure 13-26**. The four halftones are used to prepare the three process color and black printing plates. These plates also are referred to as *printers*.

Figure 13-26. This is an enlargement of a halftone separation dot structure within a four-color separation. Each separation is used to print one color. When two or more colors overlap, a new color is created.

The exposures creating the four different halftones are each altered through the use of color separation filters. The *red filter* is used to reproduce the cyan printer. Cyan ink (red light absorber) will represent the image of the red light absorbed by the original, when printed in positive form. When the eye sees the cyan ink, it only identifies green and blue light reflection because the red light from the paper is absorbed by the ink layer. See **Figure 13-27**.

The *green filter* is used in the reproduction of the magenta printer. Magenta ink (green light absorber) will represent the image of the green light absorbed by the original, when printed in positive form. For the eye to see magenta, the green light must be absorbed by the ink, and only the red and blue reflected.

The *blue filter* is used to reproduce the yellow printer, because it represents only a blue light image on the negative. When the blue light image is printed in positive form on the paper with yellow ink (blue light absorber), only the red and green light rays will stimulate the eye and allow the brain to identify the color yellow.

The *black printer* is produced by partial exposure of the film through each of the previously used filters (blue, green, and red). A single exposure technique using a yellow or orange filter may also be used.

Narrow and wide band filters

To be more specific, the normal color separation filters include the No. 25-red, No. 47-blue, and the No. 58-green. The specific numbered filters are considered to be pure and are referred to as narrow band filters. The ***narrow band filter*** is considered to be monochromatic (passing only *one* color of light). For color separation work, the narrow band filter reproduces only pure colors. For example, when photographing a clean green that flows into an off shade of green (grayish green), the narrow band filter only reproduces the pure green value. The use of narrow band filters is beneficial if color correction systems are limited.

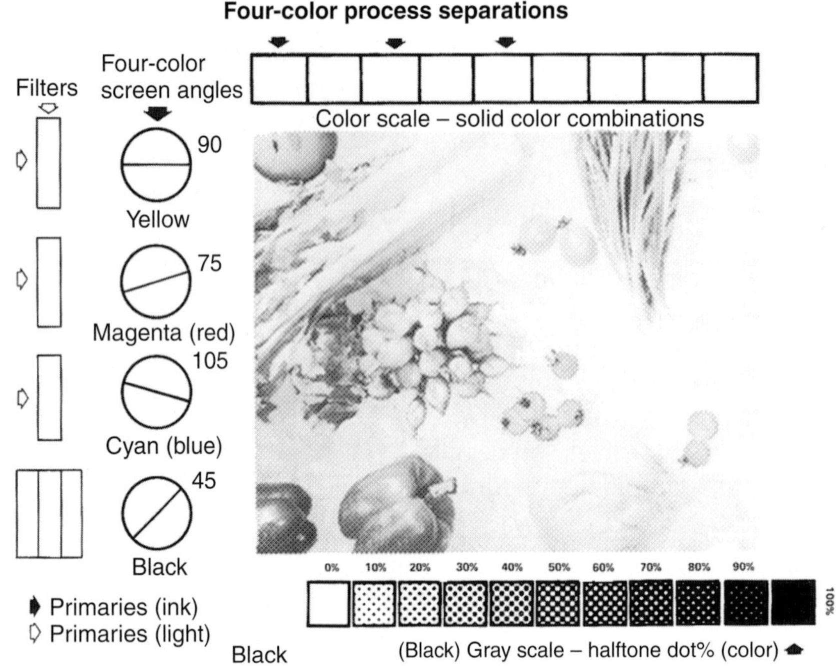

Figure 13-27. This chart shows the filters used for making color separations.

Wide band filters are color separation filters that are used to reproduce broader parts of the light spectrum. Some examples of wide band color separation filters include the No. 23-red or 29-red, No. 61-green, and No. 49B-blue. If wide band filters are used, it is recommended that the color separation system have a good masking technique.

Screen angles for color reproduction

Color reproduction uses four halftone negatives, each representing a different screen angle. The rotation of screen angles is designed to eliminate or minimize the undesirable moiré pattern. Each of the four screen angles is assigned to one of the separation colors.

Yellow is assigned to the 90° angle for two reasons. The first reason is that the 90° screen angle is only 15° away from the 75° and 105° angles that represent a moiré. The slight moiré is not noticeable when a light yellow pigment is used. The second reason is that the human eye aligns images either on a horizontal or vertical format, and the light yellow dot structure is not as visible. The normal screen angle assignments are illustrated in **Figure 13-28.**

When printing separations containing considerable amounts of flesh tones and brown, it is suggested that the magenta and black angles be exchanged. The 45° angle of the magenta when imposed with the yellow at 90° provides a very pleasing 45° pattern. Since there is often a minimal amount of black in the flesh tones, its conversion to a 75° angle is less objectionable.

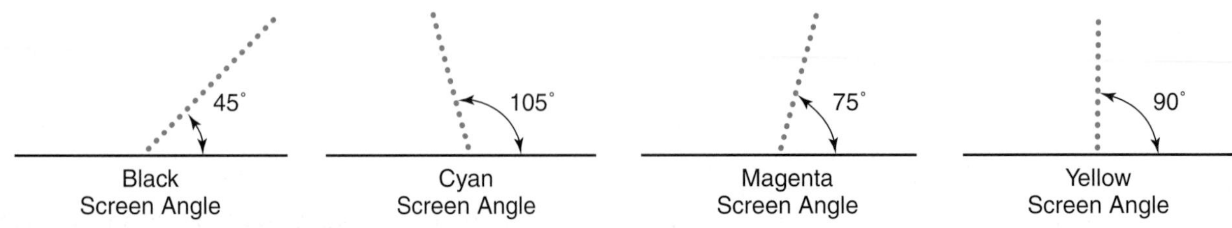

Figure 13-28. These are the normal screen angle assignments for color separations.

Black printer

In pure color reproduction theory, the three process color inks each subtract one color of the visible spectrum and reflect the other two. The difficulty with this theory lies in ink impurities. The inks used in the pressroom do not entirely absorb one part of the spectrum, and only reflect a percentage of the other two parts. For this reason, when the three subtractive primary pigments are overlapped, they do not produce black, but a dark brown color.

The process black printer serves a dual purpose. First, the *black printer* is used to extend the shadow details or density ranges. Printing a black ink density over the three primary colors will improve and enhance the shadow details of the reproduction. Second, the black ink provides fine detail outlines and simplifies register problems of the three primary color overprints. See **Figure 13-29.**

Figure 13-29. Effect of the black printer. A—The shadow areas of a three-color separation lack detail. B—The shadow areas in a four-color separation (using the black printer) have greater detail.

Direct screen color separation

Direct screen color separation is created when the halftone screening process is completed during the same color separation exposure. This is considered to be one of the fastest and most cost-effective techniques for creating color separations. The direct screen exposure can be color-corrected with masking techniques, or can be done with no color correction and the use of narrow band filters.

Depending on the original used and the aim points selected, pleasing color reproductions can be accomplished without color correction or masking. The systems of color correction are normally used to ensure facsimile reproduction of the original.

Direct screen separations can be accomplished by contact methods in a vacuum frame. This is the simplest technique and the equipment required is relatively inexpensive. The use of a contact frame will also assist in production when the cameras or enlargers are busy, as separations can be *ganged* (photographed) together. See **Figure 13-30.**

Figure 13-30. The contact frame and light source can be used for making direct screen color separations.

Another advantage of the contacting method is the filter requirements are not as critical as in the process camera. Older filters once used on the process camera can be used in the contact frame. Over time, filters tend to warp, change thickness, and fade in color. They should be discarded after a period of time. One major drawback to the contact method of direct screen separation is the one-to-one (1:1) size ratio during reproduction.

Direct camera separations are commonly produced on a process camera or a direct screen enlarger. The advantage to using these two pieces of equipment is the lens or optical system. Incorporating a lens will allow for changes in reproduction size, unlike the contact frame. These lenses are designed to photograph flat copy, either reflection or transparent, and are fully color-corrected to avoid lateral color aberration.

Indirect color separation

Indirect color separation requires two separate photographic operations. First, the original is color-separated through the appropriate filters, then the halftone screen is incorporated.

If a color correction system is used, masks are made from the original. Later the masks are used to produce the color separations on continuous tone film. The color-corrected continuous tone separation negatives can be modified or further corrected if necessary. The negatives are then converted to halftone positives using a contact screen.

The advantage of this system over the direct screen method is that size of the final film can be further reduced or enlarged during the screening phase. The indirect method is more complex and time-consuming, however, and it uses more film. See **Figure 13-31**.

The indirect method of color separation can be accomplished in a contact frame as well as with a process camera or enlarger. For the separation work, the use of continuous tone emulsions will require total darkness or altered safelighting conditions. The halftone screen exposures can be completed with ortho film and will require normal red safelights.

Special Effects

Many unusual special effects can be created photomechanically, by either a modification or conversion using standard techniques. These modifications and special effects are a designer's effort to capture an audience's attention.

For designers to properly use special effects, they must understand the photomechanical processes involved. Due to the processes involved, some original artwork lends itself to the desired effect better than other artwork. For this purpose, the designer and reproduction people must understand the limitations of the effects.

One of the simplest special effects is the use of special screens to produce a pattern on the halftone reproduction. Often, the special effect techniques, such as duotones as posterizations, are inexpensive attempts at imitating four-color process reproduction. Without the expense and time factor of color separations, many reproduction facilities can offer the client the impact of color through these special effects.

In some cases, the client will furnish only black-and-white photographs. Then the designer will find that more effect is needed to convey a message to an audience. This is where the applications of special effects photography becomes important to the industry.

Special screens

In addition to the normal square, elliptical, and round dot screens, there are special design, tint, or texture screens that can be used. *Steel etch, mezzo tint, straight line, wavy line*, and *concentric circle* are just a few of the more common special effect halftone screens that can be used. See **Figure 13-32**. The large assortment of special effect hard dot and contact screens provide the designer an easy and inexpensive means to create a new dimension, or to add appeal to the halftone.

Often, the use of tint and texture screens act as a background to an overprint. Type matter or a dense image may be photomechanically superimposed over a soft background. The same basic exposure tests must be done to work with these contact screens. **Figure 13-33** shows several special effect screens.

Duotone techniques

The *duotone* is a special effect that consists of making a two-color halftone reproduction from a single color image. Each halftone has a different screen angle and tone range of the continuous tone original. There are four different classifications of duotones.

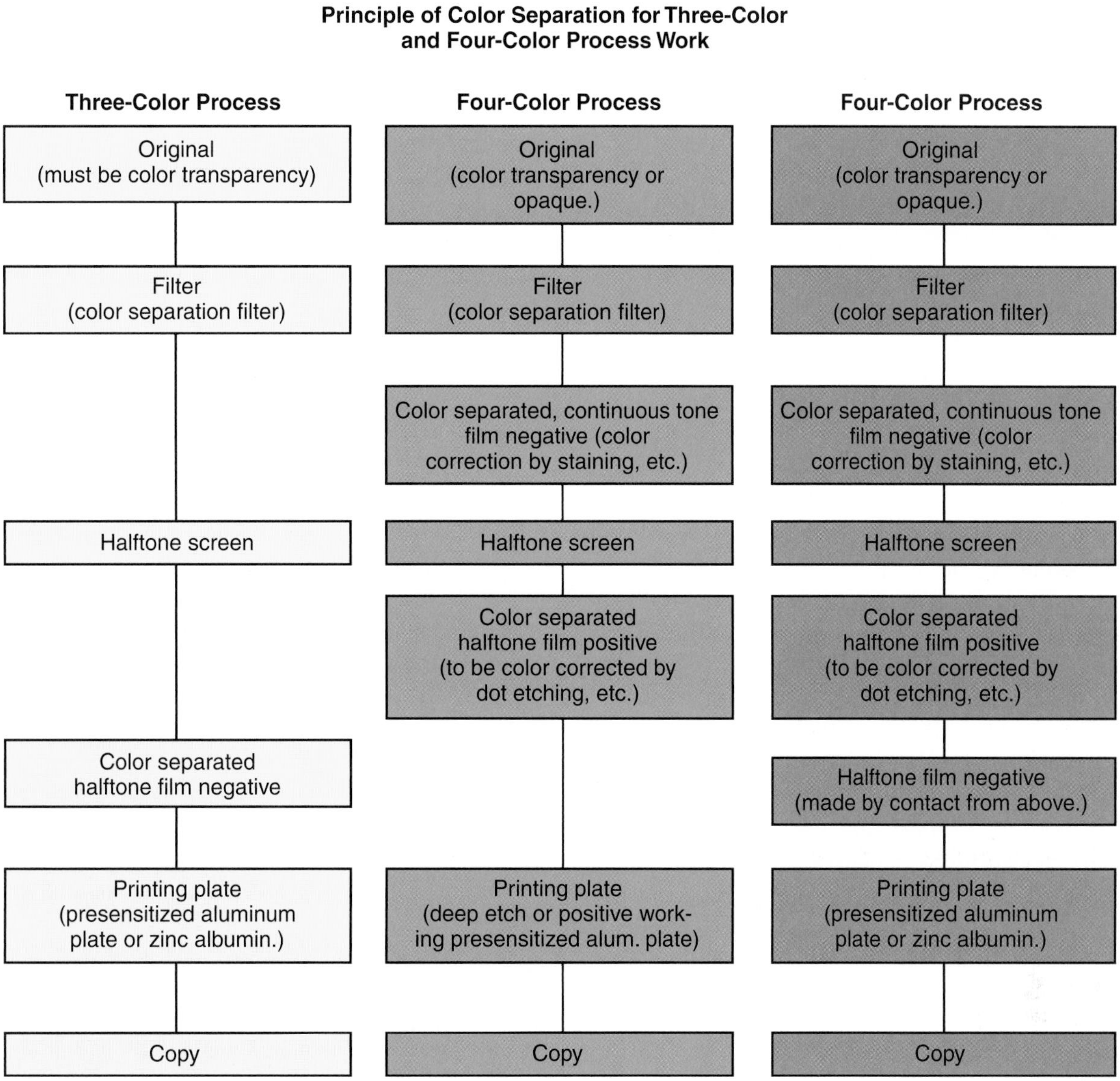

Principle of Color Separation for Three-Color and Four-Color Process Work

Three-Color Process	Four-Color Process	Four-Color Process
Original (must be color transparency)	Original (color transparency or opaque.)	Original (color transparency or opaque.)
Filter (color separation filter)	Filter (color separation filter)	Filter (color separation filter)
	Color separated, continuous tone film negative (color correction by staining, etc.)	Color separated, continuous tone film negative (color correction by staining, etc.)
Halftone screen	Halftone screen	Halftone screen
	Color separated halftone film positive (to be color corrected by dot etching, etc.)	Color separated halftone film positive (to be color corrected by dot etching, etc.)
Color separated halftone film negative		Halftone film negative (made by contact from above.)
Printing plate (presensitized aluminum plate or zinc albumin.)	Printing plate (deep etch or positive working presensitized alum. plate)	Printing plate (presensitized aluminum plate or zinc albumin.)
Copy	Copy	Copy

Figure 13-31. This diagram details the indirect color separation method.

Figure 13-32. Special effects screens, such as the mezzotint, can be used to alter an image.

Figure 13-33. There is a wide range of special effect screens available.

- A *two-impression black duotone*, sometimes referred to as a double-black.
- A *one color plus black duotone.*
- A *color on a second color duotone.*
- A *fake duotone*, usually constructed with a color tint screen value and a normal halftone overprint.

The designer can use duotones to create a mood or simulate process color separations. Duotone colors can add warm tones to a normal black-and-white illustration.

The difficulties in producing a desired effect or a successful duotone come from the camera operator's abilities in evaluating tone values. The camera operator is given a continuous tone original from which to make a full-tone normal halftone and a second skeleton or shadow detail halftone. The density value, where the skeleton or detail halftone starts to overlap the normal halftone, is the critical judgment or decision.

Another factor contributing to the success of a duotone is the choice of colors. In the realm of special effects, there are no hard rules, but past experience can offer suggestions to the novice.

For example, blues and greens will combine well with black for seascapes. But the designer must remember that a seashore in California is often sunny, depicting the color blue. The seascape in New England may be cloudy, and better represented with green hues. Warm hues, such as yellows and reds, are often appropriate for sunsets or sunrises.

Duotone production

The procedures used in the production of a duotone are similar to the normal halftone. The major difference will be in the angle of the halftone screen or original copy. To prevent a moiré pattern when printing two screen images at the same angle, rotate either the contact screen or original artwork. The contact screen can be purchased in different screen angles or as a circular screen to eliminate the need for measuring rotation.

It is best to rotate the screen rather than the copy because smaller film sizes can be used and the copyboard will not be moved. The screen angle difference between the two halftones should be 60° for elliptical dot screens and 30° for conventional or square dot screens.

Remember that for any multiple exposure of the same original, the copyboard percentage must *not* change. Even the slightest movement can cause registration problems. After exposing the two halftone images, process the film. Proof the final film negatives using any negative acting prepress proofing system.

Using a magnifying lens, determine if the dot structure creates the desired effect. The use of a reflection gray scale located next to the original copy during reproduction will assist in the final evaluation. See **Figure 13-34**.

Figure 13-34. This is a final printed duotone and a gray scale.

Two impression black duotones

The major reason for two impression black duotones is for exact facsimile reproduction of an original continuous tone photograph. Many professionally produced photographs have a maximum density of 1.85 and higher. The normal single impression of black ink, produces a press sheet density of about 1.40 to 1.60. The two-impression black duotone will more closely represent the tonal range of the original photo.

The first halftone negative should be exposed to reproduce nearly the entire range of the original. The highlight, midtones, and nearly all shadows should be represented on the first run. The second halftone negative should be extremely dense and reproduce only the midtones to the darkest shadows of the original. The overprint technique will improve the printed density value in the shadows.

To determine exposure times for the two halftones, simply calibrate the exposure computer as for a normal halftone. In evaluating the original, locate the whitest highlight and the almost darkest shadow. These density figures will be used with the exposure computer to determine the first halftone exposure requirements.

For the second, black printer (shadow detail halftone), select a midtone value on the original to be used for the main exposure requirement and the darkest shadow density for the flash exposure. The detail halftone should *not* reproduce the highlight values. This is to prevent white tones from becoming muddy or too dense.

One-color plus black duotone

The one-color plus black duotone is often referred to as a *true color duotone*. This is perhaps the most common duotone used in design work. The use of color with black details creates moods and almost simulates four-color process reproduction. The creative judgment of the designer or camera operator becomes more critical with this type of duotone.

The procedures used in the production of a one-color plus black duotone are the same as outlined for the two impression black duotone. The first halftone will represent the entire tonal range of the original from highlight to shadow, and will be the assigned color. The second halftone will represent a selected midtone to shadow range. As the black printer, it will add the details. See **Figure 13-35**.

Color on a second color duotone

Using process color inks, the designer and camera operator can create a visually stimulating effect. The choice of colors will depend upon the desired results. The selection of color hues should exhibit contrast to ensure all the details are visually reproduced. The technique for the process of color-on-color duotones is the same as for color-on-black.

Figure 13-35. This is an example of a one-color plus black duotone.

Fake duotone techniques

Fake duotone is a technique of producing a two-color reproduction from a single halftone and a halftone screen tint, instead of producing a true duotone from two different halftone negatives. The fake duotone simulates a color and black duotone or a color-on-color duotone. It is an inexpensive way to add color appearance on the printed work. See **Figure 13-36**.

The original photograph should have good contrast because the highlight value will be the background screen tint value. In a fake duotone, the full-tone halftone (black) overprints a 10%-20% screen tint (color). The fake duotone is practical for layouts requiring many duotone images.

Posterization

Posterization is the technique of changing a black-and-white, continuous tone photo into a multicolor or multitone reproduction. In this process, the continuous tone original must be

Figure 13-36. This is an example of a fake duotone. Compare it to Figure 13-35.

Figure 13-37. When making a posterization, the original image must have good contrast and plenty of detail.

converted into selected tone values. These selected tone values should enhance the details of the original continuous tone. The abstract reproduction should attract the attention of an individual by virtue of color or contrast.

The success of the posterization technique will greatly depend upon the proper selection of the original continuous tone photograph. See **Figure 13-37**. An ideal black-and-white photograph should have good contrast, with fine line detail. Photo texture or grain can also be useful for posterization.

Posterization classifications

There are four classifications of posterization. They are classified by the selected number of tone values or colors of ink. A posterization may involve different colors of ink or different tone values using a hard dot tint screen. The number of tone values or colors can include the paper substrate for the posterization. For the purposes of this description, the paper surface or color will be considered a tone or color value.

- **Two-tone posterization**. A line reproduction of a continuous tone original that is printed on a white or colored sheet of paper. See **Figure 13-38**.
- **Three-tone or three-color posterization**. Consists of two reproductions of the original, each having a different density, that will overprint the paper value. See **Figure 13-39**.
- **Four-tone or four-color posterization**. A reproduction of the original using three

Figure 13-38. This two-tone posterization is a line reproduction of a continuous tone original.

Figure 13-39. This is an example of a three-tone posterization.

films, each with a different density. The density of these films can be controlled by either exposure or development. The three films can be represented on the paper with colors of ink or tint screen values.

- **Multiple-tone posterization**. Posterization with more than four tones or colors. These are created using techniques similar to three-tone and four-tone posterizations. However, the most popular posterizations, from the design and economy standpoint, are the three-tone and four-tone posterizations.

Posterization techniques

There are three different techniques for reproducing a photomechanical posterization of a continuous tone photograph. Alternative posterization methods use screen tints or positives.

Using percentages of basic line exposure. Probably the simplest method of producing a posterization is to use different percentages of the basic line exposure and controlled processing. This technique is the easiest and fastest of the three methods. However, it does not afford predictable results in the separation of tone values.

Select a suitable black-and-white photograph with good contrast, fine detail, and a subject matter that is recognizable *without* all the middle tone values. For the purposes of explanation, the example of a four-tone posterization will be identified as the white paper plus yellow, red, and black ink. The required line exposures will be based on a percentage of the normal basic line exposure.

For the four-tone posterization, three film negatives will be required. The exposures will be at 50%, 150%, and 300% of the normal line exposure. For example, if the normal line exposure is 20 seconds

(20 units) at f/22, the exposures required to make the different tone values in this posterization would be 10 units, 30 units, and 60 units.

After making the three different film exposures, process the film following manufacturer's recommended time and temperature. Agitation can be controlled by processing all three sheets of film simultaneously. After washing and drying the film, examine the density differences on a light table. See **Figure 13-40**.

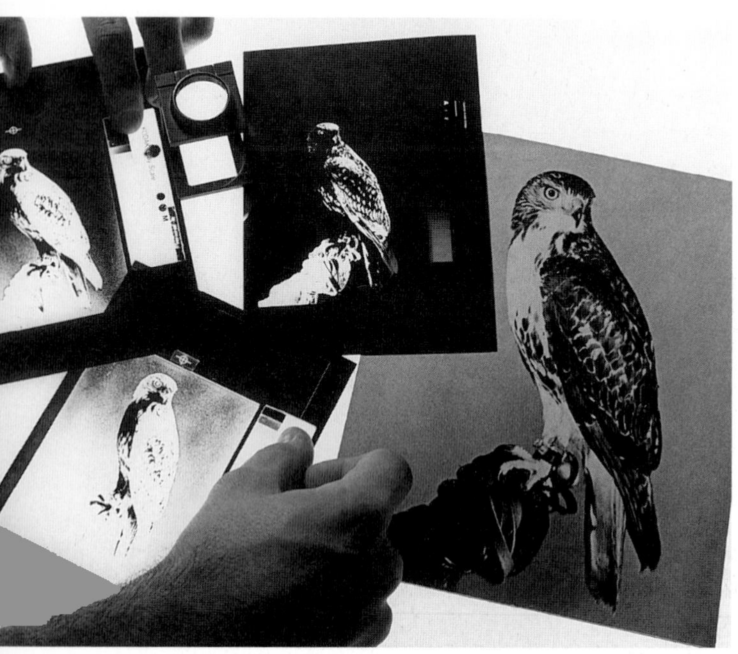

Figure 13-40. Before making a posterization, the negatives must be evaluated by measuring their densities.

To determine the success of the four-tone posterization, proof the film negatives with any negative-acting prepress proof system. The negative with the least density (50% exposure) will be assigned the lightest color pigment (in this case, yellow). The 150% exposure negative with medium density will be red and the darkest negative will be for the black or detail printer. Mount the prepress color proof on the selected paper stock for final evaluation. A color key proof can be used to make the final evaluation of the posterization. See **Figure 13-41**.

Using a reflection gray scale and inspection processing. The second method of producing a posterization involves a reflection gray scale. It will

Figure 13-41. A color key proof can be used to make the final evaluation of the posterization.

allow the camera operator more control in determining the starting point for tone values.

The selected original is evaluated prior to reproduction with the tone values on the gray scale. The camera operator will select a highlight value on the photo where the first color (yellow) of a four-tone posterization will appear. Next, the selected highlight value is matched to a gray scale step. This will later become the quality control step used when processing the film. See **Figure 13-42**. Use the same cross-evaluation technique to identify the midtone and shadow values.

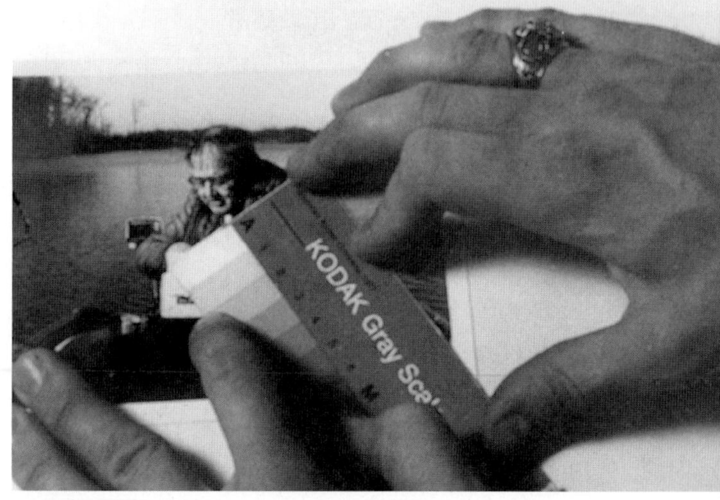

Figure 13-42. A gray scale can be used to match the selected highlight densities when making a posterization.

When making the posterization, the basic line exposure time will be given for all three pieces of film (highlight, midtone, and shadow). To process the film, use the selected gray scale steps in determining length of development for each negative. After processing is complete, evaluate the negatives on a light table. Remember that opaquing or scribing of images can be done on line reproductions to enhance the results.

Again, the use of a prepress proofing system will allow for final evaluation of the posterization on the selected paper stock, which is the fourth-tone value in this case. The lightest pigment color should usually be assigned to the negative with the least density or development time.

Using reflection density values and a halftone calculator. The third method of producing a posterization will provide the most control and consistency in results through the use of a halftone calculator. Refer to Figure 13-19.

In this procedure, evaluate the original photo with either a reflection gray scale or a reflection densitometer to determine a density value for the different tone values. For example, if the camera operator selects a midtone value for a tint or color, then that color or tint will appear on any location in the reproduction where the density value or higher values appear.

To use a halftone calculator, first calibrate the device by rotating the dials to align the basic line exposure with the normal gray scale density step used for processing, usually around 0.30 for density (4th step). After precalibrating the halftone calculator with the normal development density and basic line exposure, identify exposure times by reading across from the different selected densities. If the calculator does not have dials as illustrated, program it with the same data. Then, follow manufacturer's instructions to call up specific density exposure combinations.

To produce the required negatives for a specific predetermined density value, use the calculated exposures and process by film manufacturer's time and temperature specifications.

Remember that in tray processing, the still development technique will bring out more details from the continuous tone copy. This method of posterization is more complicated than the two previous methods. However, it is more accurate in the multiple color or tint screen posterizations. For the final evaluation, use the same information and proofing techniques described for the other two posterization methods.

Using tint screens. This is an alternative posterization method, because most posterizations are created for color applications. Tint screens are substituted if color is too expensive or not a part of the design. Hard dot tint screens, *not* halftone contact screens, come in different percentages and may create the illusion of specific gray tones.

A 10% tint screen (light gray) may be used in place of a light pigment such as yellow ink. The 40% tint can be used as a midtone and a solid black for fine details. The dot percentage represents the ink value on paper. If tint screens are used, the percentage values must be far enough apart to differentiate the tone values.

The tint screens must be rotated or angled to prevent the visually distasteful moiré pattern. Some examples of incorrect screen angles and the resulting moiré patterns are pictured in **Figure 13-43**. The use of an angle indicator will help to align the rows of dots. A 30° rotation or angle difference is suggested. **Figure 13-44** shows how a 30° triangle can be used to set the screen angle.

Using positives. Another alternative effect can be created in the posterization using film positives contacted from the line negatives. In selected cases, the positives will fill in the background areas with color or tint values. The use of positives can create very abstract and different effects. However, this should be reserved for specific design applications.

To make the positive, first select the line negative that best enhances the desired effect. Then, make a contact in the vacuum frame. Position a

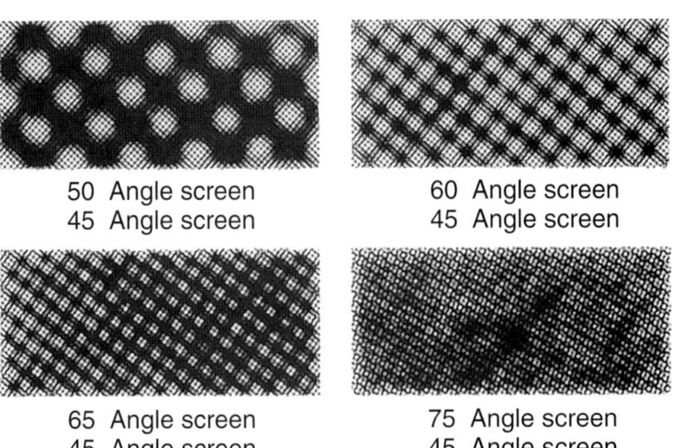

Figure 13-43. These screen angles have created unwanted moiré patterns.

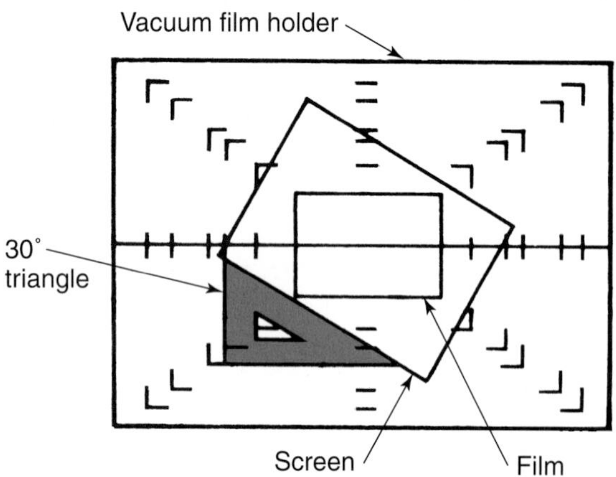

Figure 13-44. A 30° triangle can be used to set the screen angle on the copyboard.

fresh piece of film with its emulsion up. Position the selected line negative with its emulsion facing up.

With the negative emulsion up, the positive will have the same film orientation as the negative. After processing the film positive, use a prepress proof to evaluate the desired effect.

Figure 13-45. A tone-line reproduction only shows an outline of the original image.

Tone-line process

The ***tone-line process*** is used to convert continuous-tone originals into line reproductions that resemble pen-and-ink sketches or other fine-line drawings. In other words, it is used to create a detailed outline reproduction of a continuous tone original. This effect will remove the gray tone values. See **Figure 13-45.**

The original tone-line process involves a line conversion technique using a continuous tone, ortho-chromatic film. Processing of this film in a continuous tone developer will yield a high-contrast negative image of the original continuous tone. Contacting this film negative with fresh ortho film then produces a line positive.

The line negative and positive, sandwiched with several sheets of mylar or acetate, are contacted to produce a spread or *fatty* on film or photographic paper. The contacting procedure involves a light source at an angle with the contact sandwich being spun on a turntable.

Another modification of this tone-line process is called a bas-relief image. The *bas-relief image* is a special effect obtained by making a positive similar to the tone-line. However, the sandwiched negative and positive images are intentionally positioned slightly *out of register*.

Yet another method of producing a tone-line image is to select a high-contrast, fine-line, continuous tone original. The original can be either color or black-and-white. Either reflection or transparent copy will work. Using either a camera or enlarger, produce four different line negatives on panchromatic high-contrast film. Each negative should be exposed to reproduce a specific density value of the original. Later, make contact positives of each of the four line negatives.

Using a light table, evaluate different combinations of a negative and positive until the desired effect is achieved. With tape or pin register, position the films base-to-base over a piece of fresh ortho film in a contact frame. Using a point light source, expose the ortho film with several thicknesses of diffusion sheeting over the tone-line films. Process the final film and the tone-line effect will be complete.

Diffusion transfer modifications

Many special effects can be created by using diffusion transfer products. Diffusion transfer modifications can include posterization, multiple exposures or transfers, and the phantom halftone. See **Figure 13-46**. The use of special effect screens can produce prescreened halftone images. The use

Figure 13-46. Using a diffusion transfer process, this phantom halftone with an overprint of text can be created.

Figure 13-47. This photo has been altered using a diffusion transfer process.

of tint screens during the different posterization exposures will produce the complete effect on one piece of photographic paper. See **Figure 13-47**.

Because of the nature of most diffusion transfer products, the receiver sheet will keep accepting the silver transfer images from new sheets of negative paper. Thus, multiple images or overprints are easy to produce with this method of reproduction.

One popular technique using a receiver sheet and two exposed negative sheets is called ***phantom halftones***, or ***ghost halftones***. To create the phantom halftone, a continuous tone image is converted through normal halftone procedures. However, the flash exposure is increased 4-5 times the calibrated exposure time. More light striking the diffusion transfer material will decrease the density to form a weak halftone image when transferred to the receiver sheet. Using a registration system, the type matter or overprint image is then photographed under normal conditions using a fresh piece of negative paper.

After carefully aligning the new exposed negative paper with the previously processed receiver sheet, reprocess the materials in the processor. Wait the recommended development time and separate the two sheets. The desired effect can then be evaluated.

Review Questions

Do not write in this book. Write your answers on a separate sheet of paper.

1. The term _____ refers to the degree of blackness or light-stopping ability.
2. What is the difference between a high-key and a low-key photo?
3. What is a *densitometer*?
4. Why must a continuous tone photo be converted into a halftone for printing?
5. A halftone screen is used to record different size dots that represent _____ values (whites), _____ values (grays), and _____ values (blacks).
6. What are the four classifications of camera copy?
7. _____ copy includes photos, oil paintings, chalk or charcoal renderings, and watercolor work.
   a. Reflection
   b. Transparent
   c. Transmission
   d. Either b or c.

8. _____ copy includes 35 mm slides or large-format transparencies.
   a. Reflection
   b. Transmission
   c. Transparent
   d. Either b or c.
9. Explain the difference between halftone-grade film and line film.
10. How do you prevent a moiré pattern?
11. Highlight dots will usually be _____% to _____% in size, the midtone will be _____% to _____%, and the shadow dots will be _____% to _____%.
12. Explain *screen dot shapes*.
13. The _____ exposure is considered a supplementary exposure used to form shadow details.
14. _____ is the process of using blue, green, and red filters to divide the many colors of an original image into the three process colors (cyan, magenta, and yellow) and black.
15. Explain the function of the red, green, and blue filters.
16. What are four types of duotones?
17. Why is it better to rotate the screen rather than the copy when making a duotone?
18. _____ is the technique of changing a black-and-white, continuous tone image into a multicolor or multitone reproduction.
19. What is the simplest method of producing a posterization?
20. Define the *tone-line process*.

Processing Photographic Material

14

Learning Objectives

After studying this chapter, you will be able to:

- Identify the equipment needed to process film.
- Summarize the chemical solutions necessary to process film.
- State the precautions to follow when mixing and working with chemicals.
- Explain manual and automatic developing processes.

Important Terms

automatic film processing
contact printing
darkroom
developer
fixer
imagesetter
manual film processing
roomlight
safelight
stop bath

A latent image is created when a light source reflects the image from the original copy through a camera lens on to a photosensitive material (film). The latent image can also be produced electronically using a scanner or digital camera, a computer, and an imagesetter. No matter how the latent image is produced on the film, it must be processed to make the image permanent.

Processing film can be done manually or automatically. In the printing industry, tray processing is the most common manual processing method. Automatic processing is intended for high-volume output and consistent quality. However, before these processing techniques are described in detail, the processing equipment should be understood completely.

Darkroom

A ***darkroom*** is a light-tight chamber in which film is handled and processed. See **Figure 14-1**. A darkroom is used to develop film, make contact prints, and do other work that cannot be done in roomlight (normal or white light). ***Roomlight*** is the normal, full spectrum light found in areas other than a darkroom. Any roomlight in the darkroom could expose and ruin the film and the latent image. A ***safelight*** is a darkroom light that has a limited spectral composition that will not expose or fog a specific film type. Safelights, as well as other darkroom equipment, are essential in processing film.

Darkroom equipment

A darkroom is usually equipped with an exposure device, processing unit (processing sink and trays, or automatic film processor), film dryer,

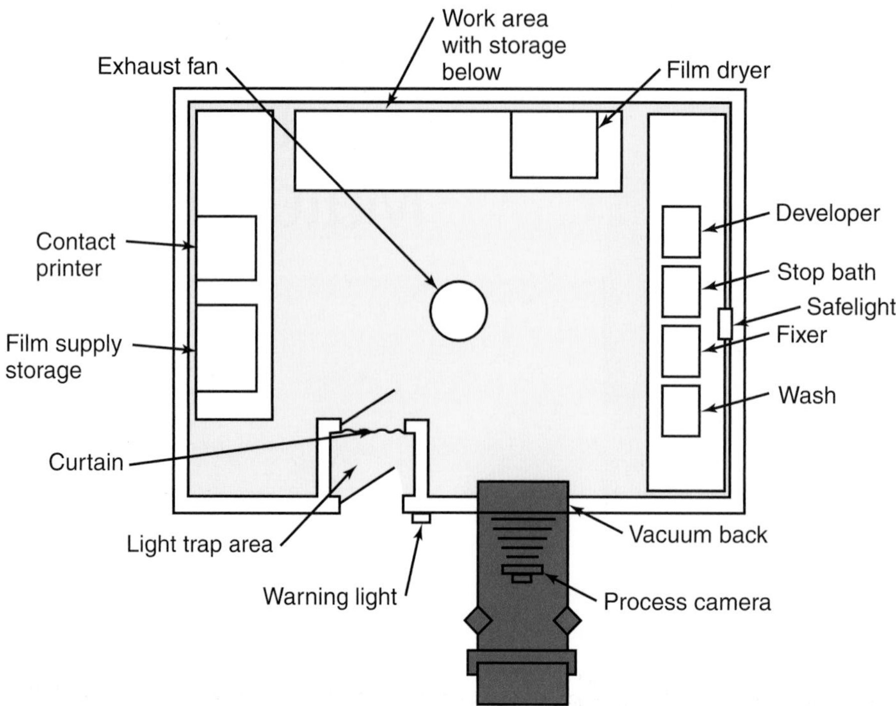

Figure 14-1. This is the general layout of a darkroom that is set up for manual film processing.

storage cabinets, work area, safelights, ventilation system, and special light-excluding entrance. A complete understanding of this equipment is essential before processing is attempted.

Exposure device

The exposure device can be a process camera (horizontal or vertical), a contact printer, or an imagesetter. Vertical cameras or contact printers are commonly used, but they require extra darkroom space. This is somewhat of a disadvantage. The horizontal process camera is referred to as the *darkroom camera,* because the *film back* (for loading, holding, and exposing film) is enclosed in the darkroom. The film back has a vacuum device for drawing the film down tight. See **Figure 14-2**. The rest of the camera is located outside the darkroom—this saves on darkroom space.

Figure 14-2. The film back of a horizontal process camera is normally located inside darkroom. The film can be loaded and unloaded in safelight area.

An ***imagesetter*** is a device that is used to output electronically-created latent images. See **Figure 14-3**. Many imagesetters are located outside the darkroom and the processor input is located in the darkroom. In this case, the exposed photographic material is contained in a light-tight cartridge, which is removed from the imagesetter and transported to the processor. Other imagesetters are combined with the processor or have the *capability* of being combined with the processor as one unit. These units are usually light-tight, so they do not have to be located in the darkroom.

Figure 14-3. This imagesetter has the capability to process eight-page imposed, punched, and plate-ready film. It also has the automatic film loading and unloading, and support for on-line film processing.
(Fuji Photo Film U.S.A., Inc.)

Processing sink

The *processing sink* holds the processing trays (containing the developing chemicals) used for *manually* processing film. Some factors to consider when buying a sink are the size of tray to be used, ease of cleaning, level of corrosion resistance, proper draining, ease of installation, and maintenance requirements. Stainless steel and fiberglass processing sinks are the two most popular types. Temperature controls are essential to maintain the proper cooling or heating of the water in the sink.

Processing trays

Processing trays hold the chemicals for manually processing film. These trays come in various sizes. Stainless steel and plastic are the most common tray materials. However, stainless steel trays can be quite expensive.

Automatic film processor

An *automatic film processor* is a mechanical device used to develop the latent image. Some of these processors feed exposed film over rollers and through baths and a dryer to produce a developed image. Others process electronically-created latent images in a similar manner, but the output may be film, paper, or plates.

Automatic processors are found in many high-volume facilities. Where consistency and control are essential, they must be considered.

Film dryer

A *film dryer* is used for rapid moisture removal from film. Dryers are available in various sizes and styles. See **Figure 14-4**. Some facilities use the simple system of hanging up film to air-dry.

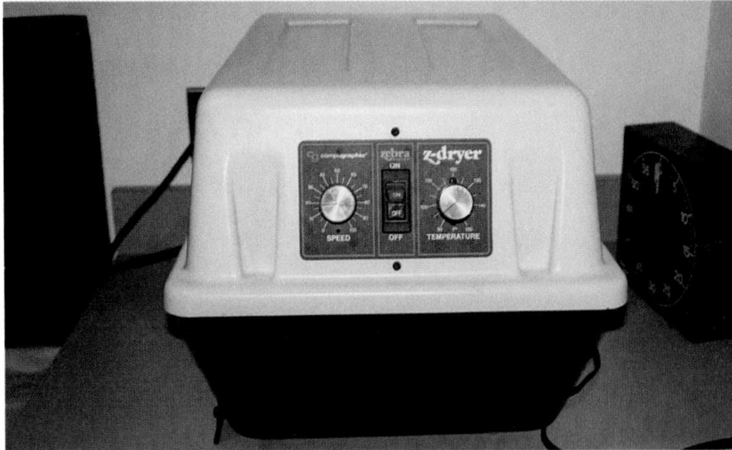

Figure 14-4. A film dryer will speed up the film processing operation.

Storage cabinets

Proper storage of chemicals and photosensitive materials is essential for an efficient and effective darkroom. Most chemicals require a cool, dry area. Film is stored in film storage cabinets or, in some cases, a refrigerator.

Store chemicals and photosensitive materials separately. Storage of both in the same area might affect film emulsions.

Work area

Sufficient countertop working area in the darkroom is very desirable. This area provides room for equipment, such as trimmers, cutters, or densitometers.

Safelight

As previously mentioned, *safelights* are darkroom lights that have a limited spectral composition to prevent exposing or fogging film.

See **Figure 14-5**. The type of safelight is determined by the specific type of film (photosensitive emulsion) that will be used in the darkroom. It may be necessary to have several different safelight filters available if different types of light-sensitive materials will be processed.

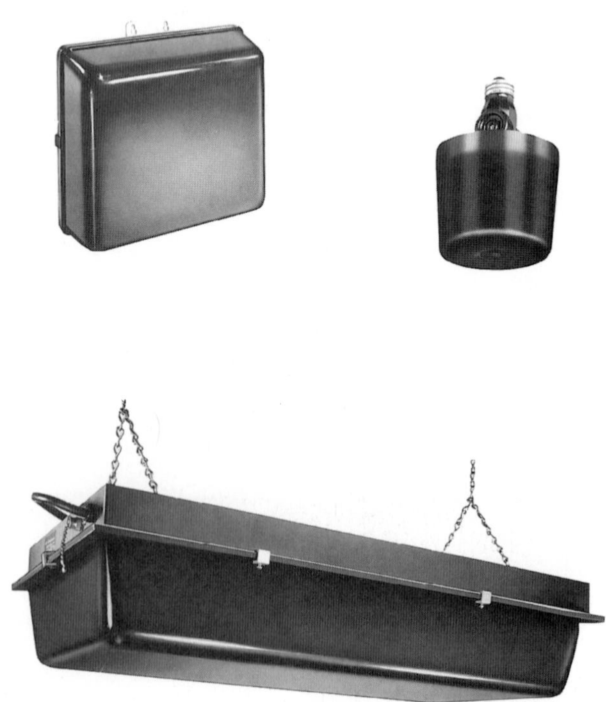

Figure 14-5. Many types of safelights are available for working with film. Selection of the correct type and color for the film being processed is important. (nuArc company, inc.)

Darkroom ventilation

Proper *ventilation* is required to prevent a buildup of chemical fumes in the darkroom. The amount of air exchange is set by federal, state, and local regulations. These regulations must be followed to be in compliance with the law. Some ventilation systems remove dust particles, as well as the chemical fumes, from the air. Dust removal is important for quality assurance and safety in the darkroom.

Do not work with darkroom chemicals in an unventilated area. Chemical fumes can be harmful if they are inhaled. Refer to Chapter 2 for more safety information.

Darkroom entrances

By definition, a darkroom is to be light-tight. So the darkroom entrance must *not* let light enter the room. There are a number of light-excluding entrance sizes and types. See **Figure 14-6**. The entrance used primarily depends on the facility.

One of the simplest accesses to a darkroom is the open passage. The *C-type* or *S-type entrance* is often used when ventilation or rapid entry and exit are considerations. However, this entrance requires extra space.

A *revolving door entrance* is also very popular. The advantage of revolving doors is they require very little space. On the other hand, they can be quite expensive.

The *double-door entrance* is another means of making the darkroom light-tight. It requires less space than an open passage, but opening both doors at one time can be a problem. Sometimes, a curtain (darkroom cloth) is used in place of one or both the doors.

A variation of the double-door entrance is the *curtain-type entrance*. This type of entrance has double doors, but also has a curtain between the two doors.

Processing Chemicals

Chemicals are necessary to process light-sensitive materials. Many different kinds of light-sensitive materials are on the market today. The manufacturers of these materials recommend processing chemicals.

Properly mixing and diluting processing chemicals, such as developer, stop bath, and fixing solution, is critical. Each manufacturer has a recommended procedure. Exact measurement is important to assure consistency. All chemical containers must be clearly labeled.

The containers for mixing and holding chemicals must be clean. Contamination can be a problem if someone is careless. If the same container and stirring rods are used for each chemical, make sure they are thoroughly cleaned before the mixing of each chemical.

Whenever mixing chemicals and water, always add the chemicals to the water. Extreme care must be taken not to splash the liquid. Developer and other chemicals often tend to irritate the skin. If possible, use tongs or wear gloves that are compatible with the solutions.

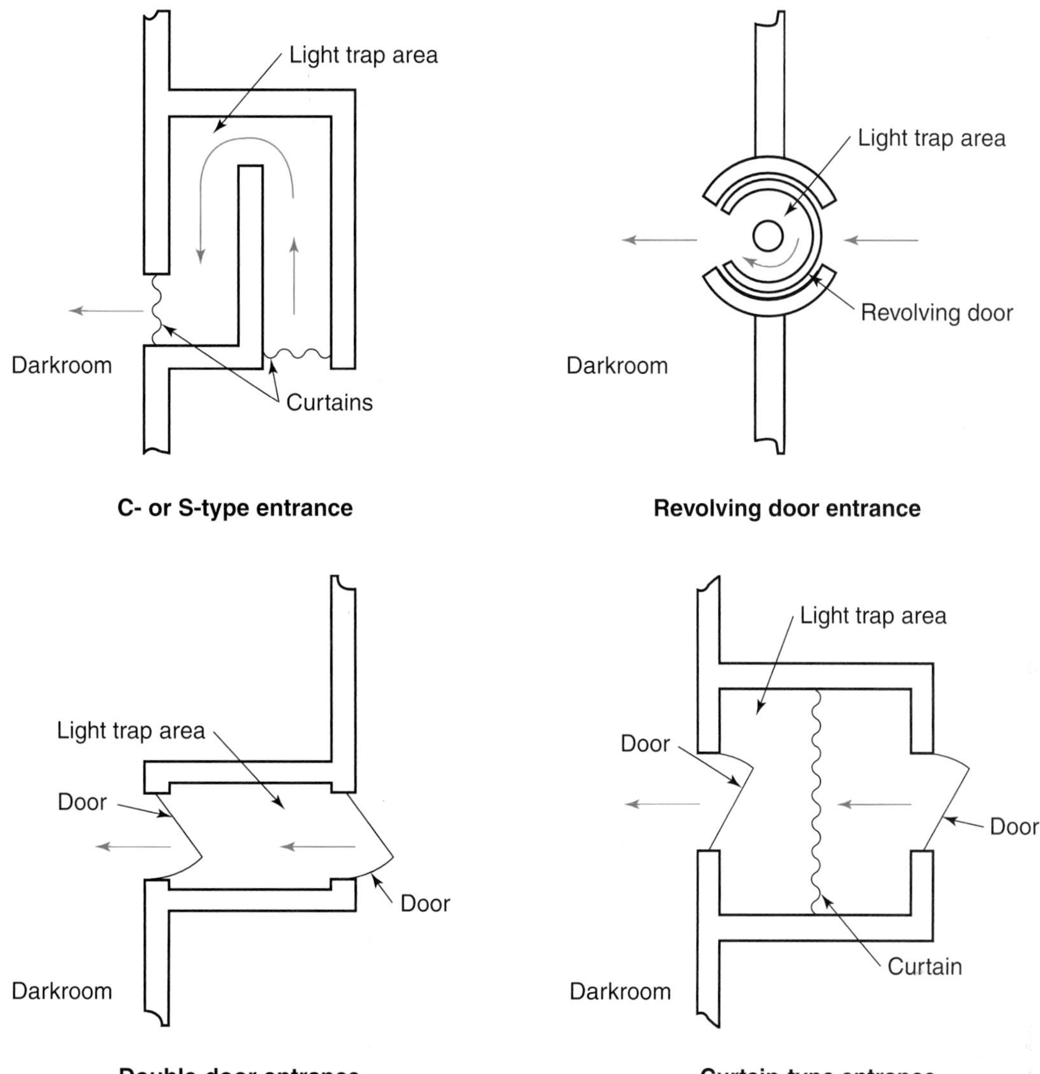

Figure 14-6. The darkroom entrance must be light-tight. There are a number of darkroom entrance configurations.

Developer solution

Several chemical ingredients, in addition to water, make up the developer solution. Each has a specific and important purpose. The developer may be purchased in either powder or liquid form, but either type must be mixed with water. When mixing, extreme care must be taken not to splash the liquid or breathe dust from the powder. The water acts as the *vehicle* to carry the other chemicals that actually develop the silver bromide crystals in the film. The water also has the function of swelling the film gelatin so the solution can easily reach the crystals.

The major ingredient is the ***developing agent***, which is a chemical compound that makes the latent image visible. This is accomplished by changing the silver halide crystals to dark black metallic silver. The developing agent works best in combination with an accelerator. An ***accelerator*** is an alkaline solution used to activate the developing agent. The development of the photographic material becomes more rapid when the alkalinity of the solution is increased.

Developing agents are very susceptible to oxidation. The oxygen in the water and air destroys the developing agent. When this occurs, developing action stops. Another chemical, called a ***preservative***, must be added to stop oxidation. A typical preservative is *sodium sulfite*.

Still another chemical, called a ***restrainer***, is necessary to lessen the fogging tendency of film. *Fogging* means that the unexposed silver crystals have a tendency to develop (turn black) in the developing solution. A typical restrainer is *potassium bromide*.

Again, proper mixing of chemicals is essential. Follow the manufacturer's instructions. Proper measurement is critical. When measuring liquids, place the vessel on a level surface and view it at eye level. See **Figure 14-7**.

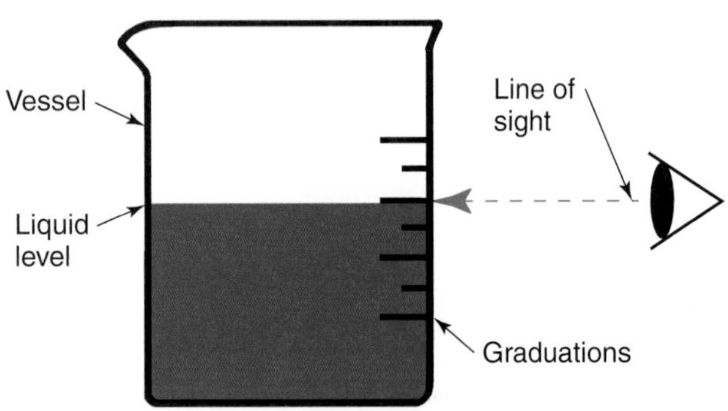

Figure 14-7. Proper measurement technique is critical when mixing processing chemicals. When measuring liquids, hold the vessel so that eye level is even with the graduations.

Once the developer solution is mixed, place the recommended amount in the developer tray. Most film manufacturers recommend that the temperature of the developer be at 68°F (20°C).

Stop bath

The ***stop bath*** is an acetic acid rinse used to neutralize the developer solution remaining on the film. To make the stop bath, use approximately 2 oz. (59 ml) of 28% acetic acid, added to 1 gal. (3.78 l) of water. Prepared liquid stop bath solutions, ready for dilution with water, are also available.

Even though acetic acid is one of the safer acids, care must still be taken when mixing chemicals. Always pour acid into water, not water into acid. This makes splashing less likely.

If a chemical is accidentally splashed in your face, it may cause painful eye or skin burns. Immediately go to the nearest eyewash station. Always wear eye protection, gloves, and a chemical apron when working with chemicals.

Fixer

A ***fixer*** is a solution that makes the developed film image permanent. The prime purpose of the *fixer* is to dissolve the remaining unexposed silver in the emulsion. The chemical that dissolves out the exposed crystals is usually *sodium thiosulfate*. Fixer is sometimes referred to as *hypo*, which comes from the chemical (potassium hyposulfite) formerly used for fixing.

A preservative, such as sodium sulfite, is used in fixer to stop the formation of sulfur compounds, and acetic acid or boric acid also may be added to help eliminate sludge.

The newly developed film emulsion is soft and easily damaged, so a hardening agent is often part of the fixer solution. The *hardener* makes the emulsion more compact and dense.

Manual Film Processing

Film processing is a critical operation because of the many variables involved. The object is to photographically convert the image with precise and predictable results. A gray scale is used as an aim point to provide quality control and assure consistency. This step will be illustrated after describing how the film is developed.

As previously mentioned, film processing can be done manually or automatically, with *tray processing* being the most common manual processing method. Although machine processing is becoming more prevalent, tray processing is still very evident in small facilities. It is still used for specialized processing and as a backup for machine processing. The steps for tray processing are develop, stop, fix, wash, and dry. See **Figure 14-8**.

Using developer

Insert the exposed film in the developer with the emulsion side up. Not all manufacturers recommend the emulsion-up method, but this eliminates the possibility of the tray scratching the film. See **Figure 14-9**. At this point, the emulsion is soft and is very susceptible to damage. Some workers first lay the film emulsion-side-down on the surface of the developer. The film is then flipped over and processing is done emulsion-up.

Agitation, time, temperature, and developer strength will all affect film processing. They are critical considerations when developing film because image areas of a black-and-white film negative should remain clear while nonimage areas must turn black.

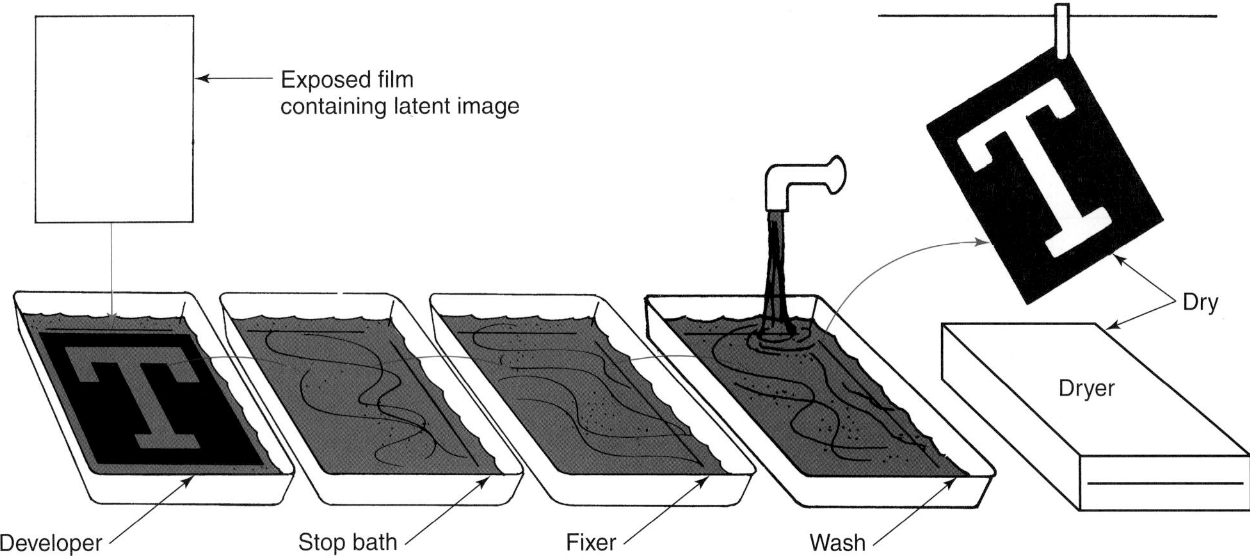

Figure 14-8. Most film processing techniques require development, stop bath, fixing, washing, and then drying. This shows the normal arrangement for manual tray processing set up.

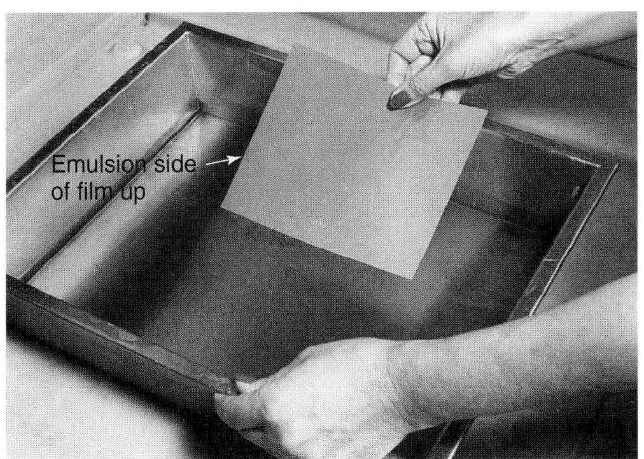

Figure 14-9. Film is normally placed in developing solution with the emulsion side up. This helps prevent scratches on emulsion from contact with the tray.

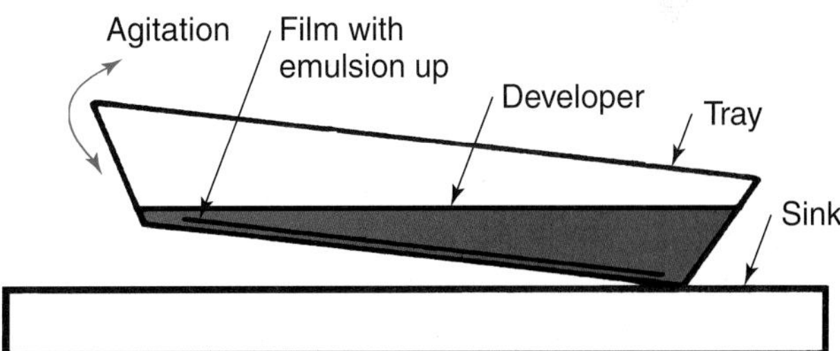

Figure 14-10. Agitation is commonly used to prevent exhausting the chemicals in some areas of the image. Agitation keeps fresh chemicals in contact with all image areas to provide full development.

Manufacturers normally recommend that the developer tray be continually rocked or moved in a circular motion. This is called *agitation*. See **Figure 14-10**. The main reason for agitation is to keep the developer strength evenly distributed during the development of the film. If the tray is left stationary, the image areas requiring more development than others will exhaust the chemicals directly in contact with them. Development in those areas would stop. Always have enough developer to completely cover the film.

The manufacturer will give the recommended development time. This development time is based on developer mixed according to their specifications. The temperature of the solution is also important. As previously mentioned, it is recommended that developer be at 68°F (20°C).

A timer can be used to make sure the film is developed for the required time. Agitation should be done until the development time has been reached (typically about 2 1/2 minutes) or the proper gray scale step (aim point) has appeared. The *gray scale* is a sensitivity guide that is developed along with the film to show when the film has reached an acceptable density. The data sheets distributed by each manufacturer will give recommended densities. A solid (black, not gray) step four, on a 12-step gray scale, might be a typical recommendation. See **Figure 14-11**.

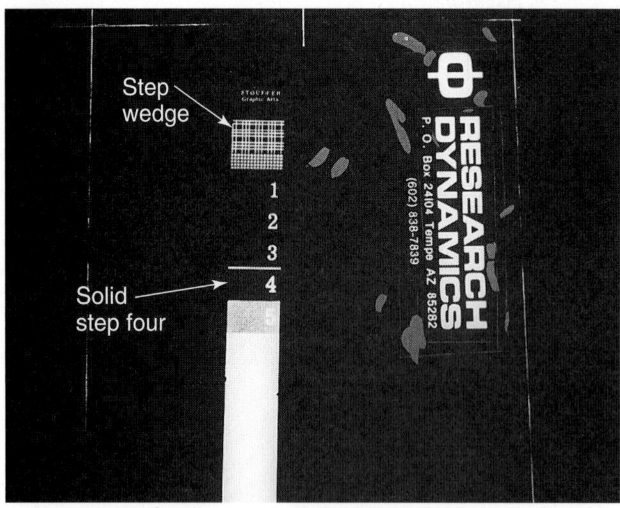

Figure 14-11. Step wedge is a control device for checking development. When the wedge is exposed and developed along with the image, a step four that is solid black should result. This is a quality control method that indicates proper exposure and development.

Figure 14-12. To avoid developer carryover, slowly slide film out of developer so that chemical drains back into tray.

Developer weakens with every processed piece of film. Manufacturers usually specify how many square inches of film can be processed in a given amount of developer. Developer also oxidizes very rapidly. While not in use, the developer tray should be covered with a piece of plastic wrap or another covering to exclude air. This will increase the life of the developer.

Proper handling of the film is also a basic requirement. Every piece of film must be developed in the same manner. Once the film is developed to the proper density, it should be removed from the developer and placed in the stop bath. Transfer as little developer as possible into the stop bath. The best way to remove the film from the developer tray is to take one of its corners and slowly draw the film over the edge of the tray. See **Figure 14-12**. This allows most of the solution to drain back into the developer tray. When tongs or gloves are used, be careful to avoid contamination of solutions. Wash your utensils thoroughly before placing them in any solution.

Still-tray development

As the name implies, *still-tray development* is a technique in which the tray is *not* agitated during the developing process. It is used for heavy and fine line work and sometimes for halftone processing.

Place the film in the developing solution with the emulsion side up. Agitate it briefly, then leave it without movement. The manufacturer of the developing solution or the film will have recommended still times. Once the development time is over, remove the film from the developer and place it in the stop bath. From this point on, the steps are identical to the agitated-tray development process.

Using stop bath

Once the film is placed in the stop bath (emulsion-side-up), five to ten seconds usually is sufficient time to stop all developing action. The time for the stop bath varies with the manufacturer.

After the stop bath, the film is placed in the fixing solution. To minimize transfer of solutions, remove the film from the tray using the same method as you did with the developer.

Using fixer

The fixer dissolves the unexposed silver halides and hardens the emulsion to help eliminate the possibility of scratching the surface. If unexposed silver were not removed by the fixer, it would turn black when exposed to light, ruining the image.

When the film is first placed in the fixer, image areas will be milky-looking. The amount of time allowed for fixing varies. Some camera operators say that double the length of time it takes for the image to clear (lose the milky appearance) is satisfactory time. In some situations, the operator will remove the film as soon as it clears. Generally, film should remain in the fixer for several minutes. Always follow the manufacturer's recommendations.

Once the image area is clear, the roomlights can be turned on if needed. The film is removed from the fixing tray and placed in the wash tray or sink.

Washing

The film must be thoroughly washed to remove the fixer residue. Discoloration will take place if the fixer is not totally removed. A constant flow of fresh water is suggested. The length of time recommended by manufacturers varies, but 20 minutes in a tank of moderately flowing water is typical. Remove the film from the wash and carefully squeegee the film to remove excess water.

Drying

Once the film is removed from the wash and squeegeed, it is either hung up to dry or placed in a film dryer. Hanging the film to dry is a very slow process. Using a powered, heated film dryer is a much quicker method. When a film dryer is used, it is important that the chemicals are fully removed, because the chemical deposits on the machine rollers can damage film. When dry, the film is ready to be used for the next step in the production process.

Automatic Film Processing

Automatic film processing uses a machine to send the photosensitive material through the same development steps used for manual processing. Some automatic film processors are used to process latent images created by a process camera or contact printer. See **Figure 14-13**. The exposed film enters the processor dry, and travels through a developer, a stop bath, a fixer, a wash, and a dryer.

Other automatic processors are used to develop electronically-created latent images being output by an imagesetter. Refer to Figure 14-3. The processing procedure is similar to that of the other automatic processors, except these may produce film, paper, or press plates.

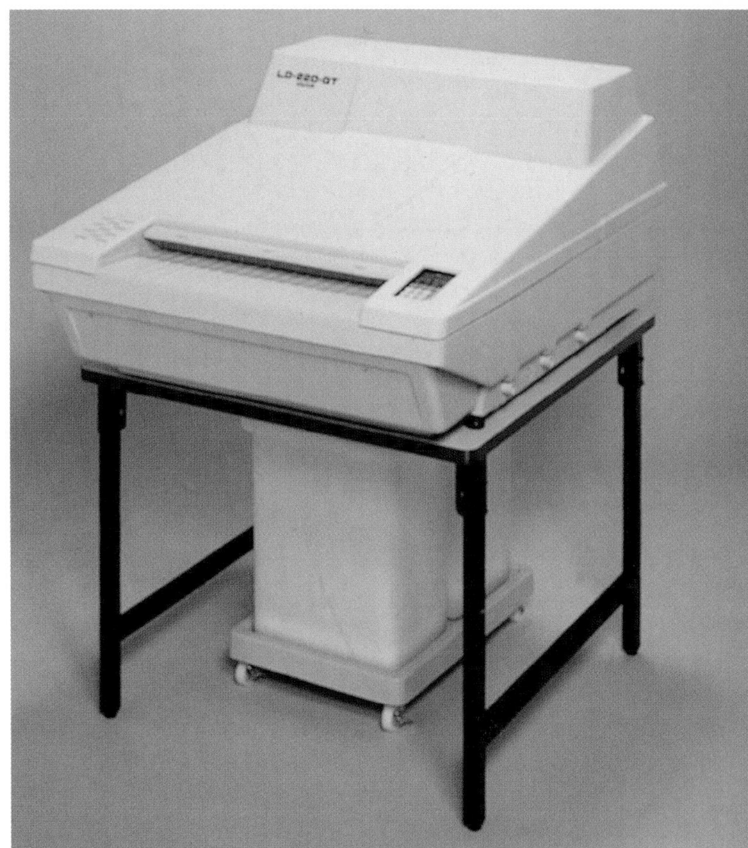

Figure 14-13. This automatic film processor is used to develop line film, contact film, and paper. It has an automatic chemical replenisher, which prevents developer fatigue and oxidation. (Screen–USA)

Automatic processors are used to produce a large quantity of high-quality film. See **Figure 14-14**. Correct machine settings are essential for assuring quality. Procedures for operating and maintaining automatic processors vary from model to model. Always refer to the operator's manual for your specific model.

Each processor is equipped with a system to control time at each step. Usually, the speed of film travel determines the time in each step. The temperature and agitation is also automatically controlled and must be properly set. The total time the film is in the machine varies from one machine to another.

To keep the developing solution and other chemicals in proper balance, many of these processors are equipped with an automatic chemical replenisher. The replenisher adds chemicals to the solutions as needed, preventing chemical fatigue

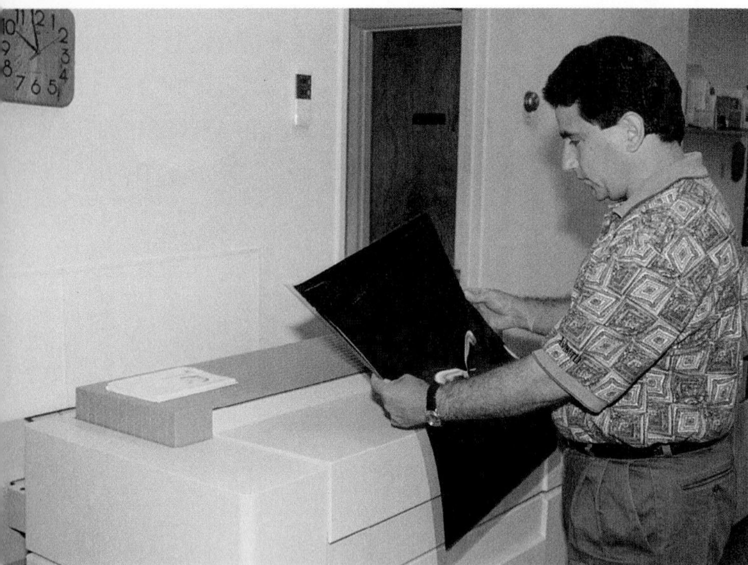

Figure 14-14. Automatic processors are capable of processing a large quantity of film with consistent, high-quality results.

and oxidation. Some automatic processors require large quantities of chemicals. This can be very costly when the volume is not sufficient to keep the processor in constant operation.

Process control strips are essential to establish the machine settings and quality control. See **Figure 14-15**. Once the specific control is attained, however, consistency will be assured. This means that every piece of photosensitive material is meeting quality standards. Any time the development of the control strip is above or below the recommended step, the automatic processor must be readjusted.

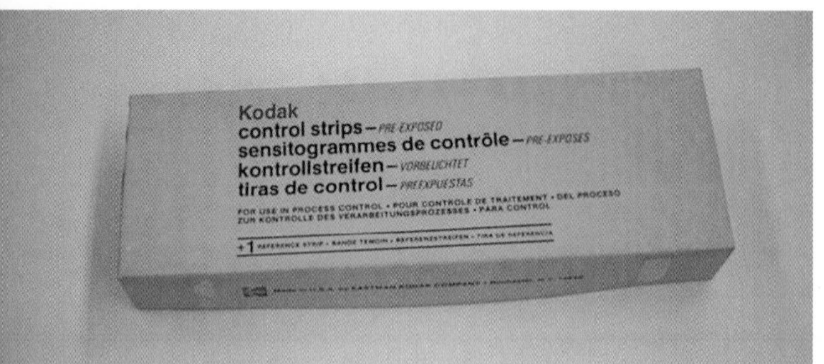

Figure 14-15. Control strips are vital in establishing proper machine operation and control of processing chemicals, temperature, speed, and other variables. Read the directions provided with the specific control strips

Contact Printing

Contact printing is one of the special photo techniques requiring processing. ***Contact printing*** results from taking an original negative or positive, placing it in physical contact with a photosensitive material, then exposing it to light. The contact is the same size as the original. The most common type of contact is the ***contact duplicate***. If the original is a negative, then a negative is created; if the original is a positive, then a positive is created. The processing of the materials can be manual or automatic. Contact printing is covered in detail in Chapter 16 of this text. In addition to normal photographic development, stabilization and diffusion transfer processes can be used for contact printing.

Stabilization

The stabilization process involves passing the exposed material through two solutions; an ***activator*** that develops the materials and a ***stabilizer*** that dissolves the unexposed emulsion. The stabilizer also acts as a fixer. The result is a permanent image on a photosensitive material.

Most stabilization processors are in the darkroom, unless a light-tight area is attached to the processor. The light-tight area acts as a darkroom for the cassette holding the exposed photosensitive paper.

Diffusion transfer

Diffusion transfer, also called ***photomechanical transfer (PMT)***, is a means of creating images directly on another carrier. Diffusion transfer is commonly used in industry to make a duplicate of a pasted-up image. Then, if the image is lost or damaged, there is another copy of the original. The final diffusion transfer image can appear on an opaque surface or a transparent base. The image can also be produced on a plate, ready for printing.

This process bypasses conventional film developing. With diffusion transfer, a negative sheet is exposed to the image on a process camera or contact printer. The negative and a receiver sheet are fed into a diffusion transfer processor. The emulsion side of the negative must face the coated side of a receiver sheet (paper, film, or aluminum plate). The negative and the receiver sheet are slightly separated as they are fed into the processor and into the processing solution. Then, they are fed together through sheet rollers. The unexposed part of the emulsion transfers to the receiver sheet. For most short-term uses, the negative and the receiver sheet are left in contact for approximately 30 seconds, pulled apart, and then used. If the print is going to be kept for an extended period of time, the receiver sheet is fed through a washing unit and drying unit.

Review Questions

Do not write in this book. Write your answers on a separate sheet of paper.

1. The area normally used to process film is called the _____.
2. Explain six factors that should be considered when purchasing a processing sink.
3. Explain the different types of darkroom entrances.
4. *True or false?* Manual processing in trays is more efficient than an automatic film processor and produces higher-quality results.
5. A(n) _____ is used for removal of moisture from developed film before it is dried.
6. How does the developer make the latent image visible?
7. What is the main reason for agitation during the developing process?
8. The _____ is an acetic solution used to neutralize the developer.
   a. fixer
   b. developer
   c. stop bath
   d. wash
9. *True or false?* When mixing acid and water, you should pour the water into the acid.
10. What is the role of the fixer?

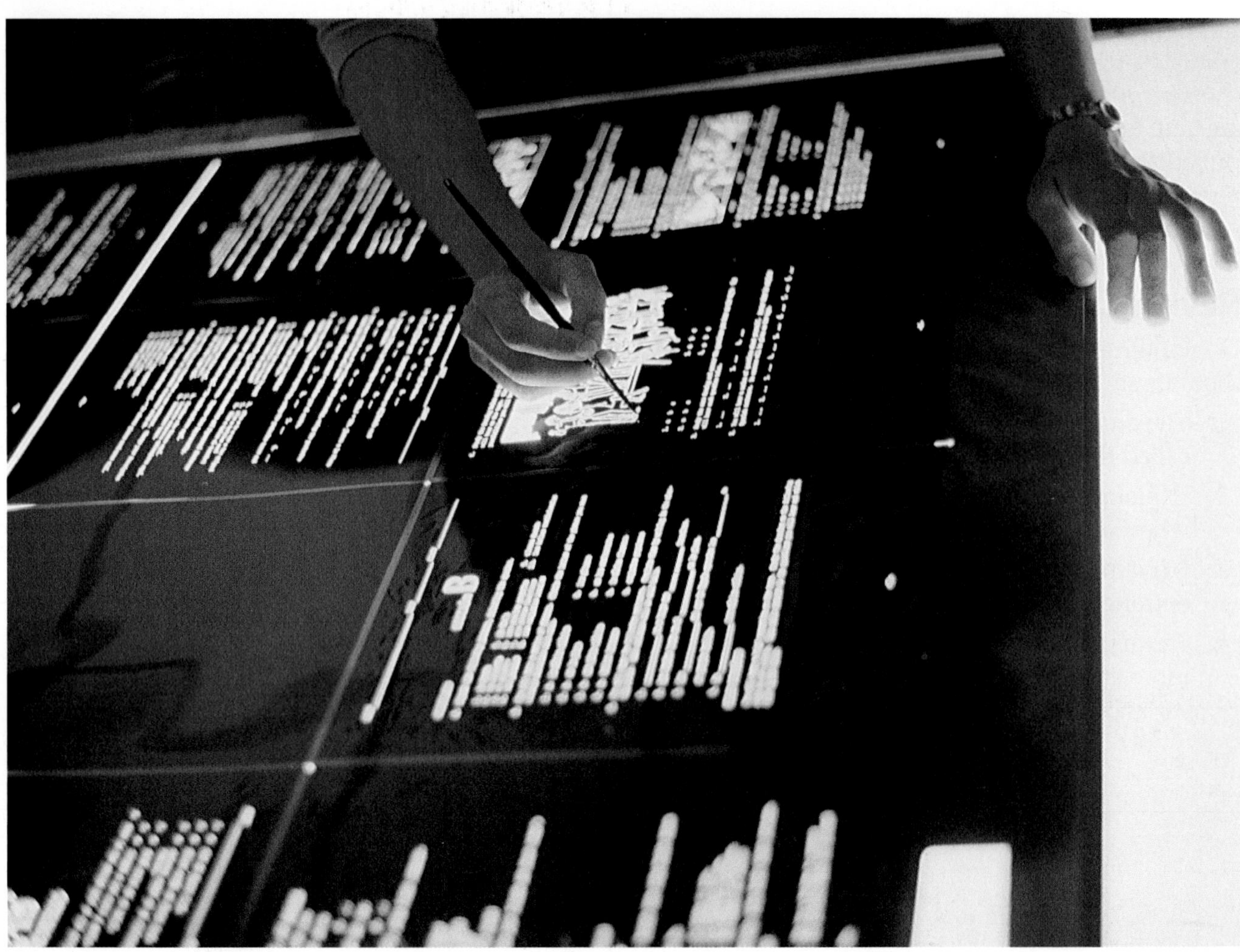

Process cameras are still used, especially in smaller print shops, to produce negatives of line art and type. Before the negatives can be stripped into flats, they often must be opaqued to eliminate pinholes caused by dust, scratches resulting from handling during processing, and other minor defects.

Stripping and Imposition 15

Learning Objectives

After studying this chapter, you will be able to:

- Define imposition and stripping.
- Explain the three basic imposition layouts used in the industry.
- Describe the materials, tools, and equipment commonly used by the stripper.
- Explain the steps required to produce a single color flat.
- Explain the importance of quality control.
- Describe when multiple-page imposition is used.
- Explain how electronic prepress operations are replacing the manual imposition and stripping processes.

Important Terms

flat
opaque
parallax error
portable document format (PDF)
registration
sheetwise imposition
signatures
step-and-repeat
work-and-tumble
work-and-turn

Lithographic ***imposition*** is the layout of various sizes and shapes of copy on a page in preparation for the photographic process. Layout is done on a ***flat***, a large support sheet that consists of assembled images (films), **Figure 15-1**. The flat is used to make the printing plate. ***Stripping*** is the physical assembly of those images on the flat. *Image assembly* requires the positioning and attaching of film to the support sheeting. The person doing the image assembly is called a ***stripper***.

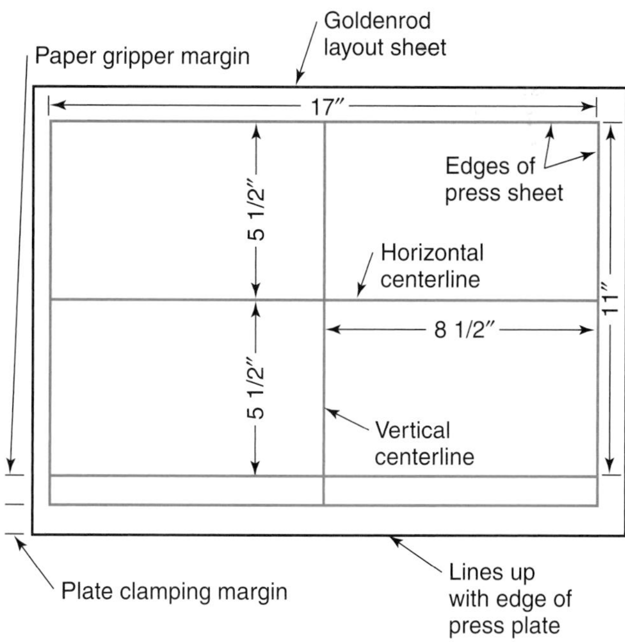

Figure 15-1. Layout lines on the base sheet of a flat help ensure accuracy during stripping and when feeding the sheets onto the press.

Making the flat is a critical part of the prepress process, since an error at this stage will show up in the final printed product. ***Prepress*** refers to the production steps carried out prior to printing. Increasingly, the term is being used to describe the application of computers to composition, color separation, and color proofing. In fact, the stripping departments in many printing facilities have changed dramatically in recent years, with computers replacing light tables and electronic applications making image assembly faster and more efficient.

Although the development of software to support the shift to digital prepress and printing has been nothing less than spectacular, many graphic communication facilities still use manual impositioning and stripping. Therefore, this chapter will examine both the traditional and electronic methods of image assembly, looking at the conventional tools and techniques, with an eye to current and future technologies.

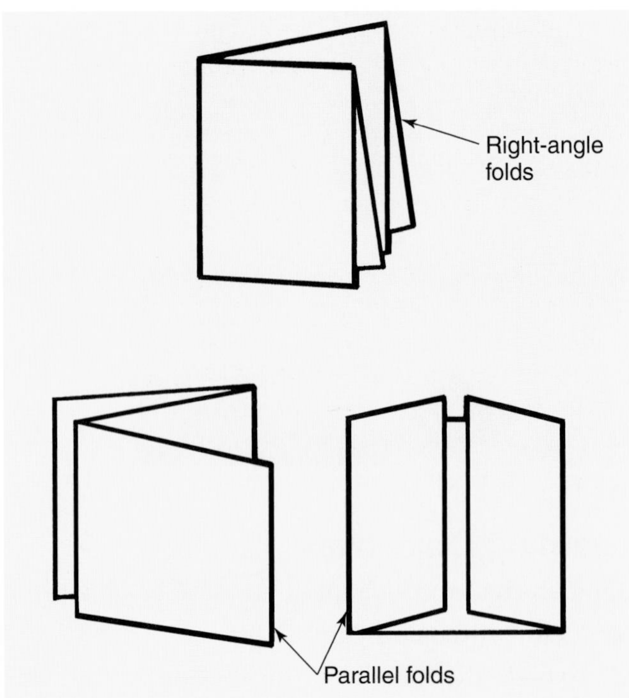

Figure 15-2. In a right-angle fold, each fold is at a right angle to the proceeding fold. In a parallel fold, all folds are parallel with each other.

Mechanics of Layout

Page position, sequence, and folding patterns are issues that arise daily in prepress operations. To assist with imposition, the stripper usually makes a "dummy."

Dummy

A ***dummy*** is a folded representation of the finished job. Right angle and parallel are the two most common types of folding, **Figure 15-2**. In the *right angle* fold, each succeeding fold is made at a right angle to the preceding one. In the *parallel* fold, all folds are parallel with each other. The first fold is made from the center out.

The final page size and fold is important. To make a dummy, use a blank press sheet that is the same size as the paper to be used for the print job. For an eight-page dummy, fold the sheet in half, then in half again. Number each page, and cut a notch through the tops of the folds, **Figure 15-3**. When the dummy is unfolded, the pages appear in proper sequence for layout, and the notches indicate the head of each page.

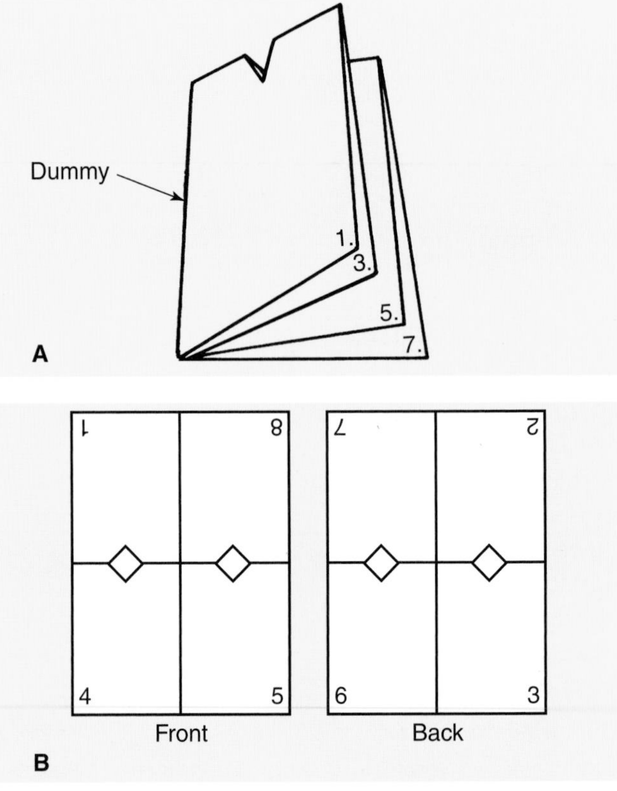

Figure 15-3. The dummy. A—The dummy is a folded and numbered representation of the printed sheet. B—When opened, the dummy indicates the correct positioning of the pages.

Signatures

To form a book or other multiple-page document, printed sheets are folded into sections that contain four, eight, 16, or 32 pages. The folded sheets are called ***signatures***.

Each signature was once a large sheet of paper printed front and back, called a press sheet. The group of pages on each side of the sheet is called a *form*. The pages on each form are laid out so that when the signature is folded, trimmed, and bound, they end up in the proper sequence and position for reading.

An eight-page signature, for example, would have four pages printed on one side and four pages printed on the other side. After printing, the sheet is folded and ready for trimming and binding.

Workers in both the stripping and bindery departments must be familiar with the parts of a signature, **Figure 15-4**:

- *Head* is the top portion or top edge of the signature.
- *Thumb edge* is the edge where you would spread the signature to turn the pages.
- *Bind edge* is the outside edge, opposite the thumb edge. It is the same as the *saddle edge* or *spine edge* that forms the backbone of the finished book.
- *Gutter* refers to the inside of the bind edge or saddle edge.
- *Open edge* is a side that is not folded, so the pages can be opened without cutting or trimming.
- *Closed edge* is a side that is folded and must be cut or trimmed to open the pages.
- *Foot* is the bottom of the signature.
- *Signature number* or *mark* is printed on the spine or saddle edge to designate the sequence of the signatures. It ensures the signatures are in the correct order for binding.
- *Folio* is the term for the page number of the signature.
- *Front folio* is the lowest page number in the signature.

Types of Imposition

Three types of imposition (or press layout) are commonly used in the industry: *sheetwise*, *work-and-turn*, and *work-and-tumble*. The type of imposition used depends on the press, the format size, and the number of pages. Before discussing press layouts, several terms should be defined.

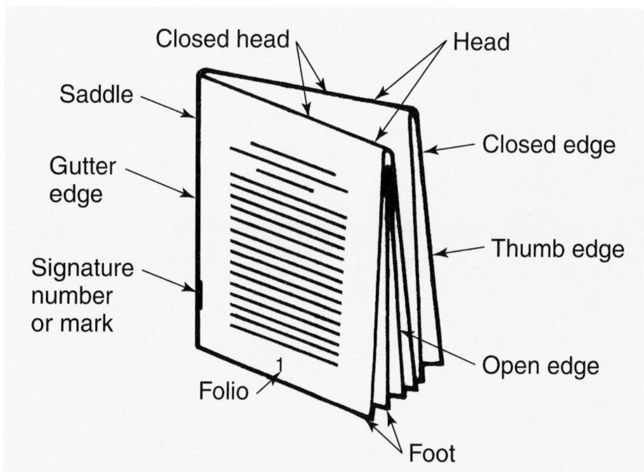

Figure 15-4. Parts of a folded signature.

One-up means one impression will be made on only one side of the final printed sheet.

Step-and-repeat means to expose the same image on a plate a number of times. Sometimes, a small form (such as a business card) will be stepped and repeated to fill the image area of the plate. Images are also stepped and repeated when a long run is required. Repeating the images reduces press time. See **Figure 15-5**.

A *combination* layout also utilizes the full area of a plate. While step-and-repeat exposes the same form, a combination is made up of various size forms on the same printed sheet.

Sheetwise

Sheetwise imposition is generally used when two sides of the sheet are to be printed with separate flats. The front side of the sheet has one image, and the back side has another image. Since the images are different, two separate printing plates and two runs are required.

The ***gripper edge***, the side of the flat that enters the press first, is the same for both plates; however, the guide edge changes. The first image uses the left guide; the backup image uses the right guide because the sheet has been turned over. In this case, pages 1, 4, 5, and 8 are printed on one side, while 2, 3, 6, and 7 are printed on the other side, **Figure 15-6**.

Work-and-turn

Work-and-turn imposition requires a sheet twice as large as needed for running the job

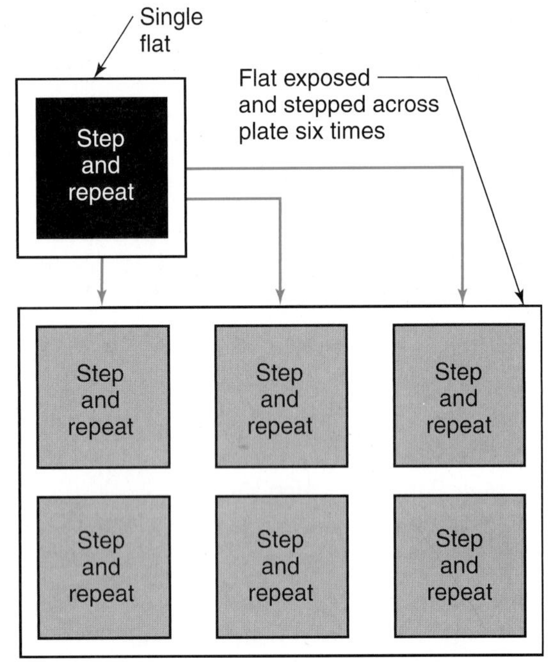

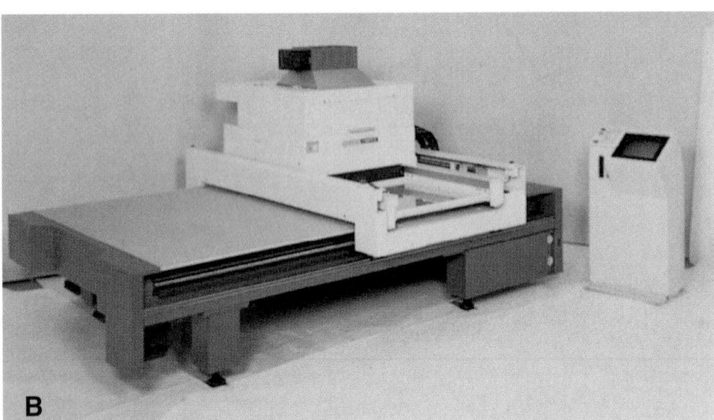

Figure 15-5. Step-and-repeat. A—Step-and-repeat produces the same image more than once on the same plate. B—A platemaker used for automated step-and-repeat exposures. (Screen-USA)

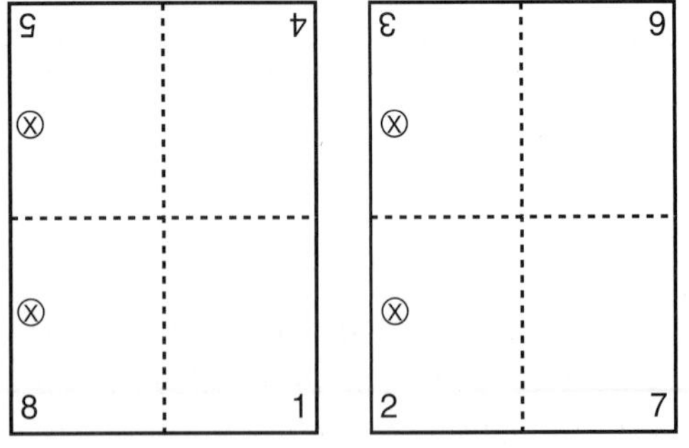

Figure 15-6. The sheetwise layout uses the same gripper edge (indicated by X marks) but different press guides.

sheetwise, **Figure 15-7**. The gripper edge is the same for both sides, but the guide edge is changed. When the sheet is turned over end-for-end, all the images printed on the first side will be repeated. The pages on the second side will properly "back up" the pages on the first side so the press sheet can be cut into two identical eight-page signatures.

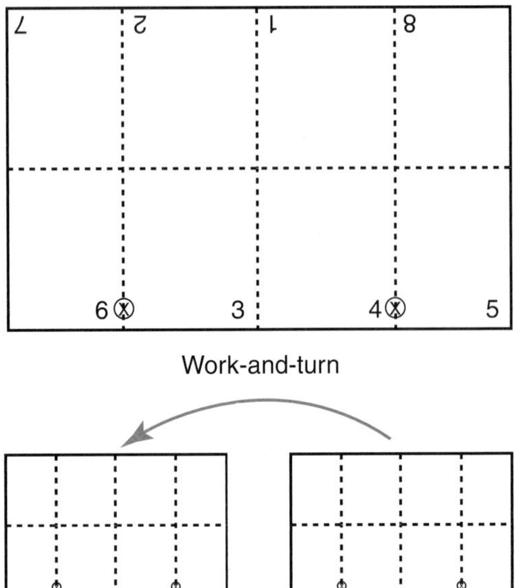

Figure 15-7. With work-and-turn, all of the images printed on one side of the sheet are also printed on the other side.

Work-and-turn saves half the time of sheetwise imposition and uses only one plate. Work-and-turn imposition requires a larger press size, however.

Work-and-tumble

Work-and-tumble imposition also requires the sheet to be twice as large as for sheetwise imposition. Work-and-tumble imposition requires different gripper edges. The top becomes one gripper edge; then, the sheet is tumbled (or flopped), and the bottom becomes the gripper edge. Only one guide edge is used. Work-and-tumble imposition uses only one plate and requires only one press makeready. See **Figure 15-8**.

The two gripper positions require the sheets to be trimmed and squared on all four sides.

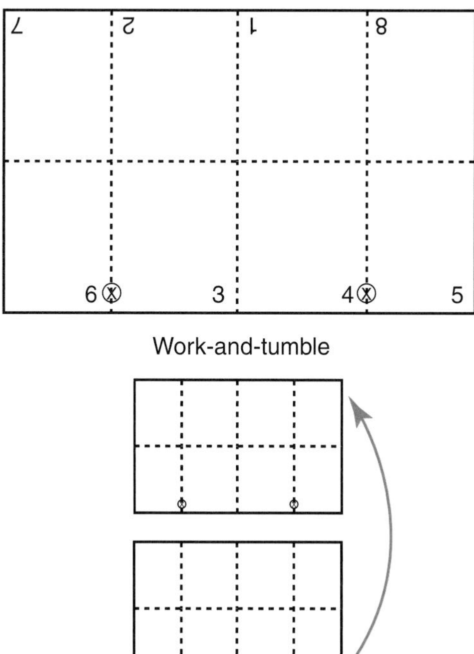

Figure 15-8. With work-and-tumble, the top and bottom of the sheet become the gripper edges.

Figure 15-9. A light table is used for stripping films onto a base sheet. Light shines through the paper and film, making image assembly easier.

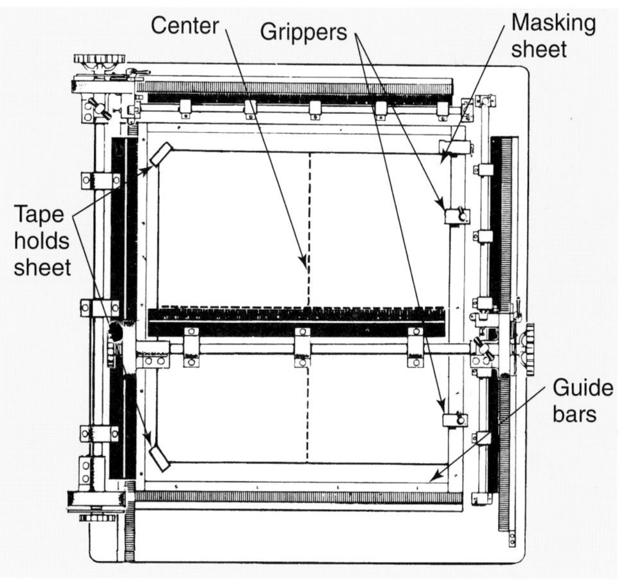

Figure 15-10. A lineup table guides the alignment of images during stripping. It is useful when working on several masking sheets with the same reference lines. (nuArc company, inc.)

Stripping Equipment and Tools

Accuracy is essential in stripping. The equipment must be high quality. It must be durable and rugged yet designed for efficiency, accuracy, and convenience.

Stripping tables

The ***stripping table*** (or *light table*) is an illuminated work surface that allows the stripper to clearly see the film, **Figure 15-9**. Illumination should be even throughout the entire working area. The glass surface should have diffused light with no evidence of hot spots (bright areas). Many stripping tables have edges that are true on all four sides for use with a T-square.

Layout tables (also called *lineup tables*) are precision pieces of equipment. They are used to accurately prepare layouts or check finished flats. See **Figure 15-10**. Many of the lineup devices are capable of making micrometer adjustments. Since manual imposition and stripping departments are being eliminated, stripping and layout tables have disappeared from many printing facilities.

Punches are devices used to make holes in perfect alignment on the masking sheet and the plate,

Figure 15-11. ***Registration*** (alignment) is controlled by holding flats in the same position during stripping and platemaking. ***Register pins*** are used to hold the punched sheets for stripping photographic materials. See **Figure 15-12**.

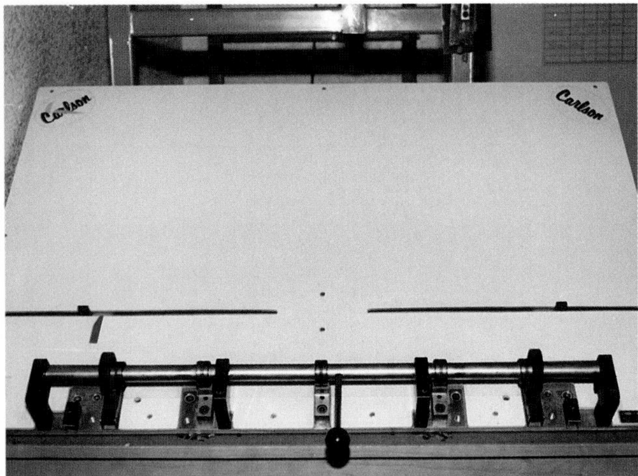

Figure 15-11. A register punch makes accurate holes in a goldenrod base sheet. It can also be used to punch alignment holes in the plate.

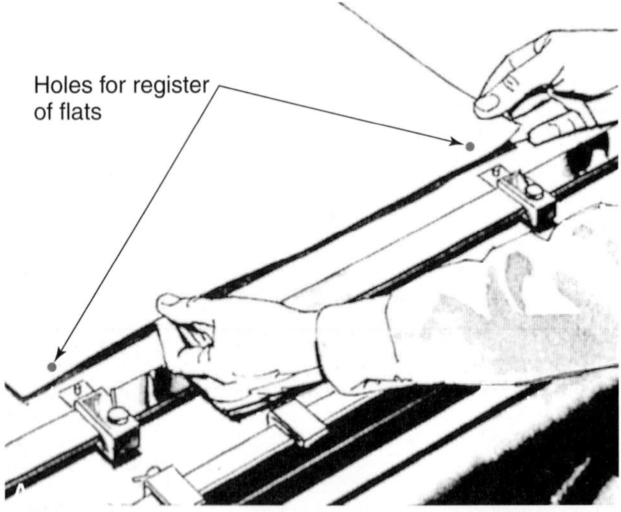

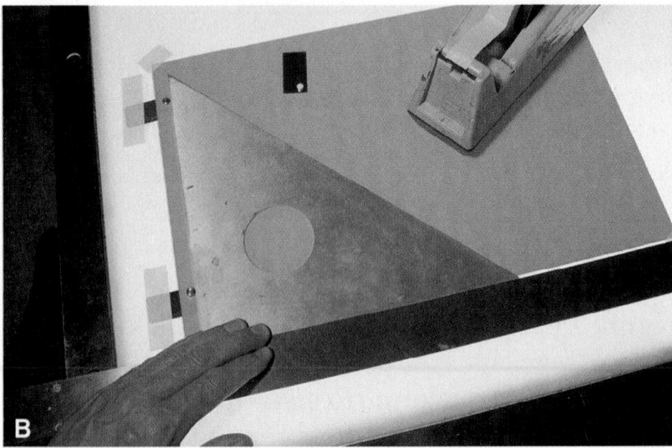

Figure 15-12. Using register pins. A—Holes punched in a base sheet ensure the flats are properly placed. B—Register pins inserted through the punched holes are taped down to keep the flats in register.

Tools and supplies

The choice of measuring devices, such as rules and scales depends upon the accuracy required for the job, **Figure 15-13**. Measuring instruments may be made of steel or plastic; steel is more common in stripping. Many scales or rules can be used as a straightedge as well as a measuring device. The straightedge must have a true smooth edge. The edge should not be affected by knives, scribers, pens, pencils, or needles.

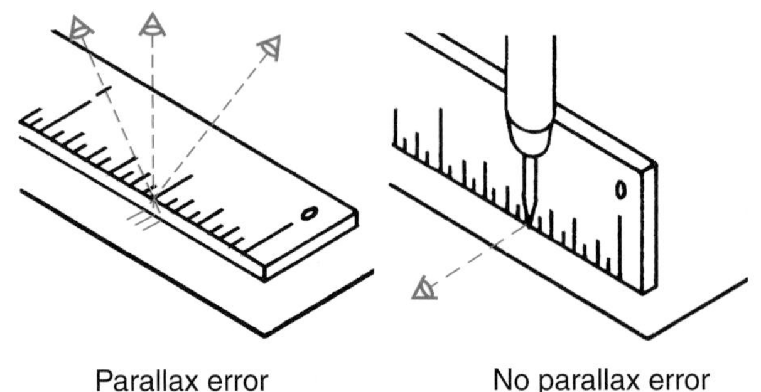

Figure 15-13. Accuracy is critical to stripping. When scribing lines or making measurements, look straight down at the scale. This view will prevent parallax error.

T-squares and triangles are used to align film and other materials, **Figure 15-14**. They also serve as a true edge for drawing layout lines, control marks, or outlines, and are useful in essentially any layout or stripping activity.

Irregular curves serve as guides for opaquing irregular shapes. Other drafting tools, such as dividers, compasses, ruling pens, and protractors are also useful to the stripper.

Figure 15-14. A stripper is using a T-square to accurately position a goldenrod sheet on a work surface.

Stripping knives, **Figure 15-15**, and sturdy scissors are essential cutting tools. Fine felt tip pens, ballpoint pens, and mechanical pencils are basic marking instruments.

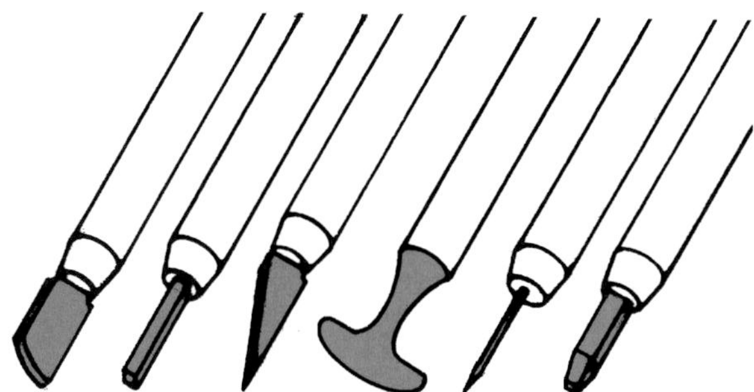

Figure 15-15. Some scribing and cutting tools used by the stripper.

Screen angle indicators are used to determine the screen angles of halftones and tints, **Figure 15-16**. When a tint or halftone area overlaps, the indicator is useful for determining the correct angle to eliminate a ***moiré*** pattern, **Figure 15-17**.

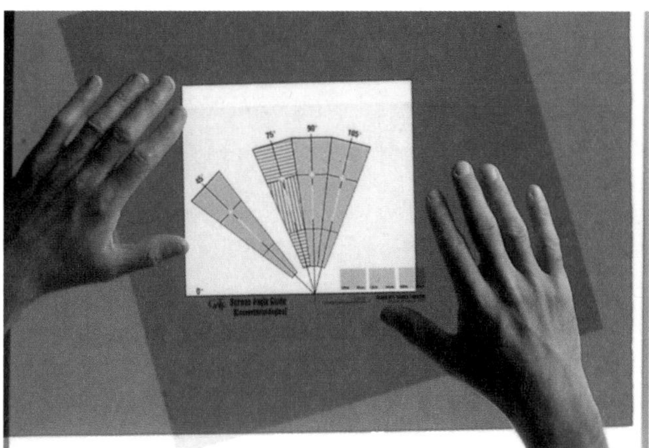

Figure 15-16. Screen angle indicators are used by the stripper to help produce a high-quality image. (Graphic Arts Technical Foundation)

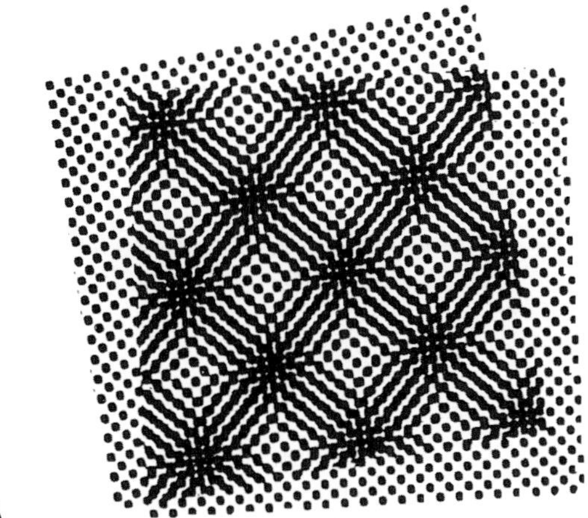

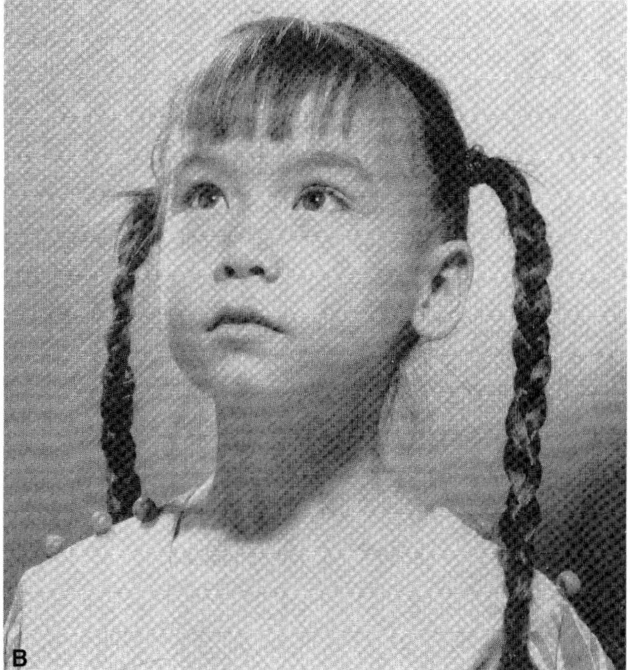

Figure 15-17. Moiré pattern. A—Incorrect screen angles can produce an undesirable dot pattern. B—A moiré pattern on an image.

Brushes are used by the stripper to ***opaque*** film. The brushes should be made of high-quality hair. Low-quality brushes are difficult to control when precision work is required. Brushes are sometimes used for other operations, such as applying rubber cement to adhere materials.

Opaquing solution is a red or black nontransparent pigment used to block out unwanted images on negatives. Water-based solutions can be diluted or thinned with water, if needed. Alcohol- and petroleum-based opaques are also available. The solution is also used to touch up details on positives. Opaquing solution is usually applied with a brush, but pens and applicators are also available, **Figure 15-18**.

Magnifiers and collimators are used to examine film, **Figure 15-19**. Magnifiers with power of 10× or 12× (10 or 12 times actual size) are typical for examining photographic and printing detail, **Figure 15-20**. The ***collimator*** is an optical instrument useful when the visible line of sight is straight. With the

Figure 15-18. Opaquing solution is used to touch up tiny imperfections on the negatives. Any unwanted light passing through a negative will cause ink to deposit on the plate and printing substrate.
(Bowling Green State University)

Figure 15-19. A stripper is using a magnifier to inspect the quality of the images for a job.

collimator, the stripper can make sure register marks are properly aligned when two or more overlays are used. Sighting with a regular magnifier cannot ensure the marks are lined up properly. The collimator eliminates ***parallax error***, an illusion that can result due to a change in the viewing angle.

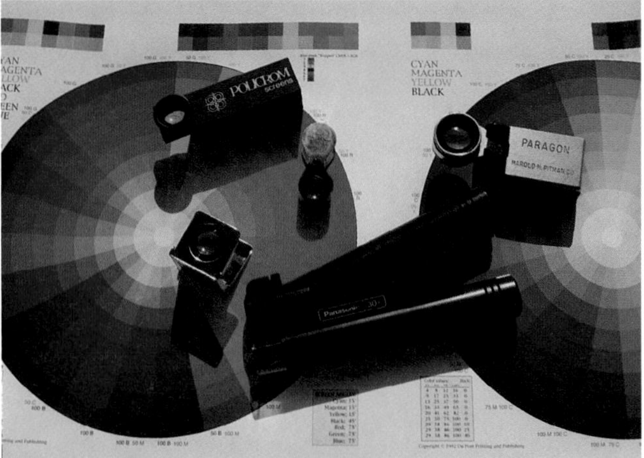

Figure 15-20. Magnifying devices are used to enlarge images for closer inspection.

Supplies used by the stripper include adhesives, ink, opaque, control marks, and cleaners. Drafting tape is recommended to hold base material, although masking, transparent, or translucent tapes are also used. Lithographer's tape is an effective medium for holding film on masking sheets. It is also used to block out areas on the negative that will not be printed. Double-coated tapes are sometimes used to adhere film to another piece of film or to the masking sheet. Nonreproducing blue ink and black ink are the two most common types used by the stripper.

Control marks, pins, tabs, and dowels, are used to correctly position multiple flats for successive exposure. Correct positioning is imperative to ensure accurate register (alignment) with each plate or proof. The tabs or pins are also valuable guides for step-and-repeat work.

Solutions are available for cleaning the films. Cleaning solutions should not leave a residue. Most commercial products are satisfactory.

Base material

A ***substrate***, or base material, is used to support photographic materials when preparing a flat. The most common support is photomask paper (***masking sheets***). Base material is available in goldenrod, orange, or red, with goldenrod the most commonly used. The color of the base material blocks ***actinic light*** emitted from mercury vapor lamps, arc lamps, or photoflood bulbs — light that will expose light-sensitive coatings.

Goldenrod paper is often purchased with preprinted guidelines (top, side, and bottom margins and a centerline) to meet the size requirement of a specific press. Goldenrod unprinted stock is available in various sizes and can be cut to meet press plate specifications, **Figure 15-21**. Often, a master sheet is laid out and used as a base for all flats. Larger presses seldom use preprinted base sheets.

Figure 15-21. Goldenrod unprinted stock can be cut to meet press plate specifications. Shelving below the light table stores supplies or work in progress. (Foster Manufacturing Co.)

Masking sheets are made of paper or vinyl. Paper base is satisfactory for many jobs but lacks stability. The paper is affected by moisture and heat, and a change of size is possible.

Goldenrod plastic (vinyl) sheet is normally used for negative-type stripping jobs requiring a high degree of accuracy. When positive film flats are used, clear plastic sheet material is needed. Because vinyl is affected by temperature, a stripper might choose an acetate or polyester sheet.

Photographic films

A stripper uses both film negatives and film positives to produce flats. On *negative* films, the black areas of the photographed subject appear transparent (white) in the final document. The white areas appear black. On *positive* films, or transparencies, the image appears exactly as it was photographed.

The thicknesses of the film will vary. The most common thicknesses are from 0.003″ to 0.007″ (0.08 mm to 0.18 mm). Generally, thin films are used when one negative is laid over another and contact printed. The materials must lie flat so the image is not distorted.

Stripping Procedures

A stripper assembles negatives and attaches them in prescribed locations to a base sheet to create a flat. The negatives held in place on the base sheet are used to make an image proof or image carrier (such as a printing plate). This section of the chapter explains how to correctly position the negatives on the base sheet and prepare them for producing an image carrier.

Stripping preparation

Preparation is the first stage of stripping. The stripper must check the negatives for opacity and opaquing. Dimensions must be checked and control marks correctly located.

The ***job ticket*** gives the imposition for a particular job and provides a checklist of general information for use by the stripper or others in the preparation department. See **Figure 15-22**.

Bleed and creep

Before starting image assembly, the stripper must be aware of two situations: *bleed* and *creep*. When any type of image extends to the edge of the printed page, it is called a ***bleed***. Allowances must be made when stripping because the printed area extends beyond the trim-page size.

When a thick, saddle-stitched book is folded, a problem called ***creep*** develops. The thickness causes the center pages to creep forward, resulting in different dimensions than the outside pages, **Figure 15-23**.

The stripper can allow for creep by requesting a complete folded dummy. The paper for the dummy must be the same paper planned for the job. Many booklets are not critical enough to consider creep. However, any time that alignment *is* required, creep must be considered.

```
TITLE:       GRAPHIC COMMUNICATION                                   JOB NUMBER
CUSTOMER:    GOODHEART-WILLCOX COMPANY                                22126 GRAPHIC      COMMUNICATION
PLANNER:     LONG                                                          VO
ISBN:                        BND: VON-BIND CASE
PLATES:      NEG             WEB: 22-3/4 LAYOUT
TRIM SIZE:   8-01/02       PAPER: 34-03/04  ROLLS
           X 11-00/00

      FORM:        1
      PAGES:      32        XX FILM GRIPPER XX           |        XX FILM GRIPPER XX
      LOW PAGE:    1           PUNCH EDGE                |           PUNCH EDGE
      COLORS:    4/C           TOP PLATE         4/C     |          BOTTOM PLATE        4/C

                  17     16    ||   9     24             |    21     12   ||   13     20
                  H      H     ||   H     H              |    H      H    ||   H      H
                  --- 3/ 8 ---                           |    --- 3/ 8 ---
                  H   1  H     ||   H     H              |    H      H    ||   H      H
KEY:                  S
L.P.=LOW PAGE     32     1     ||   8     25             |    28     5    ||   4      29
   S =SPINE ID
   H =HEAD OF            L.P.                            |                     L.P.
      PAGE
                         L.P.                            |                     L.P.
                  31     2     ||   7     26             |    27     6    ||   3      30
                  H      H     ||   H     H              |    H      H    ||   H      H
                  --- 3/ 8 ---                           |    --- 3/ 8 ---
                  H      H     ||   H     H              |    H      H    ||   H      H
             3                 3              3       3                   3                  3
             /    18     15    /    10    23  /       /   22     11       /   14     19      /
            16                 8             16      16                   8                 16

                          BOTTOM PLATE           4/C     |           TOP PLATE          4/C
                           PUNCH EDGE                    |           PUNCH EDGE
A        CUN32          XX FILM GRIPPER XX               |       XX FILM GRIPPER XX
```

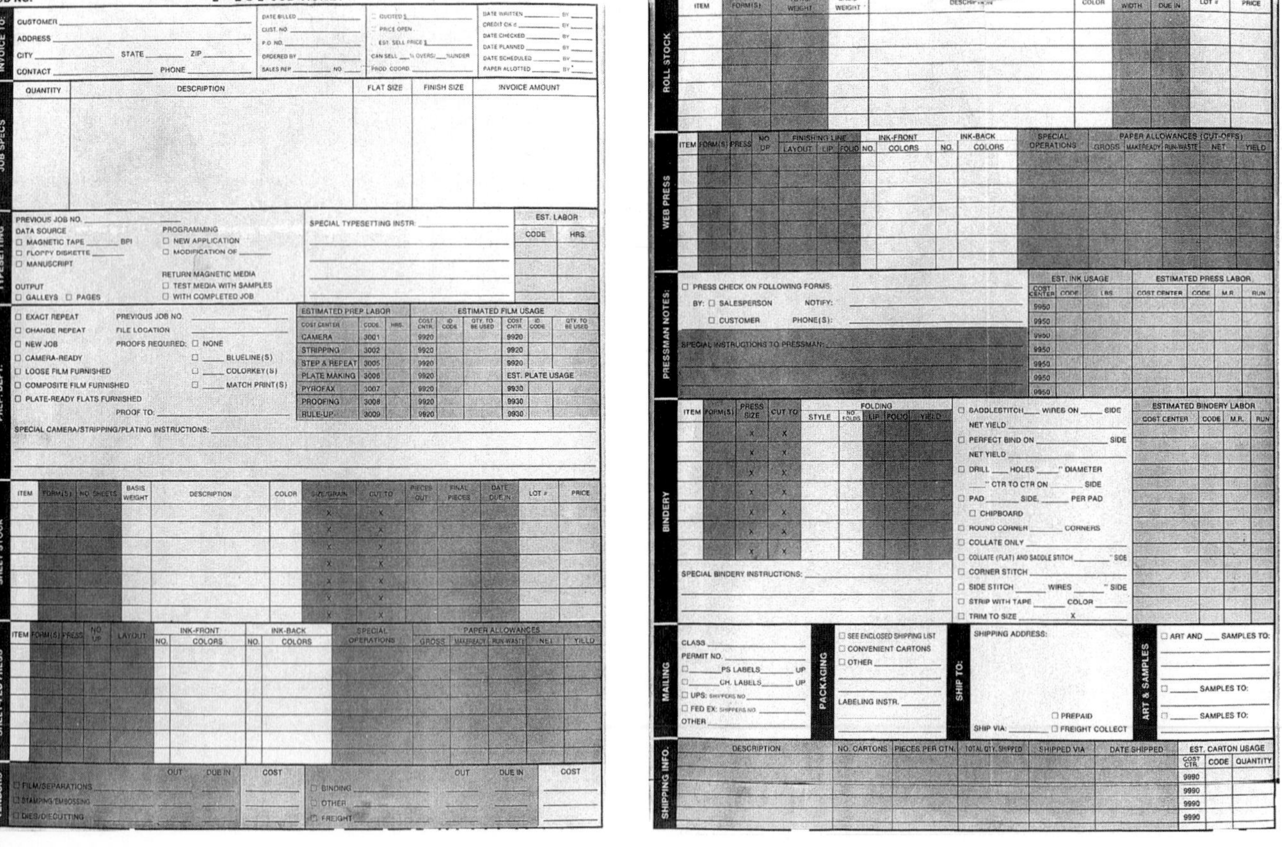

JOB NO. JOB TICKET DUE DATE:

INVOICE TO: CUSTOMER / ADDRESS / CITY / STATE / ZIP / CONTACT / PHONE / DATE BILLED / CUST. NO. / P.O. NO. / ORDERED BY / SALES REP / NO. / QUOTED $ / PRICE OPEN / EST. SELL PRICE $ / CAN SELL % OVERS/ % UNDER / PROD. COORD. / DATE WRITTEN / CREDIT OK'd / DATE CHECKED / DATE PLANNED / DATE SCHEDULED / PAPER ALLOTTED / BY

JOB SPECS: QUANTITY / DESCRIPTION / FLAT SIZE / FINISH SIZE / INVOICE AMOUNT

TYPESETTING: PREVIOUS JOB NO. / DATA SOURCE / ☐ MAGNETIC TAPE BPI / ☐ FLOPPY DISKETTE / ☐ MANUSCRIPT / OUTPUT / ☐ GALLEYS ☐ PAGES / PROGRAMMING / ☐ NEW APPLICATION / ☐ MODIFICATION OF / RETURN MAGNETIC MEDIA / ☐ TEST MEDIA WITH SAMPLES / ☐ WITH COMPLETED JOB / SPECIAL TYPESETTING INSTR. / EST. LABOR / CODE / HRS.

PREP. DEPT.: ☐ EXACT REPEAT / PREVIOUS JOB NO. / ☐ CHANGE REPEAT / FILE LOCATION / ☐ NEW JOB / PROOFS REQUIRED: ☐ NONE / ☐ CAMERA-READY / ☐ BLUELINE(S) / ☐ LOOSE FILM FURNISHED / ☐ COLORKEY(S) / ☐ COMPOSITE FILM FURNISHED / ☐ MATCH PRINT(S) / ☐ PLATE-READY FLATS FURNISHED / PROOF TO: / SPECIAL CAMERA/STRIPPING/PLATING INSTRUCTIONS:

ESTIMATED PREP LABOR			ESTIMATED FILM USAGE					
COST CENTER	CODE	HRS.	COST CNTR.	ID CODE	QTY. TO BE USED	COST CNTR.	ID CODE	QTY. TO BE USED
CAMERA	3001		9920			9920		
STRIPPING	3002		9920			9920		
STEP & REPEAT	3005		9920			9920		
PLATE MAKING	3006		9920			EST. PLATE USAGE		
PYROFAX	3007		9920			9930		
PROOFING	3008		9920			9930		
RULE-UP	3009		9920			9930		

SHEET STOCK: ITEM / FORM(S) / NO. SHEETS / BASIS WEIGHT / DESCRIPTION / COLOR / SIZE GRAIN / CUT TO / PIECES OUT / FINAL PIECES / DATE DUE IN / LOT # / PRICE

SHEET-FED PRESS: ITEM / FORM(S) / PRESS / NO. UP / LAYOUT / INK-FRONT NO. COLORS / INK-BACK NO. COLORS / SPECIAL OPERATIONS / PAPER ALLOWANCES GROSS / MAKEREADY / RUN WASTE / NET / YIELD

VENDORS: OUT / DUE IN / COST / ☐ FILM/SEPARATIONS / ☐ STAMPING/EMBOSSING / ☐ DIES/DIECUTTING / ☐ BINDING / ☐ OTHER / ☐ FREIGHT

ROLL STOCK: ITEM / FORM(S) / TOTAL WEIGHT / BASIS WEIGHT / DESCRIPTION / COLOR / ROLL WIDTH / DATE DUE IN / LOT # / PRICE

WEB PRESS: ITEM / FORM(S) / PRESS / NO. UP / FINISHING LINE LAYOUT / LIP / FOLIO / INK-FRONT NO. COLORS / INK-BACK NO. COLORS / SPECIAL OPERATIONS / PAPER ALLOWANCES (CUT-OFFS) GROSS / MAKEREADY / RUN WASTE / NET / YIELD

PRESSMAN NOTES: ☐ PRESS CHECK ON FOLLOWING FORMS: / BY: ☐ SALESPERSON / NOTIFY: / ☐ CUSTOMER / PHONE(S): / SPECIAL INSTRUCTIONS TO PRESSMAN: / EST. INK USAGE: COST CENTER / CODE / LBS. (9950) / ESTIMATED PRESS LABOR: COST CENTER / CODE / M.R. / RUN

BINDERY: ITEM / FORM(S) / PRESS SIZE / CUT TO / FOLDING STYLE / NO. FOLDS / LIP / FOLIO / YIELD / ☐ SADDLESTITCH WIRES ON SIDE / NET YIELD / ☐ PERFECT BIND ON SIDE / NET YIELD / ☐ DRILL HOLES " DIAMETER / " CTR TO CTR ON SIDE / ☐ PAD SIDE PER PAD / ☐ CHIPBOARD / ☐ ROUND CORNER CORNERS / ☐ COLLATE ONLY / ☐ COLLATE (FLAT) AND SADDLE STITCH " SIDE / ☐ CORNER STITCH / ☐ SIDE STITCH WIRES " SIDE / ☐ STRIP WITH TAPE COLOR / ☐ TRIM TO SIZE X / SPECIAL BINDERY INSTRUCTIONS: / ESTIMATED BINDERY LABOR: COST CENTER / CODE / M.R. / RUN

MAILING: CLASS / PERMIT NO. / ☐ PS LABELS UP / ☐ CH. LABELS UP / ☐ UPS: SHIPPERS NO. / ☐ FED EX: SHIPPERS NO. / OTHER

PACKAGING: ☐ SEE ENCLOSED SHIPPING LIST / ☐ CONVENIENT CARTONS / ☐ OTHER / LABELING INSTR.

SHIP TO: SHIPPING ADDRESS: / ☐ PREPAID / SHIP VIA: / ☐ FREIGHT COLLECT

ART & SAMPLES: ☐ ART AND SAMPLES TO: / ☐ SAMPLES TO: / ☐ SAMPLES TO:

SHIPPING INFO.: DESCRIPTION / NO. CARTONS / PIECES PER CTN. / TOTAL QTY. SHIPPED / SHIPPED VIA / DATE SHIPPED / EST. CARTON USAGE: COST CTR. / CODE / QUANTITY (9990)

B

Figure 15-22. Job tickets. A—Job ticket for an imposition layout. B—General job ticket that includes a prepress department checksheet.

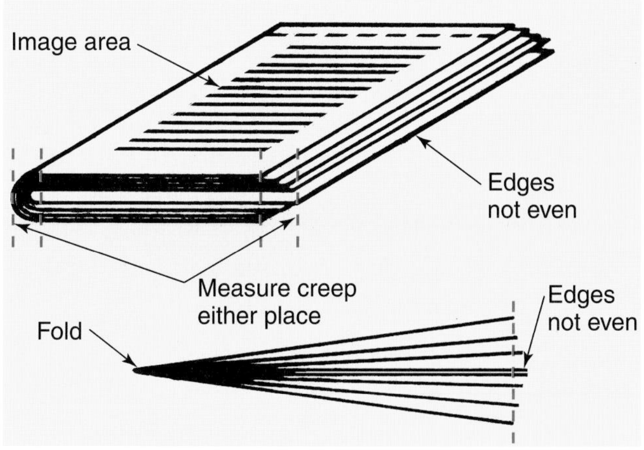

Figure 15-23. The thickness of a folded signature can cause the center pages to creep forward, resulting in different dimensions than the outside pages.

Single-page stripping

Assembling line and halftone images to create a single page is commonly referred to as ***single-page imposition***. The flat must be prepared according to the specifications of each press. Most of the duplicator-type presses have preprinted masking sheets. These goldenrod sheets cover the plate size for a specific press. All reference lines are located on the preprinted masking sheets. Since most larger presses do not have preprinted sheets, a plain goldenrod sheet may be used. See **Figure 15-24.**

Follow these guidelines for single-page stripping:

1. Square the sheet. The goldenrod sheet must be squared and fastened to the light table with masking tape.
2. Locate the gripper edge or margin.
3. Locate the plate bend. Every press requires that a portion of the leading edge of the plate be inserted into a plate-holding device. The three types of holding devices are pin bar, slotted or serrated, and clamp. The inserted portion of the plate is called the ***plate bend allowance*** and varies with each press, **Figure 15-25.**
4. Consider ***gripper allowance,*** **Figure 15-26.** Allowance must be made on the flat and a visual indication given that no printing can occur in this area. The allowance size will vary with the press, but 1/4″ to 3/8″ is most common. Since images cannot be printed in this area, the stripper must allow for any work that extends or bleeds.

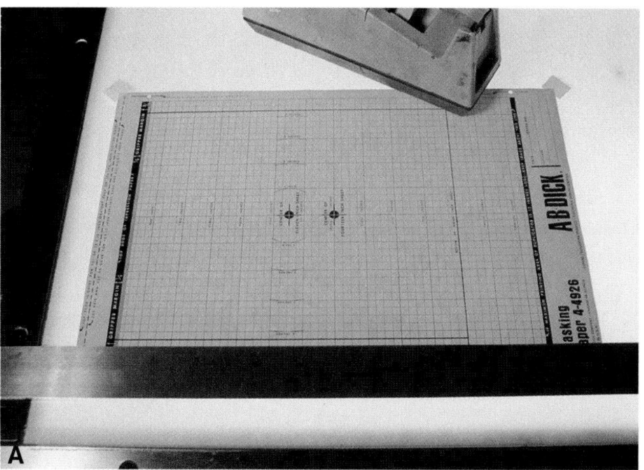

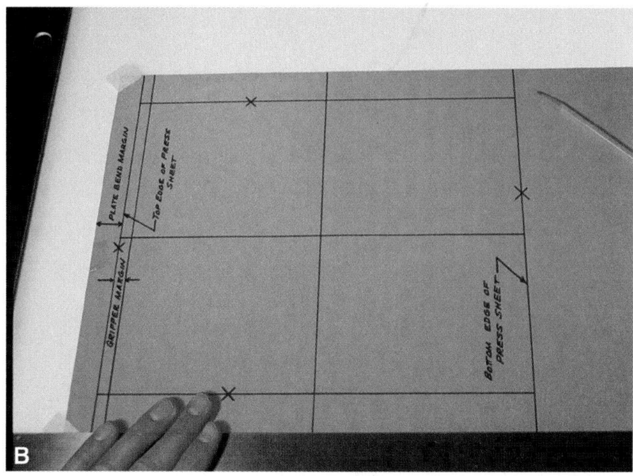

Figure 15-24. Masking sheets. A—Preprinted masking sheets match the plate size of a specific press. B—For larger presses, reference lines are ruled on plain sheets.

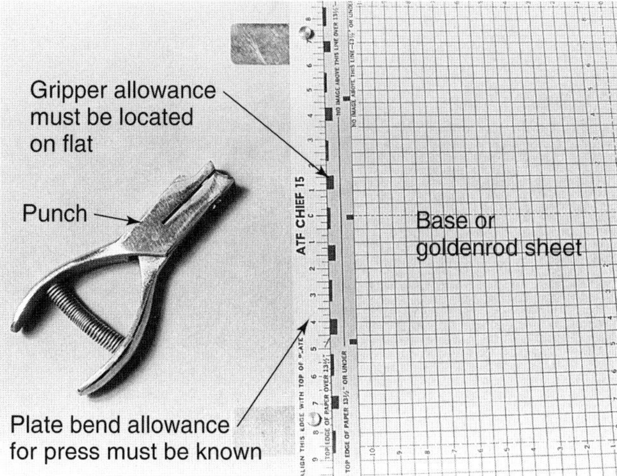

Figure 15-25. Allowances are provided on a goldenrod sheet for press grippers and plate bend. Allowances vary with the type of printing press.

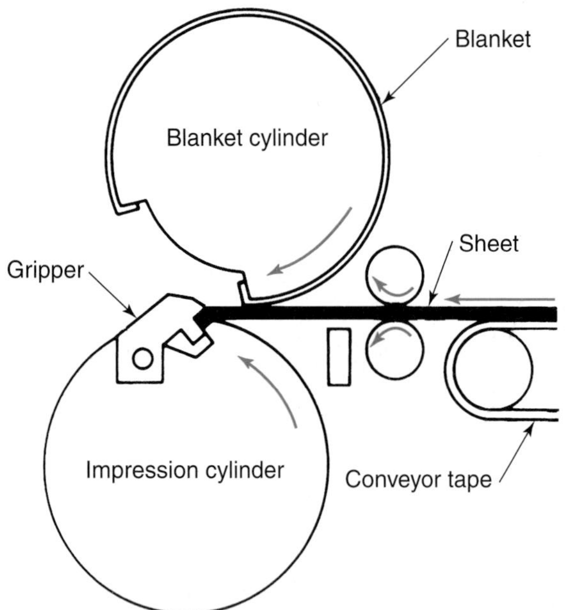

Figure 15-26. Grippers hold the sheet as it goes through the press. The stripper must allow for gripper room on the flat.

5. Know the maximum sheet size the press will run. The press manual is the best source of information. If necessary, draw margins on the masking sheet.
6. Locate the control or reference lines. ***Control lines*** are essential to accurately position the negatives, **Figure 15-27.** Control lines also assist in registering the flat on the plate. Trim and registration marks are sometimes printed on the press sheet. These marks are also important to the bindery operation.
7. Cut a V-shaped notch in the lead edge of the flat. The notch is called a ***tick mark*** and identifies the gripper edge.
8. Trim the negatives. Allow at least 1/2″ of film to remain around the image area. The extra edge is necessary for taping the negative to the goldenrod sheet, **Figure 15-28.** Negatives should not overlap on the flat, so less than 1/2″ edge may sometimes be necessary.
9. Strip the first negative, either emulsion side up or emulsion side down. Both techniques are described next.

Emulsion-up stripping

With the emulsion of the negative facing up, position the negative on or *over* the goldenrod flat. The base side should be toward the goldenrod. When looking at the negative, the image will be wrong-reading, **Figure 15-29**. Attach the negative using lithographic tape.

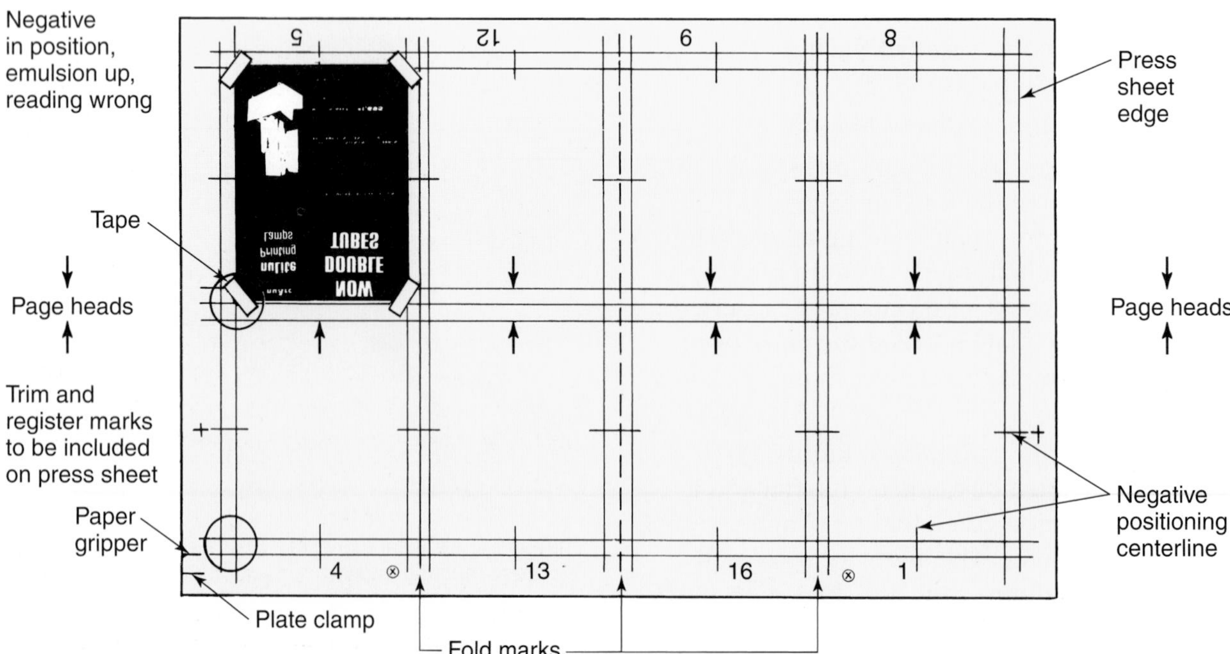

Figure 15-27. Basic layout lines of concern to the stripper.

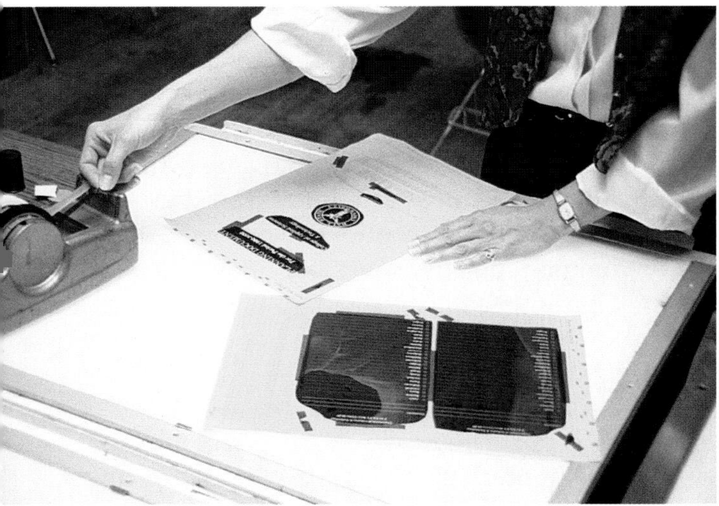

Figure 15-28. Negatives should be trimmed with enough margin left for taping them to the goldenrod sheet.

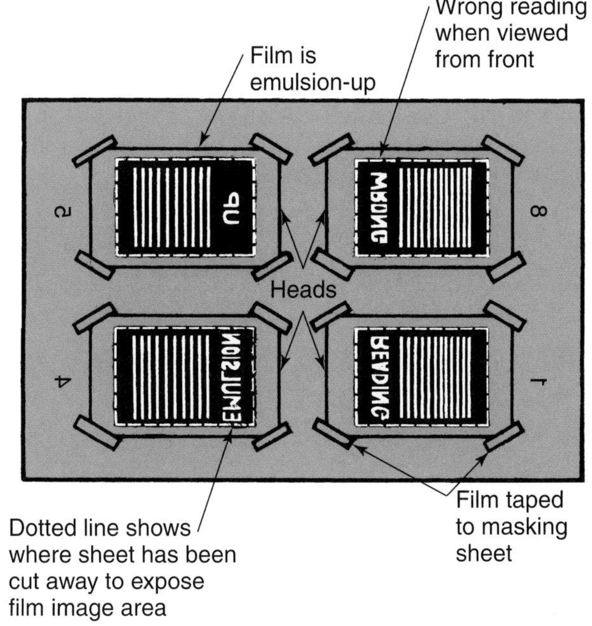

Figure 15-29. Film in this flat has been stripped emulsion-up.

With emulsion-up stripping, the film is easily taped and removed. This method is recommended with film positives. However, stripping is awkward, alignment is difficult, and reference lines can be obscured by the film. Also, the emulsion is more easily damaged.

Emulsion-down stripping

With the emulsion of the negative facing down, place the negative *under* the goldenrod sheet. The base side of the film should be placed next to the goldenrod. This technique requires a small opening be cut in the goldenrod sheet, **Figure 15-30**. The stripper inserts the negative in the position indicated by the layout.

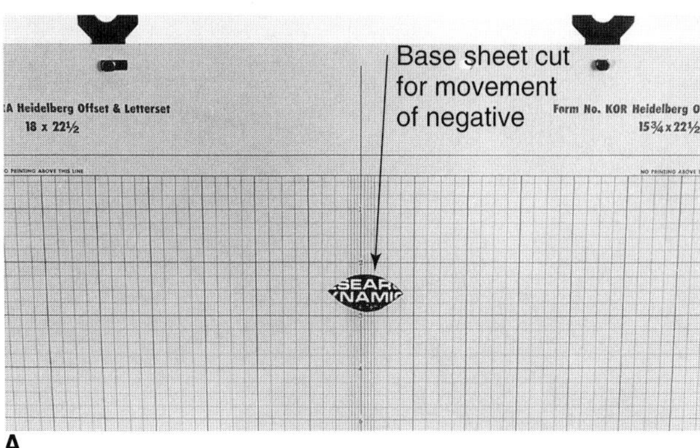

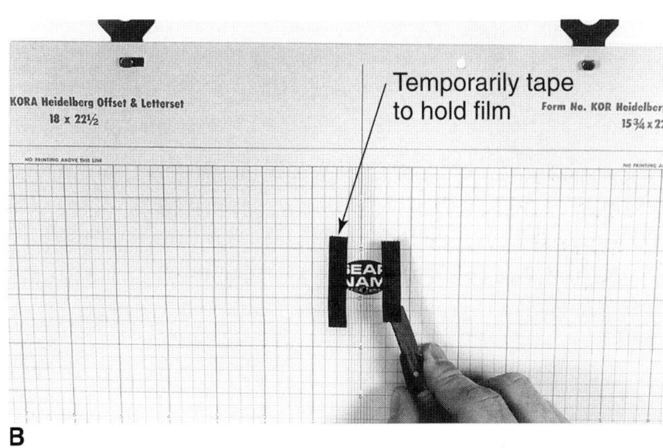

Figure 15-30. Positioning negatives in emulsion-down stripping. A—A small opening cut in the goldenrod sheet allows the negative to be moved into proper alignment. B—Strips of tape hold the negative in place so the flat can be turned over. The negative is then secured in position.

When the negative is positioned properly, tape is placed across the opening to hold it in place. The flat is turned over and the negative is fully secured with lithographer's tape.

With emulsion-down stripping, reference lines are easy to see, and the base side of the film is up for opaquing. See **Figure 15-31**. This method is recommended with film negatives. Emulsion-down stripping makes the film more difficult to tape and remove, however.

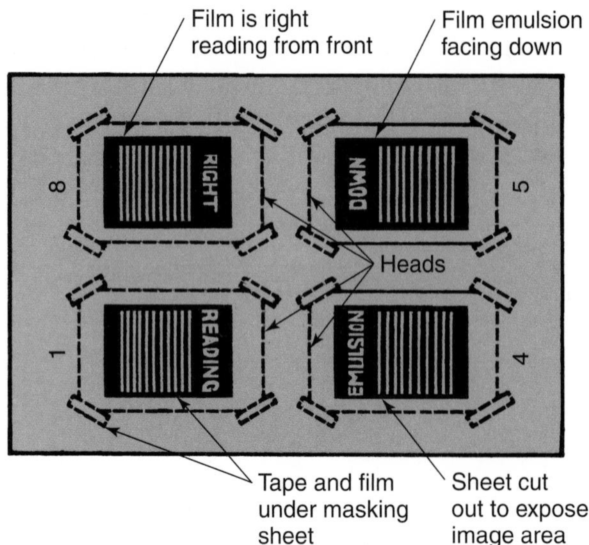

Figure 15-31. Film in this flat has been stripped emulsion-down.

Cutting masking materials

To uncover the images for printing, openings called "windows" must be cut in the masking material, **Figure 15-32**. Because the base of the film is toward the goldenrod sheet, the negative is less likely to be damaged. Care still must be taken to avoid cutting through the negative when cutting the masking sheet. Practice with a sharp knife before making the first cut on the flat.

Figure 15-32. Windows or holes are cut into the goldenrod sheet to allow light to pass through the clear parts of the negatives. (NAQP)

Quality control devices

The quality of images and the accuracy of registration are best determined by the use of quality control devices. Developed by the Graphics Arts Technical Foundation, these devices are stripped onto the nonimage areas of the flat. Directions for use are given with each control device.

A common quality control device is a ***star target***, **Figure 15-33.** The star target is a circular pattern of wedges used to detect slurring (smearing) of ink. Other devices are a sensitivity guide, a gray scale used to gauge film or plate exposure; a dot gain scale use to gauge the dot areas on halftones; a slur gauge; and a color gauge to maintain accuracy of color reproduction, **Figure 15-34**.

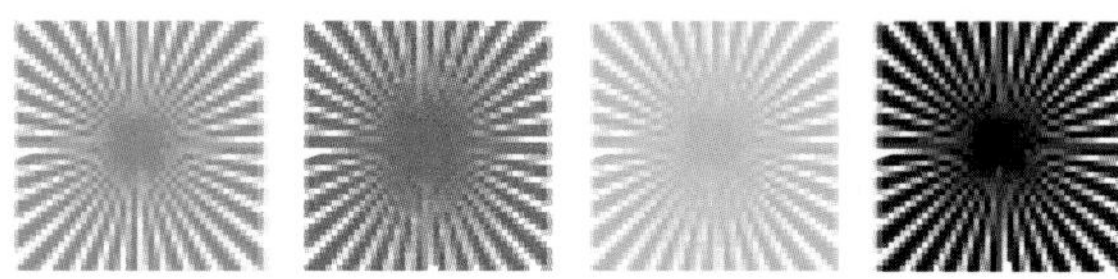

Figure 15-33. A star target is a quality control device used to detect ink slurring. (Graphic Arts Technical Foundation)

Figure 15-34. A color gauge is a quality control device.

Opaquing

Once the windows have been cut in the masking material, some unwanted light-emitting areas could appear. Pinholes can occur in the negative because of a dirty copyboard or original. An opaquing solution covers the pinholes or other defects and blocks out light, **Figure 15-35**. Without proper opaquing, ink spots will appear on the printed image any place unwanted light passes through a negative and exposes tiny spots on the printing plate.

Figure 15-35. A stripper must opaque any imperfections in negatives to block unwanted light from reaching the plate or proofing material.

Opaquing on the *base* side rather than the *emulsion* side of the film is recommended. It is easier to scratch off unwanted opaque on the base side, and the stripper does not risk damaging the emulsion. There is also less chance of image distortion, **Figure 15-36**.

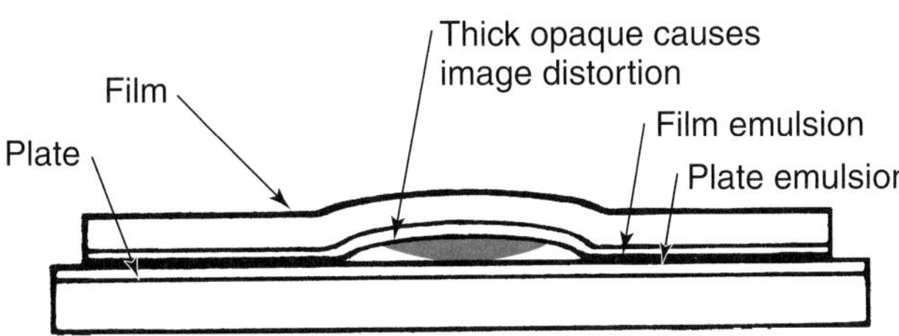

Figure 15-36. If opaque is applied too thickly, the film could be held away from the plate emulsion during burning, causing distortion.

Opaquing is usually the last photoconversion step. Then, the flat is ready for proofing. All specifications should be double-checked.

Complementary flats

Complementary flats are stripped with negatives that are exposed in successive ***burns*** (exposures) onto the same plate. More than one flat is used when several negatives must be pieced close together, for example, a halftone with close-fitting captions. Complementary flats are also suggested when the plate exposure times vary. In **Figure 15-37**, the line work is stripped in one flat while the halftones are stripped in the second flat.

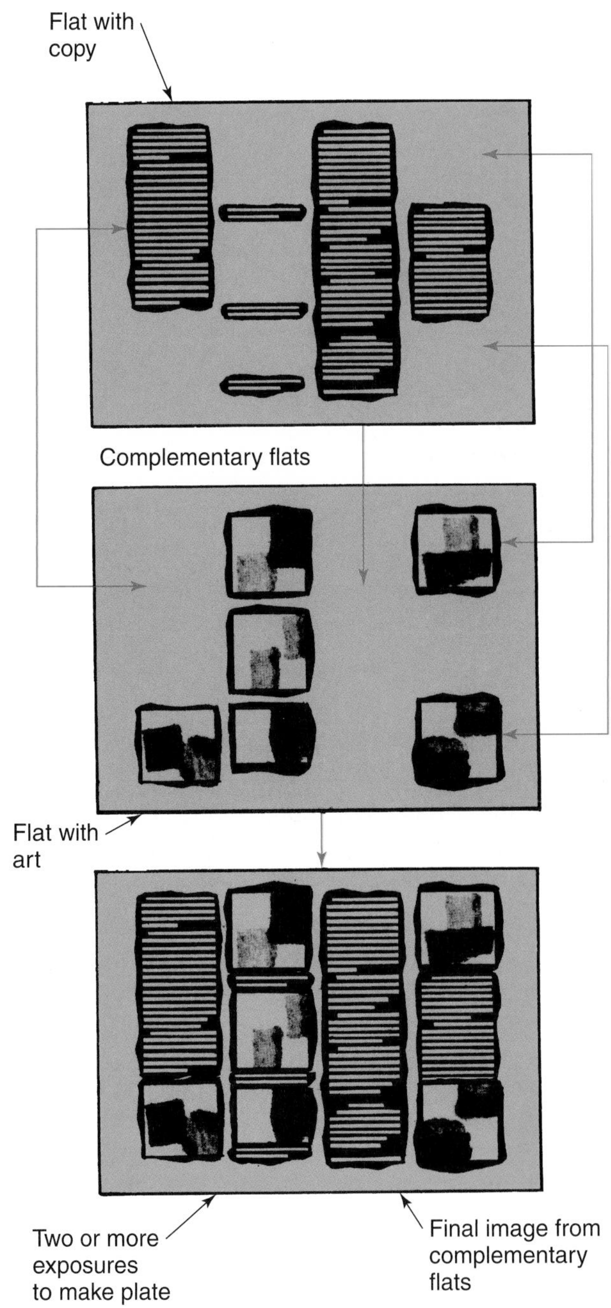

Figure 15-37. Complementary flats are used when images are extremely close together. Each flat is exposed onto the same plate separately. (nuArc company, inc.)

The flats are held down using the register-pin method. This ensures each goldenrod sheet is in the same location for stripping and platemaking, **Figure 15-38**.

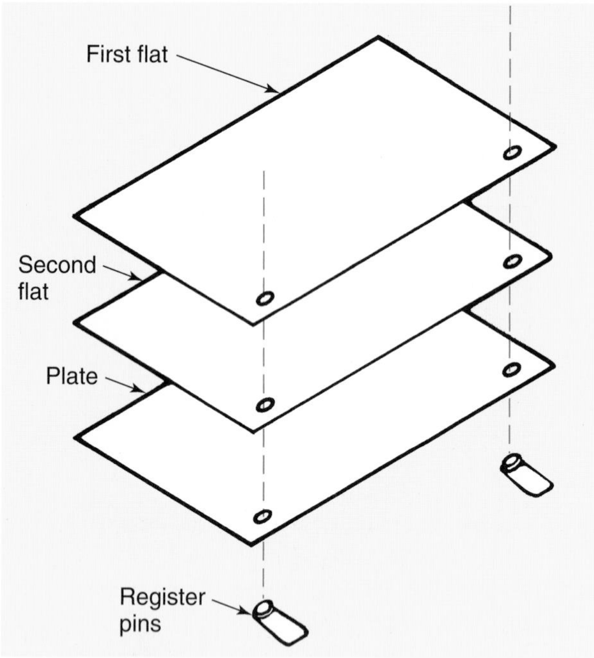

Figure 15-38. Register pins fit through holes punched in the plate and flats. Pins keep the flats in alignment when exposing the plate.

Rubilith™ is a thin, red plastic film on a clear base, often used as masks for halftones. The masking sheet is punched and placed over the pins. The lineup material becomes the guide for cutting the windows in the "ruby" film. The window area is opened by peeling off the ruby film.

The same cutting procedure can be completed with a sheet of goldenrod stock. The windows are cut in the goldenrod sheet. Refer to Figure 15-32. This system can be used to attach halftone materials, tints, or other material requiring complementary flats.

Multiple-page stripping

Assembling line and halftone images to print several pages is called ***multiple-page imposition***, **Figure 15-39**. The number of pages stripped into the flat will typically be 2, 4, 6, or 8, depending upon the size of the signature to be printed. A 32-page signature, for example, would require four 8-page flats.

Figure 15-39. Negatives for two pages have been stripped into this flat.

Color stripping

To reproduce process color negatives and positives, a separate flat is required for each color, **Figure 15-40**. Sometimes the job calls for simple color work. If the colors do not overlap, a single flat can be used. When each color plate is being exposed, the other colors are masked out, as in **Figure 15-41**. Accurate register is very important.

Registering color flats

The multiple-flat process is used in many situations besides complementary text and halftone flats. Most often, it is used in process color work, when flats for three or four colors must be precisely registered.

Two techniques are commonly used to register more than one flat for color work. The first technique is stripping up to a drawn layout. All other flats are keyed to the first master flat.

The second technique uses a proof, such as a blue-line flat, as a key. When goldenrod is used as the base for the key, the technique is similar to stripping a single-color flat.

As in single-color printing, the layout must be drawn. Very often, the black printer negatives are positioned and used as the key. Once the key flat is finished, each color is positioned over the key flat one at a time.

The greatest challenge in multiflat exposure is registration. Each flat must be accurately positioned, and the control marks must line up perfectly. A collimating magnifier is used to sight down directly over the register marks. Once all of the

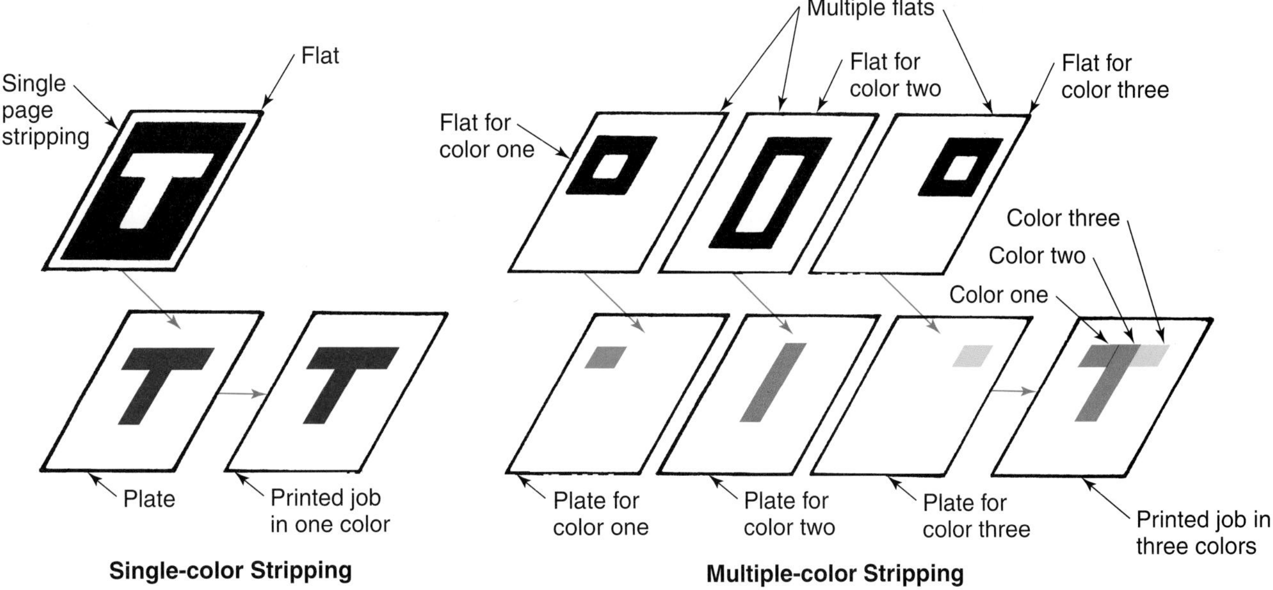

Figure 15-40. Compare single- and multiple-color stripping.

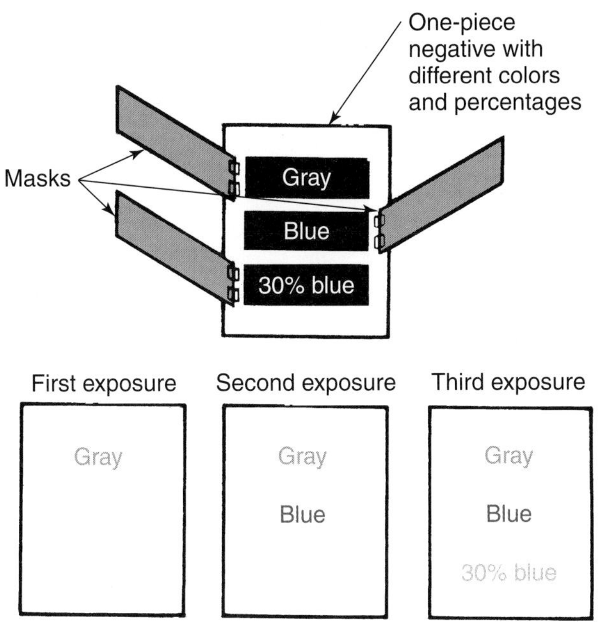

Figure 15-41. Flaps can be used to expose different color images or plates at different times. This saves the stripper from making a separate flat for each color.

negatives have been checked and fastened down to the goldenrod, the windows are cut to allow light to pass through when burning the plate.

Stripping on a clear base

Whenever a clear base is used for negative flats, the goldenrod windows are cut to accurately correspond to the negative placement. Some strippers prefer this system because visibility is increased.

Since film positives are the opposite of negatives, the image areas are opaque and the nonimage areas are clear. A clear stripping base is used. A sheet on which the reference lines are located is put down first. All the sheets are punched to ensure register. The same technique is used for positive flats as was used for negative flats.

After the flats are completed, they must be carefully checked and proofed. The type of proof will vary according to the requirements of the customer. Complementary and multiple flats are proofed before the plates are exposed.

Electronic Imposition and Stripping

Electronic stripping using a computer, display screen, and mask cutting machine to automatically generate flats was considered state-of-the-art only a few years ago. In this technology, the mouse, in conjunction with the menu keypad, is used to produce different shapes on the display screen, **Figure 15-42**. The resulting electronic data is used to run a mask cutting machine or other output device such as an imagesetter, **Figure 15-43**. The output film is a single sheet with all the images in the proper location. In many cases, the film is ready to be used to produce a plate for the press. Less

Figure 15-42. A mouse, control keypad, and viewing screen allow this operator to make and size masks electronically. (Screaming Color-Chapter One)

sophisticated systems use a machine to cut conventional mask overlays for the flat. More advanced systems go directly from electronically scanned data to the printing plate.

Figure 15-43. Electronic stripping methods can allow an imagesetter to output film with all images properly positioned, ready for exposing a printing plate. (Orbotech, Inc.)

Imposition software

One revolution in prepress operations has been the introduction of imposition software. Traditional imposition with stripping done by hand is time-consuming, labor-intensive, and costly. Imposition software significantly reduces all three expenditures by automating the prepress process for electronically published documents, **Figure 15-44**.

Software programs enable users to impose, preview, edit, proof, color separate, and print in a single application. Plates can be quickly created and saved as templates of unlimited size. Strippers can override templates and create a library of custom layouts. Settings can be defined for gutter widths, paper-stock thickness, binding methods, bleed amount, and trim-page sizes. Layouts may be combined, blank pages inserted, and the forms precisely positioned onto a sheet of final film. Compensation for creep is done automatically.

Portable document format

Computer-to-plate and computer-to-press technologies are advances in the printing industry requiring a totally digitized workflow, from creation of a document to its publication. Desktop publishing, using a combination of desktop computer hardware, peripherals, and sophisticated software, allows users to create, manipulate, and store text, graphic images, and entire documents prior to printing. New applications of these ***front-end platforms*** continue to revolutionize the printing industry.

Portable document format (PDF) files are quickly becoming the industry standard for delivering digital documents. PDF files are compressed,

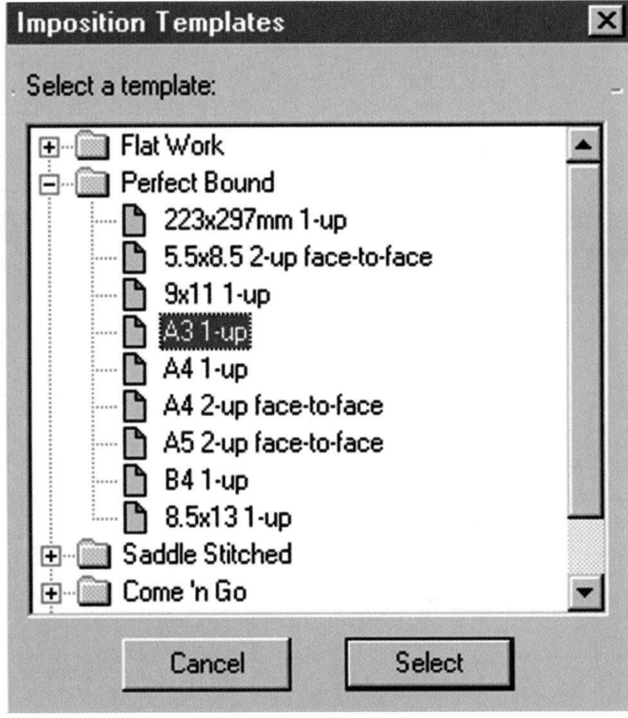

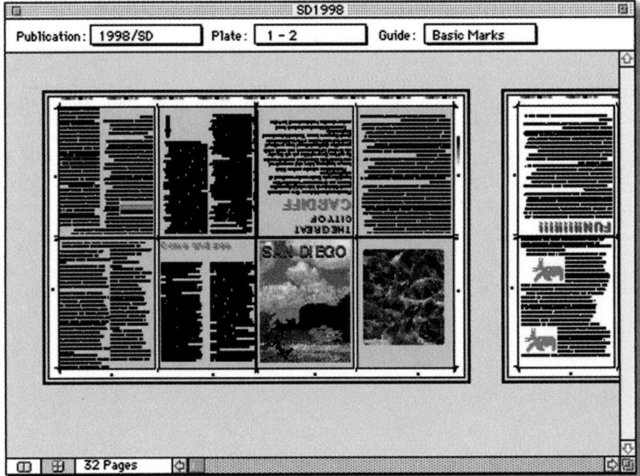

Figure 15-44. Imposition software. A—Plate styles are saved as templates. B—Screen shows the publication as imposed plates. (DK&A, Inc.)

and their small size makes them ideal for electronic distribution. As described in Chapter 9, PDF files are platform and media independent. They preserve the document's original layout, fonts, and graphics as one unit for electronic transfer and viewing. Compatible software "reads" and prints the file. Publishers frequently use a digital master file to distribute documents over electronic mail, the World Wide Web, CD-ROM, or other media. Recycling content into other media is easier and faster with PDF than with PostScript™, the workflow system that has dominated print production since 1985.

The job ticket is as important to the electronic prepress process as it is to the manual process. Attached to every PDF file, the job ticket travels with the file wherever it goes, allowing operators along the way to record, store, and manage information. The job ticket specifications can be easily viewed and modified by everyone who has access to the file. See **Figure 15-45.**

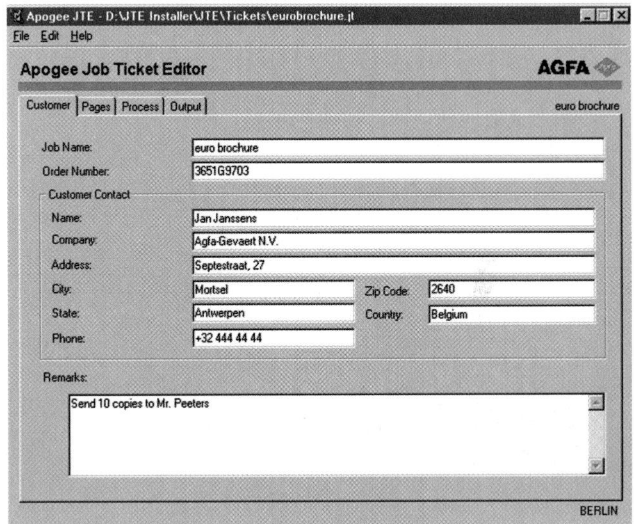

Figure 15-45. Part of a new digital workflow system, this job ticket is attached to every PDF file to automatically lead the job through the prepress process. (Agfa)

When the file is ***rasterized*** (converted to a grid of small dots known as *pixels*), the Raster Image Processor (RIP) will take the job ticket instructions and carry out the imposition order, color separations, and other image assembly procedures conventionally done by hand.

PDF publishing also eliminates the film-proofing stage. A viewing tool allows the designer to zoom in on the pixels and edit them before output to the imagesetter or proofer.

Review Questions

Please do not write in this book. Write your answers on a separate sheet of paper.

1. Define *imposition* and *stripping*.
2. Why is a flat needed?
3. When is step-and-repeat desirable?

4. Describe the three types of press layout commonly used in the industry.
5. _____ is/are used by the stripper to block out unwanted images on negatives.
   a. Tabs
   b. Double-coated tape
   c. Opaque solution
   d. Lithographer's tape
6. What would happen if a stripper failed to opaque a small flaw or mark on a negative?
7. The _____ is used to eliminate parallax error when checking alignment of images.
8. Since film positives are opposites of negatives, the image areas are _____ and the nonimage areas are _____.
9. When any type of image extends completely to the edge of the printed page, it is called a _____.
10. What causes creep?
11. What is *gripper allowance*?
12. How are image quality and accurate registration maintained on the flats?
13. _____ are stripped with material that will be exposed in successive "burns" onto the same plate.
14. _____ enable users to impose, preview, edit, proof, color separate, and print in a single computer application.
15. What is the name of the computer file format that is quickly becoming the industry standard for delivering digital documents?

Contact Printing 16

Learning Objectives

After studying this chapter, you will be able to:

- Explain the process of contact printing.
- Identify the equipment needed for contact printing.
- Determine the proper exposure for various light sources and contact printing materials.
- Describe various contact printing methods.
- Make a contact duplicate.
- Make a spread and a choke.

Important Terms

chokes
contact
contact duplicate
contact printing
contact printing frame
drawdown time
lateral reversal
point light source
spreads
vacuum frame

This chapter discusses how contact printing can be used to reproduce or modify images. The tasks presented in this chapter are changing dramatically. Electronic imaging has replaced most of these manual applications. However, contact printing is still performed for such things as duplicating and proofing.

Contact Printing

Once a negative or positive is produced, a need may exist to develop new films from those originals. These new films can be made by contacting the original to another light-sensitive material. ***Contact printing*** is a process that produces a photographic print by exposing a light-sensitive material (film, photographic paper, or plates) held against a negative or positive in a contact printing frame. The positive or negative is actually in *physical contact* with the film or photo paper during the exposure. The result is a ***contact print***, often referred to as a contact, which is a same-size negative or positive reproduction. An accurate 1:1 size reproduction is assured because of the nature of the contact printing process.

The following list is not exhaustive, but it does indicate some of the applications for which contact printing is used:

- Making negatives from positives.
- Making positives from negatives.
- Changing contrast and tonal values.
- Making proofs and plates.
- Producing spreads and chokes.
- Making screen tints.
- Making step-and-repeat images.

- Making original screened separation negatives for direct screen color work.
- Creating masks.
- Using duplicating film.

Some plants will have a separate area for contact printing. This area usually is in the darkroom, but the location will vary. When selecting a location, care must be taken so that objects in the surrounding area do not reflect light. Also, air currents should not pass over the contact printing frame. The frame should not be placed in a passage or high traffic area.

One of the major problems in the contacting area is controlling dust. Keeping everything dust-free, especially glass surfaces of the contact frame, is essential for quality assurance. Inspection for cleanliness should be part of the initial setup procedure.

Contact Printing Equipment

The three pieces of equipment that make up a basic contact printing system are the contact frame, a light source, and a timer. See **Figure 16-1**. The contact printing frame holds the negative or positive against the light-sensitive material with vacuum pressure, the controlled light source is used to expose the light-sensitive material, and the timer is use to measure the exposure.

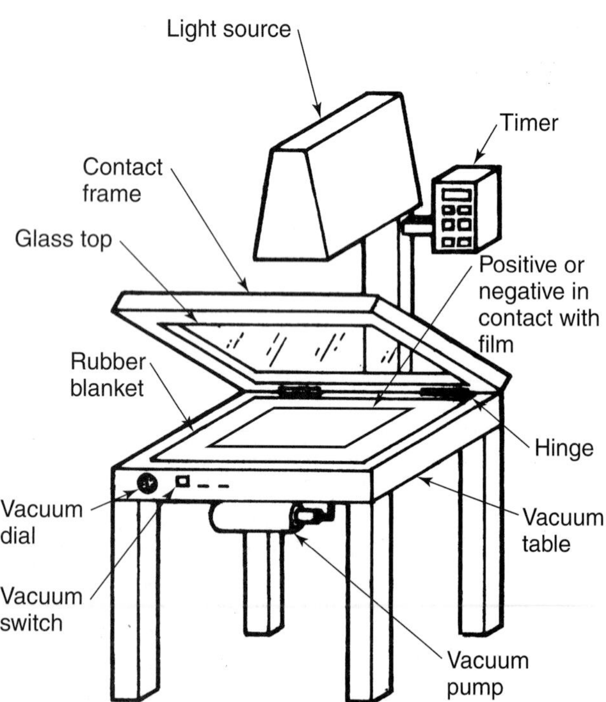

Figure 16-1. Shown is a contact printing frame with a glass top, vacuum system, light source, and light control device (timer).

Contact printing frame

A ***contact printing frame*** is a device that uses a vacuum or a spring action to hold the image and light-sensitive materials together. Frame size selection should be based on the plant requirements. The frame size should be at least 4″ to 5″ larger than the largest film to be used in the facility.

Most applications for contact printing require the use of a vacuum type contact printer, or *vacuum frame*. The three types of vacuum frames commonly used in industry are the glass top (covered), acetate overlay, and open-faced types.

The *glass top frame* is the most common. See **Figure 16-2**. A glass top contact printing frame requires that the glass must be cleaned frequently (preferably before each exposure). Care must be taken not to scratch or break the glass. Glass can refract (bend) light, especially if it is dirty or covered with a residue left by a glass cleaner. A recommended graphic arts glass cleaner must be used with a soft cloth or special material to clean the contact frame glass.

The drawdown of the vacuum must be sufficient to allow trapped air to escape from between the materials in the frame. ***Drawdown*** is the

Figure 16-2. The glass top frame is most common type of vacuum contact printer. (nuArc company, inc.)

amount of time required to remove all air from a vacuum frame to allow the original and the film to achieve uniform contact before exposure.

The rubber blanket used on the glass frame must be pliable enough to conform to the glass when under vacuum. Refer to Figure 16-1. The bead around the edge of the blanket also must be uniform. An uneven bead will not hold a good vacuum. The surface texture of the blanket can cause undesirable patterns on exposed film. Because of this, a backing sheet might be needed. The backing sheet should exhaust air freely. The backing sheet will also help avoid problems with alignment when using register pins.

The *acetate overlay frame* is similar to the glass frame, because the image and light-sensitive material are covered before vacuum is applied. However, the drawdown time for the acetate overlay frame is less than for the glass frame. Proper cleaning of the overlay is important, just as it is with glass.

The *open-faced vacuum frame* does not have a cover over the vacuum surface, so cleaning the cover material is eliminated. Multiple exposures are easier using the open-faced frame. However, problems can arise when trying to expose several small pieces of film onto one large, single sheet. To achieve a good vacuum, the uppermost piece of film must extend at least 1″ beyond any lower films.

Vacuum systems

The *vacuum system* is used by the contacting frame to hold the film or photosensitive material in place. The suction of the vacuum system forces contact between surfaces to ensure good reproduction. See **Figure 16-3**.

The pump must maintain a designated amount of vacuum. Most pumps are the oil-less type that require little maintenance. However, some units have sealed bearings while others require periodic lubrication. The manufacturer's recommendations should be followed to ensure proper performance of the vacuum unit.

Most of the systems have a *bleed valve* to release vacuum. The vacuum gauge is usually in inches of mercury (in. Hg) or kilopascals (kPa). The vacuum generally required for proper drawdown is between 15 in. Hg and 25 in. Hg (50 kPa and 85 kPa).

Proper drawdown is viewed at an angle. The backing sheet must be sealed against the glass or overlay. If air pockets are trapped, release the vacuum, and restart the drawdown.

Sometimes, Newton's rings (colored rings) will appear. When they appear between the top film and the glass, good contact is being made. If Newton's rings appear between the contact materials and the material to receive the image, they will appear on anything contacted after that stage. Under these conditions, they are undesirable.

Light source

Light sources used for contact printing may be point light sources, high-intensity lights, or broad lights. These light sources are generally considered to be roomlight (white light).

Point light source

The ***point light source*** forms a narrow cone of light, which is beneficial when using emulsion-to-base exposures because it ensures a close

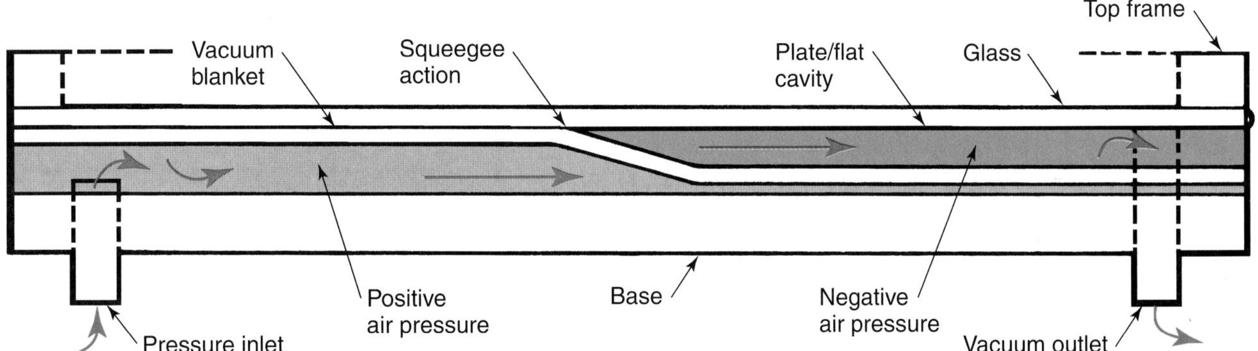

Figure 16-3. The vacuum pump draws air out of vacuum frame, which results in positive air pressure forcing the blanket up against the glass. This pushes the light-sensitive material and film image upward to create good contact with glass. (Teaneck Graphics)

application of dot-for-dot reproduction. See **Figure 16-4**. Point light sources are used with high-speed films, which do not require a large amount of light for exposure.

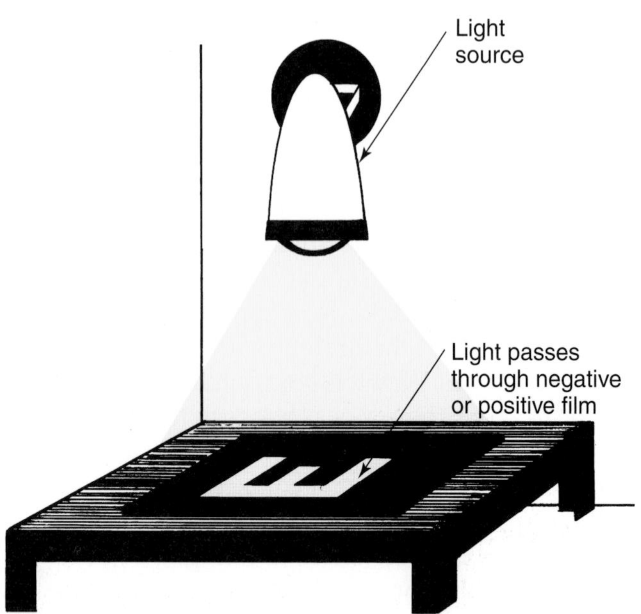

Figure 16-4. A small cone of light is formed by a point light source. This provides the most accurate reproduction since light passes straight down through the image area and onto light-sensitive material.

This point light source also lends itself to applications using filters. A typical point source setup has a constant voltage regulator, a three-stepped transformer, an accurate timer, and a lamp housing that is capable of holding a filter. A multiple-filter turret-style lamp housing might also be used in place of the single filter holder. If color separation work is involved, the multiple-filter setup would be used.

High-intensity light source

The *high-intensity light source* brought contact printing out of the darkroom and into a yellow-light environment. The advantages of the use of this type of light source are that the operators have a better view of what is taking place and they are not curtailed by the confinement of the darkroom. High-intensity light sources are commonly used to expose printing plates.

Whatever high-intensity light source is used, an integrator is a basic requirement because line voltage fluctuations can cause a change in the amount of light that strikes the light-sensitive material. An *integrator* will make adjustments to ensure that a consistent amount of light strikes the contact frame surface with each exposure.

Broad light source

A ***broad light source*** is widely distributed light coverage and less directional than a point light source. Broad lights are commonly used for altering line and image widths and dot sizes by contacting intermediate materials.

If a diffusion sheet is placed in the filter holder of a point light source, it will have the same effect. See **Figure 16-5**. A broad light allows for some dust on the glass or acetate overlay of the contact frame, since the light undercuts (flows around) the unwanted particles.

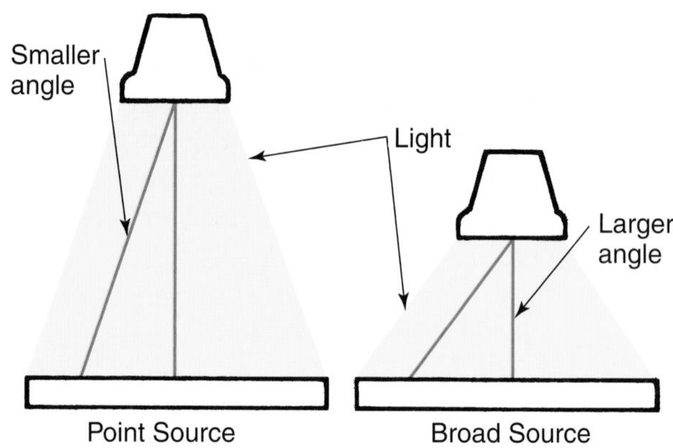

Figure 16-5. A broad light source hits the image at a larger angle than does the point light source. The broad light source can be used to alter the reproduction image.

Contact Printing Considerations

There are a number of considerations that should be kept in mind when contact printing. These considerations should become part of your working routine.

- If using a glass top or acetate overlay contact printing frame, make sure the glass or acetate is free of dust, finger prints, tape residue, opaquing solution, etc.
- Avoid scratching the frame's surface with razor blades when removing tape residue.
- Use an approved backing sheet, and place the film in the frame with the desired side facing up.

- Always include a target control aid appropriate to the work being conducted.
- Be careful not to place fingerprints on the photosensitive material. See **Figure 16-6**.

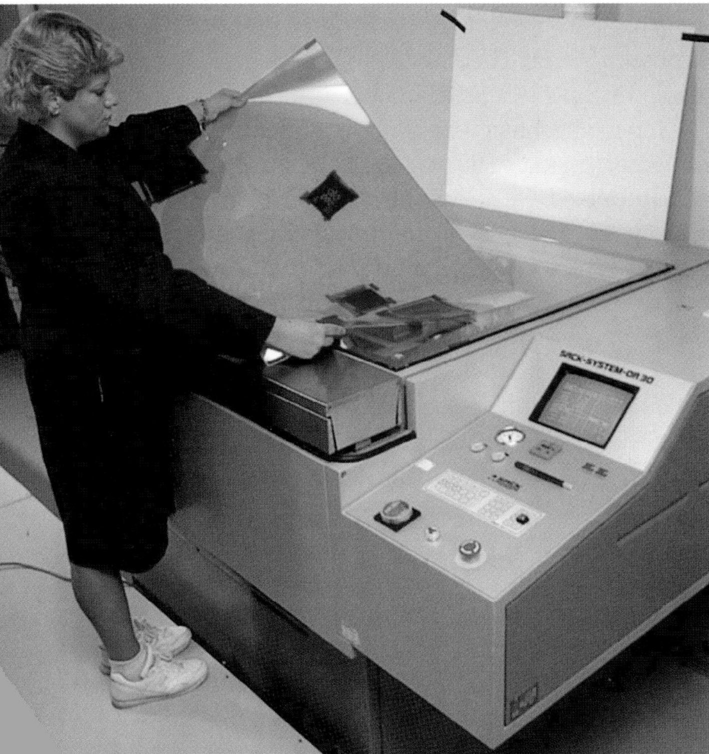

Figure 16-6. A modern contact printer in use. Be sure to place film in the printer with correct side up. Always work carefully to avoid leaving fingerprints on the glass or film and to prevent scratching the glass or film. (Screaming Color-Chapter One)

- Make sure the exposed film is dust-free.
- Position the exposed film so you do not scratch the film emulsion.
- Apply the vacuum slowly and visually inspect for good contact or drawdown, if possible
- Make certain the vacuum gauge reads properly.
- Before exposing, wait until all air is exhausted between films and overlays. For less critical work, delay at least 30 seconds after the vacuum gauge has reached maximum reading. Wait up to 2 minutes for the more demanding jobs. This delay is very important.
- Make sure the frame is evenly lighted over the entire surface.
- Set the timer to the established values for the type of work and film being used.
- Process exposed film according to an established format for the type of film and application intended. Both manual and automatic processing are suitable for films used for contacting. Refer to Chapter 14.

Exposures for Contact Printing

Proper *exposure for contact printing* is determined by light intensity and time. Variations in either lighting or time will change the final product. The intensity of the light source is based on the following factors:

- Bulb wattage.
- Light reflectors used.
- Consistency of the light.
- Distance between the light source and film. The light intensity, or brightness, is inversely proportional to the square of distance. This means that light falling on a object 2′ from a light source is only 1/4 as intense as the light on an object 1′ from the light. Light on an object 4′ from the light is only 1/16 as intense. **Figure 16-7** shows that the greater the distance between the light source and film, the less intense the exposure.

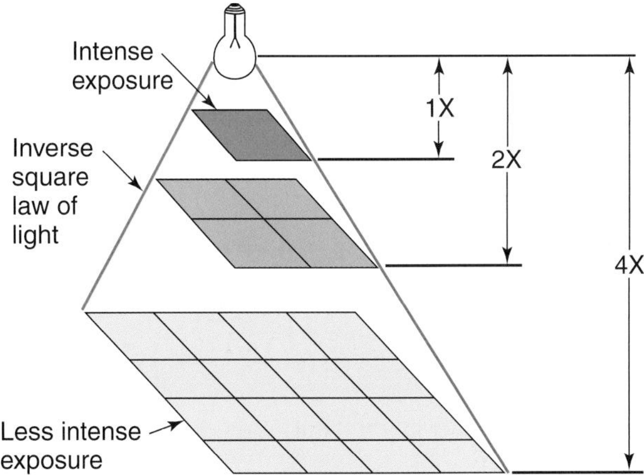

Figure 16-7. Light intensity, or brightness, decreases rapidly as the distance between the light source and the film increases.

The time (duration) of the exposure is typically controlled by a timer. The timer must be able to produce the same exposure each time the contact frame is used. Short exposures tend to be difficult to control. In such situations, the use of a neutral density (ND) filter is recommended. An ***ND filter*** reduces the amount of light transmitted, giving greater time for controlling the exposure.

Because a light source may be powerful enough and high enough in ultraviolet rays to cause eye damage, never look directly into it.

Determining exposure

An *exposure test* should be conducted periodically to check for changes in conditions. Light sources age and lose intensity. This can change the exposure time if a light integrator is not a part of the system. Changing to a different type of film, different film manufacturer, new emulsion number, or even a new box of film may require an exposure test to determine a new basic exposure time.

The correct exposure will produce an accurate image size on the contact or duplicate with a minimum number of defects. Fine serifs in type and the correct size of halftone dots are indicators of a proper exposure. Improper exposure will result in low-density film, pinholes, and inaccurate reproduction of the original.

Step-off method

The *step-off method* consists of a series of progressive exposures made on a single sheet of film. Refer to Chapter 12, Figures 12-28 and 12-29. By moving a mask across the frame at fixed intervals, a stepped effect will be produced on the processed film. The exposure time is determined by viewing the step-offs. The most representative image is chosen and the time is calculated. This determines the basic exposure for that specific application. If the correct exposure appears to be between two different steps, an additional step test may be required. Use the steps in question as the low and high for the second exposure test.

Other methods can be used to test for the best exposure time. They include the use of a density guide or a projection exposure indicator.

Once the basic exposure has been determined for the specific type of film and contacting conditions, then an exposure control device, such as a gray scale, will help maintain quality. See **Figure 16-8**. Most film manufacturers produce control devices that should be utilized when exposing their specific products. There are some differences among control devices, but their main goal is to allow the operator to control the process, rather than the *process* controlling the *operator*. By becoming more familiar with the different devices available and the specific purposes and applications of each, an operator will become much more proficient at contact printing. Establishing standards within the facility itself and maintaining set procedures will reduce time and costs in the long run. Different operators in the same facility will be working together, rather than against each other.

Sometimes too much attention is given to results from the control devices rather than the actual film being reproduced. Remember that exposure control devices are an aid, *not* the end result or final product.

Contact Image Orientation

The contact operator must be aware of the three types of image orientation. These are emulsion-to-emulsion, base-to-emulsion, and emulsion-to-base. See **Figure 16-9**.

Figure 16-8. Two exposure control variations—a standard gray scale and a contact printing scale. The exposure control device is stripped into a film flat as close to images as possible. Remember to position control device emulsion to correspond to other components.

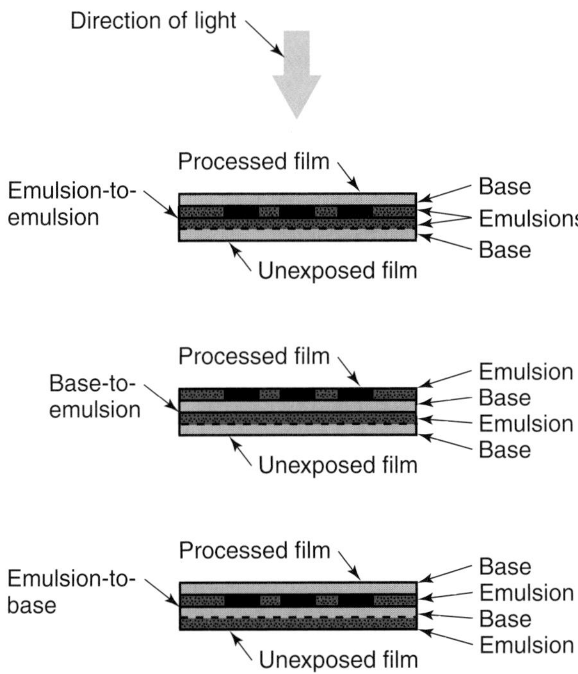

Figure 16-9. These are the three emulsion positions used for contacting. Emulsion-to-emulsion is most accurate.

One of the most common types of film contact printing is a reversal of image orientation. It is made with an *emulsion-to-emulsion* exposure. In this case, the *original* negative would be wrong-reading when viewed from the emulsion side and right-reading when viewed from the base side. The finished product of an emulsion-to-emulsion exposure would result in a right-reading positive when viewed from the emulsion side.

If the final negative or positive is to be used for platemaking, the correct image orientation requires the emulsion to be *toward* the plate. This is a very important point to remember.

An emulsion-to-emulsion contact requires that the emulsion of the unexposed film faces the light source. The emulsion of the processed film, which is placed on top, faces the exposed film. This procedure will give the *highest quality* reproduction. A ***negative working film*** (one where exposure increases density) is required for this type of process.

Contact reversal

The ***contact reversal*** process is used to produce negatives from positives and vice versa. It is accomplished by placing an orthochromatic contact film with the emulsion up in the contact frame. The film negative or positive is placed over the orthochromatic film with the emulsion side up. Once exposed, the film is processed in the same manner as other orthochromatic films. See **Figure 16-10**.

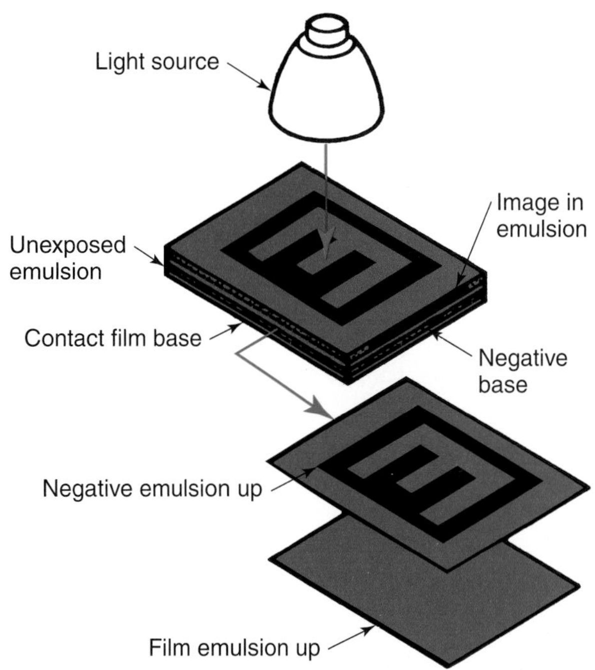

Figure 16-10. The process of making a contact film reversal.

Contact duplicates

A ***contact duplicate***, or ***dupe***, is the result of a process that makes the same image as the original, such as a negative to produce another negative. The unexposed areas of duplicating film remain black when developed. This makes the duplicate the same as the original.

To make a left-to-right reading duplicate the same as the original, the emulsion of the duplicate and original must face in the *same* direction. When the emulsion of the duplicate film and the original are facing *each other*, the resulting duplicate will be a ***lateral reversal***.

Contacting films

Much of the film used for contact printing is *daylight film*. This does *not* mean it can be handled in daylight. However, daylight film can be handled in a yellow light environment without exposure. This makes it ideal for use with a contact frame because of improved visibility in the work area.

If duplicates of an original (either negative or positive) are required, use a *duplicating film*. This film is ***positive-working***, which means that light or exposure subtracts density from the film (exposed areas become clear film). *Dupes* are commonly made when a multiple number of copies are needed on one press sheet. Processing duplicating film is the same as with regular lithographic film, and require the same care in handling.

Contact Masking Materials

Care should be taken when choosing masking materials for applications involving contact printing and duplicating film. The film has an exposure threshold. This threshold might be exceeded by multiple exposures if a high-quality masking material is not employed.

Masking material can be checked by first determining the maximum number of exposures that will be given to the film, then multiplying it by the time per exposure. This will give the total or maximum exposure of light.

Cover the exposed film with the masking material and expose for the maximum calculated time. If the processed film shows exposure through the mask, then the masking material is not appropriate for that given task. Care should be taken in selecting the right masking material for the specific job.

Spreads and Chokes

A ***spread (fatty)*** is made by a contact printing process that makes the original image slightly larger. The light source spreads out to expose more of the light-sensitive material. A ***choke (skinny)*** is made by a contact printing process that makes the original image slightly smaller. The light source angles inward to expose less image area. Spreads are made from *negative film images* while chokes are made from *positive film images*. See **Figure 16-11**.

Both spreads and chokes create an overlap of the images. When an image's outline is complex, contacting is usually used to create the overlap, rather than using handwork. The amount of choke or spread should be specified for any given job, and may be influenced by the type of press used to print the image. If lettering is involved, the width should be considered when specifying the amount of overlap. Spreads and chokes are measured with control guides.

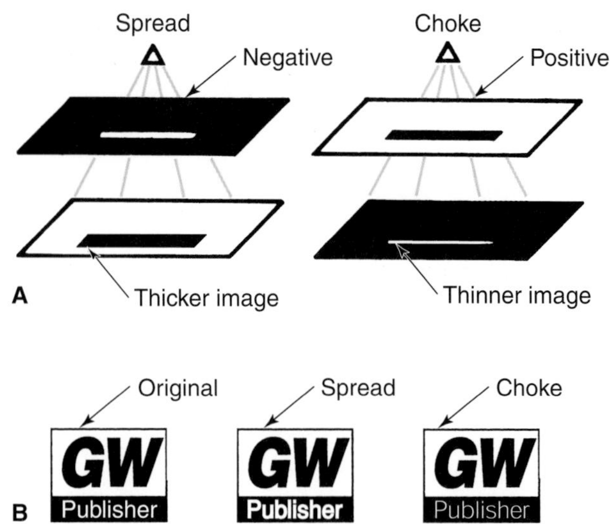

Figure 16-11. A—Light can be used to enlarge and spread or reduce and choke an image. B—An original image and its spread and choked versions.

When making spreads or chokes, the light is spread as it passes through the layer of film. Therefore, it does not produce an accurate image, but instead a somewhat larger or smaller one depending on the method or orientation of materials. See **Figure 16-12**.

By placing a diffuser sheet on top of the contact printing frame, the natural tendency of light to spread is multiplied and the image is undercut. Exposure times are increased in order to achieve this undercutting. *Diffuser sheets* are usually frosted acetate, matte drafting film, or 1/8″ white rigid plastic. Sometimes, the amount of spread or choke is such that spacer sheets (commonly acetate) are placed between the layers of the film sandwich in order to provide even greater undercutting of the image.

The spread and choke practice is also used in electronic imaging. In this case, it is referred to as *trapping*. Refer to Chapter 11 for more details on trapping.

Contact Frame Screening

A continuous tone negative or positive can be converted to a halftone in a contact printing frame by using a contact screen. The technique is similar to

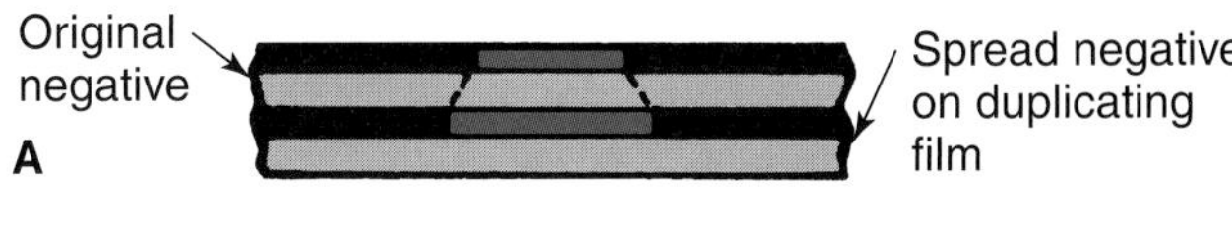

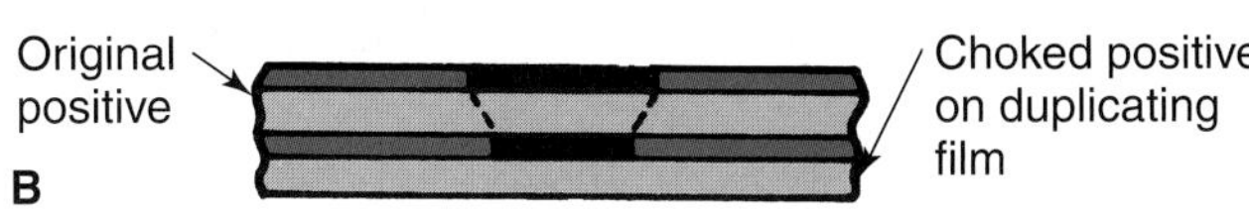

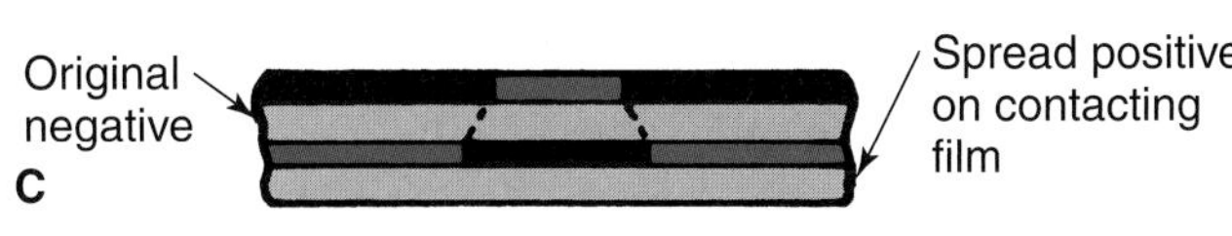

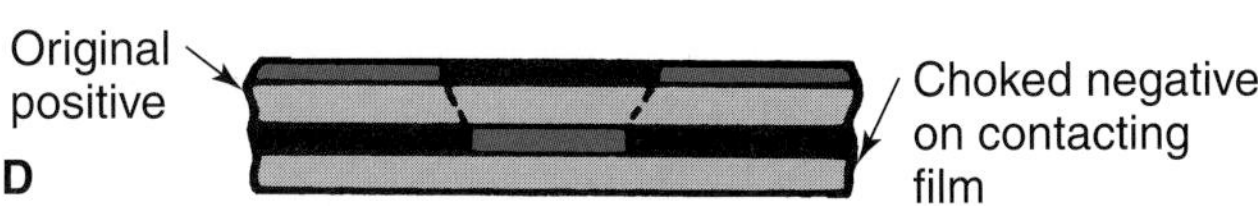

Figure 16-12. The techniques for making spreads and chokes. A—This orientation of the original negative will make spread negatives on duplicating (positive-working) film. B—This orientation of the original positive will make a choked positive on duplicating film. C—This orientation of the original negative will make a spread positive on contacting (negative working) film. D—This orientation of the original positive will make a choked negative on contacting film.

the regular process camera procedure. A white light source is used to make the main exposure, while a flash exposure is also used to extend the contrast range. The correct exposure is determined by the step-off method, which was discussed in Chapter 12.

Review Questions

Do not write in this book. Write your answers on a separate sheet of paper.

1. Define *contact printing*.
2. List four reasons for contact printing.
3. Explain how a vacuum contact frame works.
4. _____ time refers to the amount of time needed for sufficient vacuum to be produced in a vacuum frame.
   a. Buildup
   b. Exposure
   c. Developing
   d. Drawdown
5. The required vacuum for contact printing generally ranges between _____.
   a. 5 in. Hg and 15 in. Hg (17 kPa and 50 kPa)
   b. 50 in. Hg and 75 in. Hg (169 kPa and 252 kPa)
   c. 15 in. Hg and 25 in. Hg (50 kPa and 85 kPa)
   d. None of the above.
6. A(n) _____ light is beneficial when using emulsion-to-base exposure orientation.
7. A broad light source is a common application for altering line image _____ and _____.
8. What is a contact reversal?
9. How can you find out if the masking material is sufficient when contacting?
10. Explain the difference between a spread and a choke.

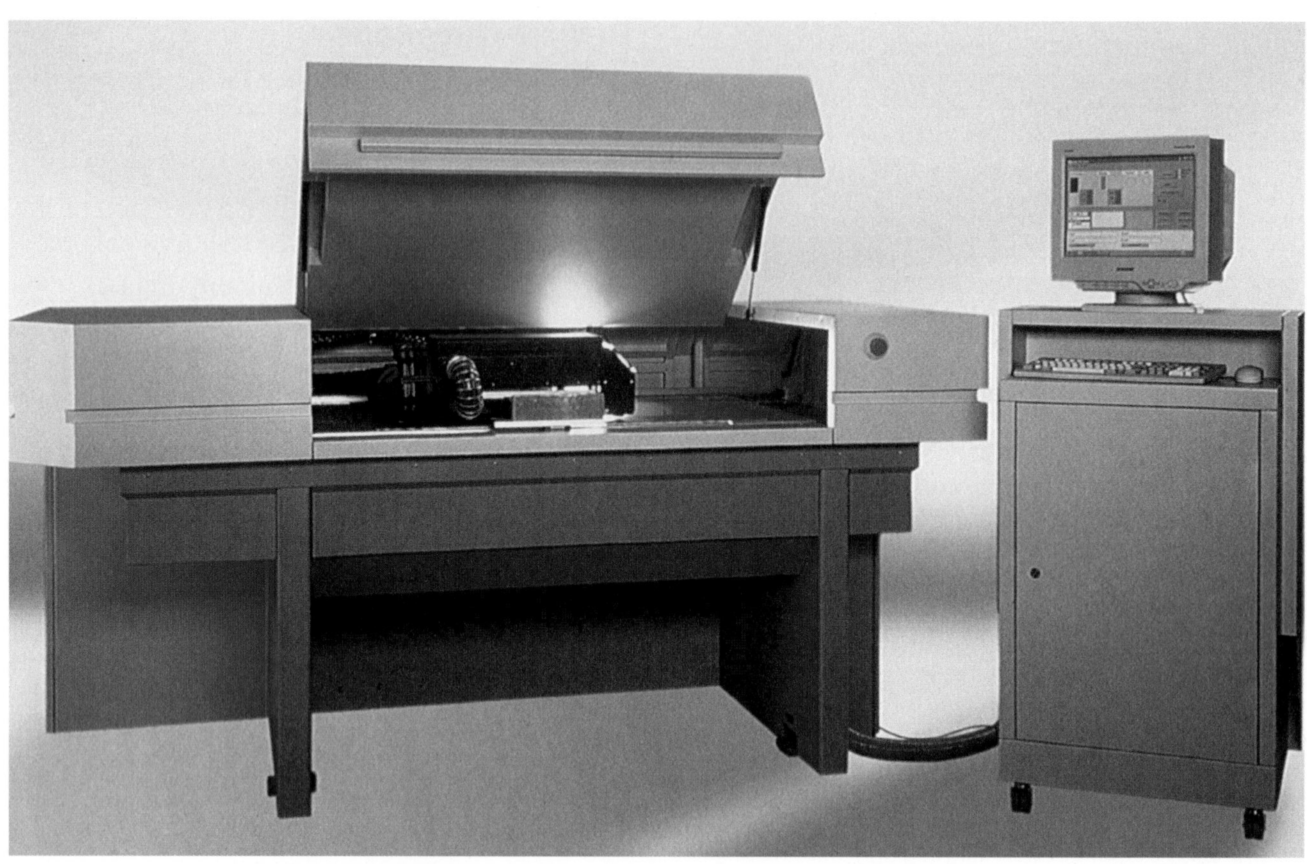

This digital platesetter uses ultraviolet light for direct imaging of conventional high-speed aluminum press plates. It was the first equipment designed to combine the use of conventional UV-sensitive plates (rather than thermal or laser plates) with the time and cost advantages of the computer to plate (CTP) method. The platesetter incorporates a UV light source and a digitally controlled screen with more than 300,000 addressable dots to form an image that can then be projected onto the plate for exposure. (basysPrint Inc.)

17 Lithographic Platemaking

Learning Objectives

After studying this chapter, you will be able to:

- Understand the use of lithography as a printing method and explain how lithographic plates are used on an offset press.
- Describe the types of equipment used in platemaking.
- Identify the main parts of a lithographic plate and explain how plates are classified.
- Demonstrate how plates are exposed and developed on a platemaker.
- Recognize the methods and equipment used in different platemaking systems.
- List common problems associated with the platemaking process.

Important Terms

automatic plate processor
computer-to-plate (CTP)
electrostatic plate
laser plate
lithography
plate
soft image
surface plate
thermal plate
waterless plate

This chapter covers the different methods used in making and processing plates and the various types of plates used in offset lithographic printing. A ***plate*** or *image carrier* is an imaged sheet designed for printing multiple copies on a press. This chapter will illustrate how different types of plates are made and introduce the various forms of equipment used in platemaking.

Lithography

Lithography is a method of printing directly from a flat surface or *plate* containing an image formed in ink. The lithographic process is also known as *planography*, which means printing from a flat surface. Lithographic printing is based on the principle that oil (or grease) and water do not readily mix. The plate (image carrier) has a *nonimage area* that receives water and repels oil or grease-based ink. The *image area* accepts grease (ink) and refuses water. **Figure 17-1** illustrates how ink and water act in lithographic printing.

Lithography was developed as a method of printing from a flat stone surface by Alois Senefelder, a German playwright, in 1796. Using a smooth piece of limestone, he drew an image with a grease-based material. When the stone was moistened, water would only be absorbed by the nonimage area of the stone; it would not adhere to the image formed in grease. When the stone was inked, only the grease-based image would accept the ink. Paper was placed on the stone, and pressure was applied to transfer the image. Images for stone lithography were drawn in reverse, since the image would transfer directly or *mirror* to the printing

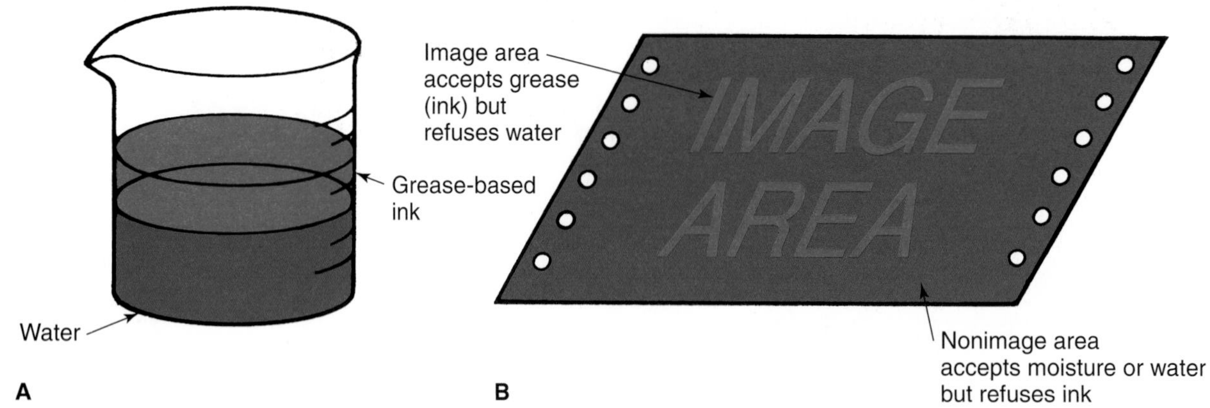

Figure 17-1. Lithography is a printing method based on the principle that oil or grease and water do not mix readily. A—If grease-based ink is poured into a container of water, the ink will normally separate and rise to the surface. B—Lithographic plates use the principle of ink and water repulsion for printing. The image area accepts ink but rejects water, while the nonimage area accepts water but rejects ink.

surface. See **Figure 17-2**. Prints were made by repeating the process of applying water and then ink to the stone.

As printing methods improved, metal replaced stone as the standard material for making lithographic plates. The development of ***offset printing*** led to the use of metal plates with printing presses.

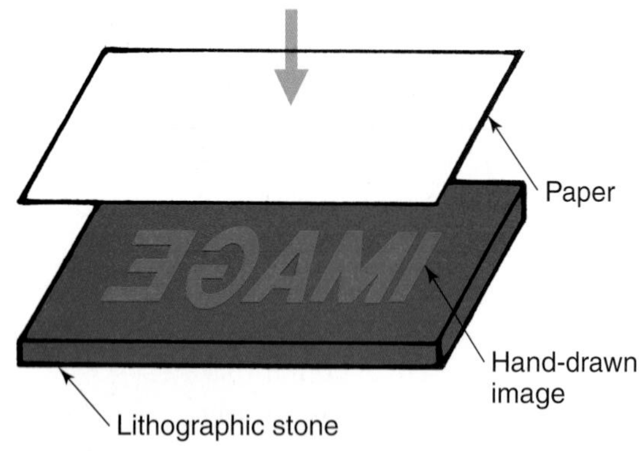

Figure 17-2. In stone lithography, images were drawn in reverse on a smooth stone surface to make prints.

The operation of an offset lithographic press involves the *transfer* of images from one surface to another. The image is *offset* from the plate to a *blanket* and is then transferred to the paper. See **Figure 17-3**. After the blanket receives the image in reverse form from the plate, the image transfers back to its original form on the substrate.

Printing methods continue to evolve as electronic platemaking and desktop publishing systems gain more use in the graphic communications industry. Traditionally, platemaking has involved the use of a plate coated with a light-sensitive material to capture images from a positive source. In this method, film is placed over the plate and the plate is exposed and then processed. In electronic platemaking, film is not used and the image is transferred from the original source directly to the plate. Automatic plate processors, combining image transfer with plate processing, are commonly used to make plates. While electronic methods of platemaking have become widely adopted, traditional platemaking techniques and equipment continue to be used in commercial applications of printing.

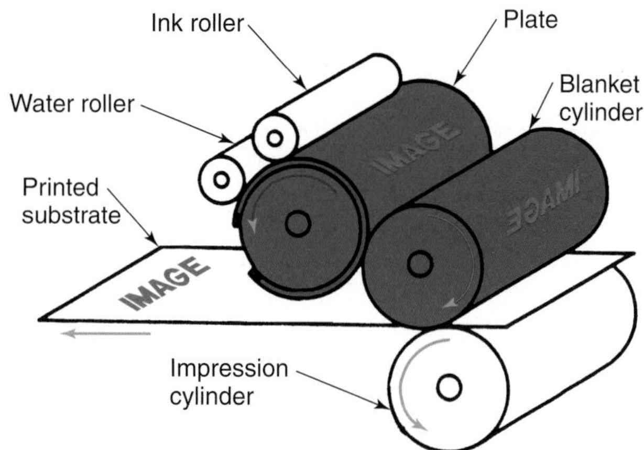

Figure 17-3. Components of an offset lithographic press. After the image is offset from the plate to the blanket, it is offset again to the substrate.

Platemaking Equipment

Platemaking requires the use of a platemaker and processing materials or an automatic plate processor. A platemaker uses a light source to expose the plate from a piece of film or camera-ready copy. The plate is placed in contact with the original image inside a glass frame called a ***vacuum frame***. After the plate is exposed, it may be developed or processed by hand using chemicals in a developing sink, or processed by an automatic plate processor.

A self-contained platemaking unit is equipped with a light source, a light control or timer, a vacuum frame, a vacuum pump, and a motor. A flip-top platemaker is one example of a self-contained unit. See **Figure 17-4**.

Figure 17-4. A flip-top platemaker used to expose plates. Exposure time is controlled electronically. (nuArc company, inc.)

The vacuum frame holds the plate and stripped flat (film mounted on a masking sheet) in close contact under the glass during exposure. The plate and flat are aligned and placed inside the frame on a rubber blanket, which is connected to a vacuum pump. The pump removes air between the blanket and the glass, sealing the plate and flat together. After the plate and flat have made close contact, the light source is turned on and the exposure is made. See **Figure 17-5**.

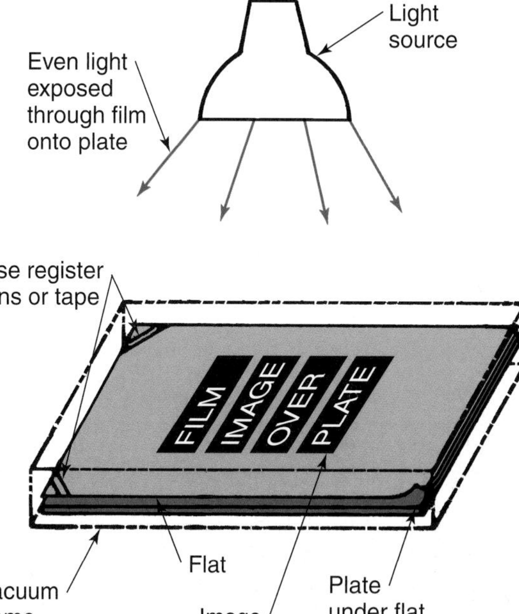

Figure 17-5. A plate is exposed once the film has been registered over the plate and a close contact has been made. The light source shines through the image on film and exposes the light-sensitive surface of the plate.

A source with light high in ultraviolet is commonly used to expose plates. The light source must provide an even illumination across the plate area; a computerized control panel on the front of the platemaker houses the controls for vacuum and exposure time.

After the plate is exposed, it is developed by hand in a developing sink. See **Figure 17-6**. The plate is processed with developing solution and rinsed with water. A water control is commonly attached to the sink and used in plate processing.

Automatic plate processors

Automatic plate processors are used to automatically prepare plates for the press. They are commonly found in small and large printing plants. See **Figure 17-7**. Processing chemicals are automatically applied and replenished when needed. Process

Figure 17-6. A developing sink is used when processing exposed plates by hand. (nuArc company, inc.)

Figure 17-7. Plate processing is increasingly being done with automatic plate processors. (3M Company)

monitoring is conducted to ensure the chemicals are at the proper strength for consistent development.

Automatic processing eliminates the task of processing plates by hand and assures consistent plate quality. The internal parts of a typical processor are shown in **Figure 17-8**. During automatic processing, the plate is transported through the unit at a determined rate of speed. It is fully developed and ready for the press when it leaves the processor. See **Figure 17-9**.

Lithographic Plates

Most of the lithographic plates in use today are still based on the principle that grease and water do not readily mix. The image and nonimage areas of a plate are kept separate chemically. This separation is necessary because the image and nonimage are essentially on the same plane.

Waterless printing plates are designed with a principle different from that used for the conventional lithographic plate. A waterless plate has a light-sensitive, ink-receptive photopolymer attached to its surface. The nonimage area is coated with an ink-repellent substance other than water.

The most common material used to make plates is aluminum. Other metals, plastic, and paper are also used as plate materials. Aluminum is widely used because it is more receptive to water than grease. It is also flexible and lightweight, and it can be easily grained.

Generally speaking, lithographic plates have three parts: the base or *plate grain*, the *plate covering*, and the *plate coating*. Plate materials and surfaces vary according to the use of the plate.

Plate grains

The ***plate grain*** of a lithographic plate is the surface texture of the plate base. It can appear very smooth or quite rough when magnified. Several types of grains are used to make plates. Each appears as a texture on the surface of the plate.

Mechanical grains include *blasted* and *brushed* grains. Blasted grain is formed by an abrasive applied by air pressure. Brushed grain is applied to the plate with abrasives and a brush. *Chemical grains* are formed by chemicals that etch into the plate. **Figure 17-10** shows several grain classifications for plates.

Paper and plastic plates are considered to be *grainless plates*. The surfaces of grainless plates are manufactured to hold moisture.

Plate coverings

The materials making up a plate can also be a combination of plastic, paper, or various metals. ***Plate coverings*** are layers of material bonded to the base of a plate. The covering assists in holding the image area on the plate surface.

Plate coatings

Plate coatings are the surface layers of light-sensitive material that form or harden when exposed to light. Plates manufactured with a

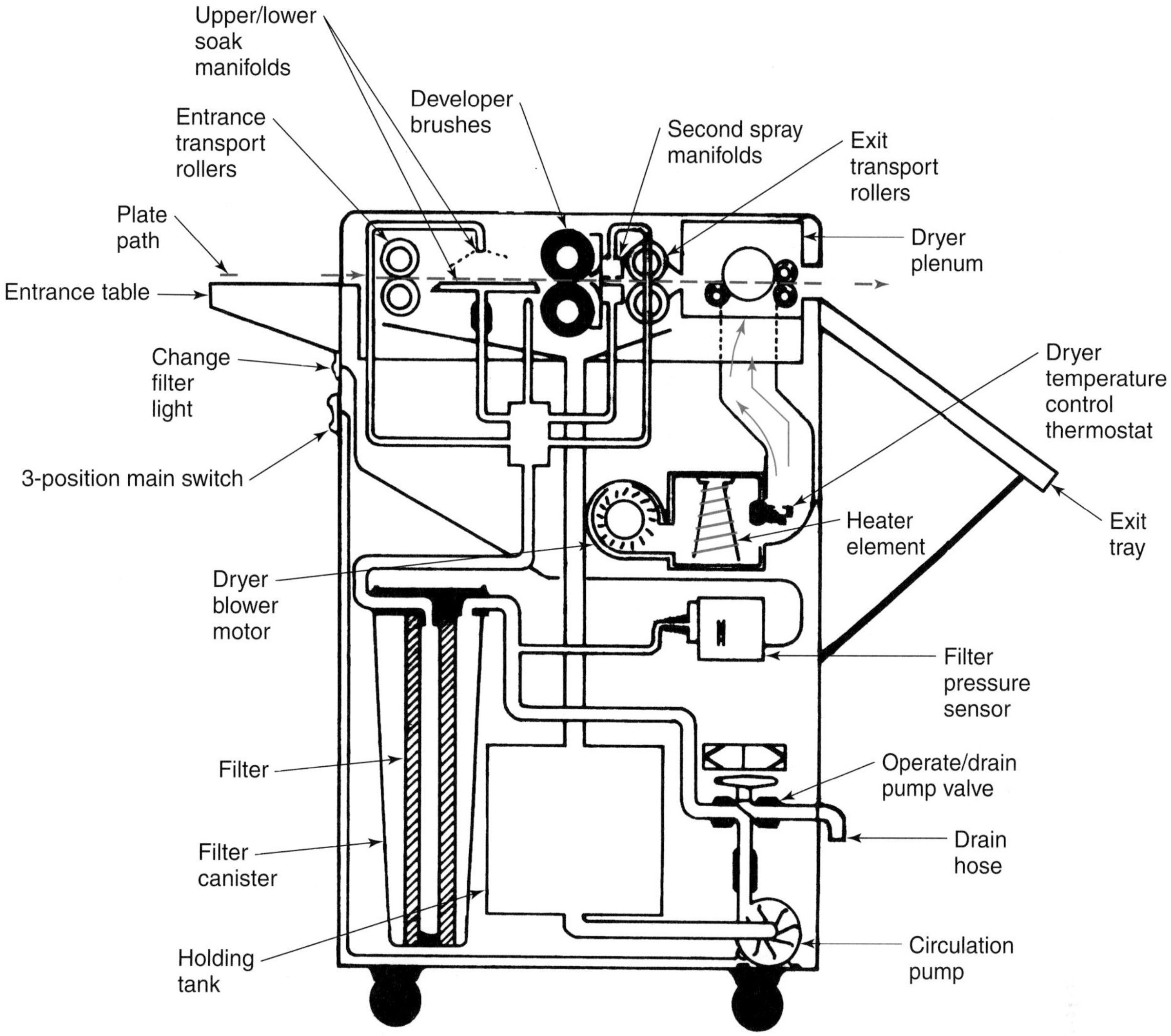

Upper/lower soak manifolds
Developer brushes
Entrance transport rollers
Second spray manifolds
Exit transport rollers
Plate path
Dryer plenum
Entrance table
Change filter light
Dryer temperature control thermostat
3-position main switch
Heater element
Exit tray
Dryer blower motor
Filter pressure sensor
Filter
Operate/drain pump valve
Filter canister
Drain hose
Holding tank
Circulation pump

Figure 17-8. Components of an automatic plate processor. Rollers feed the plate through the processor as it is developed and dried.

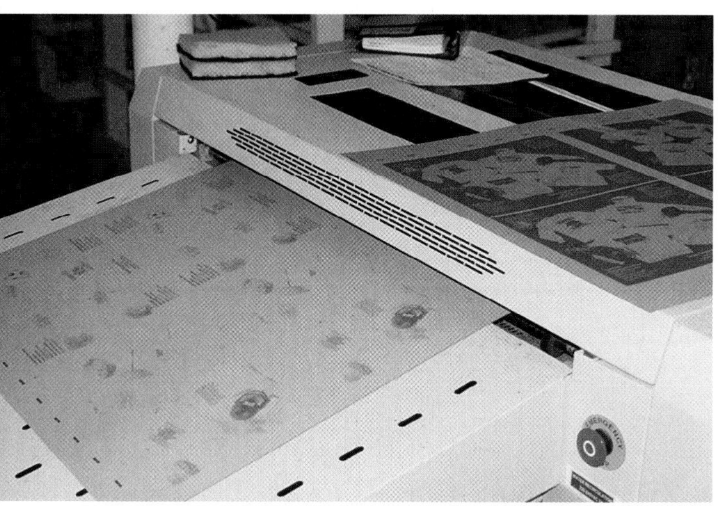

Figure 17-9. A finished plate emerges from the automatic plate processor, ready for printing.

light-sensitive material to capture images are *presensitized*. Different types of coatings are used for various platemaking applications.

Diazo coating is one of the most commonly used. When a plate is exposed and active light strikes a diazo coating, the image area becomes inactive. The nonimage areas remain active and can be removed during plate processing. The inactive image area remains as a part of the plate for printing the image.

Photopolymers are plastic coatings on plates that are designed to produce long-lasting images without requiring added protection. When light strikes the coating, the coating hardens and forms a strong image area.

Silver halide coatings contain silver salts and are used with diffusion transfer plates, which are

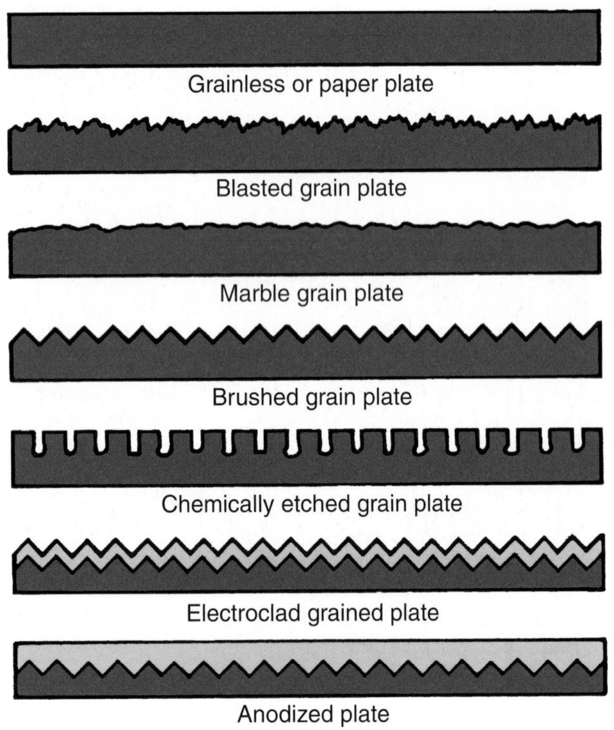

Figure 17-10. Different types of grain used to form a surface texture on a plate.

exposed from a negative. The image areas are converted to metallic silver when light strikes the plate surface and when the plate is developed.

Electrostatic plates have carbon powders or liquids applied to the surface. The coating is fixed on the plate *electrostatically* (using a static electrical charge). Although the surface of the plate is not coated with a light-sensitive material, light is used during the platemaking process to neutralize an electrical charge in nonimage areas.

Plate classifications

Presensitized plates coated with light-sensitive material are called surface plates because of the coating on the surface of the plate. ***Surface plates*** are classified as negative-acting, positive-acting, additive, or subtractive plates.

Negative-acting plates are plates with image areas that harden when exposed to light. Negative film stripped on a flat is used to expose the image onto the plate.

Positive-acting plates are those in which the area exposed by light becomes the nonimage area. Positive film is contacted to the positive-acting plate to transfer the image. After exposure, the exposed nonimage area is removed in processing.

Additive plates have a developing solution added to the image during processing. Although additive plates are presensitized, developer is used to make the image more receptive to ink and more durable.

Subtractive plates are presensitized plates that are processed after exposure by removing the plate coating from the nonimage area.

Handling plates

Lithographic plates must be handled carefully when they are processed and mounted on a printing press. Fingerprints or dirty roller marks will appear on the plate if proper care and cleanliness are not practiced at all times.

Lithographic plates are designed with a means of being attached to the plate cylinder of a printing press. Plates are classified by holding as straight bar, pinbar, or serrated (slotted). See **Figure 17-11.** All three types of plates are commonly used with duplicator presses, but larger presses normally use straight bar plates.

A *straight bar* is a clamping device that is used to hold a plate over the entire press cylinder length. Pinbar and serrated plates have punched holes that

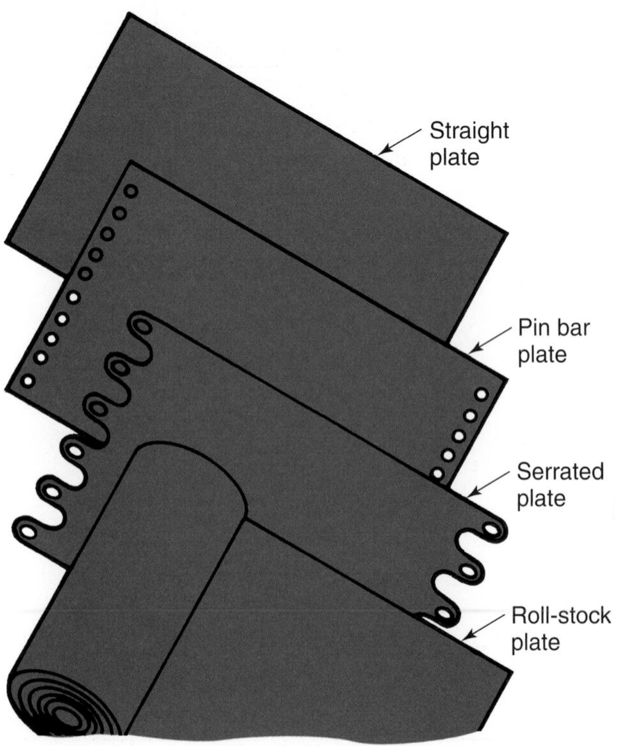

Figure 17-11. Plates use different methods for attachment to a press.

are positioned with fittings on the leading and trailing edges of the press cylinder. If too much tension is put on the plate, the holes or slots will tend to elongate.

Platemaking

The manual techniques used in making and processing lithographic plates vary depending on the type of plate used, processing methods, and printing applications. While the use of computers and desktop publishing has resulted in a shift to electronic platemaking, traditional platemaking methods from manual exposure to hand processing continue to be used in the graphic communications industry.

Exposing and processing plates

Presensitized plates are ready for exposure and are commonly used with traditional platemaking systems. There are four steps used in hand-processing a plate: exposure, development, rinsing the plate, and gumming the plate. See **Figure 17-12**. The following is a typical procedure used to expose and process a plate:

1. Remove the plate from its package, making sure not to scratch the surface. Because the plate has a light-sensitive coating, it must not be exposed to white light. Plates should be used in a darkroom or under safe lighting conditions. The corners of printing plates are very sharp. Extreme care must be taken to prevent cuts or injuries. Severe lacerations can result from carelessly handled plates.

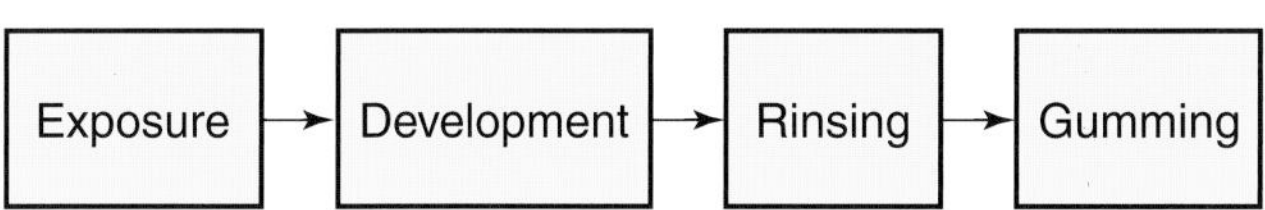

Figure 17-12. Processing plates by hand involves four steps.

2. Position the plate in the vacuum frame of the platemaker. The flat and the plate must be lined up and registered. After the flat is positioned properly over the plate, clean the glass and close the vacuum frame. See **Figure 17-13**.

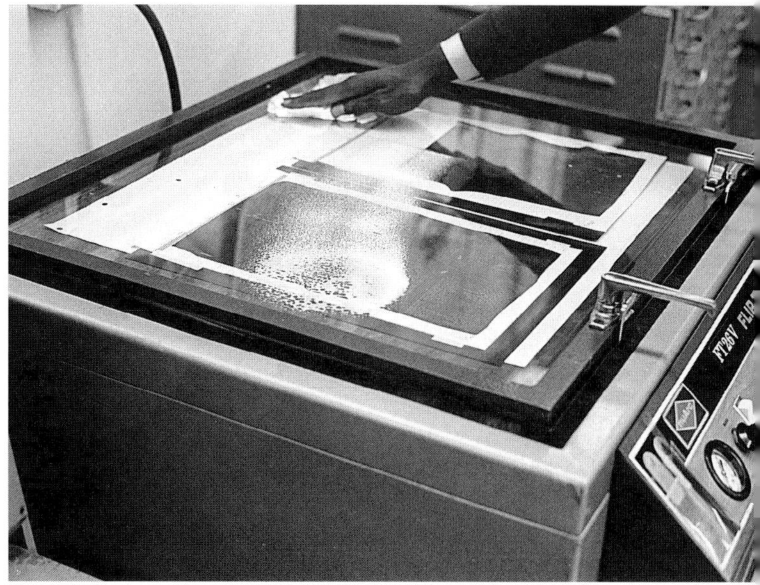

Figure 17-13. The vacuum frame glass must be cleaned before making the exposure.

3. Turn on the vacuum to pull the plate against the flat. Allow 20 to 30 seconds to make sure the air has escaped and a good contact has been established.

4. Determine the exposure time and expose the plate. Most plate manufacturers provide a recommended exposure time. A sample exposure can also be made using an exposure sensitivity strip. See **Figure 17-14**.

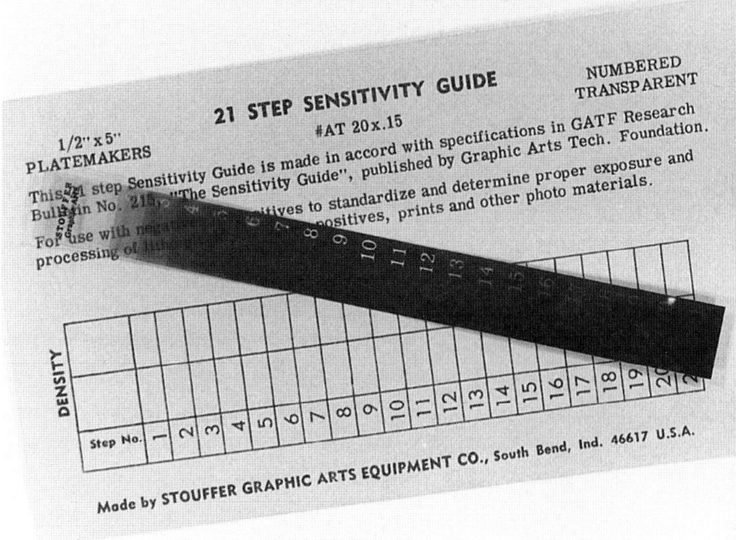

Figure 17-14. A sensitivity guide is used to check the correct exposure of a plate.

5. Remove the plate and prepare for processing. Clamp the plate in place on the developing table or sink. Absorbent paper is often placed between the plate and the surface of the developing area.

6. Develop the plate. Dampen a developer pad with developing solution and pour a small amount on the plate. Using the weight of the pad, spread the developer over the entire area of the plate. Pressure is not required in most cases. Allow the developer to stand for approximately 20 seconds, then lightly rub the entire plate with the pad. Use a figure-eight motion. See **Figure 17-15**.

Figure 17-15. Developing solution is rubbed over the plate with a pad to bring out the image. (3M Company)

7. Rinse the plate with water and use a squeegee to remove any excess moisture. Take care not to scratch the plate.

8. Apply a protective gum to the plate with a damp sponge. Remove any excess with a disposable wipe or cloth, then buff the entire plate surface dry. See **Figure 17-16**.

9. Place the plate in proper storage. Plates are commonly hung from a bar or storage racks, **Figure 17-17**. They may also be stored flat, if a protective sheet is inserted between each plate.

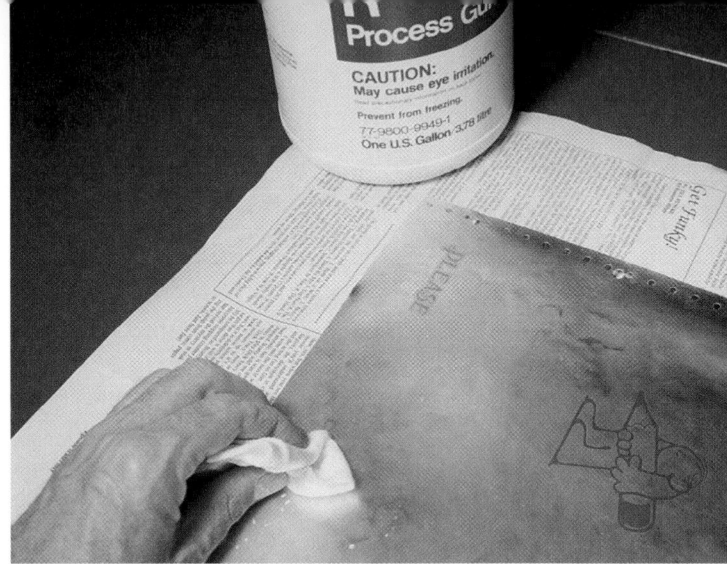

Figure 17-16. A protective gum is applied to the plate after development.

Figure 17-17. Plates hung for storage. Plates can also be stored flat if they are separated by protective sheets. (Foster Manufacturing Company)

10. Wash the developing pad, the gum sponge, and any other supplies used. The developing area must be thoroughly cleaned.

Platemaking Systems

Numerous advances have been made in the production of lithographic plates for offset printing in recent years. Automatic processing machines and electronic platemaking systems have replaced many of the manual techniques previously used to make plates. Newer systems involve the production of presensitized plates and vary depending on the type of plate used. This section of the chapter will present several of the most commonly used surface plates and different platemaking systems.

Photo direct plates

Photo direct plates are carriers that are imaged directly from a flat or camera-ready copy. The images on photo direct plates are commonly projected through a lens to the light-sensitive surface. Photo direct platemaking systems typically are fully automatic, computerized systems. See **Figure 17-18**.

Figure 17-18. A photo direct platemaking system images the plate and processes it automatically. (3M Company)

In this system, the camera-ready copy is placed face up on a copyboard, **Figure 17-19**. An automatic registration control allows the operator to position the copy accurately and easily. Photo direct systems are often equipped with automatic centering, which positions copy for enlarging or reducing. The operator inputs the information on the control panel located in front of the system.

The photo direct plate system eliminates the use of a film intermediate. After the plate is exposed, it is automatically processed and then ready to be mounted on the press. See **Figure 17-20**.

Thermal plates

Thermal plates are carriers that can be imaged optically or digitally through the use of heat. Heat, not light, is used to expose thermal plates. The base of the plate is metal and is similar to that of a conventional lithographic plate.

Figure 17-19. The original image or mechanical is placed on the copyboard for exposure in a photo direct platemaking system. (3M Company)

The coating of a thermal plate is a heat-sensitive polymer. A thermal plate can be processed automatically through aqueous processing, a method using water-based chemicals.

Another thermal platemaking system, using a red laser diode as the imaging device, uses paper or film-based plates. See **Figure 17-21**. The plate material is supplied in rolls and automatically cut to length after exposure. Developing is performed by an in-line processor. The system is temperature-controlled and the developing chemicals are automatically replenished.

Laser plates

Laser plates are imaged digitally by a laser platemaking system. Images from the flat or pasted-up material are scanned, and the digitized information is imaged directly to the polyester plate. Each line is exposed to the plate by the laser. Once all of the images of a page are on the plate, the plate is automatically processed. Due to static electricity, some toner is scattered over the plate by the printer. The plate must be cleaned and buffed before it is used on a press.

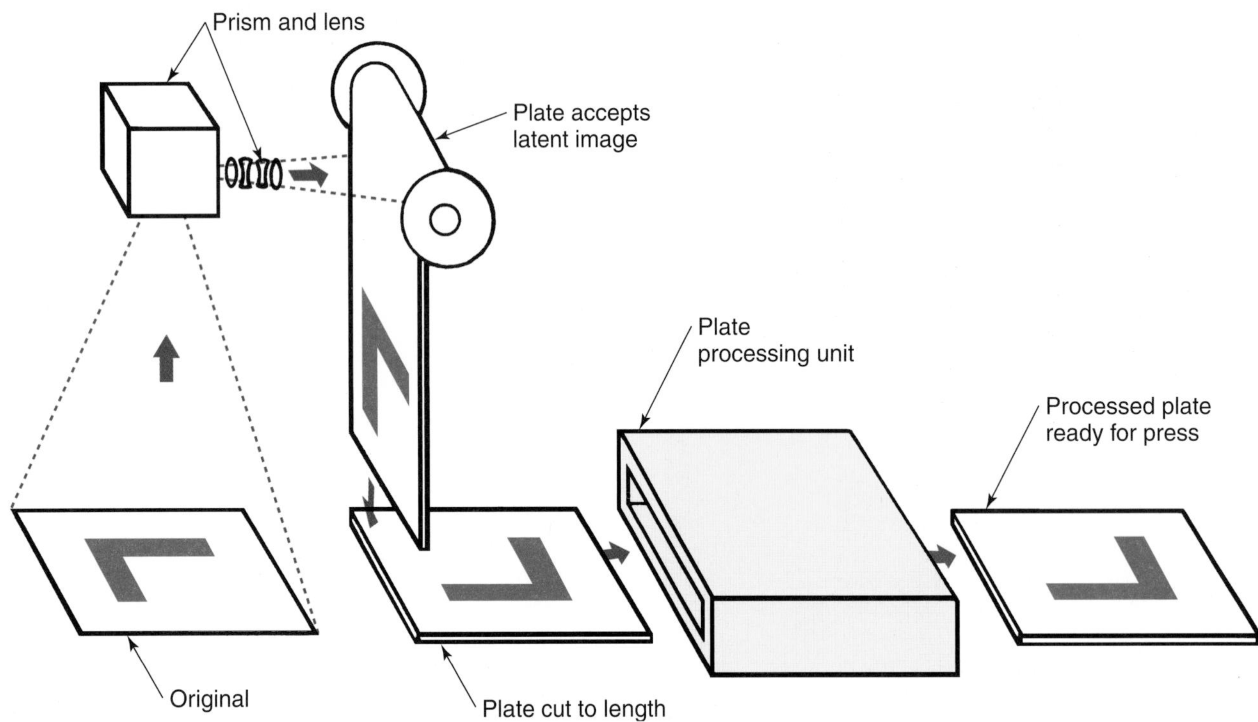

Figure 17-20. The different processes used by a photo direct platemaking system. The original image is reflected through the prism and lens onto the light-sensitive plate. The plate is then cut to length and fed through the processing unit. It emerges ready for use on the press.

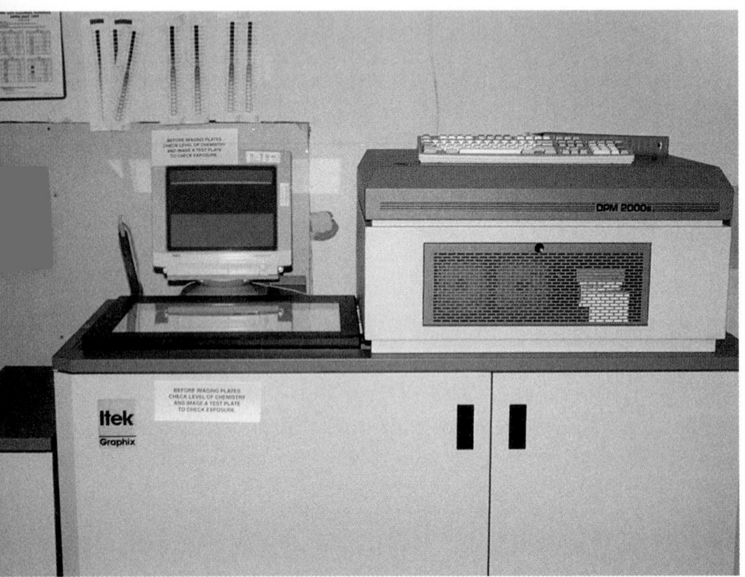

Figure 17-21. A thermal platemaking system used to image plates digitally.

Computer-to-plate (CTP)

Computer-to-plate (CTP) is an electronic platemaking system that uses an *imagesetter* to accept digital files directly from a computer and image light-sensitive or heat-sensitive plates. The use of CTP technology, also known as *direct-to-plate*, is growing steadily in the printing industry. The system is an electronic network that eliminates the use of film as an intermediate, and it produces plates with high resolution. A typical CTP system can produce imaged plates with resolutions up to 4000 dpi (dots per inch). See **Figure 17-22**.

Several different types of plates and imagesetters can be used in CTP applications. Silver-based polyester plates, photopolymer plates, metal plates, and thermal (heat-sensitive) plates are all used in CTP. Light-sensitive plates can be imaged with a low-powered, visible light laser. Heat-sensitive, polymer-coated plates are imaged by an infrared laser.

The equipment used in a CTP system is illustrated in **Figure 17-23**. Images that are created electronically and paginated on a desktop publishing system are scanned and converted to digital files, a process known as *electronic prepress*. PostScript™ language is commonly used in conjunction with desktop software and output devices to interpret digital files.

The platemaking component or *imagesetter* is an output device that produces an imaged plate containing text and graphics. After an electronic page

Figure 17-22. A computer-to-plate (CTP) system is used to image high-resolution plates. (Gerber Systems Corporation)

design is produced in prepress, it is transferred digitally to a raster image processor (RIP), which processes the file and transmits the information to the imagesetter. When the plate is imaged, it is automatically processed and is then ready for the press.

A typical CTP network includes a digital color proofing system and an electronic color correction system. A *color proof* is a prepress version of the final printed product. After a proof of the design is produced and evaluated, electronic color correction can be used to adjust the computer file before the file is sent to the imagesetter and the plate is made.

The use of CTP technology is becoming more prevalent in the graphic communications industry.

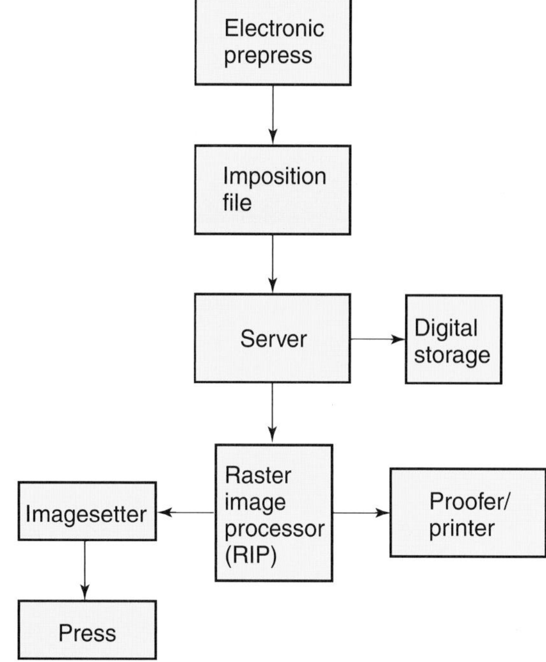

Figure 17-23. A CTP system is an electronic network that produces plates directly from a computer.

By eliminating the use of film negatives and flats and by outputting plates directly from a computer, CTP presents several advantages over traditional platemaking. A CTP system results in higher productivity and better image quality.

Waterless plates

Waterless plates are presensitized plates that use an ink-repellent substance instead of water to separate the nonimage area from the image area. Waterless plates are manufactured as both negative-acting and positive-acting plates. They are designed to be used on a lithographic press without a dampening solution.

The nonimage area of the plate is covered with an ink-repellent silicone rubber layer, while the image area is slightly recessed and coated with an ink-receptive polymer. The plate is designed differently from a conventional lithographic plate. See **Figure 17-24**.

After the plate is exposed, it may be developed by hand or by an automatic processor. Special chemicals are used to develop the plate. The plate does not require gumming, if used within a month of processing. Although the surface is resistant to

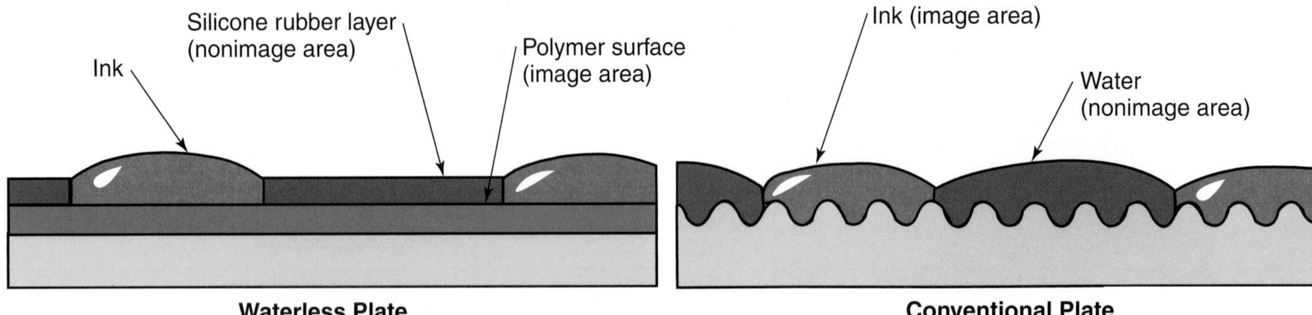

Figure 17-24. A comparison between a waterless plate and a conventional lithographic plate. Waterless plates are designed with an ink-repellent substance other than water to form the nonimage area. The image area is slightly below the nonimage area and is receptive to ink. (Polychrome Corporation)

oxidation, it is recommended the plate be cleaned and stored with a protective sheet to prevent scratching.

Electrostatic plates

Electrostatic plates are light-sensitive plates that are imaged by a charge of electrostatic energy. When the plate is exposed and light strikes the nonimage area, the positive charge is eliminated from that area. The *image* area remains positively charged and receptive to ink. A resin powder, which is negatively charged, is then applied to the image area and fused.

Electrostatic platemakers are designed to process electrostatic plates automatically. See **Figure 17-25.**

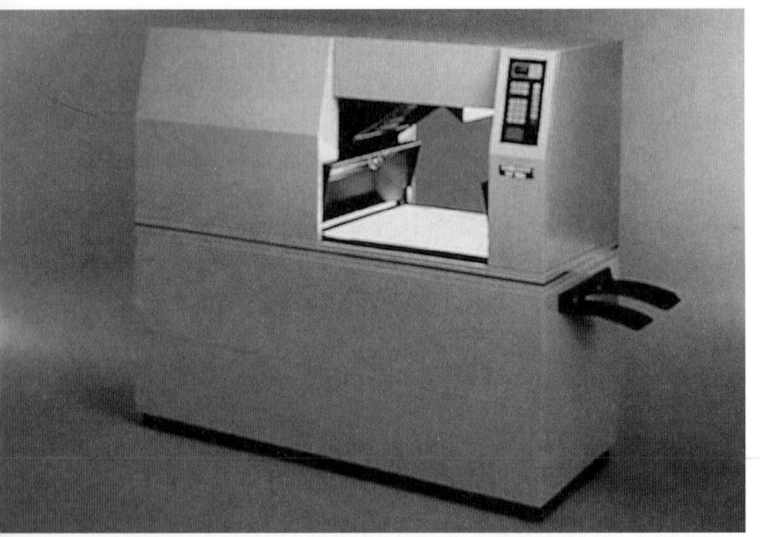

Figure 17-25. An electrostatic platemaker. (Multigraphics)

Platemaking Variables

The materials and equipment used in traditional platemaking systems must be properly applied to ensure the quality of a plate. Electronic platemaking and CTP systems have eliminated many of the variables commonly encountered in manual platemaking, but traditional methods continue to be used and have a critical effect on image quality.

Using equipment

Selecting the correct equipment is one of the most important steps in the platemaking process. The components of a platemaker must be used properly when imaging plates.

A good vacuum frame is essential for proper drawdown and good contact between the plate and the flat. The vacuum frame must also be located at the right distance from the light source to assure proper exposure. If the frame is too close to the light source, overexposure of the plate may result. When the distance between the frame and the light source is too great, underexposure may occur.

Contact is an important variable to be considered in using the vacuum frame. When exposing the plate, it is essential that the film intermediate be in firm, even contact with the plate. A soft, pliable vacuum blanket assists in assuring good contact. If good contact is not made, the image will be larger than the original because of the light escaping under the edges and exposing the plate.

Film that is improperly stripped on the flat or an excessive amount of tape may also cause poor contact. See **Figure 17-26.**

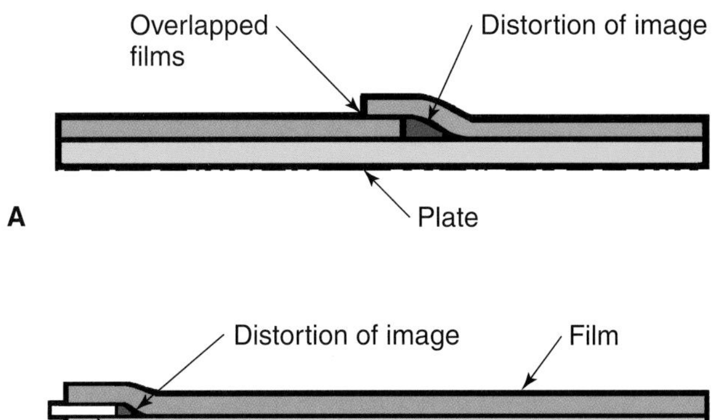

Figure 17-26. An improperly stripped flat can result in poor contact with the plates. A—Overlapped film causes a distorted image to result. B—An excess of tape prevents complete contact between the film and the plate.

Soft image

One of the most frequent problems affecting the quality of a plate is a ***soft image***. This occurs when the outside edges of an image contain less density or tone quality than that of the inside portion of the image. A soft image is a common problem when working with halftones. In a soft image, the dots making up the image appear to be *vignetted*.

To process a good lithographic plate, the flat or film intermediate must be of high quality. It is imperative that the film intermediate closely represent the original copy.

The softness of an image can be checked with *darkfield illumination*. This technique involves viewing the intermediate image with a black background and a light source. If the intermediate image has a dense center and there is less density around the edges, a soft image will commonly result.

Scumming

Scumming occurs when ink adheres to the nonimage area of a plate. This condition is the result of an excess of ink or a lack of water on the plate. Scumming may be caused by a poorly developed plate, an over-inked press, or a lack of dampening solution applied by the press.

To eliminate scumming, the plate should be thoroughly cleaned and regummed. The dampening system or ink operation on the press may also need to be adjusted.

Gum blinding

Gum blinding is caused by an excess of gum on the image area and results in image loss. When gum blinding occurs, the image will not accept ink. This condition is usually evident at the beginning of a press run. When gum is applied to the plate, any excess material must be removed and the surface must be buffed dry.

Review Questions

Please do not write in this text. Write your answers on a separate sheet of paper.

1. Explain the process of lithographic printing.
2. A _____ _____ is used to provide contact between the plate and the original image for exposure on a platemaker.
3. Which of the following materials can be used in the manufacture of lithographic plates?
   a. Aluminum.
   b. Plastic.
   c. Paper.
   d. All of the above.
   e. None of the above.
4. What are the three parts of a lithographic plate?
5. Two types of mechanical grain applied to plates are _____ and _____ grain.
6. Name two types of plate coatings.
7. Plates that are manufactured with a light-sensitive material to capture images are _____.
8. When a positive-acting plate is exposed, the area struck by light becomes the _____ area.
9. What are the four steps used in hand processing a lithographic plate?
10. Thermal plates can be imaged _____ or _____ through the use of heat.
11. Which type of platemaking system scans images as digital data and transfers them directly to the plate?
12. Which plate has a coating of resin powder applied to its surface?
    a. Waterless.
    b. Silver halide.
    c. Diazo.
    d. Electrostatic.

13. A _____ _____ is a condition in which the outside edges of an image contain less density than that of the inside portion of the image.
14. What is scumming?
15. _____ _____ is caused by an excess of gum on the image area and results in image loss.

Specialized offset presses have been developed to meet specific needs of printers and their customers. This web offset press is designed specifically for the printing operations geared to rapid production of short-run, single-color books. It permits quickly and easily changing web width for different jobs. (Strachan Henshaw Machinery, Inc.)

Lithographic Press Systems

18

Learning Objectives

After studying this chapter, you will be able to:

- Distinguish between lithographic sheet-fed and web-fed presses.
- Identify the five fundamental systems used in a lithographic press.
- Demonstrate how a substrate travels through the press.
- Explain the function of each press cylinder in a printing system.
- Describe how dampening and inking systems prepare a plate for printing.
- Compare the equipment used by delivery systems on sheet-fed and web-fed presses.

Important Terms

blanket cylinder
dampening system
delivery system
feeding system
impression cylinder
inking system
plate cylinder
printing system
sheet-fed press
web-fed press

Offset lithography continues to be the dominant technology in the graphic communications industry. This chapter covers the different types of presses and press operations used in commercial printing operations. Offset lithographic printing is done on both sheet-fed and web-fed presses. This chapter will introduce the five fundamental systems of a press and explain how each system functions. The next chapter covers the operation of offset presses.

Lithographic Presses

Lithography is a process of printing or *transferring* images from one surface to another. The lithographic system of printing from plates on a press is commonly referred to as an *offset* or *indirect* method. In the operation of a lithographic press, the image on a plate is offset from one cylinder to another. See **Figure 18-1**.

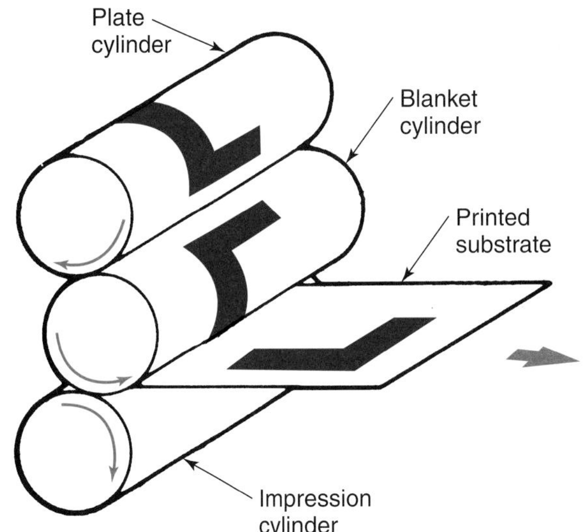

Figure 18-1. Offset lithographic printing is a method of transferring an image from one press cylinder to another.

During the printing process, the plate is dampened, then inked. The plate has an *image area* that accepts ink and repels water and a *nonimage area* that accepts water and repels ink. This design is based on the principle that ink, a grease-based substance, does not mix readily with water; ink adheres to the image area only. When the plate is placed on a press, the image in ink is transferred from the plate cylinder to a blanket, which in turn transfers the image to the substrate. See **Figure 18-2**.

Because the image is printed directly or *mirrored* from the plate to the blanket, it appears in reverse form on the blanket. When the image is offset again from the blanket to the substrate, it returns to its original form as it appears on the plate.

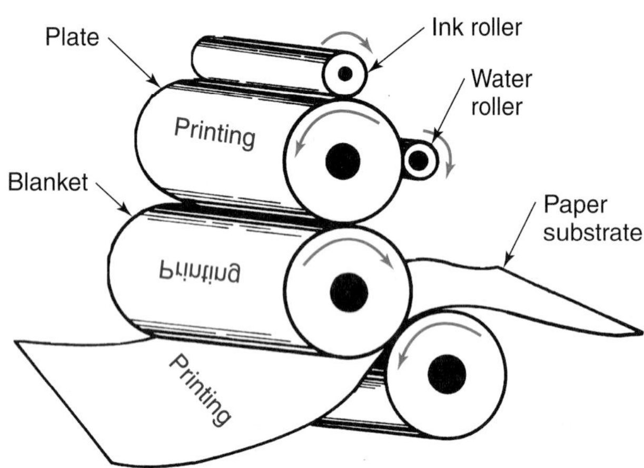

Figure 18-2. In offset lithography, the plate is dampened with water and then inked. The inked image is offset from the plate to the blanket, which then transfers the image to the paper substrate. (A.B. Dick Company)

Lithographic presses are classified as either *sheet-fed presses* or *web-fed presses*, based on how paper is fed through the system. See **Figure 18-3.**

A ***sheet-fed press*** prints on individual sheets of paper as they are drawn through the system. Sheets are removed from a stack, one at a time, and fed through the press. See **Figure 18-4.**

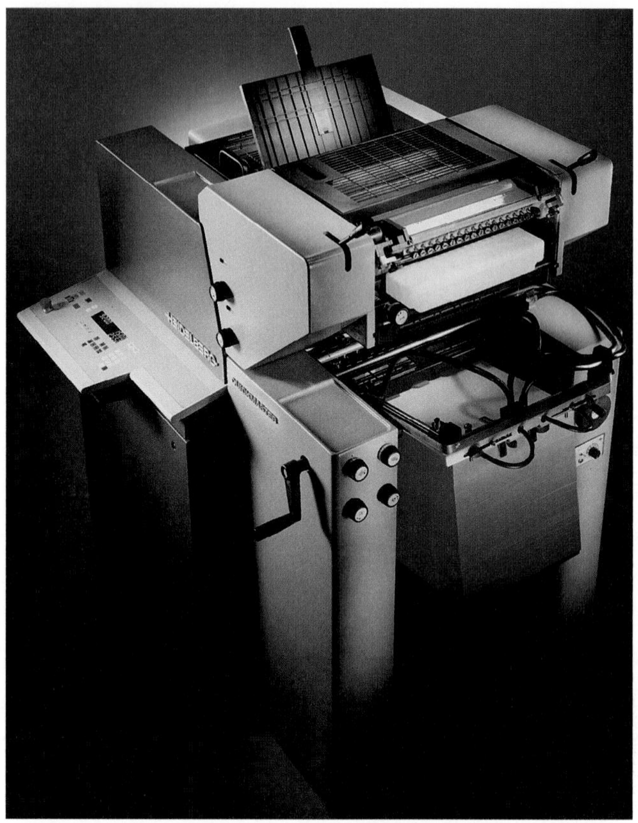

Figure 18-4. A sheet-fed press feeds and prints paper one sheet at a time. (Heidelberg USA)

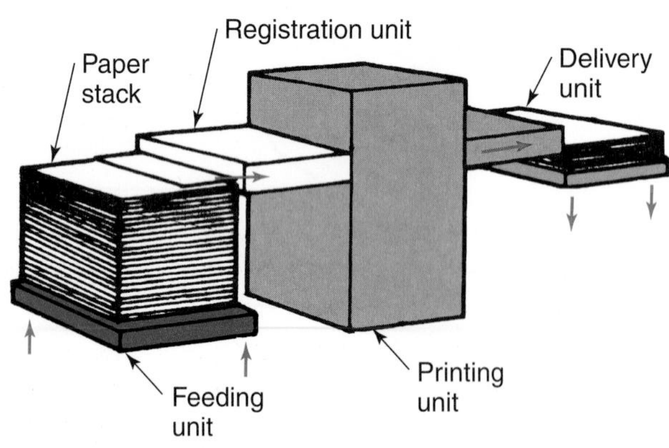

Sheet-fed press

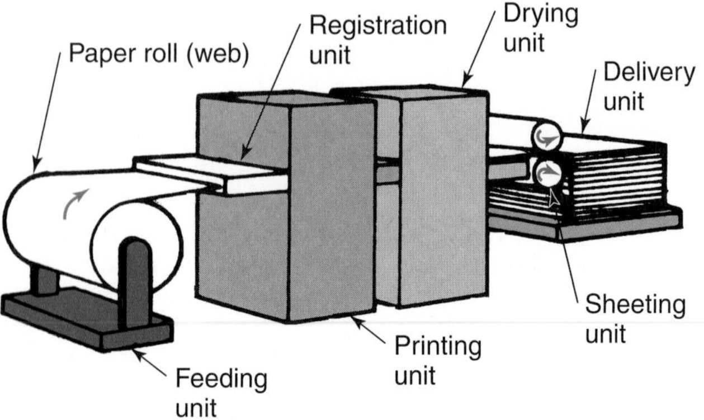

Web-fed Press

Figure 18-3. A comparison of sheet-fed and web-fed press designs.

A ***web-fed press*** prints on one long, continuous web of paper that is drawn into the press from a roll. As the roll unwinds, images are printed on the web and the entire length of paper winds through the press. See **Figure 18-5**.

Figure 18-5. A web-fed press prints on a continuous roll of paper called a web that feeds through the entire system. (Heidelberg USA)

Lithographic Press Systems

The operation of a lithographic press, whether sheet-fed or web-fed, can be divided into five systems, each of which must perform a basic function. See **Figure 18-6**. The five basic press systems are the *feeding system, printing system, dampening system, inking system*, and *delivery system*. The rest of this chapter will discuss these systems and illustrate how each one works.

The feeding system is the mechanism that sends the paper (substrate) into the press. The printing system consists of the equipment used to offset the image from the plate to the substrate. The dampening system feeds water or fountain solution to the plate. The inking system feeds ink to the plate. The delivery system removes the paper from the press and stacks it for finishing operations.

The components making up each press system will vary, depending on the design of the press. Each system must be working properly for the press to accurately print images on the substrate.

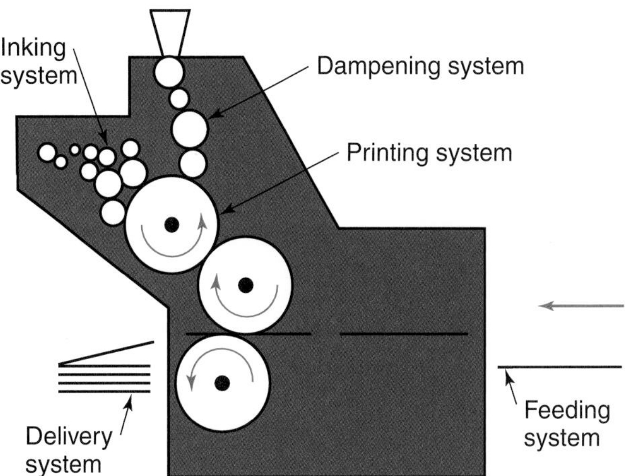

Figure 18-6. Five basic systems are used in the operation of a lithographic press.

Feeding Systems

Paper is fed, printed, and delivered differently depending on the type of press used. Feeding systems, discussed next, are classified as *sheet-feeding systems* and *web-feeding systems*.

Sheet-feeding systems

On a sheet-fed press, sheets of paper are typically stacked on a feeding platform and removed one at a time by the press. Most of today's printing duplicators and presses are equipped with automatic feeders to operate at high production speeds. The feeding system is divided into three operations. A stack of paper is placed by hand on the feeding platform, which serves as a guide for feeding each sheet into the press separately. Air-producing ***sheet separators*** positioned along the upper edges of the paper stack are used to separate the top sheet from the rest of the pile. Each sheet is then transported to the register unit, which positions or *registers* the paper for insertion to the press. This process is known as *successive sheet feeding*. No two sheets overlap when they are fed, as shown in **Figure 18-7A**.

Some presses allow sheets to partially overlap when paper enters the press. This method, known as *stream feeding*, is typically used with high-speed presses. See **Figure 18-7B**.

Some sheet-feeding systems are classified as continuous-feeding. A press equipped with a continuous-feeding system can remain running when the platform is reloaded with paper. This system increases production since the press does not need to be stopped for reloading.

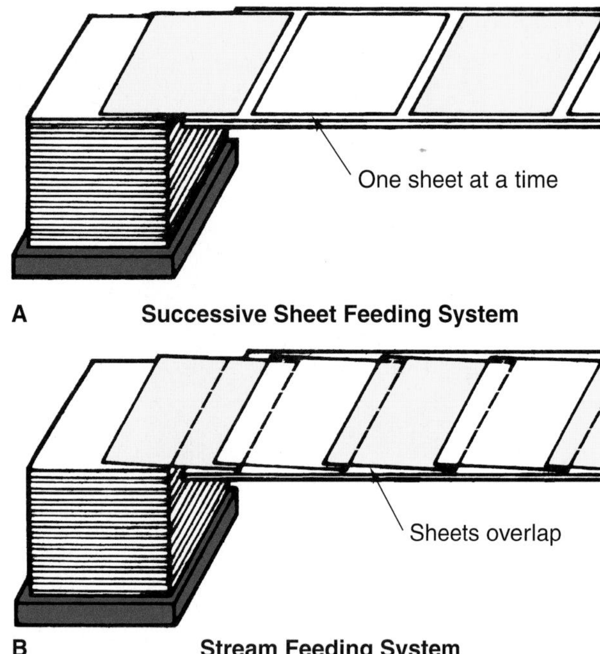

Figure 18-7. Sheet-fed presses can use a successive sheet feeding system or a stream feeding system. A—In successive feeding, one sheet at a time is fed through the press. B—Stream feeding allows sheets to partially overlap when they are fed for greater press speeds.

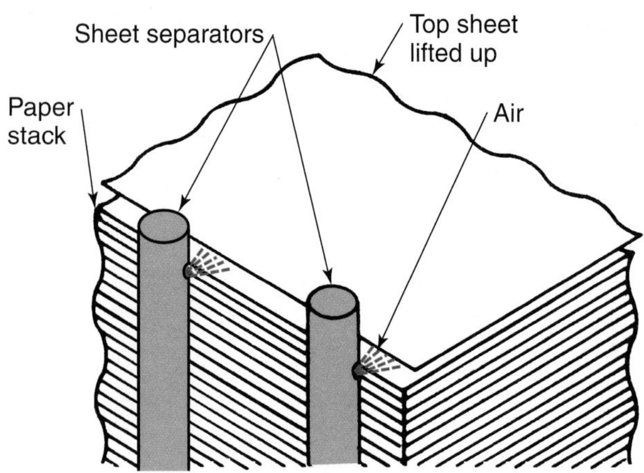

Figure 18-8. Sheet separators provide a flow of air to help guide one sheet at a time into the press.

In general, if the paper is positioned properly on the platform and aligned with the feeding system, the sheets will be fed correctly without causing a jam or misfeed. Any variation in the system could force the operator to stop the press. Most manufacturers of stock provide an indication of how different grades of paper should be stacked.

When the press is running, the paper stack must remain at a certain height on the platform for best operation. Operating height can be monitored manually or with a control device. Some feeding systems are equipped with gauges that provide readings for operating heights of stock.

Sheet separation

The separation of sheets on a platform is typically controlled by airflow. Air nozzles serving as ***sheet separators*** direct streams of air toward the edges of the paper to separate the sheets. This system helps assure that the top sheet of the stack can be picked up and transferred to the next press operation. See **Figure 18-8**.

Sheet separators may be located near the lead edges of the stack or on the sides. The location of sheet separators depends on the design of the press.

Sheet separation may also be aided by the use of thin brass or spring-steel devices known as *fingers*. See **Figure 18-9**.

Paper is held in alignment on the platform by sheet guides, which are located on the sides and rear edges of the stack. Rear guides are typically weighted to assist in separating one sheet at a time.

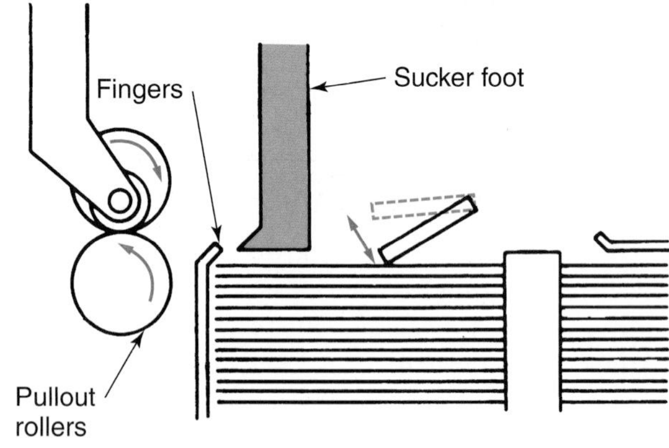

Figure 18-9. Fingers are devices that help to separate sheets for feeding.

Sheet transfer

Sheets are commonly transferred from the stack and fed to the press by ***sucker feet***, also known as *suckers*. Sucker feet are devices that provide a vacuum to remove sheets and position them for access to the press-feeding pullout rollers. On smaller presses, the sucker feet are positioned at the leading edge of the sheet. See **Figure 18-10.** Sucker feet may also be located at the rear edges of a sheet. The rear feet draw the paper forward to the pullout rollers, **Figure 18-11**.

The amount of vacuum provided by sucker feet must be adjusted for each type of stock. A typical sheet-fed press equipped with sucker feet is shown in **Figure 18-12**.

Once a sheet is directed to the pullout rollers by the sucker feet, it is then guided to the register unit for entry to the press. To ensure that only one sheet passes through, the system is equipped with a control device called a ***double-sheet detector***. Double-sheet detectors sense paper thickness. When the sensor detects excess thickness, indicating multiple sheets, it activates a solenoid. The solenoid opens a deflector plate for removal of the sheets. See **Figure 18-13**.

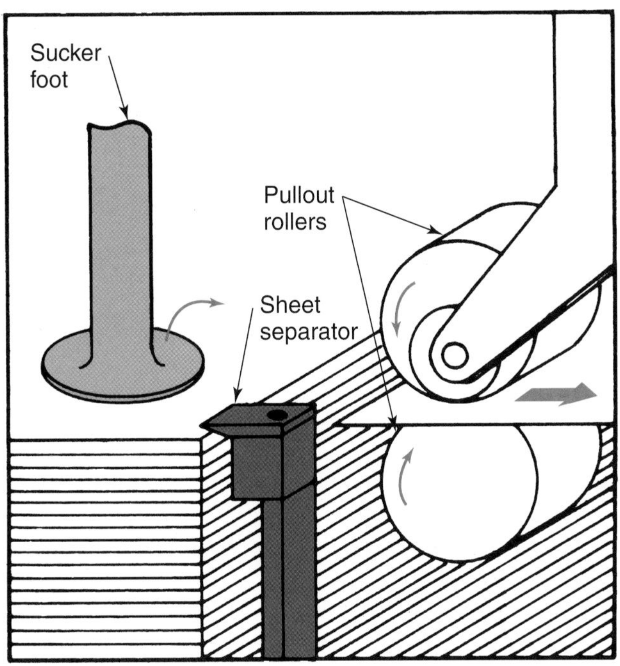

Figure 18-10. Sucker feet are used to lift and guide sheets of paper to the pullout rollers in a feeding system.

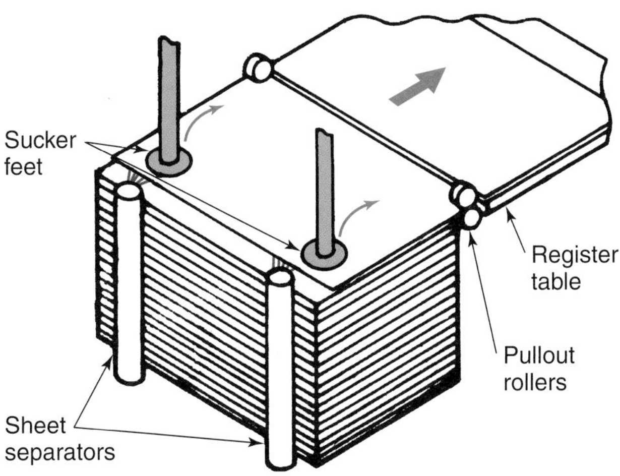

Figure 18-11. Sucker feet located at the rear edges of the paper draw sheets forward from the stack.

Figure 18-12. A typical sheet-fed press equipped with sucker feet to feed paper for printing.

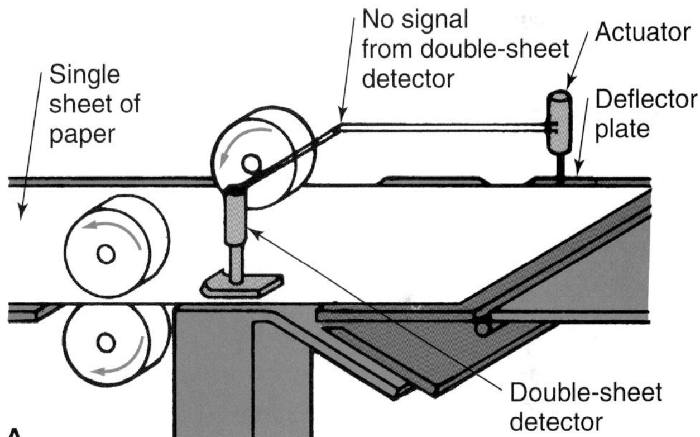

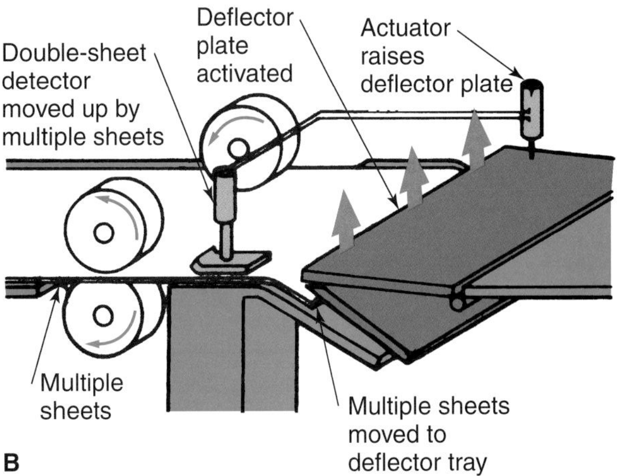

Figure 18-13. A double-sheet detector senses paper thickness as sheets are fed through the system. A—When a single sheet is fed, the detector remains inactive. B—When it senses excess thickness, the detector activates the deflector plate for removal of the paper.

Register unit

A ***register unit*** is a mechanism that aligns the sheet for printing. The unit consists of a register table that carries each sheet to the register stop, where paper is aligned with the printing system of the press. The register table uses conveyor tapes to carry sheets of paper to the register stop for entry to the press. See **Figure 18-14**.

Figure 18-14. A register table equipped with conveyor tapes carries sheets of paper to be registered for printing.

Proper registration of the paper is critical to the operation of the press. Register units vary in design, but they must provide a means to feed the paper and align it in the same position for printing each time. The most common register units have side guides for positioning. See **Figure 18-15**.

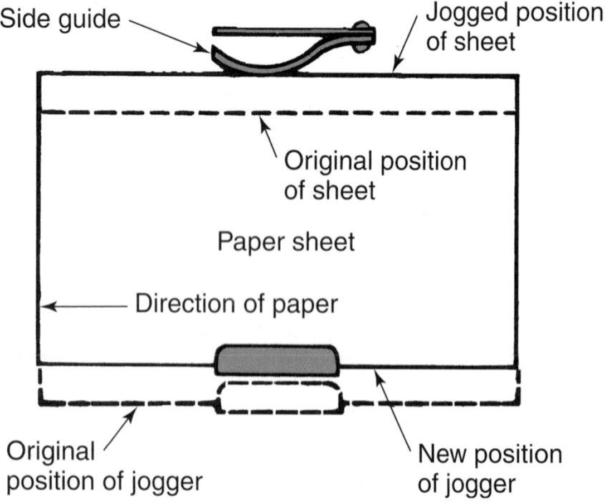

Figure 18-15. Joggers move paper into position against the side guides when it is fed to the register unit.

When a sheet of paper is fed through the register unit, it comes into contact with the register stop. The paper is then aligned square with the printing system, ready to be captured by the grippers on the impression cylinder. See **Figure 18-16**.

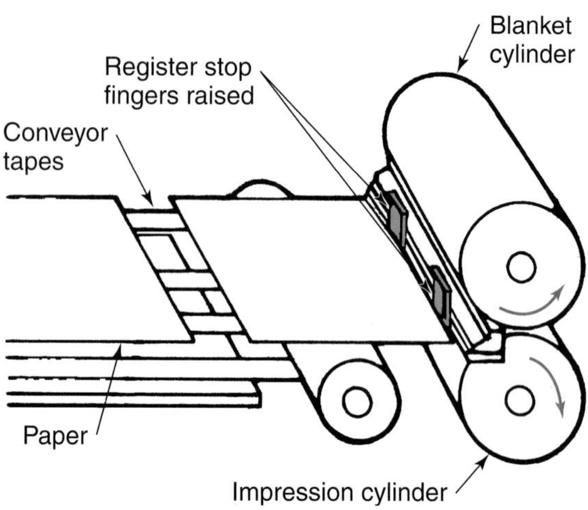

Figure 18-16. The register stop places paper in register, ready to pass through the printing system.

Web-feeding systems

Web-fed presses are equipped with feeding systems that are designed differently from those used with sheet-fed presses. Printing on a web-fed press is done on a continuous roll of paper that winds through a series of rollers. See **Figure 18-17**.

The movement of paper through a web-fed press is controlled by a paper tension device. Since a continuous web of paper is fed through the press, its tension must be closely regulated. Improper web tension can alter the registration of paper and affect print quality. In some cases, improper tension can cause the web to break and force shutdown of the press.

A ***brake mechanism*** is one of the most commonly used tension control devices on a web-fed press. See **Figure 18-18**. The brake mechanism is attached to the paper roll and is designed to produce a slight amount of friction or *drag* on the web.

Web splicer

When a new roll of paper must replace an existing roll while the press is running, a ***web splicer*** is used to splice or *bond* the end of the existing roll to the start of a new roll. Splicing allows the web to

Figure 18-17. Paper travels through a web-fed press as one continuous web. The web winds through a series of rollers as it is printed. (Tensor Group, Inc.)

Figure 18-18. A brake mechanism provides the correct tension as the web is fed from the roll on a web-fed press unit like this one. (Tensor Group, Inc.)

remain intact while it is being printed. Webs must be spliced accurately; an improper paper splice could cause a web break. Two types of web splicers commonly used are the *zero-speed splicer* and the *flying splicer*.

A ***zero-speed splicer*** uses a set of rollers called a *festoon* to draw out slack from the web before a splice is made. The festoon unit allows the new roll to be spliced to the old one while the press uses up the slack. See **Figure 18-19**. When a splice is made, the two paper rolls are stopped, but the press continues to run from the web stored on the festoon.

The festoon rollers move up and down during the press run. As the web is fed through the press, the festoon unit draws out slack and moves up. When the web roll runs out of paper, the web rollers are stopped, and the festoon unit moves down to feed the press. The end of the new roll can then be taped to the end of the old roll. After the splice is made, the new roll is rotated up to speed before the paper from the festoon rollers is used up, keeping the press in operation.

A ***flying splicer*** is a device that bonds a new roll of paper to the existing web without stopping any operations on the press. Neither web roll is stopped while the splice is made. The process is illustrated in **Figure 18-20**. An adhesive such as double-sided tape is applied to the end of the new web to make the splice.

When the existing web roll is nearly empty, the splicing unit rotates the new roll toward the existing roll and accelerates it to match the speed of the moving web. When the new web meets the moving web, the two ends are spliced together and the old web is cut. The new web becomes the moving web and is rotated into the running position previously occupied by the old web.

Figure 18-19. This web-fed press is equipped with a zero-speed splicer unit. The unit contains festoon rollers that allow web slack to build up for use on the press when a new web is attached and a splice is made.

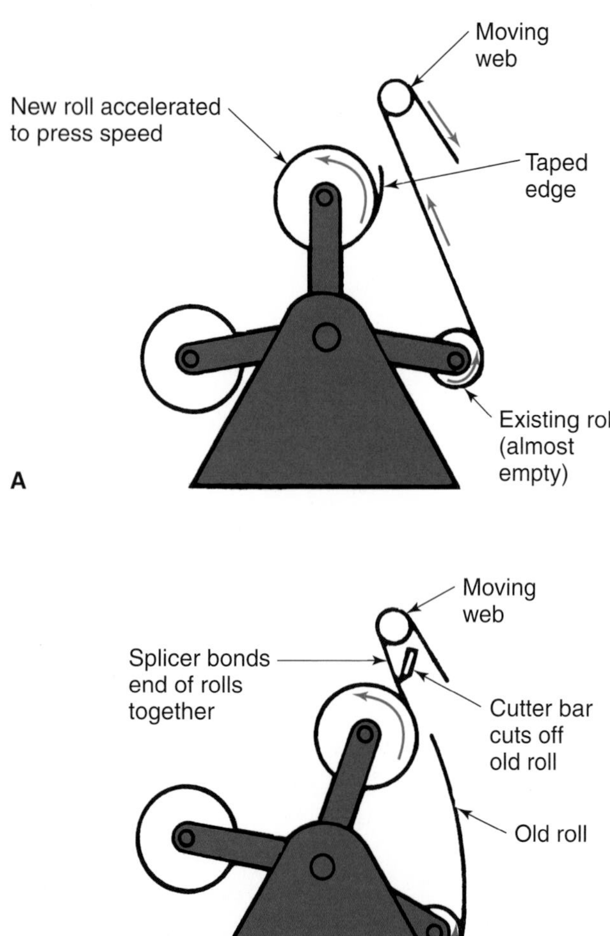

Figure 18-20. A flying splicer allows the press to remain in operation when a new roll is spliced to the moving web. A—When the existing roll of paper is nearly used up, the new roll is accelerated to the speed of the press. Double-sided tape is applied to the end of the new roll to make the splice. B—The splicer rotates the new roll to meet the moving web and cuts away the old roll. The new roll is then moved into operating position.

Web break detector

A ***web break detector*** is a device that automatically shuts down the press if the web snaps or tears. Modern web-fed presses operate at tremendous speeds; a web break can be disastrous. A break could cause the incoming ribbon of paper to jam and wrap around the printing rollers, severely damaging the press.

A web break detector uses a sensor to detect a break in the web. If a break occurs, the detector will kill power to the press instantly. It will also activate a mechanism that cuts off the incoming web before it reaches the printing system. Any incoming paper is therefore not allowed to enter the press.

Printing Systems

The ***printing system*** of a lithographic press consists of a group of cylinders that transfer images from the printing plate to the substrate. The components of a printing system are the *plate cylinder*, the *blanket cylinder*, and the *impression cylinder*, **Figure 18-21.**

The printing system accepts paper from the feeding system and uses the dampening and inking systems to print images from the plate. On an offset press, images are offset from the plate cylinder to the blanket cylinder, and then offset again as paper contacts the impression cylinder. The equipment making up a three-cylinder printing system is discussed next.

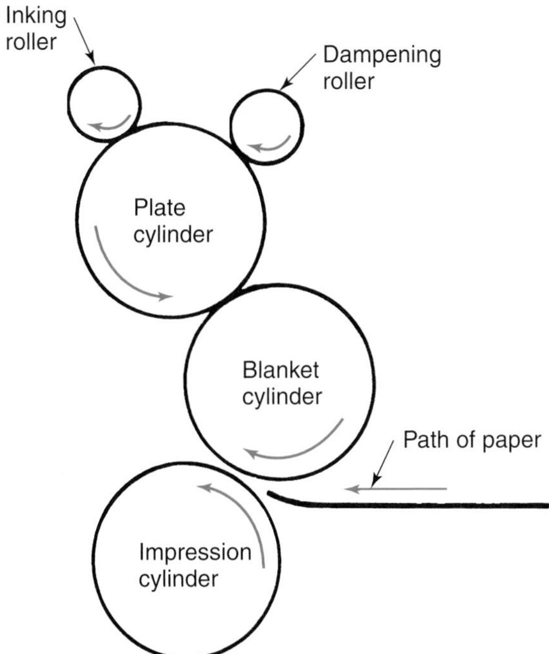

Figure 18-21. The three components that make up a printing system are the plate cylinder, the blanket cylinder, and the impression cylinder.

Plate cylinder

The ***plate cylinder*** holds the printing plate on the press. The components of a plate cylinder include the body, bearers, bearings, and a gear that drives the cylinder. See **Figure 18-22**.

A plate cylinder has a series of clamps that hold the plate in place. Plates are classified as serrated, straight, pinbar, or punched, depending on how they are held on a plate cylinder. See **Figure 18-23**. The cylinder clamps are used to tighten or loosen the plates. Proper tension must exist between the plate and the plate cylinder; excessive tension can place too much stress on the plate and cause it to crack or tear. Insufficient tension can affect registration and print quality.

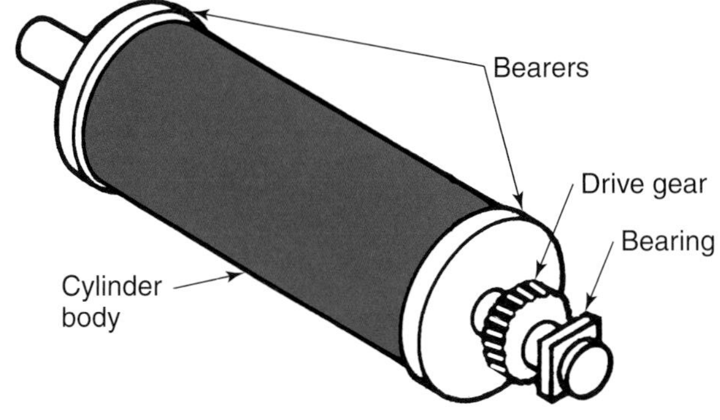

Figure 18-22. The basic parts of a plate cylinder.

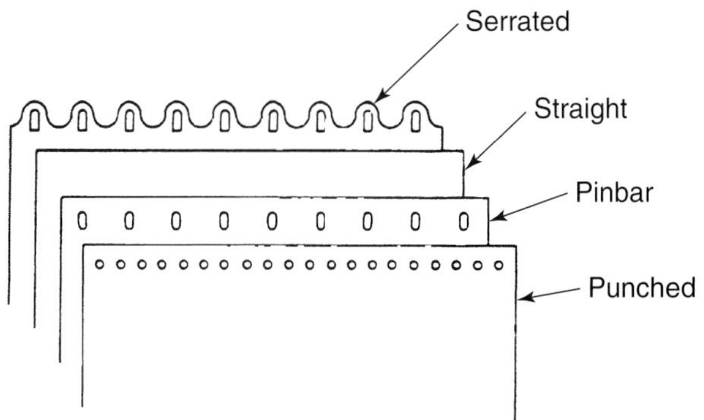

Figure 18-23. Different attaching methods for plates.

The vertical space that lies between the surface of the plate cylinder bearers and the cylinder body is known as the ***undercut***. See **Figure 18-24**. The undercut allows for the thickness of the plate and *packing*. The size of the undercut can be determined by measuring the difference between the diameter of the cylinder bearers and the diameter of the cylinder body. See **Figure 18-25**.

Since the bearers of the cylinders ride on each other, the plate and blanket cylinders are commonly packed to achieve proper image transfer. The size of the undercut is usually stamped on the cylinder body. Undercut can also be measured with a cylinder packing gauge. See **Figure 18-26**.

Blanket cylinder

The ***blanket cylinder*** holds the image-receptive blanket on the press. The blanket cylinder serves as

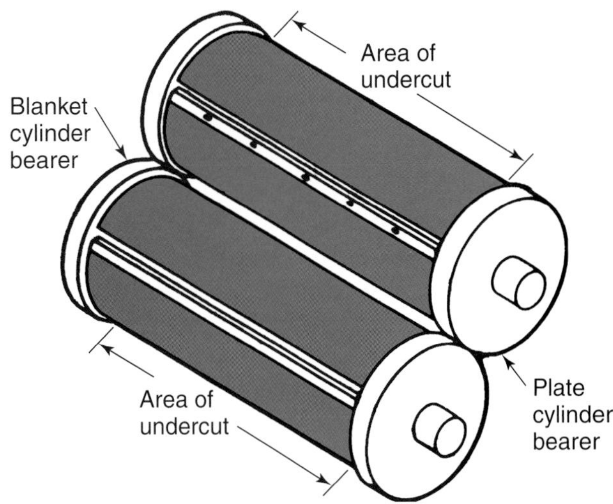

Figure 18-24. Cylinder surfaces are undercut from the bearers to allow for plate and blanket thickness and packing.

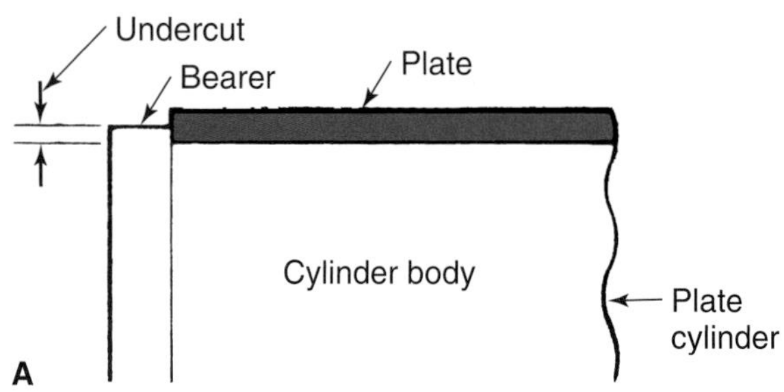

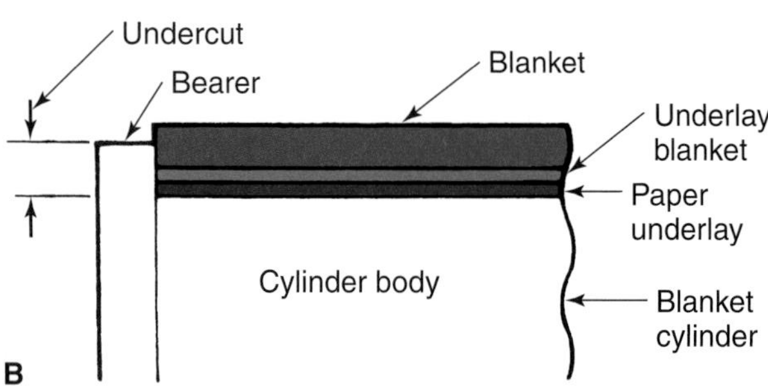

Figure 18-25. The undercut of a plate or blanket cylinder is equal to the difference between the diameter of the bearers and the diameter of the cylinder body. A—The plate cylinder body is undercut to allow for the thickness of the plate and packing. B—The blanket cylinder is undercut to allow for blanket thicknesses and packing.

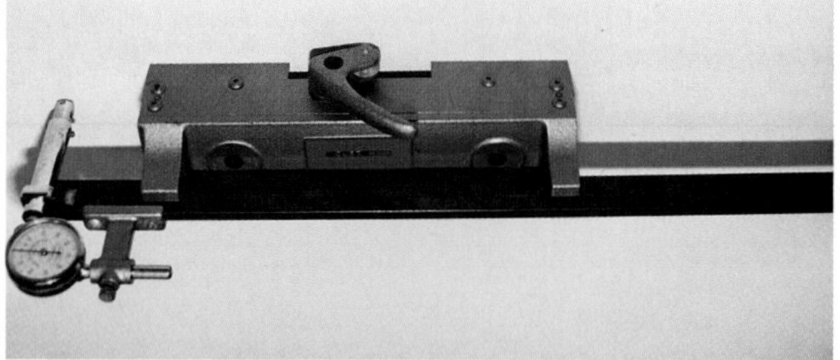

Figure 18-26. A cylinder packing gauge can be used to measure the amount of undercut on a press cylinder.

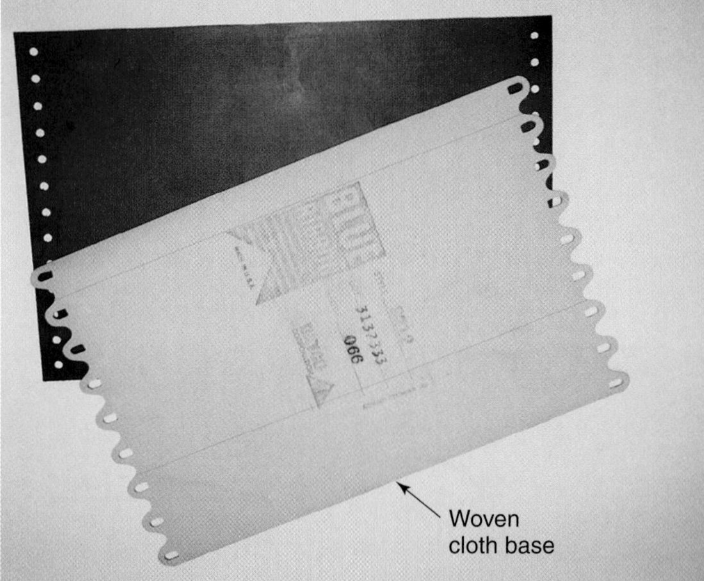

Figure 18-27. Press blankets stretch to fit the blanket cylinder. The resilient surface of the blanket accepts the inked image from the plate.

an *intermediate* between the plate cylinder and the impression cylinder. During printing, the blanket receives the image in reverse from the plate and then offsets the image to the substrate in its original orientation.

The blanket cylinder consists of the same components that make up the plate cylinder. The blanket cylinder body holds the blanket in place with a set of clamps. Blankets are elastic and are designed to stretch around the cylinder. Blanket surfaces are commonly made of rubber and supported by a woven cloth base. See **Figure 18-27**.

Blanket sizes vary, depending on the size of the press. To allow for the thickness of the blanket and packing between the cylinders, the blanket cylinder is undercut. The undercut serves the same function as the undercut of a plate cylinder.

Impression cylinder

The ***impression cylinder*** brings the stock to be printed into contact with the blanket cylinder. As paper travels between the impression cylinder and the blanket cylinder, the image is transferred from the blanket to the paper. The impression cylinder carries the substrate from the feeding system and feeds it to the delivery system. See **Figure 18-28**.

The impression cylinder serves as the base component of a three-cylinder system. It applies the pressure needed to transfer the image from the blanket cylinder to the substrate. As paper passes between the cylinders, the impression cylinder must provide the correct amount of *gap* between the paper and the blanket to make the impression.

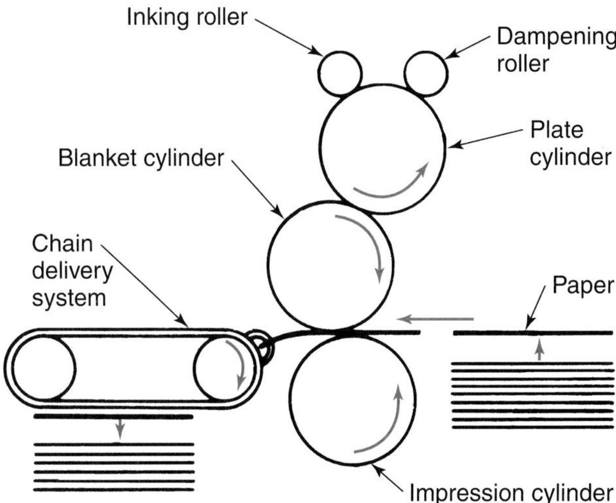

Figure 18-28. The impression cylinder brings the paper into contact with the blanket cylinder and provides the pressure needed to offset the image. (A.B. Dick Company)

Two-cylinder system

Most presses operate with a three-cylinder printing system, but other systems are also used. A ***two-cylinder system*** is a press design that combines the printing operations of the plate cylinder and impression cylinder into one cylinder. See **Figure 18-29**.

The combination cylinder serves as the main cylinder and is twice the circumference of the blanket cylinder. When each impression is made, the blanket cylinder revolves twice, while the combination cylinder makes one revolution. The combination cylinder is divided into two operations or *segments* as it revolves. In the first half of the turn, the image is offset from the plate segment of the cylinder to the blanket cylinder. In the second half of the turn, paper contacts the impression segment of the cylinder and the blanket cylinder and accepts the image.

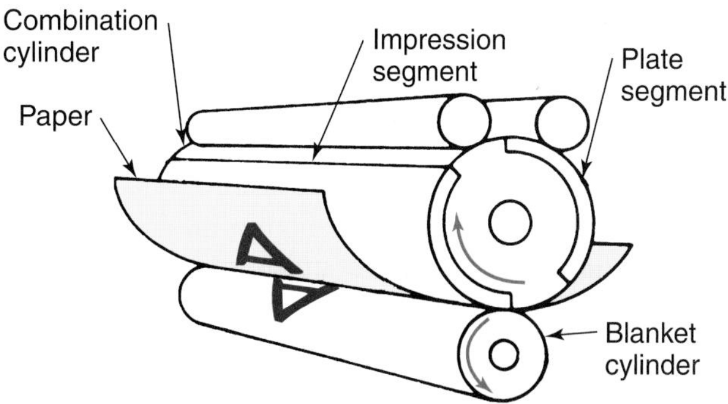

Figure 18-29. A two-cylinder system combines the plate and impression segments of the press into one cylinder. (A.B. Dick Company)

Perfecting press

A ***perfecting press*** is a printing system that prints both sides of the substrate at once. As shown in **Figure 18-30**, a perfecting press consists of two plate cylinders and two blanket cylinders. The pairs of cylinders are arranged above and below the path of the substrate. The substrate comes into contact with both blanket cylinders; the upper cylinder prints one side of the substrate, while the lower cylinder prints the other side simultaneously.

Common impression cylinder

A ***common impression cylinder*** is a press design commonly used for multicolor printing on web-fed

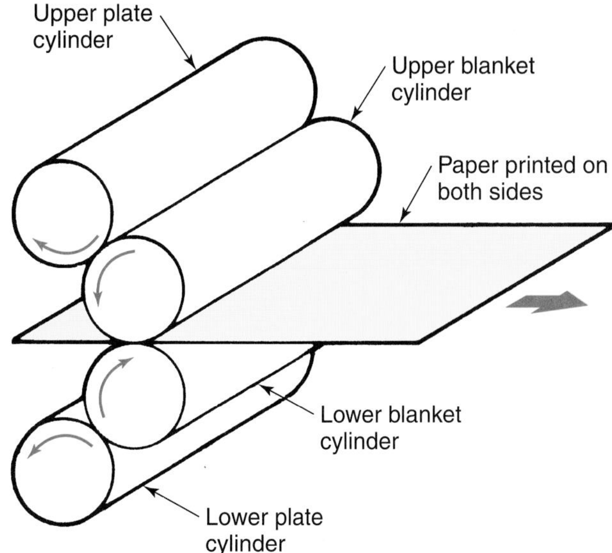

Figure 18-30. A perfecting press is equipped with two plate cylinders and two blanket cylinders to print both sides of the substrate at once.

presses. One large impression cylinder is central to the printing system, **Figure 18-31**. The cylinder is surrounded by a group of printing units, each of which is made up of a plate cylinder, a blanket cylinder, and inking and dampening systems. Each printing unit prints a separate color on the web as it travels between the blanket cylinders and the common impression cylinder.

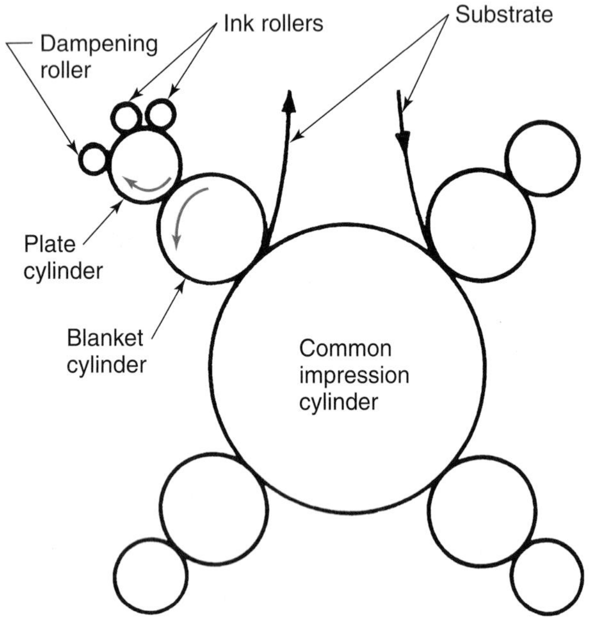

Figure 18-31. A common impression cylinder joined with a group of printing units is commonly used for multicolor printing on a web-fed press.

dampening system are a dampening fountain, a fountain roller, a ductor roller, a distributor roller, and a form roller. See **Figure 18-32**.

During the printing process, fountain solution is supplied to the *dampening fountain* by a bottle or similar reservoir. To keep the solution at the same level, many presses use a bottle that works by gravity feed to refill the fountain.

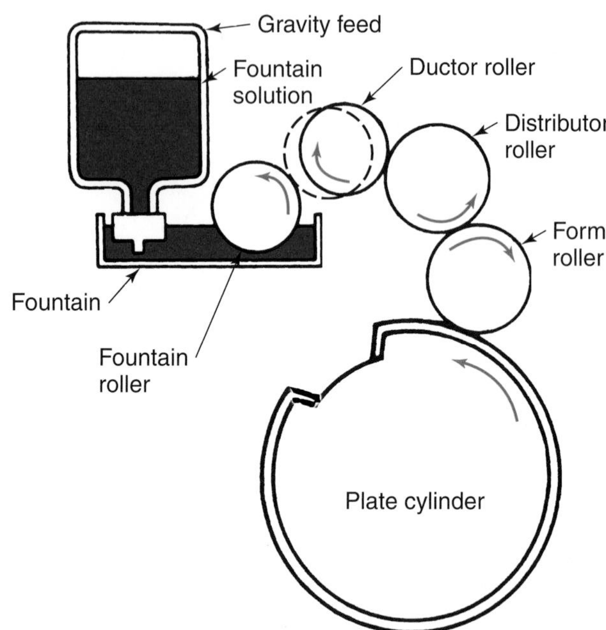

Figure 18-32. In a conventional dampening system, rollers are used to carry fountain solution from a fountain to the plate.

Dampening Systems

A ***dampening system*** is a group of rollers designed to apply moisture to the nonimage area of the plate. Before the plate is inked, the nonimage area is coated with fountain solution to separate it from the image area. When the plate is inked, only the image area is receptive to ink; the nonimage area repels ink.

The two most common types of dampening systems used on a press are *conventional dampening systems* and *continuous dampening systems*.

Conventional dampening systems

A conventional dampening system uses a series of rollers to distribute fountain solution from the fountain to the plate when the plate is positioned on the press. The basic components of a conventional

The *fountain roller* revolves in the fountain to draw out the solution. It transfers the fountain solution to the *ductor roller*, which moves back and forth and makes intermittent contact with the fountain roller. The movement of the ductor roller controls the amount of fountain solution that is transferred to the rest of the system. Refer to Figure 18-32.

The ductor roller is often covered with a ***molleton cover***, a cloth tube that fits over the body of the roller and helps it retain the fountain solution. Because water is not easily absorbed by the surface of a roller, the molleton cover is used to keep the ductor roller coated with fountain solution. Molleton covers help absorb and transfer the solution.

As the ductor roller rotates, it carries the fountain solution to the *distributor roller*. The distributor roller is used to spread the solution evenly across the rollers and prepare the solution for placement on the plate. The number of distributor rollers used in a dampening system varies. Distributor rollers are classified as *rotating* rollers and *oscillating* rollers. A rotating roller turns steadily in one direction to distribute the solution. An oscillating roller or *vibrator* moves from side to side while rotating to achieve a more even distribution of the fountain solution.

The distributor roller transfers the solution to the *form roller*, which applies the solution to the plate. Different systems may use one or more form rollers; they are typically covered with a molleton to retain moisture.

Dampening system rollers should be regularly cleaned and adjusted to ensure that the correct levels of pressure exist between each roller. Excessive pressure between the rollers can cause the rollers and plate surfaces to wear. Molleton covers must also be cleaned and rinsed thoroughly on a regular basis to remain effective.

Continuous dampening systems

A continuous dampening system is a system of rollers that distributes a continuous flow of fountain solution to the plate. The system eliminates the use of a ductor roller. See **Figure 18-33**. A *transfer roller* used in place of the ductor roller makes direct contact with the fountain roller to distribute the solution.

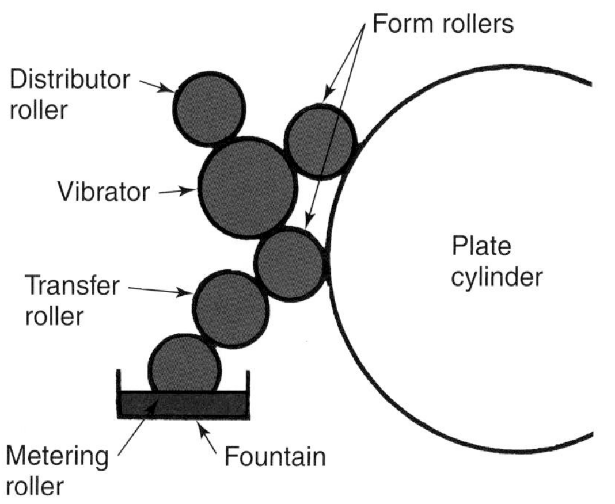

Figure 18-33. A continuous dampening system applies moisture to the plate with a continuous alignment of rollers. A transfer roller carries fountain solution from a metering roller to the rest of the system.

A *metering roller* is commonly used in a continuous dampening system. It serves the same purpose as the fountain roller but can be adjusted to control the flow of solution when it makes contact with the transfer roller. This presents an advantage over other dampening systems by allowing the system to respond quickly to changes in fountain settings. When the press is in operation, the operator can adjust the flow of solution if there is not enough reaching the plate.

A ***brush system*** is a continuous dampening system that uses a *brush roller* to transfer solution from the fountain roller to the rest of the system. The brush roller is used in place of a transfer roller to control the flow of solution, **Figure 18-34**. The brush roller draws solution from the fountain roller and spreads it accurately to a distributor roller, which transfers the solution to the form roller.

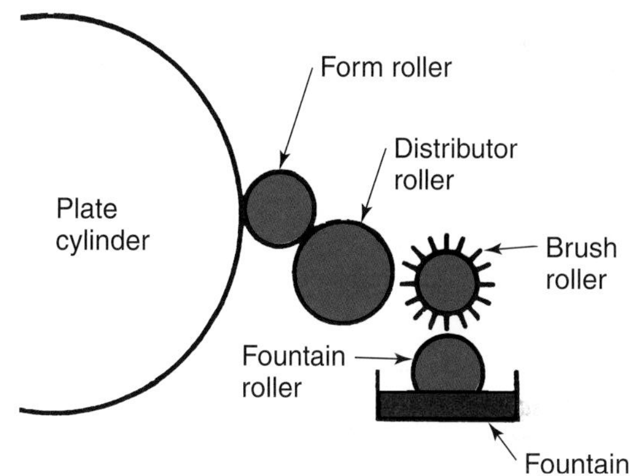

Figure 18-34. In a brush system, a brush roller spreads the fountain solution and is part of a continuous series of rollers.

Fountain solution

The fountain solution used in a dampening system must be properly mixed to provide a consistent dampening material for the plate surface. The fountain solution is normally a combination of water, an acidic substance, and gum arabic. Water serves as the main ingredient of the solution; it is applied to the nonimage area of the plate and is used to repel ink.

Because ink is applied repeatedly to the plate, the fountain solution is also responsible for separating the nonimage area from the image area and ensuring that the nonimage area remains receptive to water. A concentration of acid and gum arabic in the solution helps prevent the nonimage area of the plate from receiving ink. The solution is designed to *desensitize* the nonimage area, or keep it from becoming image receptive.

Fountain solutions are commonly identified by their ***pH value***, a measurement that indicates the acidity or alkalinity of the solution. A ***pH scale*** provides numeric pH values ranging from 0 to 14, with 7 designated as neutral. See **Figure 18-35**. A pH value less than 7 describes a solution that is acidic, with a reading of 0 representing the highest acidity. A pH value above 7 indicates an alkaline solution, with a value of 14 representing the highest alkalinity. Each successive pH value is 10 times the previous value; for example, a solution with a pH reading of 3.0 is 10 times more acidic than a solution with a pH reading of 4.0.

Plates have a recommended pH value that is used when mixing the fountain solution. Most plates are designed to use solutions with a pH reading between 4.0 and 5.5. Some presses are equipped with devices that automatically monitor the pH value of the fountain solution.

Solutions with a controlled pH level result in higher printing quality and reduce wear on the plate. A solution with a low pH reading can cause emulsification (ink loss) and plate damage. A solution with a high pH reading reduces the ability of the plate to repel ink and can cause scumming (excess ink in the nonimage area).

Waterless Presses

A ***waterless press*** is an offset lithographic press system that eliminates the use of a dampening system during the printing process. A waterless press prints with waterless plates, which are designed differently from conventional plates. The surface of a waterless plate is a layer of silicone rubber that repels ink and keeps the nonimage area separate from the image area. The image area is recessed; it lies just below the plate surface and has an ink-receptive photopolymer coating. The silicone plate surface serves the same function that is provided by the fountain solution in a dampening system.

The inking system used by a waterless press is temperature-controlled. As ink is applied to the plate, the surface is designed to repel a certain thickness of ink. The system must regulate the temperature of the ink to maintain the correct thickness. Several rollers in the system contain hollow tubes that are filled with water to remove excess heat. Water circulates through the rollers and cools the ink as it is transferred to the plate.

The use of waterless lithography is becoming more common in the graphic communications industry. Waterless presses present several advantages over conventional presses that use dampening systems. Waterless plates provide greater image quality by producing a higher *density* of ink when they are offset. The procedures involved in formulating fountain solutions and maintaining a dampening system are also eliminated, saving the press operator setup time when running the press.

Inking Systems

An ***inking system*** consists of a set of rollers that carries a thin film of ink to the image area of a plate. See **Figure 18-36**. The inking system or *ink train* is

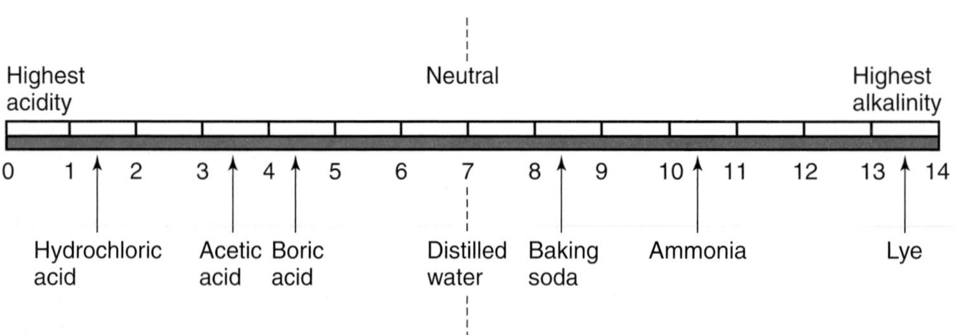

Figure 18-35. A pH scale is used to measure the acidity or alkalinity of a solution. The scale ranges from 0-14, with 7 indicating a neutral solution. A value above 7 indicates an alkaline solution; a value below 7 represents an acidic solution. (A.B. Dick Company)

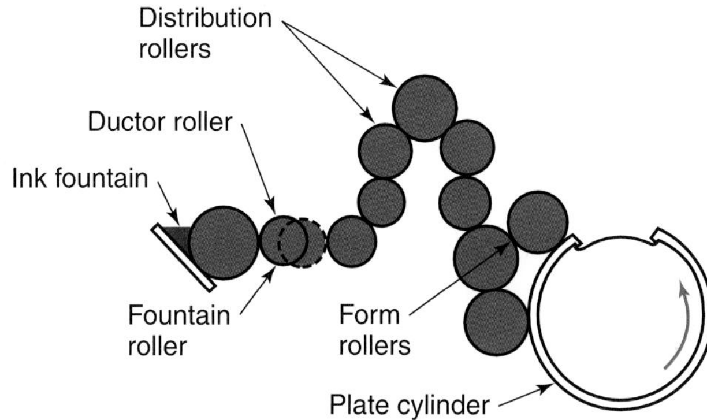

Figure 18-36. Ink is applied to the plate by a series of rollers that make up the inking system.

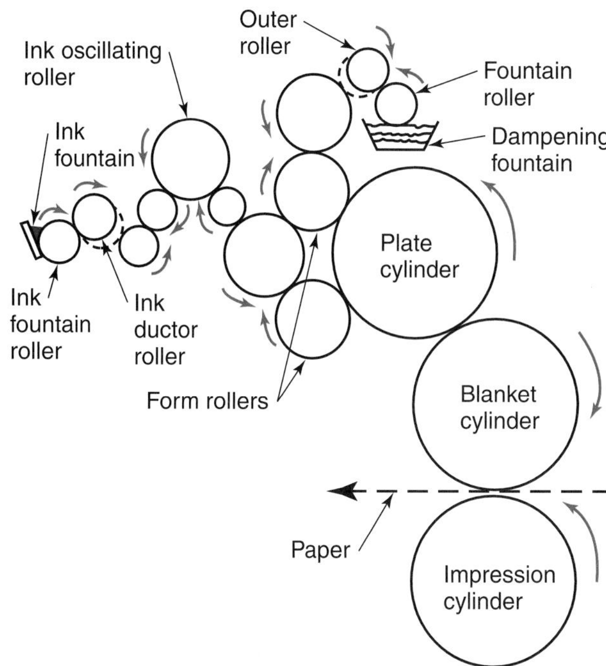

Figure 18-37. An inking and dampening system is a combined design that carries both ink and fountain solution to the plate. (A.B. Dick Company)

responsible for maintaining a consistent flow of ink to the plate surface. A typical system includes an ink fountain, a fountain roller, a ductor roller, and a combination of distributor rollers and form rollers.

Ink is supplied to the system by an *ink fountain*. On larger presses, an *ink agitator* may be used to help maintain a consistent ink flow. An agitator is a revolving device that moves along the fountain and stirs the ink to keep it at the same flow level.

The *fountain roller* transfers ink from the fountain to the *ductor roller*, a movable roller that makes intermittent contact with the fountain roller and the *distributor roller* or *vibrator*. The ink is then distributed by one or more distributor rollers to the *intermediate rollers* or directly to the *form rollers*. The form rollers place the final film of ink on the plate.

The number of distributor, intermediate, and form rollers used in an inking system varies according to the press. The number of rollers in the design provides an indication of the quality of the system. The greater the number of rollers, the more uniform the distribution of ink to the plate.

Inking and dampening system

Inking systems are joined with dampening systems on some duplicators to form a combined ***inking and dampening system***. See **Figure 18-37**. The two systems are linked to apply both ink and fountain solution to the plate. In an integrated system, the entire set of inking and dampening rollers is first inked. Fountain solution is then added to the dampening fountain and fed to the system. Because ink is first distributed to the entire system, fountain solution *rides* on the top of each roller after it is added. The form rollers connect the two systems and carry the ink and fountain solution directly to the plate.

Delivery Systems

A ***delivery system*** removes the printed substrate from the printing system of the press and prepares it for finishing operations. Delivery systems on sheet-fed presses are designed differently from those used on web-fed presses. On a sheet-fed press, the delivery system removes sheets of paper and places them into a stack called the *delivery pile*. On a web-fed press, the delivery system conducts a number of additional operations.

Sheet-fed delivery systems

A *sheet-fed delivery system* removes sheets after they are printed and stacks them onto an outfeed table or tray. Sheet-fed delivery systems vary in design and use.

The most common delivery system used on a sheet-fed press is a chain delivery system. See **Figure 18-38**. As a sheet of paper leaves the printing system, it is directed to the ***delivery pile*** by a pair of chains that serve as conveyor belts. Two delivery

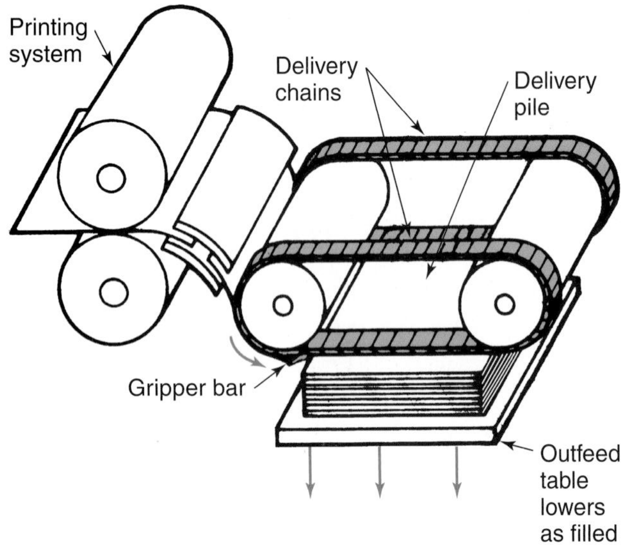

Figure 18-38. A chain delivery system driven by a pair of chain conveyor belts directs printed stock to a delivery pile.

bars extending between the chains contain grippers that grasp the sheet and guide it through the system. See **Figure 18-39**. The gripper bars are positioned along the length of the chains so one set of grippers pulls a sheet from the printing unit at the same time the other set of grippers delivers a sheet to the delivery pile. The pile is stacked on top of the outfeed table.

When a sheet is released by the gripper bars, it is aligned in the delivery pile by guides positioned along the sides of the pile. See **Figure 18-40.** Proper alignment of the sheets is critical. The delivery pile must be uniformly arranged so that the paper can be trimmed or folded after it is stacked. Two stationary guides and two jogging guides place each sheet in position and straighten the stack. The stationary guides are on two sides of the paper. The jogging guides are adjustable and move or *jog* the paper into place as it is fed to the pile. See **Figure 18-41**. As the sheets build up, the outfeed table slowly drops under the weight of the pile. Refer to **Figure 18-38**.

Other delivery systems use a tray to hold the paper after it is printed. Duplicators are commonly

Figure 18-39. Gripper bars are used to guide printed sheets through a chain delivery system.

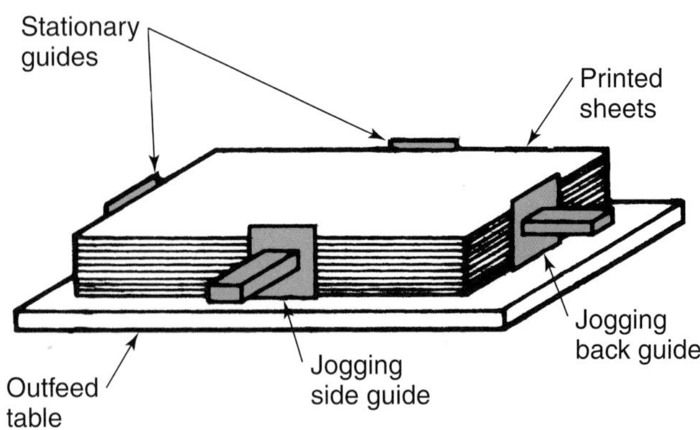

Figure 18-40. Guides are positioned to align delivered paper on the outfeed table.

Figure 18-41. Jogging guides can be adjusted to align the edges of the stack as paper is delivered.

equipped with an ejector system that uses rollers to feed the paper from the printing system to the delivery tray. See **Figure 18-42**. Paper guides align the edges of the paper when it reaches the tray.

Web-fed delivery systems

A *web-fed delivery system* is designed to provide a series of finishing operations in addition to the actual delivery of paper. The feeding and delivery systems used with web-fed presses are designed much differently from those used with sheet-fed presses. After the paper is printed, it is transferred to a group of units that make up the delivery system.

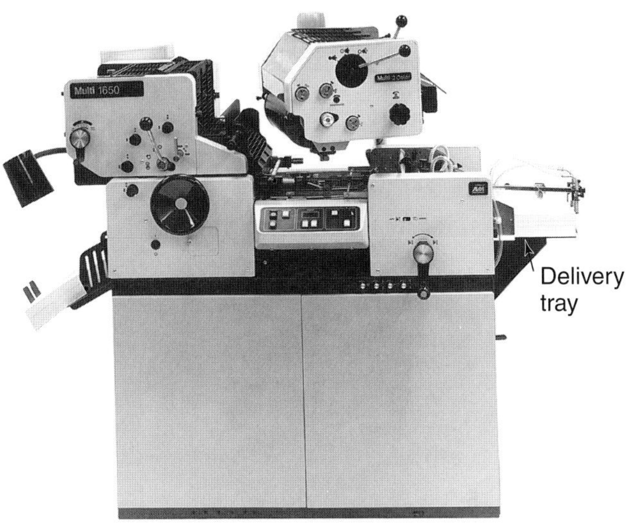

Figure 18-42. An offset duplicator uses a delivery tray to receive paper after it is printed.

Different delivery systems are used on various web-fed presses. A typical system includes a *dryer*, *chiller*, and *folder*. See **Figure 18-43**.

The dryer unit dries the ink printed on the web. The dryer operates at high temperatures and removes much of the moisture from the ink through evaporation. The web is then cooled by the chiller unit, which lowers the temperature on the web surface and hardens the ink. The system may also include a moisturizing unit to restore web moisture that is lost in the drying and chilling processes.

Once the web passes through the dryer and chiller units, it is transferred to the folder, where it is trimmed and folded into signatures. A signature is a folded sheet that is commonly printed on both sides and trimmed. A typical folder folds sheets using a ***former board***, a curved or triangular plane that serves as the folding surface. See **Figure 18-44**.

Other folder units are equipped with a series of rollers that produce folded signatures. A *jaw folder* uses a blade to feed the web through the system. As the web travels through the rollers, it is automatically folded and cut into signatures. The finished signatures are then delivered by a conveyor system to a delivery table.

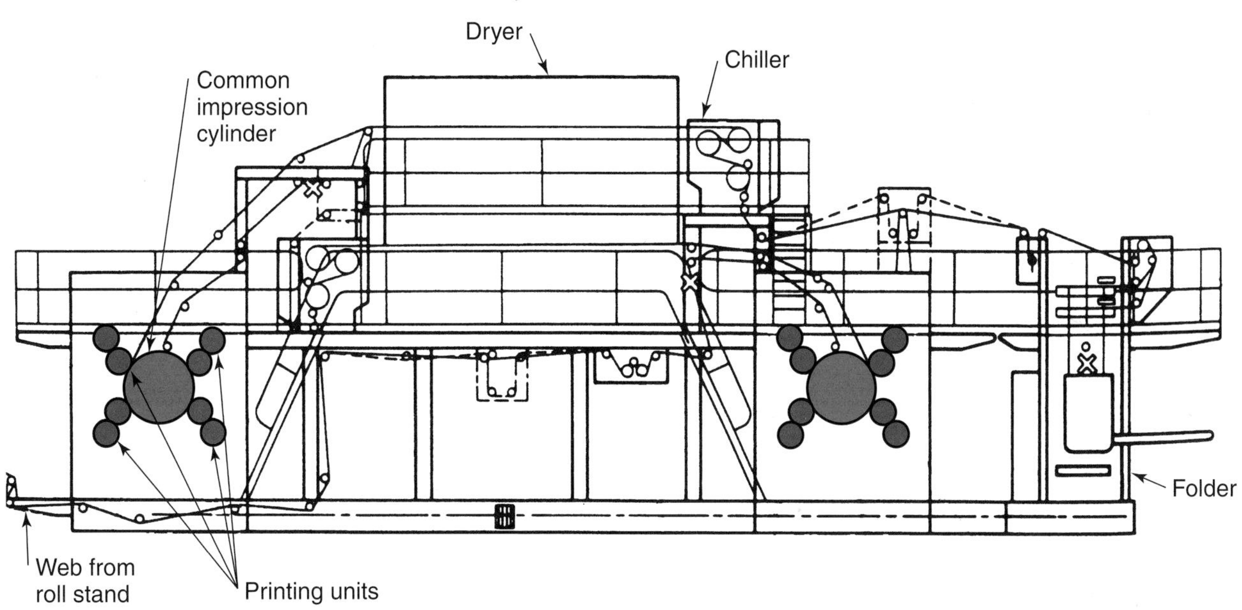

Figure 18-43. The delivery system of a web-fed press is commonly equipped with separate dryer, chiller, and folder units. (Baker Perkins Limited)

Figure 18-44. A former board is used to make the first fold in the paper web. The folder unit cuts the paper web and makes additional folds to form the signature. (King Press Corporation)

Review Questions

Please do not write in this text. Write your answers on a separate sheet of paper.

1. What are the five basic systems of a lithographic press?
2. Name two components that are used by a feeding system to separate paper and feed sheets one at a time to a sheet-fed press.
3. A _____ is a control device that prevents more than one sheet of paper from entering the press.
4. Which portion of a feeding system positions the paper and carries it to be registered for printing?
5. Name two types of splicer units that are typically used on a web-fed press.
6. How does a web break detector work?
7. What are the three cylinders that make up the printing system of a typical lithographic press?
8. The vertical space that lies between the surface of the plate cylinder bearers and the cylinder body is called the _____
9. The _____ applies the pressure needed to transfer the image from the blanket cylinder to the substrate.
10. A _____ is a printing system that prints both sides of a sheet at once.
11. A web-fed press design in which one cylinder is surrounded by a group of printing units is called a _____ cylinder.
12. What are the two most common types of dampening systems used on a press?
13. A _____ is a cloth tube that fits over the body of a dampening roller to help it retain fountain solution.
14. Which of the following would be an acceptable pH value for a fountain solution?
    a. 9
    b. 1
    c. 4.5
    d. 3.5
15. What are three finishing units commonly used by the delivery system of a web-fed press?

19 Lithographic Press Operation and Troubleshooting

Learning Objectives

After studying this chapter, you will be able to:

- Identify the different types of equipment and fundamental principles used to operate a sheet-fed offset press.
- Describe how to set up and operate the feeding system of a press.
- Demonstrate the procedures used to prepare and adjust the press cylinders in a printing system.
- Prepare and maintain fountain solutions for use in a dampening system.
- Operate and make adjustments to an inking system.
- Summarize the components and operational methods used in a press delivery system.
- Recognize common problems related to the operation of an offset press and make corrections to the system.

Important Terms

chain delivery system
hickeys
ink keys
misting
pH scale
picking
piling
scumming
setoff
slurring

The fundamental operating systems and equipment used by sheet-fed and web-fed offset presses were introduced in the previous chapter on lithographic press systems. This chapter will cover the different methods used in the operation of a sheet-fed press. While press designs vary and different operational methods are required for each type of press, many systems are designed with the principles common to the operation of a typical sheet-fed press. A press operator familiar with the design of a sheet-fed press can use many of the same guidelines and techniques when operating other presses.

The operation of an offset press is commonly divided into five systems. Each press has a *feeding system*, a *printing system*, a *dampening system*, an *inking system*, and a *delivery system*. The first section of this chapter will cover the different methods of preparing and operating each press system. Although waterless press systems without dampening units are increasingly being used by commercial printers, the majority of presses in operation today still use dampening systems. For this reason, this chapter will cover the five traditional offset press systems. The second part of the chapter will present common troubleshooting techniques used in the maintenance of an offset press.

Offset Presses

Offset presses are used in printing applications throughout the graphic communications industry and are classified as *sheet-fed presses* and *web-fed presses*. Sheet-fed presses print on individual sheets of paper as they are fed through the press. Web-fed presses print on an entire web or paper roll that travels continuously through the press. While the feeding and delivery systems designed for sheet-fed presses differ from those used by web-fed presses, each type of press uses many of the same operating procedures.

Sheet-fed presses are used in many different commercial printing operations. A ***duplicator*** is a small sheet-fed press used for short printing runs and can produce more than 10,000 impressions per hour (iph). See **Figure 19-1**. Duplicators are often found in small commercial print shops and in-plant printing operations.

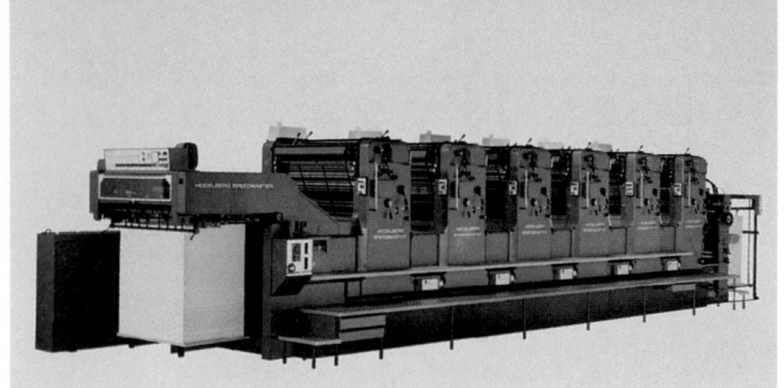

Figure 19-2. Large sheet-fed presses used in multicolor printing are equipped with several printing units, each of which prints a separate color. The knowledge gained from using a small sheet-fed press can be used to operate larger presses like this one. (Heidelberg USA)

Figure 19-1. A duplicator is a small sheet-fed press commonly used for in-house printing applications.

Many of the same control devices used on large sheet-fed presses are common to duplicators. Some of the knowledge gained from operating a duplicator can be used to run larger presses.

Sheet-fed presses used for multicolor printing are considerably larger than duplicators, **Figure 19-2**. Larger sheet-fed and web-fed presses are typically equipped with several printing units, each of which is used to print a separate color. Different dampening and inking systems operate with each printing unit, and numerous control devices are used by operators to make adjustments to each system.

Although setup methods and operations vary depending on the type of press used, this chapter will focus on the operation of a sheet-fed press. As discussed in the last chapter, the feeding and delivery units used by web-fed presses are designed to feed an entire web of paper through the system and typically operate automatically. Sheet-fed presses commonly involve more manual operations for each press system.

Offset press operation

In the operation of an offset press, five different systems must be set up and adjusted to prepare it for printing. Each system performs a different function as paper is fed through the press and printed.

Paper is drawn to the press from the feeding system, which consists of a feeding platform, a group of devices that help separate and transfer sheets of paper, and a register unit that aligns the paper for printing. The feeding system is controlled by a series of guiding and registration devices that are adjusted when the system is set up. Paper is transferred from the feeding system to the printing system, which offsets images from an inked plate to the printing substrate. A three-cylinder printing system consists of a plate cylinder, a blanket cylinder, and an impression cylinder. Images are offset from the plate to a blanket, and offset again to the substrate as paper travels between the impression cylinder and blanket cylinder. See **Figure 19-3**. Each cylinder must be properly aligned and *packed* to provide the amount of pressure necessary to transfer images to paper.

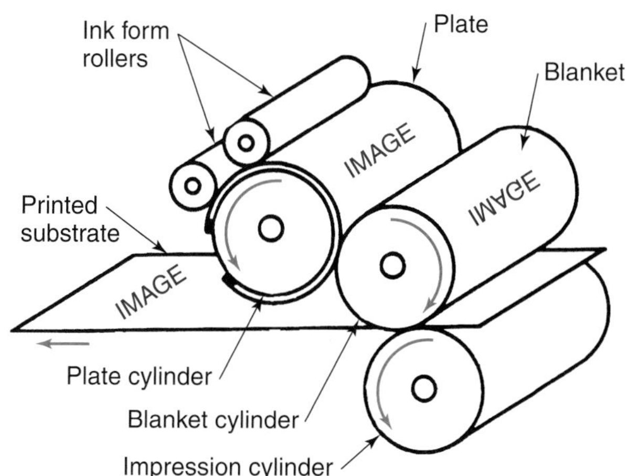

Figure 19-3. Images are first offset from a plate to a blanket and then offset again to paper in offset lithographic printing.

When the plate is positioned on the press, water or fountain solution is applied to the plate surface by the dampening system and ink is applied by the inking system. The plate contains a nonimage area that accepts fountain solution and repels ink and an image area that accepts ink and repels fountain solution. This process is based on the principle that ink, a grease-based substance, does not readily mix with water. The separation of the image area from the nonimage area permits only the inked image to be offset during printing. The dampening and inking systems consist of a series of rollers and must be set up to provide the correct proportion of fountain solution and ink to the plate; on some presses, the two systems are combined into a single unit. When the press is in operation, adjustments are sometimes necessary to maintain a consistent flow of fountain solution and ink.

After the image is printed, paper is transferred from the printing system and stacked for postpress operations by the delivery system. A typical delivery system uses chain conveyor belts and gripper bars to pull sheets of paper to an outfeed table or delivery pile. Pile guides are set to align the paper on the delivery pile, where sheets are stacked for such operations as folding, trimming, and binding.

Each system in an offset press must be set up and maintained for consistent operation by the press operator. Paper must be guided properly through the system as it is fed, printed, and delivered. Presses are commonly equipped with a computerized control unit that allows the operator to set up the press by entering and reading data on a display. See **Figure 19-4**. The computer collects, controls, and analyzes information about the various functions of the press.

Other offset presses are equipped with operating devices that must be adjusted manually. Before a press is used, each system must be checked and set up according to specifications of the press. The next part of this chapter will present the different equipment and operating methods used in running a press.

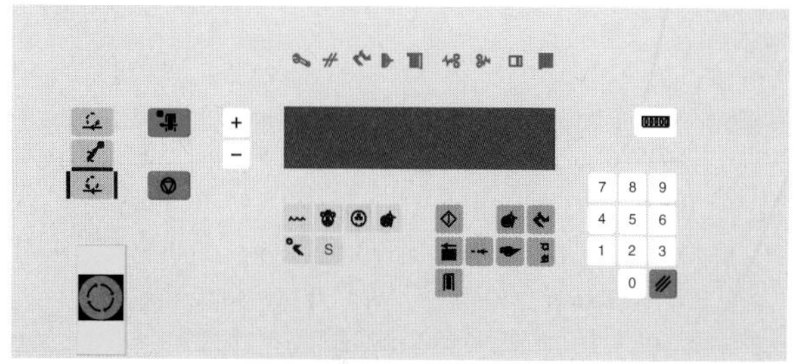

Figure 19-4. A computerized control panel is used by the operator to make automatic adjustments to the press. (Heidelberg USA)

Feeding System Operation

The *feeding system* consists of the equipment used to feed individual sheets of paper to the press. The feeding system transfers paper to the printing system through the use of mechanical guides and registration devices. As paper leaves the feeding system, it is aligned and registered with the printing system. Making the proper adjustments to the feeding system is critical when setting up the press.

The location and types of control devices in a feeding system vary, depending on the press design. The typical components of a feeding system are a feeding platform, paper guides, sheet separators, sucker feet, pullout rollers, a double-sheet detector, and a register unit. See **Figure 19-5**.

When paper is placed on the platform, it is aligned into a uniform stack by the paper guides. The platform is typically lowered by hand; when the stack is at the right height, the top sheet should be in position to enter the registration unit. Sheet separators positioned along the edges of the paper are used to separate the top sheet from the rest of the stack by producing streams of air. Each sheet is then directed to the pullout rollers by the sucker feet, a set of vacuum devices that remove paper from the

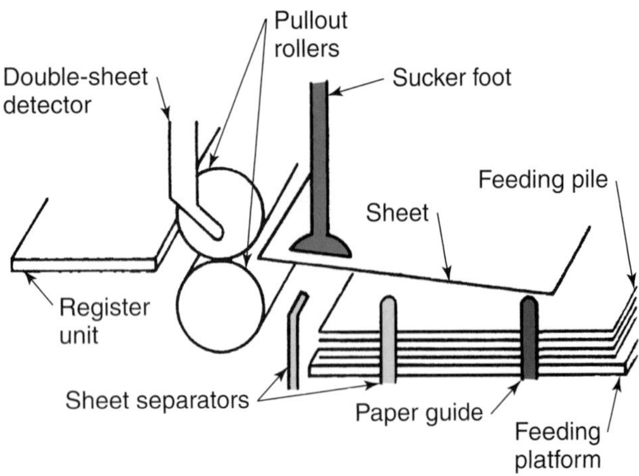

Figure 19-5. Typical components of a sheet-fed press feeding system.

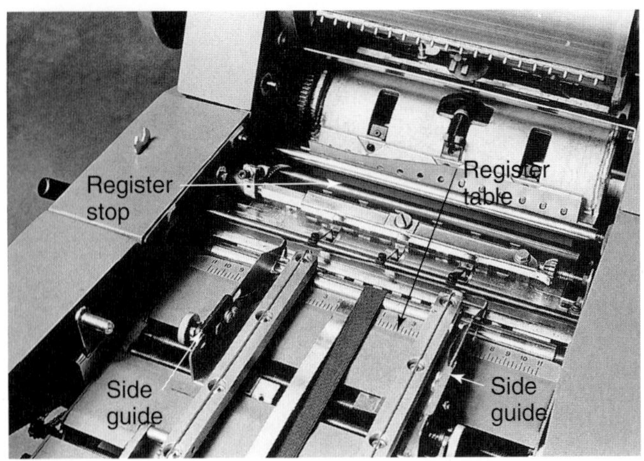

Figure 19-7. Paper is placed in register with the press by side guides once it reaches the register stop.

stack. See **Figure 19-6**. When the rear edge of one sheet leaves the pile, the sucker feet pick up the next sheet.

As the paper passes through the pullout rollers, it comes into contact with the double-sheet detector, a device that senses paper thickness and prevents more than one sheet of paper from entering the press. When more than one sheet is fed through the pullout rollers, the double-sheet detector activates and opens a deflector plate to remove the excess paper.

The register table uses a set of conveyor tapes to carry the paper to the register stop; when the paper reaches the stop, it is registered with the printing system by the side guides. See **Figure 19-7**. The paper is then ready to be printed.

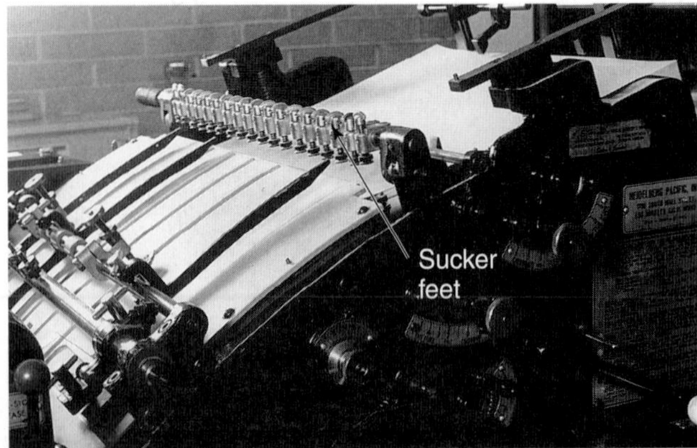

Figure 19-6. Sucker feet draw sheets of paper from the feeding pile to the register unit.

Feeding system setup

Proper setup of the feeding system is a critical part of operating the press. Paper must be registered correctly when it leaves the feeding system in order to receive a consistent transfer of images from the printing system. Proper setup is also essential in eliminating misfeeds. The following is a typical procedure for setting up and operating a feeding system on an offset press.

The press operator must have a thorough understanding of all press operations before setting up and running a press. Any adjustments to the press must be made when the press is not in operation. The operator must practice correct safety procedures when using the press; damage to the press or injury can result if the recommended procedures are not followed.

1. Lower the feeding platform to the operating height by turning the elevator handle and adjust the paper guides to match the sheet size of the paper. Fan the paper and stack it on the platform, jogging it into place to meet the guides. Next, adjust the pile height and align the paper just below the sucker feet. During operation of the press, the pile must remain at the same height as sheets are drawn off for printing. See **Figure 19-8**. The elevator control knob is used to set the pile height. Turning the knob clockwise lowers the pile height, while turning it counterclockwise raises the pile height. Once the pile height is set, the platform will rise automatically to maintain the height of the pile when the press is in operation.

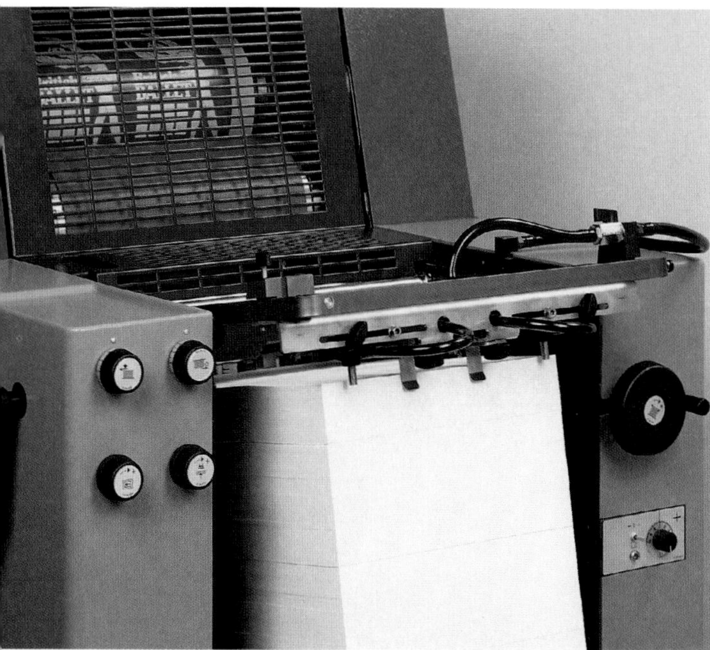

Figure 19-8. The feeding pile is set to remain at the same height during operation of the press. (Heidelberg USA)

2. Adjust the sheet separators to control the flow of air separating the top sheet from the rest of the pile. The sheet separators or fingers are typically located at the front and rear edges of the stack. They can be moved up or down, and forward or backward. The amount of air flow should also be adjusted in relation to the size and weight of the paper.
3. Position the sucker feet so they are parallel to the bar controlling the operating height of the feeding platform. The sucker feet are typically arranged in a single row on a bar located above the paper. See **Figure 19-9**. The sucker feet must be close enough to remove individual sheets of paper; too much suction will draw more than one sheet of paper from the stack. Any sucker feet on the bar that extend beyond the edges of the sheet must be turned off. The amount of vacuum provided by the sucker feet can also be adjusted for the type of stock used.
4. Adjust the pullout rollers and the double-sheet detector. The pressure between the rollers must be sufficient to draw each sheet of paper to the register table. The pressure can be checked by pulling a thin strip of paper through each set of rollers. When the strips are pulled through, there should be a slight amount of resistance. The pressure or resistance felt between the rollers must be equal. The pressure can be adjusted by tightening or loosening the control knobs on the side of each roller. After paper is fed through the pullout rollers, its thickness is monitored by the double-sheet detector. See **Figure 19-10**. If more than one sheet of paper is detected, a deflector plate opens to remove the paper.

Figure 19-9. The sucker feet must be set parallel to the feeding pile height control bar. (Heidelberg USA)

Figure 19-10. The double-sheet detector is set to monitor paper thickness as sheets pass through the system. (Heidelberg USA)

5. Set up the register unit by positioning the side guides. Paper is transferred from the pullout rollers to the register unit by a set of conveyor tapes that run along the register table. When a sheet of paper reaches the register stop, the side guides bring the paper into register with the printing system. Refer to Figure 19-7. The register stop consists of a group of fingers that stop the paper before it is guided into position. After the paper is registered, the fingers

rise or drop to allow the paper to pass to the printing system. The side guides are located on both sides of the paper on the register table; one of the guides is designated as an active guide, while the other is designated as the stationary guide. The active guide *jogs* the paper into register when it reaches the register stop. To set the active guide, a handwheel is used to manually advance the press until the guide reaches its most inward position on the register table. See **Figure 19-11**. The guide can be repositioned after loosening a screw attached to the assembly; it is then adjusted along a measuring scale to match the width of the paper. The stationary guide remains in a fixed position and meets the edge of the paper opposite the active guide. When a sheet of paper reaches the register stop, it is guided into position to accept the image when it passes between the blanket cylinder and the impression cylinder.

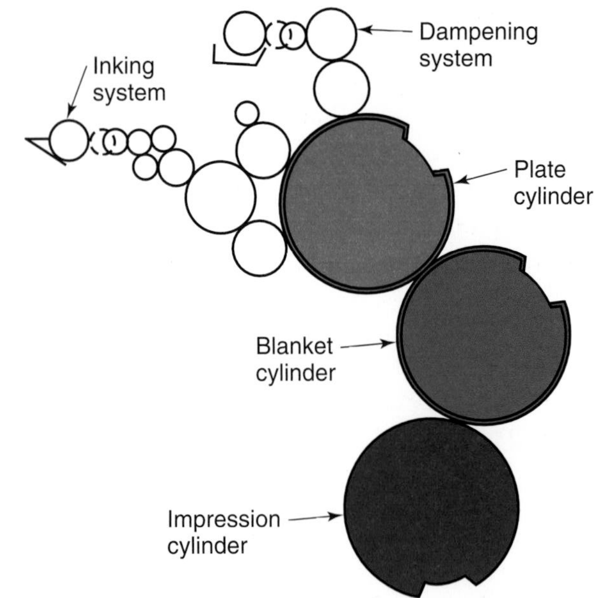

Figure 19-12. A three-cylinder printing system consists of a plate cylinder, a blanket cylinder, and an impression cylinder.

Figure 19-11. A handwheel is used to manually advance the press when setting up the register unit. (Heidelberg USA)

Printing System Operation

The ***printing system*** of an offset press is a group of cylinders that draws paper from the feeding system and prints or *offsets* images from a printing plate. The printing system is the main unit of the press. A three-cylinder system is made up of a plate cylinder, a blanket cylinder, and an impression cylinder. See **Figure 19-12**. During operation of the press, the cylinder bearers *ride* on each other as images are transferred from one cylinder to another. The plate cylinder provides the holding surface for the plate. The blanket cylinder holds the blanket, which serves as a printing intermediate between the plate and the printing substrate. The impression cylinder provides the pressure necessary to transfer the image from the blanket to the substrate as it revolves against the blanket cylinder. The impression cylinder also serves the function of grasping paper from the feeding system after the paper is registered. Grippers located along a bar on the impression cylinder are used to draw the paper when it reaches the register stop, **Figure 19-13**. As paper is transferred, it travels between the impression cylinder and the blanket cylinder. Images are offset from the plate to the blanket, which offsets the image again to the paper as it feeds through the system.

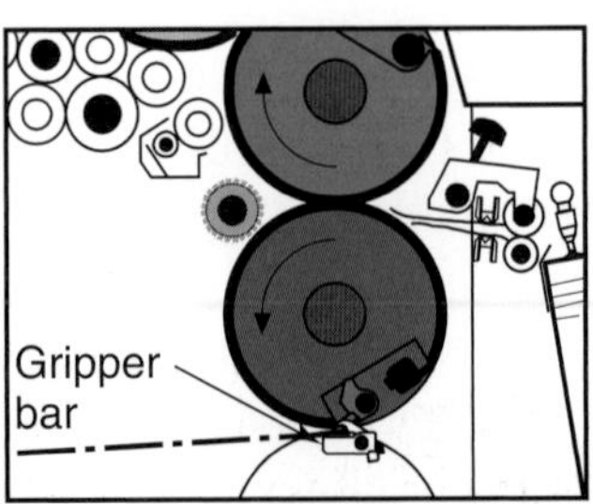

Figure 19-13. A gripper bar grasps the edges of the paper as it makes contact with the impression cylinder. (Heidelberg USA)

The printing system operates in connection with the dampening and inking systems of the press. When a plate is positioned on the plate cylinder, fountain solution is applied to the nonimage area of the plate surface and ink is applied to the image area. Only the inked image is transferred from the plate to the blanket during printing. An even distribution of fountain solution and ink must reach the plate surface during a press run.

The printing system cylinders must be set up properly before operating the press. The plate must be positioned correctly on the plate cylinder and the blanket must be mounted properly on the blanket cylinder. Plates are commonly *punched* at the ends and attached to pinbar fittings on the plate cylinder. See **Figure 19-14**. The plate cylinder has two pinbars, one to hold the lead edge of the plate and one to hold the tail end. When the plate is mounted, it is attached to the lead pinbar and then wrapped around the cylinder to meet the tail pinbar. A set of clamps lock the plate in place. Blankets are typically designed with the same punched fittings used by plates and are attached to lead and tail pinbars on the blanket cylinder.

When a press is in operation, the correct level of pressure between cylinders must exist for images to transfer to the paper. The surfaces of the plate and blanket cylinders are *undercut* from the cylinder bearers to allow for different thicknesses of plates and blankets. See **Figure 19-15**. The ***undercut*** is the vertical space that lies between the cylinder body and the cylinder bearer surface. It is designed to provide space for the plate and blanket and any extra packing sheets that must be used to supply added cylinder pressure.

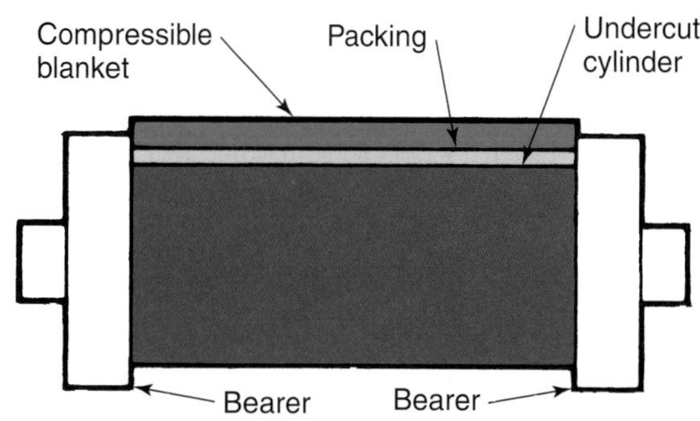

Figure 19-15. The undercut surface of a cylinder body lies below the cylinder bearers, allowing for packing when different plate and blanket thicknesses are used.

The operation of the printing system has a direct effect on the appearance of the image when it is printed. The cylinders must provide enough pressure to offset images and the plate and blanket must be mounted correctly. The following is a typical procedure for setting up each cylinder in a three-cylinder printing system.

Plate cylinder setup

1. Clean off the plate cylinder, removing any foreign particles or moisture, before mounting the plate. Using the handwheel on the operating side of the press, turn the press until the lead clamp of the cylinder is in position to receive the lead edge of the plate. See **Figure 19-16**. With the clamp bar open, mount the plate on the lead pinbar and then tighten

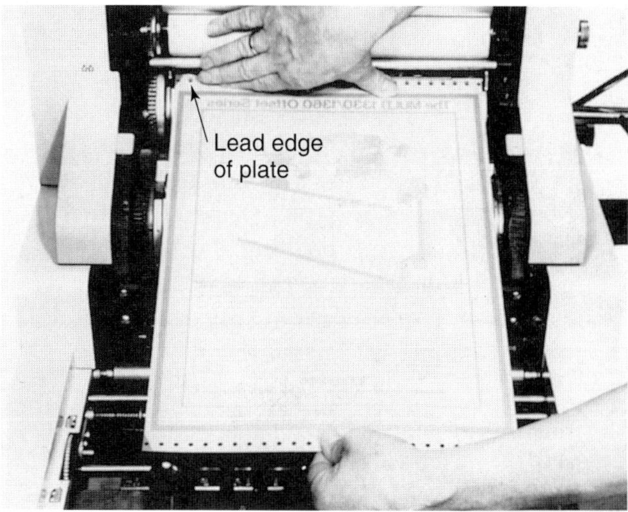

Figure 19-14. Plates are mounted on a press by engaging the lead and tail pinbar fittings of the plate cylinder.

Figure 19-16. A mounted plate is held in place by lead and tail clamps on the plate cylinder. (Heidelberg USA)

the lead clamp. Holding the tail end of the plate securely, use the handwheel to rotate the press until the tail clamp is in position to receive the tail end of the plate. Release the tail clamp and position the plate fittings over the tail pinbar. When the pins are inserted, tighten the tail clamp to lock in the plate.

2. Rotate the plate cylinder to adjust the printed appearance of the image. Some presses are equipped with a control device that can be used to adjust the plate cylinder and raise or lower the image when it is printed. If the image is too high or too low on the plate, it may not offset to the correct position on the paper. To adjust the position of the image, loosen the plate cylinder locknut and turn the handwheel to rotate the cylinder. A scale is used to indicate the location of the image; the direction of the turn determines whether the image is raised or lowered. See **Figure 19-17**. After adjusting the offset position of the image, retighten the cylinder.

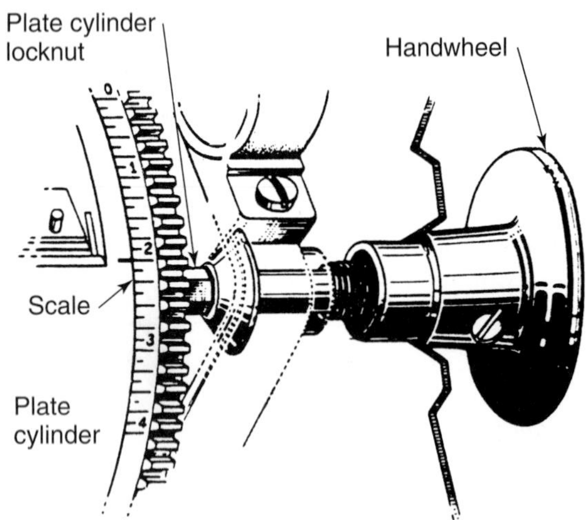

Figure 19-17. A printed image can be raised or lowered when it is offset from the plate by adjusting the position of the plate cylinder. (Multigraphics)

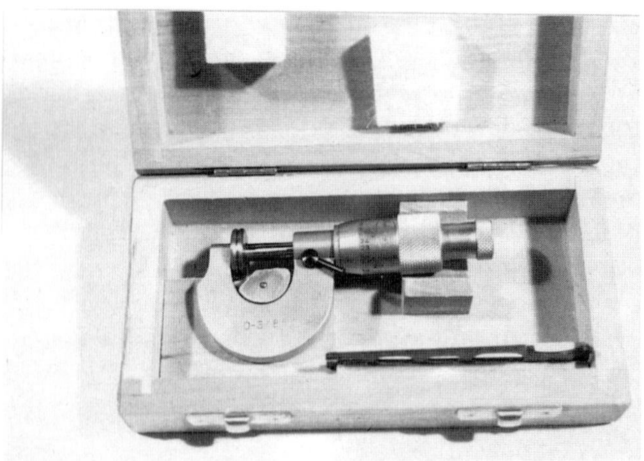

Figure 19-18. A micrometer may be used to measure the thickness of a blanket when calculating the amount of packing needed.

Blanket cylinder setup

1. Measure the thickness of the blanket and determine the amount of packing needed to pack the cylinder. A *micrometer* is commonly used to measure blanket thickness. See **Figure 19-18**. Next, determine the amount of undercut of the blanket cylinder; it is typically indicated on the cylinder body or listed in the press operating manual. When positioned on the press, the blanket commonly extends above the bearers to meet the plate on the plate cylinder. The distance that the blanket should extend above the blanket cylinder bearers is generally recommended by the press manufacturer. To calculate the amount of packing needed, first subtract the blanket thickness from the undercut. The resulting figure is the distance from the blanket surface to the bearers; adding this figure to the recommended distance past the bearers gives the total thickness for blanket packing.

   Blanket and plate packing thickness can also be determined by using a ***cylinder packing gauge***, **Figure 19-19**. The gauge can be used to measure the amount of pressure or *squeeze* that exists between the cylinders when the plate and blanket are both mounted on the press. To provide the pressure necessary to transfer images, the total thickness of the plate, blanket, and packing should exceed the combined undercut of the plate and blanket cylinders. The amount of squeeze typically ranges from 0.002″ to 0.004″.

2. Clean the surface of the blanket cylinder and mount the blanket. After inspecting the cylinder for any loose particles or moisture, the blanket can be mounted. Blankets commonly have a rubber surface and are punched with the same fittings used to mount plates on the press. Using the press handwheel, rotate the

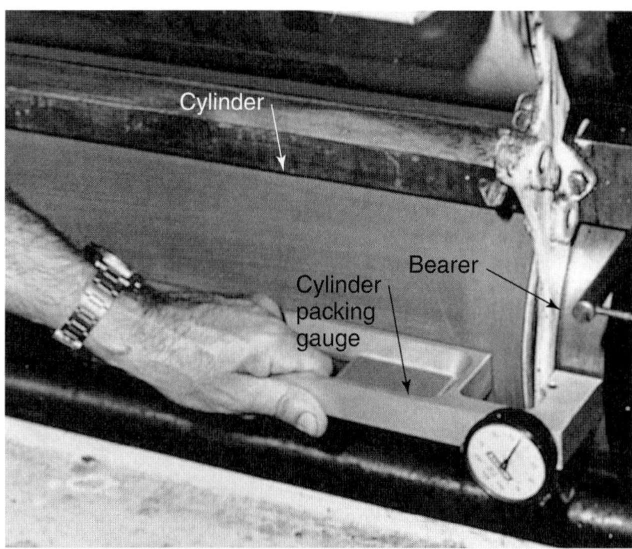

Figure 19-19. A cylinder packing gauge is used to measure plate or blanket thicknesses and packing between the cylinders. (Baldwin Technology)

blanket cylinder far enough to that the lead edge of the blanket can be positioned in the lead cylinder clamp. Attach the blanket and tighten the clamp. If any packing sheets are to be used, place them under the blanket. The sheets should fit entirely under the blanket without extending past the edges. Holding the blanket in place, turn the handwheel and rotate the cylinder until the tail end of the blanket can be positioned with the tail cylinder clamp. Attach the blanket and tighten the clamp. See **Figure 19-20**.

3. Clean the blanket after operating the press. The blanket surface must be free of ink, any foreign materials, and moisture from previous use. A recommended ink solvent is typically used as a blanket wash; after the wash is applied, the blanket is wiped clean. Some presses are equipped with an automatic washing system to clean the blanket, **Figure 19-21**. The system uses a set of rollers to feed washing solution to the blanket. When the system is operated, a dampening roller transfers washing solution from a filled container to a metering roller. The metering roller carries the solution to an oscillating roller, which moves back and forth to apply solution to the blanket. After the blanket is cleaned, it should be wiped dry and placed in storage until needed for further use.

Figure 19-20. A blanket is held in place on the cylinder by clamps. (Heidelberg USA)

Figure 19-21. This automatic washing system can be used to clean the blanket after a press run. (Heidelberg USA)

Impression cylinder setup

1. Clean the cylinder surface. The impression cylinder must be free of any substances or residue that will affect the pressure needed to transfer the image from the blanket cylinder to the paper. A cloth dampened with ink solvent can be used to clean the impression cylinder. After cleaning the cylinder, wipe it dry.
2. Test the impression provided by the impression cylinder and adjust the cylinder pressure as needed. The impression cylinder provides the pressure necessary to make the impression when images are offset. After running a number of sheets through the press, the system may require an adjustment to improve the quality of the impression. On some presses, the impression cylinder is spring-loaded and designed to adjust to the pressure of the system. Other presses are equipped

with a manual control device that can be used to adjust the impression. The adjustment varies the amount of pressure between the blanket and the impression cylinder. To adjust the impression cylinder pressure, turn off the press and loosen the cylinder locking screw by hand. Next, turn the adjusting screw to adjust the impression. Turning the adjusting screw clockwise will increase the pressure, while turning it counterclockwise will decrease the pressure. After making the adjustment, tighten the cylinder locking screw and resume operation of the press.

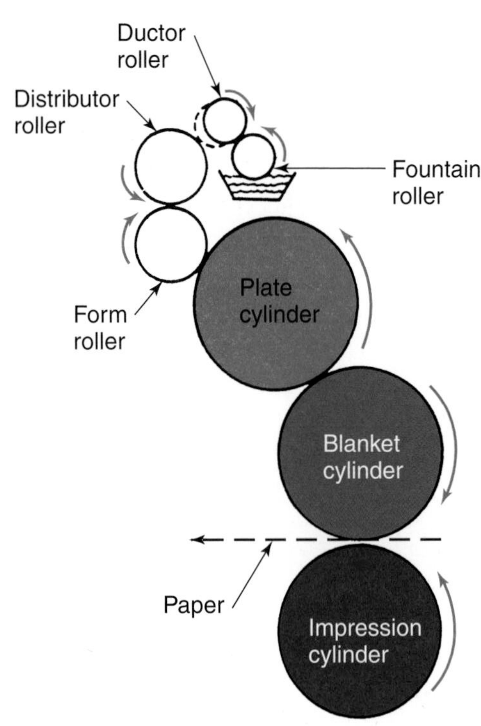

Figure 19-22. A group of rollers is used to carry fountain solution to the plate in a dampening system. (A.B. Dick Company)

Dampening System Operation

A ***dampening system*** is an assembly of rollers that feeds fountain solution to the plate surface during operation of the press. When a plate is mounted on the plate cylinder, fountain solution is applied to keep the nonimage area of the plate both ink repellent and separate from the image area. The dampening system must be set up to provide a steady flow of fountain solution to the plate. Dampening systems vary in design, but a typical system consists of a dampening fountain, a fountain roller, a ductor roller, a distributor roller, and a form roller. Different dampening systems may be equipped with a combination of rollers. See **Figure 19-22**. Some presses are equipped with a combined inking and dampening unit, in which ink and fountain solution are fed together across the rollers to the plate.

A conventional dampening system uses a rotating ductor roller to transfer fountain solution intermittently across the rollers. Fountain solution is carried from the fountain by a fountain roller, which transfers the solution to the ductor roller. The ductor roller moves back and forth between the fountain roller and the distributor roller to transfer the solution. The distributor roller carries the solution to the form roller, which makes direct contact with the plate and applies the solution to the plate surface.

In many conventional dampening systems, the ductor and form rollers are covered with a *molleton*, a cloth sleeve that fits over the body of the roller. See **Figure 19-23**. Because most rollers are made of metal or rubber, fountain solution does not adhere easily to the roller surface. Molleton covers are used to help rollers absorb and retain the solution as it is carried to the plate. They must be cleaned regularly or replaced to keep the rollers receptive to fountain solution.

Figure 19-23. Molleton covers are used with dampening rollers to absorb and retain fountain solution as it is transferred to the plate.

A continuous dampening system, **Figure 19-24**, supplies a continuous flow of fountain solution to the plate. The system does not use a ductor roller; each successive roller makes contact and the fountain solution is spread continuously through the system. A metering roller is commonly used to monitor the flow of solution from the fountain. It can be set to control the flow at different rates during use of the press.

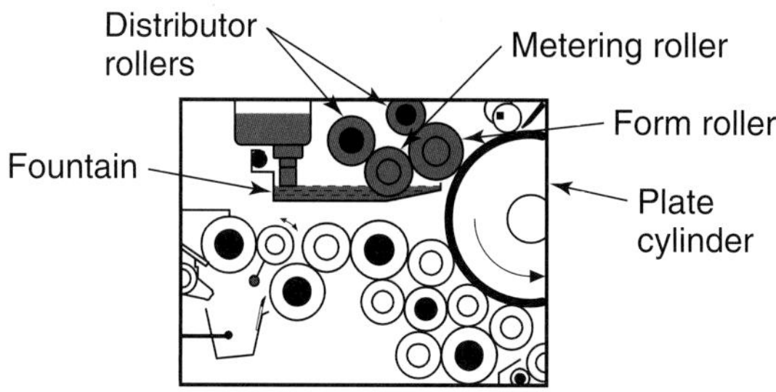

Figure 19-24. A continuous dampening system uses a metering roller to transfer a continuous flow of dampening solution to the plate. (Heidelberg USA)

Fountain solution

Fountain solutions are formulated for use with specific types of plates on the press. Water serves as the base ingredient of the solution. A typical fountain solution consists of water, gum arabic, and an acidic concentrate. Water is used to repel ink when the fountain solution is applied to the nonimage area of the plate; a mix of gum arabic and acid is used to keep the nonimage area *desensitized,* or free from receiving the image. Because the plate surface is repeatedly coated with ink, the nonimage area must remain desensitized. The chemicals making up the fountain solution must be in correct proportion with the water. The solution must contain enough water to repel ink and enough acid to desensitize the nonimage area. Different fountain solutions are recommended for use with plates by different plate manufacturers. In many cases, the acidic concentrate is supplied by a manufacturer and is mixed with distilled water to produce the solution. Whether the fountain solution is purchased or mixed by the operator of the press, it must be prepared based on the type of plate used.

Fountain solutions are commonly identified by their ***pH value,*** a measurement that indicates the acidity or alkalinity of a solution. A ***pH scale*** is a range of numeric pH values from 0-14, with the midpoint value of 7 designated as neutral. A solution with a pH value below 7 is considered acidic, with a value of 0 representing the highest acidity. A solution with a pH value above 7 is considered alkaline, with 14 representing the highest alkalinity. Each successive pH value is 10 times the previous value. For example, a solution with a pH value of 4.0 is 10 times as acidic as a solution with a pH value of 5.0. A solution with a pH value of 3.0 is 100 times as acidic as a solution with a pH value of 5.0. A small difference in pH values can have a significant impact on the strength of the fountain solution.

Recommended pH values for fountain solutions to be used with plates commonly range between 4.0 and 5.5. Several methods are used to measure the pH value of a solution. Two of the most common measuring devices are *litmus paper* and an *electronic pH meter*. See **Figure 19-25.**

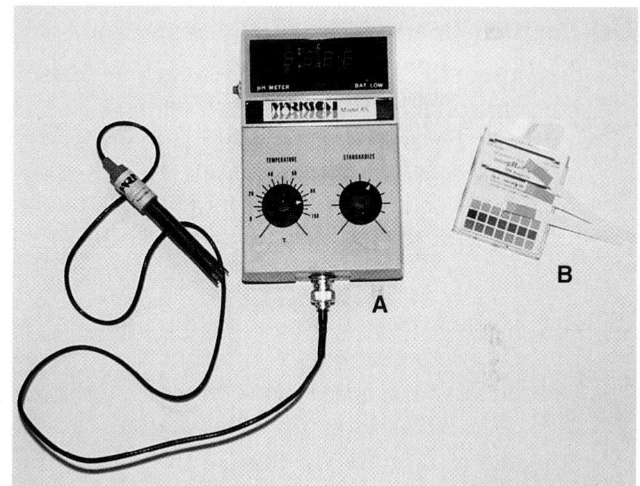

Figure 19-25. Fountain solution pH values can be measured with an electronic pH meter or litmus paper. A—A pH meter provides a digital readout of pH values through the use of a probe. B—When litmus paper is dipped into the solution, the paper changes color and is compared to a range of color tones to determine the pH value.

When a strip of litmus paper is dipped into the fountain solution, it will change in color or darkness depending upon the level of acidity present. The paper is then removed from the solution and compared to a standardized scale that contains varying shades of color. Each color tone is marked with a pH value. The scale darkness that most closely matches the darkness of the litmus paper equals the pH value.

An electronic pH meter provides a much more accurate means of measuring pH values. When a probe attached to the meter is submerged into the fountain solution, a digital readout gives the pH value. The meter must be calibrated before it is used. Measuring the pH value of distilled water should produce a reading of 7 (neutral). After the meter is calibrated, it can be used to measure the fountain solution pH.

The fountain solution should be checked regularly and reformulated if necessary. The solution pH can change after a press run. The type of paper and ink used can also have an effect on the pH value of the solution. The fountain solution must keep the nonimage area of the plate water-receptive and desensitized. A fountain solution that is too acid can make the nonimage area image-sensitive, which allows it to be ink receptive. A solution with a high acidity can also damage the plate.

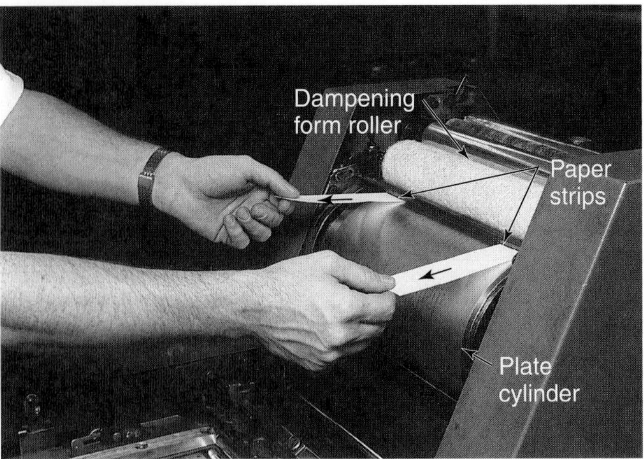

Figure 19-26. Roller pressure can be checked by pulling two thin strips of paper between each set of rollers.

Dampening system setup

1. Formulate the fountain solution and measure the solution pH. The solution must be prepared for a specific type of plate; use a blend of chemicals recommended by the plate manufacturer. After the solution is mixed properly, fill the bottle that feeds the dampening fountain.
2. Adjust the flow of fountain solution to the press. A metering roller is typically set to control the flow. On some dampening systems, the speed of the fountain roller can be adjusted to monitor the flow of the solution.
3. Check the level of pressure between the dampening rollers. To ensure that an even flow of fountain solution is transferred from the fountain to the plate, the level of pressure between the rollers might require adjustment. The pressure between each set of rollers can be checked by positioning two thin strips of paper on either side of the rollers and pulling the strips through. See **Figure 19-26.** The resistance felt from each strip should be the same. If the pressure is not even, adjust one of the rollers to increase or decrease the pressure. The devices used to adjust roller pressure vary, depending on the type of press. A locknut on the side of the roller is typically loosened and an adjustable screw is turned to change the roller pressure. When adjusting roller pressure, each dampening roller should be checked.
4. Clean the dampening system after operating the press. A combined inking and dampening system is typically equipped with an automatic washing system. See **Figure 19-27.** When the rollers are placed in the cleanup position, distributor rollers carry washing solution across the entire system. With other dampening systems, the rollers must be removed and cleaned manually. When using a conventional dampening system with molleton covers, the covers must be removed from the rollers and cleaned after each press run. Solvent can be used to remove any ink that appears on the covers or roller surfaces.

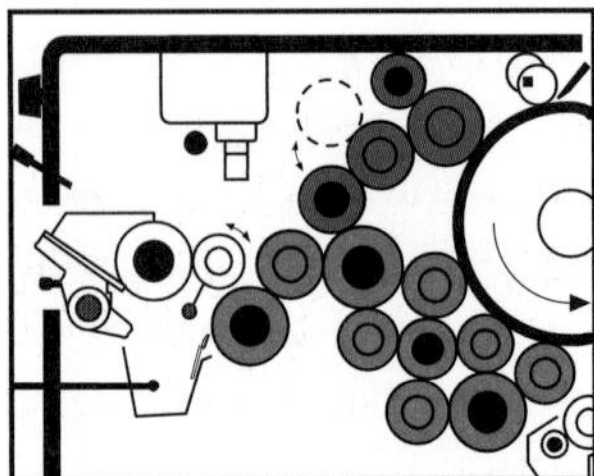

Figure 19-27. The rollers in a combined inking and dampening system are typically cleaned together by an automatic washing unit. (Heidelberg USA)

Inking System Operation

An ***inking system*** consists of the equipment used to transfer ink to the plate surface. Inking systems are made up of an assembly of rollers that carries ink from a fountain to the plate. The number of rollers in different systems varies, but the components of a typical unit are an ink fountain, a fountain roller, a ductor roller, and a series of distributor and form rollers. See **Figure 19-28**. When ink is fed through the system, the form rollers make final contact with the plate and apply ink directly to the plate surface.

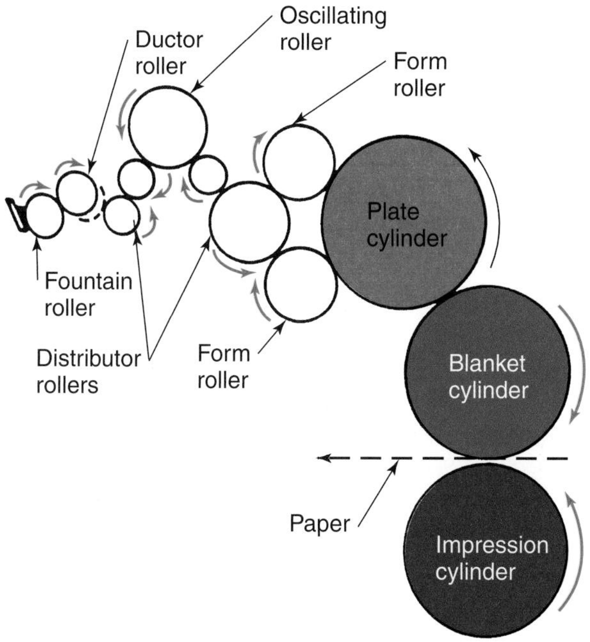

Figure 19-28. An inking system uses a series of rollers to carry ink to the plate. (A.B. Dick Company)

The fountain contains the supply of ink that is carried to the press, **Figure 19-29**. A fountain roller draws ink from the fountain and transfers it to the ductor roller, which rotates back and forth, making intermittent contact with the fountain roller and distributor roller. Refer to **Figure 19-28**. Ink is then transferred from the distributor rollers to the form rollers, which place the ink on the plate. During the printing process, the plate is coated with fountain solution before it is inked; on some presses, the two processes are combined and performed by a single inking and dampening unit. In this design, ink is applied first to the entire set of inking and dampening rollers. Fountain solution is then added to the fountain and drawn out by the system. Since the rollers are first inked, fountain solution *rides* on the inked surface of each roller as it is transferred to the plate. While the ability of the ink to repel water allows the fountain solution to remain separate from the ink, the correct proportion of the two fluids must be maintained to keep the nonimage and image areas of the plate separate.

Figure 19-29. Ink is supplied from an ink fountain for transfer to the press. (Heidelberg Harris)

The inking system or *ink train* must be set to apply an even film of ink across the rollers to the plate. A number of control devices are used to operate an inking system. The ink fountain is equipped with an adjustable blade that regulates the flow of ink from the fountain to the rollers. A line of thumbscrews along the length of the blade, called ***ink keys***, are used to adjust the position of the blade. See **Figure 19-30**. The blade controls the thickness of

Figure 19-30. Ink keys are used to control ink thickness by adjusting the amount of gap that exists between the fountain blade and the ink roller surface. (Heidelberg USA)

the ink as it is drawn by the fountain roller. A small gap separates the blade from the roller surface; when the ink keys are loosened, the gap widens and the blade allows more ink to pass from the fountain. When the keys are tightened, the gap closes and the blade permits less ink to be drawn.

Ink distribution can also be controlled by adjusting the speed of the fountain roller. Setting a higher speed releases more ink to the system, while setting a lower speed releases less ink. As the fountain roller rotates in the fountain, it stirs the ink to keep it moving at a consistent flow. Larger presses are equipped with an ***ink agitator***, a device that revolves in the fountain while the system is in operation. See **Figure 19-31**. The agitator is used to maintain a consistent flow of ink to the rollers.

When ink is drawn from the fountain, the pressure between the rollers must be sufficient to split the ink into a thin, even film. The pressure between the ink rollers can be checked by using the same technique employed to check dampening roller pressure. When two thin strips of paper are pulled through the ends of each pair of rollers, the resistance felt from each strip should be the same.

A more accurate technique is commonly used to check the level of pressure between the ink form rollers and the plate. Because the form rollers make direct contact with the plate, the pressure between the two surfaces plays a critical part in the final placement of the ink. Inking systems typically use two to four form rollers to ink the plate; to check the form roller pressure, turn on the inking system and coat the rollers with an even layer of ink. With the plate mounted on the plate cylinder, position the plate so it is in line with the form rollers. Lower the form rollers to make contact with the plate and examine the resulting ink stripes formed by the rollers. The stripes should be evenly spaced and measure approximately 1/8″ to 3/16″ (1.18 mm to 4.76 mm) in width along their entire length. See **Figure 19-32**.

If the stripes are too wide or too narrow, or if they appear uneven from end to end, the plate will receive a disproportionate amount of ink and portions of the image may not print correctly. When the stripes are too wide, the roller pressure is excessive, resulting in plate wear and uneven images.

Figure 19-31. An ink agitator helps maintain a consistent flow of ink from the fountain on large presses. (Baldwin Technology)

Figure 19-32. After the form rollers are inked and lowered onto the plate, the resulting ink stripes should be evenly spaced and should have a uniform length and width.

The form roller pressure can be adjusted by tightening or loosening the body of each roller. Different inking problems can occur when the correct roller pressure is not applied, **Figure 19-33.**

Inking system setup

1. Inspect and clean the system and place ink in the fountain. Before inking the unit, inspect the rollers and make sure they are clean and free of any dried ink, lint, or dust. Solvent can be used to remove ink from the rollers; the fountain and fountain roller should also be washed with solvent. Once the system is clean, the fountain can be filled with ink. Use ink that is compatible with the fountain solution, the press, and the stock being printed. An ink knife is commonly used to remove the ink from a can, **Figure 19-34.** Use the knife to remove and discard any dried ink from the top of the can, then fill the fountain.

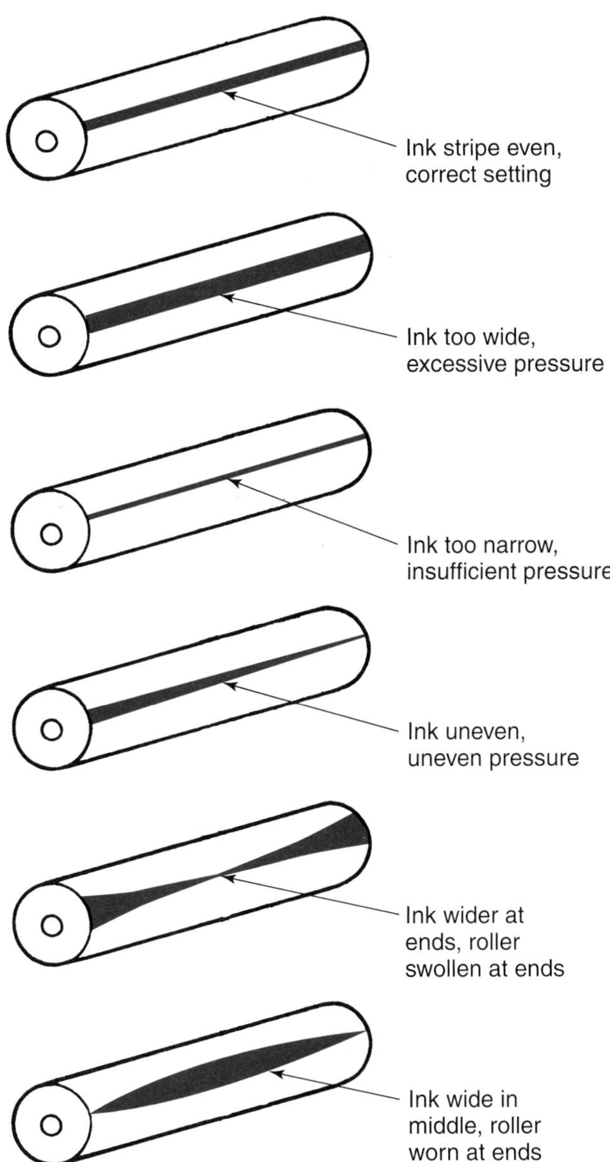

Figure 19-33. Different inking problems caused by excessive or insufficient roller pressure.

Figure 19-34. An ink knife is used to remove ink from the can and fill the fountain. (Van Son Holland Ink Corporation)

2. Adjust the ink keys to produce an even flow of ink to the rollers. To decrease the flow of ink, the keys are turned *clockwise*. To increase the flow of ink, the keys are turned *counter-clockwise*. Ink thickness can also be adjusted to different levels along the width of the fountain as the ink is transferred, **Figure 19-35.** If one side of the plate requires more ink to print than another portion of the plate, the keys controlling the corresponding area of the fountain can be adjusted to apply a greater amount of ink. A plate that contains a large halftone image, for example, may require more ink for the halftone portion than another portion containing type.

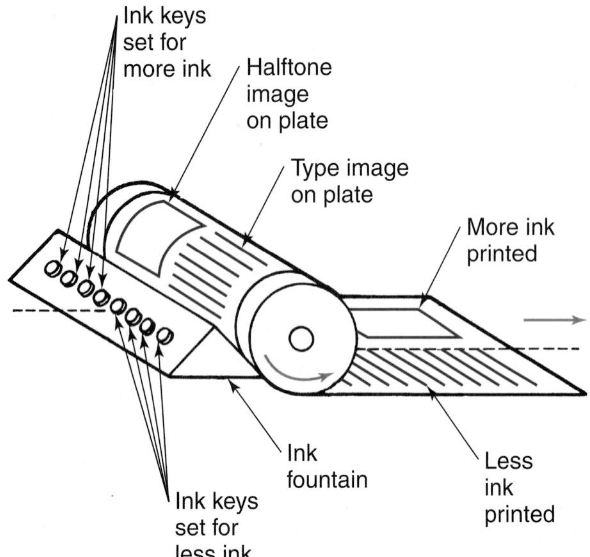

Figure 19-35. The ink keys can be adjusted to provide a greater flow of ink from different parts of the fountain to the plate.

3. Adjust the speed of the fountain roller and ink the entire set of rollers. The fountain roller speed is typically controlled by an adjustable knob. While setting the speed, observe the movement of ink across the rollers and readjust the ink keys to provide an even flow. On some presses, the ductor roller can also be set to make the necessary amount of contact with the fountain roller.
4. Check the pressure between the form rollers and the plate. After inking the rollers, bring the form rollers into contact with the plate and observe the ink stripes that form on the plate surface. The stripes should run parallel and appear even in width. If the stripes appear to be uneven, adjust the pressure by tightening or loosening the rollers.
5. Clean the ink fountain and system rollers after the press run. To clean the fountain, remove excess ink with a knife and use a cloth dampened with solvent to wash off any dried ink deposits. The ink rollers are typically cleaned with blanket or roller wash. The rollers should be cleaned thoroughly with solvent; any leftover ink must be removed before it dries. Because ink tends to spread to the ends of the system by the oscillating movement of the distributor rollers, the roller ends must be carefully examined for ink buildup.

Some presses are equipped with automatic washing systems. A combined inking and dampening system can be moved into cleanup position and cleaned automatically. Solvent is carried by the distributor rollers and applied to the entire set of inking and dampening rollers. Refer to **Figure 19-27.**

Delivery System Operation

A ***delivery system*** transfers printed sheets from the press and stacks them for finishing operations. As a sheet is drawn from the impression cylinder, it is carried to the delivery pile by a group of components that make up the system. Delivery systems used by sheet-fed presses are designed much differently from web-fed delivery systems. The delivery system of a web-fed press draws a continuous length of paper from a web or *roll* through the press, rather than individual sheets of paper. Because this chapter is concerned with the operation of a sheet-fed press, the following discussion will focus on the equipment used by a sheet-fed delivery system.

Most sheet-fed presses use a *chain delivery system* to remove and stack paper as it leaves the press. See **Figure 19-36**. A chain delivery system consists of a pair of chain conveyor belts that drive two or more gripper bars to transfer paper from the press to the

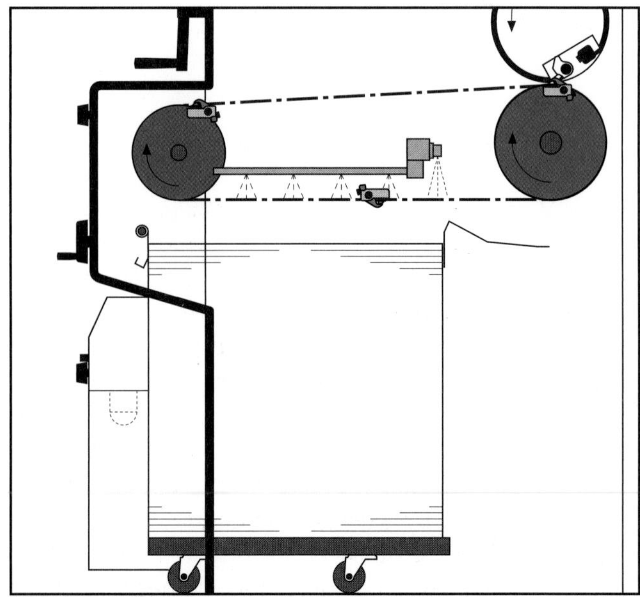

Figure 19-36. Most sheet-fed presses are equipped with a chain delivery system to remove and stack paper after it is printed. (Heidelberg USA)

delivery pile. The gripper bars extend between the chains at different points; as one set of grippers grasps the front edges of the paper from the impression cylinder, another set releases a sheet of paper to the delivery pile. See **Figure 19-37**. The grippers are operated by a cam. As the grippers approach the impression cylinder, they pass over a cam and are forced open to grasp the paper. The grippers then close and carry the paper to the delivery pile, where they open again to release the paper.

Figure 19-37. Paper is drawn through the delivery system by gripper bars that are mounted on chains. While one set of grippers pulls a sheet from the press, another set releases a sheet to the delivery pile. (Davidson International)

When paper is transferred from the gripper bars to the delivery pile, stationary and jogging guides are used to align the stack on the outfeed table. Refer to Figure 19-37. The guides are set to the sheet size of the paper. The stationary guides are located along one or two sides of the paper; the jogging guides are adjustable and located along the remaining edges. The jogging guides move or *jog* the paper into place as it is transferred to the delivery pile. Setting the jogging guides in the correct position is a critical step in preparing the delivery system. Each sheet must be aligned and stacked in the same position on the delivery pile. As the pile grows, the outfeed table drops. The outfeed table is also known as a *receding table* because it can be set to lower automatically at a certain rate.

Some presses are equipped with a *drying system* to prevent ink from being offset from one sheet of paper to the next as paper is stacked on the delivery pile. When sheets of paper are stacked, the printed side of one sheet meets the unprinted backside of the next sheet and smudging or *setoff* can occur. Two different types of drying devices are commonly used with delivery systems to prevent ink setoff. In one design, printed sheets are sprayed with an antioffset powder or liquid that dries the ink and prevents it from being transferred. The powder or liquid is sprayed between the delivery of each sheet. Another system uses a source of heat to dry the ink as sheets of paper are moved to the delivery pile.

Many delivery systems use *static eliminators* to prevent the buildup of static electricity as paper is delivered and stacked. Static electricity can cause sheets to cling together as they are delivered. As paper passes through the system, it contacts an anti-static bar or strands of tinsel that remove static buildup. See **Figure 19-38**. This process helps keep each sheet separate and aids in the alignment of the stack.

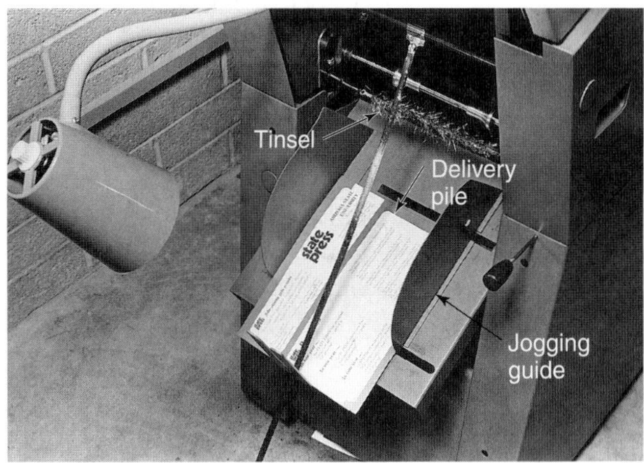

Figure 19-38. Tinsel is used to eliminate static electricity from paper as it is fed to the delivery pile.

When paper is drawn to the delivery pile from the press, it must be transferred correctly through each part of the delivery system. Each sheet must be guided into the same position when it leaves the press to prevent damage to the paper. When paper reaches the delivery pile, it must be arranged in a uniform stack for such finishing operations as folding, trimming, and packaging. The delivery system represents the final operating stage of the press; each component must be set up to guide the paper into the same position every time.

Delivery system setup

1. Adjust the chain delivery grippers to accommodate the type of stock being printed and the speed of the press. In a chain delivery system, two or more gripper bars are used to transfer paper from the impression cylinder to the delivery pile. The grippers open to grasp paper as it leaves the impression cylinder; when the paper reaches the delivery pile, the grippers open again to release it. The opening of the grippers is controlled by a cam mounted on a shaft extending between the chains. As the gripper bars revolve along the chains, the grippers are forced open when they come into contact with the cam. To adjust the opening position of the grippers for releasing paper, set the cam dial. A higher setting will allow the grippers to hold each sheet longer before releasing it. Such a setting, used with light stock, will help provide better stacking of the sheets. A higher setting should also be used for lower press speeds. When using heavy stock, the cam should be adjusted to a lower setting to provide an earlier release point for the paper. A lower setting will help keep each sheet separate as paper is released and can also be used when operating the press at higher speeds.
2. Adjust the stationary and jogging guides to match the sheet size. To set the guides, feed a sheet of paper through the press and stop it just before it is released to the delivery pile. Adjust each guide to meet the edges of the paper. The jogging guides are typically adjusted by loosening a thumbscrew and moving the guide into place. Once the guides are in position, retighten the thumbscrews.
3. Align the feeding system with the delivery system. Because the press is designed to run hundreds or thousands of sheets, adjustments may be necessary to ensure the feeding and delivery systems are operating consistently. While running the press, observe both systems and determine whether each is functioning properly. Adjustments can be made by turning the press handwheel and manually advancing the press to bring the systems into alignment. Adjustments may also be needed to reset other components in the delivery system, depending on the source of the problem.
4. Set the receding table control. The outfeed table can be set to lower at various rates, depending on such factors as the speed of the press and the type of stock used. A control knob or handle is typically used to adjust the receding table speed. It should be set so the receding table lowers at the same rate that the feeding platform moves up.

Offset Press Troubleshooting

The operation of an offset press involves many procedures and variables that determine the quality of the printed product. Printing problems are often encountered by press operators because of the different conditions that occur as a result of working with a high volume of materials. Because of the potential for printing problems, troubleshooting and maintenance play a critical part in operating a press. See **Figure 19-39**. Regular press maintenance helps increase production and printing quality.

Figure 19-39. Making the right adjustments to the press can play a key role in troubleshooting printing problems.

Many of the setup procedures discussed in this chapter have a direct effect on image quality; every press component must be functioning properly to achieve consistent production. Operating a press requires a thorough knowledge of the five press systems and the techniques used to prepare and maintain each system. Because the systems are interdependent, each press function affects the entire operation.

Printing problems can often be attributed to various factors that must be considered while operating the press. During a press run, the operator must be able to recognize different problems, understand how they are caused, and determine how they can be solved.

Any printing problem that occurs must be carefully analyzed and understood before adjustments are made to the press. Different problems can be associated with a number of causes. Poorly printed materials can result from such conditions as a failure of the plate to keep the nonimage and image areas separate, improper packing of the plate or blanket, a disproportionate combination of ink and fountain solution, or insufficient roller pressure. The numerous control devices and settings used on the press can make it difficult to identify the exact cause of the problem. When analyzing a problem, the operator should consider the different variables associated with the problem and then decide which steps to take to adjust the press. Thorough analysis can help the operator identify the source or cause of the problem.

While printing problems vary and can be attributed to a number of factors, they can generally be classified as either *ink* problems or *press* problems. Most printing problems are related to the proper distribution of ink, the amount of ink used, and the printed appearance of the ink. Other problems relate to different areas of the press and typically require adjustments to specific parts of the system. While newer presses are equipped with automatic control devices that allow operators greater control over image quality, manual adjustments are often necessary to correct a printing problem. Troubleshooting charts are commonly used by operators to analyze and solve printing problems. The following troubleshooting guides offer a list of common ink and press problems, along with typical causes and corrections.

Troubleshooting Guide: Ink Problems	
Chalking: Condition that occurs when dried ink is easily rubbed off or lost from the sheet, often resulting from an improper bonding of ink with paper.	
Cause	Correction
1. Insufficient amount of ink drier.	Add drier as suggested by manufacturer.
2. Ink absorbed by paper before setting properly.	Add gum or binding agent to control absorption.
3. Job printed with improper ink for stock used.	Overprint paper with varnish.
Hickeys: Ink spots surrounded by a white background.	
Cause	Correction
1. Particles of dried ink.	Remove dried ink when skimming ink from can. Clean press and remove all dried ink from fountain and rollers. Use rubber form rollers as *hickey pickers* to remove unwanted particles that can print as hickeys.
2. Dust specks or other contaminants.	Improve cleanliness in pressroom.
3. Slitter or paper dust.	Check feeding pile for loose edges.
Misting: Condition that occurs when a fine spray of ink is produced by the movement of the ink rollers.	
Cause	Correction
1. Ink film too soft.	Stiffen ink with body gum or varnish.
2. Press speed too high.	Reduce press speed.
3. Excess flow of ink.	Adjust ink flow from fountain.
4. Ink rollers damaged or "out of round."	Inspect rollers and replace if necessary.
5. Poor lateral distribution of ink on rollers.	Adjust roller pressure or oscillating motion of vibrator roller.

Troubleshooting Guide: Ink Problems (continued)

Piling: A buildup of ink on the ink rollers, plate, or blanket.	
Cause	Correction
1. Ink too stiff or tacky.	Reduce tack by adding a reducing compound.
2. Emulsified ink.	Clean up press and use proper balance of ink and fountain solution.
3. Improperly ground ink.	Reformulate ink.
4. Blanket packed improperly.	Repack blanket.
Poor ink distribution: An uneven dispersion of ink, resulting in an excess of ink film in one area of the ink rollers.	
Cause	Correction
1. Ink rollers glazed.	Deglaze or replace rollers.
2. Ink rollers "out of round."	Regrind or replace rollers.
3. Ink too stiff or tacky.	Add an ink-reducing compound to the ink supply.
4. Uneven ink fountain distribution.	Adjust ink keys.
Poor ink trapping: The misregistration of color images in multicolor printing, a condition that occurs when a second color prints with a higher tack than the first color printed.	
Cause	Correction
1. Excess tack in overprinted ink.	Reduce tack of ink that fails to trap. Reformulate each color of ink.
2. Insufficient drier used on first color printed.	Change drier.
3. Ink and fountain solution out of balance.	Reduce ink feed in problem areas, then minimize use of fountain solution.
4. Too much time taken after printing first color.	Perform additional color runs as soon as possible.
Slow drying: Condition that occurs when ink fails to cure quickly enough after printing, delaying multicolor printing runs.	
Cause	Correction
1. Fountain solution too acidic.	Check pH and ajust value to between 4.0 and 5.5.
2. Insufficient amount of ink drier.	Add drier to ink.
3. Wrong ink used with paper.	Use proper ink for grade of stock.
4. Low temperature in pressroom.	Raise temperature to improve drying ability.

Troubleshooting Guide: Press Problems	
Blinding: Condition in which the image area of the plate will not accept ink.	
Cause	Correction
1. Excess gum in fountain solution.	Check solution and reformulate using procedure recommeded by manufacturer.
2. Fountain solution too acidic.	Check pH and adjust value to between 4.0 and 5.5.
3. Excess plate-to-blanket pressure.	Check roller pressure with cylinder packing gauge and repack blanket.
4. Glazed rollers.	Deglaze or replace rollers.
5. Improper ink tack.	Reformulate ink to match stock.
6. Contamination of plate during platemaking.	Thoroughly clean and rinse plate and regum surface.
Ghosting: Condition that occurs when a solid image prints unevenly or a faint, second image appears next to the original.	
Cause	Correction
1. Glazed or hardened ink rollers.	Clean or replace rollers.
2. Excess fountain solution.	Adjust balance of ink and fountain solution.
3. Embossed or engraved blanket.	Replace blanket.
4. In multicolor printing, ink loss due to varying solids.	Minimize fountain solution or use opaque inks.
Image loss: An area of missing lines or halftone dots that make up the image.	
Cause	Correction
1. Blanket wearing thin under pressure.	Repack blanket.
2. Glazed blanket surface.	Clean or replace blanket.
3. Swollen blanket.	Remove packing or replace blanket.
4. Smashed blanket.	Fill in smashed area or replace blanket.

Troubleshooting Guide: Press Problems (continued)

Ink roller stripping: Failure of ink rollers to absorb ink.	
Cause	Correction
1. Fountain solution pH too acidic.	Adjust pH to between 4.0 and 5.5.
2. Excess use of fountain solution.	Adjust fountain solution setting.
3. Ink rollers are desensitized.	Clean and etch rollers.
4. Glazed ink rollers.	Deglaze rollers.
Misregistration: A condition that occurs when two overprinted images or color elements do not align when printed.	
Cause	Correction
1. Excess ink tack.	Reduce tack.
2. Curled or wrinkled paper stock.	Reduce humidity of pressroom.
3. Printing pressures stretch paper stock.	Adjust impression (cylinder pressure).
4. Image improperly positioned on plate.	Remake plate with image in register.
5. Plate mounted improperly.	Reposition plate on plate cylinder.
6. Loose blanket.	Reattach blanket.
Mottling: Uneven amounts of ink in the solid portion of the image, causing printed sheet to appear cloudy.	
Cause	Correction
1. Failure of ink to be absorbed uniformly by paper.	Formulate ink to grade of stock.
2. Excess fountain solution.	Adjust balance of ink and fountain solution.
3. Ink not resistant to water.	Add varnish to increase tack.
Picking: The lifting of paper fibers by the ink during printing.	
Cause	Correction
1. Excess ink tack.	Reduce tack with a reducing compound.
2. Excess blanket-to-impression cylinder pressure.	Repack blanket or reduce cylinder pressure.
3. Poor quality of paper.	Use a better grade of stock.
4. Tacky blanket surface.	Clean or replace blanket.
Plate wear: Gradual disappearance of the image area from the plate surface.	
Cause	Correction
1. Excess form roller pressure.	Check pressure by inking plate and observing ink stripes.
2. Excess pressure between plate and blanket.	Check roller pressure with cylinder packing gauge and repack blanket.
3. Fountain solution too acidic.	Check pH and adjust value to between 4.0 and 5.5.
4. Insufficient amount of ink.	Adjust ink keys.
5. Dried gum on plate.	Clean plate with water and solvent and regum surface.
6. Abrasive residue or debris from blanket or stock.	Clean blanket or check paper.
Scumming: Buildup of ink film on nonimage area of plate.	
Cause	Correction
1. Ink too soft.	Add varnish to increase tack.
2. Excess use of ink.	Adjust balance of ink and fountain solution.
3. Sensitized nonimage area of plate.	Remake plate.
4. Incorrect fountain solution pH.	Check pH and adjust value to between 4.0 and 5.5.
5. Glazed blanket.	Clean or replace blanket.
6. Excessive printing pressure	Reduce plate-to-blanket and blanket-to-impression cylinder pressures.
7. Glazed or dirty ink rollers.	Clean or replace rollers.
8. Dirty dampening rollers.	Clean or replace rollers.
Setoff: The transfer of ink from one sheet to the back of another on a delivery pile.	
Cause	Correction
1. Too much ink carried to paper.	Readjust ink keys.
2. Excess acid in fountain solution.	Change pH value of solution to recommended level.
3. Insufficient amount of ink drier.	Add drier to ink.
4. Improper ink for stock.	Change ink to match stock.
5. Sheets clinging from static electricity.	Use static eliminators with delivery system.
6. Delivery pile too high.	Reduce pile height.

Troubleshooting Guide: Press Problems (continued)

Slurring: An unwanted accumulation of halftone dots that result in a smeared image, commonly caused by slippage or improper contact between the cylinders at the time of impression.	
Cause	Correction
1. Slippage in the impression phase.	Reduce impression cylinder pressure.
2. Excessive pressure between plate and blanket.	Adjust pressure.
3. Excess ink on coated stocks.	Adjust ink keys to reduce ink feed.
4. Piling of ink on paper.	Change paper or use a moisture-resistant stock.
5. Loose-fitting plate on cylinder.	Reattach plate.
6. Excessive tack; paper sticks to blanket at trail edge.	Add reducing varnish to ink or use ink with lower tack.

Tinting: Unwanted color tint in background of image, commonly caused by emulsification of ink in the fountain solution.	
Cause	Correction
1. Ink fails to repel water.	Add varnish to soft ink to increase tack.
2. Improper fountain solution pH.	Adjust pH value to between 4.0 and 5.5.
3. Ink and fountain solution out of balance.	Clean press and adjust mix of ink and fountain solution.
4. Plate not properly desensitized.	Prepare new plate.

Review Questions

Please do not write in this text. Write your answers on a separate sheet of paper.

1. Offset presses used in the graphic communications industry are classified as _____ and _____ presses.
2. A _____ is a small sheet-fed press used in short printing runs.
3. When preparing a feeding system, the height of the feeding pile should be set so the top sheet rests just below the _____ .
4. What are the two functions of the impression cylinder in a printing system?
5. Plates and blankets mounted on a press are held in place by a set of _____.
6. The undercut surface of a press cylinder allows for _____ to adjust for different plate and blanket thicknesses.
7. Which roller makes intermittent contact with the fountain roller and distributor roller to transfer fountain solution in a dampening system?
8. What are two devices used to measure the pH value of a fountain solution?
9. What are *ink keys*?
10. Describe a common process used to check the pressure between the ink form rollers and the plate.
11. A chain delivery system uses _____ to draw paper from the press and release it to the delivery pile.
12. What is a *hickey*?
13. _____ is a buildup of ink on the ink rollers, plate, or blanket.
14. _____ is a printing problem that occurs when two overprinted images or color elements do not align when printed.
15. List three possible causes and corrections for each of the following printing problems: Chalking, misting, picking, scumming, and setoff.

Relief Printing 20

Learning Objectives

After studying this chapter, you will be able to:

- Explain the basic principles of relief printing and describe traditional printing techniques.
- Demonstrate the typical procedures used in hot type composition.
- Understand the use of flexography as a printing method and recognize modern applications of relief printing.
- Identify the different types of plates and platemaking methods used in relief printing.
- List three types of relief presses and the traditional procedures involved in their operation.

Important Terms

chase
drawsheet
duplicate plate
form
furniture
letterpress
original plate
photoengraving
photopolymer plate
platen press

Relief printing is a traditional printing method in which images are printed from a raised surface. In relief printing, commonly referred to as ***letterpress***, the elements making up the image are *in relief* (or raised) above the surface. The nonimage or nonprinting area is recessed and lies below the surface, **Figure 20-1**. After the image carrier or *plate* is inked, the raised surface is pressed against paper to print the image. This process differs from lithographic printing, a method in which the image and nonimage areas lie on the same plane. Lithographic printing relies on the fact that water (fountain solution) and greasy ink do not readily mix.

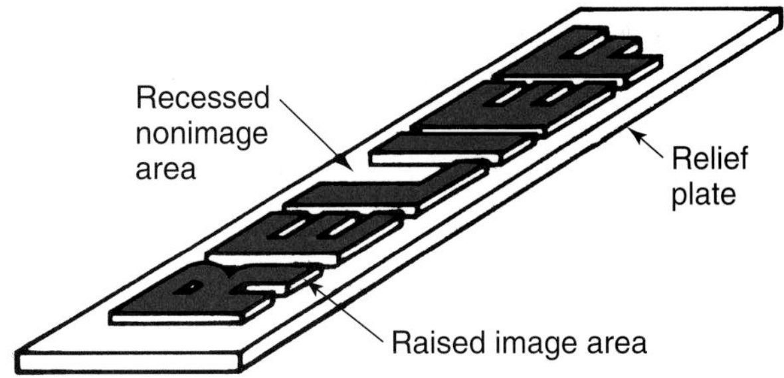

Figure 20-1. The relief process prints images from a raised surface that accepts ink. The nonimage area is recessed and lies below the raised image.

Although relief printing has essentially been replaced by offset lithography as the standard commercial printing process, applications of relief printing are still used in different areas of the graphic communications industry. A basic understanding of letterpress printing can provide a valuable background of knowledge for using other printing methods. This chapter will cover the different types of equipment and procedures traditionally used in letterpress, along with relief printing techniques that continue to be used today.

Principles of Relief Printing

Relief printing was the first printing method to be developed and was the dominant form of printing in the world from the 1400s until the middle of this century. The first applications of relief printing can be traced to as far back as the eighth century in China, where images were carved into wood and printed, but modern relief printing methods originated in the mid-1400s in Germany when Johannes Gutenberg invented movable type.

Gutenberg's ***movable type*** consisted of individual pieces or *blocks* of metal type, each of which was distinguished by a letter raised from the surface of the body. See **Figure 20-2**. The metal type was called *movable type* because the pieces could be positioned to form different words for printing; movable metal type has also been referred to as *hot metal* or *foundry* type because of the casting process used to make each piece. Movable type was originally cast by first making a mold of the letter and then pouring molten metal into it. The mold was produced by cutting a piece of metal into the shape of a letter and punching it into a soft metal called a matrix. The matrix (mold) could then be used to make multiple copies of each letter.

Figure 20-2. Movable type is traditionally used in relief printing. Each piece of type contains a letter raised from the surface.

Prior to the invention of movable type, books were either hand-lettered or printed from carved wooden plates. Using letterpress, multiple copies of books could be printed, making them available to more people. Gutenberg used movable type to print copies of the Christian Bible. Written in Latin, the Gutenberg Bible remains one of the most famous texts ever published. Its printing helped lay the groundwork for modern printing practices.

Hot type composition

Hot type composition involves the arrangement of hot metal (movable) type for relief printing on a press. The term refers to the use of hot or *molten* metal to cast movable type. In traditional hand composition, pieces of type are set by hand in a *composing stick*. See **Figure 20-3**. Characters are aligned to form words, sentences, paragraphs, or an entire page. Each character is a letter raised from the surface of a block of metal. Because letterpress printing is a *direct* method of printing, the letters are in reverse form on each piece of type. See **Figure 20-4**. When the characters are inked and pressed against paper, they are printed to read correctly.

Figure 20-3. A type form consists of movable type that is set by hand in a composing stick.

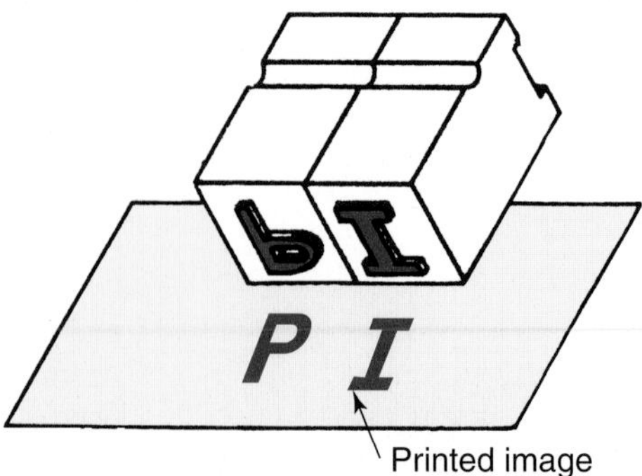

Figure 20-4. In letterpress printing, letters appear in reverse on each piece of type. When the letter is printed, the resulting image reads correctly.

Once the composing stick is filled to a set line length with type, the block of type (called a *form*) is removed and placed in a holding tray called a *galley*. The form is then tied together with a piece of string and aligned against two edges of the galley to print a *proof*. A roller is typically used to ink the form; paper is then placed over the form and pressure is applied with the roller to make the proof. The proof is checked for any mistakes or imperfections that can be corrected prior to printing.

After the proof is printed and checked for accuracy, the form is removed from the galley and placed on an *imposing table*. To hold the type in position for printing on a press, several pieces of equipment are used to *lock up* the form. Some of the typical components used in lockup are a *chase*, *furniture*, *reglets*, and *quoins*.

A ***chase*** is a metal frame that serves as a support device for the form. It is placed on the imposing stone and the form positioned near its center. Once the chase is centered around the form, blocks of wood or metal called ***furniture*** are placed around the form to fill in the empty areas and lock up the chase. **See Figure 20-5.** ***Reglets*** are thin pieces of wooden furniture that are inserted to eliminate small amounts of space that exist between the borders of the chase and the form. Locking devices called ***quoins*** are also positioned between pieces of furniture. A quoin key is used to tighten the quoins. When tightened, they expand to lock the furniture against the chase and the form.

Figure 20-5. Wooden or metal furniture is placed inside the chase to lock up the type form for printing.

In traditional letterpress printing, the chase holds the form when it is printed on a hand-operated or power-operated press. A typical small hand-operated platen press is shown in **Figure 20-6.** Discussed later in this chapter, a platen press prints images by bringing the surface of an inked type form into direct contact with paper.

Figure 20-6. Hand-operated platen presses were widely used to print from hot metal type.

Relief printing applications

Hot metal type and traditional relief printing methods have limited use today in commercial operations. Letterpress printing is used to some extent in printing packaging materials, **Figure 20-7.**

Letterpress equipment is also used in finishing operations such as embossing, ticket numbering, perforating, and die cutting. After paper is printed, it can be die-cut into a special design using letterpress equipment. The printed material is trimmed to a final shape by pressing it against a die mounted on a press. See **Figure 20-8.**

Flexography

Flexography is a modern relief process that prints from a curved or *flexible* plate containing images raised from the surface. Flexographic plates are most commonly made from rubber or plastic; when mounted on the press, the plate is wrapped

Figure 20-7. Packaging materials and numbered tickets are examples of products that use applications of letterpress printing.

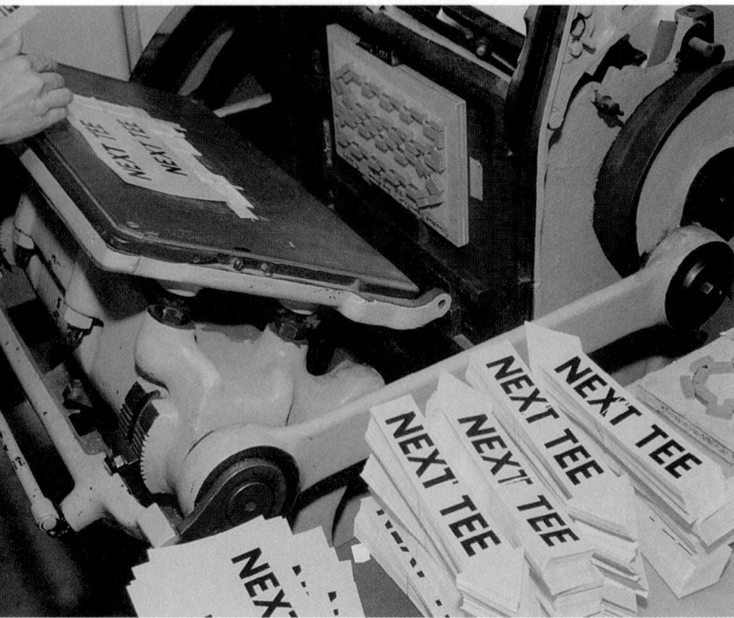

Figure 20-8. Die cutting is a letterpress equipment application for cutting printed materials into special designs.

around a plate cylinder. Flexographic printing, which is covered in more detail in the next chapter, is the only relief process that still has widespread use in the graphic communications industry.

Flexography is most commonly used to print packaging materials. Flexible rubber or plastic plates mounted on a press are inked and pressed against a printing substrate to produce images. Flexographic printing is used to print products such as grocery bags, labels, and folding cartons, as well as paperback books and newspapers.

Flexography offers several advantages to other forms of printing. Flexographic plates made from rubber are highly durable and can be used to print a large number of materials, **Figure 20-9**. Another advantage presented by flexographic plates is the ability to use fast-drying, water-based inks. Water-based inks are less harmful to the environment than solvent-based inks, which produce fumes as they dry.

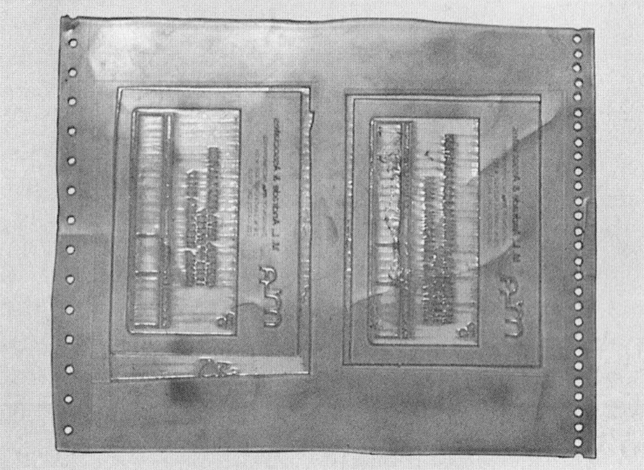

Figure 20-9. Rubber plates used in flexographic printing are highly durable and designed for long press runs.

Although flexographic printing technology has replaced many of the procedures and equipment previously used in letterpress, many of the principles associated with modern printing originated in letterpress printing. The development of flexible plates, for example, can be directly related to traditional relief printing methods. The next section of this chapter will discuss the different types of plates used in relief printing.

Relief Plates

As letterpress printing methods evolved, type forms were eventually used to make secondary image carriers or *plates*. The hand-set composition of individual pieces of movable type was a very time-consuming process that often took weeks to accomplish. The production of secondary plates was initiated to reduce wear on the form and allow printers to produce more than one copy of a form at a time. In many cases, the original form served as a master plate and was then used to make duplicates. As a result, plates traditionally used in relief printing are classified as *original* and *duplicate plates*.

An ***original plate***, also called a *master* or *primary* plate, is the original form of composed characters. Original plates can be used directly for printing or to make a duplicate plate. A ***duplicate plate*** is a copy of the original; it is used for long press runs when one plate is expected to wear out before the printing is completed. Duplicates made from a master can also be sent to different locations for printing. Two of the most common types of duplicate plates used in relief printing are *stereotypes* and *electrotypes*.

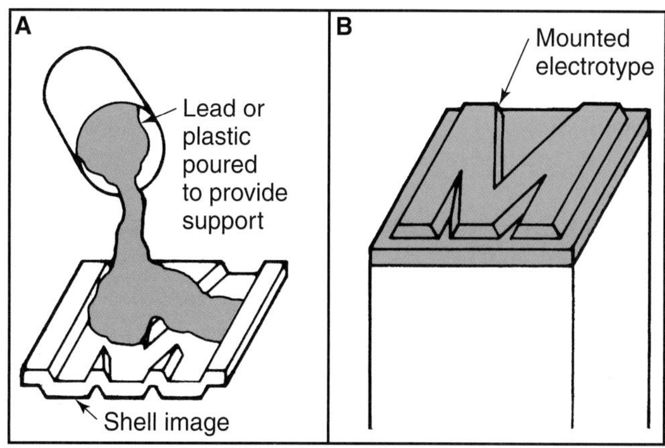

Figure 20-10. Electrotypes are duplicate plates that are formed through an electrochemical process. A—A shell containing the image is produced from a mold of the original form and is backed with a layer of lead or plastic. B—The newly formed plate is mounted on a base for printing.

Stereotypes

A ***stereotype*** is cast by pouring molten type metal (an alloy of lead, tin, and antimony) into a mold or *mat* made from the original type form. The mat is produced by placing a blank rubber or paper sheet over the form and applying pressure to form an *intaglio* image (one that appears in reverse from the original). To produce plates for use on high-speed newspaper presses, the mats were curved to the same diameter as the press cylinders. The resulting curved plates could be locked in place on the cylinders for web-fed printing.

Electrotypes

An ***electrotype*** is produced from a mold through an electrochemical process. After a mold is made from the original type form, the intaglio image is sprayed with silver. The silver coating is a conductive material that forms a thin layer on the surface of the mold. The surface is then electroplated with a layer of copper or nickel to form a shell. When the shell that forms the relief image is removed from the mold, it is backed with a layer of lead or plastic to provide support. The electrotype is then attached to a base and ready to be printed, **Figure 20-10.**

Photoengraving

The early use of hot metal to make duplicate plates led to more efficient platemaking techniques over time. For many years, line art images had to be first carved by hand when they were printed along with type forms. This process changed in the 1800s when photochemical processes such as *photoengraving* were first used to reproduce printing plates. ***Photoengraving*** is a platemaking method that produces relief images by exposing a light-sensitive plate coating through a *negative* (a film version of the original image). After exposure, the nonimage portion of the plate is etched away with acid to produce the relief image. This process allows picture images to be reproduced by converting the two-dimensional image of a negative into a three-dimensional relief image.

Photoengraved plates are made up of line or halftone images, or a combination of both. Exposure is made when a negative containing the original image is placed face down and contacted to meet the plate. This allows the plate to receive a wrong-reading version of the image. When the plate is used on a press, the image is transferred to the printing substrate in its original form.

The image area of the plate is formed when the light-sensitive coating is exposed. When the plate is developed, the unexposed coating of the nonimage area is washed away. The raised relief surface is produced when the nonimage area is etched to a designated depth with an acid.

While the basic principles used in relief printing changed little after the invention of movable type, newer platemaking procedures continued to emerge as the printing industry grew. Different materials and procedures have been applied to make photoengraved plates. The most common materials used in the manufacture of relief plates today are rubber and plastic.

Rubber plates

Rubber plates are the flexible relief plates commonly used in flexographic printing. Rubber plates contain a raised image area that is formed from a mold or matrix. As discussed earlier, rubber plates are designed to wrap around the plate cylinder of a press.

When rubber plates are imaged, a matrix is first produced from the original image. The original is placed on top of the matrix material inside a hydraulic press, and the two are forced together through heat and pressure to form the matrix. When a sheet of rubber is placed over the matrix on the press, heat and pressure are applied to vulcanize the rubber and form a duplicate plate.

Rubber plates present several advantages over other plates used in relief printing. Rubber plates have a softer surface than metal plates and are compressible; they are designed to provide a smooth transfer of ink to materials with a rough surface, such as folding cartons and grocery bags. Plastic plates are growing in use and have replaced rubber plates as the most common plates used in flexography. Photopolymer plates, discussed next, are plastic plates that do not require a mold to be made from the original copy.

Photopolymer plates

Photopolymer plates are light-sensitive plastic image carriers that are widely used in flexographic printing. The plate surface contains a hard, sensitized plastic coating or *polymer* that is bonded to a backing or base, **Figure 20-11**. Photopolymer plates are flexible and designed for long use. They are typically used to print packaging materials.

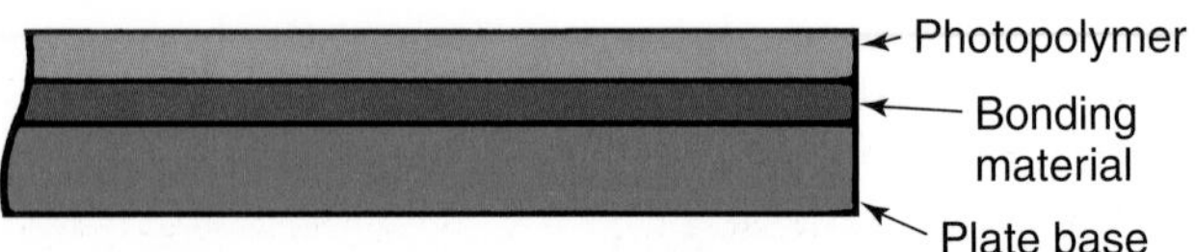

Figure 20-11. Photopolymer plates have a sensitized plastic surface layer that hardens after exposure to ultraviolet light.

When a photopolymer plate is exposed through a negative by ultraviolet light, the polymer coating hardens to form a raised image area. The nonimage area remains soft and is *washed out* (etched) through processing with a water-based solution. After exposure and development, the plate undergoes a drying process. The plate is then reexposed to ultraviolet light for additional hardening of the relief image. This process strengthens the plate for extended use on the press. The basic steps used in exposing and processing a photopolymer plate are shown in **Figure 20-12**.

Photopolymer plates can also be imaged directly by lasers through the use of computer-to-plate (CTP) technology. This process eliminates the use of film as an intermediary when the plate is made. Images are scanned and transferred directly to the plate by a computer; the plate is then processed automatically or developed by washing out the nonimage area.

Relief Presses

While the use of letterpress has sharply declined, it lasted as the dominant form of printing well into this century and continues to be used in a few applications. In traditional letterpress, a chase containing the type form or plate is mounted on the press and positioned for printing. The surface of the plate is inked and pressed against the printing substrate to transfer the image.

Three types of presses have commonly been used in the relief printing process. Letterpress can be conducted on a *platen press*, a *flatbed cylinder press*, or a *rotary press*. See **Figure 20-13**. The different equipment and operating procedures used with each type of press are discussed next.

Platen press

A ***platen press*** produces printed materials by pressing a locked-up form or plate containing the image against a *platen*, the printing surface that holds the paper. Originally, hand-operated platen presses were used extensively by print shops. During press operation, sheets of paper were fed by hand and printed individually. Power-operated presses were later developed to feed, print, and deliver sheets automatically. See **Figure 20-14**.

A platen press is equipped with a number of devices that are commonly used to prepare it for printing. Press designs vary, but the typical

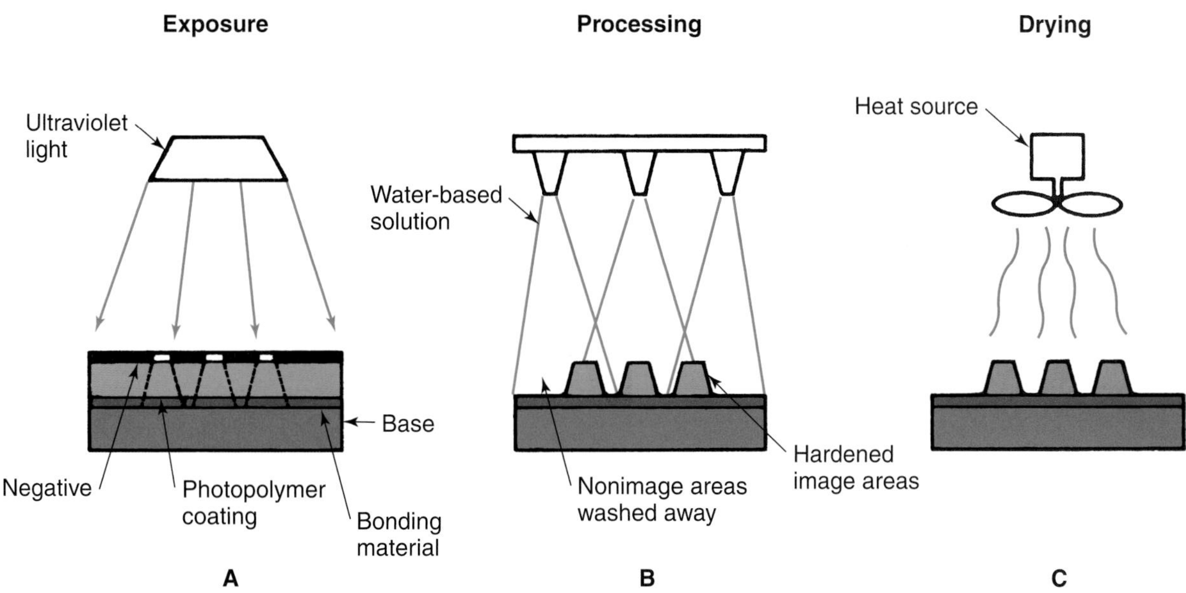

Figure 20-12. The basic procedures used in exposing and processing a photopolymer plate. A—A negative is placed over the plate and the exposure is made from a source of ultraviolet light. B—During processing, a water-based solution is applied to wash out the nonimage area. The image area has hardened and is raised from the surface. C—A drying process is used to remove moisture from the plate before it is exposed again to strengthen the image.

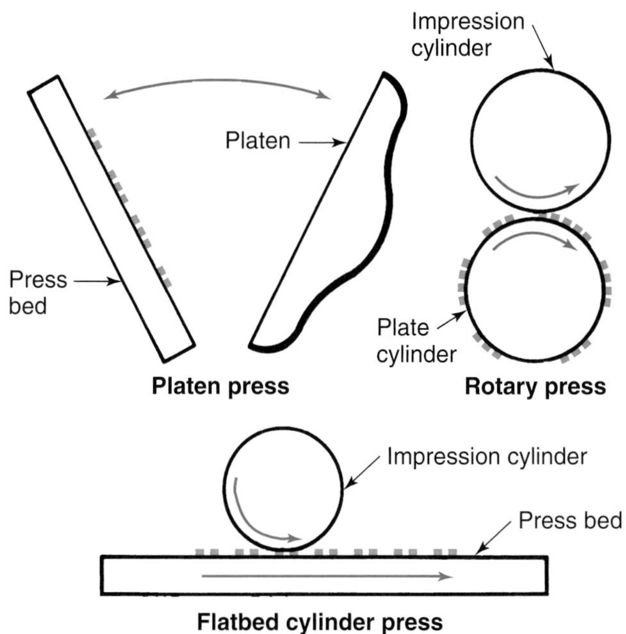

Figure 20-13. The three types of presses most commonly used in relief printing are the platen press, the flatbed cylinder press, and the rotary press.

Figure 20-14. A traditional power-operated platen press.

components of a platen press are a *feedboard*, a *bed*, a *platen*, *bails*, *grippers*, and a *delivery board*. After the type form is locked up in a chase, it is placed in the bed of the press and locked in position. During the printing process, paper is stacked onto the feedboard and transferred to the platen. Once the type form is inked by a set of form rollers, the form and platen are pressed together to make the impression. Ink is supplied to the rollers by an *ink disk*. After the paper is printed, each sheet is removed from the platen and placed on the delivery board.

To prepare the press for printing, the platen is *dressed* with packing sheets. Each sheet is attached to the platen and held in place by the bails, a pair of locking arms that clamp the sheets in place. The packing is used to provide enough pressure between the surface of the platen and the form to transfer the image. Sheets used for packing include *tympan paper*, *hanger sheets*, and a *pressboard*. To pack the platen, hanger sheets are first attached and clamped down by the lower bail. A sheet of tympan paper, also called a ***drawsheet***, is then placed on top of the hanger sheets and clamped under the lower bail; it serves as the holding surface for the paper and can be used to make a test impression. See **Figure 20-15**. With the drawsheet and hanger sheets in place, the pressboard (a heavy piece of stock) is positioned under the rest of the packing, but is not locked by either bail. The drawsheet is then clamped under the top bail.

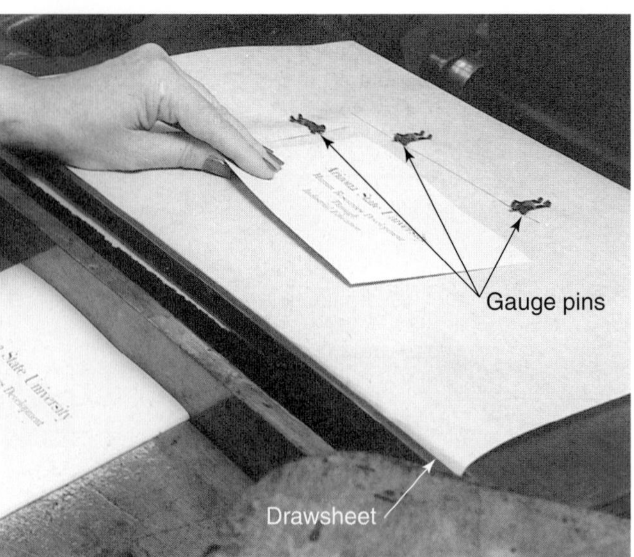

Figure 20-16. Gauge pins are used to position paper on the drawsheet on a hand-fed platen press.

Figure 20-15. A drawsheet is a piece of tympan paper that serves as the holding surface for the printing substrate on the platen press.

As each sheet is transferred from the feedboard to the platen, it must be aligned in the correct position to receive the image when it is printed. Sheets are aligned on the drawsheet by two bars of grippers, mechanical devices that close around the edges of the paper when it reaches the platen. The grippers must be located so they guide each sheet into position without touching the type form. If the grippers make contact with the type form, the type will be smashed.

On hand-fed platen presses, paper is aligned on the drawsheet by *gauge pins*. See **Figure 20-16**. The location of the gauge pins is determined by printing a test impression on the drawsheet and placing a sheet of paper over the image. The pins are inserted to fit the dimensions of the paper; they are typically positioned at the top and left sides. When paper is placed on the platen, the gauge pins are used to hold each sheet in the desired position for printing. After the gauge pins are set, the test impression can be removed from the drawsheet with solvent.

Flatbed cylinder press

A ***flatbed cylinder press*** prints by producing contact between a flat surface or *bed* supporting the plate and a revolving impression cylinder that carries sheets of paper. See **Figure 20-17**. A chase holding the plate or type form is mounted on the bed; when paper on the cylinder rolls over the bed, it receives the image from the inked form. The impression cylinder uses a set of grippers to grasp and deliver paper as it travels through the press. The pressure between the cylinder and the type is used to transfer the image.

Many of the same devices and techniques that are associated with platen presses are used to operate flatbed cylinder presses. A typical sheet-fed cylinder press is equipped with devices that draw and feed paper through the system automatically. Some cylinder presses are designed to print from flexographic plates and are used in multicolor printing.

Figure 20-17. A flatbed cylinder press. Paper is printed as contact is made between the impression cylinder and the press flatbed.

Rotary press

A ***rotary press*** prints the substrate as it travels between an impression cylinder and a plate cylinder, **Figure 20-18**. The impression cylinder draws paper to the printing unit and releases it after it is printed. The image carrier used by a rotary press is a *curved* plate that is mounted on the plate cylinder. Rotary presses typically use duplicate plates for long press runs and operate at high speeds. They are designed as sheet-fed systems and web-fed systems and are commonly used in magazine and newspaper publishing, where longer runs are required.

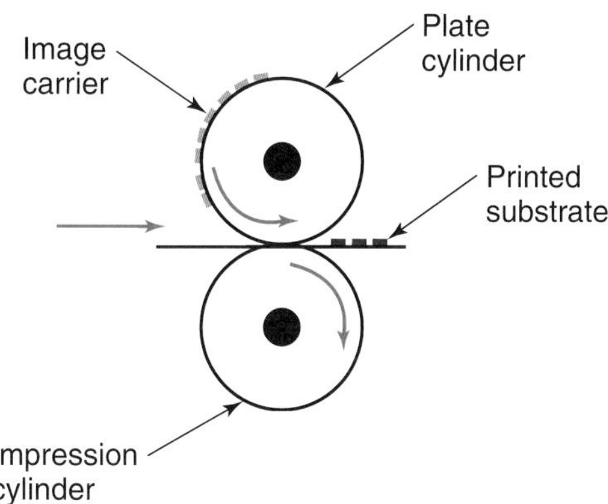

Figure 20-18. A rotary press is designed to print paper as it passes between a plate cylinder and an impression cylinder.

Rotary presses used in multicolor printing are equipped with several printing units, each of which contains a separate plate cylinder that prints a single color. In this design, a common impression cylinder is surrounded by several printing units; the common cylinder provides the pressure needed to transfer images from each plate to the paper as it is fed through the system.

Web-fed rotary presses are designed to print high volumes of materials on a web or continuous *roll* of paper. The web winds through each system during operation of the press, **Figure 20-19**. Rotary presses used in flexographic printing are equipped with different feeding, printing, drying, and delivery systems.

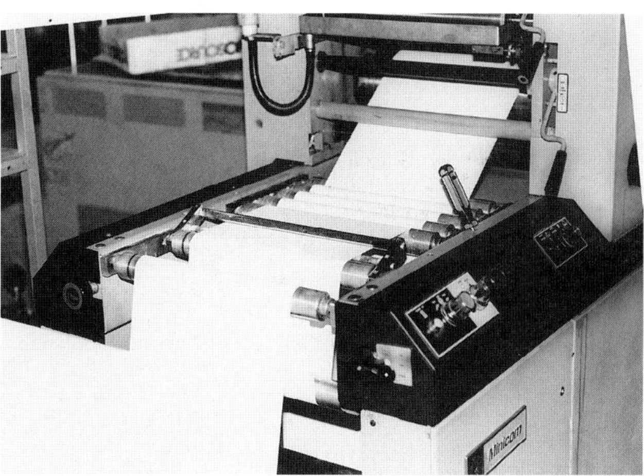

Figure 20-19. This web-fed rotary press prints on a continuous web (roll) of paper and is designed to operate at high speeds.

Review Questions

Please do not write in this text. Write your answers on a separate sheet of paper.

1. Relief printing or letterpress is a process that prints images from a _____ surface.
2. Hand composition involves the traditional arrangement of _____ in a composing stick. .
3. What is a chase?
4. List three finishing applications of letterpress equipment.
5. Flexographic printing is most commonly used to print _____ .

6. Name the two traditional classifications of relief plates.
7. Define *photoengraving*.
8. Describe the process used to make a photopolymer plate.
9. List the three types of presses traditionally used in relief printing.
10. What two cylinders make up the printing unit of a rotary press?

Flexographic Printing 21

Learning Objectives

After studying this chapter, you will be able to:

- Describe the flexographic process.
- Recognize various types of presses used in flexography.
- Identify the types of substrates, inks, and plates used in flexography.

Important Terms

anilox roll
doctor blade
flexography
inline
matrix
photopolymer plates
plate elongation
repeat length
viscosity
Zahn cup

Overview of Flexography

With the burgeoning demand for high quality graphics on packaging products, flexography has grown to be a giant among the printing processes. Corrugated boxes are the largest market for flexography. It is also used to print candy wrappers, shopping bags, milk cartons, cereal boxes, gift wrap, wallpaper, and many other goods, including polyethylene for clear, flexible packaging.

Flexography is a method of direct rotary printing that uses flexible relief image plates of rubber or photopolymer material. The plates are affixed to cylinders of various repeat lengths and inked by a cell-structured ink metering roll. A fast-drying, fluid ink is carried to plates that print on nearly any substrate.

Flexography was originally known as *aniline printing* because of the aniline dyes used to color the ink. However, aniline dyes and their harsh solvents left an odor on the product and came to be considered toxic. Eventually, the Food and Drug Administration banned their use on food packaging. Chemists began developing new inks and alcohol solvents as replacements. The name aniline printing remained until 1958, when the process became known as flexography. In 1980, the United States Clean Air Act spurred the development of water-based inks using low-solvent or no-solvent inks. Today, flexography is often chosen because of the ability to print with clean, water-based, or no-solvent ultraviolet inks.

Press Developments

Europe was the leader in printing press engineering until the mid-1940s, when press manufacturers in the U.S. became competitive with European firms. Today, flexographic press design is globally competitive.

Flexographic presses are often part of an entire manufacturing process, **Figure 21-1**. Presses range in web width from 2″ to 110″. Many machines have the ***inline*** ability to slit, laminate, number, perforate, die-cut, emboss, and sheet. Unlike offset lithography or letterpress, flexography uses only one roll to apply ink to the printing plates. Lithographic and letter presses use many rollers to split and work the paste ink into a thin film. Paste inks dry very slowly compared to flexographic inks which evaporate in microseconds. This makes them ideal for printing on polyethylene, the material used for plastic grocery bags and similar products.

An ink fountain pan holds the ink, which is usually water-based. The fountain roll, a soft or hard rubber roller, transfers the ink to the next roller in the chain, the anilox roll. See **Figure 21-2**. A skidding action occurs between the two contacting rollers, because the fountain roll runs at a slower speed than the anilox roll. Many presses slow the fountain roll to increase the doctoring (shearing) action between the two. The ***anilox roll*** is the heart of the flexography system. The roll surface is engraved with cells that carry ink up to the plate cylinder.

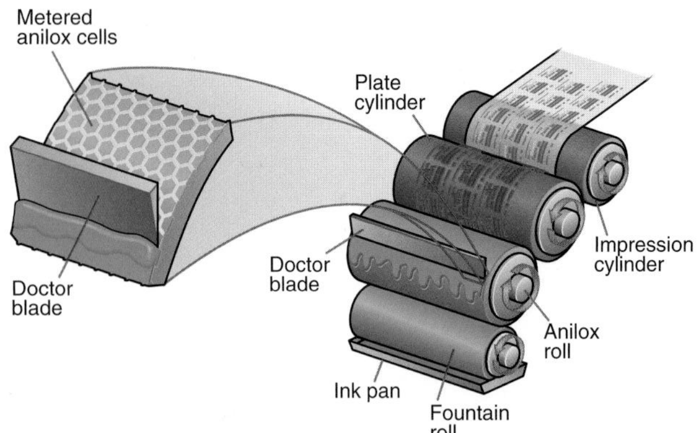

Figure 21-2. The flexographic ink delivery system uses an anilox roll engraved with tiny cells. (Agfa)

An image carrier (plate) mounted on the plate cylinder is made of rubber or photopolymer, **Figure 21-3**. The anilox roll inks the relief image plate with a continuous metered supply of ink. The substrate is fed, under controlled tension, against the impression cylinder. The fast-drying ink prints on the absorbent or nonabsorbent substrate and dries instantly.

A two-roll system for removing excess ink was used for many years until the ***doctor blade*** was introduced. The blade angle is used to "doctor" or clear excess ink from noncell areas. The doctor blade produces excellent, even inking of the cells in the anilox roll.

Figure 21-1. Flexographic presses are widely used for printing packaging and labels. This is a seven-station, narrow-web label press. (Mark Andy, Inc.)

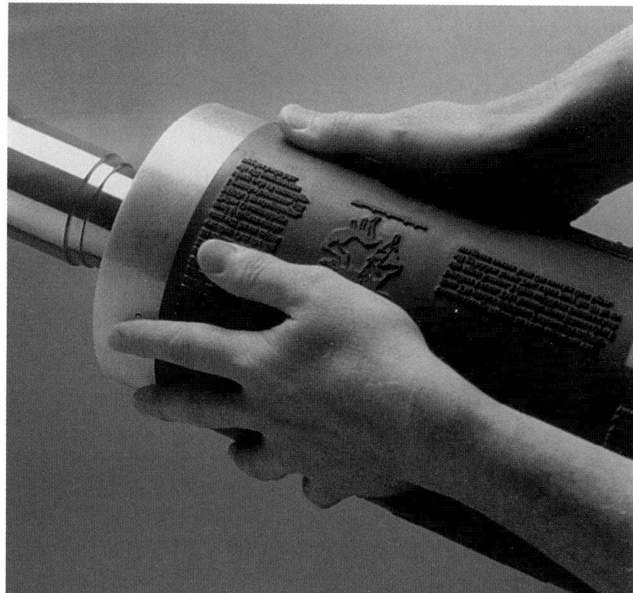

Figure 21-3. Rubber or polymer are used for the raised flexographic plate. (Strachan Henshaw Machinery, Inc.)

The latest improvement in the flexographic inking system is the enclosed (chambered) double doctor blade system, **Figure 21-4**. Two blades are used against the anilox roller. The prime blade doctors the anilox roll. The opposite blade is called a trailing or containment blade. The ends of the enclosed unit have special wipers that prevent ink from coming out of the enclosed system. The dual doctor ink chamber eliminates the need for a fountain roller and pan. New presses are being built with the chambered system, while many existing presses are being retrofitted for it.

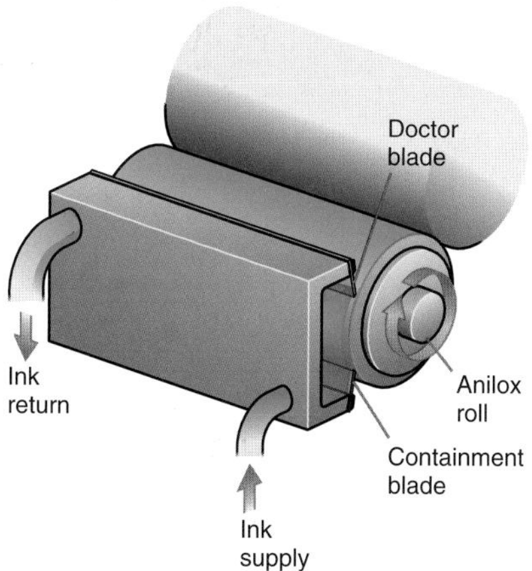

Figure 21-4. The dual doctor ink chamber system is becoming common on presses. (Agfa)

Flexographic Press Types

The design of the flexographic printing unit allows press manufacturers to build presses in any one of three configurations: the stack press, the central impression cylinder press, and the inline press.

Stack press

The stack press was the first type of flexographic press and was used with aniline inks. One printing station is positioned above the other. A two- or three-foot allowance between the stations gives the web time to dry before the next color is printed. A typical stack-type press prints three colors down and three colors up on the web, **Figure 21-5**. Since the moving web is unsupported between the printing stations, pliant materials like polyethylene plastic can stretch between stations and cause register problems. However, unstretchable substrates, such as thick paper, can hold register from station to station. Heavier gauge plastics can also be printed, providing they have little stretch.

Stack presses with good web tension controls are used for work that does not require tight register. Fewer stack type presses are being manufactured today because other press types have proven better.

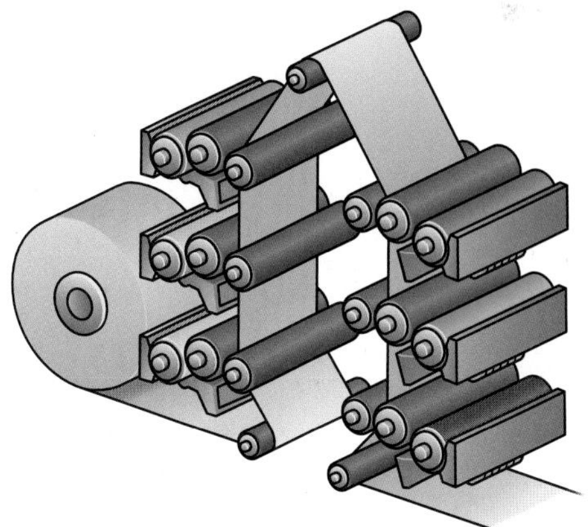

Figure 21-5. The stack press was the first type developed for flexographic printing. (Agfa)

Central impression cylinder presses

In the central impression cylinder press (CIC), the web travels around a central drum from one print station to the next, **Figure 21-6**. The moving

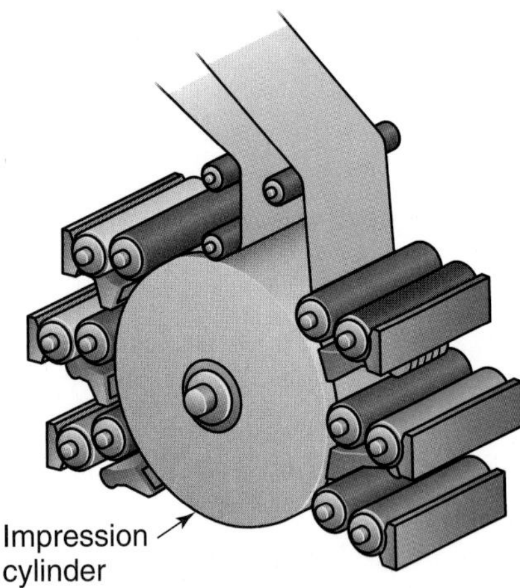

Figure 21-6. The central impression cylinder type of flexographic press supports the substrate by direct contact with the cylinder. (Agfa)

web is supported between stations, so the press is ideal for stretchable films with close register. The CIC drum (or bull drum) does not allow the web to stretch. See **Figure 21-7**.

CIC presses originally had four stations around the drum. Today's presses, with full drums up to 96″ in diameter, allow for six to eight colors. Each drum has an accurate gear that times and controls the turning of all print stations and keeps them in register.

CIC presses are limited to one-sided printing. Because of their accuracy, CIC presses are ideal for printing on stretchable plastic film packaging.

Inline press

The inline flexographic press has separate print stations placed in a straight line, **Figure 21-8**. Each section has its own dryer. The stations are connected to one another by a long central shaft that keeps the stations in register. A single print station is similar to a gravure press print station, **Figure 21-9**.

Two sides can be printed in one pass with the aid of a turnover bar. Printing stations can be added to an inline press at any time to increase the number of colors it can print. Because of the distance the web must travel from one station to the next, inline register problems can occur. Sensitive tension-control devices must be used to keep the web in tight register. Some inline presses are extremely wide-web machines, feeding webs up to 110″, with repeat lengths up to 110″. These presses are used to print linerboard for corrugated boxes before corrugation takes place. See **Figure 21-10**.

Many inline presses are designed to print narrow-web labels and forms 6″ to 18″ wide, **Figure 21-11**. Narrow-web inline presses have six to eight color stations. They also are capable of die

Figure 21-7. The CIC press is capable of producing high quality, close register work. Note: Guards have been removed from this press to show details. (Paper Converting Machine Company)

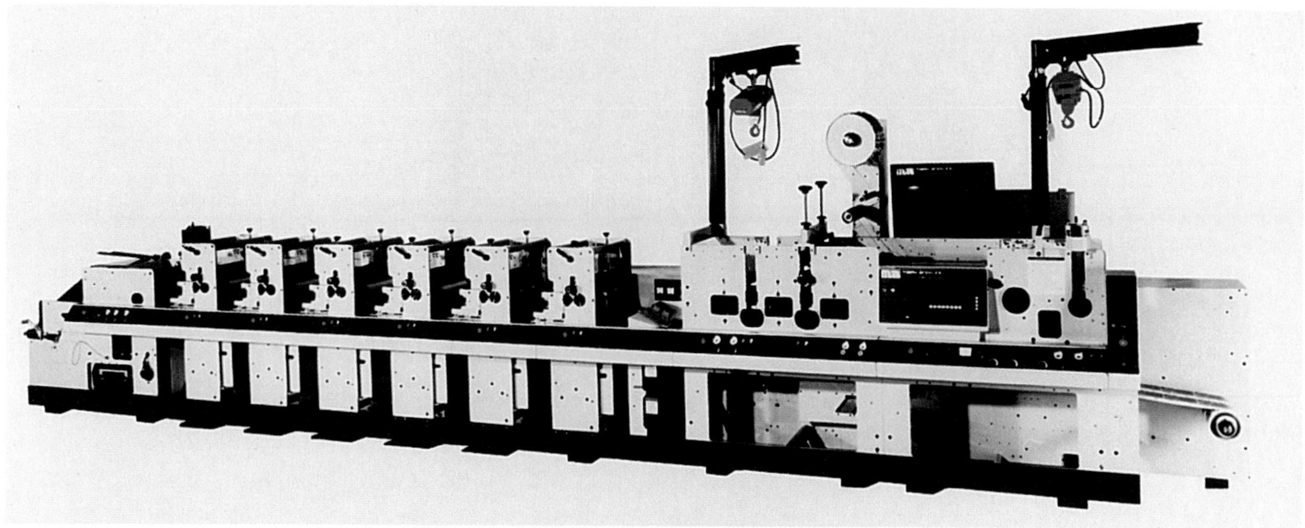

Figure 21-8. This inline web label press has six print stations. (Mark Andy, Inc.)

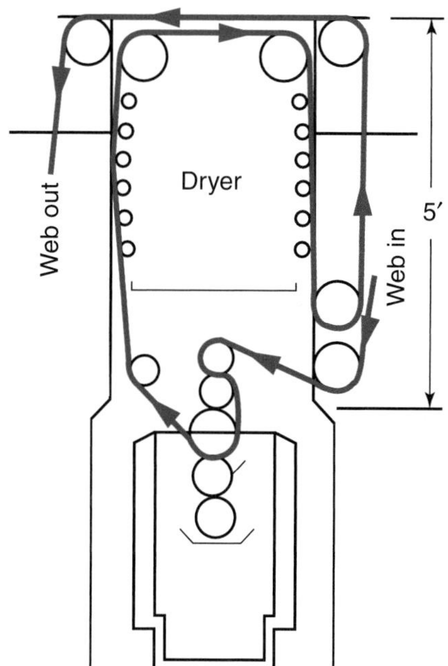

Figure 21-9. A single print station of an inline press, showing the path of the web.

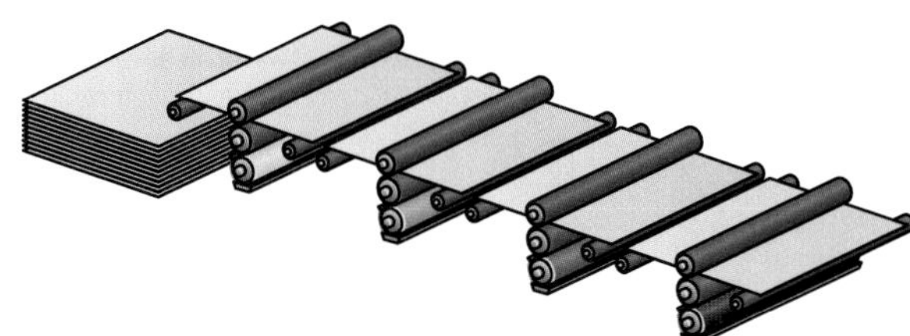

Figure 21-10. A corrugated press is a type of inline press used for printing large sheets (up to 120″ wide) of linerboard for paper box manufacture. (Agfa)

cutting, slitting, sheeting, numbering, and embossing. Most flexographic label shops use these smaller presses to print pressure-sensitive labels.

Flexographic presses are rotary printing machines. The cylinders print on every revolution (or repeat length) to a moving web of substrate material. This very action makes for high press speeds, **Figure 21-12**. It is not uncommon for wide-web presses printing polyethylene to run at speeds of 750 feet per minute. Label presses can print up to 500 feet per minute. Press speed is relative to the type of work being done. Some jobs require lower speeds to print properly.

The advent of fully automated, computerized presses is not far off. Press controls are becoming more sophisticated, and numerous improvements have made flexography comparable to offset and gravure.

Flexographic Plates

Flexographic presses use flexible plates (image carriers) that conform to uneven surfaces. The plates have raised or relief images, much like letterpress plates. In fact, letterpress photoengravings are used to vulcanize rubber into the relief-type plates. Besides rubber molding, flexographic plates can be produced by exposing and processing photopolymer materials, and by laser imaging.

Molded rubber plates

Molded rubber plates are created in a multistep process. The original photoengraving is etched from

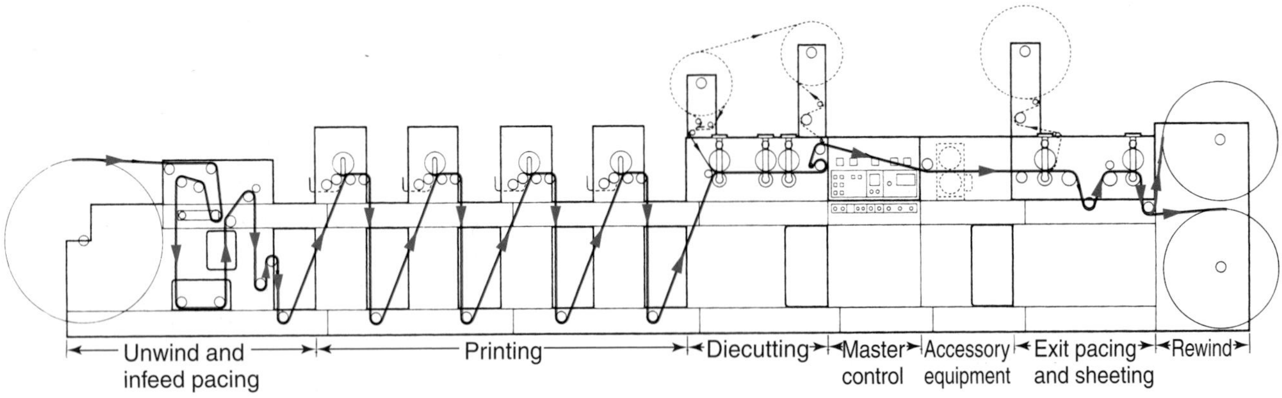

Figure 21-11. A narrow-web inline press with four color stations. (Flexographic Technical Association, Inc.)

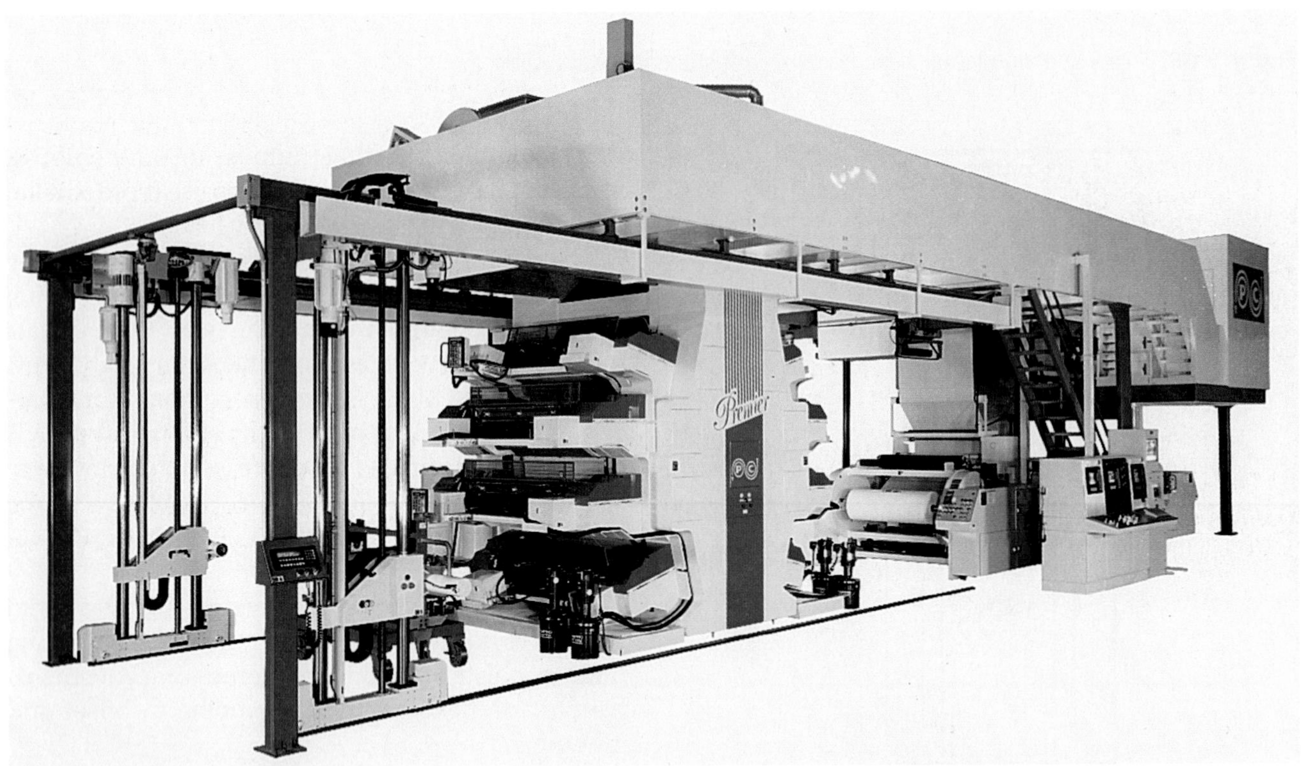

Figure 21-12. Every revolution of the plate cylinder creates the same image on a substrate. (Paper Converting Machine Company)

magnesium or made from a UV-sensitive polymer. A phenolic resin ***matrix*** (also called a "mat" or mold) captures the details of the original plate, **Figure 21-13**. A hydraulic press generates the heat and pressure needed to mold the matrix board and plates. The mat can be used to make many rubber plates; hence, it is called a duplicate platemaking process.

The original photoengraving is placed on top of the matrix board. Steel bearers on each side of the

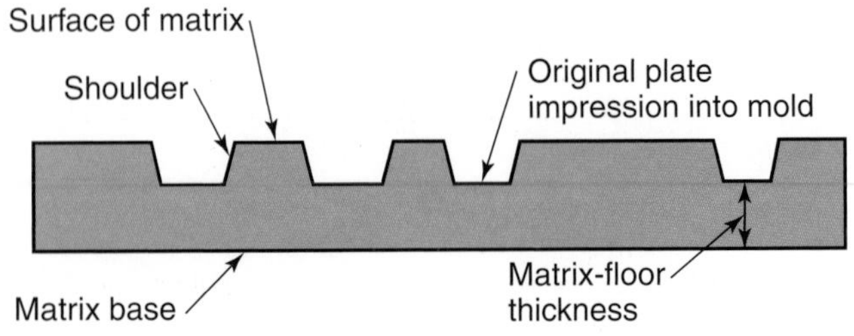

Figure 21-13. Matrix (mold) material is etched or formed to create a reverse image.

mold stop the press at the proper distance to produce the desired plate thickness. Upper and lower platens (rams) are heated to 307°F (153°C) and a pressure of 300 psi to 1000 psi (2070 kPa to 6900 kPa) is applied. The matrix board melts slightly and forms the mold. After 15 minutes, the press is opened, and the original plate is removed. All details of the original plate are impressed into the matrix.

When the matrix cools, a sheet of unvulcanized rubber is placed over the matrix, **Figure 21-14**. Cloth coated with silicone is placed on top of the matrix and rubber to prevent the rubber from sticking to the upper ram of the molding press. The press is closed, applying heat and pressure that cause polymerization to occur and the rubber to vulcanize. See **Figure 21-15**. The press is opened, and the plate is removed from the matrix. When the plate is mounted onto a cylinder, it prints onto the substrate as a readable image.

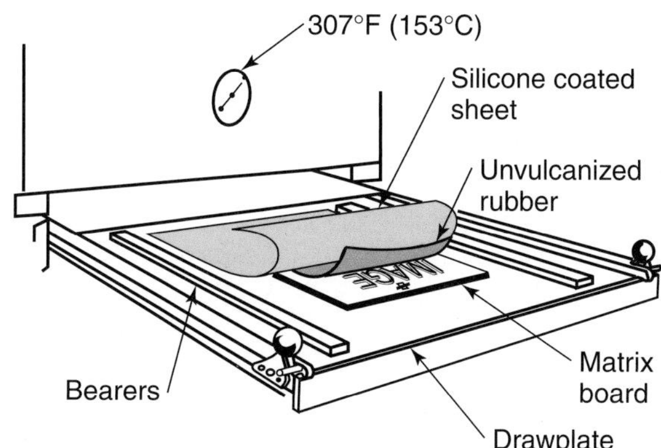

Figure 21-14. A molding press forces unvulcanized rubber into the recessed areas of the matrix, where it is cured (vulcanized) by heat and pressure.

Rubber plate molding is a continuous process in flexography plants. Many jobs for wide-web cylinders require making numerous plates from the same mold. The process has its limitations. Some small details and fine type styles may not reproduce well. The quality of process halftones is limited, as well. Even though rubber plates have excellent ink transfer, their use has decreased since the perfection of photopolymer plates.

Photopolymer plates

During the 1970s, chemists developed formulations of polymers (flexible plastic materials) that react to ultraviolet light and then solidify. Several companies produced sheet material with a nonstretchable base which, after UV exposure, can be washed out, leaving a sharp relief image on its surface. ***Photopolymer plates*** became a standard in flexography.

Photopolymer plates have advantages over molded rubber plates. Photoengravings and molding boards are not required. Subsequently, a hydraulic molding press is unnecessary. The entire platemaking operation can easily be done by the printer rather than sent out to a subcontractor. See **Figure 21-16**.

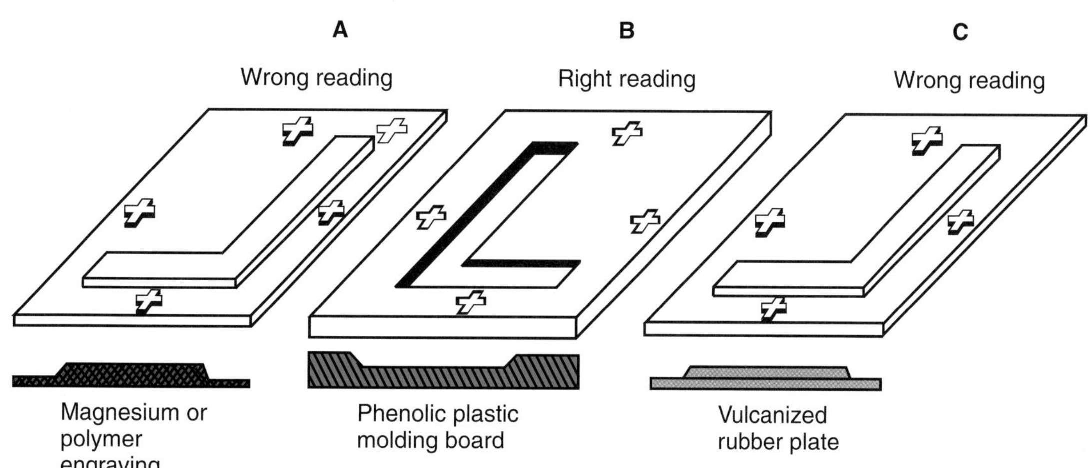

Figure 21-15. The sequence for making a duplicate rubber plate. A—The original is wrong-reading (reversed). B—The mold is right-reading. C—The plate is wrong-reading so it will print correctly on the substrate.

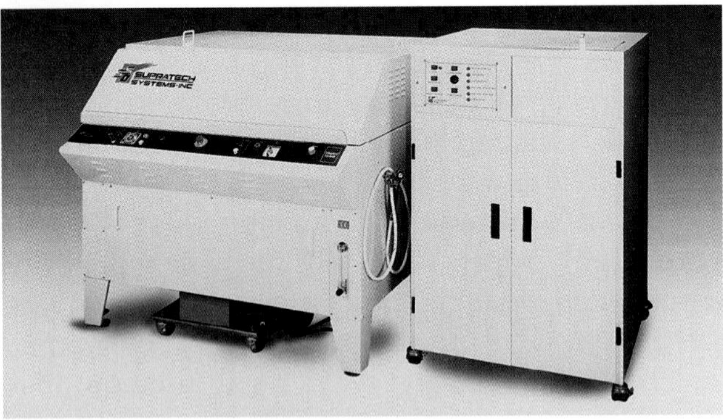

Figure 21-16. A platemaking system for processing photopolymer plates. The plates are washed out with water. (Supratech Systems, Inc.)

The platemaking process begins with a laterally reversed (letterpress-type) negative on matte emulsion-based film. Matte-based film allows air to flow across the smooth polymer surface. The image area of the plate is exposed by UV light through the film negative. The UV light causes a reaction with a photo initiator in the plate material and sets off a cross-linking within the polymer that causes it to harden.

After UV exposure, the unexposed polymer material is washed out (etched) with water or another chemically reactive liquid. Once dry, the plate is exposed to intense UV light which finishes the cross-linking phase. The finished relief plate feels like a rubber plate because the polymer contains a large amount of gum rubber, **Figure 21-17**.

Figure 21-17. The rubber-like photopolymer plate has a nonstretchable plastic base that keeps it stable. (Supratech Systems, Inc.)

Polymer material holds very fine screen size dots; excellent printing results are obtained with 200-line process screens. Photopolymer plate costs generally are higher than rubber plate costs, but the fine detail held by the polymer plates usually offsets the difference. Polymer plates also have a longer life than rubber plates.

Polymers eventually will dominate the flexographic industry. Costs are being reduced by a trend to print from thinner plates that use less polymer. Less polymer needs to be etched away; therefore, less time is needed to produce the plates. Thin plates stretch less when placed on cylinders. Thin plates also print sharper images because they compress less on impression.

Laser plates

Computer-to-plate (also called direct-to-plate) processing transfers images directly from the computer to the plate, thus eliminating film. Some photopolymer plates can be directly imaged by lasers. In recent years, laser-engraved rubber cylinders have been used to print wallpaper and other continuous pattern jobs.

Plate Stretch

Because flexographic plates are made with soft material, they tend to stretch when mounted on the plate cylinder and may distort images and text. A circle, for example, may stretch to look like an oval, **Figure 21-18**. Allowance must be made for ***plate elongation.***

The amount a plate stretches depends on the thickness of the plate and the diameter of the cylinder. Stretch can easily be calculated using the

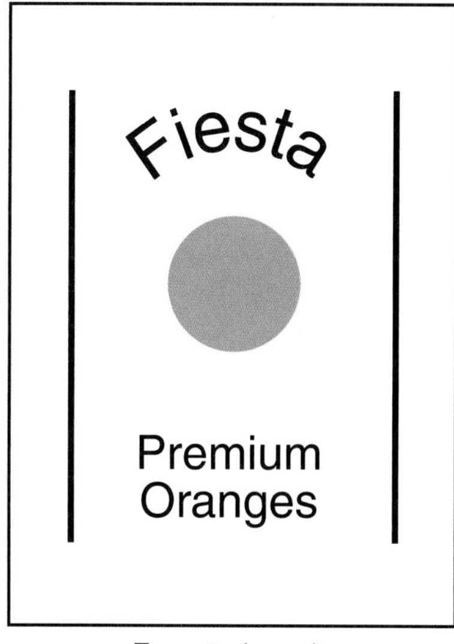

Expected result

Plate elongation occurs around the cylinder

Printed piece without compensation for elongation

Figure 21-18. If compensation is not applied by distorting the original art, the round image will print as an oval.

formula $\pi \times 2T \div RL$, where T is the plate thickness and RL is the repeat length of the cylinder.

Compensation is applied by distorting (shortening) the original image in the curve direction. Flexographic software programs that allow for distortion are available for computer-generated art. In direct-to-plate imaging, compensation is not needed if the imaging is applied directly to a curved plate.

Plate Mounting

Flexographic plates must be accurately mounted on press cylinders. Registration to other plates on other cylinders is important. To accomplish accurate mounting, a mounting machine is used.

In the flexographic pin-register system, punched holes in the plate are fitted to pins on the mounting machine. Each cylinder is mounted with the same pin locations, and perfect register is quickly attained. Some narrow-web mounters use microscopes and small targets on two sides of the plates. The plates are carefully aligned with the dots, and excellent register is obtained.

The latest type of mounter is the television-monitored microscope camera/plate machine. Two TV monitors show enlarged dot areas on both ends of the cylinder. The microdots on the plate are then projected by the camera to the TV monitors, achieving dot-for-dot register.

When both sets of dots are lined up, the plate is adhered with sticky-back mounting tape, a two-sided adhesive with a cloth center. One side sticks to the metal cylinder; the other holds the plate in place, **Figure 21-19**. Sticky-back tape comes in several thicknesses. The diameter of the cylinder determines the required thickness of the tape. Most printers use 0.015″ or 0.020″ thickness. The total plate height should be 0.002″ larger than the pitch circle diameter of the press drive gear.

Anilox Rolls

While the plates are an important link in the flexographic printing process, the manner in which the plates are inked is critical. The anilox roll applies ink evenly and consistently to the relief image of the plate. The amount of ink applied to the plate surface directly affects the quality and sharpness of the image produced. The surface of the anilox roll is

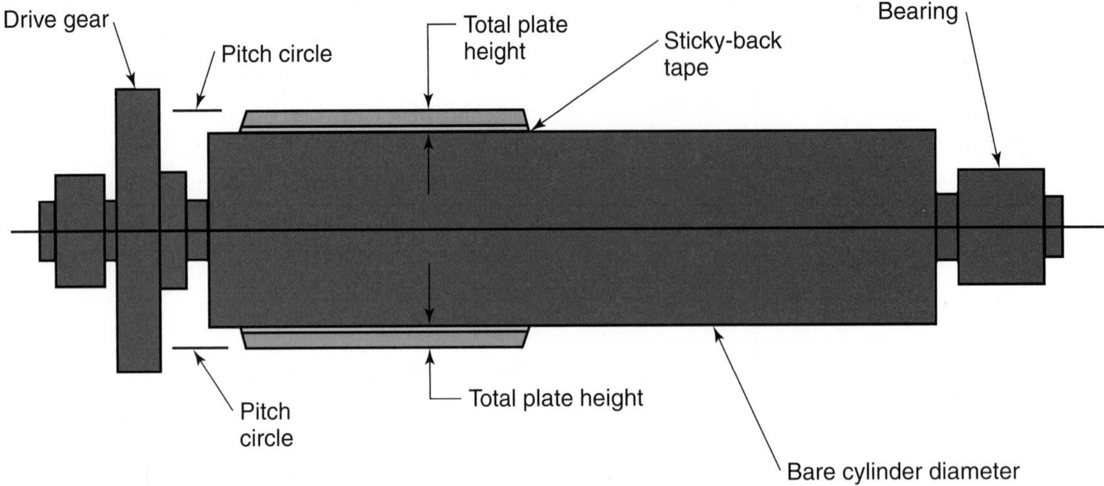

Figure 21-19. Sticky-back mounting tape is used to adhere the plate to the cylinder.

engraved with cells, **Figure 21-20**. The ink capacity of each cell is calculated in billions of cubic microns. The larger the cells, the greater the volume of ink carried to the plates. Typically, the cells on the anilox are engraved at 45° angles. Laser-engraved cells have 30° or 60° angles. The number of cells per square inch (cpi) varies.

Proper screen ruling is crucial and should be correlated with anilox cell count. Anilox cells come in screen ruling sizes from 65 to 1200 lines. The higher the screen ruling, the higher the resolution, because there are more dots per square inch. The surface of an anilox roll with a 500-line screen engraving has 250,000 (500 × 500) cpi. A 1200-line screen has 1,440,000 cpi engraved into its surface.

Figure 21-20. Engraved cells cover the entire surface of the anilox roll. The cells carry the ink.

Why must anilox rolls use certain screen sizes? For anilox rolls to ink fine process dots on a plate, several cells must contact each dot surface. The four-time rule of thumb applies. If you are printing a 150-line screen plate, use four times the screen size, or a 600-cell anilox roll. If you want to gain finer inking, a 700- or 800-cell anilox roll can be used to control print density. See **Figure 21-21**.

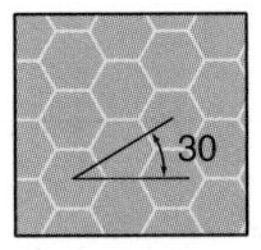

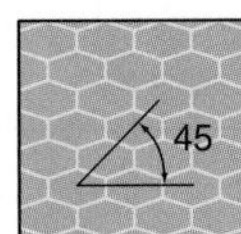

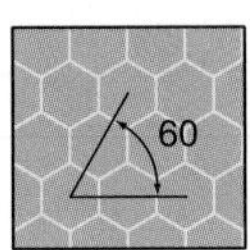

Cells are engraved on an anilox roll at one of three angles: 30 , 45 or 60 .

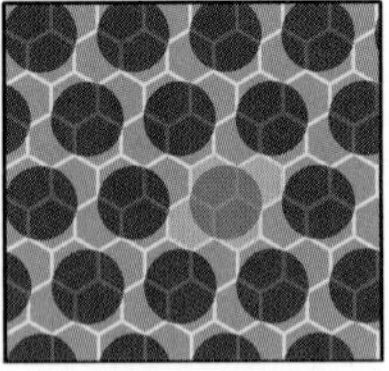

Ideally, the anilox should contain a minimum of 4 cells for every halftone dot.

Figure 21-21. Anilox cell angles should be 30°, 40°, or 60°. (Agfa)

In flexography, the amount of ink delivered to the plate is regulated by varying the screen size and the capacity of the anilox rolls. To increase ink volume, an anilox with a lower screen size is positioned on the press. The cells are larger and hold more ink as the cells per square inch decrease in number.

The emergence of the laser has changed the manner in which anilox rolls can be engraved. The versatile laser process cleanly engraves ceramic-coated steel rollers with screen sizes up to 1200 cpi. The plasma-coated ceramics are hard and long-wearing.

Print Cylinders

Flexography and gravure share some advantages. The printing cylinders are completely round, permitting them to print continuous patterns, such as wallpaper and gift wrapping.

The cylinders are also removable. Because each press is adjustable, a wide range of repeat-length cylinders can be used. ***Repeat length*** equals one revolution of a press cylinder. Therefore, flexographic presses can print the exact repeat length of a job with minimum waste.

Each flexographic press is made to fit a certain pitch size. *Pitch* refers to the drive gears on the cylinders. For example, a 1/4″ circular pitch press has a range of repeat lengths 7″ to 28″. Each cylinder size increases by 1/4″ increments, for example 7 1/2″, 7 3/4″, 8″, 8 1/4″, etc.

Three plate systems—integral, demountable and sleeve—are available to the flexographer. The *integral* type is a one-piece cylinder and shaft with a circumference matched to the plate cylinder. Each revolution is a repeat length of the image. This cylinder is very expensive but very accurate.

The *demountable* cylinder has a sleeve of steel or aluminum; the circumference depends on the repeat length of the image. This system requires that the gears and bearings correspond to the cylinder diameter. They are installed to match the cylinder during mounting.

The *sleeve* system is lightweight and can accommodate a variety of repeat images. A single mandrel can be used to accommodate a single sleeve in a range of repeat image lengths. The plate cylinder mandrels are hollow and fitted for compressed air. To place the sleeve on the mandrel, air is forced into the sleeve to slightly expand it, so that it can be positioned on the mandrel. Once on the mandrel, the air pressure is released and the cylinder contracts to create a tight fit. To remove the sleeve, the reverse takes place.

Flexography plants store an array of cylinders, although few have all the cylinder sizes their presses will run. Typically, plants store repeat sizes that fit the general sizes of the types of work they do.

The bare cylinder diameter of all flexographic cylinders is undercut (made smaller in diameter) to accommodate the thicknesses of the plate and the sticky-back tape. Refer to Figure 21-19.

Cylinders must run true to their centers by standard tolerances. A cylinder should not wobble (be out-of-round) by more than 0.001″ for general-type printing. A closer tolerance of 0.0005″ is needed for process-type printing.

Press Makeready

After plates are mounted onto cylinders, they are brought to the press and placed in the proper stations. Required aniloxes are installed. Each station is fed ink. Press adjustments are made, and the job begins to print. Registration is achieved by moving cylinders into a timed position. After final approval of a press web sample, the job is run.

Each type and size of press has its own makeready procedures. Generally, the larger the press, the longer the time needed to change jobs. New systems have been developed that allow anilox rolls to be changed in minutes.

Because of their smaller cylinders and anilox rolls, narrow-web label presses require less changeover time than wide-web presses. Some presses have a slide-out print station that can be changed over in seconds.

Flexographic newspaper presses are engineered for short run times. Plate register systems allow quick plate-changing and register control. Many times the second turn of the press produces saleable copy.

Flexographic Inks

Flexography and gravure printing use inks that are more fluid than paste inks. Since the ink is free-flowing, it is easily pumped into print stations and dries in microseconds.

The press operator is responsible for regulating ink ***viscosity***, the internal resistance of an ink to flow. Resistance is measured by a gravitational flow device, called a viscometer. A ***Zahn cup*** is one such device and resembles a test tube. Viscosity is measured by the time (in seconds) it takes for the volume of the cup to be emptied. Ratings are on a scale of 1 to 5.

To better understand viscosity, look at the relative viscosity of two common liquids. Water flows at the rate of 15.2 seconds, #2 Zahn cup. Heavy cream flows at 20 seconds, #2 Zahn cup. The higher the viscosity, the longer it takes the fluid to flow out of the viscometer. Always report measurements in the seconds it takes for the cup to empty, as well as the type of cup used. There are over 20 types of viscosity cups made for industry and lab use.

Flexographic ink viscosities are between 19 and 55 seconds, #2 Zahn cup. The press operator thins the ink with solvent to acquire the proper viscosity. Most polyethylene films are printed with 21 second ink, #2 Zahn cup.

The higher the ink viscosity, the thicker the film left on the substrate. High-viscosity inks print fewer impressions. They also dry slowly, in turn, slowing down the press to allow time for drying between stations.

Proper viscosity of inks is an important consideration to produce sharp, clean images. In large flexographic printing plants where precise measurement and control of viscosity, pH, and temperature are critical for controlling ink costs, a viscosity control system may be utilized, **Figure 21-22**.

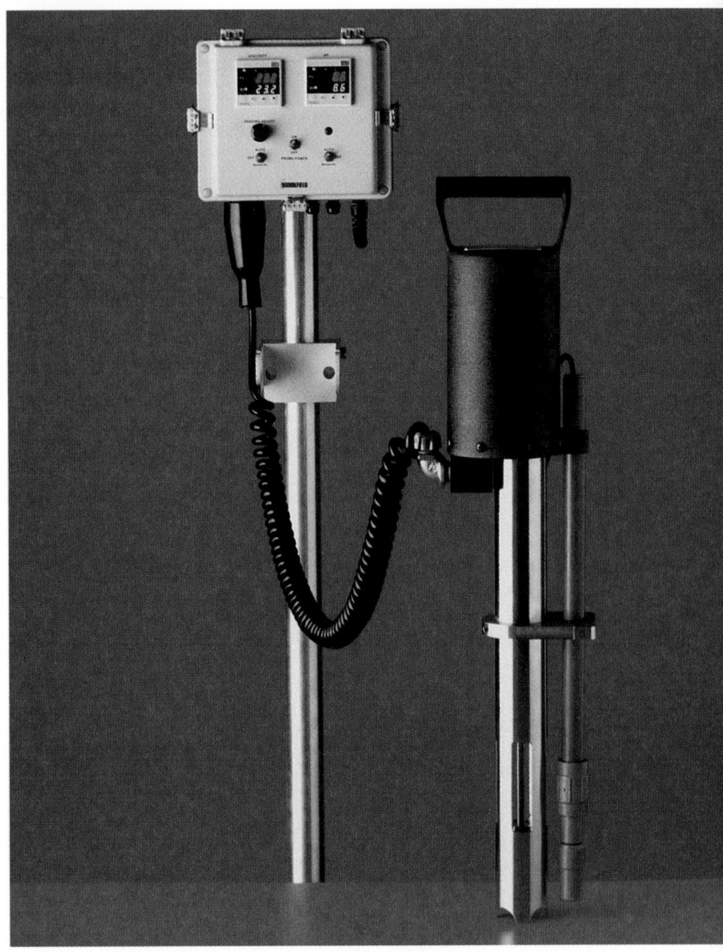

Figure 21-22. A viscometer system that features centralized monitoring and control of viscosity and pH. (Brookfield Engineering Laboratories, Inc.)

Types of inks

Three types of flexographic inks are widely used in the graphic communications industry today: alcohol-based-inks, polyamide inks, and water-based inks.

Alcohol-based inks come in a full range of dyes. Pigmented inks are also available.

Polyamide inks are solvent-type inks requiring alcohol and acetates to dissolve their resins. Polyamide inks are widely used for general purpose printing. These inks print successfully on nearly any substrate, including absorbent or nonabsorbent plastics. However, both alcohol and polyamide inks emit volatile organic compounds (VOCs). Printers that continue to use solvent-type inks must install complex pollution control devices to catch and neutralize all VOC emissions from their plants.

Although water-based inks have been used in flexography for over 60 years, they are gaining wider use in the wake of stiff environmental laws. Water-based inks must maintain a critical pH. Viscosity ranges from 20 to 40 seconds, #2 Zahn cup. Water-based inks may or may not adhere to some substrates as well as solvent inks do. However, research continues to produce water-based inks that do print well on nonabsorbent materials.

Inks cured by ultraviolet light are readily used in flexographic printing. These high-viscosity inks have been adapted from the letterpress UV paste inks. Many printers are using UV-cured coatings for all types of printing.

Strengths and Weaknesses

Flexography has emerged and continues to grow as a major printing process. This chapter has depicted the use of flexography on large presses; however, it is possible to experience the process using a small press, **Figure 21-23**.

Figure 21-23. A small press like this one allows students to experience working with flexography.

Like any printing process, flexography has its strengths and weaknesses. Flexographic presses can do many inline operations, such as laminating, die-cutting, gluing, and folding. Flexography is capable of printing on a wide variety of absorbent and non-absorbent substrates, including stretchable plastics. Many plate sizes allow for a wide range of printing image sizes. In addition, the process works well with water-based inks. Conversely, imaging of very small type can be a problem. Short runs are not economical. Dot gain is evident. Generally, printing standards have not been established.

Review Questions

Please do not write in this book. Write your answers on a separate sheet of paper.

1. List at least two types of products commonly printed by the flexographic process.
2. What is the heart of the flexographic inking system?
3. What device scrapes the ink off the anilox roll?
4. List three main types of flexographic presses.
5. Flexographic image carriers are commonly made from what two materials?
6. How is plate elongation compensated?
7. What material holds the flexographic plate to the print cylinder?
8. The internal resistance of a liquid to flow is called _____.
9. What is a common type of viscometer?
10. List the three types of flexographic ink.

Electromechanical engraving is the most widely-used method of preparing gravure cylinders. In this set-up, the multiple engraving heads at right are responding to electronic signals from the multiple scanning stations at left. (Linotype-Hell)

Gravure Printing

22

Learning Objectives

After studying this chapter, you will be able to:

- Identify applications of gravure printing.
- Describe the four basic steps in gravure printing.
- Describe the advantages and disadvantages of gravure.
- Indicate the reproduction requirements essential for printing a finished product with gravure.
- Summarize the methods of cylinder imaging.
- Explain the electrostatic assist process.
- Describe the properties of gravure inks.

Important Terms

color correction
electroplating
electrostatic assist
gravure
halftone gravure
intaglio
reflection copy
ribbons
rotogravure
stylus

Development of Gravure

For hundreds of years, artists have used sharp, pointed tools to cut images in metal plates. Before printing, the image carrier is covered with ink, and the ink fills in the etched images. The excess ink is removed from the image carrier. Paper is pressed against the plate, and the image is transferred to the paper.

Sinking words, pictures, or designs into a printing plate or cylinder is a process known as ***intaglio*** (pronounced "in-tal-yo"). Because the plates are hand-engraved, the intaglio process lends itself to line illustrations or type. Paper money, postage stamps, and stock certificates are some of the products printed by this process today, **Figure 22-1**.

The Gravure Process

Intaglio was the forerunner to modern ***gravure*** printing. Like intaglio, gravure prints from images that are etched below the surface of the image carrier. Today, printing techniques are quite different, and most images are placed on the printing plate or cylinder with electronically controlled cutting devices or with laser imaging technology. The use of acid to etch the images into the image carrier has almost disappeared in commercial applications in the United States.

Karl Klietsch (pronounced "Klic") is considered the inventor of modern gravure printing. With the advent of his grain screen photogravure etching process in 1878, printing continuous tone illustrations became possible. Klietsch further refined the process using a crossline screen and a sheet of light-sensitive (carbon) tissue. By 1890, the first rotary cylinder gravure press was built.

Figure 22-1. This intaglio plate is used to print postage stamps. (U.S. Bureau of Engraving and Printing)

Rotogravure printing uses a metal cylinder as the image carrier. The engraved image area is recessed below the nonimage surface. The press rotates and prints continuously, at high speed, on both web and sheetfed stock.

The gravure process has four basic steps, as shown in **Figure 22-2**.

1. Ink is deposited on the surface of the image carrier and collects in microscopic ink wells below the surface.
2. Excess ink is removed from the nonimage area.
3. The substrate is pressed against the image.
4. The substrate absorbs or attracts the ink to produce a printed image.

The paper, usually fed by a web traveling about 30 mph (48 km/h), acts like a blotter, absorbing the ink from the microscopic ink wells. The cylinder can have as many as 22,500 ink wells per square inch. The amount of ink absorbed into the surface of the substrate depends on the size and depth of the ink wells, **Figure 22-3**.

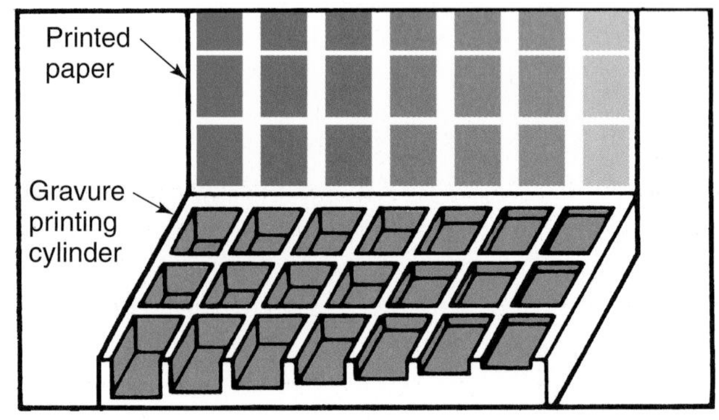

Figure 22-3. Magnified ink wells. Deep wells produce darker, denser image areas. Shallow wells produce lighter, less dense image areas.

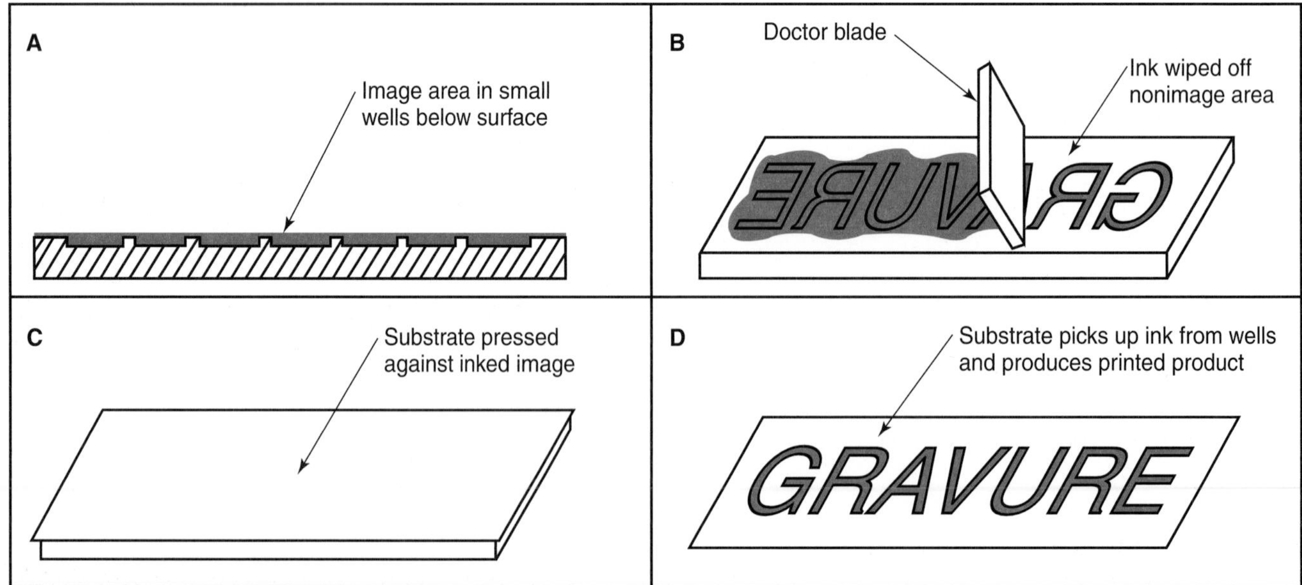

Figure 22-2. Basic steps for printing with gravure. A—Side view of an image carrier shows ink collected in tiny ink wells recessed below the nonimage surface. B—A doctor blade is slid across the image carrier to remove excess ink. C—The substrate is pressed against the inked image. D—The substrate absorbs the ink for a printed image.

Gravure as an industry

Gravure is responsible for 15% to 18% of the printing done in the United States. The U.S. Department of Commerce has identified gravure printing as an industry in itself, with its own North American Industry Classification System (NAICS) classification code number: *NAICS 323111, Commercial Gravure Printing*. Gravure printing is currently a $12 to $14 billion industry, employing tens of thousands of people.

The gravure industry is divided into three major markets: publication/advertising, packaging, and specialty products. Products typical of the publication/advertising market are newspaper supplements, magazines, catalogs, advertising and promotional material, coupons, and stamps. Examples of packaging products are folding cartons; wrapping paper; flexible packaging, such as nylon, cellophane, and foil; and labels. Specialty printing products include wall and floor coverings, automobile windshield and glass tints, plastic containers, decorative laminates (furniture and counter tops), and sanitary tissues.

Advantages and disadvantages of gravure

The main advantage of gravure printing is its simplicity. Gravure or rotogravure is a direct printing process that does not have to contend with ink and water balance, as does offset lithography. By eliminating the production variables typical of other printing processes, gravure presses can run at higher speeds.

Letterpress is a direct printing process that requires pressure for the transfer of the image. Gravure image-transfer, on the other hand, requires pressure but also utilizes the natural tendency of the paper to absorb ink from the tiny ink wells in the cylinder.

Gravure is capable of consistent, high-quality reproduction at a low per-unit cost on extremely long press runs. The microscopic cell structure of the image carrier results in the appearance of nearly continuous tone on the press sheet. Furthermore, the long life of the gravure cylinder sustains high-quality reproduction. The inks used in gravure printing dry rapidly, allowing for faster press speeds.

The main disadvantage of gravure is inherent in the printing cylinder. If an engraved gravure cylinder is damaged during shipping or production, the entire cylinder or set of cylinders may have to be re-engraved. Previously, the time involved in the preparation of the gravure cylinder made prepress operations more costly than for other printing processes. Direct digital engraving has lowered platemaking costs and drastically reduced lead time from weeks to a few hours.

Gravure Prepress Considerations

Several factors must be considered at the prepress stage. These include art preparation, page makeup, color reproduction, film preparation, and image carrier configuration. While most artwork is currently being produced digitally, about 10% is still done on boards.

Art preparation requirements

Direct digital input bypasses the traditional methods of art and copy preparation. If necessary, a scanner can be used to digitize any art and copy prepared on flexible board stock. Artwork placed on flexible stock can be scanned on a flatbed scanner, or it can be mounted to the copy drum of a rotary color scanner. Board layouts requiring color separation should be no thicker than 1/8″ (3 mm). Multilayered paste-ups can cause focusing problems with the scanner.

Both line work and continuous tone images are reproduced with a screen pattern. Because the screen pattern will disrupt fine lines, medium- or bold-faced styles are recommended with 8-point or smaller type. Small sans serif type styles reproduce better than small type in styles containing a hairline serif structure.

Reproduction films used in gravure, like those in offset lithography, will not reproduce light blue guide lines. Type matter should be proofed for consistent density and image structure. If possible, typesetting should be output directly to film. The film should equal the quality or density level required of the engraver.

Continuous tone and color requirements

Continuous tone photographs or copy should be selected for reproduction based on average contrast and good tonal separation. To avoid a loss in quality, photographs should not be enlarged more than 500% or reduced to less than 20% of original size.

Reproductions for four-color gravure can be in the form of transparency copy or reflection copy. Transparencies produce the sharpest image. Common transparency sizes are 35 mm, 2 1/4″ × 2 1/4″, 4″ × 5″, and 8″ × 10″. Transparencies with balanced tones reproduce better than light ones. A photograph that has been produced using slow-speed film will have a smaller grain pattern than one produced with high-speed film.

Digital cameras are capable of producing high-quality photographic images — today, many photographic images are produced utilizing digital technology. The same requirements regarding quality of the photograph apply to both conventional photography and digital images. For excellent results, the original must have high-quality features.

Reflection copy includes such items as color photographs, watercolor or oil-based paintings, or any other opaque copy. In reproduction, white light is reflected from the copy and passed through filters before striking unexposed film. When reflection is a problem, as with original oil paintings, a color transparency can be made for reproduction.

Color correction should be done before reproduction to compensate for impurities in the printing ink. Today, most separation and color-correction work is done electronically, but dot etching is still used in some cases. Dot etching is a manual correction technique that can be done on either the film separations or the plates.

Color evaluation and viewing of both originals and reproductions should be performed under uniform lighting conditions. The gravure industry uses the American National Standards Institute standard of 5000 Kelvin lighting for viewing.

Image carrier configurations

The three basic gravure image carrier configurations are flat, cylinder, and split cylinder, **Figure 22-4.**

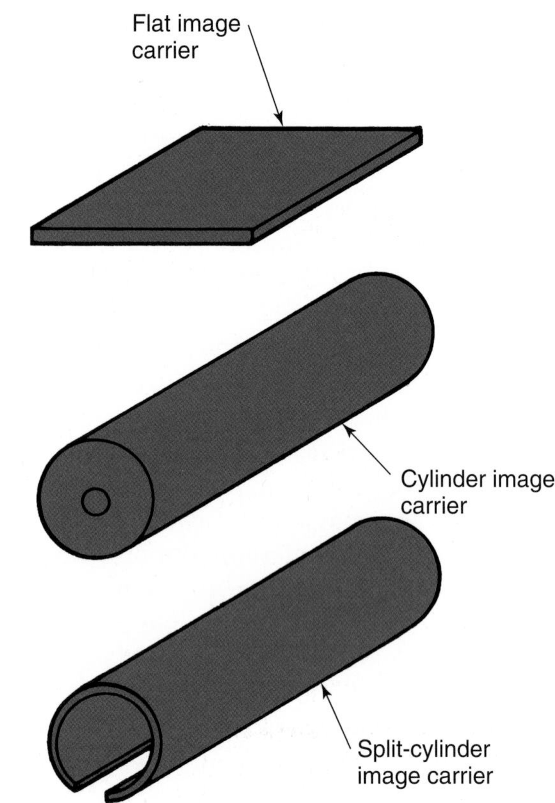

Figure 22-4. Basic image carrier configurations. The cylinder is able to produce a continuous image.

The flat image carrier is used on sheetfed presses. It is used for limited runs requiring high-quality results, such as printing stock certificates and limited editions of fine art originals.

A split cylinder (or wrap-around plate) is thicker than an offset plate. However, like the offset plate, it is flexible and designed to bend around a cylinder. In the U.S., sheet-fed gravure is used primarily for limited runs. In Europe and Asia, there is much greater use of this method. Some wrap-around presses have as many as six printing units. They cannot produce an edgeless or continuous design because they incorporate a clamping gap to hold the plate on the cylinder.

The cylinder is the most popular image carrier for gravure because it can print a *continuous* pattern. It is used for printing packaging, publications, and such products as laminates for furniture and floor coverings. A cylinder can be constructed either integral with or mounted on a shaft, **Figure 22-5**. Because of its popularity, the cylinder image carrier is the configuration that will be examined in this chapter.

Gravure Cylinder Engraving

Traditionally, cylinders have been produced using continuous tone films, carbon tissue, and chemical etching. At present, cylinder imaging is

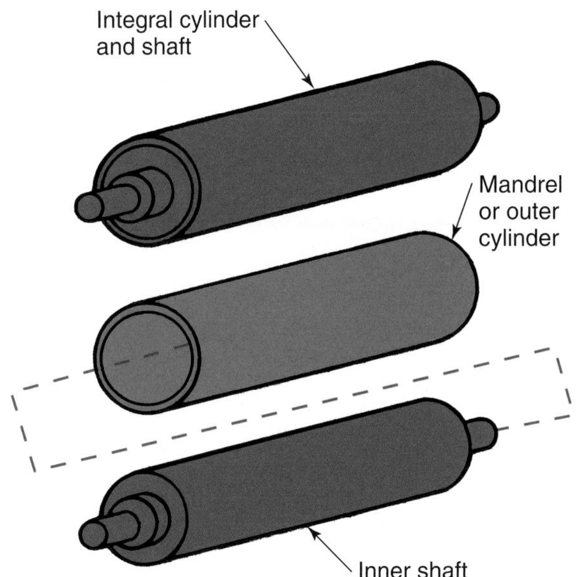

Figure 22-5. A gravure cylinder can be integral with the shaft. More commonly, however, a mandrel or outer cylinder is mounted on an inner shaft.

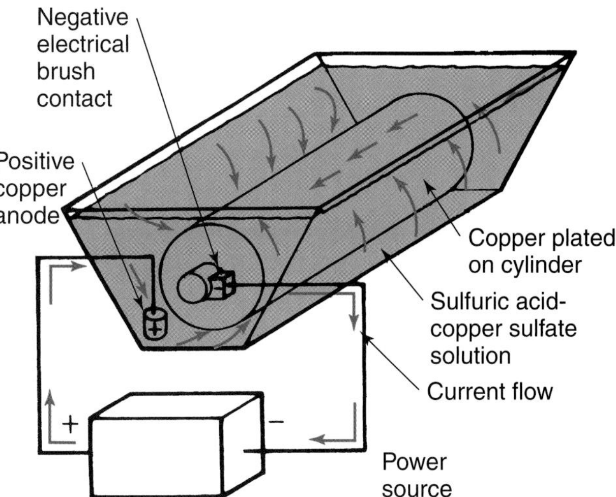

Figure 22-6. In the copper-plating process, the cylinder is submerged in an acid and copper sulfate solution. An electrical current is fed through the solution and the cylinder, causing the copper to electroplate onto the surface of the cylinder.

almost exclusively done by direct digital input to cylinder production devices — electronic and laser. The image is engraved by a cutting mechanism or a laser beam.

Gravure base cylinder

The quality of the final image depends on the construction and preparation of the cylinder. Base cylinder refers to the gravure cylinder before it is imaged. The base is made of steel or aluminum and is ground and polished to a tolerance of 0.001″ (0.025 mm).

The base is copper-plated to an additional thickness of 0.006″ to 0.030″ (0.15 mm to 0.76 mm). The copper plating is applied by an electrical-chemical process known as ***electroplating***, **Figure 22-6**.

The copper plating is oversized approximately 0.006″ (0.15 mm) in thickness, then ground down to its final diameter. A 1000-grit abrasive is used to polish the copper-coated cylinder smooth. The copper plating is tested for hardness, tensile strength, grain structure, and percent of elongation. See **Figure 22-7**.

There has been experimentation with a variety of alternate plate materials, including plastics, photopolymers, and ceramics. Success to date has not warranted changing to newer materials. Laser imaging has had success in using zinc as an image carrier material.

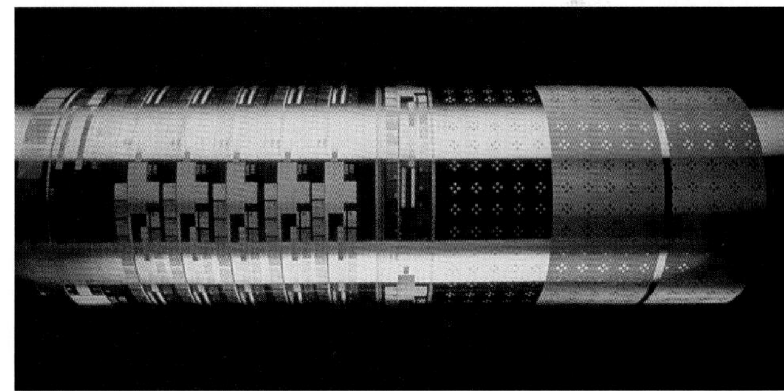

Figure 22-7. A copper-plated gravure cylinder. (Max Daetwyler Corporation)

Cylinder imaging methods

Transferring the image to the cylinder is accomplished using two major processes: electromechanical engraving and chemical engraving. In recent years, laser engraving has experienced some success. Research has been discontinued on a promising technique called Electron Beam Engraving.

Engraving techniques

Max Daetwyler Corporation (MDC) has acquired the assets of Ohio Electronic Engravers. MDC manufactures high-speed electromechanical engravers and direct laser engravers.

The MDC Laserstar direct laser engraves images into a zinc material that is chrome-plated using traditional chrome tanks and polishers. This technology is being adopted in both publication and packaging gravure markets. The advantages of the direct laser method are: quicker imaging, repeatability, significant ink savings, and greater stability (no mechanical tools). Research is taking place using polymer material as an image carrier, and there is one engraving head from MDC (called tranScribe®) that gives an intaglio look.

Publication engravers usually use multiple heads for engraving page formats or ribbons. Packaging or product engravers usually use a single head so that multiple images will match up. Very small gravure cells do not release ink well. For instance, to get a 3% dot on paper may require a 20% cell on the cylinder.

Electromechanical engraving method

Direct digital electromechanical engraving produces the most reliable cylinder for the press. Electromechanical engraving essentially replaced chemical engraving during the 1980s. Today, direct digital accounts for 95% of all cylinder-making in the United States.

In direct digital engraving, the gravure cylinder is prepared using scanned data to drive an engraving machine, **Figure 22-8**. The scanner and the engraver are electronically linked. The scanner reads the original copy and converts it to electronic data or pulses.

Electronic circuits feed the digital information, stored in the computer file, to the engraving unit. A computer-controlled engraver receives the electronic pulses that are generated by the computer file, prompting a diamond ***stylus*** cutting tool or a laser device to form tiny ink wells on the image carrier surface. The diamond stylus vibrates at approximately 4500 oscillations per second. See **Figure 22-9.**

The strength and duration of the impulses picked up from the scanning drum control the depth and size of the ink cell structure. The precision oscillating or cutting frequency is controlled by a quartz crystal, the type used in wristwatches.

Most of these machines have multiple engraving heads that work simultaneously. It takes about 40 minutes to engrave four ***ribbons*** (rows) of pages.

Figure 22-8. The image processing workstation is the heart of this fully automated direct digital engraving system. (Max Daetwyler Corporation)

Figure 22-9. This high-frequency engraving head is cutting an image into a copper-plated gravure cylinder. The diamond stylus moves in and out to cut ink wells to the correct size and depth. (Max Daetwyler Corporation)

Multiple-head machines are used for publications printing. For packaging and product printing, single-head machines are the norm.

Chemical Engraving

Chemical engraving accounts for a small percentage of the gravure cylinder market in the U.S. and worldwide. The market share has dropped because of the continued growth of direct digital engraving.

The use of carbon tissue and chemical engraving is essentially nonexistent in the U.S. today, because of the environmental issues involved. Only 2% of the engraving is done by direct etching.

Laser-beam engraving method

Since being introduced in the late 1970s, the use of lasers for engraving has been limited. The cylinder was originally coated with plastic, and the laser functioned as a cutting tool. The laser vaporized the plastic to form the cells. An epoxy coating was used because the highly polished copper reflected 95% of the laser output, leaving only 5% for engraving.

Copper did not prove to be a suitable metal for use with the laser. Later developments have demonstrated that zinc is a more suitable metal base for laser engraving.

Cylinder evaluation and finishing

Once the gravure cylinder is etched or engraved, it must be closely inspected. Under 12× or greater magnification, the ink cell structure is checked for flaws. Cylinder correction can be accomplished by spot plating, burnishing with charcoal, lacquering, or other methods.

Once correction (if necessary) is completed, the cylinder is chrome-plated to increase the life of the image carrier. Plating is typically 0.0003″ (0.008 mm) thick. Chromium is harder than copper and can better withstand the friction of the doctor blade.

Proofing of completed cylinders is an expensive process, but can be done if the customer requires it to be done. Less on-press proofing is done today because the cylinder engraving process has become more accurate and turn-around times have become shorter.

Clients have developed greater confidence in digital proofs as the digital process has become more predictable, **Figure 22-10.** The proof must meet the client's approval.

Figure 22-10. A quality control technician examines a digital proof to make sure the final product will meet the customer's specifications.
(Max Daetwyler Corporation)

Halftone gravure technology

Halftone gravure, also called offset gravure, uses halftone color separations to produce films for the gravure process. It was introduced as a way to allow advertising agencies and gravure printers to use films prepared for the offset process in gravure, instead of having to produce a set of expensive continuous-tone separations.

The gravure industry developed the technology in order to use a generic or universal halftone film for both offset work and gravure work. However, the use of halftone gravure has diminished as digital technology has brought about the reality of filmless engraving. It is now possible to bring images directly from a prepress system into a computer for electronic engraving.

Gravure Printing Press

Next to the flexographic press, the gravure press has one of the simplest reproduction methods. Unlike offset, the gravure press does not require a dampening system. Cheaper grades of paper can be run at higher press speeds without the threat of web tear.

Press configuration

Gravure printing typically uses a web-fed or rotary press, **Figure 22-11.** Publication presses are rated at speeds of up to 3500 fpm. Packaging presses are rated at speeds up to 2500 fpm. Realistic operating ranges are from 2800–3300 fpm in publication presses and 600–1500 fpm in packaging. A press running at 2000–2500 feet per minute has a web that is traveling around 30 miles per hour.

Printing units

The gravure press is made up of a number of printing units, each containing a printing cylinder. The web is fed through each unit, **Figure 22-12.** The combination of printing units can range from 4 to 16 or more. The number of units depends on the number of pages being printed and the amount of color work being produced.

Cylinder action

At each unit, the cylinder is immersed in a trough or fountain of ink. As the cylinder turns, its tiny ink wells fill with ink. Modern gravure printing presses can have cylinders over 150″ (3810 mm) in width.

Figure 22-11. This multicolor gravure press prints from a web. (Bobst Group, Inc.)

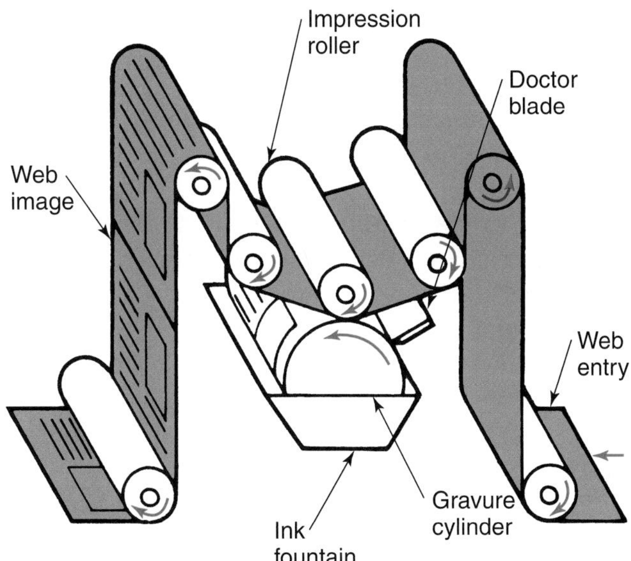

Figure 22-12. Movement of the web through a gravure printing unit.

Doctor blade

The doctor blade removes excess ink from the raised, nonimage area of the cylinder. Blade thickness is typically 0.006″ (0.15 mm) with a set angle of 20°. The blade can be stainless steel or plastic, but is usually made of blue spring steel. Both thickness and set angle can vary.

Impression roller

An impression roller is used to press the paper or substrate against the printing cylinder. The impression roller usually supplies between 100 lbs. to 200 lbs. per linear inch of pressure at the printing nip point. Impression rollers are made of rubber, neoprene, and other synthetic products.

Impression rollers should be tested for the degree of hardness as determined by the printing substrate. Resilience and solvent resistance are important to the continued quality of printing.

Substrates

Gravure printing is done on a wide variety of substrates, including inexpensive paper stocks. Paper should be evaluated by strength and ink absorption. Packaging and specialty products typically use such substrates as film, cellophane, cloth, plastic, and corrugated board. The gravure press runs about a 32-pound newsprint stock and a 35- to 40-pound coated stock for publication work.

Electrostatic assist

Many gravure printing presses use a process known as ***electrostatic assist*** to improve ink transfer to the substrate, especially when the surface is hard or has poor ink receptivity. If ink transfer is incomplete or inconsistent, highlights or light tone values will have a speckled appearance, or color reproduction may shift in hue. In electrostatic assist, electrical charges between the impression roller (negative) and the printing cylinder (positive) create a force that achieves a nearly complete release of ink from the etched cells. See **Figure 22-13.**

Warning: Precautions should be taken to prevent fires on the gravure press when electrical charges are exposed to volatile solvent-based inks.

Gravure process inks

The process color inks used in gravure printing differ in both hue and composition from the average offset lithography and letterpress inks.

Classification of gravure inks

The classification is a guide and as such cannot encompass all technologies and technical variants used to address the needs and demands of the ever

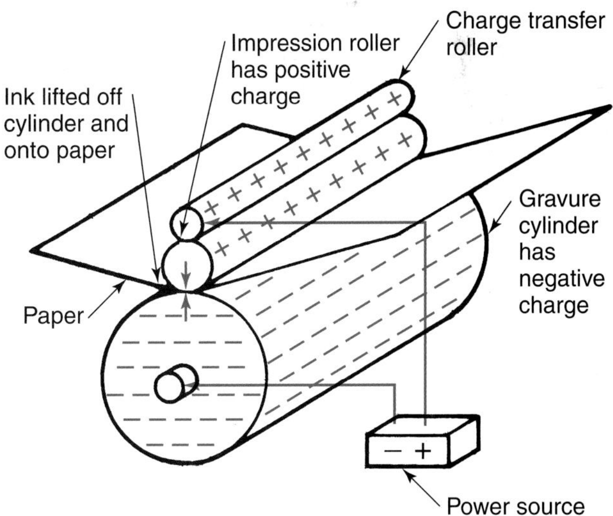

Figure 22-13. In electrostatic assist, a power source feeds a positive charge to the transfer roller which, in turn, transfers the charge to the impression roller and the paper. The gravure cylinder receives a simultaneous negative charge. A magnetic force is created, helping to pull ink out of the wells onto the substrate.

changing gravure market. It is important to utilize technical information and proper handling information furnished by the manufacturer.

These are the classifications:

- Type A: This type of ink is mostly used for newspaper supplements, catalogs, advertising inserts, and similar publication work.
- Type B: This ink is formulated mainly for publication printing on coated stock.
- Type C: These inks are principally used for package printing on foil, paperboard, coated and uncoated paper, metallized paper, and some types of fabrics.
- Type D: These inks work well when printing on plastic film.
- Type E: These inks are often used on paper and paper board, shellac or nitrocellulose primed foil, and many coated papers and boards.
- Type M: These inks are made from polystyrene resins that are used to produce low-cost top lacquers.
- Type T: High gloss type of ink, but the health and safety hazards associated with chlorinated rubber has almost eliminated its use.
- Type V: These inks are used to print on vinyls. Decorative products, which include labels, cartons, shrink sleeves, and wall coverings are typical examples.
- Type W: These are water-based inks that are primarily used in package printing and product gravure.
- Type X: Inks not associated any of the listed types are classified as Type X (Miscellaneous).

Ink standards

Standards were adopted in 1984 for halftone gravure. The original objective was to establish a universal film, which could be used for both gravure and offset printing. For this to work, the gravure and offset ink colors had to be similar, and the decision was made to modify the gravure coated paper Group V inks to be more similar to the offset SWOP colors.

The gravure yellow was made greener and cleaner, the red became bluer (more like a magenta), and the gravure blue, greener (more like cyan). The resulting ink, formulated for coated paper, was designated as Group 6/SWOP.

The gravure Group I inks are designed for use on newsprint and supercalendered papers used mainly for supplement, insert, or tabloid work. SWOP standards do not exist for uncoated paper.

All publication gravure today is essentially using SWOP standards. The SWOP standards are not very applicable in packaging and product gravure, however.

Common properties of gravure ink are opacity, drying speed, gloss, and fineness of pigment grind. Gravure inks are thinner than those used in other printing processes. The ink viscosity (weight) is much lower than most inks. They are usually diluted with 50% or more solvent.

Solvent-based gravure inks are considered highly volatile. The gravure pressroom should be isolated from unnecessary traffic. Ventilation must be ample, and fumes should be filtered through beds of charcoal to absorb the odors and vapors. Petroleum shortages, rising costs, and regulation by the U.S. Environmental Protection Agency has increasingly forced the printing industry to substitute water-based inks for solvent-based inks.

Inks should never run too low in the press fountain, or air entrapment and foaming may occur. Like any other process inks, gravure inks contain impurities. Pressroom results determine the color correction requirements used in color separation.

Review Questions

Please do not write in this book. Write your answers on a separate sheet of paper.

1. In what printing process are images manually etched or engraved onto a printing plate?
   a. Gravure
   b. Rotogravure
   c. Intaglio
   d. Offset lithography
2. Write the four basic steps in gravure printing.
3. List at least three advantages of gravure printing.
4. List the common properties of gravure ink.
5. Why is the cylinder a popular image carrier configuration?
6. What are the methods of cylinder imaging?
7. Why is a gravure cylinder chrome-plated?
8. *True or false?* Halftone gravure is not compatible with electromechanical engraving.
9. What is the purpose of electrostatic assist?
10. Why must precautions be taken on a gravure press during electrostatic assist?

High production rates can be achieved by large, automated screen process presses such as this flatbed cylinder press. This type of press is used primarily for long runs on flat substrates, such as plastic or paper. (The Lehigh Press, Inc.)

Screen Printing

23

Learning Objectives

After studying this chapter, you will be able to:

- Describe various applications of screen printing.
- Select the proper screen fabric.
- Select and prepare screen frames as support devices.
- Prepare and attach fabric to a frame.
- Cut and prepare stencils by hand.
- Prepare photographic stencils.
- Indicate the uses for each type of screen printing press.

Important Terms

burned edges
cell distortion
durometer
filament
mesh count
percent open area
retarders
sawtoothing
squeegee
tensiometer

Screen printing is the process of forcing ink through a porous fabric and the open areas of a stencil to produce an image. It has been known by several names: serigraphy, mitography, silk screen, stencil printing, and screen process. Only two terms are commonly used today: *serigraphy* in the field of fine arts and *screen printing* in the graphic communications industry.

Screen printing can be a very simple process, requiring only a few inexpensive tools and materials, or it can be extremely complex, requiring an array of sophisticated equipment and production techniques. The deciding factors are the complexity and level of quality required in the finished piece.

History of Screen Printing

Screen printing is one of the oldest printing processes. Its origin is difficult to prove, but the Chinese, Egyptians, and Japanese all are credited with first using a stencil process. The Japanese combined a screen with a stencil, cutting a stencil from two sheets of paper and sandwiching silk or hair between the sheets to form a screen. Printing with stencils spread to Europe in the fifteenth century and eventually to the American colonies.

In America, many people contributed to the process through experimentation. In 1914, a multicolor screen printing process was perfected by John Pilsworth, a San Francisco commercial artist. In 1929, Louis F. D'Autremont, a screen printer in Ohio, developed the first material for knife-cut stencils. His stencil, called Profilm, was difficult to cut and adhere.

Several years later Joe Ulano, a New York screen printer, developed his own knife-cut stencil material, called Nufilm. D'Autremont and Ulano became involved in a court battle over patent rights, which was eventually settled in favor of D'Autremont. However, Ulano's Nufilm was a better, more easily used stencil, and it became the industry standard.

With a working stencil available, paint manufacturers saw a potential market for their products, and screen printing was established as an industrial process. The applications for screen printing were limited by the availability of hand-cut stencils and inks. During World War II, screen printing began to have wider applications, in particular for identifying military vehicles and related equipment.

Modern screen printing developed in the 1940s and 1950s as new materials and production techniques were introduced. Today, rapid technological advances continue to improve the process and lead to expanded markets.

Screen Printing Applications

The hallmark of screen printing is its diverse applications, **Figure 23-1**. Posters, plastic bottles, drinking glasses, soda bottles, mirrors, metal surfaces, wood, textiles, printed circuit boards, product displays, and vinyl binders are just a few of its applications. End products are as diverse as a football jersey or a traffic sign.

Figure 23-1. Screen printing is used on a variety of products. (John Walker)

Screen printing is an extremely versatile process. Frequently, it is the *only* process that can do the job. Like any process, it has advantages and disadvantages.

The advantages of screen printing are:

- Images can be printed on a wide variety of substrates.
- The production process is relatively easy.
- Capital expenditures are low compared to other printing processes.
- Images can be printed with glitter, flock, and other decorative finishes.
- The ink film is very resilient due to the extreme thickness of the ink deposit (up to 100 times as thick as other printing processes).

Several disadvantages are:

- Rate of production is slow.
- Ink mileage is poor.
- Details and fine line images may be difficult to print.

The designer creates images in much the same way as with other printing processes. Manual techniques are still used in the industry, but many designs are generated on the computer. Drawing and page composition programs are readily available. The designer may also use existing digitized material. A common output device is the imagesetter. (Refer to Chapters 5-7 for detailed information.)

Screen Printing Process

The basic equipment needed for screen printing is screen fabric, a frame, a stencil, ink, a squeegee, and a substrate.

First, porous fabric is stretched across the frame. Next, a stencil is adhered to the fabric, blocking out portions of the fabric and leaving open the desired image areas. Ink is poured onto the fabric and forced through the image areas using a rubber or plastic blade called a ***squeegee***. The ink is deposited on a substrate below, producing an image of the cut stencil, **Figure 23-2**. Multiple prints are accomplished by repeating the squeegee action on a new substrate.

Squeegees

A hand-held squeegee has a smooth wooden or aluminum handle and a rubber blade. Squeegee blades are usually 3/16″ to 3/8″ thick and 2″ high.

Figure 23-2. Screen printing. A—Hold the squeegee at a 45° angle, press down, and pull it across the image. At the end of the stroke, use the squeegee to scoop up the ink and return it to the top of the frame. B—The image is transferred from the stencil to the substrate below the frame. (Bowling Green State University, Visual Communication Technology Program)

Squeegee blades are rated by hardness, as determined by a ***durometer***. A durometer reading of 60 is considered soft, 70 medium, and 80 hard. A #70 medium squeegee blade is recommended for general use.

Blades are also distinguished by material used. Neoprene blades (black) are the least durable and require frequent sharpening. Plastic blades (tan) are most frequently used and provide good durability and easy sharpening. Amber (or orange) and translucent polyurethane blades provide maximum durability; however, they are sometimes difficult to sharpen. See **Figure 23-3**.

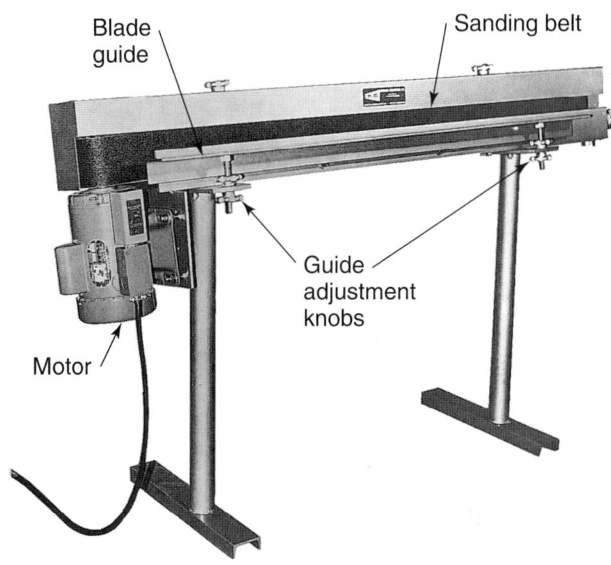

Figure 23-3. This squeegee blade sharpening machine uses a long sanding belt to grind new edges on used blades. (Advance Graphics Equipment)

Different substrates require different blade edges, **Figure 23-4**. The six squeegee blade shapes are:

- *Squared-edge.* Used for flat surfaces and general-purpose printing.
- *Squared-edge with rounded corners.* Gives extra-heavy ink deposits on flat substrates. Used when a light color will be printed on a dark substrate.
- *Rounded-edge.* Used primarily in textile printing where an extra-heavy ink film is required.

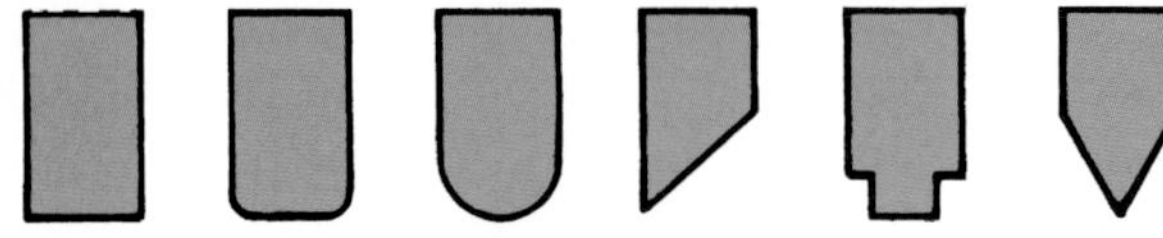

Figure 23-4. Squeegee blade shapes used for printing on various substrates.

- *Single-sided beveled edge.* Used for printing on glass.
- *Double-sided beveled edge with flat point.* Used for printing on ceramics.
- *Double-sided beveled edge.* Used for printing on cylindrical objects such as bottles and containers.

Machine squeegees are similar to hand squeegees. The machine squeegee handle is rectangular and has a thicker profile, **Figure 23-5.**

Squeegee blades lose their shape with use. Always keep squeegee edges sharp. Problems associated with dull squeegee blades include:

- Bubbles in the ink film.
- Poor edge definition in print.
- Excessive ink film thickness.
- Loss of detail.
- Spread images.
- Poor ink mileage.

Figure 23-5. A squeegee on a screen printing press is automatically pulled across the image.

Screen inks

Selecting the proper ink is critical to the production of screen-printed images. The type of ink depends upon the type of stencil being used, the substrate, and the intended product. Should the ink be resistant to ultraviolet rays from the sun? Is moisture-resistance important? These and other questions must be answered before the proper ink can be selected. Additional concerns include resistance to fading, chipping, and scratching; chemical resistance to acids and alkalis, and the ability to withstand the effects of vacuum forming.

Screen solvents

Screen printing solvents are classified as thinners, retarders, and washups. ***Thinners*** are solvents added to ink to change the viscosity (thickness) of the ink. Thinners do not affect drying time.

The viscosity of thinned ink should resemble pancake syrup or 40-weight motor oil at room temperature. High ink viscosity may cause a mesh pattern to appear in the printed ink film.

Retarders are solvents added to ink to change (thin) the viscosity *and* slow (retard) the drying time. Retarders are necessary with some fast-drying inks that may clog mesh openings in the screen fabric. This is an especially important factor in warm climates, where solvent evaporation and drying is accelerated.

Washup solvents are used to remove ink from the screen. They are inexpensive, and their only function is to dissolve ink.

Warning: Prolonged exposure to solvent fumes can be harmful. Provide adequate ventilation and air exchange.

Drying systems

At one time, large drying racks were used to air-dry substrates. Modern oven drying systems allow much faster drying and more efficient use of floor space. Three methods of heat transfer are utilized for oven drying an ink film: conduction, convection, and radiation.

Conduction occurs when heat is generated within an object by contact with a heat source. *Convection* heating involves using warm air that transfers its heat to the object. *Radiation* heating occurs when heat is generated within an object by exposure to radiation. The popularity of radiation heating is growing with the formulation of new inks that can be cured (dried) by infrared or ultraviolet radiation.

Most modern drying systems use a conveyor, **Figure 23-6**. The speed of the conveyor belt determines the length of time the ink is subjected to heat transfer. Faster-drying inks use a faster conveyor belt speed, and vice versa.

Figure 23-6. A conveyor carries screen-printed items, such as these shirts, through the drying oven.

Figure 23-7. Wood and metal alloy are the most common materials used to manufacture screen printing frames. (Bowling Green State University, Visual Communication Technology Program)

Screen Frames

The screen frame serves several important functions. A frame:

- Provides a means of attaching fabric at the proper tension.
- Provides rigidity and dimensional stability.
- Resists mechanical stress and warpage.
- Resists chemical action and corrosion.
- Provides a means for register.

Frame materials

Materials used to manufacture screen frames include wood, metal alloy, steel, and plastic. Wood and metal alloy are the most common, **Figure 23-7**.

Wood frames

Although metal alloy frames have achieved wide use, wood frames are still popular for general screen printing applications. A hardwood such as maple is ideal, but pine is most frequently used because of its low cost.

Wood frames may be constructed using screws, corrugated fasteners, dowels, splines, or nails. Whatever technique is used, it is wise to remember that frames are continuously subjected to mechanical and chemical stress.

The constant deluge of water on the frame and fasteners is one such chemical stress. Avoid metal fasteners when possible; rust and corrosion will cause the frame joints to loosen and weaken. Wood frames should be glued using an adhesive that is not water-soluble. A waterproof sealer should be applied before the frame contacts moisture.

Wood frames may be constructed, or they may be purchased assembled or ready-to-assemble. As frame size increases, frame sidewall dimensions should also increase to withstand the mechanical strain of the fabric after tensioning. A larger frame also has less tendency to warp.

As a rule of thumb, frame sizes up to 15″ × 15″ should be constructed of 1 1/8″ × 1 1/8″ frame lumber. Sizes up to 24″ × 24″ should be constructed of 1 5/8″ ×1 5/8″ frame lumber. Beyond this size, frame lumber 2″ × 2″ or larger should be used.

Metal alloy frames

Metal alloy frames provide greater rigidity and dimensional stability than wood frames and are essential in commercial screen printing. While not susceptible to chemical attack from water, these frames have poor resistance to acids and soda solutions.

Metal alloy frames are available in a variety of styles and sidewall dimensions. Most have built-in mechanical clamps for attaching and stretching the screen fabric.

Metal alloy is rigid enough for frame sizes up to 36″ × 36″. For larger frames, steel is preferred. Some frames are constructed using a combination of metal and wood. The fabric may be glued to the wooden part of the frame.

Frame profiles

If fabric tension causes the frame to bend inward, the fabric tension will be varied, causing the image to lose register or become distorted.

To compensate for the inward pull, some screen printers intentionally deflect frame sidewalls inward when attaching fabric, **Figure 23-8**. After the tensioned fabric is attached, the frame automatically relaxes, resulting in an outward pull of the frame sidewalls to balance the inward pull of the tensioned fabric.

Print size

Maximum print size is determined by the inside dimensions of the screen frame. Generally, the non-image area should be twice the size of the image area. An ideal frame size is four times the image area. Such dimensions are necessary for two reasons: proper flexibility of the fabric without excessive squeegee pressure and proper ***off-contact distance*** (distance from the screen to the substrate).

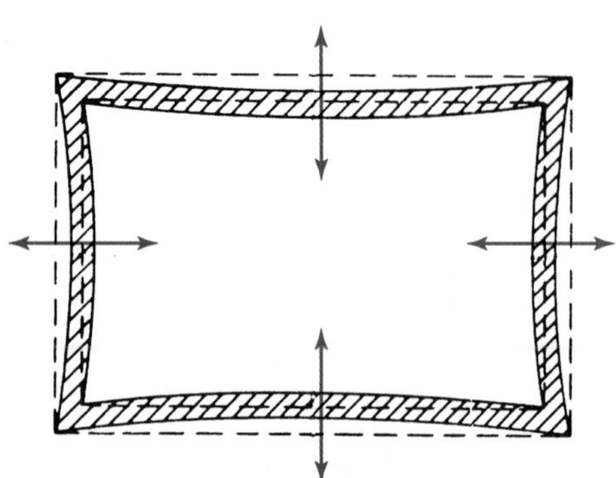

Figure 23-8. An inward deflection of the frame causes an outward pull on the fabric, which produces fabric tension. (Screen Printing Association International)

Screen Fabrics

Screen fabrics are classified according to filament, mesh count, strength, and weave pattern.

Filaments

Filaments are threads. A fabric may be either multifilament or monofilament, **Figure 23-9**. ***Multifilament*** means there are several strands of material per filament. For example, sewing thread may have multiple strands. ***Monofilament*** means each filament is a single strand of material, or one thread. Fishing line is monofilament.

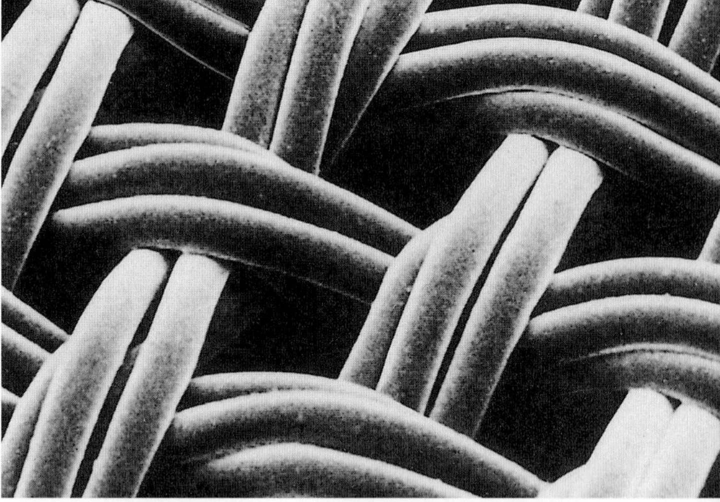

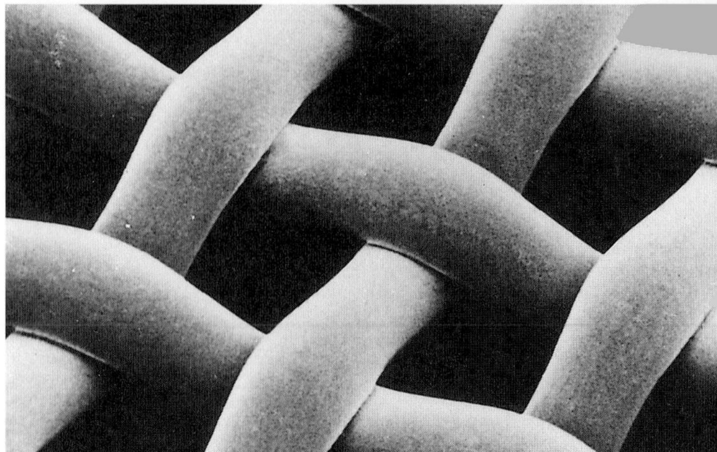

Figure 23-9. Compare the magnified views of a multifilament fabric and a monofilament fabric. (Autotype USA)

Multifilament fabrics usually print a slightly uneven ink film. The unevenness is due to the irregular size and shape of the cells caused by the differing cross sections of each thread. Multifilament fabrics lose some dimensional stability as a result of the stretching (elongation) associated with their "rope" construction.

Monofilament fabrics provide better ink film thickness uniformity and dimensional stability than multifilaments. However, monofilaments cost more than multifilaments and are not as durable.

Mesh count

Fabric ***mesh count*** is specified by the number of threads (or strands) per linear inch. The higher the mesh count, the better the reproduction of fine details. A high mesh count also minimizes ***sawtoothing***, a distortion in the design contours that causes a notched effect. As mesh count increases, fabric strength and durability decrease.

The mesh count in multifilament fabrics is specified by digits ranging from 5 to 25. Mesh count per linear inch is estimated by multiplying the digit by 10. Thus, if the mesh number is 12, the mesh count per linear inch is 120 (12 × 10 = 120). This number is only *approximate* because little standardization exists between manufacturers. A 12-mesh fabric, for instance, could have 115 to 129 threads per linear inch.

Monofilament fabrics are specified by *actual* thread count. A 160-mesh fabric has exactly 160 threads per linear inch. The same is true for metal mesh.

Fabric strength

Fabric strength is directly related to thread diameter. The strength of multifilament fabrics is specified by X, XX, or XXX. Single X is the smallest diameter; double X is stronger than single X; triple X is the largest diameter and yields the strongest fabric. As mesh count increases, thread diameter must decrease or no porous areas (open cells) will exist, **Figure 23-10**.

Monofilament fabrics use a different system to specify strength. Either the actual thread diameter will be given, expressed in thousandths of an inch, or a letter rating will be given: S = small, T = medium, and HD = heavy-duty. In general, most screen printers select XX-multifilament and T-monofilament fabrics.

Figure 23-10. Magnified view of open cells in the image area on screen fabric.

Weave patterns

Weave pattern determines how the vertical and horizontal threads are woven into the fabric. Threads that run horizontally are called ***weft threads***. Threads that run vertically are called ***warp threads***.

Three weave patterns used for screen fabrics are shown in **Figure 23-11**. The *plain* or *taffeta weave* is a general-purpose weave used in most situations requiring good strength and sharp detail.

The *gauze weave* is strong, so it is generally selected for extremely long runs. With this weave, the squeegee must move parallel to the double threads. Fine details cannot be printed due to the double threads.

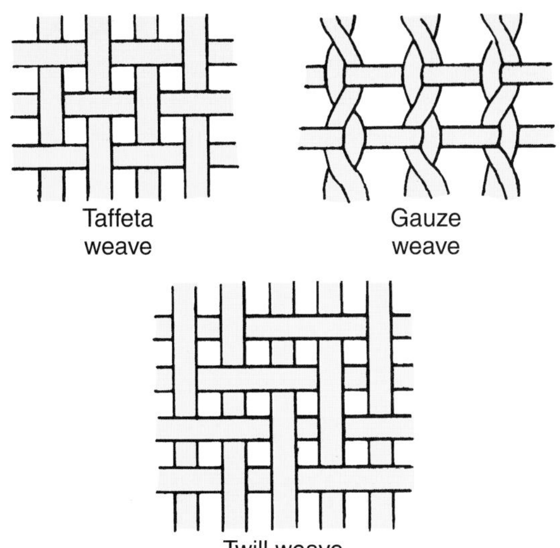

Figure 23-11. Three types of fabric weaves used for screen printing. (Screen Printing Association International)

The *twill weave* causes uneven ink film thickness and poor edge definition, resulting in a more pronounced sawtooth effect. Twill weave fabrics are not capable of producing fine details.

Ink film thickness and uniformity are related to weave pattern. ***Percent open area*** is the percentage of area per square inch through which ink can pass. The greater the percent open area, the thicker the ink film and the weaker the fabric.

Cell size is the distance across individual open areas between adjacent threads. It is specified in thousandths of an inch. As cell size increases, the percent open area increases, and fabric strength decreases.

Types of Fabric

Three types of fabric are used as screens: natural, synthetic, and metal mesh. Natural fabrics are always multifilament. Synthetic fabrics may be either multifilament or monofilament. Metal mesh is always a monofilament. Natural fabrics are seldom used in industry today. Instead, most screen printers prefer synthetic and metal fabrics.

Silk

Silk is a natural fabric once used by most screen printers, giving rise to the term *silk screen*. Today, it is only used by serigraphers. Silk has good durability and dimensional stability. It cannot be used with certain chemicals.

Polyester

Polyester is a synthetic fabric available as a multifilament or monofilament. The fabric has wide applications in almost all areas of screen printing and can be used with any stencil. It is very durable in both multifilament and monofilament forms, but is slightly better as a multifilament. Monofilament polyester has better ink film uniformity and the best dimensional stability of any natural or synthetic fabric. Polyester, particularly monofilament, is very popular.

Nylon

Nylon is a synthetic fabric available only as a monofilament. Nylon has relatively good dimensional stability if used in a climate-controlled environment. It is the most durable of the natural or synthetic fabrics, and adapts well when printing on rough-textured or uneven substrates. Its flexibility makes it suitable for printing on concave or convex surfaces.

Metal mesh

Metal mesh is a monofilament. Typically, it is stainless steel, but it may also be bronze, copper, or brass. It is used for printing with heated inks on plastic or when the ultimate in dimensional stability is required. Metal mesh is durable yet fragile. Any kinks or deformities usually require replacement of the mesh.

Metalized polyester

Metalized polyester is a hybrid monofilament fabric with a nickel-plated coating. The metallic surface is about 3µ (microns) thick. The coating increases dimensional stability for printing critical tolerances, as with electronic circuit board printing. Each thread is "welded" in position. Metalized polyester is more durable than metal mesh and not as susceptible to kinks or deformities.

Fabric Attaching and Tensioning

In practice, attaching and tensioning (stretching) the fabric to the frame is carried out in one operation. The fabric can be attached to the frame in four ways: stapling, cord and groove, mechanical clamping, and adhesive bonding.

Stapling

Staples are the least desirable means for attaching and tensioning fabric, **Figure 23-12**. Staples are placed in the center of each side of the wood frame. The fabric is stretched to a near corner and stapled. Gradually pull and tension the fabric while installing the staples. Finish the side by placing the staples at an angle, about 1/8″ apart. Then, the opposite side is pulled and stapled. The remaining side is finished in the same way.

Avoid stapling when other techniques are available since uniform fabric tension is difficult to achieve. Staples puncture and tear the fabric. Tears weaken the weave and can lead to premature fabric failure. Staple tape may be helpful, but it will not solve the basic problems associated with the process.

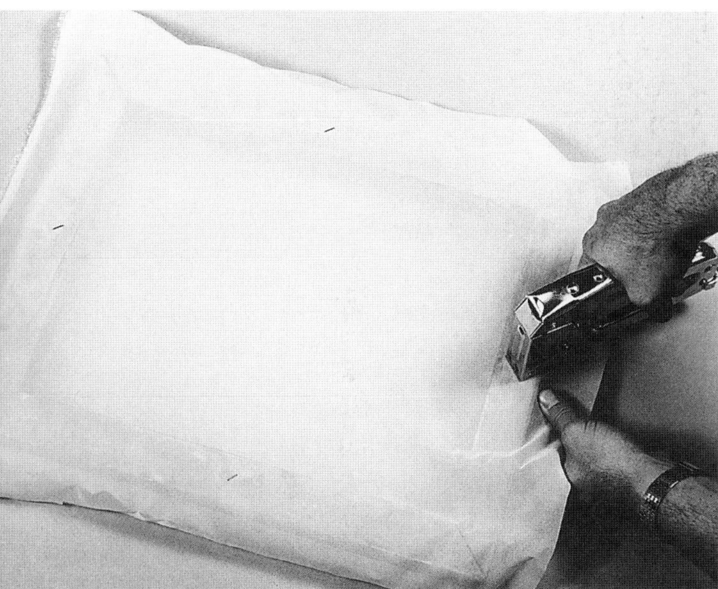

Figure 23-12. Staples can be used to attach and tension screens for low-quality printing.

Cord and groove

The cord and groove method is popular in small screen applications where printing requirements are not critical. A cotton or plastic cord is forced into a groove in the frame, **Figure 23-13**.

As the cord moves down into the groove, the fabric is stretched across the frame. Grooved-frame lumber and cord are available from a variety of manufacturers, or frames can be made by the printer.

Cords of varying sizes are available. Care should be taken to correctly match cord diameter and groove width so a tight fit is obtained without causing damage to the frame or fabric. A groove depth one and one-half times the cord diameter is recommended.

Mechanical clamping

Mechanical clamps are available on many aluminum frames. The fabric is clamped in position on all four sides. Then, screws are turned to force the movable clamps outward, resulting in fabric tension.

With mechanical clamping, the fabric may be tensioned to exact specifications. The screw threads should be lubricated periodically to prevent corrosion and wear.

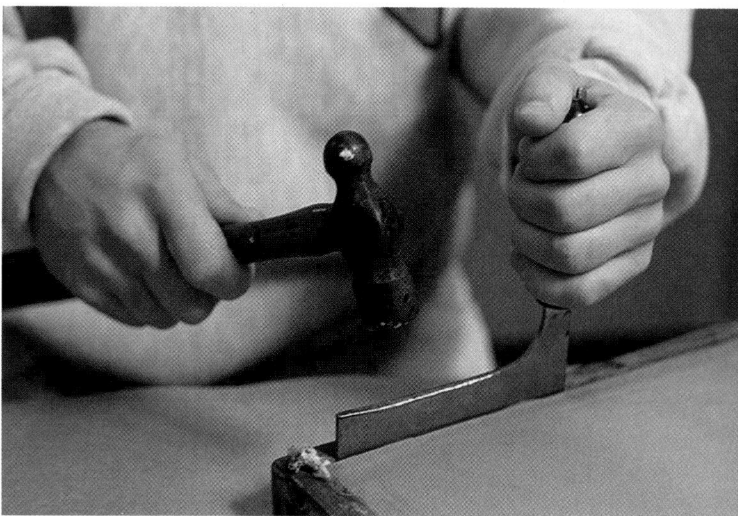

Figure 23-13. Fabric is being stretched using the cord and groove method. As the cord and fabric are forced into the groove, tension is placed on the fabric. (Bowling Green State University, Visual Communication Technology Program)

Adhesive bonding

To attach fabric to a frame with adhesive, a stretching machine is necessary. Stretching machines may be mechanical or pneumatic, **Figure 23-14**.

With a stretching machine, fabric may be tensioned to exact specifications without cell distortion. ***Cell distortion*** is the result of tensioning the fabric in one direction without stretching it equally in the other direction, **Figure 23-15**. Cell distortion is

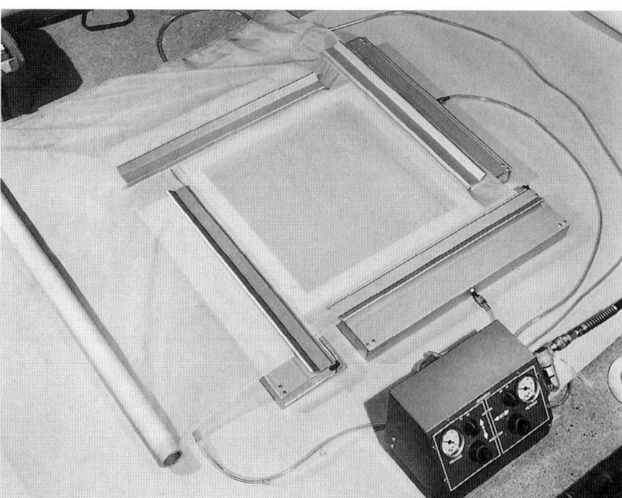

Figure 23-14 An automatic or pneumatic fabric stretching machine. Controlled air pressure is used to pull the fabric in all directions, resulting in an even stretch. (Autotype USA)

always present when using means other than a stretching machine.

Stretching machines are generally used for high-volume printing, which compensates for the high initial cost of the machine. They are also used when fine detail and ink film uniformity are critical, such as printed circuit boards and four-color process printing.

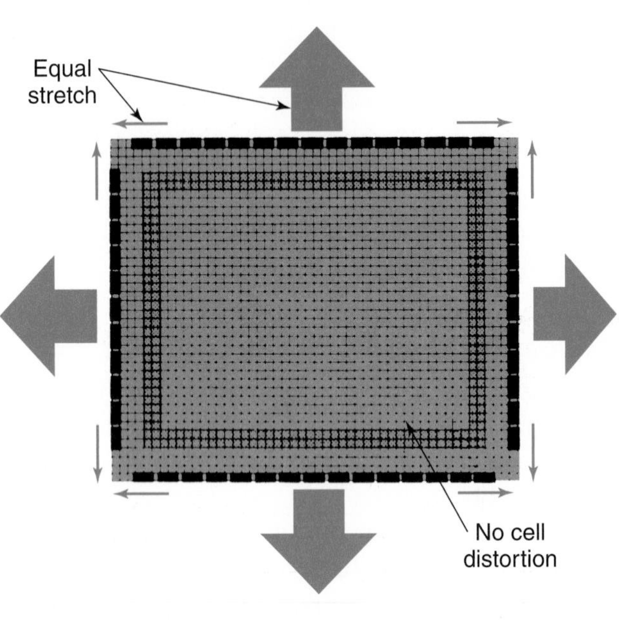

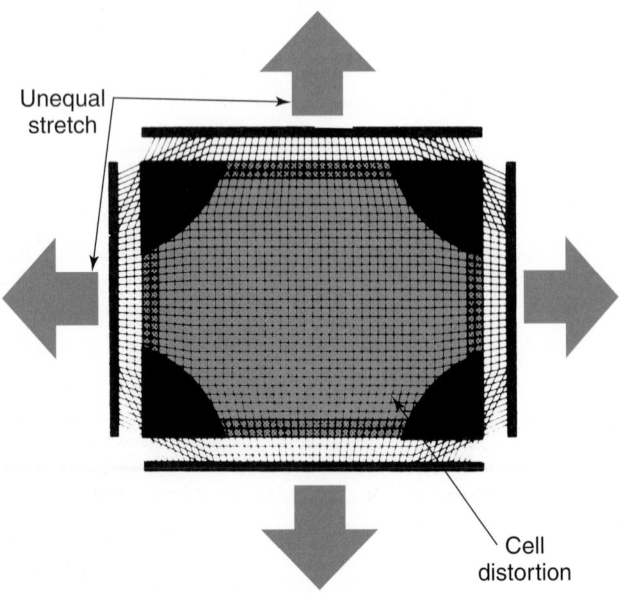

Figure 23-15. With equal tension applied, cells or openings in the fabric are not distorted. (Tetko, Inc.)

Measuring fabric tension

Screen tension, or tightness, can be accurately measured in two ways: by finding the percent of fabric stretch or by using a tension meter.

Percent stretch is a simple technique that entails taking very accurate measurements before and during tensioning. Then, the percent of increase is found.

For example, a fabric at rest before tensioning is measured and marked at 10″, the inside measurement of the frame being 10″ × 10″. As the fabric is tensioned, measurements are taken until the original 10″ distance is stretched to 10 1/2″.

Marking and measuring should be done in at least six different locations. It should be done adjacent and parallel to each of the four frame sides, and in the middle of the frame, horizontally and vertically. To find the percent increase, divide the original measurement (10″) by the stretched measurement (10 1/2″ or 10.5″). The result (1.05) is then multiplied by 100 to determine the percent increase (105%). Perform the calculation for each of the locations. For proper tensioning, the percent stretch should be equal for all measurements.

The percent stretch procedure can be used when stretching fabric by cord and groove, mechanical clamp, or a stretching machine.

When using a tension meter, measurements are taken from all areas of the fabric. A ***tensiometer*** measures tension in Newtons per centimeter. The reading is compared to other areas of the fabric and to the manufacturer's specifications, **Figure 23-16**.

Relax time between tensioning and measuring is important to allow the fabric to reach equilibrium at the new tension level. Tensiometers are used in conjunction with mechanical or pneumatic stretching machines.

Fabric treatment

For the stencil and fabric to adhere to each other, the fabric must be cleaned chemically, mechanically, or both. Proper cleaning removes surface grease, airborne contaminants, and residue.

Chemical treatment alters the adhesion characteristics of the fabric and allows for better bonding between the stencil and fabric. Mechanical treatment changes the physical properties of the fabric to enhance the bond between stencil and fabric. Usually, chemical and mechanical treatments are done only once with new fabric. Repeated use of

Figure 23-16. A tensiometer measures fabric stretch. (Bowling Green State University, Visual Communication Technology Program)

these treatments will degrade the fabric and cause premature fabric failure.

Cleaning the fabric is usually referred to as "degreasing" and should be completed just before a new stencil is adhered to the fabric. The following treatments are suggested:

- *Silk.* No mechanical or chemical treatment. Degrease with a 2% solution of trisodium-phosphate (TSP) or other caustic soda.
- *Nylon.* No mechanical treatment. Chemically treat once with a 5% solution of metacresol (cresylic acid). Remove from the screen with cold water. Degrease with a 5% solution of trisodium-phosphate (TSP) or other caustic soda.
- *Polyester.* If a monofilament, mechanically treat with silicon carbide to roughen the threads. Do not use household cleaners, which damage threads and clog mesh. Treat only once if the fabric is new. Multifilament polyester does not require mechanical treatment or chemical treatment. Degrease with a 5% solution of acetic acid, and rinse with cold water.
- *Stainless steel mesh.* No mechanical treatment. Flame-treating is optional; always following the manufacturer's directions. Degrease with a 5% solution of trisodium-phosphate (TSP) or other caustic soda.

Always wear skin and eye protection when handling and using chemicals. Follow all safety precautions indicated on chemical containers.

Stencils

By properly selecting and tensioning the fabric, the printer is able to reproduce images with quality edge definition, image resolution, ink film thickness, and ink uniformity. The stencil, however, determines whether the quality available in the selected fabric will be attained. No matter how fine the fabric mesh or accurate the tension, an incorrect or improperly processed stencil will not produce the desired results.

Knife-cut stencils

The three types of knife-cut stencils are paper, water-soluble, and lacquer-soluble. Each has its own applications.

Paper stencils

Paper stencils are cut from thin, durable types of paper, such as vellum. They are inexpensive and can produce excellent results. The amount of detail depends on the stencil cutter's talent. Generally, paper stencils are used for simple designs, especially if the production run is limited, **Figure 23-17**.

After the stencil is cut, it is placed beneath the screen frame. Ink is spread across the fabric. The tack (stickiness) of the ink causes the stencil to adhere to the underside of the fabric.

Water-soluble stencils

Water-soluble stencils consist of a plastic support sheet coated with a water-soluble gelatin. The gelatin is cut and removed from the image area to produce a stencil. Be careful not to cut into or remove the plastic support.

After stripping away the gelatin, position the stencil under the frame, with the gelatin side in contact with the underside of the fabric. Use a wet sponge to moisten the remaining gelatin portions of the stencil in small sections.

Adhering should take place diagonally, from corner to corner. After a suitable drying time, the base support is peeled off, leaving the adhered gelatin stencil. See **Figure 23-18**.

Figure 23-17. A paper stencil on a screen press. (Bowling Green State University, Visual Communication Technology Program)

After printing and ink removal are completed, the stencil may be removed with a warm-water spray. If a spray unit is not available, let the stencil soak in warm water until it can be flushed from the fabric. Water-soluble stencils cannot be used with water-based inks.

Lacquer-soluble stencils

Lacquer-soluble stencils are essentially the same as water-soluble stencils, except they must be adhered to the screen using a lacquer-based solvent. They are composed of a lacquer-soluble material coated onto a plastic or paper support sheet.

Cut the stencil, taking care not to remove any of the support sheet. After stripping away all image area material, position the stencil beneath the frame. The lacquer side must be in contact with the underside of the fabric. Using a cloth wetted with a lacquer-adhering liquid (solvent), wet the stencil.

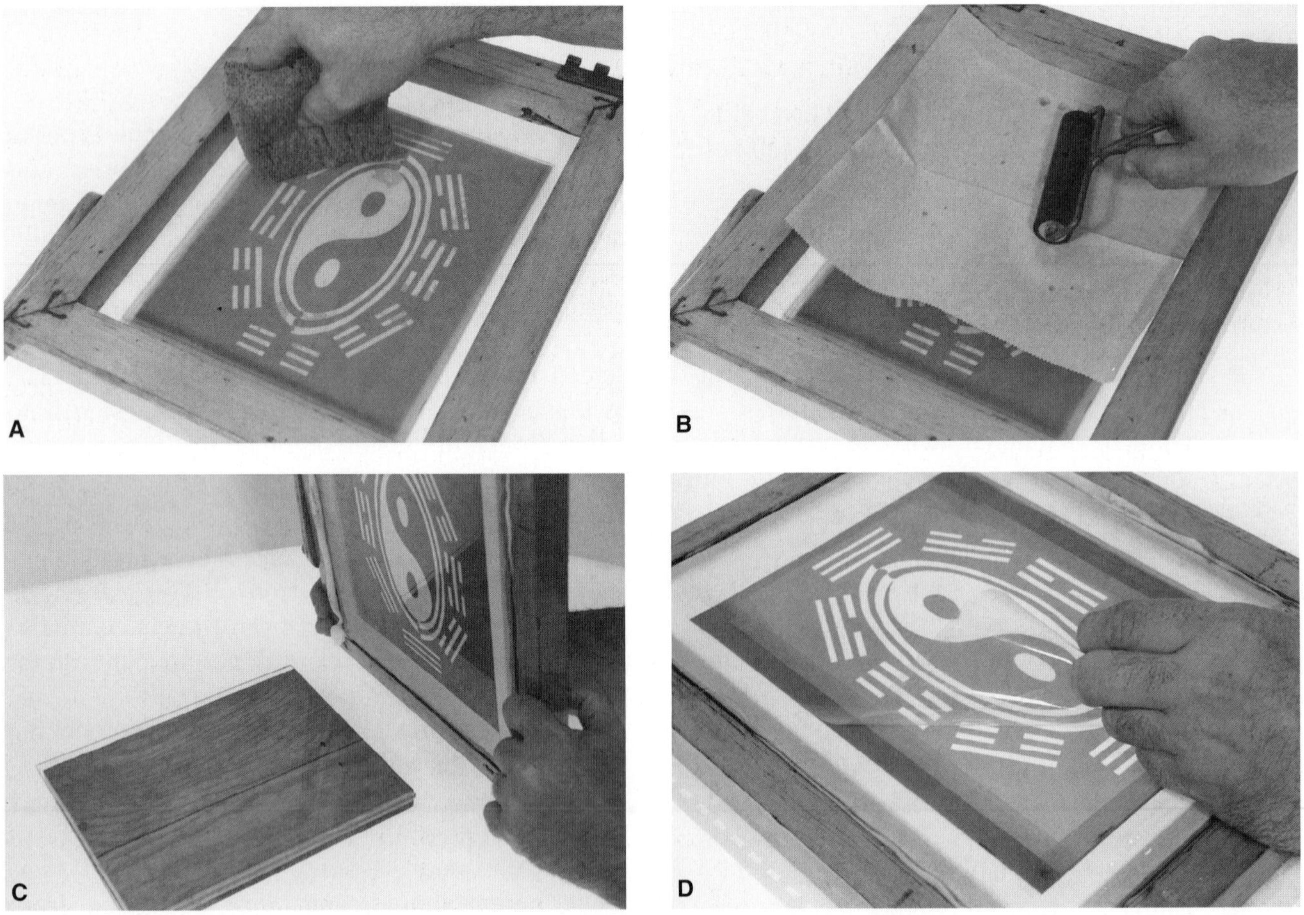

A

B

C

D

Figure 23-18. Steps in adhering a water-soluble stencil. A—The stencil is positioned in the frame and moistened with a damp sponge. B—Excess water is absorbed by a paper towel. C—The stencil is air-dried. D—The base support is peeled from the stencil.

Next, dab small sections of the stencil with a dry cloth, working diagonally from corner to corner. After a suitable drying time, peel off the base support, leaving the adhered stencil.

After use, the stencil may be removed from the screen using lacquer thinner. Lacquer-soluble stencils produce excellent results but cannot be used with lacquer-based inks. They are ideal for use with water-based inks.

Burned edges

Both water-soluble and lacquer-soluble stencils can produce imperfect images if ***burned edges*** are present. Burned edges are the result of poor cutting or adhering techniques, **Figure 23-19**. If the backing sheet is cut, solvent will collect in the cut and melt (burn) the cut edge.

Other causes of burned edges are:

- Cutting with a dull knife.
- Poor fabric and stencil contact during adhering.
- Using new fabric which has not been degreased.
- Using old fabric that is not clean.
- Using the wrong adhering liquid or adhering technique.
- Using rough, abrasive rags to apply adhering liquid.
- Failure to dry the screen immediately after adhering.
- Failure to keep the stencil clean while cutting.
- Kinks and creases in the stencil.

Photographic stencils

Photographic stencils provide the detail, durability, and flexibility needed for the majority of screen-printing applications. They are light-sensitive and are generally exposed using a positive film image; however, a newer technique is available. This system, called the computer-to-screen system, produces a high-resolution screen stencil. The positive image is placed on an emulsion-coated screen.

Positives used to prepare photographic stencils must block light in the image areas and allow light to pass through the nonimage areas. Diffusion-transfer positives are suitable if the density is adequate to prevent exposure in the image areas.

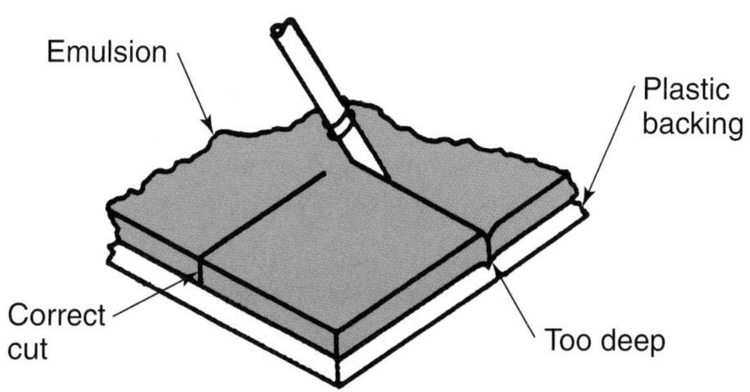

Figure 23-19. Cutting too deeply may groove the backing sheet. Solvent can collect in the groove and burn the stencil.

Other types of positives include contact film positives made from film negatives, high-speed duplicating film positives exposed on a process camera, and rubylith masking film.

For most applications, the film positive must be right-reading on the emulsion side. The exceptions are when printing a textile transfer or a transparent substrate, such as glass. When printing on a transparent substrate, it may be desirable to see a right-reading image when viewing the image through the substrate from the unprinted side.

Photographic stencils are classified as indirect, direct, or direct-indirect.

Indirect stencils

Indirect stencils are exposed off the screen fabric. In other words, they are not in direct contact with the fabric. Indirect water-soluble stencils are used for relatively short production runs, and they reproduce fine detail well. Indirect stencils adhere particularly well to multifilament fabrics. Degreasing and mechanical treatment of monofilament polyester is essential if good adhesion is to be obtained. Indirect stencils have excellent ***mesh-bridging capability***, the ability to bridge diagonally across a cell.

An indirect stencil has three layers: a light-sensitive gelatin, a plastic support, and an intermediate adhesive to keep the gelatin and base together until adhered to the fabric. The stencil is exposed in a contact frame (usually a lithographic platemaker) through the base, emulsion-side down, and in contact with the stencil base.

After exposure, the stencil is placed in a hardening solution for a minimum of 1 1/2 minutes. After the stencil hardens, it is washed with a warm-water spray. The softened stencil is placed base side down on a flat buildup. The screen fabric is wetted, and the substrate side of the screen is brought into contact.

Unprinted newsprint or paper towels are used to remove excess water. After blotting five or six times with a cloth, the stencil is allowed to dry. Fans or blowers are ideal to speed drying.

A blockout solution may be applied to cover unwanted image areas on the stencil, **Figure 23-20**. It is applied to the substrate side of the screen before or after the stencil has dried. Use caution to prevent the blockout liquid from filling the image area.

Figure 23-20. Blockout liquid is being used to cover the open area between the stencil and frame. (Bowling Green State University, Visual Communication Technology Program)

Direct stencils

Direct stencils are exposed after a light-sensitive emulsion has been applied to the screen frame. Direct stencils (or photographic emulsions) are favored for their durability on long runs. By impregnating the fabric, direct emulsions can withstand abrasion and chemical action over time. When properly coated, they have nearly the mesh-bridging capability of indirect stencils.

Direct stencils are composed of a polyvinyl alcohol suspension and a sensitizer. Two common sensitizers are bichromate and diazo (ammonium or potassium bichromate).

If bichromated sensitizers are used, the direct emulsion must be sensitized, coated, dried, exposed, and washed within 24 hours. Coated screens using bichromated emulsions lose their sensitivity to light over time. Bichromated emulsions, if properly processed, have the shortest exposure time.

Warning: Bichromates are toxic. Adequately ventilate the area. Wear appropriate gloves and eye protection.

Diazo emulsions are nontoxic and biodegradable, two reasons for their popularity. They are also safer to handle than biochromates. Diazo-sensitized direct emulsions may be stored up to six weeks in a closed container, longer if refrigerated. Coated screens may be stored for three or four weeks before exposure.

Diazo emulsions are half as sensitive to light as bichromated emulsions; therefore, they require twice the exposure time. A variety of diazo direct emulsions are available for use with water-based or solvent-soluble inks.

A scoop coater is used to coat a screen with the photographic emulsion, **Figure 23-21**. Sensitized emulsion is poured into the scoop and applied to both sides of the screen fabric. Multiple coats are necessary to obtain a high-quality print.

An intermediate drying time should be used. The emulsion will shrink as it dries. If enough shrinkage occurs, thread profiles will appear on the substrate side of the emulsion, and the ink will seep out of the image area during printing. The results will be poor edge definition and a loss of resolution when printing fine-detailed images. It is important that the coating be thicker than the fabric. The substrate side of the emulsion should be smooth.

A deep-bottom vacuum frame is used to expose a direct emulsion. The screen is positioned with the positive on the substrate side. The film emulsion should be in contact with the screen emulsion.

Exposure to light, **Figure 23-22**, causes a chemical reaction. Areas struck by light become hardened and insoluble in water. The unexposed image area remains soluble and can be washed using a warm water spray.

After the direct emulsion dries, a blockout solution can be applied to uncoated areas. ***Pinholes*** caused by dust or other airborne contaminants should also be retouched, **Figure 23-23**.

Reclaiming solutions are used to remove direct emulsions from the screen fabric. Originally,

Figure 23-21. A photographic emulsion is being coated directly on the screen using a scoop coater. (Bowling Green State University, Visual Communication Technology Program)

Figure 23-22. Exposing a direct stencil in a vacuum frame. (Bowling Green State University, Visual Communication Technology Program)

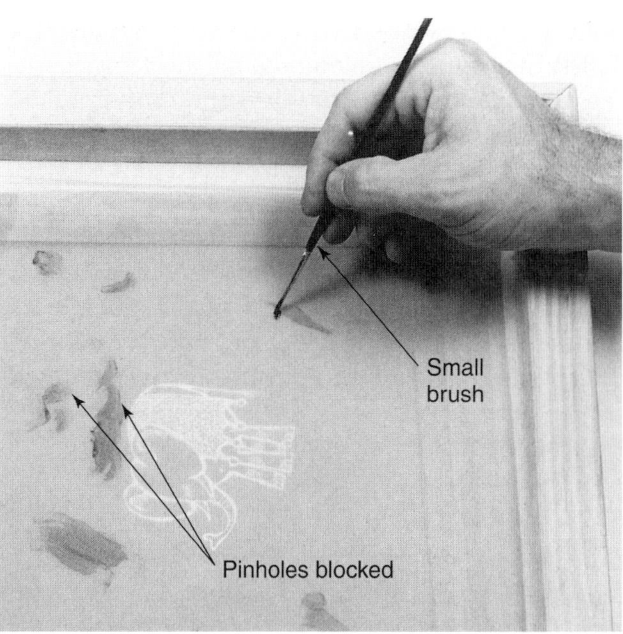

Figure 23-23. A small brush can be used to fill pinholes caused by dust or other contaminants.

undiluted household bleach was used. Better reclaimers are available today, and bleach should be avoided.

Apply the reclaiming solution to a screen that is free of ink, and wait several minutes. The direct emulsion will gradually change color. It can be removed using a warm- or hot-water spray. Special high-pressure screen washers are available to aid in the removal of the emulsion from the fabric mesh.

Direct-indirect stencils

Direct-indirect stencils (sometimes called direct-film stencils) are a combination of the two stencil techniques and materials. Direct-indirect stencils can be either emulsion-adhering or water-adhering.

With *emulsion-adhering stencils*, a dry film or unsensitized gelatin on a polyester base is in contact with the substrate side of the fabric. A bichromate or diazo-sensitized direct emulsion is spread across the screen with a squeegee.

The direct emulsion is forced into the fabric mesh. As it softens the dry gelatin film, the indirect portion of the stencil is adhered and sensitized. After the direct emulsion dries, the polyester base support is stripped away, and the stencil is exposed. The stencil is exposed just like the direct emulsion.

With *water-adhering stencils* (also called *capillary-system stencils*), the dry gelatin is already light-sensitive. Water is spread across the screen to soften the stencil, allowing the gelatin to adhere to the screen fabric. After the direct emulsion dries, the polyester support is stripped away. The stencil is exposed in the same way as the direct emulsion.

A direct-indirect stencil is a compromise. Direct-indirect stencils last longer than indirect stencils. However, they cannot match the detail that indirect stencils provide. Direct-indirect stencils do not last as long as direct emulsion stencils. However, they can resolve and print a finer image with more detail.

Photographic stencil exposure calibration

All photographic stencils require a specific exposure. Calibration test images are used to determine the correct exposure, **Figure 23-24**. With any change in fabric, mesh count, stencil, or exposure device, a new exposure time should be determined.

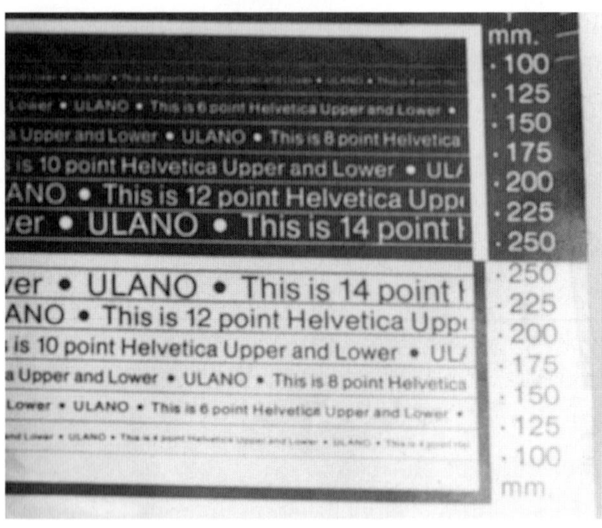

Figure 23-24. A test image is used for the proper exposure calibration of photographic stencils.

Indirect Stencil	
Underexposed	Overexposed
• Stencil becomes too thin after washout. • Excessive pinholes. • Early failure of stencil. • Images spread.	• Stencil fails to adhere to fabric. • Images choke. • Stencil is difficult to remove.

Direct Emulsion Stencil	
Underexposed	Overexposed
• Stencil is soft in nonimage areas. • Stencil becomes too thin after washout. • Images spread. • Early failure of stencil. • Excessive sawtoothing at edges of image (poor mesh bridging).	• Stencil is difficult to wash out. • Loss of detail (such as serifs). • Images choke. • Stencil is difficult to remove.

Direct-Indirect Stencil	
Underexposed	Overexposed
• Stencil is soft in nonimage areas, or washes away completely. • Squeegee side of stencil becomes too thin. • Images spread. • Early failure of stencil. • Excessive sawtoothing at edges of image (poor mesh bridging).	• Stencil is difficult to wash out, or washes out completely due to high pressure required. • Loss of details (such as serifs). • Images choke. • Stencil is difficult to remove.

Figure 23-25. Common exposure problems for three types of stencils.

Whenever a colored screen fabric is used to reduce light scatter within a direct or direct-indirect stencil, the exposure time must be increased by 1/3 to 1/2. **Figure 23-25** lists some common problems associated with improper stencil exposure.

Fabric and Stencil Compatibility

The fabric and stencil must be compatible to get the best image resolution and edge definition. Indirect stencils are best-suited to a multifilament polyester fabric, although they can be used successfully with any fabric. Direct emulsions and direct-indirect stencils work well with any fabric, but are typically used with a colored (dyed) monofilament polyester when printing critical detail.

As light strikes each fabric thread, rays scatter to adjacent areas of the stencil. As a result, small, detailed images can be lost. Ruby, orange, or yellow fabrics reduce the chance of exposure in the image areas due to light refraction. The threads of dyed fabrics act as a safelight filter, refracting wavelengths of light to which the stencil is sensitive. Colored monofilament polyester should always be used when printing halftones or process color reproductions.

Printing Halftone and Process Color

Whenever a screened (halftone) image is to be printed, the screen fabric tension, frame stability, and proper stencil processing become even more important in producing an acceptable product.

Using conventional process color angles, the fabric mesh count should be five to six times higher than the screen ruling of the halftone dots. This ratio should eliminate a moiré pattern between halftone screen and fabric mesh. The angle between the halftone ruling and the fabric thread should be 22.5° for the least noticeable interference pattern between lines of halftone dots and fabric mesh.

Screen Printing Presses

Screen printing requires specialized equipment. The type of substrate determines the degree of automation. *Semiautomatic* presses require the operator to hand-feed the substrate into the printing position. The printed substrate may or may not be removed automatically. Once adjusted, the machine carries out all printing functions. *Automatic* presses infeed and outfeed automatically.

There are several types of screen printing presses:

- *Flatbed press.* Hand tables, semiautomatic, and automatic presses are common types of flatbed screen printing presses. See **Figure 23-26.** The image carrier frames are clamped in place. Most production-type presses have vacuum tables or beds that hold the substrate in place during the printing process. A squeegee is pulled across the screen, forcing the ink through the open portion of the screen. On the return, the screen is coated with ink. This is called a flood coat.
- *Cylinder press.* The cylinder press is used to print on substrates that are round, oval, or tapered. Bottles, pails, glasses, and toys are a few of the common objects using this type of printing press. The substrate is carried on the impression cylinder and the screen carrier supports the image; both of these rotate while the squeegee remains stationary. Some of these presses are fully automated, some are semiautomated, while others are manually operated.

Figure 23-26. A multicolor screen printing press for textiles.

- *Rotary press.* The rotary press has three main components: a fine wire rotary screen, a squeegee, and an impression cylinder. The squeegee remains stationary while the rotary screen mesh revolves. The rotary screen is the image carrier. Ink is continually pumped into the cylinder and the squeegee forces the ink onto the substrate (which could be gift wrap stock, a textile, or vinyl wall covering). Each cylinder unit carries an ink color or a clear coating.

Review Questions

Please do not write in this book. Write your answers on a separate sheet of paper.

1. What are some typical applications of screen printing?
2. Describe the basic printing process for screen printing.
3. ________ are solvents added to screen ink to alter viscosity and slow drying time.

4. This type of fabric is used for printing heated inks or when the ultimate of dimensional stability is needed.
   a. organdy
   b. nylon
   c. polyester
   d. metal mesh
5. Chemical treatment alters the _____ characteristics of the fabric, and mechanical treatment changes the _____ of the fabric.
6. This is the least desirable way of holding fabric on a wooden frame.
   a. staples
   b. adhesive
   c. mechanical clamp
   d. cord and groove
7. What are two ways of finding fabric tension?
8. List the steps in preparing a knife-cut stencil.
9. This type of photographic stencil is used for long runs because of its durability.
   a. indirect
   b. direct
   c. direct-indirect
10. The precision flatbed press is used for printing what type of product?

Huge paper mills like this one at Escanaba, Michigan, produce paper used for various printing processes. This mill specializes in coated papers for textbooks, such as this one, and produce more than one-half million tons per year. (Mead Publishing Paper Division)

Substrates 24

Learning Objectives

After studying this chapter, you will be able to:

- Explain how paper is manufactured.
- Identify the basic characteristics of various types of paper.
- Describe the applications of coated and uncoated papers.
- Explain the basic size and basis weight of paper.
- Determine various paper weights.
- Summarize the characteristics of plastic substrates.

Important Terms

basic size
basis weight
calendering
fourdrinier
grade
grain
lignin
opacity
ream
totally chlorine free (TCF)

Substrates include any material with a surface that can be printed or coated. Although the most common printing substrate is paper, substances such as plastic, metal, and wood are also classified as substrates.

Matching the substrate to the job is critical. A high-quality layout, plate, ink, and printing technique will be wasted if a low-quality substrate is used. On the other hand, expensive stock should not be used to print low-quality products such as newspapers or sale flyers. Salespeople, designers, strippers, press operators, and finishing and binding personnel must have knowledge of the characteristics of paper and its applications. Its misuse can be very costly.

More than one thousand different grades of paper are listed in The Paper Buyer's Encyclopedia. Another valuable source of information is a paper merchant's catalog.

Papermaking History

Most paper is manufactured using machine technology, although some paper is still hand-made. The use of hand-made papers is usually limited to special applications, such as fine art reproductions, or limited editions of books printed and bound by craft workers using hand methods.

Some historical highlights of papermaking are:

- 105 A.D. — Ts'ai Lun, a Chinese official, mixed the bark of the mulberry tree with linen and hemp to make a crude form of paper.
- 500 A.D. — The Mayans produced paper using fig tree bark.

- 751 A.D. — The Arabs captured several Chinese papermakers and learned their art. Papermaking spread to Europe as a result of the Crusades and the Moorish conquest of northern Africa and Spain.
- 1400 A.D. — Papermaking by hand flourished.
- 1690 A.D. — The first paper mill in America was established near Philadelphia by William Rittenhouse and William Bradford.
- 1798 A.D. —Nicholas Louis Robert of France invented a machine with an endless wire screen to produce paper in rolls. The machine was financed by two English merchants, the Fourdrinier brothers, and named the American fourdrinier machine.

Most of the paper manufactured in the United States today is made on the ***fourdrinier***. It can produce continuous sheets of paper up to 33′ (10 m) wide at speeds faster than 3000′ (900 m) per minute. Some fourdrinier machines are more than 350′ (110 m) long. The mechanical principles of the original machine have remained nearly unchanged. Other inventions have occurred, but many are simply refinements.

Significant improvements in papermaking in recent years include thermomechanical pulping, synthetic wires and felts, twin-wire machines, and the use of computers to control pulping and papermaking operations. Paper manufacturers have also worked to improve pollution control and energy conservation in the industry.

Making Paper

For centuries, the principle raw materials used in papermaking were cotton and linen fibers obtained from rags. Some cotton and linen fibers are still used for high-quality writing papers, business letterhead papers, art papers, and documents that will be kept for years. However, wood fibers (***cellulose***) are the raw materials used to make most paper today.

Pine, fir, spruce, aspen, beech, birch, maple, and oak are typical species harvested for papermaking. The length of the tree fibers varies and determines, among other characteristics, the strength of the paper.

Papermaking is a complex manufacturing process. It uses both chemical and mechanical means to reduce wood fibers to *pulp*, which is the material used to ultimately produce paper in sheet form. See **Figure 24-1**.

Chipping

Harvested logs are cut to uniform length, debarked, **Figure 24-2**, and sent to a chipper or grinder. The ***chipper*** cuts the logs into 3/8″ to 3/4″ chips, **Figure 24-3**. After the chips are screened for size, they are put in a huge cooking kettle called a ***digester***.

Making pulp

In the chemical pulpmaking process, chemicals in the sealed, pressurized digester break down the binding material (***lignin***) present in the cellulose fibers. The cellulose fibers, which once resembled soda straws, become pulp, a mass of soft, spongy matter. The pulp is blown into a pit where the chemicals are washed away.

The mechanical pulpmaking (groundwood) process uses grinding wheels to reduce the logs to fiber. The byproduct is pulp with high opacity but relatively low strength.

Sizing and fillers

Sizing is added to the pulp slurry to make the paper more resistant to moisture. Rosin is a common sizing material. Alum is added as a binding agent.

Fillers are needed to improve a paper's opacity, brightness, smoothness, and ink receptivity. Two common fillers are clay and titanium dioxide.

Dyes, pigments, and bleach

Dyes and pigments are added to produce colored substrates, while bleach makes the pulp white, **Figure 24-4**. Coloring or bleaching additives are mixed in vats called ***pulpers***. The pulp goes through a final beating and refining stage before it is pumped to a stock chest.

Removing water

A jordan machine refines the fiber slurry until it is about 99% water and 1% fiber and other solids. At this point, the paper is known as ***furnish***. The

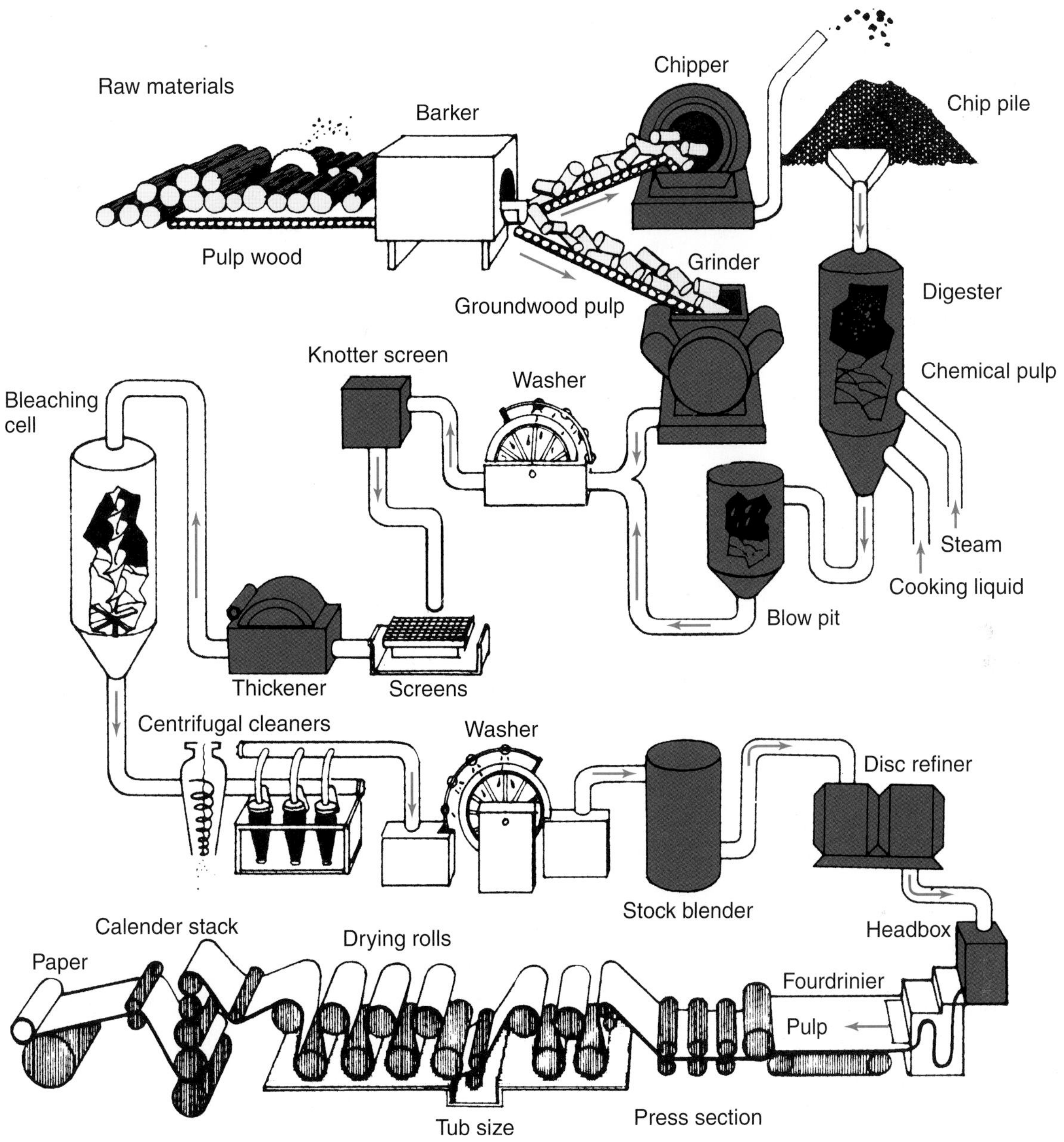

Figure 24-1. Major steps in the manufacture of paper. A modern papermaking operation requires a large investment in equipment and raw materials.

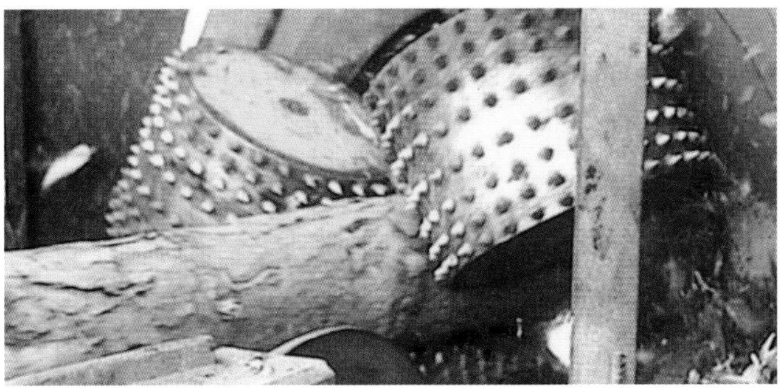

Figure 24-2. This huge machine rotates logs inside a toothed chamber to remove the bark. (Southern Forest Products Assn.)

solution is pumped into the headbox of the papermaking machine.

The pulp furnish is evenly dispersed on the fourdrinier wire, **Figure 24-5**. The wire screen vibrates as it travels along an endless belt, aligning the fibers in the direction of travel. A continuous web of paper is formed in the process. Gravity and suction remove about 35% of the water.

Some papers are given a ***watermark***, a translucent identifying design impressed in the paper while it is still wet. The symbols or images are created by rearranging the fibers with a dandy roll. See **Figure 24-6**.

Figure 24-3. A chipper reduces large logs to tiny bits of wood. (International Paper Co.)

Figure 24-4. Pulp selected for bleaching is treated with chlorine to whiten the paper fibers. Federal and state laws on clean air and water have created an interest in totally chlorine free (TCF) papers. (International Paper Co.)

Figure 24-5. The fourdrinier wire section of the paper-making process. Wet paper fibers ride on an endless wire screen. This is known as the "wet end" of the machine. Water drains off as the fibers move toward the dryers. (Mead Publishing Paper Division)

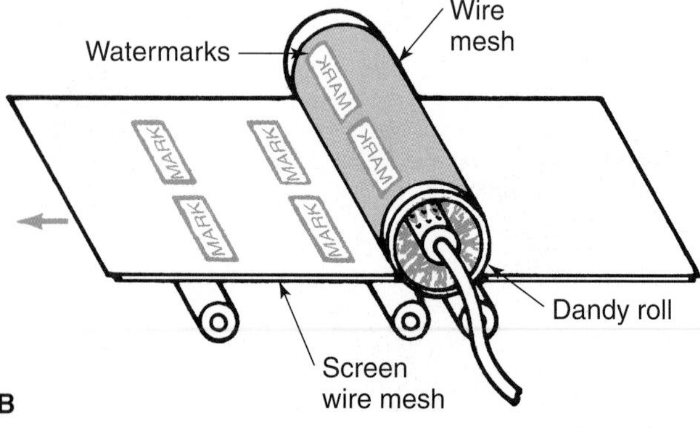

Figure 24-6. Creating a watermark. A—The watermark is simply a rearrangement of paper fibers. It identifies the grade of paper or the trademark of a company. B—A dandy roll is used to place the watermark on the paper.

Drying

When the furnish leaves the screen, it enters the press section, which removes more water. Then, the paper enters a dryer section consisting of large temperature-controlled rollers. More moisture is removed. Coatings are applied as the paper moves through the machine, **Figure 24-7**.

At some stage of the drying process, the paper must be calendered. ***Calendering*** is the process of flattening and smoothing the paper surface by passing it between a series of rollers. ***Supercalendering*** uses heated steel rollers and pressure to form a very smooth, high-gloss finish, **Figure 24-8**.

Rolling

The untrimmed paper is wound into rolls. Some rolls are rewound, slit, and cut into lengths to make flat packages of paper. Others remain as rolls for use in web-fed presses, **Figure 24-9**.

Paper Types

Adhesive-coated, safety, bond, carbonless, offset, duplicator, cover, ledger, index, newsprint, and recycled are some of the many types of paper. A general understanding of the characteristics and applications of various papers is important.

Figure 24-7. Many of the papers used today for magazine and book publishing are coated for better reproduction of color and fine-screened halftones. Coating is applied on the papermaking machine. (Mead Publishing Paper Division)

Figure 24-8. Heated supercalender rolls are used to smooth and polish the paper surface to a high gloss. (Mead Publishing Paper Division)

Figure 24-9. On the machine in the background, rolls of paper are being rewound after being slit to different widths. Some of these rolls may later be cut into sheets and packaged; others will be used on web-fed presses. (Mead Publishing Paper Division)

Coated and uncoated papers

Coated paper is a broad classification of paper that has a mineral substance applied to its surface. Clay, stain white, and other substances can be used to produce coated papers. Coated papers typically have a smoother, stronger surface than uncoated papers. Finishes may be high-gloss, dull-coated, or matte-coated. They are more expensive than uncoated papers but yield better reproduction of images.

Coated papers are rated by brightness. A No. 1 rated paper is suitable for high-quality jobs, such as sales literature. Material intended to convey a prestigious image might use a matte finish, while high gloss might be used to convey a bright and exciting image. No. 1 paper produces very bright color through the use of transparent inks. Printed material the end user would not save indefinitely, such as catalogs or posters, is typically printed on No. 2 or No. 3. Groundwood sheets are often No. 4 or No. 5.

Uncoated paper, as implied, does not have a mineral layer applied over the surface and tends to have a textured feel. Uncoated paper textures (laid, woven, and linen) are suited to printed pieces that will be written on, such as stationery. Uncoated papers also enhance legibility, making them good choices for text-intensive printed material, such as textbooks or novels.

Adhesive-coated

The stock is coated with an adhesive material that is permanently tacky or is activated by water or heat. Labels are a common product that use this type of substrate. The heat-seal type of paper uses heat to melt the coating so that it will stick to another surface. Stock with a coating that is permanently tacky is commonly called *pressure-sensitive.* These stocks require contact and pressure to make them adhere to another surface.

Safety

This stock typically is used for printing checks. The specifications are very rigid, because the stock must expose any attempted alteration of the document. If someone tries to alter it by erasure or by using chemicals, the paper would automatically display a change in the design or color. Some other documents using safety paper include bonds, deposit slips, coupons, tickets, certificates of title, warrenties, and legal forms.

Bond paper

Bond paper is a broad classification of quality paper used for business forms, letterheads, stationery, and many other products. Characteristics of bond paper include strength, good ink receptivity, and erasability.

Bond paper is used extensively for printers connected to desktop computers. Laser printers can provide acceptable quality using the same paper designed for photocopying machines. Paper for use in inkjet printers has a coating formulated to accept the dye-like inks used by these printers.

Bond paper is made from cotton or rag fiber, or from chemical wood pulps. It has an even, hard finish on both sides. Rag bond is the most expensive type of paper and often has a watermark.

Duplicator paper

Duplicator paper is an inexpensive bond designed for use in photocopying machines and laser printers. Duplicator paper should never be used as a stock for offset lithography or other forms of printing. Its surface strength and other qualities are not suitable for use "on press."

Carbonless paper

Carbonless paper is used to make multipart business forms that will be written on or used in some type of *impact printer* (a device, such as a typewriter, that makes a physical impression by striking the paper). Carbonless paper starts with a base stock similar to ordinary bond. The paper is coated with encapsulated colorless dyes and/or a receptor coating that reacts with the dye to produce an image. The capsules are broken when pressure is applied, releasing the dye onto the sheet below. The receptor coating develops the image.

Carbonless business forms have a variety of applications. Checks, vouchers, shipping labels in clear plastic envelopes, and continuous forms for impact-type printers are common uses.

Offset paper

Offset paper is designed specifically for use on offset printing presses. It has good opacity, rapid ink absorption, and permanence. It can be coated or uncoated. Offset paper is used for a wide variety of products, such as books, form letters, magazines, manuals, and advertisements. See **Figure 24-10**.

Figure 24-10. Books and many other printed products are produced using offset paper, often on web-fed presses like this one. (Heidelberg Harris)

Offset paper is sometimes called *book paper* because both have similar properties and construction methods. Book and offset papers are made from various materials, including chemical wood pulp, mechanical wood pulp, recycled papers, and even straw. Frequently, two or more of these raw materials are combined to make offset paper.

Impregnated offset paper receives a mineral film to smooth and strengthen the surface for better image reproduction. It is sometimes called *pigmentized offset paper*.

Text paper is an expensive grade of offset or book paper. Depending upon its surface smoothness, it can be both attractive and functional. Smooth text paper is used for accurate reproduction of halftones. Rougher surfaces are used when halftone reproduction quality is not important.

Cover paper

Cover paper is a thick or heavy paper, typically used for the covers of books, catalogs, brochures, manuals, and similar publications. Sometimes, two layers of cover paper are bonded together to produce double thickness. When pasted together, it can be sold by caliper or thickness.

Ledger paper

Ledger paper (also called *record paper*) has a smooth, matte finish that resists erasing. It easily accepts pen and is both strong and durable. Ledger paper is used for accounting notepads, bookkeeping forms, business ledger sheets, and financial statement forms.

Index paper

Index paper is a thick, stiff, smooth paper, frequently two-ply or greater. Index stock may be coated or uncoated. Its most common uses are index cards and postcards, so it must be sturdy enough to withstand frequent handling. *Bristol paper* is similar to index paper.

Newsprint paper

Newsprint is one of the lowest grades of printing paper. It is made by the groundwood or mechanical method of papermaking. Newsprint has very short fibers which enable the paper to be folded easily in any direction. When new, it has a grayish-white color, but it turns yellow and becomes brittle with age. Since newsprint absorbs ink readily, a drying system on the press is not needed.

Recycled paper

Tightened access to forest resources, depleted landfill space, changes in consumer awareness and preferences, and government restrictions have all contributed to the trend toward buying and using recycled paper. ***Recycled paper*** is made from old or used paper products, **Figure 24-11**. There are different grades of recycled paper. High grades can be made into quality printing paper. Low grades can be made into newsprint, cartons, and other products.

The recycled paper arena is dynamic. Guidelines relating to the manufacture of recycled paper are continually being reviewed by the United States Environmental Protection Agency (EPA). The federal government has established minimum-content standards for the paper it purchases. According to U.S. EPA guidelines, printing and writing paper purchased by the federal government must contain at least 50% total recycled fiber content, with 30% postconsumer material by 1999. The federal government standard is being adopted by states and is becoming the *de facto* industry standard.

Recycled papers may contain preconsumer waste, postconsumer waste, or both. ***Preconsumer paper waste*** is material generated by industrial manufacturing processes (mill broke, wood chips, other mill waste) that is not sold to the consumer and would otherwise be disposed of in a landfill. ***Postconsumer paper waste*** is used materials (office paper, newspapers, old magazines, mixed waste paper, corrugated boxes) that have served their intended purpose and are separated from other waste to be recycled into new paper. The greater the percentage of postconsumer material in the paper, the less resource-intensive its production.

Figure 24-11. Corrugated packaging is a major user of fiber from recycled paper. (Sonoco Products Co.)

In 1992, the Federal Trade Commission issued guidelines for the use of environmental marketing claims, such as those for recycled or recyclable products, so consumers can understand labeling and not be deceived. Printers must label recycled products clearly and prominently, and indicate what portion of the product consists of recycled content, **Figure 24-12**. If a product is not 100% recycled, it must be labeled according to the percentage of recycled matter it contains. Printers are warned against using the term "recyclable" since the guidelines on that term vary from state to state, thereby making mislabeling easy.

De-inking and bleaching

Before paper can be reused, it is subjected to chemical and mechanical processes to return it to a pure condition. ***De-inking*** is the process of removing inks, fillers, and coatings from waste paper. The mixture is reduced to cellulose fibers suspended in a water slurry.

After the waste paper is de-inked, the fibers are bleached. ***Bleaching*** is the use of chlorine bleach to give recycled (as well as new or "virgin") paper a bright white appearance. It is currently a topic of hot debate.

For years, chlorine gas, known as ***elemental chlorine***, has been used to bleach paper pulp and to separate pulp from lignin. During the 1980s, Europeans discovered that the industrial effluent from chlorine is linked directly to the creation of dioxin, a man-made carcinogen that passes up the food chain easily.

In 1994, the EPA issued a draft report concluding that dioxin can create adverse health

Figure 24-12. A product must be labeled to indicate the percentage of recycled matter it contains. The recycled content of this product came entirely from postconsumer waste.

effects, even at low levels. The findings prompted the agency to begin developing air- and water-emission standards for the pulp and paper industry.

Alternatives to elemental chlorine bleaching have been implemented widely in Europe and, to a lesser extent, in the U.S.

Elementally chlorine-free (ECF) bleaching. ECF bleaching is an alternative process that utilizes chlorine dioxide or sodium hypochlorite instead of chlorine gas as a bleaching agent. Even though chlorine dioxide has "chlorine" in its name, its chemistry is very different from chlorine gas.

In the bleaching process using chlorine gas, chlorine tends to combine with lignin to create chlorinated organics (dioxins) that end up in mill effluent. In contrast, chlorine dioxide typically breaks apart the lignin, leaving behind organic compounds that are soluble in water and similar to naturally occurring substances. By substituting chlorine dioxide at levels of 70% to 100%, mills may be able to reduce the level of chlorinated organics found in wastewater by 80% to 90% and reduce dioxins to undetectable levels.

Using oxygen or other nonchlorine bleaching processes is another alternative to eliminate the formation of dioxins. No matter what process is used, though, most of the fibers contained in recycled paper were originally bleached in chlorine. Once chlorine is in the paper, it cannot be washed out. Therefore, the real need for eliminating chlorine still must be addressed.

Totally chlorine-free (TCF). One answer to the chlorine-bleaching problem is to use unbleached (slightly brown) paper products known as ***totally chlorine-free (TCF)***.

Adoption of TCF printing has been much more widespread in Europe than in the U.S. Currently, 40% of European mills are operating TCF. The markets there are spurred by greater consumer awareness of chlorine issues and tighter regulations of chlorinated chemicals. In the U.S., TCF use is expected to reach 10% by the year 2000.

Paper Applications

Some papers are adaptable to different applications, while others are very limited in their use. The applications of paper to various printing processes will be discussed next.

Paper for gravure

Newsprint produced for gravure printing typically contains mineral fillers and a calendered surface. Mail-order catalogs are a good example of this type of stock. When high-quality gravure printing is desired, the paper used contains mineral filler, but also a larger percentage of short-fiber chemical pulp.

Paper surfaces may be relatively soft, since gravure ink is not tacky. This eliminates the problem of ink picking fibers from the surface of the paper. Coated surfaces are widely used in gravure. Compressibility of paper is important because the gravure cells must make contact with the paper surface.

Because gravure is used in packaging, the stock must have dimensional stability, thickness must be controlled, and moisture content must be considered. The reaction of the stock to the process is critical in the high-production speeds required of gravure.

Paper for offset lithography

In offset lithography, fuzz, lint, and dust must be strictly limited. See **Figure 24-13**. A wide variety of papers can be printed by the lithographic process, but any paper must have sufficient fiber-bonding strength to prevent the pulling of fibers from the

Figure 24-13. Papers used for offset lithography, whether printed on a small duplicator or a large web-fed press, must have a surface resistant to having fibers pulled loose by tacky ink. Loose fibers can cause specks and other defects in the printed product.

stock by tacky ink. Because of the surface contact and tackiness of the ink, special coatings are applied to the paper.

Moisture is another consideration. The paper surface must not become weakened by moisture, or fibers will pick off with each successive impression.

Surface irregularity is not critical in offset lithography. The blanket is resilient and should return to its original shape, even if the paper has an irregular surface. Of course, limitations do exist.

Paper for flexography

Flexography is ideal for printing packaging materials because the soft plates can transfer ink to almost any kind of substrate. Kraft linerboard and coated kraft are used in corrugated boxes. Other paper and paperboard substrates include folding cartons, labels, gift wrap, and paperback books. Newsprint, corrugated linerboard, and paperboard are relatively rough and very absorbent. Calendered and coated papers are the smoothest and least absorbent. They also exhibit high ink holdout.

Digital printing paper

In digital printing, errors in paper selection can cause such problems as misregistration and ink rub-off. The high speeds and temperatures of digital printing equipment require specially formulated papers, some of which are laser-compatible or laser-guaranteed, as well.

For medium- and high-speed black and white or color digital printers, smooth-finished laser papers have superior toner adhesion and excellent performance at high speeds and high temperatures. These printers typically print on papers ranging from 16-lb. bond to 60-lb. cover and 110-lb. index.

Dry-toner digital presses run well with smooth, bright papers from 24-lb. bond to 80-lb. cover stock, coated or uncoated.

Wet-toner digital presses require a special coating on substrates for optimal toner adhesion. A variety of substrates will work, from 50-lb. text to transparencies to labels, as long as they are coated.

Paper Characteristics

Paper made by the machine method has ***grain***, which is determined by the direction in which the pulp fibers lie. Direction of grain becomes important when feeding the paper through the press and during some finishing procedures.

Grain direction

The underlined dimension on a package of paper specifies the direction of the grain, **Figure 24-14**. Another way to find grain direction is to tear a sheet of paper in one direction and then the other. The straightest tear is *with* (parallel to) the grain, **Figure 24-15**.

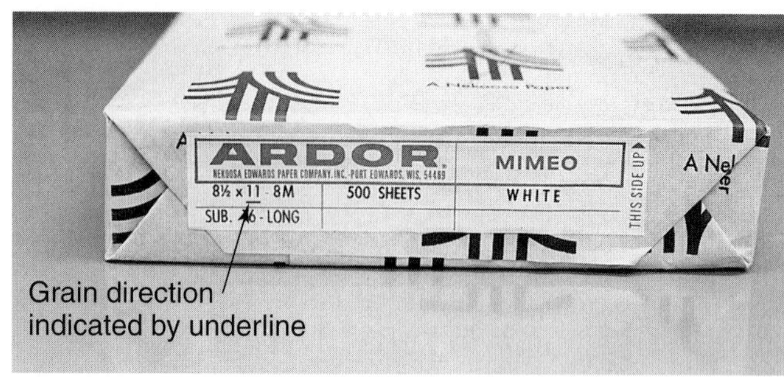

Figure 24-14. The underlined dimension on this package of duplicator paper tells the direction of the paper grain.

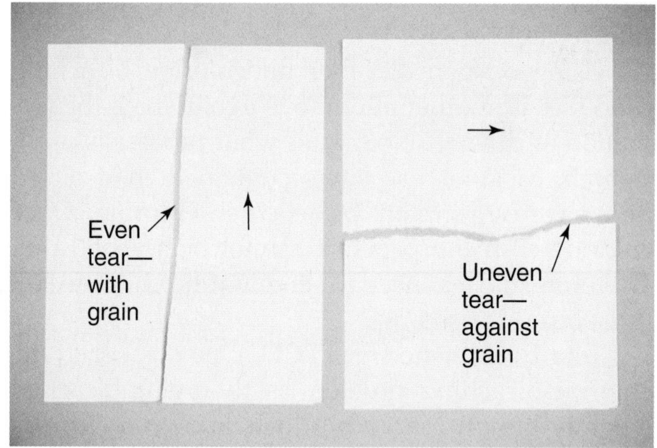

Figure 24-15. An easy way to tell paper grain direction is to tear two sheets in different directions. The straightest tear is parallel to the direction of grain.

A third means of finding grain direction is to cut two strips of paper, each in a different direction. Lay the strips over a rod or straight surface. The sheet that curves the most is *across* (at right angles to or opposite) the grain.

Grain may also be found by dampening one side of the sheet. The dampened paper will curl *with* the grain. Usually, a sheet of paper will fold easier and form a more even edge with the grain.

In most cases, sheets are fed through a press with the grain parallel to the cylinder of the offset press. The stock is referred to as ***grain long***. During binding, the grain should be parallel to the binding edge so the fibers will not break.

Paper flatness

Paper flatness refers to how well the paper remains straight or unwarped. Flatness is a basic requirement if the stock is to feed through a sheet-fed press without problems.

Paper is naturally *hygroscopic;* the cellulose fibers seek the moisture in the surrounding area. Most paper is shipped with 4% to 6% moisture content. In a facility with an air temperature of 70°F to 75°F (21°C to 24°C), that equates to 42% to 48% relative humidity.

Wavy paper edges indicate a greater amount of moisture in the edges than inside the sheet, **Figure 24-16**. Sometimes the opposite occurs, resulting in tight edges and a sheet that curls up or down.

Paper handling must be closely supervised. Relative humidity and paper moisture are critical to smooth operation of the press. Packages of paper should be kept closed until needed to keep moisture out. Also, paper must be square and free of dust, lint, and dirt.

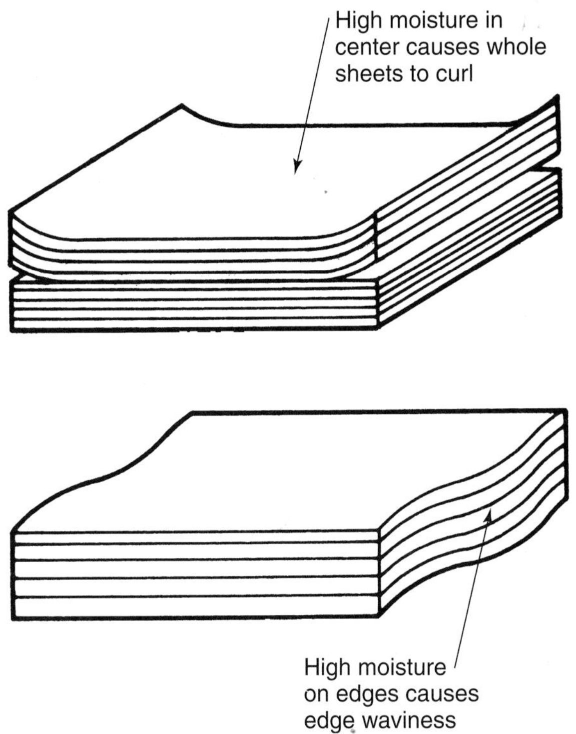

Figure 24-16. High moisture content can make paper warp or become wavy.

Paper size and weight

All paper has a grade, a basic size, and a basis weight. The types of paper — book, writing, cover, index, Bristol, and newsprint — are also known as ***grades***. Each grade has certain characteristics and uses. The choice of paper grade depends on the intended use.

Basic size, specified by length and width, varies with grade, **Figure 24-17**. The basic size of bond paper is 17″ × 22″. One ream weighs 16 or 20 lbs.; 16-lb. stock is thinner than 20-lb. stock. The basic size of book paper is 25″ × 38″. The substance weight of book paper is 2 1/2 times the weight of bond with 2 1/2 times the surface area.

Cover paper has a basic size of 20″ × 26″. It is a durable stock with many textures. It comes in 60-lb. to 80-lb. weights. The basic size of index stock is 25 1/2″ × 30 1/2″. It is a heavy stock and often identified by the number of plies. One-ply equals 90-lb. stock; two-ply equals 110-lb. stock; three-ply equals 140-lb. stock.

Kind of Paper	Square Inches	Basic Size
Bond, ledger, writing	374	17″ × 22″
Cover	520	20″ × 26″
Newsprint	864	24″ × 36″
Book, offset, text	950	25″ × 38″
Index, bristols	778	25 1/2″ × 30 1/2″

Figure 24-17. Some common types of paper and their basic sizes.

Basis weight is the weight in pounds of one ream of basic-sized stock. A ***ream*** has 500 sheets. Usually paper is referred to by its ream weight, for example, 20-lb. bond or 70-lb. book. Twenty-pound bond means that 500 sheets of 17″ × 22″ writing paper weigh 20 pounds.

If the letter M appears after the weight, it means per 1000 sheets. For example, 25 × 38 – 140M means 1000 sheets of 25″ × 38″ book paper weigh 140 pounds, **Figure 24-18**.

Substance weight is the actual weight of the ream. Papers have many basic sizes and basis weights. Therefore, the thickness of a ream of stock can vary based on its substance weight.

Equivalent weight is the weight of one ream of paper that is of a size larger or smaller than the basic size. Use the following formula to find the *equivalent weight* of paper, referring to Figure 24-17 for the basic size.

Type	Basic Size	Weights
Writing	17″ × 22″	26 32 40 48 56 64 etc.
Cover	20″ × 26″	100 120 130 160 180 etc.
Book	25″ × 38″	60 70 80 90 100 120 140 160 etc.
Index bristol	25 1/2″ × 30 1/2″	117 144 182 222 286 etc.

Figure 24-18. Some typical weights of paper for common sizes.

$$\frac{\text{Length} \times \text{Width of sheets} \times \text{Basis weight}}{\text{Length} \times \text{Width of basic size}} = \text{Equivalent weight}$$

Example: What is the equivalent weight of a ream of 28″ × 34″ ledger paper, 32-lb. stock?

$$\frac{28 \times 34 \times 32}{17 \times 22} = 81.4 \text{ lbs.}$$

To find the *total weight* of a number of sheets, use the following formula:

$$\frac{\text{Weight of 1000 sheets} \times \text{Number of sheets}}{1000} = \text{Total weight}$$

Example: What is the total weight of 1475 sheets of 17″ × 22″ – 56M, 28-lb. stock?

$$\frac{56 \times 1475}{1000} = 82.6 \text{ lbs.}$$

To find the *basis weight* (when the sheet size and ream weight are known) use the following formula:

$$\frac{\text{Basic size} \times \text{Ream weight}}{\text{Length} \times \text{Width of sheet}} = \text{Basis weight}$$

Example: What is the basis weight of a ream of book paper 23″ × 29″, with a ream weight of 56 pounds?

$$\frac{25 \times 38 \times 56}{23 \times 29} = \frac{53{,}200}{667} = 80 \text{ lbs.}$$

Paper in rolls

The length and weight of paper in rolls can be calculated by applying the factors shown in **Figure 24-19** to the appropriate formula.

Paper Computation Factors		
Type	**Basic size**	**Factor**
Business papers	17″ × 22″	374
Book papers	25″ × 38″	950
Cover papers	20″ × 26″	520
Printing bristols	22 1/2″ × 28 1/2″	641
Tag, news, conv.	24″ × 36″	864
Index bristols	25 1/2″ × 30 1/2″	778

Figure 24-19. A factor is derived by multiplying the dimensions of the basic size of a type of paper. For example, the basic size of business papers (bond) is 17″ × 22″, which equals 374. (Inter-City Paper Co.)

To find the *length* of paper in a roll of known width and net weight (not including wrapper and core), use the following formula:

$$\frac{41.67 \times \text{Roll weight} \times \text{Factor}}{\text{Roll width} \times \text{Basis weight}} = \text{Length}$$

Example: How many feet of paper are in a 1000-lb. roll of 35″-wide offset book, 75-lb. stock?

$$\frac{41.67 \times 1000 \times 950}{35 \times 75} = 15{,}080'$$

To find the *approximate weight* of rolls on a 3″ inner diameter (ID) core, use the following formula:

$$(\text{Roll diameter})^2 \times \text{Width} \times \text{Roll factor}^* = \text{Approximate weight}$$

*Roll factors:

Bond	0.021
Smooth Finish Offset	0.022
Vellum Finish Offset	0.018
C2S Web Offset	0.032

Example 1: What is the approximate weight of a 34 1/2″-wide, 40″-diameter roll of coated web paper?

$$(40 \times 40) \times 34.5 \times 0.032 = 1766 \text{ lbs.}$$

Example 2: What is the approximate weight of a 17 1/2″-wide, 40″-diameter roll of vellum offset?

$$(40 \times 40) \times 17.5 \times 0.018 = 504 \text{ lbs.}$$

Sometimes it is necessary to figure out how many pieces of paper can be cut out of a large sheet. A typical stock cutting sheet is shown in **Figure 24-20**.

To figure the number of pieces per sheet, the dimensions of the desired cut piece are written below the dimensions of the uncut sheet. First, each dimension of the cut size is divided into its corresponding full-sheet dimension. The resulting whole numbers (fractions are dropped) are multiplied to find the number of pieces that can be cut from the sheet. The computation is done two ways. In one, the dimensions are divided vertically; in the other, division is done crosswise (diagonally).

An example of the two methods is shown in **Figure 24-21**. Stock size is 25″ × 38″, while the desired cut size is 6″ × 9″. The results would be that 16 pieces can be obtained using the vertical method and 12 pieces using the cross method.

It is more economical to cut the short dimension of the piece out of the short dimension of the sheet (the number obtained using the vertical method). However, this is true only if it is satisfactory to have the grain run the long way on the piece.

If the grain had to run parallel to the short (6″) dimension of the piece, it would yield only 12 pieces (as determined using the cross method).

Sometimes, it is possible that the ***trim*** (the paper left over when cutting a sheet into smaller pieces) can be used for another job. To find out, utilize the same type of formula.

Metric paper sizes

In many countries, the SI metric system is used for specifying paper size. The letters A and B each designate a different series. The sizes in each series are numbered 0 to 8 and represent the number of times a sheet can be folded to obtain a particular size. The sizes in a series are proportionate; any smaller size is always half the next larger size.

In the A series, A0 has an area of 1 m^2. The sheet is not a true square but has a proportion of 5:7, **Figure 24-22**. Using 1 m^2 as a starting point, the subsequently smaller sizes are determined by halving the larger size, **Figure 24-23**.

The B series is divided the same as the A series. However, the sizes fall between the A series measurements and are used for unusual situations. Standard metric sizes of paper are listed in **Figure 24-24**. The nearest metric equivalent to the

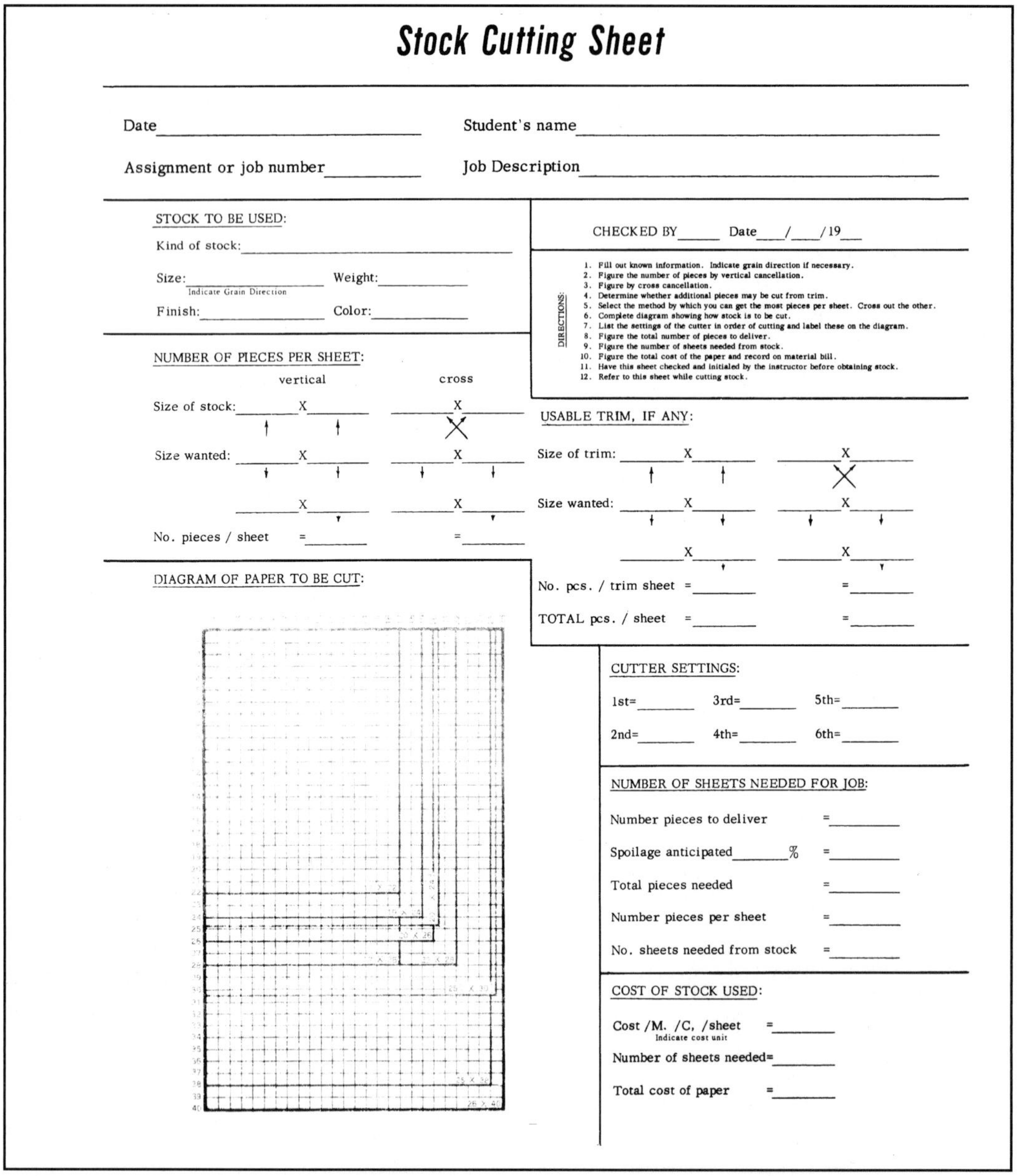

Stock Cutting Sheet

Date ____________ Student's name ____________

Assignment or job number ________ Job Description ____________

STOCK TO BE USED:

Kind of stock: ____________

Size: ________ (Indicate Grain Direction) Weight: ________

Finish: ________ Color: ________

CHECKED BY ______ Date ___/___/19__

DIRECTIONS:

1. Fill out known information. Indicate grain direction if necessary.
2. Figure the number of pieces by vertical cancellation.
3. Figure by cross cancellation.
4. Determine whether additional pieces may be cut from trim.
5. Select the method by which you can get the most pieces per sheet. Cross out the other.
6. Complete diagram showing how stock is to be cut.
7. List the settings of the cutter in order of cutting and label these on the diagram.
8. Figure the total number of pieces to deliver.
9. Figure the number of sheets needed from stock.
10. Figure the total cost of the paper and record on material bill.
11. Have this sheet checked and initialed by the instructor before obtaining stock.
12. Refer to this sheet while cutting stock.

NUMBER OF PIECES PER SHEET:

	vertical	cross
Size of stock:	____ X ____	____ X ____
Size wanted:	____ X ____	____ X ____
	____ X ____	____ X ____
No. pieces / sheet	= ____	= ____

USABLE TRIM, IF ANY:

Size of trim:	____ X ____	____ X ____
Size wanted:	____ X ____	____ X ____
	____ X ____	____ X ____
No. pcs. / trim sheet	= ____	= ____
TOTAL pcs. / sheet	= ____	= ____

DIAGRAM OF PAPER TO BE CUT:

CUTTER SETTINGS:

1st= ____ 3rd= ____ 5th= ____

2nd= ____ 4th= ____ 6th= ____

NUMBER OF SHEETS NEEDED FOR JOB:

Number pieces to deliver = ____

Spoilage anticipated ____ % = ____

Total pieces needed = ____

Number pieces per sheet = ____

No. sheets needed from stock = ____

COST OF STOCK USED:

Cost /M. /C. /sheet (Indicate cost unit) = ____

Number of sheets needed= ____

Total cost of paper = ____

Figure 24-20. A stock cutting sheet form. (Central Missouri State University)

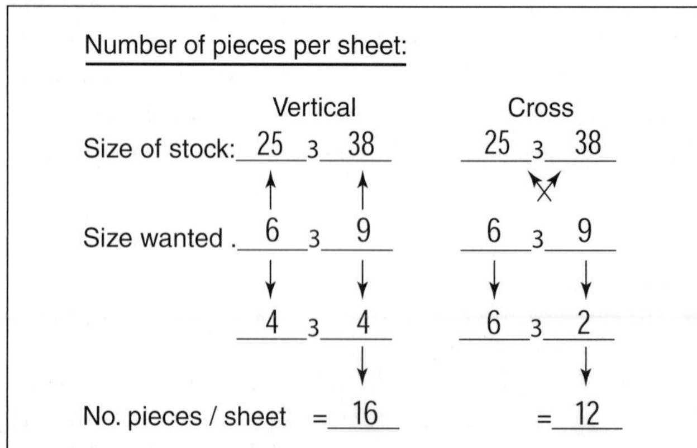

Number of pieces per sheet:

	Vertical	Cross
Size of stock:	25 3 38	25 3 38
Size wanted .	6 3 9	6 3 9
	4 3 4	6 3 2
No. pieces / sheet	= 16	= 12

Figure 24-21. How to determine the number of pieces per sheet.

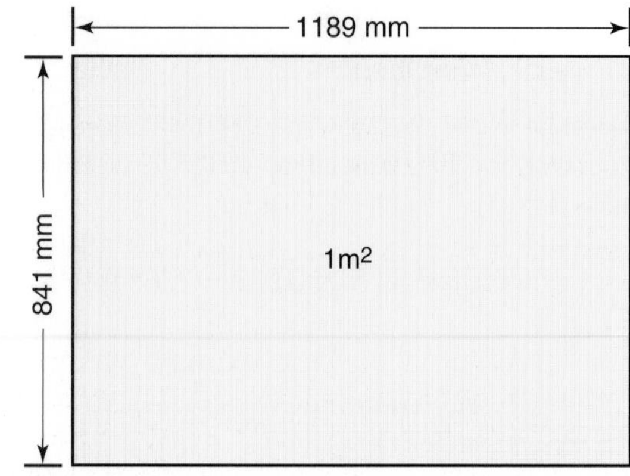

Figure 24-22. Size A0 is the basis for metric paper sizes. It is 1 m^2 in area, with a rectangular shape in a 5:7 proportion.

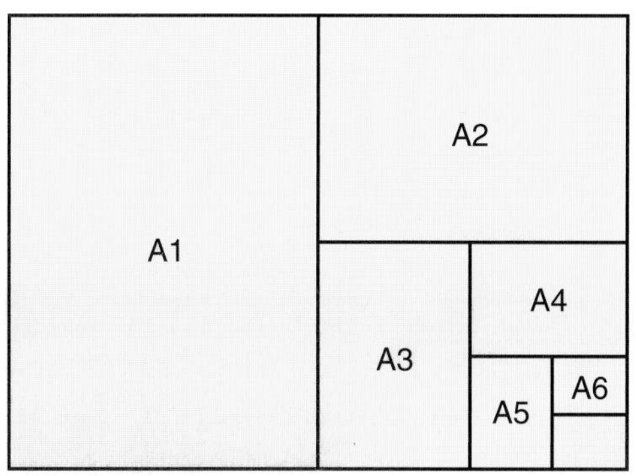

Figure 24-23. Metric paper sizes are simply halves of larger sizes.

Designation	mm	Index
A0	841 × 1189	33.11 × 46.81
A1	594 × 841	23.39 × 33.11
A2	420 × 594	16.54 × 23.39
A3	297 × 420	11.69 × 16.54
A4	210 × 297	8.27 × 11.69
A5	148 × 210	5.83 × 8.27
A6	105 × 148	4.13 × 5.83
A7	74 × 105	2.91 × 4.13
A8	52 × 74	2.05 × 2.91
B0	1000 × 1414	39.37 × 55.67
B1	707 × 1000	27.83 × 39.37
B2	500 × 707	19.68 × 27.83
B3	353 × 500	13.90 × 19.68
B4	250 × 353	9.84 × 13.90
B5	176 × 250	6.93 × 9.84
B6	125 × 176	4.92 × 6.93
B7	88 × 125	3.46 × 4.92
B8	62 × 88	2.44 × 3.46

Figure 24-24. Alphanumeric designations, sizes, and indices for the metric-size paper sheets. An index is the decimal equivalent in inches.

8 1/2″ × 11″ standard sheet used in the United States is the A4 size. It is 210 mm × 297 mm (8.27″ × 11.69″).

Qualities of Paper

There are several physical qualities that can be used to make judgments about which paper is most well-suited for a particular printing job. These are color, smoothness, strength, brightness, and opacity.

Color

Paper color and ink color must be compatible. White paper is essential for full- or four-color printing. It reflects all the colors of the spectrum, while colored paper does not. Colored paper can create a process color value that is undesirable, producing a finished piece that may not be what the customer expected.

Smoothness

Smoothness and texture both greatly affect ***printability***, or how well images show fine detail. Smoothness varies with paper type. A smooth sheet requires a very thin film of ink to produce sharp images. The opposite is true for rough papers.

Strength

The ***tensile strength*** of paper is determined by how well the inner fibers are bonded together. A roll of paper that cannot feed through a web press without breaking easily has loosely bonded fibers and low strength.

Print strength (or *pick strength*) is determined by how well the surface of the paper is bonded together. A low print strength could allow bits of fiber to be lifted off the paper surface by high-tack inks. *Hickeys* or specks would appear on the printed image. Coated stock normally has higher print strength than uncoated stock.

Brightness

Brightness is determined by how well the paper surface reflects light. Paper brightness affects the contrast of the printed image. A bright paper makes colors, particularly black, stand out more.

Transparent ink on a bright paper also produces exceptional color rendition. More light reflects up through the ink layers to produce stronger colors.

Opacity

Opacity refers to the ability of light to pass through a sheet of paper. It is also the ability to see through the sheet. Poor opacity produces an undesirable result called ***show-through***. The image on the back side of the sheet can be seen through the paper, and is a distraction to the reader. Examine stock carefully to make sure show-through will not occur. A heavyweight paper has high opacity, whereas a thin paper tends to have low opacity.

Envelopes

Envelopes come in many styles and sizes for a variety of applications. Envelopes used for postal purposes have a minimum size requirement of 3 1/2″ × 5″. Any size over 6 1/8″ × 11 1/2″, or thicker than 1/4″, is subject to additional postage fees. **Figure 24-25** illustrates common envelope styles.

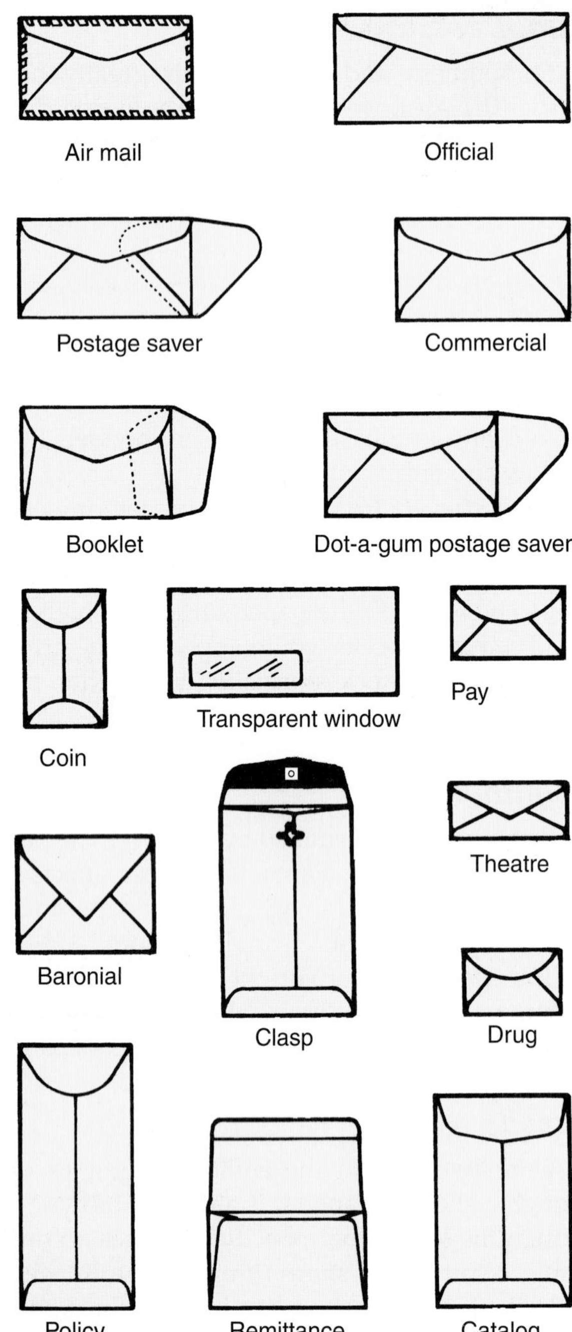

Figure 24-25. Typical envelope styles. (Carpenter-Offutt Paper Co.)

- The *commercial envelope* is typically used to send correspondence. The No. 10 size (4 1/8″ × 9 1/2″) is the most widely used.
- The *window envelope* has an opening that allows the address to appear through the clear opening. This is a time-saving and convenient feature.
- The *baronial envelope* is used mostly for invitations, announcements, and greeting cards.
- The *booklet envelope*, with its opening on the side, is used to hold house publications and direct mail pieces.
- The *clasp envelope* is used to mail bulky materials. The manner of fastening will vary, but it is strong and can take abuse.

Figure 24-26 lists common envelope sizes. Envelope company catalogs provide more detailed information.

Other Substrates

Paper is not the only substrate used in the graphic communications industry. Printing on foil is common in the packaging industry. Metal and plastic have many applications, as well. Because of their use in so many products, plastic substrates will be discussed here.

Plastic substrates

Plastic has many variations. Sometimes it is a thin film. Other times it is a sturdy yet flexible material. Another plastic might be stiff or even rigid. Plastic substrates are blended from various ***petrochemicals*** (petroleum-based chemicals) and other compounds. Most plastic substrates are available in both roll and sheet form.

Polyester

Polyester is one of the strongest plastic films used as a printing substrate. It has high clarity, toughness, durability, and good dimensional stability. It must be treated to prepare its surface for offset printing. Polyester substrates are used for decals, labels, and signs.

Copolyester

Copolyester is an extruded and dull-finished plastic substrate. It has a high degree of dimensional stability, clarity, and formability. It is available in matte finish or transparent colors. Copolyester is a comparatively inexpensive plastic substrate. Book report covers, overhead projector overlays, and flip charts are a few of its applications.

Size	Dimensions (inches)		
Office and Commercial			
5	3 1/6	x	5 1/2
6 1/4	3 1/2	x	6
6 3/4	3 5/8	x	6 1/2
7	3 3/4	x	6 3/4
7 3/4	3 7/8	x	7 1/2
8 5/8	3 5/8	x	8 5/8
9	3 7/8	x	8 7/8
10	4 1/8	x	9 1/2
11	4 1/2	x	10 3/8
12	4 3/4	x	11
14	5	x	11 1/2
Baronial			
4	3 5/8	x	4 11/16
5	4 1/8	x	5 1/8
5 1/2	4 3/8	x	5 5/8
5 3/4	4 5/8	x	5 15/16
Booklet			
2 1/2	4 1/2	x	5 7/8
3	4 3/4	x	6 1/2
5	5 1/2	x	8 1/8
6	5 3/4	x	8 7/8
6 1/2	6	x	9
7	6 1/4	x	9 5/8
7 1/2	7 1/2	x	10 1/2
9	8 3/4	x	11 1/2
9 1/2	9	x	12
10	9 1/2	x	12 5/8
Clasp			
0	2 1/2	x	4 1/4
5	3 1/8	x	5 1/2
10	3 3/8	x	6
15	4	x	6 3/8
11	4 1/2	x	10 3/8
25	4 5/8	x	6 3/4
35	5	x	7 1/2
14	5	x	11 1/2
50	5 1/2	x	8 1/4
55	6	x	9
63	6 1/2	x	9 1/2
68	7	x	10
75	7 1/2	x	10 1/2
80	8	x	11
83	8 1/2	x	11 1/2
87	9 3/4	x	11 1/4
90	9	x	12
93	9 1/2	x	12 1/2
94	9 1/4	x	14 1/2
95	10	x	12
97	10	x	13
98	10	x	15
105	11 1/2	x	14 1/2
110	12	x	15 1/2

Figure 24-26. Common envelope sizes and dimensions.

Lexan polycarbonate film

Lexan® polycarbonate film is a high-gloss substrate with good dimensional stability, good heat resistance, and excellent light transmittance. Low-haze polycarbonate film can be printed on offset presses without pretreatment. It is easily die cut and embossed. Lexan is used for decals, nameplates, membrane switch panels, overlays, and product identification.

Rigid vinyl

A *rigid vinyl* substrate has good stability and is available in calendered gloss or matte finish. It comes in white translucent, white opaque, and standard opaque colors. Rigid vinyl is commonly used for identification cards or credit cards, but it is also used for shelf signs or labels, danglers, wall signs, and pocket calendars. Rigid vinyl is easily die cut and ***thermoformed*** (formed by heat and pressure) into shapes.

High-impact polystyrene

High-impact polystyrene is a versatile and economical plastic substrate. It is offset-printable and available in translucent and opaque colors. It is used for point-of-purchase display signs and toys.

Cellulose acetate

Cellulose acetate is the plastic film that was first used as a printing substrate. It provides outstanding clarity but poor dimensional stability and tear-resistance. Its soft surface is receptive to a wide variety of inks. Cellulose acetate is used for folders, book jackets, and overhead projector transparencies.

Clear-oriented polyester

Clear-oriented polyester is the cheapest plastic substrate available. It tears and scratches easily but provides good clarity. It is used for short-term display signs, labels, visual aids, and similar products.

Kimdura

Kimdura® is a white opaque or translucent polypropylene film substrate. It serves as a "synthetic paper" that has been treated for offset printing. It is tough and durable, and can withstand repeated folding. Kimdura has good dimensional stability and a waterproof printing surface. It is used for posters, brochures, catalogs, children's books, outdoor maps, globes, menus, and instructional manuals.

Reemay

Reemay® is a spunbonded polyester that is acrylic-coated on both sides. It is bright white. Reemay feels like fabric and can be sewn and grommeted. It is used for banners and similar applications and has excellent UV-resistance.

Tyvek

Tyvek® is a strong spunbonded polyolefin plastic substrate. It has a smooth surface, good dimensional stability, good UV-resistance, and excellent opacity. Tyvek is treated with an antistatic agent to facilitate sheet handling. It is commonly used for envelopes, tags, labels, maps, and book coverings.

Review Questions

Please do not write in this book. Write your answers on a separate sheet of paper.

1. List three common materials used as printing substrates.
2. Most paper manufactured in the U.S. is made on what machine?
3. What is the raw material used to make paper?
4. _____ is added to the pulp to make paper moisture-resistant. _____ are added to improve opacity, brightness, smoothness, and ink receptivity.
5. _____ paper is smoother, stronger, and yields a better image than _____ paper.
6. What are two alternatives to using chlorine gas to bleach paper?
7. What characteristic is associated with machine-made papers?
8. How many sheets are in a ream of paper?
9. What is the formula for determining basis weight?
10. How many sheets of 8″ × 10″ can be cut out of a 17″ × 22″ sheet?
11. What color of paper is essential for true process color reproduction?
12. Pick or print _____ is an important factor affecting hickeys or specks on the printed image.
13. The _____ of paper affects whether the paper will exhibit an undesirable problem called _____.
14. The process that impresses a translucent design in paper is:
    a. watermarking.
    b. calendering.
    c. furnishing.
    d. embossing.
15. Which plastic substrate is typically used to make identification cards and credit cards?

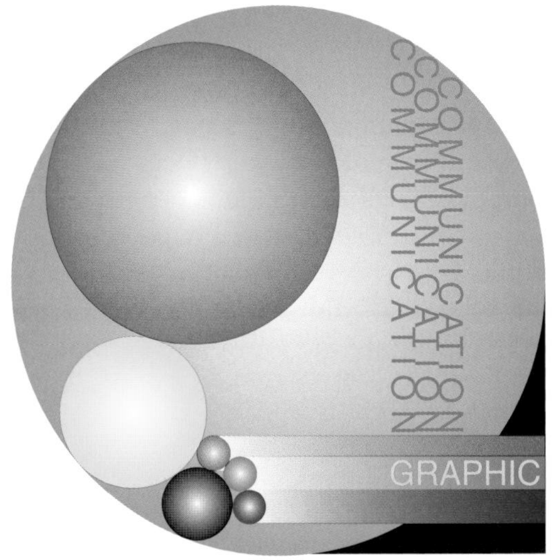

Ink 25

Learning Objectives

After studying this chapter, you will be able to:

- Summarize the various properties of ink.
- Define commonly used terms relating to ink.
- Identify the characteristics of inks used for different printing processes.
- Describe the characteristics of some specialized inks.
- Describe how to mix and match ink.
- Explain how ink characteristics affect the printed product.

Important Terms

inkometer
pigment
polymerization
reflection densitometer
scumming
setoff
strike-through
tack
thixotropy
vehicle

Ink is the most common coating used to place a printed image on a substrate. Various inks are manufactured for use with the many printing processes and substrates available today. Inks have several properties that can affect printing quality. They must flow properly, have the correct stickiness (tack), be permanent, dry properly, and have a workable consistency for the press rollers. This chapter will discuss the characteristics of printing inks and summarize how ink can affect a print job.

Ink Ingredients

Ink formulation refers to the amount and type of ingredients used in a particular printing ink. Three ingredients are essential to the formulation of printing inks: vehicle, pigment, and additives.

The ***vehicle*** is a binding agent that holds the ink together. It also acts as a carrier for the *pigment* (color). A vehicle is often a solvent-resin or oil-resin combination, although soy-based paste inks are also widely used. Compounds, additives, oxidant agents, wetting agents, and antifoaming agents may be added, as well.

The ***pigment*** provides the color in an ink. A wide range of opaque or transparent pigments is available. Pigments are usually used dry and ground into a vehicle. They can also be used ***flush***, as a paste dispersed in a vehicle. Dyes also may be used as coloring agents, particularly in flexographic inks.

Additives are ingredients added to ink to impart special characteristics. For example, certain additives reduce body tack, while others help make ink water-resistant. Driers, lubricants, waxes, and starches are common additives.

Driers accelerate drying, which permits the stacking of printed sheets without causing ***setoff***, the transfer or smearing of ink. See **Figure 25-1**. Various devices or systems can assist with drying. Infrared (IR) radiation is used to accelerate oxidation. Ultraviolet (UV) radiation assists in curing. Spray powders are sometimes dispersed over the surface of the printed sheet to eliminate direct contact.

Ink is a chemical product and must be handled properly. Certain inks require special handling. Always follow the manufacturer's instructions.

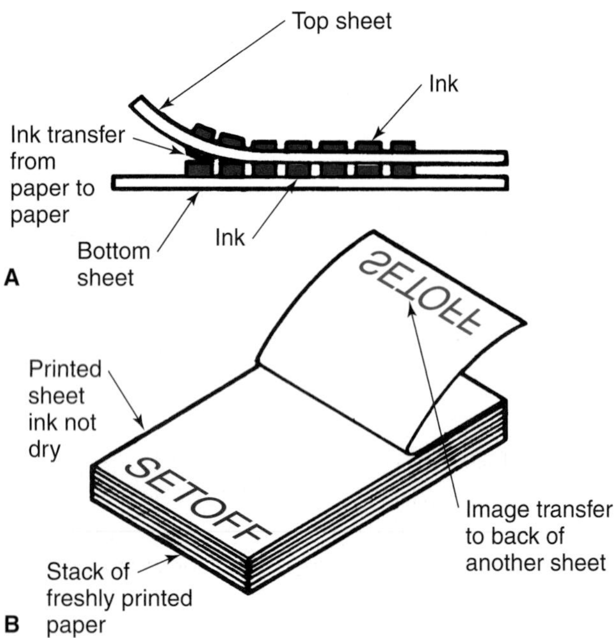

Figure 25-1. Setoff occurs when printed sheets output from a press are stacked on top of each other. Setoff is usually caused by improper drying of ink, but it can also be caused by excessively thick ink film, paper stacked too high, or an improper substrate and ink combination. A—How setoff occurs. B—The result of setoff.

Ink Properties

Color strength, body, stability, length, tack, and drying are common properties of ink.

Color strength

Color strength is the ability of an ink to cover a substrate. Strong colorants produce vivid, sharp images and give good coverage. Weak colorants are generally not desirable. Pigments or dyes must be compatible with the ink base and carefully selected for the end use. Metallic, fluorescent, and pearl pigments are used to create special effects.

A transparent ink has weak color strength and is used when it is desirable for an image to show through the ink. Transparent inks are used in four-color printing where all colors of the spectrum are produced by overprinting the four process colors.

Ink body

Ink body refers to an ink's consistency, thickness, or fluidity. Some inks are stiff and thick, while others are thin and fluid. The thickness or fluidity of an ink can affect press operation considerably.

Inks used in relief or offset lithographic printing are very stiff, but flow more freely after being worked (mixed) by the press rollers. Gravure inks are formulated to be thin so they flow easily onto the substrate from the microscopic ink wells of the gravure cylinder.

With lithography, high ink body tends to thicken the deposit of ink on the substrate. A thinner ink does the opposite. High-speed presses use soft-bodied (more flowing) ink, while slower presses use heavy-bodied (less flowing) ink. Ink must be formulated for a specific printing process.

Thickness and fineness gauges

An ***ink thickness gauge*** is a device used to measure the thickness of the ink film on the press. The measurement is taken on the steel roller of the ink train of the press. The ink film gauge measurements are in mils (thousandths of an inch). An ***ink fineness gauge*** measures the pigment particle size in the ink with a very high degree of accuracy.

Ink stability

Ink stability, or ***thixotropy***, is the tendency of an ink to flow more freely after being worked. In relief printing, the press rollers work the ink by squeezing and depositing it on the press rollers before printing. Stirring or agitating ink tends to break down its internal cohesiveness. Ink that is agitated in the fountain flows more easily and distributes more evenly on the press rollers.

Many large presses have vibrators to work the ink. The motion helps keep the ink stable and fluid while it is in the fountain. Lack of motion causes the ink to become stiff and unable to transfer properly.

Ink length

Ink length refers to the elasticity of an ink and its ability to form a filament or strand. The filament can be long or short, **Figure 25-2**.

If the ink forms a long filament, it will have a tendency to fly out on a high-speed press. *Long inks*, such as those used on newsprint, flow more rapidly than short inks. *Short inks* flow poorly and have the consistency of butter.

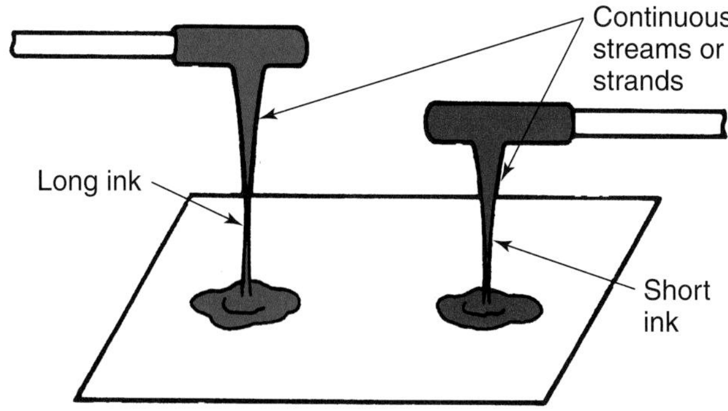

Figure 25-2. To form filaments, a rod is placed in ink, tapped on a surface, and then lifted. An ink that produces long filaments is called a "long" ink. "Short" inks produce shorter filaments.

Ink tack

Ink tack refers to stickiness of the ink. It is a measurement of cohesion between the ink film and the substrate. The term is generally used when describing paste inks, such as those used in relief printing. When ink leaves the fountain, it should "split" (have limited tack). If ink does not split (has too much tack), it cannot be transferred from one roller to another, to the plate and blanket, or from the roller to a surface of the substrate.

An ***inkometer*** measures the tack of an ink to determine if it is too great for the surface strength of the paper. Too much tack can cause the paper to rupture, resulting in picking, splitting, or tearing. See **Figure 25-3**.

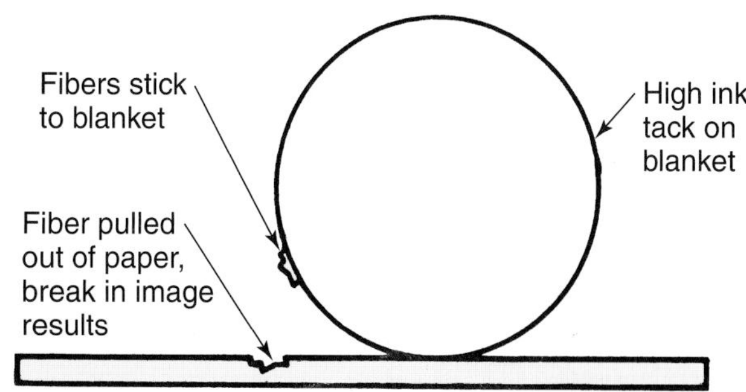

Figure 25-3. Picking can result when ink tack is not matched to stock. High tack can pull off fibers of paper.

Ink drying

An ink's ability to dry is important to the quality of the final product. Some common means of drying ink are absorption, evaporation, oxidation, polymerization, and precipitation, **Figure 25-4**.

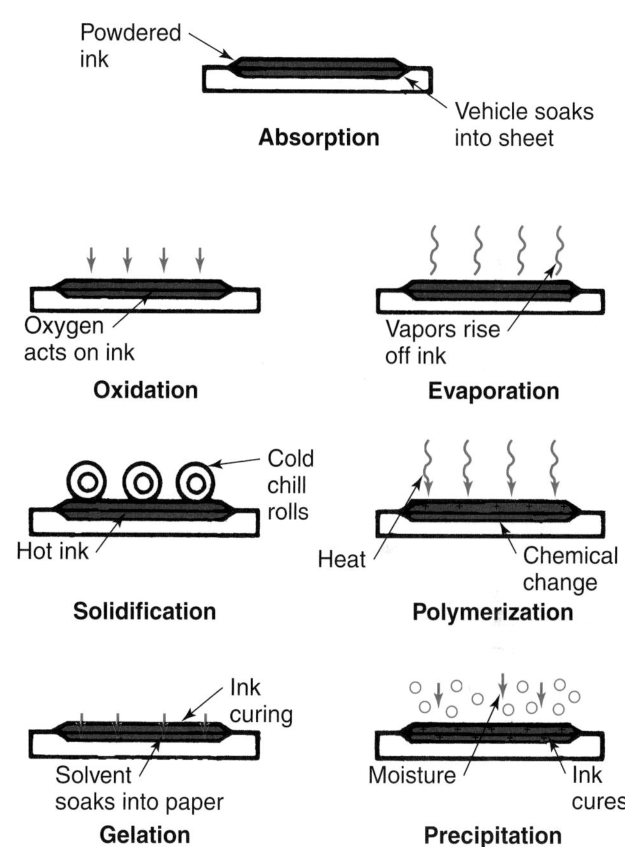

Figure 25-4. Inks dry in a number of ways.

- *Absorption-drying ink*, also called *penetrating ink*, dries when the solvent is drawn into the paper. The ink does not dry hard but remains on the surface as a powder-like substance. Newspapers are a good example of inks that dry by absorption or penetration. If you rub your fingers over newsprint, a black powder will deposit on your skin.

- *Evaporation-drying inks* dry as the solvent is evaporated into the surrounding air, leaving a solid film of resin on the paper. Evaporation-drying inks are used in flexography, gravure, web offset, and other processes where fast drying time is important. Solvent-evaporative inks consist of resins, solvents, and additives. Specific types include poster inks, lacquers, and textile dyes.
- *Oxidation-drying inks* dry by absorbing oxygen from the surrounding air. Letterpress and offset printing commonly use oxidation-drying inks.
- *Polymerization-drying inks* dry by a chemical reaction that causes molecules in the ink to combine. Oxygen thickens the ink into a gel-like consistency, allowing the ink to be handled without smearing before it is fully dried. Polymerization inks can be used to print on metal.
- *Chemical-reaction inks* consist of resins, solvents, additives, and a drying-oil catalyst. These inks cure and dry by evaporation of the solvent and by oxidation. Specific types of ink include enamel, vinyl, epoxy, and polyester.
- *Precipitation-drying inks,* also called *moisture-set inks,* dry by reacting with water. Steam or water is sprayed on the ink after printing, causing the ink to set quickly. Glycol in the ink combines with the water and is absorbed into the paper.

Other ink-related terms

Other ink-related terms you should know include:

- *Permanent* or *colorfast ink* maintains its color with exposure to sunlight. It will not easily fade and is suitable for posters, signs, and other similar applications.
- *Resistant ink* is a very stable ink that can withstand exposure to forces that would fade other inks. It can tolerate sunlight, chemicals, heat, moisture, and gases without fading.
- *Fugitive ink* will fade and lose its color after prolonged exposure to sunlight. It is useful for temporary signs and posters.
- *Viscosity* refers to how easily an ink will flow. High viscosity ink is thick and resists flow. Low viscosity ink is fluid and flows more easily. See **Figure 25-5.**

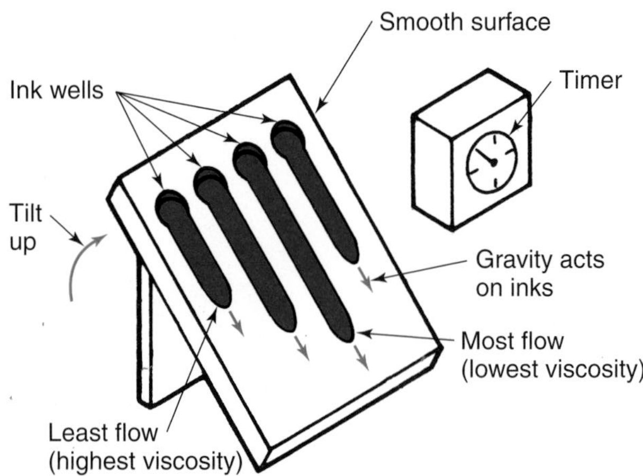

Figure 25-5. Viscosity is a measure of the thickness or fluidity of an ink. A basic method for comparing viscosity is to place the inks in small wells hollowed out of a flat surface. Tilt the surface upward so the inks flow out of the wells. The ink with the most (fastest) flow has the lowest viscosity; the ink with the least (slowest) flow has the highest viscosity. Flows can be timed to get accurate viscosity readings.

- *Lake* is an ink colorant formed when a soluble dye is converted to a pigment in a white base.
- *Toner* is a strong, concentrated ink colorant. Toner primarily consists of pure pigment ground and mixed into linseed oil.
- *Job black* refers to normal black ink used for a typical press run of average quality.
- *Halftone black* is a higher quality black ink designed for reproducing fine detail in halftone screen images.
- *Watercolors* are inks with a very flat or dull finish. They are water-based and do not contain varnish or oil.
- *Metallic inks* contain metal powders, such as aluminum or bronze, blended with an appropriate vehicle.
- *Cleaning white* is used to wash a press before changing from a dark to a light color.

- *Liquid tack reducer* cuts an ink's tack and body. It can be used to correct problems like picking and linting.
- *Paste tack reducer* cuts tack but does not affect ink body.
- *Gloss/matte finishes* are the visual effect of ink formulation. Gloss is achieved by the smoothness of the ink deposited on the substrate as well as the volume of dried ink the substrate retains. The surface of the substrate also contributes to gloss. Matte ink is achieved by the addition of flattening agents. The agents create microscopically irregular surfaces, which the eye sees as matte.
- *Slow-dry additive* can be used to lengthen ink drying time or skinning time in the fountain.
- *Spray powder* can be placed on ink after printing to prevent setoff. A special press attachment sprays the powder onto the printed images, **Figure 25-6.**

Figure 25-6. A powder sprayer for small- to medium-sized presses. (Accel Graphic Systems)

- *Ink mill* is a machine with steel rollers for crushing the ink ingredients into a fine substance.
- *Nontoxic compounds* must be used when dried ink has direct contact with food or edible materials.
- *Fluorescent inks* are special colored ink pigments that glow under black light.
- *Opaque inks* are capable of hiding the color of the stock on which an image is being printed.
- *Vegetable-base inks* are replacing those based on petrochemical (mineral) oils. Vegetable oils have replaced mineral oils for mostly environmental reasons. Petrochemical solvents and oils emit environmentally toxic volatile organic substances (VOCs). In addition, ink wastes must be classified as "hazardous waste" and disposed of according to strict federal and state regulations.

Ink Formulation

Special formulas are used to produce inks that are compatible with certain printing processes. Scientists, engineers, and technicians are all involved in the highly competitive business of formulating inks.

The characteristics of ink formulation are determined by the plates, press units, and type of substrate. The types of ink used in producing images using the four basic printing processes are discussed next.

Relief inks

Several types of inks are used to place an image on a substrate by raised surfaces, or relief. Letterpress inks for covering the face of electrotypes, foundry type, and similar printing surfaces are generally quite tacky and viscous (thick). These inks usually dry by oxidation. However, the inks used to print on substrates, such as newsprint, dry by evaporation if heat is applied to the inked surface. Drying oils are used as vehicles to support the pigment. The pigment is often purchased in paste form.

Flexographic inks are fast-drying and used for printing on a variety of substrates, including paper, cloth, plastic, and metal. Alcohol-based flexographic inks dry by evaporation while water-based flexo inks dry by evaporation or absorption.

Typical kinds of relief printing ink include rotary, quick-set, moisture-set, water-washable, news, and job. The inks are formulated for various types of presses and stocks for printing books, magazines, labels, packaging, or other commercial applications. *Job ink* is found in many commercial letterpress facilities, since it can be used on a wide variety of presses and papers. The quality of the ink varies with the types of images being printed. Linework ink does not need to be as high quality as halftone ink.

Gravure inks

The cells of a gravure plate or cylinder are recessed. Ink must be pulled from the cells and deposited on a substrate. Inking the cells is known as ***flooding***. A doctor blade removes the ink from the surface of the nonimage areas of the cylinder or plate. Gravure inks are very fluid and dry rapidly, mainly by evaporation. The printing substrate must be capable of absorbing the ink from the cells.

Many gravure inks are highly volatile and require certain precautions against fire. The area must be properly ventilated. Local, state, and federal requirements for pollution control, including solvent drainage, must be strictly followed. Many facilities have installed a solvent-recovery system.

Screen printing inks

Screen printing inks are thicker than inks for other processes. They are formulated to flow evenly when forced through the screen by the squeegee. Screen clogging can be a problem with screen printing inks; therefore, the solvent must not evaporate too quickly.

Conventional screen process inks contain pigments, binders, and solvents. The ***colorant*** (pigment) is held together by the binder, which also assists in adhering the ink to the substrate. The solvents dissolve the resins and form a pliable material.

Screen ink formulas vary greatly, since substrates are numerous. Typical substrates include paper, cloth, plastics, metal, and glass. It is important to communicate clearly with ink suppliers and vendors to select the screen ink that best meets the product's requirements.

Lithographic inks

The image area of a lithographic (also called planographic) plate is neither raised nor recessed. It is a flat surface with an image area that accepts ink. The nonimage areas are receptive to moisture.

Inks formulated for offset lithography must have high color strength. In lithography, the ink film placed on the substrate has less thickness than the ink film used in relief printing. A balance between ink and moisture is essential for complete and even ink transfer to the plate and substrate, **Figure 25-7**.

Figure 25-7. A compressible inner layer on these offset ink rollers eliminates roller distortion throughout the nip and distributes ink more evenly. (American Roller Company)

Lithographic inks dry by oxidation; therefore, it is essential that the ink set quickly. Moreover, the pigment must not bleed in water. Formulation of lithographic inks varies greatly since many types of substrates are used in sheet-fed and web-fed presses. Vehicles must be oxidative. Additives include soluble resins, drying and semi-drying oils, and varnishes.

Inks that dry (cure) by ultraviolet radiation (UV-curable inks) are used in lithographic facilities. Thermal-curing inks are also used. The thermal technique uses low amounts of solvents and requires heat and a catalyst.

The amount of moisture absorbed in the ink is critical. The vehicle for lithographic ink must be water-resistant, although the ink may accept 20% to 25% moisture before it emulsifies. Once emulsified, the surface will no longer distribute the ink throughout the inking system of the press. Too much moisture eliminates the tack needed for ink to transfer from one roller to another. The ink must split at the nip point of the press rollers, **Figure 25-8**.

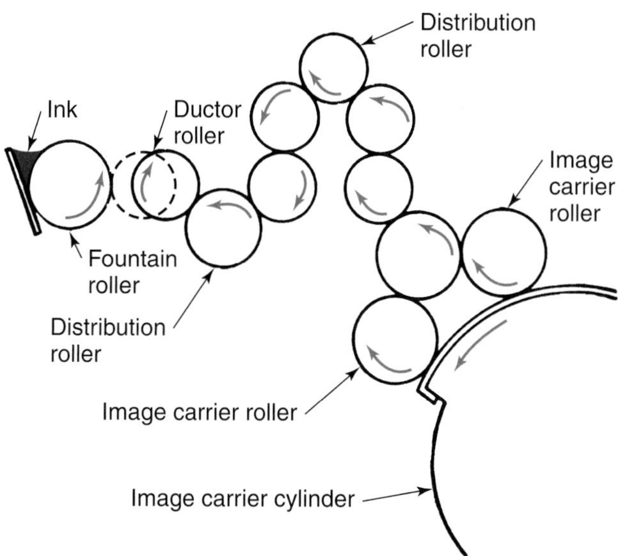

Figure 25-8. Ink formulation is critical to how well an ink splits and transfers from one press roller to the next.

Figure 25-9. Vacuum-sealed tubes in this ink-dispensing system prevent oxygen from contacting the ink and causing skinning. (Van Son Holland Ink)

Litho ink problems

A number of ink problems are associated with offset lithographic printing. Litho ink mixes with moisture to form an ink-in-water emulsion. This results in a problem known as ***tinting***, in which a slight tint of ink is left on the nonimage area of the printed sheet.

Scumming is the second problem that arises when the nonimage area of the plate accepts ink. There are two main causes of scumming: too much ink or too little fountain solution reaching the plate.

Most inks today contain a combination of vehicles that prevent the ink from ***skinning*** in the can or drying overnight if left on the press. Automated ink-dispensing systems also reduce costly ink waste by metering the precise amount of ink into the fountain, **Figure 25-9**.

Specialized Inks

Lithography is the most widely used printing process and has spurred a demand for specialized litho inks. While the majority of inks used are process colors in the main-line ink formulations, many specialized inks have been developed to satisfy specific needs.

Vegetable oil inks

A substantial portion of color inks in use now are *vegetable-oil based*, **Figure 25-10**. Vegetable oils have replaced mineral oils for mostly environmental reasons. Petrochemical solvents and oils emit environmentally toxic volatile organic substances (VOCs). The level of VOCs must be

Figure 25-10. Soy and other vegetable-based inks, which are free of environmentally harmful substances, are replacing solvent-based inks. (National Soy Ink Information Center)

controlled to meet local, state, and federal standards. The formula for determining the level of VOCs (by weight) is:

$$\text{VOCs} = \frac{\text{Total weight of formula} \quad \text{Water weight} \quad \text{Weight of nonvolatile compounds}}{\text{Total weight of formula}}$$

Apart from environmental benefits, vegetable inks have several technical benefits, such as cleaner and sharper printing and brighter colors. Transference, rub-resistance, and ink mileage are improved, as well. The price of vegetable oil color inks is comparable to the price of mineral oil color inks. Black ink, however, has less apparent technical benefits and a higher cost.

Vegetable-based inks do not dry as fast or as hard as conventional inks. As formulations for conventional inks become more environmentally safe, the popularity of vegetable-based inks may decline.

Sheetfed inks

Sheetfed inks contain a high proportion of vegetable oil, most commonly linseed oil. They contain about 5% to 10% petroleum distillates to allow acceptable press speeds. Sheetfed inks are suitable for use on eight-color perfecting machines, which require an ink that sets at exactly the correct speed.

Laser-proof inks

Electrostatic printing uses laser-proof inks for printing on laser printers and copiers. The image is fixed on the paper by heat up to 410°F (210°C) and pressure. The inks must be formulated to withstand intense heat without evaporating and to resist softening and transfer to the drum.

Hexachrome

Conventional yellow, magenta, and cyan have been brightened by the addition of fluorescent colors to produce a specialized ink called Hexachrome™ by Pantone. It is suited for six- and seven-color process printing. Colors are brighter than are possible with standard four colors; however, press performance is compromised because of the presence of fluorescent pigments.

Proofing inks

Despite the growth of digital proofing, wet proofs are still needed when accurate contract proofs are required. Proofing inks are formulated to compensate for the porosity that occurs on proofing press rollers, which are frequently washed with strong solvents. In addition to being stable, these inks are able to control dot gain.

Metallic inks

Metallic inks contain metal powders, such as aluminum and bronze, blended with an appropriate vehicle. New gold and silver inks are free of heavy metals, a concern in food and toy packaging. Water-based metallic inks that deliver superior brilliance have been developed for use on multicolor presses.

UV-curable inks

Ultraviolet curable inks consist of resins, monomers, additives, and photoinitiators. These inks do not dry; instead they cure (there is no solvent evaporation). As ultraviolet light strikes the ink, a chemical reaction, called ***polymerization***, occurs which converts the ink from a liquid to a solid. Specific types of UV-curable inks are available for paper, plastic sheets, plastic bottles, and other substrates.

UV curing is comparable in cost to solvent- and water-based systems. The environmentally friendly aspect of UV technology may be the most important factor in the growth of UV inks. VOCs are less than 1% in UV inks, and UV-printed papers can be repulped and recycled. An odor problem associated with curing has had a limiting effect on the use of UV inks with food packaging.

Waterless inks

Waterless inks have attracted the attention of print shops because they allow for faster makeready and also dry quickly. Higher color density and good adhesion to nonabsorbent plastic substrates make them attractive, as well. Waterless inks have high viscosity and thickness. Raising the temperature during printing allows a waterless ink to flow more readily. See **Figure 25-11**.

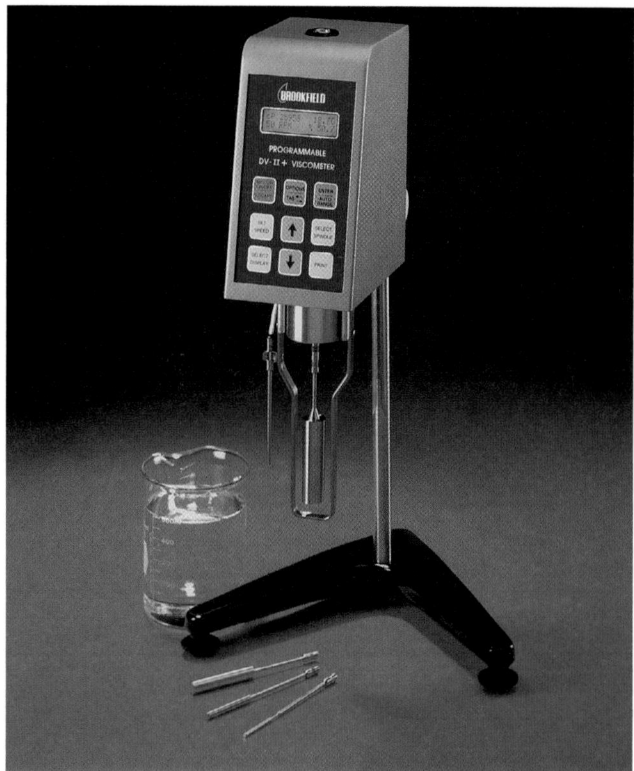

Figure 25-11. A viscometer is useful in determining the effect of temperature on the viscoelastic properties of ink used in waterless printing. (Brookfield Engineering Laboratories, Inc.)

Hybrid inks

The development of this ink came about because printers wanted a material with the qualities of UV ink at lower cost. It is very expensive for a printer to dedicate one press to UV inks. The hybrid inks can be used on a conventional press, which is then retrofitted with UV lighting stations. These energy-cured inks can perform as well or better than conventional inks. Most conventional inks don't dry quickly, but when hybrid inks are used, the image is dry when it arrives at the delivery end of the press.

Mixing, Matching, and Proofing

Mixing systems are available for all types of printing inks. These systems are used to blend basic inks. The inks are weighed to a prescribed amount based on information on a cataloged color selector.

The basic equipment for manual color mixing and matching consists of a hard, smooth surface; mixing knives or spatulas, scales, a color chart, and a record card. See **Figure 25-12**.

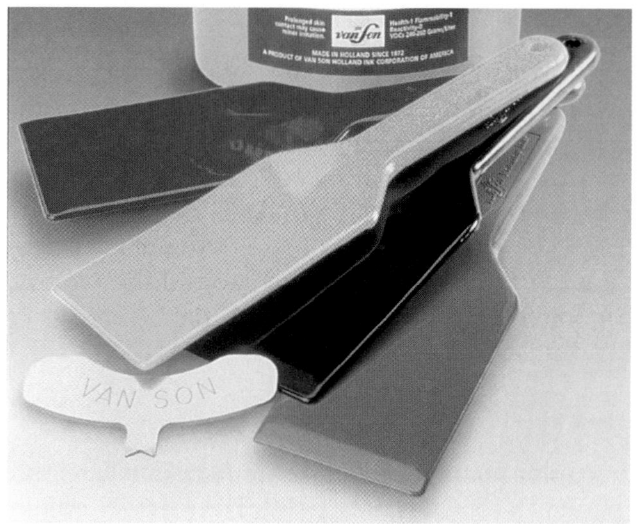

Figure 25-12. Spatulas or mixing knives are used to mix ink by hand. (Van Son Holland Ink)

Color matching can be done by visually evaluating the color and substrate. The selection of pigments and dyes requires the eye of a talented and knowledgeable colormatcher. Small adjustments are made to bring the color to exact specifications.

Another color matching technique is to read the color values of a sample using a ***spectrophotometer***, **Figure 25-13**. This computer-controlled instrument measures the relative intensity of radiation through the spectrum based on the sample.

Figure 25-13. Accurate matches between digital color proofs and color samples can be made using a spectrophotometer. (Iris Graphics, Inc.)

Figure 25-14. Color matching charts or manuals are used to match inks with sample colors. (Van Son Holland Ink)

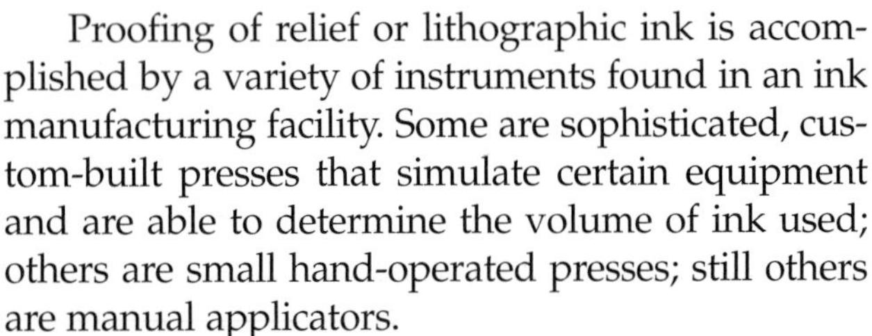

Proofing of relief or lithographic ink is accomplished by a variety of instruments found in an ink manufacturing facility. Some are sophisticated, custom-built presses that simulate certain equipment and are able to determine the volume of ink used; others are small hand-operated presses; still others are manual applicators.

Custom-built presses are available for flexographic proofing. Proofs can also be done manually using a ***brayer***, a small, hand-held roller used to spread ink with both a rubber plate-type roller and a metering steel roll. It simulates the "squeegee" application of ink on a full-size flexographic press. Gravure can be proofed very successfully on custom-built proofing presses and press-simulating instruments.

Mixing and matching procedures

Color manuals or charts are available from ink manufacturers, **Figure 25-14**. The charts contain samples of ink on coated and uncoated stock.

Before mixing, make sure the area is clean. Weigh out the designated amount of each ink on a scale, according to the manufacturer's specifications. (Be sure to include the weight of the paper placed on the scale pan.) Place the inks on a glass plate or smooth surface, and thoroughly mix them with an ink spatula until the color is uniform. Tap some of the ink onto the stock to be used, and compare the color with the sample. Continue selecting and weighing the ink according to the color system, until the color matches the sample perfectly.

Use only small amounts of ink to mix a trial batch. After the ink is thoroughly mixed, pull a proof. Compare the proof with the sample. When matching a tint, the color should be added to a white base in very small quantities until the desired tint is reached.

Ink mileage

How much ink is needed for a specific job? Finding the ***ink mileage*** is not easy, but it is crucial. Running out of ink can be disastrous. Tables can provide the approximate number of square inches that a given amount of ink will cover. For example, full strength lithographic inks cover between 350,000 sq. in./lb. and 450,000 sq. in./lb. on coated, sheet-fed stock. On uncoated sheets, coverage is between 280,000 sq. in./lb. and 360,000 sq. in./lb. Absorption may result in a mileage loss of 20% or more.

When calculating the amount of ink needed, include the ink for makeready as well as the amount left in the ink fountain and on the rollers. See **Figure 25-15**.

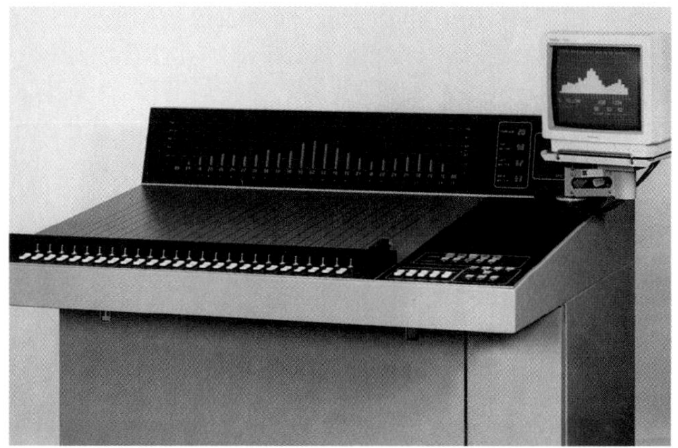

Figure 25-15. This remote ink control system can interface with computer-to-plate systems, plate scanners, imagesetters, and scanning densitometers, resulting in shorter makeready time and better color consistency. (Essex Products Group)

Several factors govern the amount of ink needed: specific gravity and color strength of the ink, stock surface, work to be printed, ink needed to prepare the press, type of press, and thickness of the ink film.

Ink can be purchased in tubes, cartridges, cans, pails, drums, and tanks, **Figure 25-16**. Ink containers should be stored in a cool, dry place and covered tightly to prevent contamination and drying. ***Livering***, a chemical change that takes place during storage, is not reversible. Flakes of dried ink should be kept out of the ink fountain.

Figure 25-16. Today's inks are engineered to meet the high-speed requirements of technologically advanced printing presses. (Van Son Holland Ink)

Ordering ink

Consider the following questions when ordering ink:

- What colors will be used for the job?
- What printing process will be used: relief, gravure, offset, screen?
- What are the product requirements? For example, must the ink be long-lasting and weather-resistant?
- What substrate will be used: paper (smooth or rough, etc.), plastic, metal?
- Is ink *cost* a consideration?

Asking these questions will help you and your ink sales representative select the appropriate ink for the job.

Ink-related Challenges

Inks can cause a wide variety of printing problems. Sometimes ink *is* at fault; other times, the ink is blamed for what is, in fact, a *press* or a *paper* problem.

Setting and drying

Set is the point at which an ink is dry enough to be lightly touched without smudging. ***Dry*** is the point at which the ink is free of volatile substances and has polymerized to a total solid state. Ink will dry relative to the substrate. On nonabsorbent substrates, ink must dry strictly by oxidation. This may take from 6 to 24 hours.

Chalking

Chalking is an ink-adherence problem that occurs when dried ink rubs off the substrate. Newspaper ink chalks by nature. Since a newspaper is only used once and then discarded, chalking does not pose a serious problem. Chalking would be unacceptable with a more permanent product, such as this textbook. Chalking can be prevented by applying a nonpenetrating varnish to the substrate surface to hold the pigment.

Adhesion in ink is relative to the printing process. Lithographic inks adhere best on porous substrates, while gravure and flexographic printing allow the use of solvents and resins that readily adhere to nonporous substrates, such as foils, vinyl, and polyester.

Strike-through

Strike-through is an ink-penetration problem that occurs when the ink soaks into the paper too deeply and shows through the opposite side of the sheet. Usually, strike-through is caused by an excessively long ink-drying time. The long drying time allows the ink to soak into the paper. A highly absorbent paper can also cause strike-through.

Strike-through should not be confused with *show-through*. Strike-through is caused by excessive ink absorption. Show-through is caused by thin or insufficiently opaque stock.

Setoff

As mentioned earlier, *setoff* occurs when wet ink transfers onto the back of a sheet that is stacked on top of the previously printed sheet. It is often incorrectly referred to as "offset." Setoff can also be caused by an excessively thick ink deposit on the paper, improper ink, paper stacked too high, or a drying system problem.

Ink sticking

Ink sticking can occur if two layers of ink film, on two different sheets, bond together. The problem is similar to setoff; both are caused by improper drying.

Plate wear

Plate wear can be caused by pigments that are not fully ground to a fine powder. The unground particles in the ink act as an abrasive, wearing away the surface of the plate. Excessive pigment can also cause plate wear. Always check the ink grind when plate wear is excessive. Excessive roller pressure or an abrasive substrate are two more reasons for plate wear.

Off color

When the color of the printed job does not match the intended color, the job is said to be ***off color***. Off-color problems have many causes. A dirty press can alter the colors of the ink. The substrate color (if it is not true white) can affect the printed color. Thickness, opacity, translucence, or other ink qualities can all affect the color of the printed product. Improper ink mixing can also result in an off-color problem.

A ***drawdown test*** can be used to check for proper ink mixing. A standard ink and the newly mixed ink are placed on the stock. Then, a thin blade is used to spread the inks down over the surface of the stock, **Figure 25-17**. After drying, the standard ink is compared to the newly mixed ink for proper color match, tone, and strength.

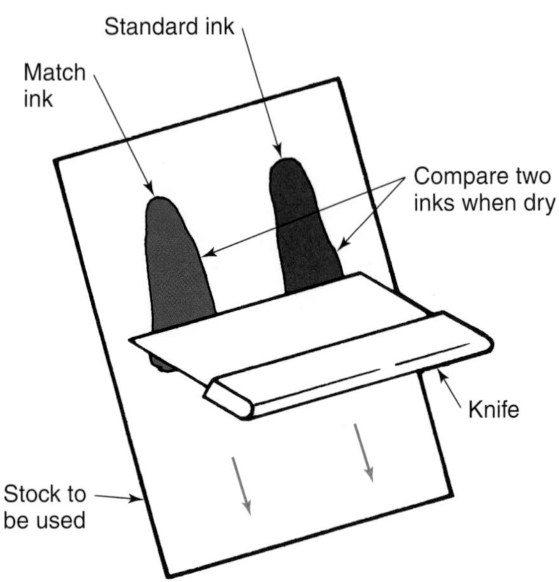

Figure 25-17. In a drawndown test, a standard ink and a mixed ink are placed on the chosen stock. A sharp blade is used to spread the inks onto the stock. After drying, ink qualities are compared.

Specking

Specking is the appearance of tiny dots next to halftone dots or line art. Specking occurs when the ink is contaminated with paper fibers or other foreign material, or when it is not properly ground. Ink film that is too thick could also cause specking.

Process Ink Analysis

Process inks (yellow, magenta, cyan, and black) differ from one ink manufacturer to another. Color bars printed under normal printing conditions may be used to evaluate a particular set of inks used in a printing facility. Most service bureaus or printers furnish test patterns, **Figure 25-18**.

A ***reflection densitometer*** is used for taking density readings from the printed control bars. This instrument measures the amount of light reflected from an object. Record the density readings on a

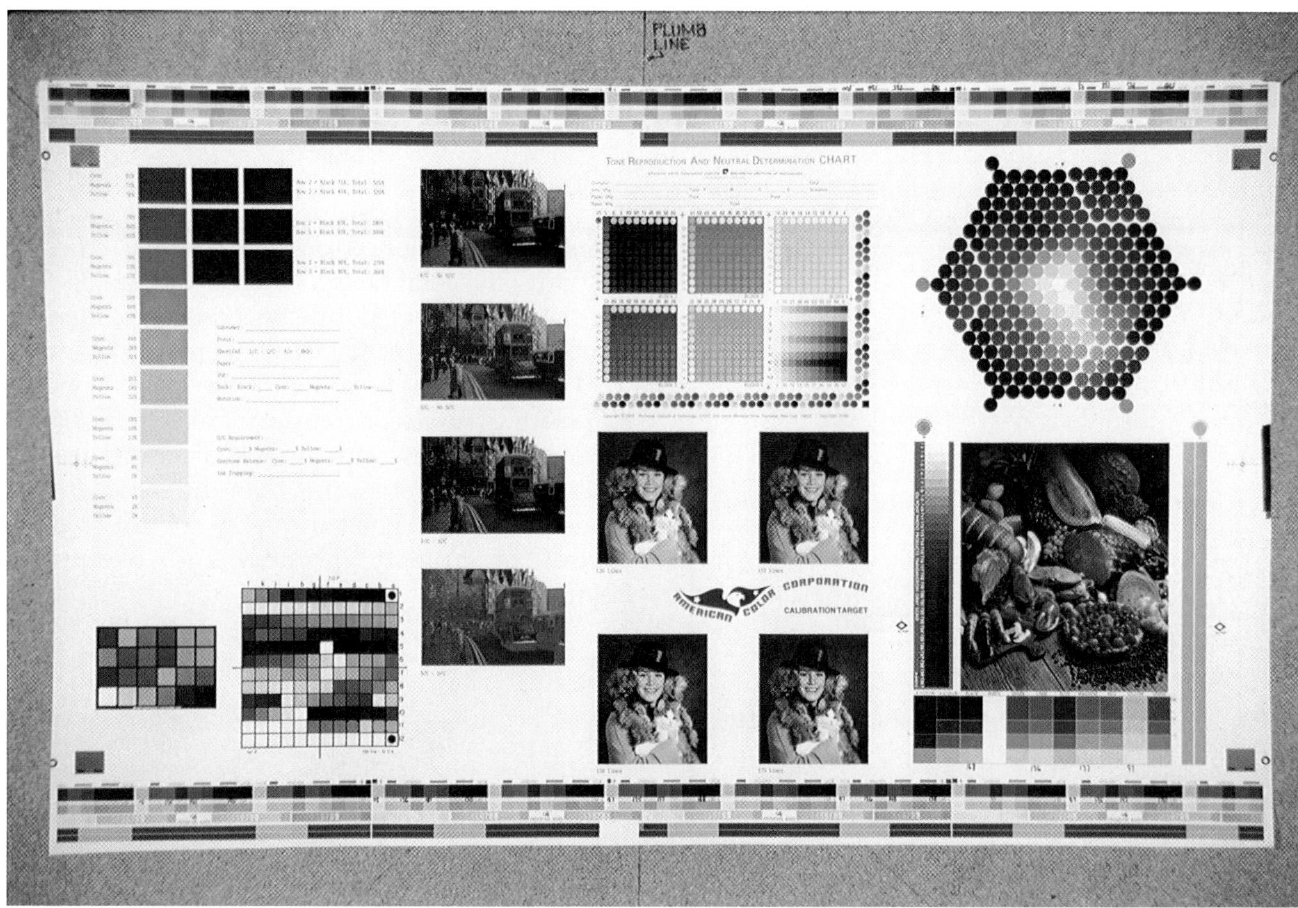

Figure 25-18. An ink analysis test pattern. (American Color Corp.)

process ink data sheet, **Figure 25-19**. The density readings can be used to determine the four principle working characteristics of a set of process inks: strength, hue, grayness, and efficiency.

Ink strength identifies the range and depth of colors that can be produced from a set of inks. Strength can be determined by visually comparing the density readings, and selecting the highest reading for the yellow, magenta, and cyan inks.

Ink hue error identifies the percentage of reflection of colored light from a specific color of ink. A hue or color is determined by the eye in terms of cone stimulation to colors of light. The color or hue of magenta ink should absorb and prevent green light from reflecting off the paper surface, and allow all of the blue and red light to reflect. The ink impurities in the magenta ink pigmentation that distort this normal reflection ratio can be measured as a percentage of hue error.

To determine the hue error for one color of ink and its red, green, and blue filter readings, use the equation:

$$\text{Hue error} = \frac{\text{Medium filter reading} - \text{Low filter reading}}{\text{High filter reading} - \text{Low filter reading}}$$

The purity of a process color is identified by a *grayness* factor. A color is considered gray when its predominant color reflects less light than the white sheet of paper it is printed on. For example, cyan should reflect 100% blue and green light, but it is considered gray in percentage because it reflects less blue than the white paper.

The lower the percentage or grayness factor, the higher the purity level. To determine the grayness factor for a given color of ink, use the equation:

$$\text{Grayness factor} = \frac{\text{Low filter reading}}{\text{High filter reading}}$$

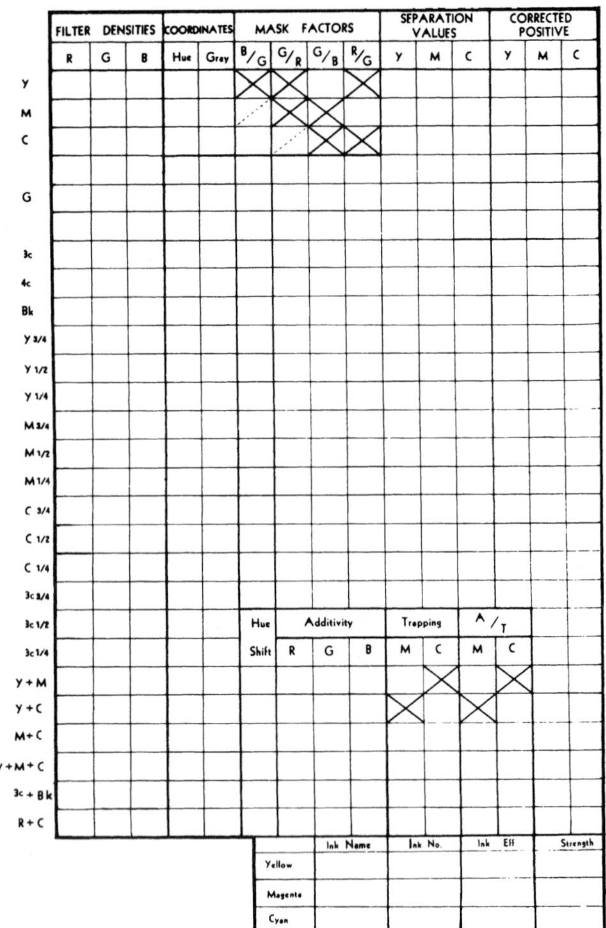

	FILTER DENSITIES			COORDINATES		MASK FACTORS				SEPARATION VALUES			CORRECTED POSITIVE		
	R	G	B	Hue	Grey	B/G	G/R	G/B	R/G	Y	M	C	Y	M	C
Y															
M															
C															
G															
3c															
4c															
Bk															
Y 3/4															
Y 1/2															
Y 1/4															
M 3/4															
M 1/2															
M 1/4															
C 3/4															
C 1/2															
C 1/4															
3c 3/4															
3c 1/2															
3c 1/4															
Y+M															
Y+C															
M+C															
Y+M+C															
3c + Bk															
R+C															

Hue Shift	Additivity			Trapping		A/T	
	R	G	B	M	C	M	C

	Ink Name	Ink No.	Ink Eff	Strength
Yellow				
Magenta				
Cyan				

Figure 25-19. A process ink data sheet can be used to record information concerning methods used to produce separations.

Ink efficiency is similar to hue error, but instead of measuring the percentage of error in the reflection of light, a positive percentage is expressed. Each color of process ink filters out its complementary additive color and reflects the other two-thirds of the spectrum. This is the measurement of efficiency — the higher the percentage of an ink's efficiency, the less color correction will be required, and the greater the gamut of possible colors that it can produce.

To determine a specific ink color efficiency percentage, use the equation:

$$\text{Ink efficiency} = 1 \quad \frac{\text{Low filter reading} + \text{Medium filter reading}}{2 \times \text{High filter reading}}$$

Color diagrams for ink evaluation and color correction

When performing process ink analysis, it is beneficial to plot the information on a ***color diagram*** for the purpose of visual evaluation or comparison. Data such as hue error or grayness factor can be calculated and plotted on one of three types of diagrams: the color hexagon, circle, or triangle. The ink data, represented by the plots, can then be visually compared to ideal colors on the diagram.

The *color hexagon* is one of the only diagrams that requires no major computations or formulas. It is one of the easiest and quickest diagrams used to plot color strength and hue differences. The hexagon is best suited for quality control or press control of primary printers and overprints, **Figure 25-20**.

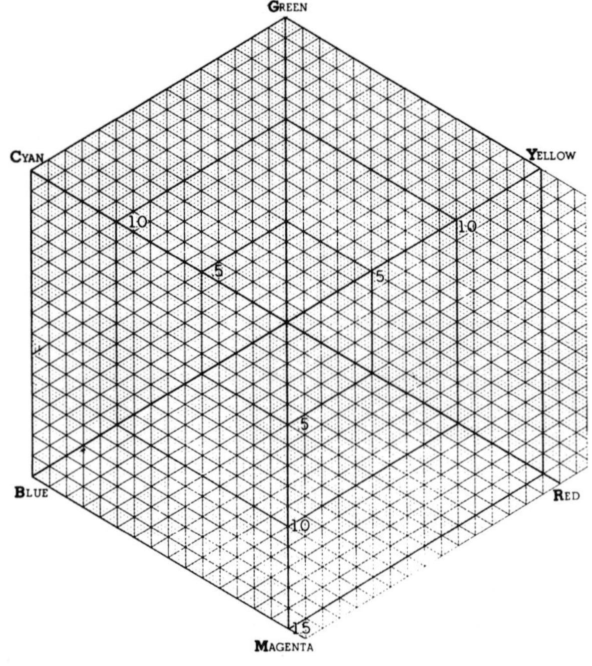

Figure 25-20. A color hexagon is used to plot color strength and hue differences to improve quality control. (Graphic Arts Technical Foundation)

The *color circle* is designed for visualizing the hue error and grayness factor of actual colors in relation to ideal colors. It is also valuable in determining the color correction system requirements for different inks and substrates. See **Figure 25-21**.

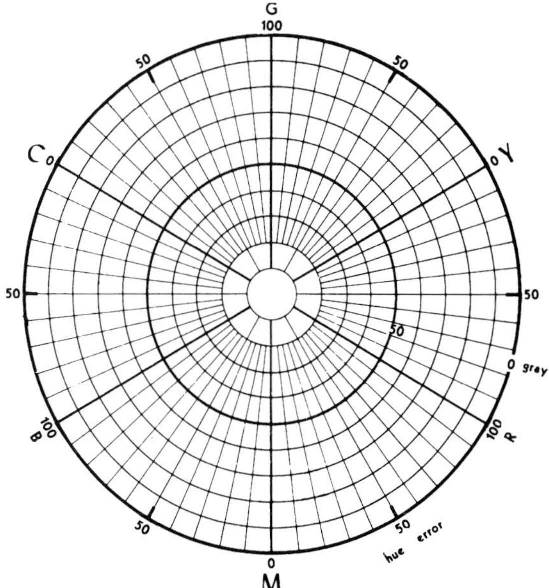

Figure 25-21. A color circle can be plotted so that hue error and grayness can be visualized and compared to ideal colors. (Graphic Arts Technical Foundation)

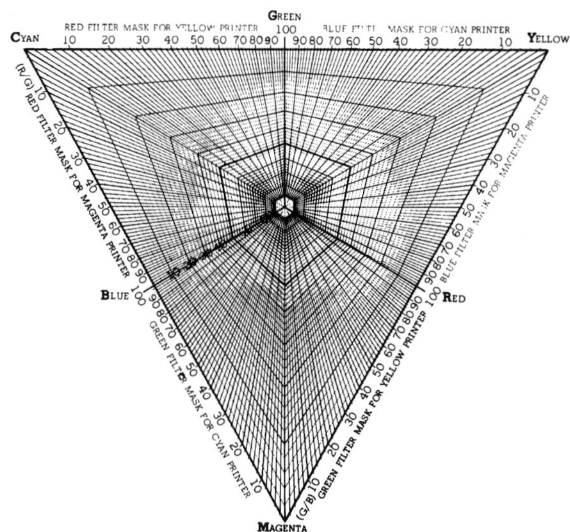

Figure 25-22. A color triangle indicates the gamut of color possibilities for a set of process inks. Mask percentages for color correction are located on the sides of the triangle. (Graphic Arts Technical Foundation)

The *subtractive color triangle* is designed to illustrate the gamut of pure color that is possible with a set of process inks. The plots of ink data can also identify under- or over-trapping and predict overprints. Mask percentages are located along the sides of the triangle to identify masking requirements for color correction of the specific inks. See **Figure 25-22**.

The color triangle has two additional applications. It can be used to analyze new batches of process ink for hue and grayness by comparing the batches to successful proofs. The triangle can also be used to plot readings from the customer's reflective original art to immediately determine whether the important colors fall within the gamut of the process inks' capabilities.

Ink impurities

The data derived from the analysis of a set of process inks will determine the exact masking or color correction requirements. Usually, the yellow pigment will be the purest. Magenta will typically contain a yellow impurity. Magenta ink can either be rubine or rhodamine in color. Rhodamine is a blue-magenta which is more expensive and produces good fleshtones. Rubine magenta is more red.

Cyan ink contains the most impurities and will usually have a major impurity of magenta. If the cyan appears to have a magenta impurity, it will also contain a certain amount of yellow that is already in the magenta. Then the cyan ink is said to have a major impurity of magenta and a minor impurity of yellow.

During color correction, the cyan printer separation will receive the least amount of correction. Because the magenta impurity or yellow impurity in the cyan ink cannot be removed, less magenta and even less yellow must be printed. The yellow impurity is in both the cyan and magenta ink; therefore, it requires the most reduction, masking, and correction. The percentage of color correction is best determined by actual ink density readings and evaluation of the four basic ink characteristics.

Review Questions

Please do not write in this book. Write your answers on a separate sheet of paper.

1. Explain the three main ingredients of ink.
2. _____ is the ink's ability to cover the substrate.
3. _____ refers to the ink's thickness or fluidity.
4. What type of press uses soft-bodied inks?
5. Define *thixotropy*.

6. This ink quality would tend to make the ink fly out on a high-speed press.
   a. Short ink.
   b. Long ink.
   c. High tack.
   d. Low tack.
7. Low ink tack could cause which of the following problems?
   a. Paper tearing.
   b. Picking.
   c. Splitting.
   d. All of the above.
   e. None of the above.
8. Describe the six ways that ink can dry.
9. _____ viscosity ink is thick and resists flow, while _____ viscosity ink is fluid and flows more easily.
10. What is the most important factor in the growth of UV ink use?
11. _____ can be found in many commercial letterpress facilities since it can be used on a wide variety of presses and papers.
12. What five factors should you consider when ordering ink?
13. *True or false?* Strike-through is an ink-penetration problem that is caused by thin stock.
14. What instrument is used to measure the amount of light reflected from an object?
15. What three types of color diagrams are used for process ink analysis?

26 Finishing and Binding

Learning Objectives

After studying this chapter, you will be able to:

- Identify the many finishing methods for completing a multipage printed product.
- Choose the most efficient finishing process for the specific job.
- Explain the types of equipment found in the finishing and binding section of a facility.
- Describe the various binding techniques.
- Summarize the processes needed for different binding techniques.

Important Terms

binding
blind embossing
casing in
die cutting
edition binding
finishing
mechanical binding
perfect binding
spiral binding
stamping

Finishing is a general term that applies to the many operations carried out during or following printing. Operations classified as finishing include cutting, folding, slitting, perforating, creasing and scoring, die cutting, embossing, stamping, numbering, drilling and punching, varnishing, and laminating. Exact finishing methods will vary depending upon the type of product and its specifications.

Binding is the process of fastening together the sheets of a product with methods including gluing, sewing, stapling, or other mechanical means. It can be considered a finishing operation, but is usually classified separately, since binding is often a operation subcontracted to a specialty house. Like finishing, binding is a general term that can be applied to slightly different tasks depending upon the type of product and the process involved. **Figure 26-1** depicts the steps involved in a perfect binding (glued softcover) operation.

Finishing and binding are as important as the printing itself. If even one finishing process is poorly done, even a very well-printed job will have little or no value. The customer might reject the job, refusing to pay for it, or demand that it be done over without additional charge. In either case, the printing company will be faced with a financial loss on the job, instead of the expected profit. This makes it extremely important that all finishing and binding processes are performed correctly.

Cutting

Making a large sheet of paper into several smaller sheets is termed ***cutting***, which should not

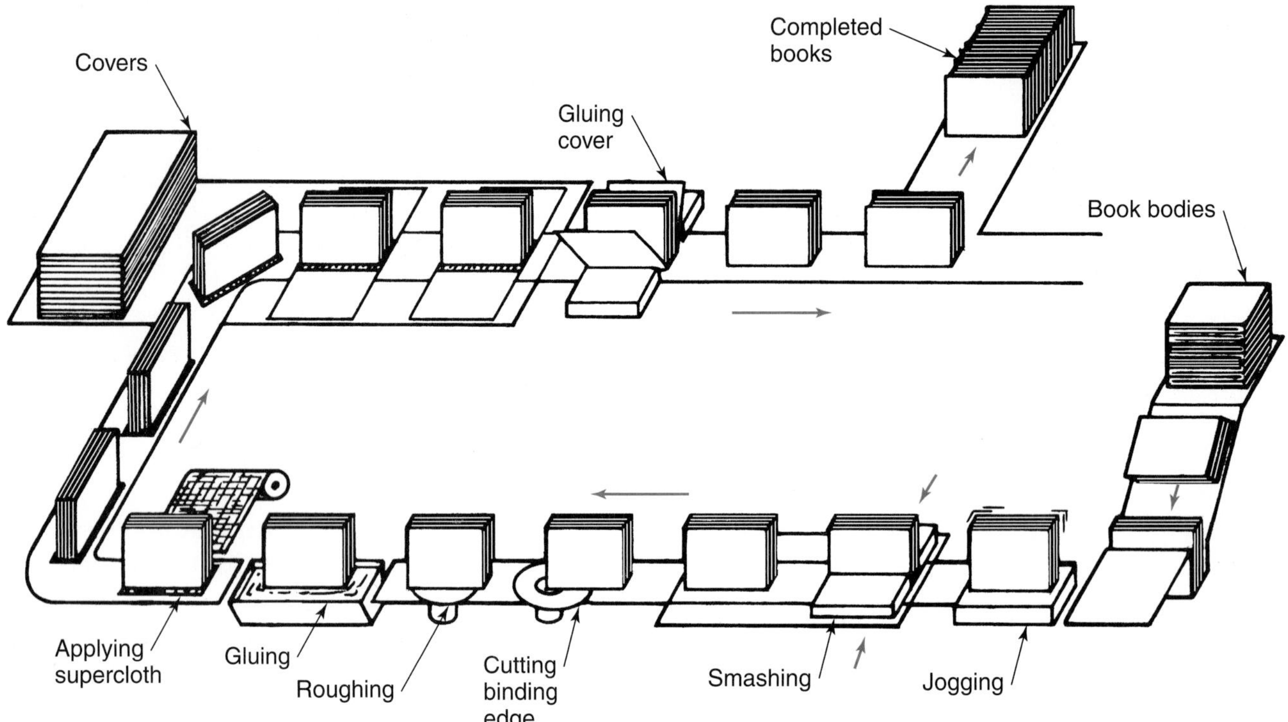

Figure 26-1. The flow of a typical perfect binding operation. Perfect binding is the process of attaching a paper cover (softcover) to the book body with glue.

be confused with trimming. ***Trimming*** is the process of cutting off uneven edges of paper, as when trimming the three sides of a book.

Guillotine cutter

The most common type of equipment used to cut paper stock is the guillotine cutter, **Figure 26-2**. The knife of a guillotine cutter is forced through the paper at a slight angle to produce an oblique shearing action, **Figure 26-3**.

The blade must be very sharp and free of nicks, since any roughness of the blade will appear as a jagged edge on the cut sheets.

Keeping blades in excellent condition is essential for quality trimming or cutting of stock. Most plants will send cutter blades out to be sharpened. Extreme care must be taken when removing or installing a cutter blade. Any blade that is out of the cutter should be placed in a *sheath* (cover) to eliminate the possibility of injury from the sharp edge.

Respect a cutter blade's sharpness. Handle a blade carefully, since it can cause severe cuts.

Specific equipment instructions should be followed. To correctly position a sharpened blade in the cutter, follow specific directions provided by the equipment manufacturer. Before making any adjustments, place a new wood or plastic ***shear stick*** in the table's groove or channel. Refer to Figure 26-3.

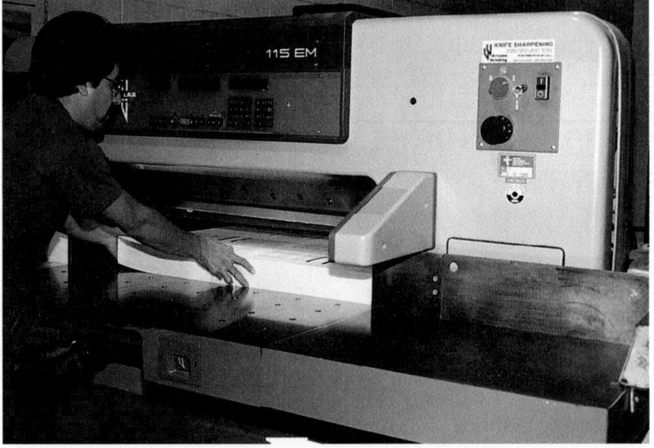

Figure 26-2. This is a powerful computer-controlled guillotine cutter. Cuts can be preprogrammed into computer memory. To help in moving and positioning large stacks of paper, the cutting table is pierced with many tiny holes through which powerful jets of air are blown. The paper stack is slightly raised from the surface by the air, making it easy to move.

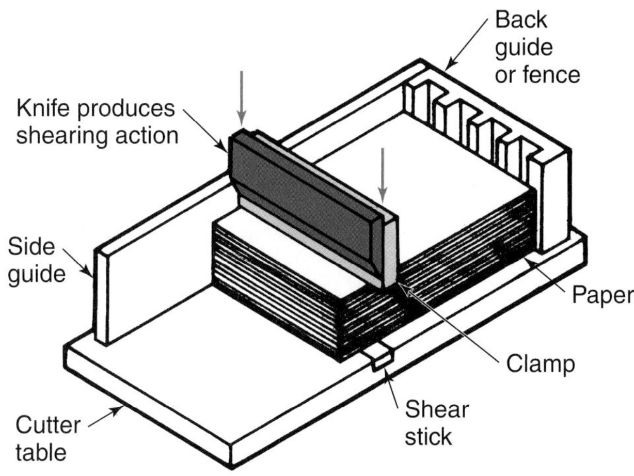

Figure 26-3. The guillotine cutter forces a blade through a stack of paper to produce shearing action.

The shear stick should be rotated or turned periodically to give a new surface under the cutting edge and produce a sharp, clean cut.

Paper cutters

Today's paper cutters come in a wide variety of sizes from tabletop models to huge floor models. The simplest type is usually hand-operated while other models have power clamps to hold the paper while it is being cut. Modern floor models have automatic clamps and are computer-programmed to make planned cuts. The cutter size is designated by the length of cut. A 30″ paper cutter will take a sheet up to 30″ in width, **Figure 26-4**.

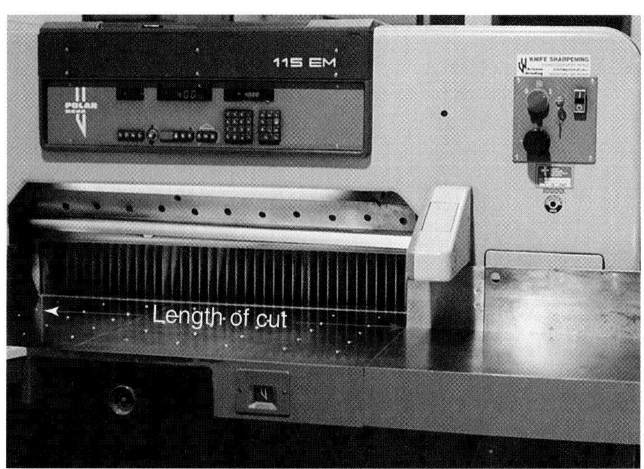

Figure 26-4. The length of cut that can be made by a paper cutter is used to designate its size. Typical sizes are 30″ and 37″, although larger and smaller models are made.

A dial gauge or digital readout indicates the distance of the back gauge to the cutting edge of the blade. A properly adjusted cutter will give very accurate cuts.

The amount of paper each cutter will cut depends on paper type, weight, and size. Six hundred sheets of narrow paper will cut much easier than 600 sheets that cover the full width of the cutter table.

Most large cutters have an *air jet bed* that allows for easy movement of heavy stacks of sheets. Air is pumped up through the table to form a cushion between the table and the paper. The air lifts the paper so it floats over the table for easy positioning, **Figure 26-5**.

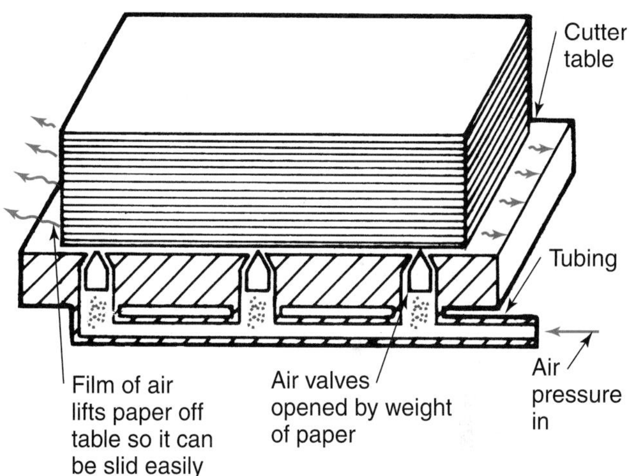

Figure 26-5. Most large cutters use an air jet bed on the table. Air flows up through holes in the table to lift paper for easy movement.

Many of today's facilities have a vacuum system to remove all of the unwanted paper. The waste stock is sucked to a receiving area, where it is baled for recycling, **Figure 26-6**. Paper dust must be held to a minimum to comply with local, state, and federal regulations.

The cutting of paper is a very exacting task. A miscut can make a job a pile of waste—a very costly mistake. Accuracy is essential when paper is cut down to the size for a given press run. Proper allowances must also be considered when bleeds and trims are specified.

Figure 26-7. Paper waste, such as trimmings from paper cutters, is usually baled for recycling.

Automatic paper cutters usually have safety features designed to prevent loss of fingers or hands. These include:

- *Nonrepeat device* (cutter blade will only come down once until reset).
- *Two-handed operation* (buttons on each side of the operator must be pressed simultaneously to make the cutter blade operate). See **Figure 26-7**.
- *Electric eye stop* (a detector that will automatically stop the descent of the cutter blade if a hand, arm, or other object is in its path).

Figure 26-7. On most large paper cutters, the operator must use both hands to press buttons that make the cutter knife operate. This system keeps hands out of the area where the cut is performed.

Whatever the cutting device, safe operation is essential. If a cutter will slice through a pile of paper like butter, what would it do to a hand? Always follow manufacturer's directions and never bypass safety devices when operating a cutter.

Folding Operations

Once images have been printed on the substrate, they are often folded. Many jobs are printed on one side and backed up with a second printing, commonly called sheetwise imposition. The single sheet might be letter-size and small enough to be folded for insertion in an envelope, or large enough to have 8 or 16 book pages on each side.

The most common folding machine for smaller sheets is the *buckle type*, **Figure 26-8**, which uses roller action to buckle-fold the paper. The stock is placed in a friction- or suction-type feeder. The adjustment on the suction-type feeder is similar to a printing unit feeder, while the friction type requires a very exact setting.

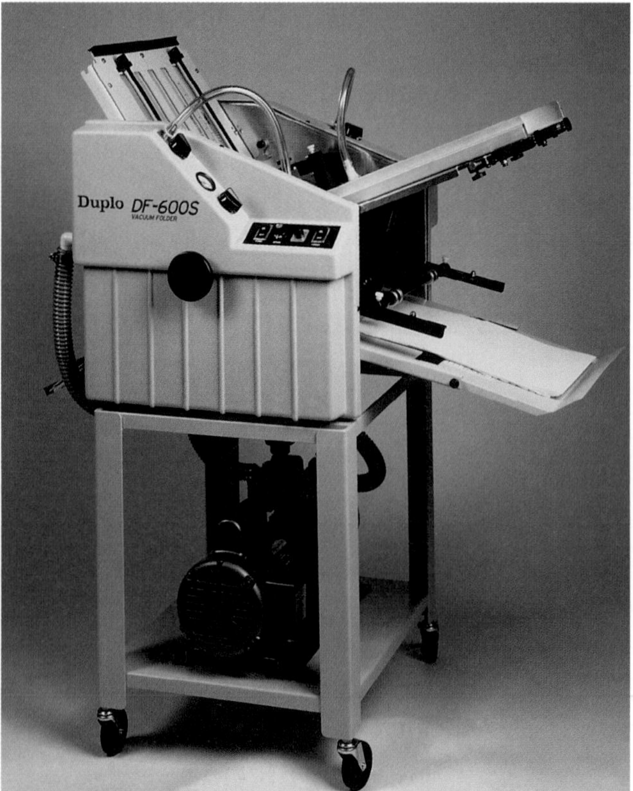

Figure 26-8. A small folder that uses a suction-type feeder. The suction is provided by a vacuum pump mounted below the folder. (Duplo USA)

As the sheet leaves the feeder, it travels on belts or rollers to two rollers that carry the sheet to the fold plate, **Figure 26-9**. As the sheet is forced against the fold plate, the sheet *buckles* and another combination of rollers folds the sheet and carries it to a delivery station or to another set of folding rollers. These rollers will place another fold if necessary. The fold will be either parallel with or at right angles to the first fold. **Figure 26-10** shows a parallel fold and a right-angle fold.

Some folders use a *folding knife* to force the paper between rollers for folding. The operation of a knife-type folder is illustrated in **Figure 26-11**.

For larger folding jobs, *floor-type folders* in a variety of sizes are commonly found in graphic communications facilities. Some of these are used for smaller sheets, such as 11″ × 17″, others for very large sheets containing up to 32 book-size pages. Some newer folders, such as the one shown in **Figure 26-12**, have computerized controls to speed up the process of setting up for different folds and different paper sizes.

The folding requirements of any project should be considered in the planning stage, since it can affect the choice of equipment and the overall production schedule. Most folds are a combination of parallel and right angle folds, such as those shown in shown in **Figure 26-13**.

Special types of folds

Some printing jobs, especially those used for advertising and promotion purposes, have special folding requirements. A few of these are described below:

- *Self-cover stitched body*. The cover is the same stock as the sheets inside the book. Sheets are folded on the long side and stitched along the spine of the book.
- *Gate-fold book*. The front and back cover have panels that are folded in toward the spine of the book.
- *Folder*. A pocket or a flap which can be on one or both sides of the inside of the cover stock.
- *Fold-out book*. A fold out in a book can fall anywhere in the book. Some books and magazines use the fold out format.

This is not a complete list but it conveys the idea that innovative types of folds require advance planning. Hand folding should be avoided, if possible, since it is a very costly operation.

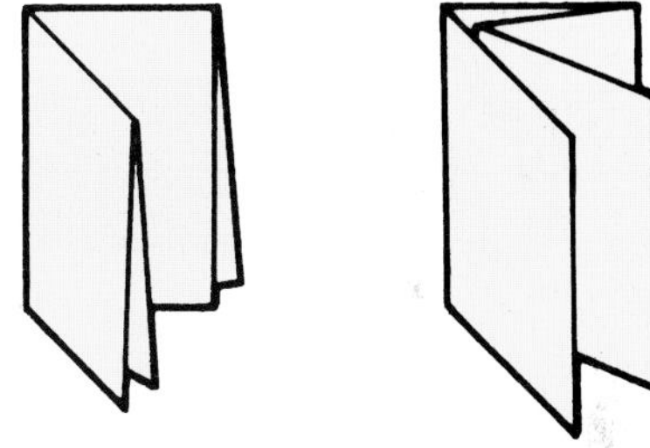

Figure 26-10. Examples of parallel and right angle folds.

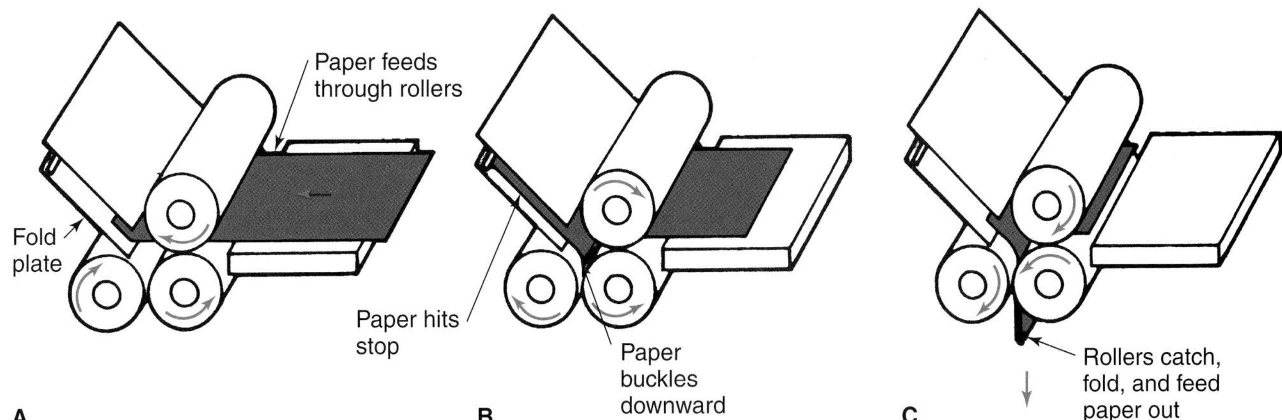

Figure 26-9. The basic operating principle of a buckle folder. A—Paper is fed into the machine by rollers. B—Paper hits the stop on the fold plate and buckles downward. C—Rollers catch the paper and feed it downward to make a fold.

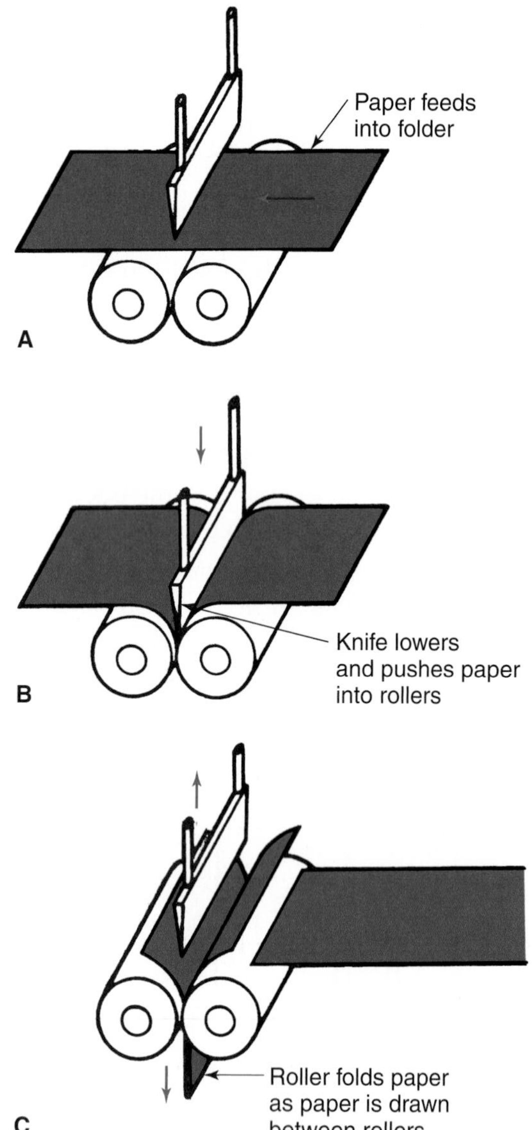

Figure 26-11. Operation of a knife type folder. A—Paper is fed into the folder by rollers. B—The folding knife comes down and pushes the paper between two rollers. C—The rollers fold and pull paper through machine.

Folding area safety

- Tie back long hair and secure any loose sleeves or similar clothing items. The rotating parts of folding machinery could grasp hair or loose clothing and pull it into the machine.
- Keep your fingers clear of pinch points, such as folding rollers.
- Handle paper carefully — the edges of sheets are very sharp and can cause painful cuts.

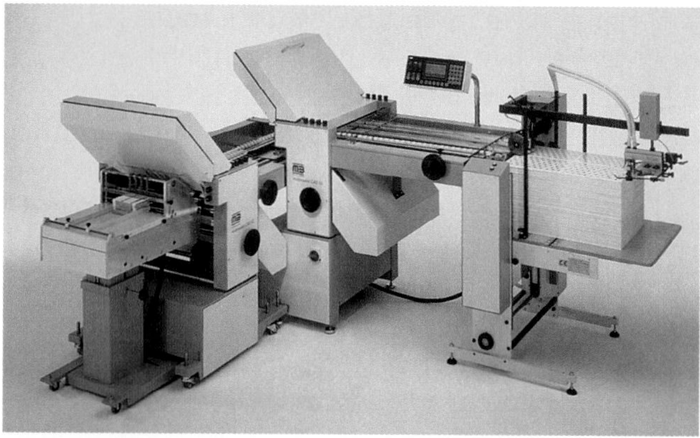

Figure 26-12. A computerized control panel on this floor model folder permits quick set-up for different paper sizes. Various attachments are available to permit use as a buckle-type folder or a combination buckle-type and knife-type folder. (Matthias Bauerle GmbH)

- Turn off any machine before making adjustments. Follow the manufacturer's prescribed procedures for adjusting machine settings.
- Lock out electrical power when performing maintenance.

Other Finishing Operations

In addition to cutting and folding, there are many other finishing operations that are used as required to produce the final product. Some of these are done "in-line" during the printing or folding processes; others are separate operations done on standalone equipment.

Perforating

Whenever it is necessary to remove a portion of the printed material, stock is perforated or "perfed." This makes it possible to readily tear off and remove a reply card on an advertising circular or a single page in a workbook. ***Perforating*** places a series of small cuts or slits in the substrate, using various types of blades or wheels, as shown in **Figure 26-14.**

Sometimes, the task can be completed while running the job on the press. This is a common practice with relief and planographic mechanical processes. The stock can also be perforated on the folder as an auxiliary process. The type of perforation and the number of teeth per inch to make the slits or holes will depend on the type of substrate used. **Figure 26-15** shows some examples of perforations.

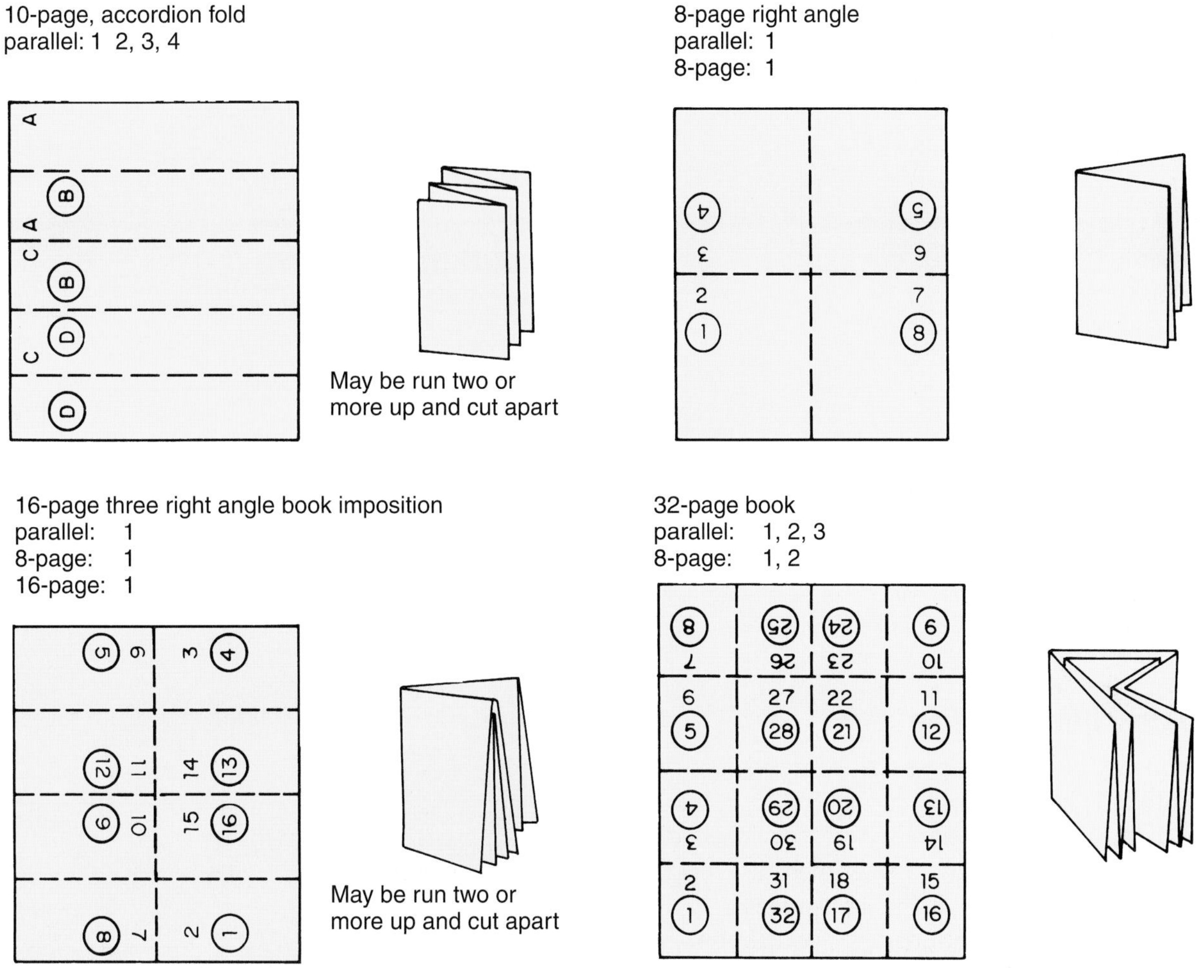

10-page, accordion fold
parallel: 1 2, 3, 4

May be run two or more up and cut apart

8-page right angle
parallel: 1
8-page: 1

16-page three right angle book imposition
parallel: 1
8-page: 1
16-page: 1

May be run two or more up and cut apart

32-page book
parallel: 1, 2, 3
8-page: 1, 2

Figure 26-13. These are a few of the common folds used in the industry.

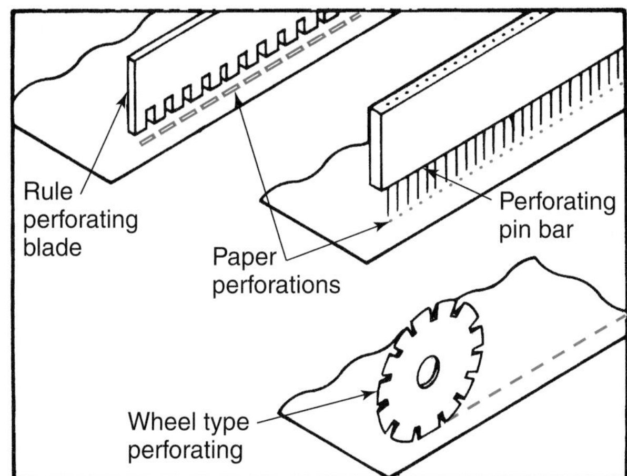

Figure 26-14. Stock can be perforated through the use of various devices on the press or the folder.

Pinhole	28T per inch
Slot	9T per inch
Slot	8T per inch
Slot	7T per inch
Slot	3 1/2T per inch
Knifecut	6 1/2T per inch
Knifecut	2 1//2T per inch
Knifecut	12T per inch

Figure 26-15. These are a few of the many different perforations that are used. (Rollem)

Slitting

Slitting is similar to perforating, but makes a continuous cut, rather than a series of slits. It is usually done by one or more sharp-edged wheels that cut the stock as it passes through the folder, **Figure 26-16**. During the folding operation, for example, a leaflet or booklet can be trimmed to finished size by slitting wheels.

Figure 26-16. Slitting is commonly done by a sharp wheel that cuts paper sheet as it exits the folder.

Creasing and scoring

Creasing is the process of compressing the substrate so it will fold more easily. This is often accomplished with a rotary creaser attached to the folder, **Figure 26-17A**. Sometimes, creasing is a separate operation using a creasing rule, **Figure 26-17B**, on letterpress equipment or specially designed finishing equipment. Rule thickness will vary with the stock.

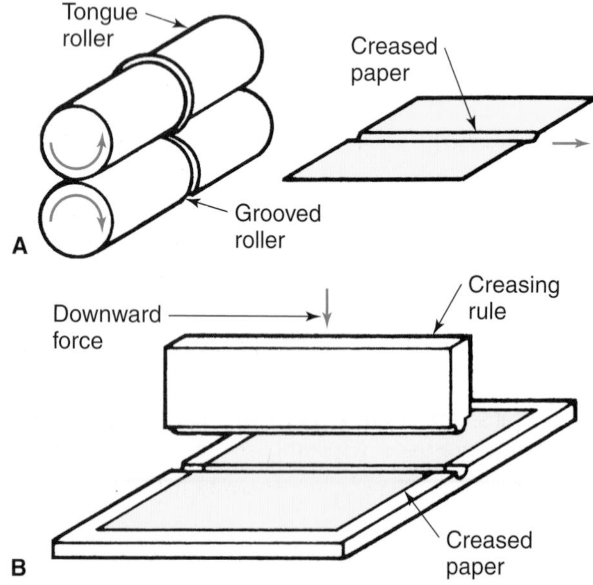

Figure 26-17. Creasing devices. A—The creasing roller method is used on a folder. B—Creasing rules are typically used on letterpress equipment.

The term *scoring* is used interchangeably with creasing in some operations, but ***scoring*** is actually a slight *cut* made in heavy stock before it is folded. The correct depth of the cut is important. Scoring is commonly done in the packaging industry, where scores are made at the fold points for cartons.

Die cutting

Whenever an irregular shape must be cut in a substrate, the method most often used to do the task is die cutting. In the ***die cutting*** process, pressure is used to force a sharp metal die (steel rule) through the stock, **Figure 26-18**.

Figure 26-18. Pressure applied to a die formed with sharp steel rules will cut irregular shapes, such as these arrows, out of a substrate. The pink material surrounding the rules is sponge rubber, which compresses and then springs back to push the cut shape out of the die.

The dies, which look somewhat like kitchen cookie cutters, are used to slice through the substrate to form tags, cards, labels, and boxes, **Figure 26-19**. Dies are also used to cut the irregular shapes after screen process printing of labels, decals, and stickers. Die cutting is not limited to paper, but can be done with many materials.

Although relief printing is no longer done by most printers, a small relief press is found in many shops because of its usefulness for die cutting and similar tasks requiring pressure. The dies used in the process consist of a base, or *dieboard*, with steel

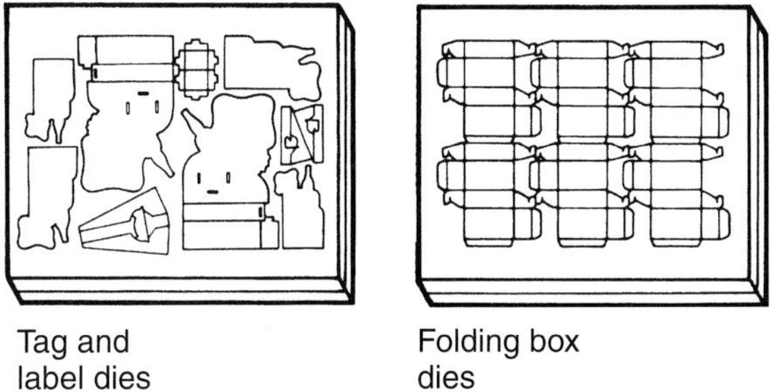

Figure 26-19. Irregular shapes can be die cut. These are examples. (Accurate Steel Rule Die Mfg., Inc.)

rules shaped and inserted in a saw kerf. Pieces of sponge rubber are glued to the dieboards on either side of the rules to release substrate material after cutting.

Embossing

Embossing is a process that creates a raised image on a substrate by pressing it between two dies, **Figure 26-20**. One die is in relief, while the other is recessed. When the two are brought together with the stock between them, the clamping force creates a raised image on the stock.

High quality embossing requires expensive dies and must be done to close tolerances, but the results can be very impressive. See **Figure 26-21**. Sometimes, an image is printed, and the stock is then embossed. In other applications, the stock itself creates the image and ink is not used. This technique is called ***blind embossing***. If an image is sunk into the substrate, rather than being raised, the process is called ***debossing***.

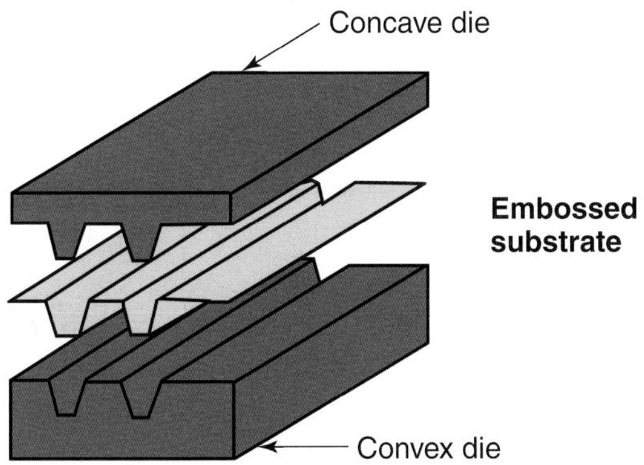

Figure 26-20. A pair of dies is used for embossing an image on a substrate.

Figure 26-21. Embossed surfaces create a very interesting pattern or design that has depth. This is an example of blind embossing, with no ink used on the raised image.

Stamping

The process called ***stamping*** or *foil stamping* is a method of transferring a thin layer of metallic tone or color to a substrate, using heat and pressure. Gold or simulated gold is commonly used as a stamping material, **Figure 26-22**. Silver and other metallics, as well as various color foils are also available. Some other colors are also available as hot stamping materials.

Stamping is a form of relief printing process. The material to be stamped is set in raised metal type or produced as a "cut" (an engraving in metal which has a raised printing area), then clamped into a holding device. The type or other material is heated, then brought into contact with a coated foil laid over the substrate. The heat and pressure transfers the color or metallic film from the foil to the substrate. Proper image transfer depends on the amount of heat and pressure, and the length of time they are applied.

In a production situation, the foil stamping unit is automated, but for small jobs, a hand-operated press like the one in **Figure 26-23** is typically used.

Numbering

The process of imprinting tickets, certificates, checks, or other items with consecutive figures (numbers) is called ***numbering***. Using a device

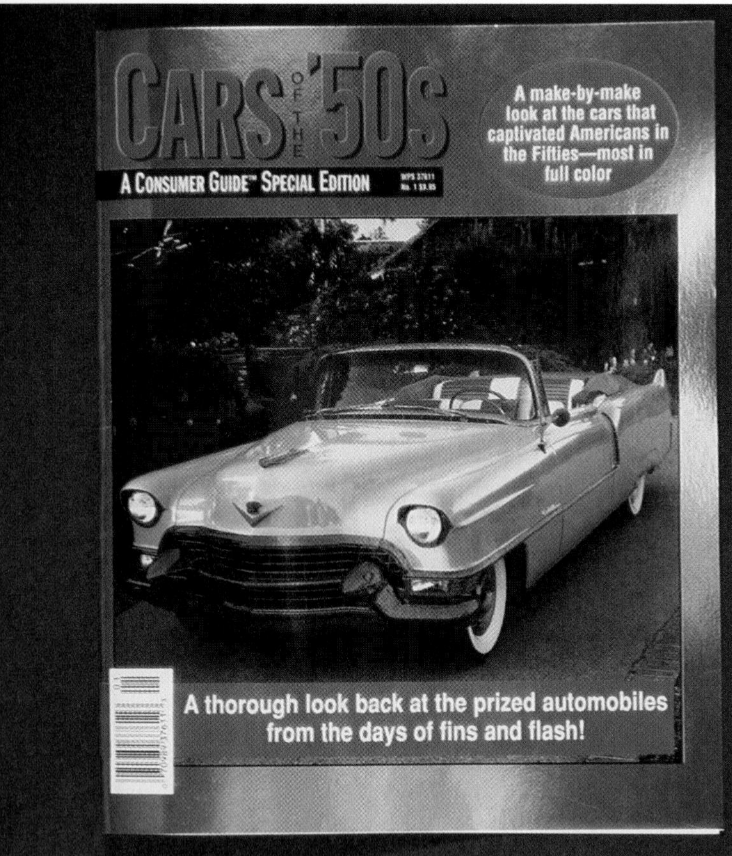

Figure 26-22. Foil stamping is used as an accenting or decorative device. It is frequently used on book covers.

Figure 26-23. A hand-operated foil stamping press. It is used for low production quantities.

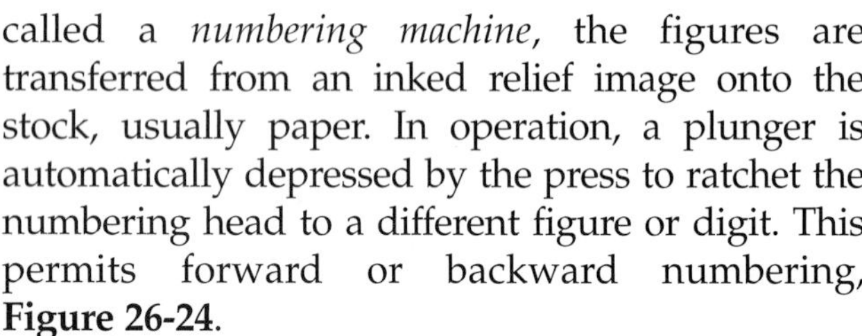

called a *numbering machine*, the figures are transferred from an inked relief image onto the stock, usually paper. In operation, a plunger is automatically depressed by the press to ratchet the numbering head to a different figure or digit. This permits forward or backward numbering, **Figure 26-24**.

Often, the numbering machine is set to start on the maximum amount, so that the last figure printed will be number 1. This prevents an overrun and places the tickets, forms, or other numbered materials in the correct numerical order.

Punching and drilling

Both punching and drilling produce holes in a substrate, but use different means to do so. ***Punching*** is done by forcing a metal rod (a punch) down through the paper to remove stock. The punch works in a shearing action with a *die* placed below the paper, **Figure 26-25**. Neither the punch

Figure 26-24. Tickets are a printed product that commonly must be numbered as a finishing operation.

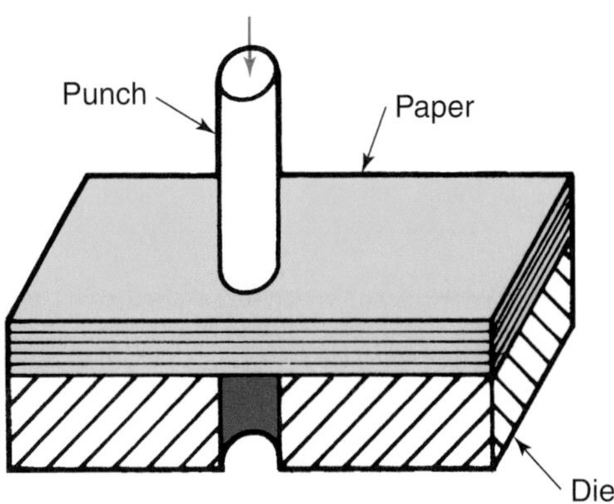

Figure 26-25. A punch forces a metal rod straight down through stock. It does not spin, as does a drill. The die located below the punch shears off stock to form a hole.

Figure 26-27. A fence at the back of the drilling machine table can be set for proper positioning of the holes being drilled. This machine is operated with a foot switch, leaving the operator's hands free to position the material.

nor the die rotate. Punching is used for such applications as producing the holes needed to do spiral binding.

Drilling uses a revolving, hollow drill bit with very sharp edges, **Figure 26-26**. After placing stock on the drill table board, the revolving drill is forced through a ***lift*** (pile) of paper. The waste stock rises through the hollow center of the drill and is ejected out of the drill top. A guide at the back of the board regulates the distance the holes are drilled from the edge of the sheet, **Figure 26-27**. Most drills have stops to assure the proper positioning for each lift to be drilled.

Figure 26-26. Paper drills have very sharp edges. Handle drills carefully when mounting or removing them.

Drills are available in various diameters. Many drilling machines have auxiliary devices as attachments. These devices make it possible to slit, round corner, or notch a lift of paper. Also available are *multiple spindle drilling machines* that make it possible to drill up to ten or more holes at one time.

The drill spindle should be protected by a guard. The high speed revolving action of the drill tends to draw hair toward it. This action is caused by static electricity. Hands and fingers must also be kept away from the revolving drill.

Varnishing

After an image has been printed on a substrate, ***varnishing*** is sometimes used to provide a clear protective surface. Usually, the coating makes the surface resistant to moisture and scuffing.

Glossy brochures, annual report covers, and similar products are typical examples of varnishing. The coating materials vary, but some of the latest coatings are epoxies that give excellent wear qualities.

Total area coverage can be accomplished by various processes but a planographic (offset) press can be used if the dampeners are removed. Letterpress and screen processes can also be used for specific varnishing jobs.

Laminating

Laminating is the bonding of two or more materials together to become one common unit. A thin film of plastic with an adhesive coating is bonded to the substrate to provide protection against abrasion and moisture. The laminate material can be applied as an in-line operation on a web press, **Figure 26-28**, or as individual sheets of various sizes. A common use of lamination is restaurant menus, which must be protected from moisture and constant handling.

Figure 26-28. Laminating material being applied at high speed on a web-fed press. The thin plastic layer protects the printed product.

The process often called ***liquid lamination*** is actually a coating method similar to varnishing. The plastic coating material is applied in liquid form and then cured into a tough protective layer by exposure to ultraviolet light. For this reason, it is sometimes referred to as a *UV-cured coating*.

Binding

After printing and such finishing steps as folding, a product may be ready for shipment or it may require *binding* to fasten the sheets or folded signatures together.

Some general or basic types of binding include the following:

- ***Adhesive binding.*** Also called *padding*, this is a classification for methods that use glue or adhesive to hold the sheets together but allow them to be removed, as in the case of notepads.
- ***Mechanical binding.*** A broad category that includes many different devices used to hold sheets together. Spiral wire, metal posts, metal or plastic rings, plastic combs, and channels that rely on friction to hold are all mechanical methods. Since separate sheets are being fastened together, this is sometimes called *loose-leaf binding*).
- ***Side stitching.*** A form of stapling in which metal wire is forced through sides of sheets and formed to hold sheets together. *Side sewing* is similar, but uses threads rather than staples to bind sheets together.
- ***Saddle stitching.*** A method in which metal wire is forced through the folded edge of a signature and formed into staples to hold the pages together. *Saddle sewing* is like saddle stitching, but is done with thread instead of wire.
- ***Perfect binding.*** Also called *softcover binding*, this method uses an adhesive to hold sheets or signatures together and to fasten the flexible cloth or paper cover onto the body.
- ***Case binding.*** The most complex and permanent form of binding, in which a rigid cover is attached to a book body that is held together by sewing. Also called *edition binding* or hard binding.
- ***Self-cover binding.*** A term used to describe using the same material for both the cover and body of the book. Self-cover books may be perfect bound, but are most often saddle stitched or side-stitched.

Many printed press sheets are very large and must be folded, gathered and collated, stitched, and trimmed. The fastening process can be divided into pamphlet binding, edition binding, perfect binding, and mechanical binding. See **Figure 26-29**.

Pamphlet binding

Most of today's magazines, catalogs, and booklets fall into the *pamphlet binding* category. One of the simplest techniques is saddle wire stitching. Sheets are folded, gathered, and stitched through the center or *saddle* of the folded sheets.

Many booklets and magazines are fastened by this method. The folded sheets are placed one over the other and then placed on the saddle of the stitcher, **Figure 26-30**. The maximum number of pages is regulated by the limit of the stitcher and/or the pamphlet thickness allowing the booklet or magazine to lie flat.

When larger publications are bound, the machine is capable of gathering the signatures and cover. They are then stitched and trimmed, **Figure 26-31**.

Gathering and collating

Gathering is a general term associated with the assembling of signatures for a book or other multipage product. As discussed previously, a *signature* is a large sheet that has been folded to form a group of pages, **Figure 26-32**.

The term *collating* usually means the assembling of single sheets. However, the term *collate* can also mean the checking of signature placement after gathering.

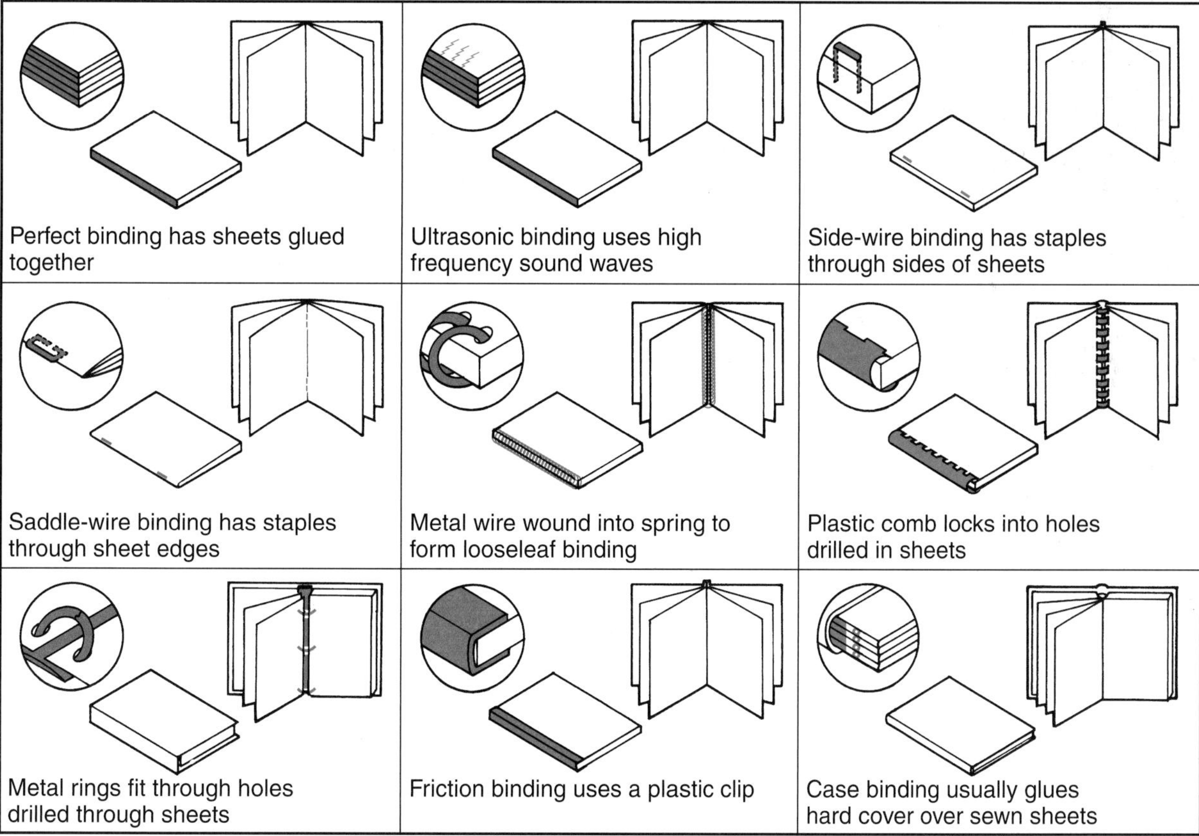

Figure 26-29. Various methods used to bind materials together after printing.

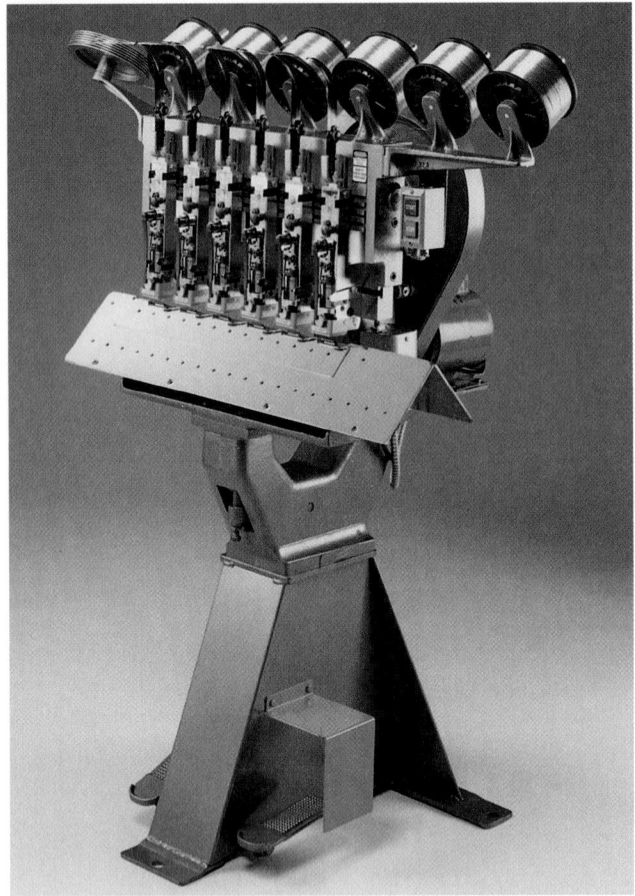

Figure 26-30. Stitching machine uses rolls of wire to produce staples that are inserted through the saddle of a signature. Signature is opened and positioned over the angled base for stitching. (Interlake Packaging Corp.)

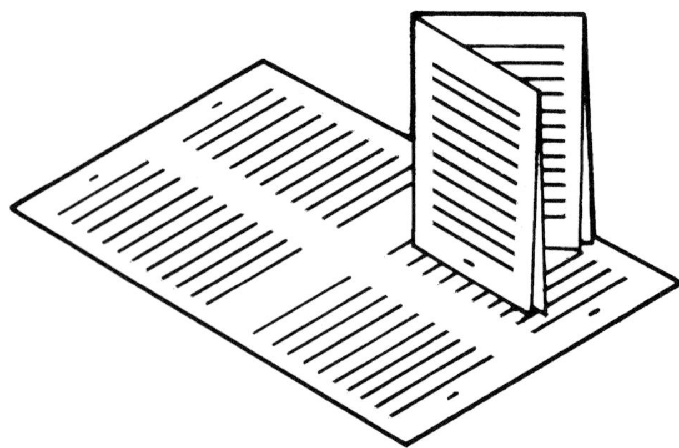

Figure 26-32. A signature is a larger sheet that is folded to produce a series of pages.

The basic process of gathering is illustrated in **Figure 26-33**. It involves using a gathering machine to stack the signatures on top of each other in the correct order. Note that one type uses a rotating gripper bar and the other uses a gripper arm. Both place the signatures on a moving conveyor. Other variations are also available. **Figure 26-34** shows a gathering machine placing book signatures in the proper sequence.

A suction feed collator with in-line folding, stitching, and trimming for creating finished booklets is shown in **Figure 26-35**. It is shown collating six stacks of pages plus a cover.

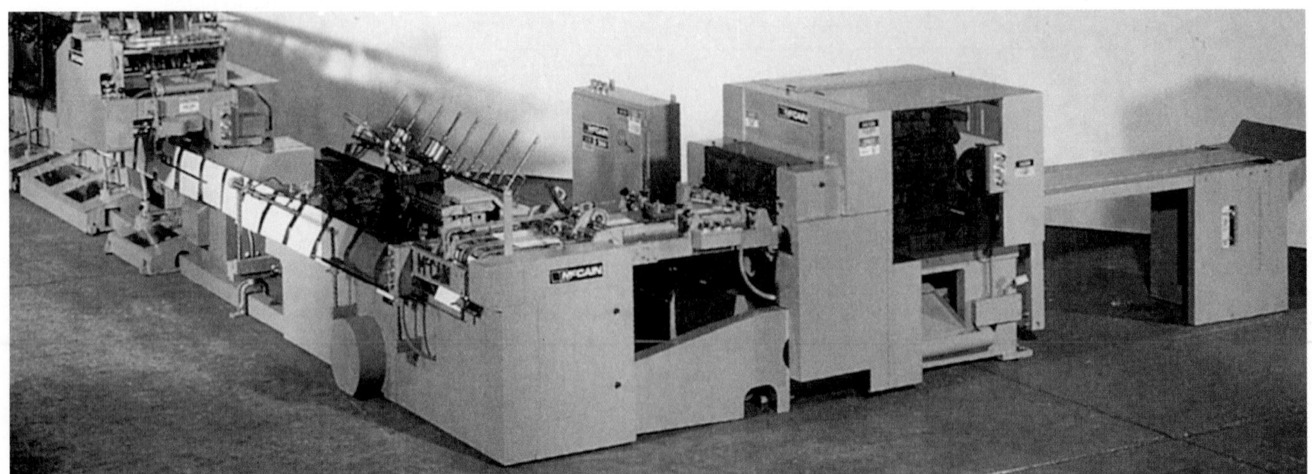

Figure 26-31. This saddle wire binding machine is used for high-volume production of magazines and booklets. (McCain Manufacturing Corp.)

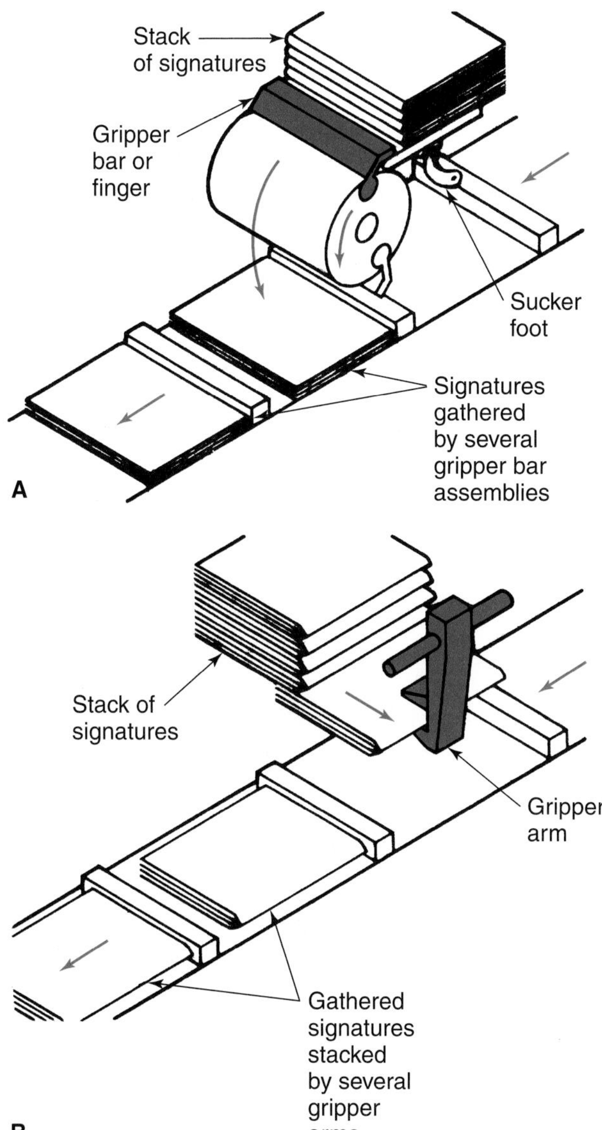

Figure 26-33. Two methods commonly used to gather signatures. A—Rotary gathering. B—Gripper arm gathering.

Figure 26-34. A gathering machine like this one places all signatures of a product in proper order for binding.

Figure 26-35. This is a suction feed collator with in-line fold, stitch, and trim units. It can be equipped with up to 18 bins and handle many different sheet sizes and paper weights. (Duplo USA)

Collating marks can be used on signatures to check the accuracy of the signature-gathering sequence. As illustrated in **Figure 26-36**, the collating marks should form a diagonal line when signatures are in the proper order. If the marks do not align, one or more signatures is out of sequence.

Stitching

Stitching is a common binding method that holds the sheets together with wire staples. It is typically used on products with fewer than 120 pages. Books with large numbers of pages are bound with other methods, such as sewing or mechanical devices.

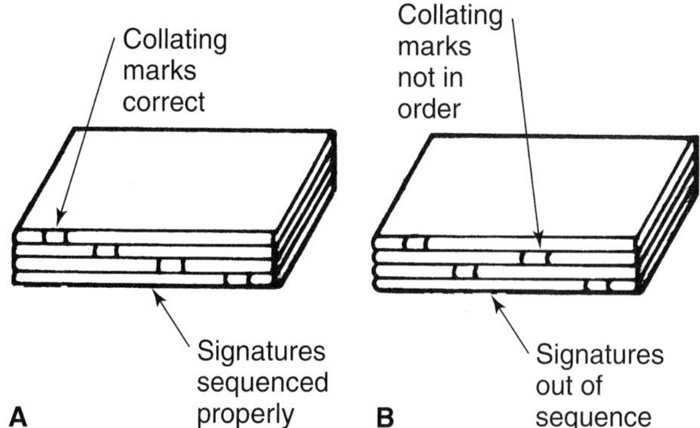

Figure 26-36. Collating marks placed on folded edges of signatures allow a visual check for proper gathering sequence. A—Marks align diagonally, showing correct signature order. As a further check, collating marks often are printed with letters or numbers in proper sequence. B—Marks not aligned diagonally. Signature order is incorrect.

Saddle stitching, **Figure 26-37**, is commonly used for booklets or magazines because they tend to lie more flat than side stitched products when opened. When the thickness of a saddle stitched product increases, the amount of ***creep*** becomes more evident. As shown in **Figure 26-38**, creep (also called ***shingling***) is a pushing out, or extension of, pages on the outer edge of the book, caused by the greater thickness at the spine. Although the finished pages will be trimmed even, an allowance for creep must be made in the prepress phase, when the pages are being laid out. If allowance is not made, page margins of the finished book will not be even. In extreme cases, type or illustrations along the outer edges could be cut off.

The side wire stitching technique is another method of fastening several signatures or many sheets, **Figure 26-39**. The cover could be of the same type of stock or a specially printed substrate. One of the drawbacks of this type of binding is that the booklet or magazine does not lie flat when opened.

Side stitch machines might be of the single head type, like the one shown in Figure 26-39, or a multiple head configuration that places several staples simultaneously. Multiple-head stitching increases binding speed or volume.

Never place a finger or hand under a stitcher head. A staple could be driven through your finger or hand if the machine is activated.

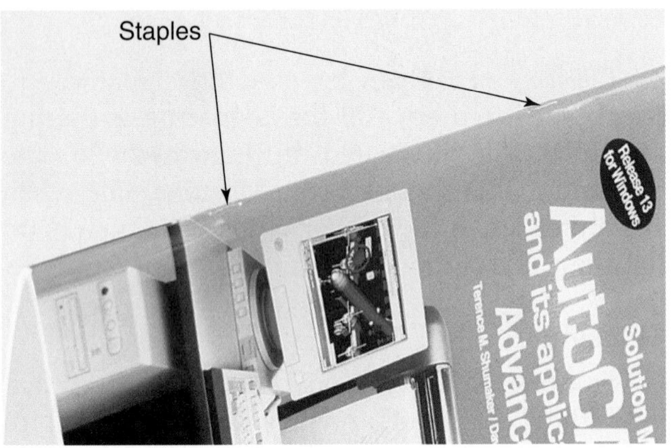

Figure 26-37. Saddle-stitching involves stapling through the folded area, or saddle, of the product. It allows a booklet to lie relatively flat when opened.

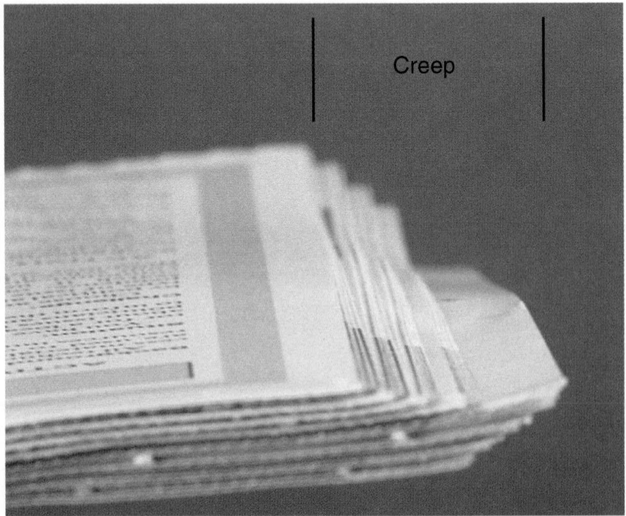

Figure 26-38. Creep, or shingling, results when saddle-stitched products become thicker. The extended page edges will be trimmed off evenly.

Figure 26-39. Side-wire stitching is used for some booklets and other products. A booklet bound by this method will not lie as flat when opened as will a saddle-stitched product.

Edition binding

Edition binding, also called *case binding*, is considered the most durable and permanent method of binding books that will be used extensively over a period of time, such as textbooks and reference volumes. The parts of a case-bound book are identified in **Figure 26-40.**

The binding process involves gathering and sewing the signatures together, then compressing (smashing) the signatures together, and trimming the edges with a three-knife trimmer, **Figure 26-41**. The book body is then glued, the spine rounded, and lining applied. The book cover is manufactured separately by wrapping and gluing a printed cover on binder's board. It is then attached to the body with an adhesive in a process called ***casing in***. The bound book is then clamped in a fixture until the adhesive dries. The steps in the binding process are shown, in order, in **Figure 26-42**.

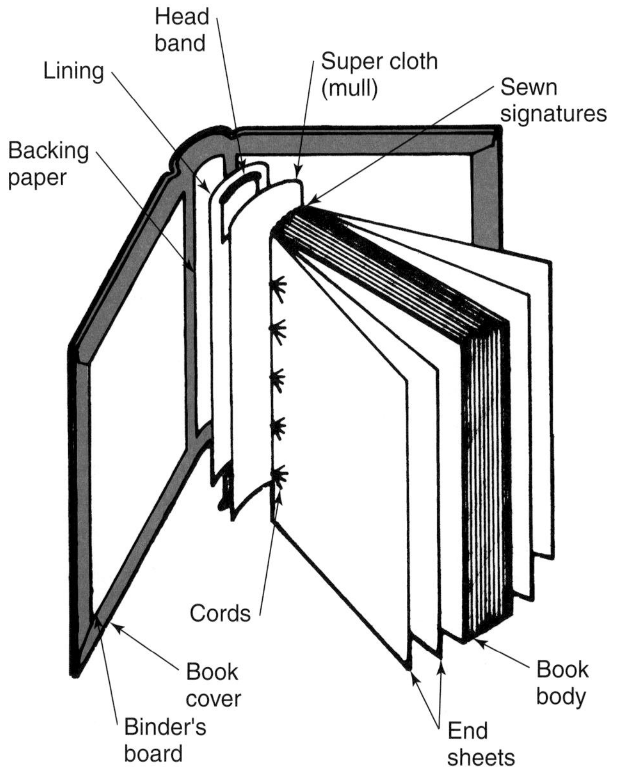

Head band
Lining
Super cloth (mull)
Sewn signatures
Backing paper
Cords
Book cover
Binder's board
Book body
End sheets

Figure 26-40. The basic parts of a case-bound (hard cover) book.

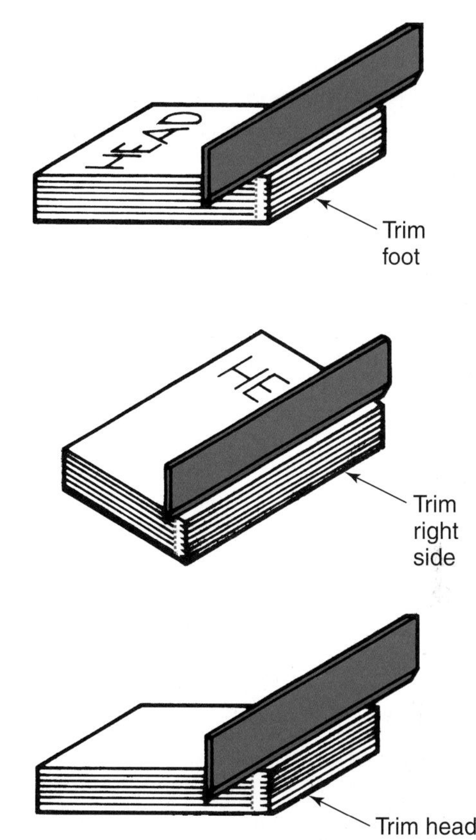

Figure 26-41. A three-knife paper trimmer cuts excess material off the foot, right side, and head of the book body after signatures are sewn together. Although the three trimming steps are shown separately here, they are completed in a single operation.

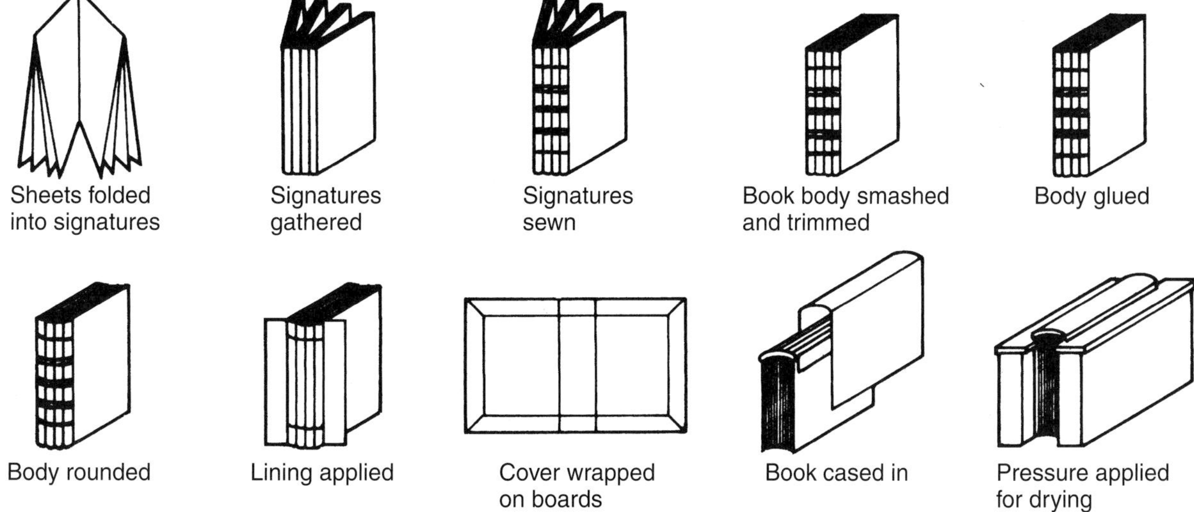

Figure 26-42. These are the major steps that occur during the edition binding of a book.

Although the vast majority of case-bound books produced today are manufactured with machine binding methods, hand-binding is still done for special volumes and other uses. Knowing how to do hand-binding is a useful skill and an aid to understanding the binding process. Step-by-step instructions for this process are contained in *Appendix 2, Hand-binding a Book*.

Perfect binding

The ***perfect binding*** process, used for producing books usually described as *softcover* or *paperback*, is a fast and relatively low-cost method. Since it eliminates the need for sewing and constructing a hard cover, it is more economical than edition binding. Perfect binding is not as long-lasting or rugged as edition binding. For this reason, it is often selected for products that will have a limited lifespan, such as telephone directories, magazines, and some books for children. Its low cost has made it popular for mass-market novels and other books where price is a competitive factor. See **Figure 26-43**.

Figure 26-43. Perfect binding is a very popular method for use with products as diverse in size as magazines, books, and telephone directories. Costs are much lower, and production much faster, than traditional edition binding.

In this process, either signatures or single sheets can be gathered or collated to form the book body. The binding equipment then grinds or saws the binding edge of the book body to roughen the surface, and a flexible glue is applied. The cover is placed on the body and clamped until the glue sets. The book is then trimmed, usually with a three knife trimmer.

Perfect bound books intended for greater permanence, such as some textbooks and reference volumes, often are bound with a system called *burst* binding. This method involves notching the spine of the book body and applying a high-strength adhesive under pressure. Another method that provides greater permanence is sewing the signatures together (like an edition-bound book) before the gluing and covering operations are performed. These methods virtually eliminate pages coming loose and falling out, which has been a problem with some softcover books in the past.

Mechanical binding

The broad category called ***mechanical binding*** consists of a number of methods that employ a mechanical device (metal spring, plastic fastener, etc.) to hold sheets together in loose-leaf form.

Plastic comb binding is commonly used for booklets that might have to be altered by adding or removing pages. Books bound with this method permit the pages to lay perfectly flat when open.

The binding method involves using a special machine, **Figure 26-44**, to punch rectangular holes along one edge of the printed material. After the sheets are punched, they are positioned over the spread or expanded plastic teeth of the fastener.

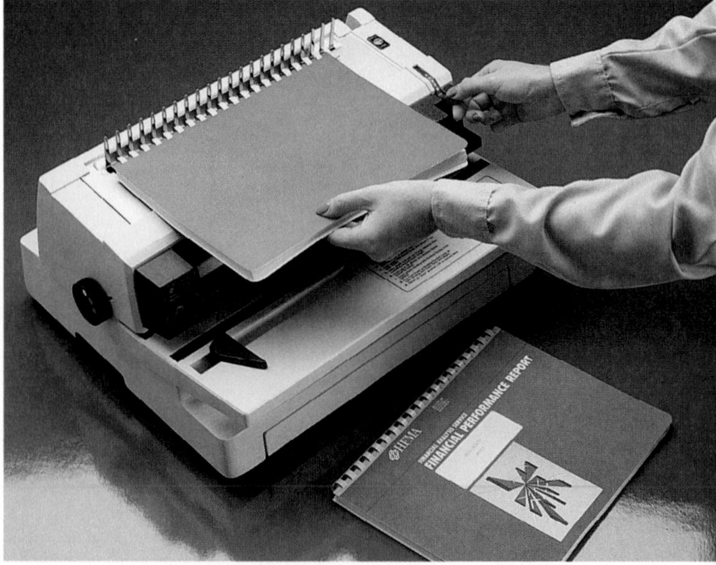

Figure 26-44. A special machine is used to punch the product and insert a plastic binding comb. The finished plastic bound book can be taken apart to easily add or remove pages. (General Binding Corp.)

When released, the plastic teeth extend through the punched holes to bind the publication. The same machine can be used to open the comb teeth so that pages can be removed or added. Combs are available in various diameters to suit the number of pages being fastened.

Spiral binding is similar to the plastic comb method, but does not allow opening the binding for the addition or removal of pages. In this method, smaller round holes are punched, then the wire is spiral fed through the booklet, using automatic equipment. The method is used for many types of products from small pocket notebooks to calendars, to books an inch or more in thickness, **Figure 26-45**. Several variations of the spiral method are used, but all follow the same principle. The diameter of each type of binding wire varies with the need.

Figure 26-45. Spiral fastening uses metal or plastic wire wound through holes to bind together loose sheets. Many different products are produced using this method.

Like most mechanical bindings, the spiral wire method allows a book to be opened flat and remain that way. The spiral allows for the tearing out of a page but not the insertion of sheets.

Packaging

In graphic communications, *packaging* basically involves wrapping, strapping, or boxing the printed pieces together for delivery to the customer. While printed products were once typically wrapped in paper and then packed in boxes, the more common method today is the use of plastic ***shrink-wrapping***. In this method, a stack of printed pieces is placed on the conveyor of a shrink-wrapping machine, **Figure 26-46**, and enclosed with a thin plastic in sheet form. The wrapped stack then passes through a heated tunnel where the plastic reacts by shrinking to form a tight, sealed package.

Figure 26-46. A shrink-wrapping machine wraps bundles of product in plastic, then passes the bundles through a heated tunnel (at left end of the machine) to shrink the plastic tightly around the product. (Doboy Packaging Machinery)

The shrink-wrapped products may then be packed in boxes of corrugated board to protect them during shipment. Other printed products, such as books, may be packed in boxes without being wrapped beforehand. Several boxes can be stacked on a pallet and then strapped in place for shipping.

An alternative to shrink-wrapping is to use a ***banding machine***, also called a loop press, to wrap and bond a plastic or metal band around a bundle of booklets, books, boxes, or other products. This holds the products together for shipping.

Larger forms of the banding machine may be used to strap stacks of boxes onto pallets to keep them securely in place during shipping. Plastic wrapping material, similar to shrink-wrap, is often used to bind a stack of boxes on a pallet into a single unit.

A ***taping machine*** is used in shipping departments to automatically apply tape to seal the tops of boxes. One is pictured in **Figure 26-47**. As the boxes are fed through the machine, a series of rollers and brushes applies the tape to the top of each box. A cutter also slices off the tape to the correct length. Two belts move the boxes through the taping machine. This helps automate the shipping department of a facility.

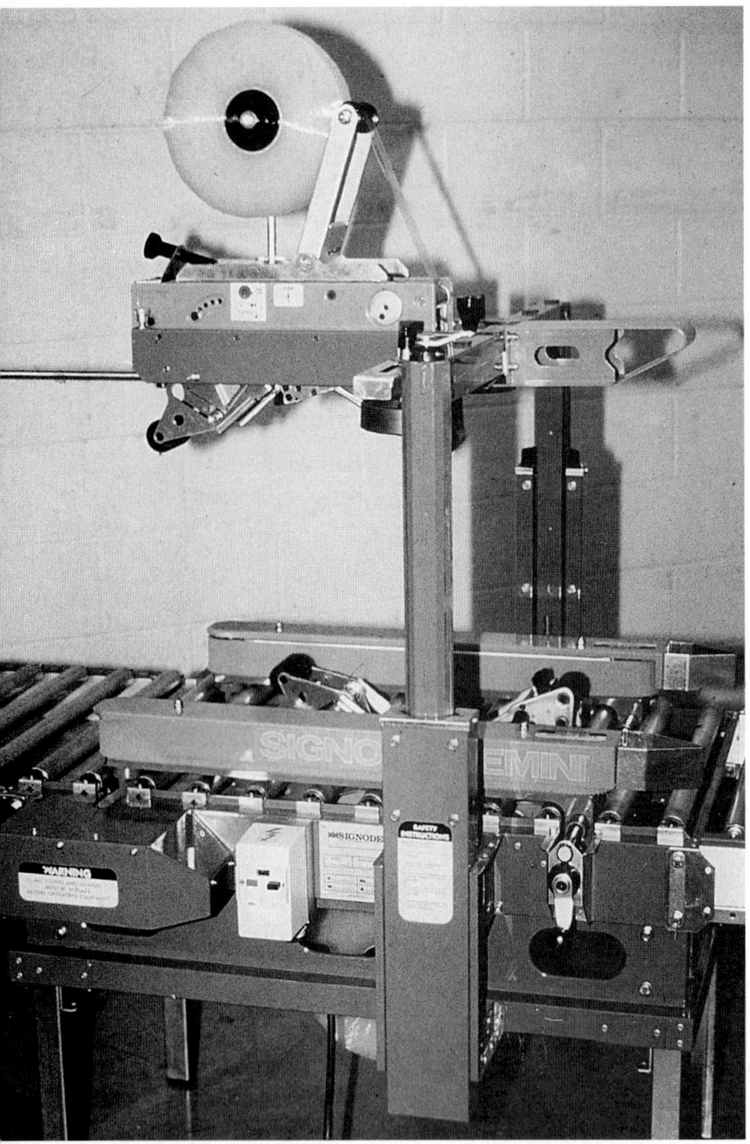

Figure 26-47. A taping machine will speed up the packaging area by automatically sealing boxes. (Signode)

Review Questions

Please do not write in this text. Write your answers on a separate sheet of paper.

1. What does the term "finishing" mean to a printer?
2. Which term refers to making three sides of a book even and square?
   a. Cutting.
   b. Scoring.
   c. Sheathing.
   d. Trimming.
3. What is a *shear stick*?
4. Explain why a folding machine operator should tie back long hair and secure loose clothing.
5. An _____ lifts heavy stacks of paper off the cutter table for easy movement.
6. How does a buckle folder work?
7. _____ is similar to cutting but it can be done by a set of wheels as the sheet passes through the folder.
8. Describe the processes and uses of pamphlet binding, edition binding, perfect binding, and mechanical binding.
9. _____ is a general term associated with the assembling of signatures.
10. Why are collating marks used?

27 The Business of Printing

Learning Objectives

After studying this chapter, you will be able to:

- Discuss the three basic types of business organization.
- Explain the relationship of business costs to printing estimates.
- List some of the areas in graphic communications that make use of computer technology.
- Compare the advantages of conventional and digital printing.
- Utilize job tickets and other business forms.
- Describe the most common trade customs in graphic communications.
- Summarize copyright laws.

Important Terms

copyright
corporation
infringement
job ticket
North American Industry Classification System (NAICS)
partnership
printing estimate
productivity
profit
single proprietorship
trade customs

Printing and publishing is a big business made up of mostly small businesses. It is a big business in terms of the dollar value of products (approaching $200 billion), the number of establishments, (more than 70,000), and the number of employees (approximately 1.5 million). More than 85 percent of commercial printing businesses, however, employ 20 or fewer people, nearly one-half of all shops have five or fewer employees, and only about 2 percent of all commercial printers employ more than 100 workers. In the publishing segment of the industry, 75 percent of business employ fewer than 20 people, and just over 6 percent have more than 100 workers.

Business Basics

A business may be organized in one of three forms — single proprietorship, partnership, or corporation. The ***single proprietorship*** is a business owned by one person. A ***partnership*** is a business owned by two or more persons. A ***corporation*** is a different form of multiple ownership with certain legal and financial advantages.

In the printing industry, with its large number of small companies, most businesses are single proprietorships or partnerships. The larger companies (and some smaller ones) are typically corporations. Single owners and most partners are actively involved in operating their businesses, while many of the stockholders (partial owners) in a corporation do not work in the business.

Organization

Every company, no matter what its size, has certain responsibilities that must be performed if it is to stay in business. These include:

- *Sales*, the job of obtaining orders for the company's products or services.
- *Business*, handling all the financial operations of the company.
- *Production*, consisting of all the activities needed to produce goods or services.
- *Administration*, coordinating and overseeing all aspects of the company.

In a large business, there might be dozens of people fulfilling each of these responsibilities. At the opposite end of the scale, a single proprietor may fill all the roles. **Figure 27-1** is a chart showing the organization of a small print shop with five employees. In this company, the owner handles both the sales and administrative responsibilities. An office manager takes care of such tasks as sending out invoices, paying bills from suppliers, and keeping business records. The production manager physically operates press equipment, and also oversees the work of the prepress worker and press helper.

As company size increases, these responsibilities are divided among a greater number of people. The company whose organization chart is shown in **Figure 27-2** has approximately 50 employees grouped into four departments. In this case, the company is a two-person partnership, with one partner serving as President (administrator) and the other as Controller (business manager). A variation on this organization might be the addition of an overall Production Manager to whom the Prepress Manager and the Plant Manager would report. The Production Manager would be responsible to the President, as are the Controller and the Sales Manager.

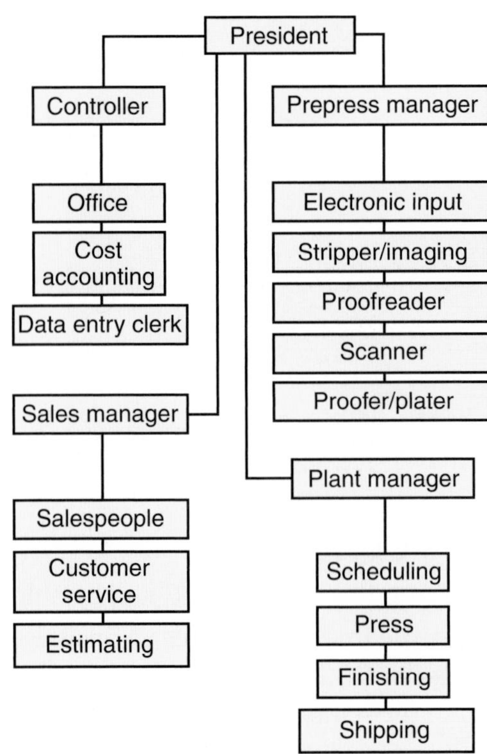

Figure 27-2. A company with approximately 50 employees would spread responsibilities to over a larger number of people. In this company, the President and the Controller are joint owners (partners).

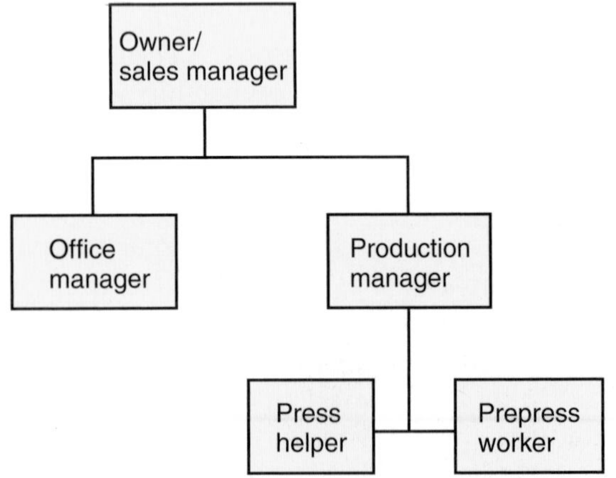

Figure 27-1. Organization of a typical small single-proprietor printing business. The owner also serves as sales manager. Often, such enterprises are family businesses, with all or most of the employees related to the owner.

Figure 27-3 is the organization chart for a printing company with 125 employees. This company is a corporation, with a Board of Directors elected by its stockholders to oversee the business. Day-to-day operation is conducted by the President, or ***Chief Executive Officer (CEO)***. Larger organizations such as this one are more complex, with a number of different levels of supervision and responsibility.

Business costs

To remain in business, a company must make a ***profit***. This means that it must receive more income from the sale of products or services than it spends for raw materials, salaries, building rent, utility

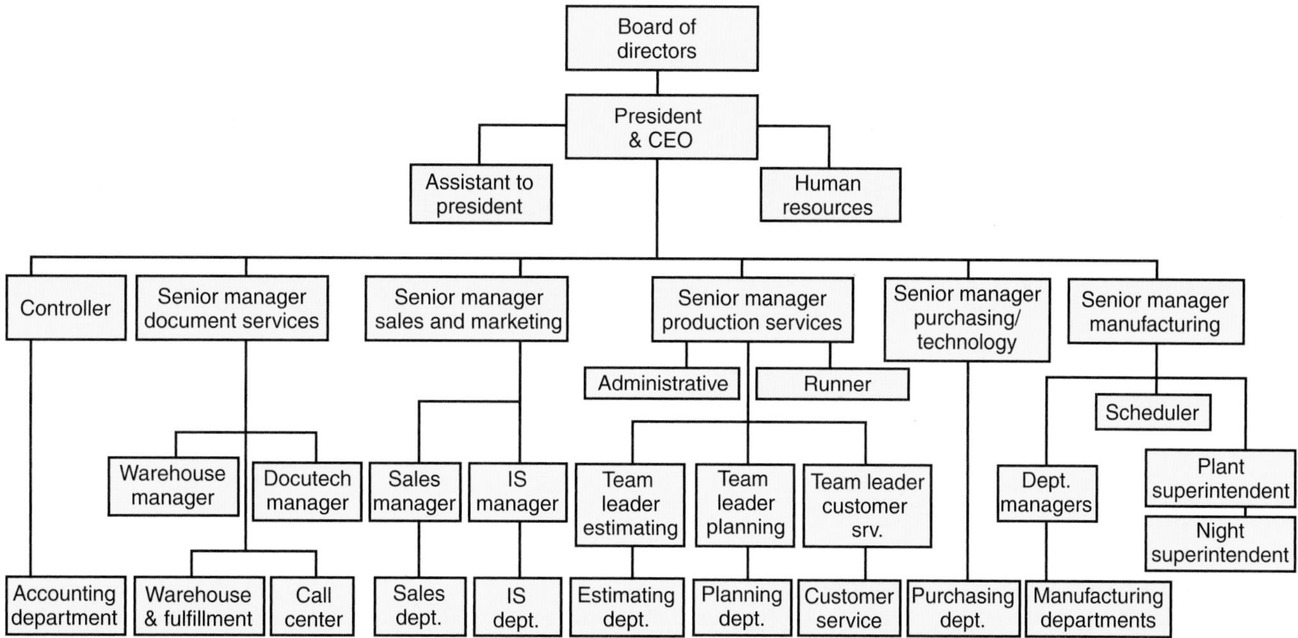

Figure 27-3. Large companies, such as this corporation with approximately 125 employees, have a more complex organization than smaller firms. As shown, there are several levels of management.

bills, and other costs of doing business. The difference between income and expenses is the profit of the business.

The key to success is identifying and controlling business costs, then setting prices that will cover the costs and provide a desired percentage of profit. A company that does not accurately determine its costs, or sets prices too low to make a profit, will soon go out of business.

Business costs can be grouped into three categories, materials costs, labor costs, and fixed costs, **Figure 27-4**.

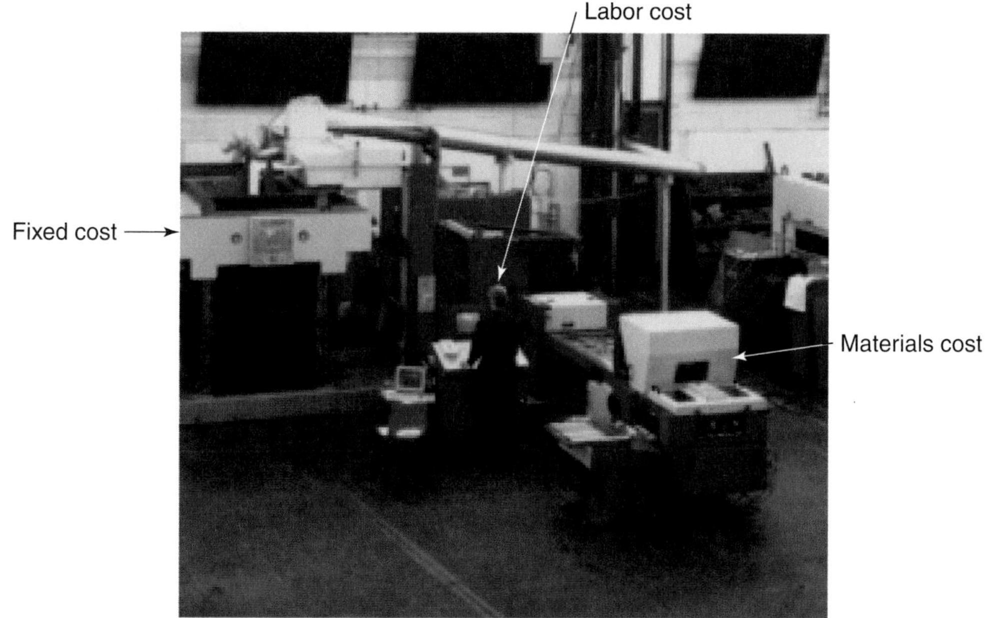

Figure 27-4. In a typical printing business, costs can be divided into three categories. Equipment, rent, and utilities are fixed costs, employees represent labor costs, and paper is a major part of materials costs. (Variquick)

- *Materials costs* are the prices paid for the items that are used up as a job is printed, primarily the paper and ink. Other items, such as packaging for the finished product, are also part of the materials cost.
- *Labor costs* are the "people costs" involved in operating the business. They include not only the hourly wages or salaries of the workers, but the cost of health insurance, paid holidays and vacations, and other fringe benefits. Services purchased from outside suppliers, such as illustrators, are also considered labor costs.
- *Fixed costs* are those that remain the same, regardless of the volume of business. For example, rent or mortgage payments on the shop premises are the same whether the printing presses are running around the clock, or the business is closed for the weekend. This cost category includes electricity, gas, telephone, and other utilities; the equipment needed to run the business; supplies ranging from copier toner to floor wax, even the cost of the company's advertisement in the telephone directory.

Accountants have various formulas for assigning a portion of the fixed costs (called "overhead") to each job that is printed. Materials costs and labor costs are more specific to the job: a particular number of worker hours was needed to produce it, along with a measurable quantities of paper, ink, and other materials.

Once a job is completed, it is a fairly simple matter to accurately determine exactly what costs were involved. It then would be just as easy to determine a price for the job that covered costs and provided a fair profit. Unfortunately, that business approach is not usually possible, since customers want to know in advance what they are going to pay for their printing.

This is where the printing estimate comes in. A ***printing estimate*** is an offer to print a particular job for a specified amount. If the customer accepts the estimate, it becomes a contract that is binding on both the printer and customer.

Printing estimates

Developing an estimate can be very simple, or extremely complicated, depending upon the circumstances. At the simple end of the scale are the jobs performed day-in and day-out by small shops and quick printers, which are usually handled with a fixed price schedule, rather than an actual estimate. These jobs are typically priced by units, such as 100 or 500 sheets, with a base price for printing and additional charges for variables such as a different paper stock or colored ink. Finishing steps, such as folding, are also covered on a price schedule.

More complicated projects require estimates that are custom-developed to meet the specifications provided by the customer. They require careful calculation of every aspect of the project, from paper cost to availability and operating cost of each piece of equipment to percentage of spoilage to final packaging and delivery.

Preparing an accurate estimate requires a precise knowledge of costs. Many successful firms have developed detailed breakdowns of their operations, building a data base of information for use in developing estimates. They are able to determine exactly how much per hour it costs to operate a specific piece of equipment, **Figure 27-5**, or how many worker hours must be allotted to carry out a particular operation.

The hourly cost rates developed by this method include a portion of the company's overhead (fixed cost) and the labor costs. Cost of materials is determined separately, since it can vary widely from one job to another. The estimate is developed using hourly cost rates, then the specific material cost for that job is added in.

For years, many printing firms (especially smaller companies or those performing varied types of printing operations) relied upon ***pricing guides*** that provided average costs for virtually every type of prepress, printing, and finishing operation. Following instructions provided in guides such as the *Franklin Offset Catalog*, an estimator could develop an estimate fairly quickly.

Although such printed pricing guides are still in use, they have been replaced in many plants by specialized ***estimating software*** used with computers, **Figure 27-6**. There are a number of

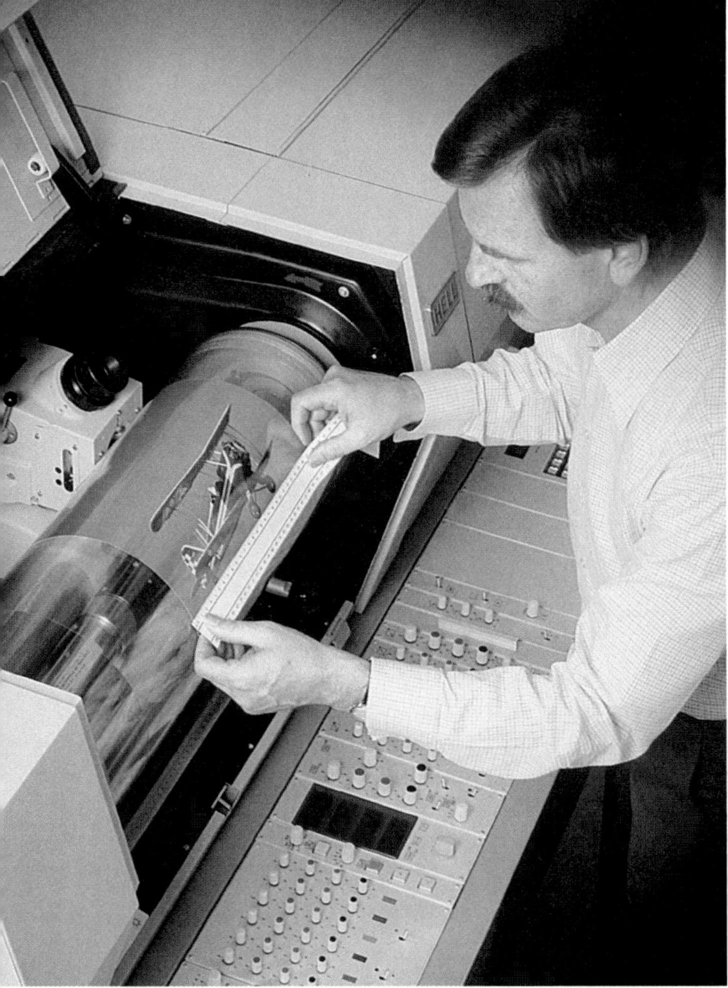

Figure 27-5. Accurate printing estimates depend upon precise costing information. The hourly cost of operating this scanner is a combination of labor costs and overhead (a percentage of fixed costs).

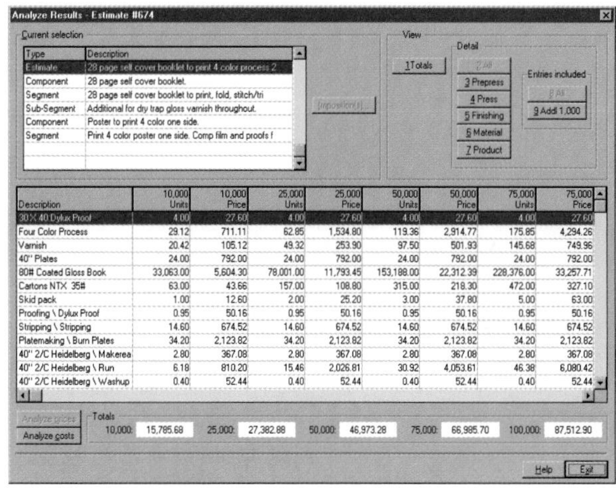

Description	10,000 Units	10,000 Price	25,000 Units	25,000 Price	50,000 Units	50,000 Price	75,000 Units	75,000 Price
30 X 40 Dylux Proof	4.00	27.60	4.00	27.60	4.00	27.60	4.00	27.60
Four Color Process	29.12	711.11	62.85	1,534.80	119.36	2,914.77	175.85	4,294.26
Varnish	20.42	105.12	49.32	253.90	97.50	501.93	145.68	749.96
40" Plates	24.00	792.00	24.00	792.00	24.00	792.00	24.00	792.00
80# Coated Gloss Book	33,063.00	5,604.30	78,001.00	11,793.45	153,188.00	22,312.39	228,376.00	33,257.71
Cartons NTX 35#	63.00	43.66	157.00	108.80	315.00	218.30	472.00	327.10
Skid pack	1.00	12.60	2.00	25.20	3.00	37.80	5.00	63.00
Proofing \ Dylux Proof	0.95	50.16	0.95	50.16	0.95	50.16	0.95	50.16
Stripping \ Stripping	14.60	674.52	14.60	674.52	14.60	674.52	14.60	674.52
Platemaking \ Burn Plates	34.20	2,123.82	34.20	2,123.82	34.20	2,123.82	34.20	2,123.82
40" 2/C Heidelberg \ Makerea	2.80	367.08	2.80	367.08	2.80	367.08	2.80	367.08
40" 2/C Heidelberg \ Run	6.18	810.20	15.46	2,026.81	30.92	4,053.61	46.38	6,080.42
40" 2/C Heidelberg \ Washup	0.40	52.44	0.40	52.44	0.40	52.44	0.40	52.44

Figure 27-6. Estimating software can simplify the process of preparing a printing estimate. This summary screen provides the estimator with pricing for various quantities of the job. With software such as this, information can be viewed many different ways before preparing and printing the estimate.
(Hagen Systems, Inc.)

different estimating programs on the market, but most operate in a similar manner. The estimator "fills in the blanks" on a screen, entering the specifics of the job, such as size, quantity, paper to be used, equipment required, and so on. The software will then calculate an estimate based on cost data, and present it for review. The estimator can then print out the estimate to be sent or delivered to the customer.

Some estimating software is designed for use on standalone desktop computers, while other programs may be intended for larger operations where a number of different sites are linked by telephone lines or even satellite systems. Some estimating programs allow outside sales personnel with laptop computers to prepare an estimate right at the customer's office or plant. Information is exchanged with the printing company's computer with a modem connection via telephone line, allowing confirmation of prices, scheduling, or materials availability.

As detailed in earlier chapters, the computer has become a major tool in almost every aspect of graphic communications, from the creative and prepress areas through all phases of production and business operations. In addition to software for estimating and business office operations (accounting, billing, purchasing, and related activities), programs have been developed to simplify personnel and equipment scheduling and to more efficiently operate equipment. See **Figure 27-7.** Some systems also use computer terminals at various workstations to gather information that can be used for more accurate cost calculations. More precise information on costs, in turn, can allow more closely calculated estimates that could provide a competitive advantage for a printer. Better cost control can also improve a company's profitability.

Figure 27-7. Computers are an integral part of almost every printing operation today. A computerized control system helps to run this large press efficiently, and can also be used to gather information needed for accurately developing cost figures. (King Press Corporation)

Job tickets

Productivity is the amount of quality work completed in a given time span. It is a key word in the printing plant. *Efficiency* (maximum output with minimum effort) and *utilization* (maximum use of people and equipment) are two factors which add up to productivity. To achieve high productivity, good *communication* is essential.

To keep track of printing jobs as they move through the plant and to convey important information to all departments, some type of ***job ticket*** is typically used, **Figure 27-8**. Job tickets are generally designed to meet the needs of a specific company or area in a company. In some plants, separate job tickets are used for sheet-fed presswork and for web-press operations. Often, tickets take the form of a jacket or pouch to hold loose papers, such as purchase orders or other forms relating to the job.

Information for a form like the one shown in Figure 27-8 would be provided by various workers. Some areas are filled out by personnel in the planning and purchasing departments, while others are filled out by sales and production people. Headings break up the form to aid in the communication process. This clearly identifies what is to be done in each special area.

Invoice to

This topmost section of the form provides room to record customer, quotation, billing, and other important business information.

Job specs

A short summary of the job particulars is recorded here. For a small job, no other information may be necessary, but a more complex project will usually have more detailed information contained in the quotation.

Type/art

The *type/art* section of this job ticket has check boxes to indicate various actions. Additional or special information or instructions can be written in the space provided.

Prep

The personnel in the prep department are informed of what needs to be done by this form. Sometimes, the job has been printed before. If so, the job may be repeated without any changes. However, if changes are to be made, the proper square on the form must be checked. The various stages are also checked to identify camera-ready copy, one piece of film, or a number of negatives or positives. *Seps* is shorthand for separations — the film necessary to print a full-color job.

Proofs

The types of proofs requested are identified on the form. Space is also provided to note whether a press check will be made, and who will be responsible for that check.

Paper

Correct paper information is extremely important. In this case, sales personnel fill out one section of the job ticket. The planning and purchasing people are responsible for listing the basis weight of the stock, as well as the supplier of the paper. Also listed are order and delivery dates, quantity and size information, and cutting requirements.

On the form used for web-press operation, the paper section differs somewhat, since the paper is in roll form. The width of the roll and the cut allowance are two different pieces of information needed to make sure enough paper is ordered.

Sheet-fed press

Specifics such as number of forms, the press to be used, and ink colors to be used on each side of the sheet are listed. The total number of sheets and various allowances for waste are recorded.

Customer ______________
Address ______________
City/State ______________
Contact ______________

Courier GRAPHICS CORP

Date In ________ Date Due ________
Art In ________ Job Due ________
Sales Rep ______________
Phone ________ Fax ________

Description ______________

Trim Size Flat ________ Folded ________
Flat ________ Folded ________
Flat ________ Folded ________
Flat ________ Folded ________

No. of pages ______________

Prepress Output from Disk ❑ ______________

Proofs Blueline ❑ Matchprint ❑ Barco ❑ ______________

Ink Colors ______________

	Form	Basis Weight	Type	Book or Cover	Finish
Paper					

Bindery ______________

Shipping ______________

Quantity ______________

Property of Courier Graphics MUST REMAIN ON PREMISES

Figure 27-8. The job ticket, form, or jacket provides space for all major departments. (Courier Graphics Corp.)

An important part of this section of the form is the *net yield*. This is the final production total or figure after the job is completed. It is an excellent follow-up tool for control.

Bindery

The bindery area of many plants is becoming more automated, but many types of operations are still done by hand. This section of the form is used to indicate all the finishing operations that are to be performed.

Vendors

If material is to be supplied or an activity performed by another company or outside contractor, the action is indicated in this section of the form.

Mailing

On mailing pieces or envelopes, special postal information (such as a bulk mail permit number) often must be printed. This section of the form is used to specify such work.

Packaging, Ship to

There are a number of ways of packaging the finished job for delivery to the customer. A small letterhead and envelope job might be packed in a sturdy box and mailed, while a large run of a multipage booklet would probably be boxed, packed on skids, and shipped by truck.

Art & samples

Some printers store artwork and other materials for the customer for use in future projects, but the originals are more often returned. Samples of the printed job may be sent to the customer, the customer's advertising agency, or other interested parties.

Matching the job to the equipment

One of the important tasks in running an efficient and profitable printing operation is matching the requirements of a job with the equipment available. Using a piece of equipment that is less suitable for a particular job can cause delays, increase waste, and cut profit margins. One common example of a choice faced by many printers today is whether to print a given job by conventional means or electronic (digital) methods.

There is frequently no clear indication of when it is better to use conventional printing or digital printing. Speed, quality, and economics are some determining factors. Run length, page count, and bindery requirements also affect optimum process and performance determination. Aspects that differentiate the economics of traditional printing and the use of digital printing are discussed in this section.

Run length and ***page count*** are primary factors in choosing the appropriate printing technology. A conventional printing vs digital printing comparison shows that per-page cost remains constant for digital printing. With conventional printing, however, per-page cost *decreases* with higher page counts and longer run lengths and *increases* with shorter page counts and shorter run lengths, **Figure 27-9**.

Conventional printing is best for longer runs, higher page counts, and higher quality. Digital printing is best for shorter runs, lower page counts, and moderate quality. There is an optimum point for each reprographic technology. With experience, users learn to optimize job requirements and printing method.

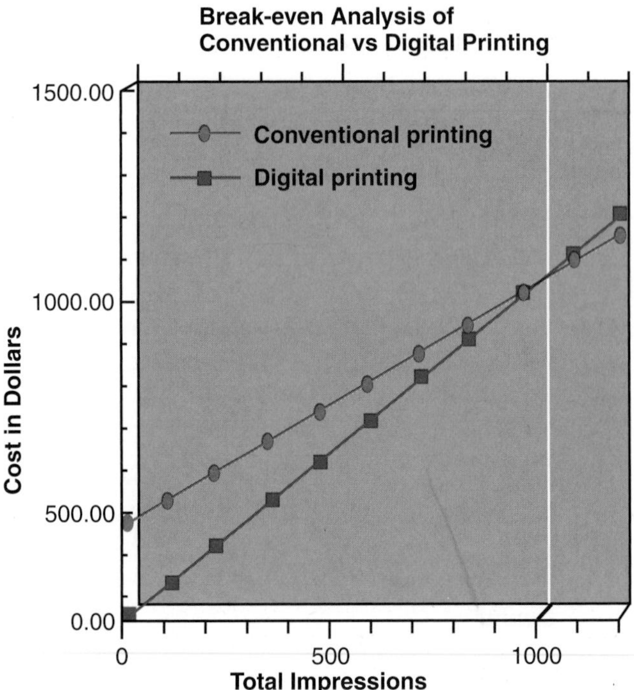

Figure 27-9. Digital color technology can be used cost effectively for short runs, although conventional printing clearly has advantage for longer runs.

Most digital systems have integrated sorting with limited in-line binding. If the desired result is complete units, then the run length and page count become critical aspects in determining the reprographic method. Since conventional printing provides for more variability and the ability to customize the manufacturing process, you will likely utilize one of the many conventional methods. Digital systems, on the other hand, have the ability to provide short run fully completed products, if product specifications conform to the options available.

The *operator skill level* for conventional press operation is high, requiring years of experience typically gained through an apprenticeship program. ***Journeyman*** press operators usually command high wages for their time and dedication to the trade.

The *digital press* operators have a much different skill set and must continually upgrade their knowledge, because the computer-based technology is constantly changing. Digital press operators are usually on a lower pay scale than journeyman conventional press operators.

Paper variety is considerably more restricted with digital presses in terms of the substrates they can handle. The conventional printing press has much greater latitude, giving it an advantage in this category. The ability of either device to handle paper *within specifications* is excellent.

Deviation from standard size paper does have an impact on digital press speed, but little impact on conventional printing. Speed then must be accounted for based on quantity plus sheet size and number of copies.

Machine costs are the overhead that must be taken into account when costing work produced on the device. Machine costs depend on quantity and number of pages. Specifically, the conventional offset process has higher initial cost, but lower per-copy costs.

Operator costs strongly favor electronic systems because the lesser trade requirements usually mean lower wages. Perhaps of greater importance is that it is common for one electronic system operator to run more than one printer. Conventional printing presses typically need one or more people for one machine. In some shops, however, it is not uncommon for one person to operate two small offset presses at the same time.

First-copy time always favors the digital printer, because makeready requirements are not needed. Likely more important is that the high-volume electronic printers have an interrupt feature that requires minimum time and bother to produce another job, even if a different paper is involved. In same situation, conventional printing presses require considerable downtime. The operator must put the job's plate back on the press, change inks, get the ink levels correct, registering the image, and so forth.

Film and *plates* are traditional printing requirements that introduce variable costs for material, labor, and time. Plating costs vary based upon press requirements, but typically require a film image, assembly time and material, and a printing plate. This cost ranges from less than a dollar for a direct-image plastic master, to many more dollars for a film negative or positive and a metal plate.

Because digital printers do *not* require a platemaking step to produce copies they have a decisive cost advantage. Once running, though, printing ink and chemistry will cost much less than the fuser and toner used in the digital press. Printing presses cost considerably more to get the first copy, but each additional copy has a much lower unit cost than the copier.

The cost break-even point between a digital printer and printing press is directly related to the platemaking processes. For example: printing presses have makeready costs, including plate cost, transfer of the master to the plate cylinder, and anywhere from three sheets of paper to several hundred before the first good copy is achieved.

Digital printers have no makeready cost — the first copy produced is the same as the second and the last. Thus the break-even point is when the cost of total copies made on the digital press equals the makeready cost on the printing press plus the lower cost per copy volume.

Multiple-page documents require added consideration to be given to the types of binding and the available equipment. Usually, bindery operations for conventionally printed sheets are done off-line. Some electronic printers can saddle stitch work on-line; others require an off-line operation. The key considerations are run length and page count.

Planning for Growth and Success

The growth and success of a graphic communications operation depends upon many factors. Every employee, every process, every supplier, every piece of equipment, all play a vital role in the growth or downfall of a company!

The location of the various departments, the placement of equipment, employee attitudes, the location of the facility geographically, these factors and many others affect business success. For this reason, careful planning is tremendously important. If a planner or manager makes mistakes, it can cost the firm time, money, and personnel.

The growth of a graphics firm primarily depends upon the finished product's cost and quality. In turn, the employees, raw materials, and equipment control the cost and quality of a printed product.

As an old saying goes, "A chain is only as strong as its weakest link." Relating to the planning of the growth or development of a graphics company, every phase of production must be well thought out and reviewed periodically. If one phase of production is a "weak link," in the chain, it can affect the final product and the future of the company.

The growth and success of a company is dependent upon many interacting factors. To help achieve growth and success, effective managers rely upon proven business and personnel practices. Some of these include:

- Using efficient, cost-effective equipment to produce better products at a lower cost.
- Developing a "team effort" mental attitude where all employees work and communicate as a cohesive unit to outperform competing companies.
- Using worker feedback to analyze and improve production steps; the person performing the task usually has the best idea of how it can be done better.
- Basing pay increases in part on company profits. This can generate peer pressure to improve job performance.
- Making it obvious that promotions and salary increases are based on job performance; use qualities like dependability, work quality, efficiency, cooperation, initiative, and innovation.
- Providing workers with the capability of advancement within the company, as a performance incentive and means of building employee morale.
- Carefully analyzing and selecting outside sources of supplies and services, weighing cost versus quality factors.
- Applying modern quality control and production control methods to all appropriate operations within the company.
- Developing and implementing a continuous training program to help employees keep up-to-date with advances in technology.

E-Commerce

It is anticipated that the Internet and the world of print will continue to have an increasingly close association. Communication (or the lack thereof) has often been a problem within the graphic communications industry from the idea through the finished product. The need for greater speed, accuracy, and accountability are essential factors in today's business environment. Improving the printer-customer communication interface is vital to improving efficiency and cutting down waste within a company. A company website can be a very valuable tool for both promoting and conducting business. Companies should look into the possibility of partnering with a service provider to create and maintain such a site.

Trade Customs

It would be time-consuming and inefficient to write a contract that covered all aspects of each new print job. In the printing industry, *trade customs* are used rather than a formal, individual contract. ***Trade customs*** are understood rules or implied laws used in the printing industry, and have been backed up by courts as binding agreements. At times, specific contracts are issued when other additional terms are desired, however.

Use of trade customs

The National Association of Printers and Lithographers (NAPL) has issued guidelines for the use of trade customs. These state that the printer should:

- Print trade customs on the back of estimates and other order acknowledgments.
- State on the order acknowledgment that all work is subject to trade customs.

Trade Customs of The Printing Industry of North America

Preamble To The Trade Customs

As the name suggests, the Printing Industry Trade Customs reflect the common business practices of the printing industry. However, "Trade Customs" are not necessarily "recommended" practices. Some printers may elect to follow them; others may not. The use of any Trade Custom must always be an independent, individual business decision. As each company drafts its own contractual provisions, it will also want to consider customer's wishes, relationships with potential customers, and other competitive issues.

It is important to note that Trade Customs having to do with rates, payment terms, and warranties may be subject to modification.

1. Quotation

A quotation not accepted within 30 days may be changed.

2. Orders

Acceptance of orders is subject to credit approval and contingencies such as fire, water, strikes, theft, vandalism, acts of God, and other causes beyond the provider's control. Canceled orders require compensation for incurred costs and related obligations.

3. Experimental work

Experimental or preliminary work performed at customer's request will be charged to the customer at the provider's current rates. This work cannot be used without the provider's written consent.

4. Creative work

Sketches, copy, dummies, and all other creative work developed or furnished by the provider are the provider's exclusive property. The provider must give written approval for all use of this work and for any derivation of ideas from it.

5. Accuracy of specifications

Quotations are based on the accuracy of the specifications provided. The provider can re-quote a job at time of submission if copy, film, tapes, disks, or other input materials don't conform to the information on which the original quotation was based.

6. Preparatory materials

Art work, type, plates, negatives, positives, tapes, disks, and all other items supplied by the provider remain the provider's exclusive property.

7. Electronic manuscript or image

It is the customer's responsibility to maintain a copy of the original file. The provider is not responsible for accidental damage to media supplied by the customer or for the accuracy of furnished input or final output. Until digital input can be evaluated by the provider, no claims or promises are made about the provider's ability to work with jobs submitted in digital format, and no liability is assumed for problems that may arise. Any additional translating, editing, or programming needed to utilize customer-supplied files will be charged at prevailing rates.

8. Alterations/corrections

Customer alterations include all work performed in addition to the original specifications. All such work will be charged at the provider's current rates.

9. Prepress proofs

The provider will submit prepress proofs along with original copy for the customer's review and approval. Corrections will be returned to the provider on a "master set" marked "O.K.," "O.K. with corrections," or "Revised proof required" and signed by the customer. Until the master set is received, no additional work will be performed. The provider will not be responsible for undetected production errors if:

*proofs are not required by the customer;
*the work is printed per the customer's O.K.;
*requests for changes are communicated orally.

10. Press proofs

Press proofs will not be furnished unless they have been required in writing in the provider's quotation. Press sheet can be submitted for the customer's approval as long as the customer is present at the press during makeready. Any press time lost or alterations/corrections made because of the customer's delay or change of mind will be charged at the provider's current rates.

11. Color proofing

Because of differences in equipment, paper, inks, and other conditions between color proofing and production pressroom operations, a reasonable variation in color between color proofs and the completed job is to be expected. When variation of this kind occurs, it will be considered acceptable performance.

12. Overruns or underruns

Overruns or underruns will not exceed 10 percent of the quantity ordered. The provider will bill for actual quantity delivered within this tolerance. If the customer requires a guaranteed quantity, the percentage of tolerance must be stated at the time of quotation.

13. Customer's property

The provider will only maintain fire and extended coverage on property belonging to the customer while the property is in the provider's possession. The provider's liability for this property will not exceed the amount recoverable from the insurance. Additional insurance coverage may be obtained if it is requested in writing, and if the premium is paid to the provider.

14. Delivery

Unless otherwise specified, the price quoted is for a single shipment, without storage, F.O.B. provider's platform. Proposals are based on continuous and uninterrupted delivery of the complete order. If the specifications state otherwise, the provider will charge accordingly at current rates. Charges for delivery of materials and supplies form the customer to the provider, or from the customer's supplier to the provider, are not included in quotations unless specified. Title for finished work passes to the customer upon delivery to the carrier at shipping point; or upon mailing of invoices for the finished work or its segments, whichever occurs first.

15. Production schedules

Production schedules will be established and followed by both the customer and the provider. In the event that production schedules are not adhered to by the customer, delivery dates will be subject to renegotiation. There will be no liability or penalty for delays due to state of war, riot, civil disorder, fire, strikes, accidents, action of government or civil authority, acts of God or other causes beyond the control of the provider. In such cases, schedules will be extended by an amount of time equal to delay incurred.

16. Customer-furnished materials

Materials furnished by customers or their suppliers are verified by delivery tickets. The provider bears no responsibility for discrepancies between delivery tickets and actual counts. Customer-supplied paper must be delivered according to specifications furnished by the provider. These specifications will include correct weight, thickness, pick resistance, and other technical requirements. Artwork, film, color separations, special dies, tapes, disks, or other materials furnished by the customer must be usable by the provider without alterations or repair items not meeting this requirement will be repaired by the customer, or by the provider at the provider's current rates.

17. Outside purchases

Unless otherwise agreed in writing, all outside purchases as requested or authorized by the customer, are chargeable.

18. Terms/claims/liens

Payment is net cash 30 calendar days from date of invoice. Claims for defects, damages, or shortages must be made by the customer in writing no later than 10 calendar days after delivery. If no such claim is made, the provider and the customer will understand the job has been accepted. By accepting the job, the customer acknowledges the provider's performance has fully satisfied all terms, conditions, and specifications.

The provider's liability will be limited to the quoted selling price of defective goods, without additional liability for special or consequential damages. As security for payment of any sum due under the terms of an agreement, the provider has the right to hold and place a lien on all customer property in the provider's possession. This right applies even if credit has been extended, notes have been accepted, trade acceptances have been made, or payment has been guaranteed. If payment is not made, the customer is liable for all collection costs incurred.

19. Liability

A. Disclaimer of express warranties: Provider warrants that the work is as described in the purchase order. The customer understands that all sketches, copy dummies, and preparatory work shown to the customer are intended only to illustrate the general type and quality of the work. They are not intended to represent the actual work performed.

B. Disclaimer of implied warranties: The provider warrants only that the work will conform to the description contained in the purchase order. The provider's maximum liability, whether by negligence, contract, or otherwise, will not exceed the return of the amount invoiced for the work in dispute. Under no circumstances will the provider be liable for specific, individual, or consequential damages.

20. Indemnification

The customer agrees to protect the provider from economic loss and any other harmful consequences that could arise in connection with the work. This means that the customer will hold the provider harmless and save, indemnify, and otherwise defend him/her against claims, demands, actions, and proceedings on any and all grounds. This will apply regardless of responsibility for negligence.

A. Copyrights: The customer also warrants that the subject matter to be printed is not copyrighted by a third party. The customer also recognizes that because subject matter does not have to bear a copyright notice in order to be protected by copyright law, absence of such notice does not necessarily assure a right to reproduce. The customer further warrants that no copyright notice has been removed from any material used in preparing the subject matter for reproduction.

To support these warranties, the customer agrees to indemnify and hold the provider harmless for all liability, damages, and attorney fees that may be incurred in any legal action connected with copyright infringement involving the work produced or provided.

B. Personal or economic rights: The customer also warrants that the work does not contain anything that is libelous or scandalous, or anything that threatens anyone's right to privacy or other personal or economic rights. The customer will, at the customer's sole expense, promptly and thoroughly defend the provider in all legal actions on these grounds as long as the provider

*promptly notifies the customer of the legal action;
*gives the customer reasonable time to undertake and conduct a defense.

The provider reserves the right to use his or her sole discretion in refusing to print anything he or she deems illegal, libelous, scandalous, improper, or infringing upon copyright law.

21. Storage

The provider will retain intermediate materials until the related end product has been accepted by the customer. If requested by the customer, intermediate materials will be stored for an additional period at additional charge. The provider is not liable for any loss or damage to store material beyond what is recoverable by the provider's fire and extended insurance coverage.

22. Taxes

All amounts due for taxes and assessments will be added to the customer's invoice and are the responsibility of the customer. No tax exemption will be granted unless the customer's "Exemption Certificate" (or other official proof of exemption) accompanies the purchase order. If after the customer has paid the invoice, it is determined that more tax is due, then the customer must promptly remit the required taxes to the taxing authority, or immediately reimburse the provider for any additional taxes paid.

23. Telecommunications

Unless otherwise agreed, the customer will pay for all transmission charges. The provider is not responsible for any errors, omissions, or extra costs resulting from faults in the transmission.

(Printing Industries of America, INC.)

Figure 27-10. These are the accepted Trade Customs used in the printing industry. Read through them carefully. (Printing Industries of America, Inc.)

- Make sure that custom-made terms and conditions are no less strict than trade customs.
- Make sure that salespersons are knowledgeable of trade customs and how they protect the printer.

The *Trade Customs of the Printing Industries of North America*, **Figure 27-10**, have been accepted by the National Association of Printers and Lithographers and the Printing Industries of America (PIA). These associations reaffirm the trade customs at their business meetings and, from time to time, create a committee to study proposed changes to the customs. One example of a recent change is the addition of a paragraph relating to responsibility for copy and images provided in electronic form.

Many companies use the traditional trade customs as written by the NAPL and PIA. However, some firms modify those customs slightly and may add *riders* or additional stipulations to them, **Figure 27-11**. Riders are important to the printer and to the customer, since they can affect the responsibilities and outcome of the job as well as the costs of the job if difficulties arise.

Standards and Specifications

Under certain circumstances, such as producing work for government agencies, printers may be required to conform to certain standards set by organizations such as ISO or ANSI. In other situations, customers may require the printer to meet specifications set by the company or by a specialized organization, such as SWOP.

International Organization for Standardization (ISO)

The International Organization for Standardization (ISO) is a worldwide federation of national standards bodies. ISO is a nongovernmental organization. It covers all fields except electrical and electronic engineering standards which is covered by another organization. The results of ISO technical work are published in the form of international standards. ISO coordinates the exchange of information on international and national standards. The ISO technical committee for graphic arts is TC130.

American National Standards Institute (ANSI)

The American National Standards Institute is an impartial organization that validates work conducted by organizations accredited as standards development groups. Standards are considered to be voluntary and not mandated. Each standard is identified with the letters ANSI and a number.

Rider

C & S Company will accept orders for printing, binding, and other book manufacturing services only upon the following understandings and agreements of Customer:

Risk of loss and insurance coverage on material supplied by Customer and on work produced and billed by C & S or delivered, including film and unfinished as well as finished books, are Customer's responsibilities. Customer releases and forever discharges C & S and its employees from any and all claims or causes of action whatsoever founded upon loss of or damage to such material or work, if such loss or damage is caused by fire or other insurable peril, whether or not attributable to the fault or negligence of C & S, its employees or agents, and whether or not Customer has obtained insurance coverage therefore. Insurable perils are those perils such as sprinkler leakage, explosion, riot/civil commotion and building collapse, in addition to fire and such other risks that
under the standard form of ALL RISKS insurance currently in use.

C & S prices are based on the present cost of materials involved and C & S
there are any changes in the cost of materials or in C & S scale of wag
any portion of this work, said increases or decr
of the work.

All applicable personal prop
sale and on the us
extra and will

Figure 27-11. A rider like this one may be added by the printer to the traditional Trade Customs. These are stipulations intended to protect both the printer and the customer. (NAPL)

Committee for Graphic Arts Technologies Standards (CGATS)

The Committee for Graphic Arts Technologies Standards (CGATS) is accredited by ANSI. The goal of CGATS is to have the entire scope of printing and publishing recognized as the national standards group. It also intends to coordinate the efforts of other bodies.

Specifications for Web Offset Publications (SWOP)

Specifications for Web Offset Publications (SWOP) are recommended specifications for the publications printing industry. The intent is to raise the quality level of publications printing. The complete set of SWOP specifications is reprinted as Appendix 1.

SIC Replacement

The Standard Industrial Classification (SIC) code is being replaced by the new six-digit ***North American Industry Classification System (NAICS)*** code. The NAICS codes will be used to collect data. This information will be used to compare data within the industry and among the members of NAFTA (North American Free Trade Agreement)—the United States, Canada, and Mexico. The NAICS codes for the printing industry are:

323 Printing and Related Activities
3231 Printing and Related Activities
32311 Printing
323110 Commercial Lithographic Printing
323111 Commercial Gravure Printing
323112 Commercial Flexographic Printing
323113 Commercial Screen Printing
323114 Quick Printing
323115 Digital Printing
323116 Manifold Business Forms
323117 Book Printing
323118 Blankbooks, Looseleaf Binder, and Device Manufacturing
323119 Other Commercial Printing
323121 Trade Binding and Related Work
323122 Prepress Services

The first two NAICS digits designate industry sectors, the third digit represents the subsector, the fourth represents the industry group level, the fifth digit identifies the international industry level, and the sixth designates the national detail. NAICS creates a standard to be used by each of the NAFTA trading partners.

Copyright Laws

A ***copyright*** is a legal protection against unauthorized reproduction of literary works (books and other printed materials), musical compositions and recordings, artworks, photographs, films and video, and dramatic works. Copyright gives authors, artists, and other copyright owners the opportunity to exclusively profit from their creations for a stated period. It protects against financial loss due to sale of their work by someone who has not paid a fee to them. In the U.S., a copyright is in effect for the life of the author or producer, plus 50 years after his or her death.

In graphic communications or printing, you are primarily concerned with copyrights on printed matter. For example, a textbook like this one, will usually have the copyright information on the page immediately following the title page. Smaller printed pieces (such as booklets) might have a copyright notice on the first page or inside the front cover. Single page items (such as posters) will usually have a copyright notice on the front side.

There are a number of forms that the copyright notice can take, but it should include the word "copyright," the abbreviation "Copr.," or the symbol ©. The word or symbol should be followed by the name of the copyright owner and the year the work was first published. See **Figure 27-12**. Sometimes, the year is omitted and/or the name is reduced to initials. This is often done to provide notice unobtrusively on artworks, photographs, or similar objects.

© Jones Publishing 1999

Copyright Jones Publishing 1999

Copr. Jones Publishing

© **JP**

Copr. JP 1999

Figure 27-12. There are a number of ways that a copyright notice can be presented.

When someone brings in materials (sign, poster, ad, etc.) and asks the printer or copy service to reproduce it, they may be asking the printer or copy service to violate copyright law. If the item bears a copyright notice, the person seeking to reproduce it should have evidence of permission —in writing— from the copyright holder.

It might be wise to have a release form for customers to sign that releases the printer from liability for ***infringement***, (unauthorized use of a copyrighted work) since conviction on a charge of copyright infringement can cost literally thousands of dollars in fines and damage awards to the copyright holder.

The factors commonly used by the courts to determine if infringement of copyright has taken place, and what kinds of monetary award might be made include:

- How the material was used.
- The type of work copied.
- The amount of the material copied.
- Content of the copied material.
- Monetary value of the copied material.

There are exceptions to the law that allow some duplication of copyrighted materials without infringement. These exceptions are known as the ***fair use*** provisions of the law. The most common example of fair use is in education. An instructor is allowed to copy a reasonable portion of a copyrighted work (for example a magazine article or book chapter) for classroom use by students. Students are also allowed to copy material while doing research.

Review Questions

Please do not write in this text. Write your answers on a separate sheet of paper.

1. What are the three forms in which a business may be organized?
2. The abbreviation CEO is usually considered to stand for _____.
   a. Chief Estimator on duty
   b. Computer Equipment Operator
   c. Chief Executive Officer
   d. Company Equipment Order Clerk
3. The portion of fixed costs assigned to each job printed is usually referred to as _____.
4. *True or false*? Digital printers have no makeready cost.
5. _____ is the amount of quality work completed in a given time span.
6. Define the term *trade customs*.
7. Which organizations have accepted the Trade Customs for the Printing Industries of North America?
8. What does the abbreviation SWOP stand for?
9. How long is a copyright in effect?
   a. 50 years
   b. For the producer's lifetime.
   c. Forever.
   d. For the producer's lifetime, plus 50 years.
10. If you are working for a printer and someone brings in a poster with a copyright notice on it, can you legally reproduce the poster?

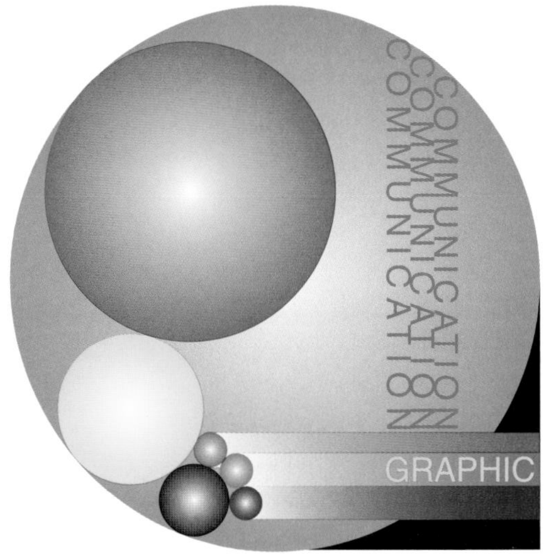

Graphic Communications Careers 28

Learning Objectives

After studying this chapter, you will be able to:

- Identify the variety of jobs available within the graphic communications industry.
- Separate skilled technical, creative, management, and support positions.
- Explain the characteristics common to positions in graphic communications.
- Describe the advantages and disadvantages of owning your own business.
- Explore a graphic communications career that matches your interests and abilities.

Important Terms

apprenticeship
career
craft-centered
electronic information transfer
entrepreneur
lifelong learning
manager
outsourcing
robotics
turnaround

The graphic communications industry encompasses a multitude of challenging positions for skilled technical, creative, management, and support personnel. Engineers and scientists can also find positions in the graphic communications industry. Entrepreneurship is yet another avenue open to someone who wants to own and operate a company. This chapter will summarize and help you more fully understand these positions.

Choosing a Career

Choosing a ***career*** is one of the most important decisions you will ever make. It can affect many aspects of your life, including level of education, income potential, working conditions, and types of coworkers. A career choice can also affect your family. It determines your geographic location, the number of hours spent on the job, possibilities for advancement, and many other considerations. Above all, your career choice can affect your satisfaction with life in general.

Job satisfaction

Job satisfaction is important. You need to feel good about your work and your future. Choosing the right career requires you to look ahead. What kind of work do you expect to be doing five years from now? Ten years from now? Which occupation will offer advancement and bring satisfaction? What areas are in demand?

First, you must know your interests and talents. Then, you need to learn the requirements of different jobs in a particular field. This will enable you to select a career that matches your aptitudes and goals.

Preparing for a Career

What are the entry-level jobs within the graphic communications industry? Most of the skill areas require at least a high school education or the equivalent (i.e., a general equivalency diploma [GED]) or vocational/technical training. See **Figure 28-1**. Ambitious students who apply for part-time work during high school can get a head start toward full-time employment after graduation.

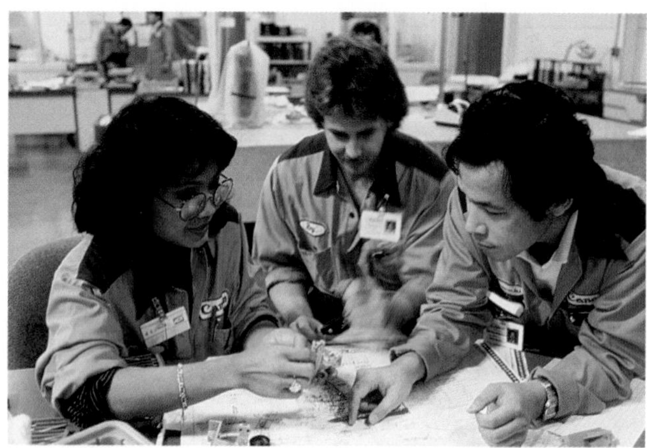

Figure 28-1. These young people are in training for positions as skilled technicians. (Canon USA, Inc.)

Figure 28-2. Many students prepare for careers in graphics and printing at a four-year educational institutions. (Bowling Green State University, Visual Communication Technology Program)

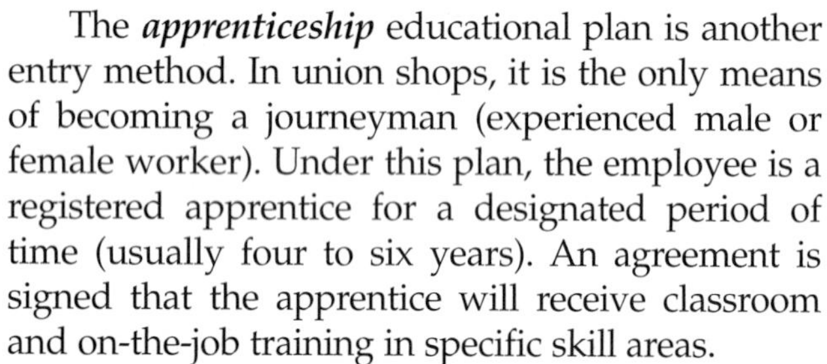

The ***apprenticeship*** educational plan is another entry method. In union shops, it is the only means of becoming a journeyman (experienced male or female worker). Under this plan, the employee is a registered apprentice for a designated period of time (usually four to six years). An agreement is signed that the apprentice will receive classroom and on-the-job training in specific skill areas.

Formal training is available in private or public post-secondary institutions. These schools provide technical education, where specific skills are being developed for jobs within an industry. Because many jobs now require higher level skills, community colleges are offering technical skills training programs. A four-year program in graphic communications is another career path, **Figure 28-2**.

Many companies have lost the opportunity for innovation and growth because of their tendency to stifle employees who suggest new approaches. Management-hiring practices that encouraged the status quo created decisionmakers who were not receptive to new ideas. The trends in progressive companies have changed, and management personnel often are hired from the ranks of university or college graduates.

Teaching or educational administration opportunities in the field of graphic communications require a college degree from an accredited institution. Positions as technologists, scientists, researchers, and engineers also require a degree.

The employment outlook in the graphic communications industry is very good for all career levels. Constantly changing technology will make necessary ongoing retraining and upgrading of skills and knowledge, a trend in education and business known as ***lifelong learning***.

Try to obtain a broad knowledge of products and processes. Courses in basic electronics and computer science should be taken during high school and college. Typesetting, quality assurance, cost analysis, inventory, color separating, production scheduling, and robot control are just a few of the careers that require the use of electronic equipment. Hiring criteria no longer indicate "computer experience is a plus;" rather, computer literacy is a *necessity*. **See Figure 28-3.**

Categories of careers

The graphic communications industry needs people with many different interests, talents, and abilities. The workforce can be organized into six general categories:

- *Skilled technical personnel* who can operate sophisticated machinery and carry out tasks that directly involve machines, materials, and products.
- *Creative personnel* who have skills in writing, art, and design.
- *Management personnel* who like to work with people and can supervise the work of others.

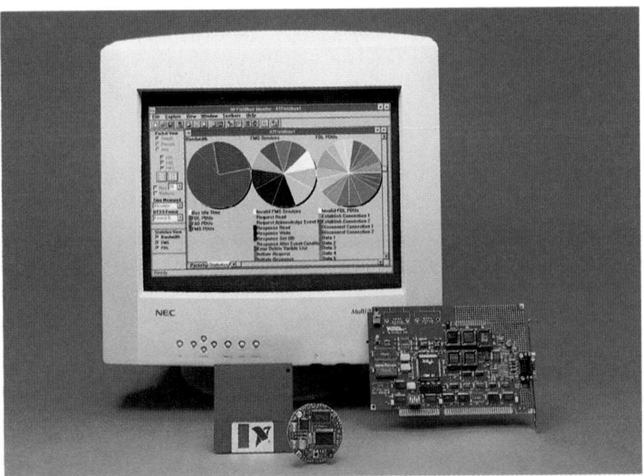

Figure 28-3. Computers and electronics are utilized in almost all areas of graphic communications.

Figure 28-4. Bindery and finishing personnel must operate and maintain various types of complex equipment.

- *Support personnel* who are the link between products and customers.
- *Engineers and scientists* with an interest in research.
- *Entrepreneurs* who are interested in starting their own businesses in one of the many areas available in the field.

Skilled Technical Positions

Skilled technical workers are involved in the prepress and press stages of production. Changes in technology have brought about changes in these career positions. Many formerly ***craft-centered*** jobs that were traditionally performed by artisans or others with manual skills, now require specialized technical skills.

Bindery and finishing personnel

Accuracy and mechanical aptitude are required of bindery and finishing personnel. Physical strength is sometimes necessary. Workers use sophisticated equipment to cut stock to size for the press or once it has been printed, **Figure 28-4**. Machine operators must have knowledge of slitting, perforating, and folding techniques. Gathering and collating operations require machine operators and setup personnel who can do accurate work. Skills in die cutting, embossing, foil stamping, and printing are also utilized.

Makeup person, stripper, opaquer

Arranging film images into position is the job of the makeup person in relief printing and the stripper in lithographic shops. This individual must have good visual perception. Drafting knowledge and proper use of drafting tools is essential.

The opaquer retouches imperfections in films but also opaques over unwanted images. Patience is essential. Electronic or computerized stripping is rapidly replacing manual stripping and opaquing procedures, making computer skills essential.

Pasteup artist

Large commercial printers, newspapers, and magazine and book publishers historically have had an art department where pasteup artists work. They are responsible for producing mechanical layouts, which are assemblies of type, art, and photographs. Although pasteup is still done, its applications are limited. Most of the layout work today is performed by graphic designers working on desktop publishing systems.

Platemaker

Several classifications of platemakers are found in the graphic communications industry. The planographic (litho) platemaker uses the flat (negatives located on a sheet by stripper) to place the image on a plate (image carrier). The plate is exposed when light passes through the clear areas of the negative or positive, and an image is developed on the image carrier or plate. The platemaker may develop the carrier by hand methods or with an automatic plate processor. A basic understanding of working with chemicals is helpful.

A photoengraver makes plates for printing by the relief (letterpress) process. The work involves the use of applied mathematics and chemistry.

A relief platemaker makes duplicate image carriers (plates) from metal, plastic, or rubber. Knowledge of how materials react to heat, pressure, and time is useful. Understanding other graphic processes is also desirable.

The use of computer-to-plate (CTP) technology is growing rapidly. Workers trained in the use of CTP systems will be needed, **Figure 28-5**.

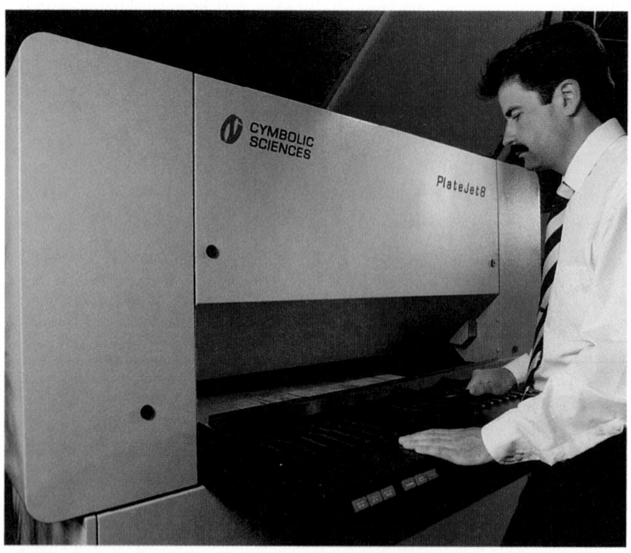

Figure 28-5. This computer-to-plate (CTP) system is capable of exposing as many as 12 full-size plates in an hour. One immediate effect of CTP technology by its users has been a reduction in the amount of overtime in prepress and pressrooms. (Cymbolic Sciences)

Pressroom personnel

No matter what printing process is involved, pressroom workers are responsible for the quality of the final printed product, **Figure 28-6**. The efforts of many individuals are needed to transfer the image from a plate to a substrate. The number of people involved depends on the type and size of the press. Some presses are small and simple to operate, but many are complex and require extensive technical knowledge.

Figure 28-6. Press operators are checking a run of a printed product. (USA Today)

Controlling ink, solutions, and paper are basic activities of pressroom workers. Quality control is imperative. Knowledge of paper, ink, and press operations is essential. Mechanical aptitude is a desirable quality.

Activities performed by lithographic press operators include positioning plates, filling the ink fountain, loading stock; controlling ink flow, fountain solution, and press speed; and inspecting finished sheets, **Figure 28-7**.

Figure 28-7. Press operators must set up, run, and maintain complex printing presses. Mechanical aptitude and knowledge of ink, paper, and solutions are important.

The web lithographic press operator must set up a press using huge rolls of paper, rather than sheets of stock, **Figure 28-8**. Press size and complexity varies. Newspaper and other large presses print on both sides of the stock, fold, and deliver a finished product with great speed. Press assistants working under experienced press operators are common on many of the large presses.

Figure 28-8. The operator of this web offset book printing press is responsible for maintaining quality on very long runs. (Strachan Henshaw Machinery, Inc.)

Figure 28-9. This technician is operating a gravure cylinder engraving machine. The finished cylinders will be transported to the pressroom. (Linotype-Hell)

The letterpress operator runs a smaller press. Common job-shop printing includes letterheads, forms, cards, and envelopes. Today, these presses are used primarily for finishing operations, such as die cutting and numbering.

The intaglio (gravure) press operator runs a press at very high speeds and usually has a crew assigned to specific responsibilities. See **Figure 28-9**.

Screen presses have a configuration uncommon to the other processes. The screen press operator must set up the press to print on a variety of materials. Knowledge of inks, screens, and image carriers is essential.

Process camera operator

The process camera operator must take visual images and transfer them onto light-sensitive materials. These intermediates are used to make the final film used in platemaking. Knowledge of lighting, optics, calculations, chemical reactions, as well as process camera operations, are basic requirements. See **Figure 28-10**.

Figure 28-10. Process camera operators must understand lighting, optics, exposure calculations, chemicals, and basic photographic techniques. (Bowling Green State University, Visual Communication Technology Program)

Duties of the process camera operator include working with line art, halftones, special effects, diffusion transfer, and color separations. Some plants require specialists in each area, but many plants require the operator be able to diversify.

A working knowledge of mathematics is preferred, as well as a basic understanding of physics, chemistry, and graphic communications processes.

Scanner operator

The scanner operator uses an electronic scanner to create digital files, film intermediates, and color separations, **Figure 28-11**. After examining the copy, the operator programs the necessary corrections into the machine. He or she evaluates the intensity of the color using a densitometer, sets the scanner dials for optimum results, and starts the machine, producing positive or negative films. Scanning is widely used today to create digital files from photographs and artwork. These files can then be manipulated electronically. Scanning operators are often classified as technicians, suggesting a knowledge of mathematics and science.

Typesetter

The typesetter inputs manuscript or copy into a computer or a phototypesetting machine. This person also may be required to use and maintain processing or developing equipment. High manual dexterity is essential for keystroking. The knowledge and aptitude to use a personal computer is a good basis for typesetting. A knowledge of photography, darkroom procedures, and typographic principles is also desirable.

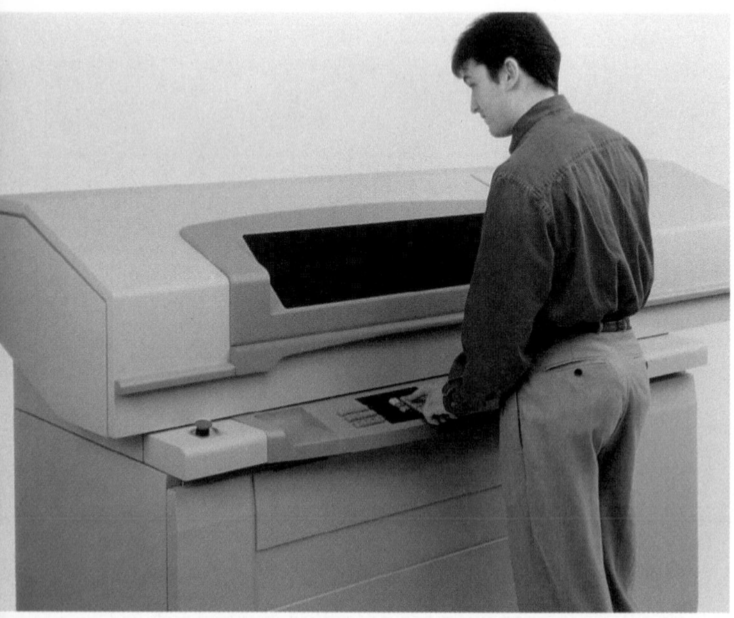

Figure 28-11. This drum scanner operator is specially trained in creating film images and color separations. (Fuji Photofilm U.S.A., Inc.)

Creative Positions

Creative people are needed in many roles within the graphic communications industry. Talented designers, editors, illustrators, writers, and photographers conceptualize and create products that go to print.

Copywriter

As the name implies, the copywriter generates the manuscript or copy, as well as other text to be printed. Creative writing talent and thorough knowledge of the language is imperative. A willingness to write on a wide variety of topics is usually needed. Many times the copywriter is not employed by the printer, but by an agency or other business firm.

Graphic designers

Graphic designers are practical artists who are responsible for planning printed pieces. Creative talent is imperative. Expressing an idea visually is the primary role of a graphic designer or artist. An appreciation for beauty and an eye for composition and color are essential traits. These traits may be natural in an individual or developed through training and experience, **Figure 28-12**.

The computer has nearly replaced the traditional cut-and-paste method of production. Desktop systems are utilized at nearly every workstation. Digital fluency is a standard job requirement, with small variations in software proficiency. Working knowledge of several of the common drawing, image editing, and page layout programs is expected. See **Figure 28-13**.

Despite the advances in computer technology, traditional artistic composition and design skills remain important. Some graphic designers design exclusively on the computer, while others may use both the computer and hand drawing or painting. As more of the workforce becomes computer literate, the future trend in hiring will focus on creative talent. Designers who are "computer-proficient," not "computer-dependent," will be sought.

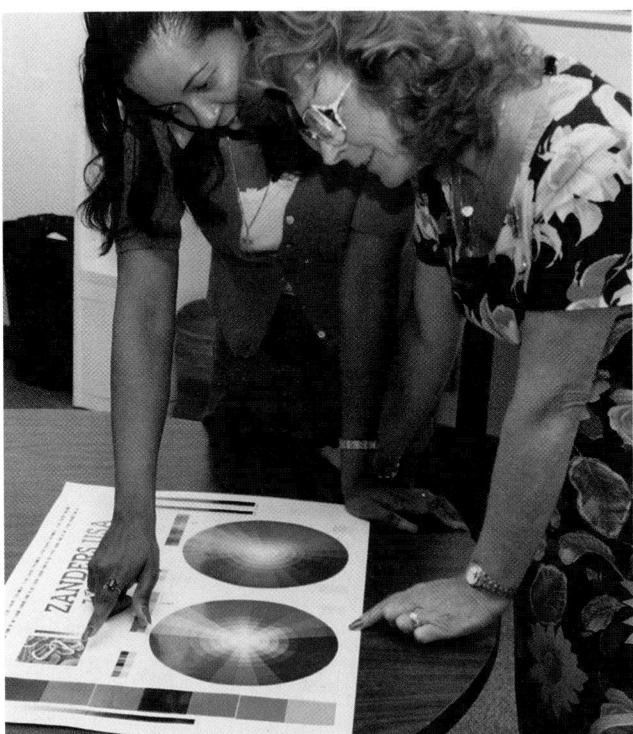

Figure 28-12. Artists must understand color theory and be able to visualize a concept.

Figure 28-13. Graphic artists use computers to design and layout text and images for print. (Hewlett-Packard Co.)

Editor

The editor prepares the written material and illustrations for publication by revising and rewriting copy and checking it for accuracy. Copy editing entails sequencing content, marking the copy for style, and ensuring consistency throughout the manuscript. A command of the language is essential. Sometimes technical expertise is also needed.

Publishers of books, magazines, and newspapers commonly employ editors. Freelance editorial work is also possible for those who prefer self-employment.

Photographer

A photographer may be called upon to take high-quality photographic illustrations for a publication. The photographer must create the image based on the customer's stated objective and parameters. A working knowledge of camera equipment and photographic techniques is expected.

Many photographers work independently, while others are employed by newspaper and magazine publishers. Advertising and public relations agencies also employ photographers.

Management Positions

Managers direct a team of workers who affect the entire organization. Part of being a good ***manager*** is being able to get work done through other people. It also requires excellent organizational abilities. See **Figure 28-14**.

Figure 28-14. Managers are part of a team. They must be able to plan, organize, and direct activities. (IBM Corp.)

Management must work in a team with other employees to accomplish the objectives of the company. Communication, cooperation, and understanding between departments are the ingredients for a productive, innovative workforce. Managers are "point people" who are responsible for ensuring that a job gets done right and on time.

Management-level employees in a graphic communications facility typically include executive officers, plant managers, plant superintendents, managing editors, production managers and schedulers, controllers, sales managers, supervisors, estimators, and planners.

Chief executive officer

The president or chief executive officer (CEO) of a company is the top administrator. He or she is the policymaker and overseer of the total operation. The president is interested in employing skilled and reliable personnel to contribute to the effective and efficient operation of the company. See **Figure 28-15**.

Figure 28-15. The chief executive officer is the highest ranking manager in a company.

Controller

The controller is responsible for the financial operation of a company. He or she ensures that the company operates by sound methods and practices. Contact with financial institutions, as well as preparing budgets, forecasts, analyses, reports, and statements are functions of this position. Working with mathematics and a thorough knowledge of accounting practices are essential.

EDP supervisor

The EDP supervisor is in charge of all the electronic data processing (EDP) functions in the plant. Knowledge of computer programming and applications is essential.

Estimator

The estimator calculates the costs used to bid or price a job. Understanding all plant operations is essential. Accurate calculations are required, since the figures will reflect the technical capabilities of the various operations as well as the cost of materials. Business and technical experience is needed.

Plant manager

The plant manager is responsible for the plant's manufacturing operations. Products must be produced on time, at the lowest possible cost, at a level of quality acceptable to the customer. Another critical concern to the plant manager is the safety and health of all employees. The ability to analyze results and understand people is important.

Plant superintendent

The plant superintendent directs all manufacturing operations of the company as well as first-line supervisors. The plant superintendent makes sure all equipment is working efficiently and kept in good condition. The position is high-pressure, requiring patience, but direct control.

Production manager

The production manager is a liaison between sales and production personnel. The production manager is in charge of cost estimates, job entry, job planning, and scheduling. Keeping accurate records and getting along with others is essential.

Production scheduler

The production scheduler sets up timetables for all jobs in an efficient and effective manner. After the job is in production, each phase must be recorded so the product can be traced at any phase of production. Being able to plan and understand the capabilities of equipment and personnel is important. The application of computer technology to production scheduling must be understood.

Quality control supervisor

The quality control supervisor sets standards for production and finished products, **Figure 28-16**. The job requires constant sampling to ensure consistent quality and to reduce waste or spoilage. Knowledge of control devices as a means to measure quality is basic to the position.

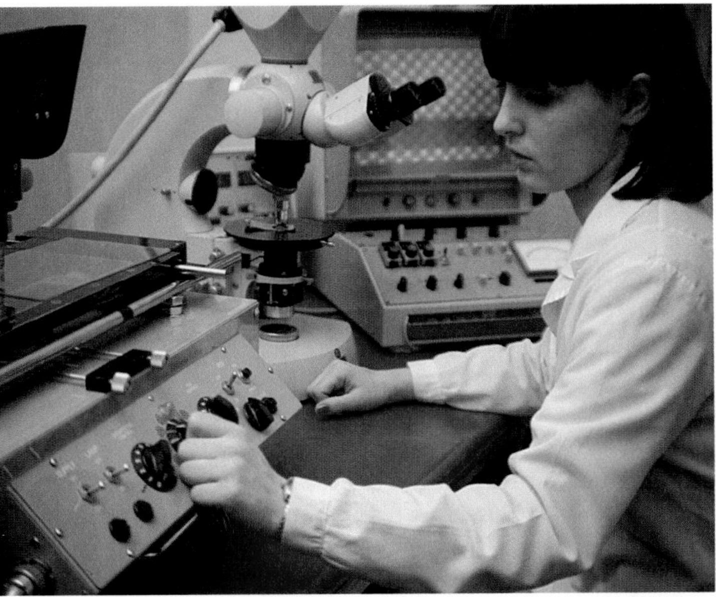

Figure 28-16. The quality control supervisor ensures that every aspect of production is within specifications.

Sales manager

The sales manager is responsible for establishing a profitable sales staff. Among the manager's responsibilities are supervising sales activities, customer relations, and budgeting; setting sales quotas and profit margins, and overseeing sales service. The sales manager must have good business acumen and leave a favorable impression upon people.

Characteristics important to being an effective member of the management team include being able to:

- Make logical decisions.
- Get work done through others.
- Communicate well with others.
- Motivate personnel.
- Apply factual information and not opinions.
- Act maturely and fairly.

The management team must be concerned with the following aspects of the business:

- Increased specialization of production equipment.
- High investment requirements for new equipment.
- Rising costs of materials and energy.
- Shortages or lead times for critical materials.
- Rapid introduction of new technology.
- High interest rates for capital equipment purchases and short-term borrowing.
- Excess production capacity.
- Slow real growth in market areas.
- Threat of increased international competition.
- Government regulations affecting manpower, fiscal and manufacturing operations, and environmental compliance.

Typically, management personnel "wear many hats." At times, the executive officer can be the chief financial officer and also have responsibilities for sales. Such a mix of duties is common to the graphic communications industry.

Support Personnel

Support personnel reinforce the work of the technical, creative, and managerial departments through two main channels: customer service and sales and marketing. These employees are the important link between products and customers.

Customer service representative

A customer service representative is the liaison between customers, management, and the sales force. Knowledge of job schedules and job progress is essential. Understanding the operation of the firm is also imperative. Good interpersonal skills, particularly on the telephone, are necessary to the position.

Sales representative

A sales representative position requires basic sales techniques, but it also requires a knowledge of printing processes. In a way, a sales representative is a trusted advisor to the customer. The representative must be able to provide the greatest product or service for the customer's investment. Meeting and being accepted by people is a prime requisite for the position. Being ambitious, highly organized, and able to project a professional image are contributors to success. See **Figure 28-17**.

Marketing coordinator

The fundamental objective of any company is to market its products or services profitably. Personnel with positions in marketing, advertising, and public relations are responsible for promotional activities, including identifying potential customers. In a mid-sized firm, a single marketing coordinator may handle all these activities. The marketing and sales departments often work together closely. Both managerial- and support-level positions are available in marketing.

Preflight technician

The preflight technician is a person who works with computers and software applications. This person is a troubleshooter. When a computer file arrives, the preflight technician goes over the file and identifies problems within the file that could prevent the job from printing successfully. The term commonly associated with this task is *preflighting*.

Color specialist

The color specialist works closely with the printer and the customer. If the customer indicates that "the green is not green enough," the color specialist checks the copy and informs the printer what changes need to be made to produce a job acceptable to the customer. A thorough knowledge of color theory, as it relates to printing processes, is essential.

Figure 28-17. Sales representatives must understand processes and be able to work with customers. (DuPont)

Engineers and Scientists

Engineers and scientists are able to find positions in research and development in the graphic communications industry. Engineers are needed to improve industrial processes, **Figure 28-18**. Positions are often product-oriented and exist to provide quality assurance.

Figure 28-18. Engineers in industrial settings work to improve processes and products. (Martin Marietta Corp.)

Scientists, particularly those with a strong background in chemistry, also are hired as researchers. They may experiment with and test equipment, inks, and printing paper. The paper and pulp industry, in particular, conducts much of its own research.

With the ever-increasing focus on environmental questions, environmental engineers and scientists are being hired by industry to ensure compliance standards are met, **Figure 28-19**.

Positions for engineering and science technicians are also available. Often, four or five technicians are hired to support the activities of a single scientist or engineer.

Educator

Educators have the great responsibility of preparing capable people for careers in the graphic communications industry. An effective educator must have an in-depth knowledge of the industry, have a strong desire to work with young people, and be a strong communicator.

Entrepreneurship

An ***entrepreneur*** is someone who starts his or her own business. In the graphic communications field, it might be a small print shop, typesetting service, silk screen facility, color separation house, or similar endeavor.

Thousands of new businesses are started every year. Small businesses provide over 50% of all jobs in the United States. Service areas, such as printing, are predicted to be in demand for many years to come.

A good entrepreneur must be a self-starter, in good health, and self-confident. He or she should be able to differentiate a calculated risk from a foolish chance. An entrepreneur must be responsible, dependable, hardworking, and able to motivate and utilize workers' talents. He or she will set specific goals and work until these goals are achieved. See **Figure 28-20**.

Advantages and disadvantages of entrepreneurship

Before deciding to start your own business, consider the advantages and disadvantages of entrepreneurship. Some possible advantages are:

- More control over income if the business is successful and grows.
- More control over job responsibilities.
- Meaningful professional relationships with talented people.
- Recognition as a leader.

Some possible disadvantages are:

- Working long hours to keep the business profitable.

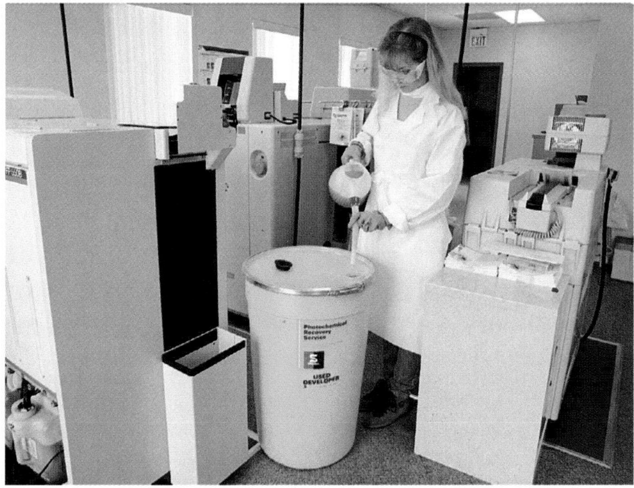

Figure 28-19. Stringent federal, state, and local waste-reclamation standards have created a need for waste management professionals with a background in science. (Safety-Kleen)

Figure 28-20. An owner of a facility has responsibilities similar to an executive officer or president of a company. Overseeing operations and accomplishing work through others is vital. (Bowling Green State University, Visual Communication Technology Program)

- Work worries go home with you.
- Success or failure are on your shoulders.
- Loss of money, even life savings, if the business fails.
- Repaying business loans for many years.
- Inconsistent or unpredictable income.
- Large amount of paperwork for recordkeeping.
- Need to discipline workers for unsatisfactory performance.

Starting the business

You can either buy an existing business or start a new one. When buying an existing business, you have the advantage of being able to check financial records to determine if it has been profitable in the past. Also, you will already have customers that know about and patronize the business. Equipment costs, facility planning, and other problems are already solved.

If you decide to start a new business, much more work is involved. You must find a suitable location, rent or build a facility, order equipment and supplies, and more. Until customers start patronizing the facility, it can be difficult to meet financial obligations. Financial backing can also be more difficult to obtain with a new business because of the high risk of failure.

To obtain information on buying or starting a business, you can contact:

- Accountants.
- Attorneys.
- Bankers.
- Business, accounting, or bookkeeping teachers.
- Chambers of Commerce.
- Computer consultants.
- Friends that own businesses.
- Insurance agents.
- Librarians.
- Realtors who might know of a business for sale or a building for lease.
- Small business assistance centers at community colleges.
- Trade associations in graphic communications.
- U.S. Small Business Administration.

Do not expect instant fame and fortune when starting a business. Instead, look realistically at the inherent advantages and disadvantages. It is easy to get excited about starting a business and overlook how much work and money is involved. You may not realize the consequences of failure. Keep in mind that there may be less stress and more money working for someone else.

Positions with Service Operations

Printing is a cooperative enterprise. One component depends on another. Since most firms do not have an integrated facility, ***outsourcing*** to service companies is essential for the completion of a product. Positions supporting the printing process are available in all service operations.

Agency or studio

An agency or studio is a type of service operation. It helps a larger company with advertising, packaging, and producing printed or media-oriented materials. Many graphic communications positions are available in agencies.

Bindery and finishing services

Specialized bindery and finishing operations are often beyond the capability of a printing facility. The operations are subcontracted to a company that has equipment capable of rapidly folding, trimming, and packaging printed products.

Composing service

Composing (typesetting) is integral to the operation of many firms, while others outsource to typographic service companies who supply their typesetting needs. Typographic processes have become very sophisticated as a result of the technological advances in the industry.

Manufacturers

The graphic communications industry depends on many types of machines and materials. Someone must manufacture and service the cameras, platemakers, processors, presses, scanners, cutters, and folders. Someone must supply inks, solutions, and paper.

Many jobs exist for people to sell and service products used by the graphic communications industry, **Figure 28-21**. Ink manufacturers, for example, supply a great service to the industry. Chemists have the important job of formulating ink so it is compatible with the press, substrate, and various other requirements of the process. Research and testing are essential for correct results.

Quick printing and copy services

The role of quick printing and copy services is to provide printing services quickly, with different levels of quality. The level of technical knowledge and skills needed depends on the job. Some operators are "button pushers," while others are highly skilled technicians operating sophisticated systems.

Positions in quick printing require employees to be versatile. They may be responsible for managing others, selling services, estimating job costs, or operating equipment. Job requirements vary with the owner or franchise, and should be made clear to prospective employees. See **Figure 28-22**

Screen process service

Screen printing drives the need for specialty-type printing facilities and workers with a wide variety of skills. Typical screen applications include sign printing, fabric imaging, printing on vinyl, and the manufacture of printed electronic circuit boards and components. See **Figure 28-23**.

Figure 28-21. Manufacturing provides the materials and machinery that equip graphic communications plants. (basysPrint Corporation)

Figure 28-22. Service companies include advertising agencies, quick printing shops, specialty printers, and composing services. These smaller companies do work for larger companies or individuals. (National Association of Quick Printers, Inc.)

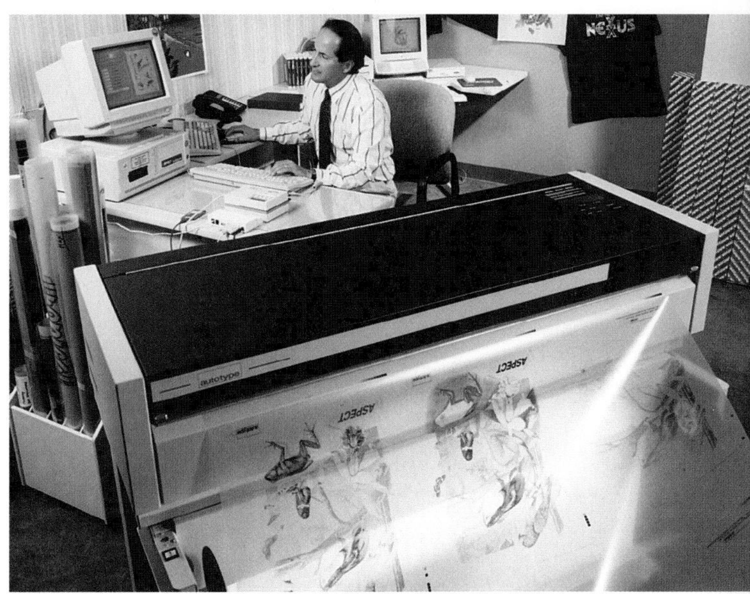

Figure 28-23. Screen process services fill a niche for such specialty products as tee-shirts with images.

Specialty printing service

Specialty printing shops do not have a wide market but provide a service for specialized products. These shops do engraving, labelmaking, and similar types of printing. Engraving, for example, is needed for producing high-quality business cards, stationery, and invitations.

Technological Growth

Changes in technology have brought about changes in traditional careers in printing. For example, the manual aspects of prepress are being replaced by a fast-paced, all-digital workflow. In fact, much of the typesetting and layout work formerly done by prepress workers is increasingly being done by customers on their personal computers.

The computerized workplace has made for faster work patterns, with clients expecting projects to be completed in short periods of time. In addition to fast ***turnaround***, the ability to function through electronically linked sites, modems, and faxes has changed how work gets done, **Figure 28-24**.

Figure 28-24. The computer terminals in this office are electronically linked to each other. Faxes, modems, and internet services link terminals around the world. (IBM Corp.)

Telecommunications and ***electronic information transfer*** over telephone lines or by satellite permits almost instant transmission of digitized (computer-coded) images and proofs around the globe. Subsequently, information management positions are being created to handle job ticketing, tracking, processing, and billing.

Beyond prepress considerations are the capabilities for multimedia. Printing customers want to tap into the mass-marketing capability of the World Wide Web, creating positions for web designers, computer graphics designers, and people in sales and marketing.

Robotics, the use of machines to do repetitive tasks, is utilized in various manufacturing venues. Robots are ideal in the bindery area of a printing plant where highly repetitive tasks are done. While many traditionally labor-intensive activities are being eliminated by robots, positions requiring higher technical skills are opening in other areas.

Our technological age has revolutionized the way we communicate and work. The field of graphic communications is in the forefront of this revolution. Diverse employment opportunities will continue to emerge in such a dynamic, global industry.

Review Questions

Please do not write in this book. Write your answers on a separate sheet of paper.

1. Name three methods for entering a career in graphic communications.
2. What is lifelong learning?
3. Why should someone preparing for a career in graphic communications take courses in basic electronics and computer science?
4. What are the six general employment categories in graphic communications?
5. How have changes in technology brought about changes in careers in prepress and press work?

6. Who is responsible for the quality of the final printed product?
7. The computer has nearly replaced the traditional cut-and-paste methods used in what position?
8. List six characteristics important to the management team.
9. Name three advantages and three disadvantages of entrepreneurship.
10. What should an entrepreneur avoid when starting a business?
11. Name seven types of service operations to which a printing firm might outsource its work.
12. How has electronic information transfer impacted communication between customers and employees in production facilities?
13. What are a few positions created by electronic information transfer and multimedia?
14. In what area of a printing plant is the use of robots ideal?
15. What two industry factors will bring about more employment opportunities in graphic communications?

Teamwork and Leadership

Solving problems often requires you to work with other people as a member of a team. A team usually consists of team members and one or more team leaders. Teamwork can help get a job done quicker than doing it alone, and it allows for more possible solutions to be considered. Problems are successfully solved using teamwork when all the members provide their ideas and abilities. Working in teams takes organization and cooperation among the team members, and the exercise of leadership skills by the team's leaders.

The team's leaders are in command of the rest of the team. The quality of their leadership determines whether the team will be a success or a failure. Important characteristics of leadership include:

- Good leaders have a vision of what must be done and look for ways to reach the team's goals.
- Good leaders are skilled communicators who are able to encourage the team members to assist each other and cooperate. They work to ensure that all the team members contribute to the team's success.
- Good leaders are willing to work as long as it takes to achieve success. They can organize and direct the team's activities.
- Good leaders are fair and honest. They take responsibility for their own actions and give credit to others when it is due.
- Good leaders know how to delegate authority. They may even assign leadership roles to other team members to get the job done as efficiently as possible.

High-speed web offset presses, such as this one at a metropolitan newspaper, are often custom-designed to meet a specific publication's needs. Web offset is extensively used for magazine and book printing, as well. (Heidelberg Harris)

Appendix 1 Specifications for Web Offset Publications

Viewing of Artwork and Proofs

Artwork, proofs, and the final printed product should be viewed and/or compared under illumination specified in the ANSI PH2.30-1989 standards. This calls for use of illumination having correlated color temperature of 5000 Kelvins (D50) and a Color Rendering Index of 90–100.

File Preparation

Type reproduction

- Thin lines, fine serifs, and medium or small type should be restricted to one color. Reproduce all colored type with a minimum of colors.
- Reverse type and line art should not be less than .007″ (equivalent to a 1/2 point rule) at the thinnest part of a character or rule. Reverse type should use dominant color (usually 70% or more) for shape of letters. Where practical, and not detrimental to the appearance of the image, make the type in subordinate colors slightly larger to minimize register problems on the production press. Small type and fine serifs should not be used for reverse type. The surrounding tone must be dark enough to ensure legibility.
- Surprinting type should not be less than .004″ (equivalent to a 1/3 point rule) at the thinnest part of a character or rule. When type is to be surprinted, the background should be no heavier than 30% in any one color, and no more than 90% total in all four colors for legibility.

Image trapping

- All supplied materials sent to the publisher must be properly trapped and, insofar as possible, the trap should be represented by the accompanying SWOP proofs. Overlap of colors should be introduced when line work abuts line work or abuts Continuous-Tone (CT) images with the dominant colors providing the image shape. Lighter colors should be spread into darker colors. This overlap should be sufficient to minimize register problems on production presses.

Vignette or fadeaway edges

- Special care should be taken with fadeaway edges where the fadeaway is made up of more than one color because color balance is difficult to maintain. In many cases, fadeaway shadows are best reproduced in black only.

Minimum printable dot (Minimum tone value)

- In offset printing, when using negative plates, normally a 2% dot will be held; when using positive plates, normally a 4% dot will be held. Input materials should be prepared with these limits in mind.

Screen rulings

- 133 lines per inch (52 lines per centimeter) is the recommended nominal screen ruling.
- Screen rulings coarser then 133 lines per inch may not be acceptable for gravure publications.
- For black-and-white reproduction, check individual publisher for screen ruling requirements.
- The use of finer screen rulings and stochastic or other alternative screening must be preapproved by the publisher and printer.

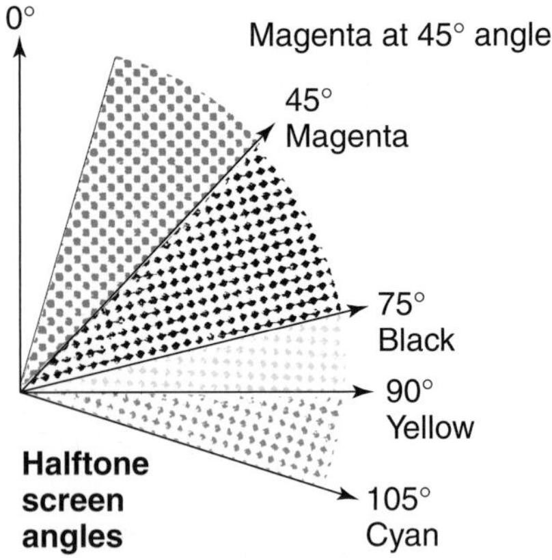

Figure A1-2. This shows magenta as the dominant color at the 45° angle.

Screen angles

- The screen angles of the colors should be 30° apart, with the yellow placed 15° from the other colors and between the cyan and magenta or the cyan and black, **Figure A1-1.** It is often acceptable to place the yellow on the same angle as the cyan or, depending on the dominant colors in the picture, on the same angle as the magenta. This alignment has the advantage of spacing all the angles by 30° and eliminating the moiré that often occurs between yellow and the other colors.
- It is desirable to have the dominant color (magenta in most cases) on the 45° angle, **Figure A1-2**. When significant Gray Component Replacement (GCR) is used, and if black becomes the dominant color, black should be printed at the 45° angle.
- Screen angles for one- and two-color printing should follow the same guidelines, with the black at 45°.
- Screen angle and ruling should be such that no moiré pattern will appear in the film, proof, or print.
- Electronic files should not include screening parameters and dot shape. When plates or film are made by the printer directly from digital files, it is the printer's responsibility to report moiré pattern problems to the agency and publisher and to help them resolve the problem whenever possible.
- For gravure publications, colors other than yellow should avoid angles between 75° and 105°.

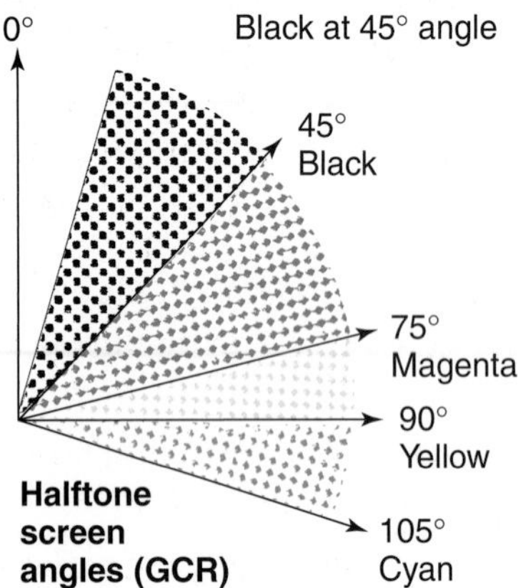

Figure A1-1. Diagram showing black at the 45° angle.

Gray balance

- Good visual gray balance, under standard viewing conditions, is essential to proper four-color printing.
- In order to reproduce black, the undercolors should be in a neutral or gray balance.
- It is important to coordinate and control the gray balance of the separations with the gray balance in proofing and printing. The tint values that produce gray balance in SWOP proofing are listed in the *Proofing* section.

Total Area Coverage (TAC): Undercolor Removal (UCR) and Gray Component Replacement (GCR)

- Total halftone dot area coverage should be checked in the film or electronic file and read in the same physical location in each color.
- The total of dot percentages in any spot in the four-color films should be no more than 300%.
- For some small image areas of a picture that carry no significant detail, Total Area Coverage (TAC) may exceed 300%. TAC in these small image areas must be less than 325%.
- When GCR is used, it is important to add color back under blacks to maintain gloss and density. This is accomplished by the use of Undercolor Addition (UCA). Percentages of tones in film should be read with a properly calibrated transmission densitometer.
- In two-color printing, Undercolor Removal (UCR) is not usually necessary, as long as the two inks are trapping properly. It is probably advantageous that only one color be solid.
- Minimum TAC for GCR:

Black Printer Percentage	Minimum 3-Color Coated Paper	Area Coverage Uncoated Paper
98	00	125
95	120	145
90	165	180
85	190	195
80	210	210
75	220	220
70	230	230

NOTES:

The values in this table are based on the densities of the single-color black being within 10 percent of a three-color overprint black. The three-color balance (cyan, magenta, yellow) remaining in dark gray colors after GCR is applied must remain neutral gray.

Final Film

Film required

- All film should be dimensionally stable and of identical thickness (0.004″ is recommended).
- The film should be supplied in one piece per color and identified by color and kind (e.g., "black positive").
- Film should be hard dot.
- No camera or etched film is acceptable.
- All opaquing should be done on the non-emulsion side of the film and should be minimal.
- The clear area (Dmin) of the film should have an ortho density of no more than 0.07.
- The black area (Dmax) of the film should have an ortho density of no less than 3.50.
- Gravure publications require type to be provided on separate films.

Image orientation

- All film should base looked at as "right-reading." Information on whether emulsion side should be "up" or "down," and whether film should be "negative" or "positive," should be obtained from the publisher.

Register marks

- Film for color ads should have four centered register marks identical in each color located approximately 1/2″ outside the "live" area of the ad. Where ads are less than full page (nonbleed), it may be necessary for the printer to remove the register marks before plating. Any removal of register marks required for page form assembly is the responsibility of the printer.
- Register marks should include solid lines at least 1/4″ long on both axes.
- The lines should be precisely the same width (thickness) in each color.

Multiple insertions

- The publisher's specified number and kind of film sets, along with the required proofs and (if required) progressives, should be supplied.
- Appropriate process control elements should be used in contacting this final film to ensure that all are identical and accurate reproductions of the master files or films. Examples are the UGRA Plate Control Wedge and the RIT Microline Resolution Target.
- Appropriate process control elements should also be used in the digital output of final films to ensure that all are identical and accurate reproductions of the master files.

Generation and Exchange of Electronic Files

Introduction

As the industry begins to exchange digital files as well as film, these files must be in a format that can be easily written and read by all systems. Further, these files must contain data that will ultimately produce film or plates that meet SWOP specifications. The goal is to be able to mix images generated from supplied electronic files and from supplied film in the same printing form. There are, however, several principles that must be followed when dealing with digital data files to ensure that they meet these goals.

General requirements

- Until remote proofing is widely implemented and robustly controlled, an approved SWOP proof (digital or analog) must be supplied for all electronic files regardless of the delivery process.
- Digital color bars should not be included directly in a live image. With all job transfers, a digital control object should be included within the file but outside the live image area. The object should include patches with tone values of 5%, 25%, 50%, 75%, and 95% for all process colors. These are used to verify the accuracy of data transfer and/or interpretation.
- The method of delivery (e.g., magnetic tape, removable disk, electronic transmission) and file formats to be used for exchange of electronic files should be agreed to by all participants.
- Electronic files should be accompanied by either an electronic or hard copy job jacket. Business information such as insertion orders, space reservation, and ad copy instructions should be transmitted using the GCA Specifications for Publisher/ Agency Communications Exchange (SPACE) and DDAP Electronic Business Information Exchange Specifications (DDAP DEBIES).
- The files should also incorporate all of the logical parameter specified by SWOP for file preparation and final film (e.g., UCR/GCR, gray balance, register marks, image trapping, etc.). Multiple sets of files may be necessary with multiple insertion orders. Check with the publisher.
- SWOP recognizes the DDAP User Requirement Specification (Version 3.2-1995) regarding editability. In the event that changes need to be made, they should only be made at the direction of the advertising agency/advertiser, with agreement of the publisher and printer.

Standard Formats

- For predictable proofing, imposition and output results, final prepress files should be exchanged as CMYK raster files using the PI compliance level of the Tag Image File Format for Image Technology (TIFF/IT) file format as defined in International Organization for Standardization (ISO) 12639. Typically, Final Page (FP), Continuous-Tone (CT), and Line Work (LW) files will be required. In some situations, High-Resolution Contone (HC) files may also be required.
- SWOP supports the work presently under way within CGATS and ISO TC 130 Committee to develop standard formats for file exchange. As additional formats are identified by the standards committees, these will be evaluated and considered for inclusion by SWOP.

Currently, the ANSI TIFF/IT P1 format is the only format recommended by the DDAP Association, with which SWOP has a working relationship.

Other Formats

- Where other file formats must be exchanged, the GCA Electronic Mechanical Specification (EMS) (2nd Edition) 118-1993 or equivalent may be used with agreement among all parties. This document provides guidelines that are particularly useful where proprietary desktop applications or native Color Electronic Prepress System (CEPS) files are used and where a mixed variety of other file types [e.g., Encapsulated PostScript (EPS), PICT or Portable Document Format (PDF) file formats] are involved. One exception to EMS is that SWOP compliant digital files must not be screened.
- Data compression shall only be used if the sender and receiver agree to the method and use of compressed files. It is the sender's responsibility to ensure that the publisher and/or the printer is aware of the compression used and has the means to decompress the file. Only lossless compression can be used: defined as a compression method that results in no (0%) data alterations.

Proofing

- All color proofs should be in exact register.
- The color guide should be an offset press proof made to SWOP specifications or an off-press proof made according to the manufacturer's SWOP Application Data Sheets.
- Proofs will change over a period of time. They should be dated and not used if it is known that a change in appearance has occurred (e.g., exposure to light over time will affect the color accuracy of a proof).

Yellow	(SWOP process yellow)
Blue	(SWOP process cyan)
Red	(SWOP Secondary Red*)
Green	(SWOP secondary green*)

Figure A1-3. These are the standard second-color inks for two-color reproduction.

Press Proofing

Inks

Standard Ink Colors

Use proofing inks that conform to the color specifications of the SWOP/NAPIM Standard Reference Proofing Process Inks. These same inks have undergone extensive testing as part of the international standards development of ISO 2846-1 and have been shown to be very similar to inks made in Europe and Japan.

Standard Second-Color Inks

Standard second-color inks for two-color reproduction are shown in **Figure A1-3**.

*The red and green are equivalent to the solid overprints of magenta/yellow and cyan/yellow respectively.

Samples of these colors are included in the SWOP Single Level Color References.

Matched Colored Inks

Matched colored inks other than standard second-color inks are often used, depending on the availability of open press cylinders. Arrangements must be made with the publisher in advance in order to run matched colors.

Paper-proofing stock

- Standard proofing paper is 60# basis weight paper of 72 (nominal) brightness. (Brightness will diminish with age.)
- The paper may be a coated groundwood stock or a sheet coated to simulate the appearance of such a groundwood stock. The designated proofing stock, *Deferiet Textweb,* is no longer in production. Stocks with similar characteristics of grade, basis weight, gloss, brightness,

and color may be acceptable, but other characteristics may require consideration. Digital proofing may require a whole new set of characteristics. Another factor for consideration is the fact that UV brighteners may cause viewing variations.

Wet proofing

- When possible, it is recommended that four-color proofing be done on a (minimum) four-color press with the ad or editorial page printing in the same direction as in the eventual press run.
- Particular attention should be paid to solid ink density, trapping, dot gain, gray balance, doubling, and other four-color print characteristics in order to ensure maximum reproducibility on the web press.

Proofer's color bars

- Proofs should carry a control bar stripped in register, positioned perpendicular to the direction of printing, covering the full width of the image area. Proofs made from separation film materials should use an original, hard-dot film control bar. Proofs made using digital proofing systems should use a digital control bar having similar content to the hard-dot film control bar.

This bar should have the following characteristics:

- A repeating pattern of solids of individual inks and two-and three-color overprints.
- Screened areas with rulings of 133 lines per inch with tint values of 25%, 50%, and 75% of each of the primary colors in physical proximity to a solid patch. Two-color overprints of the same 25%, 50%, and 75% are also recommended.
- Target areas visually sensitive to slur and dot gain to assist the proofer.
- A gray bar which has three color tints running parallel to, and designed to match in neutrality and weight, black tints of three different values, when viewed under 5,000 K lighting conditions, must be included in proofing.

Gray Balance			
Black	Cyan	Magenta	Yellow
75%	75%	63%	63%
50%	50%	39%	39%
25%	25%	16%	16%

Figure A1-4. These are the values of the gray balance portion of the proofing bar.

The gray balance portion of the GATF/SWOP Proofing Bar has the values shown in **Figure A1-4**.

- A control element for evaluating correct plate exposure from films.

Note: Use only the original films as supplied by the manufacturer for exposing the control bars on plates. Contacting or duplicating this film will lead to aberrations in sensitive areas and is unacceptable. Computer-to-plate (CTP) digital control bars should include the above general characteristics, but may require additional features for controlling digital plate systems.

Film material and digital control bars as described above may be obtained from the Graphic Arts Technical Foundation (GATF). Specify: "GATF/SWOP Proofing Bar" for film and "GATF/SWOP Digital Proofing Control Bar" for digital output.

Solid ink density and color

- SWOP specifications recommend the use of Status T densitometers for measuring process control parameters such as density, Total Dot Gain/Tone Value Increase and Print Contrast. Solid-color verification and control can be achieved using either Status T densitometry or colorimetric measurement in accordance with CGATS.4 and CGATS.5 along with the proper use of the SWOP Color References.
- Ink density and color in proofing should be controlled by the use of the SWOP Color References, available from the IPA.
- Proofers should control ink density so that the density values on dry proofs fall between the Hi and Lo references. When the SWOP Single Level Color Reference is used, the Status T densities should fall within plus or minus 0.07 of the density value of that reference.

The SWOP Color References are printed on SWOP specified paper using SWOP proofing inks. The inks have been verified as being accurate in color to SWOP specifications by the SWOP/NAPIM Proofing Ink Verification Program. Two types of color references are available on a subscription basis from the IPA. These provide physical references for both density and color measurement.

Total dot gain/tone value increase

- In order to ensure properly balanced tone reproduction, it is recommended that Total Dot Gain at 50% from file or film to print should be as shown in **Figure A1-5.**
- It is preferable to run on the high side of the target value (within tolerance) rather than the low side to allow for an easier match by production presses.
- In order to help obtain proper gray balance, included in this specification is the restriction that gain values of the three colors (Y, M, C) should not differ from each other by more than 4% from their target value. That is: if either cyan or magenta is +2% (22%) in dot gain, yellow deviation should not be greater than –2% (16%), **Figure A1-6.**

Another way to explain this specification is: after adding two percentage points to the measured yellow dot gain value, process colors (Y, M, C) should not differ by more than 4 percentage points.

	Target Value	Tolerance
Yellow	18%	15–21%
Magenta	20	17–23
Cyan	20	17–23
Black	22	19–25

Figure A1-5. The numbers represent the recommended amount of dot gain at 50% from file or film to print.

	Target Value	Example	From Target
Cyan	20%	22%	+2%
Magenta	20	20	0
Yellow	18	16	–2

Figure A1-6. The three colors shown should not differ from each other more than 4% from their target area.

Print contrast (not a specification)

- Print Contrast, which is an important characteristic in printing, should be controlled in press proofing. Based on data collected during the 1993 and 1995 SWOP Calibration Kit press runs, the recommended values (absolute, includes paper) are:

Yellow	25–35%
Magenta & Cyan	30–40%
Black	27–45%

Progressive proofs and cover sheets

- Progressive proofs are no longer required by most publications. A SWOP press proof or off-press proof is all that is required in most cases.
- When progressives are supplied to a publication they should include the four single-color sheets, a three-color and a four-color sheet.
- All proofs and progressives (when used) should match one another and be consistent in ink amount.
- The press or off-press proof or progressive should include the name, address, and phone number of the prepress service supplier and, if possible, the name of the person or persons who should be contacted in case of a problem. A cover sheet can be used to provide this information.
- The number of proofs or progressives required is usually specified by the individual publisher.
- Proofs and progressives should not be stapled or otherwise damaged in any area that might interfere with the densitometer reading of the color bars.

Two-color and black-and-white proofing

- A press proof or off-press proof should be furnished with each black-and-white or two-color film set delivered. A photographic print of the black film with a color overlay may be acceptable to certain publications. Check individual publishers for specifications regarding acceptability of proofs, screen ruling, and number of proofs required.

Off-Press Proofing

SWOP recognizes the use of analog and digital (halftone and non-halftone) off-press proofs when in conformance with the manufacturer's SWOP Application Data Sheet. SWOP does not *certify* the accuracy of any off-press proofing system. The end user takes the responsibility to determine if any given system is acceptable within their work flow.

Manufacturers of off-press proofing systems must file a SWOP Application Data Sheet that will provide users with directions for producing their proof as closely as possible to the appearance of a SWOP press proof. Application Data Sheets for each conventional and digital off-press proofing system are available through SWOP, Inc.

The Application Data Sheet presents manufacturer's recommendations for density, dot gain, sequence, colorants and substrate, to provide the best match to SWOP press proofs.

SWOP has established a method to verify a proofs conformance to the manufacturer's Application Data Sheets. Users may contact GATF for necessary procedures for this verification process.

- The appearance of an off-press proof used in this application must closely simulate SWOP press proofing. The proofer is responsible for following the appropriate SWOP Application Data Sheet.
- Note that when off-press proofs are made in conformance with the manufacturer's SWOP Application Data Sheet, it does not necessarily mean that a *perfect* match to a SWOP press proof has been achieved. In addition, it should be recognized that different off-press proofing systems may not perfectly match one another.
- SWOP Calibration Kits, including Certified Press Proofs, are available from GATF. In addition, electronic files of the pictorials and test targets used in the SWOP Calibration Kit are available from NPES on CD-ROM as ISO 12640. These tools may be used to help determine the relationship (subjective or objective) between the Certified Press Proof and the proofing system in use.

Off-press proof cover sheet

- The off-press proof should be accompanied by a cover sheet or equivalent (e.g., label) stating the proofing product or system used and the name, address, and contact person of the prepress service supplier.
- The sheet should also contain information relating to conformance with the manufacturer's Application Data Sheet.

Control bar

- All off-press proofs should include a color bar. This color bar should be a 133-line screen on all halftone proofs—analog or digital. All color bars should include a solid and 25%, 50%, and 75% tones of each process color, solid overprints and at least one gray balance patch (cyan = 50%, magenta & yellow = 39%). Two-color overprints at 25%, 50%, and 75% are also recommended. This color bar could take the form of a manufacturer's color control guide, a GCA/GATF Proof Comparator or a GATF/SWOP Proofing Bar or their digital equivalents. An exposure control element may also be included where appropriate.

Solid density and color

- Aim for off-press proofing densities and colorants are based on the SWOP Hi-Lo Color References. Because of process differences (lamination, gloss, sequence, colorants, etc.), an off-press system's values may differ slightly from the Hi-Lo Color References and should be identified in the Application Data Sheets.

Dot gain and gray balance

- Aims for tone reproduction are based on SWOP press-proofing. Imaging characteristics of the various technologies can result in slightly different color and tonal renditions but must result in an acceptable and consistent match to the visual appearance of a SWOP press proof. Applicable values for Total Dot Gain/Tone Value Increase are listed in each manufacturer's Application Data Sheets.
- It is important that off-press proofs achieve a gray balance that matches SWOP press proofing as closely as possible.

Sequence

- Users of off-press proofing materials will note that manufacturers of these products often specify a particular sequence of colorant application. This is not necessarily the same as the press proofing or production printing sequence.

Substrate

- The proofing substrate is defined as the receiver material and should be measured in non-image areas including any subsequent layers applied by the proofing system.
- The appearance of the off-press proofing substrate should closely match SWOP proofing paper.
- Each manufacturer specifies the substrate to be used in their Application Data Sheet.

Verification/Conformance/Tolerances

- Fully processed samples of actual off-press proofs containing color pictures and a SWOP approved control bar may be sent to GATF/SWOP Off-Press Proofing Verification Program, c/o GATF.
- Submitted proofs will be compared visually and instrumentally for conformance to data contained in the manufacturer's Application Data Sheet, and a report will be generated. A fee will be charged by GATF for measurement, analysis and reports issued.
- The verification procedure does not constitute the endorsement of any proofing system or product by SWOP.

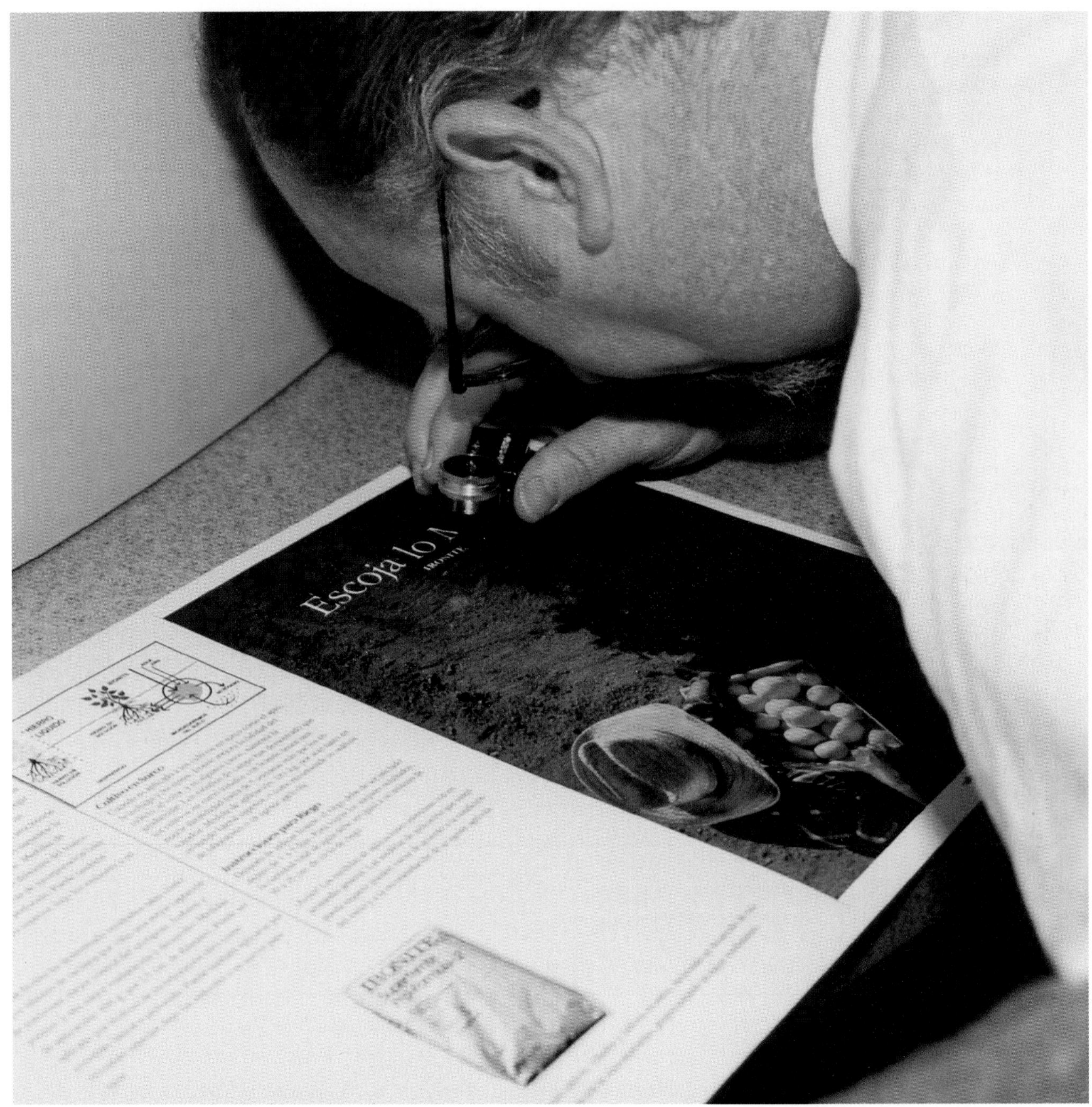

In today's highly competitive graphic communications environment, excellent quality control is a vital requirement for success. Close adherence to standards and specifications is a necessity.

Appendix 2 Hand-binding a Book

High production bookbinding facilities use automatic machines to make a finished product. Although this summary describes a slow hand operation, some facilities still do hand-binding for short runs and special editions. Hand-binding is also used for the repair of old, valuable library books. The material presented in this Appendix will also help you better understand book construction.

Making the book body

1. Select ten sheets of 11″ × 17″ stock (newsprint or bond). Make two right-angle folds in each sheet to create 8-page (5 1/2″ × 8 1/2″) signatures. The fold should be sharp.
2. Clamp the ten signatures between two pieces of plywood. Starting at the *left* end, mark the stack of signatures at the following intervals: 1″, 2 1/2″, 3 1/2″, 5″, 6″, and 7 1/2″, as shown in **Figure A2-1**.
3. Make a saw cut across all signatures at the marked positions. The saw cut should be deep enough to just cut through the signature folds, **Figure A2-2**.

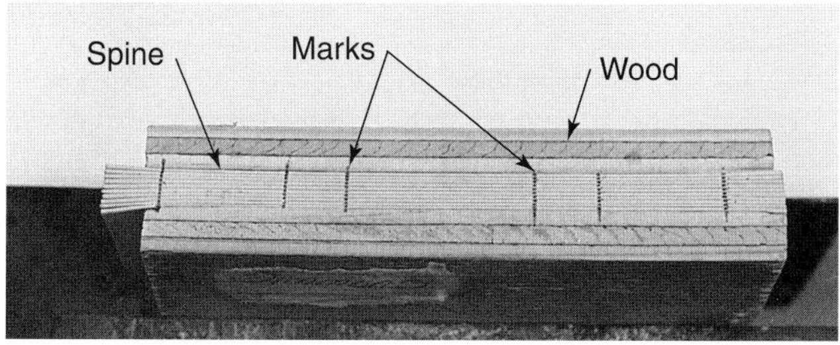

Figure A2-1. To hand bind a book, first mark the edges of the signatures.

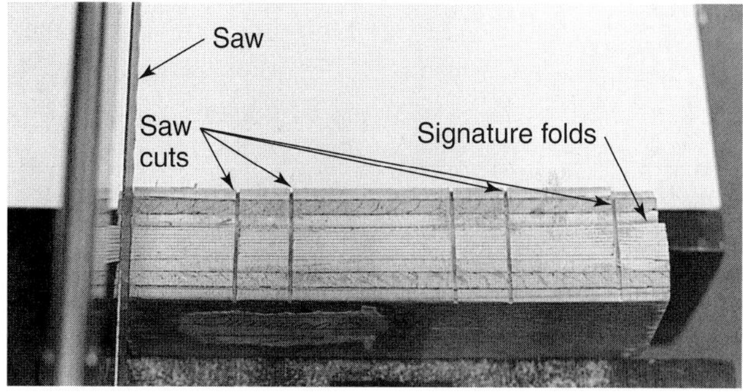

Figure A2-2. Use a saw to make a small cut into the spine at each of your marks.

4. Position the first signature on the platform of the sewing frame with the head or top-of-page fold to the left, **Figure A2-3**. Tack the sewing tapes onto the frame. The spine marks closest to the center identify the tape locations. Sew with a linen or other type of thread

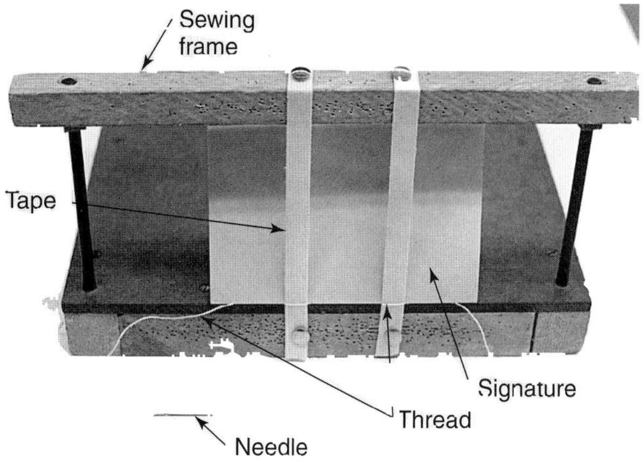

Figure A2-3. Position the first signature in the frame. Sew the tapes to the signature

and a large sewing needle. Insert the needle from the outside through the first saw cut. Leave at least a 3″ tail of thread. Determine the amount of thread needed by measuring one length and multiply it by the number of signatures. Continue sewing in and out until finished with the first signature,

5. Place the second signature on top the first, oriented in the same direction. Insert the needle through the saw cut opposite the final cut of the first signature. Continue sewing each cut. When finished, tie the first and second signatures with the loose end of the thread from the first signature, **Figure A2-4**. The third signature and those thereafter require another step. Rather than tying one signature to another, a kettle stitch is used to fasten at the end of the signature. The *kettle stitch* is a looping of the needle end of the thread under the stitch made through the prior signature. The last signature must be tied. **Figure A2-5** shows how signatures of the book are sewn together.
6. The *spine* of the book is glued with bookbinder's glue. When the spine glue is dry, apply a ribbon of glue to one side of the folded edge of the *end sheets*, **Figure A2-6**. The end sheets are usually made of slightly heavier stock and placed on both sides of the combined signatures (forming the first and last pages of the book body).

Figure A2-5. The completed set of sewn signatures, showing how the thread holds them together.

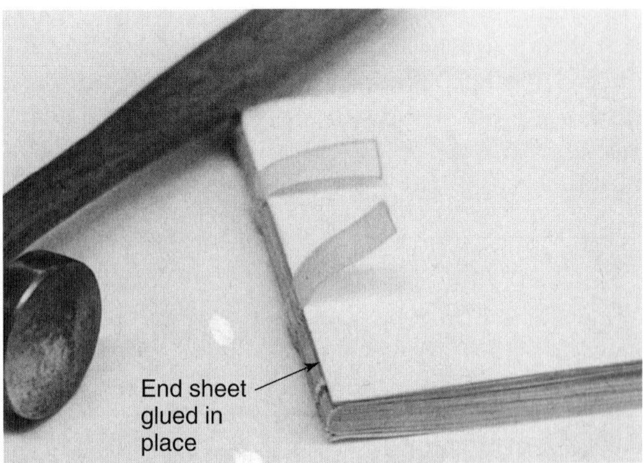

Figure A2-6. End sheets are glued to the first and last pages of the book body.

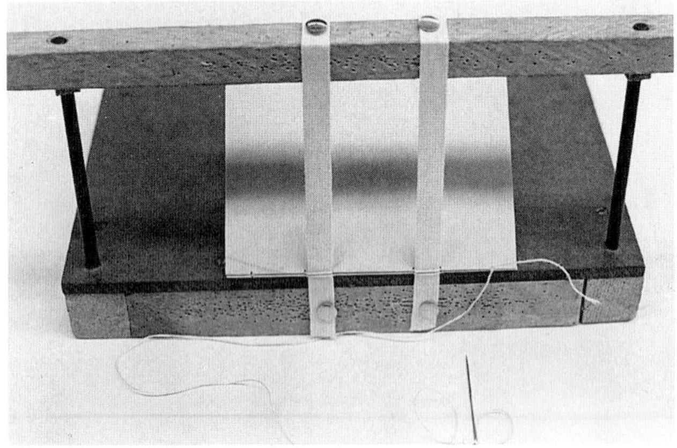

Figure A2-4. Sew and attach the first signature to the second. Continue until all signatures are sewn.

7. Trim the top, bottom, and outside edge of the book to final size with a hand or power guillotine cutter. Next, round and shape the spine or back edge of the book. See **Figure A2-7**.
8. Glue the headbands to the top and bottom of the book, **Figure A2-8**. The *headbands* are the finishing touch to hide the glue and folded portion of each signature when the book is completed. They should be cut to fit the width of the rounded and shaped back.

Figure A2-7. The spine of the book is forced into a rounded shape.

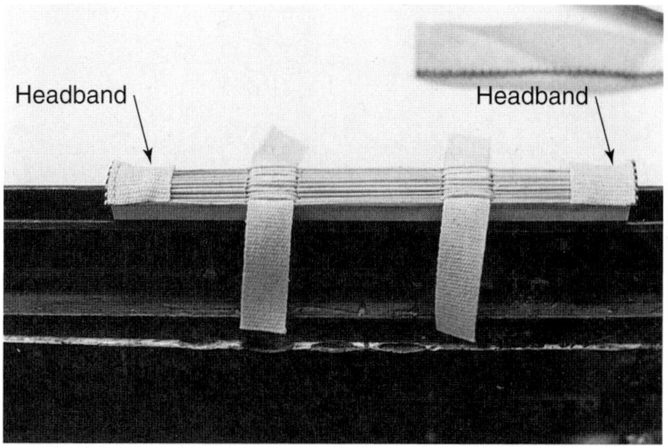

Figure A2-8. The fabric headbands are glued to the top and bottom of the spine for a better finished appearance.

9. Cut supercloth approximately 1/2″ shorter than the length of the spine. It should extend 1″–2″ on each side of the spine, **Figure A2-9.** Center the supercloth horizontally and vertically and adhere it to the back of the book, using bookbinder's glue.
10. Cut a piece of thin paper the size of the spine and position it over the glued supercloth. Allow the glue to dry before casing the book.

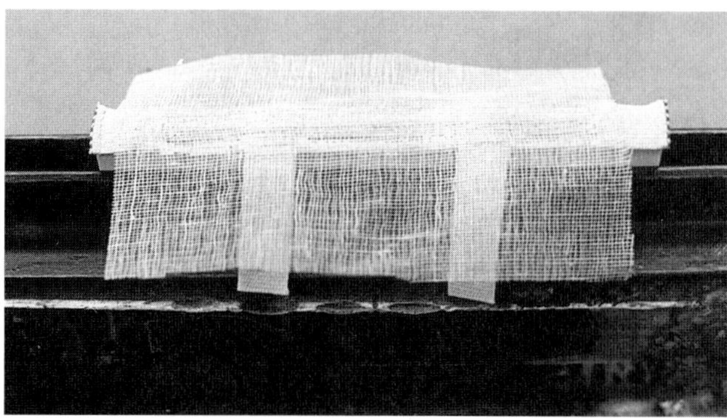

Figure A2-9. The supercloth must be cut to size and glued to the spine of the book.

Making the case

11. Cut two pieces of bookbinder's board. The size of the board pieces is determined by first measuring from the shaped spine to the opening edge of the book, then adding 1/8″. Next, measure the distance from the top to the bottom of the book body and add 1/4″.
12. Position the boards on each side of the book body. Moisten two pieces of gummed tape large enough to extend over the book spine and onto the two pieces of board. Position the boards on the book body and tape them together as shown in **Figure A2-10.** Position the boards carefully—accuracy is important to producing a well-bound book.

Figure A2-10. Glued paper tape can be used to hold the boards in position to allow for spine width.

13. Remove the taped boards from the book body and open them out flat. Stretch the boards so that the tape is tight, then measure horizontally and vertically. Add 2″ to both the length and width measurements, and cut a piece of bookbinder's cloth or paper to that size.
14. Position the taped boards on the wrong side of the cloth or paper so that the distance around the outside is equal, **Figure A2-11**. Mark around the edges of each board piece, then remove the gummed tapes.

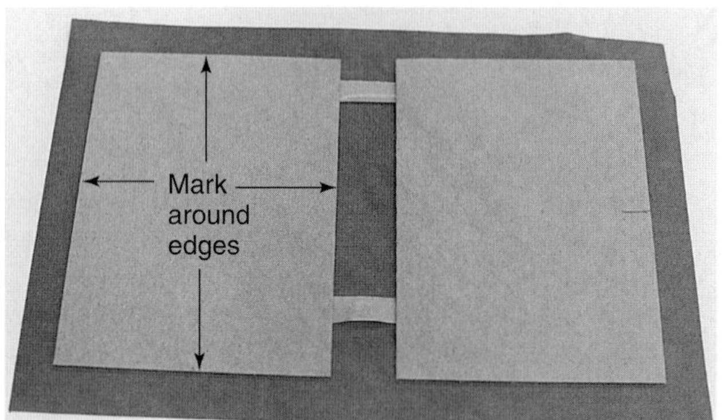

Figure A2-11. Position the binder's board on the cloth or paper. Mark around the edges of each board to establish proper position.

15. Cover one side of each board with a thin coat of bookbinder's glue. Position them on the cloth or paper, using the marks you made in Step 14. Press the boards firmly in place.
16. Cut a paper strip. It should be the exact length of the boards and the exact width of the rounded back. The grain of the paper should run lengthwise. Center the strip between the boards and glue it in place, **Figure A2-12**.
17. Wrap the cloth or paper onto the boards using the *library corner* technique shown in **Figure A2-13**. First, glue and fold all four corners. Then, attach the sides, one by one, beginning with the long sides. Fold the material over the edge and stretch it into position. Sometimes, the case is clamped in a book press until the glue is dry.

Figure A2-12. Glue a paper strip in place, centered between the case boards.

Figure A2-13. Fold over the corners of the material and glue them to the boards. Fold and glue the long sides, then the short sides, to finish the cover ("case").

Casing-in

18. Cut two pieces of waxed paper larger than the book page size. Place the waxed paper between the end sheets and the adjoining book pages.
19. Cut the sewing tapes to match the edges of the supercloth. Apply bookbinder's glue to the outside surface of the two end sheets. Make sure the tapes are glued to the end sheets and coated with a thin film of glue. Carefully position one side of the cased cover against one of the glued end sheets, **Figure A2-14**. Repeat the operation with the second end sheet and the other side of the cover.

Figure A2-14. Carefully position one side of the cover on an end sheet and glue them together. Repeat with the other cover and end sheet.

20. Close the book and crease it for the hinges. Carefully position the press boards on both sides of the book. The metal parts of the press boards must fit into the hinges of the book.

21. Place the book in the book press and close it, **Figure A2-15**. Allow the glue to dry for 8 hours.

Figure A2-15. Place the book in the book press with the press boards in position.

Glossary of Technical Terms

A

A/D converter: Device used to convert analog data to digital data.

Absorption: The ability of paper to take up liquids such as ink.

Accelerator: An alkaline solution use to activate a developing agent.

Accordion fold: The folding of paper using two or more parallel folds.

Achromatic colors: Colors without hue (white, grays, black).

Achromatic vision: People who are blind to all colors possess this type of vision. They only see in shades of white, gray, and black.

Actinic light: Light that will expose light-sensitive emulsion on film or plates.

Activator: A solution, used in the stabilization process, that develops the exposed photographic material.

Adaptation: Adjustment that the eyes make to their sensitivity of light.

Additive color formation: Theory based on mixing red, green, and blue light in various combinations to create a color reproduction or image.

Additive primary colors: Red, green, and blue. When mixed together in varying combinations and intensities, these three colors of light can produce any other color. Usually referred to as the *RGB system.*

Additives: Ingredients such as driers, lubricants, waxes, and starches that are added to ink to impart special characteristics, improve desirable properties, or suppress undesirable properties.

Adhesive binding: A method that uses glue or adhesive to hold sheets together but allows them to be removed, as in the case of notepads. Also called *padding*.

Adjacency: Overlap or spacing of neighboring pixels in an array.

Adjacency effect: The property of the eye that causes the same color to look different when surrounded by or adjacent to other colors. A color will appear brighter if surrounded by dark colors, or darker when surrounded by light colors. This color-vision effect is called *chromatic induction* or *simultaneous contrast*; the visual influence of a highly saturated color on a nearby color.

Adobe Acrobat™: Popular *document file (PDF)* format. Through PDFs, users can read electronic versions of printed documents that maintain the attributes (bold and italic type and other formatting choices) assigned to a printed original.

Adobe PostScript™: Adobe Systems, Inc. tradename for a page description language that enables imagesetters developed by different companies to interpret electronic files from any number of personal computers ("front ends") and off-the-shelf software programs.

Adobe Type Manager™ (ATM): Application that creates bitmapped fonts in any size or style from PostScript outline fonts. ATM also converts missing font sizes and improves fonts printed on nonPostScript output devices.

Adobe Type Reunion™: Application that collects style variations in a pull-down menu and lists style variations of a typeface in a pop-up menu. Also unifies a type family into a list that makes *true* typeface selection easier.

Afterimage: An image that viewer continues to see after the actual object is no longer in sight. Because of cone fatigue in our eyes, the color and shape of the afterimage may be complementary to the color and shape of the actual object. The image is created by the eyes' attempt to restore equilibrium.

Aliasing: The process in which smooth curves and other lines become jagged because an image is enlarged or the resolution of the graphics device or file is reduced.

Amplitude modulation: See *Spot screening.*

Analog: The principal feature of something in analog form is that it is continuous.

Analog charge: The series of electrical impulses into which a CCD converts light.

Angstrom: Unit of measure used for wavelength of light. Ten angstroms equal one nanometer. Symbol is Å.

Anilox roll: A metal or ceramic roll engraved with cells that carry ink to the plate cylinder.

Anti-offset spray: A fine powdered starch spray used to eliminate setoff from the previously printed sheet.

Antialiasing: Software technique for diminishing the jagged edges of an image that should be smooth. It reduces the prominence of *jaggies* by surrounding them with intermediate shades of gray or color.

Antihalation backing: A biodegradable dye coating on the back of most films that absorbs light so it will not reflect back to the emulsion and produce a shadow or double image.

Aperture: The actual opening created by the diaphragm.

Apprenticeship: A method of job training in which an employee in a union shop receives classroom training and on-the-job experience as a means of becoming an experienced journeyman.

APR: See *Automatic picture replacement.*

Array: A group of light-sensitive recording elements, often arranged in a line. Used as a scanner light-sensing device.

Art knife: Very sharp knife, with interchangeable blades, for making precise cuts in typeset copy, masking films, and other materials. The pointed tip of the blade can also be used to shift or position small elements during pasteup.

Artwork: The graphic elements (line art and photographs) used in producing printed products.

Ascender: The part of a letter that extends above the body height.

ASCII: The American Standard Code for Information Interchange. A system that assigns a specific binary word (see byte) to represent individual letters, numbers, punctuation marks, and symbols. This provides a way to digitally store and process information.

ASCII file: A text file containing no special formatting.

ASCII protocol: A simplified method of text file transfer with no allowances for error or flow control.

Automatic film processor: A mechanical device used to develop the latent image on photographic material. It moves exposed photosensitive material through the same development steps used for manual processing.

Automatic picture replacement (APR): Scitex process that replaces a low-resolution image in a document with its corresponding high-resolution image.

Automatic trap: Trap set by building art with common colors. See also *Trapping.*

Autotracing: A feature found in some graphics programs that allows conversion of bitmapped images into an object-oriented format.

B

Backup: To copy files to a second medium (disk or tape) as a precaution in case the first medium fails or is destroyed. The copy itself is also called a backup.

Banding machine: Device that is used to wrap and bond a plastic or metal band around a bundle of booklets, books, boxes, or other products. This holds the products together for shipping.

Bank: A compositor's workstation used to hold a job case when hand-setting foundry type.

Barrier guards: Machine guards that can be hinged or moved.

Base cylinder: A gravure cylinder before it is copper-plated, polished, and etched.

Base font: Term used to describe the multiple master font itself.

Base line: An imaginary line drawn along bottom of body height letters.

Base material: The layer of film that supports the emulsion. It is commonly made from plastic or a special grade of paper. Most of today's graphic films use a polyester base.

Baseline grid: A nonprinting set of guidelines on each page of a page composition program. Included on the grid are guidelines for margins, columns, gutters and other basic page elements.

Basic main exposure: The best exposure time for reproducing the camera-ready copy for a specific camera.

Basic size: The standard length and width, in inches, of a grade of paper.

Basis weight: The weight, in pounds, of a ream of paper cut to its basic size.

Bezier curve: A vector graphic, named after French mathematician Pierre Bezier, that is defined mathematically by two endpoints and two or more other points that control its shape.

Binary: A notation system that uses only two numbers or digits: 1 and 0. Since a computer recognizes two states, the binary system can be used to describe those states: 1 is used to represent "on" and 0 represents "off."

Binding: The process of joining together multiple pages of a printed product by various means including sewing, stapling, spiral wire, and adhesives.

Bit: See *Byte.*

Bit depth: Number of bits used to represent each pixel. The greater the bit depth, the more colors or grayscales can be represented. For example, a 24-bit color scanner can represent 224 (16.7 million) colors. Also referred to as *tonal resolution.*

Bitmap: An image represented by an array of picture elements, each of which is encoded as a single binary digit. Alternative term: bit image.

Bitmapped images: Graphics files that contain a map of *pixels* (tiny rectangular picture elements), each of which is assigned characteristics such as color and brightness, to make up the image. Artwork created by a paint program is a bitmapped image, so is a continuous tone image (photograph) that has been digitized by use of a scanner.

Black letter: A classification of type consisting of faces that resemble the hand-drawn lettering of German monks in the Middle Ages.

Blanket: A resilient material that is coated on fabric. The size varies according to the press cylinder size. The blanket is attached to a cylinder and used as an image transfer material from the plate cylinder to the substrate.

Blanket cylinder: A printing system component that holds the image-receptive blanket on the press and receives the image from the plate cylinder.

Bleaching: A chemical treatment to whiten wood pulp.

Bleed: An image that extends to the edge of a printed page after the page is trimmed.

Blind embossing: An embossing process in which the stock itself creates the image and ink is not used.

Blind image: The image on an offset lithographic plate does not print an inked image on the blanket.

Blinding: Condition in which the image area of the printing plate will not accept ink.

Blueline proof: Proof produced from imageset film. A photographic procedure is used in which light-sensitive compounds are applied to paper, plastic, or metal sheets. The substrate is then exposed to intense blue and/or ultraviolet light and developed with ammonia vapors or an alkaline solution to form an image. The images and text on the proofs are usually blue in color. Also referred to as *diazo proof.*

Blue-sensitive film: Film that is highly sensitive to only the blue portion of the spectrum.

Body height: The distance from top to bottom of lowercase letters, not including the ascenders and descenders. Also called *x-height.*

Body type: Type sizes that range from 4-point through 12-point that are used for setting straight matter.

Book publishing and printing: Graphic communications industry segment that produces *trade books* (general interest nonfiction and fiction) sold in bookstores and other retail locations, and *textbooks* providing instruction on a great variety of subjects.

Brake mechanism: A tension control device designed to produce a slight amount of drag on the web as it travels through a web-fed press.

Brayer: A small, hand-held roller used to distribute ink on a proof press.

Brightness: Often referred to as lightness or luminosity, brightness can be defined as a value indicating how light or dark a color is. For paper classification, the percent reflectance of blue light only, centering on the wavelength of 457 nm.

Broad light source: A contact printing light source that has a wide angle of coverage.

Brush system: A continuous dampening system that uses a brush roller to transfer fountain solution from the fountain roller to the rest of the system.

Buffer: Temporary storage area that enables the manipulation of data before it is transferred to internal or external storage.

Bump exposure: A no-screen, or line shot, of the continuous tone camera copy that will enhance the highlight details by *reducing* the size of dots with the additional exposure. Its purpose is to shorten the screen range to compensate for camera copy with a density range *less than* the screen range. Also referred to as *nonscreen highlight exposure.*

Burn: To expose the image on a printing plate with a light source.

Burned edges: An imperfection in a water- or lacquer-soluble stencil in which solvent collects in an improperly cut area of the stencil and melts (burns) the edge.

Burnish: To rub down a dry transfer image onto a base sheet with a smooth wood, plastic, or metal tool.

Burnisher: Roller or beveled-edge stick used to apply firm pressure to copy or artwork being adhered to the base sheet when preparing a mechanical.

Byte: A binary word, or group of eight individual 1s and 0s (called *bits*) or binary digits.

C

Calendering: Passing paper between rollers to increase the smoothness and gloss of the paper's surface.

Calibrate: To adjust the scale on a measuring instrument, such as a *densitometer*, to a standard for specific conditions.

Calibration: A process by which a scanner, monitor, or output device is adjusted to provide a more accurate display and reproduction of images.

Calibration bars: See *Color control bar.*

Calligraphy: The art of hand-drawing letters, also known as "manuscript writing."

Caliper: The thickness of a sheet of paper.

Camera bed: The main support for the other camera parts. It determines the sturdiness of the camera. Also referred to as the *frame.*

Camera-processor: A process camera and a developer combined into a single unit.

Camera-ready copy: A pasted-up page or other material in final form, ready for the photomechanical techniques that convert it to film.

Caps: Designates material to be set in all capital letters.

Caret: An upside-down v symbol used to mark the location of an error in typeset copy.

Case: The cover of a hardbound (casebound) book.

Case binding: The most complex and permanent form of binding, in which a rigid cover is attached to a book body that is held together by sewing. Also called *edition binding* or hard binding.

Casing in: In edition binding, the process of attaching the separately manufactured book cover to the body with an adhesive.

Cathode ray tube (CRT): A large vacuum tube, much like a television screen, used to generate images with the most sophisticated phototypesetting machines. A computer monitor is also a CRT.

CCD: See *Charged-coupled device.*

CD-R (compact disc-recordable): Polished metal platter capable of storing digital information. CD-Rs can only be recorded once, but read many times.

CD-ROM (compact disc-read only memory): Polished metal platter capable of storing digital information. CD-ROMs are read-only (once written, information cannot be erased).

CD-RW (compact disc-rewritable): Polished metal platter capable of storing digital information. CD-RWs can be written to and read over and over again.

Cell distortion: The result of stretching fabric openings unequally in two directions.

Cell size: The distance across individual open areas between adjacent threads.

Cellulose: The raw material used to make paper.

Chalking: Condition that occurs when dried ink is easily rubbed off or lost from a printed sheet.

Channel: Color separation of a bitmap image.

Character compensation: A method of tight-setting copy by electronically reducing the width of each character and space very slightly, thus reducing the white space between characters.

Characteristic curve: A graphic representation of the relationship between exposure and density. It indicates how a given film reacts to light and development. Also referred to as a *D log E chart.*

Characterization: Describes the color limitations or color profile of a particular device.

Characterization profiles: See *ICC color profile.*

Characters: The individual visual symbols, such as letters, numerals, and punctuation marks, in a particular typeface.

Charge-coupled device (CCD): An array of light-sensitive solid-state receptors that react electronically when exposed to light. It is the technology used most often in desktop scanners. A light-sensitive chip commonly built into image capturing devices (such as scanners and digital cameras) that converts light into a corresponding electrical charge.

Chase: A metal frame that serves as a support device for the type form on a relief printing press.

Chemical fog: The slight amount of density increase in the unexposed areas of film caused by the action of the developer. Also referred to as *developmental fog.*

Chief Executive Officer (CEO): The person with day-to-day responsibility for operating a corporation.

Chipper: A machine that cuts logs into chips.

Choke: A print made in a contact printing frame that makes the original image slightly smaller. The light source angles inward to expose less image area. Also referred to as a *skinny.*

Choke trap: Trap performed by spreading the background under the foreground object. See also *Trapping.*

Chroma: A term used in the Munsell system to indicate the extent to which the color is diluted by white light. The chroma value shows the amount a given hue deviates from a neutral gray of the same value.

Chromalin proof: A type of prepress proof.

Chromatic adaptation: The adjustment our eyes make to color conditions. For example, if you were reading next to a lamp that emits light with a yellow cast, your eyes would quickly adapt to the point that the yellow color would not even be noticeable.

Chromatic colors: Grouping that includes all colors except for white, grays, and black.

Chromatic induction: The property of the eye that causes the same color to look different when surrounded by or adjacent to other colors. A color will appear brighter if surrounded by dark colors, or darker when surrounded by light colors.

Chromaticity: A quality of color that includes hue and saturation (chroma), but not brightness (lightness); color specification indicated by dominant wavelength and purity.

Chromaticity coordinates: The ratios of each of the tristimulus values of a color to the sum of the tristimulus values. In CIE systems, they are designated by x, y, and z. Also referred to as *trichromatic coefficients* or *trilinear coordinates.*

CHRP: See *Common Hardware Reference Platform.*

Cicero: A unit of print measure used in the European didot point system. One cicero is equal to 12 didot points or 0.1776″.

CIE: Commission Internationale de l'Eclairage or the International Commission on Illumination: In 1931, the CIE established a worldwide color measurement standard. The system is a mathematical model of human color perception. Numerical values are used to quantify the responses of the average human eye to different wavelengths of light.

Clip art: Preprinted artwork designed to be cut and pasted up on the mechanical.

CMOS APS (complementary metal oxide semiconductor): Active light sensor chip that is finding use in low-end digital cameras.

CMYK: See *Subtractive color.*

Coated paper: Paper with a mineral substance applied to it for a smoother, stronger surface.

Collate: The gathering of sheets or signatures, usually after they are printed.

Collimator: An optical instrument used by the stripper to make sure register marks are properly aligned when two or more overlays are used. The collimator eliminates *parallax error*.

Color: A visual sensation produced in the brain when the eye views various wavelengths of light. Color viewing is a highly subjective experience that varies from individual to individual. In the graphic arts industry, lighting standards and color charts help ensure the accuracy of color reproduction.

Color balance: Specific combination of yellow, magenta, and cyan needed to produce a neutral gray in the color separation process.

Color blindness: The inability of some people to tell colors apart. It is caused by a deficiency in the vision system.

Color constancy: The tendency to perceive inaccurate nature-specific and object-specific colors as true.

Color control bar: A device printed in a trim area of a press sheet to monitor printing variables such as trapping, ink density, dot gain, and print contrast. It usually consists of overprints of two- and three-color solids and tints; solid and tint blocks of cyan, magenta, yellow, and black; and additional aids such as resolution targets and dot gain scales. Also referred to as *color control strip*, *proofing bar*, or *color bar*.

Color control strip: See *Color control bar*.

Color correction: Adjusting images to optimize values for highlight and shadow, neutral tones, skin tones, and sharpness, used to compensate for impurities in the printing ink and color separation.

Color depth: The number of distinct colors that can be represented by a piece of hardware or software. Color depth is sometimes referred to as *bit depth* because it is directly related to the number of bits used for each pixel. A 16-bit video adapter, for example, has a color depth of 216 (about 16.7 million) colors.

Color diagram: A visual representation of color data, used for process ink analysis.

Color electronic prepress system (CEPS): A computer-based image manipulation and page makeup system for graphic arts applications. CEPS replaces manual correction techniques previously accomplished with duplicate transparencies and emulsion stripping.

Color gamut: The range of colors that can be formed by all possible combinations of the colorants in a color reproduction system. See also *Palette*.

Color Key™: A color proofing system that generates a set of process-color transparent film positives from separation negatives so that registration and screen-tint combinations can be checked before actual press proofs are produced.

Color management module (CMM): Color transformation engine that translates data from one device's color space to another.

Color management software (CMS): Program designed to provide a monitor display in RGB color that will better match the CMYK printed material. The resulting display is termed *WYSIWYP*, or "What You See Is What You Print."

Color management system (CMS): An electronic prepress tool that provides a way to correlate the color-rendering capabilities of input devices (scanners, digital cameras), color monitors, and output devices (digital proofers, imagesetters, and color printers) to produce predictable, consistent color.

Color permanence: See *Color retention*.

Color printer: Printer capable of printing more than one color. Most color printers are based on the CMYK color model, which prints in four basic colors: cyan, magenta, yellow, and black.

Color quality index: See *Color rendering index*.

Color rendering index: A measure of the degree to which a light source influences color perception. Objects are illuminated under a nonstandard light source (such as fluorescent light) and then under a standard source (such as 5000 Kelvin) and the differences in color are compared. Also referred to as *color quality index*.

Color retention: The ability of a color to resist fading or otherwise deteriorating after exposure to light. Also referred to as *colorfastness*, *color permanence*, or *color stability*.

Color sensitivity: A measure of how receptive a material is to the colors of light.

Color separation: Process of dividing the colors of a multicolored original into the printing primaries (CMY) and black (K). The CMYK color separations are made into film and used to prepare printing plates.

Color space: The three-dimensional area where three color attributes, such as hue, value, and chroma, can be depicted, calculated, and charted.

Color stability: See *Color retention*.

Color strength: The amount of pigment in an ink that determines how well the ink will cover the substrate.

Color temperature: The degree to which a black body must be heated to produce a certain color radiation; it is the method of rating the quality of a light source.

Color wheel: A visual tool that illustrates the basics of color.

Colorant: Chemical substance that gives color to such materials as ink, paint, crayons, and chalk. The *colorants* that dissolve in liquids are called *dyes*. Colorants that do not dissolve but spread through liquids or other substances as tiny solid particles are called *pigments*.

Colorfastness: How well a printed substrate retains its color under normal storage conditions and resists change as it ages or is exposed to light, heat, or other environmental influences. Also referred to as *color permanence*, *color retention*, or *color stability*.

Colorimeter: Color measurement device that measures and compares the hue, purity, and brightness of colors in a manner that simulates how people perceive color.

Colorimetry: The science of determining and specifying colors.

Combination densitometer: Color measurement device that identifies both reflection and transmission densities.

Commercial printing: An important segment of the graphic communications industry, encompassing all sizes and types of printing operations. These range from small local shops with one or two employees to large companies with several plant locations and hundreds or thousands of employees. This industry segment is dominated by one printing process, offset lithography.

Common Hardware Reference Platform (CHRP): Prototype system that allows users to run software written for either the Macintosh or PC platforms. It would also make possible the connection of peripheral devices, such as printers, originally designed for either platform.

Common impression cylinder: A web-fed press design in which one cylinder is surrounded by a group of printing units. Each printing unit prints a separate color on the web.

Compact disk (CD): See *CD-ROM* .

Comparison proofing: Proofing done primarily by one person to find such major problems as copy deletion, incorrect sequence, or copy duplication. It is most suitable for small jobs with little copy.

Compass: An adjustable device that can be used to draw circles of various sizes. It can be used with a lead (pencil) point, an inking (pen) point, or a swivel knife blade used to cut overlay film.

Complementary colors: Any two colors that lie directly opposite each other on the color wheel.

Complementary flats: Multiple flats that are exposed successively onto the same plate.

Composing stick: A device used to hold foundry type when performing hand composition. The stick has a movable knee that can be set to the determined line length.

Composition: The process of setting type for printed communication. The term *composition* also can be used to refer to the production and organization of all images to be printed as in *page composition.*

Compositor: A person who sets type; also referred to as a *typesetter.*

Comprehensive layout: A detailed layout showing how the printed piece will look when finished.

Compression: Reducing the size of a file for storage purposes or to enhance the speed of data transfer by eliminating the redundancies and other unnecessary elements from the original. See also *Data compression; Lossy compression; Lossless compression.*

Computer graphics: Graphic material from computer systems. This process also often involves integrating text and art and completing page layout on the computer before outputting it to a laser printer or imagesetter.

Computer graphics interface: A hardware-independent link between a device driver and higher level graphics programs. Alternative term: *virtual device interface.*

Computer graphics metafile: A hardware-independent data structure for storing and transferring two-dimensional graphic information.

Computer-to-plate (CTP): Technology that uses imaging systems that take fully-paginated digital materials and expose this information to plates in platesetters or imagesetters without creating film intermediates. Also referred to as *direct-to-plate (DTP)* or *digital-to-plate.*

Condensed typefaces: Those intended to get more words in less space by narrowing the width (but not height) of the characters. They are used rather than going to a smaller typeface.

Cones: Light-sensitive nerve cells of the retina that help us perceive light and color. Cones detect both intensity and wavelength (color), responding to red, green, or blue. Colors are perceived according to which cones are stimulated by wavelengths of the light entering the eye.

Constructive interference: Brightening of light that occurs when the crests of more than one light wave pass through the same point at the same time.

Contact: A same-size negative or positive reproduction that is the result of the contact printing process. See *Contact printing.*

Contact duplicate: A photographic process in which a negative or positive image is duplicated. If the original is a negative, then a negative results and if the original is a positive, then a positive results.

Contact film: Film used to make positives from negatives or to make negatives from film positives. It is considered to be a blue-sensitive film.

Contact printing: Process that produces a photographic print by exposing a light-sensitive material (film, photographic paper, or plate) held against a negative or positive in a contact printing frame. The resulting copy is the same size as the original.

Contact printing frame: A device used for contact printing that utilizes a vacuum or a spring action to hold the image and light-sensitive materials together. See *Contact printing.*

Contact reversal: A contact printing process is used to produce negatives from positives or vice versa.

Contact screen: A series of uniform vignetted (soft) dots printed on a flexible support base.

Continuous spectrum: Spectrum of colors that is created when sunlight passes through a prism. The spectrum blends smoothly from one color to the next.

Continuous tone: An image with an infinite number of tone gradations between the lightest highlights and the darkest shadows.

Continuous-drop: Type of ink-jet printing system.

Contrast: The variation of elements in a printed product.

Control lines: Markings on originals and along the margins of negative film flats to aid in color registration and correct alignment.

Control strips: Continuous wedges of film with graduated densities that are preexposed under exacting conditions. They are used to test the development solution in automatic processors.

Conversion: Step of color management systems that performs color correction between imaging devices.

Copy: The text elements (words) used in producing printed products.

Copyboard: A glass-covered frame at one end of a process camera that holds the original image while it is being shot.

Copyboard controls: Controls used for positioning the copyboard in relation to others parts of the process camera.

Copyfitting: The process of fitting together copy and illustrations in a specific amount of space.

Copyholder: Member of a two-person proofreading team who follows the original manuscript or a printout.

Copyright: A legal protection against unauthorized copying of creative works, providing the producer with exclusive rights for his or her lifetime plus 50 years.

Cornea: A transparent window at the front of the eye that refracts light to the retina.

Corporation: A form of business organization with multiple owners. Owners may have varying number of shares of stock in the business, and often are not directly involved in its operation.

Counter: The nonprinting area surrounding a letter or inside the loop of a letter, such as **d** or **p**.

Craft-centered: Refers to work performed by artisans or others with manual skills.

Creasing: The process of compressing the substrate so that it will fold more easily; often done with a rotary creaser attached to the folder.

Creep: A pushing out or extension of pages on the outer edge of a saddle-stitched book, caused by the greater thickness at the spine. An allowance for creep must be made in the prepress phase. Also called *shingling*.

CREF: Acronym for Computer Ready Electronic File.

CREF II guidelines: Guidelines published by the Scitex Graphic Arts Users Association to improve prepress productivity.

Crop: Marks that indicate what portion of the original pictorial material is to be used.

Cross-platform: Refers to applications, formats, or devices that work on different platforms.

Cursive: A typeface, designed to simulate handwriting, in which the letters are not joined.

Customized printing: Printing that allows assembly and printing of documents that are particular to selected audiences.

Cutting: The process of making a large sheet of paper into several smaller sheets. Compare with *trimming*.

D

Dampening system: A group of rollers designed to apply moisture to the nonimage area of the printing plate.

Dark adaptation: Adjustment that the eyes make in their sensitivity to light. If the eyes experience low light for some time, the cones and rods grow more sensitive and light appears brighter.

Darkroom: A light-tight chamber in which film is handled and processed.

Data compression: A software or hardware process that reduces the size of images so that they occupy less storage space and can be transmitted faster and easier. This process is accomplished by removing the bits that define blank spaces and other redundant data, and replacing them with a smaller algorithm that represents the removed bits. Data must be decompressed before it can be used.

Data conversion: Technique of changing digital information from its original code so that it can be recorded by an electronic device using a different code. Data created in one software format may be converted to another before printing. Data must also be converted for various output devices, such as when RGB colors are converted to CMYK.

Data file: Images that are stored electronically.

Daylight film: Film that is used with a very high-intensity light source, because it has emulsion that is not very sensitive to light. Most of these films are intended to be used for emulsion-to-emulsion contacting.

De-inking: The process of removing inks, fillers, and coatings from waste paper.

Debossing: The reverse of embossing, so that the image is sunk into the substrate, rather than being raised.

Decibels (dB): A unit for expressing the intensity of sound.

Decompression: A reversal of the data compression process.

Definition: The sharpness or distinction of the printed image.

Delivery pile: A uniform stack of paper that accepts sheets from the delivery system of a sheet-fed press.

Delivery system: A press system that removes the printed substrate from the printing system and prepares it for finishing operations.

Delta Pulse Code Modification (DPCM): Lossy compression technique that measures one set of bits and then measures differences from that set. The differences are then encoded into fewer bits.

Densitometer: An electronic instrument that uses a photocell to accurately measure the amount of light reflected from or through different tone values.

Densitometry: The measurement of density.

Density: The light-stopping ability of a material. The ability to hold back or block light.

Density capacity: The theoretical maximum density allowed by a given film (emulsion).

Descender: The part of a letter that extends below the body or baseline.

Design: The application of proper methods to produce a product that is both artistic and functional.

Design axis: Variable typeface attribute (weight, width, style, optical size). The base design determines the range of variations available.

Desktop color separations 1:0 (DCS 1:0): File format that creates five separate files, one for each process color (CMYK), and a data or master file. DCS 1:0 is also referred to as *five-file format*.

Desktop color separations 2:0 (DCS 2:0): File format that is an EPS graphic saved as a single file and can include up to six plates (cyan, magenta, yellow, black, and two spot colors) and a master image. The master file is used for composite printing. The DCS format supports grayscale, RGB, spot color, and CMYK color models. DCS can contain both bitmap and object-oriented information.

Desktop publishing system: A computerized system commonly used in the graphic communications industry to produce type and images.

Destructive interference: A dimming of light that occurs when the crest of one wave crosses the same point as the trough of another wave. The trough reduces the height of the crest, leaving the spot very dim or even dark.

Detail printer: The black printer in a set of color separations.

Developing agent: The part of the developer solution (a chemical compound) that makes the latent image visible.

Development by inspection: Development method in which the operator examines the film for proper processing. The operator processing the film looks for an acceptable highlight dot first, and then checks for the acceptable shadow dot in reference to the original artwork or photograph.

Device-dependent format: A format specifically related to a particular device or program. It usually hampers the conversion of data from other device-independent or device-dependent formats for output to various devices and media.

Device-independent format: A format not specifically related to any particular device that allows data to be converted without the loss of information to other device-independent or device-dependent formats. Examples are PDF or a device-independent display list.

Dialog box: A computer software feature that permits the operator to input information, such as specifying an action, inputting a measurement, or selecting a color.

Diaphragm: The adjustable opening mounted behind or between the elements of a camera lens. It is used to control the amount of light that reaches the film.

Diazo proof: See *Blueline proof.*

Dichroic fog: A deposit of silver particles that are suspended in the developer solution and appear to leave a purplish coating on the emulsion. This is a problem typically caused by developer contaminated by fixer.

Dichromatic vision: Most color blind people have this type of vision and can see only yellows and blues. They confuse reds with greens, and some reds or greens with some yellows.

Didot point system: The standard system of print measurement used in Europe. The didot point is equal to 0.0148″. Twelve didot points equal one cicero (0.1776″).

Die cutting: A process in which pressure is used to force a sharp metal die (steel rule) through the stock. It is used to make irregular shapes.

Diffraction: Phenomenon that occurs when light waves spread out into curving waves.

Diffraction grating: Optical device used to study colors in light. The grating uses thousands of thin slits to diffract light and separate it into its component parts.

Diffusion transfer process: A reproduction process in which a negative sheet is exposed to the image on the process camera. The negative and a receiver sheet are fed into a diffusion transfer processor. It is capable of making a line positive, screened positive, or lithographic printing plate using a process camera.

Digester: A pressurized kettle that breaks down the lignin in the cellulose fibers as part of the papermaking process.

Digital: The method used to represent information in a computer system. The information is stored and processed in *binary* form, as a series of on and off (the *presence* or *absence* of an electrical charge) states. The numerals 1 and 0 are conventionally used to represent the on and off states.

Digital bluelines: Two-sided digital position proof for eight-page impositions (sixteen-page signatures).

Digital camera: A camera that uses a CCD or CMOS APS sensor to convert light into electrical signals and then into digital data. Images from digital cameras can be integrated immediately into a design or layout program.

Digital Data Exchange Standards (DDES): An established set of protocols, formats, and values that allow the exchange of data between equipment made by different manufacturers.

Digital film: Term used to describe a removable storage device known as a *PCMCIA card*.

Digital prepress: A computer-centered process that consists of preparing content (text and graphics), then composing pages (design/layout), and outputting the finished file to an imagesetter, directly to a platemaker, or directly to a digital press

Digital printing: Any reproduction technology that receives electronic files and uses spot (or dots) for replication. Ink, toner, ink-jet, or any other dye- or pigment-based transfer system may be used.

Digital proofs: Proofs generated by outputting files on a high-resolution, high-quality printer.

Digital-to-paper: Printing technology that is the printing of images directly on the press from electronic files. Eliminates the time-consuming and costly preparation of film, plates, and inks. Also referred to as *totally electronic printing (TEP)*.

Digital-to-plate: See *Computer-to-plate.*

Dingbats: See *Pi characters.*

Direct digital color proof (DDCP): Proof printed directly from computer data to paper or another substrate without creating separation films first. Proof made with computer output device, such as laser or ink-jet printer.

Direct screen color separation: A color separation that is created when the halftone screening process is completed during the color separation exposure. It is considered to be one of the fastest and most cost-effective techniques for creating color separations. See *Color separation.*

Direct screen photographic color separation: A method in which process camera, contact printing frame, or enlarger is used to make color separation exposures through a photographic mask and a halftone screen onto high-contrast panchromatic film. Color-corrected halftone separation negatives are produced in one step, eliminating the need to screen tone values separately.

Direct-to-plate (DTP): See *Computer-to-plate.*

Discrete cosine transform (DCT): Lossy compression algorithm that analyzes each pixel block, identifies color frequencies, and removes data redundancies.

Disk (floppy and hard): A flexible ("floppy") disk stores input data and is removable; while the hard disk is a storage device that is a permanent part of the computer.

Disk drive: The device that rotates the disk.

Display type: Type sizes above 12-point, used to emphasize the importance of a message and capture the reader's attention.

Distributed printing: Method of sending electronic files to multiple locations for output. Commonly used for localized editions of newspapers and magazines.

Doctor blade: In gravure, a thin metal blade that clears excess ink from the noncell areas of the anilox roll.

Dot: The single element of a halftone.

Dot etching: Manual alteration of the dot structure to correct color. Also a contacting technique used to spread or choke the dot structure.

Dot gain: Optical increase in the size of a halftone dot during prepress operations or the mechanical increase in halftone dot size that occurs as the image is transferred from plate-to-blanket-to-paper in lithography.

Dot-gain calibration: Method(s) of controlling or minimizing dot gain.

Dot pitch: A measurement of the vertical distance between rows of pixels on a monitor, stated in decimal fractions of a millimeter. The image quality becomes crisper as the fraction becomes smaller. A common dot pitch measurement on monitors for general computer use is 0.28.

Dots per inch (dpi): Measuring units for image resolution; the number of dots a printing device can generate in one linear inch. It is also used to describe pixels per inch in a bitmapped image.

Double-sheet detector: A control device that prevents more than one sheet of paper from entering the press.

dpi: See *Dots per inch.*

Drafting tape: Mounting tape similar to masking tape, but with a less-sticky adhesive, so it can be pulled off paper without damage. In paste-up work, drafting tape is commonly used to hold a base sheet to a drawing board.

Draw program: Graphics program that enables the user to draw, store, and merge images into documents. Draw programs use *vector graphics* instead of raster graphics. Also referred to as *illustration/design program.*

Drawdown: The amount of time required to remove all air from a vacuum frame to allow the original and the film to achieve uniform contact before exposure.

Drawdown test: A method of checking for proper ink mixing by placing a small amount of ink on paper, and then using a blade to spread it and produce a thin ink film.

Drawing board: A working surface used in layout that provides an area where the mechanical can be taped down for paste-up.

Drawsheet: A sheet of tympan paper that provides the holding surface for paper to be printed on a platen press.

Drilling: Piercing operation that uses a revolving, hollow drill bit with very sharp edges. The waste stock rises through the hollow center of the drill. Compare with *punching.*

Drop-on-demand: Method of ink-jet printing.

Dropdown menu: A list that extends downward from the menu bar on the computer display screen. The list consists of choices that can be used to create or modify documents.

Drum scanner: The drum, or rotary, scanner scans images mounted on a rotating drum. The drum spins quickly in front of a stationary reading head. As the drum rotates, the originals are illuminated by a light source that pans slowly across the front of the drum. Light is transmitted through, or reflected from, the original, then passed through an aperture to the PMT light sensors where the color measurements are made.

Dry: The point at which the ink is free of volatile substances and has polymerized to a total solid state.

Dual-dot halftone screen: Halftone screen that has a secondary ruling to reproduce extremely fine details in the middle tones and shadows.

Dummy: A representative layout of a printed piece showing the folds, page numbers, and positions of text and illustrations.

Duplicate: The act of making the same image as the original, such as a negative to produce another negative. Also referred to as *duping.*

Duplicate plate: In relief printing, a secondary plate or copy of the original type form of composed characters.

Duplicating film: Film that is used to make a duplicate of the negative or positive.

Duplicator: A small sheet-fed press typically used for short printing runs.

Durometer: A measure of a rubber squeegee blade's hardness.

DVD: Digital Versatile Disk, a very high capacity disk that is increasingly used for data storage in the graphics industry.

Dye sublimation printing: Printing technology that uses digital data to control a thermal printhead to melt spots of dry ink on a ribbon and transfer them to a receiver. When *sublimable dye* replaces solid ink, the thermal head converts the dye spots to gas spots which condense on the receiver.

Dylux: A type of prepress proof.

Dynamic range: The gradations from light to dark that a digital imaging device can read or produce.

E

E gauge: A device used to measure point sizes and leading of printed type.

Editing: The final preparation of the author's or writer's manuscript for publication. It involves checking the text, line art, and photographs. *Content* editing involves checking the material to make sure it is up-to-date, technically accurate, organized in a logical sequence, and covers all important ideas. *Copy* editing is done to correct spelling and punctuation, to mark for style, and to assure proper grammar.

Edition binding: See *Case binding*.

Electromagnetic spectrum: The entire range of wavelengths of electromagnetic radiation, extending from gamma rays (very short) to radio waves (very long). The wavelengths are usually measured in nanometers (nm).

Electron charge deposition printing: Printing process that produces images with negative charges from an electron cartridge transferred onto a heated nonconductive (dielectric) surface using magnetic toner. Used mainly for single or spot color printing because the pressure of image transfer and cold fusion toner fixing can distort the substrate. Also known as *ion deposition* or *ionography*.

Electronic color separation: The process of separating the process colors and black (CMYK) with an electronic (computer-assisted) imaging system.

Electronic imaging system: A combination of computer hardware and software designed for image handling and the assembly of text and images into page layouts.

Electronic information transfer: Sending digital information instantly via telephone lines and satellites.

Electronic page composition: A computer-based method of combining and arranging text and line art to assemble the final page. Pages are then output to an imagesetter to produce camera-ready copy, actual negatives, or even the printing plates themselves. This method has replaced mechanical paste-up in many printing operations.

Electronic scanning: See *Scanner.*

Electrophotographic printing: Printing system that uses drums or metal plates coated with chargeable photoconductors that discharge to the nonimage areas after exposure to light. The image receives toners in the charged area, transfers to a substrate, and fuses or fixes by heat, solvent vapor, or other fixing method.

Electroplating: An electrical-chemical process of applying copper plating to a gravure cylinder.

Electrostatic assist: A process in which a power source feeds electrical charges between the impression roller (negative) and the printing cylinder (positive), creating a force that achieves a nearly complete release of ink from the etched cells.

Electrostatic plates: Light-sensitive plates that are imaged by a charge of electrostatic energy.

Electrostatic printing: A printing method that uses the forces of electric current and static electricity. It is commonly found in office copying machines. Machines capable of producing copies in multiple colors have become common in recent years.

Electrotype: A duplicate relief plate that is produced from a mold through an electrochemical process.

Elemental chlorine: Chlorine gas used to bleach paper pulp and to separate the pulp from lignin.

Elements of design: The fundamental elements used by the graphic designer. Elements of design include lines, shapes, mass, texture, and color.

Elements of layout: The fundamental elements used by the layout artist to make a composition. The elements of layout include body type, display type, illustrations, and white space.

Em quad: In foundry type, a nonprinting type block that is a square of the type size, typically used to indent the beginning of a paragraph.

Embossing: A process that creates a raised image on a substrate by pressing it between two dies.

Emulsion: Chemical compounds that form a light-sensitive coating on the base material. It is usually made up of silver halides suspended in a gelatin.

Emulsion sensitivity: A measure of how light-sensitive material reacts to light exposure. It is rated by an arbitrary numerical system known as ISO. The higher the ISO rating assigned to a film emulsion, the faster the film will react to a light exposure.

En quad: In foundry type, a spacing element half an em quad in width, typically used to separate words.

Encapsulated PostScript (EPS): A file format used to transfer PostScript image information from one program to another.

Enlargement. Process used when the images must be increased in size.

Entrepreneur: Someone who starts his or her own business.

Equivalent weight: The weight of one ream of paper of a size that is larger or smaller than the basic size.

Erasable optical (EO) disks: Optical disks that can be read, written to, and erased just like magnetic disks. EO disks can be erased up to around 1000 times before their recording capabilities deteriorate. Also referred to as CD-RWs (compact disc-rewritable).

Ergonomics: The science of fitting the job to the worker.

Error-diffusion screening: Screening method that places dots randomly.

Estimating software: A computer program that accepts quantity, cost, and other information and calculates price estimates.

Expanded typefaces: Those intended to fill more space without going to a larger point size. Also called *extended faces*, they consist of letters that have been made wider without increasing their height.

Exposure-determining device: An instrument used to decide the different exposures required to make a good halftone, or facsimile reproduction, of the original continuous tone copy.

Extended job ticket: An electronic document that contains all of the instructions required for processing a job. It includes data such as customer information, proofing directives, trapping, imposition and ripping parameters, and even finishing and shipping instructions. May also contain the description of user preferences that will guide the actions of the adaptive software.

Extension: See *File extension*.

Eye span: The width of body type a person can see with one fixation (sweep or adjustment) of the eye muscles. The normal eye span is about one and one-half alphabets.

F

f-stop: The fixed aperture at which the diaphragm of the camera can be set.

Fair use: Provision of the copyright law that allows limited copying for certain uses, such as education and research.

Family: See *Typeface family*.

Feeding system: A press system that transfers individual sheets of paper to the press and places them in register.

Felt side: The smoother side of a piece of paper.

Field camera: Portable digital camera that is capable of stopping motion. RGB data is usually gathered in a single exposure with a single CCD array. Most field cameras use interpolation schemes to produce moderately high RGB resolution.

Field effect imaging: High-speed, high-quality color printing composed of variable density pixels. Uses a write head to generate powerful electrostatic fields across a thin-film insulator surface. These fields cause the pickup of pixel-sized ink bits whose thickness is proportional to the strength of the fields. The writing surface carries these ink bits to a print surface where the full ink amount is transferred to the print substrate.

Filament: A single thread.

File extension: A three-letter suffix added primarily to Windows file names to describe the contents of the file.

Fillers: Inorganic materials, such as clay or titanium dioxide, added to the papermaking furnish to improve opacity, brightness, smoothness, and ink receptivity.

Film: A material that is chemically altered after it is exposed to light. It is made up of a protective overcoating, an emulsion, a base material, and an antihalation backing.

Film back: The hinged assembly on the process camera used to hold a sheet of film flat in the focal plane.

Film dryer: A machine that uses forced air for rapid moisture removal from film.

Film scanner: Specially designed CCD scanners that allow the user to capture images from various types of film.

Film-base-plus-fog density: The value indicating the amount of chemical (developmental) fog. It is found by developing an unexposed film emulsion, and taking a transmission densitometer reading (value) to determine the exact amount of fog (density) added to the film base as a result of the development. See *Chemical fog*.

Filter: A colored material, usually glass or acetate, that blocks some wavelengths of the light spectrum (color) and lets others through. It can be used on a process camera to photograph color line copy and convert the color image to black, or it can be used to drop out specific line colors and leave the area white.

Filters: In imaging programs, *filters* are used to apply special effects to bitmap images.

Finishing: A general term that applies to the many operations carried out during or following printing, such as cutting, folding, slitting, perforating, creasing and scoring, die cutting, embossing, stamping, numbering, drilling and punching, varnishing, and laminating.

Five-file format: Same as the *Desktop Color Separations 1:0 (DCS 1:0)* file format. It creates five separate files, one for each process color (CMYK), and a data or master file.

Fixer: A solution that makes the developed image on a film permanent by dissolving or neutralizing the remaining unexposed silver halides.

Flash exposure: A supplementary exposure used to strengthen the dots in the shadows of negatives, thereby lengthening the screen's tonal reproduction range.

Flat: A large support sheet to which images (films) have been attached (stripped) for exposure onto a printing plate.

Flatbed cylinder press: A relief press that prints on paper as it travels between a flat surface (bed) and an impression cylinder.

Flatbed scanner: Electronic imaging device in which images are placed on the glass bed, or scan area, with or without some type of holder.

Flexography: A relief printing process that uses flexible (usually plastic) printing plates. Flexography is extensively used in packaging, and is achieving growing use in printing newspapers and other long run jobs.

Flooding: In gravure printing, the process of inking the cells of the plate or cylinder.

Floor horizontal camera: A horizontal process camera with a large bed that mounts on the floor of the facility.

Floppy disk: Portable, inexpensive, and fairly reliable storage device consisting of a thin magnetized disk encased in hard plastic. A high-density 3 1/2″ floppy disk can hold 1.44 Mb of data.

Floppy disk drive: Disk drive that functions in the same way as a hard disk drive but uses a removable disk known as a *floppy disk.*

Flush: Term describing the dispersing of a pigment in an undried state (a paste) into a vehicle for ink.

Flying splicer: A splicer unit that bonds a new web to the existing web without stopping any operations on a web-fed press.

FM screening: See *Stochastic screening.*

Focal length: The distance from the optical center of the camera lens, to the surface that supports the film (focal plane).

Focal plane: The plane on a camera where the images transmitted by the lens are brought to sharpest focus. Also referred to as the *film plane.*

Foil stamping: See *Stamping.*

Font: In computer-based or phototypesetting composition methods, a font consists of all the characters that make up a specific typeface. In foundry type, where each character is on a separate piece of metal, a font consists of different quantities of each character in one size and style of type.

Font set: The font list for a document. Font sets can be created for individual jobs and activate only the set needed.

Font Sneak: Standalone Mac-only software that supports EPS files and reports to the user all fonts used by the document. It reports any fonts used by the document that are not currently installed and offers the user several font collection options.

FontMinder™: Font utility software that can help manage and collect fonts used within a job.

For position only (FPO): Copies of photos/artwork placed on a mechanical or in electronic layout to show their placement, but not for reproduction.

Form: A guide for determining how images on a signature will be laid out to meet folding, trimming, and bindery requirements. Also, a block of metal type produced by a compositor.

Formal balance: A design principle that is achieved when the elements of a design are of equal weight and are positioned symmetrically.

Former board: A curved or triangular plane that serves as the folding surface on a web-fed press.

Forms printers: Companies that design and print special paper forms used in many businesses.

Foundry type: Individual pieces of metal type that could be aligned with type containing other letters to form words and sentences for printing on paper.

Four-color process printing: The overprinting of the four process colors (yellow, magenta, cyan, and black).

Fourdrinier: A paper machine that forms a continuous web of paper on a moving, endless wire belt.

Fovea: The most sensitive part of the retina of the eye. It is located at the center of the macula. It is packed with cone cells and is the area of sharpest vision.

FPO: See *For position only.*

Frequency: The lines per inch (lpi) in a halftone screen.

Frisket: A masking material.

Front-end platform: The combination of desktop computer hardware, peripherals, and software that allow users to create, manipulate, and store documents prior to printing.

Furnish: The slurry of fillers, sizing, and colorants in a water suspension from which paper is made.

Furniture: Wood or metal spacers arranged around a block of type in a chase to position the type for printing.

G

Galley: In composition for relief printing, a three-sided metal tray used to store type forms (blocks of hand-set type or Linotype slugs) before they are assembled into page form. Also used as a term for a long strip of paper containing a proof of typeset material.

Gamma: A measure of film contrast resulting from length of development.

Gamma correction: Compressing or expanding the ranges of dark or light shades in an image.

Gamut: Common expression for the entire (greatest possible) range of color that can be shown on a computer display or reproduced by another output device.

Gamut alarm: Warning used by many imaging or page composition programs to indicate the presence of colors that are out of the printing range.

Gamut compression: Technique used to compress colors to fit into a smaller color gamut. The compression gives the illusion that all color chroma, saturation, and value are present.

Gamut reduction: See *Gamut compression.*

Gathering: Assembling printed signatures.

GCR: See *Gray Component Replacement.*

Ghosting: Condition that occurs when a solid image prints unevenly or a faint, second image appears next to the original.

Gigabyte: One billion bytes, abbreviated Gb.

Goldenrod: The sheet of stock that is used as the support material for the flat.

Grades: Categories or classes of paper.

Grain: The direction or structure of paper fibers.

Grain short: Indicates that the grain runs across the paper.

Graphic communications: A general term for the exchange of information in a visual form, such as words, drawings, photographs, or a combination of these. More specifically, a term describing printing and related industries.

Graphical User Interface (GUI): A method of representing computer operations and programs on the screen with small pictures (icons) that can be selected with a mouse to preform activities. The GUI is considered far easier and more rapid to use than the command method, which involved typing directions from the keyboard.

Graphics interchange format (GIF): Bitmapped graphics file format that supports color and various resolutions. Also includes data compression.

Gravure: A method of printing from cells or depressions that are engraved below the nonimage area of the printing cylinder.

Gray balance: The measures of cyan, magenta, and yellow required to create a gray scale without producing a dominant hue. The values for yellow, magenta, and cyan that produce a neutral gray with no dominant hue when printed at a normal density.

Gray component replacement (GCR): The removal of equal amounts of cyan, magenta, and yellow areas of a four-color halftone and replacement of these colors with a higher proportion of black. This produces a clearer, less muddy effect.

Gray scale: A continuous tone strip used to visually gauge exposure of an image.

Grayscaling: The process of converting a continuous-tone image to an image in shades of gray.

Gripper allowance: The unprinted space allowed at the edge of a printing sheet.

Gripper edge: The side of the flat that enters the press and is held by the mechanical fingers of the press gripper.

Ground glass: A piece of grained, matte, or frosted glass mounted onto the back of the process camera with hinges or on rails. It is used to view and focus on the original copy before it is exposed as a latent image on film.

Guillotine cutter: A cutting device that slices through a stack of paper.

Gum blinding: An excess of gum on the image area of a plate, resulting in image loss.

H

Hairline: A thin line or element of the character.

Half-page scanners: See *Hand-held scanners.*

Halftone dots: Dots on a contact screen. They are specified as percentages of ink density on a printed sheet. The highlight dots will usually be 5% to 10% in size, the midtone dots ranging from 30% to 70%, and the shadow dots around 90% to 95%.

Halftone exposure calculator: A device used to determine exposures for halftone reproduction. Also referred to as *halftone calculator* or *exposure computer.*

Halftone gravure: A gravure method that uses halftone separations rather than continuous tone separations for image reproduction.

Halftone screen process: The procedure of converting a continuous tone original into a dot structure.

Halftone-grade film: Film used to create halftones. It is considered to be more sensitive and dimensionally stable than *line film.*

Hand-held scanner: Small electronic imaging devices that the user moves across the paper or image by hand. Also referred to as *half-page scanners* because they can scan only 2″–5″ at a time.

Hard copy: The visual material output by a computer or printer.

Hard disk: Aluminum disk coated with a magnetic material that is used within a hard disk drive. See *Hard disk drive.*

Hard disk drive: Device that reads data from and writes data to a hard disk. Hard disk drives are usually built into the computer system. The hard disk drive contains one or more permanent aluminum hard disks coated with a magnetic material. The aluminum disks rotate very quickly as a read/write head moves over the surface, which contains densely packed magnetic tracks. The read/write head is used to write or read information as the magnetic tracks spin past it.

Hardware: A computer and its associated devices.

Heavy elements: The darker strokes of a type character that give it identity.

Hewlett-Packard PCL (Printer Control Language): A PCL developed by printer manufacturer Hewlett-Packard.

Hickeys: Printing imperfections that appear as dried ink spots surrounded by a white background.

High-key photograph: Photo that contains the most important details in the highlights, or lighter tones.

Highlights: Tones with the lightest value. In halftone, the area with the smallest dots.

Hinting: Application that optimizes how type prints at small point sizes on printers with a resolution of 600 dpi or lower.

Histogram: In graphic form, the *histogram* appears as a horizontal display of highlight, midtone, and shadow values corresponding to the number of pixels affected in each part of the tonal scale.

Horizontal camera: A process camera that has a horizontal (side-to-side) optical axis. Also referred to as the *darkroom camera*.

Hot type composition: The traditional arrangement of movable type or hot metal into a form for relief printing.

HTML (HyperText Markup Language): Coded text documents used on the Internet's World Wide Web.

HTTP (HyperText Transfer Protol): The standard that allows the exchange of information on the World Wide Web.

Hue: The color of an object perceived by the eye, and determined by the dominant light wavelengths reflected or transmitted.

Hue, saturation, and brightness (HSB): The eye differentiates colors according to these three basic criteria. *HSB* is a color model used in the graphic arts industry. This color model describes a color's appearance in relationship to its environment.

Huffman method: Lossless data compression technique in which adjacent bits are replaced with codes of varying lengths. For example, this method would encode the fact that zero occurs 20 times rather than using 20 zeros.

I

ICC color profiles: Profiles based on the CIELAB color space and used as standards for describing the color characterizations of different devices. ICC color profiles contain information on the device's color space and the compensation required to bring the device to its ideal level of performance.

Icon: An image that appears on the computer screen to represent a file or a function.

Illustration/design program: Graphics program that enables the user to draw, store, and merge images into documents. Design programs use *vector graphics* instead of bitmapped graphics. Also referred to as a *draw program*.

Illustrations: The elements of layout that include the ornamentation, photographs, and artwork, such as line art.

Image assembly: The process of electronically assembling line and halftone negatives or positives into pages. See *Stripping*.

Image carrier: A press plate or other intermediate used to transfer identical images onto a substrate.

Image editor: Powerful software that permits manipulation of almost any aspect of a bit-mapped image such as cropping, changing color and contrast, adding or removing visual information, or combining images into a new illustration.

Image loss: An area of missing lines or halftone dots that make up the printed image.

Image manipulation program: Graphics program that provides a variety of special features for altering bitmapped images.

Imagesetter: An electronic device used to output fully paginated text and graphic images at a high-resolution onto photographic film, paper, or plates.

Impactless printing: Term for several types of printing (such as ink jet or electrostatic) that do not require direct contact between an image carrier and the substrate.

Imposition: The layout of various sizes and shapes of copy on a page in preparation for the photographic process.

Impression cylinder: A printing system component that brings the paper to be printed in contact with the blanket cylinder.

In-plant printing: Term for printing facilities operated by companies whose business is not the production of printed materials.

Incident beam: A beam of light coming toward a surface.

India ink: An ink used in technical pens. It produces a very dense black line.

Indirect screen photographic color separation: A two-step process in which continuous-tone separations are produced from full-color originals, and halftone negatives or positives are made from the continuous-tone separations. In the first step, the color values are separated; in the second step, tone values are screened. See *Color separation*.

Informal balance: A design principle that is achieved by changing the value, size, or location of elements in a design.

Infringement: A copyright violation.

Ink: A colored coating specially formulated to reproduce an image on a substrate.

Ink agitator: A revolving device that is used to maintain a consistent flow of ink from the ink fountain.

Ink body: Term that describes the consistency of an ink.

Ink darkness: A factor that affects the contrast of printed materials. Darkness depends on the ink's covering power—complete coverage hides the surface of the paper.

Ink fineness gauge: A device that measures the pigment particle size in an ink.

Ink formulation: The amount and type of ingredients used in a particular printing ink.

Ink keys: Adjustable devices used to control the flow of ink from the ink fountain to the printing plate.

Ink length: The elasticity of ink. It is referred to as long or short.

Ink mileage: The surface area that can be covered by a given quantity of ink.

Ink mist: Tiny droplets of ink thrown into the air by rapidly rotating press rollers.

Ink sticking: A press problem that occurs when two layers of ink film, on two different sheets, bond together.

Ink thickness gauge: A device that measures the thickness of the ink film on the press rollers.

Ink-jet printing: Printing method that is direct-to-paper technology with no intermediate image carrier. It uses digital data to control streams of very fine dye drops to produce images directly on paper. Types of ink-jet printers include *continuous-drop*, *drop-on-demand*, and *bubblejet.*

Inking and dampening system: A combined system of rollers that applies both ink and fountain solution to the plate during operation of the press.

Inking system: A group of rollers designed to carry ink to the image area of the printing plate.

Inkometer: An instrument that measures the tack of a printing ink.

Inline: Done as a continuous process on a single piece of equipment.

Input device: A piece of equipment used to enter information into a computer for processing. A keyboard is the most common input device.

Intaglio: A printing process in which words, pictures, or designs are engraved into a printing plate or cylinder.

Intelligent character recognition (ICR): A sophisticated form of optical character recognition (OCR) in which the computer determines the probable meaning of a character, not by looking for an exact match with a character pattern stored in memory, but by analyzing the shape of the character. ICR is, therefore, able to interpret a wide range of different typefaces and point sizes, differing from OCR, which is restricted to the specific face and point size combinations stored in memory.

Intermediate colors: On the color wheel, yellow-green, blue-green, blue-violet, red-violet, red-orange, and yellow-orange.

International Color Consortium (ICC): Organization established in 1993 by leading manufacturers to create a cross-platform standard for color management.

International Standards Organization (ISO): International organization composed of national standards bodies from over 75 countries. ISO has defined a number of computer standards, the most important of which is perhaps OSI (Open Systems Interconnection), a standardized architecture for designing networks.

International System of Units: See *SI Metric.*

Internet: International computer network that grew out of the Advanced Research Projects Agency Network (Arpanet) developed by the U.S. Department of Defense during the 1950s. It has evolved to become a text-based network serving users from all over the world.

Interpolation: Mathematical technique used to increase the apparent resolution of an image. Increases image resolution by adding data in intermediate shades of gray or color to surrounding areas.

Intranet: An internal computer network within a corporation, organization, or institution. Based on the same network protocols as the Internet.

Ion deposition: See *Ionography.*

Ionography: Printing process that produces images with negative charges from an electron cartridge transferred onto a heated nonconductive (dielectric) surface using magnetic toner. Used mainly for single or spot color printing because the pressure of image transfer and cold fusion toner fixing can distort the substrate. Also known as *ion deposition* or *electron charge deposition printing*.

Iris: An opaque diaphragm that contracts to control the amount of light that enters the eye. The iris is the colored portion of the eye. The pupil is located in the center of the iris.

Iris proofs: Proofs produced by a proprietary ink-jet printing process that produces four-color proofs directly from the digital files.

ISO series: The series of standard paper and envelope sizes established by the International Organization for Standardization (ISO).

IT8 reflective target: Standard color reference tool used to calibrate input and output devices.

Italic: A slanted type, modeled on a form of handwriting. It was developed and first used by Aldus Manutius, a printer in Italy. Most Roman and sans serif faces have a companion italic of the same design.

J

Jaggies: Stairlike lines on an image that appear where there should be smooth straight lines or curves.

Job: The collection of all input files and processing instructions, including fonts, graphics, images, data dictionaries, etc., required to produce the finished product whether it will be a printed piece or electronic document.

Job case: A storage drawer with individual compartments for the letters and spacing material used in handsetting foundry type.

Job ticket: A work order that gives the imposition for a particular job and provides a checklist of general information for use by the stripper or others in the prepress department.

Jog: To align a stack of paper so that all edges are even.

Joint Photographic Experts Group (JPEG): This compression scheme, based on the discrete cosine transform (DCT) lossy compression algorithm, is a standard on the Internet. JPEG allows the user to control the compression ratio and reproduction quality at the point of compression. It can also incorporate other algorithms, such as one-dimensional modified Huffman compression for lossless compression.

Journeyman: A member of the printing trades who has completed an apprenticeship and is considered fully qualified.

Justify: To adjust letter-spacing and word-spacing so that lines of type in a block are all equal in length, resulting in even left and right margins.

K

Kerning: A typesetting technique in which space between certain pairs of characters is tightened to improve appearance and readability.

Keyboard: The input device commonly found at a variety of workstations (computers, typesetters, etc.).

Kilobyte (Kb): A unit composed of 1024 bytes, often used to designate computer file length.

Kilogram: The standard unit of mass in the SI Metric system.

Kilometer: The standard unit of length in the SI Metric system.

Knockout: Clean break between design elements.

L

Laminating: Process in which thin film of plastic with an adhesive coating is bonded to a printed substrate to provide protection against abrasion and moisture.

Laser plates: Carriers that are imaged digitally by a laser platemaking system.

Lateral reversal: A duplicate created when the emulsion of the copy film and the original are facing each other.

Layers: In image editing programs, a method used to create multiple levels of artwork in the same document. The layers can be thought of as clear acetate sheets stacked on top of each other. Each sheet contains one or more objects. Where there are no objects, the layer is transparent and you can see through it to the layer below.

Layout: The sketch or plan for the finished page followed by a pasteup artist when assembling a mechanical.

Layout base sheet: The pasteup surface or board used in layout.

Layout table: A precision piece of equipment used for arranging and locating the type, illustrations, and line art that compose a flat. It often has lineup devices capable of making micrometer adjustments. Also called a *lineup table.*

Leading: The vertical distance separating each line of typeset copy, measured in points from one line to the next. (Pronounced *"ledding."*)

Legibility: A measure of how difficult or easy it is to read printed matter.

Lempel-Ziv-Welch (LZW): Lossless data compression technique in which adjacent bits are replaced with codes of varying lengths.

Lensboard: The support that holds the lens in alignment with the optical axis of the camera.

Lensboard controls: Controls used for positioning the lensboard and making other adjustments to the lens on process cameras.

Letterpress: See *Relief printing.*

Letterspacing: Changing the spacing between typeset letters, for better appearance or to fit copy in a given space.

Lifelong learning: Upgrading and updating one's job skills and knowledge to keep pace with technological changes in a field.

Lift: Term describing a pile of paper, usually the amount cut or drilled in a single operation.

Ligatures: Joined letter combinations, such as *fi, ff, fl, ffi,* or *ffl,* found in some typefaces.

Light elements: The hairlines or other less-dark strokes that tie together the heavy elements of a type character.

Light integrator: A device used to regulate the intensity and the length of an exposure according to a predetermined setting. It controls the amount of light striking the film.

Light table: A working surface used in layout for the placement of transparent images.

Light spectrum: The electromagnetic wavelengths visible to the human eye.

Lignin: A glue-like substance that bonds wood fibers together.

Line art: A drawing with no grays or middletones. Traditionally, black lines on white paper. In computer publishing, an object-oriented graphic. While scanned-in line art is bitmapped, line art created (mathematically) in the computer is a vector, or object-oriented graphic.

Line gauge: A device used to measure type sizes and line lengths in picas or inches.

Line length: The distance from the left to right sides of a line or body of copy, usually measured in picas. Also called *line width.*

Line spacing: See *Leading.*

Lines: Design elements that form the shapes of an image.

Lines per inch (lpi): The screen ruling is the number of ruled *lines per inch (lpi)* on a halftone screen.

Linotype: The most common type of mechanical linecasting machine. It permitted the compositor to use a keyboard to quickly assemble brass letter molds, or matrices, then cast an entire line of type. After the line was cast, the matrices were automatically distributed into storage channels for reuse.

Liquid lamination: A coating method similar to varnishing. The plastic coating material is applied in liquid form and then cured into a tough protective layer by exposure to ultraviolet light. Also called *UV-cured coating.*

Liter: The standard unit of capacity in the metric system.

Lithography: A method of printing directly from a flat surface or plate containing an image formed in ink.

Livered: A chemical change in the body of an ink that occurs during storage.

Lockout device: A key or combination-type lock used to hold an energy isolating device in the safe position to prevent the machine from energizing.

Lookup tables: Chart stored in computer memory that lists the dot sizes needed to produce given colors.

Loose register: Alignment used when copy does not need to be positioned with extreme accuracy, such as images that are next to each other but printed in different colors.

Loose-set: Term describing wider than normal letterspacing.

Lossless algorithm: A mathematical formula for image compression that assumes that the likely value of a pixel can be inferred from the values of surrounding pixels. Because lossless compression algorithms do not discard any of the data, the decompressed image is identical to the original.

Lossless compression: Refers to data compression techniques in which no data is lost. The PKZIP compression technology is an example of lossless compression. For most types of data, lossless compression techniques can reduce the space needed by only about 50%.

Lossy algorithm: A mathematical formula for image compression in which the data in an image that is least perceptible to the eye is removed. This improves the speed of data transfer but causes a slight degradation in the decompressed image.

Lossy compression: Refers to data compression techniques in which some amount of data is lost. Lossy compression technologies attempt to eliminate redundant or unnecessary information. Most video compression technologies, such as JPEG, use a lossy compression.

Low-key photograph. Contains primarily shadows, or darker tones.

Lowercase: The smaller, body-type letters in a typeface. In abbreviated form, usually noted as "lc."

lpi: See *Lines per inch.*

Ludlow: A type of linecasting machine that was used primarily to set larger point sizes for use as display type.

M

Machine guards: Metal or plastic enclosures that cover moving machine parts and protect the operator from being cut, squashed, or hit by flying fragments. Guards also protect the equipment from foreign objects.

Macintosh: A computer platform introduced by Apple in 1984. The Macintosh achieved popularity rapidly because of its ease of use and ability to generate high-quality graphic images.

Macula: A small hollow in the middle of the retina of the eye. The cones are concentrated in the macula and diminish in concentration toward the edges of the retina.

Magnetic disk: A disk is a round plate on which data can be encoded. On a magnetic disk, data is encoded as microscopic magnetized needles on a disk's surface. You can record and erase data on a magnetic disk any number of times. Magnetic disks come in a number of different forms, including *hard* and *floppy*.

Magneto-optical (MO) drive: Disk drive that combines magnetic disk technologies with CD-ROM technologies. Like magnetic disks, MO disks can be read, written to, and removed. However, their storage capacity can be more than 200 megabytes. In terms of data access speed, they are faster than floppies and CD-ROMs, but not as fast as hard disk drives.

Magnetography: Printing technology that converts an electronic image to a magnetic charge on a drum that then attracts magnetized toner. Because the toners are dark and opaque, magnetography is suited for spot color but not process color.

Magnifiers: Viewing devices for inspecting small areas on images. The 8× and 10× magnifiers are common.

Main exposure: The primary exposure made through a halftone screen to produce a halftone negative. Its main purpose is to reproduce the highlight, midtone, and shadow details of the original.

Main exposure test: An exposure used to determine the main exposure for a specific camera, halftone screen, and type of film. It is usually two to three times a normal line shot of a reflection density guide, or gray scale.

Main memory: Type of computer memory that can be accessed randomly. That is, any byte of memory can be accessed without touching the preceding bytes. It is the most common type of memory found in computers and other devices such as printers. Commonly referred to as *RAM*.

Makeup: Assembling all images into a completed page.

Manuscript: A style of hand lettering used by the scribes of Germany, France, Holland, and other countries in the Middle Ages.

Masking film: A material with a thin ruby- or amber-colored emulsion on a thicker sheet of clear plastic. The colored emulsion blocks light, creating a clear area when a film negative is exposed. For this reason, it is used to make windows, solid areas, color overlays, and dropouts during pasteup. Unwanted colored areas are cut with an art knife and peeled off. The remaining color film is positioned on an overlay for the mechanical.

Masking sheet: A type of base material used to support photographic materials when preparing a flat.

Masks: In image editing programs, a method used to isolate an area to keep it from being affected while applying color changes, filters, or other effects to the rest of the image. Semitransparent masks enable the user to partially affect an area of an image.

Mass: A measure of volume that adds definition to shapes in a visual presentation.

Master page: A page composition program feature that can be set up to include the page geometry, typography, and other elements of a page that will recur in a document. Several different master pages may be used within a single document.

Matchprint proofs: Industry-standard contract proof produced from the actual film that will create the printing pages. This enables accurate evaluation of the film for trapping, moiré, and other conventional printing problems.

Material Safety Data Sheet (MSDS): A document, produced by a chemical manufacturer, that summarizes the physical properties of a particular chemical and the health and safety hazards associated with its use.

Matrix: A mold used with molten metal to produce individual pieces of foundry type. In molded-rubber platemaking, a phenolic resin mold that captures the details of the original plate.

Maximum resolution: Maximum number of pixels that a computer screen can represent in both horizontal and vertical dimensions.

Mechanical: A completed page of type on photographic paper and illustrations, adhered to a base sheet, that is used to produce a photographic negative. The negative, in turn, is used to produce a printing plate.

Mechanical binding: A broad category that includes many different devices used to hold sheets together. An example is *loose-leaf binding*.

Mechanical shading: A form of line art that requires more attention because of the fine details and intricate nature of the images. Like line art, it will contrast the image and nonimage areas by the use of only light colors (white) and dark colors (black). Includes tints, textures, and some coarse or stippling airbrush techniques.

Megabyte: One million bytes, usually abbreviated Mb.

Memory: Internal storage in a computer that comes in the form of chips (integrated circuits).

Menu: A display on the monitor that allows the operator to select functions using the mouse or keyboard.

Mercury vapor lamp: Light source that produces radiation by passing an electrical current through gaseous mercury. At one time, these lamps were the primary means of exposing sensitive printing plates.

Mesh count: The number of threads (or strands) per linear inch in a fabric.

Mesh-bridging capability: The ability of a stencil to bridge diagonally across an individual fabric cell.

Metal halide lamp: Mercury lamp that has metal halide additives.

Metric conversion chart: A table of equivalencies used to convert US Conventional and metric values from one system to another.

Metric prefixes: Word prefixes that indicate multiples or divisions of measuring units in the metric system.

Metric system: The most commonly used system of weights and measures in the world, recognized as the international standard.

Midtones: Tones with gray values. Also referred to as *middle tones*.

Minus leading: See *Negative leading*.

Misregistration: Printing problem that occurs when two overprinted images or color elements do not align.

Misting: Condition that occurs when a fine spray of ink is produced by the movement of the ink rollers on a press.

Modem: A device used with a computer to send and receive files electronically over telephone lines.

Moiré pattern: A visually undesirable dot-exaggerating effect that occurs when two different screen patterns are randomly positioned or superimposed.

Molleton cover: A cloth tube that fits over the body of a dampening roller and helps it retain fountain solution.

Monochromatic colorimeter: Color measurement device that does not measure types of color but more specifically measures the intensity of a particular color. Unlike the *trichromatic colorimeter*, it does not depend on the perception of color by the eye.

Monochromatic: A single color or shades of a single color.

Monofilament: Consisting of a single strand of material; one thread.

Monotype: A composing machine that produced individual cast letters, rather than a line of type. This was a two-part system with a keyboard and a separate metal caster.

Mottling: A blotchy or cloudy appearance of an image instead of a smooth, continuous appearance.

Mouse: A hand-held device used to position the cursor on the computer screen.

Movable type: Individual type characters, usually cast in metal, that can be assembled into words, then later taken apart and reassembled into different words. The term was used, beginning in the 1400s, to distinguish this typesetting method from block printing, in which the message to be printed was carved as a unit onto a wood block.

Multifilament: Made up of several strands of material.

Multiple master font: Adobe System that allows a user to create variations on a base design. Each multiple master font consists of the *base font* (the multiple master font itself) and one or more *instances* of the font.

Multiple-page imposition: Assembling line and halftone images to form several pages.

Munsell system: Color system that identifies color's three attributes as *hue, value,* and *chroma* (HVC). The vertical dimension is called value, the circumferential dimension is called hue, and the radial dimension is called chroma. Chroma indicates the intensity or strength of a color and its saturation. The colors are spaced at subjectively equal visual distances.

N

Nanometer: Measuring unit used for electromagnetic wavelengths. The nanometer is equal to one billionth of a meter.

Narrow-band filter: A filter used in color separation process to reproduce only pure colors. Also referred to as a *monochromatic filter.*

Near-complementary color: A color that harmonizes with colors that lie next to its complement on the color wheel. Such as red with blue-green or yellow-green.

Negative leading: The practice of reducing spacing below the type size resulting in lines that are set very close together vertically.

Negative-working: A film that responds to light by increasing density as exposure increases. Exposed areas are black after development.

Network: A computer system that allows exchange of data between workstations.

Newspaper printing: A segment of the graphic communications industry that involves publishing and printing daily or weekly newspapers.

Newton's rings: Undesirable color patterns that result from interference between the exposure light and its reflected beam from the closely adjacent surface. Commonly referred to as "Newton rings."

Nip point: The point of contact where two cylinders, gears, or rollers meet or come close to one another.

Noise: Unwanted electronic or optical signals that cause interference in the reproduction of data or images.

Nonimaging: The term which indicates that the exposure affects the entire emulsion surface uniformly and does *not* record the original image or copy.

Nonimpact printing: An electronic device that places an image on a substrate without touching it.

Nonpareil: Measuring unit on a line gauge that is equal to one-half pica. A pica is equal to 0.166"; a nonpareil is 0.083".

Novelty: A typeface designed primarily to command special attention, express a mood, or provide a specific appearance for a theme or an occasion. Also called "decorative" or "occasional" typefaces.

Numbering: The process of imprinting tickets, certificates, checks, or other items with consecutive figures (numbers), using a device that transfers the figures from an inked relief image.

O

Object-oriented: Term that is generally used to describe a system that deals primarily with different types of objects, and where the action you can take depends on what type of object you are manipulating. For example, an object-oriented draw program may allow you to draw many types of objects such as circles, squares, or triangles. Applying the same action to these objects, however, would produce different results. If the action applied were to make the objects three-dimensional, for instance, the result would be a sphere, a box, and a pyramid, respectively.

Object-oriented images: Images that are produced by a draw program. They are able to be defined in terms of mathematical parameters (*Bezier curves*), giving the artist or designer control over shape, placement, line width, and pattern. Because the object is defined geometrically, shapes will not break up when enlarged or reduced.

Oblique: In electronic composition, the term used to describe a simulated italic character produced by slanting an upright Roman typeface.

OCR (optical character recognition): System used to translate the bitmap image of text created by a scanner into ASCII characters.

Off color: When the color of the printed job does not match the intended color.

Off-contact distance: Position of the screen slightly above the substrate. The squeegee is drawn across the screen, exerting pressure on the stencil and bringing it in contact with the substrate.

Offset printing: A printing method in which inked images are offset or transferred from one surface to another.

Oil mounting: Method in which transparent originals are coated with a small amount of mounting oil or gel to reduce scratches and imperfections before mounting on the drum of a drum scanner.

Old English: A text typeface often used for such applications as diplomas, certificates, and religious materials.

Oldstyle Roman: A group of typefaces that have a rugged appearance, with relatively little contrast between heavy and light elements. They reflect the earliest Roman designs.

On-demand printing: Short-run, distributed, just-in-time printing, no matter how it is produced.

Opacity: The quality of a paper that does not allow print from the opposite side to show through. See *Show-through.*

Opaque: To apply a red or black nontransparent pigment to pinholes in negatives to prevent unwanted light from passing through while burning a plate.

Open press interface (OPI): An industry-standard convention that defines how to embed instructions in a PostScript output file to tell the RIP and/or server where and how to merge the various text and graphics components of a page. OPI enables the user to work with low-resolution preview images in the page-makeup programs, and keep the high-resolution graphic images closer to the output device. This maximizes workstation productivity and minimizes network traffic.

Optical character readers (OCR): Equipment that scans, interprets, and converts any copy or graphic elements to a machine-readable format.

Optical character recognition (OCR): Technique in which any printed, typed, or handwritten copy or graphic images are scanned by an electronic reader that converts the information into a form that can be read, interpreted, and displayed by computers.

Optical density: Light-stopping or light absorption ability of an image or surface material.

Optical disk drives: Drive that uses a laser to read and write to optical disks.

Optical disks: Storage medium from which data is read and written to by lasers. Types of optical disks include *CD-ROMs, WORM, erasable (EO)*, and *CD-RWs*.

Optical scanner: See *Scanner.*

Original plate: In relief printing, the original type form of composed characters, used directly for printing or to make a duplicate plate.

Orthochromatic film: Film that is sensitive to a wide range of the spectrum but not sensitive to red. Therefore, a red bulb is used as the safelight in the darkroom when handling orthochromatic films. Also referred to as *ortho films.*

Out-of-register: Term that refers to images that are visibly out of alignment due to layout error or misalignment during printing.

Outline font: See *Vector font.*

Output device: A piece of equipment used to display or transfer information processed by a computer. Monitors and printers are examples.

Outsourcing: Sending a product to a service company for specified work needed to complete a product.

Overhead horizontal camera: A horizontal process camera that has the camera bed and copyboard attached to the overhead framework.

Overlay: A transparent or translucent sheet attached to the mechanical base sheet. It is often the base for the second color material.

Overprinting: When image elements are specified to be printed over or on top of other colors.

Overrun: Number of copies that have been run above the requested amount.

P

Packing: The material used to apply the proper pressure for printing.

Page composition: The process of properly arranging the various elements or components (such as type and illustrations) that will make up a printed page. Also called *page layout.*

Page composition program: Program that enables the user to format pages of text and graphics. Also referred to as *page layout program.*

Page count: The number of pages in a printed job.

Page description language (PDL): In an electronic publishing system, a format for describing the layout and contents of a page and the page's position within the larger document. Both PostScript and more modern versions of PCL are object-oriented, meaning that they describe a page in terms of geometrical objects such as lines, arcs, and circles. Alternative terms: *page descriptor, document descriptor.*

Page layout: See *Page composition.*

Pagemaker™: Popular page composition program.

Paint: Feature of image manipulation programs that allows the user to create and color images. Various tools also allow the user to fill in and erase colors, as well as assign and adjust color values and gradations.

Paint program: Software that allows the creation and limited editing of bit-mapped images. More extensive manipulation of these images is usually done with image editing software.

Palette: In some computer software, a modified form of menu that can be resized and positioned on the screen to suit the operator's preferences. When displayed, it will always remain visible, overlaying any other images on the screen. Also, the finite set of distinct colors that can be displayed by a video, printing, or computer system. See *Color gamut.*

Panchromatic film: Film that has color sensitivity closest to the human eye. This film will reproduce the total range of the visible spectrum. Also referred to as *pan film.*

Paper caliper: A device used to measure paper thickness.

Paper flatness: How well a sheet of paper remains straight or unwarped for feeding through a sheet-fed press.

Paper sizes: Measurements that describe the length and width dimensions of paper. Sizes are expressed in inches or metric units.

Parallax error: An illusion resulting from an apparent shift in alignment due to a change in the viewing angle.

Partnership: A form of business organization with two or more owners. Partners may or may not share ownership equally.

Paste-up method: The traditional means of preparing a mechanical by adhering page elements to a base sheet.

Pasteboard: Area of the display screen that is used in page composition programs for temporary storage of layout elements (such as a piece of art or a section of typeset material) before moving them onto the page.

PCMCIA (Personal Computer Memory Card International Association) cards: Removable storage medium originally designed for adding memory to portable computers. The PCMCIA standard has been expanded several times and the cards are now suitable for use with many types of devices, including digital cameras and scanners. Also known as *PC cards* or *digital film.*

Percent open area: Percentage of area per square inch in a fabric through which ink can pass.

Percent stretch: A technique for measuring screen tension that entails taking very accurate measurements before and during tensioning.

Perfect binding: Method that uses an adhesive to hold sheets or signatures together and to fasten the flexible cloth or paper cover onto the body. Also called *softcover binding.*

Perfecting press: A printing system that prints both sides of the substrate at once.

Perforating: Operation that places a series of small cuts or slits in the substrate, using various types of blades or wheels on the press or folder.

Periodical printing: That segment of the graphic communications industry consisting of plants that are designed primarily to print magazines.

Personal protective devices: Clothing or equipment worn for protection from potential bodily injury associated with chemical use or machine operation. Devices worn in graphic communication plants include safety glasses, face shields, plastic or rubber gloves, earplugs, dust masks, respirators, and safety shoes.

Petrochemicals: Petroleum-based chemicals.

pH scale: A measuring scale used to determine the acidity or alkalinity of a solution. The pH scale is numbered from 0-14, with 7 designated as neutral. A pH value below 7 indicates an acidic solution; a value above 7 indicates an alkaline solution.

pH value: A measurement that indicates the acidity or alkalinity of a solution, as measured on the pH scale.

Phantom halftone: A technique using a diffusion transfer receiver sheet and two exposed negative sheets, where a weak halftone image is created and type or another image overprinted. Also referred to as *ghost halftone.*

Phosphor: Chemicals, coated on the inside of video monitor screens, which emit light when stimulated by electrons coming from the cathode.

Photo CD™: File format for storing digital photographs developed by Eastman Kodak Co. See *Compact disk.*

Photo cropping: A method of indicating what portion of the print is to be used or reproduced.

Photo direct plates: Image carriers that are imaged directly from camera-ready copy or a paste-up.

Photo-density range: The density difference between the highlight value and shadow value. Also referred to as *copy-density range.*

Photocomposing: The most common form of cold composition, using a phototypesetting machine.

Photocomposition: The generation of type using photographic paper or film exposed to light.

Photoconversion: The general term for processes that use light to place the original image onto a light-sensitive material. It includes the use of process cameras to make negatives and screened (halftone) images, digital cameras and scanners used for image capture, and exposure units for platemaking.

Photoengraving: A platemaking method that produces relief images by exposing a light-sensitive plate coating through a negative.

Photopolymer plates: Plastic relief plates commonly used in flexographic printing. The surface of a photopolymer plate contains a light-sensitive polymer coating that hardens after exposure.

Photographic masking: Method of color manipulation that is accomplished by creating film images from an original using filters.

Photomechanical transfer (PMT): See *Diffusion transfer.*

Photometer: Instrument for measuring luminous intensity, luminous flux, illumination, or brightness.

Photometry: Branch of science that deals with measurement of the intensity of light. Also the practice of using a *photometer.*

Photomultiplier tubes (PMTs): Light-sensing tubes composed of highly sensitive photocells that transform variations in light into electric currents. The photocells create the input signals to the computing circuits in electronic scanners.

Photopigments: Light-sensitive chemicals in the cones of the human eye. Photopigments respond to red, green, or blue light.

Photopolymer plates: Relief printing plates made of flexible plastic cured by UV light.

Photosites: The hundreds or thousands of photosensitive elements of a CCD. Also known as *well sites.*

Pi characters: In fonts for computer or phototypesetting, such symbols as stars, asterisks, arrows, percent signs, or checkmarks. In foundry type, such special characters are called sorts or dingbats.

Pica: One of the principal units of measure used in the graphic communications industry. A pica is equal to 0.166″. Six picas almost equals one inch (0.996″).

Picking: The lifting of paper fibers caused by the tackiness of ink during the printing process.

PICT file format: File format developed by Apple Computer. PICT files are encoded in QuickDraw commands and can hold both object-oriented images and bitmapped images.

Picture box: In QuarkXPress, a closed figure of any shape (from rectangular to freeform) used to position an illustration.

Pigments: Colorants in the form of fine, solid particles that do not dissolve but spread through liquids or other substances. They have varying degrees of resistance to water, alcohol, and other chemicals and are generally insoluble in the ink vehicle.

Pinholes: Imperfections on a photographic negative or stencil caused by dust and other airborne contaminants.

Pixel: Acronym for "picture element," the tiniest image component in a digital imaging or display system. On a computer monitor (CRT) screen, pixels are equivalent to the tiny dots of phosphor (arranged in rows and columns) that glow to display the image.

Pixel swapping: Trading the pixels of one area with pixels in another.

Pixelize: The electronic function by which pixel size can be increased to enable easy manipulation in creating special effects.

PKZIP: Lossless data compression technique. Files are often referred to as zip files and decompressing them is called unzipping. Files that have been compressed with PKZIP usually end with a .ZIP extension. Zip files that end with an .EXE extension are self-extracting files which can be unzipped simply by opening the file.

Plastic comb binding: A mechanical binding method commonly used for booklets that might have to be altered by adding or removing pages. Books bound with this method permit the pages to lay perfectly flat when open.

Plate: An image carrier used for printing multiple copies on a press.

Plate bend allowance: A portion of the leading edge of the plate that is inserted into a plate-holding device.

Plate coatings: Layers of light-sensitive material on the surface of plates that form or harden when exposed to light.

Plate coverings: Layers of material bonded to the plate base material, used to help hold the image area in place.

Plate cylinder: A printing system component that holds the plate on the press.

Plate elongation: The physical stretching of an image carrier when mounted on the plate cylinder, which may distort images and text.

Plate grain: The surface texture of a plate base.

Plate wear: The wearing away of the surface of a plate by coarse particles in the ink.

Platen press: A relief press that prints by pressing a type form or plate against a platen, the surface that holds the paper to be printed.

Platesetter: The platemaking component of a computer-to-plate (CTP) system, used to image plates containing paginated text and graphics.

Platform: The *platform* of an electronic imaging system is the computer system, or *hardware*, that is used to operate the *software*. The platform defines the standard around which a system can be developed. Popular platforms include the PC (IBM personal computer) and the Apple Macintosh.

PMT: See *Photomultiplier tubes.*

Point: One of the principal units of measure used in the graphic communications industry. A point is equal to 0.0138″. Twelve points equal one pica.

Point size: A vertical measurement used to identify or specify the size of a typeface. Measurement is from the top of the ascender space to the bottom of the descender space.

Point system: The system of print measurement used throughout the graphic communications industry in the United States. The standard units in the point system are the point and pica.

Point-and-shoot camera: Digital camera that is usually highly-automated.

Polymerization: A chemical reaction that occurs when UV light strikes an ink, converting the ink from a liquid to a solid.

Portable document format (PDF): A file format developed by Adobe Systems for representing documents in a manner that is independent of the original application software, hardware, and operating system used to create those documents. A PDF file can describe documents containing any combination of text, graphics, and images independently of output device or resolution. It is ideal for delivering entire documents over electronic mail, the World Wide Web, CD-ROM, or other media.

Positive-working: A film that responds to light by decreasing density as exposure increases. Exposed areas are clear after development.

Postconsumer paper waste: Used paper products that have served their intended purpose and are separated from solid waste for recycling into new paper.

Posterization: The technique of changing a black-and-white, continuous tone picture into a multicolor or multitone reproduction.

PostScript™: See *Adobe Postscript.*

PostScript language: A programming language commonly referred to as page description language, that has been adopted as a de facto standard by the graphic arts industry. Developed by Adobe Systems, the PostScript language differs from other programming languages as it was specially designed for describing text and graphics on a printed page.

PostScript printer typeface file: One of two component files used for printing PostScript Type 1 fonts.

PostScript Type 1 fonts: See *Type 1 fonts.*

ppi: Pixels per inch.

Preconsumer paper waste: Scrap material generated by the papermaking process.

Preflighting: The process of checking documents for completeness in order to avoid unnecessary or unsuccessful processing steps. Missing fonts, missing graphics and images, and PostScript errors are detected early in production to avoid wasted resources and time.

Prepress: The production steps that are carried out prior to printing.

Prescreened images: Camera copy that already contains a screen or dot pattern. Also referred to as a *preprinted halftone.*

Presensitized plate: An image carrier that has been coated with a light-sensitive material.

Preservative: A chemical that stops oxidation of the developing agent. A typical preservative is sodium sulfite.

Press proofs: Proof generated with a *proof press*. One of the best verification proofs; also very slow and expensive.

Pressrun: Operating the press to print the designated number of copies.

Pricing guides: Printed reference sources that provide printers with average cost information as an aid to developing estimates.

Primary colors: Colors that can be used to generate secondary colors. In the additive system, these colors are red, green, and blue (RGB). In the subtractive system, these colors are cyan, magenta, and yellow (CMY). On the color wheel, the colors are red, green, and yellow.

Principles of design: The basic guidelines used by a design artist. The principles of design are balance, contrast, unity, rhythm, and proportion.

Print engine: A small computer inside a laser printer that translates the output of the computer into a bit-mapped image for printing.

Print strength: How well a paper surface resists lifting of its fiber by high-tack inks. Also called *pick strength.*

Printability: How well fine details are reproduced in a printed image.

Printing system: A group of cylinders used to transfer images from the printing plate to the substrate. In a lithographic press, the printing system consists of a plate cylinder, a blanket cylinder, and an impression cylinder.

Printing: A process involving the use of a specialized machine (a *printing press*) to transfer an image from an image carrier to a substrate, usually paper. Most often, printing involves making duplicates (the printed product) in large quantities.

Printing estimate: An offer to print a particular job for a specified amount.

Process camera: Device used to make enlargements, reductions, and same-size reproductions of originals for use in page composition or stripping work. The camera may be used to produce a *film negative* (opposite original), a *film positive* (film like original), or a *print* (photo like original).

Process color printing: The printed reproduction of full-color photographs using the transparent inks of cyan, magenta, yellow, and black (CMYK).

Process colors: The three ink colors (cyan, magenta, and yellow) used for printing full color materials. Black ink is usually used as well.

Processing sink: Sink in a photographic darkroom used to hold the trays of chemicals during manual processing of film.

Processing trays: Stainless steel or plastic trays of various sizes that hold the chemicals for manually processing film.

Processor: A machine for developing photopaper. It uses chemicals to make the image on the paper or film visible and permanent.

Productivity: The amount of quality work completed in a given time span.

Profit: In business, the amount of money remaining after subtracting costs from income.

Proof: A prototype of the printed job made photomechanically from plates (a press proof), photochemically from film and dyes, or digitally from electronic data (prepress proofs). Prepress proofs serve as samples for the customer and guides for the press operators. Press proofs are approved by the customer and/or plant supervisor before the actual pressrun.

Proof press: Printing machine used to produce photomechanical proofs. It has most of the elements of a true production machine but is not meant for long press runs.

Proofreader's marks: Widely used symbols that show when something in typeset copy is to be taken out, added, or changed.

Proofreading: Process of checking for typesetting errors and marking them for correction.

Proportion: The relationship between elements in an image.

Proportional scale: A measuring device used to determine the correct reproduction percentage for the enlargement or reduction of images.

Protective coating: A material that helps keep a film emulsion from being scratched and marred while being handled.

Pulp: The soft, spongy substance produced by the chemical or mechanical breakdown of cellulose fibers for use in papermaking.

Pulpers: Vats in which coloring or bleaching additives are added to pulp.

Pulsed xenon lamp: The primary light source found in graphic communication facilities. These lamps are an excellent light source with spectral output close to daylight.

Punches: Mechanisms that are used to make holes in perfect alignment on the masking sheet and the plate.

Punching: Piercing operation done by forcing a metal rod (a punch) down through the paper to remove stock. The punch works in a shearing action with a *die* placed below the paper. Compare with *drilling*.

Purple line or purple boundary: On the CIE chromaticity diagram, the line formed after connecting the *spectrum locus* curve endpoints. Colors on this line are mixtures of pure 380 nm (violet) and 770 nm (red) light.

Q

Quad: A term used to designate the spacing between letters or words.

Quantization: Lossy compression technique; filtering process that determines the amount and selection of data to eliminate, making it possible to encode the data with fewer bits.

QuarkXPress™: Popular page composition program.

Quartz-iodine lamp: An incandescent lamp with a tungsten filament surrounded by iodine and inert gases, all enclosed in a quartz bulb.

Quick printing: A subdivision of commercial printing, consisting of shops specializing in rapidly completing short-run printing and photocopying work for business customers.

Quoins: Expanding metal locking devices used to wedge a type form and furniture in place in a chase.

R

RAID (Redundant Array of Independent Disks): The RAID configuration connects a number of high-capacity hard disk drives together to act as a single huge hard drive. It provides increased storage capacity, file-access speeds, and data-transfer rates, varying degrees of data protection, and failure-proofing the storage subsystem.

Random access memory (RAM): Type of computer memory that can be accessed randomly. That is, any byte of memory can be accessed without touching the preceding bytes. It is the most common type of memory found in computers and other devices such as printers.

Rapid access film: One type of film used to make negatives with the process camera. It is also used to produce contact negatives and film positives.

Raster: An image composed of a set of horizontal scan lines that are formed sequentially by writing each line following the previous line, particularly on a television screen or computer monitor.

Raster graphics: Images that use a grid of small squares (pixels) to represent graphics. The image is represented as rows and columns of dots on this grid. The value of each dot is stored in one or more bits of data. Each pixel is encoded as a single binary digit. Also referred to as *bitmap*.

Raster image processor (RIP): The device that interprets all of the page layout information for the marking engine of the imagesetter. PostScript or another page description language serves as an interface between the page layout workstation and the RIP.

Rasterization: The process of converting mathematical and digital information into a series of dots by an imagesetter for the production of negative or positive film.

Rasterize: To convert image data into a pattern of dots (pixels) for the production of film.

Readability: See *Legibility*.

Reader: Member of a two-person proofreading team who follows the camera-ready copy, a printout, or computer display.

Ream: Five hundred sheets of paper.

Receiver sheet: Material used to receive an image from the negative during the diffusion transfer process.

Recording film: Film that has been developed to be used with imagesetters and scanners. This film creates very sharp stochastic and/or halftone dots. It also creates sharp line images.

Recycled paper: Paper made from old or used paper products.

Reduction: Process used when the original copy is larger than the final work.

Reference image: Color reference tool used to calibrate input and output devices. See also *IT8 reflective target*.

Reflected beam: A beam of light after it has bounced off a surface.

Reflection copy: An original that will reflect different amounts of light from the different tone values of the original. Examples are photographs, oil paintings, chalk or charcoal renderings, and watercolor work.

Reflection densitometer: Instrument used to accurately determine different tone values, such as the highlights and shadows of an original. See *Densitometer*.

Reflection densitometer: A device that reads reflected light to measure the density of an image.

Reflection density guide: Measuring instrument used to visually compare the example density to the image density. It has precalibrated density steps that are assigned a numerical value, which represent the photo-density range. Also referred to as *gray scale*. See *Photo-density range*.

Reflex paper: A light-sensitive material that is used for making a same-size, positive proof of an original copy without the use of a process camera.

Refresh rate: The speed with which the screen is redrawn. The refresh rate controls the amount of detectable screen *flicker*.

Register marks: Control devices that assure the proper positioning of overlays on the base sheet of a mechanical.

Register pins: Fasteners used to hold punched flats for stripping.

Register unit: A feeding system mechanism that places paper in register for printing on a press.

Registration: The proper alignment of images on a press sheet or printing plate.

Reglets: Thin pieces of wooden furniture placed around a metal type form, used to eliminate small amounts of space in a chase.

Regulator: A device that controls voltage in a process camera to keep it constant.

Relief printing: The process of printing from a raised surface. Ink is applied to the raised image, then transferred to the paper or other substrate. *Letterpress* and *flexography* are both relief printing processes.

Removable cartridge devices: Hard disk drive that is removable.

Repeat length: Distance equal to one revolution of a press cylinder.

Repurposing: Reusing content intended for one medium by reformatting it for another. Examples include the application of content originally used for printed materials to CD-ROM, Web pages, and corporate intranets.

Resolution: An image's sharpness or clarity; the number of pixels per unit of linear measurement on a video display or the number of dots per inch (dpi) in printed form.

Restrainer: A chemical in the developing solution that is added to lessen the fogging tendency of film.

Retarders: Solvents added to ink to change (thin) the viscosity and (retard) slow the drying time.

Retina: A layer of light-sensitive cells at the back of the eye. When light reaches the eye, it is focused onto the retina.

Retouching: Tools used in image manipulation programs to modify images in ways similar to methods used in darkroom photography. For example, the user is able to *dodge* areas that are too dark and lack detail, or *burn* areas to increase "exposure" to areas that are too light. Retouching tools also include features for adjusting color, contrast, hue, and saturation.

Reverse type: White characters on a solid black or color background.

RGB: See *Additive color*.

Rhythm: The use of elements in an image to create visual movement and direction.

Ribbons: Rows of pages engraved on a cylinder.

Robotics: The use of machines to do repetitive tasks, particularly in manufacturing.

Rods: Light-sensitive nerve cells of the retina that help us perceive light and color. There are about twelve million rods in the human eye. The rods detect light intensity and are most sensitive to black, white, and shades of gray.

Roman: A type style based on the capital letters cut into stone monuments by the ancient Romans. Nicolas Jenson developed Roman lowercase letters that would merge readily into word forms. Jenson's designs were the models used by type designers for hundreds of years.

Roomlight: The normal, full spectrum light found in areas other than a darkroom.

Rosettes: The pattern that is formed by color halftone images when printed in register.

Rotary press: A relief press that prints on paper as it travels between an impression cylinder and a plate cylinder.

Rotary scanner: See *Drum scanner.*

Rotofilm: A presensitized film on which an image is exposed. After development, the film is mounted on a gravure cylinder to serve as a mask during chemical etching. Seldom used today in the U.S.

Rotogravure: Another term for gravure printing, so named because the engraved cylinder rotates during printing.

Rough layout: A redrawn version of a thumbnail sketch, closely resembling the final layout.

Rubber plates: Flexible relief plates commonly used in flexographic printing.

Rubber stamp: A rubber plate with raised letters, usually used with an ink pad to manually print single images or short messages. It can be considered a form of relief printing.

Run length: The number of copies of a job that are to be printed.

Run-length encoding (RLE): Compression method that encodes digital data to reduce the amount of storage needed to hold the data without any loss of information. Each coded item consists of a data value and the number of adjacent pixels with the same data value (strings of the same character are encoded as a single number).

S

Saddle sewing: Binding process like saddle stitching, but done with thread instead of wire.

Saddle stitching: A method in which metal wire is forced through the folded edge of a signature and formed into staples to hold the pages together.

Safelights: Darkroom lights that have a limited spectral composition to avoid exposing (fogging) film.

Sans serif: The classification for typefaces without serifs (stroke endings). This typeface classification is second only to Roman in popularity. Sans serif typefaces usually have heavy and light elements that are approximately the same thickness.

Saturation: Attribute of color that defines its degree of strength or difference from white. It can also be defined as the extent to which one or two of the three RGB primaries predominates in a color.

Sawtoothing: A distortion in a design contours that causes a notched effect.

Scaleable font: See *Vector font*.

Scaling: The process of reducing or enlarging an image.

Scan area: Area of drum scanner (removable or stationary drum) or flatbed (glass bed or platen) scanner on which images are placed for scanning.

Scanner: Electronic imaging device that measures color densities of an original, stores those measurements as digital information, manipulates or alters the data, and uses the manipulated data to create four color separations. Scanners use either a CCD array or PMTs to capture the image as a raster or bitmapped graphic.

Scoring: A slight cut made in heavy stock before it is folded.

Screen angles: Angular relationships of line screens used in making color separations for four-color printing.

Screen flicker: Rapid changes in light intensity produced by a monitor screen.

Screen printing: A printing process that uses a squeegee to force ink through a porous fabric covered by a stencil that blocks the nonimage areas. The ink pressed through the open image areas produces the image on a substrate.

Screen ruling: The number of ruled grid lines per inch on a halftone screen.

Screen tint: Reproduction screen used to provide a tint percentage of a solid color.

Screens: Ruled screens used to change continuous tone photographs into dotted halftones for printing.

Script: A typeface, designed to simulate handwriting, in which the letters are joined.

SCSI (Small Computer Systems Interface): Standard used to identify cables used for data transmission.

Scumming: A condition in lithography when the nonimage areas of the plate begin to accept ink.

Secondary colors: Colors that are produced by mixing pairs of the primary colors. On the color wheel, they are identified as orange, green, and violet.

Selective compression: Reducing the size of certain parts or areas of a file for storage purposes or to enhance the speed of data transfer by eliminating the redundancies and other unnecessary elements from the original.

Self-cover binding: A term that describes using the same material for both the cover and body of the book. Self-cover books may be perfect bound, but are most often saddle stitched or side-stitched.

Sensitometry: The study and measurement of the sensitivity of photographic materials, in relationship to exposure and development.

Separation plates: Special outputs for each color on a page created by page composition software, similar in purpose to the physical overlays used in paste-up to prepare material for color printing.

Sequential-access: Reading or writing data records in sequential order; that is, one record after the other.

Serif: The thickened tips or short finishing-off strokes at the top and bottom of a Roman typeface character.

Set: The point at which an ink is dry enough to be lightly touched without smudging.

Set size: The width of a typeset character. Electronic composition makes it possible to change the set size of characters.

Setoff: A condition that results when wet ink on the press sheets transfers to the back of other sheets in a stack.

Shade: Gradation of color that results from adding black to a color. For example, if black is added to red, the color maroon is created. Maroon is a shade of red. In ink manufacture, shade is a common synonym for hue.

Shading film: A material similar to masking film, but with a patterned emulsion. Used to create patterned areas on the mechanical.

Shadows: Darkest parts of an image or photograph, represented as the largest dots in a halftone.

Shapes: Elementary forms that define specific areas of space.

Shear stick: A wood or plastic stick placed in a groove or channel on the table of a paper cutter. The stick helps to produce a sharp, clean cut.

Sheet separators: Air-producing devices that separate the top sheet from the rest of the pile in a feeding system.

Sheet-fed press: A lithographic press that prints paper one sheet at a time as it is fed through the system.

Sheetwise imposition: A printing layout that uses separate flats and plates to print the front and back of a single press sheet. Different pages appear on each side of the sheet.

Shingling: See *Creep*.

Show-through: An undesirable result of poor opacity in which the image on one side of a sheet of paper is seen on the other side.

Shrink-wrapping: A packaging method in which a stack of printed pieces is enclosed with a thin plastic in sheet form. The wrapped stack is heated, causing the plastic to shrink and form a tight, sealed package.

SI Metric: The modern version of the metric system, based on seven internationally recognized units of measure.

Side sewing: A binding method, similar to side stitching, but using threads rather than staples to bind sheets together.

Side stitching: A form of stapling in which metal wire is forced through sides of sheets and formed to hold sheets together.

Signatures: Folded sheets that form multiple-page sections of a book. Each signature contains four, eight, 16, or 32 pages.

Silverless materials: Light-sensitive materials that do not contain silver halides.

Simultaneous contrast: The property of the eye that causes the same color to look different when surrounded by or adjacent to other colors. A color will appear brighter if surrounded by dark colors, or darker when surrounded by light colors.

Single proprietorship: A business owned by one person.

Single-page imposition: Assembling line and halftone images to create a single page.

Sizing: Material, such as rosin, that is added to pulp slurry to make the paper stronger and more moisture-resistant.

Skeleton printer: A black printer that enhances detail and contrast in the midtones and shadows of a four-color separation.

Slitting: An operation similar to perforating that makes a continuous cut, rather than a series of slits. It is usually done by sharp-edged wheels that cut the stock as it passes through the folder.

Slug: An entire line of type produced by a hot metal typesetting machine. Slugs are more easily assembled into columns and pages for printing than individual pieces of type

Slurring: An unwanted accumulation of halftone dots, resulting in a smeared image. Slurring is commonly caused by slippage or improper contact between the cylinders at the time of impression.

Small caps: Capital letters smaller than the normal caps of the font.

Smoothing: Technique used by some printers to make curves look smoother. Most printers that support smoothing implement it by reducing the dot size of the dots that make up a curved line. Some printers can alter the horizontal alignment of dots to minimize jaggies. See *Aliasing, Antialiasing.*

Smoothness: Freedom from surface irregularities. As a quality of paper, smoothness affects the visibility of printed images.

Soft image: A loss of image that occurs when the outside edges of an image contain less density or tone quality than that of the inside portion of the image.

Software: The programs used to accomplish various tasks with a computer.

Sorts: See *Pi characters.*

Spacebands: Wedge-shaped devices that spread open as pressure is applied from the bottom, used to justify a line of matrices in a hot-metal linecasting machine.

Spatial resolution: The capability of a digital imaging device to address data in two dimensions—horizontal and vertical.

Specifications: The overall layout guidelines relating to such information as type style, type size, line width, color use, and page organization.

Specking: Tiny dots that appear near an image area, caused by paper fibers or other foreign material in the ink.

Spectrodensitometer: Color measuring instrument that serves all the functions of a spectrophotometer, densitometer, and colorimeter in one device. Besides measuring color value and optical density, many of these instruments can also be used to measure paper attributes and special colors.

Spectrophotometer: Instrument capable of measuring light of different colors or wavelengths. When used for measurement in the graphic communications industry, a spectrophotometer converts this data to CIE color specifications. Spectrophotometers are the most accurate type of color measurement device. A spectrophotometer uses a prism or diffraction grating to spread the light and slits to isolate narrow bands of light between 1 nm and 10 nm.

Spectrophotometric curves: Data from a spectrophotometer that provides a contour or envelope that describes the reflection or transmission characteristics of a sample. The spectrophotometric curve is the most precise means for specifying colors.

Spectrophotometry: The science of measuring color by analyzing the reflection or transmission of samples at specified points across the electromagnetic spectrum.

Spectrum: The series of color bands formed when a ray of light is dispersed by refraction; the rainbow-like display of colors resulting when a ray of white light is passed through a prism.

Spectrum locus: Horseshoe-shaped curve that results when the chromaticity coordinates of visible light are plotted on the CIE chromaticity diagram. By definition, since all visible colors comprise mixtures of these wavelengths, all visible colors must occur within the boundary formed by this curve.

Spellcheck: A feature of a word processing program, used to automatically check the spelling of each word in a document. Misspelled words can be corrected with one keystroke or mouse click.

Spiral binding: A mechanical binding method in which small round holes are punched through the pages and metal or plastic wire is spiral fed through them.

Split complementary color: Color that harmonizes with colors that lie next to its complement on the color wheel, such as red with blue-green or yellow-green.

Spontaneous combustion: Ignition by rapid oxidation without an external heat source.

Spot screening: Screening method in which dots are laid in a grid pattern based on the color tone. The spacing between the dot centers is held constant, but the dot size (amplitude) is varied to produce different shades or tones. Also known as *amplitude modulation.*

Spread: A print made in a contact printing frame that makes the original image slightly larger. The light source spreads out to expose more of the light-sensitive material. Also referred to as a *fatty.*

Spread trap: Trap created by spreading the foreground over the background color. Typically used when a lighter object is knocked out of a darker background.

Squeegee: A rubber or plastic blade used to force ink through the open areas of a screen-printing stencil.

Stabilization: A process in which the exposed photographic material is passed through two solutions; an activator and a stabilizer. The result is a permanent image on a photosensitive material. See *Activator* and *Stabilizer.*

Stabilizer: A solution used during stabilization process that dissolves the unexposed emulsion. It also acts as a fixer. See *Fixer.*

Stamping: The process of transferring a thin layer of metallic tone or color to a substrate, using heat and pressure. Also called *foil stamping.*

Star target: A quality control device used to detect slurring of ink.

Stem: The vertical part of the character.

Step tablet: See *Gray scale.*

Step-and-repeat: To expose the same image on a plate a number of times.

Step-off method: A method used to determine the basic main exposure, where various areas of a piece of film are exposed for different lengths of time. Also referred to as a *test exposure.*

Stereotype: A duplicate relief plate that is cast by pouring molten metal into a mold or mat made from the original type form of composed characters.

Still development: Development process that requires a period of about 45 seconds where no agitation takes place in the developing tray. This allows the shadow dot structure to develop faster than the highlight dot structure.

Stochastic screening: Halftone method that creates the illusion of tones by varying the number (frequency) of micro-sized dots (spots) in a small area. Unlike conventional halftone, the spots are not positioned in gridlike pattern. Instead, the placement of each spot is determined as a result of a complex algorithm that statistically evaluates and distributes spots under a fixed set of parameters. With first-order stochastic screening, both the number and size of dots vary. Also referred to as *FM dots* or *FM screening*.

Stock: Substrates to be printed.

Stop bath: An acetic acid rinse used to neutralize the developer solution remaining on the film. It is the second step of development.

Storage: Memory that exists on tapes or disks.

Straight matter: See *Body type*.

Stress: The slant or tilt of a character.

Strike-on composition: A simple and rapid means of generating camera-ready text, using a typewriter or similar device to print words on paper.

Strike-through: An ink-penetration problem that occurs when the ink soaks into the paper too deeply and shows through the opposite side of the sheet.

Stripper: The prepress professional responsible for *image assembly*.

Stripping: The physical assembly of film negatives and positives on a flat for platemaking. Also called *image assembly*.

Stripping table: An illuminated work surface that allows the stripper to clearly see the film.

Stroke: The thickness of a line forming a character element.

Studio camera: Digital camera characterized by high- or ultra-high resolution and excellent noninterpolated color rendition. Most of the high-end digital camera backs designed for commercial use fall into this category. These designs are most often based on trilinear scanning CCD arrays and single-array three- or four-exposure backs that make individual RGB exposures.

Style sheets: Formatting tools used in page composition programs that combine a number of attributes, such as type size, alignment, and other factors.

Stylus: A diamond cutting tool used to form the tiny ink wells on the metal surface of a gravure cylinder.

Subiaco face: An early version of the Roman typeface, used for several books and named for the town where the printing was done.

Substance weight: The actual weight of a ream of paper.

Substrate: Any material with a surface that can be printed or coated.

Subtractive color: The combining of inks in the colors cyan, magenta, yellow, and black to produce the printed image. Usually referred to as the *CMYK system*.

Subtractive primary colors: Cyan, magenta, and yellow (CMY).

Successive contrast: Color-vision effect that causes the viewer to see afterimages. After gazing for some time at a green square and then closing his or her eyes, the viewer will see a red square as an afterimage. This experiment may be repeated with any color and the afterimage will always be of the complementary color.

Sucker feet: Devices that provide a vacuum to remove sheets from a stack and position them for access to the press.

Suitcase file: One of two component files used to make up a PostScript type family.

Supercalendering: Using heated steel rollers and pressure to form a very smooth, high-gloss finish on paper.

Supplementary exposure: Additional exposure used to increase contrast, shadow detail, or highlight detail. See *Flash exposure* and *Bump exposure*.

Surface plates: Presensitized plates coated with light-sensitive material.

Sweet spot: A 3″ or 4″ area in the center of a flatbed scanner. Unless the original is small enough and centered directly in the sweet spot, resolution quality will decrease toward the outer edges of the image.

SWOP: Specifications for Web Offset Publications.

Symantec Suitcase™: Font utility software that enables easier font activation or deactivation. It also enables the designation of *font sets*.

T

T-square: A paste-up and layout tool consisting of a thin straightedge blade fastened to a perpendicular head. It was used to align images, as a knife guide when cutting elements, and as a support and guide for a pen or pencil when drawing straight lines.

Tack: The stickiness of an ink, measured by its ability to split between two surfaces.

Tagged image file format (TIFF or TIF): A file format for exchanging bit-mapped images (usually scans) between applications.

Tagged image file format for image technology (TIFF/IT-P1): A device-dependent file format used for describing four-color documents, including specification for printing presses. TIFF/IT-P1 is a raster-based input format designed to be used with high-end CEPS systems that is favored by the magazine industry. The P1 component was added when the format was accepted by the International Standards Organization (ISO) for consideration as an international standard.

Tagout device: A prominent warning device, such as a tag, securely fastened to an energy isolating device, to indicate that electrical power is off and must remain off until the tag is removed.

Tape drives: Device, like a tape recorder, that reads data from and writes it onto a tape.

Taping machine: Device used in shipping departments to automatically apply tape to seal the tops of boxes.

Technical ink pen: Tool commonly used to make camera-ready illustrations and draw lines while preparing mechanicals. It is available in a range of specific nib sizes.

Template: In a page composition program, a reusable form that incorporates all the master pages and other formatting for a document. Also, a pierced guide, usually made from plastic, used to do lettering or to draw circles, ellipses, electrical symbols, and other specialized shapes.

Tensile strength: The amount of stress that will break paper.

Tensiometer: An instrument that measures screen fabric tension.

Terabyte (Tb or TB): Equal to approximately one billion kilobytes; often used to measure optical disk storage capacity.

Tertiary color: Color created by mixing two secondary colors. The tertiary colors on the color wheel are yellow-green, blue-green, blue-violet, red-violet, red-orange, and yellow-orange.

Text: Words, sentences, paragraphs. Also see *Black letter* and *Body type*.

Text box: In QuarkXPpress, a closed figure of any shape (from rectangular to freeform) used to position text.

Text composition: The process of generating copy that will be used in a printed product. Today, text composition is generally done on a computer and the file imported into a page composition program.

Text face: See *Black letter.*

Text filter: A feature of a page composition program that allows formatting of text done in the original word processing document to be retained when it is imported.

Text path: In QuarkXPpress, a means of positioning text that allows for various forms of typographic manipulation.

Texture: A projection of emphasized structure or weight.

Thermal plates: Image carriers that can be exposed optically or digitally through the use of heat.

Thermal transfer printing: Printing technology that uses digital data to control a thermal printhead to melt spots of dry ink on a ribbon and transfer them to a receiver. When *sublimable dye* replaces solid ink, the thermal head converts the dye spots to gas spots which condense on the receiver.

Thermoformed: Formed by heat and pressure.

Thinners: Solvents added to ink to change the viscosity (thickness) of the ink. They do not affect drying time.

Thixotropy: The tendency of ink to flow more freely after being worked.

Thumbnail sketches: Simple, rapidly drawn designs of a layout.

Tick mark: A V-shaped notch in the lead edge of the flat that identifies the gripper edge.

Tight register: Alignment of images that must be very accurate, most often used in printing multiple colors. Sometimes referred to as *hairline register*.

Tight set: Term describing narrower than normal letterspacing.

Tint: Created by adding white to a color. When white is added to red, it results in pink. Pink is a tint of red.

Tint screen: Screen used in the platemaking process to create the uniform tone pattern. It contains a hard dot structure that is specified by a dot percentage.

Tinting: Problem that occurs when ink pigment particles bleed into the dampening solution, causing a slight tint of ink to appear on the nonimage area of the printed sheet.

Tonal resolution: The number of bits of color or grayscale information that can be recorded per pixel. Also referred to as *bit depth*.

Tone: The degree of lightness or darkness of a color. The tone of a color may be lowered or heightened by adding some of its complement. Also, the degree of lightness or darkness in any given area of a photographic print.

Tone compression: The reduction in density (or tonal range) that occurs naturally in the printed reproduction of an original. It is possible to compensate for tone compression to improve the quality of the reproduction.

Tone curve adjustment: The use of curves to make tonal adjustments to an image.

Tone-line process: The process used to convert continuous-tone originals into line reproductions that resemble pen-and-ink sketches or other fine-line drawings. It is used to create a detailed outline reproduction of a continuous tone original.

Toner: In a laser printer or photocopier, the positively charged powder that is attracted to the negatively charged image dots to make up the image of the page. Heated rollers fuse (melt) the powder dots onto the paper to produce a permanent image.

Tool palette: The most often used palette in a page composition program. It displays icons for the tools that the operator can use to perform many different layout functions.

Tooth: The surface characteristic of a paper that allows it to take ink.

Totally chlorine free (TCF): Refers to unbleached paper with a slightly brown appearance.

Totally electronic printing (TEP): Term that refers to the use of a reimageable image carrier or no image carrier for the transfer of toner or ink-jet ink to paper. Ink-jet is a direct-to-paper technology with no intermediate image carrier. Toner-based reproduction requires a drum or belt to create the toned image and then transfer it to paper. The toner-based image carrier must create a new image for every reproduction and is thus reimageable.

Toxin: A poisonous substance.

Tracking: A feature of computer typesetting programs that allows control of letter and word spacing together.

Trade customs: Understood rules or implied laws that apply to a relationship between a printer and customer.

Transitional Roman: Typefaces that are a remodeling of Oldstyle faces. There is greater contrast between the heavy and light elements, and the characters are wider than the equivalent Oldstyle characters. Baskerville, a Transitional Roman, was the first typeface designed to print on smooth paper.

Transmission densitometer: Color measurement device that measures the fraction of incident light conveyed through a negative or positive transparency without being absorbed or scattered. See *Densitometer.*

Transparent copy: An original that allows light to pass through. Also referred to as *transmission copy.*

Transpose: To exchange the placement of a letter, word, or sentence.

Trapping: Method used to create a small area of overlap (*trap*) between colors to compensate for potential gaps; how well one color overlaps another without leaving a white space between the two or generating a third color.

Triangle: Three-sided plastic or metal tool used to aid in drawing vertical and slanted lines on layouts and mechanicals. The two most common types are the 30° triangle and the 45° triangle.

Trichromatic: Consisting of or using three colors.

Trichromatic colorimeter: Color measurement device that allows the user to match a patch of light by combination of the three primary colors. Even though this instrument relies on the perception of the eye, it is a useful device for color measurement.

Trim: The paper that is left over after cutting a sheet into smaller pieces.

Trim marks: Marks positioned on the original copy to be used as a guide to indicate where cuts should be made.

Trimming: The process of cutting off uneven edges of a product after printing. Compare with *cutting.*

Tristimulus reading: Densitometer reading made through all three color separation filters and *not* one specific part of the light spectrum.

Tristimulus values: Set of three numbers used to designate the amounts of red, green, and blue light in an image.

TrueType fonts: An outline font technology developed jointly by Microsoft and Apple. Because TrueType support is built into all Windows and Macintosh operating systems, anyone using these operating systems can create documents using TrueType fonts.

Tungsten filament lamp: An incandescent lamp with a filament of tungsten metal surrounded by gases, all enclosed in a glass bulb.

Turnaround: The completion time for a product from its inception.

Two-cylinder system: A press system that combines the printing operations of the plate cylinder and impression cylinder into one.

Two-person proofing system: A method that requires the reader to work with an assistant (copyholder). This is the most common proofreading method when accuracy and speed are important. It is frequently used with larger jobs.

Type 1 fonts: PostScript format for outline fonts where each character in a typeface is stored as a PostScript language program. Outline fonts take up less memory than bitmapped fonts; they do not suffer in appearance or legibility when scaled to different sizes; they can be easily rotated, outlined, or filled with patterns; and they produce smooth curves even at large sizes when used as display fonts.

Type high: The height of letterpress type (0.918″).

Type metal: A low-melting-point alloy of lead, tin, and antimony used to cast foundry type.

Type sizes: Measurements that describe the size of printed type, commonly expressed in points.

Typeface family: A grouping consisting of all the variations of one style of type.

Typeface series: The range of sizes of each typeface in a family. The common type sizes used in printing are 6, 8, 10, 12, 14, 18, 24, 36, 48, 60, and 72 point.

Typefaces: Distinctive designs of visual symbols used to compose a printed page.

Typographer: A print designer who determines how a manuscript should be expressed in type as well as other details of reproduction.

Typography: The art of expressing ideas in printed form through the selection of appropriate typefaces. Also, the art or craft of setting type professionally.

U

Uncoated paper: Paper that does not have a mineral layer applied over the surface, so it has a slightly textured feel.

Undercolor addition (UCA): The inverse function of *undercolor removal*. Undercolor addition is used with *gray component replacement* to produce better shadow quality.

Undercolor removal (UCR): Technique used to reduce the yellow, magenta, and cyan dot percentages in neutral tones by replacing them with increased amounts of black ink. See also *Gray component replacement, Undercolor addition.*

Undercut: The vertical distance between the surface of the cylinder bearers and the cylinder body. The undercut allows for the thickness of the plate or blanket and packing.

Unit: A measure that results from splitting the em into uniform narrow widths. The number of units per em varies with the composing method.

Unity: The proper balance of all elements in an image so that a pleasing whole results and the image is viewed as one piece.

UNIX: An operating system that runs on a variety of computers.

Unsharp masking (USM): The increase of tonal contrast where light and dark tones come together at the edges of the images.

Uppercase: The capital or larger letters in a typeface. The abbreviation "caps" is often used to describe uppercase letters.

US Conventional system: The standard system of weights and measures used in the United States. Also known as the "English system."

V

Vacuum frame: A glass frame used to hold the film and plate in tight contact for exposure on a platemaker.

Value: Term used in the Munsell system of color notation to describe the lightness or darkness of a color. It is shown on the central axis as nine visible steps. The darkest value is at the bottom and the lightest value is at the top. The value of pure black is designated as 0/, pure white as 10/, and middle gray is 5/.

Variable printing: Variable printing means that customized and personalized printing can be produced for target marketing purposes. Customized means that documents can be assembled that are particular to selected audiences; personalized, that each unit is particular to a specific person.

Varnishing: A coating applied after printing to provide a clear protective surface.

Vector: In computer graphics, a line that is defined by its start and end point.

Vector font: Font represented in an object-oriented graphics language such as PostScript or TrueType. The representation of the font defines the shape of each character (typeface) but not the size. Also referred to as *scaleable font* or *outline font*.

Vector graphics: Mathematical descriptions of images and their placement. In electronic publishing, vector graphics information is transferred from a design workstation to a *raster image processor (RIP)* that interprets all of the page layout information for the marking engine of the imagesetter. PostScript, or another page description language, serves as an interface between the page layout workstation and the RIP.

Vehicle: The liquid component in ink that serves as a binding agent.

Vertical camera: A process camera that has a vertical (up and down) optical axis. The copyboard and filmholder are perpendicular to the optical axis. Also referred to as a *gallery camera*.

Video card: Board that plugs into a computer to give it display capabilities. Also referred to as a *video adaptor*.

Video display terminal: A computer monitor.

View file: A low-resolution electronic file containing the actual data used to form the final output page. Its primary use is to drive (display an image) on the workstation's color monitor. The view file can be output to continuous-tone material to provide a low-resolution proof of a quality slightly better than that displayed on the workstation monitor.

Viewing booth: Booth or area with color-balanced lighting (5000 K) so that anyone viewing the same printed materials will be seeing them under the same lighting conditions. Images are viewed at a 90° to reduce glare.

Viscosity: The internal resistance of an ink to flow. It is the opposite of fluidity.

Visibility: A legibility factor that results from the contrast of a dark typeface against the light reflected by the paper.

Visible light: The range of wavelengths of the electromagnetic spectrum (400 nm-770 nm) that cause the sensation of vision.

Volatile organic compounds (VOCs): Toxic substances contained in blanket and roller washes, fountain solutions, plate cleaners, glaze removers, degreasers, and film cleaners. VOCs evaporate into the atmosphere, contributing to the development of such environmental hazards as ground-level ozone (smog) and other health concerns.

W

Waistline: An imaginary line drawn along top of body height letters.

Warp threads: Threads that run vertically, at a 90° angle to the weft threads.

Washup solvents: Solvent used to dissolve ink from a screen.

Waste stream: The solid, liquid, or contained gaseous material that is produced and disposed of, incinerated, or recycled by a facility.

Waterless plates: Presensitized plates that use an ink-repellent substance other than water to separate the nonimage area from the image area.

Waterless press: An offset lithographic press system that eliminates the use of a dampening system during the printing process.

Watermark: A translucent design impressed in paper.

Web: A roll of paper threaded through the printing units of a web-fed press.

Web break detector: A device that automatically shuts down the press if the web snaps or tears.

Web splicer: A device used to bond a new roll to the end of an existing web on a web-fed press.

Web-fed press: A lithographic press that prints with one long, continuous web of paper that is fed from a roll.

Weft threads: Threads that run horizontally, at a 90° angle to the warp threads.

Weight: The degree of boldness of the printing surface of a letter. The readable image might have a light, medium, bold, or extra-bold printing surface.

Well sites: The hundreds or thousands of photosensitive elements of a CCD. Also known as *photosites.*

White point: A movable reference point that defines the lightest area in an image displayed on a cathode ray tube (CRT) causing all other areas to be adjusted accordingly.

White space: The areas of the layout that are void of printed images.

Wide-band filter: Color separation filter that is used to reproduce a broader section of the light spectrum. Compare to *narrow-band filter.*

Widow: A very short word, or part of a word, forming the final line of a paragraph.

Window: A clear area in a film negative for positioning of a halftone, created by positioning masking film on the mechanical.

Windows: A Graphical User Interface designed to give the PC platform the same ease of use as the Macintosh platform.

Windows Metafile (WMF): The Windows 95/NT version of the PICT file format.

Word processing software: A highly efficient tool for creating and editing text that has allowed desktop computers to replace phototypsetters in composing text for graphic communications applications.

Word processor: A program or computer that enables the user to perform word processing functions such as creating, storing, retrieving, and editing text.

Wordspacing: Changing the spacing between typeset words, for better appearance or to fit copy in a given space.

Work-and-tumble: A printing method in which one flat is prepared, but the sheet is tumbled (or flopped) so the gripper edge changes when the second side is printed. Only one plate and press makeready are needed.

Work-and-turn: A printing method in which one plate surface is used for printing both sides of a sheet without changing the gripper edge.

Workflow: The many steps and complex processes involved in the production of printed materials. Efficient workflow in a print production environment starts before the job arrives at the shop and ends when the job is billed. It requires jobs to be produced at the right time with all the right elements by the most appropriate equipment available.

Workmarks: Lines and guides on the base sheet used for pasteup, including corner or trim marks, center marks and fold lines. These marks are helpful to the pasteup artist and the stripper.

World Wide Web: An interconnected network of computer networks that allows you to access documents across globe.

WORM (Write-Once, Read Many): Polished metal disk capable of storing digital information. WORM disks can be recorded to once, but read innumerable times.

WYSIWYG: "What You See Is What You Get." The display method used by word processing and page layout programs, in which the monitor display closely matches the printed output.

WYSIWYP: "What You See Is What You Print." See *Color management software.*

X

x-height: The height of the lowercase "x." Also called *body height.*

XY scanning: Scanning technology that optimally positions its scanning head along an XY axis. The scanner head slides both up and down and side-to-side beneath the bed.

Z

Zahn cup: A gravitational flow device used to measure the viscosity of ink.

Zero-speed splicer: A splicer unit on a web-fed system that uses a set of festoon rollers to draw out slack from the web and feed the press while a splice is being made.

Index

A

B

C

E

F

G

H

I

J

K

L

M

Q

R

S

U

V

W

X

Y

Z